W9-BZE-474

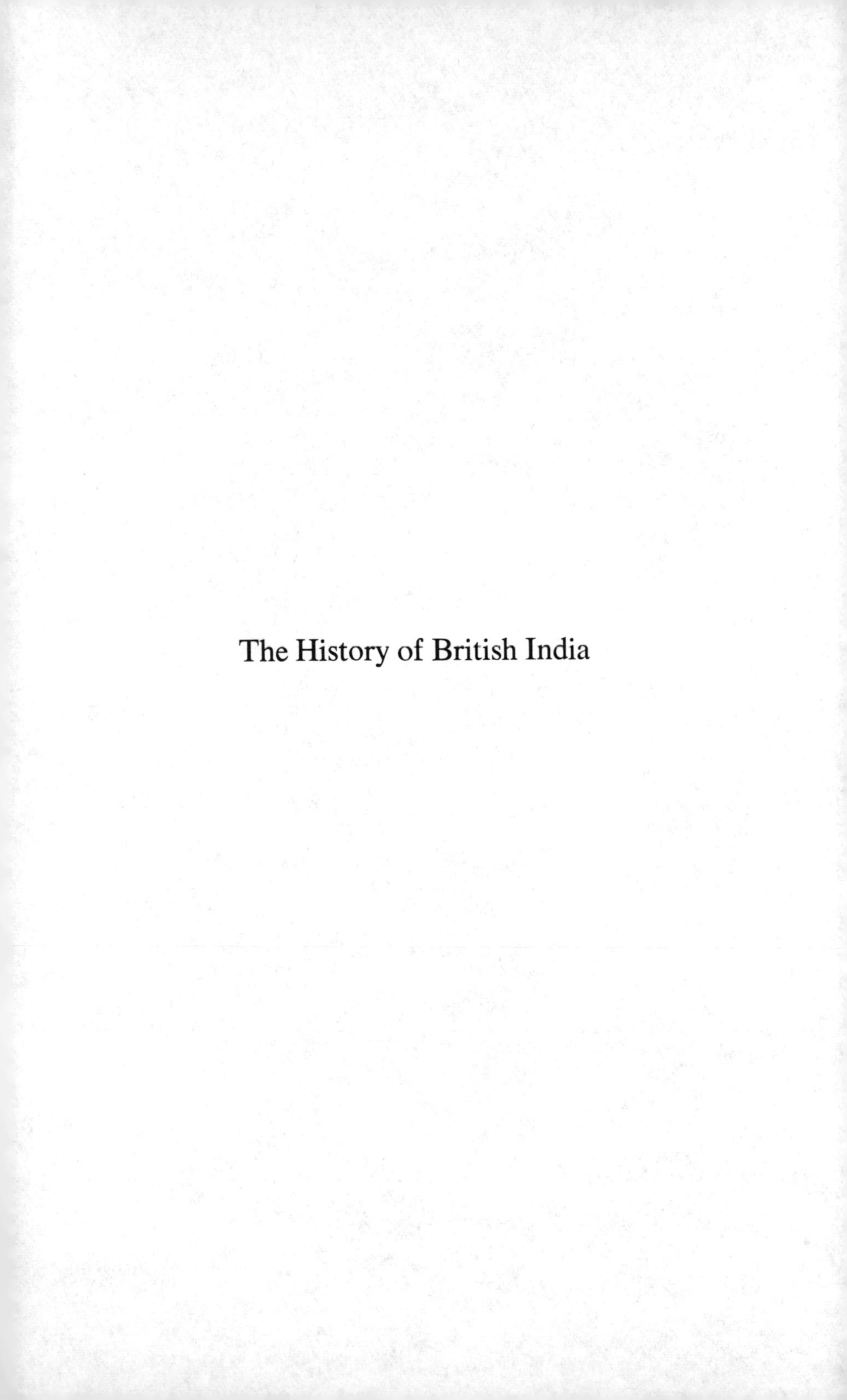

The History of British India

The History of British India

by James Mill, Esq.

Notes by Horace Hayman Wilson

Introduction by

John Kenneth Galbraith

Volumes I & II

1968
Chelsea House Publishers
New York

Library of Congress Catalogue Card Number: 68-29832

Reprinted from a copy in the collections of
The New York Public Library
Astor, Lenox and Tilden Foundations.

John Mill's India
by
John Kenneth Galbraith

With *A Pilgrim's Progress* and possibly *The Education of Henry Adams*, James Mill's *The History of British India* must be one of the most famous unread books in the English language. Everyone knows he was working on it while he was rearing and educating his more famous son. It is intimately a part of the legend of John Stuart Mill. Many, reading of the Mills, must have thought it a work they might one day read. For a long while few have.

Partly this has been because of inaccessibility. The available editions have been on deep library shelves. The one here reprinted with annotation by Horace Hayman Wilson dates from the 1850's, and the original was in a type well designed to try the eyes. The ample and important footnotes were all but microscopic. And, of course, it is a work of formidable length and thoroughness. It is not for the person who wants to read and run.

In recent times, also, it has fallen under the heavy cloud which covers colonialism. Right-thinking men disapprove of colonialism; accordingly, they do not much read or write its history. This would be a very poor time to bring out the definitive work on the Belgians in the Congo or on the French in Senegal. All of this is unfortunate and a very poor reason for ignoring this classic of British and Indian history.

In the first place, it is a great piece of English prose. It is not an easy book but it is stylish and lucid. It draws on what may well have been the richest scholarship of the day—James Mill's enormous erudition was divided, one imagines, more or less equally between his famous book and his famous son. And there are passages whose organ tones are worthy of Gibbon or Macaulay and which all but put Churchill to shame. Consider these early paragraphs.

> From the time when Vasco de Gama distinguished his nation by discovering the passage round the Cape of Good Hope, a whole century had elapsed, during which, without a rival, the Portuguese had enjoyed, and abused, the advantages of superior knowledge and art, amid a feeble and half-civilized people. They had explored the Indian Ocean, as far as Japan; had discovered its islands, rich with some of the favourite productions of nature; had achieved the most brilliant conquests; and, by their commerce, poured into Europe, in unexampled profusion, those commodities of the East, on which the nations at that time set an extraordinary value.
>
> The circumstances of this splendid fortune had violently attracted the attention of Europe. The commerce of India, even when confined to those narrow limits which a carriage by land had prescribed, was supposed to have elevated feeble states into great ones; and to have constituted an enviable part in the fortune even of the most opulent and powerful; to have contributed largely to support the Grecian monarchies both in Syria and Egypt; to have retarded the downfall of Constantinople; and to have raised the small and obscure republic of Venice to the rank and influence of the most potent kingdoms. The discovery therefore of a new channel for this opulent traffic, and the happy experience of the Portuguese, inflamed the cupidity of all the maritime nations of Europe, and set before them the most tempting prospects.

One wonders how anyone, in a matter of five sentences, could more successfully have conveyed the excitement and the sense of high drama with which the great trading adventures on the Indies were launched.

British rule in India is also one of the greatest achievements of the last three hundred years. The attitudes which make it, for the moment, an unfashionable subject of study and interest will pass. And this will be true in India as elsewhere. The British succeeded the Moghul dynasty—that of Babur, Akbar, Jahangir and Shan Jahan which established itself in India from central Asia upon the defeat of Ibrahim Lodi (also a member of an alien dynasty) at Panipat in 1526. The Indians have now adopted the Moghuls as their own. Although they did not, as did their predecessors, exchange their old kingdom for the new, British Administration was a model of compassion and concern for the masses as compared with the despotism and anarchy it replaced. Without forgetting the excesses of Clive and his contemporaries in Bengal, in most of India the British were unquestionably regarded as liberators. To this day what was

British India is appreciably more prosperous than those parts that remained under the rule of the princes. But independence was won in India as elsewhere by cultivating animosity against the imperial power. And there was much snobbishness, insult and indignity to nourish it. This is remembered. But in time these memories will fade and the accomplishments will be featured.

These accomplishments were great. British rule in India was, first of all, an extraordinary exercise in the art of administration. A mere handful of men—the Indian Civil Service (ICS) never had as many as a thousand European members—carried the responsibility for government with the support of a few regiments of British and a rather larger number of Indian troops. This was brought about by selecting men carefully, impressing them with the importance of their task, paying them well and then giving them large responsibility and the commensurate authority. Not only were the collection of revenue, the maintenance of order and the administration of justice in the hand of the Collector (the regional administrator) but when famine threatened or Muslims and Hindus clashed in the villages the problem was his. Youngsters in their twenties governed hundreds of thousands of people. They did so within a stern framework of law. And while there were doubtless petty tyrants and perhaps a very few thieves, nearly all were honest, dedicated and rather austere men. Certainly they were the best rulers India had ever had. Many gave their lives. It is a common observation on British rule that it did very little—it was law and order government and nothing more. This is unjust. It irrigated vast areas against the threat of famine and built a comprehensive railway system to get the food from the places of surplus to those of deficit. It began to build an educational system and it provided the other conventional services of Nineteenth Century governments. At the time not many other governments did more and few others did as much as well. It was not democratic. But democratic government at the time might have been worse or more likely impossible. This was the best of despotisms.

British rule in the Nineteenth Century was much better on the whole than in the Eighteenth Century. The present book is the basic document on Eighteenth Century administration. It was also influential in what happened in the next period. For Mill's criticisms of British administration, enumerated here in detail, were influential in reforms that followed. And so was Mill himself for one consequence of the book was his employment by the company in which—as I shall note presently—he came to have an influential role. This was also the book that the diligent read as they prepared for examinations; or to take ship for the subcontinent; or which they read during the course of the long journey there. These latter uses were of mixed advantage and of adverse consequences for this book.

However erudite he might be, James Mill had some serious shortcomings when it came to writing about the civilization of India. For one thing he never set foot in the country of which he wrote at such length. In the preface he argues that this was an advantage; had he visited India he could have seen only a small corner of that vast land and for this he would have sacrificed his larger view. This is defensive pleading without doubt. It would have been a warmer, more sympathetic book had Mill seen something of Indian civilization for himself. Also Mill did not know the relevant Indian languages, and translations at the beginning of the Nineteenth Century were much less commonly available than now. He excuses himself on this but he would not have excused any man who essayed to comment on the Greek or Latin poets without a knowledge of Greek or Latin. He discusses the *Mahabharata* under this handicap and the further and more serious one that, at the time, it had not been rendered into English.

He had two other faults. To this day men regularly return from India in one or two extreme states of mind. Either they are enraptured by everything Indian or they wish to see nothing again of the country and its sloth and misery. So it was also in Mill's time and without having been to India, Mill threw in his lot enthusiastically with the second party. He was determined to show that Indian culture is barren, perverse and objectionable and he was determined to prove this to be so in all particulars. He made clear his suspicion of those who confessed their admiration. Their scholarly credentials and good sense were in doubt. Nor did he allow understatement to conceal his dislike of everything Indian. "The Brahmins," he advised, "are the most audacious, and perhaps the most unskillful fabricators, with whom the annals of fable have made us acquainted." Taking issue with admirers on a less exalted manner he observed, "From the frequency with which the Hindus perform religious ablutions, the Europeans prone from partial appearances to draw flattering conclusions, painted them, at first, as in the colours of so many other virtues, so likewise in those of cleanliness. Few nations are surpassed by the Hindus, in the total want of physical purity, in their streets, houses, and persons."

More than simple bias is involved here. Mill was the prophet of a faith which made it difficult, perhaps impossible, for him to understand the civilization of India. He was a Benthamite and not for one season or one country. If a man's moral worth was measured by the practical utility of his actions in England, so it was in India. If one tested policy by the greatest good for the greatest number in Europe, so also among the masses of Asia. If one realized the greatest good by competitive individualism in one place, so in the other. And by these tests there was little in the indigenous culture of India that passed. As one measured government in Westminster so in the capital of the Nizam or Nabob. Caste, accommodation to the hot climate, the conservatism of an agricultural economy, the social customs of the villages, the inherently predatory character of landlords and rules were all outside the range of Mill's faith and hence unworthy of any effort at comprehension.

Nor can everything be blamed on utilitarianism. He also had a tendency remarkable even in an Englishman or Scotsman of his time to measure religion, marriage customs, manners, even the personal hygiene mentioned above by his own standards. No carefully nurtured sense of humility kept him from knowing what was right. And his education notwithstanding, Mill was in many ways a very narrow man. He was a fine writer; accordingly, one must grant him a feeling for the graces of English and classical prose and verse. This apart, he must have been nearly devoid of aesthetic sense. In consequence the magic of Indian temple architecture and sculpture escapes him entirely. And so does the art and architecture of the rulers. Nominally Mill's bias is directed against the Hindus but in practice it embraces also the ruling Muslim dynasties. The last of these, the Moghuls, were among the greatest patrons of architecture and painting the world has known and one, Shah Jahan, who built, along with much else, the Taj Mahal and the Red Fort in Delhi and supported one of the world's great schools of painters, is rivaled only by the Medicis. None of these achievements, were they known to Mill, were deemed worthy of more than passing mention. Most are not mentioned.

What redeems these faults? In the first place only a comparatively small part of the book is about Indian India. Most of it is about British India and here Mill's Benthamite faith coupled with his uncompromising honesty and candor are not handicaps but advantages. He judges British rule in India by the standards of the time and he judges it with all of the moral authority and certainty of a man of belief. Nothing is more sacred than his own convictions; one cannot imagine that many were spared. A few years before Mill wrote, affairs in the Kingdom of Oudh (the important state centered on Lucknow on the Ganges plain) being in their typically shocking condition, the then Governor-General, Sir John Shore, evicted the ruler who had but recently succeeded to the throne. The mismanagement of affairs was a highly cooperative enterprise in which many participated but the Governor-General had been persuaded that Nabob was the focus of the trouble. Mill tells as follows of the background of the action. "Great industry and skill had been employed in prepossessing the mind of the Governor-General with the most unfavourable opinion of the young Nabob, as a man between whose character and the interests of the English an irreconcileable contrariety was placed." He then goes on to describe the means by which the ruler was deposed. It was accepted by all that he was the son of the old Nabob and a menial woman of the seraglio. But he had been acknowledged by his father and under Muslim custom and law this was sufficient. But now it was further held that his mother went home at night to a husband and that he had been purchased unborn for five hundred rupees as a putative son by the old Nabob who felt himself insufficiently supplied with progeny. Contemplating this transaction, Mill in a fine concluding passage attributes innocence, stupidity and injustice to the exalted British official without pausing for breath.

It is impossible to read the account of this transaction, drawn up by the Governor-General, and not to be impressed with a conviction of his sincerity, and his desire to do justice. But it is easy to perceive also how much his understanding was bewildered; and impossible not to confess that he decided against the unfortunate Nabob the great question of a kingdom, upon evidence upon which a court of English law would not have decided against him a question of a few pounds.

Standards that might be meaningless or even bigoted when brought to bear on Hindus and Muslims were not at all bad for judging the conduct of Eighteenth and Nineteenth Century Englishmen.

The other redeeming feature in this edition is Mill's editor, Horace Hayman Wilson, who also continued the history from where Mill had left it. An orientalist and professor at Oxford, Wilson was as persuaded of the depth and subtlety of Indian culture as was Mill of its sterility. And while he is not without respect for Mill in his particular areas of competence, Wilson did not believe that these extended to oriental languages, literature, art, manners, philosophy and religion. He not only felt obliged to correct Mill in these matters but, as any reader of his comments will quickly sense, rejoiced in the opportunity. Accordingly in this book, we have not only Mill's views, but those of his editor. Until he is well into the history of the British in India no one should neglect the footnotes in this book marked "W"[1]

Let me now say a word about the author.[2]

James Mill was born in 1773 near Montrose in Scotland of poor parents—his father was a cobbler and a small landholder. But though poor, his parents were ambitious for their son and his mother in particular determined that he should have a good education. After attending local schools he went to the University of Edinburgh under the patronage of Sir John and

[1] Although Wilson's footnotes cannot be accepted uncritically either, scholars have generally thought him a valuable defender of Indian culture against the narrow strictures of Mill. And, as the reader will discover, this is a service he undoubtedly renders. But there are also errors in Wilson's footnotes. These, in turn, seem to have been related to his habit of using the work of other scholars as a ladder for himself. My views of Wilson have, in this respect, been usefully corrected by two diligent Idian scholars, Gerald and Natalie Sirkin. *cf.* Natalie P. R. Sirkin, "Horace Hayman Wilson and Gamesmanship in Indology," *Asian Studies*, August, 1965.

[2] For a more detailed biographical sketch, on which I have drawn here, see Donald Winsch, ed., *James Mill: Selected Economic Writings* (Chicago, 1966). This in turn draws on Alexander Bain's biography, *James Mill: A Biography*. (London, 1882).

Lady Jane Stuart with whom he is assumed to have lived more or less as a member of the family. It was in Edinburgh that he began to develop what was to be his enduring passion for the Greeks. It was his intention to prepare for the Church, not from any known interest in its work but because it was an accepted means of social and economic advance by impoverished Scotch youth at the time as for many years thereafter. He served as an itinerant preacher for a time but in 1802 abandoned this vocation and went to London with Sir John Stuart.

Mill's early years in London were less than happy. Initially he practiced journalism, became editor of two literary journals, did a translation and began his career as an essayist. But before long he had sufficient income to contemplate marriage and therewith his life took a sharp turn for the worse. He ignored and probably disliked his wife although this did not prevent him from having nine children by her of whom John Stuart, named for his patron, was the oldest. The burden of providing for this vast brood darkened the middle years of Mill's life and, presumably, affirmed his agreement with his friend Thomas Malthus on the dangers of over-population. It was intensified because after 1805 he gave up his other regular sources of income to concentrate on the present history. He expected, when beginning the work, to complete it in three or four years. It took twelve. He sustained himself and his family during these years with miscellaneous journalism, editing, translations and hack literary work. He also in these years produced, among other more substantial works, his notable pamphlet, *Commerce Defended*, in which he strongly attacked the notion that the economic interests of the nation are safe-guarded by the landowning classes, a position which was sharply at odds with earlier and more tolerant attitudes toward the landlords.

As work on *The History of British India* continued, a new and powerful influence entered Mill's life in the form of Jeremy Bentham. This association began in 1818 and was in every respect symbiotic. Mill was audience, editor and exponent of Bentham's ideas. Bentham found in Mill an avid disciple for his doctrines, one whose mind was extensively prepared by his own reading and thought. To further the association Bentham bought a house for Mill and his family not far from his own and helped him with the rent. They went together to the country and in 1814 had their first quarrel over Mill's evident preference for the company of Joseph Hume.

The present history was finished in 1818, at about the time when the association with Bentham was coming gradually to an end. The book brought a sharp change in Mill's life for, its criticism of British government in India notwithstanding, it led to his employment by the East India Company. The Company paid him well and Mill rose rapidly in its service. His financial problems came to an end; by 1821 his salary was £ 1000 a year and he was able to consider himself quite rich. Though his responsibilities were considerable he was able to discharge them in six hours of work a day. In the remainder of his time he engaged in a wide range of discussions on the problems of the day, wrote and revised his *The Elements of Political Economy* (1821) and contributed his notable injunctions to public virtue as defined by himself to the Westminister Review. During these years he saw also coming to maturity the most notable achievement of his life, one for which, with some reason, he took full credit, namely his son John Stuart Mill. His son (with mellower wisdom) succeeded him not only as political economist and utilitarian philosopher but also in employment at India House. James Mill died in 1836.

One will ask what is the meaning of this book for modern India—or for modern India and Pakistan. It is, without wishing to exaggerate, very great. Both of these lands are profoundly Asian; it was a measure of the power as well as the quality of their culture that it kept its character and integrity through two centuries of strong British rule. India, as Gandhi insisted, is to be found in its villages. I do not suppose that a transmigratory visitor returning to a village in Bihar or Orissa after an absence of a thousand years would find much that had changed. But there is also a superstructure that is immensely British. I have mentioned the Civil Service. The parliament, police, law courts, the army, universities, the newspapers and the industrial and commercial life are all profoundly according to the British model. This book is a chronicle, possibly the best that we have, of the transplant of this model. It is not only an admirable and even unique document on economic, political and cultural imperialism, but it is the early history of the institutions of government, education and economic life that are most conspicuous to the visitor in India to this day.

The book has another high relevance. People often asked me what book they should read before going to India. I always suggest E. M. Forster's *Passage to India.* If one knows this great novel, nothing about the subcontinent comes as a surprise. It pictures as no other the clash of the two cultures and the uncertainty and ambiguity of the life of those who live between the two. This is the thing which continues to impress one after a long stay in India. Indian society exists between the two worlds and has the insecurity which comes from an uncertain identification with each. So does Indian administration. So does Indian diplomacy. So also her approach to economic development and modern technical achievement. When the Japanese adopt they adopt—confidently and fearlessly. So one senses do the Chinese. But India is far more likely to remain in suspense.

Mill, I think, provides the clue. The Japanese could select as could the Chinese. Economic organization, technology, the industrial ethic were taken over completely. Language, art, other culture, social and family life could remain in the traditional mold. But in India the powerful and dominating culture of which Mill was such a superb and supremely confident exponent offered much less choice. Benthamite concepts of government and economics were believed to be the natural order of things. So were English manners, English ethics, English social customs, even English food. So, of course, was the English language itself. It was not so much that they were imposed as that their superiority was taken for granted. Having to adopt much, the Indians adopted fearfully and often rather badly. They wished to conform, but they sought also to stay apart. Here in this great book we see, in marvelous panoply, how great was the task. Accordingly, we see the sources of the insecurity which Forster so wonderfully evokes. We see why today Indians often seem more westernized than they are. We see the sources of the underlying commitment of traditional attitudes and values which the visitor—the modern engineer, agronomist, politician—is so often so disconcerted to discover in what he thought were wholly westernized, wholly modern men. We see the reasons that

Europeans and Americans often find Indians, as they say, difficult. They are unprepared for an underlying commitment to a traditional culture for which, in other Asian countries, they would be wholly braced. The story of the tasks which Eighteenth Century Englishmen took on in India in all their variety and complexity will carry the reader through this book. But in getting the measure of the imperial task the reader will win an understanding, as a result, of the psychology and behavior of modern India or, more precisely, of behavior and thought in that thin but dominant stratum of Indian society which was juxtaposed to the Raj.

THE HISTORY OF

BRITISH INDIA.

BY JAMES MILL, ESQ.

FIFTH EDITION WITH NOTES AND CONTINUATION,

BY HORACE HAYMAN WILSON, M.A., F.R.S.

MEMBER OF THE ROYAL ASIATIC SOCIETY, OF THE ASIATIC SOCIETIES OF PARIS, BOSTON AND CALCUTTA, AND OF THE ORIENTAL SOCIETY OF GERMANY; OF THE IMPERIAL INSTITUTE OF FRANCE, AND THE IMPERIAL ACADEMIES OF VIENNA AND ST. PETERSBURGH; OF THE ROYAL ACADEMIES OF BERLIN AND MUNICH, ETC., ETC.; AND BODEN PROFESSOR OF SANSCRIT IN THE UNIVERSITY OF OXFORD.

VOLUME I.

LONDON:
JAMES MADDEN, 8, LEADENHALL STREET;
PIPER, STEPHENSON AND SPENCE,
PATERNOSTER ROW.

M.DCCC.LVIII.

LONDON:
PRINTED BY WERTHEIMER AND CO.,
CIRCUS PLACE, FINSBURY CIRCUS.

CONTENTS.

BOOK II.—OF THE HINDUS.

PREFACE OF THE EDITOR.

IN the Preface to the History of British India, Mr. Mill has claimed for himself the merits of patient and laborious investigation, and of original and independent judgment. The claim is substantiated by his work. His history is remarkable for extensive and diligent research, and for opinions which are peculiar either to the author, or to the school of which he was a distinguished disciple.

Whilst, however, the historian of British India has derived the facts which he relates from numerous and diversified sources of information, and has investigated those sources with undeniable industry and unquestionable talent, it is not to be imagined that his labours have in every instance been rewarded with success, or that he has left nothing unexplored. He has himself taken pains to guard against such an expectation. He acknowledges that his opportunities of consulting published authorities were sometimes transient and precarious, that in some things, the unpublished documents of which he had need were not accessible to him; and that in the latter portion of his work, which may be regarded as almost contemporary history, he was in want of much personal information which he believed to exist, and which might have rendered his narrative richer, and perhaps more accurate in matters of detail. To supply in some degree the omissions, and to correct the inaccuracies which have arisen from these causes, as far as additional materials supply the means, is one of the objects of the present publication. Many of the documents, and much of the personal information which Mr. Mill desiderated, have been given to the public since he wrote, and various valuable works, comprehending periods and transactions of which he treats, have furnished facilities for clearly understanding, and definitively appreciating much that was dark and doubtful at the date of his inquiries. Of these publications, it is sufficient here to specify the works of Sir John Malcolm, the biographies of Clive and Munro, and the Indian portion of the despatches of Marquis Wellesley and the Duke of Wellington.

Besides the defects occasioned by incomplete materials, the History of British India presents inaccuracies both of fact and opinion, which have risen from the author's imperfect knowledge of the country, and unacquaintance with any of the languages spoken in it. He has taken great pains to prove that these deficiencies are of no consideration, and that his never having been in India, and his possessing but a slight and elementary acquaintance with any of the languages of the East, are to be regarded rather as qualifications than disqualifications for the task which he had undertaken. His arguments are ingenious: they will carry conviction but to few. It is true that residence in a country, command of its dialects, conversancy with its literature, are but humble elements in the formation of the historical character; but they are elements, and cannot be discarded without injury to the consistency and completeness of the whole. It is also true, that there are many circumstances in the position of the servants of the East India Company, which are unpropitious to the development and cultivation of the talent and knowledge requisite to constitute a historian of India; but, although these circumstances may counterbalance, in the individuals themselves, the benefits derivable from personal observation, they do not therefore invalidate the reality of those benefits, or render local knowledge altogether valueless. It may be without reservation conceded, that no one person of the many who have been engaged in official duty in India, or who have earned distinction as oriental scholars, has yet brought to the attempt to write a history of India the same degree of fitness as Mr. Mill; yet it cannot but be felt, that had Mr. Mill himself passed but a short time in the country, or been but moderately versed in any department of its literature, his history would have been exempt from many of those blemishes by which its perfectness is now impaired, and its utility diminished.

Personal knowledge of a country, and especially of India, possesses one great recommendation, of which Mr. Mill does not seem to have been aware. It secures one important historical requisite, of the want of which his pages present many striking examples. It enables the historian to judge of the real value of that evidence to which he must have recourse for matters that are beyond the sphere of his own observation. Mr. Mill justly argues, that it is only by combining the observations of a number of individuals, that a comprehensive knowledge of any one subject can be acquired, and that in so extensive and complicated a subject as India, a very small portion can fall under the cognizance of any single observer. Yet it should be considered, that although the subject be diversified in its details, it is in substance the same. Amidst all the varieties of the picture, there are many features in common, and he to whom those features are familiar, will be able to judge of the fidelity with which they are delineated by another and will thence be able to infer the power and disposition of the artist, to portray with truth and skill the lineaments which are less intimately known to himself. He will be in a situation to estimate with accuracy the opportunities which the author of an account of any part of India may have enjoyed, of gathering authentic information; he will be in the way of learning something of the narrator's pursuits, habits, occupation, and prepossessions, and will by daily experience be prepared for the many circumstances by which observation is biassed, and opinions are instilled. He will know what to credit, what to mistrust, what to disbelieve. He will be qualified to select the pure metal from the dross, to separate the false from the true. An incompetency to perform this most essential part of the duties of a careful and critical historian is constantly apparent in the citations which Mr. Mill was made, either in his text or his notes, from writers on

India. He commonly attaches the greatest weight to the authorities which are least entitled to confidence, or adduces from those of a higher order, the passages which are least characterized by care and consideration. Numerous instances of Mr. Mill's mistaken estimate and partial application of authority are pointed out in the present publication. To have specified all, would have swelled the annotations to a disproportionate and inconvenient bulk. A local knowledge of India on the part of its historian, would have obviated the necessity of most of these animadversions.

Acquaintance with the languages and literature of India would have preserved Mr. Mill from some other mistaken conclusions. He states it as his conviction, that even when he wrote, a sufficient stock of information had been collected in the languages of Europe to enable an inquirer to ascertain every important point in the history of India. As far as this assertion may be considered applicable to the European part of Indian history, it is inconsistent with the deficiencies which he has himself indicated. It is still more incorrect when applied to the history of the Hindus and the Mohammedans of Hindustan. Many very important accessions have been acquired in both these respects since the publication of the history of British India, but many more remain to be supplied, before it can be asserted with truth, that every important point in the history of India has been ascertained. In the Journals of the several Asiatic Societies, and the publications of various Hindu scholars, information almost entirely new and of exceeding interest, has been obtained within the last few years, relating to the religion, philosophy, and ancient history of the Hindus, whilst their later fortunes have been richly illustrated by the history of the Marathas, and the Annals of Rajasthan: until, however, some of the Puránas, and the chief portion of the Vedas, shall have been translated, it is not safe to speculate upon the scope and character of the primitive institutions of the Hindus, and for more recent periods, it is still essential to extend investigation into those chronicles of the native states which are known to have existence. The whole of the Mohammedan history of India, when Mr. Mill wrote, was restricted to a single compilation, loosely if not incorrectly translated, and to a few fragmentary notices snatched from oblivion by the industrious curiosity of European orientalists. We have now a more trustworthy translation of Ferishta, and in the autobiography of Baber, and in other publications, much more copious and serviceable contributions to our knowledge of the transactions of the Mohammedans in India: but every epoch of their rule abounds with original authorities, many of which are of great merit, and the principal of these must be translated or consulted before we can venture to affirm that we have, in the languages of Europe, materials sufficient for the determination of every important point in the Mohammedan history of India.

From these remarks it will be apparent, that with regard to the facts of his history, the sources of his information were more scanty and less pure than the historian suspected. Exceptions even more comprehensive may be taken to his opinions. In many instances, the intensity of his prejudices has dimmed the clearness of his perception, and blunted the acuteness of his intelligence. However unconscious of deserving the imputation, he is liable to the censure which he has pronounced upon one class of candidates for popular approbation. He is a zealot for a party; he panegyrizes its leader; he places its principles in the fairest light; he labours to bring odium upon the principles and practices of his opponents; he advocates, in a word, the theoretical views of Mr. Bentham, and tries all measures and all institutions by a scale constructed according to the notions of that writer upon law and government. As long as the opinions thus prompted, are put forth as abstract propositions, or affect conclusions irrelevant to the main subject of the composition, it has not been thought necessary to controvert them, but when they are employed as standards by which to try the conduct of the East India Company and of their servants, either in their commercial or political connexion with India, it has been occasionally attempted to demonstrate their unsoundness, their inapplicability, or their injustice.

Of the proofs which may be discovered in Mr. Mill's history of the operation of preconceived opinions, in confining a vigorous and active understanding to a partial and one-sided view of a great question, no instance is more remarkable than the unrelenting pertinacity with which he labours to establish the barbarism of the Hindus. Indignant at the exalted, and it may be granted, sometimes exaggerated descriptions of their advance in civilization, of their learning, their sciences, their talents, their virtues, which emanated from the amiable enthusiasm of Sir William Jones, Mr. Mill has entered the lists against him with equal enthusiasm, but a less commendable purpose, and has sought to reduce them as far below their proper level, as their encomiasts may have formerly elevated them above it. With very imperfect knowledge, with materials exceedingly defective, with an implicit faith in all testimony hostile to Hindu pretensions, he has elaborated a portrait of the Hindus which has no resemblance whatever to the original, and which almost outrages humanity. As he represents them, the Hindus are not only on a par with the least civilized nations of the Old and New World, but they are plunged almost without exception in the lowest depths of immorality and crime. Considered merely in a literary capacity, the description of the Hindus in the History of British India, is open to censure for its obvious unfairness and injustice; but in the effects which it is likely to exercise upon the connexion between the people of England and the people of India, it is chargeable with more than literary demerit: its tendency is evil; it is calculated to destroy all sympathy between the rulers and the ruled; to preoccupy the minds of those who issue annually from Great Britain, to monopolize the posts of honour and power in Hindustan, with an unfounded aversion towards those over whom they exercise that power, and from whom they enforce that honour; and to substitute for those generous and benevolent feelings, which the situation of the younger servants of the Company in India naturally suggests, sentiments of disdain, suspicion, and dislike, uncongenial to their age and character, and wholly incompatible with the full and faithful discharge of their obligations to Government and to the people. There is reason to fear that these consequences are not imaginary, and that a harsh and illiberal spirit has of late years prevailed in the conduct and councils of the rising service in India, which owes its origin to impressions imbibed in early life from the History of Mr. Mill. It is understood, that had he lived to revise the work, he would probably have modified some of the most exceptionable passages in this part of it, and it has been an especial object of the present edition, to show that the unfavourable views which Mr. Mill exhibits of the civilization and character of the Hindus, are always extreme, and are not unfrequently erroneous and unjust.

It may be thought inconsistent with the unfavourable opinions thus avowed of the History of British India in such important particulars, to have engaged in preparing a new edition of it for the public; but, notwithstanding the imputations which have been urged to its disavantage, the editor regards the history of Mr. Mill as the most valuable work upon the subject which has yet been published. It is a composition of great industry, of extensive information, of much accuracy on many points, of unrelaxing vigour on all; and even where the reader may not feel disposed to adopt the views it advocates, he will rarely fail to reap advantage from the contemplation of them, as they are advanced to illustrate the relations between India and Great Britain. The vast importance of that connexion is never lost sight of; and in describing the steps by which it was formed, or speculating on the means by which it may be perpetuated, a lofty tone of moral and political principle is maintained; which, even when we may think that the principles are unfairly applied, is entitled to our respect, which, in a great number of instances, commands unhesitating acquiescence and which is well worthy of imitation by all to whom the interests of our Indian empire are matters, either of theoretical reasoning, or of practical administration. In dwelling upon the defects of the work, it has been intended only to explain the motives of those endeavours which have been made to remedy them; and it is hoped, that in the annotations which have been inserted, such correctives will have been provided, as may obviate the evil consequences of what the editor apprehends to be mistaken or mischievous, without impairing the utility, or detracting from the credit of that which he believes to be correct and instructive.

PREFACE OF THE AUTHOR.

IN the course of reading and investigation, necessary for acquiring that measure of knowledge which I was anxious to possess, respecting my country, its people, its government, its interests, its policy, and its laws, I was met, and in some degree surprised, by extraordinary difficulties, when I arrived at that part of my inquiries which related to India. On other subjects, of any magnitude and importance, I generally found, that there was some one book, or small number of books, containing the material part of the requisite information; and in which direction was obtained, by reference to other books, if, in any part, the reader found it necessary to extend his researches. In regard to India, the case was exceeding different. The knowledge, requisite for attaining an adequate conception of that great scene of British action, was collected no where. It was scattered in a great variety of repositories, sometimes in considerable portions, often in very minute ones; sometimes by itself, often mixed up with subjects of a very different nature: and, even where information relating to India stood disjoined from other subjects, a small portion of what was useful lay commonly embedded in a large mass of what was trifling and insignificant; and of a body of statements, given indiscriminately as matters of fact, ascertained by the senses, the far greater part was in general only matter of opinion, borrowed, in succession, by one set of Indian gentlemen from another.[1]

In bestowing the time, labour, and thought, necessary to explore this assemblage of heterogeneous things, and to

[1] The difficulty arising from this source of false information was felt by the very first accurate historian.

Οἱ γαρ ανθρωποι τας ακοας των προγεγενημενων, και ην επιχωρια σφισιν η, ὁμως αβασανιστως παρ' αλληλων δεχονται. Thucyd. lib. i. c. κ'. Other excellent observations to the same purpose are found in the two following chapters.

separate, for my own use, what was true and what was useful, from what was insignificant and what was false, I was led to grieve, that none of those who had preceded me, in collecting for himself a knowledge of Indian affairs, had been induced to leave his collection for the benefit of others; and perform the labour of extracting and ordering the dispersed and confused materials of a knowledge of India, once for all. The second reflection was, that, if those who preceded me had neglected this important service, and in so doing were not altogether free from blame, neither should I be exempt from the same condemnation, if I omitted what depended upon me, to facilitate and abridge to others the labour of acquiring a knowledge of India; an advantage I should have valued so highly, had it been afforded by any former inquirer.

In this manner, the idea of writing a History of India was first engendered in my mind. I should have shrunk from the task, had I foreseen the labour in which it has involved me.

The books, in which more or less of information respecting India might be expected to be found, were sufficiently numerous to compose a library, some were books of travels, some were books of History. Some contained philological, some antiquarian, researches. A considerable number consisted of translations from the writings of the natives in the native tongues; others were books on the religion of the people of India; books on their laws; books on their sciences, manners, and arts.

The transactions in India were not the only transactions of the British nation, to which the affairs of India had given birth. Those affairs had been the subject of much discussion by the press, and of many legislative, executive, and even judicial proceedings, in England. Those discussions and proceedings would form of course an essential part of the History of British India; and the materials of it remained to be extracted, with much labour, from the voluminous records of British literature, and British legislation.

The British legislature had not satisfied itself with deliberating, and deciding; it had also inquired; and, inquiring, it had called for evidence. This call, by the fortunate publicity of parliamentary proceedings, brought forth the records of the councils in India, and their correspondence, with one another, with their servants, and with the constituted authorities in England; a portion of materials, inestimable in its value; but so appalling by its magnitude, that many years appeared to be inadequate to render the mind familiar with it.

Such is a short and very imperfect description of the state of the materials.[1] The operations necessary to draw from them a useful history, formed the second subject of consideration. To omit other particulars, which will easily present themselves, and are common to this with all undertakings of similar nature, a peculiar demand, it is evident, was presented for the exercise of discrimination, that is, of criticism, in a chaotic mass, of such extent, where things relating to the subject were to be separated from things foreign to it; where circumstances of importance were to be separated from circumstances that were insignificant; where real facts, and just inferences, were to be separated from such as were the contrary; and above all things where facts really testified by the senses, were to be descriminated from matters, given as testified by the senses, but which, in truth, were nothing but matters of opinion, confounded with matters of fact, and mistaken for them, in the minds of the reporters themselves.[2]

[1] "Il y avoit plus de choses là-dessus qu'on ne le croyoit communement, mais elles étoient noyées dans une foule de recueils immenses, en langues Latine, Espagnole, Angloise, et Hollandoise, où personne ne s'avisoit de les aller chercher; dans une quantité de routiers très-secs, très ennuyeux, relatifs à cent autres objects, et dont il seroit presque impossible de rendre la lecture intéressante. Les difficultés ne touchent guère ceux qui ne les essayent pas." Hist. des Navigations aux Terres Australes, par M. le Président de Brosse.

[2] "L'on ne sent trop," says Mr. Gibbon, "combien nous sommes porté à mêler nos idées avec celles que nous raportons." Mémoire sur la Monarchie des Médes, Gibbon's Miscel. Works, iii. 61. Ed. 8vo. This infirmity of the human mind, a fact of great importance, both in speculation and in action, the reader, who is not already acquainted with it, will find very elegantly illustrated in one of the chapters of the second volume of the work of Mr. Dugald Stewart, on the Philosophy of the Human Mind. Vol. ii. note B., to which more particular reference is made in Book ii. chap. ix. of the present work. Many examples of it will present themselves in the course of this

A history of India, therefore, to be good for any thing, must, it was evident, be, what, for want of a better appellation, has been called, "A Critical History."[1] To criticise means, to judge. A critical history is, then, a *judging* history. But, if a judging history, what does it judge?

It is evident that there are two, and only two, classes of objects, which constitute the subject of historical judgments. The first is, the matter of statement, the things given by the historian, as things really done, really said, or really thought. The second is, the matter of evidence, the matter by which the reality of the saying, the doing, or thinking, is ascertained.

In regard to evidence, the business of criticism visibly, is, to bring to light the value of each article, to discriminate what is true from what is false, to combine partial statements, in order to form a complete account, to compare varying, and balance contradictory statements, in order to form a correct one.

In regard to the matter of statement, the business of criticism is, to discriminate between real causes and false causes; real effects and false effects; real tendencies and falsely-supposed ones; between good ends and evil ends;

---

history; for as it is a habit peculiarly congenial to the mental state of the natives, so a combination of circumstances has given it unusual efficacy in the minds of those of our countrymen by whom India has been surveyed.

[1] The idea of a critical history is not very old. The first man who seems to have had a distinct conception of it, says, "Je traiterai mon sujet en critique, suivant la règle de St. Paul, *Examinez toutes choses, et ne retenez que ce qui est bon.* L'histoire n'est bien souvent qu'un mélange confus de faux et de vrai, entassé par des écrivains mal instruits, crédules, ou passionnés. C'est au lecteur attentif et judicieux d'en faire le discernement, à l'aide d'une critique, qui ne soit ni trop timide, ni téméraire. Sans le secours de cet art, on erre dans l'histoire, comme un pilote sur la mer, lorsqu'il n'a ni boussole, ni carte marine." Beausobre, Hist. de Manich. Disc. Prélim. p. 7.

The same writer has also said, what is not foreign to the present purpose, "Une histoire critique ne pouvant être trop bien justifiée, j'ai eu soin de mettre en original, au bas des pages, les passages qui servent de preuve aux faits que j'avance. C'est un ennuyeux travail, mais je l'ai cru necessaire. Si l'on trouve les citations trop amples et trop abcndantes, c'est un superflu qui n'a coûté qu'à moi, et le lecteur peut bien m'en pardonner la dépense." Id. Ibid. Pref. p. 24.

A great historian of our own has said: "It is the right, it is the duty of a critical historian to collect, to weigh, to select the opinions of his predecessors; and the more diligence he has exerted in the search, the more rationally he may hope to add some improvement to the stock of knowledge, the use of which has been common to all." Gibbon's Miscel. Works, iv. 589.

means that are conducive, and means not conducive to the ends to which they are applied.

In exhibiting the result of these several judgments, the satisfaction, or the instruction of the reader, is very imperfectly provided for, if the reasons are not adduced. I have no apology therefore to make, for those inductions, or those ratiocinations, sometimes of considerable length which were necessary to exhibit the grounds upon which my decisions were founded. Those critical disquisitions may be well, or they may be ill performed; they may lead to correct, or they may lead to erroneous conclusions; but they are, indisputably, in place; and my work, whatever had been its virtues in other respects, would have remained most imperfect without them.[1]

There will be but one opinion, I suppose, with regard to the importance of the service, which I have aspired to the honour of rendering to my country; for the public are inclined to exaggerate, rather than extenuate, the magnitude of the interests which are involved in the management of their Indian affairs. And it may be affirmed, as a principle not susceptible of dispute, that good management of any portion of the affairs of any community is almost always proportional to the degree of knowledge respecting it diffused in that community. Hitherto the knowledge of India enjoyed by the British community has been singularly defective. Not only among the uneducated, and those who are regardless of knowledge, but among those who are solicitous to obtain a competent

[1] Even those strictures, which sometimes occur, on institutions purely British, will be all found, I am persuaded, to be not only strictly connected with measures which relate to India, and which have actually grown out of those institutions; but indispensably necessary to convey complete and correct ideas of the Indian policy which the institutions in question contributed mainly to shape. The whole course of our Indian policy having, for example, been directed by the laws of parliamentary influence, how could the one be explained without adducing, as in the last chapter of the fourth volume, and in some other places, the leading principles of the other? The result of all the judicial inquiries, which have been attempted in England, on Indian affairs, depending in a great degree on the state of the law in England, how could these events be sufficiently explained, without adducing, as in the chapter on the trial of Mr. Hastings, those particulars in the state of the law of England on which the results in question appeared more remarkably to depend? The importance of this remark will be felt, and, I hope, remembered, when the time for judging of the use and pertinence of those elucidations arrives.

share of information with respect to every other branch of the national interests, nothing is so rare as to meet with a man who can with propriety be said to know anything of India and its affairs. A man who has any considerable acquaintance with them, without having been forced to acquire it by the offices he has filled, is scarcely to be found.

The same must continue to be the case till the knowledge of India is rendered more accessible. Few men can afford the time sufficient for perusing even a moderate portion of the documents from which a knowledge of India, approaching to completeness, must have hitherto been derived. Of those, whose time is not wholly engrossed, either by business or by pleasure, the proportion is very moderate whom the prospect of a task so heavy, and so tedious, as that of exploring the numerous repositories of Indian knowledge, would not deter. And, with respect to the most important of all the sources of information, the parliamentary documents, they were not before the public, and were by the very nature of the case within the reach of a number comparatively small.

But though no dispute will arise about the importance of the work, I have no reason to expect the same unanimity about the fitness of the workman.

One objection will doubtless be taken, on which I think it necessary to offer some observations, notwithstanding the unfavourable sentiments which are commonly excited by almost any language in which a man can urge pretensions which he may be suspected of urging as his own; pretensions which, though they must exist in some degree in the case of every man who writes a book, and ought to be encouraged, therefore, rather than extinguished, had better, in general, be understood, than expressed.

This writer, it will be said, has never been in India; and, if he has any, has a very slight and elementary acquaintance with any of the languages of the East.

I confess the facts, and will now proceed to mention the considerations which led me, notwithstanding, to conclude that I might still produce a work of considerable utility, on the subject of India.

In the first place, it appeared to me, that a sufficient stock of information was now collected in the languages of Europe, to enable the inquirer to ascertain every important point in the history of India. If I was right in that opinion, it is evident, that a residence in India, or a knowledge of the languages of India, was, to express myself moderately, not indispensable.

In the next place, I observed, that no exceptions were taken to a President of the Board of Control, or to a Governor-General, the men intrusted with all the powers of government in India, because they had never been in India, and knew none of its languages.

Again, I certainly knew, that some of the most successful attempts in history had been made, without ocular knowledge of the country, or acquaintance with its languages. Robertson, for example, never beheld America, though he composed its history. He never was in either Germany or Spain, yet he wrote the history of Charles the Fifth. Of Germany he knew uot so much as the language; and it was necessary for him to learn that of Spain, only because the docnments which it yielded were not translated into any of the languages with which he was acquainted. Tacitus, though he never was in Germany, and was certainly not acquainted with the language of our uncultivated ancestors, wrote the exquisite account of the manners of the Germans.

But, as some knowledge may be acquired by seeing India, which cannot be acquired without it; and as it can be pronounced of hardly any portion of knowledge that it is altogether useless, I will not go so far as to deny, that a man would possess advantages, who, to all the qualifications for writing a history of India which it is possible to acquire in Europe, should add those qualifications which can be acquired only by seeing the country and conversing with its people. Yet I have no doubt of being able to make out, to the satisfaction of all reflecting minds, that the man who should bring to the composition of a history of India, the qualifications alone which can be acquired in Europe, would come, in an almost infinite degree, better fitted for the task, than the man who should bring to it the qualifications alone which can be acquired in India; and that the business of acquiring the one set of qualifications is almost wholly incompatible with that of acquiring the other.

For, let us inquire what it is that a man can learn, by going to India, and understanding its languages. He can treasure up the facts which are presented to his senses; he can learn the facts which are recorded in such native books as have not been translated; and he can ascertain facts by conversation with the natives, which have never yet been committed to writing. This he can do; and I am not aware that he can do any thing further.

But, as no fact is more certain, so none is of more importance, in the science of human nature, than this; that the powers of observation, in every individual, are exceedingly limited; and that it is only by combining the observations of a number of individuals, that a competent knowledge of any extensive subject can ever be acquired. Of so extensive and complicated a scene as India, how small a portion would the whole period of his life enable any man to observe!

If, then, we may assume it as an acknowledged fact, that an account of India, complete in all its parts, at any one moment, still more through a series of ages, could never be derived from the personal observation of any one individual, but must be collected from the testimony of a great number of individuals, of any one of whom the powers o perception could extend but a little way, it follows, as a necessary consequence, that a man best qualified for dealing with evidence, is the man best qualified for writing the history of India. It will not, I presume, admit of much dispute, that the habits which are subservient to the successful exploration of evidence are more likely to be acquired in Europe than in India.

The man who employs himself in treasuring up, by means of perception and the languages, the greatest portion of knowledge in regard to India, is he who employs the greatest portion of his life in the business of observing and in making himself familiar with the languages. But the mental habits which are acquired in mere observing, and in the acquisition of languages, are almost as different as any mental habits can be, from the powers of combination, discrimination, classification, judgment, comparison, weighing, inferring, inducting, philosophizing in short: which are the powers of most importance for extracting the precious ore from a great mine of rude historical materials.

Whatever is worth seeing or hearing in India, can be expressed in writing. As soon as every thing of importance is expressed in writing, a man who is duly qualified may obtain more knowledge of India in one year in his closet in England, than he could obtain during the course of the longest life, by the use of his eyes and ears in India.

As soon as the testimony is received of a sufficient number of witnesses, to leave no room for mistake from the partial or the erroneous statements which they may have separately made, it is hardly doubtful, that a man, other circumstances being equal, is really better qualified for forming a correct judgment on the whole, if his information is totally derived from testimony, than if some portion of it is derived from the senses. It is well known, how fatal an effect on our judgments is exerted by those impulses, called partial impressions; in other words, how much our conceptions of a great whole are apt to be distorted, and made to disagree with their object, by an undue impression, received from some particular part. Nobody needs to be informed, how much more vivid, in general, is the conception of an object which has been presented to our senses, than that of an object which we have only heard another man describe. Nobody, therefore, will deny, that of a great scene, or combination of scenes, when some small part has been seen, and the knowledge of the rest has been derived from testimony, there is great danger, lest the impression received from the senses should exert an immoderate influence, hang a bias on the mind, and render the conception of the whole erroneous.

If a man were to lay down the plan of preparing himself for writing the history of India, by a course of observation in the country, he must do one of two things. Either he must resolve to observe minutely a part; or he must resolve to take a cursory review of the whole. Life is insufficient for more. If his decision is to observe minutely; a very small portion comparatively is all that he will be able to observe. What aid can he derive from this, in writing a history, has partly been already unfolded, and may for the rest be confided to the reflections of the intelligent reader.

What I expect to be insisted upon with greatest emphasis is, that, if an observer were to take an expansive view of India, noting, in his progress, those circumstances alone which are of greatest importance, he would come with peculiar advantage to the composition of a history; with lights capable of yielding the greatest assistance in judging even of the evidence of others. To estimate this pretension correctly, we must not forget a well-known and important law of human nature. From this we shall see, that a cursory view, of the nature of that which is here described, is a process in the highest degree effectual, not for removing error, and perfecting knowledge, but for strengthening all the prejudices, and confirming all the prepossessions or false notions, with which the observer sets out. This result is proved by a very constant experience; and may further be seen to spring, with an almost irresistible necessity, from the constitution of the human mind. In a cursory survey, it is understood, that the mind, unable to attend to the whole of an infinite number of objects, attaches itself to a few; and overlooks the multitude that remain. But what, then, are the objects to which the mind, in such a situation, is in preference attracted? Those which fall in with the current of its own thoughts; those which accord with its former impressions; those which confirm its previous ideas. These are the objects to which, in a hasty selection, all ordinary minds are directed, overlooking the rest. For what is the principle in the mind by which the choice is decided? Doubtless that of association. And is not association governed by the predominant ideas? To this remains to be added, the powerful influence of the affections; first, the well-known pleasure which a man finds, in meeting, at every step, with proofs that he is in the right, inspiring an eagerness to look out for that source of satisfaction; and, secondly, the well-known aversion which a man usually has, to meet with proofs that he is in the wrong, yielding a temptation, commonly obeyed, to overlook such disagreeable objects.

He who, without having been a percipient witness in India, undertakes, in Europe, to digest the materials of Indian history, is placed, with regard to the numerous individuals who may have been in India, and of whom one has seen and reported one thing, another has seen and reported another thing, in a situation very analogous to that of the judge, in regard to the witnesses who give their evidence before him. In the investigation of any of those complicated scenes of action, on which a judicial decision is sometimes required, one thing has commonly been observed by one witness, another thing has been observed by another witness; the same thing has been observed in one point of view by one, in another point of view by another witness; some things are affirmed by one, and denied by another. In this scene, the judge, putting together the fragments of information which he has severally received from the several witnesses, marking where they agree and where they differ, exploring the tokens of fidelity in one, of infidelity in another; of correct conception in one, of incorrect conception in another; comparing the whole collection of statements with the general probabilities of the case, and trying it by the established laws of human nature, endeavours to arrive at a complete and correct conception of the complicated transaction, on which he is called to decide. Is it not understood, that in such a case as this, where the sum of the testimony is abundant, the judge, who has seen no part of the transaction has yet, by his investigation, obtained a more perfect conception of it, than is almost ever possessed by any of the individuals from whom he has derived his information?[1]

But, if a life, in any great degree devoted to the collection of facts by the senses and to the acquiring of tongues, is thus incompatible with the acquisition of that knowledge, and those powers of mind, which are most conducive to a masterly treatment of evidence; it is still less compatible with certain other endowments, which the discharge of the highest duties of the historian imperiously demands. Great and difficult as is the task of extracting perfectly the light of evidence from a chaos of rude materials, it is yet not the most difficult of his operations, nor that which requires the highest and rarest qualifications of the mind. It is the business of the historian not merely to display

[1] The Indians themselves have a striking apologue to illustrate the superiority of the comprehensive student over the partial observer.

"One day in conversation," says Mr. Ward, "with the Sungskritu, head pundit of the College of Fort William, on the subject of God, this man, who is truly learned in his own Shastrus, gave the author, from one of their books, the following parable:—In a certain country, there existed a village of blind men, who had heard of an amazing animal called the elephant, of the shape of which, however, they could procure no idea. One day an elephant passed through the place; the villagers crowded to the spot where the animal was standing; and one of them seized his trunk, another his ear, another his tail, another one of his legs. After thus endeavouring to gratify their curiosity, they returned into the village, and sitting down together, began to communicate their ideas on the shape of the elephant, to the villagers; the man who had seized his trunk said, he thought this animal must be like the body of the plantain tree; he who had touched his ear was of opinion, that he was like the winnowing fan; the man who had laid hold of his tail, said he thought he must resemble a snake; and he who had caught his leg declared, he must be like a pillar. An old blind man, of some judgment, was present, who, though greatly perplexed in attempting to reconcile these jarring notions, at length said—You have all been to examine the animal, and what you report, therefore, cannot be false: I suppose, then, that the part resembling the plantain tree must be his trunk; what you thought similar to a fan must be his ear; the part like a snake must be the tail; and that like a pillar must be his leg. In this way, the old man, uniting all their conjectures; made out something of the form of the elephant." A View of the History, Literature, and Religion of the Hindoos. By the Rev. W. Ward. Introduction p. lxxxvii. London Ed. 1817.

the obvious outside of things; the qualities which strike the most ignorant observer, in the acts, the institutions, and ordinances, which form the subject of his statements. His duty is, to convey just ideas of all those objects; of all the transactions, legislative, administrative, judicial, mercantile, military, which he is called upon to describe. But in just ideas of great measures what is implied? A clear discernment, undoubtedly, of their causes; a clear discernment of their consequences; a clear discernment of their natural tendencies; and of the circumstances likely to operate either in combination with these natural tendencies, or in opposition to them. To qualify a man for this great duty hardly any kind or degree of knowledge is not demanded; hardly any amount of knowledge, which it is within the competence of one man to acquire, will be regarded as enough. It is plain, for example, that he needs the most profound knowledge of the laws of human nature, which is the end, as well as instrument, of every thing. It is plain, that he requires the most perfect comprehension of the principles of human society; or the course, into which the laws of human nature impel the human being, in his gregarious state, or when formed into a complex body along with others of his kind. The historian requires a clear comprehension of the practical play of the machinery of government; for, in like manner as the general laws of motion are counteracted and modified by friction, the power of which may yet be accurately ascertained and provided for, so it is necessary for the historian correctly to appreciate the counteraction which the more general laws of human nature may receive from individual or specific varieties, and that allowance for it with which his anticipations and conclusions ought to be formed. In short, the whole field of human nature, the whole field of legislation, the whole field of judicature, the whole field of administration, down to war, commerce, and diplomacy, ought to be familiar to his mind.[1]

[1] "Aux yeux d'un philosophe, les faits composent la partie la moins intéressante de l'histoire. C'est la connoissance de l'homme; la morale, et la politique qu'il y trouve, qui la relèvent dans son esprit." Gibbon, Mém. Sur la Monarchie des Mèdes, Misc. Works, iii. 126. Ed. 8vo.

What then? it will be said, and most reasonably said; do you hold yourself up, as the person in whom all these high qualifications are adequately combined? No. And I am well assured, that by not one of those by whom I shall be criticised, not even by those by whom I shall be treated with the greatest severity, will the distance between the qualifications which I possess, and the qualifications which are desirable in the writer of a history, be estimated at more than it is estimated by myself. But the whole of my life, which I may, without scruple, pronounce to have been a laborious one, has been devoted to the acquisition of those qualifications; and I am not unwilling to confess, that I deemed it probable I should be found to possess them in a greater degree, than those, no part of whose life, or a very small part, had been applied to the acquisition of them. I was also of opinion, that if nobody appeared, with higher qualifications, to undertake the work, it was better it should be done imperfectly, better it should be done even as I might be capable of doing it, than not done at all.

Among the many virtues which have been displayed by the Company's servants, may justly be enumerated the candour with which they themselves confess the necessity under which they are laid, of remaining to a great degree ignorant of India. That they go out to their appointments at a time of life when a considerable stock of general knowledge cannot possibly have been acquired, is a fact which nobody will dispute. And they are the foremost to declare, that their situation in India is such, as to preclude them from the acquisition of local knowledge. Notwithstanding the high degree of talent, therefore, and even of literary talent, which many of them have displayed, more than some very limited portion of the history of India none of them has ventured to undertake.[1]

[1] The following words are not inapplicable, originally applied to a much more limited subject. De quibus partibus singulis, quidam separatim scribere maluerunt, velut onus totius corporis veriti, et sic quoque complures de unaquaque earum libros ediderunt: quas ego omnes ausus contexere prope infinitum mihi laborem prospicio, et ipsa cogitatione suscepti muneris fatigor. Sed durandum est quia cœpimus, et si viribus deficiemur, animo tamen perseverandum. Quinct. Inst. Or. lib. 4. Procem.

"When we consider," said Lord Teignmouth, in his celebrated Minute on the Revenues of Bengal, "the nature and magnitude of our acquisitions, the characters of the people placed under our dominion, their difference of language, and dissimilarity of manners; that we entered upon the administration of the government ignorant of its former constitution, and with little practical experience in Asiatic finance, it will not be deemed surprising that we should have fallen into errors; or if any should at this time require correction.—If we further consider the form of the British Government in India, we shall find it ill calculated for the speedy introduction of improvement. The members composing it are in a state of constant fluctuation, and the period of their residence often expires, before experience can be acquired, or reduced to practice. Official forms necessarily occupy a large portion of time; and the constant pressure of business leaves little leisure for study and reflection, without which no knowledge of the principles and detail of the revenues of this country can be attained. True information is also procured with difficulty, because it is too often derived from mere practice, instead of being deduced from fixed principles." [1]

Lord William Bentinck, after being Governor of Fort St. George, and President of the Council at Madras, expresses himself in very pointed terms. "The result of my own observation, during my residence in India, is, that the Europeans generally know little or nothing of the customs and manners of the Hindoos. We are all acquainted with some prominent marks and facts which all who run may read: but their manner of thinking; their domestic habits and ceremonies, in which circumstances a knowledge of the people consists, is, I fear, in great part wanting to us. We understand very imperfectly their language. They, perhaps, know more of ours; but their knowledge is by no means sufficiently extensive to give a description of

[1] No. 1. Appendix to the Fifth Report of the Select Committee of the House of Commons, on the Affairs of the East India Company, in 1810. This passage the Committee have thought of sufficient importance to be incorporated in their Report.

subjects not easily represented by the insulated words in daily use. We do not, we cannot associate with the natives. We cannot see them in their houses, and with their families. We are necessarily very much confined to our houses by the heat. All our wants and business, which would create a greater intercourse with the natives, is done for us; and we are in fact strangers in the land."[1]

Another servant of the Company, Sir Henry Strachey, distinguished both by his local experience, and by general knowledge, remarking upon the state of judicature, under the English government in India, says, "Another impediment, though of a very different nature from those I have mentioned, and much more difficult to remove, is to me too palpable to be overlooked:—I mean, that arising from Europeans in our situation being necessarily ill qualified, in many points, to perform the duties required of us, as judges and magistrates. This proceeds chiefly from our very imperfect connexion with the natives; and our scanty knowledge, after all our study, of their manners, customs, and languages." "We cannot study the genius of the people in its own sphere of action. We know little of their domestic life, their knowledge, conversation, amusements, their trades, and casts, or any of those national and individual characteristics, which are essential to a complete knowledge of them." "The difficulty we experience in discerning truth and falsehood among the natives may be ascribed, I think, chiefly, to our want of connexion and intercourse with them; to the peculiarity of their manners and habits, their excessive ignorance of our characters; and our almost equal ignorance of theirs."[2]

[1] Observations of Lord William Bentinck, printed in the Advertisement, prefixed to the "Description of the Character, &c., of the People of India," by the Abbé J. A. Dubois, Missionary in the Mysore. If any one should object to the testimony of this Ruler, as that of a man who had not been bred in India, it is to be remembered that the testimony is adduced, as expressing his own opinion, by the translator of that work, whose knowledge of India is not liable to dispute; and given to the world as the opinion of the Court of Directors, to whom the manuscript belonged, and under whose authority and direction, it was both translated and published.

[2] Fifth Report, ut supra, p. 534, 562. "It is a fact," says another enlightened observer, "which, however singular and unfortunate, is yet founded in

One or two things I may venture to affirm that I have done.

I have performed the business of research, with a labour, and patience, which it would not be easy to surpass. And I believe there is no point, of great importance, involved in the History of India, which the evidence I have adduced is not sufficient to determine. I am, at the same time, aware, that in regard to some things there are documents which were not within my reach; and, concerning the latter part of the history, in particular, that there are individuals in England, possessed of information, which, in several places, would have rendered the narrative richer, and perhaps more accurate, in matters of detail. If I shall be found to have performed, with any tolerable success, what I had the means of performing, the liberality which dis-

---

truth, that those persons from whom correct information on these subjects might justly be expected, are generally the least able, from the peculiar circumstances of their situation, to supply it; I mean the Company's servants. —During the early period of their residence in the East, every hour must be employed, in the acquisition of the languages, in the study of the laws of the country, and the manners of the natives: whilst the latter years of their service are still more unremittingly engrossed, in the discharge of the irksome and arduous duties of their profession." Considerations on the Present Political State of India. By Alexander Fraser Tytler, late Assistant-Judge in the Twenty-four Pergunnahs, Bengal Establishment, Preface, p. xii. See other passages to the same purpose, Introduction, p. iv. v. xi.; also i. 77, 357, 415. And Mr. Tytler quotes with peculiar approbation the passages already given from the Minute of Lord Teignmouth.

"I must beg you always to bear in mind, that when an English gentleman undertakes to give an account of Indian manners and habits of private life, he labours under many disadvantages. The obstacles which prevent our ever viewing the natives of India in their domestic circles are great and insuperable; such as the restrictions of caste on their side, rank and situation in ours, &c. We do not intermarry with them, as the Portuguese did; nor do we ever mix with them, in the common duties of social life, on terms of equality. What knowledge we have of their domestic arrangements has been gained chiefly by inquiry, &c." Letters written in a Mahratta camp, &c. by T. D. Broughton, Esq., p. 3.

See to the same purpose, Sir John Malcolm, Sketch of the Political History of India, &c., p. 449.

After adverting to certain erroneous notions on Indian subjects, Lieutenant Moor, the well-informed author of the "Narrative of the Operations of Captain Little's Detachment," observes: "Other opinions, equally correct and entertaining, are indulged by the good people of England; which it is vain to oppose, for the party 'was told so by a gentleman who had been in India, perhaps a voyage or two; but these, however respectable in their profession, are surely not the persons to receive information from, on the subject of the political characters of the East; no more (nor indeed much less) than some gentlemen who may have *resided* a few years in India; for we can easily admit the possibility of a person spending many years of his life in the cities of Calcutta, Madras, or Bombay, without knowing much more of the politics, prejudices, &c. of interior states or countries, than if he had never stirred out of London, Dublin, or Edinburgh." p. 196.

tinguishes the gentlemen of India gives me reason to hope, that many of those who are possessed of useful information, but whom it was impossible for me to find out, will not be unwilling to contribute their aid to the improvement of the History of British India.

Having thus placed before me the materials of Indian history in a state, I believed, of greater fulness and completeness, than any preceding inquirer, I followed the course of my own thoughts in the judgments which I formed; not because I vainly imagined my thoughts more valuable than those of all other men, but because the sincere and determined pursuit of truth imposed this rigid law. It would not allow me to give for true the opinion of any man, till I had satisfied myself that it was true; still less to give the opinion of any man for true, when I had satisfied myself that it was not true.

Mr. Locke has declared; that he who follows his own thoughts in writing, can hope for approvers in the small number alone, of those who make use of their own thoughts in reading; that, by the rest, "a man is not permitted, without censure, to follow his own thoughts in the search of truth, when they lead him ever so little out of the common road."

If this is the severe condition, under which a man follows his own thoughts, in writing even on abstract and general truths, how much harder must be the lot of him who follows them, in writing of the actions and characters of powerful men, and bodies of men? Conscious, however, that I had been faithful in forming my opinions, I believed that I lay under an indispensable obligation to be faithful in expressing them: "to give them without violation of modesty, but yet with the courage of a man unwilling to betray the rights of reason;" and with that manly plainness, which the sincerity of the historical character appeared to require.

I could not overlook the probable consequences. "La perfection d'une Histoire," says a great judge, "est d'être désagréable à toutes les sectes, et à toutes les nations;

car c'est une preuve que l'auteur ne flatte ni les uns, ni les autres, et qu'il a dit à chacun ses vérités."[1]

He who desires to obtain a considerable portion of immediate applause, has two well-known, and well-trodden paths before him.

The first is, to be a zealot for some particular and powerful party; to panegyrize its leaders; attack its opponents; place its principles and practices in the fairest possible light; and labour to bring odium upon the principles and practices of its opponents. This secures the loud and vehement applause of those who are gratified; and the vehement applause of a great party carries, by contagion, along with it, all, or the greater part of those, who are not very strongly engaged by their interests or passions on the opposite side.

The next of the easy ways to the acquisition of fame, consists of two principal parts. The first is, "to wanton in common topics, where a train of sentiment generally received enables a writer to shine without labour, and to conquer without a contest."[2] The second is to deal for ever in compromise; to give up the half of every opinion and principle; go no further in favour of any side of any question, than may be reconcileable in some degree with the good opinion of those who oppose it; and having written as much on one side, as to extract applause from one set of persons, to turn immediately and write as much on the other, as will extract applause from the opposite sort. This is done, without glaring marks of inconsistency, by avoiding all close encounter with the subject, and keeping to vague and general phrases. And in this manner, by a proper command of plausible language, it is easy to obtain reputation with all parties; reputation, not only of great talents, but of great moderation, great wisdom, and great virtue.[3]

[1] Bayle, Eclaircissemens, sur le Dictionnaire.

[2] Rambler, No. ii.

[3] Some considerabfe reputations have been acquired, by praising every thing in one's own country. And there are many persons who sincerely insist upon it, that a writer ought always to contrive to put his country in the right: and that it is a proof of his not being a friend to it, if he ever puts it

If my book were possessed of a much greater share of the titles to applause, than even the partialities of the writer allow him to ascribe to it; I have travelled so very wide of those beaten paths to success, that my only chance for it depends, I cannot fail to perceive, upon the degree in which real liberality, that is, strength of mind, is diffused in the community. I have done enough, doubtless, to secure to myself the malignity of the intemperate, and the narrow-minded, of all parties. I have encouraged myself, however, with the belief, that civilization, and the improvement of the human mind, had in this country attained a sufficient elevation to make a book be received as useful, though it neither exaggerated, nor extenuated the good, or the evil, of any man, or combination of men: to afford a multitude, in every party, far enough removed from the taint of vulgar antipathies, to yield to an author, who spoke with sincerity, and who though he has not spoken with a view to gratify any party, or any individual, most assuredly has never spoken with a view to hurt any, a compensation for the hostilities of the lower and more ungenerous portion of every party.

Though I am aware of many defects in the work which I have ventured to offer to the public; and cannot forget how probable it is, that more impartial and more discerning eyes will discover many which are invisible to mine, I shall yet appeal from the sentence of him, who shall judge of me solely by what I have not done. An equitable and truly useful decision would be grounded upon an accurate estimation of what I have done, and what I have not done, taken together.

It will also deserve to be considered, how much was in the power of any individual to compass. In so vast a subject, it was clearly impossible for one man to accomplish every thing. Some things it was necessary to leave that

---

in the wrong. This is a motive which I utterly disclaim. This is the way, not to be a friend to one's country, but an enemy. It is to bring upon it the disgrace of falsehood and misrepresentation, in the first instance; and, next, to afford it all the inducement, in the writer's power, to persevere in mischievous, or in disgraceful courses.

others might be taken; some things it was necessary to handle but slightly, that others might be treated with greater attention. The geography, for example, alone, would have occupied a life-time. To nicety in the details of geography, I was, therefore, unable to aspire. I followed without much criticism, the authors whom I was consulting, and was only careful to give, with correctness, that outline and those particulars, which were necessary for understanding completely the transactions recorded in my work. To compensate as far as possible, for that which in this department, I myself was unable to perform, I was anxious to afford the reader the advantage of Mr. Arrowsmith's map, by far the finest display which has yet been made of the geography of India; and in any discrepancy, if any should appear, between the text and that reduction of his noble map, which is prefixed to the second volume, I desire the reader to be guided rather by the geographer than by the historian.

In the orthography of Indian names, I should not have aimed at a learned accuracy, even if my knowledge of the languages had qualified me for the task. I have not been very solicitous even about uniformity in the same name; for as almost every author differs from another in the spelling of Eastern names, it appeared to me to be not altogether useless, that, in a book intended to serve as an introduction to the knowledge of India, a specimen of this irregularity should appear.

There is another apparent imperfection, which I should have more gladly removed. In revising my work for the press, some few instances have occurred, in which I have not been able to verify the references to my authorities. This rose from one of the difficulties of my situation. Unable to command at once the large and expensive number of books, which it was necessary for me to consult, I was often dependent upon accident for the period of my supply; and, if not provided with the best channels of information, obliged to pursue my inquiries, at the moment, in such as I possessed. It was often, in these cases, useful, for the sake of memory, and of following out the thread of research, to quote, in the first instance, at second hand. When I afterwards obtained the better authority, it was a matter of anxious care to adjust the reference; but I have met with some instances in which I am afraid the adjustment has not been performed. I mention this, to obviate cavils at the appearance of inaccuracy, where the reality does not exist; inaccuracy in form, rather than in substance; for I have no apprehension that those who shall trace me with the requisite perseverance will accuse me of wanting either the diligence, or the fidelity of an historian; and I ought not to have undertaken the task, if I had not possessed the prospect of obtaining, sooner or later, the means of carrying it to completion.

GLOSSARY.

ADAWLUT. Justice, equity; a court of justice. The terms Dewanny Adawlut, and Foujdarry Adawlut, denote the civil and criminal courts of justice. See Dewanny and Foujdarry.

AMEER, MEER, EMIR, a nobleman.

AMEER UL OMRAH. Noble of nobles, lord of lords.

ANNA. A piece of money, the sixteenth part of a rupee.

AUMEEN. Trustee, commissioner. A temporary collector or supervisor, appointed to the charge of a country on the removal of a Zemindar, or for any other particular purpose of local investigation or arrangement.

AUMIL. Agent, officer, native collector of revenue. Superintendent of a district or division of a country, either on the part of the government, Zemindar, or renter.

AUMILDAR. Agent, the holder of an office. An intendant and collector of the revenue, uniting civil, military, and financial powers, under the Mohammedan government.

AURUNG. The place where goods are manufactured.

BALA-GHAUT. Above the Ghauts, in contradistinction to Payeen Ghaut, below the Ghauts. The terms are generally applied to the high table land in the centre of India, towards its southern extremity.

BANYAN. A Hindu merchant, or shopkeeper. The term Banyan is used in Bengal to denote the native who manages the money-concerns of the European, and sometimes serves him as an interpreter. At Madras, the same description of persons is called Dubash, which signifies one who can speak two languages.

BATTA. Deficiency, discount, allowance. Allowance to troops in the field.

BAZAR. Daily market, or market place.

BEGA. A land measure equal, in Bengal, to about the third part of an acre.

BEGUM. A lady, princess, woman of high rank.

BICE, VAISYA. A man of the third Hindu cast, who by birth is a trader, or husbandman.

BRAHMEN, BRAHMIN, BRAHMAN, BRAMIN. A divine, a priest; the first Hindu cast.

BRINJARRIE, BINJARY, BENJARY, BANJARY. A grain merchant.

BUNGALOW. The name used, in Bengal, for a species of country-house, erected by Europeans.

CALY YUG, CALYOOGUM. The present or fourth age of the world, according to the chronology of the Hindus.

CASTE, CAST. A tribe, or class of people.

CARAVAN-SERAI. The serai of the caravan. See Serai and Choultry.

CAWZI, CAZI, KAZY. A Mohammedan judge, or justice, who also officiates as a public notary, in attesting deeds, by affixing his seal. The same as the officer we name Cadi, in Turkey.

CAUZY-UL-CAZAUT. Judge of judges; the chief judge, or justice.

CHANDALA. One of the names for the most degraded Hindu caste.

CHOKY, CHOKEE. A chair, seat; guard, watch. The station of a guard or watchman. A place where an officer is stationed to receive tolls and customs.

CHOULTRY. A covered public building, for the accommodation of passengers.

CHOUT. A fourth; a fourth part of sums litigated. Mahratta chout; a fourth of the revenues, exacted as tribute by the Mahrattas.

CHOBDAR. Staff-bearer. An attendant on a man of rank. He waits with a long staff, plated with silver, announces the approach of visitors, and runs before his master, proclaiming aloud his titles.

CHUNAM. Lime.

CIRCAR. Head of affairs; the state or government; a grand division of a province; a head man; a name used by Europeans in Bengal, to denote the Hindu writer and accountant, employed by themselves, or in the public offices. See Sircar.

COLLURIES, COLEREES. Saltworks, the places where salt is made.

COOLIES, COOLY. Porter, labourer.

COSS. A term used by Europeans, to denote a road-measure of about two miles, but differing in different parts of India.

CRORE. Ten millions.

CSHATRIYA, KSHATRIYA, CHETTERIE, KHETERY. A man of the second or military caste.

CUTCHERRY. Court of justice; also the public office where the rents are paid, and other business respecting the revenue transacted.

CUTWAL, KATWAL. The chief officer of police in a large town or city, and superintendent of the markets.

DAR. Keeper, holder. This word is often oined with another, to denote the holder of a particular office or employment, as Chob-dar, staff-holder; Zemin-dar, landholder. This compound word, with *i*, *ee*, *y*, added to it, denotes the office, as Zemindar-ee.

DAROGAH. A superintendent, or overseer; as of the police, the mint, &c.

DAUM, DAM. A copper coin, the fortieth part of a rupee.

DECCAN. Literally, the south. A term employed by Mohammedan writers to denote the country between the rivers Nerbuddah and Crishna.

DECOITS. Gang-robbers. *Decoity*, gang-robbery.

DEWAN, DUAN. Place of assembly. Native minister of the revenue department; and chief justice, in civil causes, within his jurisdiction; receiver-general of a province. The term is also used, to designate the principal revenue servant under an European collector, and even of a Zemindar. By this title, the East India Company are receivers-general of the revenues of Bengal, under a grant from the Great Mogul.

DEWANNY, DUANNEE. The office, or jurisdiction of a Dewan.

DEWANNY COURT OF ADAWLUT. A court for trying revenue, and other civil causes.

DOAB, DOOWAB. Any tract of country included between two rivers.

DROOG. A fortified hill or rock.

DUBASH. See Banyan.

DURBAR. The court, the hall of audience; a levee.

FAQUEER, FAKIR. A poor man, mendicant, a religious beggar.

FIRMAUN, PHIRMAUND. Order, mandate. An imperial decree, a royal grant, or charter.

FOUJDAR, FOJEDAR, PHOUSDAR, FOGEDAR. Under the Mogul government, a magistrate of the police over a large district, who took cognizance of all criminal matters within his jurisdiction, and sometimes was employed as receiver-general of the revenues.

FOUJDARRY, FOJEDAREE. Office of a Foujdar.

FOUJDARRY COURT. A court for administering the criminal law.

GHAUT. A pass through a mountain: applied also to a range of hills, and the ford of a river.

GHEE. Clarified butter, in which state they preserve that article for culinary purposes.

GHIRDAWAR, GIRDWAR. An overseer of police, under whom the *goyendas*, or informers, act.

GOMASHTAH. A commissioner, factor, agent.

GOOROO, GURU. Spiritual guide.

GOYENDA. An inferior officer of police; a spy, informer.

GUNGE. A granary, a depôt, chiefly of grain for sale. Wholesale markets, held on particular days. Commercial depôts.

GURRY. A name given to a wall flanked with towers.

HARAM. Seraglio, the plaee where the ladies reside.

HIRCARRA, HARCARRAH. A guide, a spy, a messenger.

HOWDA. The seat of great men fixed on an elephant, not much unlike the body of a sedan in shape.

JAGHIRE, JAGHEER, JAGIR. Literally, the place of taking. An assignment, to an individual, of the government share of the produce of a portion of land. There were two species of jaghires; one, personal, for the use of the grantee; another, in trust, for some public service, most commonly, the maintenance of troops.

JAMMA, JUMMA. Total amount, collection, assembly. The total of a territorial assignment.

JAMMABUNDY, JUMMABUNDY. A written schedule of the whole of an assessment.

JEEL. A shallow lake, or morass.

JINJAL. A large musket, fixed on a swivel; used in Indian forts, and fired with great precision.

JUG. See Yug.

JUNGLE, JANGLE. A wood, or thicket; a country overrun with shrubs, or long grass.

KHALSA. Pure, unmixed. An office of government, in which the business of the revenue department is transacted: the exchequer. Khalsa lands, are lands, the revenue of which is paid into the exchequer.

KHAN, CAWN. A title, similar to that of Lord.

KHILAUT, KELAUT. A robe of honour, with which princes confer dignity.
KILLADAR, KELLADAR. Warder of a castle; commander of a fort.
KIST. Stated payment, instalment of rent.
KUSHOON, CUSHOON. A body of military, corresponding nearest to our term brigade; varying from one to six or eight thousand.

LAC. One hundred thousand.
LASCAR. Properly a camp-follower, but applied to native sailors and artillerymen.

MAAL, MAHL, MEHAL, MHAL. Places, districts, departments. Places, or sources of revenue, particularly of a territorial nature; lands.
MAHA. Great.
MOCURRERY. As applied to lands, it means lands to let on a fixed lease.
MOFUSSIL. Separated, particularized; the subordinate divisions of a district, in contradistinction to Saddur, or Suddur, which implies the chief seat of government.
MOFUSSIL DEWANNY ADAWLUT. Provincial court of civil justice.
MOLUNGEE. Manufacturer of salt.
MOOFTY, MUFTEE. The Mohammedan law-officer who declares the sentence.
MONSOON. The rainy season. The periodical winds and rains.
MOULAVY, MOULAVEE. A learned and religious man, an interpreter of the Mohammedan law.
MOONSHEE. Letter-writer, secretary. Europeans give this title to the native who instructs them in the Persian language.
MOSQUE. A Mohammedan temple.
MUSNUD. The place of sitting: a seat; a throne, or chair of state.
MUTSEDDEY, MUTSEDDEE. Intent upon. Writer, accountant, secretary.

NABOB, NAWAB. Very great deputy vicegerent. The governor of a province under the Mogul government.
NAIB. A deputy.
NAIB NAZIM. Deputy of the Nazim, or Governor.
NAIG, NAIK. A petty military officer.
NAIR. Chief. The Nairs are a peculiar description of Hindus, on the Malabar coast.
NAZIM. Composer, arranger, adjuster. The first officer of a province, and minister of the department of criminal justice.
NIZAM. Order, arrangement; an arranger.
NIZAM UL MULK. The administrator of the empire.
NIZAMUT. Arrangement, government; the office of the Nazim, or Nizam.
NIZAMUT ADAWLUT. The court of criminal justice.

NULLA. Streamlet, water-course.
NUZZER. A vow, an offering; a present made to a superior.

OMRAH. A lord, a grandee, under the Mogul government.

PAGODA. A temple; also the name of a gold coin, in the south of India, valued at eight shillings.
PALANKEEN. A litter in which gentlemen in India recline, and are carried on the shoulders of four men.
PARIAH. A term used by Europeans in India to denote the outcasts of the Hindu tribes.
PATAN. A name applied to the Afghaun tribes.
PESHWA, PAISHWA. Guide, leader. The prime minister of the Mahratta government.
PEON. A footman, a foot soldier; an inferior officer or servant employed in the business of the revenue, police, or judicature.
PERGUNNAH. A small district, consisting of several villages.
PESHCUSH. A present, particularly to government, in consideration of an appointment, or as an acknowledgment for any tenure. Tribute, fine, quit-rent, advance on the stipulated revenues.
PETTAH. The suburbs of a fortified town.
POLLIGAR, POLYGAR. Head of a village district. Military chieftain in the Peninsula, similar to hill-Zemindar in the northern circars.
POLLAM. A district held by a Polligar.
POTAIL. The head man of a village. The term corresponds with that of Mocuddim and Mundul in Bengal.
POTTAH. A lease granted to the cultivators on the part of government, either written on paper, or engraved with a style on the leaf of the fan palmira tree.
PUNDIT. A learned Brahmen.
PURANA, POORAN. Literally ancient: the name given to such Hindu books as treat of creation in general, with the history of their gods and ancient heroes.
PYKE, PAIK. A foot messenger. A person employed as a night-watch in a village, and as a runner or messenger on the business of the revenue.

RAJA. King, prince, chieftain, nobleman; a title in ancient times given to chiefs of the second or military Hindu tribe only.
RAJEPOOT. Literally, son of a king. The name of a warlike race of Hindus.
RANA. A species of raja

RANNY, RANEE. Queen, princess, wife of a rajah.

ROY ROYAN. A Hindu title given to the principal officer of the Khalsa, or chief treasurer of the exchequer.

RUPEE. The name of a silver coin; rated in the Company's accounts, the current rupee at 2*s.*; the Bombay rupee at 2*s.* 3*d.*

RYOT. Peasant, subject; tenant of house or land.

SAYER. What moves; variable imposts' distinct from land rent or revenue; consisting of customs, tolls, licences, duties on goods, also taxes on houses, shops, bazaars, &c.

SEPOY. A native soldier.

SERAI. The same as Choultry.

SHASTER. The instrument of government or instruction; any book of instruction, particularly containing divine ordinances.

SHROFF, SHROF. A banker, or money-changer.

SIRCAR. A government; a man of business.

SIRDAR. Chief, captain, head man.

SOUCAR. A merchant, or banker; a money-lender.

SUBAH. A province such as Bengal. A grand division of a country, which is again divided into circars, chucklas, pergunnahs, and villages.

SUBAHDAR. The holder of the subah, the governor or viceroy.

SUBAHDARY. The office and jurisdiction of a subahdar.

SUDDER. The breast; the fore-court of a house; the chief seat of government, contradistinguished from Mofussil, or interior of the country; the presidency.

SUDDER DEWANNY ADAWLUT. The chief civil court of justice under the Company's government, held at the presidency.

SUDDER NIAZMUT ADAWLUT. The chief criminal court of justice, under the Company's government.

SUDRA, SHUDRA, SOODER. A Hindu of the fourth, or lowest tribe.

SUNNUD. A prop, or support; a patent charter, or written authority for holding either land or office.

TALOOKDAR, A holder of a talook, which is a small portion of land; a petty land-agent.

TANK. Pond, reservoir.

TANNAHDAR. A petty police office.

TEEP. A note of hand; a promissory note given by a native banker, or money-lender, to Zemindars and others, to enable them to furnish government with security for the payment of their rents.

TEHSILDAR. Who has charge of the collections. A native collector of a district, acting under a European or Zemindar.

TOPASSES. Native black Christians, the remains of the ancient Portuguese.

TOPE. A grove of trees.

TUNCAW, TUNKHA. An assignment on the revenue, for personal support, or other purposes.

TUMBRIL. A carriage for the gun ammunition.

VACKEEL, VAQUEEL. One endowed with authority to act for another. Ambassador, agent sent on a special commission, or residing at a court. Native law pleader, under the judicial system of the Company.

VIZIR, VIZIER. Under the Mogul government, the prime minister of the sovereign.

VEDAS, VEDS, BEEDS. Science, knowledge. The sacred scriptures of the Hindus.

YOGIES, JOGIES. Hindu devotees.

YUG, JUG, YOOG. An age; a great period of the Hindus; also a religious ceremony.

ZEMINDAR. From two words signifying, earth, land, and holder or keeper. Land-keeper. An officer who, under the Mohammedan government, was charged with the superintendence of the lands of a district, financially considered; the protection of the cultivators, and the realization of the government's share of its produce, either in money or kind.

ZEMINDARRY. The office or jurisdiction of a Zemindar.

ZENANA. The place where the ladies reside.

ZILLAH. Side, part, district, division. A local division of a country having reference to personal jurisdiction.

N.B. The explanations of the above terms are taken, for the most part, from the Glossary attached to the Fifth Report of the Committee of the House of Commons on Indian affairs, appointed in 1810.

HISTORY

OF

BRITISH INDIA.

BOOK I.—From 1527 to 1707.

Commencement of the British Intercourse with India; and the Circumstances of its Progress, till the Establishment of the Company on a durable Basis by the Act of the Sixth of Queen Anne.

BOOK I.
CHAP. I.

TWO centuries have elapsed, since a few British merchants humbly solicited permission of the Indian princes to traffic in their dominions.

The British power at present embraces nearly the whole of that vast region, which extends from Cape Comorin to the mountains of Tibet, and from the mouths of the Brahmapootra to the Indus.

In the present undertaking, it is proposed to collect, from its numerous and scattered sources, the information necessary to convey correct and adequate ideas of this empire, and of the transactions through which it has been acquired; and, for that purpose:—

I. To describe the circumstances in which the intercourse of the British nation with India commenced, and the particulars of its early progress, till the era when it could first be regarded as placed on a firm and durable basis:

II. To exhibit as accurate a view as possible of the character, the history, the manners, religion, arts, literature and laws of the extraordinary people with whom this intercourse had thus begun; as well as of the physical circumstances, the climate, the soil, and productions, of the country in which they were placed :

III. To deduce to the present times (1805) a history of that part of the British transactions, which have had an immediate relation to India; recording the train of events; unfolding the constitution of that Body, half political, half commercial, through which the business has been ostensibly performed; describing the nature, the progress, and effects of its commercial operations; exhibiting the legislative proceedings, the discussions and speculations, to which the connexion of Great Britain with India has given birth; analyzing the schemes of government which she has adopted for her Indian dominions; and attempting to discover the character and tendency of that species of relation to one another in which the mother country and her eastern dependencies are placed.

The subject forms an entire, and highly interesting, portion of the British History; and it is hardly possible that the matter should have been brought together, for the first time, without being instructive, how unskilfully soever the task may have been performed. If the success corresponded with the wishes of the author, he would throw light upon a state of society, curious, and commonly misunderstood; upon the history of society, which in the compass of his work presents itself in almost all its stages and all its shapes; upon the principles of legislation, in which he has so many important experiments to describe; and upon interests of his country, of which, to a great degree, his countrymen have remained in ignorance, while prejudice usurped the prerogatives of understanding.

CHAPTER I.

From the Commencement of the Efforts to begin a Trade with India, till the Change of the Company from a Regulated to a Joint-stock Company.

THE Portuguese had formed important establishments in India, before the British offered themselves as competitors for the riches of the East.

From the time when Vasco de Gama distinguished his

nation by discovering the passage round the Cape of Good Hope, a whole century had elapsed, during which, without a rival, the Portuguese had enjoyed, and abused, the advantages of superior knowledge and art, amid a feeble and half-civilized people. They had explored the Indian Ocean, as far as Japan; had discovered its islands, rich with some of the favourite productions of nature; had achieved the most brilliant conquests; and, by their commerce, poured into Europe, in unexampled profusion, those commodities of the East, on which the nations at that time set an extraordinary value.

The circumstances of this splendid fortune had violently attracted the attention of Europe. The commerce of India, even when confined to those narrow limits which a carriage by land had prescribed, was supposed to have elevated feeble states into great ones; and to have constituted an enviable part in the fortune even of the most opulent and powerful: to have contributed largely to support the Grecian monarchies both in Syria and Egypt; to have retarded the downfall of Constantinople; and to have raised the small and obscure republic of Venice to the rank and influence of the most potent kingdoms. The discovery therefore of a new channel for this opulent traffic, and the happy experience of the Portuguese, inflamed the cupidity of all the maritime nations of Europe, and set before them the most tempting prospects.

An active spirit of commerce had already begun to display itself in England. The nation had happily obtained its full share of the improvement which had dawned in Europe; and the tranquil and economical reign of Elizabeth had been favourable both to the accumulation of capital, and to those projects of private emolument on which the spirit of commerce depends. A brisk trade, and of considerable extent, had been carried on during the greater part of the sixteenth century with the Netherlands, at that time the most improved and commercial part of Europe. The merchants of Bristol had opened a traffic with the Canary Islands; those of Plymouth with the coasts of Guinea and Brazil: the English now fished on the banks of Newfoundland; and explored the sea of Spitzbergen, for the sovereign of the waters: they engrossed by an exclusive privilege the commerce of Russia: they took an

BOOK I. CHAP. I.

1527.

active part in the trade of the Mediterranean: the company of merchant-adventurers pushed so vigorously the traffic with Germany and the central parts of Europe, as highly to excite the jealousy of the Hans Towns: and the Protestant inhabitants of the Netherlands and France, flying from the persecutions of their own oppressive and bigoted governments, augmented the commercial resources of England by the capital and skill of a large importation of the most ingenious and industrious people in Europe.[1]

In these circumstances, the lustre of the Portuguese transactions in the East peculiarly attracted the admiration of the English. Already a most adventurous spirit of navigation was roused in the nation. The English were the first who had imitated the example of the Spaniards in visiting the New World. In 1497, Cabot, with a small squadron, explored the coast of America, from Labrador to Virginia, and discovered the islands of Newfoundland and St. John.[2] An English merchant, named Robert Thorne, who had been stationed for many years at Seville in Spain, and had acquired particular knowledge of the intercourse which the Portuguese had opened with the East, presented a project to Henry VIII. about the year 1527, the accomplishment of which he imagined would place his countrymen in a situation no less enviable than that of the Portuguese. As that nation had obtained a passage to India by a course to the south-east, and pretended a right, which they defended by force, to its exclusive occupation, he supposed that his countrymen might reach the same part of the globe by sailing to the north-west, and thus obtain a passage at once expeditious and undisputed.[3] What effect this representation produced on the mind of Henry is not accurately known. But two voyages in the course of his reign were undertaken for the discovery of a north-west passage, one about this period,[4] and another ten years later.[5]

[1] Anderson's History of Commerce in the reign of Elizabeth, passim. See also Hakluyt's Voyages, ii. 3, 96. Ibid. iii. 690. Guicciardini's Description of the Netherlands. Sir William Temple. Camden, 408.

[2] Hakluyt, iii. 4. Rymer's Fœdera, xii. 595. Anderson's History of Commerce, published in Macpherson's Annals, ii. 11. Robertson's History of America, iv. 138.

[3] Hakluyt, iii. 129. Harris's Collection of Voyages, i. 874.

[4] Hakluyt, ut supra.

[5] Ibid. 131.

1567.

Nothing can more clearly prove to us the ardour with which the English coveted a share in the riches supposed to be drawn from the East, than the persevering efforts which they made to discover a channel from which the Portuguese should have no pretence to exclude them. Two attempts in the reign of Henry, to obtain a passage by the north-west, having failed, their exploring fancy anticipated a happier issue from a voyage to the north-east. A small squadron, under the direction of Sir Hugh Willoughby, was fitted in the reign of Edward VI.; and, sailing along the coast of Norway, doubled the North Cape,[1] where it was encountered by a storm. The ship of Sir Hugh was driven to an obscure spot in Russian Lapland, where he and his crew perished miserably by the climate. The other principal vessel found shelter in the harbour of Archangel, and was the first foreign ship by which it was entered. So well did Chancellour, its captain, improve the incident, that he opened a commercial intercourse with the natives, visited the monarch in his capital, stipulated important privileges for his countrymen, and laid the foundation of a trade which was immediately prosecuted to no inconsiderable extent. This voyage but little damped the hopes of obtaining a north-east passage to the riches of India. Some vigorous attempts were made by the company in whose hands the commerce with Russia was placed;[2] the last of them in 1580, when two ships were sent out to explore the passage through the Straits of Waygatz. After struggling with many perils and difficulties from the ice and the cold, one of the vessels returned unsuccessful; of the other no intelligence was ever received.

Before this hope was abandoned, the project of obtaining a passage by the north-west was ardently resumed. No fewer than six voyages were made in the course of a few years. Two barks of twenty-five tons each, and a pinnace of ten, sailed under Martin Frobisher in the year 1567, and entered Hudson's Bay, which they at first imagined was the inlet about to conduct them to the golden shore. The same navigator was encouraged to make a second attempt in the same direction in 1576. As he brought home some minerals, which were supposed to be

[1] Hakluyt, i. 226, etc.
[2] Anderson's History of Commerce, in Macpherson, ii. 166.

BOOK I. CHAP. I.

1567.

impregnated with gold, the attention of government was excited; and, after two years, Frobisher was sent out with fifteen of the Queen's ships, miners for the supposed ore, and 120 persons as the rudiments of a colony. Having spent his provisions, and lost one of his ships, but not having found the expected passage, nor left his settlers, he returned with 300 tons of the supposed treasure, which proved to be only a glittering sand.[1] The nation persevered in its hopes and its enterprises. A few years afterwards, Captain John Davis sailed as far as 66° 40′ north, and discovered the straits distinguished by his name. In a second voyage, undertaken in 1586, he explored in vain the inlet which he had thus discovered, and after a few years was enabled to proceed in a third expedition, which had no better success than the preceding two.[2]

After the defeat of so many efforts to discover a new passage to India, the English resolved to be no longer deterred by the pretensions of the Portuguese. A voyage to China by the Cape of Good Hope was undertaken in 1582. Four ships proceeded to the Coast of Brazil, fought with some Spanish men-of-war, and were obliged to return for want of provisions.[3] Another expedition, consisting of three ships, was fitted out in 1596, the commander of which was furnished with Queen Elizabeth's letters to the Emperor of China. This voyage proved eminently unfortunate. The ships were driven upon the coast of Spanish America, where only four men were preserved alive from the effects of storms, famine, and disease.[4]

Amid these unsuccessful endeavours two voyages were accomplished, which animated the hopes of the nation, and pointed out the way to more fortunate enterprises. Francis Drake, the son of a clergyman in Kent, who at a tender age had been put an apprentice to the master of a slender bark trading to the coast of Holland and France, had early evinced that passionate ardour in his profession which is the usual forerunner of signal success.[5] He gained the

[1] Hakluyt. Anderson, ut supra, ii. 145, 158, 159.

[2] Hakluyt. Anderson, ut supra, ii. 175, 180, 185.—M. It is scarcely necessary to add to these the attempts which have been made within the last few years to determine the practicability of the north-west passage, by the voyages of Captains Ross and Parry.—W.

[3] Anderson, ut supra, ii. 171.

[4] Purchas, b. iii. sect. 2. Anderson, ii. 210.

[5] Hakluyt, iii. 440. Harris's Collection of Voyages, i. 14. Camden's Annals, 301, &c.

1577.

affections of his master, who left him his bark at his death: at the age of eighteen he was purser of a ship which sailed to the Bay of Biscay: at twenty he made a voyage to the coast of Guinea; in 1565 he ventured his all in a voyage to the West Indies, which had no success; and in 1567 he served under his kinsman Sir John Hawkins, in his unprosperous expedition to the Bay of Mexico. In these different services, his nautical skill, his courage, and sagacity, had been conspicuously displayed. In 1570 his reputation enabled him to proceed to the West Indies with two vessels under his command. So vehemently was he bent on executing some great design, that he renewed his visit the next year, for the sole purpose of obtaining information. He had no sooner returned than he planned an expedition against the Spaniards, executed it with two ships and seventy-three men, sacked the town of Nombre de Dios, and returned with great treasure. It is said that, in this voyage, he saw from the top of a high tree, that is, fancied he saw, across the American isthmus, the Southern Ocean, and became inflamed with the desire of reaching it in a ship of England.

For this expedition he prepared on a great scale; obtaining the commission of the Queen, and the command of five vessels, one of 100 tons, another of eighty, one of fifty, another of thirty, and a pinnace of fifteen; the whole manned with 164 select sailors. The historians of his voyage are anxious to display the taste and magnificence, as well as judgment, of his preparations; expert musicians, rich furniture, utensils of the most curious workmanship, vessels of silver for his table, and many of the same precious metal for his cook-room.

The expedition sailed from Plymouth on the 13th of December, 1577. Having passed the Straits of Magellan, and ravaged the western coast of Spanish America, Drake feared the encounter of a Spanish fleet, should he attempt to return in the same direction, and formed the bold design of crossing the Pacific Ocean, and regaining England by the Cape of Good Hope.

With one ship, the only part of the fleet which remained, he steered along the coast of America to the latitude of 38° north, and then entered upon that immense navigation, in which Magellan, the only circumnavigator who preceded

BOOK I. CHAP. I. 1577.

him, had sustained so many disasters. No memorable occurrence attended the voyage. Of the islands which have been discovered in the Pacific Ocean none were observed till he approached the Asiatic coast. Fixing his attention on the Moluccas, of which the fame had been circulated in Europe by the rich spices thence imported by the Portuguese, he passed, with little observation, the more eastern part of the numerous islands which stud the Indian seas, and held his course for Tidore. From intelligence, received on the passage, he waved his intention of landing on that island, and steered for Ternate, the sovereign of which he understood to be at enmity with the Portuguese.

His intercourse with that island forms a remarkable epoch in the history of the British nation in India, as it was the beginning of those commercial transactions which have led to the greatest results. The King, having received assurances that his new visitants came with no other intention than that of trading with his country, gave them a very favourable reception. This monarch possessed considerable power, since the English navigators were informed that he ruled over seventy islands, besides Ternate, the most valuable of all the Moluccas; and in the visits which they paid to his court they were eye-witnesses of no contemptible magnificence. They exchanged presents with him, and received him on board: they traded with his subjects, laid in a cargo of valuable spices, and acquainted themselves with the nature and facilities of a commerce which was the object of admiration and envy in Europe.

Not satisfied with the information or the commodities which they received on one island, they visited several, being always amazed at their prodigious fertility, and in general delighted with the manners of the inhabitants. Among other places they landed in the great island of Java, famous afterwards as the seat of the Dutch government in India. They held some friendly intercourse with the natives, and departed with a tolerable knowledge both of the character of the people, and the productions of the country.

They now spread their sails for that navigation between Europe and India, to which the Portuguese claimed an exclusive right, and by which they monopolized the traffic

1580.

with India. Those discoverers had craftily disseminated in Europe terrific accounts of dangers and horrors attending the navigation round the Cape of Good Hope. As the voyage of the English proved remarkably prosperous, they were surprised and delighted with the safety and ease which seemed to them to distinguish this envied passage, and conceived a still more lofty opinion of the advantages enjoyed by the nation that engrossed it. After leaving Java, the first land which they touched was the Cape of Good Hope. They landed once more at Sierra Leone, on the African coast, and received supplies which sufficed for the remainder of the voyage.

They arrived at Plymouth on Monday, the 26th of September, 1580, after a voyage of two years, ten months, and a few days; exhibiting to the wondering eyes of the spectators the first ship in England, and the second in the world, which had circumnavigated the globe. The news quickly spread over the whole kingdom, which resounded with applause of the man who had performed so daring and singular an enterprise. Whoever wished to be distinguished as the patron of merit, hastened to confer some mark of his admiration on Captain Drake. The songs, epigrams, poems, and other pieces, which were composed in celebration of his exploits, amounted to several collections.[1] The Queen, after some delay, necessary to save appearances with the Spanish court, which loudly complained of the depredations of Drake, though as reprisals perhaps they were not undeserved, paid a visit in person to the wonderful ship at Deptford; accepted of an entertainment on board, and conferred the honour of knighthood on its captain; observing, at the same time, that his actions did him more honour than his title.[2]

We may form some conception of the ardour which at that time prevailed in England for maritime exploits, by

[1] Harris is not satisfied with the merit of those productions, which reached not, in his opinion, the worth of the occasion; and seems to be rather indignant that no modern poet has rivalled the glory of Homer, "by displaying in verse the labours of Sir Francis Drake.

[2] Her Majesty appears to have been exquisitely gracious. The crowd which thronged after her was so great, that the bridge, which had been constructed between the vessel and the shore, broke down with the weight, and precipitated 200 persons into the water. As they were all extricated from their perilous situation without injury, the Queen remarked that so extraordinary an escape could be owing only to the Fortune of Sir Francis Drake. Harris, i. 20

BOOK I. CHAP. I. 1586.

the number of men of rank and fortune, who chose to forego the indulgences of wealth, and to embark their persons and properties in laborious, painful, and dangerous expeditions. Among them we find such names as those of the Earls of Cumberland and Essex, of Sir Richard Greenville, Sir Walter Raleigh, Sir Humphry Gilbert, Sir Robert Dudley, who prepared squadrons at their own expense, and sailed to various parts of the world. No undertaking of this description was attended with more important circumstances than that of Thomas Cavendish.

This gentleman, descended from a family of distinction, and inheriting a large estate in the county of Suffolk, had been early fired with a passion for maritime adventure. In a vessel of his own, he had accompanied Sir Richard Greenville in his unsuccessful voyage to Virginia; and now sold or mortgaged his estate, to equip a squadron with which he might rival the glory of Drake. It consisted of three ships, the largest of 140 tons, one of sixty, and a bark of about forty, the whole supplied with two years' provisions and manned with 126 officers and sailors, of whom several had served in the celebrated expedition of Drake.

They sailed from Plymouth on the 21st of July, 1586. Their voyage through the Straits of Magellan, and the depredations which they proceeded to commit along the western coast of the American continent, not only in the spirit of avarice, but even of wanton devastation, form no part of our present subject, and may without regret be left to other recorders. They had reached the coast of California, and nearly 24° of northern latitude; when, having taken a very rich Spanish ship, and completed their schemes of plunder, they commenced their voyage across the Pacific Ocean. They left the coast of America on the 19th of November, and came in sight of Guam, one of the Ladrone Islands, on the 3rd of January. From this island they were visited by sixty or seventy canoes full of the inhabitants, who brought provisions to exchange for commodities, and so crowded about the ship, that the English, when they had finished their traffic, discharged some of their fire-arms to drive them away.[1] With the Philippines, to which they

[1] I am sorry to observe that no great respect for human life seems to have been observed in this proceeding; since, directly implying that the guns had been charged with shot, and levelled at the men, the historian of the voyage

1588.

next proceeded, they opened a more protracted intercourse, having cast anchor at one of the islands, where they lay for nine days, and carried on an active trade with the inhabitants.

The cluster of islands, to which the Europeans have given the name of the Philippines, was discovered by Magellan. Philip II., shortly after his accession to the Spanish throne, planted there a colony of Spaniards, by an expedition from New Spain; and a curious commerce had from that time been carried on across the Great Pacific, between this settlement and the dominions of Spain in the new world. To Manilla, the capital of the Philippine colony, the Chinese who resorted thither in great numbers, brought all the precious commodities of India; and two ships were sent annually from New Spain, which carried to the Philippines the silver of the American mines, and returned with the fine productions of the East. The impatience, however, of the natives under the Spanish yoke, was easily perceived. When they discovered that the new visitors were not Spaniards, but the enemies of that people they eagerly testified their friendship; and the princes of the island, where Cavendish landed, engaged to assist him with the whole of their forces, if he would return and make war upon the common adversary.

This adventurous discoverer extensively explored the intricate navigation of the Indian Archipelago, and observed the circumstances of the new and extraordinary scene with a quick and intelligent eye. He visited the Ladrones; shaped a course among the Philippines, which brought the greater part of those islands within his view; passed through the Moluccas; sailed along that important chain of islands, which bounds the Indian Archipelago from the Strait of Malacca to the extremity of Timor; and passing the Strait of Bally, between the two Javas,[1] cast anchor on the south-west side of the great island of that

jocosely remarks, "that 'tis ten to one if any of the savages were killed, for they are so very nimble that they drop immediately into the water, and dive beyond the reach of all danger, upon the least warning in the world." Harris's Collection of Voyages, i. 27.

[1] That is, between Java and the island of Bali. De Barros observes that the distinction of two Javas is unknown to the Javanese; and the accounts of Java Major and Java Minor, given by Europeans, are inconsistent with each other. The Java Minor of Marco Polo seems to have been the east coast of Sumatra, but Little Java is now applied exclusively to Bali. Raffles, History of Java, i. p. 3.—W.

BOOK I. CHAP. I.

name, where he traded with the natives for provisions, and formed a sort of treaty, stipulating a favourable reception when his visit should be renewed.

1588.

He sailed for the Cape of Good Hope on the 16th of March, careful to treasure up information respecting a voyage, which was now the channel of so important a commerce. He made astronomical observations; he studied the weather, the winds, and the tides; he noted the bearing and position of lands; and omitted nothing which might facilitate a repetition of the voyage to himself or his countrymen. He passed the Cape with prosperous navigation about the middle of May, and, having touched at St. Helena to recruit his stores, he landed at Plymouth on the 9th of September, 1588. In the letter which, on the very day of his arrival, he wrote to Lord Hunsdon, then Chamberlain to Queen Elizabeth, he says, "I navigated to the islands of Philippines, hard upon the coast of China, of which country I have brought such intelligence as hath not been heard of in these parts: a country, the stateliness and riches of which I fear to make report of, lest I should not be credited. I sailed along the islands of Moluccas, where, among some of the heathen people, I was well entreated, and where our countrymen may have trade as freely as the Portugals, if they themselves will."

The tide of maritime adventure which these splendid voyages were so well calculated to swell, flowed naturally towards India, by reason of the fancied opulence, and the prevailing passion for the commodities, of the East. The impatience of our countrymen had already engaged them in a circuitous traffic with that part of the globe. They sailed to the eastern shores of the Mediterranean Sea, where they found cargoes of Indian goods conveyed over land: and a mercantile company, denominated the Levant Company, was instituted, according to the policy of the age, to secure to the nation the advantages of so important a commerce.[1] The Company which, after the discovery of the port of Archangel, had been formed to carry on the trade with Russia, had opened a communication with Persia, and thence imported the commodities of India: Mr. Anthony Jenkinson, an active and enterprising agent

[1] Monson's Naval Tracts. Hakluyt. Anderson's History of Commerce, published in Macpherson's Annals, ii. 169, 198. Rymer's Fœdera.

1593.

of the Russia Company, sailed down the Volga, in 1558, to the Caspian Sea, which he crossed into Persia, and at Boghar,[1] a city of some importance, found merchants not only from various parts of the Persian empire, but from Russia, and China, and India. This voyage he performed seven times; and opened a considerable trade for raw and wrought silk, carpets, spices, precious stones, and other Asiatic productions. In 1563, there was business enough to require the presence of three agents at Casbin, the seat of the Persian court; and the traffic flourished for several years.

Accidental circumstances contributed to enliven the admiration excited by the Indian trade. During that expedition to the coast of Spain, on which Sir Francis Drake was sent, by Queen Elizabeth, to harass the Spanish shipping, and prevent, as far as possible, the preparations for the Invincible Armada, he took one of the Portuguese ships from India, known at that time by the name of Carracks. The value of her cargo inflamed the imaginations of the merchants; and the papers which she carried afforded information respecting the traffic in which she was engaged.[2] A still more important capture of the same sort was made in 1593. An expedition fitted out for the West Indies by Sir Walter Raleigh, and commanded by Sir John Burroughs, encountered near the Azores, the greatest of all the Portuguese Carracks, a vessel of 1,600 tons, carrying 700 men, and thirty-six brass cannon; and, after an obstinate contest, carried her into Dartmouth. This was the largest vessel which had ever been seen in England, laden with spices, calicoes, silks, gold, pearls, drugs, porcelain, ebony, &c.; and stimulated the impatience of the English to be engaged in so opulent a commerce.[3]

Some members of the Turkey or Levant Company

[1] This is not, as might be inferred, from the way in which it is mentioned, a city of Persia, but Bokhara, the capital of the kingdom so named; independent of Persia at the time of Jenkinson's visit. The trade of Bokhara, according to him, was inconsiderable: merchants from Russia, Persia, and Balkh resorted thither; but they brought few commodities, and took still fewer. The trade of Persia was then more valuable; but Bokhara has become, in modern times, the chief mart of Central Asia. Murray's Asia, i. 321. Burnes's Journey to Bokhara.—W.

[2] This is not a conclusion merely drawn from the circumstances of the case, which however would sufficiently warrant it; but stated on the testimony of Cambden, who related what he heard and saw. Cambden's Annals. Anderson's History of Commerce.

[3] Anderson's History of Commerce, in Macpherson's Annals, ii. 201.

BOOK I. CHAP. I. 1593.

finished about the same time an expedition to India.[1] They had carried some cloth, tin, and other goods from Aleppo to Bagdad, which they next conveyed down the Tigris to Ormus in the Persian Gulf, and thence transported to Goa, the great mart between the Portuguese and Indians on the coast of Malabar. From this place they commenced an extensive survey of the adjoining countries; repaired to Agra, at that time the capital and residence of the Mogul Emperor; visited Lahor; traversed Bengal; travelled to Pegu and Malacca; and, returning by sea to Ormus, retraced their steps to Aleppo, whence they sailed for England bearing with them important and extensive information respecting the countries they had explored. Intelligence now poured itself into the nation by a variety of channels. An Englishman of the name of Stevens, had sailed with the Portuguese from Lisbon to Goa, by the Cape of Good Hope, and wrote an account of his voyage, which was read with avidity, and contributed to swell the general current of enterprise which now ran so vehemently toward India.[2]

The first application which was made to Government, was by a memorial, in the name of "divers merchants," addressed to the Lords of Council, in 1589, for the royal permission to send three ships, and as many pinnaces, on a voyage to India. They enumerated the different places at which the Portuguese had already effected settlements, on the coasts of Malabar and Coromandel, in Malacca, and in the Banda and Molucca islands, places from which it seemed to be tacitly understood that other nations were bound to abstain. But they added, that the islands and shores of the Indian Ocean presented many other places, open to the enterprise of English merchants, an intercourse with which might yield the greatest advantage.[3]

[1] They returned to London in 1591. Anderson, ut supra, ii. 198.—M. The travellers were Messrs. Fitch, Newberry, Leedes, and Storey: they travelled to India, by way of Syria and Persia, in 1583. Storey became a monk at Goa, Leedes entered into the service of the emperor Akbar, and Newberry died on his way home by the Punjab. Fitch visited various parts of the East, and returned to England in 1591: he published an account of his travels. They took with them, letters from Elizabeth to the Great Mogul, and the Emperor of China. Hakluyt, ii. 375.—W.

[2] Harris's Voyages, i. 875.

[3] This Memorial is preserved in the State Paper Office, and a short account of it has been given us by Mr. Bruce. Annals of the East India Company, i. 109.

1599.

What reception this application received, is unknown. But the unfortunate expedition of Captain Raymond; remarkable as being the first of which India was the immediate destination, though its object was not trade, so much as plunder, by cruising against the Portuguese; was fitted out in 1591. Disease had made such ravages among the crews, before they reached the Cape of Good Hope, that one of the vessels was sent home with the sick; and the rest, two in number, had not long doubled the Cape, when the principal ship was lost in a storm. Captain James Lancaster, in the remaining vessel, after a disastrous voyage, sailed to the West Indies, where he lost the ship, and with great difficulty found means to return in a French privateer.[1]

While the English fluctuated between desire and execution in this important enterprise, the Dutch, in 1595, boldly sent four ships to trade with India by the Cape of Good Hope.[2] This exploit added fuel, at once, to the jealousy, and to the ambition of the English. In 1599, an association was formed, and a fund subscribed, which amounted to 30,133*l.* 6*s.* 8*d.*, and consisted of 101 shares; the subscriptions of individuals varying from 100*l.* to 3,000*l.* It was agreed to petition the Queen for a warrant to fit out three ships, and export bullion, and also for a charter of privileges. A committee of fifteen, the origin and foundation of a Court of Directors, were chosen to manage. The approbation of the government was readily signified; but as a treaty was then pending with Spain, policy appeared to counsel delay. The subscribers, known by the name of the adventurers, were impatient, and presented a memorial, distinguishing the places with which the Spaniards and Portuguese had established an intercourse, from others to which, without any ground of complaint on the part of those nations, the English might with unspeakable advantage resort. The council replied, that "it was more beneficiall for the generall state of merchandise to entertayne a peace, then that the same should be hindered, by the standing wth ye Spanishe comissions, for the mayntayning of this trade, to forgoe the opportuncty

[1] Anderson's History of Commerce, in Macpherson's Annals, ii. 190. Harris's Voyages, i. 875.

[2] Anderson, ut supra, ii. 209. Harris's Voyages, i. 920.

BOOK I. CHAP. I.

1600.

of the concluding of the peace."[1] The memorial was referred to Sir Foulke Greville, who made a favourable report: and in the course of the same year, the Queen sent John Mildenhall[2] overland, by Constantinople, on an embassy to the Great Mogul.

It was attended with little success. The Portuguese and Venetian agents exerted themselves to raise suspicions against the designs of the English, and effectually obstructed the endeavours of the ambassador.

Towards the end of the year 1600, the efforts of the adventurers were renewed; and the consent of government was obtained to proceed in preparations for an Indian voyage, while the patent of incorporation was still under consideration. Meanwhile, an application was made from government, with what views does not appear, for the employment of Sir Edward Michelbourne in the expedition. The answer of the committee, though petitioners for a favour not yet conceded, affords a curious specimen of their independence, and of the mode of thinking of the times. They stated it as their resolution "not to employ any *gentleman* in any place of charge," and requested "that they may be allowed to sort theire business with men of their own qualitye, lest the suspicion of employm[t] of *gentlemen* being taken hold uppon by the generalitie, do dryve a great number of the adventurers to withdraw their contributions."[3] The adventure was prosecuted with ardour. On the 8th of October, the five following ships were already provided; the Malice Scourge of 200 men, and 600 tons burthen; the Hector, of 100 men, and 300 tons; the Ascension, of 80 men, and 260 tons; the Susan, of 80 men, and 240 tons; and a pinnace of 40 men, and 100 tons. To provision these ships for twenty months, the cost was computed at 6,600*l.* 4*s.* 10*d.*; and the cargo, consisting of iron and tin, wrought and unwrought, of lead, cloths, and some smaller articles, chiefly intended as

[1] Minutes, etc. (Indian Register Office). Bruce's Annals, i. 112.

[2] John Mildenhall, a merchant, was sent with a letter from the Queen to the Emperor Akbar, whilst the establishment of the Company was under discussion. He left Aleppo in 1600, but did not reach Agra till 1603. After a residence of three years, he obtained a firmaun from Jehangir. He returned to England some time about 1607: from thence he went back to Agra, where he turned Roman Catholic, and died in June, 1614. Orme, Fragments, 341.—W.

[3] Minutes of a General Court of Adventurers, preserved in the Indian Register Office. Bruce's Annals, i. 128.

1600.

presents, was estimated, exclusive of bullion, at 4,545*l*. It was determined that thirty-six factors or super-cargoes should be appointed for the voyage, divided into separate classes, rising one above another in trust and emoluments. Captain James Lancaster, whose difficult return from a predatory expedition has already been mentioned, was chosen to command the fleet; and on the 31st of December, the charter of privileges was obtained.[1]

This charter, the origin of a power so anomalous and important as that which was afterwards accumulated in the hands of the East India Company, contained nothing which remarkably distinguished it from the other charters of incorporation, so commonly in that age bestowed upon trading associations. It constituted the adventurers a body politic and corporate, by the name of "the Governor and Company of Merchants of London, trading to the East Indies;" and vested them with the usual privileges and powers. The plan which they had already adopted for the management of their affairs, by a committee of twenty-four, and a chairman, both to be chosen annually, was confirmed and rendered obligatory. With a reservation in favour of the rights granted to other associations, and with prohibition extending to all such places as might be already occupied by the subjects of states in amity with her Majesty, and whose objection to rivals should be declared, the privilege of trading to the East Indies, that is, to all places beyond the Cape of Good Hope and the Straits of Magellan, was bestowed upon the Company, with power to export in each voyage 30,000*l*. in gold and silver; also English goods for the first four voyages exempt from duties, and to re-export Indian goods in English ships under the same privilege to the end of the charter. According to the principle of the times, the charter was exclusive: prohibiting the rest of the community from trading within the limits assigned to the Company, but granting to them the power, whenever they pleased, of bestowing licenses for that purpose. It was granted for a period of fifteen years; but under condition that, if not found to be advantageous to the country, it might be annulled at any time under a notice of two years: if advan-

[1] Bruce's Annals, i. 129—136. Anderson's History of Commerce, in Macpherson's Annals, ii. 216. Harris's Collection of Voyages, i. 875.

BOOK I. CHAP. I.

tageous, it might, if desired by the Company, be renewed for fifteen years.

1600.

The ardour of individuals, where any thing is to be risked, is more easily excited than upheld. Though the list of subscribers, while the scheme of Indian adventure was yet in contemplation, had been readily filled up, the calls of the committees for the payment of the instalments were very imperfectly obeyed. Even when the charter was obtained, it was either understood to confer no power of compelling payment, or the directors were afraid to make use of it. Instead of exacting the stipulated sums, and trading upon the terms of a joint-stock company, the subscribers who had paid were invited to take upon themselves the expense of the voyage, and, as they sustained the whole of the risk, to reap the whole of the profit.

The sums which were thus advanced amounted to 68,373*l.* which greatly exceeded the capital originally subscribed. Of this, 39,771*l.* was expended in the purchase and equipment of ships—the four, excluding the pinnace, which were taken up by the committee of original adventurers: 28,742*l.* was expended in bullion: and 6,860*l.* in goods; consisting partly of British commodities, cloth, lead, tin, cutlery, glass, &c.; partly of foreign, as quicksilver, Muscovy hides, &c. The choice of Captain Lancaster to command the fleet was renewed; and it sailed from Torbay on the 2d of May, 1601, carrying letters of recommendation from the Queen to the sovereigns of the different ports to which it might resort.[1]

[1] Bruce's Annals, i. 146. "But forasmuch," says Sir William Monson (Naval Tracts, iii., Churchill's Collection of Voyages, 475), "as every innovation commonly finds opposition, from some out of partiality, and from others as enemies to novelty; so this voyage, though at first it carried a great name and hope of profit, by the word India, and example of Holland, yet was it writ against." He then exhibits the objections, seven in number, and subjoins an answer. The objections were shortly as follows; the answers may be conceived :—

1. The trade to India would exhaust the treasure of the nation by the exportation of bullion.
2. It would consume its mariners by an unhealthy navigation.
3. It would consume its ships by the rapid decay produced in the southern seas.
4. It would hinder the vent of our cloth, now exported in exchange for the spices of the foreign merchants.
5. It was a trade of which the returns would be very slow.
6. Malice to the Turkey Company was the cause of it, and jealousy and hatred from the Dutch would be the unhappy effect.
7. It would diminish the Queen's customs by the privilege of exporting bullion duty free.

These objections, with the answers, may also be seen in Anderson's History of Commerce, *ad an.*

A first and experimental attempt was naturally unproductive of any remarkable result: but the first voyage of the East India Company was not discouraging. The first place in India to which they repaired was Acheen, a principal city in the island of Sumatra, at which they were favourably received. They formed a treaty of commerce with the chief or sovereign of the place; obtained permission to erect a factory; and, having taken on board a quantity of pepper, set sail for the Moluccas. In the Straits of Malacca they captured a Portuguese vessel of 900 tons burthen, carrying calicoes and spices, which sufficed to lade the fleet. They diverted their course, therefore, to Bantam in the island of Java; where the Captain, delivering his letters and presents, and meeting with a favourable reception, left some agents, the first rudiments of the Company's factories; and returned to England, where he arrived, in September, 1603, with a handsome profit to his owners on the capital of the voyage.[1]

In the course of ten years from 1603 to 1613, eight other voyages were fitted out, on similar terms. The first, in 1603, under the command of Captain Middleton, consisted of the ships which had but just returned from the preceding voyage; and the capital subscribed was 60,450*l.*; of which 48,148*l.* was laid out in the preparation and provision of the ships; 11,160*l.* in bullion, and 1,142*l.* in goods. The second, in 1606, consisted of three ships commanded by Captain Keeling, with a capital of 53,500*l.*; of which 28,620*l.* was for the equipment of the fleet, 17,600*l.* was in bullion, and 7,280*l.* in goods. The third, in 1607, consisted of two ships, 33,000*l.* capital; 14,600*l.* of which was for the ships, 15,000*l.* in bullion, and 3,400*l.* in goods. The fourth voyage, in 1608, had but one ship; 13,700*l.* subscription; expense of equipment, 6,000*l.*; bullion, 6,000*l.*; goods, 1,700*l.* The fifth, in 1609, had three ships, larger than in any former voyage; capital subscribed, 82,000*l.*; cost of shipping, 32,000*l.*; the investment, 28,500*l.* bullion, and 21,500*l.* goods. The sixth voyage, in 1610, had four ships; and subscription, 71,581*l.*; divided into 42,300*l.* for shipping, 19,200*l.* bullion, 10,081*l.* goods. The seventh, in 1611, of four vessels, had 76,375*l.* subscription, expended

[1] Harris, i. 875. Anderson, ut supra, ii. 217, 218. Bruce's Annals, i. 151, 152.

BOOK I. CHAP. I. 1603-13.

48,700*l.* on the fleet, had 17,675*l.* in bullion, and 10,000*l.* in goods. The eighth, in 1612, had one ship, and subscription, 7,200*l.*; divided into 5,300*l.* for the vessel, 1,250*l.* bullion, and 650*l.* in goods. All these voyages, with one exception, that in 1607, of which both the vessels were lost, were prosperous: the clear profits, hardly ever below 100 per cent., being in general more than 200 on the capital of the voyage.[1]

The years in which these voyages were performed were not without other incidents of considerable importance. In 1604, the Company were alarmed by a license, in violation of their charter, granted to Sir Edward Michelborne and others, to trade to "Cathaia, China, Japan, Corea, and Cambaya, &c." The injury was compensated in 1609, when the facility and indiscretion of King James encouraged the Company to aim at a removal of those restrictions which the more cautious policy of Elizabeth had imposed. They obtained a renewal of their charter, confirming all their preceding privileges, and constituting them a body corporate, not for fifteen years, or any other limited time, but for ever; still, however, providing that, on experience of injury to the nation, their exclusive privileges should, after three years' notice, cease and expire.

The earliest of the Company's voyages were exclusively directed to the islands in the Indian Ocean, as Sumatra, Java, and Amboyna, the returns being raw silk, fine calicoes, indigo, cloves, and mace. In 1608, the factors at Bantam and in the Moluccas reported that the cloths and calicoes imported from the continent of India were in great request in the islands; and recommended the opening of a trade at Surat and Cambaya, to supply them with those commodities, which might be exchanged, with extraordinary profit, for the spices and other productions of the islands. To profit by these advantages, the fleet which sailed under the orders of Sir Henry Middleton, in 1609, was directed to steer for the western coast of the Asiatic continent, where they made several attempts to establish a commercial intercourse. At Aden and Mocha they were opposed by the Turks; who surprised one of the ships, and made the Captain and seventy men prisoners. On the

[1] Bruce's Annals, i. 152—163.

coast of India their endeavours were frustrated by the influence of the Portuguese. A fleet which sailed in 1611 had better success. Attacked at Swally, a place at no great distance from Surat, by a large Portuguese armament, it made a successful defence;[1] and, notwithstanding the intrigues and efforts of the Portuguese, obtained a favourable reception at Surat. The English now succeeded in forming a commercial arrangement. They obtained permission to establish factories at Surat, Ahmedabad, Cambaya, and Goga, which were pointed out, by the agents of the Company, as the best situations; and agreeing to pay a duty of 3½ per cent., received assurance, that this should be the only exaction to which their merchandise should be subject; that protection should be afforded to their factories; and that their property, even in the case of the death of their agents, should be secured till the arrival of another fleet. A firmaun or decree of the Emperor, conferring these privileges, was received on the 11th of January, 1613; and authorised the first establishment of the English on the continent of India, at that time the seat of one of the most extensive and splendid monarchies on the surface of the globe.[2]

CHAPTER II.

From the Change of the Company into a Joint Stock Company, in 1612, *till the Formation of the third Joint-Stock in* 1631-2.

HITHERTO the voyages of the East India traders had been conducted on the terms rather of a regulated than a joint-stock company; each adventure being the property

[1] The action, or rather series of actions, with the Portuguese, was fought between the 22nd of October, and the 27th of November, 1612. The English force consisted of two vessels, the Dragon and Osiander; the former a large, the latter a small vessel: the Dragon was commanded by Captain Best. The Portuguese squadron consisted of four galleons, of which the largest carried thirty-eight guns; and a number of small vessels, without cannon, but intended to assist in boarding. In the several encounters which took place, the Portuguese were defeated, with considerable loss of men, and injury to the vessels; and, ultimately, left Captain Best to remain unmolested at Swally, and renew the intercourse with the factory at Surat. The event of the fight raised the reputation of the English in the opinion of the natives, and contributed to accelerate the delivery of the confirmation of a treaty, previously adjusted between Captain Best and the governor of Ahmedabad. The confirmation was presented in form, in December, in 1612; but a more solemn confirmation of it, in the shape of an imperial firmaun, does not seem to have been received till January, 1613. Orme's Fragments, 332.—W.

[2] Bruce's Annals, i. 164.

BOOK I. CHAP. II. 1613-16.

of a certain number of individuals, who contributed to it as they pleased, and managed it for their own account, subject only to the general regulations of the Company. Whether this was more adapted or not, to the nature of commerce, and the interests of the nation, it was less favourable to the power and consequence of a Governor and Directors, than trading on a joint-stock, which threw into their hands the entire management and power of the whole concern. Accordingly, *they* exerted themselves to decry the former method, and, in 1612, were enabled to come to a resolution, that in future, the trade should be carried on by a joint-stock only.[1]

It still appears to have been out of their power to establish a general fund, fixed in amount, and divided into regular shares; the capital was still raised by a sort of arbitrary subscription, some individuals, whose names stood as members of the Company, advancing nothing, others largely. They now, however, subscribed, not each for a particular adventure, with an association of his own choosing, but all into the hands of the Governor and Directors, who were to employ the aggregate as one fund or capital for the benefit of those by whom it was advanced. On these terms 429,000*l.* was raised, which the Directors thought proper to divide for the purpose of four separate adventures or voyages, to be undertaken in as many successive years. The voyages were regulated, and composed as follows:

Year.	Vessels.	Investment. Bullion.	Goods.
1613	8	18,810*l.*	12,446*l.*
1614	8	13,952	23,000
1615	6	26,660	26,065
1616	7	52,087	16,506

The purchase, repair, and equipment of the vessels amounted to 272,544*l.*, being the remainder of the stock.

The profit of these voyages was far from setting the management of a court of Directors, as compared with that of individuals taking charge of their own affairs, in a favourable light. The average of the profits on the eight voyages which preceded, leaving out of the account the small adventure of what is called the Company's fourth

[1] Bruce, i. 165.

voyage, wholly unfortunate, was 171 per cent. The average of the profit on the four voyages in question, was only 87½ per cent.[1]

As the power of the Portuguese in the East carried the usual consequences of power along with it, among other things, an overbearing and insolent spirit, they had already embroiled themselves with the Mogul government: an event favourable to the English, who were thus joined with that government in a common cause. At the same time the splendid achievements of the English, against an enemy whom the governments of India were ill able to resist, raised high their reputation for prowess in war. A Portuguese fleet burned the towns of Baroach and Goga: and a powerful armament arrived at Swally with the Portuguese Viceroy, in January, 1614; which attacked the English; but was defeated, with a loss of 350 men. To improve these favourable circumstances, an agent of the Company repaired to the Mogul court, where he was well received, and obtained a royal firmaun for a general and perpetual trade; and in the same year took place the celebrated royal embassy of Sir Thomas Roe. The character of an ambassador, and the respect attached to it by the discernment of more enlightened nations, were but little understood at the court of the Mogul. On that occasion the choice of the English Ambassador was happy: Sir Thomas was a man of discernment, and temper, and made the most of the circumstances in which he was placed; though he soon discovered that it was bad policy by which he had been sent. He obtained redress of some of the grievances of which the English merchants complained; and concluded, though with difficulty, a sort of treaty, in which liberty was promised them of trading and establishing factories in any part of the Mogul dominions; Surat, Bengal, and Sindy being particularly named.[2]

Besides his other services, Sir Thomas bestowed advice upon the Company. "At my first arrival," says he, "I understood a fort was very necessary; but experience teaches me we are refused it to our own advantage. If the Emperor would offer me ten, I would not accept of one."

[1] Bruce, i. 166.

[2] Bruce, i. 171, etc. Sir Thomas Roe's Journal and Letters. Churchill, i. 770—809.

BOOK I. CHAP. II. 1613-16.

He then states his reasons: first, he adduces evidence that it would be of no service to their trade: "secondly, the charge," he says, "is greater than the trade can bear; for to maintain a garrison will eat out your profit; a war and traffic are incompatible. By my consent you shall never engage yourselves but at sea, where you are like to gain as often as to lose. The Portugueses, notwithstanding their many rich residences, are beggared by keeping of soldiers; and yet their garrisons are but mean. They never made advantage of the Indies since they defended them: observe this well. It has also been the error of the Dutch, who seek plantations here by the sword. They turn a wonderful stock; they prole in all places; they possess some of the best: yet their dead pays consume all the gain. Let this be received as a rule, that if you will profit, seek it at sea, and in quiet trade; for, without controversies, it is an error to affect garrisons and land wars in India.

"It is not a number of ports, residences, and factories that will profit you. They will increase charge, but not recompense it. The conveniency of one, with respect to your sails, and to the commodity of investments, and the well employing of your servants, is all you need." If Sir Thomas had lived to the present day, he might have urged the trade with China as proof, by experiment, of the proposition he advanced.

"The settling your traffic here will not need so much help at court as you suppose. A little countenance and the discretion of your factors will, with easy charge, return you most profit; but you must alter your stock. Let not your servants deceive you; cloth, lead, teeth, quicksilver, are dead commodities, and will never drive this trade; you must succour it by change.

"An ambassador lives not in fit honour here. A meaner agent would, among these proud Moors, better effect your business. My quality, often, for ceremonies, either begets you enemies, or suffers unworthily. Half my charge shall corrupt all this court to be your slaves. The best way to do your business in it is to find some Mogul, that you may entertain for 1000 rupees a year, as your solicitor at court. He must be authorised by the king, and then he will serve you better than ten ambassadors. Under him you must allow 500 rupees for another at your port, to follow the

Governor and customers, and to advertise his chief at court. These two will effect all; for your other smaller residencies are not subject to much inconveniency."

The permission to the Company's servants to trade privately on their own account, which afterwards produced so many inconveniences, was, it seems, even at this early period, a source of abuse. "Concerning this, it is my opinion," says Sir Thomas, "that you absolutely prohibit it, and execute forfeitures, for your business will be the better done. All your loss is not in the goods brought home; I see here the inconveniences you think not of: I know this is harsh to all men, and seems hard. Men profess they come not for bare wages. But you will take away this plea, if you give great wages to their content; and then you know what you part from: but then you must make good choice of your servants, and use fewer."

Sir Thomas tells the Company that he was very industrious to injure the Dutch. "The Dutch," he says, "are arrived at Surat from the Red Sea, with some money and southern commodities. I have done my best to disgrace them; but could not turn them out without further danger. Your comfort is, here are goods enough for both."[1] If so, why seek to turn them out?

One of the objects at which the adventurers from England most eagerly aspired, was a share in the traffic of the Spice Islands. The spices, from their novelty, were at that time a favourite object of consumption to those, the supply of whose wants is so naturally but thoughtlessly regarded by the dealer as peculiarly profitable, the rich and the great: and the commerce, brilliant as compared with that of other nations, which the enterprise and diligence of the Dutch now carried on with the East, almost entirely consisted of those commodities. The English, by their connexion with Sumatra and Java, had their full share in the article of pepper; but were excluded from cinnamon, cloves, nutmegs, and all the finer spices. Agents were now

[1] Churchill, i. 106—108. He gives another account of his endeavours to injure the Dutch, in the following words:—"The 10th, 11th, and 12th, I spent in giving the prince advice that a Dutch ship lay before Surat, and would not declare upon what design it came, till a fleet arrived; which was expected with the first fit season. This I improved to fill their heads with jealousies of the designs of the Dutch, and the dangers that might arise from them; which was well taken: and, being demanded, I gave my advice to prevent coming to a rupture with them, and yet exclude them the trade of India."—Ibid. 774.

1617.

sent from Bantam to Amboyna, Banda, and other islands, who fired the jealousy and cupidity of the Dutch. Defeated in their endeavours at all the places where the Dutch had already established themselves, the English projected, as a last resource, a factory at Macassar, of which the produce was only rice, but which might serve as a magazine for spices collected from the neighbouring islands.[1]

In the year 1617, or the year of the last of the four voyages in which the general subscription had been employed, the Company's agents reported; That Surat was the place at which the cloths of India could best be obtained, though nothing could there be disposed of in return, except China goods, spices, and money: That large quantities of Indian wove goods might be sold, and gold, camphor, and benjamin obtained, at the two factories of Acheen and Tekoo, on the island of Sumatra: That Bantam afforded a still larger demand for the wove goods of India, and supplied pepper for the European market: That Jacatra, Jambee, and Polania, agreed with the two former places in the articles both of demand and supply, though both on a smaller scale: That Siam might afford a large vent for similar commodities, and would yield gold, silver, and deer-skins for the Japan market: That English cloth, lead, deer-skins, silks, and other goods, might be disposed of at Japan for silver, copper, and iron, though hitherto want of skill had rendered the adventures to that kingdom unprofitable: That, on the island of Borneo, diamonds, bezoar stones, and gold, might be obtained at Succadania, notwithstanding the mischief occasioned by the ignorance of the first factors; but from Banjarmassin, where the same articles were found, it would be expedient, on account of the treacherous character of the natives, to withdraw the factory: That the best rice in India could be bought, and the wove goods of India sold, at Macassar: And that at Banda the same goods could be sold, and nutmegs and mace procured, even to a large amount, if the obstruction of European rivals were removed.[2]

Surat and Bantam were the seats of the Company's principal establishments.

In the year 1617-18, a subscription was opened for a new

[1] Bruce, i. 174, 178.

[2] Ibid., i. 188.

BOOK I. CHAP. II. 1618.

fund, and was carried to the large amount of 1,600,000*l.* This was denominated the Company's Second Joint-stock. They were now, we are told, possessed of thirty-six ships, from 100 to 1,000 tons burthen; and the proprietors of stock amounted to 954.[1] But as the accounts of the Company have never been remarkable for clearness, or their historians for precision,[2] we are not informed whether these ships belonged to the owners of the first joint-stock, or to the owners of the second; or if to both, in what proportion; whether the 954 proprictors of stock were the subscribers to both funds, or to the last only; whether any part of the first joint-stock had been paid back to the owners, as the proceeds came in; or whether both funds were now in the hands of the Directors at once, employed for the respective benefit of the respective lists of subscribers: two trading capitals in the same hands, employed separately, for the separate account of different associations. That such was the case, to a certain extent, may be concluded from this, that of the last of the voyages, upon the first of the funds, the returns were not yet made. We shall see that, afterwards, the Directors had in their hands, at one and the same time, the funds of several bodies of subscribers, which they were bound to employ separately, for the separate benefit of each; that they, as well as their agents abroad, experienced great inconvenience in preserving the accounts and concerns separate and distinct; and that the interests and pretensions of the several bodies were prone to interfere.

The new subscription was divided into portions for three separate voyages.

The passion, naturally, of the Company's agents, at the different stations abroad, was to grasp at everything, with

[1] Sir Jeremy Sambrooke's Report on East Indian Trade (MS. in East India Register Office) quoted by Bruce, i. 193.

[2] This remark is somewhat severe, and cannot in all cases be merited. In the present instance there seems to be no difficulty in understanding what is intended. It is clear, from the whole tenor of the statements regarding the Company's commercial proceedings at this period, that each voyage was a separate transaction, and the cost of the equipment was charged to the capital embarked in that particular adventure alone. There was no transfer of stock from one set of adventurers to another, at least until the adventure was closed. All that is here meant, therefore, seems to be, that at this period there were thirty-six ships and 954 persons engaged in the trade with India, including the ships and individuals then actually concerned in adventures not brought to a conclusion; it does not imply that the individuals and ships specified were restricted to the new joint-stock association.—W.

BOOK I. CHAP. II. 1618.

little regard to the narrowness of the funds upon which their operations depended. In one point of view this was advantageous: while the ground was yet imperfectly explored, it yielded a wider field for selection. The factors at Surat were captivated with the project of a trade to Persia: it promised a vent for English woollens to a large amount, and would furnish silk and other goods, which, both in Europe and in India, might sell to the greatest advantage. Sir Thomas Roe dissuaded the speculation; on the ground, that the Portuguese were already in possession of the commerce, and that it would cost the Company more to protect themselves in it, than they could hope to gain by it. The views of the factors, because the most flattering, were the most persuasive; agents were sent to the court of Persia; grants of privileges were obtained; and a trade was opened, which experience proved to be of little importance.

The rivalship between the East India Company and the other nations of Europe includes, for a considerable time, the principal incidents of the Company's history. The Portuguese, on the pretence of discovery, had long maintained an exclusive claim to the passage by the Cape of Good Hope: they had, partly by conquest, partly by agreement, made themselves masters of Goa, Bombay, and other places, on the Malabar coast; of Aden, at the entrance of the Red Sea; of Ormus, in the Persian Gulf; of part of the Malay coast, in the Straits of Malacca; of the Molucca islands; and of the coasts of Ceylon, the most valuable of all the eastern islands: they were possessed of factories in Bengal and in Siam; and they had erected the city of Macao on the coast of China.

The Dutch, while subject to the crown of Spain, had been accustomed to repair to Lisbon for the productions of the East; which, even at that early period, they were employed in distributing to the rest of Europe. When they broke the chains of their ancient masters, one of the means which Philip employed to distress them was, to deprive them of the commerce of his dominions. Prevented from obtaining Indian commodities by traffic with the subjects of Philip, they became ruinous competitors for the trade with India itself.

At the time when the Dutch commenced their voyages

1618.

to the East, the crown of Spain was engaged in enterprises of so much importance in other quarters, and so much engrossed with the contemplation of its splendid empire in the New World, that the acquisitions, in the East Indies, of the Portuguese, now become its subjects, were treated with comparative neglect. The Dutch, accordingly, who entered upon the trade to India with considerable resources and the utmost ardour, were enabled to supplant the Portuguese in the spice trade, and, after a struggle, to expel them from the Molucca islands. That celebrated people, now freed from the oppression of a bad government, were advancing in the career of prosperity with great and rapid strides. The augmentation of capital was rapid, in Holland, beyond what has often been witnessed in any other part of the globe. A proportional share of this capital naturally found its way into the channel of the India trade, and gave both extent and vigour to the enterprises of the nation in the East; while the English, whose country, oppressed by misgovernment, or scourged with civil war, afforded little capital to extend its trade, or means to afford it protection, found themselves unequal competitors with a people so favourably situated as the Dutch.

During that age, the principles of public wealth were very imperfectly understood, and hardly any trade was regarded as profitable but that which was exclusive. The different nations which traded to India, all traded by way of monopoly; and the several exclusive companies treated every proposal for a participation in their traffic, as a proposal for their ruin. In the same spirit, every nation which obtained admittance into any newly-explored channel of commerce endeavoured to exclude from it all participators, and considered its own profits as depending on the absence of all competition.

The Dutch, who were governed by the same prejudices as their contemporaries, and actuated, at least in that age, with rather more perhaps than the usual intensity of the appetite for gain, beheld, with great impatience, the attempts of the English to share with them in the spice trade. While contending for their independence against the power of Spain, and looking to England for support, they were constrained to practise moderation and forbearance; and during this time the English were enabled to

BOOK I. CHAP. II. 1618.

form a connexion with Sumatra, to establish themselves at Bantam, and obtain a share in the traffic of pepper, which being a commodity so generally produced in the East, could not easily become the subject of monopoly. But before the English made efforts on any considerable scale to interfere with the trade of the further India, where the finer spices were produced, the power and confidence of the Dutch had greatly increased.

That people were more effectual opponents than the Portuguese, between whom and the English the interference was not so direct. The chief settlements of the Portuguese on the continent of India were on the Malabar coast, at a great distance from Surat, which was the principal seat of the English: it was in the Persian trade alone that much incompatibility of interest existed: and feeble, in India, as the English at that time were, it is remarkable that they were an overmatch at sea for the Portuguese; and hardly ever encountered them without a brilliant victory, or at least decided advantages. The case was different in regard to the Dutch: the pretensions of the English to the spice trade interfered with the very vitals of the Dutch commerce in the East; and the fleets which the prosperous enterprise of the new republic enabled it to maintain were so far superior to those which the restricted means of the English Company allowed them to send, that contention became altogether hopeless and vain.

It was not till the year 1617-18, that the hostility of the two nations displayed itself in operations of force; the Dutch, in those places where they had formed establishments, having in general been able, by intrigue and artifice, to defeat the attempts of their rivals. The English took possession of two small islands, called Polaroon and Rosengin, which were not formally occupied by the Dutch, but intimately connected with some of their possessions. The Dutch raised pretensions to them, and attacked the English. The English had, however, so well fortified themselves, that the Dutch found it impracticable at the first attempt to expel them; but they found the means, partly by force, and partly by artifice, to get possession of two English ships, on their voyage to these islands; carried them to a Dutch settlement, and refused to deliver

1618.

them up, till every pretension to the Spice Islands was renounced.[1]

The proceedings of the Dutch, though regarded by the English as in the highest degree unjust and rapacious, were founded on pretensions, not inferior to those on which the English Company endeavoured to convert claims into rights ; and on pretensions which it is clear, at any rate, that the Dutch themselves regarded as valid and equitable ; since they presented them to the English monarch, as the ground of complaint against his subjects, and of a demand for his interference to prevent the recurrence of similar injuries. In a memorial to James, in 1618, the Dutch Company set forth, that, at their own cost and hazard, they had expelled the Portuguese from the Spice Islands, and had established a treaty with the natives, on the express condition of affording the natives protection against the Portuguese, and enjoying the exclusive advantage of their trade ; that the agents of the English Company, however, had interfered with those well-established rights, and had not only endeavoured to trade with the natives, but to incite them against the Dutch.

To these complaints the English Company replied, by an enumeration of injuries, from the resistance, the intrigues, and violence of the Dutch, in places where no factories of theirs had ever existed. But they also enumerated among their grievances, the hostilities experienced at Tydore and Amboyna, places to which the pretensions of the Dutch applied in all their force.[2] And if the ideas are admitted, which then prevailed, and on which the English as confidently grounded themselves as any other nation ; ideas importing that, in newly-discovered countries, priority of occupancy constituted sovereignty, and that the will of the natives was to be counted for nothing ; the English could not make out a right to the trade of the Moluccas ; for though Polaroon and Rosengin might not, by actual occupancy, have accrued to the Dutch, they form part of a narrow and closely-connected cluster of islands, of which the Dutch had seized the principal, and with the security of which the presence of the English in

[1] Bruce, i. 199.

[2] Memorial of the Dutch East India Company to King James, and Reply of the London East India Company thereto, in the year 1616 (East India Papers in the State Paper Office), quoted, Bruce, i. 202.

BOOK I. CHAP. II. 1619.

any of the rest could as little be reconciled, as the security of Great Britain could be reconciled with the dominion of Ireland by the French. With respect to Java, and the settlements at Bantam and Jacatra, the English had an equitable plea, of which they appear not to have availed themselves; they might have insisted on the consent of the Dutch, who had not resisted their early settlement on that island, now sanctioned by time.

After a tedious interchange of hostilities, in which intrigue and force were combined (the practice of buying up the pepper, at prices higher than the English could afford, forming one of the principal subjects of English complaint), it was agreed between the two governments in Europe, at that time allies, to institute a mutual inquiry, and form an arrangement respecting the claims of their subjects in the East. Commissioners were appointed; and, after repeated conferences, a treaty was concluded at London, on the 17th July, 1619. It was stipulated, that there should be a mutual amnesty, and a mutual restitution of ships and property; that the pepper trade at Java should be equally divided; that the English should have a free trade at Pullicate, on the Coromandel coast, on paying half the expenses of the garrison; and that of the trade of the Moluccas and Bandas they should enjoy one-third, the Dutch two, paying the charges of the garrisons in the same proportion. Beside these conditions, which regarded their opposite pretensions, the treaty included arrangements for mutual profit and defence. Each Company was to furnish ten ships of war, which were not to be sent in the European voyages, but employed in India for mutual protection; and the two nations were to unite their efforts to reduce the duties and exactions of the native governments at the different ports. To superintend the execution of this treaty a council was appointed, to be composed of four members of each Company, called the *Council of Defence*. And the treaty was to be in force during twenty years.[1]

This solemn engagement is a proof, if there was not another, of the imperfection which still adhered to the art of legislation. The principal stipulations were so vague, and the execution of them dependent on so many unas-

[1] Rymer's Fœdera, xvii. 170. Bruce, i. 212.

1619.

certained circumstances, that the grounds of dispute and contention were rather multiplied than reduced. For these evils, as far as they were foreseen, the Council of Defence seems to have been devised as the remedy. But experience taught here what experience has uniformly taught, that in all vague arrangements the advantages are reaped by the strongest party. The voice of four Englishmen in the Council of Defence was but a feeble protection against the superior capital and fleets of the Dutch. The English, to secure their pretensions, should have maintained a naval and military force superior to that of their opponents. In that case, they would have been the oppressors; the Dutch would have been expelled from the spice trade; the spice trade would have rested with the English, who would have overlooked the continent of India, because their capital would not have sufficed to embrace it; the continent would have been left to the enterprise of other nations; and that brilliant empire, established by the English, would never, it is possible, have received a commencement.

In consequence of this treaty, by which the English were bound to send a fleet of ten ships to India, a larger fund was this year raised than had been provided for any preceding voyage: 62,490*l.* in the precious metals, and 28,508*l.* in goods, were exported with the fleet. The return was brought back in a single ship, and sold at 108,887*l.*[1]

In the interval between the time of concluding the treaty and the establishment of the *Council of Defence* at Jacatra, the Dutch had committed various acts of oppression on the English; and, when the council began its operations, the Dutch, after executing some of the least important conditions of the treaty, endeavoured to evade the rest. They consented to restore the ships taken from the English, but not the goods or stores taken by individuals; on the pretext, that the Company could not be responsible for any acts but their own; though, if the letters may be credited of the English factors at Jacatra, they exploded the same pretension when it was urged against themselves: They refused to admit the English to their share of the pepper trade, till indemnified for certain fortifications, and for the expenses incurred by them at the siege of Bantam: They insisted that at Jacatra, and all other places where

[1] Bruce, i. 213.

BOOK I. CHAP. II.

1620.

they had erected fortifications, they possessed the rights of sovereignty; and that the English could claim no permission to reside there except under the Dutch laws: They set forth the large expense they had incurred in fortifications on the Spice Islands; the maintenance of which they estimated at 60,000*l.* per annum; and of all this they required the English to advance their due proportion, before they could be admitted to the stipulated share of the trade. The English objected, that some of the fortifications were at places where no produce was obtained, and that none of them were useful but for defence against the Spaniards and Portuguese, with whom they were not at war. On the whole it may be remarked, that if there were fortifications at places where none were required, the English had a right to decline paying for the blunders of the Dutch; but as they claimed a share of the trade upon the foundation of the Dutch conquests, and would not have been admitted to it, without a war, had not those conquests taken place, it was a less valid plea, to say that they were not at war with the Spaniards and Portuguese. In framing the treaty, no distinction was made between past and future expenses. The English intended to bind themselves only for a share of the future: the Dutch availed themselves of the ambiguity to demand a share of the past; and in all these pretensions they acted with so high a hand, that the English commissioners of the Council of Defence reported the impracticability of continuing the English trade, unless measures were taken in Europe to check the overbearing and oppressive proceedings of the Dutch.[1]

In the circle of which Surat was the centre, as the English were more than a match for their antagonists, they had a better prospect of success. In 1620, two of the Company's ships, which sailed from Surat to Persia, found the port of Jasques blockaded by a Portuguese fleet, consisting of five large and sixteen smaller vessels. Unable to cope with so disproportionate a force, they sailed back to Surat; where they were joined by two other ships. Returning with this reinforcement, they attacked the Portuguese, and, after an indecisive action, entered the port. The Portuguese retired to Ormus, but, after refitting, came back for

[1] Bruce, i. 223.

1622.

revenge. An obstinate conflict ensued, in which the English were victorious over a vast superiority of force. Such an event was calculated to produce a great impression on the minds of the Persians.

The English and Persians agreed to attack with joint forces the Portuguese on the island of Ormus, which that nation in the days of its prosperity had seized and fortified. The English furnished the naval, the Persians the military force: and the city and castle were taken on the 22nd of April, 1622. For this service the English received part of the plunder of Ormus, and a grant of half the customs at the port of Gombroon; which became their principal station in the Persian Gulf. The agents of the Company at Bantam, who were already vested with the superb title of President and Council, and with a sort of control over the other factories, condemned this enterprise; as depriving them of the ships and effects, so much required to balance the power, and restrain the injustice of the Dutch.[1]

The domestic proceedings of the Company at this period were humble. In 1621-22, they were able to fit out only four ships, supplied with 12,900*l.* in gold and silver, and 6253*l.* in goods: the following year, they sent five ships, 61,600*l.* in money, and 6,430*l.* in goods; in 1623-24, they equipped seven vessels, and furnished them with 68,720*l.* in money, and 17,340*l.* in goods. This last was a prosperous year to the domestic exchequer. Five ships arrived from India with cargoes, not of pepper only, but of all the finer spices, of which, notwithstanding the increasing complaints against the Dutch, the Company's agents had not been prevented from procuring an assortment. The sale of this part alone of the cargoes amounted to 485,593*l.*; that of the Persian raw silk to 97,000*l.*; while 80,000*l.* in pursuance of the treaty of 1619, was received as compensation money from the Dutch.[2]

Other feelings were the result of demands, by the King, and by the Duke of Buckingham, Lord High Admiral, of shares, to the one as droits of the crown, to the other as droits of the admiralty, of the prize-money, gained by the various captures of the Company, particularly that of Ormus. The Company, who deemed it prudent to make little oppo-

1 Bruce, i, 237, 238.
2 Accounts in the Indian Register Office. Bruce, i. 225, 234, 24

BOOK I. CHAP. II. 1623.

sition to the claims of the King, objected, as having acted not under letters of marque from the Admiral, but under their own charter, to those of the Duke of Buckingham. The question was referred to the Judge of the Admiralty court; witnesses were examined, to ascertain the amount of the prize-money, which was estimated at 100,000*l.* and 240,000 reals of eight.[1] The Company urged the expense of their equipments, the losses they had sustained, the detriment to their mercantile concerns, by withdrawing their ships from commerce to war. All possible modes of solicitation to the King and the Admiral were employed; but the desire for their money was stronger than their interest. Buckingham, who knew they must lose their voyage, if the season for sailing was passed, made their ships be detained; and the Company, to escape this calamity, were glad of an accommodation. The Duke agreed to accept of 10,000*l.*, which he received. A like sum was demanded for the King, but there is no direct evidence that it ever was paid.

The animosities between the English and Dutch were now approaching to a crisis in the islands. The English complained of oppression, and were so weak as to find themselves at the mercy of their rivals. They represented that, in the execution of the joint articles of the treaty, they were charged with every item of expense, though their voice was entirely disregarded in the disposal of the money, in the employment of the naval and military force, and even in the management of the trade; that, instead of being admitted to their stipulated share of the spice commerce, they were almost entirely extruded from it; and that, under the pretext of a conspiracy, the Dutch had executed great numbers of the natives at Banda, and reduced Polaroon to a desert.[2] At last arrived that event, which made a deep and lasting impression on the minds of Englishmen. In February, 1623, Captain Towerson and nine Englishmen, nine Japanese, and one Portuguese sailor, were seized at Amboyna, under the accusation of a conspiracy to surprise the garrison, and to expel the Dutch; and, being tried, were pronounced guilty, and executed. The

[1] East India Papers in the State Paper Office. Bruce, i. 241.

[2] The Dutch, in their vindication, stated that the English intrigued with the Portuguese, and underhand assisted the natives in receiving the Portuguese into the islands. See Anderson's History of Commerce, in Macpherson's Annals, ii. 305.

1623.

accusation was treated by the English as a mere pretext, to cover a plan for their extermination. But the facts of an event, which roused extreme indignation in England, have never been exactly ascertained. The nation, whose passions were kindled, was more disposed to paint to itself a scene of atrocity, and to believe whatever could inflame its resentment, than to enter upon a rigid investigation of the case. If it be improbable, however, on the one hand, that the English, whose numbers were small, and by whom ultimately so little advantage could be gained, were really guilty of any such design as the Dutch imputed to them; it is on the other hand equally improbable that the Dutch, without believing them to be guilty, would have proceeded against them by the evidence of a judicial trial. Had simple extermination been their object, a more quiet and safe expedient presented itself; they had it in their power at any time to make the English disappear, and to lay the blame upon the natives. The probability is, that, from certain circumstances, which roused their suspicion and jealousy, the Dutch really believed in the conspiracy, and were hurried on, by their resentments and interests, to bring the helpless objects of their fury to a trial; that the judges before whom the trial was conducted, were in too heated a state of mind to see the innocence, or believe in any thing but the guilt, of the accused; and that in this manner the sufferers perished. Enough, assuredly, of what is hateful may be found in this transaction, without supposing the spirit of demons in beings of the same nature with ourselves, men reared in a similar state of society, under a similar system of education, and a similar religion. To bring men rashly to a trial whom a violent opposition of interests has led us to detest, rashly to believe them criminal, to decide against them with minds too much blinded by passion to discern the truth, and to put them to death without remorse, are acts of which our own nation, or any other, was then, and would still be, too ready to be guilty. Happy would it be, how trite soever the reflection, if nations, from the scenes which excite their indignation against others, would learn temper and forbearance in cases where they become the actors themselves!

One of the circumstances, the thought of which most

BOOK I. CHAP. II. 1623.

strongly incited the passions of the English, was the application of the torture. This, however, under the Civil Law, was an established and regular part of a judicial inquiry. In all the kingdoms of continental Europe, and in Holland itself, the torture was a common method of extorting evidence from supposed criminals, and would have been applied by the Dutch judges to their own countrymen. As both the Japanese, who were accused of being accessaries to the imputed crime, and the Englishmen themselves, made confession of guilt under the torture, this, however absurd and inhuman the law, constituted legal evidence in the code of the Dutch, as well as in the codes of all the other continental nations of Europe. By this, added to other articles of evidence which would have been insufficient without it, proof was held to be completed; and death, in all capital cases, authorized and required. This was an ancient and established law; and as there are scarcely any courses of oppression to which Englishmen cannot submit, and which they will not justify and applaud, provided only it has ancient and established law for its support, they ought, of all nations, to have been the most ready to find an excuse and apology for the Dutch.[1]

[1] The English had not been so long strangers to the torture themselves, that it needed to excite in their breasts any emotions of astonishment. "The rack itself," says Hume in his History of Elizabeth, v. 457, "though not admitted in the ordinary execution of justice, was frequently used upon any suspicion, by authority of a warrant from a secretary or the Privy Council. Even the Council in the Marches of Wales were empowered, by their very commission, to make use of torture whenever they thought proper. There cannot be a stronger proof how lightly the rack was employed, than the following story, told by Lord Bacon. We shall give it in his own words: 'The Queen was mightily incensed against Haywarde on account of a book he dedicated to Lord Essex, thinking it a seditious prelude to put into the people's head boldness and faction: [*to our apprehension, says Hume, Haywarde's book seems rather to have a contrary tendency; but Queen Elizabeth was very difficult to please on that head.*] She said, she had an opinion that there was treason in it, and asked me if I could not find any places in it that might be drawn within the case of treason? . . . . . . Another time when the Queen could not be persuaded that it was his writing whose name was to it, but that it had some more mischievous author, she said, with great indignation, that she would have him racked to produce his author.' . . . . . . Thus," continues Hume, "had it not been for Bacon's humanity, or rather his wit, this author, a man of letters, would have been put to the rack for a most innocent performance"—The truth is, that the Company themselves, at this very time, were in the regular habit of perpetrating tortures upon their own countrymen, and even their own servants—of torturing to death by whips or famine. Captain Hamilton (New Account of the East Indies, i. 362) informs us, that before they were entrusted with the powers of martial law, having no power to punish capitally any but pirates, they made it a rule to whip to death, or starve to death, those of whom they wished to get rid. He produces (ib. 376) an instance of a deserter at Fort St. George, "whipt," as he expresses it, "out of this world into the next." The power, too, of executing as for piracy, the same author complains, was

From the first moment of acting upon the treaty, the Dutch had laid it down, as a principle, that at all the places where they had erected fortifications, the English should be subject to the Dutch laws; and though the English had remonstrated, they had yet complied.

It was in vain, that the English President and Council at Java, on hearing of the massacre, as they called it, remonstrated in terms of the utmost indignation, and even intimated their design of withdrawing from the island. In their representations to the Court of Directors at home, they declared, what might have been seen from the beginning, that it was impossible to trade on a combination of interests with the Dutch; and that, negotiation being fruitless, nothing but a force in the islands, equal to that of their rivals, could ensure to their countrymen a share of the trade.

When the news of the execution at Amboyna arrived in England, the people, whose minds had been already inflamed against the Dutch, by continual reports of injustice to their countrymen, were kindled into the most violent combustion. The Court of Directors exerted themselves to feed

made use of to murder many private traders. "That power (he says, ib. 362), of executing pirates is so strangely stretched, that if any private trader is injured by the tricks of a Governor, and can find no redress—if the injured person is so bold as to talk of *lex talionis*, he is infallibly declared a pirate." He gives an account of an attempt of an agent of the Company, and a creature of the Governor of Fort St. George, to swear away his life by perjury at Siam. (Ib. ii. 183.)—These parallels are presented, not for the sake of clearing the one party at the expense of the other; but, by showing things as they were, to give the world at last possession of the real state of the case.—M.

It is not impossible that there was amongst the English on Amboyna some wild scheme for the seizure of the island. The Japanese were soldiers of the garrison, and their position rendered their co-operation of an importance more than equivalent to the smallness of their numbers. At the same time, the conspirators were punished with a severity wholly unjustifiable. It is no extenuation of the cruelty of the Dutch, to argue that the English in India, in those days, were guilty of similar atrocities; the fact is not proved, and the probability may be questioned: no instance of such savage barbarity can be quoted against any of the English factories or governments, and particular acts of severity towards deserters and pirates are not to be confounded with the deliberate cruelties of a public body. Even with regard to individual instances, however, the evidence is defective; Hamilton wrote from recollection, according to his own admission, and his accusations are, for the most part, general and vague. It is elsewhere noticed by our author, also, that he was an interloper, and that his testimony, when unfavourable to the Company, must be received with caution. His assertions cannot be admitted, as conclusive or unsuspicious. The conduct of the Council of Amboyna admits of no doubt, and no plea of precedent or necessity can be justly heard in its palliation. The Dutch writers themselves acknowledge, that it would have been much better to have sent the accused to Europe for trial, even by the English courts. Vies des Gouverneurs Hollandois, in the Histoire Générale des Voyages xvii. 33,—W.

BOOK I. CHAP. II.

1623.

the popular fury. They had a hideous picture prepared, in which their countrymen were represented expiring upon the rack, with the most shocking expressions of horror and agony in their countenance and attitudes, and the most frightful instruments of torture applied to their bodies. The press teemed with publications, which enlarged upon the horrid scene at Amboyna; and to such a degree of rage were the populace excited, that the Dutch merchants in London became alarmed, and applied to the Privy Council for protection. They complained of the inflammatory publications, more particularly of the picture: which, being exposed to the people, had contributed to work them up to the most desperate resolutions. The Directors, when called before the Privy Council to answer these complaints, denied that they had any concern with the publications, but acknowledged that the picture was produced by their order, and was intended to be preserved in their house as a perpetual memorial of the cruelty and treachery of the Dutch. The Directors were aware that the popular tide had reached the table of the council room, and that they had nothing to apprehend from confessing how far they had been instrumental in raising the waters.[1]

Application was made to the King, to obtain signal reparation from the Dutch government for so great a national insult and calamity. The whole nation was too violently agitated to leave any suspicion that the application could be neglected. A commission of inquiry was formed of the King's principal servants, who reported in terms confirming the general belief and indignation, and recommended an order, which was immediately issued, for intercepting and detaining the Dutch East India fleets, till satisfaction was obtained. With great gravity the Dutch government returned for answer; that they would send orders to their Governor General in the Indies, to permit the English to retire from the Dutch settlements without paying any duties; that all disputes might be referred to the council of Defence; that the English might build forts for the protection of their trade, provided they were at the distance of thirty miles from any fort of the Dutch; that the "administration, however, of politic government, and particular jurisdiction, both civil and criminal, at all such

[1] East India Papers in the State Paper Office. Bruce, i. 256.

places as owe acknowledgment to the Dutch," should remain wholly in their hands; and that to the Dutch belonged the exclusive right to the Moluccas, Bandas, and Amboyna.[1]

This was an undisguised assumption of all the rights for which their subjects were contending in India. It is remarkable enough that the English East India Company, who were highly dissatisfied with the other parts of this answer, declared their acceptance of the first article, which permitted their servants to retire from the Dutch settlements. And here, for the present, the matter rested.

In 1624, the Company applied by petition, to the King, for authority to punish his servants abroad, by martial as well as municipal law. It appears not that any difficulty was experienced in obtaining their request; or that any parliamentary proceeding for transferring unlimited power over the lives and fortunes of the citizens, was deemed even a necessary ceremony. This ought to be regarded as an era in the history of the Company.[2]

In the year 1624-5, the Company's voyage to India consisted of five ships, but of the amount of the capital with which they were supplied, no account, it should seem, remains. In 1625-26, it consisted of six ships; and in 1626-27, of seven; further information wanting as before.[3] In the last of these years, we gain the knowledge, collaterally, of one of those most important facts, in the Company's history, which it has been their sedulous care to preserve concealed, except when some interest, as now, was to be served by the disclosure. Sir Robert Shirley, who had been ambassador at the court of Persia, made application to the King and Council to order the East India Company to pay him 2000*l.*, as a compensation for his exertions and services in procuring them a trade with Persia. The Company, beside denying the pretended services, urged their inability to pay; stating that they had been obliged to contract so large a debt as 200,000*l.*; and that their stock had fallen to 20 per cent. discount, shares of 100*l.* selling for no more than 80*l.*[4]

The Company's Persian trade was not prosperous, under the caprice and extortions of the Persian magistrates. At Java their agents, tired out with the mortifications and

[1] Bruce, i. 258. [2] Ibid. i. 252. [3] Ibid. 252, 265, 271.
[4] East India Papers in the State Paper Office. Bruce, i. 272.

BOOK I. CHAP. II. 1627.

disasters to which they were exposed from the Dutch, retired to the island of Lagundy, in the Straits of Sunda; having abandoned both Bantam and Jacatra, at which the Dutch, under the name of Batavia, had now established their principal seat of government. The island of Lagundy was found to be so unhealthy, that in less than a year, the imprudent English were anxious to return. Their distress was so great, that out of 250 individuals 120 were sick; and they had not a crew sufficient to navigate a ship to any of the English factories. In these circumstances the Dutch lent them assistance, and brought them back to Batavia.[1] On the coast of Coromandel some feeble efforts were continued. The Company had established factories at Masulipatam and Pullicat; but the rivalship of the Dutch pursued and obliged them to relinquish Pullicat. In 1624-5, they projected an establishment in the kingdom of Tanjore, but were opposed by a new rival, the Danes. At Armegaum, however, situated a little to the south of Nellore, they purchased in the succeeding year, a piece of ground from the chief of the district; erected and fortified a factory; and, suffering oppression from the native government at Masulipatam, they withdrew the factory in 1628, and transferred it to Armegaum.[2]

Shortly after the first application to James on account of the injury at Amboyna, that monarch died. In 1627-8, the application was renewed to Charles, and three large Dutch Indiamen from Surat, which put into Portsmouth, were detained. The Company, watching the decline of the royal authority, and the growing power of the House of Commons, were not satisfied with addressing the King, but in the year following presented, for the first time a memorial to the Commons. They represented that by their failure in the spice trade, and the difficulties they experienced in opening a trade for wove goods on the coast of Coromandel, they were nearly driven from all their factories; and assigned as causes, partly the opposition of the native powers, but chiefly the hostility of the Dutch. The narrowness of their own funds, and their unskilful management by the negligent Directors of a joint-stock, far more powerful causes, they overlooked or suppressed. They set forth, however, the merits of the Company, as towards the nation, in terms repeated to the present day: they employed many seamen:

[1] Bruce, i. 262, 264, 268. [2] Ibid. 264, 269, 290.

BOOK I. CHAP. II.

1628.

they exported much goods; as if the capital they employed would have remained idle; as if it would not have maintained seamen, and exported goods, had the East India Company, or East India traffic, never existed.[1]

The detention of the ships, and the zeal with which the injury seemed now to be taken up in England, produced explanation and remonstrance on the part of the Dutch. They had appointed judges to take cognizance of the proceedings at Amboyna, even before the parties had returned from Europe. Delay had arisen from the situation of the judges, on whom other services devolved, and from the time required to translate documents written in a foreign tongue. The detention of the ships, the property of private individuals altogether unconcerned with the transaction, might bring unmerited ruin on them, but could not accelerate the proceedings of the judges. On the other hand, by creating national indignation, it would only tend to unfit them for a sober and impartial inquiry. And, were the dispute allowed, unfortunately, to issue in war, however the English in Europe might detain the fleets of the Dutch, the English Company must suffer in India far greater evils than those of which they were now seeking the redress. At last on a proposal that the States should send to England commissioners of inquiry, and a promise that justice should be speedily rendered, the ships were released. It was afterwards recommended by the ministry, that the East India Company should send over witnesses to Holland to afford evidence before the Dutch tribunal; but to this the Company objected, and satisfaction was still deferred.[2]

In 1627-28, the Company provided only two ships and a pinnace for the outward voyage. They deemed it necessary to assign reasons for this diminution, dreading the inferences which might be drawn. They had many ships in India which, from the obstructions of the Dutch, and the state of their funds, had been unable to return: though the number of ships was small, the stock would be large, 60,000*l.* or 70,000*l.* in money and goods; and they hoped to bring home all their ships richly laden the following year. In 1628-29, five ships went out; two for the trade with India, and three for that with Persia; and though no account

[1] Bruce, i. 276, 277, 282. Anderson, in Macpherson's Annals, ii. 351.
[2] Bruce, i. 285, 287.

BOOK I. CHAP. II. 1629.

is preserved of the stock with which they were supplied, a petition to the King remains for leave to export 60,000*l.* in gold and silver in the ships destined to Persia. In the succeeding year four ships were sent to Persia, and none to India. Of the stock which they carried with them no account is preserved.[1]

As the sums in gold and silver which the Company had for several years found it necessary to export, exceeded the limits to which they were confined by the terms of their charter, they had proceeded annually upon a petition to the King, and a special permission. It was now, however, deemed advisable to apply for a general license, so large as would comprehend the greatest amount which on any occasion it would be necessary to send. The sum for which they solicited this permission was 80,000*l.* in silver, and 40,000*l.* in gold; and they recommended as the best mode of authenticating the privilege, that it should be incorporated in a fresh renewal of their charter; which was accordingly obtained.[2]

Notwithstanding the terms on which the English stood with the Dutch, they were allowed to re-establish their factory at Bantam after the failure of the attempt at Lagundy: a war in which the Dutch were involved with some of the native princes of the island, lessened, perhaps, their disposition, or their power, to oppose their European rivals. As Bantam was now a station of inferior importance to Surat, the government of Bantam was reduced to an agency dependent upon the Presidency of Surat, which became the chief seat of the Company's government in India. Among the complaints against the Dutch, one of the heaviest was that they sold European goods cheaper, and bought India goods dearer, at Surat, than the English; who were thus expelled from the market. This was to complain of competition, the soul of trade. If the Dutch sold so cheap and bought so dear as to be losers, all that was necessary was a little patience on the part of the English. The fact was, that the Dutch, trading on a larger capital, and with more economy, were perfectly able to outbid the English both in purchase and sale.

The English at Surat had to sustain, at this time not only the commercial rivalship of the Dutch, but also a powerful

[1] Bruce, i. 278, 293. [2] Ibid. 298.

effort of the Portuguese to regain their influence in that part of the East. The Viceroy at Goa, had in April, 1630, received a reinforcement from Europe, of nine ships and 2000 soldiers, and projected the recovery of Ormus. Some negotiation to obtain the exclusive trade of Surat was tried in vain with the Mogul Governor; and in September, an English fleet of five ships endeavouring to enter the port of Swally, a sharp, though not a decisive action, was fought. The English had the advantage; and after sustaining several subsequent skirmishes, and one great effort to destroy their fleet by fire, succeeded in landing their cargoes.[1]

CHAPTER III.

From the Formation of the third Joint-Stock, in 1632, *till the Coalition of the Company with the Merchant Adventurers, in* 1657.

IN 1631-32, a subscription was opened for a third joint-stock. This amounted to 420,700*l.*[2] Still we are left in darkness with regard to some important circumstances. We know not in what degree the capital which had been placed in the hands of the Directors by former subscriptions had been repaid; not even if any part of it had been repaid, though the Directors were now without funds to carry on the trade.

With the new subscription, seven ships were fitted out in the same season; but of the money or goods embarked, no account remains. In 1633-34, the fleet consisted of five ships; and in 1634-35, of no more than three, the money or goods in both cases unknown.[3]

During this period, however, some progress was made in extending the connexions of the Company with the eastern coast of Hindustan. It was thought advisable to replace the factory at Masulipatam not long after it had been removed; and certain privileges, which afforded protection from former grievances, were obtained from the King of Golconda, the sovereign of the place. Permission was given by the Mogul Emperor to trade to Piplee in

[1] Bruce, i. 296, 304, 300, 302.

[1] Papers in the Indian Register Office. Sir Jeremy Sambrooke's Report on the East India Trade. Bruce, i. 306.

[3] Bruce, i. 306, 320, 323.

BOOK I. CHAP. III. 1635.

Orissa; and a factor was sent to Masulipatam. For the more commodious government of these stations, Bantam was again raised to the rank of a Presidency, and the eastern coast was placed under its jurisdiction. Despairing of success in the contest with the Dutch for the trade of the islands, the Company had, for some time, despatched their principal fleets to Surat; and the trade with this part of India and with Persia now chiefly occupied their attention. From servants at a vast distance, and the servants of a great and negligent master, the best service could not easily be procured. For this discovery the Directors were indebted, not to any sagacity of their own, but to a misunderstanding among the agents themselves; who, betraying one another, acknowledged that they had neglected the affairs of their employers to attend to their own; and, while they pursued with avidity a private trade for their private benefit, had abandoned that of the Company to every kind of disorder.[1]

As pepper was a product of the Malabar coast, a share was sought in the trade of that commodity, through a channel, which the Dutch would not be able to obstruct. A treaty was concluded, between the English and Portuguese, in 1634-35, and confirmed with additional articles the following year, in which it was ordained that the English should have free access to the ports of the Portuguese, and that the Portuguese should receive from the English factories the treatment of friends.[2]

The Company, like other unskilful, and for that reason unprosperous, traders, had always competitors of one description or another, to whom they ascribed their own want of success. For several years they had spoken with loud condemnation of the clandestine trade carried on by their own servants; whose profits, they said, exceeded their own. Their alarms, with regard to their exclusive privilege, had for some time been sounded; and would have been sounded much louder, but for the ascendency gained by the sentiments of liberty, the contentions between Charles and his parliament being already high;[3] and the hope that their monopoly would escape the general wreck,

[1] Bruce, i. 306, 320, 324, 327.

[2] Ibid. 325, 334.

[3] Some inaccuracy of expression occurs in the text. There was not any Parliament from 1628 to 1640, but there was much public discontent at the time in question, especially on the subject of Ship-money.—W.

with which institutions at variance with the spirit of liberty were threatened, only if its pretensions were prudently kept in the shade. The controversy, whether monopolies, and among others that of the Company, were injurious to the wealth and prosperity of the nation, had already employed the press: but, though the Company had entered boldly enough into the lists of argument, they deemed it their wisest course, at the present conjuncture, not to excite the public attention by any invidious opposition to the infringements which private adventure was now pretty frequently committing on their exclusive trade.

An event at last occurred, which appeared to involve unusual danger. A number of persons, with Sir William Courten at their head, whom the new arrangements with the Portuguese excited to hopes of extraordinary profit, had the art, or the good fortune, to engage in their schemes Endymion Porter, Esq., a gentleman of the bedchamber to the King, who prevailed upon the sovereign himself to accept of a share in the adventure, and to grant his license for a new association to trade with India. The preamble to the license declared that it was founded upon the misconduct of the East India Company, who had accomplished nothing for the good of the nation, in proportion to the great privileges they had obtained, or even to the funds of which they had disposed. This was probably the general opinion of the nation; nothing less seeming necessary to embolden the King to such a violation of the charter. Allowing the contrariety to the interests of the nation, the consequences were not so ruinous, but that the stipulated notice of three years might have been given, and a legal end been put to the monopoly. The Company petitioned the King, but without success. They sent, however, instructions to their agents and factors in India, to oppose the interlopers, at least indirectly. An incident occurred, of which they endeavoured to avail themselves to the utmost. One of their ships from Surat reported that a vessel of Courten's had seized and plundered two junks belonging to Surat and Diu, and put the crews to the torture. The latter part at least of the story was, in all probability, forged; but the Directors believed, or affected to believe, the whole. In consequence of the outrage, the

BOOK I. CHAP. III. 1637-38.

English President and Council at Surat had been imprisoned, and the property of the factory confiscated to answer for the loss. A memorial was presented to the King, setting forth, in the strongest terms, the injuries which the Company sustained by the license to Courten's Association, and the ruin which threatened them unless it were withdrawn. The Privy Council, to whom the memorial was referred, treated the facts alleged, as little better than fabrication, and suspended the investigation till Courten's ships should return.[1]

The arrival of Courten's ships at Surat seems to have thrown the factory into the greatest confusion. It is stated as the cause of a complete suspension of trade on the part of the Company, for the season, at that principal seat of their commercial operations.[2] The inability early and constantly displayed by the Company, to sustain even the slightest competition, is a symptom of inherent infirmities.

In 1637-38, several of Courten's ships returned, and brought home large investments, which sold with an ample profit to the adventurers. The fears and jealousies of the Company were exceedingly raised. They presented to the crown a petition for protection; placing their chief reliance, it should seem, on the lamentable picture of their own distresses. Their remonstrance was, however, disregarded; a new license was extended to Courten's Association, continuing their privileges for five years; and, to form a line between them and the Company, it was ordained, that neither should they trade at those places where the Company had factories, nor the Company trade at any places at which Courten's Association might have erected establishments.[3]

The Directors, as if they abandoned all other efforts for sustaining their affairs, betook themselves to complaint and petition.[4] They renewed their addresses to the throne. They dwelt upon the calamities which had been brought upon them by competition; first, that of the Dutch, next, that of Courten's Association. They endeavoured to stimulate the jealousy of the King, by reminding him that the redress which he had demanded from the States General

[1] Bruce, i. 329, 387. [2] Ibid. 342. [3] Ibid. 345, 349.
[4] Ibid. 349, 350, 353.

1638.

had not been received: and they desired to be at least distinctly informed what line of conduct in regard to their rivals they were required to pursue. The affairs of the King were now at a low ebb; and this may account in part for the tone which the Company assumed with him. A committee of the Privy Council was formed, to inquire into their complaints; and had instructions to inquire, among other particulars, into the means of obtaining reparation from the Dutch, and of accomplishing a union between the Company and Courten's Association. One thing is remarkable, because it shows the unfavourable opinion, held by that Privy Council, of the mode of trading to India by a joint-stock Company. The Committee were expressly instructed "to form regulations for this trade, which might satisfy the noblemen and gentlemen who were adventurers in it; and to vary the principle on which the India trade had been conducted, or that of a general joint-stock, in such a manner as to enable each adventurer to employ his stock to his own advantage, to have the trade under similar regulations with those observed by the Turkey and other English Companies."[1]

The committee of the Privy Council seem to have given themselves but little concern about the trust with which they were invested. No report from them ever appeared. The Company continued indefatigably pressing the King, by petitions and remonstrances. At last they affirmed the necessity of abandoning the trade altogether, if the protection for which they prayed was not afforded. And now their importunity prevailed. On the condition that they should raise a new joint-stock, to carry on the trade on a sufficient scale, it was agreed that Courten's license should be withdrawn.[2]

On this occasion, we are made acquainted incidentally with an important fact; that the Proprietors of the third joint-stock had made frequent but unavailing calls upon the Directors to close that concern, and bring home what belonged to it in India.[3] For the first time, we learn that payment was demanded of the capital of those separate funds, called the joint-stocks of the Company. Upon this occasion a difficult question might have presented itself.

[1] Bruce, i. 353, 354. [2] Ibid. 355, 361, 362. [3] Ibid 363.

BOOK I. CHAP. III. 1642.

It might have been disputed to whom the immoveable property of the Company, in houses and in lands, both in India and in England, acquired by parts indiscriminately, of all the joint-stocks, belonged. Amid the confusion which pervaded all parts of the Company's affairs, this question had not begun to be agitated: but to encourage subscription to the new joint-stock, it was laid down as a condition, "That to prevent inconvenience and confusion, the old Company or adventurers in the third joint-stock should have sufficient time allowed for bringing home their property, and should send no more stock to India, after the month of May."[1] It would thus appear, that the Proprietors of the third joint-stock, and by the same rule the Proprietors of all preceding stocks, were, without any scruple, to be deprived of their share in what is technically called the *dead stock* of the Company, though it had been wholly purchased with their money. There was another condition, to which inferences of some importance may be attached; the subscribers to the new stock were themselves, in a general court, to elect the Directors to whom the management of the fund should be committed, and to renew that election annually.[2] As this was a new Court of Directors, entirely belonging to the fourth joint-stock it seems to follow that the Directors in whose hands the third joint-stock had been placed, must still have remained in office, for the winding up of that concern. And, in that case, there existed, to all intents and purposes, two East India Companies, two separate bodies of Proprietors, and two separate Courts of Directors, under one charter.

So low, however, was the credit of East India adventure, under joint-stock management, now reduced, that the project of a new subscription almost totally failed. Only the small sum of 22,500*l.* was raised. Upon this a memorial was presented to the King, but in the name of whom; whether of the new subscribers, or the old; whether of the Court of Directors belonging to the old joint-stock, or of a Court of Directors chosen for the new, does not appear. It set forth a number of unhappy circumstances, to which was ascribed the distrust which now attended

[1] Preamble to a subscription for a new joint-stock, for trade to the East Indies, 28th January, 1640 (East India Papers in the State Paper Office), Bruce, i. 364.

[2] Ibid.

1642.

joint-stock adventures to India;[1] and it intimated, but in very general terms, the necessity of encouragement, to save that branch of commerce from total destruction.

In the meantime a heavy calamity fell upon the Proprietors of the third joint-stock. The King having resolved to draw the sword for terminating the disputes between him and his people; and finding himself destitute of money; fixed his eyes, as the most convenient mass of property within his reach, on the magazines of the East India Company. A price being named, which was probably a high one, he bought upon credit the whole of their pepper, and sold it again at a lower price for ready money.[2] Bonds, four in number, one of which was promised to be paid every six months, were given by the farmers of the customs and Lord Cottington for the amount; of which only a small portion seems ever to have been paid. On a pressing application, about the beginning of the year 1642, it was stated, that 13,000*l.* had been allowed them out of the duties they owed; the remainder the farmers declared it to be out of their power to advance. A prayer was presented that the customs, now due by them, amounting to 12,000*l.*, might be applied in liquidation of the debt; but for this they were afterwards pressed by the parliament. The King exerted himself to protect the parties who stood responsible for him; and what the Company were obliged to pay to the parliament, or what they succeeded in getting from the King or his sureties, nowhere appears.[3]

About the period of this abortive attempt to form a new joint-stock, a settlement was first effected at Madras; the only station as yet chosen, which was destined to make a figure in the future history of the Company. The desire of a place of strength on the coast of Coromandel, as a security both to the property of the Company and the persons of their agents, had suggested, some years ago, the

[1] The principal of these was the ascendancy of the Dutch in India; an ascendancy, of the reality and consequences of which no doubt can be reasonably entertained, when the state of England, both at home and abroad, is remembered. The disputes, also, which divided the king and parliament, and the general agitation of men's minds, must be considered unpropitious to the investment of capital in any commercial speculation. It is not just, therefore, to insinuate that the failure of the subscription was wholly ascribable to the mismanagement of the Directors of prior joint-stock enterprises.—W.

[2] See Bruce, i. 371. The quantity was, 607,522 bags, bought at 2*s.* 1*d.* per pound; total, 63,283*l.* 11*s.* 1*d.*: sold at 1*s.* 8*d.* per pound; total, 50,626*l.* 17*s.* 1*d.*

[3] Bruce, i. 379, 380.—M. In all probability, nothing was recovered.—W.

BOOK I. CHAP. III. 1678.

fortification of Armegaum. On experience, Armegaum was not found a convenient station for providing the piece goods,[1] for which chiefly the trade to the coast of Coromandel was pursued. In 1640-41, the permission of the local native chief to erect a fort at Madraspatam was, therefore, eagerly embraced.[2] The works were begun, and the place named Fort St. George; but the measure was not approved by the Directors.[3]

Meanwhile the trade was languishing, for want of funds. The agents abroad endeavoured to supply, by loans, the failure of receipts from home.[4]

An effort was made in 1642-43 to aid the weakness of the fourth joint-stock by a new subscription. The sum produced was 105,000*l.*; but whether including or not including the previous subscription does not appear. This was deemed no more than what was requisite for a single voyage: of which the Company thought the real circumstances might be concealed under a new name. They called it, the *First General Voyage*.[5] Of the amount, however, of the ships, or the distribution of the funds, there is no information on record. For several years, from this date, no account whatever is preserved of the annual equipments of the Company. It would appear, from instructions to the agents abroad, that, each year, funds had been supplied; but from what source is altogether unknown. The instructions sufficiently indicate that they were small; and for this the unsettled state of the country, and the distrust of Indian adventure, will sufficiently account.

In 1644, the Dutch followed the example of the English in forming a convention with the Portuguese at Goa. Though it is not pretended that in this any partiality was shown to the Dutch, or any privilege granted to them which was withheld from the English, the Company found

[1] *Piece Goods* is the term which, latterly at least, has been chiefly employed by the Company and their agents, to denote the muslins and woven goods of India and China in general.

[2] The date of the grant from Sri Ranga Raya, Raja of Chandragheri, by whom the ground was given, is the 1st of March, 1639. The chief of the factory of Armegaum, who removed thence to Madras, was Mr. Day, who was invited by the Naik, or local governor, to change the seat of the settlement. In compliment to the latter, the new station was named after his father, Chenappa-patan; by which, or its abbreviation, Chenna-patan, the town is known to the natives. Hamilton's Gazeteer.—W.

[3] Bruce, i. 377, 393. [4] Ibid. 385. [5] Ibid. 389, 390.

themselves, as usual, unable to sustain competition, and complained of this convention as an additional source of misfortune.[1]

1648.

In 1647-48, when the power of the parliament was supreme, and the King a prisoner in the Isle of Wight, a new subscription was undertaken, and a pretty obvious policy was pursued. Endeavours were used to get as many as possible of the members of parliament to subscribe. If the members of the ruling body had a personal interest in the gains of the Company, its privileges would not fail to be both protected and enlarged. An advertisement, which fixed the time beyond which ordinary subscribers would not be received, added, that, in deference to members of parliament, a further period would be allowed to them, to consider the subject, and make their subscriptions.[2]

It appears not that any success attended this effort; and in 1649-50, the project of completing the fourth joint-stock was renewed, partly as a foundation for an application to the Council of State, partly in hopes that the favours expected from the Council would induce the public to subscribe.[3]

In the memorial, presented on this occasion to the ruling powers, Courten's Association was the principal subject of complaint. The consent of the King, in 1639, to withdraw the license granted to those rivals, had not been carried into effect; nor had the condition on which it had been accorded, that of raising a respectable joint-stock, been fulfilled. The destruction, however, to which the Association of Courten saw themselves at that time condemned, deprived them of the spirit of enterprise: with the spirit of enterprise, the spirit of vigilance naturally disappeared: their proceedings from the time of this condemnation had been feeble and unprosperous: but their existence was a grievance in the eyes of the Company; and an application which they had recently made for permission to form a settlement on the island of Assada, near Madagascar, kindled anew the Company's jealousies and fears. What the Council proposed to both parties was, an agreement. But the Assada merchants, so Courten's Association were now denominated, regarded joint-stock management with so much aversion, that, low as the condition was to which they had fallen,

[1] Bruce, i. 407, 412, 423. [2] Ibid. 423. [3] Ibid. 434.

BOOK I. CHAP. III. 1650.

they preferred a separate trade on their own funds to incorporation with the Company.[1] To prove, however, their desire of accommodation, they proposed certain terms, on which they would submit to forego the separate management of their own affairs.

Objections were offered on the part of the Company; but, after some discussion, a union was effected, nearly on the terms which the Assada merchants proposed.[2] Application was then made for an act to confirm and regulate the trade. The parliament passed a resolution, directing it to be carried on by a joint-stock; but suspending for the present all further decision on the Company's affairs.[3] A stock was formed, which, from the union recently accomplished, was denominated *the united joint-stock*; but in what manner raised, or how great the sum, is not disclosed. All we know for certain is, that two ships were fitted out in this season, and that they carried bullion with them to the amount of 60,000*l.*[4]

The extreme inconvenience and embarrassment which arose from the management, by the same agents, in the same trade, of a number of separate capitals, belonging to separate associations, began now to make themselves seriously and formidably felt. From each of the presidencies complaints arrived of the difficulties, or rather the impossibilities, which they were required to surmount; and it was urgently recommended to obtain, if it were practicable, an act of parliament to combine the whole of these separate stocks.[5] Under this confusion, we have hardly any information respecting the internal transactions of the Company at home. We know not so much as how the Courts of Directors were formed; whether there was a body of Directors for each separate fund, or only one body for the whole; and if only one Court of Directors, whether they were chosen by the voices of the contributors to all the separate stocks, or the contributors to one only; whether, when a Court of Proprietors was held, the owners of all the separate funds met in one body, or the owners of each separate fund met by themselves, for the regulation of their own particular concern.[6]

[1] Bruce, i. 435, 436. [2] Ibid. 437, 438. [3] Ibid. 439, 440.
[4] Ibid. 440. [5] Ibid. 441.
[6] If we hear of committees of the several stocks; the bodies of Directors were denominated committees. And if there were committees of the several

BOOK I. CHAP. III.

1652.

In 1651-52,[1] the English obtained in Bengal the first of those peculiar privileges, which were the forerunners of their subsequent power. Among the persons belonging to the factories, whom there was occasion to send to the Imperial Court, it happened that some were surgeons; one of whom is particularly named, a gentleman of the name of Boughton.[2] Obtaining great influence, by the cures which they effected, they employed their interest in promoting the views of the Company. Favourable circumstances were so well improved, that, on the payment of 3000 rupees, a government license for an unlimited trade, without payment of customs, in the richest province of India, was happily obtained.[3]

On the Coromandel coast, the wars, which then raged among the natives, rendered commerce difficult and uncertain; and the Directors were urged by the agent at Madras to add to the fortifications. This they refused, on the ground of expense. As it was inconvenient, however,

stocks, how were they constituted? Were they committees of Proprietors, or committees of Directors? And were there any managers or Directors besides?

[1] An attempt was made to establish a factory at Patna, in 1620. In 1624, a firmaun was obtained from Shahjehan Keber, permitting the English to trade with Bengal, but restricting them to the port of Piplee in Midnapore, but the regular connexion of the Company with Bengal did not commence till 1642; when a factory was established by Mr. Day, at Balasore. Bruce, i. 301. Stewart's History of Bengal. Hamilton's Hindustan.—W.

[2] This is not quite correctly described. The surgeons of the Company's ships had been occasionally employed by Mohammedans of rank at Surat and other places, and had acquired credit. Whilst Shah Jehan was in the Dekhan, one of his daughters was dreadfully burnt; and, at the recommendation of the vazir, Asad Khan, an express was sent to Surat for an English surgeon. The factory despatched Mr. Gabriel Boughton, who was fortunate enough to cure the princess, and thereby acquired that favour with the emperor which he used to procure the privilege of free trade for the English. He was afterwards in the service of Prince Shuja, whilst in the government of Bengal, and was thus enabled to secure attention to the firmaun of the emperor. Bruce, i. 106. Stewart, History of Bengal, 251. There is a material difference of dates in the two authorities; Bruce places Mr. Boughton's mission in 1645, Stewart in 1636: the latter, however, evidently confounds the privileges procured by Boughton with the permission previously granted to the English to visit the port of Piplee. According to Bruce, the firmaun for free trade with Bengal was not granted till 1651-52; but even this is not correctly denominated a firmaun. In 1676 the Company's agent writes, "there doth not appear that there ever was any firmaun or royal command; but only a nishan or letter from Prince Shujah, and parwanas or warrants from the governors of the province;" and he expresses his fear that the trade will be ruined for want of such authority, and the plea for exaction afforded by the charge that the English had traded custom-free for many years, without any right to be exempted. It was therefore determined to make an effort to obtain an imperial firmaun; and it was at last procured from Aurangzeb in 1680, after a disbursement of bribes to his officers of 50,000 rupees. By this the trade of the English was made custom-free in all places except Surat.—W.

[3] Bruce, i. 460, 463.

BOOK I. CHAP. III.

to keep the business of this coast dependent on the distant settlement of Bantam, Fort St. George was erected into a presidency in 1653-54.[1]

1654.

When the disputes began, which ended in hostilities between Cromwell and the Dutch, the Company deemed it a fit opportunity to bring forward those claims of theirs which, amid the distractions of the government, had lain dormant for several years. The war which succeeded, favourable to the British arms in Europe, was extremely dangerous, and not a little injurious, to the feeble Company in India. On the appearance of a Dutch fleet of eight large ships off Swally, in 1653-54, the English trade at Surat was suspended. In the Gulf of Persia, three of the Company's ships were taken, and one destroyed. The whole of the coasting trade of the English, consisting of the interchange of goods from one of their stations to another, became, under the naval superiority of the Dutch, so hazardous, as to be nearly suspended; and at Bantam, traffic seems to have been rendered wholly impracticable.[2]

As Cromwell soon reduced the Dutch to the necessity of desiring peace, and of submitting to it on terms nearly such as he thought proper to dictate, a clause was inserted in the treaty concluded at Westminster in 1654, in which they engaged to conform to whatever justice might prescribe regarding the massacre at Amboyna. It was agreed to name commissioners, four on each side, who should meet at London, and make an adjustment of the claims of the two nations. One remarkable, and not an ill-contrived condition was, that if the appointed commissioners should, within a specified time, be unable to agree, the differences in question should be submitted to the judgment and arbitration of the Protestant Swiss Cantons.[3]

The Commissioners met on the 30th of August, 1654. The English Company, who have never found themselves at a loss to make out heavy claims for compensation, whether it was their own government, or a foreign, with which they had to deal, stated their damages, ascertained by a series of accounts, from the year 1611 to the year 1652, at the vast amount of 2,695,999*l.* 15*s.* The Dutch, however, seem to have been a match for them. They too had their claims for compensation, on account of joint expenses

[1] Bruce, i. 454, 462, 484. [2] Ibid. 458, 482, 484, 485. [3] Ibid. 48.

1654.

not paid, or injuries and losses sustained, amounting to 2,919,861*l.* 3*s.* 6*d.* It is impossible to pronounce with accuracy on the justice, comparative or absolute, of these several demands. There is no doubt that both were excessively exaggerated. But if we consider, that, under the domineering ascendancy which the Protector had acquired, it was natural for the English to overbear, and expedient for the Dutch to submit; while we observe, that the award pronounced by the Commissioners, allotted to the English no more than 85,000*l.*, to be paid by two instalments, we shall not find any reason, distinct from national partiality, to persuade us, that the balance of extravagance was greatly on the side of the Dutch. All the satisfaction obtained for the massacre of Amboyna, even by the award of the same Commissioners, was 3,615*l.*, to be paid to the heirs or executors of those who had suffered.[1] Polaroon was given up to the English, but not worth receiving.

Various occurrences strongly mark the sense which appears to have been generally entertained, of the unprofitable nature of joint-stock. That particular body of proprietors, including the Assada merchants, to whom the united joint-stock belonged, presented to the Council of State, in 1654, two separate petitions; in which they prayed, that the East India Company should no longer proceed exclusively on the principle of a joint-stock trade, but that the owners of the separate funds should have authority to employ their own capital, servants, and shipping, in the way which they themselves should deem most to their own advantage.[2] The power and consequence of the Directors were threatened; and they hastened to present those pleas, which are used as their best weapons of defence to the present day. Experience had proved the necessity of a joint-stock; since the trade had been carried on by a joint-stock during forty years. Such competitions as those with the Portuguese and the Dutch could only be supported by the strength of a joint-stock. The equipments for the India trade required a capital so large

1 Bruce, i. 491.

2 The reasons on which they supported their request, as stated in their petition, exhibit so just a view of the infirmities of joint-stock management, as compared with that of individuals, pursuing their own interests, that they are highly worthy of inspection as a specimen of the talents and knowledge of the men by whom joint stock was now opposed. See Bruce, i. 518.

BOOK I. CHAP. III. 1654.

as a joint-stock alone could afford. The failure of Courten's experiment proved that voyages on any other principle could not succeed. The factories requisite for the Indian trade could be established only by a joint-stock, the East India Company having factories in the dominions of no less than fourteen different sovereigns. The native princes required engagements to make good the losses which they or their subjects might sustain at the hands of Englishmen; and to this a joint-stock company alone was competent.

On these grounds, they not only prayed that the trade by joint-stock should be exclusively continued; but that, as it had been impracticable for some time to obtain sufficient subscriptions, additional encouragement should be given by new privileges; and, in particular, that assistance should be granted sufficient to enable them to recover and retain the Spice Islands.[1]

In their reply, the body of petitioners, who were now distinguished by the name of Merchant Adventurers, chiefly dwelt upon the signal want of success which had attended the trade to India, during forty years of joint-stock management. They asserted, that private direction and separate voyages would have been far more profitable; as the prosperity of those open Companies, the Turkey, Muscovy, and Eastland Companies, sufficiently proved. They claimed a right by agreement, to a share in the factories and privileges of the Company in India; and stated that they were fitting out fourteen ships for the trade.[2] They might have still further represented, that every one of the arguments advanced by the Directors, without even a single exception, was a mere assumption of the thing to be proved. That the trade had, during forty years, or four hundred years, been carried on by a joint-stock, proved not that, by a different mode, it would not have yielded much greater advantage; if the trade had been in the highest degree unprosperous, it rather proved that the management had been proportionally defective. The Directors asserted, that in meeting competition, private adventure would altogether fail; though with their joint-stock they had so ill sustained competition, that Courten's Association had threatened to drive them out of every market in which they had appeared, and they themselves had repeatedly and solemnly declared

[1] Bruce, i. 492, 493.

[2] Ibid, 494.

1655.

to government, that unless the license to Courten were withdrawn, the ruin of the East India Company was sure. With regard to *mercantile* competition, at any rate, the skill and vigilance of individuals, transacting for their own interest, was sure to be a more powerful instrument than the imbecility and negligence of joint-stock management; and as to *warlike* competition, a few ships of war, with a few companies of marines, employed by the government, would have yielded far more security than all the efforts which a feeble joint-stock could make. The failure of Courten's Association was sufficiently accounted for by the operation of particular causes, altogether distinct from the general circumstances of the trade; the situation, in fact, in which the jealousy and influence of the Company had placed them. Factories were by no means so necessary as the Company ignorantly supposed, and interestedly strove to make others believe; as they shortly after found to their cost, when they were glad to reduce the greater number of those which they had established. Where factories were really useful, it would be for the interest of all the traders to support them. And all would join in an object of common utility in India, as they joined in every other quarter of the globe. As to the native princes, there was no such difficulty as the Company pretended: nor would individual merchants have been less successful than the directors of a joint-stock, in finding the means of prosecuting the trade.

These contending pretensions were referred to a committee of the Council of State; and they, without coming to a decision, remitted the subject to the Protector and Council, as too difficult and important for the judgment of any inferior tribunal.[1]

Nothing could exceed the confusion which, from the clashing interests of the owners of the separate stocks, now raged in the Company's affairs. There were no less than three parties who set up claims to the Island of Polaroon, and to the compensation money which had been obtained from the Dutch; the respective proprietors of the third, fourth, and united joint-stocks. The proprietors of the third joint-stock claimed the whole, as the fourth joint-stock and united stock were not in existence at the time when the debt obtained from the Dutch was incurred;

[1] Bruce, i. 503.

BOOK I. CHAP. III. 1655.

and they prayed that the money might be lodged in safe and responsible hands, till goverment should determine the question. The owners of the two other stocks demanded that the money should be divided into three equal shares, for the three several stocks, and that they should all have equal rights to the Island of Polaroon.

Five arbitrators, to whom the dispute was referred, were chosen by the Council of State. In the meantime, Cromwell proposed to borrow the 85,000*l.* which had been paid by the Dutch, and which could not be employed till adjudged to whom it belonged.

The Directors, however, had expected the fingering of the money, and they advanced reasons why it should be immediately placed in their hands. The pecuniary distresses of the Company were great. The different stocks were 50,000*l.* in debt; and many of the Proprietors were in difficult circumstances. From gratitude to the Protector, however, they would make exertions to spare him 50,000*l.*, to be repaid in eighteen months by instalments, provided the remaining 35,000*l.* were immediately assigned them, to pay their most pressing debts, and make a dividend to the Proprietors.[1] It thus appears, that these Directors wanted to forestall the decision of the question, and to distribute the money at their own pleasure, before it was known to whom it belonged. At the same time, it is matter of curious uncertainty who these Directors were, whom they represented, by what set or sets of Proprietors they were chosen, or to whom they were responsible.

While this dispute was yet undecided, the Merchant Adventurers, or Proprietors of the united stock, obtained a commission from the Protector to fit out four ships for the Indian trade, under the management of a committee.[2] We are made acquainted upon this occasion with a very interesting fact. The news of this event being carried to Holland, it was interpreted, and understood, by the Dutch, as being an abolition of the exclusive charter, and the adoption of the new measure of a free and open trade. The interests of the Dutch Company made them see, in this supposed revolution, consequences very different from those which the interests of the English Directors made them behold or pretend that they beheld in it. Instead

[1] Bruce, i. 503, 504.

[2] Ibid. 508,

1657.

of rejoicing at the loss of a joint-stock in England, as they ought to have done, if by joint-stock alone the trade of their rivals could be successfully carried on; they were filled with dismay at the prospect of freedom, as likely to produce a trade with which competition on their part would be vain.[1]

Meanwhile the Company, as well as the Merchant Adventurers, were employed in the equipment of a fleet. The petition of the Company to the Protector for leave to export bullion, specified the sum of 15,000*l.*, and the fleet consisted of three ships. They continued to press the government for a decision in favour of their exclusive privileges; and in a petition which they presented in October, 1656, affirmed, that the great number of ships sent by individuals under licenses, had raised the price of India goods from 40 to 50 per cent., and reduced that of English commodities in the same proportion. The Council resolved at last to come to a decision. After some inquiry, they gave it as their advice to the Protector to continue the exclusive trade and the joint-stock; and a committee of the Council was, in consequence, appointed to consider the terms of a charter.[2]

While the want of funds almost annihilated the operations of the Company's agents in every part of India; and while they complained that the competition of the ships of the Merchant Adventurers rendered it, as usual, impracticable for them to trade with a profit in the markets of India, the Dutch pursued their advantages against the Portuguese. They had acquired possession of the island of Ceylon, and in the year 1656-57, blockaded the port of Goa, after which they meditated an attack upon the small island of Diu, which commanded the entrance into the harbour of Swally. From the success of these enterprises they expected a complete command of the navigation on that side of India, and the power of imposing on the English trade duties under which it would be unable to stand.[3]

1 Thurloe's State Papers, iii. 80. Anderson says, "The merchants of Amsterdam, having heard that the Lord Protector would dissolve the East India Company at London, and declare the navigation and commerce to the Indies to be free and open, were greatly alarmed; considering such a measure as ruinous to their own East India Company." Anderson's History of Commerce, in Macpherson's Annals, ii. 459. See Bruce, i. 518.

2 Bruce, i. 514—516.

3 Ibid, 522—529.

BOOK I.
CHAP. IV.

1658.

CHAPTER IV.

From the Coalition between the Company and the Merchant Adventurers, till the Project for a new and a rival East India Company.

AFTER the decision of the Council of State in favour of the joint-stock scheme of trading to India, the Company and the Merchant Adventurers effected a coalition. On the strength of this union a new subscription, in 1657-58, was opened, and filled up to the amount of 786,000*l.*[1] Whether the expected charter had been actually received is not ascertained.[2]

The first operation of the new body of subscribers was the very necessary one of forming an adjustment with the owners of the preceding funds. A negociation was opened for obtaining the transfer of the factories, establishments, and privileges in India. After the lofty terms in which the Directors had always spoken of these privileges and possessions, when placing them in the list of reasons for opposing an open trade, we are apt to be surprised at the smallness of the sum which, after all, and "though situated in the dominions of fourteen different sovereigns," they were found to be worth. They were made over in full right for 20,000*l.*, to be paid in two instalments. The ships, merchandise in store, and other trading commodities of the preceding adventurers, were taken by the new subscribers at a price; and it was agreed that the sharers in the former trade, who on that account had property in the Indies, should not traffic on a separate fund, but, after a specified term, should carry the amount of such property to the account of the new stock.[3] There was, in this manner, only one stock now in the hands of the Directors, and

[1] Bruce, i. 529.

[2] Bruce, upon whose authority this transaction is described, states the matter rather differently; he says: "That the charter was granted in this season will appear, from the reference made to it in the petition of the East-India Company, though no copy of it can be discovered among the records of the state or of the Company."—loc. cit. In a letter from Fort St. George to the factory of Surat, dated 12th July, 1658, it is stated that the Blackmoore, which had arrived from England on the 12th of June, had "posted away with all haste, after His Highness the Lord Protector had signed the Company's Charter."—W.

[3] Bruce, i. 529, 530.

1659.

they had one distinct interest to pursue; a prodigious improvement on the preceding confusion and embarrassment, when several stocks were managed, and as many contending interests pursued at once.

Some new regulations were adopted for the conduct of affairs. The whole of the factories and presidencies were rendered subordinate to the President and Council at Surat. The presidencies, however, at Fort St. George and at Bantam were continued; the factories and agencies on the Coromandel coast and in Bengal being made dependent on the former, and those in the southern islands on the latter.[1]

As heavy complaints had been made of trade carried on, for their own account, by the agents and servants of the Company, who not only acted as the rivals, but neglected and betrayed the interests, of their masters, it was prohibited, and, in compensation, additional salaries allowed.[2]

After these preliminary proceedings, the first fleet was despatched. It consisted of five ships; one for Madras carrying 15,500*l.* in bullion; one for Bengal; and three for Surat, Persia, and Bantam.[3] The following year, that is the season 1658-59, one ship was consigned to Surat, one to Fort St. George, and two to Bantam. The latter were directed to touch at Fort St. George to obtain coast clothes for the islands, and to return to Bengal and Fort St. George to take in Bengal and Coromandel goods for Europe. Instructions were given to make great efforts for recovering a share of the spice trade.[4] Bantam, however, was at this time blockaded by the Dutch, and no accounts were this year received of the traffic in the southern islands.[5]

The operations of the new joint-stock were not more prosperous than those of the old. Transactions at the several factories were feeble and unsuccessful For two years, 1659-60, and 1660-61, there is no account of the Company's equipments; and their advances to India were no doubt small.[6] "The embarrassed state of the Company's

[1] Bruce, i. 532. [2] Ibid. [3] Ibid, 533.

[4] Bruce, 539, 540. The state of interest, both in India and England, appears incidentally in the accounts received by the Company from the agents at Surat, in the year 1658-59. These agents, after stating the narrowness of the funds placed at their disposal, recommend to the Directors rather to borrow money in England, which could easily be done at 4 per cent., than leave them to take up money in India at 8 or 9 per cent. Ibid, 542

[5] Bruce, 544. [6] Ibid, 549—551.

BOOK I. CHAP. IV. 1661.

funds at this particular period," says Mr. Bruce, "may be inferred from the resolutions they had taken to relinquish many of their out-stations, and to limit their trade in the Peninsula of India to the presidencies of Surat and Fort St. George, and their subordinate factories."[1]

Meanwhile Cromwell had died, and Charles II. ascended the throne. Amid the arrangements which took place between England and the continental powers, the Company were careful to press on the attention of government a list of grievances, which they represented themselves as still enduring at the hands of the Dutch; and an order was obtained, empowering them to take possession of the island of Polaroon. They afterwards complained that it was delivered to them in such a state of prepared desolation, as to be of no value.[2] The truth is, it was of little value at best.

On every change in the government of the country, it had been an important object with the Company to obtain a confirmation of their exclusive privileges. The usual policy was not neglected, on the accession of Charles II.; and a petition was presented to him for a renewal of the East India charter. As there appears not to have been, at that time, any body of opponents to make interest or importunity for a contrary measure, it was far easier to grant without inquiry, than to inquire and refuse; and Charles and his ministers had a predilection for easy rules of government. A charter, bearing date the 3rd of April, 1661, was accordingly granted, confirming the ancient privileges of the Company, and vesting in them authority to make peace and war with any prince or people, not being Christians; and to seize unlicensed persons within their limits, and send them to England.[3] The two last were important privileges; and, with the right of administering justice consigned almost all the powers of government to the discretion of the Directors and their servants.

It appears not that, on this occasion, the expedient of a new subscription for obtaining a capital was attempted. A new adjustment with regard to the privileges and dead stock in India would have been required. The joint-stock was not as yet a definite and invariable sum, placed beyond the power of resumption, at the disposal of the

[1] Bruce, i. 555. [2] Ibid, 553, 554. [3] Ibid, 557.

Company, the shares only transferable by purchase and sale in the market. The capital was variable and fluctuating; formed by the sums which, on the occasion of each voyage, the individuals, who were free of the Company, chose to pay into the hands of the Directors, receiving credit for the amount in the Company's books, and proportional dividends on the profits of the voyage. Of this stock 500*l*. entitled a proprietor to a vote in the general courts; and the shares were transferable, even to such as were not free of the Company, upon paying 5*l*. for admission.[1]

Of the amount either of the shipping or stock of the first voyage upon the renewed charter we have no account; but the instructions sent to India prescribed a reduction of the circle of trade. In the following year, 1662-63, two ships sailed for Surat, with a cargo in goods and bullion, amounting to 65,000*l*., of which it would appear that 28,300*l*. was consigned to Fort St. George. Next season there is no account of equipments. In 1664-65, two ships were sent out with the very limited value of 16,000*l*. The following season, the same number only of ships was equipped; and the value in money and goods consigned to Surat was 20,600*l*.; whether any thing in addition was afforded to Fort St. George does not appear; there was no consignment to Bantam. In 1666-67, the equipment seems to have consisted but of one vessel, consigned to Surat with a value of 16,000*l*.[2]

With these inadequate means, the operations of the Company in India were by necessity languid and humble. At Surat the out-factories and agencies were suppressed. Instructions were given to sell the English goods at low rates, for the purpose of ruining the interlopers. The Dutch, however, revenged the private traders; and, by the competition of their powerful capital, rendered the Company's business difficult and unprofitable.[3] On the Coromandel coast the wars among the native chiefs, and the overbearing influence of the Dutch, cramped and threatened to extinguish the trade of the English. And at Bantam, where the Dutch power was most sensibly felt, the feeble

1 Anderson's History of Commerce, in Macpherson's Annals, ii. 495, 605.
2 Bruce, ii. 108, 119, 152, 186.
3 Ibid. 110, 138, 157, 158, 174.

BOOK I. CHAP. IV. resources of their rivals hardly sufficed to keep their business alive.[1]

1662-67. During these years of weakness and obscurity, several events occurred, which, by their consequences, proved to be of considerable importance. The island of Bombay was ceded to the King of England as part of the dowry of the Infanta Catharine; and a fleet of five men of war commanded by the Earl of Marlborough, with 500 troops commanded by Sir Abraham Shipman, were sent to receive the possession. The armament arrived at Bombay on the 18th of September, 1662; but the governor evaded the cession. The English understood the treaty to include Salsette and the other dependencies of Bombay. As it was not precise in its terms, the Portuguese denied that it referred to anything more than the island of Bombay. Even Bombay they refused to give up, till further instructions, on the pretext that the letters or patent of the King did not accord with the usages of Portugal. The commander of the armament applied in this emergency to the Company's President, to make arrangements for receiving the troops and ships at Surat, as the men were dying by long confinement on board. But that magistrate represented the danger of incurring the suspicion of the Mogul government, which would produce the seizure of the Company's investment, and the expulsion of their servants from the country. In these circumstances the Earl of Marlborough took his resolution of returning with the King's ships to England; but Sir Abraham Shipman, it was agreed, should land the troops on the island of Angedivah, twelve leagues distant from Goa. On the arrival of the Earl of Marlborough in England, in 1663, the King remonstrated with the government of Portugal, but obtained unsatisfactory explanations; and all intention of parting with the dependencies of Bombay was denied. The situation, in the meantime, of the troops at Angedivah proved extremely unhealthy; their numbers were greatly reduced by disease; and the commander made offer to the President and Council at Surat, to cede the King's rights to the Company. This offer, on consultation, the President and Council declined; as well because, without the authority of the King, the grant was not valid, as because,

[1] Bruce, ii. 130, 159.

in their feeble condition, they were unable to take possession of the place. After Sir Abraham Shipman and the greater part of the troops had died by famine and disease, Mr. Cooke, on whom the command devolved, accepted of Bombay on the terms which the Portuguese were pleased to prescribe: renounced all claim to the contiguous islands; and allowed the Portuguese exemption from the payment of customs. This convention the King refused to ratify, as contrary to the terms of his treaty with Portugal; but sent out Sir Gervase Lucas to assume the government of the place. As a few years' experience showed that the government of Bombay cost more than it produced, it was once more offered to the Company: and now accepted. The grant bears date in 1668. Bombay was "to be held of the King in free and common soccage, as of the manor of East Greenwich, on the payment of the annual rent of 10*l.* in gold, on the 30th of September, in each year;" and with the place itself was conveyed authority to exercise all political powers, necessary for its defence and government.[1]

Subtorfuges of a similar kind were invented by the Dutch to evade the cession of the island of Polaroon. The Governor pretended that he could not deliver up the island without instructions from the Governor of Banda; and the Governor of Banda pretended that he could not give such instructions without receiving authority from the Governor-General of Batavia. After much delay and negotiation, the cession was made in 1665; but not, if we believe the English accounts, till the Dutch had so far exterminated the inhabitants and the spice-trees, that the acquisition was of little importance. On the recommencement, however, of hostilities between England and Holland, the Dutch made haste to expel the English, and to reoccupy the island. And by the treaty of Breda, both Polaroon and Damm, on which the English had attempted an establishment, were finally ceded to the Dutch.[2]

In the beginning of 1664, Sivajee, the founder of the Mahratta power, in the course of his predatory warfare against the territories of the Mogul Sovereign, attacked the city of Surat. The inhabitants fled, and the Governor

[1] Bruce, ii. 104, 106, 126, 134, 141, 155, 168, 199. Macpherson's Annals, ii. 503.
[2] Ibid. 132, 161, 184,

BOOK I. CHAP. IV. 1663-68.

shut himself up in the castle. The Company's servants, however, taking shelter in the factory, stood upon their defence, and having called in the ships' crews to their aid, made so brave a resistance that Sivajee retired after pillaging the town. The gallantry and success of this enterprise so pleased the Mogul government, as to obtain its thanks to the President, and new privileges of trade to the Company.[1] The place was again approached by the same destructive enemy in 1670, when the principal part of the Company's goods was transported to Swally, and lodged on board the ships. The English again defended themselves successfully, though some lives were lost, as well as some property in their detached warehouses.[2]

[1] Scant justice is done to the Company's servants in this brief notice of a conduct highly remarkable for cool and resolute courage. Sivajee's approach to within fifteen miles of Surat was announced on the morning of the 5th of January, upon which the Governor retired into the castle, and the inhabitants fled from every part of the city except that adjacent to the factory. In the evening the Mahrattas entered, and part blockaded the castle, whilst the rest plundered and set fire to the houses. During that night and the following day repeated demands and menaces were sent to the factory, but they were all met with terms of defiance. "We replied to Sivajee," says the despatch to the Court dated the 26th January, 1664, "we were here on purpose to maintain the house to the death of the last man, and therefore not to delay his coming upon us." It does not appear that any organized attack was made upon the factory, but the Mahrattas assembled in considerable numbers before it, and broke into an adjoining house. To prevent their establishing themselves in a situation from which they might offer serious annoyance, a sally was made from the factory which had the effect of dislodging the assailants, and putting them to flight, with some loss and three men wounded on the part of the English; this success was followed up with spirit—the plundered house was occupied—several sorties were made, and pushed even to the gates of the castle, and the neighbourhood for near a quarter of a mile round was cleared of the enemy. No further attempts were made to molest the factory or its vicinity during the three days that Sivajee continued in possession of the town, and the inhabitants of the quarter in which the factory was situated "were very thankful in their acknowledgments, blessing and praising the English nation," to whose valour they ascribed their exemption from the calamities which had desolated the rest of the city. The governor presented Sir G. Oxenden with a dress of honour, and recommended the interests of the Company to Aurungzeb.

The emperor in the first instance remitted the customs at Surat for one year in favour of all merchants, and subsequently granted a perpetual remission of a portion of the duties to the English in particular. The despatch from Surat states the proportion to be one half, but the translation of the Husb-ul-hookum, in the Records, says a half per cent.; and in the firmaun granted on the 26th June, 1667, the amount is stated at one per cent. out of three, the ordinary impost. A more important provision of the firmaun is exemption from all transit charges on any pretext whatever.—W.

[2] Bruce, ii. 144, 145, 284.—M. According to Orme, the English and Dutch factories were free on this, and on the former irruption, from either molestation or demand.—Fragments, 14, 25. A very extraordinary statement, as he had access to the public records, which tell a very different story. On this occasion, as on the former, the English factory was defended with spirit, "the enemy," says the letter from Surat, "found such hot service from our house, that they left us." Subsequently a parley was held with "the Captain of the Brigade," who agreed to refrain from further molestation, and "the house was quiet for two days." On the third day they again appeared before the factory,

At this period occurred one of the first instances of refractory and disobedient conduct on the part of the Company's servants. This is a calamity to which they have been much less frequently exposed, than, from the distance and employment of those servants, it would have been reasonable to expect. The efforts of the Directors to suppress the trade, which their agents carried on for their own account, had not been very successful. Sir Edward Winter, the chief servant at Fort St. George, was suspected of this delinquency, and in consequence recalled. When Mr. Foxcroft, however, who was sent to supersede him, arrived at Fort St. George, in June, 1665, Sir Edward, instead of resigning, placed his intended successor in confinement, under a pretext which it was easy to make, that he had uttered disloyal expressions against the King's government. Notwithstanding remonstrances and commands, he maintained himself in the government of the place till two ships arrived, in August, 1668, with peremptory orders from the Company, strengthened by a command from the King, to resign; when his courage failed him, and he complied. He retired to Masulipatam, a station of the Dutch, till the resentment excited against him in England should cool; and his name appears no more in the annals of the Company.[1]

In Bengal the English factory at Hoogly[2] had been involved in an unhappy dispute with the Mogul government,

"threatening that they would take or burn it to the ground.; but Mr. Master stood in so resolute a posture that the Captain, not willing to hazard his men, with much ado kept them back, and sent a man into the house to advise Mr. Master what was fit to be done." In consequence of this communication a complimentary present was sent to Sivajee by two of the Company's servants; he received them kindly, "telling them that the English and he were very good friends, and putting his hand into their hands told them that he could do the English no wrong, and that this giving his hand was better than any 'Coul' to oblige him thereto." Sivajee was in fact desirous to conciliate the English, in order to induce them to return to Rajapore, where they had formerly had a factory, which they had abandoned in consequence of his exactions. The loss of their trade had injured the town of Rajapore, and diminished the Mahratta's revenue from it. Sivajee immediately afterwards left Surat. The French had saved their factory, by paying a contribution. The Dutch factory was without the town, and was not attacked; and these circumstances, with the interview between Sivajee and the English, inspired the Mogul Government with considerable distrust of the Europeans at Surat.—W.

[1] Bruce, ii. 179, 245.

[2] The English were first permitted to establish a factory at Hoogly, 1640, in the early part of Shah Shuja's government of Bengal. Hamilton. Stewart, 252. Bruce says, the agents and factors at Fort St. George, sent Captain Brockhaven, to attempt to establish a factory at Hoogly, about 1650; i. 454.—W.

BOOK I. CHAP. IV. 16 3-68.

on account of a junk which they imprudently seized on the river Ganges. For several years this incident had been used as a pretext for molesting them.[1] In 1662-63, the chief at Madras sent an agent to endeavour to reconcile them with Meer Jumlah, the Nabob of Bengal; and to establish agencies at Balasore and Cossimbuzar.[2] The Company's funds, however, were too confined to push to any extent the trade of the rich province of Bengal.

The scale was very small on which, at this time, the Company's appointments were formed. In 1662, Sir George Oxenden was elected to be "President and chief Director of all their affairs at Surat, and all other their factories in the north parts of India, from Zeilon to the Red Sea," at a salary of 300*l.* and with a gratuity of 200*l.* per annum as compensation for private trade. Private trade in the hands of their servants, and still more in those of others, the Company were now most earnestly labouring to suppress. Directions were given to seize all unlicensed traders and send them to England; and no exertion of the great powers intrusted to the company was to be spared, to annihilate the race of merchants who trenched upon the monopoly, and to whom, under the disrespectful name of interlopers, they ascribed a great part of their imbecility and depression.[3]

Their determination to crush all those of their countrymen who dared to add themselves to the list of their competitors, failed not to give rise to instances of great hardship and calamity. One was rendered famous by the altercation which in 1666 it produced between the two houses of parliament. Thomas Skinner, a merchant, fitted out a vessel in 1657. The agents of the Company seized his ship and merchandise in India, his house, and the island of Barella, which he had bought of the King of Jambee.[4] They even denied him a passage home; and he was obliged to travel over land to Europe. The sufferer failed

[1] It could not have been used for many years, as it occurred only in 1660-61; and Shuja, who invariably encouraged the English, governed Bengal in 1659. He then took up arms to assert his claim to the throne. After he was defeated by Mir Jumla, that general detained some English boats laden with saltpetre, at Rajmahal, and it was in reprisal that the English seized one of his boats at Hoogly: the difference was speedily adjusted. Stewart, 286.—W.

[2] Bruce, i. 560; ii. 110, 131.

[3] Ibid. ii. 107—109.

[4] Jambi is a district on the east coast of Sumatra, with a navigable river; the island of Barella is not noticed by Marsden, History of Sumatra. It is the Pulo Brawl of the Records, a barren and unoccupied island, about eight leagues in compass. The Company's agents write, that no good was to be done with the island, unless people were sent to plant it.—W.

not to seek redress, by presenting his complaint to the government, and after some importunity it was referred first to a committee of the Council, and next to the House of Peers. When the Company were ordered to answer, they refused to acknowledge the jurisdiction of the Peers, on the ground that they were only a court of appeal, and not competent to decide in the first resort. The objection was overruled. The Company appealed to the House of Commons; the Lords were highly inflamed; and, proceeding to a decision, awarded to the petitioner, 5,000*l*. The Commons were now enraged in their turn; and being unable to gratify their resentments upon the House of Peers, which was the cause of them, they were pleased to do so upon the unfortunate gentleman who had already paid so dearly for the crime (whatever its amount) of infringing the Company's monopoly. He was sent a prisoner to the Tower. The Lords, whom these proceedings filled with indignation, voted the petition of the Company to the Lower House to be false and scandalous. Upon this the Commons resolved that whoever should execute the sentence of the other house in favour of Skinner, was a betrayer of the rights and liberties of the Commons of England, and an infringer of the privileges of their house. To such a height did these contentions proceed, that the King adjourned the parliament seven times; and when the controversy after an intermission revived, he sent for both houses to Whitehall, and by his personal persuasion induced them to erase from their journals all their votes, resolutions, and other acts relating to the subject. A contest, of which both parties were tired, being thus ended, the sacrifice and ruin of an individual appeared, as usual, of little importance: Skinner had no redress.[1]

Another class of competitors excited the fears and

[1] Macpherson's Annals, ii. 493.—M. If Skinner's claims were just, and were yet disregarded, the blame rests not with those who disputed his claims, but those who gave judgment in his favour, with the House of Lords; and whatever hardship he personally sustained, was the act, not of the East India Company, but of the House of Commons. The Company, in any case, are free from culpability. As to their conduct in seizing his ship and property, it may be doubted if the case is accurately stated by Macpherson, the only authority here followed. Thomas Skinner was preceded at Jambi by his brother, Frederick Skinner, as agent of the merchant adventurers. On the union of the two Companies, he was directed to transfer his agency to persons sent out by them. After some little delay, he assented, and quitted Jambi, making over his assets to the united stock, together with his debts, which amounted to 24,000 dollars. The property then, whatever it might have been, was not

BOOK I. CHAP. IV. 1663-68.

jealousies of the Company. Colbert, the French minister of finance, among his projects for rendering his country commercial and opulent, conceived, in 1664, the design of an East India Company. The report which reached the Court of Directors in London represented the French as fitting out eight armed vessels for India, commanded by Hubert Hugo, whom in their instructions to the settlements abroad, the Directors described as a Dutch pirate. The hostilities of the Company were timid. They directed their agents in India to afford these rivals no aid or protection, but to behave towards them with circumspection and delicacy. The subservience of the English government to that of France was already so apparent, as to make them afraid of disputes in which they were likely to have their own rulers against them.[1]

The war which took place with Holland in 1664, and which was followed, in 1665, by a temporary quarrel with France, set loose the powers of both nations against the Company in India. The French Company, however, was too much in its infancy to be formidable; and the Dutch, whose mercantile competition pressed as heavily during peace as during war, added to the difficulties of the English, chiefly by rendering their navigation more hazardous and expensive.

A fact, an enlightened attention to which would probably have been productive of important consequences, was at this time forced upon the notice of the Company. One grand source of the expenses which devoured the profits of their trade was their factories, with all that mass of dead stock which they required, houses, lands, fortifications, and equipments. The Dutch, who prosecuted their interests with vigilance and economy, carried on their trade in a great many places without factories. Upon re-

Skinner's, but that of the united Company; but it seems to have been in the possession of Thomas Skinner, and to have been recovered from him by the aid of the Sultan of Jambi, whether legally or not, may be questioned: but Skinner was certainly not dispossessed of his property "for the crime of infringing the Company's monopoly." That he was harshly treated by the Commons, is undeniable; but he was not the only person for whose captivity sympathy should have been excited. The Lords were as little lenient as the Commons; and in reprisal for Skinner's incarceration, ordered Sir Samuel Barnadiston, and three other members of the Court of Directors, into confinement. Parliamentary History, v. iv. 422.—W.

[1] Raynal, Hist. Philos. et Polit. des Etabliss., etc., dans les Deux Indes, ii. 183. Ed. 8vo. Génève, 1781. Bruce, ii. 137, 150, 167. Macpherson's Annals, ii. 516.

ceiving instructions to make preparations and inquiry for opening a trade with Japan, Mr. Quarles Brown, the Company's agent at Bantam, who had been at Japan, reported to the Court, that it would be necessary, if a trade with Japan was to be undertaken, to follow the plan of the Dutch; who procured the commodities in demand at Japan, in the countries of Siam, Cambodia, and Tonquin, not by erecting expensive factories, but by forming contracts with the native merchants. These merchants, at fixed seasons, brought to the ports the commodities for which they had contracted, and though it was often necessary to advance to them the capital with which the purchases were effected, they had regularly fulfilled their engagements.[1] Even the Company itself, and that in places where their factories cost them the most, had made experiments, and with great advantage, on the expediency of employing the native merchants in providing their investments. At Surat, in 1665-66, "the investments of the season were obtained by the employment of a native merchant, who had provided an assortment of pepper at his own risk, and though the Dutch had obstructed direct purchases of pepper, the agents continued the expedient of employing the native merchants, and embarked a moderate assortment."[2] Factories to carry on the traffic of Asia, at any rate on the scale, or anything approaching to the scale, of the East India Company, were the natural off-spring of a joint-stock; the Managers or Directors of which had a much greater interest in the patronage they created, which was wholly their own; than in the profits of the company, of which they had only an insignificant share. Had the trade to India been conducted from the beginning, on those principles of individual adventure and free competition, to which the nation owes its commercial grandeur, it is altogether improbable that many factories would have been established. The agency of the native merchants would have performed much; and where it was not sufficient, the Indian trade would have naturally divided itself into two branches. One set of adventurers would have established themselves in India,

[1] Letters from the Agent and Council of Bantam (in the East India Register Office), Bruce, ii. 163.
[2] Bruce, ii. 178, from a letter from the President and Council of Surat.

BOOK I. CHAP. IV. 1663-68.

by whom investments would have been provided for the European ships, and to whom the cargoes of the European goods would have been consigned. Another class of adventurers, who remained at home, would have performed the business of export and import from England, as it is performed to any other region of the globe.[1]

The time, however, was now approaching when the weakness which had so long characterised the operations of the English in India was gradually to disappear. Notwithstanding the imperfections of the government, at no period, perhaps, either prior or posterior, did the people of this country advance so rapidly in wealth and prosperity, as during the time, including the years of civil war, from the accession of James I. to the expulsion of James II.[2] We are not informed of the particular measures which were

[1] It is very unlikely that any such results would have taken place, or that a trade with India would have been formed, or if formed, would have been perpetuated by any other means than those actually adopted. The Portuguese and Dutch had territorial possessions and fortified factories; and without similar support, it would have been impossible for the English to have participated in the profits of the commerce of the East. Even with these resources, the Dutch succeeded in expelling the English from the Archipelago; and it is very little probable, that they would have suffered a single English adventurer to carry on a trade with any part of India from whence they could so easily exclude him. Principles of individual adventure and free competition, would have availed but little against the power and jealousy of our rivals; and it was necessary to meet them on equal terms, or to abandon the attempt. But it was not only against European violence, that it was necessary to be armed; the political state of India rendered the same precautions indispensable. What would have become of "individual adventure" at Surat, when it was pillaged by the Mahrattas? And what would have been the fate of the English commerce with Madras and Bengal, on the repeated occasions on which it was menaced with extinction, by the rapacity and vindictiveness of the native princes? Had, therefore, the anti-monopoly doctrines been more popular in those days than they were, it is very certain that the attempt to carry them into effect, would have deprived England of all share in the trade with India, and cut off for ever one main source of her commercial prosperity. It is equally certain, that without the existence of such factories as were "the natural offspring of a joint-stock;" without the ample resources of a numerous and wealthy association; and without the continuous and vigorous efforts of a corporate body, animated by the enjoyment of valuable privileges, and the hope of perpetuating their possession by services rendered to the state, we should never have acquired political power in India, or reared a mighty empire upon the foundations of trade.—W.

[2] Sir William Petty, who wrote his celebrated work, entitled "Political Arithmetic," in 1676, says: "1. The streets of London showed that city to be double what it was forty years before; great increase was also manifested at Newcastle, Yarmouth, Norwich, Exeter, Portsmouth, and Cowes; and in Ireland, at Dublin, Kingsale, Coleraine, and Londonderry. 2. With respect to shipping, the navy was triple or quadruple what it was at that time; the shipping of Newcastle was 80,000 tons, and could not then have exceeded a quarter of that amount. 3. The number and splendour of coaches, equipages, and furniture, had much increased since that period. 4. The postage of letters had increased from one to twenty. 5. The king's revenue had tripled itself." See too, Macpherson's Annals, ii. 580.

pursued by the Directors for obtaining an extension of funds; but the increase of capital in the nation was probably the principal cause which enabled them, in the year succeeding the acquisition of Bombay, to provide a grander fleet and cargo than they had ever yet sent forth. In the course of the year 1667-68, six ships sailed to Surat, with goods and bullion to the value of 130,000*l.*; five ships to Fort St. George, with a value of 75,000*l.*; and five to Bantam, with a stock of 40,000*l.* In the next season we are informed that the consignments to Surat consisted of 1,200 tons of shipping, with a stock of the value of 75,000*l.*; to Fort St. George, of five ships, and a stock of 103,000*l.*; and to Bantam, of three ships and 35,000*l.* In the year 1669-70, 1,500 tons of shipping were sent to Surat, six ships to Fort St. George, and four to Bantam, and the whole amount of the stock was 281,000*l.* The vessels sent out in 1670-71 amounted to sixteen, and their cargoes and bullion to 303,500*l.* In the following year four ships were sent to Surat, and nearly 2,000 tons of shipping to Fort St. George; the cargo and bullion to the former, being 85,000*l.*, to the latter, 160,000*l.*; shipping to the amount of 2,800 tons was consigned to Bantam, but of the value of the bullion and goods no account seems to be preserved. In 1672-73, stock and bullion to the amount of 157,700*l.* were sent to Surat and Fort St. George. On account of the war, and the more exposed situation of Bantam, the consignment to that settlement was postponed. In the following year, it appears that cargoes and bullion were consigned, of the value of 100,000*l.* to Surat; 87,000*l.* to Fort St. George; and 41,000*l.* to Bantam.[1]

Other events of these years were of considerable importance. In 1667-68, appears the first order of the Company for the importation of tea.[2] Attempts were now recommended for resuming trade with Sumatra.[3] In 1671-72, considerable embarrassment was produced at Surat by the arrival of a French fleet of twelve ships, and a stock computed at 130,000*l.* The inconsiderate purchases and sales of the French reduced the price of

[1] Bruce, ii. 201, 206, 209—224, 227, 230—256, 258, 259—278, 281, 282, 283—293, 296, 297—312, 313—327, 328, 331.

[2] Ibid, 210. The words of this order are curious, "to send home by these ships 100 lb. waight of the best tey that you can gett."

[3] Ibid, 211.

BOOK I. CHAP. IV. 1674.

European goods, and raised that of Indian; but these adventurers exhibited so little of the spirit and knowledge of commerce, as convinced the Company's agents that they would not prove formidable rivals.[1]

As England and France were now united in alliance against the Dutch, the Company might have exulted in the prospect of humbling their oppressors, but the danger of a new set of competitors seems effectually to have repressed these triumphant emotions. In 1673, the island of St. Helena, which had several times changed its masters, being recaptured from the Dutch, was granted anew and confirmed to the Company by a royal charter.[2]

The funds which, in such unusual quantity, the Directors had been able to supply for the support of the trade in India, did not suffice to remove, it would appear that they hardly served to lighten, the pecuniary difficulties under which it laboured. To an order to provide a large investment, the President and Council at Surat, in 1673-74, replied, that the funds at their disposal were only 88,228*l.* and their debts 100,000*l.* besides interest on the same at 9 per cent.; and in November, 1674, they represented that the debt arose to no less a sum than 135,000*l.*; and that all returns must in a great measure be suspended till, by the application of the funds received from Europe, the Company's credit should be revived.[3]

Of the sort of views held out at this period to excite the favour of the nation towards the East India Company, a specimen has come down to us of considerable value. Sir Josiah Child, an eminent member of the body of Directors, in his celebrated Discourses on Trade, written in 1665, and published in 1667, represents the trade to India as the most beneficial branch of English commerce; and in proof of this opinion he asserts, that it employs from twenty-five to thirty sail of the most warlike mercantile ships of the kingdom, manned with mariners from 60 to 100 each; that it supplies the kingdom with saltpetre, which would otherwise cost the nation an immense sum to the Dutch; with pepper, indigo, calicoes, and drugs, to the value of 150,000*l.* or 180,000*l.* yearly, for which it would otherwise pay to the same people an exorbitant price; with materials for export to Turkey, France, Spain, Italy,

[1] Bruce, ii. 302. [2] Ibid. 232, 334. [3] Ibid. 337, 342, 366.

and Guinea, to the amount of 200,000*l.* or 300,000*l.* yearly, countries with which, if the nation were deprived of these commodities, a profitable trade could not be carried on.

These statements were probably made with an intention to deceive. The imports, exclusive of saltpetre, are asserted to exceed 400,000*l.* a year; though the stock which was annually sent to effect the purchases, and to defray the whole expense of factories and fortifications abroad, hardly amounted in any number of years preceding 1665, to 100,000*l.*, often to much less; while the Company were habitually contracting debts, and labouring under the severest pecuniary difficulties.[1] Thus early, in the history of this Company, is it found necessary to place reliance on their accounts and statements, only when something very different from the authority of their advocates is found to constitute the basis of our belief.

It will be highly instructive to confront one exaggerated statement with another. About the same time with the discourses of Sir Josiah Child, appeared the celebrated work of De Witt on the state of Holland. Proceeding on the statement of Sir Walter Raleigh, who in the investigation of the Dutch fishery, made for the information of James I. in 1603, affirmed, that "the Hollanders fished on the coasts of Great Britain with no fewer than 3,000 ships, and 50,000 men; that they employed and sent to sea, to transport and sell the fish so taken, and to make returns thereof, 9,000 ships more, and 150,000 men; and that twenty busses do, one way or other, maintain 8,000 people;" he adds, that from the time of Sir Walter Raleigh to the time at which he wrote, the traffic of Holland in all its branches could not have increased less than one third. Allowing this account to be exaggerated in the same proportion as that of the East India Director, which the nature of the circumstances, so much better known, renders rather improbable; it is yet evident, to what a remarkable degree the fisheries of the British coasts, to which the Dutch confined themselves, constituted a more important

1 The pecuniary difficulties were chiefly encountered in India, and might have explained the apparent disagreement between the value of the imports and the stock sent out to effect their purchase, the fact being that the stock sent out was inadequate to the purchase, and the investments were paid for by money taken up in India, the great profit made on their sale more than covering the interest of the debt.—W.

BOOK I. CHAP. IV. 1675-82.

commerce than the highly vaunted, but comparatively insignificant business of the East India Company.[1] The English fishery, at the single station of Newfoundland, exceeded in value the trade to the East Indies. In the year 1676, no fewer than 102 ships, carrying twenty guns each, and eighteen boats, with five men to each boat, 9,180 men in all, were employed in that traffic; and the total value of the fish and oil was computed at 386,400*l.*[2]

The equipments, in 1674-75, were, five ships to Surat with 189,000*l.* in goods and bullion; five to Fort St. George with 202,000*l.*; and 2,500 tons of shipping to Bantam with 65,000*l.*: In 1675-76, to Surat, five ships and 96,500*l.*; to Fort St. George, five ships and 235,000*l.*; to Bantam, 2,450 tons of shipping and 58,000*l.*: In 1676-77, three ships to Surat, and three to Fort St. George, with 97,000*l.* to the one, and 176,600*l.* to the other; and eight ships to Bantam, with no account of the stock. The whole adventure to India, in 1677-78, seems to have been seven ships and 352,000*l.*; of which a part, to the value of 10,000*l.* or 12,000*l.*, was to be forwarded from Fort St. George to Bantam: In 1678-79, eight ships and 393,950*l.*: In 1679-80, ten ships and 461,700*l.*: In 1680-81, eleven ships and 596,000*l.*: And, in 1681-82, seventeen ships, and 740,000*l.*[3]

The events affecting the East India Company were still common and unimportant. In 1674-75, a mutiny, occasioned by retrenchment, but not of any serious magnitude, was suppressed at Bombay. In trying and executing the ringleaders, the Company exercised the formidable powers of martial law. The trade of Bengal had grown to such importance, that, instead of a branch of the agency at Fort St. George, an agency was now constituted in Bengal itself. Directions were forwarded to make attempts for opening a trade with China; and tea, to the value of 100 dollars, was in 1676-77, ordered on the Company's account. Be-

[1] An anonymous author, whom Anderson in his History of Commerce quotes as an authority, says, in 1679, that the Dutch herring and cod fishery employed 8,000 vessels, and 200,000 sailors and fishers, whereby they annually gained five millions sterling; besides their Iceland, Greenland, and Newfoundland fisheries, and the multitude of trades and people employed by them at home. Macpherson's Annals, ii. 596. See in the same work, ii. 547, and 552, a summary of the statements of Child and De Witt. For ampler satisfaction the works themselves must be consulted.

[2] Anderson's History of Commerce. Macpherson's Annals, ii. 579.

[3] Bruce, ii. 356, 360, 361—375, 379—392, 393, 395—406, 409, 410—435, 438, 439—446, 451, 453—459, 465, 468.

side the ordinary causes of depression which affected the Company at Bantam, a particular misfortune occurred in 1667. The principal persons belonging to the factory having gone up the river in their prows, a number of Javanese assassins, who had concealed themseves in the water, suddenly sprung upon them, and put them to death.[1]

In 1677-78, "the Court," says Mr. Bruce, "recommended temporising expedients to their servants, with the Mogul, with Sivajee, and with the petty Rajahs; but at the same time they gave to President Augier and his council discretionary powers, to employ armed vessels, to enforce the observation of treaties and grants:—in this way, the Court shifted from themselves the responsibility of commencing hostilities, that they might be able, in any questions which might arise between the King and the Company, to refer such hostilities to the errors of their servants."[2] This cool provision of a subterfuge, at the expense of their servants, is a policy ascribed to the Company, in this instance, by one of the most unabashed of their eulogists. We shall see, as we advance, in what degree the precedent has been followed.

The difficulties which now occurred in directing the operations of the various individuals employed in the business of the East India Company began to be serious. The Directors, from ignorance of the circumstances in which their servants were placed, often transmitted to them instructions which it would have been highly imprudent to execute. The functionaries abroad often took upon themselves, and had good reasons for their caution, to disregard the orders which they received. A door being thus opened for discretionary conduct, the instructions of the Directors were naturally as often disobeyed for the convenience of the actors abroad, as for the benefit of the

[1] Bruce, ii. 367, 466, 396, 404. [2] Ibid, 400.—M.

There is a clause in these instructions omitted, which it is but justice to the Directors to re-insert. They enjoined their servants " to endeavour by their conduct to impress the natives with an opinion of the probity of the English in all commercial dealings." With regard to the object of the Court in giving discretionary powers to the President and Council of Surat, to enforce the observation of treaties and grants, it is not very candid to limit it to leaving an opening by which they might escape responsibility. Their own distance from the scene of action rendered some such discretionary authority in their servants indispensable, as is admitted a few lines further on.—W.

BOOK I. CHAP. V. 1683.

Company at home. The disregard of their authority, and the violation of their commands, had been a frequent subject of uneasiness and indignation to the Directors. Nor was this all. From discordant pretensions to rank and advancement in the service, animosities arose among the agents abroad. Efforts were made by Directors for the cure of these troublesome, and even dangerous, diseases. Seniority was adopted as the principle of promotion; but nomination to the important office of a Member of Council at the Agencies, as well as Presidencies, was reserved to the Court of Directors.[1]

CHAPTER V.

From the Project of forming a new and rival Company, till the Union of the two Companies by the Award of Godolphin, in the year 1711.

THE Company were now again threatened by that competition with their fellow-citizens, which they have always regarded as their greatest misfortune. From the renewal of their charter, shortly after the accession of Charles II., their monopoly had not been disturbed, except by a few feeble interlopers, whom they had not found it difficult to crush. In the year 1682-83, the design was disclosed of opening a subscription for a new joint-stock, and establishing a rival East India Company. The scheme was so much in unison with the sentiments of the nation, and assumed an aspect of so much importance, that it was taken into consideration by the King and Council. It had so much effect upon the views of the Company, though for the present the Council withheld their sanction, that, in Mr. Bruce's opinion,[2] it introduced into their policy of 1682-83 a refinement, calculated and intended to impose upon the King and the public. It induced them to speak of the amount of their equipments, not, as usual, in terms of exact detail, but in those of vague and hyperbolical estimate. What we know of their adventure of that year is only the information they forwarded to their Indian

[1] Bruce, ii. 355, 374, 459, 453.

[2] Ibid. 275—M. Bruce's words are "a new practice, probably a refinement in policy," ii. 477.—W.

stations, that the stock to be sent out would exceed one million sterling. In the course of the next season they equipped four ships to Surat. Of that year we only further know that 100,000*l.* in bullion was intended for Bengal. In 1684-85, information was forwarded to Surat, in general terms, that the tonnage and stock would be considerable. Five ships sailed for Fort St. George and Bengal, with 140,000*l.* in bullion. Of other circumstances nothing is adduced: and for several succeeding years no statement of the tonnage and stock of the annual voyages appears.[1]

Under the skill which the Court of Directors have all along displayed in suppressing such information as they wished not to appear, it is often impossible to collect more than gleanings of intelligence respecting the Company's debts. At the present period, however, they appear to have been heavy and distressing. In 1676, it was asserted by their opponents in England that their debts amounted to 600,000*l.*;[2] and we have already seen that, in 1674, the debt of Surat alone amounted to 135,000*l.*[3] In 1682-83, the Directors authorised the Agency in Bengal to borrow 200,000*l.*, and in 1683-84, it is stated that the debt upon the dead stock at Bombay alone amounted to 300,000*l.*[4] It seems highly probable that at this time their debts exceeded their capital.

In a war between the King of Bantam and his son, in which the English sided with the one,[5] and the Dutch with the other, the son prevailed; and expelled the English from the place. The agents and servants of the factory took shelter at Batavia, and the Dutch Governor made offer of his assistance to bring the property of the Company from Bantam. As the English, however, accused the Dutch of being the real authors of the calamity, they declined the proposal, as precluding those claims of redress which the Company might prosecute in Europe. Various efforts were made to regain possession of Bantam, but the Dutch from this time remained sole masters of Java.[6]

Upon the loss of Bantam, the Presidency for the govern-

1 Bruce, ii. 476, 481—496, 506—528, 531.

2 Anderson's History of Commerce. Macpherson's Annals, ii. 579.

3 Supra, p. 95. 4 Bruce, ii. 482, 499.

5 There is no proof that the English took any part in the dispute, nor is it likely. They were not sufficiently strong to provoke the enmity of the Dutch.—W.

6 Bruce, ii. 492.

BOOK I. CHAP. V. 1683-85.

ment of the Eastern Coast, which had hitherto, with a fond desire for the traffic of the islands, been stationed at that place, was removed to Fort St. George.[1]

The nation becoming gradually more impatient under the monopoly, the numbers multiplied of those who ventured to break through the restraint which it imposed on the commercial ardour of the times.[2] The Company, not satisfied with the power which they had already obtained of common and martial law, and of seizing, with their property, and sending to England, as many of their countrymen as their interests or caprice might direct, still called for a wider range of authority: and, under the favour of government which they now enjoyed, obtained the powers of Admiralty jurisdiction, for the purpose of seizing and condemning, safe from the review of the courts of municipal law in England, the ships of the interlopers.[3] The servants of the Company were now invested with unlimited power over the British people in India.

Insurrection again appeared at Bombay, and assumed a very formidable aspect. The causes were such as have commonly, in the Company's affairs, been attended with similar effects. Efforts had been made to retrench expenses; unpleasant to the Company's servants. The earliest experiment of the Company in territorial sovereignty agreed with the enlarged experience of succeeding times: the expense of the government exceeded the revenue which the population and territory could be made to yield. The Directors, new to the business of government, were disappointed; and having first laboured to correct the deficit by screwing up the revenue, they next attempted the same arduous task by lessening the expense. By the two operations together, all classes of their subjects were alienated: first, the people, by the weight of taxation; next, the instruments of government, by the diminution of their

[1] Bruce, ii. 502.

[2] It would appear, from the way in which these interlopers are spoken of, that they were unconnected merchants seeking only to carry on trade with India on the principles of individual adventure and free competition. It seems, however, that they attempted more than this, representing themselves as a new Company chartered by the King, whose purpose it was to deprive the old of their privileges. They endeavoured also to establish themselves permanently at various places in the Dekhan, and offered to the King of Golconda 15,000 Pagodas for permission to erect a Fort at Armagaon. It was not without cause, therefore, that the Company regarded them with fear, and endeavoured to suppress their commerce.—W.

[3] Bruce, ii. 496.

profits. Accordingly Captain Keigwin, commander of the garrison at Bombay, was joined by the troops and the great body of the people, in renouncing the authority of the Company, and declaring by proclamation, dated December 27, 1683, that the island belonged to the King. Keigwin was by general consent appointed Governor; and immediately addressed letters to the King and the Duke of York, stating such reasons as were most likely to avert from his conduct the condemnation to which it was exposed.[1]

The President and Council at Surat, conscious of their inability to reduce the island by force, had recourse to negotiation. A general pardon, and redress of grievances, were promised. First three commissioners were sent; afterwards the President repaired to Bombay in person. But neither entreaties nor threats were of any avail.[2]

As soon as intelligence arrived in England, the King's command was procured, directing Captain Keigwin to deliver up the island; and instructions were forwarded to proceed against the insurgents by force. When Sir Thomas Grantham, the commander of the Company's fleet, presented himself at Bombay, invested with the King's commission, Keigwin offered, if assured of a free pardon to himself and adherents, to surrender the place. On these terms, the island was restored to obedience.[3] For the more effectual coercion of any turbulent propensities, the expedient was adopted of removing the seat of government from Surat to Bombay. Nor could the humble pretensions of a President and Council an longer satisfy the rising ambition of the Company. The Dutch had established a regency at Batavia and Columbo. It was not consistent with the grandeur of the English Company to remain contented with inferior distinction. In 1687, Bombay was elevated to the dignity of a Regency, with unlimited power over the rest of the Company's settle-

1 Bruce, ii. 512. Governor Child is accused by Hamilton of wanton and intolerable oppressions; and that author states some facts which indicate excessive tyranny. New account of the East Indies, i. 187—199.

2 Bruce, ii. 515.

3 The first was surrendered on the 20th November, 1684, upon stipulations which secured entire immunity to the mutineers, with leave to return to Europe or remain at their pleasure. In the interval, a civilian, Dr. St. John, had been sent out with a Commission from the King, and one from the Company, to preside in all judicial proceedings at Bombay.—W.

BOOK I. CHAP. V.

ments.[1] Madras was formed into a corporation, governed by a mayor and aldermen.[2]

1685-87.

The English had met with less favour, and more oppression, from the native powers in Bengal, than in any other part of India.[3] In 1685-86, the resolution was adopted of seeking redress and protection by force of arms. The greatest military equipment the Company had ever provided was sent to India. Ten armed vessels, from twelve to seventy guns, under the command of Captain Nicholson, and six companies of infantry, without captains, whose places were to be supplied by the Members of Council in Bengal, were despatched, with instructions to seize and fortify Chittagong as a place of future security, and to retaliate in such a manner upon the Nabob and Mogul as to obtain reparation for the injuries and losses which had been already sustained. In addition to this force, the Directors, in the following year, made application to the King for an entire company of regular infantry with their officers; and power was granted to the Governor in India to select from the privates such men as should appear qualified to be commissioned officers in the Company's service. By some of those innumerable casualties, inseparable from distant expeditions, the whole of the force arrived not at one time in the Ganges; and an insignificant quarrel between some of the English soldiers and the natives, was imprudently allowed to bring on hostilities, before the English were in a

[1] The seat of Government had been transferred from Surat to Bombay in the preceding year. Bruce, ii. 553. The policy of placing the British Indian authorities under one head, is too obvious to be ascribed merely to the rising ambition of the Company.—W.

[2] Bruce, ii. 526, 540, 584, 591. It was debated in the Privy Council, whether the charter of incorporation should be under the King's or the Company's seal. The King asked the Chairman his opinion, who replied, "that no person in India should be employed by immediate commission from his Majesty, because, if they were, they would be prejudicial to our service by their arrogancy, and prejudicial to themselves, because the wind of extraordinary honour in their heads would probably make them so haughty and overbearing, that we should be forced to remove them." Letter from the Court to the President of Fort St. George (ibid, 591). Hamilton, ut supra (189—192). Orme's Historical Fragments, 185, 188, 192, 198.

[3] Mr. Orme is not unwilling to ascribe part of the hardships they experienced to the interlopers, who, seeking protection against the oppressions of the Company, were more sedulous and skilful in their endeavours to please the native governors. Historical Fragments, 185.—M. This was, no doubt, true to some extent, but the difficulties were, in a still greater degree, attributable to the administration of Shaistah Khan, as Subahdar of Bengal, whose insatiable desire of accumulating wealth, led him to a system of extortion, which descended through all his subordinates, and of which the English trade was the especial object.—W.

BOOK I. CHAP. V. 1685-87.

condition to maintain them with success. They were obliged to retire from Hoogly,[1] after they had cannonaded it with the fleet, and took shelter at Chutanuttee, afterwards Calcutta, till an agreement with the Nabob, or additional forces, should enable them to resume their stations. The disappointment of their ambitious schemes was bitterly felt by the Court of Directors. They blamed their servants in Bengal in the severest terms, not only for timidity, but breach of trust, as having turned the resources of the Company, which ought to have been effectually employed in obtaining profitable and honourable terms from the Nabob and Mogul, to their own schemes of private avarice and emolument.[2] A hollow truce was agreed to by the Nabob, which he only employed for preparing the means of an effectual attack. The English under the direction of Charnock, the Company's agent, made a gallant defence. They not only repulsed the Nabob's forces in repeated assaults, but stormed the fort of Tanna, seized the island of Injellee, in which they fortified themselves, and burnt the town of Balasore, with forty sail of the Mogul fleet; the factories, however, at Patna and Cossimbuzar were taken and plundered. In September, 1687, an accommodation was effected, and the English were allowed to return to Hoogly with their ancient privileges. But

[1] These circumstances are so summarily narrated as to be inexactly told. "Three English soldiers had quarrelled with the Peons of the Nawab, and had been wounded; a company of soldiers was called out in their defence, and finally the whole of the troops. The native forces collected to oppose them were routed, the town was cannonaded by the ships, and the Foujdar was compelled to solicit a cessation of arms, which was granted on condition of his furnishing means of conveying the Company's goods on board their vessels. Before the action took place orders had come from Shaistah Khan to compromise the differences with the English, but their claims had now become so considerable, amounting to above 66 lacs of rupees, or nearly 700,000*l.*, that it was not likely they expected the Nawab's acquiescence. They remained at Hoogly till the 20th of December, and then, "considering that Hoogly was an open town, retired to Chutanuttee, or Calcutta, from its being a safer situation during any negotiation with the Nabob or Mogul." Negotiations were accordingly opened and terms agreed upon, when, in February, the Nawab threw off the mask, and a large body of horse appeared before Hoogly. Bruce, ii. 581.—W.

[2] As here represented, it does not appear why the Court was dissatisfied with the conduct of affairs in Bengal, an indistinctness arising from the extreme compression of the original account in Bruce; the chief object of the armament was the occupation of Chittagong; the Court considered that the truce granted to the Foujdar of Hoogly, and the negotiation entered into with the Nawab, had given to the latter time to strengthen his troops at Chittagong, and place it out of danger, their servants proposing, by their claims for compensation, to make good personal losses, rather than vindicate the rights of the Company. Bruce, ii. 594.—W.

BOOK I. CHAP. V. 1687.

this was a termination of the contest ill-relished by the Court of Directors. Repeating their accusations of Charnock and their other functionaries, they sent Sir John Child, the governor of Bombay, to Madras and Bengal, for the purpose of reforming abuses, and of re-establishing, if possible, the factories at Cossimbuzar and other places, from which they had been driven by the war. A large ship, the Defence, accompanied by a frigate, arrived from England under the command of a captain of the name of Heath, with instructions for war. The Company's servants had made considerable progress by negotiation in regaining their ancient ground; when Heath[1] precipitately commenced hostilities, plundered the town of Balasore, and proceeded to Chittagong, which he found himself unable to subdue. Having taken the Company's servants and effects on board, agreeably to his orders, he sailed to Madras; and Bengal was abandoned.[2]

These proceedings, with the rash and presumptuous behaviour of Sir John Child on the western side of India, exasperated Aurengzebe, the most powerful of all the Mogul sovereigns, and exposed the Company's establishments to ruin in every part of India. The factory at Surat was seized; the island of Bombay was attacked by the fleet of the Siddees; the greater part of it was taken, and the governor besieged in the town and castle. Aurengzebe issued orders to expel the English from his dominions. The factory at Masulipatam was seized; as was also that at Vizagapatam, where the Company's agent and several of their servants were slain. The English stooped to the most abject submissions. With much difficulty they obtained an order for the restoration of the factory

[1] The Defence arrived in India in October, 1688, and took the Company's servants and property on board at Calcutta in the following month. The attack on Balasore was made on the 29th of November, and in opposition to the advice of the agent and Council on board the fleet: after its failure, the ships proceeded to Chittagong, where it was determined to address the Nawab before commencing hostilities. Without waiting for a reply, or commencing military operations, Captain Heath sailed from Chittagong, and after a fruitless attempt to effect a settlement in Aracan, conveyed the Company's property and servants to Madras, where they arrived in March, 1689. Bruce, ii. 648.—W.

[2] These events occurred under the government of the celebrated imperial deputy, Shaistah Khan; "to the character of whom (says Mr. Stewart, History of Bengal, 300,) it is exceedingly difficult to do justice. By the Mohammedan historians he is described as the pattern of excellence; but by the English he is vilified as the oppressor of the human race. Facts are strongly on the side of the Mohammedans."—W

at Surat, and the removal of the enemy from Bombay. Negociation was continued, with earnest endeavours, to effect a reconciliation. The trade of the strangers was felt in the Mogul treasuries; and rendered the Emperor, as well as his deputies, not averse to an accomodation. But the interruption and delay sustained by the Company made them pay dearly for their premature ambition, and for the unseasonable insolence, or the imprudence of their servants.[1]

During these contests, the French found an interval in which they improved their footing in India. They had formed an establishment at Pondicherry, where they were at this time employed in erecting fortifications.[2]

The equipments for 1689-90 were on a reduced scale; consisting of three ships only, two for Bombay, and one for Fort St. George. They were equally small the succeeding year. We are not informed to what the number of ships or value of cargo amounted in 1691-2. In the following year, however, the number of ships was eleven; and was increased in 1693-4, to thirteen. In the following year there was a diminution, but to what extent does not appear. In each of the years 1695-6 and 1696-7, the number of ships was eight. And in 1697-8 it was only four.[3]

It was now laid down as a determinate object of policy, that independence was to be established in India; and dominion acquired. In the instructions forwarded in 1689, the Directors expounded themselves in the following words: "The increase of our revenue is the subject of our care, as much as our trade:—'tis that must maintain our force, when twenty accidents may interrupt our trade; 'tis that must make us a nation in India;—without that we are but as a great number of interlopers, united by his Majesty's royal charter, fit only to trade where nobody of

[1] Bruce, ii. 558, 569, 578, 594, 608, 620, 630, 639, 641, 646, 650. The lively and intelligent Captain Hamilton represents the conduct of Sir John Child at Surat as exceptionable in the highest degree. But the Captain was an interloper, and though his book is strongly stamped with the marks of veracity, his testimony is to be received with same caution on the one side as that of the Company on the other. New account of India, i. 199—228.—M.

Bruce and Stewart give translations of the original orders from the Company's Records. The factory at Surat was fined 150,000 rupees, and Mr. Child was ordered to be turned out and expelled. Bruce, ii. 639. Hist. Bengal App. vi. and vii. Sir John (Mr.) Child, an able and enterprizing servant of the Company, and the chief of all their establishments in India, had previously died.—W.

[2] Bruce, ii. 655.

[3] Ibid, iii. 75, 87, 122, 139, 181. 203, 231.

BOOK I. CHAP. V. 1689-98.

power thinks it their interest to prevent us;—and upon this account it is that the wise Dutch, in all their general advices which we have seen, write ten paragraphs concerning their government, their civil and military policy, warfare, and the increase of their revenue, for one paragraph they write concerning trade."[1] It thus appears at how early a period, when trade and sovereignty were blended, the trade, as was abundantly natural, became an object of contempt, and by necessary consequence, a subject of neglect. A trade, the subject of neglect, is of course a trade without profit.[2]

This policy was so far gratified, about the same period, that Tegnapatam, a town and harbour on the Coromandel coast, a little to the south of Pondicherry, was obtained by purchase, and secured by grant from the country powers. It was strengthened by a wall and bulwarks, and named Fort St. David.[3]

A fact of much intrinsic importance occurs at this part of the history. Among the Christians of the East, the Armenians, during the power of the successors of Constantine, had formed a particular sect. When the countries which they inhabited were overrun by the Mahomedan arms, they were transplanted by force, in great numbers, into Persia, and dispersed in the surrounding countries. Under oppression, the Armenians adhered to their faith; and addicting themselves to commerce, became, like the Jews in Europe, the merchants and brokers in the different countries to which they resorted.[4] A proportion of them made their way into India, and by their usual industry and acuteness, acquired that share in the business of the country which was the customary reward of the qualities they displayed. The pecuniary pressure under which the Company at this time laboured, and under which, without ruinous consequences, the increase of patronage could not

[1] Bruce, iii. 78.

[2] The anxiety of the Directors to maintain a trade "without profit," would be somewhat inexplicable, if it was true, but the injuries to which that trade had been exposed from European competition and native exactions, had sufficiently proved that it could not be carried on without the means of maintaining an independent position in India.—W.

[3] Bruce, iii. 120.

[4] See, in Gibbon, viii. 357 to 360, a train of allusions, as usual, to the history of the Armenians; and in his notes a list of its authors.—The principal facts regarding them, as a religious people, are collected with his usual industry and fidelity by Mosheim, Ecclesiast. Hist. iii. 493, 494, 495, and 412, 413.

be pursued, constrained the Directors to look out for economical modes of conducting their trade. They accordingly gave instructions, that, instead of multiplying European agents in India, natives, and especially Armenians, should be employed: "because," to use the words of Mr. Bruce, copying or abridging the letters of the Court, "that people could vend English woollens, by carrying small quantities into the interior provinces, and could collect fine muslins, and other new and valuable articles, suited to the European demands, *better* than any agents of the Company could effect, under any phirmaund or grant which might be eventually purchased."[1]

The prosperity which the nation had enjoyed, since the death of Charles I., having rendered capital more abundant, the eagerness of the mercantile population to enter into the channel of Indian enterprise and gain had proportionably increased; and the principles of liberty being now better understood, and actuating more strongly the breasts of Englishmen, not only had private adventure, in more numerous instances, surmounted the barriers of the company's monopoly, but the public in general at last disputed the power of a royal charter, unsupported by Parliamentary sanction, to limit the rights of one part of the people in favour of another, and to debar all but the East India Company from the commerce of India. Applications were made to Parliament for a new system of management in this branch of national affairs; and certain instances of severity, which were made to carry the appearance of atrocity, in the exercise of the powers of martial law assumed by the Company, in St. Helena and other places, served to augment the unfavourable opinion which was now rising against them.[2]

The views of the House of Commons were hostile to the Company. A committee, appointed to investigate the subject, delivered it as their opinion on the 16th January, 1690, that a new Company should be established, and established by Act of Parliament; but that the present Company should carry on the trade exclusively, till the new Company were established.[3] The House itself, in

[1] Bruce, iii. 88.

[2] Ibid. 81; Macpherson's Annals, ii. 618; and Adam Smith, Wealth of Nations, iii. 132, who with his usual sagacity brings to view the causes of the principal events in the history of the Company.

[3] Bruce, iii. 82.

BOOK I. CHAP. V. 1689-98.

1691, addressed the King to dissolve the Company, and incorporate a new one; when the King referred the question to a committee of the Privy Council.[1]

In the mean time the Company proceeded, in a spirit of virulence, to extinguish the hated competition of the general traders. "The Court," says Mr. Bruce, transcribing the instructions of 1691, "continued to act towards their opponents, interlopers, in the same manner as they had done in the latter years of the two preceding reigns; and granted commissions to all their captains, proceeding this season to India, to seize the interlopers of every description, and to bring them to trial before the Admiralty Court at Bombay;—explaining, that, as they attributed all the differences between the Company and the Indian powers to the interlopers, if they continued their depredations on the subjects of the Mogul or King of Persia, they were to be tried for their lives as pirates, and sentence of death passed; but execution stayed till the King's pleasure should be known."[2]

The cruelty which marks these proceedings is obvious; and would hardly be credible if it were less strongly attested. The Company seized their opponents, and carried them before their own Admiralty Courts, that is, before themselves, to judge and pass sentence in their own cause, and inflict almost any measure of injury which it suited minds, inflamed with all the passions of disappointed avarice and ambition, to perpetrate. They accused their competitors of piracy, or of any other crime they chose; tried them as they pleased, and sentenced them even to death: accounting it an act of mercy that they did not consign them to the executioner before the royal pleasure was known;—as if that pleasure could be as quickly known in India, as it could in England;—as if the unfortunate victim might not remain for months and years in the dungeons of the Company, in a climate, where a sentence of imprisonment, for any length of time, to a European constitution, is a sentence of almost certain death; and where he could hardly fail to suffer the pains of many executions, beside the ruin of his affairs, in a land of strangers and enemies, even if his wretched life were protracted till his doom, pronounced at the opposite side of

[1] Macpherson's Annals, ii. 648. [2] Bruce, iii. 102.

the globe, could be known. Mr. Bruce, with his usual alacrity of advocation, says, "This proceeding of the Court rested upon the opinion of the twelve Judges, which was, that the Company had a right to the trade to the East Indies, according to their charter."[1] Because the Judges said they had a right to the trade to the East Indies, they assumed a right to be judges and executioners of their fellow-subjects, in their own cause. This was a bold conclusion. It was impossible that, under any colour of justice, the powers of judicature intrusted to the Company, by kingly without parliamentary authority, even if allowed, could be extended beyond their own servants, who voluntary submitted to their jurisdiction. Over the rest of their fellow-subjects, it was surely sufficient power, if they were permitted to send them to England, to answer for their conduct, if challenged, before a tribunal which had not an overbearing interest in destroying them.

The King of 1693, like the King of any other period, preferred power in his own hands to power in the hands of the parliament, and would have been pleased to retain without participation the right of making or annulling exclusive privileges of trade. Notwithstanding the resolution of the committee of the House of Commons, that parliament should determine whatever regulations might be deemed expedient for the Indian trade, a new charter

[1] Bruce, iii. 103. Sir Josiah Child, as Chairman of the Court of Directors, wrote to the Governor of Bombay, to spare no severity to crush their countrymen who invaded the ground of the Company's pretensions in India. The Governor replied, by professing his readiness to omit nothing which lay within the sphere of his power, to satisfy the wishes of the Company; but the laws of England, unhappily, would not let him proceed so far as might otherwise be desirable. Sir Josiah wrote back with anger: "That he expected his orders were to be his rules, and not the laws of England, which were a heap of nonsense, compiled by a few ignorant country gentlemen, who hardly knew how to make laws for the good of their own private families, much less for the regulating of companies, and foreign commerce" (Hamilton's New Account of India, i. 232). "I am the more particular," adds Captain Hamilton, "on this account, because I saw and copied both those letters in anno 1696, while Mr. Vaux [the Governor to whom the letters were addressed] and I were prisoners at Surat, on account of Captain Evory's robbing the Mogul's great ship, called the Gunsway." Bruce, iii. 233.—M.

Mr. Mill here forgets the caution he had recommended, a few pages before, in regard to Captain Hamilton's testimony. No doubt the servants of the Company in India, were little inclined to exercise forbearance towards the interlopers; but the picture here delineated is exaggerated. Captain Hamilton, an interloper, trafficked in India for ten years, and could not have encountered very serious opposition: his imprisonment was the act of the Mogul government.—W.

BOOK I. CHAP. V.

1693.

was granted by letters patent from the crown, as the proper mode of terminating the present controversies. The principal conditions were, that the capital of the Company, which was 756,000*l.*, should be augmented by 744,000*l.*, so as to raise it to 1,500,000*l.*; that their exclusive privileges should be confirmed for twenty-one years; that they should export 100,000*l.* of British produce annually; that the title to a vote in the Court of Proprietors should be 1000*l.*; and that no more than ten votes should be allowed to any individual.[1]

The pretensions, however, of the House of Commons, brought this important question to a different issue. Towards the close of the very same season, that assembly came to a vote, "that it was the right of all Englishmen to trade to the East Indies, or any part of the world, unless prohibited by act of parliament:"[2] and William knew his situation too well to dispute their authority.

The Company laboured under the most pressing embarrassments. Though their pecuniary difficulties, through the whole course of their history, have been allowed as little as possible to meet the public eye, what we happen to be told of the situation at this time of the Presidency at Surat affords a lively idea of the financial distresses in which they were involved. Instead of eight lacks of rupees, which it was expected would be sent from Bombay to Surat, to purchase goods for the homeward voyage, only three lacks and a half were received. The debt at Surat already amounted to twenty lacks; yet it was absolutely necessary to borrow money to purchase a cargo for even three ships. A loan of one lack and 80,000 rupees was necessary to complete this small investment. To raise this sum, it was necessary to allow to individuals the privileges of the contract which subsisted with the Armenian merchants.[3] And after all these exertions the money could only be obtained by taking it up on loans from the Company's servants.[4]

[1] Bruce, iii. 133—135. Macpherson's Annals, ii. 649. [2] Ibid. 142.

[3] We know not the terms of that contract, nor how a participation in its privileges could be granted to individuals without a breach of faith toward the Armenian merchants.—M.

Why should a breach of contract be imputed to the Company's servants, when it is not known what the terms of the contract were; what reason, indeed, is there to suppose that there was any contract at all?—W.

[4] Bruce, iii. 167.

The Company meanwhile did not neglect the usual corrupt methods of obtaining favours at home. It appeared that they had distributed large sums of money to men in power, before obtaining their charter. The House of Commons were, at the present period, disposed to inquire into such transactions. They ordered the books of the Company to be examined; where it appeared that it had been the practice, and even habit of the Company, to give bribes to great men; that, previous to the revolution, their annual expense, under that head, had scarcely ever exceeded 1,200*l.*; that since the revolution it had gradually increased; and that in the year 1693, it had amounted to nearly 90,000*l.* The Duke of Leeds, who was charged with having received a bribe of 5000*l.*, was impeached by the Commons. But the principal witness against him was sent out of the way, and it was not till nine days after it was demanded by the Lords that a proclamation was issued to stop his flight. Great men were concerned in smothering the inquiry; parliament was prorogued; and the scene was here permitted to close.[1]

As the science and art of government were still so imperfect as to be very unequal to the suppression of crimes; and robberies and murders were prevalent even in the best regulated countries in Europe; so depredation was committed on the ocean under still less restraint, and pirates abounded wherever the amount of property at sea afforded an adequate temptation. The fame of Indian riches attracted to the Eastern seas adventurers of all nations; some of whom were professed pirates; others, men preferring honest trade, though, when they found themselves debarred from this source of profit, by the pretensions and power of monopoly, they had no such aversion to piracy as to reject the only other source in which they were allowed to partake. The moderation which, during some few years, the Company had found it prudent to observe in their operations for restraining the resort of private traders to India, had permitted an increase of the predatory adventurers. As vessels belonging to Mogul subjects fell occasionally into the hands of plunderers of the English nation, the Mogul government, too

[1] Macpherson's Annals, ii. 652, 662; 10,000*l.* is said to have been traced to the king.

OOK I. CHAP. V.

1698.

ignorant and headlong to be guided by any but the rudest appearances, held the Company responsible for the misdeeds of their countrymen; and sometimes proceeded to such extremities as to confiscate their goods, and confine their servants. The Company, who would have been justified in requiring aid at the hands of government for the remedy of so real a grievance,[1] made use of the occasion as a favourable one for accumulating odium upon the independent traders. They endeavoured to confound them with the pirates. They imputed the piracies, in general, to the interlopers, as they called them. In their complaints to government they represented the interlopers, and the depredations of which they said they were the authors, as the cause of all the calamities to which, under the Mogul government, the Company had been exposed. The charge, in truth, of piracy, became a general calumny, with which all the different parties in India endeavoured to blacken their competitors; and the Company itself, when the new association of merchants trading to India began to rival them, were as strongly accused of acting the pirates in India, as the individual traders had been by themselves.[2]

Such was the situation of the Company in England, and in India, when the influence of the rival association threatened them with destruction. In the year 1698, both parties were urging their pretensions with the greatest possible zeal, when the necessities of the government pointed out to both the project of bribing it by the accommodation of money. The Company offered to lend to government 700,000*l.* at 4 per cent. interest, provided their charter should be confirmed, and the monopoly of India secured to them by act of parliament. Their rivals, knowing on how effectual an expedient they had fallen, resolved to augment the temptation. They offered to advance 2,000,000*l.* at 8 per cent., provided they should be

[1] Would they have obtained any such remedy? It is very improbable, in the temper of the times. The grievance, it is admitted, was real: the Company had been armed by the nation with powers to protect themselves, and it could scarcely be expected that they should prefer the delay and uncertainty of an unnecessary appeal.—W.

[2] Bruce, iii. 146, 186. "Sir Nicholas Waite [Consul of the Association] addressed a letter," says Mr. Bruce, "to the Mogul, accusing the London Company of being sharers and abettors of the piracies, from which his subjects, and the trade of his dominions, had suffered; or, in the Consul's coarse language, *of being thieves and confederates with the pirates.*"—Ibid. 337.

1698.

invested with the monopoly, free from obligation of trading on a joint-stock, except as they themselves should afterwards desire.[1]

A bill was introduced into parliament for carrying the project of the new association into execution. And the arguments of the two parties were brought forward in full strength and detail.[2]

On the part of the existing Company, it was represented: That they possessed charters; that the infringement of charters was contrary to good faith, contrary to justice, and in fact no less imprudent than it was immoral, by destroying that security of engagements on which the industry of individuals and the prosperity of nations essentially depend. That the East India Company, moreover, had property, of which to deprive them would be to violate the very foundation on which the structure of society rests; that they were the Lords-Proprietors, by royal grant, of Bombay and St. Helena; that they had in India, at their own expense, and by their own exertions, acquired immoveable property, in lands, in houses, in taxes and duties, the annual produce of which might be estimated at 44,000*l*. That, at great expense, they had erected fortifications in various parts of India, by which they had preserved to their country the Indian trade; and had built factories and purchased privileges of great importance to the nation; enterprises to which they could have been induced by nothing but the hope and prospect of national support. That the resources and abilities of the Company were proved, by the estimate of their quick and dead stock; and that a capital of two millions would be raised immediately by subscription. That the project, on the contrary, of the new association made no provision for a determinate stock; and the trade, which experience proved to require an advance of 600,000*l*. annually, might thus be lost to the nation, for want of sufficient capital to carry it on. That justice to individuals, as well as to the public, required the continuance of the charter, as the property and even subsistence of many families, widows, and orphans, was involved in the fate of the Company: In short, that humanity, law, and policy, would all be

1 Anderson's History. Macpherson's Annals, ii. 694. Bruce, iii. 252, 253.
2 Bruce, iii. 253. Macpherson, ii. 694.

BOOK I. CHAP. V.

equally violated by infringing the chartered rights of this admirable institution.[1]

1698.

The new association replied; That it was no infringement of good faith or justice, to annul, by a legislative act, a charter which was hostile to the interest of the nation; because that would be to say, if a government has once committed an error, that it is not lawful to correct itself; it would be to say that, if a nation has once been rendered miserable, by erroneous institutions of government, it must never try to rescue itself from its misery. That the practical rule of the British government, as many precedents abundantly testified, had been, to set at nought the pretended inviolability of charters, as often as they were proved to be unprofitable or injurious. That not only had charters been destroyed by act of parliament, but even the judges at law (so little in reality was the respect which had been paid to charters) had often set them aside, by their sole authority, on the vague and general ground that the King had been deceived in his grant. That, if any chartered body was entitled to complain of being dissolved, in obedience to the dictates of utility, it was certainly not the East India Company, whose charter had been originally granted, and subsequently renewed, on the invariable condition of being terminated after three years' notice, if not productive of national advantage. To display the property which the Company had acquired in India, and to pretend that it gave them a right to perpetuity of charter, was nothing less than to insult the supreme authority of the state; by telling it, that, be the limitations what they might, under which the legislature should grant a charter, it was at all times in the power of the chartered body to annul those limitations, and mock the legislative wisdom of the nation, simply by acquiring property. That, if the Company had erected forts and factories, the question still remained, whether they carried on the trade more profitably by their charter than the nation could carry it on if the charter were destroyed. That the nation and its constituted authorities were the sole judge in this controversy; of which the question whether the nation or the Company were most

[1] Bruce, iii. 253. Anderson's History of Commerce; Macpherson, ii. 694, 695.

BOOK I. CHAP. V. 1698.

likely to fail in point of capital, no doubt formed a part. That if inconvenience, and in some instances distress, should be felt by individuals, this deserved consideration, and, in the balance of goods and evils, ought to be counted to its full amount; but to bring forward the inconvenience of individuals, as constituting in itself a conclusive argument against a political arrangement, is as much as to say that no abuse should be ever remedied; because no abuse is without its profit to somebody, and no considerable number of persons can be deprived of customary profits without inconvenience to most, hardship to many, and distress to some.[1]

The new associators, though thus strong against the particular pleas of their opponents, were debarred the use of those important arguments which bore upon the principle of exclusion; and which, even in that age, were urged with great force against the Company. They who were themselves endeavouring to obtain a monopoly could not proclaim the evils which it was the nature of monopoly to produce. The pretended rights of the Company to a perpetuity of their exclusive privileges, for to that extent did their arguments reach, were disregarded by everybody, and an act was passed, empowering the King to convert the new association into a corporate body, and to bestow upon them the monopoly of the Indian trade. The charters, the property, the privileges, the forts and factories of the Company in India, and their claims of merit with the nation, if not treated with contempt, were at least held inadequate to debar the legislative wisdom of the community from establishing for the Indian trade whatever rules and regulations the interest of the public appeared to require.[2]

The following were the principal provisions of the act: That the sum of two millions should be raised by subscription for the service of government: that this subscription should be open to natives or foreigners, bodies politic or corporate; that the money so advanced should bear an interest of 8 per cent. per annum: that it should be lawful for his Majesty, by his letters patent, to make the sub-

[1] Bruce, iii. 253, 254. Anderson's History of Commerce; Macpherson, ii. 695.
[2] Bruce, iii. 295. Macpherson, ii. 696.

BOOK I. CHAP. V. 1698.

scribers a body politic and corporate, by the name of the "General Society": that the subscribers severally might trade to the East Indies, each to the amount of his subscription: that if any or all of the subscribers should be willing and desirous, they might be incorporated into a joint-stock Company: that the subscribers to this fund should have the sole and exclusive right of trading to the East Indies: that on three years' notice, after the 29th of September, 1711, and the repayment of the capital of 2,000,000*l.*, this act should cease and determine: that the old or London Company, to whom three years' notice were due, should have leave to trade to India till 1701: that their estates should be chargeable with their debts: and that if any furtheir dividends were made before the payments of their debts, the members who received them should be responsible for the debts with their private estates to the amount of the sums thus unduly received.

This measure, of prohibiting dividends while debt is unpaid, or of rendering the Proprietors responsible with their fortunes to the amount of the dividends received, befitted the legislative justice of a nation.

A clause, on the same principle, was enacted with regard to the New Company, that they should not allow their debts at any time to exceed the amount of their capital stock; or, if they did, that every proprietor should be responsible for the debts with his private fortune, to the whole amount of whatever he should have received in the way of dividend or share after the debts exceeded the capital.[1]

This good policy was little regarded in the sequel.

In conformity with this act a charter passed the great seal, bearing date the 3rd of September, constituting the subscribers to the stock of 2,000,000*l.* a body corporate under the name of the "General Society." This charter empowered the subscribers to trade, on the terms of a regulated Company, each subscriber for his own account. The greater part, however, of the subscribers desired to trade upon a joint-stock: and another charter, dated the 5th of the same month, formed this portion of the subscribers, exclusive of the small remainder, into a joint-

[1] Statute 9 & 10 Will. III., c. 44.

1698.

stock Company, by the name of "the English Company trading to the East Indies."[1]

"In all this very material affair," says Anderson, "there certainly was a strange jumble of inconsistencies, contradictions and difficulties, not easily to be accounted for in the conduct of men of judgment."[2] The London Company, who had a right by their charter to the exclusive trade to India till three years after notice, had reason to complain of this injustice, that the English Company were empowered to trade to India immediately, while they had the poor compensation of trading for three years along with them. There was palpable absurdity in abolishing one exclusive company, only to erect another; when the former had acted no otherwise than the latter would act. Even the departure from joint-stock management, if trade on the principle of individual inspection and personal interest had been looked to as the source of improvement, might have been accomplished, without the erection of two exclusive companies, by only abolishing the joint-stock regulation of the old one. But the chief mark of the ignorance of parliament, at that time, in the art and science of government, was their abstracting from a trading body, under the name of loan to government, the whole of their trading capital: and expecting them to traffic largely and profitably when destitute of funds. The vast advance to government, which they feebly repaired by credit, beggared the English Company, and ensured their ruin from the beginning.

The old, or London Company, lost not their hopes. They were allowed to trade for three years on their own charter; and availing themselves of the clause in the act, which permitted corporations to hold stock of the New Company, they resolved to subscribe into this fund as largely as possible; and under the privilege of private adventure, allowed by the charter of the English Company, to trade, separately, and in their own name, after the three years of their charter should be expired. The sum which they were enabled to appropriate to this purpose was 315,000*l*.[3]

1 Macpherson's Annals, ii. 699. Bruce, iii. 257, 258. Preamble to the Stat. 6 Anne, c. 17.
2 Anderson's History of Commerce; Macpherson, ii. 700.
3 Bruce, iii. 256, 257. Macpherson, ii. 700. Smith's Wealth of Nations, iii. 133.

BOOK I. CHAP. V. 1698-99.

In the instructions to their servants abroad they represented the late measures of parliament as rather the result of the power of a particular party than the fruit of legislative wisdom: "The Interlopers," so they called the New Company, "had prevailed by their offer of having the trade free, and not on a joint-stock;" but they were resolved by large equipments (if their servants would only second their endeavours) to frustrate the speculations of those opponents: "Two East India Companies in England," these are their own words, "could no more subsist without destroying one the other, than two kings, at the same time regnant in the same kingdom: that now a civil battle was to be fought between the Old and the New Company; and that two or three years must end this war, as the Old or the New must give way; that, being veterans, if their servants abroad would do their duty, they did not doubt of the victory; that if the world laughed at the pains the two Companies took to ruin each other, they could not help it, as they were on good ground and had a charter."[1]

When the time arrived for paying the instalments of the subscriptions to the stock of the New Company, many of the subscribers not finding it easy to fulfil their engagements, were under the necessity of selling their shares. Shares fell to a discount, and the despondency, hence arising, operated to produce still greater depression.[2]

The first voyage which the New Company fitted out, consisted of three ships with a stock of 178,000*l*.[3] To this state of imbecility did the absorption of their capital reduce their operations. The sum to which they were thus limited for commencing their trade but little exceeded the interest which they were annually to receive from government.

With such means the New Company proved a very unequal competitor with the Old. The equipments of the Old Company, for the same season, 1698-99, amounted to thirteen sail of shipping, 5,000 tons burthen, and stock estimated at 525,000*l*. Under the difficulties with which they had to contend at home, they resolved by the most submissive and respectful behaviour, as well as by offer of services, to cultivate the favour of the Mogul. Their endeavours were not unsuccessful. They obtained a grant of

[1] Bruce, iii. 257. [2] Ibid. 259, 260. [3] Ibid. 265.

the towns of Chuttanuttee, Govindpore, and Calcutta, and began but cautiously, so as not to alarm the native government, to construct a fort. It was denominated Fort William; and the station was constituted a Presidency.[1]

To secure advantages to which they looked from their subscription of 315,000*l.* into the stock of the English Company, they had sufficient influence to obtain an act of parliament,[2] by which they were continued a corporation, entitled, after the period of their own charter, to trade, on their own account, under the charter of the New Company, to the amount of the stock they had subscribed.[3]

The rivalship of the two Companies produced, in India, all those acts of mutual opposition and hostility which naturally flowed from the circumstances in which they were placed. They laboured to supplant one another in the good opinion of the native inhabitants and the native governments. They defamed one another. They obstructed the operations of one another. And at last their animosities and contentions broke out into undissembled violence and oppression. Sir William Norris, whom the New Company, with the King's permission, had sent as their ambassador to the Mogul court, arrived at Surat in the month of December, 1700. After several acts, insulting and injurious to the London Company, whom he accused of obstructing him in all his measures and designs, he seized three of the Council, and delivered them to the Mogul Governor, who detained them till they found security for their appearance. The President and the Council were afterwards, by an order of the Mogul government, put in confinement; and Sir Nicholas Waite, the English Company's Consul at Surat, declared, in his correspondence with the Directors of that Company, that he had solicited this act of severity, because the London Company's ser-

[1] The chief agent of the Company, Job Charnock, had taken possession of Chutanutty, in the contests with the Nawab, in 1687; and, upon the restoration of tranquillity, returned to it in 1690. The Foujdar of Hoogly sought to induce the English to return there; but they obtained leave to build a factory at Calcutta, which they preferred, as more secure and accessible to shipping. Subsequently, permission was procured from Azeem-us-shan, the grandson of Aurungzeb, and Governor of Bengal, to purchase the rents of the three villages named in the text, from the Zemindars, who were then in charge of the collections, amounting to 1195 rupees, 6 annas, annually. The ground was, no doubt, very thinly occupied, and in great part overrun with jungle; giving to the Company, therefore, lands sufficient for the erection of their factory and fort. Stewart, App. xi. p. 541.—W.

[2] Bruce, iii. 264, 268, 300.

[3] Ibid. 293, 326, 350.

BOOK I. CHAP. V. 1700.

vants had used treasonable expressions towards the King; and had made use of their interest with the Governor of Surat to oppose the privileges which the Ambassador of the English Company was soliciting at the court of the Mogul.[1]

As the injury which these destructive contentions produced to the nation soon affected the public mind, and was deplored in proportion to the imaginary benefits of the trade; an union of the two Companies was generally desired, and strongly recommended. Upon the first depression, in the market, of the stock of the New Company, an inclination on the part of that Company had been manifested towards a coalition. But what disposed the one party to such a measure, suggested the hope of greater advantage, and more complete revenge, to the other, by holding back from it. The King himself when he received, in March, 1700, the Directors of the London Company, on the subject of the act which continued them a corporate body, recommended to their serious consideration an union of the two Companies, as the measure which would most promote, what they both held out as a great national object, the Indian trade. So far the Company paid respect to the royal authority, us to call a General Court of Proprietors for taking the subject into consideration; but after this step they appeared disposed to let the subject rest. Towards the close, however, of the year, the King, by a special message, required to know what proceedings they had adopted in consequence of his advice. Upon this the Directors summoned a General Court, and the following evasive resolution was voted. "That this Company, as they have always been, so are they still ready to embrace every opportunity by which they may manifest their duty to his Majesty, and zeal for the public good, and that they are desirous to contribute their utmost endeavours for the preservation of the East India trade to this kingdom, and are willing to agree with the New Company upon reasonable terms." The English Company were more explicit; they readily specified the conditions on which they were willing to form a coalition; upon which the London Company proposed that seven individuals on each side should

[2] Bruce, iii. 260—370, 374—379, 410.

1702.

be appointed, to whom the negotiation should be intrusted and by whom the terms should be discussed.[1]

As the expiration approached of the three years which were granted to the London Company to continue trade on their whole stock, they became more inclined to an accommodation. In their first proposal they aimed at the extinction of the rival Company. As a committee of the House of Commons had been formed, "to receive proposals for paying off the national debts, and advancing the credit of the nation," they made a proposition to pay off the 1,000,000*l.* which government had borrowed at usurious interest from the English Company, and to hold the debt at five per cent. The proposal, though entertained by the committee, was not relished by the House; and this project was defeated.[2] The distress, however, in which the Company was now involved, their stock having within the last ten years fluctuated from 300 to 37 per cent.,[3] rendered some speedy remedy indispensable. The committee of seven, which had been proposed in the Answer to the King, was now resorted to in earnest, and was empowered by a General Court, on the 17th of April, 1701, to make and receive proposals for the union of the two companies.

It was the beginning of January, in the succeeding year, before the following general terms were adjusted and approved: That the Court of twenty-four Managers or Directors should be composed of twelve individuals chosen by each Company; that of the annual exports, the amount of which should be fixed by the Court of Managers, a half should be furnished by each Company; that the Court of Managers should have the entire direction of all matters relating to trade and settlements subsequently to this union; but that the factors of each Company should manage separately the stocks which each had sent out previously to the date of that transaction; that seven years should be allowed to wind up the separate concerns of each Company; and that, after that period, one great joint-stock should be formed by the final union of the funds of both. This agreement was confirmed by the

1 Bruce, iii. 290, 293, 355.
2 Ibid. 124.
3 Anderson's History of Commerce; Macpherson, ii. 705.

BOOK I. CHAP. V.

General Courts of both Companies on the 27th April, 1702.[1]

1702.

An indenture tripartite, including the Queen and the two East India Companies, was the instrument adopted for giving legal efficacy to the transaction. For equalizing the shares of the two Companies, the following scheme was devised. The London Company, it was agreed, should purchase at par as much of the capital of the English Company, lent to government, as added to the 315,000*l.* which they had already subscribed, should render equal the portion of each. The dead stock of the London Company was estimated at 330,000*l.*; that of the English Company at 70,000*l.*; whereupon the latter paid 130,000*l.* for equalizing the shares of this part of the common estate. On the 22nd July, 1702, the indenture passed under the great seal; and the two parties took the common name of *The United Company of Merchants trading to th East Indies.*[2]

On the foundation on which the affairs of the two Companies were in this manner placed, they continued with considerable jarrings and contention, especially between the functionaries in India, till the season 1707-8, when an event occurred which necessitated the accommodation of differences, and accelerated the completion of the union. A loan of 1,200,000*l.*, without interest, was exacted of the two Companies for the use of government. The recollection of what had happened, when the body of private adventurers were formed into the English East India Company, made them dread the offers of a new body of adventurers, should any difficulty be found on their part. It was necessary, therefore, that the two Companies should

[1] Bruce, iii. 424—426. Of the subtleties which at this time entered into the policy of the Company, the following is a specimen. Sir Basil Firebrace, or Firebrass, a notorious jobber who had been an interloper, and afterwards joined with the London Company, was now an intriguer for both Companies. At a general Court of the London Company, on the 23rd April, 1701, this man stated that he had a scheme to propose, which he doubted not would accomplish the union desired; but required to know what recompence should be allowed him, if he effected this important end. By an act of the Court, the committee of seven were authorized to negotiate, with Sir Basil, the recompence which he ought to receive: and after repeated conferences with the gentleman, they proposed to the Court of Committees, that if he effected the union, 150,000*l.* of the stock of the Company should be transferred to him on his paying 80*l.* per cent. In other words, he was to receive 20 per cent. on 150,000*l.* or a reward of 30,000*l.* for the success of his intrigues. Ibid. See also Macpherson, ii. 663.

[2] Bruce, iii. 486—491.

lay aside all separate views, and cordially join their endeavours to avert the common danger.

It was at last agreed, that all differences subsisting between them should be submitted to the arbitration of the Earl of Godolphin, then Lord High Treasurer of England; and that the union should be rendered complete and final upon the award which he should pronounce. On this foundation, the act, 6th Anne, ch. 17, was passed; enacting that a sum of 1,200,000*l.* without interest should be advanced by the United Company to government, which, being added to the former advance of 2,000,000*l.* at 8 per cent. interest, constituted a loan of 3,200,000*l.* yielding interest at the rate of 5 per cent. upon the whole; that to raise this sum of 1,200,000*l.* the Company should be empowered to borrow to the extent of 1,500,000*l.* on their common seal, or to call in moneys to that extent from the Proprietors; that this sum of 1,200,000*l.* should be added to their capital stock; that instead of terminating on three years' notice after the 29th of September, 1711, their privileges should be continued till three years' notice after the 25th of March, 1726, and till repayment of their capital: that the stock of the separate adventures of the General Society, amounting to 7,200*l.*, which had never been incorporated into the joint-stock of the English Company, might be paid off, on three years' notice after the 29th of September, 1711, and merged in the joint-stock of the United Company; and that the award of the Earl of Godolphin, settling the terms of the Union, should be binding and conclusive on both parties.[1]

The award of Godolphin was dated and published on the 29th of September, 1708. It referred solely to the winding up of the concerns of the two Companies; and the blending of their separate properties into one stock, on terms equitable to both. As the assets or effects of the London Company in India fell short of the debts of that concern, they were required to pay by instalments to the United Company the sum of 96,615*l.* 4*s.* 9*d.*: and as the effects of the English Company in India exceeded their debts, they were directed to receive from the United Company the sum of 66,005*l.* 4*s.* 2*d.*; a debt due by Sir Edward Littleton in Bengal, of 80,437 rupees and 8 anas, remaining to be dis-

1 Bruce, iii. 635—639; Stat 6. A. c. 17.

1708.

charged by the English Company on their own account. On these terms, the whole of the property and debts of both Companies abroad became the property and debts of the United Company. With regard to the debts of both Companies in Britain, it was in general ordained that they should all be discharged before the 1st of March 1709; and as those of the London Company amounted to the sum of 399,795*l.* 9*s.* 1*d.* they were empowered to call upon their Proprietors, by three several instalments, for the means of liquidation.[1]

As the intercourse of the English nation with the people of India was now destined to become, by a rapid progress, both very intimate, and very extensive, a full account of the character and circumstances of that people is required for the understanding of the subsequent proceedings and events.

The population of those great countries consisted chiefly of two Races: one, who may here be called the Hindu; another the Mahomedan Race. The first were the aboriginal inhabitants of the country.[2] The latter were subsequent invaders; and insignificant, in point of number, compared with the first.

The next two Books will be devoted to the purpose of laying before the reader all that appears to be useful in what is known concerning both these classes of the Indian people. To those who delight in tracing the phenomena of human nature; and to those who desire to know completely the foundation upon which the actions of the British people in India have been laid, this will not appear the least interesting department of the work.

[1] Bruce, iii. 667 to 679. Macpherson, iii. 1, 2.

[2] This, as far as probabilities authorize an inference, is an error; the aborigines of India are apparently represented by the various barbarous tribes still inhabiting the mountains and forests, and following rude religious practices, that are no parts of the primitive Hindu system.—W.

BOOK II.

OF THE HINDUS.

CHAPTER I.

Chronology and Ancient History of the Hindus.

BOOK II. CHAP. I.

RUDE nations seem to derive a peculiar gratification from pretensions to a remote antiquity.[1] As a boastful and turgid vanity distinguishes remarkably the oriental nations, they have in most instances carried their claims extravagantly high. We are informed, in a fragment of Chaldaic history, that there were written accounts, preserved at Babylon, with the greatest care, comprehending a term of fifteen myriads of years.[2] The pretended duration of the Chinese monarchy, is still more extraordinary. A single king of Egypt was believed to have reigned three myriads of years.[3]

[1] Mr. Gibbon remarks (Hist. Decl. and Fall of the Roman Empire, i. p. 350), that the wild Irishman, as well as the wild Tartar, can point out the individual son of Japhet from whose loins his ancestors were lineally descended.—According to Dr. Keating (History of Ireland, 13), the giant Partholanus, who was the son of Seara, the son of Esra, the son of Sru, the son of Framant, the son of Fathacian, the son of Magog, the son of Japhet, the son of Noah, landed on the coast of Munster, the 14th day of May, in the year of the world 1978. The legends of England are not less instructive. A fourth or sixth son of Japhet, named Samothes, having first colonized Gaul, passed over into this island, which was thence named Simothea, about 200 years after the flood; but the Samothians being some ages afterwards subdued by Albion, a giant son of Neptune, he called the island after his own name, and ruled it forty-four years. See the story, with some judicious reflections, in Milton's History of England (Prose Works of Milton, iv. 3. Ed.1806). "The Athenians boasted that they were as ancient as the sun. The Arcadians pretended that they were older than the moon. The Lacedemonians called themselves the sons of the earth, &c., such, in general, was the madness of the ancients on this subject! They loved to lose themselves in an abyss of ages which seemed to approach eternity." Goguet, Origin of Laws, v. i. b. 1, ch. 1, art. 5. See the authorities there quoted.

[2] Eusebii Chronicon, p. 5. Syncelli Chronograph. p. 28. Bryant's Ancient Mythology, iv. 127, 8vo. edit.

[3] Syncelli Chronicon, p. 51. Herodotus informs us (lib. ii. c. 2), that the Egyptians considered themselves as the most ancient of mankind, till an experiment made by Psammetichus convinced them that the Phrygians alone preceded them. But the inhabitants of the further Peninsula of India make the boldest incursions into the regions of past times. The Burmans, we are

The present age of the world, according to the system of the Hindus, is distinguished into four grand periods, denominated yugs. The first is the Satya yug, comprehending 1,728,000 years; the second the Treta yug, comprehending 1,296,000 years; the third the Dwapar yug, including 864,000 years; and the fourth the Cali yug, which will extend to 432,000 years. Of these periods, the first three are expired; and, in the year 1817 of the Christian era, 4,911 years of the last. From the commencement, therefore, of the Satya yug, to the year 1817, is comprehended a space of 3,892,911 years, the antiquity to which this people lay claim.[1]

The contempt with which judicious historians now treat the historical fables of early society, must be indulged with caution when we explore the ancient condition of Hindustan; because the legendary tales of the Hindus have hitherto, among European inquirers, been regarded with particular respect; and because, without a knowledge of them, much of what has been written in Europe concern-

---

informed by Dr. Buchanan (As. Res. vi. 181), believe that the lives of the first inhabitants of their country lasted one *assenchii*, a period of time of which they thus communicate an idea: "If for three years it should rain incessantly over the whole surface of this earth, which is 1,203,400 juzana in diameter, the number of drops of rain falling in such a space and time, although far exceeding human conception, would only equal the number of years contained in one assenchii."

[1] Sir William Jones's Discourse on the Chronology of the Hindus (As. Res. ii. 111, 8vo. Ed.) also that on the Gods of Greece, Italy, and India (Ibid. i. 221.)—See, too, Mr. Bentley's Remarks on the principal Eras and Dates of the ancient Hindus (Ibid. v. 315); and the Discourse of Captain F. Wilford on the Chronology of the Hindus, in the same volume, p. 24.—Consult, also, Mr. Marsden's Discourse on the Chronology of the Hindus (Phil. Trans. lxxx. 568.) These authors, having all drawn from the same sources, display an appearance of uniformity and certainty in this part of the Hindu system. It is amusing to contemplate the wavering results of their predecessors. Mr. Halhed, in the preface to his Translation of the Code of Gentoo Laws, thus states the number of years, and thus spells the names of the epochs; 1. The Suttee Jogue, 3,200,000 years; 2. The Tirtah Jogue, 2,400,000 years; 3. The Dwapaar Jogue, 1,600,000 years; 4. The College Jogue, 400,000. Colonel Dow marks the Suttee Jogue at 14,000,000; the Tirtah Jogue at 1,080,000; the Dwapaar Jogue 72,000; and the Collee Jogue, 36,000 years. (History of Hindostan, i. 2). M. Bernier, whose knowledge of India was so extensive and accurate, gives, on the information of the Brahmens of Benares, the Satya yug at 2,500,000 years, the Treta at 1,200,000, the Dwapaar at 864,000, and assigns no period to the Cali yug. (Voyages, ii. 160.)—Messrs. Rogers and le Gentil, who received their accounts from the Brahmens of the Coast of Coromandel, coincide with Sir William Jones, except that they specify no duration for the Cali yug. (Porte Ouverte, p. 179; Mém. d'Académ. des Sciences pour 1772, tom. ii. part 1, p. 17)—The account of Anquetil Duperron agrees in every particular with that of Sir W. Jones; Recherches Historiques et Géographiques sur l'Inde, Lettre sur les Antiquités de l'Inde. The four ages of the Mexicans bear a remarkable resemblance to those of the Hindus, and of so many other nations. "All the nations of Anahuac (says Clavigero, History of Mexico, B. vi. sect. 24), distinguished four ages of time by as many suns. The first, named Atona-

ing the people of India, cannot be understood.[1] It is necessary, therefore, to relate, that at the commencement of the Satya yug, or 3,892,911 years ago, lived Satyavrata, otherwise denominated Vaivaswata, and also the seventh Menu. He had escaped with his family from an universal

tiuh, that is, the sun (or the age) of water, commenced with the creation of the world, and continued until the time at which all mankind perished in a general deluge along with the first sun. The second, Tlaitonatiuh, the age of earth, lasted from the deluge until the ruin of the giants, &c. The third, Ehécatonatiuh, the age of air, lasted from the destruction of the giants till the great whirlwinds, &c. The fourth, Tletonatiuh, commenced at the last-mentioned catastrophe, and is to last till the earth be destroyed by fire."—M.

There is no other concurrence of the Hindu and Mexican systems than the number of four, which was common to all antiquity. The Hindu system is wholly mythological, and admits of a ready explanation; it originates in the descending arithmetical progression of 4, 3, 2, 1, according to the notions of diminishing virtue in the several ages, applied to a cycle of 12,000 divine years, each of which is equal to 360 years of mortals; and 12,000 multiplied by 360 is equal to 4,320,000, the whole period of the four yugs, Vishnu Purana, p. 24.—This chronology also, it must be remembered, is not the expression of national vanity—it is the Hindu theory of the age of the world. The Hindus make no pretensions to a higher antiquity than that of other races of mankind. The four ages, and countless successions of them, are the phases of universal creation, not only of national existence.—W.

[1] The reader will by and bye be prepared to determine for himself how far the tales of the Brahmens deserve exemption from the sentence which four great historians have, in the following passages, pronounced on the fanciful traditions of early nations. "The curiosity," says Mr. Hume, "entertained by all civilized nations, of inquiring into the exploits and adventures of their ancestors, commonly excites a regret that the history of remote ages should always be so much involved in obscurity, uncertainty, and contradiction, * * * The fables which are commonly employed to supply the place of true history ought entirely to be disregarded; or, if any exception be admitted to this general rule, it can only be in favour of the ancient Grecian fictions, which are so celebrated and so agreeable, that they will ever be the objects of the attention of mankind." (Hume's History of England, i. ch. 1.)—"Nations," says Robertson, "as well as men, arrive at maturity by degrees, and the events which happened during their infancy or early youth cannot be recollected, and deserve not to be remembered. * * * Every thing beyond that short period, to which well-attested annals reach, is obscure; an immense space is left for invention to occupy; each nation, with a vanity inseparable from human nature, hath filled that void with events calculated to display its own antiquity and lustre. And history, which ought to record truth, and teach wisdom, often sets out with retailing fictions and absurdities." (Robertson's History of Scotland, i. b. 1.)—Mr. Gibbon, speaking of a people (the Arabians) who in traditions and antiquity bear some resemblance to the Hindus, says, "I am ignorant, and I am careless, of the blind mythology of the Barbarians." (History of the Decline and Fall of the Roman Empire, ix, 244, 8vo. edit.) Of a people still more remarkably resembling the Hindus he says, "We may observe, that after an ancient period of fables, and a long interval of darkness, the modern histories of Persia begin to assume an air of truth with the dynasty of the Sassanides," (Ibid. i. 341.)—Quæ ante conditam condendamve urbem, poeticis magis decora fabulis quam incorruptis rerum gestarum monumentis traduntur ea nec affirmare nec refellere in animo est." *Livii Prefat.*—M.

This disdain of the early records of nations may sometimes be suspected to veil a distaste for dry, laborious, and antiquarian research. That it is much easier to depreciate than inquire we need not go beyond these pages for proof.—W.

BOOK II. CHAP. I.

deluge, which had destroyed the rest of the human species.[1] Of his descendants, were two royal branches: the one denominated the children of the sun; the other, the children of the moon. The first reigned at Ayodhya or Oude; the second at Pratisht'hana or Vitora. These families, or dynasties, subsisted till the thousandth year of the present or Cali yug, at which time they both became extinct; and a list of the names of the successive princes is presented in the Sanscrit books.[2]

Satyavrata, the primitive sire, prolonged his existence and his reign through the whole period of the Satya yug or 1,728,000 years.[3] From this patriarchal monarch are enumerated, in the solar line of his descendants, fifty-five princes, who inherited the sovereignty till the time of Rama. Now it is agreed among all the Brahmens that Rama filled the throne of Ayodhya at the end of the Treta yug. The reigns, therefore, of these fifty-five princes, extending from the beginning to the end of that epoch, filled 1,296,000 years, which, at a medium, is more than 23,000 years to each reign. During the next, or Dwapar yug, of 864,000 years, twenty-nine princes are enumerated, who must, at an average, have reigned each 29,793 years. From the beginning of the present, or Cali yug, to the time when the race of solar princes became extinct, are reckoned 1000 years, and thirty princes. There is a wonderful change, therefore, in the last age, in which only thirty-three years, at a medium, are assigned to a reign.[4]

1 The coincidence in the tradition respecting Satyavrata, and the history of Noah, are very remarkable, and will be further noticed hereafter.

2 Sir William Jones, As. Res. ii. 119, 120, 127.

3 Sir Wm. Jones, Ibid. 126. He was the son of Surya (or *Sol*), the son of Casyapa (or *Uranus*), the son of Marichi (or *Light*), the son of Brahma, "which is clearly," says Sir Wm. Jones, "an allegorical pedigree." The Hindu pedigrees and fables, however, being very variable, he is, in the opening of the fourth book of the Gita, called, not the son of the Sun, but the Sun himself. Sir Wm. Jones, Ibid. 117. In a celestial pedigree the Hindus agree with other rude nations. There is a curious passage in Plato respecting the genealogy of the Persian kings. They were descended, he says, from Achæmenes, sprung from Perseus the son of Zeus (Jupiter). Plat. Alcib. i.—M.

There is no variability in the account of Vaivaswata's genealogy, nor is he confounded with the Sun in the Gita. Mr. Mill has evidently supposed Vaivaswat, the Sun, to be the same name as Vaivaswata its patronymic derivative, in the passage to which he refers. With regard to the duration of the life of Vaivaswata, it must be remembered that the Manus are not men, although finite beings; they exist throughout a kalpa, a much longer period than that of a Satya yug.—W.

4 Compare the list of princes in the several yugs, exhibited in the Discourse of Sir Wm. Jones, As. Res. iii. 128 to 136, with the assigned duration of the yugs. The lineage of the lunar branch, who reigned in Pratisht'hana, or Vitora, during exactly the same period, is in all respects similar, excepting

Beside the two lines of solar and lunar kings, a different race, who reigned in Magadha, or Bahar, commence with the fourth age. Of these, twenty in regular descent from their ancestor Jarasandha extended to the conclusion of the first thousand years of the present yug, and were cotemporary with the last thirty princes of the solar and lunar race.[1] At the memorable epoch of the extinction of those branches, the house of Jarasandha also failed; for the reigning prince was slain by his prime minister, who placed his son Pradyota on the throne. Fifteen of the descendants of this usurper enjoyed the sovereignty, and reigned from the date of his accession 498 years, to the time of Nanda, the last prince of the house of Pradyota. He, after a reign of 100 years, was murdered by a Brahmen, who raised to the throne a man of the Maurya race, named Chandragupta. This prince is reckoned, by our Oriental antiquarians, the same with Sandracottas or Sandracuptos, the cotemporary of Alexander the Great. Only nine princes of his line succeeded him, and held the sceptre for 137 years. On the death of the last, his commander in chief ascended the throne, and, together with nine descendants, to whom he transmitted the sovereignty, reigned 112 years. After that period the reigning prince was killed, and succeeded by his minister Vasudeva. Of his family only four princes are enumerated; but they are said to have reigned 345 years.[2] The throne was next usurped by a race of Sudras, the first of whom slew his master, and seized the government. Twenty-one of this race, of whom Chandrabija was the last, reigned during a space of 456 years.[3] The conclusion of the reign of this

---

that the number of princes, in the first two ages, is in this line fewer by fifteen than in the line of solar princes. From this it has been supposed, that a chasm must exist in the genealogy of those princes; but surely without sufficient reason; since, if we can admit that eighty-five princes in the solar line could outlive the whole third and fourth ages, amounting to 2,160,000 years, we may, without much scruple, allow that seventy princes in the lunar could extend through the same period.—M.

1 The reigns of those princes, therefore, must have been fifty years at an average.—M.

Some authorities make the number twenty-one, some thirty-nine, the latter making the average less than twenty-six years.—W.

2 This is a blunder made by the compiler of the Bhagavata: other authorities concur in stating the period to be only forty-five years.—Vishnu Purana 471.—W.

3 As. Res. ii. 137—142.—M.

The dynasty comprises, according to the Vishnu Purana, thirty kings; and twenty-nine are named in the Matsya Purana, and several of the names are identifiable in old inscriptions, or in Chinese writings.—Vishnu Purana, 473.—W.

BOOK II. CHAP. I.

prince corresponds therefore with the year 2648 of the Cali yug, and with the year 446 before the birth of Christ.[1] And with him, according to Sir William Jones, closes the authentic system of Hindu chronology.[2]

It is a most suspicious circumstance in the pretended records of a nation, when we find positive statements for a regular and immense series of years in the remote abyss of time, but are entirely deserted by them when we descend to the ages more nearly approaching our own. Where annals are real, they become circumstantial in proportion as they are recent; where fable stands in the place of fact, the times over which the memory has any influence are rejected, and the imagination riots in those in which it is unrestrained. While we receive accounts, the most precise and confident, regarding the times of remote antiquity not a name of a prince in after ages is presented in Hindu records. A great prince named Vicramaditya, is said to

[1] According to the Brahmens, 4911 years of the Cali yug were elapsed in the beginning of April, A.D. 1817, from which deducting 2648, the year of the Cali yug in which the reign of Chandrabija terminated, you have 2663, the number of years which have intervened since that period, and which carry it back to 446 years before Christ.

[2] As. Res. ii. 142, 3.—We have been likewise presented with a genealogical table of the great Hindu dynastics by Captain Wilford (As. Res. v. 241), which he says is faithfully extracted from the Vishnu Purana, the Bhagavat, and other Puranas, and which, on the authority of numerous MSS. which he had collated, and of some learned Pundits of Benares, whom he had consulted, he exhibits, as the only genuine chronological record of Indian history which had yet come to his knowledge. But this differs in numerous particulars from that of the learned Pundit Radhacant, exhibited by Sir William Jones, and which Sir William says "that Radhacant had diligently collected from several Puranas." Thus it appears that there is not even a steady and invariable tradition or fiction on this subject: At the same time that the table of Captain Wilford removes none of the great difficulties which appear in that of Sir W. Jones. The most remarkable difference is exhibited in the line of the solar princes, whose genealogy Captain Wilford has taken from the Ramayan, as being, he thinks, consistent with the ancestry of Arjuna and Crishna, while that given by Sir William Jones and Radhacant, he says, is not.—The reader may also compare the *Rajuturungu*, a history of the Hindus compiled by Mrityoonjuyu, the head Sanscrit Pundit in the College of Fort William; translated and published in the first volume of "An Account of the Writings, Religion, and Manners of the Hindus," by Mr. Ward, printed at Serampore, in four volumes 4to. 1811.—M.

Sir William Jones's list was evidently extracted from the Bhagavat only. Wilford's lists are more varied and authentic. The work of Mrityoonjuya is not of any authority. The subject is most clearly set forth in the text of the Vishnu Purana, and the variations are specified in the notes. There is no doubt that the genealogies of the Puranas have been compiled from older authorities, and that their differences are chiefly attributable to the degree of care with which the common authorities have been consulted and represented. The latter series are sufficiently consistent, and are corroborated in many cases by collateral evidence, and the earlier dynasties, when the chronology is corrected, are in all probability much more authentic than has been sometimes supposed.—W.

have extended widely his conquests and dominion, and to have reigned at Magadha 396 years after Chandrabija. From that time even fiction is silent.[1] We hear no more of the Hindus and their transactions, till the era of Mahomedan conquest; when the Persians alone become our instructors.[2]

After the contempt with which the extravagant claims to antiquity of the Chaldeans and Egyptians had always been treated in Europe, the love of the marvellous is curiously illustrated by the respect which has been paid to the chronology of the Hindus.[3] We received indeed the accounts of the Hindu chronology, not from the incredulous historians of Greece and Rome, but from men who had seen the people; whose imagination had been powerfully affected by the spectacle of a new system of manners, arts, institutions, and ideas; who naturally expected to augment the opinion of their own consequence, by the greatness of the wonders which they had been favoured to behold; and whose astonishment, admiration, and enthusiasm, for a time, successfully propagated themselves. The Hindu statements, if they have not perhaps in any instance gained a literal belief, have almost universally been regarded as very different from the fictions of an unimproved and credulous people, and entitled to a very serious and profound investigation. Yet they are not only carried to the wildest pitch of extravagance, but are ut-

1 Sir Wm. Jones, As. Res, ii. 142.

2 Since the text was published, much historical information has been obtained from various sources, rendering this statement inaccurate. Buddhist annals and ancient inscriptions have confirmed the identity of Chandragupta and Sandrocottus, and, with the correction of the chronology thus obtained, it is proved that the Puranik accounts bring down the traditional history of the Hindus in Gangetic Hindustan, to the eighth and ninth centuries. In the south of India original accounts of different dynasties are preserved from an early to a very recent period, and the chronicles of Rajputana, assuming the appearance of authenticity in the first ages of Christianity, offer a connected narrative to times long subsequent to the establishment of the Mohammedans in India. These various records are illustrated and confirmed by coins and inscriptions discovered and deciphered only within the last few years, see As. Researches, vol. xv. et seq. Trans. Royal As. Soc. Tod's Rajasthan. Mackenzie Collections. Turnour's Mahawanso. Calcutta Quarterly Oriental Magazine and Review, Madras Journal of Literature, Journal of the Royal Asiatic Society, and especially the Journal of the As. Society of Bengal.—W.

3 Mr. Halhed seems, in his pref. to Code of Gent. Laws, to be very nearly reconciled to the Hindu Chronology: at any rate he thinks the believers in the Jewish accounts of patriarchal longevity have no reason to complain, p. xvii. He has since, however, made a confession at second hand, of an alteration in his belief as to the antiquity of the Hindus. See Maurice's History of Hindostan, i. 88.

BOOK II. CHAP. I.

terly inconsistent both with themselves and with other established opinions of the Brahmens.[1]

Of this a single specimen will suffice. The character which the Brahmens assign to the several yugs is a remarkable part of their system. The Satya yug is distinguished by the epithet of golden; the Treta yug by that of silver; the Dwapar yug by that of copper; and the Cali yug is denominated earthen.[2] In these several ages the virtue, the life, and the stature of man, exhibited a remarkable diversity. In the Satya yug, the whole race were virtuous and pure; the life of man was 100,000 years, and his stature 21 cubits. In the Treta yug, one third of mankind were corrupt; and human life was reduced to 10,000 years. One half of the human race were depraved in the Dwapar yug, and 1000 years bounded the period of life. In the Cali yug, all men are corrupt, and human life is restricted to 100 years.[3] But though in the Satya yug men lived only 100,000 years, Satyavrata, according to the chronological, fiction, reigned 1,728,000 years; in the Treta yug, human life extended only to 10,000 years, yet fifty-five princes reigned, each at a medium, more than 23,000 years; in the Dwapar yug, though the life of man was reduced to 1000 years, the duration of the reigns was even extended, for twenty-nine princes held each the sceptre in this period for 29,793 years.[4]

[1] The character is not correct. The extravagance has never been denied, except by a few of the first and least competent inquirers. There is no inconsistency, nor are the statements, representing as they do, the belief and traditions of all the most interesting nations of antiquity, unworthy of investigation.—W.

[2] See Sir Wm. Jones, Discourse on the Gods of Greece, Italy, and India, As. Res. i. 236. The similarity between the Hindu description of the four yugs, and that of the four ages of the world by the Greeks, cannot escape attention. We shall have occasion to notice many other very striking marks of affinity between their several systems.—M.

It is to be observed, however, that the terms golden, and the rest, are not Hindu epithets of the four ages.—W.

[3] I have followed Mr. Halhed in the number of years (see Preface to Code of Gentoo Laws), through a derivative authority, because his statement is the highest, and by consequence the least unfavourable to the consistency of the Hindu chronology. In the Institutes of Menu (ch. i. 83), human life for the Satya yug is stated at 400 years, for the Treta yug at 300, the Dwapar 200, and the Cali yug at 100 years.—M.

The duration of the life of a Manu is not bounded by the limits of an age, as previously remarked; the reigns of particular kings, in a great degree mythological personages, are also exempt from ordinary rules. The inconsistency arises from our attempts to adjust the system to a scale by which it was never designed to be measured.—W.

[4] There is a very remarkable coincidence between the number of years specified in this Hindu division of time, and a period marked in a very curious fragment of the Chaldean History. The Cali yug, it appears from the text

The wildness and inconsistency of the Hindu statements evidently place them beyond the sober limits of truth and history; yet it has been imagined, if their literal acceptation must of necessity be renounced, that they at least contain a poetical or figurative delineation of real events, which ought to be studied for the truths which it may disclose. The labour and ingenuity which have been bestowed upon this inquiry, unfortunately have not been attended with an adequate reward. No suppositions, however gratuitous, have sufficed to establish a consistent theory. Every explanation has failed. The Hindu legends still present a maze of unnatural fictions, in which a series of real events can by no artifice be traced.[1]

The internal evidence which these legends display, afforded, indeed, from the beginning, the strongest reason to anticipate this result. The offspring of a wild and ungoverned imagination, they mark the state of a rude and credulous people, whom the marvellous delights; who cannot estimate the use of a record of past events; and whose imagination the real occurrences of life are too familiar to

---

amounts to 432,000 years, and the aggregate of the four yugs, which the Hindus call a Maha yug, or great yug, amounts to a period expressed by the same figures, increased by the addition of a cypher, or 4,320,000. Now Berosus informs us, that the first king of Chaldea was Alorus, who reigned ten sari, that a sarus is 3,600 years; that the first ten kings, whose reigns seem to have been accounted a great era, reigned 120 sari, which compose exactly 432,000 years, the Hindu period. See Eusebii Chronic. p. 5, where this fragment of Berosus is preserved; Syncelli Chronograph. p. 28. See also Bryant's Analysis of Ancient Mythology, iii. 95 to 126, for a most learned and ingenious commentary on this interesting fragment.

[1] A learned author pronounces them inferior even to the legends of the Greeks, as evidence of primeval events. "Oriental learning is now employed in unravelling the mythology of India, and recommending it as containing the seed of primeval history; but hitherto we have seen nothing that should induce us to relinquish the authorities we have been used to respect, or make us prefer the fables of the Hindus or Guebres, to the fables of the Greeks." Vincent, Periplus of the Erythrean Sea, part i. 9. It may be added, that if the Greeks, the most accomplished people of antiquity, have left us so imperfect an account of the primitive state of their own country, little is to be expected from nations confessedly and remarkably inferior to them.—M.

These opinions are, to say the least of them, premature. Judgment is uttered confidently upon research whilst in its veriest infancy:—we are not even yet in a position to pronounce definitively on the subject, for the principal authorities are still unexamined. The Vishnu Purana will contribute some authentic materials, but one or two other Puranas, the Ramayana, the Mahabharata, and the Vedas, ought to be translated, and must be carefully studied, before it will be safe to decide upon the value of the elucidation which Hindu literature may afford to the History of India or of the East. In the mean time the study has not been barren; the political divisions of ancient India are beginning to take a definite and distinct outline, and new connexions between nations hitherto little suspected, have been fully admitted, upon the indisputable testimony of affinity of speech.—W.

BOOK II. CHAP. I.

engage.[1] To the monstrous period of years which the legends of the Hindus involve, they ascribe events the most extravagant and unnatural; events not even connected in chronological series; a number of independent and incredible fictions. This people, indeed, are perfectly destitute of historical records.[2] Their ancient literature affords not a single production to which the historical character belongs. The works in which the miraculous transactions of former times are described are poems. Most of them are books of a religious character, in which the exploits of the gods, and their commands to mortals, are repeated or revealed. In all, the actions of men and those of deities are mixed together, in a set of legends, more absurd and extravagant, more transcending the bounds of nature and of reason, less grateful to the ima-

[1] That propensity which so universally distinguishes rude nations, and forms so remarkable a characteristic of uncivilized society—of filling the ages that are past with fabulous events and personages, and of swelling every thing beyond the limits of nature, may be easily accounted for. Every passion and sentiment of a rude people is apt to display itself in wild and extravagant effects. National vanity follows the example of the other passions, and indulges itself, unrestrained by knowledge. in such fictions as the genius of each people inspires. *Datur hæc venia antiquitati, ut miscendo humana divinis, primordia urbium augustiora faciat.* (Liv. Pref.) Of an accurate record of antecedent events, yielding lessons for the future by the experience of the past, uncultivated minds are not sufficiently capable of reflection to know the value. The real occurrences of life, familiar and insipid, appear too mean and insignificant to deserve to be remembered. They excite no surprise, and gratify no vanity. Every thing, however, which is extraordinary and marvellous, inspires the deepest curiosity and interest. While men are yet too ignorant to have ascertained with any accuracy the boundaries of nature, every thing of this sort meets with a ready belief; it conveys uncommon pleasure; the faculty of inventing is thus encouraged; and fables are plentifully multiplied. It may be regarded as in some degree remarkable, that, distinguished as all rude nations are for this propensity, the people of the East have far surpassed the other races of men in the extravagance of their legends. The Babylonians, the Arabians, the Syrians, the Egyptians, have long been subject to the contempt of Europeans, for their proneness to invent and believe miraculous stories. Lucian deems it a sarcasm, the bitterness of which would be universally felt, when he says of an author, infamous for the incredible stories which he had inserted in his history, that he had attained this perfection in lying, though he had never associated with a Syrian. (Quom. Cons. Hist.) The scanty fragments which have reached us of the histories of those other nations, have left us but little acquainted with the particular fables of which they compose their early history. But our more intimate acquaintance with the people of southern Asia has afforded us an ample assortment of their legendary stories.

[2] "There is no known history of Hindoostan (that rests on the foundation of Hindu materials or records) extant, before the period of the Mahommedan conquests." Rennel's Memoir, Introduction, xl. The Hindus have no ancient civil history, nor had the Egyptians any work purely historical. Wilford on Egypt and the Nile, As. Res. iii. 296.—M.

This has already been shown to be not strictly true, and genealogies and chronicles are found in various parts of India, recorded with some perseverance, if not much skill.—W.

gination and taste of a cultivated and rational people, than those which the fabulous history of any other nation presents to us. The Brahmens are the most audacious, and perhaps the most unskilful fabricators, with whom the annals of fable have yet made us acquainted.[1]

The people of Hindustan and the ancient nations of Europe came in contact at a single point. The expedition of Alexander the Great began, and in some sort ended, their connexion. Even of this event, so recent and remarkable, the Hindus have no record: they have not a tradition that can with any certainty be traced to it. Some particulars in their mythological stories have by certain European inquirers been *supposed* to refer to transactions of Alexander, but almost any part as well as another of these unnatural legends may, with equal propriety, receive the same distinction.[2] The information which we

[1] If the authority of a Sanscrit scholar be wanted to confirm this harsh decision, we may adduce that of Captain Wilford, who, in his Discourse on Egypt and the Nile, As. Res. iii. 29, thus expresses himself: "The mythology of the Hindus is often inconsistent and contradictory, and the same tale is related many different ways. Their physiology, astronomy, and history, are involved in allegories and enigmas, which cannot but seem extravagant and ridiculous; nor could any thing render them supportable, but a belief that most of them have a recondite meaning; though many of them had, perhaps, no firmer basis than the heated imagination of deluded fanatics, or of hypocrites interested in the worship of some particular deity. Should a key to their eighteen Puranas exist, it is more than probable that the wards of it would be too intricate, or too stiff with the rust of time, for any useful purpose."

"The Hindu system of geography, chronology, and history, are all equally monstrous and absurd." Wilford on the Chronol. of the Hindus, As. Res. v. 241.

Another Oriental scholar of some eminence, Mr. Scott Waring, says, in his Tour to Sheeraz, p. iv. "that the Hindu mythology and history appear to be buried in impenetrable darkness."—M.

Mr. Waring is no authority, and Wilford, in a great degree, was bewildered in a labyrinth of his own creating.—W.

[2] Dr. Robertson (Disquis. concerning Anc. India, note viii. p. 301) says, "That some traditional knowledge of Alexander's invasion of India is still preserved in the northern provinces of the peninsula, is manifest from several circumstances." But these circumstances, when he states them, are merely such as this: that a race of Rajahs claim to be descended from Porus, or rather from a prince of a name distantly resembling Porus, which European inquirers *conjecture* may be the same. The other circumstance is, that a tribe or two, on the borders of ancient Bactria, *are said* to represent themselves as the descendants of some Greeks left there by Alexander. The modern Hindus, who make it a point to be ignorant of nothing, pretend, when told of the expedition of Alexander, to be well acquainted with it, and say, "That he fought a great battle with the Emperor of Hindoostan, near Delhi; and, though victorious, retired to Persia, across the northern mountains: so that the remarkable circumstance of his sailing down the Indus, in which he employed many months, is sunk altogether." Major Rennel, Memoir, p. xl.—M.

The modern Hindus are much less inclined to make it a point to be ignorant of nothing, than modern Europeans. If any modern Hindu ever pretended to have heard of Alexander, he probably did so with reason, having gained some vague notions from Mohammedan writers. He certainly did not acquire it

BOOK II. CHAP. I.

have received of the Greek invasion from the Greeks themselves, is extremely scanty and defective. The best of their writings on the subject have been lost, but we have no reason to suppose that their knowledge of the Hindus was valuable. That of the modern Europeans continued very imperfect, after they had enjoyed a much longer and closer intercourse with them than the Greeks. In fact, it was not till they had studied the Indian languages, that they acquired the means of full and accurate information. But the Greeks, who despised every forieign language, made no exception in favour of the sacred dialect of the Hindus, and we may rest satisfied that the writings of Megasthenes and others contained few particulars by which our knowledge of the Brahmenical history could be improved.[1]

From the scattered hints contained in the writings of the Greeks, the conclusion has been drawn, that the Hindus, at the time of Alexander's invasion, were in a state of manners, society, and knowledge, exactly the same with that in which they were discovered by the nations of modern Europe; nor is there any reason for differing widely from this opinion. It is certain that the few features of which we have any description from the Greeks, bear no inaccurate resemblance to those which are found to distinguish this people at the present day. From this resemblance, from the state of improvement in which the Indians remain, and from the stationary condition in which their institutions first, and then their manners and character, have a tendency to fix them, it is no unreasonable supposition, that they have presented a very uniform appearance during the long interval from the visit of the Greeks to that of the English. Their annals, however,

---

from his own, and there is no occasion to marvel at the omission. Important as we may consider Alexander's invasion, it was a matter of very trifling interest to the Hindus. It was confined to the extreme western frontier; it lasted for a short time; it left no permanent impression. In all probability, it was not heard of, at the time of its occurrence, beyond the Sutlej; and if it had been, it would have been regarded as the temporary predatory incursion of a barbarian. Repeated notices of such incursions are found in the Puranas, and in the Chronicle of Kashmir; but are not deemed worthy of a detailed description.—W.

[1] It affords a confirmation of this, that the Greeks have left us no accounts, in any degree satisfactory, of the manners and institutions of the ancient Persians, with whom they had so extended an intercourse; or of the manners and institutions of the Egyptians, whom they admired, and to whom their philosophers resorted for wisdom.

from that era till the period of the Mahomedan conquests, are a blank.

With regard to the ancient history of India, we are still not without resources. The meritorious researches of the modern Europeans, who have explored the institutions, the laws, the manners, the arts, occupations and maxims of this ancient people, have enabled philosophy to draw the picture of society, which they have presented, through a long revolution of years. We cannot describe the lives of their kings, or the circumstances and results of a train of battles. But we can show how they lived together as members of the community, and of families; how they were arranged in society; what arts they practised, what tenets they believed, what manners they displayed; under what species of government they existed; and what character, as human beings, they possessed. This is by far the most useful and important part of history; and if it be true, as an acute and eloquent historian has remarked "that the sudden, violent, and unprepared revolutions incident to barbarians, are so much guided by caprice, and terminate so often in cruelty, that they disgust us by the uniformity of their appearance, and it is rather fortunate for letters that they are buried in silence and oblivion,"[1] we have perhaps but little to regret in the total absence of Hindu records.[2]

Whatever theory we adopt with regard to the origin of mankind, and the first peopling of the world, it is natural to suppose, that countries were at first inhabited by a very small number of people. When a very small number of men inhabit a boundless country, and have intercourse only among themselves, they are by necessary consequence barbarians. If one family, or a small number of families,

1 Hume's History of England, i. 2.

2 "Tout homme de bon entendement, sans voir une histoire, peut presque imaginer de quelle humeur fut un peuple, lorsqu'il lit ces anciens statuts et ordonnances; et d'un même jugement peut tirer en conjecture quelles furent ses loix voyant sa manière de vivre." Etienne Pasquier, Recherches de la France, liv. iv., chap. 1. The sage President de Goguet, on a subject remarkably similar, thus expresses himself: "The dates and duration of the reigns of the ancient kings of Egypt, are subject to a thousand difficulties, which I shall not attempt to resolve. In effect, it is of little importance to know the number of their dynasties, and the names of their sovereigns. It is far more essential to understand the laws, arts, sciences, and customs of a nation, which all antiquity has regarded as a model of wisdom and virtue. These are the objects I propose to examine, with all the care and exactness I am capable of." Origin of Laws, Part I., Book I., chap. i. art. 4.

BOOK II. CHAP. I.

are under the necessity of providing for themselves all the commodities which they consume, they can have but few accommodations, and these imperfect and rude. In those circumstances the exigencies of life are too incessant, and too pressing, to allow time or inclination for the prosecution of knowledge. The very ideas of law and government, which suppose a large society, have no existence: men are unavoidably ignorant and unrefined; and if much pressed with difficulties, they become savage and brutal.[1]

[1] There is a remarkable passage in Plato, at the beginning of the third book, De Legibus, in which he describes the effects which would be produced on a small number of men left alone in the world, or some uncultivated part of it. He is describing the situation of a small number of persons left alive by a flood, which had destroyed the rest of mankind.—'Οι τοτε περιφυγοντες την φθοραν σχεδον ορειοι τινες αν ειεν νομεις, εν κορυφαις που σμικρα ζωπυρα του των ανθρωπων γενους διασεσωμενα.—Και δη τους τοιουτους γε αναγκη που των αλλων απειρους ειναι τεχνων, και των εν τοις αστεσι προς αλληλους μηχανων.—Ουκουν οργανα τε παντα απολλυσθαι, και ει τι τεχνης ην εχομενον σπουδαιας εὑρημενον, η πολιτικης, η και σοφιας τινος ἑτερας, παντα ερρειν ταυτα εν τῳ τοτε χρονῳ φησομεν (Plat. p. 804). The Hindus appear to have had similar opinions, though without the reasons.

"We read in the Mahad-himalaya-c'handa, that after a deluge, from which very few of the human race were preserved, men became ignorant and brutal, without arts or sciences, and even without a regular language." Wilford, on Egypt and the Nile, As. Res. iii. 324.

There is nothing more remarkable in the traditions of nations, than their agreement respecting the origin of the present inhabitants of the globe. The account of the deluge in the religious books of the Jews, may very well be taken as the archetype of the whole. On this subject, I willingly content myself with a reference to a book of singular merit, "The Analysis of Ancient Mythology," by Jacob Bryant; in which, after making ample allowance for some forced etymologies, and much superstition, the reader will find an extent of learning, a depth of research, and an ingenuity of inference, unrivalled among the inquirers into the early history of the human race. Sir William Jones, who regretted that Mr. Bryant's knowledge of Oriental literature had not enabled him to bring evidence more largely from its stores, and that he had not pursued a plan more strictly analytical, has prosecuted the same inquiry in a series of Discoveries, addressed to the Asiatic Society, on the Hindus, the Arabs, the Tartars, the Persians, the Chinese, &c., and on the Origin and Families of Nations; and by a different plan, and the aid of his Oriental literature, has arrived at the same conclusions.

All inquirers have been struck with the coincidence between the story of Noah, and that of the Hindu primeval sire Satyavrata. We may suspect that there has been a little Brahmenical forcing to make it so exact as in the following passage:—Mr. Wilford says, "It is related in the Padma-Puran, that Satyavrata, whose miraculous preservation from a general deluge is told at length in the Matsya, had three sons, the eldest of whom was named Jyapeti, or Lord of the Earth. The others were C'harma and Sharma, which last are, in the vulgar dialects, usually pronounced C'ham and Sham, as we frequently hear Kishn for Crishna. The royal patriarch (for such is his character in the Puráns), was particularly fond of Jyapeti, to whom he gave all the regions to the north of Himalaya, in the snowy mountains, which extend from sea to sea, and of which Caucasus is a part. To Sharma he allotted the countries to the south of those mountains: But he cursed C'harma; because when the old Monarch was accidentally inebriated with a strong liquor made of fermented rice, C'harma laughed: and it was in consequence of his father's imprecation that he became a slave to the slaves of his brothers." As. Res. iii. 312, 313. The following statement by the same inquirer is confirmed by a variety of authorities:—"The first descendants of Swayambhava (another name for Sat-

If we suppose that India began to be inhabited at a very early stage in the peopling of the world, its first inhabitants must have been few, ignorant, and rude. Uncivilized and ignorant men, transported, in small numbers, into an uninhabited country of boundless extent, must wander for many ages before any great improvement can take place. Till they multiplied so far as to be assembled in numbers large enough to permit the benefits of social intercourse, and of some division of labour, their circumstances seem not susceptible of amelioration. We find, accordingly, that all those ancient nations, whose history can be most depended upon, trace themselves up to a period of rudeness. The families who first wandered into Greece, Italy, and the eastern regions of Europe, were confessedly ignorant and barbarous. The influence of dispersion was no doubt most baneful, where the natural disadvantages were the greatest. In a country overgrown with forest, which denies pasture to cattle, and precludes husbandry, by surpassing the power of single families to clear the land for their support, the wretched inhabitants are reduced to all the hardships of the hunter's life and become savages. The difficulties with which those families had to struggle who first came into Europe, seem to have thrown them into a situation but few degrees removed from the lowest stage of society. The advantages of India in soil and climate are so great, that those by whom it was originally peopled might sustain no further depression than what seems inherent to a state of disper-

yavrata) are represented in the Puranas as living in the mountains to the north of India, toward the sources of the Ganges, and downwards as far as Serinagara and Hari-dwar. But the rulers of mankind lived on the summit of Meru, towards the north: where they appear to have established the seat of justice, as the Puranas make frequent mention of the oppressed repairing thither for redress." Wilford on Chron. of Hind., As. Res. v. 260. "The Mexicans," says Clavigero, Hist. of Mexico, b. vi. sect. 1, "had a clear tradition, though somewhat corrupted by fable, of the creation of the world, of the universal deluge, of the confusion of tongues, and of the dispersion of the people; and had actually all these events represented in their pictures (their substitute for writing). They said that when mankind were overwhelmed with the deluge, none were preserved but a man and woman, named Coxcox and Xochiguebzal, who saved themselves in a little bark, and landing upon a mountain, called Colhuacan, had there a great many children, who were all born dumb; but that a dove at last, from a lofty tree, imparted to them languages; all, however, differing so much, that they could not understand one another."—M.

It is scarcely fair to cite Wilford, for what he has himself taken pains to particularise as unworthy of credit; the whole story of the patriarch and his sons being the pure invention of his Pandit, as he has explained. As. Researches, v. viii. p. 254.—W.

sion. They wandered probably for ages in the immense plains and valleys of that productive region, living on fruits, and the produce of their flocks and herds, and not associated beyond the limits of a particular family. Until the country became considerably peopled, it is not even likely that they would be formed into small tribes. As soon as a young man became, in his turn, the head of a family, and the master of cattle, he would find a more plentiful subsistence beyond the range of his father's flocks. It could only happen, after all the most valuable ground was occupied, that disputes would arise, and that the policy of defence would render it an object for the different branches of a family to remain united together, and to acknowledge a common head.[1]

When this arrangement takes place, we have arrived at a new stage in the progress of civil society. The condition of mankind, when divided into tribes, exhibits considerable variety, from that patriarchal association which is exemplified in the history of Abraham, to such combinations as are found among the Tartars, or that distribution into clans, which, at no distant period, distinguished the people of Europe. The rapidity with which nations advance through these several states of society chiefly depends on the circumstances which promote population. Where a small number of people range over extensive districts, a very numerous association is neither natural nor convenient. Some visible boundary, as a mountain or a river, marks out the limits of a common interest; and jealousy or enmity is the sentiment with which every tribe is regarded by every other. When any people has multiplied so far as to compose a body, too large and unwieldy to be managed by the simple expedients which connected the tribe, the first rude form of a monarchy or political system is devised. Though we have no materials from the Hindus, which yield us the smallest assistance in discovering the time which elapsed in their progress to this point of maturity, we may so far accede to their claims of antiquity, as to allow that they passed through this first stage in the way to civilisation very quickly; and, perhaps, they acquired the first rude form of a national polity at fully as

[1] There is a short, but not irrational, sketch of the progress of society in some of the Puranas. See Vishnu Purana, 44.—W.

early a period as any portion of the race.[1] It was probably at no great distance from the time of this important change that those institutions were devised, which have been distinguished by a durability so extraordinary; and which present a spectacle so instructive to those who would understand the human mind, and the laws which, amid all the different forms of civil society, invariably preside over its progress.

CHAPTER II.

Classification and Distribution of the People.

THE transition from the state of tribes to the more regulated and artificial system of a monarchy and laws is not sudden; it is the result of a gradual preparation and improvement. That loose independence, which suits a small number of men, bound together by an obvious utility, scattered over an extensive district, and subject to few interferences of inclination or interest, is found productive of many inconveniences, as they advance in numbers, as their intercourse becomes more close and complicated, and as their interests and passions more frequently clash. When quarrels arise, no authority exists to which the parties are under the necessity of referring their disputes. The punishment of delinquents is provided for by no preconcerted regulation. When subsistence, by the multiplication of consumers, can no longer be obtained without considerable labour, the desire to encroach upon one another adds extremely to the occasions of discord: and the evils and miseries which prevail, excite at last a desire for a better regulation of their common affairs. But slow is the progress made by the human under-

[1] The cautious inquirer will not probably be inclined to carry this era very far back. "The newness of the world," says the judicious Goguet (vol. iii. dissert. 3) "is proved by the imperfection of many of the arts in the ancient world, and of all the sciences which depend upon length of time and experience." By the newness of the world, he means the newness of human society. In examining the remains of organized bodies which have been extricated from the bowels of the earth, vegetables are found at the greatest depth; immediately above them small shell-fish, and some of the most imperfect specimens of the animal creation; nearer the surface quadrupeds, and the more perfectly organized animals; lastly man, of whom no remains have ever been found at any considerable depth. The inference is, that compared with the other organized beings on this globe, man is a recent creation. See Parkinson's Organic Remains.

standing, in its rude and ignorant state. No little time is spent; first, in maturing the conviction that a great reformation is necessary; and next, in conceiving the plan which the exigency requires. Many partial remedies are thought of and applied; many failures experienced; evils meanwhile increase, and press more severely; at last men become weary and disgusted with the condition of things, and prepared for any plausible change which may be suggested to them. In every society there are superior spirits, capable of seizing the best ideas of their times, and, if they are not opposed by circumstances, of accelerating the progress of the community to which they belong. The records of ancient nations give us reason to believe that some individual of this description, exalted to authority by his wisdom and virtue, has generally accomplished the important task of first establishing among a rude people a system of government and laws.

It may be regarded as a characteristic of this primary institution of government, that it is founded upon divine authority. The superstition of a rude people is peculiarly suited to such a pretension. While ignorant and solitary, men are perpetually haunted with the apprehension of invisible powers; and, as in this state only they can be imposed upon by the assumption of a divine character and commission, so it is evidently the most effectual means which a great man, full of the spirit of improvement, can employ, to induce a people, jealous and impatient of all restraint, to forego their boundless liberty, and submit to the curb of authority.[1]

No where among mankind have the laws and ordinances been more exclusively referred to the Divinity, than by

[1] There is scarcely an exception to this rule. Minos often retired into a cave, where he boasted of having familiar conversations with Jupiter: Mneues, the great legislator of Egypt, proclaimed Hermes as the author of his laws: it was by the direction of Apollo that Lycurgus undertook the reformation of Sparta; Zuleucus, the legislator of the Locrians, gave out that he was inspired by Minerva: Zathruspes, among the Arimaspians, pretended that his laws were revealed to him by one of their divinities: Zamolxis boasted to the Getes of his intimate communications with the goddess Vesta: the pretensions of Numa among the Romans are well known. (See Goguet, Origin of Laws, part II. book I. ch. i. art. 9.) The Druids, among the ancient Britons and Gauls, were at once the legislators, and the confidants of the Divinity. Odin, who was himself a Divinity, and his descendants, who partook of his nature, were the legislators of the Scandinavians. "The legislators of the Scythians," says Mallet (Introd. to Hist. of Denmark, ii. 43), "represented God himself as the author of the laws which they gave to their fellow-citizens."

those who instituted the theocracy of Hindustan. The plan of society and government, the rights of persons and things, even the customs, arrangements, and manners, of private and domestic life; everything, in short, is established by divine prescription. The first legislator of the Hindus, whose name it is impossible to trace, appears to have represented himself as the republisher of the will of God. He informed his countrymen that, at the beginning of the world, the Creator revealed his duties to man, in four sacred books, entitled Vedas; that during the first age, of immense duration, mankind obeyed them, and were happy; that during the second and third they only partially obeyed, and their happiness was proportionally diminished; that since the commencement of the fourth age disobedience and misery had totally prevailed, till the Vedas were forgotten and lost;[1] that now, however, he was commissioned to reveal them anew to his countrymen, and to claim their obedience.[2]

The leading institutions of the Hindus bear evidence that they were devised at a very remote period, when society yet retained its rudest and simplest form.[3] So long as men roam in the pastoral state, no division of classes or of labour is known. Every individual is a shepherd, and every family provides for itself the commodities with which it is supplied. As soon as the cultivation of land, which yields a more secure and plentiful subsistence, occupies a great share of the common attention, the inconvenience of this universal mixture of employments is speedily felt. The labours of the field are neglected, while the cultivator is engaged at the loom, or repelling the incursions of an enemy. His clothing and lodging are inadequately provided for, while the attention of himself and his family are engrossed by the plough. Men quit

1 The whole of this is imaginary; there is no such legislation, there are no such assertions in Hindu tradition. W.

2 As we see them in Manu comprehending an artificial system of monarchy and law, they must have been, according to Mr. Mills's own showing (p. 177), the result of a gradual preparation and improvement: he is at variance with himself in the attempt here commenced, and pertinaciously pursued, to prove that the institutions of the Hindus belong to the rudest and simplest form of society.—W.

3 This is a necessary supposition, as the generation to whom the Vedas were first presented must have known that they had no previous acquaintance with them, and could not believe that they had remained familiar to mortals from the period of their first revelation.

not easily, however, the practices to which they have been accustomed; and a great change in their manners and affairs does not readily suggest itself as a remedy for the evils which they endure. When the Hindus were lingering in this uneasy situation, it would appear that there arose among them one of those superior men, who are capable of accelerating the improvement of society. Perceiving the advantage which would accrue to his countrymen from a division of employments, he conceived the design of overcoming at once the obstacles by which this regulation was retarded; and, clothing himself with a Divine character, established as a positive law, under the sanction of Heaven, the classification of the people, and the distribution of occupations. Nor was it enough to introduce this vast improvement; it was right to secure that the original members of the different classes should be supplied with successors, and that the community should not revert to its former confusion. The human race are not destined to make many steps in improvement at once. Ignorant that professions, when once separated, were in no danger of being confounded, he established a law, which the circumstances of the time very naturally suggested, but which erected a barrier against further progress; that the children of those who were assigned to each of the classes, into which he distributed the people, should invariably follow the occupation of their father through all generations.

The classification instituted by the author of the Hindu laws is the first and simplest form of the division of labour and employments. The priest is a character found among the rudest tribes; by whom he is always regarded as of the highest importance. As soon as men begin to have property, and to cultivate the ground, the necessity of defenders is powerfully felt; a class, therefore, of soldiers, as well as a class of husbandmen, becomes an obvious arrangement. There are other services, auxiliary to these, and necessary to the well-being of man, for which it still remains necessary to provide. In a state of great simplicity, however, these other services are few, and easily performed. We find accordingly that the Hindu legislator assigned but one class of the community to this department. The Hindus were thus divided into four orders or castes. The first were the Brahmens or priests; the second, the Cshatriyas or soldiers; the third, the husbandmen or Vaisyas; and the fourth, the Sudras, the servants and labourers.[1] On this division of the people, and the privileges or disadvantages annexed to the several castes, the whole frame of Hindu society so much depends, that it is an object of primary importance, and merits a full elucidation.

[1] There is an instructive passage in Plato (De Repub. lib. ii.), in which he ascribes the origin of political association and laws to the division of labour; *Γιγνεται πολις, ως εγ᾽ῷμαι, επειδαν τυγχανει ἡμων ἑκαστος ουκ αυταρκης, αλλα πολλων ενδεης.* From this cause, he says, men are obliged to associate, one man affording one accommodation, another another, and all exchanging the accommodations which each can provide, for the different accommodations provided by the rest. It is curious that, in limiting the simplest form of a political association, he makes it to consist of four or five classes of men. *Αλλα μεν πρωτη γε και μεγιστη των χρειων, ἡ της τροφῆς παρασκευη, δευτερα δε οικησεως, τριτη εσθητος και των τοιουτων.* * * * *Ειη δ' αν η γε αναγκαιοτατη πολις εκ τεταρων η πεντε ανδρων.*—That sagacious contemplator of the progress of society, Millar, describing the ancient state of the Anglo-Saxons, remarks that the people of England were then divided into four great classes; the artificers and tradesmen, husbandmen, those who exercised the honourable profession of arms, and the clergy. He adds, "From the natural course of things it should seem that, in every country where religion has had so much influence as to introduce a great body of ecclesiastics, the people, upon the first advance made in agriculture and in manufactures, are usually distributed into the same number of classes or orders. This distribution is accordingly to be found not only in all European nations, formed upon the ruins of the Roman empire; but in other ages, and in very distant parts of the globe. The ancient inhabitants of Egypt are said to have been divided into the clergy, the military people, the husbandmen, and the artificers. The establishment of the four great *castes*, in the country of Indostan, is precisely of the same nature." Millar's Historical View of the English Government, book i. ch. xi. In Egypt the people were divided by law in the same hereditary manner as in Hindostan. It is highly worthy of observation that, notwithstanding all the revolutions and changes to which Egypt has been subject, some remains of the division into castes are yet visible. "La distinction par familles se retrouve encore dans les villes; l'exercice des arts et métiers est héréditaire, le fils imite les procédés de son père, et ne les perfectionne pas." Le Général Reynier, De l'Egypte, p. 59. It is worthy of observation that the Colchians and Iberians were also divided into four castes, whose rank and office were hereditary and unchangeable. Herodot. lib. ii. cap. civ. cv. Strabo, lib. ii. 765. See also Bryant's Ancient Mythology, v. 102, 107. In some situations this step in civilisation, natural and simple as it may appear, is not easily made. How long have the wandering Arabs remained without it? What an improvement would the bare institution of the Hindu classes be upon their condition? and what merit would the legislator have, who should introduce it? The same observation is applicable to the Tartars.

There is a passage in Herodotus which leads us to conclude, that the distinction of castes existed among the Medes at the commencement of the monarchy. He says, lib. i. cap. ci., *Εστι Μηδων τοσαδε γενεα. Βουσαι, Παρητακηνοι, Στρουχατες, Αριζαντοι, Βουδιοι, Μαγοι.* He says nothing to fix the meaning of the word *γενεα*. But we know that the *Μαγοι* were the priests, and hence there is matter of proof to make us suppose, that the other names, in like manner, express separate castes, or hereditary classes and professions.

The Persian Monarch Jemsheed is said to have divided the Persians into four classes. Malcolm's Hist. of Persia, i. 205.

In like manner among the Peruvians, "Les citoyens," to use the language of Carli (Lettres sur l'Amérique, let. xiii.), "furent distribués en classes ou tribus. * * Il n'étoit pas permis, ni par mariage, ni par changement d'habita-

BOOK II.
CHAP. II.

I. The priesthood is generally found to usurp the greatest authority, in the lowest state of society. Knowledge, and refined conceptions of the Divine nature, are altogether incompatible with the supposition, that the Deity makes favourites of a particular class of mankind, or is more pleased with those who perform a ceremonial service to himself, than with those who discharge with fidelity the various and difficult duties of life. It is only in rude and ignorant times that men are so overwhelmed with the power of superstition as to pay unbounded veneration and obedience to those who artfully clothe themselves with the terrors of religion.[1] The Brahmens among the Hindus have acquired and maintained an authority, more exalted, more commanding, and extensive, than the priests have been able to engross among any other portion of mankind. As great a distance as there is between the Brahmen and the Divinity, so great a distance is there between the Brahmen and the rest of his species. According to the sacred books of the Hindus, the Brahmen proceeded from the mouth of the Creator, which is the seat of wisdom; the Cshatriya proceeded from his arm; the Vaisya from his thigh, and the Sudra from his foot; therefore is the Brahmen infinitely superior in worth and dignity to all other human beings.[2] The Brahmen is declared to be the Lord of all the classes.[3] He alone, to a great degree, engrosses the regard and favour of the Deity; and it is through him, and at his

---

tion, de confondre une classe avec l'autre." In Lett. xiv. it is added, "L'éducation consistoit à apprendre aux enfans rôturiers le métier que chaque père de famille exerçoit," &c. Clavigero, too, respecting the Mexicans, tells us (Hist. of Mexico, book vii. sect. v.), "The sons in general learned the trades of their fathers, and embraced their professions," &c.

In Plato's Timæus (p. 1044, Ed. Ficin. Francof. 1602), is a curious passage, which asserts that the same division of professions, which still existed among the Egyptians, existed, at a period long antecedent, among the Athenians: *Πρωτον μεν το των ἱερεων γενος, απο των αλλων χωρις αφωρισμενον· μετα δε τουτο, το των δημιουργων, ὁτι καθ' αὑτο ἑκαστον αλλῳ δε ουκ επιμιγνυμενον δημιουργει· το τε των νομεων και των θηρευτων· το τε των γεωργων· και δη το μαχιμον γενος, απο παντων των γενων κεχωρισμενον, οἱς ουδεν αλλο πλην τα περι τον πολεμον ὑπο του νομου προσεταχθη μελειν.*

[1] It was in the dark ages that the Romish priesthood usurped so many privileges. Our ancestors were barbarous when the Druids exercised over them an unlimited authority. The soothsayers and priests among the Greeks and Romans lost their influence as knowledge increased. Among the rude inhabitants of Mexico and Peru, the authority of the priest equalled or superseded that of the king, and was united in the same person.

[2] Laws of Menu, ch. i. [3] Ibid. x.

intercession, that blessings are bestowed upon the rest of mankind. The sacred books are exclusively his; the highest of the other classes are barely tolerated to read the word of God; he alone is worthy to expound it. The first among the duties of the civil magistrate, supreme or subordinate, is to honour the Brahmens.[1] The slightest disrespect to one of this sacred order is the most atrocious of crimes. "For contumelious language to a Brahmen," says the law of Menu,[2] "a Sudra must have an iron style, ten fingers long, thrust red hot into his mouth; and for offering to give instruction to priests, hot oil must be poured into his mouth and ears." The following precept refers even to the most exalted classes: "For striking a Brahmen even with a blade of grass, or overpowering him in argument, the offender must soothe him by falling prostrate."[3] Mysterious and awful powers are ascribed to this wonderful being. "A priest, who well knows the law, needs not complain to the king of any grievous injury; since, even by his own power, he may chastise those who injure him: his own power is mightier than the royal power; by his own might therefore may a Brahmen coerce his foes. He may use without hesitation the powerful charms revealed to Atharvan and Angiras; for speech is the weapon of a Brahmen: with that he may destroy his oppressors."[4] "Let not the king, although in the greatest distress, provoke Brahmens to anger; for they, once enraged, could immediately destroy him with his troops, elephants, horses, and cars. Who without perishing could provoke those holy men, by whom the all-devouring flame was created, the sea with waters not drinkable, and the moon with its wane and increase? What prince could gain wealth by oppressing those, who, if angry, could frame other worlds and regents of worlds, could give being to other gods and mortals? What man, desirous of life, would injure those, by the aid of whom worlds and gods perpetually subsist; those who are rich in the knowledge of the Veda? A Brahmen, whether learned or ignorant, is a powerful Divinity; even as fire

1 Laws of Menu, ch. vii.

2 Ibid viii. 271, 2. "From his high birth alone, a Brahmen is an object of veneration even to deities; his declarations to mankind are decisive evidence; and the Veda itself confers on him that character." Ibid xi. 85.

3 Ibid. x. 206.

4 Ibid xi. 31, 32, 33.

is a powerful Divinity, whether consecrated or popular. Thus, though Brahmens employ themselves in all sorts of mean occupations, they must invariably be honoured; for they are something transcendently divine."[1] Not only is this extraordinary respect and pre-eminence awarded to the Brahmens; they are allowed the most striking advantages over all other members of the social body, in almost everything which regards the social state. In the scale of punishments for crimes, the penalty of the Brahmen, in almost all cases, is infinitely milder than that of the inferior castes. Although punishment is remarkably cruel and sanguinary for the other classes of the Hindus, neither the life nor even the property of a Brahmen can be brought into danger by the most atrocious offences. "Neither shall the king," says one of the ordinances of Menu,[2] "slay a Brahmen, though convicted of all possible crimes. Let him banish the offender from his realm, but with all his property secure, and his body unhurt." In regulating the interest of money, the rate which may be taken from the Brahmens is less than what may be exacted from the other classes.[3] This privileged order enjoys the advantage of being entirely exempt from taxes: "A king, even though dying with want, must not receive any tax from a Brahmen learned in the Vedas."[4] Their influence over the government is only bounded by their desires, since they have impressed the belief that all laws which a Hindu is bound to respect are contained in the sacred books; that it is lawful for them alone to interpret those books; that it is incumbent on the king to employ them as his chief counsellors and ministers, and to be governed by their advice. "Whatever order," says the code of Hindu laws,[5] "the Brahmens shall issue conformably to the Shaster, the magistrate shall take his measures accordingly."[6] These prerogatives and privileges, important and extraordinary as they may seem, afford, however,

[1] Laws of Menu, ch. ix. 313—319.

[2] Ibid. viii. 380. [3] Ibid. viii. [4] Ibid vii. 133.

[5] Halhed, Preface to the Code of Gentoo Laws.

[6] The Druids among the ancient Britons, as there was a striking similarity in many of the doctrines which they taught, also possessed many similar privileges and distinctions to those of the Brahmens. Their persons were inviolable; they were exempt from taxes and military service; they exercised the legislative, the judicial, and, with the exception of commanding armies in the field, almost the whole of the executive powers of government. Cæsar, De Bell. Gal. lib. vi. 13, 14. Henry's Hist. of Great Britain, i. 302, 317.

but an imperfect idea of the influence of the Brahmens in the intercourse of Hindu Society. As the greater part of life among the Hindus is engrossed by the performance of an infinite and burdensome ritual, which extends to almost every hour of the day, and every function of nature and society, the Brahmens, who are the sole judges and directors in these complicated and endless duties, are rendered the uncontrollable masters of human life. Thus elevated in power and privileges, the ceremonial of society is no less remarkably in their favour. They are so much superior to the king, that the meanest Brahmen would account himself polluted by eating with him, and death itself would appear to him less dreadful than the degradation of permitting his daughter to unite herself in marriage with his sovereign. With these advantages, it would be extraordinary had the Brahmens neglected themselves in so important a circumstance as the command of property. It is an essential part of the religion of the Hindus, to confer gifts upon the Brahmens. This is a precept more frequently repeated than any other in the sacred books. Gifts to the Brahmens form always an important and essential part of expiation and sacrifice.[1]

[1] See the laws of Menu, passim. "The organs of sense and action, reputation, a heavenly mansion, life, a great name, children, cattle, are all destroyed by a sacrifice offered with trifling presents: let no man, therefore, sacrifice without liberal gifts." Ibid. xi. 40. "Let every man, according to his ability, give wealth to the Brahmens detached from the world and learned in Scripture; such a giver shall attain heaven after this life." Ibid. xi. 6. "Having reckoned up the persons whom the Brahmen is obliged to support, having ascertained his Divine knowledge and moral conduct, let the king allow him a suitable maintenance from his own household; and, having appointed him a maintenance, let the king protect him on all sides, for he gains from the Brahmen whom he protects a sixth part of his virtue." Ibid. xi. 22, 23. "Of that king in whose dominions a learned Brahmen is afflicted with hunger, the whole kingdom will in a short time be afflicted with famine." Ibid. vii. 114.

The Brahmens are occasionally exhorted to observe some decorum and measure in their pursuit of gifts. Laws of Menu, iv. 186. "Should the king be near his end through some incurable disease, he must bestow on the priests all his riches accumulated from legal fines; and, having duly committed his kingdom to his son, let him seek death in battle; or, if there be no war, by abstaining from food."

"The influence of priestcraft over superstition is no where so visible as in India. All the commerces of life have a strict analogy with the ceremonies of religion; and the Brachman has inculcated such a variety of strange persuasions, that the Gentoo finds himself every hour under the necessity of consulting his spiritual guide. The building of a pagoda, and maintaining within it a set of priests, is believed the best action which human virtue is capable of. Every offence is capable of being expiated by largesses to the Brachmans, prescribed by themselves according to their own measures of avarice and sensuality." Orme, On the Government and People of Indostan, 432.

"Since the Brahmen sprung from the most excellent part, since he was the

BOOK II. CHAP. II.

When treasure is found, which, from the general practice of concealment, and the state of society, must have been a frequent event, the Brahmen may retain whatever his good fortune places in his hands; another man must surrender it to the king, who is bound to deliver one-half to the Brahmens.[1] Another source of revenue at first view appears but ill assorted with the dignity and high rank of the Brahmens; by their influence it was converted into a fund, not only respectable but venerable, not merely useful but opulent. The noviciates to the sacerdotal office are commanded to find their subsistence by begging, and even to carry part of their earnings to their spiritual master. Begging is no inconsiderable source of priestly power.[2]

The duties of the Brahmens may be summed up in a few words. They are, to read the Vedas; to teach them

---

first born, and since he possesses the Veda, he is by right the chief of this whole creation.

Him, the Being who exists of himself, produced in the beginning from his own mouth, that having performed holy rites, he might present clarified butter to the Gods, and cakes of rice to the progenitors of mankind, for the preservation of this world:

"What created being then can surpass him, with whose mouth the Gods of the firmament continually feast on clarified butter, and the manes of ancestors, on hallowed cakes?

"Of created things, the most excellent are those which are animated; of the animated, those which subsist by intelligence; of the intelligent, mankind: and of men, the sacerdotal class;

"Of priests, those eminent in learning: of the learned, those who know their duty; of those who know it, such as perform it virtuously; and of the virtuous, those who seek beatitude from a perfect acquaintance with scriptural doctrine.

"The very birth of Brahmens is a constant incarnation of Dherma, God of Justice; for the Brahmen is born to promote justice, and to procure ultimate happiness.

"When a Brahmen springs to light, he is born above the world, the chief of all creatures, assigned to guard the treasury of duties, religious and civil.

"Whatever exists in the universe is all in effect, though not in form, the wealth of the Brahmen: since the Brahmen is entitled to it all by his primogeniture and eminence of birth." Laws of Menu, i. 93—100.

[1] Laws of Menu, ch. viii. The law is laid down somewhat differently in Halhed's Code: when a man finds any thing belonging to another, the magistrate is to be informed, and if the finder is a Brahmen, he keeps the whole; from others a part goes to the magistrate; and from a Sooder all but two twelfths. Halhed's Gentoo Laws, ch. 21, sect. 2.

[2] Laws of Menu, ch. ii. The mendicity of the priests seems to have been a general instrument of priestly imposture. It was so among the Romans; and no unproductive one. See Apuleius, Metam. i. viii. p. 262. Cicero, in his Book of Laws, proposes to restrain the begging trade of the priests.—Stipem sustulimus, nisi eam quam ad paucos dies propriam Idæ Martis excepimus: Implet enim superstitione animos, exhaurit domos. Cic. de Legib. l. ii. 9, 16. The Popish mendicants are a notorious instance. See Middleton's Letter from Rome, in Works of Dr. Conyers Middleton, iii. 116.

to the young Brahmens; and to perform sacrifices and other religious acts.[1]

II. Among the castes of the Hindus, the next in dignity and rank to the priestly tribe, is that of the Cshatriyas, or the military class. In the rude and early state of society, as man has provided few securities against the evils with which he is assailed, and his wisdom has enabled him to draw few general rules respecting the order of their recurrence, he lives in a perpetual expectation of unhappy events, as well from nature, as from his fellow-men; and fear is the passion which chiefly usurps the government of his mind. The priest soothes his imagination, in regard to the first and most awful source of his apprehensions, by undertaking to procure for him the favour of the mysterious powers of nature. The soldier, from whom he expects protection against the ravages

[1] See the Laws of Menu, passim. "To Brahmens were assigned the duties of reading the Veda, of teaching it, of sacrificing, of assisting others to sacrifice, of giving alms, and of receiving gifts." Menu, i. 88.—M.

Notwithstanding the view given in the text of the position of the Brahman in Hindu society, is founded upon authentic texts, yet, upon the whole, it is calculated to produce wrong impressions. The Brahmans are not priests in the ordinary acceptation of the term, nor have they, as Brahmans only, such influence in society as is here ascribed to them. The Brahmans, in the early stages of Hindu society, were an order of men who followed a course of religious study and practice during the first half of their lives, and spent the other in a condition of self-denial and mendicity. They conducted for themselves, and others of the two next castes, sacrifices, and occasionally great public ceremonials; but they never, like the priests of other pagan nations, or those of the Jews, conducted public worship, worship for individuals indiscriminately, worship in temples, or offerings to idols. A Brahman who makes offerings to idols is held as degraded, and unfit to be invited to religious feasts. Menu, ii. 152, 180.—Again, though acceptance of gifts is one mode of subsistence, Brahmans are prohibited from taking gifts indiscriminately, habitually, or excessively, and from receiving any reward for teaching, or any fixed wages or reward for sacrifices. Ibid. iii. 156; iv. 33, 186, 214, etc.—If possessed of wealth, a Brahman is enjoined to give liberally, and whatever property he may possess, he is commanded to abandon it in the prime of manhood, for a life of religious solitude and meditation. Ibid. vi. 2, et seq.—The whole tenor of the rules for the conduct of a Brahman is to exclude him from everything like worldly enjoyment, from riches, and from temporal power. Neither did the Brahmans, like the priests of the Egyptians, keep to themselves a monopoly of spiritual knowledge. The Brahman alone, it is true, is to *teach* the Vedas; but the two next orders, the Kshatriya and Vaisya, are equally to study them, and were, therefore, equally well acquainted with the law and the religion. Even the Sudra was, under some circumstances, permitted to read and teach; for it is said, "a believer in scripture may receive pure knowledge even from a Sudra." Menu, ii. 238.—In modern times the Brahmans, collectively, have lost all claim to the character of a priesthood. They form a nation, following all kinds of secular avocations, and where they are met with in a religious capacity, it is not as Brahmans merely, but as being the ministers of temples, or the family Gurus, or priests of the lower classes of the people, offices by no means restricted, though not unfrequently extended, to the Brahmanical caste, and agreeably to the primitive system virtually destructive of Brahmanhood.—W.

of hostile men, is the second object of his veneration and gratitude; and in the history of society, it will be generally found, that the rank and influence of the military order are high, in proportion as the civilization of the people is low.[1] To all but the Brahmens, the caste of Cshatriyas are an object of unbounded respect. They are as much elevated above the classes below them, as the Brahmens stand exalted above the rest of human kind. Nor is superiority of rank among the Hindus an unavailing ceremony. The most important advantages are attached to it. The distance between the different orders of men is immense and degrading. If a man of a superior class accuses a man of an inferior class, and his accusation proves to be unjust, he escapes not with impunity; but if a man of inferior class accuses a man of a superior class, and fails in proving his accusation, a double punishment is allotted him.[2] For all assaults, the penality rises in proportion as the party offending is low, the party complaining high, in the order of the castes. It is, indeed, a general and remarkable part of the jurisprudence of this singular people, that all crimes are more severely punished in the subordinate classes; the penality ascending, by gradation, from the gentle correction of the venerable Brahmen to the harsh and sanguinary chastisement of the degraded Sudra.[3] Even in such an affair as the interest of money on loan, where the Brahmen pays two per cent., three per cent. is exacted from the Cshatriya, four per cent. from the Vaisya, and five per cent. from the Sudra. The sovereign dignity, which usually follows the power of the sword, was originally appropriated to the military class, though in this particular it would appear that irregularity was pretty

[1] To this observation I know not that any exception can be adduced, which is not resolvable into the influence of a government purely or chiefly military. This, however, is the effect of art, or of forced circumstances, not of nature or of reason. It is Mandeville, I think, who remarks, that fear is the origin of the admiration which has been generally bestowed upon the profession of arms; and in confirmation of this observes, that it is the most timid sex by whom the military character is the most admired. Mr. Hume has remarked, that it is the most timid sex, also, who are the most devoted to superstition and the priests.

[2] Halhed's Code, ch. xv. sect. 2. "If a man of an inferior caste," says the Gentoo Code, "proudly affecting an equality with a person of superior caste, should speak at the same time with him, the magistrate in that case shall punish him to the extent of his abilities."—Ibid.

[3] See the Laws of Menu, and Halhed's Gentoo Code, passim. The case of theft is an exception to this, the higher classes being punished the most severely.

early introduced. To bear arms is the peculiar duty of the Cshatriya caste, and their maintenance is derived from the provision made by the sovereign for his soldiers.[1]

III. The Vaisyas are the third caste of the Hindus. Their duties are to tend cattle, to carry on merchandise, and to cultivate the ground. They are superior only to the Sudras, who owe to them, however, the same awful respect and submission, which it is incumbent on them to pay to the military class.

IV. As much as the Brahmen is an object of intense veneration, so much is the Sudra an object of contempt, and even of abhorrence, to the other classes of his countrymen.[2] The business of the Sudras is servile labour, and their degradation inhuman. Not only is the most abject and grovelling submission imposed upon them as a religious duty, but they are driven from their just and equal share in all the advantages of the social institution. The crimes which they commit against others are more severely punished than those of any other delinquents, while the crimes which others commit against them are more gently punished than those against any other sufferers.[3] Even their persons and labour are not free. "A man of the servile caste, whether bought or unbought, a Brahmen may compel to perform servile duty; because such a man was created by the Self-existent for the purpose of serving Brahmens."[4] The law scarcely permits them to own pro-

[1] There are several notices in Hindu tradition, of a collision between the Brahmans and Kshatriyas. And it is singular enough, that the cause of dispute never appears to have been secular rank or power. The Brahmans are never described as seeking kingly dignity; but the Kshatriyas contend for admission into the Brahmanical order.—W.

[2] The law does not justify the term 'abhorrence.' In what follows, Mr. Mill has collected the extreme texts, and has passed over all the favourable or qualifying passages. The condition of a Sudra, in the Hindu system, was infinitely preferable to that of the helot, the slave, or the serf of the Greek, the Roman, and the feudal systems. He was independent, his services were optional: they were not agricultural, but domestic and personal, and claimed adequate compensation. He had the power of accumulating wealth, or injunctions against his so doing would have been superfluous. He had the opportunity of rising to rank, for the Puranas record dynasties of Sudra kings; and even Manu notices their existence, iv. 61.—He might, as we have seen above, study and teach religious knowledge, and he might perform religious acts. "As a Sudra, without injuring another man, performs the lawful acts of the twice-born; even thus, without being censured, he gains exaltation in this world, and the next." Menu, x. 128. See also verses 121 to 131; and Vishnu Purana, 292, and note.—No doubt the Sudra was considered, in some degree, the property of the Brahman; but he had rights and privileges, and freedom, much beyond any other of the servile classes of antiquity.—W.

[3] See the Laws of Menu, and Halhed's Gentoo Code, passim.

[4] Ibid. ch. viii. 413.

perty; for it is declared that "no collection of wealth must be made by a Sudra, even though he has power, since a servile man, who has amassed riches, gives pain even to Brahmens."[1] "A Brahmen may seize, without hesitation, the goods of his Sudra slave; for as that slave can have no property, his master may take his goods."[2] Any failure in the respect exacted of the Sudra towards the superior classes is avenged by the most dreadful punishments. Adultery with a woman of a higher caste is expiated by burning to death on a bed of iron. The degradation of the wretched Sudra extends not only to every thing in this life, but even to sacred instruction, and his chance of favour with the superior powers. A Brahmen must never read the Veda in the presence of Sudras.[3] "Let not a Brahmen," says the law of Menu, "give advice to a Sudra; nor what remains from his table; nor clarified butter, of which part has been offered; nor let him give spiritual counsel to such a man, nor inform him of the legal expiation for his sin: surely he who declares the law to a servile man, and he who instructs him in the mode of expiating sin, sinks with that very man into the hell named Asamvrita."[4]

[1] Laws of Menu, ch. x. 129.

[2] Ibid. viii. 417. If he be distressed for susistence, says the gloss of Culluca.

[3] Ibid.

[4] Laws of Menu, ch. viii. 80, 81. "If," says the Gentoo Code, "a man of the Sooder reads the beids of the Shaster, or the Pooran, to a Brahman, a Chehter, or a Bin, then the magistrate shall heat some bitter oil, and pour it into the aforesaid Sooder's mouth; and if a Sooder listens to the beids of the Shaster, then the oil, heated as before, shall be poured into his ears, and arzees and wax shall be melted together, and the orifice of his ears shall be stopped up therewith. If a Sooder gets by heart the beids of the Shaster, the magistrate shall put him to death. If a Sooder always performs worship and the jugg, the magistrate shall put him to death. If a Sooder gives much and frequent molestation to a Brahmen, the magistrate shall put him to death." (Halhed's Code of Gentoo Laws, ch. xxi., sect. 7.) It is among the most barbarous tribes, that we in general find the principle of subordination abused to the greatest excess. Perhaps no instance is equal to that which exhibits itself among the Hindus. "Among the Natchez," says Robertson (Hist. America, ii. 139), a powerful tribe now extinct, on the banks of the Mississippi, a difference of rank took place, with which the northern tribes were altogether unacquainted. Some families were reputed noble, and enjoyed hereditary dignity. The body of the people was considered as vile, and formed only for subjection. This distinction was marked by appellations, which intimated the high elevation of the one state, and the ignominious depression of the other: the former were called *Respectable;* the latter, the *Stinkards*."—"To be a servant," says Millar (Distinction of Ranks, ch. v. sect. 1), "in these primitive times, was almost universally the same thing as to be a slave. The master assumed an unlimited jurisdiction over his servants, and the privilege of selling them at pleasure. He gave them no wages beside their maintenance; and he allowed them to have no property, but claimed to his own use whatever, by their labour, or by any other means, they happened to acquire.—Thus the

Although the adherence of each class to the particular employment assigned to it was secured by the most rigid laws, and the severest penalties, there were extraordinary cases in which a limited departure was permitted. When a Brahmen cannot obtain subsistence by the proper business of his order, he may apply himself to that of the Cshatriya or the Vaisya, but must never become so far degraded as to engage in that of the Sudra. The Cshatriya and Vaisya, in like necessitous circumstances, may have recourse respectively to the business of the class or classes below them, even that of the Sudra, but are strictly interdicted from profaning the employment of any class above them. The Sudra having, originally, no inferior class, was probably abandoned to his necessities, though afterwards, in the employments of the mixed classes, a resource was opened also for him.[1] In this arrangement, as usually happens in the laws of the Hindus, the advantages are all on the side of the superior orders. The Brahmen has open to him, if need be, the occupations of all the respectable classes; he can overload them with additional numbers in the season of distress, a season at which it is natural for them to be overloaded without him, while his own occupation is exempt from the encroachment or competition of any other description of men. The Cshatriya, while he has the occupations open to him of two of the castes, is liable to the interference of one of them only. The Vaisya, on the other hand, can have recourse to none but the lowest of employments, that of the Sudra, while he is liable to be straitened in his own occupation by the interference and competition of both the orders above him. The unfortunate Sudra, who has no resource, may be driven from his employment and his means of subsistence, mediately or immediately, by all the other classes of the community.[2]

---

practice of domestic slavery appears to have been early established among the nations of antiquity; among the Egyptians, the Phœnicians, the Jews, the Babylonians, the Persians, the Greeks, and the Romans.—The same practice obtains at present among all those tribes of barbarians, in different parts of the world, with which we have any correspondence."

[1] Laws of Menu, ch. x. passim. Mr. Colebrooke on the Indian Classes. Asiatic Researches, v. 63.

[2] The Sudra has a resource not permitted to the others—emigration; a sufficient proof of his personal liberty. "Let the three first classes invariably dwell in these before-mentioned countries; but a Sudra, distressed for subsistence, may sojourn where he pleases." Manu, ii. 24.—W.

BOOK II. CHAP. II.

This distribution of the whole people into four classes only, and the appropriation of them to four species of employment; an arrangement which, in the very simple state of society in which it must have been introduced, was a great step in improvement, must have become productive of innumerable inconveniences, as the wants of society multiplied. The bare necessaries of life, with a small number of its rudest accommodations, are all it prepares to meet the desires of man. As those desires speedily extend beyond such narrow limits, a struggle must have early ensued between the first principles of human nature and those of the political establishment. The different castes were strictly commanded to marry with those only of their own class and profession; and the mixture of the classes from the union of the sexes was guarded against by the severest laws.[1] This was an occurrence, however, which laws could not prevent. Irregularities took place; children were born, who belonged to no caste, and for whom there was no occupation. No event could befall society more calamitous than this. Unholy and infamous, on account of that violation of the sacred law to which they owed their unwelcome birth, those wretched outcasts had no resource for subsistence, excepting either the bounty of the established classes, to whom they were objects of execration and abhorrence; or the plunder of those same classes, a course to which they would betake themselves with all the ingenuity of necessitous, and all the atrocity of much injured, men. When a class of this description became numerous, they must have filled society with the greatest disorders. In the preface of that compilation of the Hindu Laws, which was translated by Mr. Halhed,[2] it is stated that, after a succession of good kings, who secured obedience to the laws, and under whom the people enjoyed felicity, came a monarch evil and corrupt, under whom the laws were violated, the

[1] This is not correct. The original system seems to have been very lax in this respect, and each caste might take wives from the caste or castes below them, as well as their own. "A Sudra woman only, must be the wife of a Sudra; she and a Vaisya of a Vaisya; they too and a Kshatriya of a Kshatriya; those too and a Brahmani of a Brahman." Manu, iii. 13. And although it was a sin for a Brahman to marry a Sudra woman, yet that such things did happen, appears from the following stanzas, 14—17, as well as passages in the tenth book.—W.

[2] Vide Halhed's Code of Gentoo Laws, preface.

mixture of the classes was perpetrated, and a new and impious race were produced. The Brahmens put this wicked king to death, and, by an effort of miraculous power, created a successor endowed with the most excellent qualities. But the kingdom did not prosper, by reason of the Burren Sunker, so were this impure brood denominated; and it required the wisdom of this virtuous king to devise a remedy. He resolved upon a classification of the mixed race, and to assign them occupations. This, accordingly, was the commencement of arts and manufactures. The Burren Sunker became all manner of artisans and handicrafts; one tribe of them weavers of cloth, another artificers in iron, and so on in other cases, till the subdivisions of the class were exhausted, or the exigencies of the community supplied. Thus were remedied two evils at once: The increasing wants of an improving society were provided for; and a class of men, the pest of the community, were converted to its service. This is another important era in the history of Hindu society; and having reached this stage, it does not appear that it has made, or that it is capable of making, much further progress. Thirty-six branches of the impure class are specified in the sacred books,[1] of whom and of their employments it would be tedious and useless to present the description. The highest is that sprung from the conjunction of a Brahmen with a woman of the Cshatriya class, whose duty is the teaching of military exercises. The lowest of all is the offspring of a Sudra with a woman of the sacred class. This tribe are denominated Chandalas, and are regarded with great abhorrence. Their profession is to carry out corpses, to execute criminals, and perform other offices, reckoned to the last degree unclean and degrading. If, by the laws of Hindustan, the Sudras are placed in a low and vile situation, the impure and mixed classes are placed in one still more odious and degrading. Nothing can equal the contempt and insolence to which it is the lot of the lowest among them to see themselves exposed. They are condemned to live in a sequestered

[1] Colebrooke on the Indian Classes, Asiatic Researches, v. 53. On this subject, however, that intelligent author tells us, that Sanscrit authorities in some instances disagree. Classes mentioned by one, are omitted by another; and texts differ on the professions assigned to some tribes. It is a subject, he adds, in which there is some intricacy.

spot by themselves, that they may not pollute the very town in which they reside. If they meet a man of the higher castes, they must turn out of the way, lest he should be contaminated by their presence.[1]

[1] "Avoid," says the Tantra, "the touch of the Chandala, and other abject classes. Whoever associates with them undoubtedly falls from his class; whoever bathes or drinks in wells or pools which they have caused to be made, must be purified by the five productions of kine." Colebrooke on the Indian Classes, Asiat. Research. v. 53. From this outline of the classification and distribution of the people, as extracted from the books of the Hindus, some of the most intelligent of our British observers appeal to the present practice of the people, which they affirm is much more conformable to the laws of human welfare, than the institutions described in the ancient books. Of this, the author is aware; so inconsistent with the laws of human welfare are the institutions described in the Hindu ancient books, that they never *could* have been observed with any accuracy; it is, at the same time, very evident, that the institutions described in the ancient books are the model upon which the present frame of Hindu society has been formed; and when we consider the powerful causes which have operated so long to draw, or rather to force, the Hindus from their inconvenient institutions and customs, the only source of wonder is, that the state of society which they now exhibit should hold so great a resemblance to that which is depicted in their books. The President de Goguet is of opinion, that a division of the people into tribes and hereditary professions similar to that of the Hindus existed in the ancient Assyrian empire, and that it prevailed from the highest antiquity over almost all Asia (part I. book I. ch. i. art. 3; Herodot. lib. i. cap. 200; Strab. lib. xvi. p. 1082; Diod. lib. ii. p. 142). Cecrops distributed into four tribes all the inhabitants of Attica. (Pollux, lib. viii. cap. 9, sect. 100; Diodorus Siculus, lib. ii. p. 33.) Theseus afterwards made them three by uniting, as it should seem, the sacerdotal class with that of the nobles, or magistrates. They consisted then of nobles and priests, labourers or husbandmen, and artificers; and there is no doubt that, like the Egyptians and Indians, they were hereditary. (Plutarch. Vit. Thes.) Aristotle expressly informs us (Polit. lib. vii. cap. 10), that in Crete the people were divided by the laws of Minos into classes after the manner of the Egyptians. We have most remarkable proof of a division, the same as that of the Hindus, anciently established among the Persians. In the Zendavesta, translated by Anquetil Duperron, is the following passage: "Ormusd said: There are three measures [literally weights, that is, tests, rules] of conduct, four states, and five places of dignity.—The states are: that of the priests; that of the soldier; that of the husbandman, the source of riches; and that of the artisan or labourer." Zendavesta, i. 141. There are sufficient vestiges to prove an ancient establishment of the same sort among the Buddhists of Ceylon, and by consequence to infer it among the other Buddhists over so large a portion of Asia. See a Discourse of Mr. Joinville on the Religion and Manners of the People of Ceylon, Asiat. Research. vii. 430, et seq.—M.

There is no distinction of caste amongst the Buddhists, although in some places an attempt may have been made to introduce some such distinction, after the Hindu model. The multiplication of castes in India, is not the enactment of any code, though it may be remotely the effect; it is the work of the people, amongst the most degraded of whom, prevails, not the shame, but the "pride" of caste. The lowest native is no outcaste, he has an acknowledged place in society; he is the member of a class; and he is invariably more retentive of the distinction than those above him. In depicturing the horrors of the system, European writers lose sight of the compensations. The veriest Chandala, who is one of a community, is less miserable, less unhappy, than many of the paupers of the civilized communities of Europe, with whom no man owns companionship or kindred; they are the true outcastes—not the Pariah or Chandala.—W.

CHAPTER III.

The Form of Government.

AFTER the division of the people into ranks and occupations, the great circumstance by which their condition, character, and operations are determined, is the political establishment; the system of actions by which the social order is preserved. Among the Hindus, according to the Asiatic model, the government was monarchical, and, with the usual exception of religion and its ministers, absolute. No idea of any system of rule, different from the will of a single person, appears to have entered the minds of them, or their legislators. "If the world had no king," says the Hindu law,[1] "it would quake on all sides through fear; the ruler of this universe, therefore, created a king, for the maintenance of this system." Of the high and uncontrollable authority of the monarch a judgment may be formed, from the lofty terms in which the sacred books describe his dignity and attributes. "A king," says the law of Menu,[2] "is formed of particles from the chief guardian deities, and consequently surpasses all mortals in glory. Like the sun, he burns eyes and hearts; nor can any human creature on earth even gaze on him. He, is fire and air; He, the god of criminal justice; He, the genius of wealth; He, the regent of waters; He, the lord of the firmament. A king, even though a child, must not be treated lightly, from an idea that he is a mere mortal: No; he is a powerful divinity, who appears in human shape. In his anger, death. He who shows hatred of the king, through delusion of mind, will certainly perish; for speedily will the king apply his heart to that man's destruction." The pride of imperial greatness could not devise, hardly could it even desire, more extraordinary distinctions, or the sanction of a more unlimited authority.[3]

[1] Laws of Menu, ch. vii. 3.

[2] Ibid. vii.

[3] Had Mr. Mill sufficiently considered several passages which he presently quotes, or to which he refers, he would have been satisfied that these descriptions of kingly power are mere generalities; and that in practice, Hindu despotism did not exist. The Raja was not above the law. "Law," says Sankara, "is the king of kings, far more powerful than they." Preface to the Digest. He was not a lawgiver: the laws to which he was amenable, as well as the meanest of his subjects, emanated from a higher: "God having created the

BOOK II. CHAP. III.

The plan, according to which the power of the sovereign was exercised in the government of the country, resembled that which has almost universally prevailed in the monarchies of Asia, and was a contrivance extremely simple and rude. In the more skilful governments of Europe, officers are appointed for the discharge of particular duties in the different provinces of the empire; some for the decision of causes, some for the control of violence, some for collecting the contingents of the subjects, for the expense of the state; while the powers of all centre immediately in the head of the government, and all together act as connected and subordinate wheels in one complicated and artful machine. Among the less instructed and less civilised inhabitants of Asia, no other plan has ever occurred to the monarch, for the administration of his dominions, than simply to divide his own authority and power into pieces or fragments, as numerous as the provinces into which it was deemed convenient to distribute the empire. To each of the provinces a viceregent was despatched, who carried with him the undivided authority and jurisdiction of his master. Whatever powers the sovereign exercised over the whole kingdom, the viceregent exercised in the province allotted to him; and the same plan which the sovereign adopted for the government of the whole, was exactly followed by the viceregent in the government of a part.[1] If the province committed to his sway was too extensive for his personal inspection and control, he subdivided it into parts, and assigned a go-

four classes, lest the royal and military class should become insupportable through their power and ferocity, produced the transcendent body of law." Ibid. He was not even permitted to administer it without legal advisers: "let not a prince, who seeks the good of his own soul, hastily and alone pronounce the law." Manu, viii. 281. The authority of the Brahmans was not a nominal restraint. In early times, they undertook to depose kings for tyranny and impiety: see the legends of Vena, Parasuráma and Devápi, Vishnu Purana, 99, 401, 458; and the Mudrá Rákshasa, Hindu Theatre, vol. ii. There were also other checks upon regal power in an hereditary nobility: "men of high lineage, whose ancestors were servants of kings." For, at a very early period, offices of state seem to have become hereditary; and the hereditary minister was often more powerful than his master. The great Kshatriyas, represented by the Samants of Prithu Rai, and the present Thakurs of Jaypur and Jodhpur, seldom allowed despotic power to their prince. See Mudra Rakshasa; Tod's Raja'sthan; Duff's Mahrattas.—W.

[1] Kæmpfer, in his History of Japan, book i. chap. v., says, "the whole empire is governed in general by the Emperor, with an absolute and monarchical power, and so is every province in particular by the prince, who, under the Emperor, enjoys the government thereof."—For the similarity of the institution in the Ottoman government, see Volney's Travels in Syria and Egypt, ii. 376.

vernor to each, whom he intrusted with the same absolute powers in his district, as he himself possessed in the administration of the greater department. Even this inferior deputy often divided his authority, in the same manner, among the governors, whom he appointed, of the townships or villages under his control. Every one of those rulers, whether the sphere of his command was narrow or extensive, was absolute within it, and possessed the whole power of the sovereign, to levy taxes, to raise and command troops, and to decide upon the lives and property of the subjects.[1] The gradations of command among the Hindus were thus regulated: the lowest of all was the lord of one town and its district; the next was the lord of ten towns; the third was the lord of twenty towns; the fourth was the lord of 100 towns; and the highest vicegerent was lord of 1000 towns. Every lord was amenable to the one immediately above him, and exercised unlimited authority over those below.[2] The following law appears to provide for their personal expenses: "Such food, drink, wood, and other articles, as by law should be given each day to the king, by the inhabitants of the township, let the lord of one town receive; let the lord of ten towns enjoy the produce of two plough-lands; the lord of twenty, that of five plough-lands; the lord of 100, that of a village or small town; the lord of 1000, that of a large town."[3] The

[1] This is not correct; even Manu separates the military from the civil authority. "Let him place a division of troops, commanded by an approved officer, over two, three, five, or a hundred districts, according to their extent," vii. 214.—W.

[2] Laws of Menu, ch. vii. 115—117. There is a very remarkable similarity between this mode of subdividing authority among the Hindus, and that adopted by the Incas of Peru. "The Incas" (says Garcilasso de la Vega, part i. book ii. ch. v.) "had one method and rule in their government, as the best means to prevent all mischiefs and disorders; which was this. That of all the people in every place, whether more or less, a register should be kept, and a division made of ten and ten, over which one of the ten, whom they called the Decurion, was made superior over the other nine; then every five divisions of this nature had a lord over them, to whom was committed the charge and care of fifty; then over two divisions of fifty, another lord, who supervised 100; so five divisions of 100 had a magistrate who commanded 500; the divisions of 100 had a leader over 1000," etc. The highest officer under the Inca was the governor of a province. Each inferior officer accounted for his conduct to the superior next above him. See, further, Acosta, Nat. and Mor. Hist. of the Indies, book vi. ch. xiii.; Carli, Lettres sur l'Amérique, let. xiii. The analogy of the Anglo-Saxon institution of tithings, or ten families; of hundreds, or ten tithings; and counties, will suggest itself to every imagination.

[2] Laws of Menu, ch. vii. 118, 119. The first of these provisions, that for the lord of one town, is not accurately ascertained; the two or five plough-lands are sufficiently distinct; but the produce of a village or large town must have been extremely uncertain and ambiguous.

expense of the government of each vicegerent was defrayed out of the taxes which he levied, and the surplus was transmitted to the superior lord, to whom he was immediately responsible. From him it was again conveyed to the governor above him, till it reached, at last, the royal treasury.

If this plan of government was unskilful and rude,[1] so was the contrivance employed for checking the abuses to which it was liable. "The affairs of these townships," says the law, "either jointly or separately transacted, let another minister of the king inspect, who should be well affected, and by no means remiss. In every larger town or city, let him appoint one superintendent of all affairs, elevated in rank, formidable in power, distinguished as a planet among stars. Let that governor, from time to time, survey all the rest in person; and, by the means of his emissaries, let him perfectly know their conduct in their several districts."[2] Of the practical state of the government abundant proof is afforded, in the passage which immediately follows. "Since the servants of the king," it is said, "whom he has appointed guardians of districts, are generally knaves, who seize what belongs to other men, from such knaves let him defend his people; of such evil-minded servants, as wring wealth from subjects attending them on business, let the King confiscate all the possessions, and banish them from his realm."[3]

At the head of this government stands the king, on whom the great lords of the empire immediately depend. He is directed by the law to choose a Council, consisting "of seven or eight ministers, men whose ancestors were servants of kings, who are versed in the holy books, who are personally brave; who are skilled in the use of weapons, and whose lineage is noble."[4] With them he is commanded perpetually to consult on the affairs of his

[1] Competent authorities opine differently; after quoting the passages of Manu, referred to in the notes of our author, Col. Briggs concludes, "these extracts afford us sufficient proof of a well-organised system of local superintendence and administration." On the Land-tax of India, 24.—W.

[2] Laws of Menu, ch. vii. 120—122. A similar officer formed a similar part of the Peruvian establishment. He was denominated *Cucuy Kioc*, which is to say, "Eye of all." Carli, Lettres sur l'Amérique, let. xiii.

[3] Menu, ut supra, 123, 124.

[4] Ibid. 54.—M.

The council of Manu does not comprise all the officers of state; and lists given in the Pancha Tantra from the Mahábhárata, specify thirty-three persons or classes of persons attached in a public or private capacity to royalty. Tr. R. As. Society, i. 174.—W.

government; but a singular mode of deliberation is prescribed to him; not to assemble his Council, and, laying before them, as in the cabinets of European princes, the subject on which the suggestions of their wisdom are required, to receive the benefit arising from the natural communication of their knowledge and views; a plan, apparently more artful and cunning, more nearly allied to the suspicious temper and narrow views of a rude period, is recommended; to consult them apart, and hear the opinion of each separately; after which, having consulted them in common, when each man is swayed by the opinion he had formerly given in private, and has a motive of interest and vanity to resist the light which might be thrown upon the subject by others, the king himself is to decide.[1] A Brahmen ought always to be his prime minister. "To one learned Brahmen, distinguished among the rest, let the king impart his momentous counsel."[2]

To provide for the defence of the country was one great branch of the duties of the sovereign, and to preside over the military force was his great prerogative and distinction. As, in the original division of the people, a fourth part of them were appropriated to the profession of arms, and destined from that alone to obtain their subsistence, the great difficulty of government must have consisted, not in obtaining troops, but in finding for them maintenance and employment. When so great a proportion of the population were set apart for the business of war, with nothing to do, from year to year, and from generation to generation, but to improve its principles, and acquire the utmost dexterity in his exercises, it appears extraordinary that the nation was not of a formidable and warlike character. Yet has India given way to every invader; "and the rudeness," says Mr. Orme,[3] "of the military art in Indostan can scarce be imagined but by those who have seen it." The precepts in the ancient and sacred books of the

[1] Laws of Menu, ch. vii. 56. Another precept to the king, respecting the mode of consulting with his ministers, is very expressive of the simplicity of the times; "Ascending up the back of a mountain, or going privately to a terrace, a bower, a forest, or a lonely place, without listeners, let him consult with them unobserved." Ibid. 147.

[2] Laws of Menu, ch. vii. 58.

[3] Orme on the Government and People of Indostan, p. 417. The same accurate and intelligent observer immediately adds: "The infantry consists in a multitude of people assembled together without regard to rank and file," etc.

BOOK II. CHAP. III.

Hindus, which lay the foundation of their military system, are few in number, simple, and rude. For the security of the royal residence, the king is directed to take up his abode[1] "in a capital, having, by way of fortress, a desert rather more than twenty miles round it, or a fortress of earth, a fortress of water or of trees, a fortress of armed men, or a fortress of mountains." Their great unskilfulness in the science of attack and defence, led them to place great dependence on fortification, as appears by a variety of their precepts. "One bowman," says Menu,[2] "placed on a wall, is a match in war for 100 enemies, and 100 for 10,000; therefore is a fort recommended." Yet their knowledge of fortification was elementary, and mostly consisted in surrounding the place with a mud wall and a ditch, or availing themselves of the natural advantages which insulated rocks, which water, or impervious thickets, could afford. The duty and advantage of maintaining at all times a powerful army are enforced in the most cogent terms. "By a king," says Menu, "whose forces are always ready for action, the whole world may be kept in awe; let him then, by a force always ready, make all creatures living his own."[3] In recommending a perpetual standing army, the preceptive part of the military doctrine of the Hindus seems in a great measure to have been summed up; for the marshalling, the discipline, the conduct of an army, in any of its branches, no instruction is conveyed. General exhortations to firmness and valour are all the additional advice of which the utility appears to have been recognised. The Hindu prince is, by divine authority, informed, that those rulers of the earth, who, "desirous of defeating each other, exert their utmost strength in battle, without ever averting their faces, ascend after death directly to heaven."[4] "Never to recede from combat," says Menu, "to protect the people, and to honour the priests, is the highest duty of kings, and ensures their felicity."[5] Of a great part of the duty which devolved upon the king, as head of the armed force, he appears to have been relieved by a deputy.[6] In times of peace, the military people seem to have been distributed over the country, under the

[1] Laws of Menu, ch. vii. 70.
[2] Ibid. vii. 74. [3] Ibid. 103. [4] Ibid. 89. [5] Ibid. 88.
[6] "The forces of the realm must be immediately regulated by the commander-in-chief." Ibid. 65.

command of the governors of provinces and of districts, for local defence, for the preservation of local tranquillity, and for the convenience of subsistence. When a general war demanded the whole force of the nation, the king commanded the governors of provinces to assemble the soldiers under their command, and repair to his standard.[1] From this circumstance it has been rashly concluded, that feudal conditions of military service, in fact a feudal government, nearly resembling that which existed in Europe, had place in Hindustan.[2]

After the care of protecting the nation from foreign aggression or from internal tumult, the next duty of the king was the distribution of justice. In the first stage of society, the leader in war is also the judge in peace; and the regal and judicial functions are united in the same person. Various circumstances tend to produce this arrangement. In the first place, there are hardly any laws: and he alone is entitled to judge, who is entitled to legislate, since he must make a law for every occasion. In the next place, a rude people, unused to obedience, would hardly respect inferior authority. In the third place, the business of judicature is so badly performed as to interrupt but little the business or the pleasures of the king; and a decision is rather an exercise of arbitrary will and power, than the result of an accurate investigation. In the fourth place, the people are much accustomed to terminate their own disputes, by their own cunning, or force, that the number of applications for judicature is comparatively small.[3] As society advances, a set of circumstances, opposite to these, are gradually introduced:

[1] Laws of Menu, ch. vii. 113–120.

[2] The laws of Menu, it is true, touch but slightly upon military arrangements, but there is no reason to believe that the Hindus cultivated the science of war less carefully than the arts of peace. Much curious illustration of this subject may be gleaned from the Mahábhárata. That they have been unfortunate in their military history, is attributable more to want of union and to mutual dissension, than any deficiency of skill or valour.—W.

[3] It is very doubtful, if this view of the progress of legislation was ever applicable to the Hindus. Certainly we have no grounds whatever for such a description. The code of Menu recognises no right or necessity in the king to make laws—the laws are administrable by judicial authorities other than the king; decisions are never the result of arbitrary will, but are enjoined to be founded on diligent investigation; and although applications for judicature might not have been numerous, yet other reasons might be assigned than the adjustment of disputes by force or cunning. We may conjecture what we please of a stage of society of which we know nothing, but it is conjecture only, and little calculated to extend real knowledge.—W.

laws are made which the judge has nothing to do but apply: the people learn the advantage of submitting to inferior authority: a more accurate administration of justice is demanded, and cannot be performed without a great application both of attention and of time: the people learn that it is for the good of the community, that they should not terminate, and that they should not be allowed to terminate, either by force or fraud, their own disputes: the administration of justice is then too laborious to be either agreeable to the king, or consistent with the other services which he is expected to render: and the exercise of judicature becomes a separate employment, the exclusive function of a particular order of men.

The administration of justice by the king in person, and in the provinces of course by his deputies, as in the subordinate districts by theirs, stands in the sacred books as a leading principle of the jurisprudence of the Hindus; and the revolution of ages has introduced a change in favour rather of the prince who abandons the duty, than of the people, for whom hardly any other instrument of judicature is provided.[1]

In the infancy of improvement, the business of the judge is much more to award punishment, than to settle disputes. The Hindu law, accordingly, represents the king, as "created for the guardianship of all, a divinity in human form, to inflict punishment according to the Shaster."[2] In conformity with these rude ideas, the most extravagant praises are bestowed upon this engine of royalty. "For the use of the king, Brahma formed, in the beginning of time, the genius of punishment with a body

[1] This is not correct. At a period not long subsequent to the Code of Manu, if not contemporary, various regulations were in force for the administration of the laws, and various courts and officers were established for the adjudication of causes, so that the king presided at pleasure only in the court of the capital, or in a court of appeal.—See Colebrooke on Hindu Courts of Justice. —Tr. R. As. Soc. ii. 166. So, also, Mr. Ellis observes: "Mr. Mill makes a considerable mistake if he supposes that in Hindu states it is, or was, the practice to administer justice only in the presence of the king. It is true, that in the Hindu Governments there was always an Aula Regia, or court at the seat of government, in which the king was supposed, according to the letter of the law, to preside in person, though he might appoint a deputy, and always had assessors; but it is doubtful how the practice was kept up, and it is certain that there were three other principal courts known to the Hindu laws, and fifteen sorts of inferior courts, all having their several jurisdictions well defined, and many of them bearing a striking resemblance to the courts of the English common law." Trans. Madras Literary Society II.—W.

[2] Halhed's Gentoo Code, preface.

of pure light, his own son, the protector of all created things. Punishment governs all mankind; punishment alone preserves them; punishment wakes while their guards are asleep; the wise consider punishment as the perfection of justice. If the king were not, without indolence, to punish the guilty, the stronger would roast the weaker, like fish, on a spit. The whole race of man is kept in order by punishment; for a guiltless man is hard to be found."[1]

For the more perfect discharge of this important duty the king is directed to associate with himself Brahmens, and counsellors capable of giving him advice.[2] Any Brahmen, or even a person of the two middle classes, may interpret the law to him; but a Sudra in no case whatever.[3] On those occasions on which it was impossible for the king to give judgment in person, he was empowered to appoint a Brahmen, who, with three assessors, might try causes in his stead.[4]

So much with regard to the constitution of the tribunals. The solemnities of jurisdiction were thus ordered to proceed: "Let the king, or his judge, having seated himself on the bench, his body properly clothed, and his mind attentively fixed, begin with doing reverence to the deities who govern the world, and then let him enter on the trial of causes."[5] The form of process was simple, and good; as it always is among a rude people. The parties were heard, generally in person; though lawyers by profession, unless in the case of certain high crimes, might appear in lieu of the principals. The application of the plaintiff might be either oral or written; but the answer was required to be in the same form; oral, if the application was oral; and

[1] Laws of Menu, ch. vii. 14—22.

[2] Ibid. ch. viii. 1.

[3] Ibid. ch. viii. 20. To learned and righteous Brahmens the magistrate shall give money, and every token of respect and consideration in the judgment seat, to have them near him; but he shall not retain fewer than ten of such Brahmens. Gentoo Code, ch. iii. sect. 1. The more sacred books of law the men by denomination *holy* were alone permitted to read. Thus the law of Menu (ch. ii. 16). "He whose life is regulated by holy texts, from his conception to his funeral pile, has a decided right to study this code, but no other person whatsoever." The more profane commentaries, however, were less confined, and the man versed in these might suffice for the common business of administering justice.

[4] Laws of Menu, ch. viii. 9, 10. The Gentoo Code, translated by Mr. Halhed, directs, that when a king in person cannot examine a cause, he substitutes a learned Brahmen; if a Brahmen cannot be found, a Cshatriya, etc., but in no case a Sudra. Gentoo Code, ch. iii. sect. 1.

[5] Laws of Menu, ch. viii 9, 10.

in writing, if it was otherwise.[1] The judge examines the witnesses; inspects, if any, the writings; and without any intricate or expensive forms proceeds directly to a decision. Punishment immediately follows conviction.[2]

One of the highest of our authorities affords a picture of the practical state of judicature in India, which, there is every reason to believe, may with immaterial variations, be applied to Hindu society, from the period at which it first attained its existing form. "No man is refused access to the Durbar, or seat of judgment; which is exposed to a large area, capable of containing the multitude.[3] The plaintiff discovers himself by crying aloud, Justice! Justice! until attention is given to his importunate clamours. He is then ordered to be silent, and to advance before his judge; to whom, after having prostrated himself, and made his offering of a piece of money, he tells his story in the plainest manner, with great humility of voice and gesture, and without any of those oratorical embellishments which compose an art in freer nations.—The wealth, the consequence, the interest, or the address of the party, become now the only considerations. He visits his judge in private, and gives the jar of oil: his adversary bestows the hog which breaks it. The friends who can influence intercede; and, excepting where the case is so manifestly proved as to brand the failure of redress with glaring infamy (a restraint which human nature is born to reverence), the value of the bribe ascertains the justice of the cause.—This is so avowed a practice, that if a stranger should inquire how much it would cost him to recover a just debt from a creditor who evaded payment, he would everywhere receive the same answer; the government will keep one-fourth and give you the rest. Still the forms of justice subsist; witnesses are heard, but brow-beaten and removed: proofs of writing are produced, but deemed forgeries and rejected, until the way is cleared for the decision, which becomes totally or partially favourable, in proportion to the methods which have been used to render it

[1] Gentoo Code, ch. iii. sect. 5.

[2] Orme on the Government, etc., of Indostan, p. 451.

[3] This publicity of judicial proceedings is common to rude nations. In the country and days of Job, the judge sat at the gate of the city, ch. ix. ver. 7. Moses alludes to the same practice, Gen. xxiii. 11; and Homer tells us it was the practice in the heroic ages of Greece, Il. lib. xviii. ver. 497.

such; but still with some attention to the consequences of a judgment, which would be of too flagrant iniquity not to produce universal detestation and resentment.—Providence has, at particular seasons, blessed the miseries of these people with the presence of a righteous judge. The vast reverence and reputation which such have acquired are but too melancholy a proof of the infrequency of such a character. The history of their judgments and decisions is transmitted down to posterity, and is quoted with a visible complacency on every occasion. Stories of this nature supply the place of proverbs in the conversations of all the people of Indostan, and are applied by them with great propriety."[1]

Such are the principal branches of the duty of the sovereign, and in these various institutions may be contemplated an image of the Hindu government. It is worthy of a short analysis. The powers of government consist of three great branches, the legislative, the judicial, and the administrative; and we have to inquire in what hands these several powers are deposited, and by what circumstances their exercise is controlled. As the Hindu believes, that a complete and perfect system of instruction, which admits of no addition or change, was conveyed to him from the beginning by the Divine Being, for the regulation of his public as well as his private affairs, he acknowledges no laws but those which are contained in the sacred books. From this it is evident, that the only scope which remains for legislation is confined within the limits of the interpretations which may be given to the holy text. The Brahmens enjoy the undisputed prerogative of interpreting the divine oracles; for though it is allowed to the two classes next in degree to give advice to the king in the administration of justice, they must in no case presume to depart from the sense of the law which it has pleased the Brahmens to impose. The power of legislation, therefore, exclusively belongs to the priesthood.

[1] Orme on the Government and People of Indostan, p. 444—446. Another of our most instructive travellers, Mr. Foster, in the Dedication prefixed to his Journey from Bengal to England, p. vii., calls Hindustan, "A land whose every principle of government is actuated by a rapacious avarice, whose people never approach the gate of authority without an offering."—This is a subject to which he often adverts; he says again (i. 7), "In Asia, the principles of justice, honour, or patriotism, as they confer no substantial benefit, nor tend to elevate the character, are seldom seen to actuate the mind of the subject."

The exclusive right of interpreting the laws necessarily confers upon them, in the same unlimited manner, the judicial powers of government.[1] The king, though ostensibly supreme judge, is commanded always to employ Brahmens as counsellors and assistants in the administration of justice; and whatever construction they put upon the law, to that his sentence must conform. Whenever the king in person, discharges not the office of judge, it is a Brahmen, if possible, who must occupy his place. The king, therefore, is so far from possessing the judicial power, that he is rather the executive officer by whom the decisions of the Brahmens are carried into effect.

They who possess the power of making and interpreting the laws by which another person is bound to act, are, by necessary consequence, the masters of his actions. Possessing the legislative and judicative powers, the Brahmens were, also, masters of the executive power, to any extent whatsoever, to which they wished to enjoy it. With influence over it they were not contented. They secured to themselves a direct and no contemptible share of its immediate functions. On all occasions, the king was bound to employ Brahmens as his counsellors and ministers; and, of course, to be governed by their judgment. "Let the king, having risen early," says the law, "respectfully attend to Brahmens learned in the three Vedas, and by their decision let him abide."[2] It thus appears that, according to the original laws of the Hindus, the king was little more than an instrument in the hands of the Brahmens. He performed the laborious part of government, and sustained the responsibility, while they chiefly possessed the power.[3]

The uncontrollable sway of superstition, in rude and

[1] This state of things then is very different from that which, a few pages back (p. 147, etc.), was described as applying, apparently, to the Hindu system; in which the king was represented as the sole source and administrator of the law.—W.

[2] Laws of Menu, ch. vii. 37.

[3] Even under a system, where the power of the altar was from the beginning rendered subservient to the power of the sword, the right of interpreting a code of sacred laws is found to confer an important authority. Hear the opinion of a recent and penetrating observer:—" L'expression vague des préceptes du Koran, seule loi écrite dans les pays Mussulmans, laisse aux docteurs une grande latitude pour les interprétations, et bien des moyens d'augmenter leur autorité. Quoique cette religion ait peu de dogmes, le fanatisme qu'elle inspire est un instrument que les prêtres savent employer avec succès." De l'Egypte, par le Gen. Reynier, p. 62.

ignorant times confers upon its ministers such extraordinary privileges, that the king and the priest are generally the same person; and it appears somewhat remarkable that the Brahmens, who usurped among their countrymen so much distinction and authority, did not invest themselves with the splendour of royalty. It very often happens that some accidental circumstances, of which little account was taken at the time, and which after a lapse of ages it is impossible to trace, gave occasion to certain peculiarities which we remark in the affairs and characters of nations. It is by no means unnatural to suppose, that to a people, over whom the love of repose exerts the greatest sway, and in whose character aversion to danger forms a principal ingredient, the toils and perils of the sword appeared to surpass the advantages with which it was attended; and that the Brahmens transferred to the hands of others, that which was thus a source of too much labour, as well as danger, to be retained in their own.[1]

So many, however, and important were the powers which this class reserved to themselves, that the kingly dignity would appear to have been reduced to that of a dependent and secondary office. But with this inference the fact does not correspond. The monuments of the Hindus, imperfect as they are, convince us, that their monarchs enjoyed no small share both of authority, and of that kind of splendour, which corresponded with their own state of society. They had two engines entrusted to them, the power of which their history serves remarkably to display: they were masters of the army; and they were masters of the public revenue. These two circum-

1 This is not a very liberal interpretation of the motives of the Brahmans, nor is it, in all probability, the correct one. We are too ignorant of the circumstances under which the system originated, to speculate upon the motives or purposes of those with whom it commenced. Apparently, however, it was contrived by a religious confederation, as the scheme best adapted to introduce order amongst semi-civilized tribes, and with no view to their own advantage or aggrandizement, or enjoyment of indolent ease. The authority of influence, of advice, the Brahmans necessarily retained, and they were the only competent expounders of the laws which they promulgated. They had no other means of protection than the character of sanctity with which they invested themselves, and which was equally necessary to ensure attention to their instructions. They laboured to deserve the opinion of sanctity by imposing burdensome duties on themselves, of a domestic and religious character, and it was probably in the true spirit of contemplative devotion, as well as from motives of prudence and policy, that they divested themselves of temporal rank. Every thing in the Hindu Institutes indicates their originating not from political but religious principles.—W.

BOOK II. CHAP. IV.

stances, it appears, were sufficient to counterbalance the legislative, and the judicative, and even a great part of the executive power, reinforced by all the authority of an overbearing superstition, lodged in the hands of the Brahmens. These threw around the sovereign an external lustre, with which the eyes of uncultivated men are easily dazzled. In dangerous and disorderly times, when every thing which the nation values depends upon the sword, the military commander exercises unlimited authority by universal consent; and so frequently is this the situation of a rude and uncivilized people, surrounded on all sides by rapacious and turbulent neighbours, that it becomes, in a great measure, the habitual order of things. The Hindu king, by commanding both the force, and the revenue of the state, had in his hands the distribution of gifts and favours; the potent instrument, in short, of patronage; and the jealousy and rivalship of the different sets of competitors, would, of their own accord, give him a great influence over the Brahmens themselves. The distribution of gifts and favours is an engine of so much power, that the man who enjoys it to a certain extent is absolute, with whatever checks he may appear to be surrounded.[1]

CHAPTER IV.

The Laws.

NEXT to the form of government, in determining the political condition of the people, is the body of law, or the mode in which the rights of individuals are expressed and secured. For elucidating this important point, in the history of the Hindus, materials are abundant. The detail, however, or even the analysis, of the Hindu code, would far exceed the bounds, to which, in a

[1] See what is observed by three great authors, Hume, Blackstone, and Paley, on the influence of the crown in England. See also what is observed by Lord Bolingbroke, on the same subject, in his Dissertation on Parties.—M.

What is here said, however, of the absolute power of Hindu princes is wholly inconsistent with much that has been previously advanced of the unbounded authority of the Brahmans; neither is quite true. Hindu princes and Brahmans are held in check by many considerations, and, in the original system, their several powers were evidently designed to control and balance each other.—W.

work like the present, this topic must be confined. An accurate conception of the character and spirit of the Hindu laws, and of their place in the scale of excellence or defect, is all I can attempt to convey.

Amid the imperfections adhering to the state of law among a rude and ignorant people, one is, that they preserve not their maxims of justice, and their rules of judicial procedure, distinct from other subjects.[1] In the law books of the Hindus, the details of jurisprudence and judicature occupy comparatively a very moderate space.[2] The doctrines and ceremonies of religion; the rules and practice of education; the institutions, duties, and customs of domestic life; the maxims of private morality, and even of domestic economy; the rules of government, of war, and of negotiation; all form essential parts of the Hindu codes of law, and are treated in the same style, and laid down with the same authority, as the rules for the distribution of justice. The tendency of this rude conjunction of dissimilar subjects is, amid other inconveniences, to confound the important distinction between those obligations which it is the duty of the magistrate to enforce, and those which ought to be left to the suggestions of self-interest, and the sanctions of morality; it is to extend coercion, and the authority of the magistrate, over the greater part of human life, and to leave men no liberty even in their private and ordinary transactions;

[1] It is not quite correct to say, that the Hindus do not preserve the ordinances of daily life, distinct from rules of judicial procedure. The original precepts as presently noticed, are classed under various titles, but these again are arranged under three great divisions; A'chára, ceremonial and moral laws; Vyavahára, jurisprudence; and Práyáschitta, religious law, expiation or punishment for crime.—W.

[2] Examine that important specimen of an original Hindu book of law, the institutes of Menu. See, too, the confession of Mr. Colebrooke in the preface to his translation of the Digest of Hindu Law on Contracts and Successions; a work compiled a few years ago, under authority of the English government, by some of the most learned and respectable of the Brahmens.—M.

There is no such confession. An extract from a letter of Sir William Jones is cited by Mr. Colebrooke, in which probably the expression alluded to occurs. "The law of contracts," it is there stated, "bears an inconsiderable proportion to the rest of the work." Nothing is said of "jurisprudence and judicature"; and Sir William Jones is speaking not of Hindu law books in general, but of a recent compilation, the Code, translated by Mr. Halhed. Mr. Colebrooke gives a very different view of the arrangement of Hindu law. "The body of Hindu law comprises a system of duties, religious and civil. Separating the topic of religious duties and omitting ethical subjects, Hindu lawyers have considered civil duties under the distinct heads of private contests and forensic practice; the first comprehends law, private and criminal, the last includes the forms of judicial procedure, rules of pleading, law of evidence, written and oral, adverse titles, oaths and ordeal" Pref. to the Digest, p. xii.—W.

while it lessens greatly the force of the legal sanction in those cases in which its greatest efficiency is required.

Another topic, which it will be convenient to detach and premise, is, the division and arrangement which the Hindus have given to the matter of law. In marking a stage of civilization, this is a very characteristic circumstance. As the human mind, in a rude state, has not the power to make a good distribution of a complicated subject, so it is little aware of its importance; little aware that this is the ground-work of all accurate thought.[1] In the Institutes of Menu, the most celebrated perhaps of all the original compends of Hindu law, the titles, as they are there denominated, or divisions of law, are eighteen, laid down in the following order:—1. Debt, on loans for consumption; 2. Deposits and loans for use; 3. Sale without ownership; 4. Concerns among partners; 5. Subtraction of what has been given; 6. Non-payment of wages or hire; 7. Non-performance of agreements; 8. Rescission of sale and purchase; 9. Disputes between master and servant; 10. Contests on boundaries; 11 and 12. Assault and slander; 13. Larceny; 14. Robbery and other violence; 15. Adultery; 16. Altercation between man and wife, and their several duties; 17. The law of inheritance; 18. Gaming with dice and with living creatures.[2] It is not easy to

[1] More importance is attached to this subject than it merits. Confessedly the laws of Manu were intended for an early stage of society, when it is more important to devise than to classify. Classification is the business of high refinement, and then, according to our author's own showing, is never very successfully performed; as observed by a competent writer on this subject, commenting on Mr. Mill's survey of Hindu law, "the most refined and enlightened countries partake with Hindostan in this symptom of barbarism. In England, till the appearance of Wood's Institutes, or Blackstone's Commentaries, the law lay over a mass of authorities, from which its principles were to be extracted by the practitioner as well as they could be. Yet who would have objected to England in the middle of the 18th century, that she had not arrived at an advanced stage of civilization, because her jurisprudence was dispersed and unmethodized. Asiatic Journal, June, 1828, p. 772. By this test, the attempt to classify would place the Hindus higher in civilisation than the English. That the later writers on Hindu law have not improved upon the method of Manu, is to be explained by the sanctity of the primitive code: it would have been irreverent to have disarranged the scheme there laid down, had it occurred to them as possible or advantageous to alter the classification.—W.

[2] Laws of Menu, ch. viii. The division and arrangement of the same subjects, in the compilation translated by Mr. Halhed, are very similar, as will appear by the following titles of the chapters:—1. Of lending and borrowing; 2. Division of inheritable property; 3. Of justice; 4. Trust or deposit; 5. Selling a stranger's property; 6. Of shares; 7. Alienation by gift; 8. Of servitude; 9. Of wages; 10. Of rent or hire; 11. Purchase or sale; 12. Boundaries or limits; 13. Shares in the cultivation of land; 14. Of cities, towns, and of the fines for damaging a crop; 15. Scandalous and bitter expressions; 16. Of assaults; 17. Theft; 18. Violence; 19. Adultery; 20. Of what concerns

conceive a more rude and defective attempt at the classification of laws, than what is here presented. The most essential and obvious distinctions are neglected and confounded. Though no arrangement would appear more natural, and more likely to strike even an uncultivated mind, than the division of laws into civil and penal, we find them mixed and blended together in the code of the Hindus. The first nine of the heads or titles, as above refer to civil law; the eleventh, twelfth, thirteenth, fourteenth, and fifteenth, to criminal law; the sixteenth and seventeenth return to civil, and the eighteenth to criminal; while the tenth relates partly to the one, and partly to the other.

Another ground of division, well calculated, as being exceedingly obvious, to strike an uncultivated mind, is the distinction of persons and things. This was the groundwork of the arrangement bestowed upon the Roman laws. It is that of the arrangement which continues to prevail in the English; rude as it is, at once the effect, and the cause, of confusion.[1] It will be seen, however, that even this imperfect attempt at a rational division was far above the Hindus.

In the order in which the titles follow one another, no principle of arrangement can be traced. The first eight of the heads may be regarded as allotted to the subject of contracts; but a more rude and imperfect division of contracts cannot easily be conceived. Not to dwell upon the circumstance of beginning with loans, one of the most remote and refined contracts, instead of the more obvious and

---

women; 21. Of sundry articles. In the elaborate Digest on the subject of Contracts and Inheritances, which has been translated by Mr. Colebrooke, the titles of the books, as far as they extend, coincide exactly with the titles in the Institutes of Menu; thus, Book 1. On loans, and their payment; Book 2. On deposits; Book 3. On the non-performance of agreements; Book 4. On the duties of man and wife. The part of the work which relates to inheritance is included in one book, and is the same with the 17th title enumerated in the Institutes of Menu.

[1] The Romans, by the ambiguity of their word *jura*, which signified either *rights* or *laws*, were enabled to use, without manifest impropriety, such expressions as *jura* of persons, and *jura* of things: for though it was absurd to talk of the *rights* of things, things having a right to nothing, yet it was not absurd to talk of the *laws* of things. In their expressions *jura personarum* and *jura rerum*, there was, therefore, only confusion of ideas, and ambiguity. The English lawyers, from two of their characteristic properties, blind imitation, and the incapacity of clearing confused ideas, have adopted the same division; though in their set of phrases, rights of persons, and rights of things, there is not only confusion and ambiguity, but gross absurdity.

simple, we may observe that the subject of purchase and sale is divided into two parts; but, instead of being treated in conjunction with one another, one occupies the third place in the list of titles, the other the eighth; and a number of heterogeneous subjects intervene. "Concerns among partners" is a title which occupies the middle place between that of "Sale without ownership," and "Subtraction of what has been given;" with neither of which it has any relation. "Nonpayment of wages or hire" stands immediately before "Nonperformance of agreements," though the latter is a general title in which the former is included. The latter, indeed, is remarkable; for it is so general that it includes the whole subject of contracts, though it is here placed as one, and the last, save one, among nine different titles or divisions of that subject. Several of the titles are nothing but particular articles belonging to some of the other divisions; and are with great impropriety made to stand as separate and primary heads. The contracts, for example, between master and servant, are part of the great subject Location, or letting and taking to hire, including services as well as things; yet are these contracts here treated of under two distinct titles: the one, "Nonpayment of wages or hire," the other, "Disputes between master and servant," and even these are separated from one another by two intervening subjects. "Concerns among partners," is an article little, surely, entitled to stand as a separate head among the primary divisions of law, since the rights of individuals in a joint property fall under the same distinctions and rules which determine their rights in other property.[1] Where one branch of one great topic, as trans-

[1] A very odd attempt at a further generalisation upon the first nine titles, appears in Mr. Colebrooke's Digest. His first book, "On Loans," corresponds exactly with the first title in the Institutes of Menu. His second book, "On Deposits," is divided into four chapters, which are exactly the 2nd, 3rd, 4th, and 5th titles in the lists of Menu. His third book, which is entitled, "On the Nonperformance of Agreements," is divided into four chapters, and these are the same with the four succeeding titles in the classification of Menu.—1. Loans; 2. Deposits; 3. Nonperformance of Agreements. These, according to the logic of the Digest, are the grand classes of contracts, and the titles which belong to them. The last of the titles, it is evident, cannot belong to any particular class: Nonperformance is incident to all classes of contracts. Either, therefore, this is an improper title altogether, or it ought to stand as the title of the whole subject of contracts: and then Nonperformance of Agreements would include *loans*, *deposits*, and everything else. Under *deposits*, the Digest includes the following sub-titles: 1. Deposits and other bailments; 2. Sale without ownership; 3. Concerns among partners; 4. Subtraction of gifts: of which the last two have no more to do with *deposits* than they have with *loans*, or any the most remote branch of the subject; and the second is either a part

fer of ownerhip is taken up, and concluded, it would appear a very necessary arrangement to pass on to another: when transfer by contract, for example, is finished, to begin with transfer by descent. Such obvious rules appear to have had no influence in the framing of the Hindu systems of law: when the subject of contracts is ended, the principal branches of criminal law are introduced; and, after these and some other topics are finished, then follows the great subject of inheritance.[1]

In order to convey, in as narrow a compass as possible, an idea of the maxims and spirit of Hindu jurisprudence, it will be convenient not to follow the mangled division of the Hindus themselves. Omitting the laws, which regulate the political order, which determine who are to govern, who are to obey, and define the terms of command and obedience; laws are conveniently distributed under the three usual heads; I. Civil laws, though *Civil* is a very objectionable term; II. Penal laws; and III. The laws of judicature, or those which fix the mode in which the judicial services are rendered. Under each of these heads, such particulars have been carefully selected from the multitude of Hindu laws, as appeared the best calculated to convey an idea of the leading qualities of the Hindu code, and of the stage of civilization at which it may appear to have been formed.

I. Under the first of these heads, Property is the great subject of law. To this we may confine our illustrations.

It is needless to remark, that the sources of acquisition, by occupancy, by labour, by contract, by donation, by descent; which are recognised in almost all states of society, are recognised in Hindustan. It is in the accuracy with which the intended effects of these incidents are defined,

---

of the first, and ought to have been included under it, as relating to the sale of things deposited, or that also has no connection with the title. Let us next contemplate the sub-titles, included under *Nonperformance of Agreements*. They are, 1. Nonpayment of wages or hire; 2. Nonperformance of Agreements, chiefly in association; 3. Rescision of purchase and sale; 4. Disputes between master and herdsman: as if these included all the agreements of which there could be nonperformance. The first and last of them, moreover, are the same thing, or the last is a portion of the first. It is needless to carry the criticism further.

[1] It is curious, though somewhat humbling, to observe how far great men may let authority mislead them. "The articles," says Dr. Robertson, "of which the Hindu code is composed, are arranged in natural and luminous order." Disquisition concerning India, Appendix, p. 217.

and in the efficiency of the means taken to secure the benefits they convey, that the excellence of one system above another is more particularly observed.

Though property in the first stage of its existence, was probably measured by occupancy, and the one ceased with the other,[1] the privilege was early conferred of alienating for a valuable consideration, or of transferring by purchase and sale. As this is a very simple compact, it appears to admit of little variety in the various stages of human improvement. In an age, however, in which the means of detecting fraudulent acquisitions, and of proving the good faith of contracts and bargains, are imperfectly known, purchases and sales, made in public, are alone considered valid. The laws of our Saxon ancestors prohibited the sale of everything above the value of twenty-pence, except in open market;[2] and it is with a pleasing kind of surprise we find, that similar circumstances have suggested a similar expedient to the people of Hindustan. "He," says the law of Menu, "who has received a chattel by purchase in open market, before a number of men, justly acquires the absolute property, by having paid the price of it."[3] The right, however, conveyed by a bonâ fide purchase, is not, among the Hindus, carried to that extent, which is found requisite in a commercial and highly civilized society. If the goods were not the property of the person by whom they were sold, the right of the purchaser becomes absolute only if he can produce the vendor. "If," says the law of Menu,[4] "the vendor be not producible, and the vendee prove the public sale, the latter must be dismissed by the king without punishment; and the former owner, who lost the chattel, may take it back, on paying the vendee half its value." This is quite sufficient to throw so much uncertainty into the great class of transactions by purchase and

[1] Lord Kames, Historical Law Tracts, p. 123, 154. Grotius de Jure Belli ac Pacis, lib. II. cap. ii. 2. Blackstone's Commentaries on the Laws of England, book II, c. i. The annotator on some of the late editions of Blackstone differs from the doctrine in the text. But that writer seems to have mistaken an important circumstance, carefully attended to by the great lawyers quoted above, that when the commodities of the earth began to be appropriated they were not without owners, but the common property of the race at large.

[2] L. L. Ethel. 10, 12. L. L. Edg. Hickes. Dissert. p. 30.

[3] Ch. viii. 201. When Abraham bought a field of Ephron to bury Sarah, the bargain was transacted in the presence of all the people. Genesis, ch. xxiii. See, too, Homer's Iliad, lib. xviii. ver. 499, &c.

[4] Ch. viii. 202.

sale, as would prove, in a civilized state of society, a ruinous obstruction of business. A manufacturer purchases a quantity of the raw material, and works it up; he would lose, in a mischievous proportion, if the owner of that material could demand the identical substance, on tendering the half of its price. In many cases, the identical substance is exported; in many it is consumed; and cannot possibly be restored.[1] Among children, and among rude people, little accustomed to take their decisions upon full and mature consideration, nothing is more common than to repent of their bargains, and wish to revoke them. Among the Hindus this has been found an affair of sufficient importance to constitute an entire head in the classification of their laws. A variety of cases are enumerated, in which, if dissatisfied with his bargain, a man may insist upon having it annulled: and in general any sale and purchase of things, not perishable, may be rescinded within ten days, at the will of either of the parties:[2] another law, altogether incompatible with an age in which the divisions and refinements of industry have multiplied the number of exchanges. The regulation, which fixes the price of things, instead of leaving it to the natural and beneficent laws of competition, conveys not a high idea of the knowledge of the Hindus. "Let the king," says the ordinance of Menu, "establish rules for the sale and purchase of all marketable things. Once in every five nights, or at the close of every half month, let him make a regulation for market prices."[3] It is a circumstance full of meaning, that, under this head of bargain and sale, is arranged the obligation of the marriage contract.[4]

[1] A curious enumeration of the cases in which the property of one man is so incorporated with that of another as to be inseparable, is given in the Roman law, under the head of *Accessio:* Inclusio, adferruminatio, intextura, inædificatio, scriptura, pictura, specificatio, commixtio, et confusio.

The English law (a few special cases excepted) gives an absolute right of property to the bonâ fide purchaser, by whatever means the commodity may have come into the hands of the vendor. If the English law, however, takes care of the purchaser, it must be owned that it is deplorably defective in the care which it takes of the party by whom the commodity is lost.

[2] Laws of Menu, ch. viii. 222, 223. See also Halhed's Code of Gentoo Laws, ch. xi. and Mr. Colebrooke's Digest of Hindu Law, book III. ch. iii.

[3] Ibid, 401, 402. It is worthy of remark, that this was a regulation, too, among the ancient Britons. Leges Wallicæ, lib. iii. 247. Henry's Hist. Brit. iv. 202.

[4] Laws of Menu, ch. viii. 224, 227.—M.

This seems to be a misapprehension of the purport of the law. It is not a question of contract, but of recission of sale, analogous to which is the invalidity of a marriage with a girl not a virgin, and who may therefore be sent

There are many occasions, on which it is useful to the owner of property, to place it in the keeping of another person, without transfer of the ownership. It may be placed, for safe-custody merely; for the sake of an operation, as with the dyer, for the benefit of his art; with the carrier, either by sea or land, for the sake of transportation; or it may be placed, as in the case of a valuable animal, for the sake of maintenance. These, and a variety of other transactions of a similar sort, are included in English law under the title of bailments.[1] In a well-regulated society, where the house of one man is nearly as secure from violence as that of another, mere deposits, unless in the case of warehousing, the object of which is convenience or economy, rather than security, form a class of transactions of little comparative magnitude. In a rude society, in which there is little or no security, and in which the means of concealing valuables is one of the great studies of life, deposits become an object of the greatest importance. In the Hindu code, other cases of bailment occupy a narrow space: the article of deposits swells, alone, to a great size, and forms an object of considerable intricacy and detail.[2] The modes of proof

---

back to her parents. As to the inference intimated that a marriage contract was a case of buying and selling, this is an error which a better recollection of Manu would have prevented. "Even a man of the servile class ought not to receive a gratuity when he gives his daughter in marriage." "Nor have we heard of the tacit sale of a daughter for a price, under the name of a nuptial gratuity," Manu ix. 98, 100. Rammohun Roy says, it is equally prohibited by the Vedas. Translation from the Vedas, p. 181.—W.

[1] On the law of bailments, the writer in the Asiatic Journal above referred to, himself a distinguished lawyer, expresses opinions in every way opposed to those of the text. "It is universally admitted that the English law of bailments is founded upon the soundest and most enlightened principles as they have been laid down and elucidated in the decisions of Westminster Hall, from Lord Holt down to Lord Mansfield. What if it shall appear certain beyond all controversy, that those principles which are comparatively of recent growth in our own law, existed for ages in the despised system of Hindu jurisprudence!" Then quoting instances in proof, he concludes, "all the requisite shades of care and diligence, and the corresponding shades of negligence and default, are carefully observed in the Hindu law of bailment, and neither in the jurisprudence nor in the legal treatises of the most civilised states of Europe are they to be found more logically expressed, or more accurately defined. In the spirit of Pyrrhus's observation on the Roman legion, one cannot refrain from exclaiming, I see nothing barbarous in the jurisprudence of the Hindus."—p. 14.—W.

[2] See Laws of Menu, ch. viii.; Halhed's Gentoo Code, iv.; Colebrooke's Digest, book II. ch. i.; Heineccii Pandect. pars III. lib. xvi. tit. 3, on the subject of deposits, and the importance of this class of transactions in the early days of Rome, with the causes of that importance.

The reader may see one of the few attempts which have been made to let in the light of common sense upon the law of England, in the Essay on Bailments, by Sir William Jones.

constitute the chief peculiarities in the provisions, and will be considered, when we speak of the third branch of jurisprudence. One rule, however, expressive of great simplicity, not to say rudeness, belongs exclusively to this article: "On failure of witnesses, to prove a deposit, let the judge actually deposit gold or precious things with the defendant, by the artful contrivance of spies. Should he restore that deposit, he is to be held innocent: if he deny it, he is to be apprehended and compelled to pay the value of both."[1]

Hiring; that is, transferring to another, for a valuable consideration, and to a definite extent, the use of any thing valuable; is a right which holds a sort of middle place between sale and bailment: and may extend to personal services as well as to commodities.[2] As this contract falls very naturally under the laws of purchase and sale,[3] it occupies a narrow space in the volumes of Hindu law, and as far as commodities are concerned, offers nothing particular for observation.[4] In the hire of personal services, three principal classes are distinguished; first, the students of the Veda, who discharge every menial office to their masters, and receive instruction in return: secondly, handicrafts, who receive either stipulated wages, or, if no agreement has been made, one tenth of the profits on their labour; thirdly, agricultural servants, who are always paid in kind; for tending cows, one tenth of the milk; for the culture of corn, one tenth of the crop.[5]

[1] Laws of Menu, ch. viii. 183.

[2] The language of English law in the case of this contract is defective, and a source of confusion. In the case of other contracts, it has one name for the act of one of the parties, another name for that of the other. Thus, in the case of exchange, one of the parties is said to sell, the other to buy; in that of a loan, one of the parties is said to lend, the other to borrow. In the present case, it often uses but one name for the acts of both parties; he who gives, and he who receives, the use, being both said to hire. The Civilians are saved from this inconvenience by the use of the Latin language; in which the act of the one party is termed *locatio*, that of the other *conductio*. To *let* and to *hire*, if uniformly employed, would answer the same purpose in English.

[3] Institut. Justin., lib. iii. tit. 25. Locatio et conductio proxima est emptioni et venditioni, iisdemque juris regulis consistit.

[4] The simplicity of some of the enactments provokes a smile: "If a person hath hired anything for a stipulated time he shall pay the rent accordingly." Gentoo Code, x. Again, "If a person, having agreed for the rent of the water of a pool, or of the water of a well, or of the water of a river, or of a house, does not pay it, the magistrate shall cause such rent and hire to be paid." Ibid.

[5] If a hired servant perform not his work according to agreement, he shall be fined, and forfeit his wages. What he has been prevented by sickness from performing, he is allowed to execute after he is well; but if he leaves unfinished, either by himself or a substitute, any part of the stipulated service,

The peculiar species of transfer which is known by the name of loan is an object of great importance in the jurisprudence of all nations. Among the Hindus it stands as the first article in the classification of legal subjects, and in the digest of Mr. Colebrooke occupies entirely one of the four books into which the compilers of that work have divided the laws of contract. From the peculiarities in the ideas and in the circumstances of the Hindus, it forms among them a subject of more than usual complexity. In an improved state of society, where the inefficiency of laws, the diffusion of wealth, and the accommodation of business, have created a mutual confidence, loans are generally contracted on the security of law, without the actual custody or deposit of the property on which they may be secured. It is only in that extremely confined and degraded species of lending, abandoned to pawnbrokers, that pledges form a regular and component part. In the more early and imperfect states of the social union, circumstances are very different. Law is both feeble and inaccurate, poverty reigns, violence prevails; and the man who is able to discharge his debts to-day may be stript of all possessions to-morrow. In these circumstances, the security of law upon the person or property of the debtor is seldom sufficient; and the deposit of some equivalent property, as a pledge, is the obvious, and, in point of fact, the common resource.[1] The doctrine of pledges forms one of the most considerable branches of this part of the Hindu code. The laws relative to them are laid down with great minuteness and solemnity; a variety of cases are distinguished; and the receipt of pledges appears to have formed a component part of a comparatively numerous and important class of transactions.[2] The responsibility of a second person, who be-

however small, he is deprived of the hire for the whole. One branch of this subject, the obligations between masters, and the servants who tend their cattle, is of so much importance, denoting a state of society approaching the pastoral, as to constitute a whole title of Hindu law. The principal object is to define those injuries accruing to the cattle, and those trespasses committed by them, for which the keeper is responsible. Laws of Menu, ch. viii. 214 to 218, and 229 to 244. Halhed's Gentoo Code, viii. ix. Colebrooke's Digest, book III. ch. ii. and iv.

[1] Lending on pledges can scarcely be regarded as proof of a state of barbarism, or the multitude of pawnbrokers in London would witness our being very low in the scale of civilisation.—W.

[2] Laws of Menu, ch. vii. Halhed's Gentoo Code, ch. 1. sect. 2. Colebrooke's Digest, part I. book I. ch. iii.

comes surety for the borrower, is another foundation on which Hindu loans are contracted, and the different species of it are not inaccurately distinguished.[1] Interest, or a consideration for property lent, appears to have been known at a very early stage of civilization.[2] As it is only interest on debts of money which is familiar to the members of a highly-civilized society, European visitors appear to have been forcibly struck with the Hindu law, which imposes an interest to be paid in kind on loans in goods, as grain, fruit, wool or hair, beasts of burden and the like.[3] Mr. Halhed says, "The different rate of interest to be paid for different articles is perhaps an institute peculiar to Hindustan; but it reflects a strong light upon the simplicity of ancient manners, before money was universally current as the medium of barter for all commodities, and is at the same time a weighty proof of the great antiquity of these laws, which seem calculated for the crude conceptions of an almost illiterate people upon their first civilization."[4] When Mr. Halhed, however, informs us that this law "reflects a strong light upon the simplicity of *ancient* manners," it is necessary to add that whatever light it reflects upon *ancient*, it reflects the same upon *present* manners, as this is not a law, anciently in force, but long ago repealed; it is a law now in operation, and as suitable as ever to the purely Hindu state of society. Mr. Halhed too is mistaken when he supposes that this is an institution peculiar to the Hindus. It was familiarly known to the Jews in the time of Moses, and was probably a common practice in the nations around Judea, as well as in Egypt, from which the Jews had recently departed.[5]

To vary the rates of interest upon the different castes is a peculiarity more naturally arising from the unfair and odious distinctions among men, created by the Hindus. The rule established in the institutes of Menu is, to take, when there is a pledge, one and a quarter per cent. per

[1] Laws of Menu, ch. viii. Colebrooke's Digest, part I. book I. ch. iv. Halhed's Gentoo Code, ch. i. sect. 3.

[2] It was perfectly familiar to the Jews at the time of their departure from Egypt; Deuteron. ch. xxiii. 20.

[3] Laws of Menu, viii. 151.

[4] Halhed, Preface to the Code of Gentoo Laws, p. 53.

[5] "Thou shalt not lend upon usury to thy brother, usury of money, usury of *victuals*, usury of *anything that is lent upon usury*. Unto a stranger thou mayest lend upon usury." Deuteron. xxiii. 19, 20.

BOOK II. CHAP. IV.

month; when there is no pledge, two per cent. per month; that is, from a Brahmen: but from a man of the military caste, three per cent.;[1] four per cent. from one of the mercantile caste; and from a man of the servile caste no less than five per cent. per month.[2] This exorbitant rate of interest affords a satisfactory criterion to judge of the opinions, which are not unfrequently advanced, of the great riches which, at some imaginary period, formerly distinguished Hindustan. The excessive accumulation, however, of interest was forbidden. Upon a loan in money, interest, beyond the amount of the principal, was not a debt;[3] upon loans in goods, for some reason which it is not easy to divine, it was permitted to take five times the amount of the principal. Compound interest too was prohibited. These were rules which would give effectual motives to the Hindu creditor to exact the regular payment of his interest, with rigid severity.[4] In the laws relating to loans, however, the most remarkable particular is the mode of enforcing payment. The creditor is commanded, first, to speak to the friends and relations of the debtor; next, to go in person and importune him, staying some time in his house, but without eating or drinking. If these methods fail, he may then carry the debtor home with him, and having seated him, as the law expresses it, before men of character and reputation, may there detain him. Should he still hold out, the creditor is next directed, to endeavour by feigned pretences to get possession of some of his goods; or, if any pledge was deposited with him, to carry it before the magistrate, who will cause it to be sold to make payment. If neither of these expedients can be used, he shall seize and confine the debtor's wife, children, cattle, buffaloes, horses, &c.; also his pots, clothes, mats, and furniture, and, seating himself at his door, there

[1] It would have been candid to have observed, that under ordinary circumstances, the Brahman and Kshatriya are prohibited from receiving any interest on money lent, although they are enjoined to pay it on money borrowed if demanded. Manu, x. 117.—W.

[2] The tribes of Burren Sunker, that is, all the mixed classes, pay at the rate of one in sixteen (or rather more than six per cent.) per month. Halhed's Gentoo Code, ch. i. sect. 1.

[3] It is curious that this, too, was a law of Egypt, at least in regard to loans upon security. Diod. Sic. lib. i. cap. 79. Goguet's Origin of Laws, part III. book I. ch. iv.

[4] For the details respecting the law of interest, consult Laws of Menu, ch. viii. 140 to 154. Halhed's Gentoo Code, ch. i. sect. 1. Colebrooke's Digest, part I. book I. ch. ii.

receive his money. Should even this proceeding fail, he is commanded to seize and bind the debtor's person, and procure by forcible means a discharge of the debt.[1] What is meant by forcible means is sufficiently explained in the following extraordinary definition. "When, having tried the debtor, the creditor carries him to his own house, and by beating or other means compels him to pay, this is called violent compulsion. By beating," adds the law, "or by coercion, a creditor may enforce payment from his debtor."[2] When the debtor is of a caste not superior to the creditor, the latter may seize and compel him to labour for the discharge of the debt. If a man owes debts to several creditors, he is commanded to discharge first one debt and then another, in the order in which they were contracted; a regulation by which one or two of his creditors may receive in full their demands, while the rest, whether few or numerous, are entirely defrauded. The equitable arrangement of an equal dividend, which we find established among nations of very limited progress in the knowledge of law, obvious and useful as it is, had not suggested itself to the rude legislators of Hindustan. When a creditor procures payment of a debt by application to the magistrate, he pays him for his interposition a twentieth part of the sum recovered.[3] By a very extraordinary regulation a punishment seems to be inflicted on the defendant in all actions for debt wherein he is cast. "A debt being admitted by the defendant, he must pay five in the hundred as a fine to the king; but if it be denied and proved, twice as much."[4] The sacred character of the Brahmen, whose life it is the most dreadful of crimes either directly or indirectly to shorten, suggested to him a process for the recovery of debts, the most singular and extravagant that ever was found among men. He proceeds to the door of the person whom he means to coerce, or wherever else he can most conve-

[1] This mode of personal seizure had place at an early age among the Egyptians; but they made sufficient advancement to abolish it. A law of king Bocchoris permitted the creditor to seize only the goods of his debtor for payment. Diod. Sic. lib. i. p. 90.

[2] Colebrooke's Digest, part I. book I. ch. vi. sect. 240, 241.

[3] For the laws respecting recovery of debt, see Laws of Menu, ch. viii. Halhed's Gentoo Code, ch. i. sect. 5. Colebrooke's Digest, part I. book I. ch. lvi.

[4] Laws of Menu, viii. 139.

niently intercept him, with poison or a poignard in his hand. If the person should attempt to pass, or make his escape, the Brahmen is prepared instantly to destroy himself. The prisoner is therefore bound in the strongest chains; for the blood of the self murdered Brahmen would be charged upon his head, and no punishment could expiate his crime. The Brahmen setting himself down (the action is called sitting in dherna), fasts; and the victim of his arrest, for whom it would be impious to eat, while a member of the sacred class is fasting at his door, must follow his example. It is now, however, not a mere contest between the resolution or strength of the parties; for if the obstinacy of the prisoner should exhaust the Brahmen and occasion his death, he is answerable for that most atrocious of crimes—the murder of a priest; he becomes execrable to his countrymen; the horrors of remorse never fail to pursue him; he is shut out from the benefits of society, and life itself is a calamity. As the Brahmen who avails himself of this expedient is bound for his honour to persevere, he seldom fails to succeed, because the danger of pushing the experiment too far is, to his antagonist, tremendous. Nor is it in his own concerns alone that the Brahmen may turn to account the sacredness of his person: he may hire himself to enforce in the same manner the claims of any other man; and not claims of debt merely; he may employ this barbarous expedient in any suit. What is still more extraordinary, even after legal process, even when the magistrate has pronounced a decision against him, and in favour of the person upon whom his claim is made, he may still sit in dherna, and by this dreadful mode of appeal make good his demand.[1]

[1] See an account of the practice of sitting in dherna, by Sir John Shore (Lord Teignmouth), Asiat. Researches, iv. 330 to 332. He tells us that, since the institution of the court of justice of Benares in 1783, the practice has been less frequent, but that even the interference of that court and of the resident had occasionally been unable to check it. He tells us, too, that some of the pundits, when consulted, declared the validity of the deed or concession extorted by dherna; but restricted that validity to such claims as are just; others denied its validity, except where the party confirmed the engagement after the coercion is withdrawn. But it is evident that these restrictions are inconsistent with the facts which Lord Teignmouth records, and are mere attempts of the pundits, according to their usual practice, to interpret their laws into as great a coincidence as possible with the ideas of the great persons by whom the questions are put to them. A regulation was made by the Bengal government in 1795 for preventing this practice. See papers, ordered to be printed by the

We have now reviewed the great peculiarities of the Hindu law, in regard to those transfers of property which partake of the nature of exchange, and in which some sort of an equivalent is given and received; it remains for us to consider those, in which the property passes from one owner to another, without any return.

The most extensive class of this species of transactions are those occasioned by the death of the owner. Men had considerably strengthened the chain by which they were connected with property, before they ceased to consider death as the cause of a perfect separation, and as leaving their possessions free to the earliest occupier. A right of succession in the children suggests itself, however, at a very early period in the progress of civilization. It is recommended by so many motives, it so happily accords with some of the strongest impulses of human nature, and is so easily engrafted upon the previous order of things, that it could not fail to be an early institution. The children, being naturally the nearest to their parent at the moment of his death, were generally able to avail themselves of the right of occupancy, and to exclude other successors by prior possession. It was the usual arrangement in early stages of society, that the different members of a family should live together; and possess the property in common.[1] The father was rather the head of a number of partners, than the sole proprietor. When he died, it was not so much a transfer of property, as a continued possession; and the copartnership was only deprived of one of its members. The laws of inheritance among the Hindus are almost entirely founded upon this patriarchal arrangement.[2] When the father dies, if the sons shall

House of Commons, 3rd June, 1813, p. 431. See also Broughton's Mahratta Camp, p. 42.—M.

There is no authority in any code or treatise of law, for these practices: the pundits might, with great propriety, differ in their views of the validity of the concession thus extorted.—W.

1 "Among barbarians, in all parts of the world, persons who belong to the same family are understood to enjoy a community of goods. In those early ages, when men are, in a great measure, strangers to commerce or the alienation of commodities, the right of *property* is hardly distinguished from the right of *using* or *possessing;* and those persons who have acquired the joint possession of any subject are apt to be regarded as the joint proprietors of it." Millar on the English Government, i. 190.

2 The whole, too, of that Title of law, "Concerns among partners," refers not so much to a joint-stock property, contributed by certain individuals for carrying on any particular business, as to the property of a number of persons, most commonly brothers or other near relations, who agree to live together,

choose to live together, the eldest, says the law, shall take the station of the head of the family, and the property is held jointly in his name.[1] "For brothers a common abode is ordained so long as both their parents live. On failure of both their parents, partition among brothers is ordained."[2] Even during the life-time of a father, a separation of the family might take place, when a division of the property, according to the strict notion of a joint interest, was made, in the proportion of two shares to the father, and one share equally to each of the sons.[3] When the division, however, of the common estate is delayed till the death of the father, the elder brother, as the new head of the family, is distinguished in the partition. He first receives one-twentieth of the inheritance, after which it is divided equally among all the brothers.[4] With a few immaterial exceptions, the principle of equal division guided succession among the Hindus. "Let the sons. after the death of the parents, equally share the assets. If all sons be equal in good qualities, they must share alike; but he who is distinguished by science and good conduct shall take a greater share than the rest."[5] The last of these clauses affords an example of that vagueness and ambiguity, the source of endless dispute, which distinguishes the laws of all ignorant people, and which forms a most remarkable feature in those of Hindustan. What is the criterion to ascertain that superiority in science and virtue, which determines the share of brothers

---

and to have all their effects in common. The multitude of the laws proves the frequency of the transactions. The old law of inheritance among the Romans was altogether founded upon the same ideas. Fundamentum successionis veteris erat conservatio familiarum. Familia enim universitas quædam videbatur, cujus princeps est paterfamilias.—Quum ergo proximi in familia essent liberi vel sui heredes, tanquam vivo patre, quodammodo domini et αυτοκληρονομοι, legibus xii. tabularum cantum fuerat; SI INTESTATO MORITUR CUI SUUS HERES NEC ESCIT AGNATUS PROXIMUS FAMILIAM HABETO. Heinec. in Inst. lib. iii. tit. i. sect. 690.

[1] Laws of Menu, ch. ix. 105.

[2] Colebrooke's Digest, part II. Book V. ch. iii. sect. 114.

[3] Halhed's Gentoo Code, ch. ii. sect. 11. Colebrooke's Digest, part II. book V. ch. ii. Mr. Halhed has remarked that the demand of the prodigal son in the Gospel for his portion, affords proof of a similar state of things among the Jews. The attentive reader will perceive many other strokes of resemblance. All the more cultivated nations of Asia appear to have reached a stage of society nearly the same.

[4] Colebrooke's Digest, book V. ch. i. sect, ii. subsect. 34. Halhed's Gentoo Code, ch. ii. sect. 12.

[5] Colebrooke's Digest, part II. book V. ch. 3, subsect. 115, 116, ch. i. sect. ii. subsect. 34.

in the division of the paternal estate? Or who is to be the judge? Equally unskilful, and pregnant with evil, is the vague and indeterminate law which declares "that all those brothers who are addicted to any vice shall lose their title to the inheritance."[1] As the interpretation of the phrase "addicted to any vice," may receive any latitude, according to the inclinations and views of the expounder, a gate is here thrown open to unlimited injustice."[2] Inconsistency, and even direct contradiction, is a characteristic of the Hindu laws, which it does not appear to have been thought even requisite to avoid; as it is expressly enacted, that when two laws command opposite things, both are to be held valid.[3] This attribute is fully exemplified in the laws of inheritance. It is declared that, "on the failure of natural heirs, the lawful heirs are such Brahmens as have read the three Vedas, as are pure in body and mind, as have subdued their passions; and they must constantly offer the cake; thus the rites of obsequies cannot fail."[4] Yet it is added, in the very next clause or sentence, "The property of a Brahmen shall never be taken as an escheat by the king; this is a fixed law; but the wealth of the other classes, on failure of all heirs the king may take."[5] Not unfrequently in rude nations, as if one misfortune ought to be aggra-

[1] In a simple state of society it might not have been difficult to appreciate and verify such grounds of exclusion. As relations became more complex, the impossibility of enforcing these exceptions was evident, and they ceased to be regarded. The comparative merit of co-heirs forms no rule for unequal partition, and is therefore 'no source of endless dispute,' or 'unlimited injustice.'—W.

[2] Laws of Menu, ch. ix. 214.—M.

It should be borne in mind, however, that this applies only to 'sacred texts,' proceeding from the impossibility of supposing either to be wrong. It does not apply to conflicting laws in general; on the contrary, any law incongruous with the code of Manu is declared invalid.—W.

[3] When there are two sacred texts, *apparently inconsistent*, both are held to be law, for both are pronounced by the wise to be valid and reconcileable. Thus in the Veda are these texts; Let the sacrifice be when the sun has arisen, and before it has risen, and when neither sun nor stars can be seen; The sacrifice, therefore, may be performed at any or all of those times. Ibid. ii. 14, 15.

[4] Laws of Menu, ch. ix. 188.

[5] Ibid. 189.—M.

There is no incompatibility or contradiction. The second clause is merely a qualification of the first, which applies to the property of a Brahman alone. "Misra and the rest hold that the first text of Manu relates to the property of Brahmanas, but the wealth of Kshatriyas and the rest shall be taken by the king alone." Digest, iii. 537. There are other texts to the same effect. It is not the part of candid criticism to contrast detached passages without reference to those by which their purport is to be explained.—W.

vated by another, those who labour under certain maladies, or bodily defects, are excluded from inheritance. This principle is fully adopted by the Hindus, and carried to an unusual and monstrous extent. All those persons who are lame, all those persons who are blind, all those who are deaf,[1] all those who are dumb, impotent, or affected with an incurable disease, as leprosy, marasmus, gonorrhœa, dysentery, are denied a share in the partition of their father's effects, and are only entitled to a maintenance from the family.[2] When a man has sons by wives of different castes, they inherit in the proportion of the mother's rank, and the son by a concubine is entitled only to one-half of the share of him who is born of a wife.[3] The laws which define proximity of kin, and fix the order of collateral succession, are numerous, minute, and in nothing remarkable.[4] It is particularly to be noted that daughters are debarred from a share in the inheritance of their fathers.[5] The woman, indeed, among the Hindus, is so restricted in the means of acquiring property, that

[1] It should be 'born' deaf. The exclusion may be regarded as harsh, but it is not arbitrary or without cause, being founded on the notion that such persons are incompetent to conduct the affairs of the household, to procreate issue, and to perform religious rites, which are essential to the preservation of the family. The persons so excluded are to be maintained by the heir, 'without stint, according to the best of his power.' Manu.—W.

[2] Colebrooke's Digest, part II. book V. ch. v. sect. 320, 321, 325, 32I, 331. In Halhed's Gentoo Code they are thus enumerated; one born an eunuch, blind, deaf, dumb, without hand, or foot, or nose, or tongue, or privy member, or fundament, and one who has no principle of religion, as well as the victims of various diseases. Gentoo Code, ch. ii. sect. 5. The law is thus stated in the Institutes of Menu; eunuchs and outcasts, persons born blind or deaf, madmen, idiots, the dumb, and such as have lost the use of a limb, are excluded from a share of the heritage. But it is just, that the heir who knows his duty should give all of them food and raiment. Laws of Menu, viii. 201, 202.

[3] Laws of Menu, viii. 149, etc. Halhed's Gentoo Code, ch. ii. sect. 2. Colebrooke's Digest, part II. book V. ch. vii.

[4] The appearance of accuracy given by minuteness of detail has sometimes been quoted as a proof of refined knowledge; but it is a proof of the very reverse. Henry tells us (Hist. of Britain, i. 320) that the laws of the Druids provided with great care for the equitable division of the effects of the family according to the circumstances of every case. The ancient laws of Wales descend to very long and particular details on this subject, and make provision for every possible case with the most minute exactness. Leges Wallicæ, lib. ii. de mulieribus, cap. i. p. 70. The refinement and niceties of the Mahomedan law of succession are perhaps still more remarkable. See Mahomedan law of succession, Works of Sir William Jones, iii. 467, and the Al Sirajiyyah, with Sir William's Commentaries, Ibid. 505. In fact, the want of skill to ascend to a general expression, or rule, which would accurately include the different ramifications of the subject, is that which gives occasion to this minuteness of detail.

[5] Those who are unmarried at the death of the father are directed to receive portions out of their brothers' allotments. Laws of Menu, ix. 118.

she is almost excluded from its rights.[1] The exceptions consist in certain presents; what was given in the bridal procession; what was given in token of love; what was received from a brother, a mother, or a father; and this property is inherited by her daughters in equal portions with her sons. If she die without issue, her property falls to her husband or to her parents, and is subject to nearly the same rules of collateral succession as are established in regard to the property of males.[2]

The idea of a joint-interest in the property of the family, while it early established the right of succession in the children, served to exclude the right of devising by will. As the property belonged to the parent in common only with his offspring, it could not be regarded as just, that he should have the power of giving it away from them after his death. It is only in stages of society considerably advanced, that the rights of property are so far enlarged as to include the power of nominating, at the discretion of the owner, the person who is to enjoy it after his death. It was first introduced among the Athenians by a law of Solon, and among the Romans, probably, by the twelve tables.[3] The Hindus have, through all ages, remained in a state of society too near the simplicity and rudeness of the most ancient times, to have stretched their ideas of property so far.[4] The power

[1] "Three persons, a wife, a son, and a slave, are declared by law to have in general no wealth exclusively their own: the wealth which they may earn is regularly acquired for the man to whom they belong." Laws of Menu, ch. viii. 416.—M.

This is by no means the case. In the absence of direct male heirs, widows succeed to a life interest in real, and absolute interest in personal property. Next, daughters inherit absolutely. Where there are sons, mothers and daughters are entitled to shares, and wives hold peculiar property from a variety of sources, besides those specified by the text, over which a husband has no power during their lives, and which descends to their own heirs, with a preference, in some cases, to females. It is far from correct, therefore, to say that women, amongst the Hindus, are excluded from the rights of property. —W.

[2] Laws of Menu, ch. ix 192—197. Colebrooke's Digest, part II., book V. ch. ix.

[3] Kames's Historical Law Tracts, i. 162.

[4] The right of devising property by will, is clearly no proof of advance in civilisation by the instances given. The Athenians, in the days of Solon; the Romans, in those of the twelve tables; and the Arabs, at the birth of Mohammed, were certainly less refined than the Hindus, at the time that the Code of Manu was compiled. The case is imperfectly weighed. It would have been very inconsistent to have given a man power to do that on his death, which he might not do whilst living. In ancestral property, the occupant had joint right only with his sons, analogously in some respects to our entailed estates, which, with all our high civilisation, we have not acknowledged to be disposable of by bequest; and, therefore, he could not have the right to bequeath at

of disposing of a man's possessions by testament, is altogether unknown to their laws.[1]

The same notion of a joint-title, in all the members of a family, to the property of the whole, had originally an effect, even upon the power of donation. Individuals were not at liberty to alienate by gift any part of the common stock. This, however, is a right which is recommended by motives more powerful and frequent than that of disposal after death, and was therefore much sooner introduced. The first instances were probably sanctioned by religious pretexts. By the laws of the Visigoths it was permitted to make donations to the church; and by those of the Burgundians a free man was allowed, after dividing his means with his sons, to make an ecclesiastical donation out of his own portion.[2] Among the Hindus the conferring of gifts upon the Brahmens, which is taught as one of the most important of religious duties, must have early familiarized the mind to gratuitous alienations; yet, notwithstanding this important circumstance, a man's power of transferring his property by gift appears subject still to extraordinary restrictions. Except in certain minor cases, the consent of his heirs is required. It is only over that part of his property which is more than sufficient to feed and clothe all his dependants, that he has an unlimited power of disposal.[3]

---

his pleasure. It is also to be recollected, that the laws of the Hindus are to be looked at, not with the eye of a jurist only, but with reference to their religious origin. One of the great objects of the descent of property, is to provide for the perpetual performance of obsequial rites to the whole body of deceased ancestors. These cannot be properly discharged by aliens to the family; and, therefore, they cannot have a valid claim to succeed. A man cannot will that a stranger shall perform his family rites, in preference to his kinsmen; and cannot, therefore, make away with property essential to their celebration. The state of the law is not a question of greater or less social refinement; it arises out of, and is inseparable from, the religious origin of the code; and would remain the same, whatever degree of social civilisation might be attained, so long as the religion was unchanged.—W.

[1] Impressed, when I began to study the history and character of the Hindus, with the loud encomiums I had been accustomed to hear on their attainments, and particularly their laws — which were represented as indicating a high state of civilisation — this fact, which is broadly stated by Mr. Halhed (Preface to the Gentoo Code, p. liii.), very forcibly struck me. Rude as the Arabs were at the time of Mohammed, their ideas of property included the right of devising by will. See Koran, ch. v.

[2] Historical Law Tracts, i. 159. How like is the regulation of the Burgundians to the rule among the Hindus for division of property to the sons during the father's life-time!

[3] Halhed's Gentoo Code, ch. vii.—M.

The law is not quite correctly stated; a man may give away even inherited personal property; he must not alienate ancestral landed property held in

II. The second class of laws, those which relate to offences and their punishment, form a subject less complicated, and of less subtle and difficult disquisition, than those which relate to the distribution of rights; it is, however, a portion of law, which, from the violent interference of human passions, is not less slow in gaining improvement.

An offence is an act by which a right is violated. The object of punishment is to prevent such acts. It is employed, under the empire of reason, only as a last resource. If offences could be prevented without punishment, punishment ought never to exist. It follows, as a necessary consequence, that as little of it as possible ought to exist.

It is equally manifest, that it would be vain to establish rights, if the necessary means were not to be used for securing them. It is therefore good to make use of punishment, as far as necessary for the securing of rights; with this precaution only, that the suffering or evil, produced by the punishment, is less, upon the whole, than that which would arise from the violation of the right.

By these maxims, as criterions, we shall endeavour to ascertain the attributes of the criminal code of the Hindus.

The misery and disorder which overspread human life, wherever self-defence rests wholly upon the individual, are the cause to which government owes its origin. To escape from those evils, men transfer to the magistrate powers sufficient for the defence of all; and agree to expect from him alone that protection, which they obtained so imperfectly from their own exertions. In the rude and violent times when this revolution takes place, it is not from a just and cool discernment of the limits of defence, prevention, and reparation, that penalties are

common; but it has not been noticed in the text, that although sons succeed in common, and may continue to hold by a joint-tenure, yet they may separate, and then each man may dispose as he likes of his own portion. This power of living as a divided family, is a sufficient reply to the barbarity of the laws which compelled undivided occupancy, and limited a man's power over his own. The ancient system probably preferred undivided possession, but it did not command it. Thus Manu says, "either let them (the brothers) thus live together, or, if they desire separate religious rites, let them live apart, since religious duties are multiplied in separate houses, their separation is therefore legal." The commentator adds, "and even laudable," ix. 111.—W.

BOOK II. CHAP. IV.

exacted. It is from the impulse of a keen resentment, that the sufferer pursues, and from a strong sympathy with that resentment, that the magistrate commonly judges and condemns. It is not so much security that is coveted, as revenge. A great injury committed can only be expiated by a great injury received. Two principles therefore universally characterize the penal code of a barbarous people: severity; and retaliation. The early laws of the Greeks and the Romans were cruel; the laws of the twelve tables, says Mr. Gibbon, like the statutes of Draco, were written in characters of blood.[1] By the laws of Moses, blasphemy, idolatry, profaning the sabbath, homicide, adultery, incest, rapes, crimes against nature, witchcraft, smiting or cursing father or mother, were punished with death, and with burning and stoning, the most cruel kinds of death.[2] Of the sanguinary character imprinted on the laws of the Egyptians, the following instance may be adduced. They thrust little pieces of reeds, about a finger's length, into all parts of the bodies of parricides; and then, surrounding them with thorns, set them on fire.[3] The barbarous punishments which prevail among the Chinese are too familiary known to require illustration. Perhaps of all the rude nations of whom we have any account, our own Saxon and German ancestors were the most distinguished for the mildness of their punishments; a singularity, however, to be accounted for, by the use of a very barbarous expedient, a compensation in money for almost every species of crime. Yet in various instances, particularly that of theft, their laws were not only severe, but inhuman.[4]

Notwithstanding the mildness which has generally been attributed to the Hindu character, hardly any nation is distinguished for more sanguinary laws. "The cruel mu-

[1] Gibbon's History of the Decline and Fall of the Roman Empire, ch. xliv.

[2] See the Books of Moses, passim.

[3] Diod. Sic. lib. i. p. 88.

[4] Wilkins, Leg. Sax. p. 2 to 20. Mr. Turner, History of the Anglo-Saxons, says, book XI. ch. viii. "The most popular of the legal punishments were the pecuniary mulcts. But as the imperfection and inutility of these could not be always disguised—as they were sometimes impunity to the rich, who could afford them, and to the poor who had nothing to pay them with, other punishments were enacted. Among these we find imprisonment, outlawry, banishments, slavery, and transportation. In other cases, we have whipping, branding, the pillory, amputation of limb, mutilation of the nose, and ears, and lips, the eyes plucked out, hair torn off, stoning, and hanging. Nations not civilized have barbarous punishments."

tilations," says Sir William Jones,[1] "practised by the native powers, are shocking to humanity."

Retaliation is another peculiarity which remarkably distinguishes the laws of that barbarous period, when the punishment of crimes is chiefly measured by the resentment of the sufferer.[2] Whatever the injury which the innocent man has sustained, a similar injury, by way of punishment, is imposed upon the guilty. Whatever the member or part of his body, with which the offender com-

[1] Charge to the Grand Jury of Calcutta, Dec. 4, 1788, Sir Wm. Jones's Works, iii. 26. Of this feature of their laws, a few examples will impress a lively conception. "The most pernicious of all deceivers," says the law of Menu, "is a goldsmith who commits frauds; the king shall order him to be cut piecemeal with razors." Laws of Menu, ch. ix. 292. "Should a wife, proud of her family and the great qualities of her kinsmen, actually violate the duty which she owes to her lord, let the king condemn her to be devoured by dogs in a place much frequented; and let him place the adulterer on an iron bed well heated, under which the executioners shall throw logs continually, till the sinful wretch be there burned to death." Ibid. viii. 371, 372. "If a woman murders her spiritual guide, or her husband, or her son, the magistrate, having cut off her ears, her nose, her hands, and her lips, shall expose her to be killed by cows." Halhed's Gentoo Code, ch. xxi. sect. 10. "Of robbers, who break a wall or partition, and commit theft in the night, let the prince order the hands to be lopped off, and themselves to be fixed on a sharp stake. Two fingers of a cutpurse, the thumb and the index, let him cause to be amputated on his first conviction; on the second, one hand and one foot; on the third, he shall suffer death." Laws of Menu, ix. 276, 277. "A thief, who, by plundering in his own country, spoils the province, the magistrate shall crucify, and confiscate his goods; if he robs in another kingdom he shall not confiscate his possessions, but shall crucify him. If a man steals any man of a superior caste, the magistrate shall bind the grass beena round his body, and burn him with fire; if he steals a woman of a superior caste, the magistrate shall cause him to be stretched out upon a hot plate of iron, and, having bound the grass beena round his body, shall burn him in the fire. If a man steals an elephant or a horse, excellent in all respects, the magistrate shall cut off his hand, and foot, and buttock, and deprive him of life. If a man steals an elephant or a horse of small account, or a camel or a cow, the magistrate shall cut off from him one hand and one foot. If a man steals a goat or a sheep, the magistrate shall cut off one of his hands. If a man steals any small animal, exclusive of the cat and the weasel, the magistrate shall cut off half his foot." Halhed's Gentoo Code, ch. xvii. sect. 3. "If a man sets fire to the tillage or plantation of another, or sets fire to a house or to a granary, or to any uninhabited spot where there is much fruit or flowers, the magistrate, having bound that person's body in the grass beena, shall burn him with fire." Ibid. xviii. "For boring the nostrils of cows belonging to priests, the offender shall instantly lose half of one foot." Laws of Menu, ch. viii. 325. The same system of mutilation prevailed in Persia. Xenophon, describing the Persian punishments, says, Πολλακις δ' ην ιδειν παρα τας τειβομενας ὁδους, και ποδων, και χειρων, και οφθαλμων στερουμενους ανθρωπους. Xenoph. Cyropæd. lib. i. p. 92. The common mode of hanging is thus described by an eyewitness: "A hook is fixed to one end of the rope, and this hook the executioner forces with all his strength into the flesh below the criminal's chin; he is then hoisted up, and the other end of the rope is made fast to the gallows." Bartolomeo's Travels, book II. ch. v. "If a magistrate has committed a crime, and any person, upon discovery of that crime, shall beat and ill-use the magistrate, the magistrate shall thrust an iron spit through him and roast him at the fire." Halhed's Gentoo Code, ch. xvi. sect. 1.

[2] "The inhuman and unequal principle of retaliation," says Mr. Gibbon, Hist. of Decl. and Fall of the Rom. Emp. ch. xliv.

mitted the crime, upon that part is the chastisement inflicted. The Hebrew law of an eye for an eye, and a tooth for a tooth, is a familiar example of what occurred among other nations. The forfeit of limb for limb, and member for member, was, among the Romans, exacted by the law of the twelve tables, unless where the offender could expiate his crime by a fine of 300 pounds of copper. The earliest legislators of Greece were so rude as to leave the punishment of crimes, undefined, to the discretion of the judge; but Zaleucus, legislator of the Locrians, who first prescribed rules on this subject, enforced so literally the maxim of an eye for an eye, that it was deemed an important reform on his laws, when it was decreed that he who struck out the eye of a person with one eye should lose both his own.[1] The Egyptians extended the principle of punishing the criminals in that part of the body which was chiefly instrumental in the guilt, to an extraordinary number of instances. He who discovered the secrets of the state had his tongue cut out; he who violated a free woman was made an eunuch; of those who counterfeited coin and seals either public or private, of those who made use of false weights and measures, and of public notaries who forged or mutilated deeds, the two hands were cut off; and calumniators were subjected to the same punishment which would have been due to those whom they falsely accused.[2] To how extraordinary a degree the spirit of retaliation moulds the penal legislation of the Hindus, a few specimens will evince. The law concerning assault and battery, in the Institutes of Menu, thus commences: "With whatever member a low-born man shall assault or hurt a superior, even that member of his must be slit or cut, more or less in proportion to the injury: this is an ordinance of Menu."[3] "If a man strikes a Bramin with his hand, the magistrate shall cut off that man's hand; if he strikes him with his foot, the magistrate shall cut off the foot; in the same manner, with whatever limb he strikes a Bramin, that limb shall be cut off; but if a Sooder strikes

[1] Strabo, lib. vi. p. 398. Potter's Antiq. book I. ch. xxvi. Blackstone's Commentaries, book IV. ch. i.

[2] Diod. Sic. lib. i. p. 88, 89.

[3] Laws of Menu, ch. viii. 279. In a style characteristically Hindu, the following, among other cases, are specified: when a man spits on another, when he urines on him, and when he breaks wind on him. The penalties I choose not to describe. See the same chapter, 280—284.

either of the three casts, Bramin, Chehteree, or Bice, with his hand or foot, the magistrate shall cut off such hand or foot."[1] "If a man has put out both the eyes of any person, the magistrate shall deprive that man of both his eyes, and condemn him to perpetual imprisonment, and fine him."[2] The punishment of murder is founded entirely upon the same principle. "If a man," says the Gentoo code, "deprives another of life, the magistrate shall deprive that person of life."[3] "A once-born man, who insults the twice born with gross invectives, ought to have his tongue slit. If he mention their names and classes with contumely, as if he say, 'Oh thou refuse of Brahmans,' an iron style, ten fingers long, shall be thrust red-hot into his mouth. Should he through pride give instruction to priests concerning their duty, let the king order some hot oil to be dropped into his mouth and into his ear."[4] "If a blow, attended with much pain, be given either to human creatures or cattle, the king shall inflict on the striker a punishment as heavy as the presumed suffering."[5] "With whatever limb a thief commits the offence, by any means in this world, as if he break a wall with his hand or his foot, even that limb shall the king amputate, for the prevention of a similar crime."[6] "A mechanic or servile man having an adulterous connexion with a woman of a twice-born class, if she was unguarded, shall lose the part offending, and his whole substance."[7] "The breaker of a dam to secure a pool, let the king punish by a long immersion under water."[8] The portion of suffering, sufficient to constitute a motive for abstaining from the crime, is all the punishment which reason authorizes; but we see nations far advanced in civilization so tardy in recognising this principle, that the excess of suffering, produced by the law of retaliation, would not, it is probable, suggest to nations, at a very early stage of civilization, the utility of repealing it. Yet no maxim more naturally recommends itself to the human mind, even before it is strong, than that all who commit the same crime should meet with equal punishment; and it requires a very slight degree of reflection to see, that when the hand or the foot is cut off

[1] Halhed's Code of Gentoo Laws, ch. xvi. sect. 1. [2] Ibid.
[3] Ibid. [4] Laws of Menu, ch. viii. 270—273.
[5] Ibid. ch. viii. 268.
[6] Ibid. ch. viii. 334. [7] Ibid. 374. [8] Ibid. ix. 279.

from one man, the punishment may be a very moderate one; when the same limb is cut off from another man, to whose subsistence it is essential, the penalty may far exceed a sentence of death.

In another class of punishments, where the principle of equality may be still more easily applied, the grossness of the violation excites considerable suprise. As among our Saxon ancestors, so among the Hindus, fines bear a very large proportion to other punishments. When reparation to the party injured should be made by the author of the wrong, the pecuniary ability of the party on whom the obligation falls can no more be regarded, than where he owes a debt. But in so far as it is the object of the law to create a motive against the occurrence of a like offence; or even to take vengeance, to inflict pain purely because pain has been occasioned; in so far it is one of the plainest dictates of reason, that where the offence is equal, the suffering or hardship imposed should be equal. Though a pecuniary mulct imposes all degrees of hardship, according to the pecuniary abilities of the man who pays, the Hindu law makes no distinction between the rich and the poor.[1] It makes, indeed, a serious distinction between the man of one class, and another: and they of the lowest are, with a very few exceptions, always the most severely fined. But if the class is the same, the same forfeit is exacted for the same offence; though one man should be too opulent to feel from it any sensible inconvenience; another should suffer all the pains and horrors of want.

From the classification of the people, and the privileges of the castes, we are prepared to expect, among the Hindus, inequalities created by distinctions of rank. They relate either to the crimes committed *against* persons of the different ranks, or the crimes committed *by* them. Inequalities of the first sort, it is found difficult to avoid even in high stages of civilization. At present, in the best governed countries of Europe, an injury done to a nobleman is treated as a crime of a deeper dye, than a similar injury

[1] There is one passage of Menu. ch. viii. 126, an incidental exhortation to the judge not to be regardless of the ability of the sufferer in the infliction of corporal or other punishment; and it is impossible but some regard must have been paid to it in practice: but defined sums are in almost all cases affixed to specific crimes, without the smallest reference to the ability of the payer.

to a person of the lowest rank.[1] If the laws should make no distinction in principle, the power of the nobleman to bring the offender to trial, and to command the partiality of the judge, would long make a very essential difference in practice. When the Hindu law, therefore, makes a gradation in the criminality of the same action, according as it is committed against the Brahman, the Cshatriya, the Vaisya, and the Sudra, it is only the excess in the difference of punishment, which is calculated to excite our surprise. With regard to offences committed *by* individuals of the different ranks, it is rare, even among the rudest people, to find the principle of unequal punishments, expressly avowed; and comparative impunity granted by law to the crimes of the great. Perjury, fraud, defamation, forgery, incest, murder, are not among us reckoned crimes more venial in the lord than in his servant. Among the Hindus, whatever be the crime committed, if it is by a Brahman, the punishment is in general comparatively slight; if by a man of the military class, it is more severe; if by a man of the mercantile and agricultural class, it is still increased; if by a Sudra it is violent and cruel. For defamation of a Brahmen, a man of the same class must be fined 12 panas; a man of the military class, 100: a merchant, 150 or 200; but a mechanic or servile man is whipped.[2] The general principle on which the penalties for this crime seem to be regulated is, that whatever fine is exacted from a man of the same class by whom you have been accused, one only half as large should be imposed upon the man of a superior class, but one double in magnitude, should the cast of the slanderer be inferior to your own. For all the more serious accusations against any of the superior orders the punishment of the Sudra is far more dreadful.[3] That the scale of punishment for crimes of assault is graduated by the same rule, the

[1] The *orthodox* judge, Blackstone, as Mr. Gibbon very *significantly* denominates him (see Hist. Decl. and Fall, &c. ch. xliv. n. 145) is quite an advocate for the superior criminality of an injury to a man of a superior rank. "If a nobleman strikes a peasant," says he, all mankind will see, that, if a court of justice awards a return of the blow, it is more than a just compensation. The execution of a needy, decrepit assassin, is a poor satisfaction for the murder of a nobleman, in the bloom of his youth, and full enjoyment of his friends, his honours, and his fortune." Commentaries on the Laws of England, book IV. ch. i.

[2] Laws of Menu, ch. viii. 260, 267.

[3] Code of Gentoo Laws, ch. xv. sect. 2. Vide supra, p. 256.

BOOK II. CHAP. IV.

following instance, out of many, will evince. "If a man of superior cast and of superior abilities to another should strike him with a weapon, the magistrate shall fine him 500 puns of cowries. If a man of an equal cast and of equal abilities with another should strike him with a weapon, the magistrate shall fine him 1000 puns of cowries. If a man of an inferior cast and inferior abilities to another should strike him with a weapon, the magistrate shall fine him 300 puns of cowries."[1] For perjury, it is only in favour of the Brahmen, that any distinction seems to be admitted. "Let a just prince," says the ordinance of menu, "banish men of the three lower classes, if they give false evidence, having first levied the fine; but a Brahmen let him only banish."[2] The punishment of adultery, which on the Brahmens is light, descends with intolerable weight on the lowest classes. In regard to the inferior cases of theft, for which a fine only is the punishment, we meet with with a curious exception, the degree of punishment ascending with the class. "The fine of a Sudra for theft, shall be eight fold; that of a Vaisya, sixteen fold; that of a Cshatriya, two and thirty fold; that of a Brahmen, four and sixty fold, or a hundred fold complete, or even twice four and sixty fold."[3] No corporal punishment, much less death, can be inflicted on the Brahmen for any crime. "Menu, son of the Self-existent, has named ten places of punishment, which are appropriated to the three lower classes; the part of generation, the belly, the tongue, the two hands; and fifthly, the two feet, the eye, the nose, both ears, the property; and in the capital case, the whole body; but a Brahmen must depart from the realm unhurt in any one of them."[4]

Punishment should be proportioned, not to the greatness of the crime, that is, the quantity of suffering it produces, but solely to the difficulty of creating an adequate motive to abstain from it: if a fine of one shilling

[1] Code of Gentoo Laws, ch. xvi. sect. 1.

[2] Laws of Menu, ch. viii. 123.

[3] Ibid. viii. 337, 338.

[4] Ibid. ch. viii. 124, 125.—M.

The banishment of a Brahman, however, is a very severe punishment, as it involves loss of caste, and consequent degradation; but in practice, and even under Hindu rule, the immunity of a Brahman, guilty of crime, does not seem to have been attended to. In the oldest of the extant dramas, the Mrichehakati, a Brahman, convicted on presumptive proof, of murder, is condemned to death.—W.

created a sufficient motive to abstain from the crime of murder, the fine of a shilling would be all the punishment which ought to exist. It must be owned, however, that the principle of punishing crimes, according to their magnitude, very naturally suggests itself; and bears a strong appearance of according with the principles of reason. Even to this early and imperfect principle, the Hindus have never ascended. While perjury, one of the most mischievous of crimes, and one against which an adequate motive is very difficult to create, is punished only with fine, and in most aggraved cases with banishment; the crime of obtaining goods on false pretences is punished with mutilation, and even with death. "If a person steals a man of an inferior cast, the magistrate shall fine him 1000 puns of cowries. If he steals an elephant or a horse excellent in all respects, the magistrate shall cut off his hand, and foot, and buttock, and deprive him of life."[1] The following places of the body are enumerated: the ear, the nose, the hand, the foot, the lip, the eye, the tongue, and some others; upon any one of which a stroke, such as to separate or cut them off from the body, is punished equally;[2] yet surely there is no comparison between the injury of depriving a man of his ear, for example, and of his tongue, or his hand. An amour with a woman of the Brahmenical caste is more dreadfully punished than parricide. Various cases of theft and robbery are accounted worthy of more shocking penalties than murder. Even Sir William Jones is constrained to say that the punishments of the Hindus "are partial and fanciful, for some crimes dreadfully cruel, for others reprehensibly slight."[3]

The principal acts erected into punishable offences by the Hindu law are, false witness, defamation, assault, theft, outrage, adultery. The species and degrees of perjury are thus distinguished: "If a witness speak falsely through covetousness, he shall be fined 1000 panas; if through distraction of mind, 250; if through terror, 1000; if through friendship, the same; if through lust, 2500; if through wrath, 1500; if through ignorance, 200 com-

1 Halhed's Gentoo Code, ch. xvii. sect. 3.

2 Ib. ch. xvi. sect. 1.

3 Preface to the Translation of the Institutes of Menu, Sir Wm. Jones's Works, iii. 62.

plete; if through inattention, 100 only."[1] The laws against reproachful expressions are numerous, and the penalties remarkably severe; a pretty satisfactory proof that the Hindus have always been abusive; as we find they continue to the present day.[2] By the term Assault, are indicated the smaller instances of personal offence and injury; on which the laws of the Hindus descend to the most minute distinctions and details. In this they present a remarkable agreement with the laws of our Gothic ancestors. Lord Kaimes, observing upon the ancient European mode of satisfying for injuries by money, remarks that "the laws of the Burgundians, of the Salians, of the Almanni, of the Bavarians, of the Ripuarii, of the Saxons, of the Angli and Thuringi, of the Frisians, of the Langobards, and of the Anglo-Saxons, are full of these compositions, extending from the most trifling injury to the most atrocious crimes. In perusing the tables of these compositions which enter into a minute detail of the most trivial offences, a question naturally occurs, Why all this scrupulous nicety of adjusting sums to delinquencies? Such a thing is not heard of in later times. But the following answer will give satisfaction:—That resentment, allowed scope among barbarians, was apt to take flame by the slightest spark; therefore, to provide for its gratification, it became necessary to enact compositions for every trifling wrong, such as at present would be the subject of mirth rather than of serious punishment: for example, where the clothes of a woman, bathing in a river, are taken away to expose her nakedness, and where dirty water is thrown upon a woman in the way of contumely."[3] The following orders of crime, in the Hindu code, present a similar, and a very remarkable picture: 1. Throwing upon the body of another, dust, or sand, or clay, or cow-dung, or anything else of the same kind, or striking with the hand or foot; 2. Throwing upon the body tears, or phlegm, or the paring of one's nails, or the gum of the eyes, or the wax of the ears, or the refuse of victuals, or spittle; 3. Throwing upon another from the navel

[1] Laws of Menu, ch. viii. 120, 121. Where the language of the text specifies the fine by naming it technically in the order of amercements, I have stated the sum, that the reader might see at a glance the proportions.

[2] See the Chapter on *Manners*.

[3] Historical Law Tracts, i. 49, 50.

downwards to his foot, spue, or urine, or ordure, or semen; 4. Throwing upon another, from the navel upwards to beneath the neck, any of the substances mentioned in the last article; 5. Throwing upon another any of the same substances from the neck upwards; 6. Assaulting with a stone, or with a piece of iron or wood; 7. Hauling by the foot, or by the hair, or by the hand, or by the clothes; 8. Seizing and binding another in a cloth, and setting one's foot upon him; 9. Raising up an offensive weapon to assault; 10. Striking with a weapon. In all these cases a further distinction is made, as the offence is committed by a superior, an inferior, or an equal, and committed against a man or a woman. The gradations too of wounds are curiously specified: 1. When no blood is shed; 2. When a little blood is shed; 3. When much blood is shed; 4. When a very great quantity; 5. When a bone is broken as well as blood is shed; 6. When a member or organ is struck off or separated.[1] Under the title "Theft," the Hindus include the various species of frauds. In all nations which have made but the first step in civilization; when the means of protecting property are very imperfectly known, and covetousness is a furious passion; the depredations of thieves are always punished with extreme severity. In the Gothic nations of Europe, when the murder even of the King inferred but a pecuniary composition, theft was punished by mutilation and death.[2] In the same manner among the Hindus, while murder is punished by the mere loss of life, some of the most atrocious instances of the cruelty of the Hindu laws were drawn as above from the punishments awarded to theft.[3] The minor cases of theft are punished by fines, and by various degrees of mutilation; but the higher species by impaling, by burning alive, and by crucifixion. By Outrage; which is sometimes denominated violence, sometimes robbery; are designated, all attacks, accompanied with violence, upon either property or person, including even murder. While the inferior species are punished by fine and by mutilation, the higher are punished by death; and some of the more heinous kinds of spoliation are avenged with all the san-

[1] See the Article Assault in the Code of Gentoo Laws, ch. xvi. sect. 1. Laws of Menu, ch. viii. 279 to 301.
[2] See Kaimes's Historical Law Tracts, i. 63, and the authorities there quoted.
[3] Supra, p. 263.

guinary fury which, among the Hindus, has dictated the higher penalties of theft.[1] Adultery is a very complicated subject. In the Hindu language it includes every unlawful species of sexual indulgence, from the least, to the most injurious, or offensive. If the laws are any proof of the manners of a people, this article affords indication of one of the most depraved states of the sexual appetite. Almost all the abuses, and all the crimes which it is possible to conceive, are there depicted with curious exactness; and penalties are devised and assigned for every minute diversity and refinement, as for acts the most frequent and familiar. There are even titles of sections in the code which cannot be transcribed with decency, and which depict crimes unknown to European laws.[2] In accordance

[1] Laws of Menu, ch. viii. 344 to 348. Code of Gentoo Laws, ch. xviii.—M. There is nothing sanguinary or furious in the verses of Manu cited; they merely command the King not to endure or dismiss unpunished, the perpetrators of atrocious violence.—W.

[2] Mr. Halhed makes so curious an apology for this article in his preface to the Code of Gentoo Laws, p. lxiii., that I am tempted to transcribe it: "The nineteenth and twentieth chapters," says he, "present us a lively picture of Asiatic manners, and in them a strong proof of their originality. To men of liberal and candid sentiments, neither the grossness of the portrait, nor the harshness of the colouring, will seem improper or indecent, while they are convinced of the truth of the resemblance; and if this compilation does not exhibit mankind as they might have been, or as they ought to have been, this answer is plain; 'Because it paints them as they were.' Vices, as well as fashions, have their spring and their fall, not with individuals only, but in whole nations, when one reigning foible for a while swallows up the rest, and then retires, in its turn, to make room for the epidemic influence of a newer passion. Wherefore, if any opinions not reconcileable to our modes of thinking, or any crimes not practised, and so not prohibited among us, should occur in these chapters, they must be imputed to the different effects produced on the human mind by a difference of climates, customs, and manners, which will constantly give a particular turn and bias to the national vices. Hence it would be a weak and frivolous argument for censuring the fifth section of this nineteenth chapter, to object that it was levelled at an offence absurd in itself, not likely to be frequent, or supposing it frequent, still to be deemed of trivial consequence; and to make this objection merely in consideration that the offence may not be usual among us, and has certainly never been forbidden by our legislature, such cavils would betray a great ignorance of the general system of human nature, as well as of the common principles of legislation; for penal laws (except for the most ordinary crimes) are not enacted until particular instances of offence have pointed out their absolute necessity; for which reason parricide was not specified among the original institutes of the celebrated law-giver of Sparta. Hence we may with safety conclude, that the several prohibitions and penalties of this fifth section were subsequent to, and in consequence of, the commission of every species of enormity therein described."—Mr. Halhed here maintains with very cogent reasons, though rather an unskilful style, that the Hindu morals are certainly as gross as the Hindu laws; that the latter grossness is, in fact, the result of the former.—M. The Code translated by Mr. Halhed, must not be confounded with that of Manu; the provisions of the former, which are the subjects of his apology, are not formally set forth in Manu. The offences denounced, whether the subject of legislation or not, were not unfamiliar to Greece and Rome, in their most polished periods, if their satirists and historians may be credited. The Gothic nations in their rudest state were apparently remarkably free from such grossness, and their purer propensities were confirmed by the diffusion amongst them of the light of Christianity.—W.

with the general spirit of Eastern nations, among whom an extraordinary value is set on the chastity of the women, its more aggravated violations are punished by the most shocking death which human cruelty has probably devised, that of burning on a heated plate of iron. The ramifications of criminality are also pursued to the most minute and trivial acts, and such as, even in the most jealous nations of Europe, would be held perfectly innocent: "He who talks with the wife of another man at a place of pilgrimage, in a forest or a grove, or at the confluence of rivers, incurs the guilt of an adulterous inclination: to send her flowers or perfumes, to sport and jest with her, to touch her apparel and ornaments, to sit with her on the same couch, are all held adulterous acts on his part."[1] Of all crimes, indeed, adultery appears, in the eyes of Hindu lawgivers, to be the greatest: and worthy of the most severe and terrible chastisement. The offences committed with the women of the higher classes by men of the lower are the acts which are looked upon as of greatest atrocity, and which rise in criminality, as the classes recede from one another, till they arrive at last at the adultery of a man of the servile with a woman of the priestly caste; a point beyond which, it is supposed, that human guilt and depravity cannot proceed.[2]

III. Conformity to the laws of the two preceding orders; denominated, for want of better terms, the Civil and the Penal; is the End. The laws of Judicature are to be regarded in the light of Means to that End. The subject, in its full extent, includes an account of, 1, the instruments made use of for producing the fulfilment of the laws of the two former kinds, and 2, the modes of using them.

The instruments made use of among the Hindus, have been already described, in giving an account of the functions of the king; who, with his Brahmen assessors, is the principal instrument. The mode of using the instruments of judicature, or the steps according to which judicature is performed, were there also briefly described. Of the matters which remain, the laws or rules respecting evidence form the only part which it is still useful to describe.

[1] Laws of Menu, ch. viii. 356, 357.
[2] Ibid. 352—386. Code of Gentoo Laws, ch. xix.

BOOK II. CHAP. IV.

Prior to the general use of writing, the chief species of evidence, applicable to judicial cases, is the speech of witnesses. It is this species which makes the principal figure in the laws of Hindustan to the present age. It is even more than doubtful whether written evidence is at all referred to by the author of the ordinances of Menu, though from himself we learn that writing had been applied to laws.[1] "On the denial," says the law, "of a debt which the defendant has in court been required to pay, the plaintiff must call a witness who was present at the place of the loan, or produce other evidence;"[2] the gloss of Culluca adds, "a note and the like:"[3] but for the use of evidence by writing not a single rule is afterwards adduced, though numerous rules are prescribed for the use of that which is delivered orally; not even a word of allusion to this novel species of evidence appears; and where the various circumstances are enumerated on which the attention of the judge ought to be fixed, while the evidence of speaking witnesses occupies a conspicuous place, the evidence of writings is entirely omitted.[4] In the compilations, however, of recent times, as in that made by order of Mr. Hastings, and translated by Halhed, the use of written evidence appears; but even there it is treated with a negligence and slightness due to a matter of subordinate importance.[5]

[1] Laws of Menu, ch. viii. 3. [2] Ibid. 52. [3] Ibid.

[4] "Let him fully consider the nature of truth, the state of the case, and his own person; and next, the witnesses, the place, the mode and the time." Ibid. 45. From these circumstances it is probable that the emendation of the commentator has been added from the more enlarged knowledge of later times.

[5] The mistake which pervades the whole of our author's view of Hindu law, has here influenced him to draw an inference wholly inaccurate. However comprehensive the Code of Manu, it is an error to suppose that it is the only ancient body of laws, and that it comprises all possible details. Those of judicial proceedings are rather indicated than explained, and the omission of any one specification does not warrant the conclusion that there was nothing to be specified. This is especially the case in the present instance, and whatever Manu may have left unsaid, great importance is attached by early writers to documentary proof. Evidence is said to consist of documents, possession, and witnesses. Again: Human evidence is threefold; documents, possession, and witnesses. Such is the opinion of eminent sages. Documents are of two sorts—official and private. Possession implies manifest occupancy. Witnesses will be treated of hereafter.—Macnaghten. Considerations on Hindu Law, 438. The censure of Hindu law on account of the absence of written testimony here advanced, is the more extraordinary, as in a few pages further on it is admitted that there are laws respecting written evidence, although there is still something to cavil at, and they are said to be few, and applied to a limited number of cases; assertions equally incorrect with that of the present text.—W.

Among the rules for evidence at the lips of witnesses, some are reasonable and good; others are not only the reverse, but indicate a state of ignorance and barbarism. The evidence of three witnesses is required for the decision of any question: "When a man has been brought into court by a suitor for property, the cause shall be decided by the Brahmen who represents the king, having heard three witnesses at least."[1] Yet it is declared in another place that "one man, untainted with covetousness, may (*in some cases*, says the gloss of Culluca) be the sole witness."[2] This apparent contradiction may perhaps be explained by a passage in the Code of Gentoo Laws, where the decision of a cause by the testimony of a single witness is made to depend upon the consent of the litigants.[3] Even from this rule the following cases are excepted: "Supposing," says the law, "a person to lend another money secretly, or secretly to intrust his money to the care of another, in such affairs one single person is a sufficient witness."[4] The different degrees of trustworthiness in different witnesses leads to mischievous rules. "Married housekeepers, men with male issue, inhabitants of the same district, either of the military, the commercial, or the servile class, are competent, when called by the party, to give their evidence."[5] The most fanciful distinction surely that ever was made by an uncultivated mind, is that between the father of male and the father of female offspring, as a source of evidence. The persons held incompetent to bear witness are a very numerous class. "Those must not be admitted who have a pecuniary interest; nor familiar friends; nor menial servants; nor enemies; nor men formerly perjured; nor persons grievously diseased; nor those who have committed heinous offences. The king cannot be made a witness, nor cooks and the like mean artificers; nor public dancers and singers; nor a priest of deep learning in Scripture; nor a student of the Vedas; nor an anchoret secluded from all worldly connexions; nor one wholly dependent; nor one

[1] Laws of Menu, ch. viii. 60. The same law is stated still more generally and absolutely, in the Gentoo Code, ch. iii. sect. 8.

[2] Ibid. ch. viii. 77.

[3] Halhed's Gentoo Code, ch. iii. sect. 8. "If the plaintiff or defendant, at their own option, appoint a single person only, not fraudulently inclined, &c., he may be a witness."

[4] Ibid.

[5] Laws of Menu, ch. viii. 62.

BOOK II. CHAP. IV.

of bad fame; nor one who follows a cruel occupation; nor one who acts openly against the law; nor a decrepid old man; nor a child; nor a wretch of the lowest mixed class; nor one who has lost the organs of sense; nor one extremely grieved; nor one intoxicated; nor a madman; nor one tormented with hunger or thirst; nor one oppressed by fatigue; nor one excited by lust; nor one inflamed by wrath; nor one who has been convicted of theft."[1] Among the persons excluded from the rank of witnesses are the female sex entirely; unless in the case of evidence for others of the same sex. Servants, too, mechanics, and those of the lowest class, are allowed to give evidence for individuals of the same description.[2] Brahmens and the king are exempted from the obligation of giving evidence, by way of privilege, though the Brahmens are admitted when they please."[3]

This enumeration of persons, whose testimony was altogether unfit to be believed, affords a proof of the great difficulty of obtaining true testimony in the age in which it was made; and holds up a dreadful picture of the state of morality to which it could be supposed to be adapted. It indicates, also, by the strange diversity of the cases which it includes, a singular want of discrimination, in the minds by which it was framed. And further; rules for the exclusion of testimony, from any person, not deprived of the ordinary exercise of the human faculties, could, however the vicious effects of custom may preserve them, be introduced, only in an age of great ignorance and barbarity, when the human mind judges in the gross, is incapable of nice discriminations, cannot assign the different value which ought to be attached to the testimony of different men, and estimates the weight of a body of evidence by the number, not the trustworthiness, of the people who deliver it.[4]

[1] Laws of Menu, ch. viii. 64—67. [2] Ibid. 68. [3] Ibid. 69—71.

[4] The imperfeceions of the Hindu law have been in this, as in all other cases, pertinaciously selected: notwithstanding these blemishes, however, its general character has received commendation from high authority. "With some trifling exceptions, the Hindu doctrine of evidence is, for the most part, distinguished nearly as much as our own, by the excellent sense that determines the competency, and designates the choice of witnesses, with the manner of examining, and the credit to be given to them, as well as by the solemn earnestness, with which the obligation of truth is urged and inculcated; insomuch that less cannot be said of this part of their law, than that it will be read by every English lawyer with a mixture of admiration and delight, as it may be studied by him to advantage."—Elements of Hindu Law, by Sir Thomas Strange, late Chief Justice of Madras, p. 309.—W.

The introduction of rules for the exclusion of evidence marks the age of false refinement, which is that of semi-barbarism, intermediate between the age of true wisdom and that of primeval ignorance. When the first judges, or arbiters, the heads of families, had to clear up any dispute, they called before them every individual of the little community or family, who appeared to know anything of the matter, and questioned them all; allowing to the statements, extracted from each, the influence, much or little, or none at all, to which they seemed entitled; and this is the course which true wisdom would recommend. In an age, however, of false refinement, which aims at excessive accuracy, but, failing in comprehensiveness, applies its rules to part only of a subject when they should include the whole, the makers of laws, perceiving that certain classes of witnesses were apt to give false testimony, and considering that false testimony misleads, resolved immediately that the testimony of such witnesses ought never to be received. Now, if the testimony of the best sort of witness had been a thing which the judges always had at command, in sufficient quantity, this might have been a rational procedure. But as this was very far from being the case; as it very often happens that the testimony of the best sort of witnesses cannot be had, or that they contradict one another; that not only some light, but full and satisfactory light, may often be obtained from the worst sort of witnesses; to determine that certain classes of persons, and among them the persons whose knowledge of the facts is naturally the most complete, shall not be used as witnesses, is merely to determine that judicature shall be performed, so far, without evidence; that the judge shall decide without knowledge; and the question of right and wrong, instead of being determined upon all the evidence that can be had, shall be determined upon a part of it only, sometimes a most insignificant part, sometimes hardly any at all.[1]

[1] "If," says Mr. Hume, "the manner of punishing crimes among the Anglo-Saxons appear singular, the proofs were not less so: and were also the natural result of the situation of those people. Whatever we may imagine concerning the usual truth and sincerity of men who live in a rude and barbarous state, there is much more falsehood, and even perjury, among them, than among civilized nations. Virtue, which is nothing but a more enlarged and more cultivated reason, never flourishes to any degree, nor is founded on steady principles of honour, except where a good education becomes general; and

BOOK II. CHAP. IV.

One of the strongest characteristics of a rude age, or of a corrupt government, is, to make laws which cannot, or ought not, to be executed; and then to give dispensations for them. "In all cases of violence, of theft and adultery, of defamation and assault," says the Hindu law, "the judge must not examine too strictly the competence of witnesses."[1]

A presumption, of the very weakest kind, is admitted as a full proof, in the following passages: "If a man brings a suit against another, saying, I have lent you several articles, and the person answers, I never received one of the articles you mention; in that case, if the plaintiff proves any one of all the articles claimed, to be in the defendant's possession, the magistrate shall cause the whole so claimed to be restored."[2] In cases of infinitely greater importance the same deceitful rule is applied. "If a man hath accused another of the murder of a man, or of a robbery, or of adultery, and should say, You have in several places been guilty of these crimes, and the defendant denies the accusation: in such a case, if the accuser can prove upon the other the commission of any one of these crimes, it shall be a proof of the whole complaint."

Of all the perverse proceedings of a superstitious mind, which the history of rude nations presents to us, few will be found more at variance with reason, than the establishment of the following law: "The witness, who has given evidence, and to whom, within seven days after, a misfortune happens from disease, fire, or the death of a kinsman, shall be condemned to pay the debt and a fine."[3]

Though there is no ground on which the infirmities of the human mind are more glaring, and more tenacious of

---

where men are taught the pernicious consequences of vice, treachery, and immorality. Even superstition, though more prevalent among ignorant nations, is but a poor supply for the defects in knowledge and education: Our European ancestors, who employed every moment the expedient of swearing on extraordinary crosses and reliques, were less honourable in all engagements than their posterity, who, from experience, have omitted those ineffectual securities. This general proneness to perjury was much increased by the usual want of discernment in judges, who could not discuss an intricate evidence, and were obliged to number, not weigh, the testimony of witnesses." History of England, Appendix I.

This subject will, one day, when the papers of Mr. Bentham are produced, be presented to the world, in all the light which full knowledge, a minute analysis, and philosophy, can bestow upon it.

[1] Menu, ch. viii. 72.

[2] Code of Gentoo Laws, ch. iii. sect. 6, p. 107.

[3] Laws of Menu, ch. viii.

existence than that of law, it is probable that the annals of legislative absurdity can present nothing which will match a law for the direct encouragement of perjury. "Whenever," says the ordinance of Menu, "the death of a man, who had been a grievous offender, either of the servile, the commercial, the military, or the sacerdotal class, would be occasioned by true evidence, from the known rigour of the king, even though the fault arose from inadvertence or error, falsehood may be spoken: it is even preferable to truth."[1] What a state of justice it is, in which the king may condemn a man to death, for inadvertence or error, and no better remedy is found than the perjury of witnesses! "Whenever a true evidence would deprive a man of his life, in that case, if a false testimony would be the preservation of his life, it is allowable to give such false testimony. If a marriage for any person may be obtained

[1] Laws of Menu, ch. viii. sect. 104.—M. This solitary passage is always seized upon by the calumniators of the Hindus as a proof of their systematic disregard of veracity—overlooking and setting aside the more numerous and earnest passages in which strict adherence to truth is enjoined, and which prove that fully as much respect was paid to it by the Hindus as by any other people whatever. Manu, viii. 80—101, is a series of verses enforcing the obligations of truth and the heinousness of false evidence, which may well be put in the scale against the single stanza to the contrary, under particular circumstances. That no other body of laws admits of any relaxation in this respect, is not exactly true. "Even the pious perjury," says Sir T. Strange, "which "the Hindu law has been supposed to sanction, is resolvable after all into no "greater liberty than what our Juries (not, indeed, with perfect approbation) "have long been allowed to take where the life of a prisoner on trial before "them is sometimes at stake." The provisions of the permission are also to be considered; a man's life is about to be sacrificed—not for intentional crime, but for an act arising out of inadvertence or error—and not from the justice, but from the rigour of the judge. In such a case a witness is permitted to give false evidence, and the motive is good; and although the act is incompatible with the sterner doctrines of our law, it is well known that something very analogous to it is not unfrequent—where in the opinion of witnesses, juries, and possibly even of judges, the punishment is unduly severe. Our author, not satisfied with the fair opportunity which the encouragement of perjury affords him, infers from the text that a judge might legally condemn a man for inadvertence or error, and therefore exclaims, What a state of justice! The words do not warrant such an interpretation; the sentence is evidently intended to be represented as unjust and rigorous; and cruel and unjust judges have existed in other countries than in India. With regard to the occasions next specified from the Gentoo Code, it is in the first place to be observed, that the Code is no authority for the ancient manners and laws of the Hindus—it is a modern work, and of a degenerate period. In the next place the cases are not without parallel, except as regards the specification of a Brahman. Our own criminals are almost compelled to plead 'not guilty,' even when they would disburden their consciences by telling the truth—and a Hindu may, therefore, be allowed to save his own life by telling a falsehood. These also, it may be observed, are not cases of perjury, or false testimony, a man's life being imperilled and his goods in danger of being spoiled, are events not likely to befall him in the character of a witness, nor are transactions with women part of legal procedure. They are not equivalent to perjury, therefore, and however reprehensible, are instances of a disregard of truth by no means peculiar to the Hindus.—W.

BOOK II. CHAP. IV.

by false witness, such falsehood may be told. If a man by the impulse of lust tells lies to a woman, or his own life would otherwise be lost, or all the goods of his house spoiled, or if it is for the benefit of a Brahmen, in such affairs falsehood is allowable."[1]

The laws respecting written evidence are few, and applied to a very limited number of cases. One distinction is recognised. "A writing," says the law, "is of two sorts; first, that which a man writes with his own hand; second, that which he procures to be written by another: of these two sorts, that which is written by a man's own hand, even without witnesses, is approved; and that written by another, if void of witnesses, is not approved."[2] The remaining rules apply, almost entirely, to the modes of supplying, by means of the oral, what is at any time defective in the quantity or quality of the matter drawn from the scriptural source.[3]

Notwithstanding the diversities of appearance which, in different ages and countries, human nature puts on, the attentive observer may trace in it an astonishing uniformity with respect to the leading particulars which characterize the different stages of society; and often a surprising coincidence in particular thoughts and observances. The trials by ordeal, in the dark ages of modern Europe; when the decision of the most important questions was abandoned to chance or to fraud; when carrying in the hand a piece of red-hot iron, or plunging the arm in boiling water, was deemed a test of innocence; and a painful or fraudulent experiment, supplanting a righteous award, might consign to punishment the most innocent, or save from it the most criminal of men; have been deemed a shocking singularity in the institutions of our barbarous ancestors. This species of evidence holds a high rank in the institutes of the Hindus. There are nine different modes of the trial by ordeal: 1, by the balance; 2, by fire; 3, by water; 4, by poison; 5, by water in which an idol has been washed; 6, by rice; 7, by boiling

[1] Halhed's Gentoo Code, ch. iii. sect. 9. [2] Ibid. 6.

[3] We know that grants of land by their princes were made in writing; and sunnuds, pottahs, and other writings, of legal import, are numerous in modern times. That so little of them is indicated in the more ancient books of law, implies a ruder period of society; though, doubtless, we cannot be sure of their being as destitute of legal writings as the few, which we possess, of their ancient monuments would give reason to suppose.—W.

oil; 8, by red-hot iron; 9, by images. The first of these, by the balance, is thus performed. The party accused is placed in the scale, and carefully weighed; after which, he is taken down, the pundits write the substance of the accusation on a piece of paper, and bind it on his forehead. At the end of six minutes he is weighed again, when, if lighter than before, he is pronounced innocent; if heavier, guilty. In the second ordeal, an excavation in the ground, nine hands long, two spans broad, and one span deep, is filled with a fire of pippal wood, into which the party must walk barefooted; proving his guilt, if he is burned; his innocence, if he escapes unhurt. The third species is rather more complicated: the person accused is made to stand in water up to his navel, with a Brahmen by his side; a soldier then shoots three arrows from a bow of cane, and a man is despatched to bring back that which was shot the farthest; as soon as he has taken it up, another man is directed to run from the brink of the water, and at the same instant the party under trial must plunge into it, grasping the foot or the staff of the Brahmen who stands by him: if he remains under the water till the two men with the arrows return, he is innocent; if he comes up, he is guilty. The fourth kind, by poison, is performed two ways: either the party swallows a certain quantity of a poisonous root, and is deemed innocent if no injury ensues; or a particular species of hooded snake is thrown into a deep earthen pot, and along with it a ring, a seal, or a coin. If the man, putting down his naked hand, cannot take this out unbitten by the serpent, he is accounted guilty. The accused, in the fifth species, is made to drink three draughts of the water in which the images of the sun and other deities have been washed; and if within fourteen days he has any indisposition, his crime is considered as proved. When several persons are suspected of theft, they chew, each, a quantity of dried rice, and throw it upon some leaves or bark of a tree; they from whose mouth it comes dry, or stained with blood, are deemed guilty: this is the sixth species of ordeal. In the seventh, a man thrusts his hand into hot oil; and in the eighth he carries an iron ball, or the head of a lance, red-hot in his hand; receiving his sentence of innocence or guilt according as he does or does not come off with safety. The ninth species is literally a casting of lots; two images of the gods, one of silver, and one of iron, are thrown into a large earthern jar; or two pictures of a deity, one on white, and the other on black cloth, are rolled up in cow-dung, and thrown into a jar: if the man, on putting in his hand, draws out the silver image, or the white picture, he is deemed innocent; if the contrary, guilty. The religious ceremonies with which these trials are performed it would be tedious and unprofitable to relate.[1]

The qualities desirable in a BODY OF LAW may all be summed up under two comprehensive titles; I. *Completeness*; II. *Exactness.*

Completeness has a reference to the matter: *Exactness* to the form.

I. A body of laws may be said to be *Complete*, when it includes everything which it ought to include; that is, when all those rights, the existence of which is calculated to improve the state of society, are created; and all those acts, the hurtfulness of which to the society is so great as to outweigh the cost, in all its senses, necessary for preventing them, are constituted offences.

II. A body of laws may be said to be *Exact*; 1, when it constitutes nothing a right, and nothing an offence, except those things precisely which are necessary to render it *Complete;* 2, when it contains no extraneous matter whatsoever; 3, when the aggregate of the powers and privileges which ought to be constituted rights, the aggregate of the acts which ought to be constituted offences, are divided and subdivided into those very parcels or classes, which beyond all others best adapt themselves to the means of securing the one, and preventing the other; 4, when it

[1] For a full account both of the law and the practice respecting the trial by ordeal, see a discourse "On the trial by Ordeal among the Hindus, by Ali Ibrahim Khan, chief magistrate at Benares," in the Asiat. Researches, i. 389. See too the Institutes of Menu, ch. viii. 114, 115, 190; Mr. Halhed's Code of Gentoo Laws, ch. iii. sect. 6, ch. ii. sect. 15, ch. xvii. sect. 4, ch. xviii., and the Translator's preface, p. 55, 56. Dr. Buchanan informs us of a shocking species of ordeal in use, in some places, in regard to those, "who, having had sexual intercourse with a person of another caste, allege that it was by mistake. If the criminal be a woman, melted lead is poured into her private parts; if it be a man, a red-hot iron is thrust up. Should they be innocent, it is supposed that they will not be injured." Journey through the Mysore, Canara, and Malabar, under the orders of Marquis Wellesley, i. 307. According to Kæmpfer, the Japanese too use a species of ordeal for the discovery of guilt. History of Japan, ch. v. 236.

defines those classes, that is, rights and offences, with the greatest possible clearness and certainty; 5, when it represses crimes with the smallest expense of punishment; and, 6, when it prescribes the best possible form of a judicatory, and lays down the best possible rules for the judicial functions.

To show in what degree the Hindu law approaches,[1] or recedes from, the standard of *Completeness*, would require a more extensive survey of the field of law, than consists with the plan of the present work.

That it departs widely from *Exactness*, in every one of the particulars wherein exactness consists, enough has already been seen to make abundantly apparent. 1. It creates a great many rights which ought to have no

[1] Of the following recapitulation of the defects of Hindu law, it may be observed that it subjects that law to a standard wholly arbitrary, the creation of the writer's own notions of perfection; tried by which all known systems of law are, as he frequently intimates, equally imperfect. It is also founded upon a very incomplete view of that law; the only authorities referred to, being Manu and the Gentoo Code. The latter, as already remarked, is a mere modern compilation—not a very careful or copious one—put together in haste—derived from sources of a very mixed character, and tainted in spirit by the corruption of modern manners, the consequence of a long period of Mahommedan domination. The translation of it by Halhed, is made through the medium of a Persian version, which Sir W. Jones characterizes as a "loose, injudicious epitome." The Code of Manu is of a different description. It is high authority; but it is not all-sufficient. "For practical purposes," says Mr. Ellis, "its use is very little, the original being a text-book of the oldest "date, without any commentary to adapt it to the circumstances of later "times. A mere text-book is considered by Indian jurists as of very little "use or authority for the actual administration of justice. It may almost be "said that the only conclusive authorities are held to be the Siddhantas, or "conclusions of the authors of the digests and commentaries."—Transactions of the Literary Society of Madras, p. 7.

There can be no doubt that the work ascribed to Manu is a very early attempt at codification, and it is the height of injustice to expect that, under such circumstances, it should be perfect. Had it been really perfect, our author's prejudiced ingenuity would, no doubt, still have detected flaws; but its imperfections may be granted, without impairing the claim of the major part of its enactments to respect and admiration. We have seen the opinion of one learned judge on one branch of their laws. We may also oppose to Mr. Mill, the authority of another; Sir Francis Macnaughten, Chief Justice in Bengal, who was by no means disposed to give unqualified approbation to this code. "I have given," he says, "some of the leading texts which relate to "the law of contracts, and, in my mind, the system, generally speaking, ap-"pears to be rational and moral. No less moral, and possibly more rational, "because it is in a great degree abstracted from the Hindoo religion, and de-"pendent upon ethics alone—upon principles which are universally admitted "—which are immutable in themselves, and which cannot but be eternal in "their duration. The merit of having being founders of their own jurispru-"dence, cannot be denied to this people, and those who are at all conversant "with the decisions of our own courts, will acknowledge the analogy which "exists between some of the doctrines and some of the texts which I have cited "from the Hindoo law. When this is not to be found, a comparison may in "several instances be made, without disadvantage to the Hindus."—Considerations on Hindoo Law, p. 404.

existence; and acts, which ought not to be erected into offences, it does so erect in great numbers. 2. It abounds in extraneous matter. 3. The division and arrangement of the matters of law are highly imperfect. 4. The definitions are so far from excluding darkness and doubt, that they leave almost everything indefinite and uncertain. 5. Punishments are not repressed, but abound; while there is the most enormous excess in the quantity of punishment. 6. The form of the judicatory is bad, as are a certain proportion of the rules for the mode of performing the judicial services.

In respect to definitions, the Hindu law is in a state which requires a few words of elucidation. Prior to the art of writing, laws can have little accuracy of definition; because, when words are not written, they are seldom exactly remembered; and a definition whose words are constantly varying is not, for the purposes of law, a definition at all. Notwithstanding the necessity of writing to produce fixed and accurate definitions in law, the nations of modern Europe have allowed a great proportion of their laws to continue in the unwritten; that is, the traditionary state; the state in which they lay before the art of writing was known. Of these nations, none have kept in that barbarous condition so great a proportion of their law as the English. From the opinion of the Hindus that the Divine Being dictated all their laws, they acknowledge nothing as law but what is found in some one or other of their sacred books. In one sense, therefore, all their laws are written. But as the passages which can be collected from these books leave many parts of the field of law untouched, in these parts the defect must be supplied either by custom, or the momentary will of the judge. Again, as the passages which are collected from these books, even where they touch upon parts of the field of law, do so in expressions to the highest degree vague and indeterminate, they commonly admit of any one of several meanings, and very frequently are contradicted and opposed by one another. When the words in which laws are couched are to a certain degree imperfect, it makes but little difference whether they are written or not. Adhering to the same words is without advantage, when these words secure no sameness in the things which they are made to signify. Further, in modern Europe, the uncertainty adhering to all unwritten laws, that is, laws the words of which have no certainty, is to some degree, though still a very imperfect one, circumscribed and limited, by the writing down of decisions. When, on any particular part of the field, a number of judges have all, with public approbation, decided in one way; and when these decisions are recorded and made known, the judge who comes after them has strong motives, both of fear and of hope, not to depart from their example. The degree of certainty, arising from the regard for uniformity which may thus be produced, is, from its very nature, infinitely inferior to that which is the necessary result of good definitions rendered unalterable by writing. But such as it is, the Hindus are entirely deprived of it. Among them the strength of the human mind has never been sufficient to recommend effectually the preservation, by writing, of the memory of judicial decisions. It has never been sufficient to create such a public regard for uniformity, as to constitute a material motive to a judge. And as kings, and their great deputies, exercised the principal functions of judicature, they were too powerful to be restrained by a regard to what others had done before them. What judicature would pronounce was, therefore, almost always uncertain; almost always arbitrary.[1]

[1] This passage has been subjected to the especial animadversions of Mr. Ellis, who makes some severe remarks upon the positiveness with which these comprehensive but ill-founded assertions are made. "The main source of "Mr. Mill's error," he continues, "seems to be sufficiently disclosed by him-"self, in the first sentence of his chapter on the Hindu laws. It is the common "one of having judged of the whole from a small part. The materials on "which he founds his opinions, seem to have been merely Sir William Jones's "Institutes of Menu, Mr. Halhed's Code of Gentoo Laws, and Mr. Colebrooke's "translation of Jagannatha Panchanana's Digest. That they were utterly "insufficient for his purpose, the section to which this note is appended suffi-"ciently shows. When he supposes that there are no definitions on Hindu "law, he has never seen, even in a translation, any one book of the second "great class of Hindu law-books, namely :—the Vyakhyánas or commentaries, "and only the translations of two very imperfect works out of the great mul-"titude of digests; and he relies mainly upon the Institutes of Menu, which "being a mere text-book, is never used as an authority in Hindu courts, but "when accompanied by an explanatory commentary, or incorporated into a "digest. It is true that the Hindus have not preserved 'Reports,' after the "English fashion, of the decisions of their courts of justice. But when the "'definitions' of the English common law are sought for, no less regard is "paid to those which are found in Lyttleton's Tenures, or perhaps in Lord "Coke's Commentary, than to those which appear in the 'reports of cases;' "and the commentaries of the Hindus are considered more decidedly by them "to be integral parts of the body of their law, than any commentary is in "England."—Trans. Literary Society of Madras, p. 12.—W.

In a JUDICATORY, the qualities desirable are: 1. intelligence; 2. good design; and that is the best judicatory in which the best securities are taken for them. In the judicatories of the Hindus, composed of the king and his Brahmens, or the Brahmens alone, there is no security for either the one or the other; and accordingly neither the one nor the other almost ever appears.

The qualities desirable in the forms of judicial procedure, are: 1. efficiency; 2. freedom from delay; 3. freedom from trouble and expense. In these several respects the system of the Hindus displayed a degree of excellence not only far beyond itself in the other branches of law, but far beyond what is exemplified in more enlightened countries. 1. The efficiency of the Hindu system of judicial procedure is chiefly impaired by those rules of evidence the badness of which has already been pointed out: 2. For preventing delay, it enjoys every requisite, in its method of immediate, direct, and simple investigation: 3. In the same method is included all that is requisite for obtaining the judicial services with the smallest portion of trouble and expense.[1]

[1] One of the most recent witnesses of the phenomena of Hindu society, who possessed extraordinary means of accurate knowledge, speaks in general upon the administration of justice among the Hindus in the following terms:—

"Without any of the judicial forms invented by the spirit of chicanery in Europe; with no advocates, solicitors, or other blood-suckers, now become necessary adjuncts of a court of justice in Europe; the Hindus determine the greater part of their suits of law by the arbitration of friends, or of the heads of the caste, or, in cases of the very highest importance, by reference to the chiefs of the whole castes of the district assembled to discuss the matter in controversy.—In ordinary questions they generally apply to the chief of the place, who takes upon himself the office of justice of the peace, and accommodates the matter between the parties. When he thinks it more fit, he sends them before their kindred, or arbitrators, whom he appoints. He generally follows the last course when the complainants are Brahmans, because persons out of their caste are not supposed capable of properly deciding differences between them. When these methods have been ineffectual to reconcile the parties, or when they refuse to submit to the decision of the arbitrators, they must appeal to the magistrates of the district, who decide the controversy without any appeal.

"The authority of the Hindu princes, as well as that of the vile emissaries whom they keep in the several provinces of their country for the purpose of harassing and oppressing them in their name, being altogether despotic, and knowing no other rule but their own arbitrary will, there is nothing in India that resembles a court of justice. Neither is there a shadow of public right, nor any code of laws by which those who administer justice may be guided. The civil power and the judicial are generally united, and exercised in each district by the collector or receiver of the imposts. This sort of public magistrates are generally known under the name of *Havildar* or *Thasildar*. They are generally Brahmans. This tribunal, chiefly intended for the collection of the taxes, takes cognizance of all affairs civil and criminal within its bounds, and determines upon all causes." Description of the Character, Manners, and Customs of the People of India, by the Abbé J. A. Dubois, Missionary in the Mysore, p. 494.

CHAPTER V.

The Taxes.

THE form of the government is one, the nature of the laws for the administration of justice is the other, of the two circumstances by which the condition of the people in all countries is chiefly determined. Of these two primary causes no result to a greater degree ensures the happiness or misery of the people, than the mode of providing for the pecuniary wants of the government, and the extent to which the agents of government, of whatever kind, are enabled to divide among themselves and their creatures, the annual produce of the land and labour of the community.

The matters of detail, which by their number and uncertainty have so exceedingly perplexed the servants of the Company, in the financial operations of the Indian government, cannot here be described. The general outline, and the more important effects, of that system of taxation which is described in the ancient books, are all that fall within the design of an account of the ancient state of the people. 1. "Of grain," says the ordinance of Menu, "an eighth part, a sixth, or a twelfth may be taken by the king;" to be determined, adds the gloss of the commentator Culluca, "by the difference of the soil, and the labour necessary to cultivate it."[1] 2. "He may also take a sixth part of the clear annual increase of trees, flesh-meat, honey, clarified butter, perfumes, medical substances, liquids, flowers, roots and fruit, of gathered leaves, pot-herbs, grass, utensils made with leather or cane, earthen pots, and all things made of stone."[2] 3. "Of cattle, of gems, of gold and silver, added each year to the capital stock, a fiftieth part may be taken by the king."[3] 4. "Having ascertained the rules of purchase and sale," says the law, "the length of the way, the expenses of food and of condiments, the charges of securing the goods carried, and the neat profits of trade, let the king oblige traders to pay taxes on their saleable commodities; after full consideration, let a king so levy those taxes continually in his

[1] Laws of Menu, ch. vii. 130. [2] Ibid. 131, 132. [3] Ibid. 130.

BOOK II. CHAP. V.

dominions, that both he and the merchant may receive a just compensation for their several acts."[1] 5. "Let the king order a mere trifle to be paid, in the name of the annual tax, by the meaner inhabitants of his realm who subsist by petty traffic: 6. By low handicraftsmen, artificers, and servile men, who support themselves by labour, the king may cause work to be done for a day in each month."[2] It is added; 7. "A military king, who takes even a fourth part of the crops of his realm at a time of urgent necessity, as of war or invasion, and protects his people to the utmost of his power, commits no sin. 8. The tax on the mercantile class, which in times of prosperity must be only a twelfth part of their crops, and a fiftieth of their personal profits, may be an eighth of their crops in a time of distress, or a sixth, which is the medium, or even a fourth in great public adversity; but a twentieth of their gains on money and other moveables is the highest tax: serving men, artisans, and mechanics, must assist by their labour, but at no time pay taxes."[3]

In these several articles is found an enumeration of all the objects of taxation; and a general expression of the modes and degrees of impost. We perceive taxes on the produce of land, taxes on the produce of labour, a tax on accumulation, a tax on sales, and poll taxes. In article 1, is exhibited a tax on the produce of land; In article 2, a tax both on the produce of land, and on the produce of labour; In article 3, is a tax on accumulation, at least in certain commodities; In article 4, is a tax on purchases and sales; In article 5, is one sort of poll tax; In article 6, is another.[4]

There are two primary qualities desirable in a system of taxation; and in them every thing is included.

The First is, to take from the people the smallest quantity possible of their annual produce.

The Second is, to take from them that which is taken with the smallest possible hurt or uneasiness.[5]

[1] Laws of Menu, ch. vii. 127, 128. [2] Ibid. 137, 138.

[3] Ibid. ch. x. 118, 120.

[4] So complete and comprehensive a system of taxation might have been received in evidence, it may be supposed, of some considerable advance in one department in civilized society.—W.

[5] The standard here devised for taxation, like that previously invented for law, is one by which no system in practice would be found free from fault, and by which it is not equitable therefore to try that of the Hindus.—W.

I. Of taking from the people more than enough of the matter of wealth, the causes are two; 1st, When the government consumes beyond the smallest amount sufficient to obtain the services which it yields: 2nd, When the collection of the taxes themselves costs more than the lowest sum at which, without sacrificing greater advantages, it is capable of being performed.

II. Of the hurt and uneasiness beyond the loss of what is taken away, which a system of taxation is liable to produce, the causes seem to be; 1. Uncertainty; 2. Inequality; 3. Impediment to production; 4. Injury to the good qualities, bodily or mental, of the people.

Of the first head and its subdivisions, no illustration is necessary; and a few words will suffice for the second.

1. Uncertainty may arise from two sources; 1. Uncertainty in the meaning of the words by which the tax is defined; 2. Uncertainty in the circumstances upon which the amount of the tax is made to depend; as if it were made to depend upon the weather, or the state of a man's health. Uncertainty in the meaning of the words opens a door to oppression and fraud, on the part of the collector. He will exact the largest sum consistent with the words, if he is not bribed; the lowest, if he is. Uncertainty, from whatever source, is a cause of uneasiness. The mind is continually haunted with the idea of the worst, and with all the fears which attend it; fears often very great and tormenting. As often as a source of chicanery is opened about the amount which the contributor should pay, a source of extortion is opened, and a source of oppression, necessary to effect the extortion.

2. Of the unequal partition of taxes, the necessary consequence is, a greater quantity of suffering than the same amount of taxes would produce, if more equally imposed; because the pain of the man who pays too much is out of all proportion greater than the pleasure of the man who pays too little. To make the burden of taxes equal, it should be made to press with equal severity upon every individual. This is not effected by a mere numerical proportion. The man who is taxed to the amount of one-tenth, and still more the man who is taxed to the amount of one-fifth or one-half, of an income of 100*l.* per annum, is taxed far more severely, than the man who is taxed to

an equal proportion of an income of 1000*l.* and to a prodigious degree more severely than the man who is taxed to an equal proportion of 10,000*l.* per annum.

3. On the mischievousness of all taxes which impede production it is needless to enlarge. It is only necessary to make them known, or rather acknowledged. 1. Of this sort are all taxes which take away any part of that property which has been already employed as capital; because there is always more or less of difficulty in replacing it from the fund destined for immediate consumption. 2. Of this sort also are all taxes which create any encouragement whatsoever, or any discouragement whatsoever, to any particular employment of capital in respect to other employments; for, as capital is always carried by a strong impulse to that employment which is the most productive, every thing which turns it out of the course which it would take of its own accord, turns so much of it out of a more, into a less productive channel.

4. That all taxes ought to be shunned which tend to lessen the amount of useful qualities in the people, will not be contradicted. Taxes upon medicines have a tendency to diminish health and strength. Taxes upon innocent amusements, as the sports of the field, have a tendency to drive the people to others that are hurtful. Taxes upon articles of consumption not hurtful, which have a tendency to supplant other that are, as tea and sugar to supplant intoxicating liquors, prompt to the consumption of the hurtful. Taxes upon law proceedings are a premium upon the practice of every species of iniquity. Lotteries are a direct encouragement to a habit of mind, with which no useful tendency can easily co-exist. And all taxes, of which the quantity due is not clear and certain, train the people, by continual practice, to a state of hardened perfection in mendacity, fraud, and perjury.

1. In the above list of the sacred ordinances concerning taxes, the first relates entirely to the tax on the produce of the soil. It offends against the rule of *certainty* to a high degree. The amount varies as one to one-half; and the variation is made to depend upon circumstances the uncertainty of which opens a boundless field to all the wretched arts of chicanery and fraud on the part of the people, and all the evils of oppression on the part of the

collectors. As the determination of the circumstances on which the amount of the assessment depends belongs of course, in such a state of society as that of the Hindus, to the agents of the treasury, a free career is afforded to all the baneful operations of favour and disfavour, of bribery and corruption. Whenever an option is granted between a less exaction and a greater, the violent propensity of all imperfect governments to excess in expense is sure in time to establish the greater. It would appear accordingly that a sixth part of the produce became the uniform tax in Hindustan; and that the indulgence in favour of the barren soils was extinguished. This is the state in which it was found by the Mohammedan conquerors.[1] And in Sacontala,[2] the king is described, at a much earlier period, as "that man whose revenue arises from a sixth part of his people's income." The source of variation and uncertainty from these causes was prodigiously enlarged by the power reserved to the king, of taking even a fourth of the crops, in times of distress. As he was himself the judge of these times of necessity, we may believe that they were of pretty frequent occurrence.[3]

2. In the second of these fiscal ordinances, a variety of products are enumerated, which, in a rude age, are either the spontaneous produce of the soil, as flowers, roots, grass; or obtained from the spontaneous produce, by some very simple process; as perfumes and medical substances, by expression; flesh-meat and honey, by killing the animals which produce them; and these as costing little in point of labour, are all taxed at the highest rate imposed upon grain. By one of these capricious arrangements which abound in the institutions of a rude people, utensils made of leather, cane, earth, and stone, in the production of which labour is the principal agent, are placed under the same exaction as the spontaneous productions of the

1 Ayeen Akbery, p. 347.

2 An ancient Sanscrit poem of the dramatic form, translated by Sir William Jones: See the beginning of the fifth act.

3 This is a wholly gratuitous assumption, and unwarranted by the text referred to, which indicates sufficiently the kind of distress intended—invasion or war. Circumstances not of the king's contrivance, and obvious to his people. Nor was there much uncertainty in the amount of the assessment in times of peace. The division of the country into townships and village communities, which appears to have existed from the time of Manu, rendered the business of valuation easy, and protected individuals from extortion.—W.

soil. The consequence must have been to render these commodities proportionably dear.

In the execution of this ordinance, there must have been excessive uncertainty, and excessive expense. What is meant by "annual increase?" The "annual increase of trees" is an absurd expression: trees grow not by the year. What shall be said of such expressions, as "the annual increase" of "clarified butter," "of flesh-meat," "of flowers"? These are not commodities, which continue accumulating, till the amount of the annual produce is seen entire at the end of the year:[1] but commodities daily brought into existence and daily consumed. To collect the tax upon such commodities, a daily visit in every family would hardly suffice. In the execution of this ordinance, the temptation to the incessant practice of all the arts of fraud, on the part of the people, and the powers of oppression bestowed upon the collectors, were well calculated to fill society with immorality and suffering.

3. In the third of the above ordinances are enumerated the principal classes of moveables known to the Hindus. It seems to be the addition made in any year to the previous stock, and not the previous stock itself, of which one-fiftieth is taken in the way of tax. In a society, full of knowledge and industry, this would have been a tax upon capital, and therefore mischievous: in Hindustan, where gold, silver, and gems, were most commonly hoarded, and not devoted to production, it would not have been easy to find a less objectionable tax. Unless in a state of society rapidly progressive, or a state in which there is excessive fluctuation of fortunes, that is, excessive misery, it would be a very unproductive tax.

4. In the words of the fourth ordinance is described a tax on all purchases and sales.[2] The circumstances on

[1] This verbal criticism is wasted. The phrase "increase of trees," is Sir William Jones's—not Manu's. The original says a sixth part of trees (that is, of their produce), of clarified butter, &c. When taxes were paid in kind, some fixed proportion of the articles of daily consumption was necessarily specified; it is clearly impossible that the rate should have been very rigorously levied, and all that is intended is to limit the demands of the purveyors.—W.

[2] The main object of the fourth law is nothing more than to establish a duty or charge of customs, and is no more objectionable than similar imposts in all countries; a further object is to enjoin due consideration of charges and expenses, and to make the customs as light as is consistent with the fair claims of the government. Nothing is said of transit duties, and the fair inference from the expression ascertaining 'the length of the way,' is, that there were no transit charges, the customs being levied only at the end of the journey.—W.

which the amount is made to depend are so uncertain, as to constitute a great seminary of fraud on the one hand, and a great office of oppression on the other. The tax is also hurtful to production, by impeding circulation; that is, the passage of property from a situation in which it is less, to one in which it is more useful. The mode in which, at least in modern times, it was chiefly raised, that of transit duties, multiplied to excess, obstructed all that encouragement to industry which is afforded by the interchange of commodities, not only between different countries, but one province and another of the same country. As often as property which has been, and is to be, employed as capital, is bought and sold, it is a tax upon capital.

5. A poll tax, when paid in money, or any other common measure of value, is chiefly objectionable on account of its inequality; as the same sum is a very different burden to different persons.

6. A poll tax paid in labour is somewhat less objectionable in point of equality, though the same portion of his time may be a much greater burden upon one man than it is upon another. It is chiefly objectionable on account of the loss of time, and of property, which it occasions to those who have it to pay. In a well-ordered society, accordingly, where every man's time and labour are disposed of to the best advantage, it has no place.

Some of these ordinances are modified, or the words rendered a little more precise, in the Gentoo Code translated by Mr. Halhed. The following are examples. If a man purchase goods in his own country, and sell them again there, one-tenth of his profit goes to the magistrate. If the purchase took place in a foreign kingdom, and the sale in his own, one-twentieth only is the share of the magistrate.[1] If a man, having purchased flowers, or roots, as ginger, radishes and the like, or honey, or grass, or firewood, from another kingdom, sells them in his own, the magistrate is entitled to one-sixth of his profits.[2] What was the reason of severe exaction in such cases does not appear. Rude times give not reasons. In the days of

[1] The political economists of Hindustan, and those of the mercantile theory in modern Europe, proceeded on different views.

[2] Halhed's Gentoo Code, ch. xxi. sect. 4. On sales of very small amount, or on those of young heifers (the cow was a sacred animal), no tax was levied.

BOOK II. CHAP. V.

Menu these taxes appear to have been much more moderate; a fiftieth of mercantile profits being the ordinary, and a twentieth the extraordinary tax.

In this system of taxation, other sources are of small importance; the revenue of the sovereign arises almost wholly from the artificial produce of the land. To understand in what manner the people of Hindustan were affected by taxation, the circumstances of this impost are all that require to be very minutely explored.

The tenure of land in Hindustan has been the source of violent controversies among the servants of the Company; and between them and other Europeans. They first sprung up amid the disputes between Mr. Hastings and Mr. Francis, respecting the best mode of taxing Bengal. And they have been carried on with great warmth, and sometimes with great acrimony, ever since. Of these controversies the account will be due, at the periods when they occur. At present it will suffice to bring to light the circumstances which appear to ascertain the ancient state of the country, in respect to the distribution of property in the land.[1]

In a state of society resembling our own, in which property is secure, and involves very extensive rights or privileges, the affections which it excites are so strong,[2] and give such a force to the associations by which the idea of it is compacted and formed, that in minds of little range, whose habits are blind and obstinate, the particulars combined together under the idea of property appear to be connected by nature, and not, without extreme injustice, to be made to exist apart.

At different times, however, very different rights and advantages are included under the idea of property.[3] At

[1] See the first volume of the continuation.

[2] It would be difficult to find any country in which the affections excited by property, are stronger than they are in India. If this be a proof of civilization, then are the Hindus an eminently civilized race.—W.

[3] The notions of the Hindus, in regard to property, have been strangely overlooked in what follows, or Mr. Mill would not have found analogies between the laws of the civilized Hindus and the practices of the barbarous nations of Africa. Had he referred to Mr. Colebrooke's translation of the Hindu law of inheritance, he would have found a much more subtle disquisition on the origin and nature of property, than that into which he has entered, and much more simply stated, showing that property originates not in written law, but in popular recognition; a conclusion precisely the same as that which he more elaborately describes as "combinations of benefits determined and chosen by the society." With regard also to the sources of property,

very early periods of society it included very few: originally, nothing more perhaps than use during occupancy, the commodity being liable to be taken by another, the moment it was relinquished by the hand which held it: but one privilege is added to another as society advances: and it is not till a considerable progress has been made in civilization, that the right of property involves all the powers which are ultimately bestowed upon it.

It is hardly necessary to add, that the different combinations of benefits which are included under the idea of property, at different periods of society, are all equally arbitrary; that they are not the offspring of nature, but the creatures of will; determined, and chosen by the society, as that arrangement with regard to useful objects, which is, or is pretended to be, the best for all.

It is worthy of remark, that property in moveables was established; and that it conveyed most of the powers which are at any time assigned to it; while, as yet, property in land had no existence. So long as men continue to derive their subsistence from hunting; so long, indeed, as they continue to derive it from their flocks and herds, the land is enjoyed in common.[1] Even when they begin to derive it partly from the ground, though the man who has cultivated a field is regarded as possessing in it a property till he has reaped his crop, he has no better title to it than another for the succeeding year.[2]

---

it would be difficult to find a more comprehensive list than that comprised in the text of Gautama; "property is by inheritance, purchase, partition, seizure or finding, and in addition by acceptance for a Brahman, conquest for a Kshatriya, gain for a Vaisya, and a Sudra, inclusive in the latter instance of wages." Colebrooke's Dayabhúga, 244. Manu has a similar description of the sources of property, showing sufficiently a complex system of society, in which such means were recognised: "there are seven virtuous means of acquiring property, inheritance, acquirement, purchase, conquest, lending at interest, husbandry or commerce, and acceptance of gifts from the good." x. 115. The Sanscrit term for property is of itself decisive of the comprehensive notions attached to it. Swatwa is the abstract of Swa, suum, or own-ship, meaning what is absolutely and unqualifiedly one's own.—W.

[1] There are no traces in the traditions of the Hindus of their ever having been a pastoral people, or a nation of hunters. The law that "the land is his by whom it is first cleared," indicates on the contrary an immigrant people, entering on the possession of an uncultivated country, and at once setting to work to clear and till it. It is a law expressively applicable to the original back woodsmen of America.—W.

[2] "Suevorum gens est longe maxima et bellicosissima Germanorum omnium. Ii centum pagos habere dicuntur. * * * Privati et separati agri apud eos nihil est; neque *longius anno* remanere uno in loco, incolendi causa licet: neque multum frumento, sed maximam partem lacte atque pecore vivunt,

In prosecuting the advantages which are found to spring from the newly-invented method of deriving the means of subsistence from the ground, experience in time discovers, that much obstruction is created by restricting the right of ownership to a single year; and that food would be provided in greater abundance, if, by a greater permanence, men were encouraged to a more careful cultivation. To make, however, that belong to one man, which formerly belonged to all, is a change, to which men do not easily reconcile their minds.[1] In a thing of so much importance as the land, the change is a great revolution. To overcome the popular resistance, that expedient which appears to have been the most generally successful, is, to vest the sovereign, as the representative of the society, with that property in the land which belongs to the society; and the sovereign parcels it out to individuals, with all those powers of ownership, which are regarded as most favourable to the extraction from the land of those benefits which it is calculated to yield. When a sovereign takes possession of a country by conquest, he naturally appropriates to himself all the benefits which the ideas of his soldiers permit.

In many of the rude parts of Africa, the property of the land is understood to reside in the sovereign; it is in the shape of a donation from him, that individuals are allowed to cultivate; and when the son, as is generally the case, succeeds to the father, it is only by a prolongation of the royal bounty, which, in some places at least, is

---

multumque sunt in venationibus." Cæsar. De Bell. Gal. lib. iv. cap. 1 Among some tribes of negroes on the coast of Africa, each individual must obtain the consent of the chief before he has liberty to cultivate a field, and is only protected in its possession till he has reaped the crop for which he has toiled. Histoire Générale des Voyages, tom. v. ch. vii. sect. 5. "Neque quisquam agri modum certum, aut fines proprios habet; sed magistratus ac principes, in annos singulos, gentibus cognationibusque hominum qui una coierunt quantum et quo loco visum est agri attribuunt; atque anno post, alio transire cogunt." Cæsar. De Bello Gallico, lib. vi. cap. 20.

. . . . . . Rigidi Getæ,
Immetata quibus jugera liberas
Fruges et Cererem ferunt,
Nec cultura placet longior annua;
Defunctumque laboribus
Æquali recreat sorte vicarius.—Hor. lib. iii. Od. 24.

[1] Yet this is evidently the familiar principle of the Hindu law, the land is his who clears it, not for a year, or for any given time, but for ever; there is no limitation.—W.

not obtained without a formal solicitation.[1] It is known, that in Egypt the king was the sole proprietor of the land; and one-fifth of the produce appears to have been yielded to him as a revenue or rent.[2] Throughout the Ottoman dominions, the Sultan claims to himself the sole property in land.[3] The same has undoubtedly been the situation of Persia, both in ancient and modern times.[4] "It is established," says the late intelligent Governor of Java, "from every source of inquiry, that the sovereign in Java is the lord of the soil."[5] And when the fact is established in regard to Java, it is established with regard to all that part of the eastern islands, which in point of manners and civilization resembled Java. It is not dis-

[1] Histoire Générale des Voyages, tom. iv. ch. xiii. p. 203. Modern Universal History, vol. xvii. p. 322. I am induced to transcribe the following passage from Mr. Park; " Concerning property in the soil; it appeared to me that the lands and native woods were considered as belonging to the king, or (where the government was not monarchical) to the state. When any individual of free condition had the means of cultivating more land than he actually possessed, he applied to the chief man of the district, who allowed him an extension of territory, on condition of forfeiture, if the lands were not brought into cultivation by a given period. The condition being fulfilled, the soil became vested in the possessor; and, for aught that appeared to me, descended to his heirs." Travels in Africa, p. 260, 261.

" All the land is said to belong to the king; but if a man chooses to clear a spot and erect a town, he may; the land is free for any of the people. If a stranger, indeed, that is, an European, should wish to settle among them, he must make a present of goods to the king." Correspondence of John Kizell, on the state of the people on the river Sherbro, Appendix to the Sixth Report of the African Institution, p. 133.

[2] Herodot. lib. ii. cap. cix, says, that Sesostris, as he was told by the priests, divided all the land of Egypt among the people, and thence raised his revenues, imposing an annual tribute on each portion; και απο τουτου τας προσοδους ποιησασθαι, επιταξαντα αποφορην επιτελειν κατ' ενιαυτον. See too, Strabo, lib. xvii. p. 1135. Diod. Sic. lib. i. sect. 2. cap. xxiv.

[3] Volney's Travels in Syria and Egypt, vol. ii. p. 402, et passim. De l'Egypte, par le Général Reynier, p. 66, 51.

[4] For information on this point, see Herodot. lib. iii. ; lib. iv. cap. xlii. ; Sir William Ouseley's Translation of Ebn Haukal, an Arabian geographer, who lived in the tenth century, p. 137 ; Institutes of Timur; Ayeen Akbery; Chardin's Travels.

[5] Gov. Raffles' Minute on Java, p. 6; also, p. 79, 108. The distribution of the land among the Peruvians was as follows: One-third part of it was dedicated to, and cultivated for, the gods; that is, the priests. Another third part the Inca reserved for himself, for the maintenance of his court and of his armies. The remaining third he distributed to the people, assigning an established portion to each family. " But no particular man," (says Acosta, Nat. and Mor. Hist. of the Indies. book VI. ch. xv.), " possessed any thing proper to himself of this third portion, neither did the Indians ever possess any, if it were not by special grace from the Inca." Garcilasso de la Vega tells us (part I. book V. ch. i.), that it was only when there was more land than sufficed for the people, that the Inca and the Sun received their full thirds; when that was not the case, these portions were diminished to augment to the proper proportion that of the people. See too Carli, Lettres sur l'Amérique, let. xv. For great services land was given in full property; Acosta, book VI. ch. xviii. ; and this is another remarkable coincidence with what existed in Hindustan.

BOOK II. CHAP. V.

puted that in China the whole property of the soil is vested in the Emperor.[1] By the laws of the Welsh, in the ninth century, all the land of the kingdom was declared to belong to the king;[2] and we may safely, says Mr. Turner, believe, that the same law prevailed while the Britons occupied the whole island.[3]

To those who contemplate the prevalence of this institution, among nations contiguous to the Hindus, and resembling them in the state of civilisation, it cannot appear surprising, that among them, too, the sovereign was the lord of the soil. The fact is, indeed, very forcibly implied, in many of the ancient laws and institutions. "Of old hoards," says one of the ordinances of Menu, "and precious minerals in the earth, the king is entitled to half by reason of his general protection, and because he is the superior lord

[1] Abbé Grosier, Desc. de la Chine; but Mr. Barrow's testimony is the most direct and satisfactory. "The emperor," says he, "is considered as the sole proprietary of the soil, but the tenant is never turned out of possession as long as he continues to pay his rent, which is calculated at about one-tenth of what his farm is capable of yielding; and though the holder of lands can only be considered as a tenant at will, yet it is his own fault if he should be dispossessed." Barrow's China, p. 397.

[2] Leges Wallicæ, Hoel. cap. 337.

[3] Turner's History of the Anglo-Saxons, vol. ii. chap. iii.—M.

The greater part of the text and of the notes here is wholly irrelevant. The illustrations drawn from Mohammedan practice, supposing them to be correct, have nothing to do with the laws and rights of the Hindus. They are not, however, even accurate; and Mr. Mill's guides have misled him. According to the Mohammedan law a conquered country is, at the moment of its subjugation, at the disposal of the conqueror; he may then either partition it amongst his followers, or allow the inhabitants to retain it on payment of a fixed portion of the produce. In either case he relinquishes the right of the soil acquired by conquest, and no other is admitted. Such was the state of things in Hindustan. Galloway on the Constitution of India, p. 31.

With regard to the right of the Hindu Raja, it is by no means analogous to those of the rulers of Egypt, or of Turkey, or of Africa, supposing them to be accurately stated in the text; and the texts which have been conceived to warrant such an inference are wrongly interpreted or understood. He is not lord of the "soil," he is lord of the earth, of the whole earth or kingdom, not of any parcel or allotment of it; he may punish a cultivator for neglect, in order to protect his acknowledged share of the crop; and when he gives away lands and villages, he gives away his share of the revenue. No donee would ever think of following up such a donation by actual occupancy, he would be resisted if he did. The truth is, that the rights of the king are a theory, an abstraction; poetically and politically speaking, he is the lord, the master, the protector of the earth (Prithvi pati, Bhumiswara, Bhúmipa), just as he is the lord, the master, the protector of men (Narapati, Naréswara, Nripa). Such is the purport of the common title of a king; but he is no more the actual proprietor of the soil than he is of his subjects; they need not his permission to buy it or to sell it, or to give it away, and would be very much surprised and aggrieved if the king or his officers were to buy or sell or give away the ground which they cultivated. In a subsequent page, the author is forced to admit, that all which is valuable in the soil, after the deduction of what is due to the sovereign, belongs of incontestable right to the Indian husbandman. p. 224.—W.

of the soil."[1] The king, as proprietor, and as fully entitled to an equitable return for the land which he has let, is empowered to punish the cultivator for bad cultivation. "If land be injured, by the fault of the farmer himself, as if he fails to sow it in due time, he shall be fined ten times as much as the king's share of the crop, that might otherwise have been raised; but only five times as much, if it was the fault of his servants without his knowledge."[2] Among other ancient memorials of Hindu institutions and manners, are certain inscriptions engraved on durable materials. Some of them are records of grants of land, commonly to favourite Brahmens; and they afford strong indication of the proprietary rights of the sovereign. The sovereign gives away villages and lands, not empty, but already occupied by cultivators, and paying rent.[3] It appears from an ordinance of Yagyawalcya, one of the most sacred of the law sages, that the kings alienated their lands within their dominions, in the same manner, and by the same title, as they alienated any portion of their revenues.[4] On this point, it is of material importance to

[1] Laws of Menu, ch. viii. 39. I have here substituted the word *supreme* for the word *paramount*, used by Sir William Jones, which has no meaning but as it relates to the feudal institutions of Europe, and is calculated to convey an erroneous idea.

[2] Laws of Menu, ch. viii. 243.

[3] See a royal grant of land, engraved on a copper plate, bearing date twenty-three years before Christ; and discovered among the ruins at Monguir, translated by Mr. Wilkins, Asiat. Researches, i. 123. "Be it known," says the inscription (p. 126), "that I have given the above-mentioned town of Meseeka, whose limits include the fields where the cattle graze, above and below the surface, with all the lands belonging to it, together with all the Mango and Modhoo trees; all its waters, and all their banks and verdure; all its *rents*, all its tolls and fines for crimes, and rewards for catching thieves. In it there shall be no molestation, no passage for troops," &c. It is here remarkable that the sovereign, as well as the proprietary, rights are given away; so indissolubly were these united in the minds and institutions of the Hindus. In the same manner in another grant of land found at Tanna, and bearing date An. Christi, 1018, the land is given away "with its herbage, wood, and water, and with power of punishing for the ten crimes." Asiat. Researches, i. 364.

[4] Let a king, *having given land*, or *assigned revenue*, cause his gift to be written for the information of good princes, who will succeed him, either on prepared cloth, or on a plate of copper, sealed above with his signet; having described his ancestors and himself, the dimensions or quantity of the gift, with its metes and bounds, if it be land, and set his own hand to it, and specified the time, let him render his donation firm." See the original, and the translation of Sir Wm. Jones, Asiat. Res. iii. 50.

The Digest of Hindu Law, translated by Colebrooke (i. 460), declares, "By conquest, the earth became the property of the holy Parasu Rama, by gift, the property of the sage Casyapa; and, committed by him to Cshatriyas, for the sake of protection, became their protective property successively held by powerful conquerors, and not by subjects, cultivating the soil." It further appears, from the same passage, that by agreement with the sovereign, and

BOOK II. CHAP. V.

remark, that, up to the time when the interests of the Company's servants led them to raise a controversy about the rights of the Zemindars, every European visitor, without one exception that I have found, agrees in the opinion, that the sovereign was the owner of the soil.[1]

---

not otherwise, a tenure of more than one year may be required; but without such agreement, the cultivator might be turned away at the end of every year, if a larger rent was offered by any other. It was highly necessary to quote this passage, though it is affirmed by Col. Wilks, to be a law manufactured by the complaisant Brahmens who made the Digest, on purpose to suit the opinions of the ruling power, at that time in love with the Zemindarry system. Col. Wilks affirms, that there is nothing whatsoever which the Brahmens cannot make to be law, on a similar occasion. And it is at least certain, that part of what they give as law has been proved to be at variance with all that appears either of their present or ancient institutions.

"That there were no hereditary estates in India; for that all the land belonged to the king, which he disposed of at pleasure." Persian authority, quoted by Stewart, Hist. of Bengal, p. 132.

[1] It is proper to adduce the more remarkable instances. The ancient Greeks who visited India expressly inform us, that the kings were the sole proprietors of the soil, and that a fourth part of the produce was actually paid them in kind as the rent or tribute. Strabo, lib. xv. p. 1030. Diod. Sic. lib. ii. p. 53.

"Diodorus, Strabo, the voyagers and travellers of later times, without any exception that has fallen within the scope of my limited reading, the authors of the Lettres Edifiantes, and the European travellers who visited the court of Aurungzebe in the latter part of the seventeenth century, Bernier, Thevenot, Chardin, Tavernier, and, I believe, Manouchi, are unanimous in denying the existence of private landed property in India." Wilks, Hist. Sketches, p. 114.

"In revenue, the Emperor doubtless exceeds either Turk or Persian, or any eastern prince; the sums I dare not name, but the reason. All the land is his, no man has a foot." Sir T. Roe to the Archbishop of Canterbury, Churchill, i. 803.

"Toutes les terres du royaume," says Bernier, "estant en propre au roi," &c. Suite de Mém. sur l'Emp. du Grand Mogul, t. ii. p. 10. See, also, p. 150, 174, 178: at p. 180, he makes the following remark; "Ces trois états, Turkie, Persie, et l'Hindoustan, comme ils ont tous osté ce *Mien* et ce *Tien*, à l'égard des fonds de terre et de la propriété des possessions, qui est le fondement de tout ce qu'il y a de beau et de bon dans le monde, ne peuvent qu'ils ne se resemblent de bien près." Montesquieu seems to have been fully aware of this important fact.—"Les lois des Indes, *qui donnent les terres aux princes*, et *ôtent aux particuliers l'esprit de propriété*, augmentent les mauvais effets du climat, c'est à dire, la paresse naturelle." Esp. des Loix, liv. xiv. ch. 6.

"All the lands in India are considered as the property of the king, except some hereditary districts possessed by Hindoo princes." Dow's Hindostan, preface, p. xiii.

"All the lands in the kingdom," says Mr. Orme (Fragments, p. 403) "belong to the king; therefore all the lands in the provinces are subject to the Nabob. With him, or his representatives, farmers agree for the cultivation of such an extent, on reserving to themselves such a proportion of the produce. This proportion is settled according to the difficulty or ease of raising the grain, and seldom exceeds a third." One-third to the cultivator, and two-thirds to the proprietor, would be accounted a rack-rent in England. Mr. Orme says again, (Ibid. p. 414), "The king, by being proprietor of the lands, sells to his subjects their subsistence, instead of receiving supplies from them." Mr. Holwell says (Interesting Historical Events, i. 220), "The rents of the lands are the property of the emperor." And again, "The tenures of the ryots are irrevocable, as long as they pay the rent; and by the laws of Hindostan, they must be twelve months in arrear before they can be ejected." Ibid.

Wherever the Hindus have remained under the influence of their ancient customs and laws, the facts correspond with the inference which would be drawn from these laws. Under the direction of the Governor-General of Bengal, a journey was undertaken, in the year 1766, by Mr. Motte, to the diamond-mines in the province of Orissa. In a narrative of his journey, he gives an account of the distribution of the land at Sumbhulpoor, which till that time had remained under the native government. Each village being rated to the government at a certain quantity of rice, which was paid in kind, the land is thus divided among the inhabitants. To every man, as soon as he arrives at the proper age, is granted such a quantity of arable land as is estimated to produce 242⅛ measures of rice, of which he must pay 60⅝ measures, or about one-fourth to the rajah or king. Mr. Motte adds; "The reserved rent of three or four villages, being one-fourth the produce of the land, is applied to the use of the rajah's household. The reserved rent of the rest is given to his relations or principal servants, who, by these means have all the inhabitants dependent on them."[1] Dr. Buchanan gives a particular account of the manner in which the crop, in those parts of India which are most purely Hindu, is divided between the inhabitants and the government. In Bengal it is not allowed to be cut down

[1] A Narrative of a Journey to the Diamond Mines of Sumbhulpoor, in the province of Orissa, by Thomas Motte, Esq., Asiat. Annual Register, i., Miscellaneous Tracts, p. 75. Mr. Motte further informs us, that every man at Sumbhulpoor is enrolled as a soldier, and is allowed half a measure of rice in the day for his subsistence, while his wife cultivates the farm. He seems to say that this subsistence is given to him by the wife from the produce of the farm. —M.

Sumbhulpore is a very unfortunate exemplification of the "ancient" system of the Hindus. The town was founded only two centuries before, by an adventurer from Upper India. Mr. Motte terms the government strictly feudal; and this explains the reason of every man's being a soldier, and the principle of the division of the lands, each man holding in fief a grant of land from his liege lord, on condition of military service. It may be doubted if Mr. Motte has given us a complete view of the system, or it would have been found that the military landlords were a distinct class from the people of the country. The latter being not Hindus at all, but Goands and Bheels; and the former alone being Hindus of the military tribe, or Rajputs, adventurers from which tribe are known to have settled in various uncultivated parts of Chattesgher, precisely on the plan of the German invaders of Britain and Gaul; the leader reserving to himself a portion of the conquered land, and distributing the rest amongst his retainers. Such a system is a very different thing from that delineated by Manu. Under any circumstances, however, it would have been most unreasonable to have had recourse to Sumbhulpore, for an illustration of the ancient laws of the Hindus, as it is the capital of a district, the greater part of which is inaccessible mountain, and impervious thicket, and in which most of the inhabitants live in a state little more civilized than that of the savages of Australia.—W.

BOOK II. CHAP. V.

till the rent or tax is first paid; but in those countries to which his journey principally relates, it is the custom, after the grain has been thrashed out in the field, to collect it into heaps and then to divide it. A heap generally consists of about 110 Winchester bushels, of which he presents the following distribution as a specimen of the partition which is usually made. For the gods, that is, for the priests at their temples, are deducted five seers, containing about one-third of a Winchester gallon each; for charity, or for the mendicant Brahmens, an equal quantity; for the astrologer and the Brahmen of the village, one seer each: for the barber, the potmaker, the washerman, and the Vasaradava, who is both carpenter and blacksmith, two seers each; for the measurer, four seers; for the Aduca, a kind of beadle, seven seers; for the village chief, eight seers, out of which he has to furnish the village sacrifices; and for the accomptant ten seers. All these perquisites are the same, whatever be the size of the heap beyond a measure of about twenty-five Winchester bushels. When these allowances are withdrawn, the heap is measured; and for every candaca which it contains, a measure equal to 5,1-20th Winchester bushels, there is again deducted half a seer to the village watchmen, two and a half seers to the accomptant, as much to the chief of the village; and the bottom of the heap, about an inch thick, mixed with the cow-dung which in order to purify it had been spread on the ground, is given to the Nirgunty, or conductor of water. These several deductions, on a heap of twenty candacas, or 110 Winchester bushels, amount to about $5\frac{1}{4}$ per cent. on the gross produce. Of the remainder, 10 per cent. is paid to the collectors of the revenue, as their wages or hire; and the heap is last of all divided into halves between the king and the cultivator.[1]

From these facts only one conclusion can be drawn, that the property of the soil resided in the sovereign; for if it did not reside in him, it will be impossible to show to whom it belonged. The cultivators were left a bare compensation, often not so much as a bare compensation, for the

[1] Buchanan's Journey through the Mysore, etc., i. 2, 3, 130, 194, 265. "This simple mode of rating lands for half their yearly produce is derived from the remotest antiquity in different parts of Hindustan, and still invariably prevails in such countries as were left unsubdued by the Mahomedans, like Tanjore, where the ancient Indian forms of administration are, for the most part, preserved entire." British India Analyzed, i. 195.

labour and cost of cultivation; they got the benefit of their labour: all the benefit of the land went to the king.[1]

Upon the state of facts, in those places where the present practices of the Hindus have not been forced into a disconformity with their ancient institutions, the fullest light has been thrown, by those servants of the Company who made the inquiries requisite for the introduction of a regular system of finance into the extensive regions in the south of India added to the British dominions during the administrations of the Marquisses Cornwallis and Wellesley. Place, Munro, Thackeray, Hodgson, were happily men of talents; sufficiently enlightened to see things which were before them with their naked eyes; and not through the mist of English anticipations. From the reports of these meritorious gentlemen, presented to their superiors, the Committee of the House of Commons, which inquired into East India affairs in 1810, have drawn the following as a general picture: "A village, geographically considered, is a tract of country, comprising some hundreds, or thousands, of acres of arable and waste land. Politically viewed, it resembles a corporation or township. Its proper establishment of officers and servants consists of the following descriptions: The *Potail*, or head inhabitant, who has the general superintendence of the affairs of the village, settles the disputes of the inhabitants, attends to the police, and performs the duty of collecting the revenues within his village: The *Curnum*, who keeps the accounts of cultivation, and registers every thing connected with it: The *Tallier* and *Totie*; the duty of the former appearing to consist in a wider and more enlarged sphere of action, in gaining information of crimes and offences, and in escorting and protecting persons travelling from one village to another; the province of the latter appearing to be more immediately confined to the

1 The missionary Dubois, with his singular opportunities of correct information, says peremptorily: "Creditors can have no hold on the real estate of their debtors, because the Hindus have no property in the soil. The lands which they cultivate are the domain of the prince, who is the sole proprietor. He can resume them at his pleasure, and give them to another to cultivate. Even the huts in which they live, built of mud and covered with thatch, are not their own. All belongs to the prince; and if a man, for any reason whatever, quits his habitation in the village, he can by no means dispose of it to another, although it were constructed by his own hands. The only property they possess is their few cows and buffaloes, and upon these no creditor is allowed to lay his hands; because, if deprived of his cattle, he would be unable to cultivate the land, whence an injury would accrue to the prince." Description, etc., of the People of India, by the Abbé Dubois, p. 496.

village, consisting, among other duties, in guarding the crops, and assisting in measuring them: The *Boundary-man*, who preserves the limits of the village, or gives evidence respecting them in cases of dispute: The *Superintendent of water-courses and tanks*, who distributes the water for the purposes of agriculture: The *Brahmen*, who performs the village worship: The *Schoolmaster*, who is seen teaching the children in the villages to read and write in the sand: The *Calendar Brahmen*, or astrologer, who proclaims the lucky, or unpropitious periods for sowing and thrashing: The *Smith* and *Carpenter*, who manufacture the implements of agriculture, and build the dwelling of the ryot: The *Potman* or potter: The *Washerman:* The *Barber:* The *Cow-keeper*, who looks after the cattle: The *Doctor:* The *Dancing Girl*, who attends at rejoicings: The *Musician*, and the *Poet*.

"Under this simple form of municipal government, the inhabitants of the country have lived, from time immemorial. The boundaries of the villages have been seldom altered: and though the villages themselves have been sometimes injured, and even desolated by war, famine, and disease, the same name, the same limits, the same interests and even the same families, have continued for ages. The inhabitants give themselves no trouble about the breaking up and division of kingdoms; while the village remains entire, they care not to what power it is transferred, or to what sovereign it devolves; its internal economy remains unchanged; the Potail is still the head inhabitant, and still acts as the petty judge and magistrate, and collector or renter of the village."[1]

These villages appear to have been not only a sort of

[1] Fifth Report, Commit. 1810, p. 85. See, in "Considerations on the State of India," by A. Fraser Tytler, i. 113, a description of a village in Bengal, which shows that the Indian continent was pervaded by this institution.

An association of a similar kind existed among the Mexicans. Robertson's America, iii. 283.

Some curious strokes of resemblance appear in the following particulars of the Celtic manners, in the highlands and islands of Scotland. "The peculiarities which strike the native of a commercial country, proceeded in a great measure from the want of money. To the servants and dependants, that were not domestics, were appropriated certain portions of land for their support. Macdonald has a piece of ground yet, called the bard's, or senachie's field. When a beef was killed for the house, particular parts were claimed as fees by the several officers, or workmen. The head belonged to the smith, and the udder of a cow to the piper; the weaver had likewise his particular part; and so many pieces followed these prescriptive claims, that the laird's was at last but little." Johnson's Hebrides.

small republic, but to have enjoyed to a great degree the community of goods. Mr. Place, the collector in the jaghire district at Madras, informs us, that "Every village considers itself a distinct society; and its general concerns the sole object of the inhabitants at large: a practice," he adds, "which surely redounds as much to the public good as theirs; each having, in some way or other, the assistance of the rest; the labours of all yield the rent; they enjoy the profit, proportionate to their original interest, and the loss falls light. It consists exactly with the principles upon which the advantages are derived from the division of labour; one man goes to market, while the rest attend to the cultivation and the harvest; each has his particular occupation assigned to him, and insensibly labours for all. Another practice very frequently prevails, of each proprietor changing his lands every year. It is found in some of the richest villages; and intended, I imagine, to obviate that inequality to which a fixed distribution would be liable."[1]

The state of taxation is described by the same committee, in the following terms: "By the custom of the Hindu government, the cultivators were entitled to one half of the paddy produce (that is, grain in the husk) depending on the periodical rains. Of the crops from the dry grain lands, watered by artificial means, the share of the cultivator was about two thirds. Before the harvest commenced, the quantity of the crop was ascertained, in the presence of the inhabitants and village servants, by the survey of persons unconnected with the village, who, from habit, were particularly skilful and expert in judging of the amount of the produce, and who, in the adjustment of this business, were materially aided by a reference to the produce of former years, as recorded by the accomptants of the villages. The quantity which belonged to the government being thus ascertained, it was received in kind, or in money." Of garden produce, of which the culture was more difficult, a smaller portion was taken; because, if field culture was taxed as much as it could bear, it seems to have been supposed that garden culture, at an equal rate of taxation, could not have been carried on.

"Such," continue the committee, "were the rights of the ryots, according to the ancient usage of the country. In consequence, however, of the changes introduced by the

1 Fifth Report, ut supra, p. 723.

BOOK II. CHAP. V.

Mohamedan conquest, and the many abuses which later times had established, the share really enjoyed by the ryots was often reduced to a sixth, and but seldom exceeded a fifth. The assessments had no bounds but those which limited the supposed ability of the husbandman. The effects of this unjust system were considerably augmented by the custom which had become common with the Zemindars, of sub-renting their lands to farmers, whom they armed with unrestricted powers of collection, and who were thus enabled to disregard, whenever it suited their purpose, the engagements they entered into with the ryots; besides practising every species of oppression, which an unfeeling motive of self-interest could suggest. If they agreed with the cultivators at the commencement of the year, for a rent in money, and the season proved an abundant one, they then insisted on receiving their dues in kind. When they did take their rents in specie, they hardly ever failed to collect a part of them before the harvest-time had arrived and the crops were cut; which reduced the ryots to the necessity of borrowing from money-lenders, at a heavy interest of 3, 4, and 5 per cent. per month, the sums requisite to make good the anticipated payments that were demanded of them. If, from calamity or other cause, the ryots were the least remiss in the discharge of their rents, the officers of the renters were instantly quartered upon them; and these officers they were obliged to maintain, until they might be recalled on the demand being satisfied. It was also a frequent practice with the renters to remove the inhabitants from fertile lands, in order to bestow them on their friends and favourites; and to oblige the ryots to assist them, where they happened to be farmers, in the tilling of their lands; and to furnish them gratuitously with labourers, bullocks, carts, and straw."[1]

The two terms, Ryot and Zemindar, introduced into this passage, are of frequent recurrence in the history of India and require to be explained. By ryots are always denoted the husbandmen; the immediate cultivators of the ground The Persian term Zemindar, introduced by the Mahomedan conquerors, was in Bengal, and certain other parts of India the name of a certain sort of middleman, between the cultivator who raised the crop, and the king, who received the

[1] Fifth Report, ut supra, p. 81, 82.

greater part of the net produce. Into the controversy respecting the nature of the interest which the Zemindar possessed in the land with respect to which he performed his function of middleman, I shall not at present enter. Another occasion will present itself for the examination of that subject. It is here sufficient to say, that in districts sometimes of greater, sometimes of less extent, a person, under the title of Zemindar, received the share of the produce, which was exacted from the ryot; either by himself, or the persons to whom he farmed the receipts; and paid it over to the sovereign, reserving a prescribed portion to himself. The Zemindar was thus, whatever else he might be, the collector of the revenue for the district to which he belonged. As the receipt of revenue, in a rude state of government, is a business most dear to the governors, the Zemindar, in order the better to secure this favourite end, was vested with a great share of the powers of government. He was allowed the use of a military force; the police of the district was placed in his hands; and he was vested with the civil branch of judicature. When his district was large, he was a sort of petty prince. In various parts of India, however, the collection of the revenue had never become fixed and hereditary in the hands of an individual, and the business was transacted between the immediate cultivators, and a man who possessed none but the characteristics of an immediate officer of government.

The committee say, that a rate of taxation much more severe than that which existed under the Hindu governments was introduced by the Mohamedan rulers, and amid the abuses of modern times. For this opinion they have no authority whatsoever. It is, therefore, a mere prejudice. The rate which they mention goes far beyond the scale of the ancient ordinances: And what reason is there to believe that the ancient Hindu governments did not, as the Mohamedan, levy assessments to the utmost limits of the supposed ability of the ryots? In those parts of India which Europeans have found still remaining under Hindu governments, the state of the people is worse, if there is any difference, than where they have been subject to the Mohamedan sway.[1]

[1] For this opinion, the writer "has no authority whatever." The contrary opinion, formed by individuals of high talent, and ample opportunities of

BOOK II. CHAP. V.

The rate established in the ancient ordinances has been regarded as evidence of mild taxation, that is, of good government. It only proves that agriculture was in its earliest, and most unproductive state; and though it paid little, could not afford to pay any more.[1] We may assume it as a principle, in which there is no room for mistake, that a government constituted and circumstanced as that of the Hindus, had only one limit to its exactions, the non-existence of any thing further to take.[2] Another thing is certain, that under any state of cultivation, but the very worst, if the whole except a sixth of the produce of a soil, so rich as that of Hindustan, had been left with the cultivator, he must have had the means of acquiring wealth, and of attaining rank and consequence; but these it is well ascertained that the ryots in India never enjoyed.[3]

Notwithstanding these proofs that the ownership in the land was reserved to the king, this conclusion has been disputed, in favour, 1st, of the Zemindars, and 2ndly, of the Ryots. The question with regard to the Zemindars may be reserved till that period of the history, when it was agitated for the sake of practical proceedings on the part of

observation, is authority. In the south of India, Hindu governments have all along been extant, as well as Mohammedan; and in the contrast between the two, the officers, whose statements are so completely disregarded, speak not from report, but from personal knowledge. To say of their deliberate affirmation, therefore, it is mere prejudice, without being able to produce any proof to that effect, is an irrational rejection of unexceptionable testimony, of which Mr. Mill would not have been guilty, had not his own prejudices been too strong for his judgment.—W.

[1] By the same rule, the Turkish government would be ranked as excellent. It takes little; but the reason is, there is nothing more which it can take. The ancient assessment on the cultivator in Persia was one-tenth; but in the days of the Indian Emperor Akbar, he was, by one means or other, made to pay more than a half. Ayeen Akbery, Ed. in 4to. p. 348.

[2] Why this principle should be taken for granted, does not appear; the contrary inference is the more probable one. The manners of the Rajas were simple: they kept up no expensive state. They were subject to fixed laws, controlled by Brahmanical influence, military independence, and popular opinion. There is no reason to believe that they ever levied to the uttermost. —W.

[3] The population in India, through so many ages, must have been kept down by excess of exaction. Even in the richest parts of India, one-half of the soil has never been under cultivation.—M.

This is a bold assertion. What proof is there that in the richest parts of India, one-half of the soil has *never* been cultivated? It is not true of the present day, that half the richest parts of Bengal are not in cultivation; and there is reason to believe, that in former times, much of the country was exceedingly populous. Greek writers talk of a thousand cities in the Punjáb alone; and remains of towns and vestiges of habitations are found in many parts of India, now covered with jungle. There is no reason to believe that the population in India was always depressed, or that it was kept down by excess of exaction.—W.

the government. The question with regard to the Ryots belongs peculiarly to this part of the work.

The circumstances, which appear to have misled the intelligent Europeans who have misinterpreted this part of the Hindu institutions, are two; first, the tenure of the ryot or husbandman; and secondly, the humane and honourable anxiety, lest the interests and the happiness of the most numerous class of the population should be sacrificed, if the sovereign were acknowledged as owner of the soil.

But, if this acknowledgment were ever so complete, it is inconsistent neither with the tenure which is claimed in favour of the ryots, nor with the means of their prosperity and happiness. And if it were, the acknowledgment of its previous existence would be no bar to a preferable arrangement; since the sovereign can have a right to nothing which is injurious to his people.

In a situation in which the revenue of the sovereign was increased in proportion to the number of cultivators, and in which a great proportion of the land continued void of cultivators, there would be a competition, not of cultivators for the land, but of the land for cultivators. If a ryot cultivated a piece of ground, and punctually paid his assessment, the sovereign would be far from any wish to remove him, because it would be difficult to supply his place. If the ryot sold the ground to another ryot, or left it to a successor, that is, put another in his place who would fúlfil the wishes of the sovereign, he, whose source of fear was the want of a cultivator, had still cause for satisfaction; and seldom, if ever, interfered.

By custom, the possession of the ryot became, in this manner, a permanent possession; whence he was not removed except when he failed to pay his assessment or rent; a possession which he could sell during his life; or leave by inheritance when he died. As far as rights can be established by prescription, these rights were established in India in favour of the ryots. And no violation of property is more flagrant than that by which the tenure of the ryot is annulled.

But, according even to European ideas, a right to cultivate the land under these, and still greater advantages, is not understood to transfer the ownership of the land.

BOOK II. CHAP. V.

The great estates in Ireland, for example, let under leases perpetually renewable, are vendible and inheritable by the leaseholders, without affecting the ownership of their lords; subject, moreover, to a very important restriction, from which the sovereigns in India were free;[1] the lords of such estates cannot raise their rents at pleasure; the sovereigns in India enjoyed this privilege, and abused it to excess. The sovereigns in India had not only the ownership, but all the benefit of the land; the ryots had merely the privilege of employing their labour always upon the same soil, and of transferring that privilege to some other person; the sovereign claimed a right to as much of the produce as he pleased, and seldom left to the ryots more than a very scanty reward for their labour.

That ownership in the land justified this extent of exaction, or implies a valid title to any power at variance with the interests of the ryots, is an erroneous inference. Without violating its obligations to the people, a government cannot spend any sum, beyond what is strictly necessary for the performance of the services, which it is destined to render: and it is justified in taking even this sum exclusively from the cultivators of the land, only if that is the mode in which all the qualities desirable in a financial system are the most completely realized.

Those who contend for the privileges of the ryots would no doubt observe, that in this mode of interpretation, we reduce the ownership of the sovereign to an empty name; and that to the admission of it, thus understood, they see nothing to object. The controversy is then at a close. The ownership of the sovereign in the soil, wherever it exists, is, by the principles which constitute the very foundation of government, reduced to the limits above described. And it is no less certain, that all which is valuable in the soil, after the deduction of what is due to the sovereign belongs of incontestable right to the Indian husbandman.[2]

[1] It is remarkable, that the king's tenants in *ancient* demesne were, in England, perpetual, on the same condition as the ryots in India. A gleba amoveri non poterint, quamdiu solvere possunt debitas pensiones. Bracton lib. i. cap. ii.

[2] The following quotations will show how completely these deductions accord with the facts which the late perfect investigation has elicited. Mr. Thackeray, in his general report, remarks, "All this peninsula, except, perhaps, only Canara, Malabar, and a few other provinces, has exhibited, from time immemorial, but one system of land-revenue. The land has been considered the property of the Circar [government], and of the ryots." The

The Hindu mode of raising the revenue of the state, wholly, or almost wholly, by taking as much as necessary

interest in the soil has been divided between these two; but the ryots have possessed little more interest than that of being hereditary tenants. If any persons have a claim to participate with government in the property of the soil, it is the ryots." (Fifth Report, ut supra, p. 992.) These ideas, and even the very words, have been adopted in the Report of the Board of Revenue. Ibid. p. 898. "Lands," says Mr. Place, "cannot be alienated without a written instrument; because both the sovereign and the subject have a mutual property in them. Each, however, may alienate his own, and the other is not affected. The sovereign may part with his interest in them: but the usufructuary right remains with the subject. And all that the latter can sell, mortgage, or give away, is the enjoyment of the profit, after paying what is due to the sovereign." (Ibid. p. 718.) Mr. Harris, in his report on Tanjore, informs us, "A meerassadar (ryot) disposes of his station in any manner he pleases. He disposes of it, too, and quits, without being bound to give, to any one, notice of his transfer and departure. Like him, his successor superintends its cultivation, and pays its revenue. Government know nothing of his relinquishment; and if they knew of it, they would not care about it here, as in Europe. The proprietorship of the land belongs to government or the landlord; and he who is intrusted with the duty of making it productive, lives upon it and cultivates it, so long as he pays its revenue, and no longer. But this occupation of it, while the superior is satisfied, has been converted by the meerassadar into a right. They have made the right a property; and they retain, sell, lend, give, or mortgage, according to their inclination, the whole or any part of it." (Ibid. 829.) Even Mr. Hodgson, who is an advocate for raising the revenue through the instrumentality of Zemindars, affirms the rights of the cultivators to be incontestable. "I make," says he, "the following inductions: 1st. that the cultivators have a right, everywhere, to pay a fixed tax for the land they occupy; 2ndly. that they have the right, universally, to occupy this land, so long as they pay the standard rent; 3rdly. that they have the right to sell or transfer, by deed, gift, or otherwise, the land they occupy, subject always to the condition of paying the standard rent; 4thly. that they exercise the right, stated in the third position, wherever the standard rent has not been increased, so as to absorb all the profit on cultivation, or arable land is sufficiently scarce to be of value in the acquisition." (Ibid. 979.)

If the writer means, by saying that the cultivator had a *right* to pay no more than a fixed rent, that it would have been right or good to pay only in that manner, I maintain the same doctrine; but if he means that the cultivator ever *enjoyed* this right, the proposition is far from true. In every other respect I assent to the propositions of Mr. Hodgson. I also agree with him when he says; "Provided the property in private estates, that is, the standard rent, and no more, be paid by these owners of private estates, I hold it to be a matter of very secondary importance to them, whether the rent is demanded of them by the ancient rajahs or polygars, the officers of Byjnuggur or Bednore government, the rajah coorg, the tehsildars of the Company, or the (to be created) zemindars of the Company." (Ibid. 980.) The collector of Tanjore also thinks it not worth inquiring what ownership the sovereign has, provided the usufruct of the ryot is well defined and secured. (Ib. 831.) See Hodgson again to the same effect. (Ib. p. 926.) We are informed by Mr. Park, that in Africa, when a permission to cultivate a spot of ground has been granted by the sovereign, it is not resumed, while the revenue or rent is paid. (Travels, p. 261.) In China, Mr. Barrow assures us, that the cultivator, though in reality a tenant at will, is never dispossessed, but when he fails to discharge the stated engagements. "So accustomed," he adds, "are the Chinese to consider the estate as their own, while they continue to pay the rent, that a Portuguese in Macao had nearly lost his life for endeavouring to raise the rent upon his Chinese tenants. (Travels in China, p. 397.) Dr. Buchanan says, "The ryots or farmers have no property in the ground; but it is not usual to turn any man away, so long as he pays the customary rent. Even in the reign of Tippoo, such an act would have been looked upon as an astonishing grievance." (Journey through Mysore, &c., i. 124.) "The genius and ten-

BOOK II. CHAP. V.

of the rent of the land, while it is the obvious expedient which first presents itself to the rudest minds, has no inconsiderable recommendation from science itself. Previous to allotment, the productive powers of the soil are the joint property of the community; and hence are a fund peculiarly adapted to the joint or common purposes and demands. If the whole of what is strictly rent were taken away, the application of labour and capital to the land would resemble the application of labour and capital to wood or iron; and the same principles, in both cases, would determine their reward.

But as the expense required for the services of government exceeds not a very small portion of the rent of the land, unless where the quantity was very minute, the greatest possible benefit is derived from the productive powers of the soil, when it is the property of individuals. The benefits of the soil have, accordingly, over the greater part of the globe, been employed, first, to supply in whole, or for the greater part, the necessities of government, next to enrich the individual occupant. The most remarkable exception to this rule is in modern Europe. After the conquests of the Gothic nations, the land was thrown in great portions into the hands of the leading men: and they had power to make the taxes fall where they chose; they took care accordingly that they should fall any where rather than upon the land; that is, upon any body rather than themselves. Further, as their influence over the sovereign made him glad to share with them what he derived from the taxes, they not only threw the burden off their own shoulders, but taxed, as they have continued to do, and sometimes in a progressive ratio, to the present hour, the rest of the community for their benefit.

---

dency of all Hindu institutions is, to render offices, as well as property, hereditary." (Wilks's Hist. Sketches, p. 231.) "The king is the general heir of all his subjects; but when there are children to inherit, they are seldom deprived of their father's estate." (Dow's Hindostan, pref. p. xiii.) Η χωρα της πολεως· αλλ' ουδεν ἡττον των κεκτημενων ἑκαστος κυριος εστι τπν ἑαυτου. (Dio Chrysostom. Orat. 31. in Rhodiac.) Anquetil Duperron was the first of the Europeans who maintained that the ownership of the land was vested in the ryots. He has written a discourse upon the subject, in his work entitled, *Recherches Historiques et Géographiques sur l'Inde.* He proves what is now acknowledged, that a man might dispose of his farm, and was seldom turned out of it, while he continued to pay his taxes or rent. There is a learned and able chapter, in support of the same opinion in "Historical Sketches of the South of India, by Col. Wilks."

The objections to the Hindu system of providing for the expenses of government, arise rather from the mode, than the essence.

By aiming at the receipt of a prescribed portion of the crop of each year; and with a very imperfect distinction of the lands of different powers, the Hindus incurred most of the evils which a bad method of raising a tax is liable to produce. They rendered the amount of the tax always uncertain, and its pressure very unequal; they rendered necessary a perfect host of tax-gatherers; and opened a boundless inlet to partiality and oppression on the one hand; to fraud and mendacity on the other. A tax consisting of any portion of the gross produce of the soil, raises the price of that produce; because the tax raised from the poorest of the cultivated land must be returned, along with the expense of cultivation, in the exchangeable value of its produce. In this manner a tax is levied upon the consumers of corn, which surpasses the sum paid to the government, and enriches the owners of the best land at the expense of the community.[1]

An expensive mode of raising the taxes is a natural effect of a rude state of society. We are informed by Sully, that the receipt into the French exchequer, in the year 1598, was only thirteen millions of French money; while the sum, dragged out of the pockets of the people, was 150 millions. "The thing appeared incredible," says the statesman: "but by the due degree of labour, I made the truth of it certain."[2] The proportion was doubtless greater in Hindustan.[3].

Receiving the taxes in kind was a practice which ensured a prodigious expense, and a waste by which nobody gained. Scarcely any other mode seems to have been known to the Hindus in the time of their ancient institutions; and to a great degree it continued down to the latest period of their history.[4] How rude and inconvenient soever this practice

1 See a Dissertation on the Principles of Taxation, the most profound, by far, which has yet been given to the world, by David Ricardo, Esq., in his work " On the Principles of Political Economy and Taxation."

2 Mém. du Sully, liv. xx.

3 It was doubtless much less, the amount was adjusted between the members of the village communities and the superintendent of the district; and the host of collectors never existed, except in the author's imagination.—W.

4 Among the Mexicans, says Dr. Robertson, " Taxes were laid upon land, upon the acquisitions of industry, and upon commodities of every kind ex-

must be regarded; we find several nations who make a considerable figure in the history of the world, who have not in this respect advanced beyond the Hindus. It may not surprise any one, that taxes were raised in kind in the ancient empire of Mexico.[1] The greater part, though not the whole, were raised in the same manner, in Persia, even in the time of Darius Hystaspes;[2] and the mixture at least, whatever the proportion, continues to the present day.[3] The whole revenue of China, with the exception of some trifling articles, is paid in kind.[4]

CHAPTER VI.

Religion.

IT is difficult to determine whether the constitution of the government and the provisions of law, or Religion, have, among the Hindus, the greatest influence upon the

posed to sale in the public markets. These duties were considerable, but not arbitrary or unequal. They were imposed according to established rules, and each knew what share of the common burden he had to bear." History of America, iii. 225, 229. The political descriptions of this admired historian are, commonly, by far too general, and thence vague. We cannot suppose that the Mexicans were more skilled in the policy of taxation than the Hindus.

[1] "As the use of money was unknown," says Robertson, (Ibid. p. 296,) "all the taxes were paid in kind, and thus not only the natural productions of all the different provinces in the empire, but every species of manufacture, and every work of ingenuity and art, were collected in the public storehouses." It is worthy of remark, that the same mode of taxing handicrafts and labourers was adopted in Mexico as in Hindustan; "People of inferior condition (Ibid.), neither possessing land nor engaged in commerce, were bound to the performances of various services. By their stated labour the crown lands were cultivated, public works were carried on, and the various houses which belonged to the emperor were built and kept in repair.

[2] It is remarkable that, in Persia, the use even of coined money was unknown till the time of Darius Hystaspes. The portion of tribute that was paid in gold and silver, was received by weight. Herodot. lib. iv. cap. clxvi. Major Rennel, not aware that this was only a portion, and a small portion, of the Persian taxes, is exceedingly puzzled to account for the diminutive amount of the Persian revenues, and at last concludes that "the value of money was *incredibly* greater at that time than at present." Rennel's Geography of Herodotus, p. 316.

[3] Ebn Haukal, translated by Sir William Ouseley, p. 136. Chardin's Travels in Persia.

[4] Abbé Grosier, p. 76; Barrow's China, p. 499. Mr. Barrow informs us that a vast number of the vessels on the canals and rivers are employed in conveying the taxes to the capital. Ibid. p. 508. In those countries on the Euxine Sea, which early attained so high a state of civilization, as to have a large export trade in grain, even the custom-house duties, or the taxes on export and import, were levied in kind. We are informed by Demosthenes, Orat. adv. Leptinem, that Leucon, king of Bosphorus, from which Athens derived her principal supplies, levied a duty of one thirtieth in kind upon all the corn shipped in his ports.

lives of individuals, and the operations of society. Beside the causes which usually give superstition a powerful sway in ignorant and credulous ages, the order of priests obtained a greater authority in India than in any other region of the globe; and this again they employed with astonishing success in multiplying and corroborating the ideas on which their power and consequence depended. Every thing in Hindustan was transacted by the Deity. The laws were promulgated, the people were classified, the government was established, by the Divine Being. The astonishing exploits of the Divinity were endless in that sacred land. For every stage of life from the cradle to the grave; for every hour of the day: for every function of nature; for every social transaction, God prescribed a number of religious observances. And meditation upon his incomprehensible attributes, as it was by far the most difficult of all human operations, so was it that glorious occupation which alone prepared the intense votary for the participation of the Divine nature.

Of so extensive and complicated a subject as the religion of the Hindus, a very general view can alone be taken here. All that is interesting to the politician and the philosopher, may, however, it is presumed, be confined within a moderate space. The task is rendered difficult by the unparalleled vagueness which marks the language of the Brahmens respecting the nature of the gods, the vast multiplicity of their fictions, and the endless discrepancy of their ideas. Hence it is, that no coherent system of belief seems capable of being extracted from their wild eulogies and legends; and if he who attempts to study their religion is disposed, like themselves, to build his faith on his imagination, he meets with little obstruction from the stubborn precision of Hindu expressions and tenets.

Nothing is more curious than to trace the ideas concerning Divine power which the natural faculties of our race suggest to them at the various stages of their career. In the very rude and imperfect state in which society originated, the human mind can hardly so far enlarge its views as to draw conclusions respecting the universe. Those operations and events of nature, which more immediately concern mankind, and on which their happiness and misery depend, no doubt engage their eager curiosity. The causes of light and darkness, of drought and rain, of the thunder, of the hurricane, of the earthquake, suggest many an anxious inquiry; but to put all the objects of nature, and all the changes which they undergo, into one group of ideas, and to ask whence did the whole proceed, seems to be an operation too complicated, and too far removed from the ordinary track of his ideas, to be one of the first that takes place in the mind of a barbarian.

With regard to that other class of questions, which more easily occur to him, his nature very readily suggests an answer. Prior to experience and instruction, there is a propensity in the imagination to endow with life whatever we behold in motion; or, in general, whatever appears to be the cause of any event. A child beats the inanimate object by which it has been hurt, and caresses that by which it has been gratified. The sun, which is the cause of day, the savage regards as a beneficent deity. A spirit resides in the storm; the woods and the waters are peopled with divinities; there is a god of plenty, and a god of want; a god of war, and a god of peace; a god of health, and a god of sickness. That this may be considered as a correct outline of the first religion which is suggested to the human mind, the laws of human nature, and the ideas which are found to prevail among rude tribes, appear sufficiently to evince.

But men are not long in making another step in their religious progress. Having made for themselves a theory with respect to the cause of the *events* which affect them, the origin too of the *things* which they perceive attracts their curiosity; and from asking the cause, first of one great object, and then of another, they come at last to put the general question, What is the cause and origin of the whole? There are very few, therefore, even among the most barbarous nations, who have not made an attempt to account for the origin of the universe, and in whose religious ideas some species of cosmogony is not involved. But, in answering the question respecting the origin of the universe, it is impossible that men should not be guided by their previous ideas. It follows, that among the divinities whom they already adored, He, whom they regarded as the most powerful, should be selected as the Maker of the world. Were they placed in circumstances of tolerable tranquillity, this potent God would probably be the sun: were they a people almost constantly plunged in the horrors of war, the god of arms would naturally be their chief divinity. Hence we see that in many nations of Asia, who at an early period seem to have been placed in favourable circumstances, the sun was supreme among the gods, and the great principle of the universe; among the turbulent and warlike tribes who inhabited the north of Europe, Odin, the god of war, was the supreme deity, and author of all things.

The Hindus had made considerable progress beyond the first and lowest stage of human society.[1] It seems common, however, to retain for a long time the ideas which are then implanted; and rather than eradicate the old, to make of them a heterogeneous compound with the new. The Greeks and the Romans did not reject their Jupiter, and Mars, their gods of the mountains, trees, and rivers, when they rose to more comprehensive views of the universe; they only endeavoured to accommodate to these primary conceptions their new apprehensions and conclusions. In like manner, the Hindus have still their Indra, or the god of firmament, Varuna, or the god of the waters, Rembha, the goddess of love, in the whole, a long and splendid catalogue of thirty-three crore.[2]

We have translations from the Hindu books of several passages containing accounts of the creation.[3] They differ from one another very widely in the minor forms and cir-

[1] This is an admission, rather incompatible with the views usually advocated by the author.—W.

[2] A crore is 100 lacs, and a lac is 100,000; so that thirty-three crore of deities is just 330 millions.—M.

This expression is not to be understood in its literal sense. It is intended only to denote an infinite number; including all the inferior spirits of heaven and earth. The objects of adoration, that are individualized, are few. Dr. Tennant is not good authority on this subject. Rembhá, is not goddess of love, but an inferior being—a nymph of Indra's court.—W.

[3] Three of these from the Vedas themselves by Mr. Colebrooke (As. Res. viii. 404, 421, 452); another account, translated from the Puranas by Mr. Halhed, is published in Maurice's History (i. 407); Mr. Wilford has given us another, derived from the same source (As. Res. iii. 358). An account of the creation is prefixed to the Gentoo code translated by Halhed; we have another in the French translation, entitled Bagavadam, of the Bhagavat. The author of the Ayeen Akbery informs us that no fewer than eighteen opinions respecting the creation were entertained in Hindustan, and presents us three as a specimen, of which the last, taken from the Surya Sidhanta, he says, is the most common. Ayeen Akbery, iii. 6. The most important of all is that which I have referred to in the text, from the institutes of Menu, ch. i. 5, &c.

cumstances; but strongly resemble in the general character, and in the principal ideas. That contained in the sacred volume which bears the name of Menu may be taken as a standard,[1] being more full and circumstantial than any of those which are given us from the Vedas; derived from a work of equal authority with the Vedas themselves, and exhibiting, as drawn up at a later period, the improvement, if any, which the ideas of the people had acquired. It is all vagueness and darkness, incoherence, inconsistency, and confusion. It is one of the most extravagant of all specimens of discourse without ideas. The fearless propensity of a rude mind to guess where it does not know, never exhibited itself in more fantastic and senseless forms.[2]

Beside accounts of what creation was, we have accounts of the mode in which the Hindu divinity performed the creation. If a man possessing refined and exalted notions of the Divine Nature were to describe the great work of creation, he would have the clearest conviction of his own incompetence; and, as Moses, he would attempt no more than by a few strokes to convey an idea of the magnitude of the task, and of the power and wisdom of him who performed it. If far removed from this degree of knowledge and reflection, he will enter without hesitation upon a minute and detailed description both of the plan, and of its execution. If, however, the society in which he lives has attained any considerable improvement, the process which he conceives will indicate some portion of human wisdom; will, at least, be such as an instructed member of that society, had he infinite power imparted to him, would devise for himself. On the other hand, if a description of the creation presents no idea but what is fantastic, wild, and irrational; if it includes not even a portion of that design and contrivance which appear in the ordinary works of man; if it carries the common analogies of production, in animal and vegetable life, to the production of the universe, we cannot be mistaken in ascribing it to a people, whose ideas of the Divine Being were grovelling.[3]

[1] It is not the best standard that could have been selected, being a rather injudicious mixture of the popular and philosophical accounts.—W.

[2] See note A. at the end of the volume.

[3] The system is not to be judged of by the only specimens within our author's reach, although, even from them, it is unjust to infer that the Hindus

"The self-existing power," says Menu, "having willed to produce various beings, first with a thought created the waters." This is not a despicable conception, but what succeeds? "He placed in these waters a productive seed." This is one of those analogies to the growth of a plant or an animal which are generally the foundation of the cosmogony of a rude people. What next? The seed becomes an egg; which is a very extraordinary product;[1] a wonderful course, too, for the self-existing power to follow in the formation of the universe. The other steps are not less amazing. In this egg the divine being deposited himself, and there he lay, in a state of inactivity, a whole year of the Creator, that is, according to the Hindus, 1,555,200,000,000 solar years of mortals.[2] At the end of this astonishing period he caused by his thought the egg to divide itself, and was himself born in the form of Brahma, the great forefather of all spirits;[3] thus, "from THAT-WHICH-IS, the first cause, was produced the divine male, famed in all worlds, under the appellation of Brahma."[4] This is celebrated in Hindu books as the great transformation of the Divine Being, from neuter to masculine, for the purpose of creating worlds; and under this masculine form of Brahma it was that he effected the rest of creation. The Hindus believe that he was engaged in it for no less than 17,064,000 years.[5] Of the two divisions of the egg from which he had just been freed, he framed the heaven above, the earth

---

had no high and noble ideas of that creative power which they describe as being alone before all things, and as calling of its own will, existence out of chaos.—W.

[1] Not at all:—the Hindus were better physiologists than the historian.—W.

[2] The length of a year of the Creator may be thus computed. A calpa, or grand period, containing the reigns of fourteen Menus, constitutes, Sir William Jones informs us (Asiat. Research. i. 237), one day of Brahma. This period comprises (see an accurate calculation, according to the books of the Hindus, in Mr. Bentley's Remarks on Ancient Eras and Dates, Asiat. Res. v. 316) 4,320,000,000 years; and such is the length of one day of the Creator. A divine year again contains 360 days; and the multiplication of these numbers produces the amount which appears in the text. Mr. Wilford (see Asiat. Research. iii. 382) makes this computation in a manner, and with a result, somewhat different. "One year of mortals," he says, "is a day and a night of the gods, and 360 of our years is one of theirs: 12,000 of their years, or 4,320,000 of ours, constitute one of their ages, and 2,000 such ages are Brahma's day and night, which must be multiplied by 360 to make one of his years."

[3] In other words, he was hatched.

[4] Vide the quotation from the Institutes of Menu, in Note A. at the end of the volume.

[5] Asiat. Research. ii. 237 and 232.

BOOK II. CHAP. VI.

beneath, and in the midst the subtle ether, the eight regions, and the permanent receptacle of waters. The creation of mind is next described; but this will be more conveniently considered when we come to appreciate the notions of the Hindus in relation to thought. The creation however of man, or at least of the Hindus, is worthy of our particular regard. "That the human race might be multiplied, he caused the Brahmen to proceed from his mouth, the Cshatriya from his arm, the Vaisya from his thigh, and the Sudra from his foot." The analogy of ordinary descent is again the foundation of this fantastic imagination; and the Hindu could picture to himself the production of a human being, even by the Deity, only in the way of a species of birth. This analogy leads to a still more extravagant conceit for the creation of other races of men, and living creatures. As if "The Mighty Power" could not produce them by his male virtue alone, "He divided his own substance, and became half male, half female. By this female the male half produced Viraj, a demigod and saint; Viraj, by the virtue of austere devotion, produced Menu, another demigod and saint." Menu again, "desirous," he says, "of giving birth to a race of men," produced ten lords of created beings; and these lords produced, at his command, "seven other Menus, and deities, and the mansions of deities, and great sages, and also benevolent genii, and fierce giants, blood-thirsty savages, heavenly quiristers, nymphs and demons, huge serpents and snakes of smaller size, birds of mighty wing, and separate companions of Pitris, or progenitors of mankind; lightnings and thunderbolts, clouds and coloured bows of Indra, falling meteors, earth-rending vapours, comets, and luminaries of various degrees; horse-faced sylvans, apes, fish, and a variety of birds, tame cattle, deer, men, and ravenous beasts with two rows of teeth; small and large reptiles, moths, lice, fleas, and common flies, with every biting gnat, and immoveable substances of distinct sorts. Thus was this whole assemblage of moveable and stationary bodies framed by those high-minded beings."[1]

But in the Hindu books we find applied to the Divinity a great variety of expressions, so elevated, that they cannot be surpassed even by those of the men who entertain the

[1] See Note B. at the end of the volume.

most sublime ideas of the Divine Nature. In the passage immediately quoted from Menu, he is described as the sole self-existing power, the soul of all beings, he whom the mind alone can perceive, who exists from eternity, and whom no being can comprehend. In a passage from the Brahmanda Purana, translated by Mr. Wilford, he is denominated "The great God, the great Omnipotent, Omniscient one, the greatest in the World, the great Lord who goes through all worlds, incapable of decay."[1] In a prayer, translated by Mr. Colebrooke, from one of the Vedas, he is called, "the pure Brahme, whom none can apprehend as an object of perception, above, around, or in the midst; the God who pervades all regions, the first-born; he, prior to whom nothing was born; who became all beings, himself the Lord of creatures; he, who made the fluid sky and solid earth, who fixed the solar orb and celestial abode, whom heaven and earth mentally contemplate; the mysterious Being, in whom the universe perpetually exists, resting on that sole support; in whom this world is absorbed, from whom it issues."[2] Without multiplying instances, it may shortly be stated that human language does not supply more lofty epithets of praise than are occasionally addressed to their deities by the Hindus.

To form a true estimate of the religion of this people, it is necessary by reflection to ascertain, what those expressions in the mouth of a Brahmen really mean. We shall incur the risk of completely deceiving ourselves, if, with the experience how naturally vague and general expressions, especially in such abstract and mental subjects, convey the most different ideas, to people in different stages of society, we take the lofty expressions of devotion in Hindu books, as full and satisfactory evidence of lofty conceptions of the Divine Nature. It is well ascertained that nations, who have the lowest and meanest ideas of the Divine Being, may yet apply to him the most sounding epithets by which perfection can be expressed.[3]

[1] Asiat. Research. viii. 352. [2] Ibid. 432.

[3] In this theory of Mr. Mill's, there is a palpable fallacy, for it involves the impossible supposition, that words are devised not only to express ideas that do not exist, but to express the very contrary of the ideas that the mind conceives. Expressions, according to this view of the subject, are lofty, not because the conceptions are lofty, but because they are base, as if we should say, 'tall,' when we meant 'short,' or 'little,' when we intended 'large.' This is utterly contradicted by every theory of language yet contrived: we must take

In tracing the progress of natural religion, through the different stages of intellectual acquirement, a very important fact is discovered; that language, on this subject, has a much greater tendency to improve, than ideas. It is well known how vile and degrading were the notions of the Divine Nature presented in the fictions of the Greek poets; insomuch that Plato deemed them unfit to be read;[1] yet the Brahmens themselves do not surpass the Greek poets in elevated expressions concerning the Deity. Orpheus, early and rude as is the period to which his poetry relates, thus describes the celestial King; "Jupiter, the sovereign; Jupiter, the original parent of all things; and Wisdom, the first procreator; and all-delighting Love: For in the mighty frame of Jupiter are all contained: One power, one godhead: He is the great Regent of all."[2] Cæsar informs

---

the sign as indicative of the thing signified, or speech would be of no more use in the interchange of thought, than the inarticulate ejaculations of the bird or brute. It is very clear, however, where Mr. Mill errs; he has lost sight of the progress of opinion, and confounded different states of social feeling. It is possible, that the loftiest epithets of Divine power, and benignity, and glory, may have lost some of their force by frequent use, and they may be directed to objects to which they cannot in truth appertain. When the terms were first employed, however, they expressed, no doubt, the ideas they were invented to express; and the Hindu priests, poets, and philosophers, by whom they were originally applied, attempted by them to convey the notions they conceived of the Divinity. Even now, in the mouth of a believing Hindu, they have not lost their purport: the object to which he addresses them, though base and mean in our eyes, is not so in his, and he imagines it to be invested with the attributes he assigns to it. But this is of little importance to the argument. It may be very true that the epithets are misapplied, that they are used as terms of course, that they exercise little influence on moral practice; the same things occur in other places than in India; but, whatever may be their practical value, they afford unequivocal proof, that at one time or other, and amongst some at least of the Brahmanical order, elevated notions of the power, and wisdom, and beneficence, of one only God, were entertained and expressed.—W.

[1] He states that the only practical inference the youth could draw from the accounts delivered by the poets concerning the gods was; to commit all manner of crimes, and out of the fruits of their villany to offer costly sacrifices, and appease the divine powers; αδικητεον και θυτεον απο των αδικηματων. De Repub. lib. 595, 6.

[2] Orphic Fragm. vi. 366. Numerous passages might be produced:

Ζευς εστιν αιθηρ, Ζευς δε γη, Ζευς δ' ουρανος·
Ζευς τοι τα παντα. Euphorion.
Ἑις Θεος εν παντεσσι. Orphic. Frag. iv. 363.
Jane pater, Jane tuens, Dive biceps, biformis,
O! cate rerum sator; O! principium Deorum.

Verses from an ancient Choriambic poem, which are quoted by Terentianus Maurus de Metris.

Ζευς ὁ προ τριων Κρονιδων. Ὁυτος εστι των ὁλων δημιουργος. Procl. in Platon. Tim. p. 95. It is almost needless to quote Homer's

Ζηνα τε μητιοεντα, Θεων πατερ' ηδε και ανδρων.

"The Araucanians [the native Indians of Chili] acknowledge a Supreme Being, the Author of all things, whom they call PILLAN, a word derived from *pulli* or *pilli*, the soul, and signifies the supreme essence; they also call him Guenu-pillan, the Spirit of heaven; Buta-gen, the Great Being; Thalcove,

us that the Druids among the ancient Gauls delivered many doctrines concerning the nature of the universe, and the powers of the immortal gods;[1] and it is remarkable that the Greeks and the Romans were forcibly struck with the similarity between the ideas of the Druids, and those of the Brahmens of India, the Magi of Persia, the Chaldeans of Assyria, and the priests of Egypt.[2] The creed of the ancient Germans, as we are informed by Tacitus, was, "that God is the Ruler of all: other things are to him subject and obedient."[3] In the ancient Scandinavian mythology the Supreme God was described as, "The author of every thing that existeth; the eternal, the ancient, the living and awful Being, the searcher into concealed things; the Being that never changeth."[4] On the statue of the Egyptian goddess Isis, was this inscription: "I am every thing past, every thing present, and every thing to come."[5] The Deity was described by Zoroaster as "The First, the Incorruptible, the Eternal, without generation, without dissolution, without a parallel, the charioteer of all which is good, inaccessible to bribes, the best of the good, the wisest of the wise.'[6] The Getes asserted their deity Zamolxis to be the true God, that besides him there was none other, and that to him they went after death, being endowed with spirits immortal.[7] Even the rude tribes of America, wandering naked in the woods, "appear," says Robertson, "to acknowledge a Divine power to be the maker of the world, and the disposer of all events. They denominate him the Great Spirit."[8] Thus it appears how commonly the loftiest *expressions* are used concerning the gods, by people whose *conceptions* of them are, confessedly, mean.[9]

---

the Thunderer; Vilvemvoe, the Creator of all; Vilpepilvoe, the Omnipotent; Mollgelu, the Eternal; Avnolu, the Infinite, &c." Molina, Civil Hist. of Chili, book II. ch. v.

A passage of Empedocles, containing the language of a pure theology, may be seen in Harris's Philos. Arrangements, ch. viii. p. 162.

1 Cæsar. de Bel. Gal. lib. vi. cap. 13.

2 See Henry's Hist. of Great Britain, i. 149; and the authorities there adduced.

3 "Regnator omnium Deus; cætera subjecta atque parentia." Tacit. de Mor. Germ. cap. xxxv.

4 See a translation from the Edda in Mallet's Introduct. Hist. Denmark, i. ch. 5, and ii. p. 7, 8.

5 Plutarch. de Iside et Osiride.

6 Euseb. Præp. Evang. lib. i. p. 42.

7 Herodot. lib. iv. cap. 93, 94.

8 Robertson's Hist. Amer. ii. 197.

9 "Ces peuples (les Romains) adorent un Dieu suprême et unique, qu'ils appellent toujours *Dieu très-grand, et très-bon;* cependant ils ont bâti un temple à une courtisanne nommée Flora, et les bonnes femmes de Rome ont

BOOK II. CHAP. VI.

This important fact, however remarkable, is founded on principles of very powerful operation in the nature of man. The timid barbarian, who is agitated by fears respecting the unknown events of nature, feels the most incessant and eager desire to propitiate the Being on whom he believes them to depend. His mind works, with laborious solicitude, to discover the best means of recommending himself. He naturally takes counsel from his own sentiments and feelings: and as nothing to his rude breast is more delightful than adulation, he is led by a species of instinct to expect the favour of his god from praise and flattery. In an uncultivated mind, how strong this sentiment is, a very superficial knowledge of human nature may convince us. Mr. Forster, in his Travels overland from India, was overtaken by a storm in the Caspian Sea; and remarks that during the danger "every man was imploring the Divine interposition in his own manner and language." "But my attention," says he, "was chiefly attracted by a Persian. His ejaculations were loud and fervent; and the whole force of his prayers was levelled at Ali; on whom he bestowed every title that could denote sanctity or military prowess. He called on him, by the name of the Friend of God; the Lord of the Faithful; the Brandisher of the invincible sword; to look down on his servant, and shield him from the impending evil. Thinking also to obtain the more grace with the father, he would occasionally launch out into the praises of his two sons."[1]

When the belief is once admitted that the Deity is pleased with panegyric, it is evident to what length the agitated and ignorant votary will speedily be carried. Whatever may be the phrases with which he begins; in a short time, the ardour of his fears incites him to invent new and stronger; as likely to prove more agreeable and prevalent. Even these, by a short use, become familiar to his mind. When they begin to be stale and feeble, he is again prompted to a new invention, and to more violent exaggerations.

Exhausting quickly the powers of his language, he has

---

presque toutes chez elles de petits dieux penates hauts de quatre ou cinq pouces; une de ces petites divinités est la déesse de tetons, l'autre celle de fesses; il y a un penat qu'on appelle le *dieu Pet*." Voltaire, Essai sur les Mœurs et l'Esprit des Nations, iv. 373.

[1] Forster's Travels, ii. 256.

other expedients in store. The god, on whom his eulogies have been lavished, is that one, among the invisible powers, on whom his interests seem more immediately to depend. This deity is at first panegyrized on account of those operations alone which belong to his own department. The sun is originally applauded only as the regent of day: the bountiful giver of light, and of all its attendant blessings. But when panegyric on this subject is exhausted, the unwearied adorer opens a new fountain of adulation. The operations of some divinity, whose department most nearly resembles that of the favourite deity, afford some circumstance which, it is imagined, might do honour to that patron god. It is accordingly, as a very artful expedient, immediately detracted from the one, and ascribed to the other. No sooner is the novelty of this new attribute decayed, than the prerogative of some other divinity is invaded, and the great object of worship is invested with a new power or function of nature. This, it is evident, is a fertile discovery. The votary has many articles to add to his list of powers and functions, before he exhausts the provinces of the whole of the gods. He proceeds incessantly, however; adding to the works and dominions of the great divinity one province after another, till at last he bestows upon him the power and functions of all the gods. He is now the supreme deity, and all the rest are subordinate. He is the king of the celestial powers; or, what is still more sublime, their author or father; He from whom their very being and powers are derived. They still, however, retain their ancient departments: and he who was god of the winds remains the god of the winds: he who was god of the waters remains god of the waters. But they are no longer independent deities; they have now a superior, and are regarded in the light of his ministers or agents.

The ingenuity of fear and desire sometimes invents a higher strain of flattery still. The power, which is delegated to so many extraordinary beings, is regarded as a deduction from that which might otherwise be wielded by the supreme. And happy is the man, who first imagines he can inform the Divinity, that no such division and diminution of his power exist: that those supposed agents or ministers are not in reality beings endowed with the powers of the Almighty; that they are those powers themselves; the different modes in which he manifests himself. After this, he is the one God. He is all in all: from him everything begins, in him everything terminates: he unites all possible attributes: like time, he has no beginning, and shall have no end: all power belongs to him, all wisdom, and all virtue. Such is the progress of the language, not of knowledge and cultivated reason, but of the rude and selfish passions of a barbarian; and all these high and sounding epithets are invented by men whose ideas of the divine nature are mean, ridiculous, gross, and disgusting.

Some of the most enlightened of the Europeans who have made inquiries concerning the ideas and institutions of the Hindus, have been induced, from the lofty epithets occasionally applied to the gods, to believe and to assert that this people had a refined and elevated religion. Nothing is more certain than that such language is far from being proof of such a religion. Yet ingenious men, from whom we have largely derived instruction, appear to have thought that no other proof was requisite; and, as on this evidence they adopted the opinion themselves, thought that others ought to receive it on the same foundation.[1]

[1] Among the similar proofs which might be produced, of sublime theological notions, may be quoted the following remarkable passage from Garcilasso de la Vega (Royal Commentaries, book II. chap. ii.). "Besides the sun, whom they worshipped for the visible God, to whom they offered sacrifice and kept festivals, the *Incas*, who were kings, and the *Amautas*, who were philosophers, proceeded by the mere light of nature, to the knowledge of the true Almighty God our Lord, Maker of Heaven and Earth, as we shall hereafter prove by their own words and testimonies, which some of them gave of the Divine Majesty, which they called by the name of *Pachacamac*, and is a word compounded of *Pacha*, which is the universe, and *Camac*, which is the soul; and is as much as he that animates the world. * * * Being asked who this *Pachacamac* was, they answered that it was he who gave life to the universe; sustained and nourished all things; but because they did not see him they could not know him; and for that reason they erected not temples to him, nor offered sacrifice, howsoever they worshippped in their hearts and esteemed him for the unknown God." And in book VIII. ch. vii. he gives us the following argument of an Inca, Topac Yupanqui, "Many say that the sun lives, and that he is the maker of all things: now it is necessary that the thing which is the cause of the being of another, should be assistant and operate in the production thereof; now we know that many things receive their beings during the absence of the sun, and therefore he is not the maker of all things. And that the sun hath not life is evident, for that it always moves in its circle, and yet is never weary; for if it had life it would require rest, as we do: and were it free, it would visit other parts of the heavens, into which it never inclines out of its own sphere: but, as a thing obliged to a particular station, moves always in the same circle, and is like an arrow which is directed by the hand of the archer." The Mexicans, too, as we are informed by Clavigero, Hist. of Mexico, book VI. sect. i. besides the crowd of their ordinary Deities, believed in "a supreme, absolute, and independent Being, to whom they ac-

Since the language employed by any people is a very fallacious test of the ideas which they entertain concerning the Divine Nature, it is necessary to investigate the circumstances, in their religious practice or belief, which enable us in any degree to define their vague expressions. Those circumstances are few; but their evidence determinate. They are the operations ascribed to the Divinity, the services reputed agreeable to him, and the laws which he is understood to have ordained. If these correspond with the ideas of infinite power, wisdom, and goodness, we may believe with certainty that the sublime language is the expression of corresponding conceptions; on the other hand, where those operations, services, and laws, are in the highest degree unworthy of a perfect nature, we may be fully assured, that the sublime language is altogether without a meaning, the effect of flattery, and the meanest of passions; and that it is directly suggested, not by the most lofty, but by the most grovelling and base, ideas of the Divine Nature.

Of the host of Hindu Divinities, Brahma, Vishnu, and Siva are the most exalted. Other nations have most frequently carried on the applause of *one* favourite deity, till they bestowed upon him alone all power in heaven and earth. The Hindus have distributed the creation and government of the universe among those three, denominating Brahma the creator, Vishnu the preserver, and Siva the destroyer.

Of the highest scene of operation in which the Divine Being can be contemplated by mortals, the creation of the universe, the conception, formed by the Hindus, is so far from corresponding with high and noble ideas of the creating power, that it is consistent only with the meanest. This itself is a criterion of a religious system from which there is no appeal.

---

knowledged to owe fear and adoration. They represented him in no external form, because they believed him to be invisible; and named him only by the common appellation of God, in their language *Teotl*, a word resembling still more in its meaning than in its pronunciation the *Theos* of the Greeks; but they applied to him certain epithets which were highly expressive of the grandeur and power which they conceived him to possess. They called him *Ipalnemoani*, that is, "He by whom we live:" and *Tloque Nahuaque*. "He who is all in himself." Clavigero adds, "But their knowledge and worship of this Supreme Being was obscured, and in a manner lost, in the crowd of deities invented by their superstition."

Of the peculiar functions of Vishnu and Siva no determinate conception appears to have been formed. They are two beings of mighty power, by whom great actions are performed; but there is no distinct separation of their provinces. Whenever, indeed, we seek to ascertain the definite and precise ideas of the Hindus in religion, the subject eludes our grasp. All is loose, vague, wavering, obscure, and inconsistent.[1] Their expressions point at one time to one meaning, and another time to another meaning;[2] and their wild fictions, to use the language of Mr. Hume, seem rather the playsome whimsies of monkeys in human shape, than the serious asseverations of a being who dignifies himself with the name of rational.[3] Vishnu is not unfrequently employed in the acts which properly belong only to a destructive power; and Siva is so far from answering to the title bestowed upon him, that he is a divinity hardly less beneficent than Vishnu himself.

In the conception which the Hindus have formed of the government of the world, the visible agency of the Deity is peculiarly required. "I have passed," says the preserving God, "many births. Although I am not in my nature subject to birth or decay, and am the lord of all created beings, yet having command over my own nature, I am made evident by my own power; and as often as

[1] The confusion is not the fault of the system but of its expounders. In the original scheme, Brahma, Vishnu, and Siva, were nothing more than mythological personifications of the power of the one first cause, to create, to preserve, and to destroy. In the course of time, the Hindus did precisely what the text asserts they did not: "they carried on the applause of one favorite deity, till they bestowed upon him alone all power in heaven and earth." Brahma, probably, Vishnu and Siva, certainly, had their respective followers, who naturally invested the deity of their preference with the attributes of all. The Vaishnavas, made Vishnu creator and destroyer, as well as preserver: and the power of creating and preserving was assigned by the Saivas to Siva. There is no confusion or contradiction of system in this. It is the opposition of opposite sects. A person undertaking to give an account of the Christian religion would make strange work if he were to amalgamate as one undivided faith, the conflicting tenets of Lutherans, Calvinists, and Romanists. With equal ignorance do we confound Vaishnava, Saiva, and Sakta doctrines.—W.

[2] This is admitted even by those whom the occasional expressions of the Hindus have most strongly convinced of the sublimity of their sentiments. Mr. Colebrooke says, "There is indeed much disagreement and consequent confusion in the gradations of persons interposed by Hindu theology between the Supreme Being and the created world." Asiat. Research. viii. 442. Even Sir William Jones is constrained to confess that the Hindu "scheme of theology is most obscurely figurative, and consequently liable to dangerous misconception; that it is filled with idle superstitions, abounds with minute and childish formalities, with ceremonies generally absurd, and often ridiculous." Pref. to Institutes of Menu.

[3] Hume's Essays, ii. 470.

there is a decline of virtue, and an insurrection of vice and injustice in the world, I make myself evident; and thus I appear from age to age, for the preservation of the just, the destruction of the wicked, and the establishment of virtue."[1] "Aty Sechen himself," says another sacred book, "all-knowing as he is, could not number the metamorphoses and different forms under which the Vishnu has appeared for the salvation of the universe."[2] Such are the Hindu ideas of the manner in which the power of the Divine Being is exerted in the government of the universe!

Of these visible appearances or incarnations of the divinity, ten, known in the Hindu mythology under the name of avatars, are peculiarly distinguished. The first, which is denominated the avatar of the fish, is thus described.[3] At the close of the last calpa, there was a general destruction, occasioned by the sleep of Brahma: his creatures in different worlds being drowned in a vast ocean. The strong demon Hayagriva came near him and stole the Vedas, which had flowed from his lips. When the preserver of the universe discovered this deed, he took the shape of a minute fish, called sap'hari. A holy king named Satyavrata then reigned. One day as he was making a libation in the river Critamala, the little fish said to him, How canst thou leave me in this river water, when I am too weak to resist the monsters of the stream, who fill me with dread? Satyavrata placed it under his protection in a small vase full of water; but in a single night its bulk was so increased, that it could not be contained in the jar, and thus again addressed the prince: I am not pleased with living in this little vase; make me a large mansion where I may dwell in comfort. The king successively placed it in a cistern, in a pool, and in a lake, for each of which it speedily grew too large, and supplicated for a more spacious place of abode; after which he threw it into the sea, when the fish again addressed him: Here the horned sharks and other monsters of great strength will devour me; thou shouldest not, O valiant man, leave me in this ocean. Thus repeatedly deluded by the fish,

[1] Bagvat-Geeta, p. 51, 52. [2] Bagavadam, p. 11.

[3] I have merely abridged the account which is given by Sir William Jones in a literal translation from the Bhagavat. Asiat. Res. i. 230.

who had addressed him with gentle words, the king said, Who art thou that beguilest me in that assumed shape? Never before have I seen or heard of so prodigious an inhabitant of the waters, who like thee has filled up, in a single day, a lake a hundred leagues in circumference. Surely thou art the great God whose dwelling was on the waves. Salutation and praise to thee, O first male, the lord of creation, of preservation, of destruction! Thou art the highest object, O supreme ruler, of us thy adorers, who piously seek thee. All thy delusive descents in this world give existence to various beings; yet I am anxious to know for what cause that shape has been assumed by thee. The lord of the universe, loving the pious man, and intending to preserve him from the sea of destruction, caused by the depravity of the age, thus told him how he was to act: In seven days from the present time, O thou tamer of enemies, the three worlds will be plunged in an ocean of death; but in the midst of the destroying waves, a large vessel, sent by me for thy use, shall stand before thee. Then shalt thou take all medicinal herbs, all the variety of seeds; and, accompanied by seven saints, encircled by pairs of all brute animals, thou shalt enter the spacious ark, and continue in it secure from the flood on one immense ocean, without light except the radiance of thy companions. When the ship shall be agitated by an impetuous wind, thou shalt fasten it with a large sea-serpent on my horn; for I will be near thee, drawing the vessel with thee and thy attendants. Thus instructed, the pious king waited humbly for the appointed time. The sea, overwhelming its shores, deluged the whole earth; and it was soon perceived to be augmented by showers from immense clouds. He, still meditating on the divine command, and conforming to the divine directions, entered the ship; when the god appeared again distinctly on the vast ocean in the form of a fish, blazing like gold, extending a million of leagues, with one stupendous horn, on which the king, as he had before been commanded, tied the ship with a cable made of a vast serpent. Afterwards the god, rising, together with Brahma, from the destructive deluge, which was abated, slew the demon Hayagriva.

Such are the operations in the government of the universe,

which the religious ideas of the Hindus lead them to ascribe to the Divine Being. The second appearance or avatar of the Preserver is of the same character, and suggested by similar views. Hiranicheren, a malignant and destructive giant, who delighted in afflicting the earth, at last rolled it up in a shapeless mass, and plunged down with it into the abyss. On this occasion there issued from the side of Brahma, a being shaped like a boar, white and exceedingly small, which in the space of one hour grew to the size of an elephant of the largest magnitude, and remained in the air. This being, Brahma discovered to be Vishnu, who had assumed a body and become visible. Suddenly, it uttered a sound like the loudest thunder, and the echo reverberated, and shook all the corners of the universe. Shaking the full-flowing mane which hung down his neck on both sides, and erecting the humid hairs of his body, he proudly displayed his two most exceedingly white tusks: then rolling round his wine-coloured eyes, and erecting his tail, he descended from the region of the air, and plunged head foremost into the water. The whole body of water was convulsed by the motion, and began to rise in waves, while the guardian spirit of the sea, being terrified, began to tremble for his domain, and cry out for quarter and mercy. At length, the power of the omnipotent having divided the water, and arriving at the bottom, he saw the earth lying, a mighty and barren stratum; then he took up the ponderous globe (freed from the water) and raised it high on his tusk, one would say it was a beautiful lotus blossoming on the tip of his tusk. In a moment, with one leap, coming to the surface, by the all-directing power of the Omnipotent Creator, he spread it, like a carpet, on the face of the water, and then vanished from the sight of Brahma.[1]

Of the third avatar we have so particular and remarkable a description, that it merits uncommon regard.[2] The soors, a species of angels, and all the glorious host of heaven, sat on the summit of Mount Meru, a fictitious mountain, highly celebrated in the books of the Hindus, meditating the disco-

[1] For an account of this avatar, see an extract from the Mahabarat, Asiat. Research. i. 154; Bartolomeo's Travels, book ii. ch. vii. The peculiar description of the boar is taken from a translation by Mr. Halhed, of a passage in the Puranas, published in Maurice's Hindustan, i. 407.

[2] It is a passage translated from the Mahabarat, by Mr. Wilkins, in one of the notes to his translation of the Bagvat-Geeta, p. 145, 146, note 76.

BOOK II. CHAP. VI.

very of the Amreeta, that is, being translated, the water of immortality: when Narayan[1] said unto Brahma, Let the ocean, as a pot of milk, be churned by the united labour of the soors and assoors; and when the mighty waters have been stirred up, the Amreeta shall be found. A great mountain, named Mandar, was the instrument with which the operation was to be performed; but the dews[2] being unable to remove it, they had recourse to Vishnu and Brahma. By their direction, the king of the serpents lifted up that sovereign of mountains, with all its forests and inhabitants; and the soors and asoors having obtained permission of the king of the tortoises, it was placed for support on his back, in the midst of the ocean. Then the soors and asoors, using the serpent Vasookee for the rope, the asoors pulling by the head, and the soors by the tail, began to churn the ocean;[3] while there issued from the mouth of the serpent, a continued stream of fire, and smoke, and wind; and the roaring of the ocean, violently agitated with the whirling of the mountain, was like the bellowing of a mighty cloud. Meanwhile, a violent conflagration was raised on the mountain, by the concussion of its trees and other substances, and quenched by a shower which the lord of the firmament poured down: whence an heterogeneous stream, of the concocted juices of various trees and plants, ran down into the briny flood. It was from this milk-like stream, produced from those juices, and a mixture of melted gold, that the soors obtained their immortality. The waters of the ocean, being now assimilated with those juices, were converted into milk, and a species of butter was produced, when the churning powers became fatigued; but Narayan endued them with fresh strength, and they proceeded with great ardour to stir that butter of the ocean. First, arose from it the moon; next, Sree, the goddess of fortune; then the goddess of wine, and the white horse, Oochisrava; afterwards the jewel Kowstoobh; the tree of plenty; and the

[1] A name of Vishnu.

[2] Dew, written otherwise Dewa, or Deva, is a general name for a superior spirit.

[3] By twisting the serpent about the mountain, like a rope, and pulling it out first towards the one end, and then towards the other; which affords us a description of their real mode of churning. A piece of wood, so formed as best to agitate the milk, was placed upright in the vessel, and a rope being twisted round it which two persons pulled alternately, one at the one end, and the other at the other, it was whirled round, and thus produced the agitation required.

cow that granted every heart's desire. Then the dew Dhanwantaree, in human shape, came forth, holding in his hand a white vessel filled with the immortal juice, amreeta; which, when the asoors beheld, they raised their tumultuous voices, and each of them clamorously exclaimed, This of right is mine! But as they continued to churn the ocean more than enough, a deadly poison issued from its bed, confounding the three regions of the world with its immortal stench, until Siva, at the word of Brahma, swallowed the fatal drug to save mankind. In the mean while a violent jealousy and hatred, on account of the amreeta, and the goddess Sree, sprung up in the bosoms of the asoors. But Narayan, assuming the form of a beautiful female, stood before them, whose minds becoming fascinated by her presence, and deprived of reason, they seized the amreeta and gave it unto her. But a dreadful battle arose between the soors and asoors, in which Narayan, quitting the female figure, assisted the soors. The elements and powers of nature were thrown into confusion by the conflict; but with the mighty aid of Narayan, and his weapon chacra, which of itself, unguided even by a hand, performed miraculous exploits, the soors obtained the victory, and the mountain Mandar was carried back to its former station. The soors guarded the amreeta with great care; and the god of the firmament, with all his immortal hands, gave the water of life unto Narayan, to keep it for their use. This was the third manifestation of the Almighty, in the preservation and government of the world.

The fourth I shall describe with greater brevity. Hirinacheren, the gigantic ruler, who rolled up the earth, and plunged with it to the bottom of the abyss, left a younger brother, Hirinakassup, who succeeded him in his kingdom, and refused to do homage to Vishnu, but persecuted his own son, who was an ardent votary of that god. I, said he am lord of all this visible world. The son replied, that Vishnu had no fixed abode, but was present everywhere. Is he, said his father, in that pillar? Then let him come forth; and rising from his seat, he struck the pillar with his foot; upon which Vishnu, bursting from it, with a body like a man, but a head like a lion, tore Hirinakassup in pieces, and placed his son upon the throne.[1]

[1] Asiat. Research. i. 154.

BOOK II. CHAP. VI.

In the fifth, the sixth, and the seventh avatars, the Preserving Power appeared in human shapes for the destruction of impious and ferocious kings, performing many heroic and many miraculous deeds. But, after the examples which have already been given, a particular description of these extravagant legends would poorly compensate the toil of a perusal. The eighth, however, is one of the most celebrated of all the incarnations of Vishnu. He was born the son of Vasudeva and Devaci, of the royal family of Cansa, and obtained the name of Crishna. But as it had been predicted to Cansa, that one born of those parents would occasion his destruction, whence he had decreed the death of all their children, Crishna was secretly withdrawn, and brought up in the family of a shepherd or herdsman. Many and wonderful were the transactions of his childhood, in which the wanton pranks of the mischievous, but amiable boy, are not less distinguished than the miraculous exploits of the god. When he grew up to youth, the indulgence of licentious love was his great occupation and enjoyment. It is a small part of the picture which I can, or which I need, to expose to view. The scenes with the young shepherdesses are painted by the Hindus in all the glowing colours of oriental poetry. A passage from a hymn, or divine song, translated by Sir William Jones, is in the following words: "With a garland of wild flowers, descending even to the yellow mantle that girds his azure limbs, distinguished by smiling cheeks, and by ear-rings that sparkle as he plays, Heri[1] exults in the assemblage of amorous damsels. One of them presses him with her swelling breast, while she warbles with exquisite melody. Another, affected by a glance from his eye, stands meditating on the lotos of his face. A third, on pretence of whispering a secret in his ear, approaches his temples, and kisses them with ardour. One seizes his mantle, and draws him towards her, pointing to the bower on the banks of Yamuna, where elegant vanjulahs interweave their branches. He applauds another who dances in the sportive circle, whilst her bracelets ring, as she beats time with her palms. Now he caresses one, and kisses another, smiling on a third with complacency; and now he chases her whose beauty has most allured him. Thus the wanton Heri frolics, in the season of sweets, among the maids

[1] A name of Vishnu.

of Vraja, who rush to his embraces, as if he were pleasure itself assuming a human form; and one of them, under a pretext of hymning his divine perfections, whispers in his ear: Thy lips, my beloved, are nectar."[1] I shall select but another instance, which is from the translation before us of the Bhagavat. "Crishna, finding himself on the banks of the Yamuna,[2] began to play on his pastoral flute. All the shepherdesses, filled with desire, ran in crowds to hear his enchanting sounds. Crishna, beholding them burning with desire, informed them that it was contrary to the order established in the world, to quit their houses to seek the embraces of a lover. He added that their families might thus, if their husbands were jealous, be thrown into disorder, and disgrace come upon themselves. He advised them accordingly to return. The women replied, that their passion, it was true, were it for an ordinary man, would be criminal; but desiring to unite themselves with the absolute master of all things, they could not believe that such an impulse was any other than meritorious. In regard to their husbands, they could have no rights which tended to the exclusion of God. Crishna, who saw the innocence of their hearts, graciously gave them entire satisfaction; and by a miracle continually renewed, in all that multitude of women, each was convinced that she alone enjoyed the Deity, and that he never quitted her an instant for the embraces of another."[3] "Crishna," says Sir William Jones, "continues to this hour the darling god of the Indian women. The sect of Hindus," he adds, "who adore him with enthusiastic and almost exclusive devotion, have broached a doctrine which they maintain with eagerness, and which seems general in these provinces;[4] that he was distinct from all the avatars, who had only a portion of his divinity; while Crishna was the person of Vishnu himself in a human form."[5] "At a more advanced age," continues Sir William, "he put to death his cruel enemy, Cansa: and having taken under his protection the king Yudhist'hir and the other Pandus, who had been grievously oppressed by the Curus, and their

1 Asiat. Research, i. 187.
2 This is spelt Emuney in the French translation.
3 Bagavadam, p. 60. This indeed was but a trifle: for with his 16,000 or 17,000 wives he could perform the same feat. See Halhed's translation of the Bhagavat, in Maurice's Hind. vol. ii.
4 He means the provinces where he then resided, Bengal, etc.
5 Asiat. Research. i. 260.

BOOK II. CHAP. VI.

tyrannical chief, he kindled the war described in the great epic poem, entitled the Mahabharat, at the prosperous conclusion of which he returned to his heavenly seat in Vaicont'ha, having left the instructions comprised in the Gita with his disconsolate friend Arjoon."[1] He was afterwards slain, being wounded bp an arrow in the foot"[2]

The ninth incarnation of Vishnu, and the last, yet vouchsafed, of the Divine appearances, was in the person of Buddha. The object of this avatar is described in the following verse of a Hindu poet; "Thou blamest, Oh wonderful, the whole Veda, when thou seest, O kind-hearted, the slaughter of the cattle prescribed for sacrifice, O Cesava,[3] assuming the body of Buddha. Be victorious, O Heri,[4] Lord of the universe!"[5] But though Buddha is, by the Hindus, regarded as a manifestation of the Divine Being, the sect of Buddhists are regarded as heretical, and are persecuted by the Brahmens. It is conjectured that, at one time, a great number of them had been compelled to fly from the country, and spread their tenets in various directions.[6] The religion of Buddha is now found to prevail over the greater part of the East; in Ceylon, in the further peninsula, in Thibet, in China, and even as far as Japan.[7] "The tenth avatar," says Sir William Jones, "we

[1] Asiat. Research. i. 261. He sometimes, however, met with severe repulses. "Calijun, a prince who resided in the western parts of India, was very near defeating his ambitious projects. Indeed, Crishna was nearly overcome and subdued, after seventeen bloody battles; and according to the express words of the Puranas, he was forced to have recourse to treachery, by which means Calijun was totally defeated in the eighteenth engagement." Wilford, on Chron. of Hindus, Asiat. Research. v. 288.

[2] Bagavadam, p. 13. "The whole history of Crishna," says Anquetil Duperron, in his Observations on the Bhagavat, in the Recherches Historiques et Géographiques sur l'Inde, "is a mere tissue of Greek and Roman obscenities, covered with a veil of spirituality, which, among the fanatics of all descriptions, conceals the most abominable enormities." Speaking of a temple of Vishnu at Satymangalam, in the Mysore, Dr. Buchanan says, "The rath, or chariot, belonging to it, is very large, and richly carved. The figures on it, representing the amours of that god, in the form of Chrishna, are the most indecent that I have ever seen." Buchanan's Journey through Mysore, etc., ii. 237.

[3] A name of Vishnu.

[4] Another name of Vishnu, vide supra, p. 247.

[5] Asiat. Research. ii. 121.

[6] "As to Buddha," says Sir William Jones (Disc. on the Gods of Greece, Italy, and India), "he seems to have been a reformer of the doctrines contained in the Vedas; and, though his good-nature led him to censure these ancient books, because they enjoined the sacrifices of cattle, yet he is admitted as the ninth avatar, even by the Brahmens of Casi."

[7] A controversy has been started, whether the religion of Buddha was derived from that of Brahma, or that of Brahma from the religion of Buddha. There seems little chance that data will ever be obtained, to prove either the

are told is yet to come, and is expected to appear mounted (like the crowned conqueror in the Apocalypse) on a white horse, with a cimeter blazing like a comet, to mow down all incorrigible and impenitent offenders who shall then be on earth."[1]

It will require the addition of but a few passages more of this wild mythology, to convey a satisfactory idea of the actions and qualities which the Hindus ascribe to their supreme deities. "It is related," says Mr. Wilford,[2] "in the Scanda,[3] that when the whole earth was covered with water, and Vishnu lay extended asleep in the bosom of Devi,[4] a lotos arose from his navel. Brahma sprung from that flower, and looking round without seeing any creature on the boundless expanse, imagined himself to be the first-born, and entitled to rank above all future beings. Resolving, however, by investigation, more fully to satisfy himself, he glided down the stalk of the lotos, and finding Vishnu asleep, asked loudly who he was. I am the first-born, answered Vishnu, waking: and as Brahma contradicted him, they had an obstinate battle, till Mahadeva, or Siva, pressed between them in great wrath, saying, It is I who am truly the first-born; but I will resign my pretensions to either of you who shall be able to reach and behold the summit of my head, or the soles of my feet. Brahma instantly ascended; but having fatigued himself to no purpose in the regions of immensity, yet loth to abandon his claim, he returned to Mahadeva, and declared that he had attained the crown of his head, calling, as his witness, the first-born cow. For this union of pride and falsehood, the angry god ordained, that no sacred rites should be per-

one or the other. Clemens Alexandrinus would lead us to believe, that the religion of Buddha, in his time must have been in high repute: Εισι δε των Ινδων, says he (Strom. lib. i. p. 352), ὁι τοις Βουττα πειθομενοι παραγγελμασι, ὁν δι ὑπερβολην σεμνοτητος ὡς Θεον τετιμηκασι. (See also Hieronym. Cont. Jovian. lib. i. cap. 26,) This divinity was not confined to the Asiatics. There was a Butus, or Buto of Egypt, a Battus of Cyrene, and a Bœotus of Greece. (See Bryant's Analysis of Ancient Mythology, iii. 170.) One of the primitive authors of the sect of Manicheans took the name of Buddas; another that of Manes; both of them names identical with the names of gods and sacred beings among the Hindus. Beausobre Hist. de Manich, liv.i. ch. i.—M.

Much additional information has been collected since this was written, and the history of Buddhism is clearly made out. See Burnouf Histoire de Bouddhisme, and Harvey's Eastern Monachism and Manual of Buddhism, &c.—W.

[1] Asiat. Research. i. 236. See also Ward's View, &c. of the Hindus, (i. 3. London Ed.) for an account of the ten avatars.

[2] Asiat, Research. iii. 374.

[3] One of the Puranas.

[5] This means literally the goddess.

BOOK II. CHAP. VI.

formed to Brahma. When Vishnu returned, he acknowledged that he had not been able to see the feet of Mahadeva, confessed him to be the first-born among the gods, and entitled to rank above them all."

After a passage such as this, who would expect to find the following? "The patriarch Atterien retired into a forest, and there performed rigorous devotion, having for his nourishment nothing but the wind, and being exposed to all the injuries of the atmosphere. One day he addressed his vows to the Eternal in these words: O thou who hast created, and who preservest the universe; O thou by whom it is destroyed; give me the knowledge of thyself, and grant me the vision of thee! Then a fire issuing from the crown of the votary's head, made all the gods tremble, and they had recourse to Vishnu, to Siva, and to Brahma. Those three divinities, completely armed and mounted, accompanied by Lacshmi, Gunga, and Seraswati, their wives, presented themselves before the saint. Prostrating himself, Atterien worshipped them, and uttered the following words: O you three Lords, know that I recognise only one God: inform me which of you is the true divinity, that I may address to him alone my vows and adorations! To this application the three Gods replied; Learn, O devotee, that there is no real distinction between us: what to you appears such is only by semblance: the Single Being appears under three forms; by the acts of creation, of preservation, and destruction: but he is One."[1] Yet this "Single" Being, this ONE God, is thus again represented, a few pages after, in the same Purana: "Even Brahma, finding himself alone with his daughter, who was full of charms and knowledge, conceived for her a criminal passion."[2] Thus are we taught by the Hindus themselves to interpret the lofty phrases which the spirit of exaggeration and flattery so frequently puts into their mouths.

Of the First-born Mahadeva, or the One, Eternal God, under one of his forms, we have the following sacred story. He was playing one day at dice with Parvati,[3] when they quarrelled, and parted in wrath to different regions. They severally performed rigid acts of devotion, but the fires which they kindled blazed so vehemently as to threaten a

[1] Bagavadam, p. 96, et seq. [2] Ib. 178.

[3] One of the names of his wife.

general conflagration. The devas,[1] in great alarm, hastened to Brahma, who led them to Mahadeva, and supplicated him to recall his consort; but the wrathful deity only answered, that she must come by her own free choice. They accordingly despatched Gunga, the river goddess, who prevailed on Parvati to return to him, on condition that his love for her should be restored. The celestial mediators then employed Camadeva,[2] who wounded Siva with one of his flowery arrows; but the angry divinity reduced him to ashes with a flame from his eye. Parvati soon after presented herself before him in the form of a Cirati, or daughter of a mountaineer, and seeing him enamoured of her, resumed her own shape.[3] Of the various passages of a similar nature, presented to us in the history of this God, I shall content myself with another, extracted by Mr. Wilford from the Scanda Purana. "There had subsisted," says he,[4] "for a long time, some animosity between Brahma and Mahadeva in their mortal shapes; and the latter, on account of his bad conduct, which is fully described in the Puranas, had, it appears, given much uneasiness to Swayambhuva, and Satarupa. For he was libidinous, going about stark-naked, with a large club in his hand. Be this as it may, Mahadeva, who was the eldest, saw his claim as such totally disregarded, and Brahma set up in his room. This intrusion the latter wanted to support; but made use of such lies as provoked Mahadeva to such a point, that he cut off one of his heads in his divine form." Such are the ideas which the Hindus entertain of the actions and character of their supreme deities; on whom, notwithstanding, they lavish all the most lofty epithets of divinity which human language can supply.[5]

[1] A general name of the inferior gods.

[2] One of the devas.

[3] See this story as extracted from the Puranas, Asiat. Researches, iii. 402.

[4] Ib. vi. 474.

[5] Much of what has been cited in the text is sectarial, intended to exalt Siva or Vishnu at the expense of the other, or of Brahma. A very great part is the invention, also, of comparatively modern times, when the manners of the Hindus had received a taint from Mahomedan licentiousness. Many of the faults, however, are, no doubt, inseparable from all mythological systems in which the passions and acts of men are attributed to divinities. It must be remembered, however, that the gods of the Hindus are, even in the opinion of the vulgar, finite beings, living for a long period, but destined to die. Nor is this notion to be taken as a proof of their unworthy conception of the divine nature; it is rather a proof that they attach the character of inferior divinity to the objects of their worship. Eternity, and all the higher attributes of godhead, are reserved for the one God, the origin of all things. If the language of panegyric ascribes them to the personifications of his power, it is less in

This theology affords a remarkable instance of that progress in exaggeration and flattery which I have described as the genius of rude religion. As the Hindus, instead of selecting one god, to whom they assigned all power in heaven and in earth, distributed the creation and administration of the universe among three divinities, they divided themselves into sects; and some attached themselves more particularly to one deity, some to another.[1]

---

their own persons than as emanations from him, and identifiable with him. This is always the prevailing idea of hymns and prayers addressed to the divinities who are the subjects of praise.—W.

[1] Mr. Paterson, in his Discourse on the Origin of the Hindu Religion, delineates a terrible picture of this Hindu controversy. The people separated, he tells us, "into sects, each selecting one of the triad, the particular object of their devotion, in preference to and exclusive of the others: the followers of Vishnu and Siva invented new symbols, each, to ascribe to their respective divinity the attribute of creation. This contention for pre-eminence ended in the total suppression of the worship of Brahma, and the temporary submission of Vishnu to the superiority of Siva; but this did not last long; the sects raised crusades against each other; hordes of armed fanatics, under the title of Sanyasis and Vairagis, enlisted themselves as champions of their respective faith; the former devoted their lives in support of the superiority of Siva; and the latter were no less zealous for the rights of Vishnu: alternate victory and defeat marked the progress of a religious war, which for ages continued to harass the earth, and inflame mankind against each other." Asiat. Research. viii. 45, 46. Dr. Buchanan informs us, "That the worshippers of the two gods (Vishnu and Siva,) who are of different sects, are very apt to fall into disputes, occasioning abusive language, and followed by violence; so that the collectors have sometimes been obliged to have recourse to the fear of the bayonet, to prevent the controversy from producing bad effects." Buchanan's Journey through Mysore, &c., i. 13. The missionary Dubois observes, that "we see the two sects striving to exalt the respective deities whom they worship, and to revile those of their opponents. . . . . The followers of Vishnu vehemently insist that he is far superior to Siva, and is alone worthy of all honour. . . . . The disciples of Siva, on the contrary, no less obstinately affirm that Vishnu is nothing, and has never done any act, but tricks so base as to provoke shame and indignation," &c. Description, &c. of the People of India, p. 58. See ,too, the Missionary Ward's View, &c. of the Hindoos.Lond. Ed. Introd. p. 27.

The preface to *(Bhagavadam)* the French translation of the Bhagavat, by M. D'Ohsonville, says, "The Indians are divided into two orthodox sects, which, however, violently oppose one another; the one asserting the supremacy of Vishnu, the other of Siva. . . . . The Puranas," it says, "differ in their interpretations of the Vedas, some of them giving the supremacy to Brahma, some to Vishnu, and some to Siva. These books are, properly speaking, pieces of controversial theology. The Brahmens, who composed them, disputing to which of their three gods the supremacy belongs, support the pretensions of each by an enormous mass of mythological legends and mystical opinions, in favour of the God whom the author adopts. All are equally supported by the authority of the Vedas."

Mr. Colebrooke, describing the different sects of the Hindus, informs us that "Sancara Acharya, the celebrated commentator on the Veda, contended for the attributes of Siva, and founded or confirmed the sect of Saivas, who worship Mahadeva as the Supreme Being, and deny the independent existence of Vishnu and other Deities. Madhava Acharya and Vallabha Acharya have in like manner established the sect of Vaishnavas who adore Vishnu as God. The Suras (less numerous than the two sects above-mentioned) worship the sun, and acknowledge no other divinity. The Ganapatyas adore Ganesa, as uniting in his person all the attributes of the Deity." Note A. on the Religious Ceremonies of the Hindus. Asiat. Research. vii.

Presently the usual consequence appeared. Whichever of the three gods any votary selected for his peculiar patron, he expected to perform to him one of the most agreeable of all possible services, by representing him as superior to the other two. This we find to have been the practice, invariably and enthusiastically. In a passage from the Scanda Purana, one of the sacred books in honour of Siva, we have seen by what legends his votaries endeavour to elevate him above Brahma and Vishnu; while he cuts off the head of the one for contesting with him the supremacy, and has it expressly yielded up to him by the other. It is not, however, sufficient that the favourite god should be only superior to the rest; whatever honour is derived from their actions, that too must be claimed for him; and he is asserted to be himself the author of all their achievements.[1]

A still higher strain of flattery succeeds. Not only must he absorb their actions, it is accounted still nobler if he can be asserted to absorb even themselves; if Siva, for example, can be affirmed, not only to be Siva, and to be at once creator, preserver, and destroyer, but can be declared to be Brahma, Vishnu, and Siva themselves. Beyond even this, a step remains. In the same manner as he absorbs the gods, he is finally made to absorb everything. He is asserted to be the universe itself. He is then all in all. We shall find this process pursued with the Hindu divinities, one after another. In another sacred book,[2] dedicated to Siva, that god is made to declare, "I have always been, and I always am, and I always will be. There is no second of whom I can say that I am he, and that he is I. I am the within of all the withins. I am in all surfaces. Whatever is I am; and whatever is not I am. I am Brahma; and I am also Brahme; and I am the causing cause. Whatever is in the east I am; and whatever is in the west I am; and whatever is in the south I am; and

[1] It is strange that this source of perplexity and contradiction did not suggest an explanation of the difficulties previously intimated. For a more detailed view of the sects of the Hindus, see Asiat. Researches, vols. xvi. and xvii.—W.

[2] The Oupnekhat, of which an ancient version into the Persian language has been found. Anquetil Duperron published first some specimens of a translation from this in the Recherches Historiques et Géographiques sur l'Inde, and has since published a translation of the whole in Latin. There is a translation of it likewise among the late Mr. Allein's manuscripts in the British Museum.

BOOK II. CHAP. VI.

whatever is in the north I am. Whatever is below I am; and whatever is above I am. I am man, and not man, and woman. I am the truth; I am the ox; and I am all other animated beings. I am more ancient than all. I am the king of kings. And I am in all the great qualities. I am the perfect being. Whatever has been, Rudra[1] is; and whatever is he is; and whatever shall be he is. Rudra is life, and is death; and is the past, present, and future; and is all worlds."[2] But if the votaries of Siva, with exaggerating devotion, thus infinitely exalt him above all; the same, or, if possible, still greater honours, do the adorers of Vishnu lavish upon that divinity. "Let it not be thought," says the Bhagavat, "that Vishnu is only one of the three divinities, or triple powers. Know that he is the principle of all. It is he who created the universe by his productive power; it is he who supports all by his preserving power; it is he, in fine, who destroys all by his destructive power. He creates under the form of Brahma, and destroys under that of Siva. The productive power is more excellent than the destructive, and the preserving more excellent than the productive. To the name of Vishnu, therefore, is attached the pre-eminence, since the title of preserver or saviour is peculiarly attributed to him."[3] In the Bhagvat-Geeta, Crishna is thus addressed: "O mighty being! who, greater than Brahma, art the prime creator! eternal god of gods! the world's mansion! thou art the incorruptible being distinct from all things transient! Thou art before all gods, and the supreme supporter of the universe! Thou knowest all things! By thee, O infinite form! the universe was spread abroad. Thou art Vayoo the god of winds, Agnee the god of fire, Varoon the god of oceans, Sasanka the moon, Prajapatee the god of nations! Reverence be unto thee before and behind, reverence be unto thee on all sides, O thou who art all in all! Infinite is thy power and thy glory! Thou includest all things, wherefore thou art all things."[4] In a

[1] One of the many names of Siva, or Mahadeva.

[2] Oupnekhat, ix.

[3] Bhagavadam, p. 8, 9.

[4] Bhagvat-Geeta, p. 94: see similar strings of praises, Ibid. pp. 84 to 88; pp. 78, 79; p. 70. At p. 80, he is denominated, "The father and the mother of this world;" which affords another curious coincidence with the phraseology of other religions. The orphic verses περι φυσεως make Jupiter the "father and mother of all things."

Παντων μεν συ πατηρ, μητηρ, &c.—Hymn. ix. ver. 18.

Sanscrit inscription, taken from a stone at Buddha Gaya, Buddha is thus addressed: "Reverence be unto thee, O god, in the form of the god of mercy; the lord of all things, the guardian of the universe. Thou art Brahma, Vishnu, and Mahesa.[1] Thou art lord of the universe! Thou art, under the proper form of all things, moveable and immoveable, the possessor of the whole."[2]

Among the numerous expressions of panegyric and adoration which the Hindus apply to their divinities, none seem to have made a deeper impression upon some of the most intelligent of our English inquirers, than the epithet ONE.[3] This has so far prevailed as to impress them with a belief that the Hindus had a refined conception of the unity of the Divine Nature. Yet it seems very clear that the use of such an epithet is but a natural link in that chain of unmeaning panegyric which distinguishes the religion of ignorant men. When one divinity has been made to engross the powers of all the rest, it is the necessary termination of this piece of flattery, to denominate

Valerius Soranus calls Jupiter "the father and mother of the gods."

> Jupiter omnipotens, regum Rex ipse Deûmque
> Progenitor, Genetrixque Deûm; Deus unus et idem.
> Apud Augustin. de Civitat. Dei, lib. iv. cap. xi. et lib. vii. cap. ix.

Synesius uses similar language:

> Συ πατηρ, συ δ'εσσι μητηρ,
> Συ δ' αρσην συ δε Θηλυς.—Synes. Hymn. iii.

Even Martial, in a sort of a Hymn, or eulogy upon Mercury, beginning

> Hermes Martia seculi voluptas,
> Hermes omnibus eruditus armis;
> &c. &c., ends thus,
> *Hermes omnia solus, et ter unus*—Mart. Ep. lib. iv. ep. 25.

"De Deo, ejusque cultu, ita Chaldæos tradidisse referunt; 1. *Esse Deum omnium regem, parentemque, cujus providentia universorum ordo atque ornatus factus est.*—Bruckeri Hist. Crit. Philosophiæ, lib. ii. cap. ii. sect. 18.

[1] Another name for Siva.

[2] Asiat, Research. i. 284, 285.

[3] Much of what follows on this subject is verbal quibbling. One, in Sanscrit, as in other languages, may no doubt imply "chief," "principal," or metaphorically denote identity of persons; but it should have been proved that the word was so used when applied to the "One" Deity. It does not signify, when so employed, the chief—or the same—but the one distinct from and above all, and from whom all things proceeded. What notions Mr. Mill would have the term express he should have explained; it is evident that he has in his instances confounded very different things; the notion of one of many with one over many, and the simple ideas of unity and supremacy, with more comprehensive ideas of other attributes. Why should the belief of one God not prevail amongst the Africans? What do we understand of oneness more than they? Why should not the Heathen nations have had some perception of this truth, although it failed to influence their practice? "The intelligent pagans acknowledged only one God according to the phrase quoted by Laertius of Thales. God is the oldest of all things, because he is unmade or unproduced, and the only thing that is so."—i. 35. "The Pagans do often characterize the Supreme God by such titles, epithets, and descriptions, as are incommunicably proper to him, thereby plainly distinguishing him from all other inferior gods." Cudworth, ii. 11.—W.

him THE ONE. Oriental scholars ought moreover to have reflected that *one* is an epithet of very common and vague application in the languages of Asia; and is by no means a foundation whereon to infer among the Hindus any conception analogous to that which we denote by the term "Unity of God." The translation of the Institutes of Menu affords us a very satisfactory example: "Then only is a man perfect when he consists of three persons united, his wife, himself, and his son; and thus have learned Brahmens announced this—the husband is even ONE with his wife."[1] Yet surely no unity of being was supposed in this triune person, *a man, his wife, and his son.* AD, we are informed by Macrobius, was among the Assyrians a word which signified *one*, and was a name conferred by them upon their chief divinity.[2] The Babylonians applied it to their principal goddess.[3] The god Rimmon, as we learn from the Bible, had the same epithet.[4] Mr. Bryant says it was a sacred title among all the Eastern nations, and originally conferred upon the sun.[5] Even the Greek poets, who have never been suspected of refined notions of the unity of God, employ it to profusion. It is applied to Jupiter, to Pluto, to the sun, to Dionysus.[6] All the gods are affirmed to be one.[7] "One power," says the Orphic poetry, "one divinity, Jupiter is the great ruler of all."[8] Plutarch informs us that Apollo was frequently denominated the *monad*, or the ONLY ONE;[9] and from the emperor Julian we learn, that the people of Edessa had a god whom they called MONIMUS, a word of the same interpretation.[10] Few

[1] Institutes of Menu, ch. ix. 45.

[2] Deo, quem summum maximumque venerantur, Adad nomen, dederunt. Ejus nominis interpretatio significat *unus*. Macrob. Satur. lib. i. cap. 23. This reduplication Mr. Bryant, with good reason, supposes to be a superlative, but is wrong in supposing it an ordinal. i. 29.

[3] Αδα, ἡδονη· και ὑπο Βαβυλωνιων ἡ Ηρα. Hesychius, ad verb. The Greeks gave it, for a feminine application, a feminine termination.

[4] Zechariah, ch. xii. ver. 11. "As the mourning of Adad Rimmon, in the valley of Megiddon."

[5] Analysis of Ancient Mythology, i. 29.

[6] Ἑις Ζευς, εἱς Αϊδης, εἱς Ἡλιος εἱς Διονυσος,
Ἑις θεος εν παντεσσι.—Orph. Frag. iv. p. 364.

[7] Πλουτων, Περσεφονη, Δημητηρ, Κυπρις, Ερωτες,
Τριτωνες, Νηρευς, Τηθυς, και Κυανοχαιτες,
Ἑρμησθ', Ἡφαιστος τε κλυτος, Παν, Ζευς τε, και Ἡρη
Αρτεμις, ηδ' Εκαεργος Απολλων, ἑις θεος εστι.—Hermesianax.

[8] Orphic. Fragm. vi. 366.

[9] Την ΜΟΝΑΔΑ τους ανδρας ονομαζειν Απολλωνα.—Plutarch. Isis et Osiris, 354.

[10] Orat. iv. p. 150. See note 2, in page 256, where Mercury is denominated the *Thrice-one*.

nations shall we find without a knowledge of the unity of the Divine Nature, if we take such expressions of it as abound in the Hindu writings for satisfactory evidence. By this token, Mr. Park found it among the savages of Africa.[1]

In pursuance of the same persuasion, ingenious authors have laid hold of the term Brahme, or Brahm, the neuter of Brahma, the masculine name of the creator.[2] This they have represented as the peculiar appellation of the one god; Brahma, Vishnu, and Siva, being only names of the particular modes of divine action. But this supposition (for it is nothing more)[3] involves the most enormous inconsistency; as if the Hindus possessed refined notions of the unity of God, and could yet conceive his modes of action to be truly set forth in the characters of Brahma, Vishnu, and Siva; as if the same people could at once be so enlightened as to form a sublime conception of the Divine Nature, and yet so stupid as to make a distinction between the character of God and his modes of action. The parts of the Hindu writings, however, which are already before us, completely refute this gratuitous notion, and prove that Brahme is a mere unmeaning epithet of

[1] "The belief of ONE GOD," says he, "and of a future state of reward and punishment, is entire and universal among them." Park's Travels in Africa, p. 273.

[2] Sir W. Jones says (Discourse on the Gods of Greece, Italy, and India), "It must always be remembered, that the learned Indians, as they are instructed by their own books, in truth acknowledge only one supreme being, whom they call Brahme, or the *Great One*, in the neuter gender; they believe his essence to be infinitely removed from the comprehension of any mind but his own; and they suppose him to manifest his power by the operation of his divine spirit; whom they name Vishnu, the *Pervader*, in the masculine gender, whence he is often denominated the first male. * * * * When they consider the Divine Power exerted in creating, or in giving existence to that which existed not before, they call the Deity Brahma, in the masculine gender also; and when they view him in the light of *Destroyer*, or rather *changer* of forms, they give him a thousand names, of which Siva, Isa or Iswara, Rudra, Hara, Sambhu, and Mahadeva, or Mahesa, are the most common." Mr. Wilford (Asiat. Research. iii. 370) says that Brahma, Vishnu, and Mahadeva, "are only the principal forms in which the Brahmens teach the people to adore Brahm, or the Great One."

[3] It is something more than supposition. "The attributes are affirmed by the Vedas to be the creating, protecting, destroying, and the like, powers of the Supreme Being. Their worship, under various representations by means of consecrated objects, is prescribed by the scripture to the human race, who, owing to the wavering nature of their minds, cannot without assistance fix the thoughts on the incomprehensible and Almighty Being." Defence of Hindoo Theism, by Sankara Sastri. Rammohun Roy, whilst he denies the necessity of the worship, equally admits the character of personified attributes attached by the Vedas themselves to Brahme, Vishnu, and Siva. Translations from the Vedas, p. 145.—W.

BOOK II. CHAP. VI.

praise, applied to various gods;[1] and no more indicative of refined notions of the unity, or any perfection of the Divine Nature, than other parts of their panegyrical devotions. We have already beheld Siva decorated with this title.[2] Vishnu is denominated the supreme Brahme in the Bhagvat-Geeta.[3] Nay, we find this Brahme, the great,

[1] This is a specimen of most perverse reasoning. Brahme is said to be a mere unmeaning epithet of praise, applied to various gods; but if it means nothing, what honour can it do them, why is it attached to them? It must have some signification, or it would not be employed. It may be absurdly used; but, undoubtedly, when God or man is called Brahme, it is intended to say, that he is something of a more elevated nature than his ordinary nature—that he is, in fact, one with that being, who, according to particular doctrines, is not only the cause of all that exists, but is all that exists. The reasonableness of the Vedanta philosophy, the fitness of sectarial panegyric, are not in question. The eulogy of any individual god by identifying him with Brahme, derives its weight entirely from the notion that besides the inferior divinities, there is a God, one, uncreated and eternal, with whom to be identified, figuratively or philosophically, is highest praise.—W.

[2] Vide supra, p. 316.

[3] Bhagvat-Geeta, p. 84. The term Para Brahme, or Great Brahme, is applied, not once, but many times to Crishna, in the Bhagavat. See Halhed's translation in Maurice's Hindostan, ii. 342, 351, 354, 360, 375, 377, 379, 380, 417, 444. "The Sri Vaishnavam Brahmens," says Dr. Buchanan (Journey through Mysore, etc., i. 144), "worship Vishnu and the gods of his family only, and all over the Deccan are almost exclusively the officiating priests in the temples of these deities. They allege Brahma to be a son of Vishnu, and Siva the son of Brahma. Vishnu they consider as the same with Para Brahma" (thus Dr. Buchanan spells it instead of Brahme), "or the Supreme Being." Yet of this Supreme Being, this Para Brahma, they believe as follows: "One of the Asuras, or demons, named Tripura, possessed a city, the inhabitants of which were very troublesome to the inhabitants of Brahma Loka. the heaven of Brahma, who attempted in vain to take the place; it being destined not to fall, so long as the women who resided in it should preserve their chastity. The angels at length offered up their prayers to Vishnu, who took upon himself the form of a most beautiful young man, and became Budha Avatara. Entering then into the city, he danced naked before the women, and inspired them with loose desires, so that the fortress soon fell a prey to the angels." Ibid. Even Vach, the daughter of Ambhrina, is decorated with all the attributes of divinity. Mr. Colebrooke gives us the following literal version of a hymn in one of the Vedas, which Vach, he informs us, "speaks in praise of herself as the *supreme and universal soul*" [the title which, it is pretended, exclusively belongs to Brahme] — "I range with the Rudras, with the Vasus, with the Adityas, and with the Viswadevas. I uphold both the sun and the ocean [metra and varuna], the firmament, and fire, etc. * * Me, who am the queen, the conferrer of wealth, the possessor of knowledge, and first of such as merit worship, the gods render, universally, present everywhere, and pervader of all beings. He, who eats food through me, as he, who sees, who hears, or who breathes, through me, yet knows me not, is lost; hear then the faith which I pronounce. Even I declare *this Self*, who is worshipped by gods and men. I make strong whom I choose; I make him Brahme, holy and wise. For Rudra I bend the bow, to slay the demon, foe of Brahma: for the people I make war on their foes; and I pervade heaven and earth. I bore the father on the head of this universal mind; and my origin is in the midst of the ocean; and therefore do I pervade all beings, and touch this heaven with my form. Originating all beings, I pass like the breeze: I am above this heaven, beyond this earth; and what is the GREAT ONE, that am I." Asiat. Research. viii. 402, 403. Mr. Colebrooke says that Vach signifies speech, and that she is personified as the active power of Brahma, proceeding from him. Ibid. There is a curious passage, descriptive of the universal soul, translated from the Vedas by Mr. Colebrooke. Several persons "deeply conversant with holy

the eternal ONE, the supreme soul, employed in rather a subordinate capacity. "The Great Brahm," says Crishna, "is my womb. In it I place my fœtus; and from it is the production of all nature. The great Brahm is the womb of all those various forms which are conceived in every natural womb, and I am the father who soweth the seed."[1] In one of the morning prayers of the Brahmens, cited from the Vedas by Mr. Colebrooke, water is denominated Brahme,[2] "The sun," says Yajnyawalcya, "is Brahme; this is a certain truth revealed in the sacred Upanishats, and in various sac'has of the Vedas. So the Bhawishya Purana, speaking of the sun: Because there is none greater than he, nor has been, nor will be, therefore he is celebrated as the supreme soul in all the Vedas."[3] Air, too receives the appellation of Brahme. Thus, says a passage in the Veda; "That which moves in the atmosphere is air, *Brahme*."[4] Thus again; "Salutation unto thee, O air! Even thou art Brahme, present to our apprehension. Thee I will call 'present Brahme:' thee I will name 'the right one:' thee I will pronounce 'the true one.' May that Brahme, the universal being entitled Air, preserve me."[5] Food, too, is denominated Brahme, so is breath, and in-

writ, and possessed of great dwellings, meeting together, engaged in this disquisition; What is our soul? and who is Brahme?" Going together for information to a profound sage, they addressed him thus: "Thou well knowest the universal soul, communicate that knowledge unto us." The sage addressed each of them, "whom he worshipped as the soul." The first answered, "the heaven." But the sage replied, that this was only the head of the soul. The second declared that he worshipped "the sun as the soul." But the sage told him, this was only the eye of the soul. The third said that he worshipped "air as the soul;" and the sage answered, that this was only the breath of the soul. The fourth declared that he worshipped "the ethereal element as the soul." But the sage replied that this was only the trunk of the soul. The fifth answered, that he worshipped "water as the soul." But the sage rejoined that this was only the abdomen of the soul. The sixth informed him that he worshipped "earth as the soul." But the sage declared that this was only the feet of the soul. The sage next proceeds to deliver his own explanation; and utters a jargon, which has not even a semblance of meaning. "He thus addressed them collectively: You consider this universal soul as it were an individual being; and you partake of distinct enjoyments. But he who worships as the universal soul, that which is known by its manifested portions, and is inferred from consciousness, enjoys nourishment in all worlds, in all beings, in all souls: his head is splendid, like that of this universal soul; his eye is similarly varied; his breath is equally diffused; his trunk is no less abundant; his abdomen is alike full; and his feet are the earth; his breast is the altar: his hair is the sacred grass; his heart the household fire; his mind the consecrated flame; and his mouth the oblation."

[1] Bhagvat-Geeta, p. 107.
[2] Asiat. Research. v. 349.
[3] An extract from a Sanscrit Commentary by Mr. Colebrooke, Asiat. Research. v. 352.
[4] Asiat, Res. viii. 417.
[5] Ibid. 456.

tellect, and felicity.[1] Nay, it is affirmed, as part of the Hindu belief, that man himself may become Brahme; thus in the Bhagvat-Geeta, Crishna declares: "A man being endowed with a purified understanding, having humbled his spirit by resolution, and abandoned the objects of the organs; who hath freed himself from passion and dislike, who worshippeth with discrimination, eateth with moderation, and is humble of speech, of body, and of mind; who preferreth the devotion of meditation, and who constantly placeth his confidence in dispassion; who is freed from ostentation, tyrannic strength, vain-glory, lust, anger, and avarice; and who is exempt from selfishness, and in all things temperate, is formed for being Brahm."[2]

Such are the proofs on which the opinion has been adopted that sublime principles run through the religion of the Brahmens.[3] I know no supposition which can be

[1] Extract from the Vedas by Mr. Colebrooke, Asiat. Research, viii 455, 456.

[2] Bhagvat-Geeta, p. 131, 132.

[3] Sir W. Jones seems to have found proofs of a pure theism almost every where. Speaking of the Arabs, he says, "The religion of the poets, at least, seems to have been pure theism; and this we may know with certainty, because we have Arabian verses of unsuspected antiquity, which contain pious and elevated sentiments on the goodness and justice, the power and omnipotence, of Allah, or *the God*. If an inscription said to have been found on marble in Yemen be authentic, the ancient inhabitants of that country preserved the religion of Eber, and professed a belief in miracles, and a future state." (As. Res. ii. 8.) Did Sir W. not know that the wildest religions abound most in miracles, and that no religion is without a belief of a future state? Did it want an inscription in Yemen to prove to us this? Sir W. finds proofs of a pure theism as easily among the Persians as among the Arabs. "The primeval religion of Iran," he says, "if we rely on the authorities adduced by Mohsani Fani, was that which Newton calls the oldest (and it may be justly called the noblest) of all religions: A firm belief that one supreme God made the world by his power, and continually governed it by his providence; a pious fear, love, and adoration of him; a due reverence for parents and aged persons: a fraternal affection for the whole human race, and a compassionate tenderness even for the brute creation." Yet under Hushang, who, it would appear, was the author of this primeval religion, he tells us, that the popular worship of the Iranians was purely Sabian. (Ibid. p. 58.) At the same time he assures us, that during his supposed Mahabadian dynasty, when this Hushangism and Sabianism existed, a Brahmenical system prevailed, "which we can hardly," he says, "doubt was the first corruption of the oldest and purest religion." (Ibid. p. 59.) By this account three different religions must have all been the prevalent religions of Persia, at one and the same time. Unless (which is not a theory with slight presumptions in its favour) we conclude that all three were originally one and the same.—Even on the most sober-minded and judicious men, the lofty language of a mean superstition is calculated to impose. The industrious and intelligent Harris, in his account of the travels of William de Rubruquis, states it as his opinion, "after all the pains that he had been able to take, in order to obtain some sort of certainty on this head," that the religion of the Tartars includes these three points: "First,—that there is one God, the fountain of being, the creator of all things, the ruler of all things, and the sole object of Divine worship. Secondly,—that all men in general are his creatures, and therefore ought to consider

employed to reconcile the inconsistencies, and to remove the absurdities, which we have found this opinion to involve, unless it be assumed that the legends of the Hindus are all allegorical: and though, in their literal interpretation, they may be altogether unworthy of a perfect being that yet a recondite and enigmatical meaning may be extorted from them, which will tally with the sublime hypothesis it is wished to entertain. Undoubtedly, if we assume to ourselves the licence of giving to the Hindu mythology a meaning to suit our own views, we may form out of it not only a sublime theology, but a sublime philosophy, or any thing we please. It might, however, have been imagined that the futility, the absurdity, of these arbitrary interpretations had been too well exposed to allow them to mislead such men as some of the advocates for the allegorical sense of the Hindu scriptures.[1] The latter Platonists, and other refiners upon the mythology of Greece and Rome, drew from it a pure system of theology, by the very same process which is adopted and recommended in regard to the fables of the Hindus. "Without a tedious detail," says Mr. Gibbon, "the modern reader could not form a just idea of the strange allusions, the forced etymologies, the solemn trifling, and the impenetrable obscurity of these sages, who professed to reveal the system of the universe. As the traditions of Pagan mythology were variously related, the sacred interpreters were at liberty to select the most convenient circumstances; and as they

each other as brethren descended from one common parent, and alike entitled to all the blessings he bestows; and that, therefore, it is great impiety to abuse those blessings, or to injure each other. Thirdly,—That in as much as the common reason of mankind hath taught them to establish property, it is necessary that it should be preserved, and that it is therefore the duty of every man to be content with his own." (See Harris's Collection of Voyages, vol. i.) Les Moskaniens m'ont tous assurés unanimement, qu'ils n'avoient jamais eu d'idoles, ni de divinités subalternes, mais qu'ils sacrifioient uniquement à un être suprême et invisible. (Pallas, Voyage, i. 126.

[1] The advocates of this interpretation are not Europeans alone. The Hindus themselves give it, and not without good authority. "It is indisputably evident that none of the metaphorical representations which arise from the metaphorical style in which the Vedas are written, were designed to be viewed in any other light than a mere allegory."—Rammohun Roy, p. 12. "Corresponding to the natures of different powers or qualities, numerous figures have been invented for the benefit of those who are not possessed of sufficient understanding."—Maharnirvana, quoted by Rammohun Roy. "For the benefit of those who are inclined to worship, figures are invented to serve as representations of God, and to them either male or female forms, and other circumstances, are fictitiously assigned."—Jamadagni, cited by Rammohun Roy, p. 34. This allegorical representation is then avowed by the Hindus themselves, as the source of their popular belief.—W.

BOOK II. CHAP. VI.

translated an arbitrary cipher, they could extract from *any* fable *any* sense which was adapted to their favourite system of religion and philosophy. The lascivious form of a naked Venus was tortured into the discovery of some moral percept, or some physical truth; and the castration of Atys explained the revolution of the sun between the tropics, or the separation of the human soul from vice and error."[1] But if a condemnation thus severe can be justly pronounced upon those who allegorize the Greek and Roman mythology, what judgment should be formed of those by whom the same mode of interpretation is applied to the fables of the Hindus?[2] The Egyptian religion is allowed on all hands to have possessed the same fundamental principles with the Hindu, and to have resembled it remarkably in its outward features: yet, of all the systems of superstition which were found within the Roman empire, Mr. Gibbon pronounces this to be "the most contemptible and abject."[3] There are satisfactory reasons for supposing that improvement in the language of the Brahmens, and refinement in the interpretations which they put upon their ancient writings, not to speak of what may have been done by their favourite practice of interpolation have been suggested by the more rational and simple doctrines of Mahomet.[4] The natural effect of acquaintance with a better creed is well described by Mr. Bryant. "It is to be observed," he says, "that when Christianity had introduced a more rational system, as well as a more

[1] Gibbon's Hist. of the Decl. and Fall of the Rom. Emp. iv. 71.

[2] The Hindu ideas are so extremely loose, vague, and uncertain, that they are materials unspeakably convenient for workmanship of this description. "The Hindu religion," says an Oriental scholar of some eminence, "is so pliant, *that there is scarcely an opinion it will not countenance.*" A Tour to Shiraz, by Edward Scott Waring, Esq. p. 3, note.—M.

Mr. Waring is no authority on Hindu subjects.—W.

[3] Gibbon's Hist. of the Decl. and Fall of the Rom. Emp. i. 52.

[4] Besides the invincible reasons afforded by the circumstances of the case, the artful pretences and evasions of the Brahmens are evidence enough. Mr. Wilford, having stated the general opinion, that the three principal gods of Egypt resolve them into one, namely, the sun, says, "The case was nearly the same in ancient India; but there is no subject on which the modern Brahmens are more reserved; for when they are closely interrogated on the title of Deva, or God, which their most sacred books give to the sun, they avoid a direct answer, have recourse to evasions, and often contradict one another and themselves. They confess, however, unanimously, that the sun is an emblem or image of the three great divinities jointly and individually: that is of Brahme, or the supreme one." Asiat. Res. iii. 372.—M.

These general assertions of Wilford are always to be received with great caution. There is no reason why the Brahmans should make a mystery of applying the word Deva to the Sun. The Sun is a god, a Deva, and Deva properly means, that which shines.—W.

refined worship, among mankind; the Pagans were struck with the sublimity of its doctrines, and tried in their turns to refine. But their misfortune was, that they were obliged to abide by the theology which had been transmitted to them; and to make the history of the Gentile gods the basis of their procedure. This brought them into immense difficulties and equal absurdities: while they laboured to solve what was inexplicable, and to remedy what was past cure. Hence we meet with many dull and elaborate sophisms even in the great Plutarch: but many more in after-times, among the writers of whom I am speaking. Proclus is continually ringing the changes upon the terms, νοος νοερος, and νοητος; and explains what is really a proper name, as if it signified *sense* and *intellect.* In consequence of this, he tries to subtilize and refine all the base jargon about Saturn and Rhea and would persuade us that the most idle and obscene legends related to the divine mind, to the eternal wisdom, and supremacy of the Deity. Thus he borrows many exalted notions from Christianity; and blends them with the basest alloy, with the dregs of Pagan mythology."[1] Such are the opinions of the greatest men respecting those attempts to allegorize a rude superstition, which some of the most celebrated of our Indian guides so vehemently recommend.[2]

[1] Bryant's Analysis of Ancient Mythology, iii. 104, 105.

[2] Mr. Halhed very judiciously condemns the project to allegorize and refine upon the Hindu mythology. "Many conjectural doctrines," says he, "have been circulated by the learned and ingenious of Europe upon the mythology of the Gentoos; and they have unanimously endeavoured to construe the extravagant fables with which it abounds into sublime and mystical symbols of the most refined morality. This mode of reasoning, however common, is not quite candid or equitable, because it sets out with supposing in those people a deficiency of faith with respect to the authenticity of their own scriptures, which, although our better information may convince us to be altogether false and erroneous, yet are by them literally esteemed as the immediate revelations of the Almighty. . . . It may possibly be owing to this vanity of reconciling every other mode of worship to some kind of conformity with our own, that allegorical constructions and forced allusions to a mystic morality have been constantly foisted in upon the plain and literal context of every Pagan mythology. . . . The institution of a religion has been in every country the first step towards an emersion from savage barbarism. . . . The vulgar and illiterate have always understood the mythology of their country in its literal sense; and there was a time to every nation, when the highest rank in it was equally vulgar and illiterate with the lowest. . . . A Hindu esteems the astonishing miracles attributed to a Brihma, a Raam, or a Kishen, as facts of the most indubitable authenticity, and the relation of them as most strictly historical." Preface to the Code of Gentoo Laws, p. xiii. xiv. On the religion of ancient nations, Voltaire says with justice' "On pourroit faire des volumes sur ce sujet; mais tous ces volumes se reduisent à deux mots, c'est que le gros du genre humain a été et sera très long-temps insensé et imbécile; et que peut-être les plus insensés de tous ont été ceux, qui ont voulu trouver

BOOK II. CHAP. VI.

Of the pure and elevated ideas of the Divine Nature, which are ascribed to the Hindus, or to any other people, an accurate judgment may be formed, by ascertaining the source from which they are derived. It will be allowed that just and rational views of God can be obtained from two sources alone: from revelation; or, where that is wanting, from sound reflection upon the frame and government of the universe. Wherever men are sufficiently improved to take a comprehensive survey of this magnificent system, to observe the order which prevails, the adaptation of means to ends, and the incredible train of effects which flow from the simplest causes; they may then form exalted notions of the intelligence to which all those wonders are ascribed.[1] If all the unrevealed knowledge which we possess respecting God, the immediate object of none of our senses be derived from his works, they whose ideas of the works are

---

un sens à ces fables absurdes, et mettre de la raison dans la folie." Voltaire, Philosophie de l'Histoire, Oeuvres Complètes, à Gotha, 1785, tom. xvi. p. 22. Mr. Wilkins, reprobating some other attempts at refinement on the Hindu text. says, "he has seen a comment, by a zealous Persian, upon the wanton odes of their favourite poet Hafiz, wherein every obscene allusion is sublimated into a divine mystery, and the host and the tavern are as ingeniously metamorphosed into their prophet and his holy temple." Bhagvat-Geeta, note 114.—M.

Every oriental scholar knows that the odes of Hafiz, as of many other Persian poets, are allegorical, and that all the rapturous love of Sufi writers is mystical philosophy relating to the separation of individualized soul from the source from whence it emanated. It is very true that explanation by allegory may have been carried sometimes to excess, but to the composition of a popular mythology many elements contribute, and none more copiously than allegory. The greater number of the Hindu fables are obvious allegories, and the foundation of the whole system, in its popular shape, is eminently allegorical. The three chief divinities are repeatedly admitted to be nothing more than personifications of the powers of God in action. With the vulgar the personifications become realities—the types become the things typified.—This is the natural progress of all idolatry, even where it has been grafted upon the simple truths of Christianity; and there is no difficulty in understanding how it should have taken this course in Hindustan.—W.

[1] That the notions of the Hindus are irrational and erroneous, may be admitted, and they are therefore offensive to minds better informed; but the subsequent designations of degrading, gross, and disgusting, are scarcely applicable; nor is any distinction here made between mythological and philosophical views, the absurdity is restricted to the former; the latter fully recognises the order of the world as the necessary consequence of its mode of development, and men are enjoined to study God in his works. "The Vedas," says Rammohun Roy, "hold out precautions against framing a deity after human imagination, and recommend mankind to direct all researches towards the surrounding objects, viewed either collectively or individually, bearing in mind their regular, wise, and wonderful combinations and arrangements." Introd. to the abridgment of the Vedant, viii. The philosophical doctrines, which invariably enjoin disregard of all external, and merely temporal existence, and the exclusive direction of the powers of mind to the study of a man's own soul, may be condemned as unwise and ill-directed, but they can scarcely be termed, with justice, mean and degrading; the end is elevated, though the means be mistaken.—W.

in the highest degree absurd, mean, and degrading, cannot, whatever may be the language which they employ, have elevated ideas of the author of those works. It is impossible for the stream to ascend higher than the fountain. The only question therefore is, what are the ideas which the Hindus have reached concerning the wisdom and beauty of the universe. To this the answer is clear and incontrovertible. No people, how rude and ignorant soever, who have been so far advanced as to leave us memorials of their thoughts in writing, have ever drawn a more gross and disgusting picture of the universe than what is presented in the writings of the Hindus.[1] In the conception of it no coherence, wisdom, or beauty, ever appears: all is disorder, caprice, passion, contest, portents, prodigies, violence, and deformity.[2] It is perfectly evident that

[1] Even Mr. Maurice says; "The Hindu notions of the mundane system ar altogether the most monstrous that ever were adopted by any beings, who boast the light of reason; and, in truth, very little reconcilcable with those sublime ideas we have been taught to entertain of the profound learning and renowned sagacity of the ancient Brahmens." Maurice, Hist. of Hindost. i. 490. I have met with nothing in Sanscrit literature in any degree to be compared with the following reflection of a Peruvian Inca, "If the heaven be so glorious, which is the throne and seat of the Pachacamac, how much more powerful, glittering, and resplendent must his person and Majesty be, who was the maker and creator of them all. Other sayings of his were these, *If I were to adore any of these terrestrial things, it should certainly be a wise and discreet man, whose excellencies surpass all earthly creatures.*" Garcilasso de Vega, Royal Commentaries of Peru, book iv. ch. 19. There is a passage which I have read since this was written (which however may well be suspected of flowing at a recent date from a foreign source) translated by Mr. Ward, from a work by Chirunjeevu, in which the inference that a God exists because the universe exists, is very distinctly expressed. Ward's View, &c. ii. 305. Lond. Ed.

[2] In my researches concerning the religious ideas of the Hindus, I was much struck with the title of a chapter or lecture in the Bhagvat-Geeta, "Display of the Divine Nature in the form of the universe." I seized it with eagerness: Here, I thought, will undoubtedly be found some reflections on the wisdom and order of the universe; I met with only the following monstrous exhibition: "Behold," says Vishnu, in the form of Crishna, to Arjoon, "behold things wonderful, never seen before. Behold in this my body the whole world animate and inanimate, and all things else thou hast a mind to see. But as thou art unable to see with these thy natural eyes, I will give thee a heavenly eye, with which behold my divine connexion."—After this, Arjoon declares, "I behold, O god, within thy breast, the dews assembled, and every specific tribe of beings. I see Brahma, that deity sitting on his lotus-throne; all the Reeshees [saints] and heavenly Ooragas [serpents]. I see thyself, on all sides, of infinite shape, formed with abundant arms, and bellies, and mouths, and eyes; but I can neither discover thy beginning, thy middle, nor again thy end, O universal lord, form of the universe! I see thee with a crown, and armed with club and chacra [the martial weapon of Crishna, a sort of discus or quoit], a mass of glory, darting refulgent beams around. I see thee, difficult to be seen, shining on all sides, with light immeasurable, like the ardent fire or glorious sun. Thou art the supreme being, incorruptible, worthy to be known! Thou art prime supporter of the universal orb! Thou art the never-failing and eternal guardian of religion! Thou art from all beginning, and I esteem the Pooroosh [literally, *man*, but here meant to express the vital soul]. I see thee without beginning, without middle, and without end; of valour infinite; of arms innu-

BOOK II. CHAP. VI.

the Hindus never contemplated the universe as a connected and perfect system, governed by general laws, and directed to benevolent ends; and it follows, as a necessary consequence, that than their religion is no other than that primary worship, which is addressed to the designing and invisible beings who preside over the powers of nature, according to their own arbitrary will, and act only for some private and selfish gratification. The elevated language, which this species of worship finally assumes, is only the refinement, which flattery, founded upon a base apprehension of the divine character, ingrafts upon a mean superstition.[1]

---

merable; the sun and moon thy eyes, thy mouth a flaming fire, and the whole world shining with thy reflected glory! The space between the heavens and the earth is possessed by thee alone, and every point around: the three regions of the universe, O mighty spirit! behold the wonders of thy awful countenance with troubled minds. Of the celestial bands, some I see fly to thee for refuge; whilst some, afraid, with joined hands sing forth thy praise. The Maharshees, holy bands, hail thee, and glorify thy name with adorating praises. The Roodras, the Adityas, the Vasoos, and all those beings the world esteemeth good; Asween and Koomar, the Maroots and Ooshmapas; the Gandhars and the Yakshas, with the holy tribes of Soors, all stand gazing on thee, and all alike amazed, The winds, alike with me, are terrified to behold thy wondrous form gigantic; with many mouths and eyes; with many arms, and legs, and breasts; with many bellies, and with rows of dreadful teeth! Thus, as I see thee, touching the heavens, and shining with such glory, of such various hues, with widely opened mouths and bright expanded eyes, I am disturbed within me; my resolution faileth me, O Vishnu! and I find no rest! Having beholden thy dreadful teeth. and gazed on thy countenance, emblem of time's last fire, I know not which way I turn! I find no peace! Have mercy, then, O god of gods! thou mansion of the universe! The sons of Dreetarashtra, now, with all those rulers of the land, Bheeshma, Drona the son of Soot, and even the fronts of our army, seem to be precipitating themselves hastily into thy mouth, discovering such frightful rows of teeth! whilst some appear to stick between thy teeth with their bodies sorely mangled. As the rapid streams of full-flowing rivers roll on to meet the ocean's bed; even so these heroes of the human race rush on towards thy flaming mouths. As troops of insects, with increasing speed, seek their own destruction in the flaming fire; even so these people, with swelling fury, seek their own destruction. Thou involvest and swallowest them altogether, even unto the last, with thy flamiug mouths; whilst the whole world is filled with thy glory, as thy awful beams, O Vishnu, shine forth on all sides!" Bhagvat-Geeta, p. 90, &c. Such is "The Display of the Divine Nature in the form of the universe!"

[1] In the grant of land, translated from a plate of copper (Asiat. Res. iii. 45), among the praises of the sovereign, by whom the donation is made, it is said, "The gods had apprehensions in the beginning of time, that the glory of so great a monarch would leave them without marks of distinction; thence it was, that Purari assumed a third eye in his forehead; Pedmachsa, four arms; Atmabhu, four faces; that Cali held a cimeter in her hand; Rama, a lotos flower; and Vani, a lyre." Sir Willam Jones, in the note, says, "The six names in the text are appellations of the gods Mahadeva, Vishnu, Brahma, and the goddesses Durga, Lacshmi, Seraswati." So that the three supreme deities, with their wives, were afraid of being eclipsed by an earthly king, and were obliged to assume new distinctions (of a very ingenious aud imposing sort!) to prevent so lamentable an occurrence.—M.

No one but the author would have pressed into the support of his theory the extravagance of adulation; he could not have supposed that the writer of the panegyric himself believed in the apprehensions which he ascribes hyperbolically to the gods.—W.

If it be deemed necessary to inquire into the principle of the Hindu superstition; or which of the powers of nature, personified into gods, they exalted in the progress of hyperbolical adoration to the supremacy over the rest, and the lordship of all things; the question is resolved by copious evidence; and on this point inquirers generally coincide. Sir William Jones has written a discourse to prove that the gods of Greece, Italy, and India are the same. But it is sufficiently proved, that the Greek and Roman deities ultimately resolve themselves into the sun, whose powers and provinces had been gradually enlarged, till they included those of all nature. It follows that the sun, too, is the principle of the Hindu religion. "We must not be surprised," says Sir William Jones, "at finding on a close examination, that the characters of all the Pagan deities, male and female, melt into each other, and at last into one or two; for it seems a well-founded opinion, that the whole crowd of gods and goddesses, in ancient Rome and modern Varanes, mean only the powers of nature, and principally those of the sun, expressed in a variety of ways, and by a multitude of fanciful names."[1] He says, too, that "the three Powers Creative, Preservative, and Destructive, which the Hindus express by the triliteral word *Aum*, were grossly ascribed by the first idolaters to the heat, light, and flame of their mistaken divinity the sun."[2] Brahma, Vishnu, and Siva, were therefore, the heat, light, and flame of the sun; and it follows as a very clear deduction, that Brahme, whose powers were shadowed forth in the characters of those three gods, was the sun himself. This conclusion, too, is established by many express texts of the Hindu scriptures, as well as by the most venerated part of the Hindu ritual. "The syllable Om (Aum) intends," says a passage from the Veda translated by Mr. Colebrooke, "every deity: It belongs to Paramesh'ti, him who dwells in the supreme abode: it appertains to Brahme, the vast one; to Deva, god; to Adhyatma, the superintending soul. Other deities belonging to those several regions, are portions of the three gods; for they are variously named and described, on account of their different operations: but in fact there is only one deity, THE

[1] On the Gods of Greece, &c., Asiat. Research. i. 267.

[2] Asiat. Research. i. 272.—M.

There is no authority for this; the notion is employed as an illustration only.—W,

GREAT SOUL. He is called the SUN; for he is the soul of all beings. Other deities are portions of him."[1] I have already quoted a very remarkable passage from Yajnyawalcya, one of the highest of all authorities, in which the sun is directly asserted to be Brahme, and to be the supreme soul, as is declared in all the Vedas.[2] Another passage, translated from a Veda by Mr. Colebrooke, says: Fire is THAT ORIGINAL CAUSE, the SUN is that; such too is that pure Brahme. Even he is the god who pervades all regions; he, prior to whom nothing was born; and who became all beings, himself the lord of creatures."[3] A passage in the Veda, translated by Sir William Jones, says, "That Sun, than which nothing is higher, to which nothing is equal, enlightens the sky, the earth, the lower worlds, the higher worlds, other worlds, enlightens the breast, enlightens all besides the breast."[4] In the Bhawishya Purana, Crishna himself says; "The sun is the god of perception, the eye of the universe, the cause of day: there is none greater than he among the immortal powers. From him this universe proceeded, and in him it will reach annihilation; he is time measured by instants." I shall add but one instance more. There is a passage in the Vedas, which is regarded by the Hindus with unspeakable veneration. It has a distinctive appellation. It is called the Gayatri, and is used upon the mightiest occasions of religion. It is denominated the holiest text in the Vedas. This extraordinary, this most sacred, this most wonderful text, is thus translated by Sir William Jones: "Let us adore the supremacy of that Divine Sun, the godhead, who illuminates all, who re-creates all, from whom all proceed, to whom all must return, whom we invoke to direct our understandings aright in our progress towards his holy seat."[5] Another version of it, and somewhat different in its phraseology, is given by Mr. Colebrooke, in his account of the first of the Vedas: "I subjoin," says he, "a translation of the prayer which contains it, as also of the preceding

[1] Ibid. viii. 397.—M.

This does not prove the converse; viz., that the Sun was ever called the Great Soul. Brahme, the Great Soul, was, according to the Vedantas, identical with the sun and with fire, as with all things, and they mutually are identical with him; but each is individually the object which is seen or worshipped, and not solely Brahme, or to be confounded with God.—W.

[2] Vide supra, p. 323.

[3] Asiat. Research. viii. 431, 432.

[4] Asiat. Research. ii. 400.

[5] Sir William Jones's Works, vi. 417.

one, (both of which are addressed to the sun), for the sake of exhibiting the Indian priests' confession of faith with its context:—"This new and excellent praise of thee, O splendid, playful Sun! is offered by us to thee. Be gratified by this my speech: approach this craving mind as a fond man seeks a woman. May that sun who contemplates and looks into all worlds be our protector!—Let us MEDITATE ON THE ADORABLE LIGHT OF THE DIVINE RULER; MAY IT GUIDE OUR INTELLECTS![1] Desirous of food, we solicit the gift of the splendid Sun, who should be studiously worshipped. Venerable men, guided by the understanding, salute the divine Sun with oblations and praise."[2] Constrained by these and similar passages, Mr. Colebrooke says: "The ancient Hindu religion, as founded on the Indian Scriptures, recognises but one God, *yet not sufficiently discriminating the creature from the Creator*."[3] This is an important admission, from one of the most illustrious advocates of the sublimity of the Hindu religion. Had he reflected for one moment, he would have seen that between *not sufficiently*, and *not-at-all*, in this case, there can be no distinction.[4]

[1] This particular passage it is, which is pointed out by Mr. Colebrooke as the gayatri.

[2] Asiat. Research. viii. 400.

[3] Ibid. 397.

[4] Nations, not behind the Hindus in civilization (the most enthusiastic of their admirers being judges) agree in these ideas. " Les nations savantes de l'Orient," says Dupuis (Origine de tous les Cultes, i. 4.) " les Egyptiens et les Phéniciens, deux peuples qui ont le plus influé sur les opinions religieuses du reste de l'univers, ne connoissoient d'autres dieux, chefs de l'administration du monde, que le soleil, la lune, les astres, et le ciel qui les renferme, et ne chantoient que la nature dans leurs hymnes et leurs théogonies." The following is a curious passage: " Eutychius, après avoir pris le Sabiisme en Chaldée, De là, dit il, il est passé en Egypte, de l'Egypte il fut porté chez les Francs, c'est à dire en Europe, d'où il s'étendit dans tous les ports de la Méditerranée. Et, comme le culte du Soleil et des Etoiles, la vénération des ancêstres, l'érection des statues, la consécration des arbres, constituèrent d'abord l'essence du Sabiisme, et que cette espèce de religion, toute bizarre qu'elle est, se trouva assez vite répandue dans toutes les parties du monde alors connu, et l'infecta jusqu' à l'Inde, jusqu' à la Chine: de sorte que ces vastes empires ont toujours esté pleins des statues adorées, et ont toujours donné la créance la plus folle aux visions de l'astrologie judiciaire, preuve incontestable de Sabiisme, puisque c'en est le fond, et le premier dogme; la conclusion est simple, que soit par tradition, soit par imitation et identité d'idées, le monde presqu'entier s'est vu, et se voit encore Sabien." Ibid. 25. Mémoires de l'Académie des Inscriptions, &c. xii. 25.—M.

Assertions in favour of a theory are here cited, as if they were authentic history. What proof is there of the progress of Sabæism here so confidently described? But as concerns the Hindus, Mr. Colebrooke's opinion needs no qualification. The want of discrimination between the creature and the Creator, is the usual progress of idolatry. The type becomes mistaken for the prototype: nor is sufficient allowance made for the mysticism that evidently pervades much of the Vedas, and gives a character other than literal to their phraseology. In truth, we are even yet too imperfectly acquainted with those works, to appreciate their doctrines correctly.—W.

In the natural progress of religion, it very frequently happens, that the spirit of adulation and hyperbole exalts admired or powerful individuals to the rank of gods. The name of the sun, or of some other divinity, is bestowed as a title, or as an epithet of inflated praise, upon a great prince, or conqueror.[1] Immediately the exploits of the hero are blended with the functions of the god; and, in process of time, when the origin of the combination is forgotten, they form a compound mass of inextricable and inconsistent mythology. Mr. Colebrooke is of opinion, that in the Vedas the elements and the planets alone are deified; that the worship of heroes was introduced among the Hindus at a later period; and makes a remarkable figure in the Puranas.[2]

Among the false refinements to which the spirit of a rude religion gives birth, it is worthy of particular remark, that abstract terms are personified, and made to assume the character of gods; such as, Health and Sickness; War and Peace; Plenty; Famine, Pestilence. When the most general abstractions, too, begin to be formed, as of space, of time, of fate, of nature, they are apt to fill the mind with a kind of awe and wonder; and appear to stretch beyond all things. They are either, therefore, apprehended as new gods, and celebrated as antecedent, and superior, to all the old; or if any of the old have taken a firm possession of the mind, they are exalted to the new dignity, and receive the name of the abstract idea which most forcibly engages the attention. Thus, among the Greeks and the Romans, Fate usurped a power over all the gods. The Parsee books represent Ormusd and Ahriman, the Good Principle and the Evil Principle, sometimes as independent beings; sometimes as owing their existence to something above them; in a manner extremely resembling the language of the Sanscrit books respecting Brahma, Vishnu, and Siva. At times, however, the Persians express themselves more precisely. "In the law of Zoroaster," says one of their sacred books, "it is positively declared that God [Ormusd] was created by Time along with all other beings:

[1] Adad, the name of the chief Assyrian deity, was held by ten Syrian kings in succession. Nicol. Damas. ap. Josephum, Antiq. lib. xii. cap. 5. Even among Christians, kings and great men have received all the general titles of the deity, *lord, majesty, highness, excellence, grace.*

[2] Asiat. Research. viii. 398, note.

and the creator is Time; and time has no limits; it has nothing above it; it has no root: it has always been, and always will be. No one who has understanding will ever say, Whence did Time come? In that grandeur wherein Time was, there was no being who could call it creator, because it had not yet created. Afterwards it created fire and water, and from their combination proceeded Ormusd. Time was the creator, and preserved its authority over the creatures which it had produced.***I said in the beginning that Ormusd and Ahriman came both from Time.[1] The Brahmens, on the other hand, rather appear to have advanced the dignity of the acknowledged divinities so far as to make it embrace the extent of the abstract ideas; and to have regarded them as the abstract ideas themselves. Thus Mr. Wilkins supposes, that Brahme represents nature; Brahma, matter; Vishnu, space; Siva, time. But this is a refinement which is very sparingly, if at all, introduced in any writings of the Brahmens, which have yet been laid open to European eyes. Direct contradictions of it, though plentifully diffused, are no proof that it is not at all a Hindu doctrine. Thus Crishna, in the Geeta, says, "I am nevertheless failing Time, the Preserver, whose face is turned on all sides";[2] a point of view in which it well agrees with the peculiar attributes of Vishnu. But in the very same discourse, Crishna says again, "I am Time, the destroyer of mankind,"[3] in which case it agrees only with the character of Siva. But it is still more remarkable that Brahma is said to have "given being to time, and the divisions of time";[4] and that space is said to have been produced from the ear of the first victim immolated by the Gods.[5] Nay, there are passages in which the Hindus acknowledge a destiny or fate which over-rules the Supreme Beings themselves. "The future condition of great beings is destined with certainty, both the nakedness of Mahadeva, and the bed of Vishnu, on a vast serpent. What is not to be, that will not be; and if an event be predoomed, it cannot happen otherwise."[6]

1 Anquetil Duperron, Zendavesta, ii. 344.

2 Bhagvat-Geeta, p. 87.

3 Ibid, p. 93.

4 Institutes of Menu, ch. i. 24.

5 A passage translated from the Veda by Mr. Colebrooke, Asiat. Research., vii. 254.

6 Hetopadesa, book I., Sir William Jones's Works, vi. 7. A personification, and mysterious deification of some very abstract idea, as Time, or Space, is by

BOOK II. CHAP. VI.

When the exaggerations of flattery are in this manner ingrafted upon the original deification of the elements and powers of nature; and when the worship of heroes and of abstract ideas is incorporated with the whole; then is produced that heterogeneous and monstrous compound which has formed the religious creed of so great a portion of the human race; but composes a more stupendous mass in Hindustan than any other country; because in Hindustan a greater and more powerful section of the people, than in any other country, have, during a long series of ages, been solely occupied in adding to its volume, and augmenting its influence.[1]

So little do men regard incoherence of thought; so little are they accustomed to trace the relations of one set of

---

no means unnatural to rude nations. It is remarkable that the Scandinavians had a notion of some mysterious power, superior to their gods; for, after the great catastrophe, in which Odin, Thor, and the other deities, lose their lives, "comes forth THE POWERFUL, THE VALIANT, HE WHO GOVERNS ALL THINGS, from his lofty abodes, to render divine justice. In his palace the just will inhabit, and enjoy delights for evermore." (See extracts from the Edda, the Sacred book of the Scandinavians, in Mallet's Introduct. to the Hist. of Denmark, vol. i. ch. vi.) That historian observes, in a style which almost appears to be copied by those to whom we owe the specimens of the Hindu religion, that a capital point among the Scythians was, the pre-eminence of "One only, all-powerful and perfect being, over all the other intelligences with which universal nature was peopled." The Scandinavians, then, were on a level with all that is even claimed for the Hindus. But these same Scandinavians draw terrible pictures of this perfect ONE; describing him as a being who even delights in the shedding of human blood; yet they call him, the Father and creator of men, and say, that "he liveth and governeth during the ages; he directeth every thing which is high, and every thing which is low; whatever is great, and whatever is small; he hath made the heaven, the air, and man who is to live for ever; and before the heaven or the earth existed, this god lived already with the giants." Ibid. But what this god was, whether matter, or space, or time, the Scandinavian monuments are too imperfect to determine.

[1] Bernier, one of the most intelligent and faithful of all travellers, who spent a number of years in great favour at the court of Aurengzebe, formed an opinion of the religion of the Hindus, with which respect was little connected, for one of his Letters he thus entitles, "Lettre, &c. touchant les superstitions, étranges façons de faire, et doctrine des Indous ou Gentils de l'Hindoustan. D'où l'on verra qu'il n'y a opinions si ridicules et si extravagantes dont l'esprit de l'homme ne soit capable." (Bernier, Suite des Mémoires sur l'Empire du Grand Mogol, i. 119.) He appears to have seen more completely through the vague language of the Brahmens respecting the divinity (a language so figurative, and loose, that if a man is heartily inclined, he may give it any interpretation) than more recent and more credulous visitors. After giving a very distinct account of the more common notions entertained of the three deities, Brahma, Vishnu, and Siva, he says, Touchant ces trois Estres j'ai vu des Missionaires Européens qui prétendent que les Gentils ont quelque idèe du mystère de la Trinité, et qui disent qu'il est expressement porté dans leurs livres que ce sont trois Personnes un seul Dieu; pour moy j'ai fait assez discourir les Pendets sur cette matière, *mais ils s'expliquent si pauvrement que je n'ai jamais pu comprendre nettement leur sentiment*; j'en ai même vu quelques-uns qui disent que ce sont trois véritables créatures très parfaites qu'ils appellent Deutas; comme nos anciens idolatres n'ont à mon avis jamais

opinions to another, and to form on any subject a consistent and harmonious combination of ideas, that while many persons of eminence loudly contend for the correctness and sublimity of the speculative, there is an universal agreement respecting the meanness, the absurdity, the folly, of the endless ceremonies, in which the practical part of the Hindu religion consists. For the illustration of this part of the subject, I shall content myself with a reference to the documents in the appendix.[1] Volumes would hardly suffice to depict at large a ritual which is more tedious, minute, and burdensome; and engrosses a greater portion of human life, than any which has been found to fetter and oppress any other portion of the human race.

No circumstance connected with a religious system more decidedly pronounces on its character, than the

---

bien expliqué ce qu'ils entendoient par ces mots de Genius, et de Numina, qui est, je pense, le même que Deuta chez les Indiens; il est vrai que j'en ai vu d'autres, et des plus sçavans, qui disoient que ces trois Etres n'estoient effectivement qu'un même consideré en trois façons, à sçavoir, en tant qu'il est Producteur, Conservateur, et Déstructeur des choses, mais ils ne disoient rien des trois personnes distinctes en un seul Dieu. Ibid. p. 173.—"The history of these gods," says Mr. Orme (Hist. of the Milit. Trans. etc. in Indostan, i. 3), "is a heap of the greatest absurdities. It is Eswara twisting off the neck of Brahma; it is the Sun who gets his teeth knocked out, and the Moon who has her face beat black and blue at a feast, at which the gods quarrel and fight with the spirit of a mob." In the Zendavesta, as translated by Anquetil Duperron, many passages are as expressive to the full of just ideas of the Divine Nature as any in the Vedas. The absurdities, too, with which they are mixed, are certainly not greater, they are many degrees less, than those with which the sublime phrases in the Vedas are mingled. The ancient magi, we are told, had a most sublime theology.—Nunquam adorabant solem: et mox addiderunt, se non adhibere aliquam adorationem soli, aut lunæ, aut planetis, sed tantum erga solem se convertere inter orandum. Hyde, p. 5. Je vois, ma sœur, says the Guèbre in Montesquieu (Lettres Persannes, Let. lxvii.), que vous avez appris parmi les Musulmans à calomnier notre sainte religion. Nous n'adorons ni les astres ni les élemens; et nos pères ne les ont jamais adorés. . . . . Ils leurs ont seulement rendu un culte religieux, mais inférieur, comme à des ouvrages et des manifestations de la divinité. Beausobre, with his usual critical sagacity, said, in regard to the pictures drawn by Hyde, Pococke, and Prideaux, of the religious system of the magi, Rien de plus beau, rien de plus orthodoxe que ce systême. Je crains seulement qu'il ne le soit un peu trop pour ces tems-là. Hist de Manich. lib. ii. ch. ii. Voltaire thus expresses himself: "On ne peut lire deux pages de l'abominable fatras attribué à ce Zoroastre, sans avoir pitié de la nature humaine. Nostradamus et le médecin des urines sont des gens raisonnables en comparaison de cet energumène. Et cependant on parle de lui, et on en parlera encore." He had, however, remarked a little before, that the book contained good precepts of morality, and asked, "Comment se pourrait-il que Zoroastre eut joint tant d'énormes fadaises à ce beau précepte de s'abstenir dans les doutes si on fera bien ou mal?" Dictionnaire Philosophique, Mot Zoroastre.

[1] See note C. at the end of the volume.

BOOK II. CHAP. VI.

ideas which it inculcates respecting merit and demerit, purity and impurity, innocence and guilt. If those qualities which render a man amiable, respectable, and useful; if wisdom, beneficence, self-command, are celebrated as the chief recommendation to the favour of the Almighty; if the production of happiness is steadily and consistently represented as the most acceptable worship of the Creator; no other proof is requisite, that they who framed, and they who understand this religion, have arrived at high and refined notions of an All-perfect being. But where, with no more attention to morality, than the exigencies and laws of human nature force upon the attention of the rudest tribes, the sacred duties are made to consist in frivolous observances, there, we may be assured, the religious ideas of the people are barbarous. The train of thought which tends to this conclusion is extremely similar to that which gives birth to other deformities in the religious system of ignorant minds. From the imbecilities which usually accompany exalted station, it is found, even when the society is considerably improved, that assiduous attendance upon the person of the great man or prince, and unwearied contrivances for the expression of devotion and respect, are the path which leads the most surely to his attention and favour.[1] To the rude mind, no other rule suggests itself for paying court to the Divine, than that for paying court to the Human Majesty; and as among a barbarous people, the forms of address, of respect, and compliment, are generally multiplied into a great variety of grotesque and frivolous ceremonies, so it happens with regard to their religious service. An endless succession of observances, in compliment to the god,[2] is supposed to afford him the most exquisite delight; while the common discharge of the beneficent duties of life is regarded as

[1] That one campaign in the court is better than two in the field, has passed into a proverb under the monarchies of modern Europe.

[2] The leading feature in the Hindu ceremonial is throughout overlooked or misstated. There are no observances "in compliment to the god," there is no form of worship prescribed in the law-books for any one divinity; the observances are all personal and domestic; they involve much less waste of time than they would appear to do, and are of a less offensive character than the public worship of Greece and Rome. This applies to the primitive system. In the actual state of the Hindu religion, public observances have been in a great degree substituted for domestic; but, even now, if the objects were worthy, the amount of time dedicated to them would not be excessive.—W.

an object of comparative indifference. It is unnecessary to cite instances in support of a representation, of which the whole history of the religion of most nations is a continual proof.

Even those inquirers who have been least aware of the grossness of the Hindu religion, have seen that wretched ceremonies constituted almost the whole of its practical part. The precepts, which are lavished upon its ceremonies, bury, in their exorbitant mass, the pittance bestowed upon all other duties taken together. On all occasions ceremonies meet the attention as the pre-eminent duties of the Hindu.[1] The holiest man, is always he, by whom the ceremonies of his religion are more strictly performed. Never among any other people did the ceremonial part of religion prevail over the moral to a greater, probably to an equal extent. Of the many rules of conduct prescribed to the householder, almost the whole concern religious observances.[2] Beside the general strain of the holy text, many positive declarations ascribe infinite superiority to rites and ceremonies, above morality. "Devotion," says Menu, "is equal to the performance of all duties; it is divine knowledge in a Brahmen; it is defence of the people in a Cshatriya; devotion is the business of trade and agriculture in a Vaisya; devotion is dutiful service in a Sudra. By reading each day as much as possible of the Veda, by performing the five great sacraments, and by forgiving all injuries, even sins of the highest degree shall soon be effaced."[3] In the following list of conditions, a small space is allotted to useful virtue. "By injuring nothing animated, by subduing all sensual appetites, by devout rites ordained in the Veda, and by rigorous mortifications[4] men obtains, even in this life, the state of beatitude."

[1] The predominance given to devotional duties in Manu, follows from the character of the work. It is a text-book of religion and law; the particular subject of "morals" is considered by the Hindus as forming a branch of literature of its own; and is therefore consistently enough only occasionally adverted to in writings dedicated to other subjects; the great duties of morality, however, are few and simple, and are not unfrequently commanded by Manu, and other legislators.—W.

[2] The performance (e.g.) of the five daily sacraments, of which no one, not even that which is falsely rendered hospitality, has, properly speaking, any reference to the duties of humanity. A few general precepts respecting the acquisition of the means of subsistence, in the modes prescribed to the different orders of the Hindus, are, in fact, of the ceremonial and religious cast. Laws of Menu, ch. iii. and iv., where the duties of the householder are described.

[3] Laws of Menu, ch. xi. 236, etc.

[4] Ibid. ch. vi. 75.

BOOK II. CHAP. VI.

"It is through sacrifices," says the Calica Purana, "that princes obtain bliss, heaven, and victory over their enemies."[1]

In conceiving the honours with which the divine powers should be treated, it is supposed that there are certain qnalities with which it is holy or unholy to approach them. As there are certain pollutions with which it would be held disrespectful to approach an earthly superior, the same sentiment, as usual, is transferred to the heavens; and the notion of a religious impurity is engendered. This is a circumstance of considerable importance. By the nature of the particulars, to which the belief of religious purity and impurity is attached, a criterion is afforded of the mental qualities which the Divine Being is supposed to possess. The causes of impurity among the Brahmens are exceedingly numerous; that they are proportionally strange, a few instances will evince. "When a child has teethed," says the law of Menu, "and when, after teething, his head has been shorn, and when he has been girt with his thread, and when, being full grown, he dies, all his kindred are impure: on the birth of a child the law is the same."[2] Among a variety of other instances it is declared, that he who has touched a Chandala, a woman in her courses, an outcast, a new-born child, a corpse, or one who has touched a corpse, is impure.[3] A Brahmen who has touched a human bone is impure. The rules of purification, which form a remarkable part of this subject, are not less exorbitant in their number, or extravagant in their forms. On the death of a kinsman, the modes of purification are various, according to various cases: one, which we may select as an example, is prescribed in the following words: "Let them eat vegetable food without factitious (that is, only with native) salt; let them bathe for three days at intervals; let them taste no flesh-meat; and let them sleep apart on the ground."[4] "Should a Brahmen touch a human bone moist with oil, he is purified by bathing; if it be not oily, by stroking a cow, or by looking at the sun, having sprinkled his mouth with water."[5] All those functions of the body, by which its offensive dis-

[1] Asiat. Res. v. 371.
[2] Institutes of Menu, ch. v. 58. [3] Ibid. 85, 87. [4] Ibid. 73.
[5] Ibid. 87.

charges are effected, or its vital powers communicated, afford occasion for the ceremonies of purification.[1] "Oily exudations, says the law of Menu, "seminal fluids, blood, dandruff, urine, feces, ear-wax, nail-parings, phlegm, tears, concretions on the eyes, and sweat, are the twelve impurities of the human frame, and for cleansing these, earth and water must be used."[2] "He who carries in any manner an inanimate burden, and is touched by any thing impure, is cleansed by making an ablution, without laying his burden down."[3] "He who has been bitten by a dog, a shakal, or an ass, by any carnivorous animal frequenting a town, by a man, a horse, a camel, or a boar, may be purified by stopping his breath during one repetition of the gayatri."[4] After the rules for the purification of living bodies, follow precepts for the purification of things inanimate. For each of a great many species, a separate mode is prescribed. Land, for example, is cleansed by sweeping, by smearing with cowdung, by sprinkling with cows' urine, by scraping, or by letting a cow pass a day and a night on it.[5] "The purification ordained for all sorts of liquids, is by stirring them with cusa grass; for cloths folded, by sprinkling with hallowed water; for wooden utensils, by planing them. The purification by sprinkling is ordained for grain and cloths in large quantities; but to purify them in small parcels, such as a man may easily carry, they must be washed."[6] These instances, selected merely as a small specimen of a great whole, will suffice to show what moral ideas are conveyed and inculcated in the notions of purity and impurity comprised in the religion of the Hindus.

As the purifications, so likewise the penances, prescribed

[1] The Hindus, among whom the idea of delicacy, in regard either to physical or moral subjects, appears never to have taken rise, describe these occasions of purification in the plainest, or in other words, the grossest terms. There is a long series of precepts about voiding the excrements (Laws of Menu, ch. iv. 45 to 52): And for purification afterwards, "Let each man," says the law, "sprinkle the cavities of his body, and taste water in due form, when he has discharged urine or feces: First, let him thrice taste water; then twice let him wipe his mouth, but a woman or servile man may once respectively make that ablution." Ibid. ch. v. 138, 139. "Having vomited, or been purged, let him bathe and taste clarified butter: for him who has been connected with a woman, bathing is ordained by law." Ibid. 144. In one instance there is a curious contrariety: it is declared (Ibid. 180), "A woman whose thoughts have been impure is purified by her monthly discharge." Yet this same peculiarity of the female constitution is a cause of impurity, from which she is separated by bathing. Ibid. 66.

[2] Laws of Menu, ch. v. 134, 135.

[3] Ibid. 143.

[4] Ibid. xi. 200.

[5] Ibid. v. 124.

[6] Ibid. 115, 118.

by the various systems of religion, afford a remarkable indication of the qualities really ascribed to the object of worship. All penance consists in suffering. In the same degree in which the object of worship is supposed to be delighted with penance, in the same degree he is delighted with human suffering; and so far as he delights in suffering, for its own sake, so far he is a malignant being: whatever epithets, in the spirit of flattery, his votaries may confer upon him. It is natural to a rude and ignorant mind to regard the object of its worship as malignant. Things appear great or little by comparison. Amid the incessant efforts which are made to ascend another step in adulation, after all the epithets of greatness and honour are lavished upon the god, to make his greatness and honour still higher, by contrast, every epithet of meanness and contempt is heaped by the worshipper upon himself and his kind. The same is the case with his happiness; which will appear the greater, the higher it is raised above that of other beings; of course, the deeper the misery of other beings. Hence it is, that the prayers and praises, addressed to the deity by rude nations, abound with the most hyperbolical expressions of human misery as well as human depravity; that, in the religion of rude minds, pleasure in general bears a strong mark of reprobation, and the voluntary creation of pain is the strongest of all recommendations to him on whom the issues of life depend. In the language of the Greeks and Romans, the gods were envious of human happiness;[1] just as the proud and haughty mind of the earthly despot, the archetype and model according to which, in certain stages of knowledge, the idea of the heavenly is regularly formed, likes not that the happiness of other people should approach to that of himself, and reaps a pleasure from their pain, both as enhancing the idea of his own happiness, and lessening the sense of his misery.[2] "A sin, involuntarily committed," says

[1] Solon asks Crœsus why he interrogates him about human happiness—Ω Κροισε, επισταμενον με το θειον παν εον φθονερον και ταραχωδες; Herod. lib. i. cap. xxxii.

[2] "'Tis evident we must receive a greater or less satisfaction or uneasiness from reflecting on our own condition and circumstances, in proportion as they appear more or less fortunate or unhappy; in proportion to the degrees of riches and power, and merit, and reputation, which we think ourselves possessed of. Now, as we seldom judge of objects from their intrinsic value, but form our notions of them from a comparison with other objects, it follows, that according as we observe a greater or less share of happiness or misery in

the sacred text of Menu, "is removed by repeating certain texts of the scripture; but a sin committed intentionally, by harsh penances of different sorts."[1] The following account of the reason for performing penances, has the effect of exposing to religious antipathy all those persons who are affected with a bodily infirmity. "Some evil-minded persons," says the same sacred volume, "for sins committed in this life, and some for bad actions in a preceding state, suffer a morbid change in their bodies: a stealer of gold from a Brahmen has whitlows on his nails; a drinker of spirits, black teeth; the slayer of a Brahmen, a marasmus; the violator of his preceptor's bed, a deformity in the generative organs; a malignant informer, fetid ulcers in his nostrils; a false detractor, stinking breath; a stealer of grain, the defect of some limb; a mixer of bad wares with good, some redundant member; a stealer of dressed grain, dyspepsia; a stealer of holy words, or an unauthorized reader of the scriptures, dumbness; a stealer of clothes, leprosy; a horse-stealer, lameness; the stealer of a lamp, total blindness; the mischievous extinguisher of it, blindness in one eye; a delighter in hurting sentient creatures, perpetual illness; an adulterer, windy swelling in his limbs. Thus, according to the diversity of actions, are born men despised by the good, stupid, dumb, blind, deaf, and deformed. Penance, therefore, must invariably be performed for the sake of expiation, since they who have not expiated their sins, will again spring to birth with disgraceful marks."[2] "Any twice-born man who has drunk spirit of rice through perverse delusion of mind, may drink more spirit in flame, and atone for his offence by severely burning his body; or he may drink boiling hot, until he die, the urine of a cow, or pure water, or milk, or clarified butter, or juice expressed

others, we must make an estimate of our own, and feel a consequent pain or pleasure. The misery of another gives us a more lively idea of our happiness, and his happiness of our misery. The former, therefore, produces delight; and the latter uneasiness." Hume's Treatise of Human Nature, ii. 174. If this principle have a real existence in human nature; and if the rude mind invariably fashion the divine mind after itself, the belief, so wonderfully common, that the Divine being is delighted with the self-inflicted torment of his worshippers, is sufficiently accounted for.

[1] Institutes of Menu, ch. xi. 46.

[2] Ibid. 48 — 54.

BOOK II. CHAP. VI.

from cow-dung."[1] A curious reason is assigned for the heinous guilt assigned to the drinking of intoxicating liquors by a Brahmen; because, "stupified by drunkenness, he might fall on something very impure, or might even, when intoxicated, pronounce a secret phrase of the Veda, or might do some other act which ought not to be done."[2] "If a Brahmen kill by design a cat, or an ichneumon, the bird chasha, or a frog, a dog, a lizard, an owl, or a crow, he must perform the ordinary penance required for the death of a Sudra;"[3] as if the crime of killing a man were the same with that of killing a frog. "Should one of the twice-born eat the food of those persons with whom he ought never to eat, or food left by a woman, or a Sudra, or any prohibited flesh, he must drink barley gruel only for seven days and nights."[4] "Having taken goods of little value from the house of another man, he must procure absolution by performing the penance santapana, or by eating for a whole day the dung and urine of cows mixed with curds, milk, clarified butter, and water boiled with cusa grass, and then fasting entirely for a day and a night."[5] The penances for venereal sin, and the description of its various species, are unfit to be transcribed.[6] Something might be said for penances, if they were attached solely to moral offences, and proportioned in painfulness to the motives to offend; because the efficacy of the punishment which is reserved to a subsequent life is commonly annihilated by remoteness. How much of this useful character belongs to the penances of the Hindus, a few passages will disclose. "He, who has officiated at a sacrifice for outcasts, or burned the corpse of a stranger, or performed rites to destroy the innocent," (a strange association of crimes!) "may expiate his guilt by three prajapatya penances."[7] "A total fast for twelve days and nights, by a penitent with his organs controlled, and his mind attentive, is the penance named paraca, which expiates all degrees of guilt."[8] "He who for a whole month

[1] Institutes of Menu, ch. xi. 91, 92. [2] Ibid. 97.
[3] Ibid. 132. [4] Ibid. 153. [5] Ibid. 165, 213.
[6] See the Institutes of Menu, ch. xi. 171 to 179, where every species of sexual abomination is deliberately specified.
[7] Institutes of Menu, ch. xi. 198. "When a twice-born man performs the penance prajapati, he must for three days eat only in the morning; for three days only in the evening; for three days food unasked, but presented to him; and for three more days, nothing." Ibid. 212.
[8] Ibid. 216.

eats no more than thrice eighty mouthfuls of wild grains, as he happens by any means to meet with them, keeping his organs in subjection, shall attain the same abode with the regent of the moon."[1] "Sixteen suppressions of the breath, while the holiest of texts is repeated with the three mighty words, and the triliteral syllable, continued each day for a month, absolve even the slayer of a Brahmen from his hidden faults."[2] "A priest who should retain in his memory the whole Rigveda would be absolved from guilt, even if he had slain the inhabitants of the three worlds, and had eaten food from the foulest hands."[3] To such a degree are fantastic ceremonies exalted above moral duties; and so easily may the greatest crimes be compensated, by the merit of ritual, and unmeaning services.[4]

But the excess to which religion depraves the moral sentiments of the Hindus is most remarkably exemplified in the supreme, the ineffable merit which they ascribe to the saint who makes penance his trade.

Repairing to a forest, with no other utensils or effects, than those necessary in making oblations to consecrated fire: and leaving all property, and all worldly duties behind him, he is there directed to live on pure food, on certain herbs, roots, and fruit, which he may collect in the forest, to wear a black antelope's hide, or a vesture of bark, and to suffer the hairs of his head, his beard, and his nails to grow continually. He is commanded to entertain those who may visit his hermitage with such food as himself may use, to perform the five great sacraments, to be constantly engaged in reading the Veda; patient of all extremities, universally benevolent, with a mind intent on the Supreme Being; a perpetual giver, but no receiver of gifts; with tender affection for all animated bodies. "Let him not eat the produce of ploughed land, though abandoned by any man, nor fruits and roots produced in a town, even though hunger oppress him.—Either let him break hard

[1] Institutes of Menu, ch. xi. 221. [2] Ibid. 214. [3] Ibid. 262.

[4] C'est une superstition très dangéreuse que le pardon des crimes attaché à certaines cérémonies...... Vous pensez que Dieu oubliera votre homicide, si vous vous baignez dans un fleuve, si vous immolez une brebis noire, et si on prononce sur vous des paroles. Un second homicide vous sera donc pardonné au même prix, et ainsi un troisième, et cent meurtres ne vous couteront que cent brebis noires et cent ablutions! Faites mieux, misérables humains, point de meurtres, et point de brebis noires. Voltaire, Dict. Philos. au mot Superstition.

fruits with a stone, or let his teeth serve as a pestle.—Let him slide backwards and forwards on the ground; or let him stand a whole day on tiptoe; or let him continue in motion rising and sitting alternately; but at sunrise, at noon, and at sunset, let him go to the waters, and bathe. In the hot season let him sit exposed to five fires, *four blazing around him with the sun above*; in the rains let him stand uncovered, *without even a mantle*, where the clouds pour *the heaviest* showers; in the cold season, let him wear humid vesture; and enduring harsher and harsher mortifications, let him dry up his bodily frame. Let him live without external fire, without a mansion, wholly silent, feeding on roots and fruit, sleeping on the bare earth, dwelling at the roots of trees. From devout Brahmens let him receive alms to support life, or from other housekeepers of twice-born classes, who dwell in the forest. Or, *if he has any incurable disease*, let him advance in a straight path, towards the invincible *north-eastern* point, feeding on water and air, till his mortal frame totally decay, and his soul become united with the Supreme."[1]

In conformity with these principles are formed those professors of mortification and piety, who are known under the modern name of Fakeers, and presented to Europeans a spectacle which so greatly surprised them. Of all the phenomena of human nature, none appears at first view more extraordinary than the self-inflicted torments of the holy saints of Hindustan. Some of them keep their hands closed till they are pierced through by the growth of the nails. Others hold them above their heads, till the power of the arms is extinguished. They make vows to remain in the standing posture for years. Three men were seen by Fryer, whose vow extended to sixteen years. One of them had completed his dreadful penance; of the rest, one had passed five years in torment, the other three.

[1] Institutes of Menu, ch. vi. 3 to 8, and 16 to 32. There is a certain stage in the progress from extreme barbarity to some degree of intellectual improvement, in which worship by self-inflicted torments seems naturally to suggest itself. Thus, the priests and people of Mexico come next, perhaps, to the Hindus, though certainly at a prodigious distance behind them, in the devotion of pain and suffering. "It makes one shudder" (says Clavigero, book vi. sect. 22), "to read the austerities which they exercised on themselves. They mangled their flesh, as if it had been insensible, and let their blood run in such profusion, that it appeared to be a superfluous fluid of the body." Their fastings, watchings, and other efforts of abstinence, were pushed to the greatest extremities. Ibid.

Their legs were prodigiously swelled, and deeply ulcerated; and became at last too weak to support their bodies, when they leaned on a pillow suspended from a tree. Others, turning their heads to gaze at the heaven over their shoulder, remain fixed in that posture, till the head can no longer be restored to its natural position, and no aliment except in the liquid state, can pass down their throats.

The ceremony, commanded by Menu, "of sitting, in the hot season, between five fires," cannot be conceived without horror. A yogee, or penitent, actually seen by Fryer, had resolved to undergo this penance for forty days, at a public festival, where an immense concourse of spectators were assembled. Early on the morning, after having seated himself on a quadrangular stage he fell prostrate, and continued fervent in his devotions, till the sun began to have considerable power. He then rose, and stood on one leg, gazing stedfastly at the sun, while fires, each large enough, says the traveller, to roast an ox, were kindled at the four corners of the stage; the penitent counting his beads, and occasionally, with his pot of incense, throwing combustible materials into the fire to increase the flames. He next bowed himself down in the centre of the four fires, keeping his eyes still fixed upon the sun. Afterwards, placing himself upright on his head, with his feet elevated in the air, he stood for the extraordinary space of three hours, in that inverted position; he then seated himself with his legs across, and thus remained sustaining the raging heat of the sun and of the fires till the end of the day. Other penitents bury themselves up to the neck in the ground, or even wholly below it, leaving only a little hole through which they may breathe. They tear themselves with whips; they repose on beds of iron spikes;[1] they chain themselves for life to the foot of a tree: the wild imagination of the race appears in short to have been racked to devise a sufficient variety of fantastic modes of tormenting themselves. The extent to which they carry the penance of fasting is almost incredible. They fix their eyes on the blazing sun till the power of vision is extinguished.[2] The following description, in the

[1] See a curious description in the Asiat. Res. v. 49, of a fakeer, seen at Benares by Mr. Duncan, who had used this bed for thirty-five years.

[2] See Fryer's Travels, pp. 102, 103.—Sonnerat's Voyage, i. 121, 149, 153, 176. Hamilton's Voyage to the East Indies, i. 274.—Voyage de Tavernier, iv. 118.

BOOK II. CHAP. VI.

drama entitled Sacontala, how much soever partaking of the hyperbolical character of oriental poetry, conveys a most remarkable image of the length of time, the patience, and steadiness, with which the devotees of the forests must have remained immoveable in their solitary positions. "You see," says one of the personages of the drama, "in that grove a pious Yogee, motionless as a pollard, holding his thick, bushy hair, and fixing his eyes on the solar orb.—Mark; his body is covered with a white ants' edifice, made of raised clay; the skin of a snake supplies the place of his sacerdotal thread, and part of it girds his loins; a number of knotty plants encircle and wound his neck; and surrounding birds' nests almost conceal his shoulders."[1] The same venerable character is thus further described in the Bhagvat-Geeta; "The Yogee constantly exerciseth the spirit in private. He is recluse, of a subdued mind and spirit; free from hope, and free from perception. He planteth his own seat firmly on a spot that is undefiled,

Mr. Richardson, in his Arabic and Persian Dictionary, under the word Fakeer, says, "Every invention of perverted ingenuity is exhausted in deforming and distorting nature." And Mr. Wilkins (Note 113, subjoined to his translation of the Bhagvat-Geeta) says, "The word zeal, in the vulgar acceptation, signifies the voluntary infliction of pain, the modes of doing which, as practised to this day by the zealots of India, are as various as they are horrible and astonishing." Bernier, who describes most of the penances alluded to in the text, mentions their standing on their hands, with the head down and the feet up: "D'autres qui se tenoient les heures entières sur leurs mains sans branler, la tête en bas et les pieds en haut, et ainsi de je ne sçai combien d'autres sortes de postures tellement contraintes et tellement difficiles, que nous n'avons de bâteleurs qui les pussent imiter; et tout cela, ce semble, par dévotion comme j'ai dit, et par motif de religion, où on n'en sçauroit seulement découvrir l'ombre." Lettre des Gentils de l'Hindoustan, p. 153, 154.

[2] Sacontala, Act vii. in Sir William Jones's Works. One of the Mohammedan travellers, whose voyages are described by Renaudot, says of these recluses, "They for the most part stand motionless as statues, with their faces always turned to the sun. I formerly saw one in the posture here described, and returning to India about sixteen years afterwards, I found him in the very same attitude, and was astonished he had not lost his eyesight by the intense heat of the sun." Renaudot's ancient Account of India and China, p. 32. Bernier describes them thus: "On en voit quantité de tout nuds assis ou couchés les jours et les nuits sur les cendres, et assez ordinairement dessous quelques uns de ces grands arbres, qui sont sur les bords des Talabs où réservoirs, ou bien dans des galeries qui sont autour de leur Deuras ou temples d'idoles. . . . . . Il n'y a Mégère d'enfer si horrible à voir que ces gens-là tout nuds avec leur peau noire, ces grands cheveux, ces fuseaux des bras dans la posture que j'ai dit, et ces longues ongles entortillés." Lettres des Gentils de l'Hindoustan, p. 151. Orme accounts in part, at least, and that very satisfactorily, for these astonishing efforts of patience and self-denial. "The many temporal advantages which the Brahmens derive from their spiritual authority, and the impossibility of being admitted into their tribe, have perhaps given rise to that number of Joguees and Facquires, who torture themselves with such various and astonishing penances, only to gain the same veneration which a Brahmen derives from his birth." Orme's Hist. Milit. Trans. Indostan, i. 4.

neither too nigh, nor too low, and sitteth upon the sacred grass which is called coos, covered with a skin and a cloth. There he, whose business is the restraint of his passions, should sit, with his mind fixed on one object alone, in the exercise of his devotion for the purification of his soul, keeping his head, his neck, and his body, steady, without motion, his eyes fixed on the point of his nose, looking at no other place around. The man who keepeth the outward accidents from entering his mind, and his eyes fixed in contemplation between his brows; who maketh the breath to pass through both his nostrils alike in expiration and inspiration, who is of subdued faculties, mind, and understanding; the Yogee, who thus constantly exerciseth his soul, obtaineth happiness incorporeal and supreme."[1] This pure state of meditation, which obtains the name of devotion, is even more exalted than that of penance. "The Yogee," says Crishna, "is more exalted than Tapaswees, those votaries who afflict themselves in performing penance, respected above the learned in science, and" (which is worthy of peculiar regard,) "superior to those who are attached to moral works."[2] "Be thou at all times," says this supreme god to Arjoon in another place, "employed in devotion. The fruit of this surpasseth all the rewards of virtue pointed out in the Vedas, in worshippings, in mortifications, and even in the gifts of charity."[3]

It is abundantly ascertained that the Hindus at one time, and that a time comparatively recent,[4] were marked with the barbarity of human sacrifices.[5] It even appears

[1] Bhagvat-Geeta, p. 60, 63.

[2] Ibid. p. 67.

[3] Ibid. p. 76.—M.

Some confusion appears here between the Ascetic, whose penance is only passive, and he whose penance is active. The Yogi merely suffers the privations incident to intensity of abstraction. The Tapaswi inflicts upon himself bodily inconveniences and sufferings, practices discouraged by Manu and the Gita.—W.

[4] It is agreed among the Sanscrit scholars that the Puranas are modern, compared with the Vedas and other ancient monuments of the Hindus. Mr. Colebrooke is of opinion that the worship of heroes is altogether unknown to the author of the Vedas; though it was evidently part of the popular belief at the time the Puranas were composed. A sacrifice, therefore, enjoined in the Puranas, must have prevailed at a pretty late period.

[5] See a translation of what is denominated "The Sanguinary chapter" of the Calica Purana, by Mr. Blaquiere, Asiat. Res. v. 371, and Wilkins's Hetopadesa, note 249, and p. 211. In the Bhawishya Purana, it is declared that the head of a slaughtered man gives Dúrga a thousand times more satisfaction than that of a buffalo. This sacrifice, however, is forbidden in the Brahma and the Bhagawat Puranas. Asiat. Res. iii. p. 260.—M.

The Calica and Bhavishya Puranas are not included in the lists of the

BOOK II. CHAP. VI.

that the remainder of that devotional service is now in existence. When it is proposed to resist, as exorbitant, the demands of government, the Brahmens erect what they denominate a koor, which is a circular pile of wood, with a cow, or an old woman on the top of it. If urged to extremity they set fire to the pile, and consume the victim, a sacrifice by which they are understood to involve their oppressor in the deepest guilt.[1] The British Government has interfered to prevent the sacrifice of children by throwing them to the sharks in the Ganges.[2]

Though the progress of improvement has brought into comparative disuse the mode of seeking divine favour by the sacrifice of a fellow-creature, horrid rites, which have too near an affinity with it, are still the objects of the highest veneration. It is one of the grandest achievements of piety, for individuals to sacrifice themselves in honour of the gods. There are solemn festivals, in which the images of certain deities are carried in procession in vast ponderous machines denominated raths, or chariots, drawn by a multitude of devotees and priests; when it is customary for numbers of the congregated people[3] to throw themselves under the wheels, and even fathers and mothers with their children in their arms. The chariot passes on, as if no impediment existed, and crushing them to death, is supposed to convey them immediately to heaven.[4] The

Puranas which are given in authentic works, and are sectarial compilations belonging to the Sakta form of worship—a form not hinted at, it is believed, in the Vedas—and taught in works alone which are undoubtedly of comparatively recent origin. These sanguinary rites seem to have been borrowed from the practices of the wild tribes bordering upon India, amongst whom human sacrifices are described by Hindu writers of the middle ages, and have been recently known to have been attempted.—W.

[1] An instance of this, in which an old woman was the victim, was attempted at Benares, so late as the year 1788. See the account by Lord Teignmouth, Asiat. Res. v. 333.

[2] Papers relating to East India affairs, ordered by the House of Commons to be printed, June 3, 1813, p. 427.

[3] It is no little exaggeration to say that, "numbers of the congregated people throw themselves under the chariot wheels." Mr. Stirling, who was resident in Orissa for four years, mentions, that during that period there were no more than three such immolations; and of them one was possibly unintentional, whilst the other two were cases of painful and incurable disease. But this practice is modern. Jagannath himself is modern, and has no place even in the Vaishnava Puranas. It is not improbable that the present shrine attained reputation as a place of pilgrimage no longer ago than a century.—W.

[4] A distinct description of this human sacrifice, performed at the feast of Juggernaut, is to be found in the voyage (i. 121) of Sonnerat, who was an eye-witness. It is also described by that faithful traveller Bernier, Lettre sur les Gentils de l'Hindoustan, p. 128. It attracted, in a peculiar degree, the attention of the Rev. Dr. Buchanan: see his work, entitled Christian Researches in Asia. The missionaries have given us several descriptions, published in the Transactions of the Missionary Societies.

practice of sacrificing themselves in the flames is a noted ceremony of the Hindus. It is sometimes executed with circumstances of studied atrocity; the victim striking himself in front with his sabre, so as to lay open his bowels to the spectators, tearing out part of his liver, cutting it off with his sabre, giving it to a relation or bystander, conversing all the time with indifference apparently complete, then with unchanged countenance leaping into the flames, and expiring without a movement.[1] In some parts of India a Brahmen devotes himself to death, by eating till he expires with the surfeit.[2] On great solemnities, the votaries strike off their own heads, as a sacrifice to the Ganges,[3] and many drown themselves in the hallowed streams.[4] Of the modes adopted by the Hindus of sacrificing themselves to the divine powers, none, however, has more excited the attention of Europeans, than the burning of the wives on the funeral piles of their husbands. To this cruel sacrifice the highest virtues are ascribed. "The wife who commits herself to the flames with her husband's corpse, shall equal Arundhati, and reside in Swarga; accompanying her husband, she shall reside so long in Swarga, as are the thirty-five

1 Such was the instance witnessed by one of the Arabian travellers of Renaudot. See Ancient Relations, p. 80.—M.

Mr. Mill is not scrupulous in his choice of authorities, when they serve his purpose, nor slow to believe what is incredible, when it is to the disadvantage of the Hindus. The Arabian travellers are witnesses whose evidence is to be received with caution, on all occasions; and it is not being very sceptical to doubt the fact of a man's cutting off pieces of his liver, and distributing them as souvenirs to his friends. In the instances that follow, he quotes from equally questionable authorities; and when he says, "that many drown themselves in hallowed streams," he improves upon his original, who only mentions that "some" annually drown themselves, at the confluence of the Jumna and Ganges. All these practices are prohibited by the Hindu law, except in the case of incurable disease, and then self-immolation is allowable only at Prayága. Even penance, which endangers life, is prohibited. Nirnaya Sindhu.—W.

2 Orme, on the Government and People of Indostan, p. 434.

3 See Richardson's Dictionary, at the word Fakeer.

4 The place where the Jumna and the Ganges meet, is a spot of peculiar sanctity. "Some of the victims of superstition," says Dr. Tennant, "annually drown themselves at the junction of the streams; and this being the most acceptable of all offerings, it is performed with much solemnity. The rapidity with which the victim sinks, is regarded as a token of his favourable acceptance by the god of the river. To secure the good inclination of the deity, they carry out the devoted person to the middle of the stream, after having fastened pots of earth to his feet. The surrounding multitude on the banks are devoutly contemplating the ceremony, and applauding the constancy of the victim, who, animated by their admiration, and the strength of his own faith, keeps a steady and resolute countenance till he arrives at the spot; when he springs from the boat, and is instantly swallowed up, amidst universal acclamations." Indian Recreations, ii. 250.

millions of hairs on the human body.[1] As the snake-catcher forcibly drags the serpent from his earth, so, bearing her husband from hell, with him she shall enjoy the delights of heaven, while fourteen Indras reign. If her husband had killed a Brahmana, broken the ties of gratitude, or murdered his friend, she expiates the crime."[2] Though a widow has the alternative of leading a life of chastity, of piety, and mortification, denied to the pleasures of dress, never sleeping on a bed, never exceeding one meal a day, nor eating any other than simple food, it is held her duty to burn herself along with her husband; and "the Hindu legislators," says Mr. Colebrooke, "have shown themselves disposed to encourage" this barbarous sacrifice.[3]

Such are the acts, by which, according to the Hindu religion, the favour of the Almighty power is chiefly to be gained; such are the ideas respecting purity and merit, which it is calculated to inspire. Yet, if any one concludes that the Hindus were unacquainted with the ordinary precepts of morality, he will be greatly deceived. "By Brahmens," says the law of Menu, "placed in the four orders, a ten-fold system of duties must ever be sedulously practised; Content; returning good for evil; resistance to sensual appetites; abstinence from illicit gain; purification; coercion of the organs; knowledge of the scripture;

[1] The Brahmens are always audacious enough to form a peremptory opinion. We have seen, before, that they never hesitated to assign a fixed number to the veins and arteries of the human body, though they are totally unacquainted with dissection. They here assign, with perfect confidence, a determinate number to the hairs on the human body.

[2] Sanscrit text, quoted by Mr. Colebrooke, in his discourse on the duties of a faithful Hindu wife, Asiat. Res. iv. 208. The custom of burning wives on the funeral piles of their husbands, was common to the Hindus with the Northern nations. See Jamieson's Scottish Dictionary, ad verb, *Bayle Fire*.—The principal among the wives of a Scandinavian chief accompanied him to the funeral pile. Mallet. Introd. Hist. Denmark, vol. i. c. 13.—The Scandinavians did not scruple to expose their children. Ibid.—Robertson, who informs us that the wives of the chiefs of the Natchez, an American tribe, were burnt along with them at their death, says that the custom arose from the excessive veneration in which they were held, as brothers of the sun, and representatives of the deity; and that from this impulse, the wives, as well as the domestics, who shared the same fate, welcomed death with exultation. Hist. of America, ii. 130.

[3] Asiat. Res. iv. 210. See the whole of that discourse, where a number of authorities are collected. The circumstances of the transaction can be so easily conceived, that, horrid as they are, I have not thought proper to describe them. The prayers and ceremonies are exactly of the usual character. See an account by Bernier, of several cases of which he was an eye-witness (Lettre sur les Gentils de l'Hindoustan, p. 131); and a variety of cases in the works of the Missionaries Ward and Dubois.

knowledge of the supreme spirit; veracity; and freedom from wrath."[1] In this enumeration of duties, though a large proportion is allowed to acts purely ceremonial and useless: yet some of the noblest virtues are included. "Action," says the same sacred code, "is either mental, verbal, or corporeal. Devising means to appropriate the wealth of other men, resolving on any forbidden deed, and conceiving notions of atheism or materialism, are the three bad acts of the mind: scurrilous language, falsehood, indiscriminate backbiting, and useless tattle, are the four bad acts of the tongue: Taking effects not given, hurting sentient creatures without the sanction of the law, and criminal intercourse with the wife of another, are three bad acts of the body; and all the ten have their opposites, which are good in an equal degree."[2] Though there is something extremely whimsical in the consequence ascribed to the following acts of injustice, yet they are with great propriety forbidden: "He who appropriates to his own use, the carriage, the bed, the seat, the well, the garden, or the house of another man, who has not delivered them to him, assumes a fourth part of the guilt of their owner."[3] The following observations are in a pure and elevated strain of morality: "Even here below an unjust man attains no felicity; nor he whose wealth proceeds from giving false evidence; nor he, who constantly takes delights in mischief. Though oppressed by penury, in consequence of his righteous dealings, let him never give his mind to unrighteousness; for he may observe the speedy overthrow of iniquitous and sinful men. Iniquity, committed in this world, produces not fruit immediately, but, like the earth, in due season; and advancing little by little, it eradicates the man who committed it. Yes; iniquity, once committed, fails not of producing fruit to him who wrought it. He grows rich for a while through unrighteousness; then he beholds good things; then it is that he vanquishes his foes; but he perishes at length from his whole root upwards. Let a man continually take pleasure in truth, in justice, in laudable practices, and in purity: let him chastise those, whom he may chastise, in a legal mode; let him keep in subjection his speech, his arm, and his appetite:

[1] Institutes of Menu, ch. vi. 91, 92.
[2] Ibid. ch. xii. 3, 5, 6, 7.
[3] Ibid. ch. iv. 202.

wealth and pleasures, repugnant to law, let him shun; and even lawful acts, which may cause future pain, or be offensive to mankind."[1]

Sir William Jones, whom it is useful to quote, because his authority may have influence with those whose opinions I am constrained to controvert, observes, that "the principles of morality are few, luminous, and ready to present themselves on every occasion."[2] Descanting on the rudeness and ignorance of the Scythian nations; "of any philosophy," he says, "except natural ethics, which the rudest society requires, and experience teaches, we find no more vestiges in Asiatic Scythia, than in ancient Arabia."[3] He was not surprised to find natural ethics, where not a vestige of philosophy was found; because "natural ethics," are what "*the rudest society requires and experience teaches.*" If we search a little further, we shall discover that nations differ less from one another in the knowledge of morality, and of its obligations (the rules of morality have been taught in all nations in a manner remarkably similar), than in the degrees of steadiness, with which they assign the preference to moral, above other acts. Among rude nations it has almost always been found, that religion has served to degrade morality, by advancing to the place of greatest honour, those external performances, or those mental exercises, which more immediately regarded the deity; and with which, of course, he was supposed to be more peculiarly delighted. On no occasion, indeed, has religion obliterated the impressions of morality, of which the rules are the fundamental laws of human society: morality has every where met with the highest applause; and no where has it been celebrated in more pompous strains, than in places where the most contemptible, or the most abominable rites, have most effectually been allowed to usurp its honours.[4] It is not so much, therefore, by the mere words

[1] Institutes of Menu, ch. iv. 170 to 177.

[2] Discourse on the Philosophy of the Asiatics. Asiat. Res. iv. 166.

[3] Discourse on the Tartars. Asiat. Res. ii. 33.

[4] Few states of society are more low and degraded than that of the Mussulmans in modern Egypt. Hear what is said of their ethics: " On remarque chez les principaux chefs de la religion, nommés en Egypte cheiks de la loi, l'astuce commune à tous les prêtres, qui, pour mieux dominer, cherchent à s'emparer de l'esprit des hommes. Leur conversation est remplie de belles sentences morales, et de grandes images poétiques qu'ils pillent dans les livres Arabes, c'est tout leur savoir; on ne doit pas chercher en eux d'autres connoissances sur la politique, les sciences, &c.; ils n'en soupçonnent pas plus l'existence que

in which morality is mentioned, that we are to judge of the mental perfections of different nations, as by the place which it clearly holds in the established scale of meritorious acts. In a moment of hyperbolical praise, it may even receive a verbal preference to ceremonies; as in one passage of the Institutes of Menu: "A wise man should constantly discharge all the moral duties, though he perform not constantly the ceremonies of religion; since he falls low, if, while he performs ceremonial acts only, he discharge not his moral duties."[1] Yet in the entire system of rules concerning duty, the stress which is laid upon moral acts, may, as we see in the case of the Hindus, bear no comparison to the importance which is attached to useless or pernicious ceremonies. Such a maxim as that which has just been quoted, can be regarded as but of little value, when it is surrounded by numerous maxims of the following tendency; "Not a mortal exists more sinful than he, who, without an oblation to the manes or gods, desires to enlarge his own flesh with the flesh of another creature."[2] "From the three Vedas, the lord of creatures, incomprehensibly exalted, successively milked out the three measures of that ineffable text beginning with the word *tad* and entitled, *savitri*, or *gayatri*; whoever shall repeat, day by day, for three years, without negligence, that sacred text

l'utilité." (De l'Egypte par le Gén. Reynier, p. 63.) Voltaire remarks, with that felicity with which he sometimes touches an important truth; "La religion de ce Siamois nous prouve que jamais législateur n'enseigna une mauvaise morale. Voyez, lecteur, que celle de Brama, de Zoroastre, de Numa, de Thaut, de Pythagore, de Mahomet, et même du poisson Oannos, est absolument la même. J'ai dit souvent qu'on jeterait des pierres à un homme qui viendrait prêcher une morale relâchée." Dictionnaire Philosophique, au mot SAMMONOCODOM.

Garcilasso de la Vega gives us a list of the moral sayings of a celebrated Inca of ancient Peru, named Pachacatec, of which the following are a specimen:

"Better is it, that thou shouldst be envied by others for being good, than that thou shouldst envy others because thou art bad.

"Envy is a cancer, which eats and gnaws into the bowels of the envious.

"Drunkenness, anger, and folly, are equally mischievous; differing only in this, that the two first are transient and mutable, but the third permanent and continuing.

"Adulterers, who take away the good reputation and honesty of another family, are disturbers of the common peace and quiet, and are as bad as thieves and robbers, and therefore to be condemned to the gallows without mercy.

"A truly noble and courageous spirit is best tried by that patience which he shows in the times of adversity.

"Impatience is the character of a poor and degenerate spirit, and of one that is ill-taught and educated." Royal Commentaries, book IV. ch. xxxvi.

[1] Institutes of Menu, ch. iv. 204.

[2] Ib. v. 52.

BOOK II. CHAP. VI.

shall hereafter approach the divine essence, move as freely as air, and assume an ethereal form."[1] "Studying and comprehending the Veda, practising pious austerities, acquiring divine knowledge, command over the organs of sense and action, avoiding all injury to sentient creatures, and showing reverence to a natural and spiritual father, are the chief branches of duty which ensure final happiness."[2] "Even three suppressions of breath made according to the divine rule, accompanied with the triverbal phrase, and the triliteral syllable, may be considered as the highest devotion of a Brahmen; for as the dross and impurities of metallic ores are consumed by fire, thus are the sinful acts of the human organs consumed by suppressions of the breath."[3] If we examine that highest degree of merit to which the imagination of the Hindu can ascend, that of the Sanyassi, or professor of austere devotion, we shall find it to consist in an absolute renunciation of all moral duties, and moral affections. "Exemption from attachments, and affection for children, wife, and home;"[4] nay, "the abandonment of all earthly attachments,"[5] form a necessary part of that perfection after which he aspires.

It is by no means unnatural for the religion of a rude people to unite opposite qualities, to preach the most harsh austerities, and at the same time to encourage the loosest morality. It may be matter of controversy to what degree the indecent objects employed in the Hindu worship imply depravity of manners; but a religion which subjects to the eyes of its votaries the grossest images of sensual pleasure, and renders even the emblems of generation objects of worship; which ascribes to the supreme God an immense train of obscene acts; which has them engraved on the sacred cars, portrayed in the temples, and presented to the people as objects of adoration, which pays worship to the Yoni, and the Lingam, cannot be regarded as favourable to chastity.[6] Nor can it be supposed, when

[1] Institutes of Menu, ch. ii. 77, 82. [2] Ibid. xii. 83. [3] Ibid. vi. 70, 71.
[4] Bhagvat-Geeta, p. 102. [5] Institutes of Menu, ch. vi. 81.
[6] See a fanciful account of the origin of this worship by Mr. Paterson, Asiat. Res. viii. 54. His description of the moral effects of this superstition is more to our purpose: "It is probable," says he, "that the idea of obscenity was not originally attached to these symbols; and, it is likely, that the inventors themselves might not have foreseen the disorders which this worship would occasion amongst mankind. Profligacy eagerly embraces what flatters its propensities, and ignorance follows blindly wherever example excites: it is therefore no wonder that a general corruption of manners should ensue, increasing in

to all these circumstances is added the institution of a number of girls, attached to the temples, whose business is dancing and prostitution, that this is a virtue encouraged by the religion of the Hindus.[1]

proportion as the distance of time involved the original meaning of the symbol in darkness and oblivion. Obscene mirth became the principal feature of the popular superstition, and was, even in after-times, extended to, and intermingled with, gloomy rites and bloody sacrifices. An heterogeneous mixture which appears totally irreconcileable, unless by tracing the steps which led to it. It will appear that the ingrafting of a new symbol upon the old superstition, occasioned this strange medley. The sect of Vishnu was not wholly free from the propensity of the times to obscene rites; it had been united in interest with that of Siva, in their league against the sect of Brahma, as was expressed by an image, called Har-Heri, half Siva, and half Vishnu. This union seems to have continued till the time when an emblem of an abstract idea, having been erected into an object of worship, introduced a revolution in religion, which had a violent and extended effect upon the manners and opinions of mankind. It was then that a gloomy superstition arose, which spread with baneful rapidity amongst mankind; which degraded the Deity into an implacable tyrant; which filled its votaries with imaginary terrors; which prescribed dreadful rites; and exacted penances, mortifications, and expiatory sacrifices." (Ibid. p. 55.) See also a picture of these religious immoralities, by Bernier, Lettre sur les Gentils, pp. 129, 130. But the writer, who, above all others, has furnished superabundant evidence of the immoral influence of the Hindu religion, and the deep depravity which it is calculated to produce, is Mr. Ward, in his "View of the History, Literature, and Religion of the Hindoos." From the facts which he records in great detail, the following are the results: "The characters of the gods, and the licentiousness which prevails at their festivals, and abounds in their popular works, with the enervating nature of the climate, have made the Hindoos the most effeminate and corrupt people on earth. I have, in the course of this work, exhibited so many proofs of this fact, that I will not again disgust the reader by going into the subject. Suffice it to say, that fidelity to marriage vows is almost unknown among the Hindoos; the intercourse of the sexes approaches very near to that of the irrational animals. . . . . But to know the Hindoo idolatry as it is, a person must wade through the filth of the thirty-six pooranus, and other popular books—he must read and hear the modern popular poems and songs—he must follow the Brahmen through his midnight orgies, before the image of Kalee, and other goddesses; or he must accompany him to the nightly revels, the jatras, and listen to the filthy dialogues which are rehearsed respecting Krishnu and the daughters of the milkmen; or he must watch him, at midnight, choking with the mud and waters of the Ganges a wealthy relation, while in the delirium of fever; or, at the same hour, while murdering an unfaithful wife, or a supposed domestic enemy; or he must look at the Brahmen hurrying the trembling half-dead widow round the funeral pile, and throwing her like a log of wood by the side of the dead body of her husband, tying her, and then holding her down with bamboo levers, till the fire has deprived her of the power of rising and running away. . . . . . This system of heathenism communicates no purifying knowledge of the divine perfections, supplies no one motive to holiness while living, no comfort to the afflicted, no hope to the dying; but, on the contrary, excites to every vice, and hardens its followers in the most flagrant crimes." (Introductory Remarks pp. 94, 95.)

[1] Notwithstanding this inference and the exaggerated pictures quoted from Mr. Ward, it may be confidently asserted that the Hindu women are most exemplary in their conduct in this respect. Even in large towns, the profligacy bears no comparison with that of London and Paris; and in the country, want of conjugal virtue is almost unknown. The form under which the Lingam is worshipped, that of a column, suggests no impure ideas, and few of the uneducated Hindus attach any other idea to it, than that it *is* Siva; they are not aware of its typical character Dancing girls are not known in Hindustan; they are confined to the temples of the south, and are not so bad or so numerous as the figurantes in European theatres. The cars, with the indecencies upon them,

Another contrast to the tortures and death which the religion of the Hindus exhorts them to inflict upon themselves, is the sacredness which it imprints upon the life of animals. Not only are the Hindus prohibited the use of animal food, except at certain peculiar sacrifices ; even the offerings to the gods consist almost entirely of inanimate objects ; and to deprive any sensitive creature of life, is a heinous transgression of religious duty. Many of the inferior creatures, both animate and inanimate, are the objects of religious veneration ; such, in particular, are the cow, the lotos, and cusa grass. Nor, in this enumeration, must the dung and urine of the cow be forgotten ; things so holy as to be of peculiar efficacy in the ceremonies of purification. To whatever origin we may ascribe this strange application of the religious principle, it has at least been very widely diffused. It is known that many negro tribes worship animals and reptiles ; and that they carry the solicitude for their preservation to a still more extravagant pitch than even the Hindus ; punishing with death those who hurt them even casually.[1] The sacred character in Egypt of the ox, and of many other animals, is too familiarly known to require any proof. The cow was oracular, and sacred among the Ammonians.[2] Not only cows, but horses, eagles, lions, bears, were divine animals among the Syrians.[3] The Egyptian priests respected as sacred the life of all animals, and animal food seems to have been interdicted not less in Egypt than in Hindustan.[4] At an early period, the Greeks, and even the Romans, punished with death the killing of an ox.[5] The

are almost restricted to Bengal and Orissa, and the temples in Hindustan are quite free from the gross representations which disgrace some of those in the south. It is not just, therefore, to accuse the Hindu religion of employing in its worship objects that imply depravity of manners. They are not necessarily or primitively comprised in its ceremonial; they have no warrant, either in the Vedas, or the Puranas, they are not to be traced in writings of an early date, they belong to a part of the prevailing system, which has sprung out of, rather than given rise to, depravity of ideas in some, not in all parts of India: and, there is every reason to believe, they are as foreign to genuine Hinduism, as to any other religion.—W.

[1] Edwards' Hist. of the West Indies, ii. 77. 4to. Ed.

[2] Bryant's Analysis of Ancient Mythology, i. 323.

[3] Lucian, De Syria Dea.

[4] The priests of Egypt, says Herodotus, account it unholy to kill any thing which has life, saving what they use in sacrifice ; Herod. Hist. lib. i. cap. 140 : and Porphyry informs us that it was not till a late period of their history that animal sacrifices were introduced. De Abstin. lib. ii. et iv.

[5] Ab hoc antiqui manus ita abstinere voluerunt, ut capite sanxerint, si quis occidisset. Varro. De Re Rustica, lib. ii. cap. 5.

worship of this species of quadrupeds appears indeed to have been common to all the idolatrous nations from Japan to Scandinavia.[1] That, in India, it was a worship directed to no moral end,[2] is evident upon the slightest inspection. To renounce the benefits which the inferior animals are fitted by nature to render to man, is not humanity, any more than swinging before an idol, by an iron hook, forced through the muscles of the back, is the virtue of self-command.[3] And that this superstition took not its rise from a sensibility to the feelings of animated creatures, is evident from the barbarous character of several of the nations where it prevails; from the proverbial cruelty suffered by the labouring animals of Hindustan; and from the apathy with which human beings are left to expire by hunger and disease while reptiles are zealously tended and fed.[4]

[1] See the satisfactory proofs adduced in the very learned and instructive, though erroneous work, of Dupuis, Origine de tous les Cultes. liv. iii. ch. viii.

[2] The worship of the cow by the Hindus is a popular error. It is held in respect for its own merits, and the bull is reverenced as the vehicle of Siva, but the latter reason is modern and sectarial. There is no trace of any form of worship for the cow in the primitive system.—W.

[3] Neither the one nor the other belong to the Hindu religion originally. The Hindus were not prohibited from eating flesh—even the flesh of the cow.

> The Vedas which enshrine our holy law,
> Direct the householder shall offer those
> Who in the law are skilled the honied meal,
> And with it flesh of ox, or calf, or goat.—See Hin. Th., i. 340.

The long note that presently follows is a series of mistakes. The practices of hospitals for insects and the like are not Hindu, they are Jain. The cruel treatment of beasts of burden or draught, by bullock or carriage drivers, is no more an illustration of national character, than the necessity of a "society for preventing cruelty to animals" in England, is indicative of general brutality amongst ourselves.—W.

[4] "Although the killing an animal of this" (the ox) "kind is by all Hindus considered as a kind of murder, I know no creature whose sufferings equal those of the labouring cattle of Hindustan." (Buchanan, Journey, &c. i. 167.) See also Ward on the Hindus, Introd. p. xliii. An hospital for the sick poor, says Dr. Tennant, was never known in India, before the establishment of the British; though there were for dogs, cats, &c. (Indian Recreations, i. 73.) The authors of the Universal History inform us gravely, on the authority of Ovington, that the Hindus have a care for the preservation of fleas, bugs, and other vermin, which suck the blood of man: for in an hospital near Surat, built for their reception, a poor man is hired now and then to rest all night upon the *kot* or bed where the vermin are put; and, lest their stinging should force him to take his flight before morning, he is tied down to the place, and there lies for them to glut themselves with human gore." (Modern Univ. Hist. vi. 262.) Anquetil Duperron, who describes a temple near Surat, full of those sacred animals, adds: "La vue de l'hôpital des animaux, entretenu par des êtres raisonnables avec tout l'ordre, le soin, le zèle même que l'on pourroit exiger d'eux, s'il étoit question de leur semblable, et cela même dans un pays, où il n'y a d'établissemens publics, ni pour les malades, ni pour les vieillards; la vue d'un pareil hôpital auroit de quoi étonner, si l'on ne sçavoit pas que la

BOOK II. CHAP. VI.

Religion consists of two great doctrines; that concerning the nature and service of God; and that concerning the nature and destination of the human soul. In the

nature se plaît aux disparates en Asie comme en Europe. (Voyages aux Indes Orient.; Disc. Prélim. Zendavesta, i. ccclxii.) "The Gentoos, though they will not kill their meat, make no conscience to work them to death, allowing them hardly food to keep them alive. Neither are they less inhuman towards their sick, a woman being brought to die among the tombs in my sight." Fryer's Travels. ch. v. sect 3. See to the same purpose, the Abbé Dubois, p. 132; Ward on the Hindoos, Introd. p. lv. It is worth observing that Milton, the universality of whose knowledge is not the least remarkable particular of his wonderful mind, was acquainted with the disgusting superstition of letting the vermin devour the man: "Like the vermin," says he, "of an Indian Catharist, which his fond religion forbids him to molest." Tetrachordon, Milton's Prose Works, ii. 122, 8vo. Edit. Tenderness to animals was a part of the religion of Zoroaster. We are informed in the Sadda, that he obtained from God a view of the regions of infernal torment, where he saw a number of kings, and among the rest one without a foot. He begged to know the reason, and God said to him; "That wicked king never performed but one good action in his life. He saw, as he was going to the chase, a dromedary tied at too great a distance from its provender, endeavouring to eat, but unable to reach it: he pushed the provender towards it with his foot. I have placed that foot in heaven; all the rest of him is here." Voltaire, Essai sur les Mœurs et l'Esprit de Nations, ch. v. The following, Porphyry tell us (De Abstin. lib. iv. p. 431), were laws of Triptolemus: 1. To honour our parents; 2. To offer nothing to the gods but the fruits of the earth; 3. Never to hurt animals. "The inhabitants of Miniana," (a place not far from Sego, in the heart of Africa) "eat their enemies, and strangers, if they die in the country. They eat the flesh of horses. But such is their veneration for the cow, that she is never killed." Park's last Mission to Africa, p. 166.

Mr. Richardson (see his Dissertation on Eastern Manners, p. 16) denies the authenticity of the fragments of the Zendavesta collected by Anquetil Duperron, on account of "the uncommon stupidity," as he is pleased to express it, "of the work itself." Yet it is in a strain remarkably resembling that of the Vedas; the same sublime praises bestowed upon the Divinity; superstitions equally gross; discourses equally childish. We must not, however, on this account question the authenticity of the Vedas and the Puranas, though we must renounce the vulgar belief of the great wisdom of the Brahmens. In truth, the stupidity, as Mr. Richardson calls it, of the Zendavesta, and its remarkable similarity to the sacred books of the Hindus, is the most striking proof of its authenticity. There is the strongest reason to conclude that the ancient Magi, and the ancient Brahmens, were people very much upon a level; and that the fame of Zoroaster for wisdom is no better founded than that of the Indian sages. There is a radical difference, he says, between the language of the Zendavesta, and the modern Persian. (Ibid.) But the same is the case with the Sanscrit, which Sir William Jones thinks, from this circumstance, can never have been vernacular in Hindustan. (See Disc. on the Hindus, Asiat. Researches, i. 422.) The language, he says, of the Zendavesta has many words, which a modern Persian could not pronounce, but there are many words in the German language which an Englishman or Frenchman cannot pronounce, though the German is the basis of the languages of both. The Zendavesta, he says, contains Arabic words; but it contains Arabic only as the Greek contains Sanscrit. In fact, the identities which can be traced in all languages is one of the most remarkable circumstances in the history of speech. Of the Vedas, a man who had unrivalled opportunities of information informs us, "They contain nothing important or rational. In fact, they have nothing but their antiquity to recommend them. As to any thing further, they include all the absurdities of Hindu paganism, not only such as it has originally been, but also the pitiful details of fables which are at present current in the country, relating to the fantastical austerities of the Hindu hermits, to the metamorphoses of Vishnu, or the abominations of the lingam. The fourth of them, called Atharvana-veda, is the most dangerous of all for a people so entirely

complicated superstition of the Hindus, the first presented many questions which it needed a considerable accumulation of evidence to solve. Of the latter a just idea may be speedily conveyed.

It is well known that the metempsychosis, or the transmigration of the soul into various orders of being, reviving in one form, when it ceases to exist in another, is the tenet of the Hindus. This is a theory well calculated to present itself to the mind of the rude inquirer, when first excited to stretch his views beyond the present term of sensation and action. The vegetable life, which expires in the plant in autumn, revives in the seed in spring. The sluggish worm, which undergoes a species of death, and buries itself in a tomb of its own formation, springs again to life, a gay and active creature, as different in appearance, as in appetites and powers. Every thing on earth is changed, nothing annihilated; and the soul of the man who expires to-day, revives in something else, to which life is at that instant imparted.

Some very obvious and very impressive appearances must have suggested the notion of the metempsychosis, since it is one of the most ancient, and one of the most general of all religious opinions. "No doctrine," says Dupuis, "was ever more universally diffused; none claims an origin so ancient. It reigned in the East, and in the West, among rude nations and polished nations: and it ascends to antiquity so high, that Burnet ingeniously declares, one would believe it to be descended from heaven; so much it appears without father, without mother, and without descent."[1] The Brahmens grafted upon it, in their usual way, a number of fantastic refinements, and gave to their ideas on this subject, a more systematic form than is usual with those eccentric theologians. They describe the mind as characterized by three qualities; good-

sunk in superstition, because it teaches the art of magic, or the method of injuring men by the use of witchcraft and incantation." (Description, &c. of the people of India, by the Abbé Dubois, p. 102. Even the *gayatri*, the most holy of all holy things, is an assemblage, says the Abbé, of unmeaning terms, " unintelligible to the Brahmens themselves. I have never met with any one who could give me a tolerable explication of it." Ibid. p. 79.

[1] Dupuis, Origine de tous les Cultes, tom. ii. par. 2, p. 181; where the reader will find authorities to prove the antiquity and diffusion of this peculiar doctrine. See, too, the learned Beausobre, Hist. de Manich. tom. ii. liv. vii. ch. 5, sect. 4. For its existence among the Mexicans, see Clavigero, book vi. sect. 1.

ness, passion, darkness. According as any soul is distinguished by one or another of those qualities in its present life, is the species of being into which it migrates in the life to come. Souls endued with goodness attain the condition of Deities; those filled with passion receive that of men; those immersed in darkness are condemned to that of beasts. Each of these conditions, again, is divided into three degrees, a lower, a middle, and a higher. Of the souls distinguished by darkness, the lowest are thrust into mineral and vegetable substances, into worms, reptiles, fishes, snakes, tortoises, cattle, shakals; the middle pass into elephants, horses, Sudras, Mlec'hchas (a word of very opprobrious import, denoting men of all other races not Hindu), lions, tigers, and boars; the highest animate the forms of dancers, singers, birds, deceitful men, giants, and blood-thirsty savages. Of the souls who receive their future condition from the quality of passion, the lowest pass into cudgel-players, boxers, wrestlers, actors, those who teach the use of weapons, and those who are addicted to gaming and drinking; the middle enter the bodies of kings, men of the fighting class, domestic priests of kings, and men skilled in the war of controversy; the highest become gandharves (a species of supposed aërial spirits, whose business is music), genii attending superior gods, together with various companies of apsarases, or nymphs. Of the souls who are characterized by the quality of goodness, the lowest migrate into hermits, religious mendicants, other Brahmens, such orders of demigods as are wafted in airy cars, genii of the signs and lunar mansions, and Daityas, another of their many orders of superior spirits; the middle attain the condition of sacrificers, of holy sages, deities of the lower heaven, genii of the Vedas, regents of stars, divinities of years, Pitris, and Sadhyas, two other species of exalted intelligences; the highest ascend to the condition of Brahma with four faces, of creators of worlds, of the genius of virtue, and the divinities presiding over the two principles of nature.[1] Besides this general description of the future allotment of different souls, a variety of particular dooms are specified, of which a few may be taken as an example. "Sinners in the first degree," says the ordinance of Menu, "having passed

[1] Institutes of Menu, ch. xii. 24, 40 to 51.

through terrible regions of torture, for a great number of years, are condemned to the following births at the close of that period. The slayer of a Brahmen must enter the body of a dog, a boar, an ass, a camel, a bull, a goat, a sheep, a stag, a bird, a Chandala, or a Pucassa. He, who steals the gold of a priest, shall pass a thousand times into the bodies of spiders, of snakes, and camelions, of crocodiles, and other aquatic monsters, or of mischievous blood-sucking demons. He who violates the bed of his natural or spiritual father, migrates a hundred times into the forms of grasses, of shrubs with crowded stems, or of creeping and twining plants, carnivorous animals, beasts with sharp teeth, or cruel brutes."[1] After a variety of other cases, a general rule is declared, for those of the four castes who neglect the duties of their order: "Should a Brahmen omit his peculiar duty, he shall be changed into a demon, with a mouth like a firebrand, who devours what has been vomited; a Cshatriya, into a demon who feeds on ordure and carrion; a Vaisya, into an evil being who eats purulent carcases; and a Sudra, who neglects his occupations, into a foul embodied spirit, who feeds on lice."[2] The reward of the most exalted piety, of the most profound meditation, of that exquisite abstemiousness which dries up the mortal frame, is peculiar: such a perfect soul becomes absorbed in the Divine essence, and is for ever exempt from transmigration.[3]

We might very easily, from the known laws of human nature, conclude, notwithstanding the language held by the Hindus on the connexion between future happiness and the virtue of the present life, that rewards and punishments, very distant and very obscure, would be wholly impotent against temptations to crime,[4] though, at the

[1] Institutes of Menu, ch. xii. 54 to 58. [2] Ib. 71, 72.

[3] Ib. ch. xii. 125.

[4] According to Mr. Ward, as presently cited, the Hindus are in this respect not dissimilar from other people, whatever be their religious faith. This is a question we are not called upon to discuss, but as far as it bears upon the Hindus, it may be remarked, once for all, that Mr. Ward, notwithstanding the epithets bestowed upon him in the text, is neither an experienced nor an admirable witness; his experience was limited to Bengal, in which the best specimens of the Hindu character are comparatively rare, and his station and circumstances brought him into contact chiefly with bad specimens even of Bengalis. Although an intelligent man, he was not a man of comprehensive views, and his views were necessarily still more narrowed by his feelings as a missionary; his testimony, therefore, although not without value, must be received with considerable distrust, and admitted only with constant qualification and correction.—W.

instigation of the priests, they might engage the people in a ceaseless train of wretched ceremonies. The fact corresponds most exactly with the anticipation. An admirable witness has said, "The doctrine of a state of future rewards and punishments, as some persons may plead, has always been supposed to have a strong influence on public morals: the Hindoos not only have this doctrine in their writings, but are taught to consider every disease and misfortune of life as an undoubted symptom of moral disease, and the terrific appearance of its close-pursuing punishment. Can this fail to produce a dread of vice, and a desire to merit the favour of the Deity? I will still further," he adds, "assist the objector; and inform him, that the Hindoo writings declare, that till every immoral taint is removed, every sin atoned for, and the mind has obtained perfect abstraction from material objects, it is impossible to be re-united to the great spirit; and that, to obtain this perfection, the sinner must linger in many hells, and transmigrate through almost every form of matter." Our informant then declares; "Great as these terrors are, there is nothing more palpable than that, with most of the Hindoos, they do not weigh the weight of a feather, compared with the loss of a roopee. The reason is obvious: every Hindoo considers all his actions as the effect of his destiny; he laments, perhaps, his miserable fate, but he resigns himself to it without a struggle, like the malefactor in a condemned cell." This experienced observer adds, which is still more comprehensive, that the doctrine of future rewards and punishments has, in no situation, and among no people, a power to make men virtuous.[1]

[1] "To this," he says, "may be added, what must have forced itself on the observation of every thoughtful observer, that, in the absence of the religious principle, no outward terrors, especially those which are invisible and future, not even bodily sufferings, are sufficient to make men virtuous. Painful experience proves, that even in a Christian country, if the religious principle does not exist, the excellence and the rewards of virtue, and the dishonour and misery attending vice, may be held up to men for ever, without making a single convert." Ward, "View, &c. of the Hindoos," Introd. p. lxxxiv. Here, however, Mr. Ward ought to have explained what he meant by the "religious principle," by which different persons mean very different things. This was the more necessary, that, having taken away all efficacy from the doctrine of future rewards and punishments, he strips religion of all power over the lives and actions of men, except in so far as good effects may be expected from the "religious principle," which, whatever else it may not be, is at any rate, in his estimation, not the expectation of future rewards and punishments.—M.

The whole of this review of the religion, as of the laws of the Hindus, is full

CHAP. VII.

Manners.

By the manners of a nation are understood the peculiar modes in which the ordinary business of human life is carried on. The business itself is everywhere essentially the same. In all nations men eat and drink; they meet, converse, transact, and sport together. But the manner in which these and other things are performed is as different as the nations are numerous into which the race is divided.

So much of the entire business of life, among the Hindus, consists in religious services, that the delineation of their religion is a delineation of the principal branch of their manners.

The singular distinctions, attached to the different classes, present another remarkable feature in the manners of this people. The lower orders, in other countries, are often lamentably debased; in Hindustan they are degraded below the brutes. With the single exception of the Vaisya caste, to whom is appropriated the business of agriculture and of barter, the whole of the productive classes, according to the standards of law and religion, are vile and odious, unworthy to eat, to drink, or to sit with a member of the classes above them.[1]

---

of very serious defects, arising from inveterate prejudices and imperfect knowledge. Every text, every circumstance, that makes against the Hindu character, is most assiduously cited, and every thing in its favour as carefully kept out of sight, whilst a total neglect is displayed of the history of Hindu belief. The doctrines of various periods and of opposing sects, have been forced into one time and one system, and the whole charged with an incongruity, which is the creation of the writer. Had he been more impartially disposed, indeed, it would not have been easy to have given an unobjectionable account of the Hindu religion, as his materials were exceedingly defective. Manu is good authority for the time to which it refers, and Mr. Colebrooke's essays furnish authentic details of particular parts of the ritual, but the different travellers who are given as authorities of equal weight, are utterly unworthy of regard. A word more on the subject of Fate, as understood by the Hindus; as it is something very different from that of other people. It is necessity, as the consequence of past acts—that is, a man's station and fortunes in his present life are the necessary consequences of his conduct in his pre-existence. To them he must submit, but not from despair. He has his future condition in his own power, and it depends upon himself in what capacity he shall be born again. He is not therefore the helpless victim of an irresistible and inscrutable destiny, but the sufferer for his own misdeeds, or the possessor of good which his own merits have secured him.—W.

[1] A very mistaken view is here taken of the condition of the "productive classes;" and on all the most important occasions of social life, they hold quite as independent and respectable a position as they do in Europe. That they

There are four remarkable periods into which, with respect to the three honourable classes, human life is divided. Of these periods, or orders, as they are denominated by the Hindus, the first is that of the student; the second, that of the householder; the third, that of the man who performs penance or other religious acts, residing continually in a forest! the fourth, that of the Sannyasi, or the ascetic absorbed in divine contemplation.[1]

The period of the student commences at the era of investiture.[2] Prior to this age, the situation of children is remarkable: even those of a Brahmen are not held superior in rank to a Sudra.[3] The condition of the student much more closely represents that of an European apprentice than that of a pupil in literature. He dwells in the house of his preceptor, and tends him with the most respectful assiduity. He is commanded to exert himself in all acts useful to his teacher;[4] and of course performs the part of an assistant in all the offices of religion.[5] "As he who digs deep with a spade comes to a spring of water, so the student, who humbly serves his teacher, attains the knowledge which lies deep in his teacher's mind." Upon the student of the priestly order a peculiar burden, or distinction, is imposed: to acquire daily his food by begging.[6]

The gift of sacred instruction is not bestowed indiscriminately; but the text, which regulates the choice of pupils, is so vague as to leave the selection nearly at the discretion of the master. "Ten persons," it is declared,

---

may not eat, drink, or intermarry with the castes above them, is no hardship to races who would not avail themselves of the privileges of such intercourse with many of the castes who are their equals. These laws of segregation are, in their case, self-imposed. European writers can little understand the prevailing feeling of the Hindus in these matters. It is pride—not shame of caste, that animates them down even to the meanest; and the sweeper is much more tenacious of his caste than the Brahman. As to "sitting" with them, let a blacksmith acquire wealth, and he will have his levee well attended by Brahmans of the most respectable descent. Instances are not wanting of this, at all the principal towns in India.—W.

[1] See Laws of Menu, ch. ii. iii. and vi.

[2] See the account of this æra, in another part of this volume.

[3] Institutes of Menu, ch. ii. 173.

[4] Ibid. 491.

[5] "Let him carry water-pots, flowers, cow-dung, fresh earth, and cusa grass, as much as may be useful to his preceptor." Ibid. 182.

[6] "The subsistence of a student by begging is held equal to fasting in religious merit." Ibid. 218. There are numerous precepts respecting the niceties of begging. Ibid. 48 to 50, and 183 to 190.

"may legally be instructed in the Veda; the son of a spiritual teacher; a boy who is assiduous; one who can impart other knowledge; one who is just; one who is pure; one who is friendly; one who is powerful; one who can bestow wealth; one who is honest; and one who is related by blood. Where virtue and wealth are not found, or diligent attention proportioned, in that soil divine instruction must not be sown; it would perish like fine seed in barren land."[1]

The instruction which is bestowed may soon be described. "The venerable preceptor, having girt his pupil with the thread, must first instruct him in purification, in good customs, in the management of the consecrated fire, and in the holy rites of morning, noon, and evening."[2] The grand object of attention and solicitude is the reading of the Veda.[3] Some classes of the Brahmens have united with their religious doctrines certain speculations concerning the intellectual and material worlds; and these speculations have been dignified with the name of philosophy; but the holy rites, and the Veda, form the great, and on most occasions the exclusive object of that higher instruction which is bestowed on the pupil of the Brahmen.

On this important occasion, as on other occasions, the attention of the Hindu is much more engaged by frivolous observances, than by objects of utility. While the directions laid down respecting the instruction of the pupil are exceedingly few and insignificant, the forms, according to which he must pay his duty to the master, are numerous, minute, and emphatically enjoined.[4]

[1] Institutes of Menu, ch. ii. 109, 112.

[2] Ibid. 69.

[3] Ibid. 70.

[4] When the student is going to read the Veda, he must perform an ablution, as the law ordains, with his face to the north; and at the beginning and end of each lesson, he must clasp both the feet of his preceptor, and read with both his hands closed. "In the presence of his preceptor let him always eat less; and wear a coarser mantle, with worse appendages: let him rise before, and go to rest after his tutor. Let him not answer his teacher's orders, or converse with him, reclining on a bed; nor sitting, nor eating, nor standing, nor with an averted face: But let him both *answer and converse*, if his preceptor sit, standing up; if he stand, advancing toward him; if he advance, meeting him; if he run, hastening after him; if his face be averted, going round to front him, *from left to right*: if he be at a little distance, approaching him; if reclined, bending to him; and if he stand ever so far off, running toward him. When his teacher is nigh, let his couch or his bench be always placed low: when his preceptor's eye can observe him, let him not sit carelessly at his ease. Let him never pronounce the mere name of his tutor, even in his absence: by censuring his preceptor, though justly, he will be born an ass. He must not serve his tutor by the intervention of another, while himself stands aloof; nor

The duration of the period of study is very indefinite. "The discipline of a student in the three Vedas may be continued for thirty-six years, in the house of his preceptor; or for half that time, or for a quarter of it, or until he perfectly comprehend them. A student, whose rules have not been violated, may assume the order of a married man, after he has read in succession a sac'ha, or branch from each of the three Vedas, or from two or from any one of them."[1] It is even permitted to pass the whole period of life in the state of a pupil; and to this, merit so exalted is ascribed, that the very highest rewards of religion are bestowed upon it. If a student anxiously desire to pass his whole life in the house of a sacerdotal teacher, he must serve him with assiduous care, till he be released from his mortal frame. That Brahmen who has dutifully attended his preceptor till the dissolution of his body, passes directly to the eternal mansion of God."[2] Should the teacher die, the student must attend upon his widow, his son, or one of his paternal kinsmen, with the same respect as to the deceased preceptor. Should none of these be living, he occupies the seat of the preceptor himself.[3]

---

must he attend him in a passion, nor when a woman is near; from a carriage or a raised seat he must descend to salute his heavenly director. Let him not sit with his preceptor to the leeward, or to the windward of him; nor let him say anything which the venerable man cannot hear." Institutes of Menu, ch. ii. 70, 71 to 199, and 201 to 203. Even to the sons and wives of the preceptor must numerous tokens of profound respect be shown. Ibid. 207 to 218. For his general conduct, "these following rules," says Menu, "must a Brahmachari, *or student in theology*, observe, while he dwells with his preceptor; keeping all his members under control, for the sake of increasing his habitual devotion. Day by day, having bathed and being purified, let him offer fresh water to the gods, the sages, and the manes; let him show respect to the images of the deities, and bring wood for the oblation to fire. Let him abstain from honey, from flesh-meat, from perfumes, from chaplets of flowers, from sweet vegetable juices, from women, from all sweet substances turned acid, and from injury to animated beings; from unguents for his limbs, and from black powder for his eyes; from wearing sandals and carrying an umbrella, from sensual desire, from wrath, from covetousness, from dancing, and from vocal and instrumental music: from gaming, from disputes, from detraction, and from falsehood; from embracing, or wantonly looking at women, and from disservice to other men. Let him sleep constantly alone." Next are forbidden several acts of sensual impurity, which are too gross to be described; and the holy text thus again proceeds: "Let him carry water-pots, flowers, cow-dung, and cusa grass, as much as may be useful to his preceptor. Having brought logs of wood from a distance, let him place them in the open air; and with them let him make an oblation to fire, without remissness, both evening and morning. Let the scholar, when commanded by his preceptor, and even when he has received no command, always exert himself in reading. Let not the sun ever rise or set while he lies asleep in the village." Institutes of Menu, ch. ii. 175 to 183, 186, 191, 219.

[1] Institutes of Menu, ch. iii. 1.

[2] Institutes of Menu, ii. 243, 244.

[3] Ibid. 247, 248. The following modes of living are pointed out to the Brahmen: 1. lawful gleaning and gathering; 2. what is given unasked; 3. what is

To the state of the student succeeds that of the married man or the housekeeper. It is at this epoch that the Hindu begins to sustain a part as a member of Society.

Marriage is a religious duty; and a duty of the highest order. Except for some grand plan of devotion, as that of remaining a student, or of becoming a fakeer, no man neglects at an early age to fulfil this sacred obligation. As the sacrament of obsequies to the manes of ancestors can be performed only by a male descendant, and as any failure in these obsequies deeply affects the spirits of the dead, to die without a son is regarded as one of the greatest of all calamities.[1]

---

asked as alms; 4. tillage; 5. traffic and money lending: even by these two last, when distressed, he may live; but service for hire is named dog-living, which he must always avoid, iv. 4, 5, 6. His hair, nails, and beard being clipped; his passions subdued; his mantle white; his body pure; let him diligently occupy himself in reading the Veda. Let him carry a staff of Venu, a ewer with water in it, a handful of cusagrass, or a copy of the Veda; with a pair of bright golden rings in his ears. He must not gaze on the sun, whether rising or setting, or eclipsed, or reflected in water, or advanced to the middle of the sky. Over a string to which a calf is tied, let him not step; nor let him run while it rains; nor let him look on his own image in water; this is a settled rule. By a mound of earth, by a cow, by an idol, by a Brahmen, by a pot of clarified butter or of honey, by a place where four ways meet, and by large trees well known in the district, let him pass with his right hand toward them, 35, 36, 37, 38, 39.

Let him neither eat with his wife, nor look at her eating, nor sneezing, or yawning, or sitting carelessly at her ease, 43.

Some precepts are ludicrous. "Let him not eat his food, wearing only a single cloth, nor let him bathe quite naked: nor let him eject urine or fæces in the highway, nor on ashes, nor where kine are grazing, nor on tilled ground, nor in water, nor on wood raised for burning, nor, *unless he be in great need*, on a mountain, nor on the ruins of a temple, nor at any time on a nest of white ants, nor in ditches with living creatures in them, nor walking, nor standing, nor on the bank of a river, nor on the summit of a mountain: nor let him ever eject them, looking at *things moved by* the wind, or a fire, or at a priest, or at the sun, or at water, or at cattle: but let him void his excrements, having covered the earth with wood, potherbs, *dry* leaves and grass, or the like, carefully suppressing his utterance, wrapping up his breast and his head: by day let him void them with his face to the north; by night, with his face to the south; at sunrise and sunset, in the same manner as by day; in the shade of darkness, whether by day or by night, let a Brahmen ease nature with his face turned as he pleases; and in places where he fears injury to life *from wild beasts or from reptiles.*" 45 to 51.

"Let not a man, desirous to enjoy long life, stand upon hair, nor upon ashes, bones, or potsherds, nor upon seeds of cotton, nor upon husks of grain," 78.

An infinite number of things relative to food are to be attended to, 207 to 225.

[1] A man is nevertheless forbidden to marry before his elder brother. Ibid. 172. But if among several brothers of the whole blood, one have a son born, Menu pronounces them all fathers of a male child, by means of that son. Ibid. 182. There is a singular importance attached to the having of a son: "By a son a man obtains victory over all people; by a son's son he enjoys immortality; and afterwards by a son of that grandson he reaches the solar abode." Ibid. 137. Kinsmen, as among the Jews, were allowed to raise up seed to one another. Not only was a widow, left without children, permitted to conceive

The ceremonies of marriage, entirely religious, have been already described. Marriages are distinguished into eight kinds: of which one half are honourable, and differ from one another only in some minute circumstances; in the fifth, the bridegroom bestows gifts upon the bride, her father, and paternal kinsman; the last three are rather species of unlawful connexion, than forms of nuptial contract; one being voluntary and by mutual consent; the other forcible when a woman is seized, "while she weeps and calls for assistance, after her kinsmen and friends have been slain in battle;" the last, "when the damsel is sleeping, or flushed with a strong liquor, or disordered in her intellect."[1] With the grand rule to prevent the intermixture of the castes, the reader is already acquainted. "For the first marriage of the twice-born classes," says the law of Menu, "a woman of the same class is recommended; but for such as are impelled by inclination to marry again, women in the direct order of the classes are to be preferred: a Sudra woman only must be the wife of a Sudra; she and a Vaisya of a Vaisya; they two and a Cshatriya, of a Cshatriya; those two and a Brahmani, of a Brahmen."[2] The Hindu law-givers, who commonly mistake minuteness for precision, and are apt to be most particular where it is least required, make rules for the choice of a wife. "In connecting a man's self with a wife. Let him," says Menu, "studiously avoid the ten following families, be they ever so great, or ever so rich in kine, goats, sheep, gold, and grain. The family which has omitted prescribed acts of religion; that which has produced no male children; that in which the Veda has not been read; that which has thick hair on the body; and those which have been subject to hemorrhoids, to phthisis, to dyspepsia, to epilepsy, to leprosy

---

by a kinsman of her husband; but even before his death, if he was supposed to be attacked by an incurable disease. Ibid. ix. 59, 162, 164. A daughter, too, when a man had no sons, might be appointed for the same purpose. Ibid. 127. In Egypt, in the same manner, a widow left without children cohabited with the brother of the deceased. Recherches Philosoph. sur les Egyptiens et les Chinois, i. 70.

[1] Institutes of Menu, ch. iii. 27 to 34. The crimes implied in the last two cases must have been frequent, to make them be distinguished formally in books of sacred law as two species of marriage.

[2] Ibid. 12, 13.

and to elephantiasis. Let him not marry a girl with reddish hair, nor with any deformed limb; nor one troubled with habitual sickness; nor one either with no hair, or too much; nor one immoderately talkative; nor one with inflamed eyes; nor one with the name of a constellation, of a tree, or of a river, of a barbarous nation, or of a mountain, of a winged creature, a snake, or a slave; nor with any name raising an image of terror. Let him choose for his wife a girl, whose form has no defect; who has an agreeable name; who walks gracefully like a phenicopteros, or like a young elephant; whose hair and teeth are moderate respectively in quantity and in size; whose body has exquisite softness."[1]

The condition of the women is one of the most remarkable circumstances in the manners of nations. Among rude people, the women are generally degraded; among civilized people they are exalted.[2] In the barbarian, the passion of sex is a brutal impulse, which infuses no tenderness; and his undisciplined nature leads him to abuse his power over every creature that is weaker than himself. The history of uncultivated nations uniformly represents the women as in a state of abject slavery, from which they slowly emerge, as civilization advances. Among some of the negro tribes on the coast of Africa, the wife is never permitted to receive any thing from the hands of her husband, or even to appear in his presence, except on her knees.[3] In the empire of Congo, where the people are sufficiently advanced to be united in a large community; and in most of the nations which inhabit the southern regions of Africa, the women are reckoned unworthy to eat with the men.[4] In such a state of society property is an advantage which it may naturally be supposed that the degraded sex are by no means permitted to enjoy. Not only among the African and other savage tribes, and the Tartars of the present day, but among the ancient inhabitants of Chaldea and Arabia, and all the nations of Europe in their ancient uncivilized state, the

1 Institutes of Menu, ch. iii. 6 to 10.

2 This important subject is amply and philosophically illustrated by Professor Millar, in his Inquiry into the Distinction of Ranks, ch. i.

3 Histoire Générale des Voyages, tom. v. liv. x. ch. iii.

4 Ibid. tom. vi. liv. xiii. ch. iii. sect. 2, and tom. iv. liv. vii. ch. xiii. sect. 1.

women were excluded from the inheritance of the family.[1] Being condemned to severe and perpetual labour, they are themselves regarded as useful property. Hence a father parts not with his daughter but for a valuable consideration; hence the general custom, among barbarous nations, as in Pegu, in Siberia, among the Tartars, among the negroes on the coast of Guinea, among the Arabs, and even among the Chinese, of purchasing the bride by a dower.[2] It is only in that improved state of property and security, when the necessities of life have ceased to create perpetual solicitude, and when a large share of attention may be given to its pleasures; that the women, from their influence on those pleasures, begin to be an object of regard. As society refines upon its enjoyments, and advances into that state of civilization, in which various corporeal qualities become equal or superior in value to corporeal strength, and in which the qualities of the mind are ranked above the qualities of the body, the condition of the weaker sex is gradually improved, till they associate on equal terms with the men, and occupy the place of voluntary and useful coadjutors.

A state of dependence more strict and humiliating than that which is ordained for the weaker sex among the Hindus cannot easily be conceived. "Day and night," says Menu, "must women be held by their protectors in a state of dependence."[3] Who are meant by their protectors is immediately explained: "Their fathers protect them in childhood; their husbands protect them in youth; their sons protect them in age: a woman," it is added, "is never fit for independence. Let husbands consider this as the supreme law, ordained for all classes; and let them, how weak soever, diligently keep their wives under lawful

[1] See Inquiry into the Distinction of Ranks, ch. i. sect. 1. They were admitted to inheritance among the Jews plainly as a novelty, and an institution unknown to their neighbours. Numbers ch. xxvii.—M.

We have seen that this was not the case amongst the Hindus, but that their right to property is fully recognised and carefully secured. See pp. 172-3.—W.

[2] See the authorities quoted by Millar, Distinction of Ranks, ch. i. sect. 1; and Goguet, Origin of Laws, i. 25, 26.—M.

Here also the law of the Hindus is the reverse of that described — if the practice sometimes conforms to it, it is apparently of modern growth, and a violation of the law. Rammohun Roy, Ancient Rights of Females, p. 278.—W.

[3] Institutes of Menu, ch, ix. 2.

restrictions."[1] "By a girl, or by a young woman, or by a woman advanced in years, nothing," says the same code, "must be done, even in her own dwelling-place, according to her mere pleasure. In childhood must a female be dependent on her father; in youth, on her husband; her lord being dead, on her sons: a woman must never seek independence."[2] The deference which is exacted towards her husband is without limits. "Though inobservant of approved usages, or enamoured of another woman, or devoid of good qualities, yet a husband must constantly be revered as a god by a virtuous wife. No sacrifice is allowed to women apart from their husbands, no religious rite, no fasting: as far only as a wife honours her lord, so far she is exalted in heaven."[3] "She who neglects her lord, though addicted to gaming, fond of spirituous liquors, or diseased, must be deserted for three months, and deprived of her ornaments and household furniture."[4] To every species of ill-usage, she is bound to submit; "neither by sale nor desertion," says the ordinance of Menu, "can a wife be released from her husband: thus we fully acknowledge the law enacted of old by the lord of creatures."[5] This is a remarkable law; for it indicates the power of the husband to sell his wife for a slave, and by consequence proves, that her condition, while in his house, was not regarded as very different from slavery. A law is even made to direct the mode in which she is beaten; "A wife, a son, a servant, a pupil, and a younger whole brother, may be corrected, when they commit faults, with a rope, or the small shoot of a cane; but on the back part only of their bodies, and not on a noble part by any means."[6]

Nothing can exceed the habitual contempt which the Hindus entertain for their women. Hardly are they ever mentioned in their laws, or other books, but as wretches of the most base and vicious inclinations, on whose nature no virtuous or useful qualities can be ingrafted. "Their husbands," says the sacred code, "should be diligently careful in guarding them; though they well know the disposition with which the lord of creation formed them; Menu allotted to such women a love of their bed, of the

[1] Institutes of Menu, ch. ix. [2] Ibid. v. 147, 148.
[3] Ibid. v. 154, 155. [4] Ibid. ix. 78. [5] Ibid. 46.
[6] Ibid. ch. viii. 299, 300. Beating their wives is a common discipline. See Buchanan's Journey, i. 247, 249.

seat, and of ornament, impure appetites, wrath, weak flexibility, desire of mischief, and bad conduct."[1] "Be there no place, be there no time, be there no one to tempt them," says the Hetopadesa, "then, O Narada, doth women's chastity appear. Women at all times have been inconstant, even among the celestials, we are told. In infancy the father should guard her, in youth her husband should guard her, and in old age her children should guard her; for at no time is a woman proper to be trusted with liberty."[2] The same author declares again; "Unto woman no man is found to be disagreeable, no man agreeable. They may be compared to a heifer on the plain, that still longeth for fresh grass. Infidelity, violence, deceit, envy, extreme avariciousness, a total want of good qualities, with impurity, are the innate faults of womankind."[3]

They are held, accordingly, in extreme degradation.[4]

[1] Institutes of Menu, ix. 16, 17.—M.

This is a specimen of unfair citation. It is made to appear as if Manu was speaking of women in general, which is not the case. He speaks of "such" women; that is, of such women as are guilty of drinking, idleness, keeping evil company, and other practices disgraceful to a married woman, iv. 13. Difficult as it is to keep "such" women under restraint, yet their husbands should be diligent in guarding them. These precepts and reflections are not directed to the conduct of the sex in general, but only of the vicious portion of it.—W.

[2] Wilkins' Hetopadesa, p. 54.

[3] Ibid. p. 78. In Halhed's Code of Gentoo Laws, the character of women is depicted in terms which, were they not strong evidence to an important point, delicacy would forbid to be transcribed: "A woman," says the law, "is never satisfied with sensual pleasures no more than fire is satisfied with burning fuel, or the main ocean with receiving the rivers, or the empire of death with the dying men and animals: in these cases therefore a woman is not to be relied on." (Gentoo Code, ch. xx.) "Women have six qualities: the first, an inordinate desire for jewels and fine furniture, handsome clothes, and nice victuals; the second, immoderate lust; the third, violent anger; the fourth, deep resentment; the fifth, another person's good appears evil in their eyes; the sixth, they commit bad actions." (Ibid.) Six faults are likewise ascribed to women, in the Institutes of Menu, but they are differently stated: "Drinking spirituous liquors, associating with evil persons, absence from her husband, rambling abroad, unseasonable sleep, and dwelling in the house of another, are six faults which bring infamy on a married woman. Such women examine not beauty, nor pay attention to age; whether their lover be handsome or ugly, they think it enough that he is a man, and pursue their pleasures. Through their passion for men, their mutable temper, their want of settled affection, and their perverse nature (let them be guarded in this world ever so well,) they soon become alienated from their husbands." Institutes of Menu, ch. ix. 13, 14, 15.—M.

The literature of most countries, even in modern times, would furnish passages abusive of the weaker sex; but no one would think of quoting occasional sarcasm as the language of universal opinion.—W.

[4] In all this, our author's usual practice prevails, of quoting every passage in favour of his own theory, and excluding every one that makes against it. A reluctant admission is subsequently made, that the Hindus have some general precepts, recommending indulgence and humanity in favour of the weaker sex; but they are passed over very lightly. If, instead of the lan-

They are not accounted worthy to partake of religious, rites but in conjunction with their husbands.[1] They are entirely excluded from the sacred books; "Women have no business with the texts of the Veda; thus is the law fully settled: having, therefore, no evidence of law, and no knowledge of expiatory texts, sinful women must be as foul as falsehood itself. To this effect many texts, which may show their true disposition, are chanted in the Vedas."[2] "A minor," says the law, "one single person, a woman, a man of bad principles, &c., may not be witnesses."[3] We have already seen, as in the most barbarous nations, that the women among the Hindus are excluded from sharing in the paternal property.[4] They are, by system, deprived of education.[5] That remarkable proof of barbarity, the wife held unworthy to eat with her husband, is prevalent in Hindustan.[6]

---

guage of law or satire, we look to the portraits of women painted by the Hindus themselves, in their tales, their plays, and poems, we shall find them invariably described as amiable, high-principled, modest, gentle, accomplished, intelligent; as exercising a very important influence upon men, and as treated by them with tenderness and respect. The English reader will find ample proofs of this in the Cloud Messenger and Hindu Theatre, and in Mr. Milman's Nala, and it may be confidently asserted, that in no nation of antiquity were women held in so much esteem, as amongst the Hindus.—W.

1 See Institutes of Menu, quoted in note 3, p. 311.

2 Institutes of Menu, ch. ix. 18, 19.

3 Halhed's Gentoo Code, ch. iii. sect. 8.

4 See ch. iv. p. 214; Menu, ch. iv, 43.—M.

The reference is incorrect; so is the law; as the passage in the first volume adverted to might have shown, had the writer remembered it. For, after stating in the text, in the same unqualified manner, that daughters are altogether debarred from a share, it is mentioned in a note, that those who are unmarried, are to receive portions out of their brothers' allotments. It is mere quibbling, therefore, to say they have no shares. But the more important question, as affecting the position of women in society, is not merely the shares of daughters; although this is artfully put forward, as if it was decisive of the rights of the whole sex; but, what rights women have in regard to property: and, as we have already shown, the laws do not very materially differ in this respect from those which are observed in the civilized countries of modern Europe.—W.

5 The Hindu women, says Mr. Forster, (Travels, i. 59,) are debarred the use of letters. The Hindus hold the invariable language, that acquired accomplishments are not necessary to the domestic classes of the female sex.

6 "The husband and wife never eat together; for the Indians consider it as indecent, and contrary to that respect which is due to the former." Bartolomeo's Travels, book i. ch. 7. Sonnerat says, "The women are ugly, slovenly, and disgusting. The husband does not permit them to eat with him. They are honourable slaves, for whom some regard is entertained." Voy. liv. iii. ch. 7. "So indelicate are the men with respect to the women," says Mr. Motte, speaking of the province of Sumbhulpoor, "that I have been introduced and obliged to show respect to a man of consequence in the morning, whose wife has, in the afternoon, brought a load of wood of her own cutting, as

BOOK II. CHAP. VII.

An almost unlimited power of rejection or divorce appears to be reserved to the husband. In the code of Gentoo laws, among various other ordinances to the same purpose, it is declared that, "a woman who dissipates or spoils her own property, or who procures abortion, or who has any intention to murder her husband, and is always quarrelling with everybody, and who eats before her husband eats, such woman shall be turned out of the house."[1] On grounds like these, a man can never be without a pretence for dismissing his wife. But on the other hand we have seen that no species of barbarous treatment, not even desertion and sale, ever absolves the woman from her obligations to her lord.[2]

---

much as she could stagger under, and sold it me for a penny." Motte's Journey to Orissa, Asiatic Annual Register, i. 76. In another part of the same Journey, p. 67, Mr. Motte says, "I was first struck with the sight of women ploughing, while their female children drove the oxen; but this is the practice through the whole mountainous country, while the men, strolling through the forests with a spear and hatchet, plunder every thing they can master. This abuse of the fair sex is characteristic of a barbarous people."

The Hindus are quite accustomed to beat their wives. Buchanan, Travels in Mysore, &c. i. 247, 249. Women in Karnata carry out the dung to the fields, in baskets on their heads. Ibid. 135, 42. The Abbé Dubois describes the following, as the common, the standard condition of conjugal life: "the young wife, beaten by her husband, and harassed by her mother-in-law, who treats her as a slave, finding no remedy for ill-usage but in flying to her father's house—recalled by fair promises of kinder treatment—the word broken—recourse had to the same remedy—but at last the children which she brings into the world, and other circumstances, compelling her to do her best, by remaining in her husband's house, with the show of being contented with her lot......... The object for which a Hindu marries is not to gain a companion to aid him in enduring the evils of life, but a slave to bear children, and be subservient to his rule." Description, &c. of the People of India, p. 145.—M.

The people amongst whom Mr. Motte travelled, as above noticed, were wild and barbarous tribes; whose usages afford no illustration of those of more civilized parts of India. The Abbé Dubois speaks also of the lower orders of a village community. Instances of brutal treatment of their women by the peasantry and lower classes in Europe, are no rarities. Europeans have never been admitted into the interior of the houses of respectable Hindoos, and are not qualified to speak of the manner in which they behave to their wives. It has happened in a few cases, that elderly women, widows and mothers, have been personally known to us; and it has generally been found, that they received great attention and deference from their sons and relations; at the same time it seems likely that the women have declined in the social scale, and that partly through fear, and partly through imitation, the rule of the Mohammedans has had a prejudicial effect upon the feelings and practices of the Hindus in all that regards the female sex.—W.

[1] Halhed's Gentoo Code, ch. xx.

[2] See above, p. 449. Even after the death of her husband, if she did not sacrifice herself to his manes, she was held inviolably bound to his memory; and, besides other penances and mortifications of the severest kind, was expressly forbidden to accept a second husband. Institutes of Menu, ch. v. 157, 158, 162, 163. The same mark of bondage and inferiority was imposed on the Athenian women during the barbarous times of Greece. Goguet, Origin of Laws, ii. 59. Mr. Richardson, who is one of the most nervous in assertion,

That polygamy was an established custom of the Hindus, we learn from various documents, and among others from the following story, which at the same time conveys no evidence of their domestic gentleness:—"In the city of Devee-kotta, there was a Brahman, whose name was Deva-Sarma. One lucky evening he found a curious dish, which he took with him into a potter's warehouse full of earthenware, and throwing himself upon a bed which happened to be there, it being night, he began to express his thoughts upon the occasion in this manner:—'If I dispose of this dish, I shall get ten kapardakas (cowries) for it; and with that sum I may purchase many pots and pans, the sale of which will increase my capital so much that I shall be able to lay in a large stock of cloth and the like; which having disposed of at a great advance, I shall have accumulated a fortune of a lack of money. With this I will marry four wives; and of these I will amuse myself with her who may prove the handsomest. This will create jealousy; so when the rival wives shall be quarrelling, then will I, overwhelmed with anger, hurl my stick at them thus!' Saying which, he flung his walking-stick out of his hand with such force, that he not only broke his curious dish, but destroyed many of the pots and pans in the shop."[1]

---

and the most feeble in proof, of all oriental enthusiasts, maintains that the women enjoyed high consideration among the Arabians and Persians, nay, among the very Tartars; so generally was civilization diffused in Asia. In proof, he tells us that the Arabian women "had a right by the laws to the enjoyment of independent property, by inheritance, by gift, by marriage settlement, or by any other mode of acquisition." The evidence he adduces of these rights is three Arabian words; which signify *a marriage portion, paraphernalia in the disposal of a wife, a marriage settlement.* (See Richardson's Dissertations on the Languages, Literature, and Manners of Eastern Nations, pp. 198, 331, 479.) But surely a language may possess three words of the signification which he assigns, and yet the women of the people who use it be in a state of melancholy degradation. In the times of Homer, though a wife was actually purchased from her father, still the father gave with her a dower. Iliad. lib. ix. ver. 147, 148. If the Tartars carry their women with them in their wars, and even consult them, "the north American tribes, says Mr. Millar, "are often accustomed to admit their women into their public councils, and even to allow them the privilege of being first called to give their opinion upon every subject of deliberation........ Yet," as he adds immediately after, "there is no country in the world where the female sex are, in general, more neglected and despised." See Distinctions of Ranks, ch. i. sect. 2. From insulated expressions, or facts, no general conclusion can safely be drawn.

[1] Wilkins' Hetopadesa, p. 248.—M. Mr. Mill here deserts his usual guide; he had better have adhered to Menu, than taken his illustration of the law or the practice from a fable intended to ridicule absurd expectations. Although permitted, polygamy is not encouraged by the ancient law, and from its being sanctioned in particular cases only, as of misconduct, aversion, or barrenness;

The Hindus were, notwithstanding, so far advanced in civilization, except in the mountainous and most barbarous tracts of the country, as to have improved in some degree upon the manners of savage tribes. They have some precepts, recommending indulgence and humanity in favour of the weaker sex. "Married women," says the law of Menu, "must be honoured and adorned by their fathers and brethren, by their husbands, and by the brethren of their husbands, if they seek abundant prosperity. Where female relations are made miserable, the family of him, who makes them so, very soon wholly perishes."[1] When particulars indeed are explained, the indulgences recommended are not very extensive. It is added, "Let those women, therefore, be continually supplied with ornaments, apparel, and food, at festivals, and at jubilees, by men desirous of wealth."[2] When it is commanded by law, as an extraordinary extension of liberality, to give them ornaments, and even apparel and food, at festivals and jubilees; this is rather a proof of habitual degradation than of general respect and tenderness. The idea, however, of purchasing a wife, as a slave, from her relations, had become odious; and though it is stated as one of the eight species of nuptial contract, it is classed among the dishonourable species, and forbidden.[3] As the necessity of such a law indicates a state of society but one remove from that in which the unhappy bride is purchased and sold; so the customary, and original purchasing gift, the bull and the cow, still remained; but it had acquired a religious character, and was at last commanded to pass by another name. "Some say," observes the law of Menu, "that the bull and cow given in the nuptial ceremony of the Rishis, are a bribe to the father; but this is untrue: a bribe indeed, whether large or small, is an actual sale of

---

Menu, ix, 77, 81, it is evident that it was not without restriction. Even the consent of the first wife seems to have been necessary. "She (the wife), who though afflicted with illness, is amiable and virtuous, must never be disgraced, though she may be superseded by another wife, with her own consent; ix. 82. By being disgraced, means the loss of consideration in the family. The first wife seems always to have held the principal rank, and to have been mistress of the household.—W.

[1] Institutes of Menu, ch. iii. 55, 57.

[2] Ib. 59.

[3] "Let no father who knows the law receive a gratuity, however small, for giving his daughter in marriage, since the man who through avarice, takes a gratuity for that purpose, is a seller of his offspring." Institutes of Menu, ch. iii. 51.

the daughter."[1] There are texts, however, which directly recognise the transaction as a purchase: "He who takes to wife," it is said, "a damsel of full age, shall not give a nuptial present to her father; since the father lost his dominion over her, by detaining her at a time when she might have been a parent."[2] The obligation of the marriage contract is stated in the Institutes of Menu, under the head of purchase and sale; and it is expressly said, "If, after one damsel has been shown, another be offered to the bridegroom, who had purchased leave to marry her from her next kinsman, he may become the husband of both for the same price: this law Menu ordained."[3] The same undoubtedly is the purport of the following sacred text: "The recitation of holy texts, and the sacrifice ordained by the lord of creatures, are used in marriages for the sake of procuring good fortune to brides; but the first gift by the husband is the primary cause of marital dominion."[4] It is to be observed, besides, that the women have no choice in their one destiny; but are absolutely at the disposal of their fathers, till three years after the nuptial age. If, until that period, the father have neglected what is reckoned one of his most sacred duties, to place his daughter in a situation to become a parent, he forfeits, through his sin, the dominion over her, and she may choose a husband for herself.[5]

It has been doubted whether immuring the women was

[1] Institutes of Menu, ch. iii. 53. [2] Ibid. ch. ix. 93.

[3] Ibid. ch. viii. 204. Our travellers find direct and avowed purchase still in practice in many parts of India. See Buchanan's Journey through Mysore, &c., i. 247. 249. "To marry, or to buy a wife, are synonymous terms in this country. Almost every parent makes his daughter an article of traffic. This practice of purchasing the young women whom they are to marry, is the inexhaustible source of disputes and litigation, particularly amongst the poorer people. These, after the marriage is solemnized, not finding it convenient to pay the stipulated sum, the father-in-law commences an action," &c. Description, &c. of the Hindus, by the Abbé Dubois, p. 137. "Apud plerasque tamen gentes dotem maritus uxori, non uxor marito offerebat. Ista sane consuetudo viguit inter Germanos, teste Tacito (*de Mor. Germ.* cap. 18)—Assyrios, teste Æliano (*Hist. Var.* iv. 1)—Babylonios, teste Herodot. (i. 116)—et Armenios, ceu patet ex *Nou.* xxi. Heineccii Antiquit. Roman. lib. ii. tit. viii. sect. 2,

[4] Institutes of Menu, ch. v. 152. The Commentator Culluca, after the words *first gift*, by his usual plan, of trying to graft the ideas of a recent period, improved a little by external intercourse, upon the original text, has foisted in the words or *troth plighted*, as if that was a gift, or, as if, had that been meant, the legislator would not have rather said *troth plighted*, than *first gift*. See what I have observed on the interpolating practices of Culluca, Note A. at the end of the volume, p. 499.

[5] Ibid. ch. ix. 88, 90, 93.

an original part of Hindu manners, or adopted in consequence of the intercourse and dominion of the Mohamedans. But they have been found in a state of seclusion and confinement beyond the range of Mohammedan influence.[1] The practice is fully recognised in the ancient writings. We are told in the Bhagavat, that on the day of the yug of Judishter, "the women who, buried in harams, were seldom permitted to see the sun, came out, on that day, to view rajah Judishter."[2] The monarch who forms the hero in the drama entitled Sacontala had many wives, and they are represented as residing in the *secret* apartments of the palace.[3] The whole spirit of the Hindu maxims indicates confinement: there are numerous precepts with respect to the guarding of women: and the punishment for vitiating those who are not guarded is always less than the punishment in the case of those that are.[4] Among these proofs of confinement are also appearances of freedom. The law of seclusion is made only for the few. Among the jealous Ottomans themselves, the great body of the community must leave their women at large, because an indigent man can neither dispense with the useful services of his wife, nor afford the cost of retaining her in confinement. In the earlier and ruder states of society, when men are in general poor, few can afford the expense of confinement; but among the Hindus, as in general among the nations of Asia, since their emerging from the rudest barbarism, it seems to have been the practice for every man, who possessed sufficient means, to keep his women guarded, in a state of seclusion.[5]

[1] Mr. Forster declares himself to have been at one time of opinion, "that the Hindoos had secluded their women from the public view, that they might not be exposed to the intemperance of the Mohammedan conquerors; but after perceiving," says he, "the usage adopted among the sequestered mountaineers, and also among the various independent Mahrattah states, I am induced to think that the exclusion of women from society prevailed in India before the period of the Afghan, or Tartar invasions." Forster's Travels, i. 310.

[2] See a translation of part of the Bhagavat by Mr. Halhed, in Maurice's Hist. of Hindostan, ii. 438.

[3] See Sacontala in Sir William Jones's Works, vi. The Rajah of Beejanuggur's harem was kept so close, that not even the nearest relations of the women received in it were ever again permitted to see them. Ferishta's Deccan, by Scott, i. 83. Nor is this mentioned as any thing unusual.

[4] Institutes of Menu, ch. viii. 374 to 385.

[5] It has, no doubt, been always the custom for the women of Hindus of rank and respectability to live in some degree apart, but not in seclusion, nor guarded with the same jealousy as by the Mohammedans. Menu provides for their being properly decorated at "festivals and jubilees;" and many of the poems and plays describe their appearance openly in public at religious and

On the coast of Malabar, where the manners differ considerably from those of the rest of the Hindus, and where the people have not reached a state of society altogether so perfect as that in some other parts of Hindustan, it would appear that the institution of marriage has never been regularly introduced. The peculiar mode in which the intercourse of the sexes is here carried on has not yet been satisfactorily explained to us; and from the differences which appear in the accounts of different authors, it probably exhibits considerable variety; but in its general character it is pretty evidently a relic of the period in which there is no law for the association of the sexes; when their intercourse is casual; when the father of the offspring is by consequence uncertain; and when the children of necessity belong to the mother. The nearest male relations of the female, her father being in this case unknown, are her brothers; who, never having children whom they can recognise as their own, naturally contract an affection for those of their sister, whom they support, and with whom they live; by consequence regard them as in some measure their own; and vest them with the property which they leave at their death. In the family of a Nair there is no wife; all the brothers and sisters live under the same roof; their mother, the only known parent, during her life, and after her death the eldest sister, manage the domestic affairs; the sisters cohabit with the men of their choice, subject only to the sacred restriction of a class not inferior to their own; the children are by the brothers regarded as their own, and inherit the property of the family.[1] This is the exact description of a people among whom the institution of marriage is unknown, and the order into which things will run of their own accord, wherever the intercourse of the sexes is ca-

other festivals and at public games, and the admission of men other than their immediate kinsmen to their presence on various occasions. Mahábhárata, Rámáyana, Vishnu Purána, Málati Mádhava, Ratnávali, &c. Even still the wives of respectable Hindus leave the inner—there is no such term as secret—apartments at pleasure, and go to bathe in the Ganges and other sacred streams.—W.

[1] Such is the account which Dr. Buchanan received from a number of the most respectable Nairs themselves, whom he assembled for the purpose of inquiring into their manners. See his Journey through Mysore, &c. ii. 411, 412. It was a practice, the continuance of which was highly convenient for the Brahmens, whose power among the inhabitants of that coast was peculiarly great. Ibid. 425. See also Mr. Thackeray's Report, Fifth Report of she Committee on India Affairs, 1810, p. 802.

BOOK II. CHAP. VII.

sual.[1] The Nairs, however, are said to have added a kind of refinement to this established custom. They contract a marriage with a particular woman. But this is entirely nominal. The woman never leaves her mother's house; her intercourse with other men is not restricted; her children belong to her brothers; and the arrangement of society is the same as if no such marriage existed. If it really takes place, and the absurdity of the thing may support a suspicion of some mistake in our informants, it must be the effect of imitation, and of the reproaches which this people have sustained from other nations. These circumstances move them to contrive a semblance of a marriage, though not in the least degree to alter the established system of manners, to which it adheres as a useless excrescence. The Nairs are only one of the castes; and there appears to be some diversity in the mode of intercourse between the sexes in the several castes. The fashion among the Nairs is the standard to which they all approach. Our information, however, of these diversities, even if they merited a fuller elucidation, is too imperfect for minute description.[2]

[1] This is not a satisfactory solution of the peculiarity. If the Nairs could be traced to the mountain regions of the Himalaya, where a similar plurality of husbands exists; it might be imagined to have originated in the circumstances by which apparently it is there continued; the difficulty of procuring food for a family in such cold and unproductive countries, and the self-imposed check, in consequence, upon population.—W.

[2] The reader will find some observations, but evidently incorrect, taken from an Arabian author, by Mr. Duncan, Asiat. Research. v. 12, 13, 14. Dr. Buchanan, too, makes some remarks on the modes of the Brahmens. Journey, ut supra, ii. 425; and mentions certain diversities between the manners of the Nairs themselves in the south, and in the north of Malabar, Ibid, 513. See, too, Bartolomeo's Travels, book ii. ch. ii. and Anquetil Duperron, Zendavesta, Discours Préliminaire, p. cxcvi. Vestiges of the same order of affairs are very widely diffused. Cecrops first instituted marriage among the Greeks; Menes, among the Egyptians. Among the Lycians, and even among the ancient inhabitants of Attica, children took their names from their mother, and not from their father. The domestic community of women among the Celtic inhabitants of Britain was a diversity, to which something very similar is said to exist among some of the castes on the coast of Malabar. "There is in the province of Madura," says the Abbé Dubois p. 3, "a caste called the Totiyars, in which, brothers, uncles, and nephews, and other kindred, when married, enjoy the wives in common." Indications of the same state are preserved by the Roman lawyers. In the island of Formosa, where the women contract a marriage for any stipulated period, the husband, during the time of the contract, passes into the family of the wife; a custom, likewise found among the people called Moxos in Peru. In the Ladrone islands, the wife is mistress of the family, turns off the husband when she chooses, and retains the children and property. In the ancient Median empire we are told that the women had several husbands; and the same is the case in some cantons of the Iroquois in North America. See the authorities quoted by Millar, Distinction of Ranks, ch. i. sect. 2, where this part of the subject is illustrated with the usual sagacity of that eminent author. See, too, Goguet's Origin of Laws, book i. ch. i. art. i. We are told by

It is not surprising, that grossness, in ideas and language, respecting the intercourse of the sexes, is a uniform concomitant of the degraded state of the women. Superficial contemplators have, in general, contented themselves with remarking, that it was a diversity of manners; or was the effect of a diversity of climate; and that what in one place was gross bore a different interpretation in another. Inquiry discovers, that grossness in this respect is a regular ingredient in the manners of a rude age; and that society, as it refines, deposits this, among its other impurities. The ancient inhabitants of our own country were as indelicate as those of the hottest regions of Asia.[1] All European witnesses have been struck with the indelicacy of the Hindus. The gross emblems and practices of their religion are already known.[2] To the indecent passages in the books of law, and the practices which they describe, exceedingly numerous, and exceedingly gross, we can here only allude.[3] Both the writings and conversation of the Hindus abound with passages which are shocking to European ears. Even in the popular and moral work, entitled

---

Herodotus, that the Massagetæ had their women in common; and a man, when he desired to be private, hung up his quiver at the door of the wagon or travelling tent. Herodot. i. 210. A people in Africa, whom he calls Nasamones were in like manner, without the rite of marriage, and a staff stuck in the ground before the tent was the signal of retirement. Ibid. iv. 172. The reader will probably not be surprised to hear, that the tradition of the casual intercourse of the sexes was preserved among the Indians of Peru. "In short," (says Garcilasso de la Vega, Royal Commentaries, book i. ch. vii.) "they were altogether savage," (meaning the inhabitants in their ancient state,) "making use of their women as they accidentally met, understanding no property or single enjoyment of them."—A woman, not married to an individual, but common to all the brothers of a family, is described as the custom of Tibet. See Turner's Embassy.—M.

It has been shown by Col. Vans Kennedy, that the charge of incorrectness attached to Mr. Duncan's observations on extracts from an Arabian author, in the beginning of this note, has been very inconsiderately preferred. Tran. Lit. Soc. of Bombay, iii. 129.

[1] Dr. Henry, in his chapter on the manners of the Anglo-Saxons, says, "It would be easy to produce many examples of rudeness and indelicacy, that were established by law, and practised, even in courts of justice (if they were not unbecoming the purity which history ought to preserve), which would hardly be believed in the present age." Henry's Hist. of Great Britain, iv. 344. He then quotes the following specimen in a note: Si mulier stuprata lege cum viro agere velit, et si vir factum pernegaverit, mulier, membro virili sinistrâ prehenso, et dextrâ reliquiis sanctorum impositâ, juret super illas, quod is, per vim, se isto membro vitiaverit. Leges Wallicæ, p. 82.

[2] Naked fakeers travel in pilgrimage about the country, and swarm around the principal temples. It is customary for women to kiss, and as it were to adore, their secret, or rather public parts.

[3] See the whole Section in Halhed's Gentoo Code, De digito in pudendum muliebre inserendo, or the various passages de concubitu virili, vel etiam concubitu bestiali.

Hetopadesa, there are parts which M. Wilkins could not translate; and he thus expresses himself on this characteristic of society among the Hindus; "The translator has carefully refined a great many indelicate expressions, which a Hindu lady, from grosser habits, might hear without a blush; and even omitted whole passages when that could not be effected but by a total change of the author's meaning."[1] Another Oriental scholar, as well as eye-witness of the manners he describes, affords us a passage which at once portrays this part of the Hindu character, and traces one of those remarkable resemblances, which run through the principal nations of Asia. "The Persian women," says Mr. Scott Waring, "like the Indian, are totally devoid of delicacy; their language is often gross and disgusting, nor do they feel more hesitation in expressing themselves before men, than they would before their female associates. Their terms of abuse or reproach are indelicate to the utmost degree. I will not disgust the reader by noticing any of them; but I may safely aver that it is not possible for language to express, or the imagination to conceive, more indecent or grosser images."[2]

Much attention has been attracted to the gentleness of

[1] Wilkins' Hetopadesa. note 82.—M. If the popularity of the Hitopadesa is an indication of a low state of moral feeling amongst the Hindus, it proves the same amongst all the nations of Europe, as it has been translated into all languages. We may observe, too, that several of these stories, which are most indelicate, have been the especial favourites of European writers, and have been reproduced in a variety of forms. See Analysis of the Panchatantra. Tr. R. As. Society, vol. i. p. 155.—W.

[2] A Tour to Sheeraz, by Edward Scott Waring, Esq. p. 62. He further says: "The same may be observed of the inhabitants of India, nor will the plea, that the false delicacy of refinement, which disqualifies us from judging of the language of nature, exempts them from censure. If the nakedness of a prostitute be more disgusting than that of an Indian, it must be allowed that their language is infinitely chaster and more refined. There are certain images which must always create disgust and aversion; and although they are familiar in the East, it is by no means evident that they are the images of nature. There may be a refinement on grossness of vice as well as an excess of delicacy, and it does not follow that the one is natural and the other unnatural." Ibid. See the Missionaries Ward and Dubois, passim,—M.

It is quite impossible that Mr. Waring could have known any thing of Persian women, except of the lower orders; and probably he knew little more of Indian women of respectability. The Missionaries are so on the watch for vice, that they often discover it where it does not exist; and their instances again are drawn from the practices of the vulgar. Without denying the charge of much that offends our notions of decency, and of much that is really reprehensible, allowance should be made for a state of society which consists of men alone. The decorum of European manners is mainly indebted to the influence of females; at the same time few Europeans have found, in their intercourse with respectable natives, any violation of delicacy either in language or behaviour.—W.

manners in this people. They possess a feminine softness both in their persons and in their address. As the inhabitants of Europe were rough and impetuous, in their rude and early state, and grew mild only as they grew civilized, the gentleness of Hindu manners has usually impressed their European visitors with a high conception of their progress in civilization. It is, perhaps, a ground of presumption, but fallacious if taken as a proof. One of the circumstances which distinguish the state of commencing civilization is, that it is compatible with great violence, as well as great gentleness of manners. Nothing is more common than examples of both. Mildness of address is not always separated even from the rudest condition of human life, as the Otaheitans, and some other of the South-Sea islanders, abundantly testify.[1] "The savages of North America are affectionate in their carriage, and in their conversations pay a mutual attention and regard," says Charlevoix, "more tender and more engaging than what we profess in the ceremonial of polished societies."[2]

The causes which seem to account for these effects are partly physical and partly moral. Where the commodities of life, by a happy union of climate and soil, are abundant,

[1] Dr. Forster, in a note to Father Paolino's (Bartolomeo) Travels, remarks a great similarity, in many respects, between the manners of the Hindus and those of the Otaheitans.

[2] Ferguson's Essay on Civil Society, part ii. sect. 2, "The Russians" (says Mr. Forster, Travels, ii. 296) "observe to their superiors an extreme submission, and their deportment is blended with a suavity of address and language, which is not warranted by their appearance, or the opinions generally formed of them." "The common people in Russia," says Lord Macartney (Account of Russia by Lord Macartney, in Barrow's Life of that lord, ii. 30), "are handsome in their persons, easy and unaffected in their behaviour; and though free and manly in their carriage, are obedient and submissive to their superiors, and of a civility and politeness to their equals, which is scarcely to be paralleled." The following passage is from a work entitled "Travels into the Crimea, [and] a History of the Embassy from St. Petersburgh to Constantinople in 1793, by a Secretary of the Russian Embassy." "In the course of my rambles I have had frequent occasions of experiencing the politeness of the Turks, which proves to me that this nation is extremely well-disposed and inclined to oblige, and that the climate alone is the cause of the idleness and indifference with which they are reproached. The Turk, when offended, or provoked to jealousy, becomes terrible, and nothing but the blood of his adversary can calm the passion which transports him. During my excursions in the environs of Constantinople I was frequently a witness of the obliging and hospitable propensities of this people. The first Turk I applied to when I wanted directions in regard to the road I was to take, always offered himself as a guide, and with the same readiness presented to me a part of his food or refreshment." "The more the Turks are known, the more they are beloved for their cordiality, their frankness, and their excessive kindness to strangers. I am not afraid to assert, that, in many respects, they may serve as models to my countrymen."—pp. 201, 237.

BOOK II. CHAP. VII.

gentleness of manners, as appears by the traditions respecting the golden or pastoral age, is by no means unnatural to men in the earliest period of improvement. The savage, involved in a continual struggle with want, who sees himself and his children every day exposed to perish with hunger, is, by a sort of necessity, rapacious, harsh, unfeeling, and cruel. The species of polity under which the national character is formed is, perhaps, to a still greater degree, the cause of the diversity which we now contemplate. Where the mind is free, and may vent its passions with little fear, the nation, while ignorant and rude, is also fierce and impetuous. Where slavery prevails, and any departure from the most perfect obsequiousness is followed with the most direful consequences, an insinuating and fawning behaviour is the interest, and thence becomes the habit of the people.

With the same causes are connected other leading features in the character of the Hindus. They are remarkably prone to flattery; the most prevailing mode of address from the weak to the strong, while men are still ignorant and unreflecting.[1] The Hindus are full of dissimulation and falsehood, the universal concomitants of oppression.[2] The vices of falsehood, indeed, they carry to a height almost unexampled among the other races of men. Judicial mendacity is more than common; it is almost universal. "Perjury," said Sir William Jones, to the Grand Jury at Calcutta, "seems to be committed by the meanest, and encouraged by some of the better sort

[1] It would be easy to produce many testimonies to the propensity of the natives to adulation. Bernier, who speaks of it in the strongest terms, gives us the following amusing instance: "Un Pendet Brahmen que j'avois fait mettre au service de mon Agah, se voulut mêler, en entrant, de faire son panégyrique; et, après l'avoir comparé au plus grands conquérans qui furent jamais, et lui avoir dit cent grossières et impertinentes flatteries, concluoit enfin sérieusement par celle-cy: 'Lorsque vous mettez le pied dans l'estrier, Seigneur, et que vous marchez à cheval avec votre cavalerie, la terre tremble sous vos pas, les huit élephans qui la supportent sur leurs têtes ne pouvant soutenir ce grand effort.' Je ne pus me tenir de rire là dessus, et je tachois de dire sérieusement à mon Agah, qui ne pouvoit aussi s'en tenir, qu'il seroit donc fort à-propos, qu'il ne montât à cheval que fort rarement pour empescher les tremblemens de terre qui causent souvent de si grands malheurs; 'Aussi est-ce pour cela même, me répondit-il sans hésiter, que je m'en fais ordinairement porter en paléky.'" Bernier, Suite des Mémoires sur l'Empire du Grand Mogol, i. 12.

[2] For a strong testimony to the extent to which dissimulation pervades the Hindu character, see Orme, on the Government and People of Hindustan, p. 428. "L'Indien qui vit sous ce gouvernement en suit les impressions. Obligé de ramper il devient fourbe." Anquetil Duperron, Voy. aux Indes Orien. Zendav. i. ccclxii.

among the Hindus and Mussulmans, with as little remorse as if it were a proof of ingenuity, or even a merit."[1]—" I have many reasons to believe, and none to doubt, that affidavits of every imaginable fact may as easily be procured in the streets and markets of Calcutta, especially from the natives, as any other article of traffic."[2] Speaking of the forms of an oath among the Hindus, he says, " But such is the corrupt state even of their erroneous religion, that if the most binding form on the consciences of men could be known and established, there would be few consciences to be bound by it."[3]

I have not enumerated the religion of the Hindus as one among the causes of gentleness which has been remarked in their deportment. This religion has produced a practice which has strongly engaged the curiosity of Europeans ; a superstitious care of the life of the inferior animals. A Hindu lives in perpetual terror of killing even an insect ; and hardly any crime can equal that of being unintentionally the cause of death to any animal of the more sacred species. This feeble circumstance, however, is counteracted by so many gloomy and malignant princi-

1 Sir Wm. Jones's Charge to the Grand Jury at Calcutta, June 10, 1787.

2 Id. June 10, 1785.

3 Id. 1787.—" La facilité que le peuple de l'Orient ont à mentir," is given by P. Paolino, as the cause of the trial by ordeal, so common in Hindustan. Voyage aux Indes Orient. par le P. Paolino (the French edition of Bartolomeo), ii. 103. Mr. Orme says, " The Gentoos are infamous for the want of generosity and gratitude in all the commerces of friendship ; they are a tricking, deceitful people, in all their dealings." On the Government and People of Hindustan, p. 434.

Dr. Buchanan ridicules the expression of Sir William Jones, when he talks of the *simple* Pandits : a race whose chief characteristic is deceit and cunning. Asiat. Res. vi. 165. M.

Most of these are exceptionable witnesses : the missionaries by their calling, and Orme and Buchanan by strong prejudices. With regard to perjury in the courts of justice, it was in some degree our own work. The form of oath imposed—the taking of an oath at all, was so repulsive to the feelings of respectable Hindus, that they have ever avoided as much as possible giving evidence at all ; and their place has been supplied by the lowest and most unprincipled, whose testimony has been for sale. " The dread of an oath prevents men of credit from giving testimony at all, even to the loss of a just cause." Treatise on swearing Hindus by the waters of the Ganges, by Kasinath Tarkapanchanana. See Oriental Magazine, March, 1826.—W.

" ' What is a Brahman ? ' I was one day asked, in a jocular way, by one of that caste, with whom I was intimately acquainted : ' He is an ant's nest of lies and impostures.' It is not possible to describe them better in so few words. All Hindus are expert in disguising the truth ; but there is nothing in which the caste of Brahmens so much surpasses them all as in the art of lying. It has taken so deep a root among them, that so far from blushing when detected in it, many of them make it their boast." Dubois, p. 177. On their propensity to adulation, see the same author, p. 178. On the fraud and perjury of the Hindus, consult Ward, ut supra, Introd. lix. and xciii.

ples, that their religion, instead of humanizing the character, must have had no inconsiderable effect in fostering that disposition to revenge, that insensibility to the sufferings of others, and often that active cruelty which lurks under the smiling exterior of the Hindu. "Although the killing of an animal of the ox kind," says Buchanan, "is by all Hindus considered as a kind of murder, I know no creature whose sufferings equal those of the labouring cattle of Hindustan."[1] No other race of men are perhaps so little friendly and beneficent to one another as the Hindus. "Dysenteries," says Dr. Tennant, speaking of the salt manufacturers, "are, at one season, peculiarly fatal. The unhappy victims of this disorder are avoided as infectious by their companions, and suffered to pine without receiving either that aid or consolation which compassion usually pays to the wretched."[2] "'The Bengalese," says another traveller, "will seldom assist each other, unless they happen to be friends or relations, and then the service that they render only consists in carrying the sufferer to the water of the Ganges, to let him die there, or be carried away by the stream."[3] Le Couteur remarks, that "men accustomed from their infancy to abstain from every kind of cruelty towards brutes, ought naturally to be humane and benevolent towards their own species; and this would infallibly be the case, if the same religion had not hardened the hearts of the superior castes; for they hold those that are born their inferiors as beings below

[1] Buchanan's Journey through Mysore, etc. i. 167.

[2] Indian Recreations, ii. 329.

[3] Stavorinus' Voyage, 1768 to 1771: Wilcock's Translation, London, 1798, p. 153. Dr. Tennant explains more fully, that only species of assistance which, according to Stavorinus, a Hindu receives even from his relations. "When a sick person's life is despaired of, he is carried by his relations to the bank of the river; and there, exposed to the storm, or the heat of the sun, he is permitted, or rather forced, to resign his breath. His mouth, nose, and ears, are closely stopped with the mud of the river; large vessels of water are kept pouring upon him; and it is amidst the agonies of disease, and the convulsive struggles of suffocation, that the miserable Hindu bids adieu to his relations, and to his present existence." Indian Recreations, i. 108. Describing the apathy with which, during a famine, the Hindus beheld one another perishing of hunger, Stavorinus says, "In the town of Chinsurah itself, a poor sick Bengalese, who had laid himself down in the street, without any assistance being offered to him by anybody, was attacked in the night by the jackals, and though he had strength enough to cry out for help, no one would leave his own abode to deliver the poor wretch, who was found in the morning half-devoured and dead." Stavorinus, ut supra, p. 153. It is highly worthy of attention, that the same inhumanity, hard-heartedness, and the greatest insensibility to the feelings of others, is described as the character of the Chinese. See Barrow's China, p. 164.

even the most worthless animals: they take away the life of a man with less scruple than we kill a fowl. To strike a cow would be sacrilege; but a Brahmen may put a man to death when he lists."[1]

It commonly happens that in a rude period of society, the virtue of hospitality, generously and cordially displayed, helps to cast into the shade the odious passions which adhere to man in his uncultivated state. The unhappy circumstances, religious and political, of the Hindu, have tended to eradicate even this, the virtue of a rude age, from his breast. After noticing, in various parts of his journey, the striking instances which he witnessed, of the want of hospitality, Dr. Buchanan says in one passage, "I mention these difficulties, which are very frequently met with by travellers in all parts of India where Europeans have not long resided, to show the inhospitable nature of its inhabitants." For one of his sepoys, who was seized with an acute disease, and left in agony by the side of the road, he could not, except by force, in a large village, obtain a cot, though he was assured there was one in every house.[2]

1 Le Couteur's Letters from India. London, 1790, p. 320. When the exactions of government press hard, Dr. Tennant says: "the ryuts (husbandmen), driven to despair, are forced to take up robbery for a subsistence; and when once accustomed to this wandering and irregular life, it becomes ever after impossible to reclaim them to industry, or to any sense of moral duty. We had yesterday a melancholy example of the daring profligacy of which they are capable: An officer who rode out only a mile beyond the piquets, was attacked by a party of five horsemen; in the midst of a friendly conversation, one stabbed him in the breast with a spear, which brought him to the ground; then the others robbed him of his watch, his horse, and every article of his clothing. In this naked state he arrived at the piquet, covered with blood; and had he not been able to walk thus far, he must have fared worse than the man who, 'between Jerusalem and Jericho fell among thieves,' since here there is no one 'good Samaritan' to pity the unfortunate." (Indian Recreations, ii. 375.)—M.

The gross exaggerations of his authorities should have made Mr. Mill more careful in his citations. It is not true, nor could it ever have been true, that a "Brahman may put a man to death, when he lists." What Dr. Tennant's evidence is to prove, except that there are robbers and murderers in India, as well as elsewhere, is not very clear.—W.

2 Buchanan, ut supra, i. 53; ii. 201, 202; iii. 300. Destitute persons, or persons in a famine, become the property of those who feed them. (Tennant's Ind. Recr. i. 131.)—M.

As Dr. Buchanan could not converse with the natives, he might have mistaken the purport of the assurances, and the case of his sepoy might have found a parallel in every village in Europe. Where would the people have endured the "forcible" abduction of their own beds for the accommodation of even a dying soldier? Dr. Tennant's exposition of the law confirms the judgment of the Edinburgh Reviewer, who states, that the facts of his book are all taken from others, and that when he endeavours to give any information from himself, he is sure to be inaccurate and contradictory. Ed. Rev. iv. p. 314.—W.

The ancient literature of the Hindus affords many proofs that no inconsiderable degree of ferocity has at all times been mingled with the other ingredients of their character. The Yadavas, a sacred race, the kindred of Crishna, in a drunken fray, took arms and butchered one another, to the utter extinction of the race.[1] One of the most remarkable stories in the celebrated book, called *Hetopadesa*, is that of a man who cut off his wife's nose, because she would not speak to him.[2] As the performance of that great religious ceremony, called a Jug, is sufficient to extort from the divinity whatever boon the true performer demands, the following law makes provision against the most cool, intense, and persevering malignity of which human nature appears to be susceptible. "If a man performs a jug to procure the death of any innocent person, the magistrate shall fine him 200 puns of cowries."[3] If the gentleness, too, of the punishment, about ten shillings,[4] be a sign, the indignation, which so atrocious a purpose excites, is far from remarkable. That murder by the most odious means, by poison, is looked upon in the same venial light, the following law bears equal testimony: "If a man, to procure the death of any innocent person, by any contrivance, causes him to drink a potion, or otherwise meditates his death, the magistrate shall fine him 200 puns of cowries."[5] The cool reflection which attends the villany of the Hindu, has often surprised the European. Mr. Holwell informs

[1] See a celebrated passage of the Mahabharat, translated by Mr. Halhed, in Maurice's Indian Hist. ii. 468.

[2] Wilkins' Hetopadesa, p. 131.—M. Mr. Mill does not state the circumstance quite correctly. To infer the general prevalence of ferocity from the narrative of a single instance is scarcely justifiable; but what is more to the purpose, is, that the same furnishes a proof of the ferocious nature of every people in Europe, for this particular story has been more popular than any other in the collection, if we may judge from its frequent repetition. Analysis of Panchatantra. Trans. Royal Asiatic Society, vol. i. p. 162.—W.

[3] Gentoo Code, ch. xxi. sect. 10.

[4] Grant on the Hindus, p. 54. Printed by order of the House of Commons. 1812.

[5] Gentoo Code, ch. xxi. sect. 10. A very intelligent servant of the East India Company, speaking of the Hindus in a situation where they had hardly ever been exposed to the influence of strangers, Sumbhulpoor, says, "The men are low in stature, but well-made, lazy, treacherous, and cruel. But to these ill qualities of the tiger, the Almighty has also, in his mercy, added the cowardice of that animal; for had they an insensibility of danger, equal to their inclination for mischief, the rest of mankind would unite to hunt them down." (Motte's Journey to Orissa, Asiat. An. Reg. i. 76.) "Pestilence or beasts of prey," says Dr. Buchanan, "are gentle in comparison with Hindu robbers, who, in order to discover concealed property, put to the torture all those who fall into their hands." (Travels through Mysore, &c. iii. 206.)

us, that, when he sat as a judge at Calcutta, he had often heard the most atrocious murders avowed and defended by the criminals, on the ground of its being now the Cali age, when men are destined to be wicked.[1]

Notwithstanding the degree to which the furious passions enter into the character of the Hindu, all witnesses agree in representing him as a timid being. With more apparent capacity of supporting pain than any other race of men; and, on many occasions, a superiority to the fear of death, which cannot be surpassed, this people run from danger with more trepidation and eagerness than has been almost ever witnessed in any other part of the globe.[2]

It is the mixture of this fearfulness with their antisocial passions, which has given existence to that litigiousness of character which almost all witnesses have ascribed to this ancient race.[3] As often as courage fails them in seeking a more daring gratification to their hatred or revenge, their malignity finds a vent in the channel of litigation. "That pusillanimity and sensibility of spirit," says Mr. Orme, "which renders the Gentoos incapable of supporting the contentions of danger, disposes them as much to prosecute litigious contests.[4] No people are of more inveterate and

[1] Remarquez que les tems les plus superstitieux ont toujours été ceux des plus horribles crimes. (Voltaire, Diction. Philos. Article Superstition.)

[2] La lacheté accompagne ordinairement la mollesse. Aussi l'Indien est-il foible et timide. (Anquetil Duperron Voyage aux Indes Orien. Zendav. p. cxvii.) This timidity admits of degrees. It is in its greatest perfection in Bengal. In the upper provinces, both the corporeal and the mental frame are more hardy. Those of the race who are habituated to the dangers of war, acquire, of course, more or less of insensibility to them. Still the feature is not only real, but prominent.

[3] Surely having recourse to law for the protection of their rights or persons, instead of taking the law into their own hands, is no proof of want of civilization. What would Mr. Mill have said if the case had been reversed, and if the Hindus had been possessed of courage enough to seek a more daring gratification of their hatred or revenge? We should have had the old and new world ransacked, for instances to exemplify the savage manners of the Hindus.—W.

[4] The fact has by no means been established, and is denied by much higher authority than Mr. Orme, who knew nothing of the people of India. Sir Thomas Munro says, "I have had ample opportunity of observing them in every situation, and I can affirm, that they are not litigious." The opinion has been hastily formed from a few instances in the Supreme courts, and from the great number of suits in the Provincial courts: the former do not warrant a general conclusion, and the latter, to be duly estimated, require the numbers of the population, and the fewness of the judges to be taken into account. The circumstances of the country are also to be considered; and the result will be, that which has been advocated in a sensible tract upon the subject, that the multitude of suits is referrible to the structure of society and state of property in India, and to the imperfection of our own systems of finance and judicature,

steady resentments in civil disputes. The only instance in which they seem to have a contempt for money, is their profusion of it in procuring the redress and revenge of injuries at the bar of justice. Although they can, with great resignation, see themselves plundered to the utmost by their superiors, they become mad with impatience, when they think they are defrauded of part of their property by their equals. Nothing can be more adapted to the feminine spirit of a Gentoo, than the animosities of a lawsuit."[1]

A modification of the same passions gives rise to another, and seemingly a strong ingredient in the Hindu character, a propensity to the war of contentious tongues. The following picture, if not finely, is at least clearly drawn. "The timidity of the Hindu may, in general, prevent his fighting, boxing, or shedding of blood; but it by no means restrains him from scolding and upbraiding his neighbours. In this respect they are the most litigious and quarrelsome of all men. Have two persons a misunderstanding? Let them meet in the street, and they will upbraid each other for an hour together, with every foul epithet of abuse which their imagination can suggest, or their language supply. A few natives engaged in one of these bickerings display a furious gesticulation: a volubility of words, and coarseness of expression, which leave the eloquence of Billingsgate far behind."[2]

---

and not to any inherent difference in the moral character or natural disposition of the people." Inquiry into the alleged proneness to litigation of the natives of India. London, 1830.—W.

[1] Orme, on the Government and People of Indostan, p. 443.—In the committee of the House of Commons, 1781, on the petition of John Touchet, &c., Charles W. Boughton Rouse, Esq. testified that "there cannot be a race of men upon the earth more litigious and clamorous than the inhabitants of Dacca." Mr. Park takes notice of the passion of the negroes in Africa for law-suits, and adds: "If I may judge from their harangues which I frequently attended, I believe that in the forensic qualifications of procrastination and cavil, and the arts of confounding and perplexing a cause, they are not always surpassed by the ablest pleaders in Europe." Park's Travels in Africa, p. 20. Dr. Robertson was sadly mistaken, when he considered the litigious subtlety of the Hindus as a sign of high civilization. See Robertson's Historic. Disq. concerning India, p. 217. Travellers have remarked that no where is this subtlety carried higher than among the wildest of the Irish.

[2] Tennant's Indian Recreations, i. 123. The following character drawn by a missionary, a man who knew them well, unites most of the particulars which I have hitherto described of the character of this remarkable people. "Les Indous sont agiles, adroits, d'un caractère doux, d'un esprit pénétrant; ils aiment les phrases et les locutions pittoresques; ils parlent avec élégance, font de longs discours, se décident, dans leurs affaires, avec une lenteur extrême, examinent attentivement, et conçoivent avec facilité; ils sont modestes

The physical temperament of the Hindus, though an effect of some of the circumstances which have operated to the formation of their minds, has reflected a strong influence on their character. Their make is slender and delicate. Their shapes are in general fine. The female form, in particular, frequently attains in India its most exquisite proportions; and "their skins," says Mr. Orme, speaking of the Hindu women, "are of a polish and softness beyond that of all their rivals on the globe." The muscular strength, however, of the Hindus is small; even less, according to the same accurate observer, than the appearance of their bodies, though expressive of weakness, would lead the spectator to infer. Their stature is in general considerably below the European standard; though such inferiority is more remarkable in the south, and diminishes as you advance toward the north.[1]

The extreme simplicity and lightness of the aliments used by the Hindu, and the smallness of his consumption, must, undoubtedly, have been among the causes of the lightness and feebleness observable in his frame. His food consists almost wholly of rice; and his drink is no thing but water: while his demands are satisfied with a pittance which appears extreme to the people of almost every other part of the world. The prohibition, by the

---

dans leurs discours, inconstans dans leurs paroles, faciles à promettre et difficiles à tenir leurs promesses, importuns dans leurs demandes, et ingrats après qu'ils les ont obtenu; humble et soumis quand ils craignent, orgueilleux et hautains quand ils sont les plus forts; paisibles et dissimulés quand ils ne peuvent se venger, implacables et vindicatifs dès que l'occasion s'en présente. J'ai vu beaucoup de familles se ruiner par des procès devant les tribunaux, seulement par esprit de vengeance." (Voyage aux Indes Orientales, par le P. Paolino, i. 293.) "Their utmost feuds," says Fryer, "are determined by the dint of the tongue: to scold lustily, and to pull one another's puckeries or turbans off, being proverbially termed a banyan fight. Nevertheless they are implacable till a secret and sure revenge fall upon their adversary, either by maliciously plotting against their life, by clancular dealing; or estate, by unlawful and unjust extortions." (Fryer's Travels, let. iii. ch. iii.)

[1] Orme, on the Effeminacy of the Inhabitants of Indostan, p. 461 to 465. Stavorinus' Voyages, p. 407. There is, however, considerable variety, as in the stature, so in the strength of the Hindus; and the one, as might be expected, follows the other. The following is a striking and important fact: "In Indostan, the common people of all sorts are a diminutive race, in comparison with those of higher castes and better fortunes; and yield still more to them in all the advantages of physiognomy. There is not a handsomer race in the universe than the Banians of Guzerat: the Haramcores, whose business is to remove all kinds of filth, and the buriers and burners of dead bodies, are as remarkably ugly." Orme, ut supra, p. 463. There cannot be more convincing proof, that a state of extreme oppression, even of stunted subsistence, has at all times been the wretched lot of the labouring classes i Hindustan.

BOOK II. CHAP. VII.

Hindu religion, of the flesh of animals for food, has been sufficiently remarked.[1] It is not such as to have produced by any means a total abstinence, but the quantity consumed is, no doubt, small. The great luxury of the Hindu is butter, prepared in a manner peculiar to himself, and called by him, ghee.[2]

But though the body of the Hindu is feeble, it is agile in an extraordinary degree. Not only in those surprising contortions and feats, which constitute the art of the tumbler, do they excel almost all the nations in the world; but even in running and marching they equal, if not surpass, people of the most robust constitutions. "Their messengers will go fifty miles a day, for twenty or thirty days without intermission." Their infantry, if totally unincumbered with burdens, which they could by no means support, will march faster, and with less weariness, than European.[3]

The delicacy of their texture is accompanied with great acuteness and sensibility in all their organs of sense. This not only gives them great advantages in some of the finest of the manual arts, as weaving, for example; the pliant fingers and exquisite touch of the Hindu being so peculiarly adapted to the handling of the finest threads: but it communicates a remarkable susceptibility to the mental organs. The Hindu is a sort of a sensitive plant. His imagination and passions are easily inflamed; and he has a sharpness and quickness of intellect which seems strongly connected with the sensibility of his outward frame.

Another remarkable circumstance in the character of the Hindus; in part, too, no doubt, the effect of corporeal

[1] There was no such prohibition; and abstinence from flesh upon principle is restricted to some tribes of Brahmans. Nor is it true, that the food of the Hindu consists almost wholly of rice. In Hindustan, his food is wheat; and rice is almost unknown. In many places wheat, or other grains, take the place of rice.—W.

[2] Orme, on the Government and People of Indostan, p. 470. Forster's Travels, i. 40. The demand of the American tribes for food was very like that of the Hindus, in point of quantity. Robertson's Hist. of America, ii. 63. The contrivances of the American Indians for food were far more ingenious, and productive of more variety, than those of the Hindus. Ibid. p. 118. It would appear from Sacontala, that anciently much scruple was not used in eating flesh. Madhavya, complaining of the hardships he sustained in the hunting party of the king, says, "Are we hungry? We must greedily devour lean venison, and that commonly roasted to a stick."

[3] Orme, on the Effeminacy of the Inhab. of Indostan, ubi supra.

weakness, though an effect in some sort opposite to that excitability which we have immediately remarked, is the inertness of disposition, with which all men have been so forcibly struck in observing the conduct of this peculiar race. The love of repose reigns in India with more powerful sway, than in any other region probably of the globe. "It is more happy to be seated than to walk; it is more happy to sleep than to be awake; but the happiest of all is death."[1] Such is one of the favourite sayings, most frequently in the mouths of this listless tribe, and most descriptive of their habitual propensities. Phlegmatic indolence pervades the nation. Few pains, to the mind of the Hindu, are equal to that of bodily exertion; the pleasure must be intense which he prefers to that of its total cessation.[2]

This listless apathy and corporeal weakness of the natives of Hindustan, have been ascribed to the climate under which they live. But other nations, subject to the influence of as warm a sun, are neither indolent nor weak; the Malays, for example, the Arabians, the Chinese.[3] The savage is listless and indolent under every clime. In general, this disposition must arise from the absence of the motives to work; because the pain of moderate labour is so very gentle, that even feeble pleasures suffice to overcome it; and the pleasures which spring from the fruits of labour are so many and great, that the prospect of them, where allowed to operate, can seldom fail to produce the exertions which they require. There is a state of barbarity and rudeness which implies, perhaps, a weak-

1 It is not true that this is a favourite saying. I never heard it uttered during a long residence in Bengal, and doubt its genuineness.—W.

2 Tennant's Indian Recreations, i. 15, 55, 102, 215. Forster's Travels, i. 192. "L'Indien est naturellement doux, mais d'une douceur de nonchalance et de paresse." Anq. Duperron, Zendavesta, Disc. Prélim. p. cxvii.

3 The Birmans, robust and active, present a striking contrast with the feeble indolence of the Hindus. Vide Symes' Embassy to Ava. "Having witnessed," says Mr. Forster, "the robust activity of the people of this country (Northern Persia) and Afghanistan, I am induced to think, that the human body may sustain the most laborious services, without the aid of animal food. The Afghan, whose sole aliment is bread, curdled milk, and water, inhabiting a climate which often produces in one day extreme heat and cold, shall undergo as much fatigue, and exert as much strength, as the porter of London, who copiously feeds on flesh-meat and ale; nor is he subject to the like acute and obstinate disorders. It is a well-known fact, that the Arabs of the shore of the Red Sea, who live, with little exception, on dates and lemons, carry burdens of such an extraordinary weight, that its specific mention to an European ear would seem romance." Forster's Travels, ii. 142, 143.

ness of mind too great to be capable of perceiving, with a clearness sufficient to operate upon the will, the benefits of labour. This, however, is a state beyond which the Hindus have long since passed; and there is but one cause, to which, among the Hindus, the absence of the motives for labour can be ascribed; their subjection to a wretched government, under which the fruits of labour were never secure.[1]

The languid and slothful habits of the Hindu appear to have prescribed even his amusements and diversions. They are almost all of the sedentary and inactive kind. The game of pucheess, which bears a resemblance to chess and draughts, and is played by two natives, reclining on their sides, with a small chequered carpet placed between them, is the favourite amusement of this indolent race. Wonderful is the patience and interest with which, we are told, they watch and plan the evolutions of this languid game.[2] The mind in vacuity droops and pines; even where the body is most gratified by repose; and in the rude state of society, when interesting objects seldom occur, the passion for play is a general resource. The Hindus, accordingly, appear to have been at all times deeply infected with the vices of gaming. In that celebrated poem, the Mahabharat, Judishter, though celebrated as a model of kingly wisdom, and his four brothers, all eminent men, are represented as losing their fortunes, and

[1] There is a curious passage, quoted by Volney, (Travels in Syria, ch. xi.) from Hippocrates, in his Treatise de Aere. Locis, et Aquis. "As to the effeminacy and indolence of the Asiatics," says the ancient, "if they are less warlike and more gentle in their manners than the Europeans, no doubt the nature of their climate, more temperate than ours, contributes greatly to this difference. But we must not forget their governments, which are all despotic, and subject every thing to the arbitrary will of their kings. Men who are not permitted the enjoyment of their natural rights, but whose passions are perpetually under the guidance of their masters, will never be found courageous in battle. To them the risks and advantages of war are by no means equal. But let them combat in their own cause, and reap the reward of their victory, or feel the shame of their defeat, they will no longer be deficient in courage. Volney remarks that the sluggishness and apathy visible among the Hindus, negroes, &c., is approached, if not equalled, by what is witnessed in Russia, Poland, Hungary, &c. Ibid. "The lower classes of people in India," says Dr. Buchanan, "are like children; and except in the more considerable places, where they meet with uncommon encouragement to industry from Europeans, are generally in such a state of apathy, that without the orders of Government, they can hardly do any thing." Buchanan's Journey through Mysore, &c. i. 270. "If we contemplate a savage nation in any part of the globe, a supine indolence, and a carelessness of futurity, will be found to constitute their general character." Gibbon, i. 356.

[2] Tennant's Indian Recreations, i. 367.

their very kingdoms, at dice. The laws, as usual, are ambiguous and contradictory. All gaming is pronounced unlawful; yet, according to the Gentoo Code, parties may game before an agent of the magistrate, to whom in that case a half of the winnings belongs.[1]

A fondness for those surprising feats of bodily agility and dexterity which form the arts of the tumbler and the juggler, is a feature in the character of the Hindu. It is a passive enjoyment which corresponds with the passiveness of his temper: and it seems in general to be adapted to the taste of all men in a similar state of society. Our Saxon ancestors were much addicted to this species of amusement; and their tumblers and jugglers had arrived at great proficiency.[2] The passion of the Chinese for those diversions is known to be excessive, and the powers of their performers almost incredible.[3] This was one of the favourite entertainments of the ancient Mexicans; and their surprising dexterity and skill seem hardly to have yielded to that of the Hindus and Chinese. Clavigero concludes a minute and interesting account of the astonishing feats of the Mexican performers, by remarking, that "the first Spaniards, who were witnesses of these and other exhibitions of the Mexicans, were so much astonished at their agility, that they suspected some supernatural power assisted them, forgetting to make a due allowance for the progress of the human genius when assisted by application and labour."[4]

A taste for buffoonery is very generally a part of the character of a rude people; as appears by the buffoons, who, under the name of fools, were entertained by our Gothic ancestors in the courts of princes and the palaces

[1] Gentoo Code, chap. i. sect. i. "So relaxed are the principles even of the richer natives, that actions have been brought by an opulent Hindu for money advanced solely to support a common gaming-house, in the profits of which he had a considerable share; and the transaction was avowed by him with as much confidence, as if it had been perfectly justifiable by our laws and his own." Charge to the Grand Jury of Calcutta, Dec. 4, 1788. Gaming is remarked as a strong characteristic of the Chinese. See Barrow's Life of Lord Macartney, ii. 415. Travels in China, p. 157. It is a remarkable passion among the Malays. See Marsden's Sumatra

[2] Turner's Hist. of the Anglo-Saxons, book viii. ch, vii.—M. Jugglers and tumblers find encouragement in civilised, as well as uncivilised nations; and our Saxon ancestors would find, on many occasions, their descendants enjoying the exhibition with quite as much interest as themselves,—W.

[3] See Barrow, and other travellers. Bell's Travels, ii. 30.

[4] Clavigero, Hist. of Mexico, book vii. sect. 46.

BOOK II. CHAP. VII.

of the great.[1] Among the Hindus, this source of amusement was an object of so much importance, as to become the subject of legislative enactment. "The magistrate," says the Gentoo Code, "shall retain in his service a great number of buffoons, or parasites, jesters, and dancers, and athletics."[2]

Story-telling, which entirely harmonizes with the Hindu tone of mind, is said to be a favourite diversion.[3] The recitations of the bards with which the people of Europe were formerly so much delighted, afforded an entertainment of the same description. The stories of the Hindus consist of the wildest fictions; and as almost all their written narratives are in verse, their spoken stories, it is probable, like the effusions of the bards, contained occasionally more or less of the measure and elevation of verse.[4] Music and dancing form a part of their entertainments; the latter, however, they enjoy as spectators chiefly, not performers.

Notwithstanding the indolence and inactivity of the Hindus, hunting, which is in general so favourite a sport of man in his uncivilized state, is capable of calling forth their most strenuous exertions. The different classes seem not only to forget their habitual languor and timidity, but their still more inveterate prejudices of caste, and join together in pursuing the tenants of the woods and mountains with an ardour, enterprise, and patience, which no other people can surpass.[5]

It is curious that avarice, which seems but little consistent with sloth, or that insecurity with regard to pro-

[1] Buffoons, under the name of fools, were retained in European courts, long subsequent to the days of Gothic princes; and in days when Mr. Mill would probably admit that civilization had made some advauce.—W.

[2] Gentoo Code, p. 118.

[3] Tennant's Indian Recreations, i. 367.—M. Story-telling is not a Hindu diversion. If in use amongst them, it has been borrowed from the Mohammedans, amongst whom it takes the place of dramatic performances. What is presently said of the 'wild fictions' which these stories relate, and the probability of their being in verse, is wholly gratuitous. In ancient times, it seems likely that their heroic poems were recited, as was practised in Greece, even in polished times.—W.

[4] Story-telling is a common amusement among the negroes of Africa. "These stories," says Mr. Park, "bear some resemblance to those in the Arabian Nights' Entertainments; but, in general, are of a more ludicrous cast." Park's Travels in Africa, p. 31.

[5] Tennant's Indian Recreations, i. 367, and other travellers. Hunting, which delights other men chiefly in their ignorant and uncivilized state, seems to delight kings in all states.

perty which so bad a government as theirs implies, forms a more remarkable ingredient in the national character of the Hindus, than in that of any other people. It is a passion congenial to a weak and timid mind, unwarmed by the social affections. They are almost universally penurious;[1] and where placed in situations in which their insatiable desire of gain can meet with its gratification, it is not easy to surpass their keenness and assiduity in the arts of accumulation.[2] "Slavery," says Mr. Orme, "has sharpened the natural fineness of all the spirits of Asia. From the difficulty of obtaining, and the greater difficulty of preserving, the Gentoos are indefatigable in business, and masters of the most exquisite dissimulation in all affairs of interest. They are the acutest buyers and sellers in the world, and preserve through all their bargains a degree of calmness, which baffles all the arts that can be opposed against it."[3] The avaricious disposition of the Hindus is deeply stamped in their maxims of prudence and morality. Thus, they say: "From poverty a man cometh to shame. Alas! the want of riches is the foundation of every misfortune.—It is better to dwell in a forest haunted by tigers and lions, than to live amongst relations after the loss of wealth."[4]

[1] Dr. Buchanan, who bears strong testimony to the prevalence of this disposition among the Hindus, says, the Nairs are a sort of an exception. He ascribes this peculiarity to the peculiar form given among them to the association of the sexes. Journey through Mysore, &c. ii. 411.

[2] The following acute observation of Helvetius goes far to account for it: "Ce que j'observe, c'est qu'il est des pays où le désir d'immenses richesses devient raisonnable. Ce sont ceux où les taxes sont arbitraires, et par conséquent les possessions incertaines, où les renversemens de fortune sont fréquens; où, comme en Orient, le prince peut impunément s'emparer des propriétés de ses sujets.—Dans ce pays, si l'on désire les trésors de Ambouleasant, c'est que toujours exposé à les perdre, on espère au moins tirer des débris d'une grande fortune de quoi subsister soi et sa famille. Partout où la loi sans force ne peut proteger le foible contre le puissant, on peut regarder l'opulence comme un moyen de se soustraire aux injustices, aux vexations du fort, au mépris enfin, compagnon de la foiblesse. On désire donc une grande fortune comme une protectrice et un bouclier contre les oppresseurs." De l'Homme, sect. viii. chap. v.

[3] Orme, on the Government and People of Indostan, p. 431.—"L'Indien qui vit sous ce gouvernment en suit les impressions. Obligé de ramper, il devient fourbe. * * * Il se permet l'usure et la fraude dans le commerce." Anquet. Duperron, Zendavesta, Disc. Prélim. p. cxvii.—"The chief pleasure of the Gentiles or Banyans, is to cheat one another, conceiving therein the highest felicity." Fryer's Travels, let. iii. chap. iii.

[4] Wilkins' Hetopadesa, p. 63. The last of these maxims is not less expressive of that want of generosity, which is so strong a feature of the Hindu character. In the ethics, however, of the Hindus, as well as their jurisprudence and theology, contradiction is endless. In the same page with the foregoing,

BOOK II. CHAP. VII.

The mode of transacting bargains among the Hindus is sufficiently peculiar to deserve description. By a refinement of the cunning and deceitful temper of a rude people, the business is performed secretly, by tangible signs. The buyer and seller seat themselves opposite to one another, and covering their hands with a cloth, perform all the most subtle artifices of chaffering, without uttering a word, by means of certain touches and signals of the fingers, which they mutually understand.[1]

The simplicity of the houses, dress, and furniture, of the Hindus corresponds with that of their diet. "The Indian houses," says Sonnerat, "display nothing of oriental magnificence."[2] Those of the poor, even in towns, are built of mud, sometimes of brick, and thatched. "Brahmens and religious people plaster the pavement, and sometimes the walls, with cow-dung; and although this act proceeds from a spirit of religion, yet it is of use in keeping out insects."[3] The furniture, which is almost nothing in the houses of the poor, is in the highest degree scanty and simple even in those of the rich. Mats or carpets for the floor, on which they are accustomed both to sit and to lie, with a few earthen and other vessels for the preparation of their victuals and for their religious ceremonies, form the inventory in general of their household goods.[4]

From the frequency and care with which the Hindus

---

is the following maxim : "He who, in opposition to his own happiness, delighteth in the accumulation of riches, carrieth burdens for others, and is the vehicle of trouble." Ibid.

[1] Tennant's Indian Recreations, ii. 232. Lord's Banyan Religion, chap. xxii. The same, or a similar mode of transacting bargains, is followed in Persia. Chardin, Voyage en Perse, iii. 122. "The merchants, besides being frequently very dexterous in the addition and subtraction of large sums by memory, have a singular method of enumeration, by putting their hands into each other's sleeve, and there, touching one another with this or that finger, or with such a particular joint of it, will transact affairs of the greatest value, without speaking to one another, or letting the standers by into the secret." Shaw's Travels in Barbary, p. 267.

[2] Sonnerat, Voyages, liv. iii. chap. 1.

[3] Ibid.; Fryer's Travels, let. iv. chap. 6.

[4] P. Paolino, Voy. Indes Orient. liv. i. ch. 7. Fryer, who represents the houses of the Moors, or Mussulmen, at Surat, as not deficient even in a sort of magnificence, says, humorously, that "the Banyans" (Hindu merchants, often extremely rich) "for the most part live in humble cells or sheds, crowding three or four families together into a hovel, with goats, cows, and calves, all chamber-fellows, that they are almost poisoned with vermin and nastiness; so stupid, that, notwithstanding chints, fleas, and musketoes, torment them every minute, they dare not presume to scratch when it itches, lest some relation should be untenanted from its miserable abode." Fryer's Travels, let. iii. chap. i.

perform religious ablutions, the Europeans, prone from partial appearances to draw flattering conclusions, painted them, at first, as in the colours of so many other virtues, so likewise in those of cleanliness. Few nations are surpassed by the Hindus, in the total want of physical purity, in their streets, houses, and persons. Mr. Forster, whose long residence in India, and knowledge of the country, render him an excellent witness, says of the narrow streets of Benares; "In addition to the pernicious effect which must proceed from a confined atmosphere, there is, in the hot season, an intolerable stench arising from the many pieces of stagnated water dispersed in different quarters of the town. The filth also which is indiscriminately thrown into the streets, and there left exposed, (for the Hindus possess but a small portion of general cleanliness) adds to the compound of ill smells so offensive to the European inhabitants of this city."[1] Dr. Buchanan informs us, that "the earthen pots in which the Hindus boil their milk, are in general so nasty, that after this operation no part of the produce of the dairy is tolerable to Europeans, and whatever they use, their own servants must prepare."[2] "The Hindoo," says Mr Scott Waring, "who bathes constantly in the Ganges, and whose heart equals in purity the whiteness of his vest, will allow this same white robe to drop nearly off with filth before he thinks of changing it. Histories, composed in the closet, of the manners of extensive nations may possess every beauty; for as *facts* do not restrain the imagination, nor impose rules on poetic license, the fancy of the historian enjoys an uninterrupted range in the regions of fiction."[3]

[1] Forster's Travels, i. 32. Of Lucknow, too, he remarks, the streets are narrow, uneven, and almost choked up with every species of filth. Ibid. p. 82. Speaking of Serinagur, he says, "The streets are choked with the filth of the inhabitants, who are proverbially unclean." Ibid. See to the same purpose, Rennel's Description of an Indian Town, Memoir, p. 58.

[2] Buchanan's Journey through Mysore, &c. ii. 14. He remarks, too, iii. 341, that the unwholesomeness of the water in many places is "in part, to be attributed to the common nastiness of the Hindus, who wash their clothes, bodies, and cattle, in the very tanks or wells from which they take their own drink; and, wherever the water is scanty, it becomes from this cause extremely disgusting to a European."

[3] Tour to Sheeraz, by Ed. Scott Waring, p. 58, note.—"Their nastiness," says Dr. Buchanan, "is disgusting; very few of the inhabitants above the Ghats being free from the itch; and their linen, being almost always dyed, is seldom washed." Travels through Mysore, &c. i. 135.—See, too, Capt. Hardwicke, Asiat. Res. vi. 330. The authors of the Universal History describe with pure and picturesque simplicity one pretty remarkable custom of the

BOOK II. CHAP. VII.

To a superficial view, it appears surprising that overstrained sentiments in regard to the ceremonial of behaviour are a mark of the uncivilized state of the human mind. The period when men have but just emerged from barbarism, and have made the first feeble steps in improvement, is the period at which formalities in the intercourse of social life are the most remarkably multiplied, at which the importance attached to them is the greatest, and at which the nice observance of them is the most rigidly exacted. In modern Europe, as manners have refined, and knowledge improved, we have thrown off the punctilious ceremonies which constituted the fine breeding of our ancestors; and adopted more and more of simplicity in the forms of intercourse. Among the inhabitants of Hindustan, the formalities of behaviour are multiplied to excess; and the most important bonds of society are hardly objects of greater reverence.[1] Some of their rules breathe that spirit of benevolence, and of respect for the weak, which begins to show itself partially at an early period of society, and still wants much of its proper strength at a late one. The distinctions of giving way on the road are thus marked in the Gentoo code; a man with sight to a man blind; a man with hearing to a man deaf; a man to a woman; a man empty-handed to a man with a burden; an inferior person to a superior; a man in health

---

Hindus. "The women scruple no more than the men to do their occasions in the public streets or highways: for which purpose at sun-rise and sun-set, they go out in droves to some dead wall, if in the city; and in case any pass by in the interim, they turn their bare backsides on them, but hide their faces. When they have done their business, they wash their parts with the left hand, because they eat with the right. The men, who exonerate apart from the women, squat like them when they make water. Although their food is nothing but vegetables concocted with fair water, yet they leave such a stink behind them, that it is but ill taking the air, either in the streets, or without the towns, near the rivers and ditches." vi. 265. Yet these authors, with the same breath, assure us that the Hindus are a cleanly people, because, and this is their sole reason, they wash before and after meals, and leave no hair on their bodies. Ibid. See to the same purpose, Fryer's Travels, let. iv. chap. vi.—M.

Notwithstanding all that is here said, or the observations cited in the text, which are either exaggerated or applicable to the poorest classes, the Hindus are a cleanly people, and may be compared, with decided advantage, with the nations of the south of Europe, both as regards their habitations and their persons. There are many of their practices which might be introduced even into the north with benefit.—W.

[1] See a curious description of the excess to which the minute frivolities of behaviour are carried both among the Moors and Hindus, by Mr. Orme, on the Government and People of Indostan, pp, 425 and 431. See, also, Laws of Menu, ch. ii. 120 to 139.

to a sick person; and all persons to a Brahmen.[1] Not a few of their rules bear curious testimony to the unpolished state of society in which they were prescribed. "If a man," says one of their laws, "having accepted another's invitation, doth not eat at his house, then he shall be obliged to make good all the expense that was incurred in consequence of the invitation."[2] When a Hindu gives an entertainment, he seats himself in the place of greatest distinction; and all the most delicate and costly of the viands are placed before him. The company sit according to their quality, the inferior sort at the greatest distance from the master, each eating of those dishes only which are placed before him, and they continually decreasing in fineness, as they approach the place of the lowest of the guests.[3]

The attachment which the Hindus, in common with all ignorant nations, bear to astrology, is a part of their manners exerting a strong influence upon the train of their actions. "The Hindus of the present age," says a partial observer, "do not undertake any affair of consequence without consulting their astrologers, who are always Brahmens."[4] The belief of witchcraft and sorcery continues universally prevalent; and is every day the cause of the greatest enormities. It not unfrequently happens that Brahmens, tried for murder before the English judges, assign as their motive to the crime, that the murdered

[1] Gentoo Code, ch. xxi. sect. 10. [2] Ibid.

[3] Tennant's Indian Recreations, i. 254,—M. Dr. Tennant speaks confidently of many things of which he must have been utterly ignorant. In a preceding passage, he compares the eloquence of Hindu vituperation to that of Billingsgate; it is very doubtful if he ever understood a syllable uttered on such an occasion. Here he describes the particulars of a Hindu entertainment, as if he had witnessed one, although it is wholly impossible that he should ever have dined with a Hindu, or been present on any such occasion; yet he is one of Mr. Mill's principal authorities.—W.

[4] Wilkins' Hetopadesa, note, p. 269. The unceremonious Fryer says, the principal science of the Brahmen is magic and theology. Travels, let. iv. ch. vi. Of the astonishing degree to which the Indians of all descriptions are devoted to astrology, see a lively description by Bernier, Suites des Mémoires sur l'Empire du Grand Mogol, i. 12 à 14. "Les rois, et les seigneurs," says he, "qui n'entreprendroient la moindre chose qu'ils n'eussent consultés les astrologues, leur donnent de grands appointements pour lire ce qui est écrit dans le ciel." Ibid. "The savages," says Mallet (Introd. to the Hist. of Denmark, i. ch. i.), "whom the Danes have found on the coast of Greenland, live with great union and tranquillity. They are neither quarrelsome, nor mischievous, nor warlike; being greatly afraid of those that are. Theft, blows, and murder, are almost unknown to them. They are chaste before marriage, and love their children tenderly. Their simplicity hath not been able to preserve them from having priests, who pass among them for enchanters; and are, in truth, very great and dexterous cheats."

BOOK II. CHAP. VII.

individual had enchanted them. No fewer than five unhappy persons in one district were tried and executed for witchcraft, so late as the year 1792.[1] The villagers themselves assume the right of sitting in judgment on this imaginary offence; and their sole instruments of proof are the most wretched of all incantations. Branches of the Saul tree, for example, one for each of the suspected individuals, inscribed with her name, are planted in water. If any of them withers within a certain time, the devoted female, whose name it bears, suffers death as a witch.[2]

[1] It is not so long since belief in witchcraft and astrology ceased to prevail in Europe, that we need to be very severe upon similar absurdities in Asia.—W.

[2] See an account of this shocking part of the manners of the Hindus in the Asiat. An. Regist. for 1801, Miscellaneous Tracts, p. 91.—M.

For some additional remarks on the tone and spirit of this chapter, see note D. in the Appendix.—W.

NOTES.

NOTE A. p. 233.

" 5. This *universe* existed only *in the first divine idea yet unexpanded, as if involved* in darkness, imperceptible, undefinable, undiscoverable *by reason*, and undiscovered *by revelation*, as if it were wholly immersed in sleep;

" 6. Then the *sole* self-existing power, himself undiscerned, but making this world discernible, with five elements and other principles *of nature*, appeared with undiminished glory, *expanding his idea, or* dispelling the gloom.

" 7. He, whom the mind alone can perceive, whose essence eludes the external organs, who has no visible parts, who exists from eternity, even he, the soul of all beings, whom no being can comprehend, shone forth in person.

" 8. He, having willed to produce various beings from his own divine substance, first with a thought created the waters, and placed in them a productive seed:

" 9. The *seed* became an egg bright as gold, blazing like the luminary with a thousand beams: and in that egg he was born himself, *in the form* of Brahma, the great forefather of all spirits.

" 10. The waters are called *nara*, because they were the production of Nara, *or the Spirit of God;* and, since they were his first *ayana, or place of motion*, he thence is named Narayana, *or moving on the waters.*

" 11. From that which is, the first cause, not the object of sense, existing *every where in substance*, not existing *to our perception*, without beginning or end, was produced the divine male, famed in all worlds under the appellation of Brahma.

" 12. In that egg the great power sat inactive a whole year *of the Creator*, at the close of which, by his thought alone, he caused the egg to divide itself.

" 13. And from its two divisions he framed the heaven *above* and the earth *beneath:* in the midst *he placed* the subtile ether, the eight regions, and the permanent receptacle of waters.

" 14. From the supreme soul he drew forth mind, existing

substantially though unperceived by sense, immaterial; and *before mind, or the reasoning power, he produced* consciousness, the internal monitor, the ruler:

" 15. And, *before them both*, he produced the great *principle of the soul, or first expansion of the divine idea;* and all vital forms endued with the three qualities of *goodness, passion, and darkness;* and the *five* perceptions of sense, and the five organs of sensation.

" 16. *Thus*, having at once pervaded, with emanations from the Supreme Spirit, the minutest portions of six principles immensely operative, consciousness and the five perceptions, he framed all creatures;

" 17. And since the minutest particles of visible nature have a dependence on those *six* emanations from God, the wise have accordingly given the name of *sarira or depending on six, that is, the ten organs on consciousness, and the five elements on as many perceptions*, to his *image or* appearance in visible nature.

" 18. Thence proceed the great elements endued with peculiar powers, and mind with operations infinitely subtile, the unperishable cause of all apparent forms.

" 19. This *universe*, therefore, is compacted from the minute portions of those seen divine and active principles, *the great soul, or first emanation, consciousness and five perceptions; a* mutable *universe* from immutable *ideas.*

" 20. Among them each succeeding element acquires the quality of the preceding: and, in as many degrees as each of them is advanced, with so many properties is it said to be endued.

" 21. He too first assigned to all creatures distinct names, distinct acts, and distinct occupations; as they had been revealed in the pre-existing *Veda.*

" 22. He, the supreme ruler, created an assemblage of inferior deities, with divine attributes and pure souls; and a number of genii exquisitely delicate: and he *prescribed* the sacrifice ordained from the beginning.

" 23. From fire, from air, and from the sun he milked out, *as it were*, the three primordial *Vedas*, named *Rich, Yajush and Saman*, for the due performance of the sacrifice.

" 24. He gave being to time and the divisions of time, to the stars also, and to the planets, to rivers, oceans, and mountains, to level plains, and uneven valleys.

" 25. To devotion, speech, complacency, desire, and wrath, and to the creation, which shall presently be mentioned; for he willed the existence of all those created things.

" 26. For the sake of distinguishing actions, he made a total difference between right and wrong, and enured these sentient creatures to pleasure and pain, *cold and heat*, and other opposite pairs.

"27. With very minute transformable portions, called *matras*, of the five elements, all this perceptible world was composed in fit order;

"28. And in whatever occupation the supreme lord first employed any vital soul, to that occupation the same soul attaches itself spontaneously, when it receives a new body again and again:

"29. Whatever quality, noxious or innocent, harsh or mild, unjust or just, false or true, he conferred on any being at its creation, the same quality enters it of course *on its future births*;

"30. As the *six* seasons of the year attain respectively their peculiar marks in due time, and of their own accord, even so the several acts of each embodied spirit *attend it naturally.*

"31. That the human race might be multiplied, he caused the *Brahmen*, the *Cshatriya*, the *Vaisya*, and the *Sudra* (so named from the *scripture, protection, wealth, and labour*) to proceed from his mouth, his arm, his thigh, and his foot.

"32. Having divided his own substance, the mighty Power became half male, half female, *or nature active and passive;* and from that female he produced VIRAJ:

"33. Know me, O most excellent of BRAHMENS, to be that person, whom the male *power* VIRAJ, having performed austere devotion, produced by himself; me, the *secondary* framer of all this *visible world.*

"34. It was I, who, desirous of giving birth to a race of men, performed very difficult religious duties, and first produced ten lords of created beings, eminent in holiness,

"35. Marichi, Atri, Angiras, Pulastya, Pulaha, Cratu, Prachetas, or Dacsha, Vasishtha, Bhrigu, and Narada:

"36. They, abundant in glory, produced seven other *Menus*, together with deities, and the mansions of deities, and *Maharshis*, or great Sages, unlimited in power.

"37. Benevolent genii, and fierce giants, blood-thirsty savages, heavenly quiristers, nymphs and demons, huge serpents, and snakes of smaller size, birds of mighty wing, and separate companies of *Pitris*, or progenitors of mankind;

"38. Lightnings and thunderbolts, clouds and coloured bows of *Indra*, falling meteors, earth-rending vapours, comets, and luminaries of various degrees;

"39. Horse-faced sylvans, apes, fish, and a variety of birds, tame cattle, deer, men, and ravenous beasts with two rows of teeth;

"40. Small and large reptiles, moths, lice, fleas, and common flies, with every biting gnat, and immoveable substances of distinct sorts." (Institut. of Menu, ch. I.)

Such is the account of the creation which is contained in one of the principal standards of Hindu faith; such is one of the chief documents from which we can draw precise ideas respecting the religious principles of the Hindus. The darkness, the vagueness, and the confusion, which reign in it, need not be remarked; for by these the Hindu mythology is throughout distinguished. The first of the propositions, as it now stands, can be adequately designated only by the familiar appellative, nonsense; the ideas are heterogeneous, and incompatible. "This universe," it is said, "existed only *in the first divine idea.*" When anything is said to exist in idea, the meaning is, that it is conceived by the mind, or, in common language, that it is an idea in the mind. This universe then, according to the above passage, was conceived by the divine mind before it was actually produced, or, in other words, it was an idea in the divine mind. This idea existed in the divine mind, "yet unexpanded." But what are we to understand by an idea in the divine mind "unexpanded?" In regard to human thought an idea may be said to be unexpanded, when something is conceived very generally and obscurely; and it may be said to be expanded, when the thing is conceived minutely, distinctly, and in all its parts. Are we then to understand by the idea of the universe being unexpanded in the divine mind, that the universe was conceived by it only generally, obscurely, indistinctly, and that it was not till creation was actually performed, that the divine idea was clear, full, and precise? How infinitely removed is this from the sublime conception which we entertain of the Divine Being; to whose thoughts all his works past, present, and to come, and every thing in the universe from eternity to eternity, are present always, essentially, perfectly, in all their parts, properties, and relations! This divine idea is still further described: it existed "as if involved in darkness." When an idea is involved in darkness, it is an idea not perfectly understood; an apprehension only compatible with the most imperfect notions of the divine nature. It existed "imperceptible." If this means by the senses, all ideas are imperceptible; if it means by the mind, it is impossible, for the very essence of an idea consists in its being perceived by the mind. It existed "undefinable, undiscoverable by reason, undiscovered by revelation, as if it were wholly immersed in sleep." What sort of an idea could that be in the divine mind which the divine mind could not define, that mind by which it was formed? If the meaning be, that it could not be defined by any other mind; neither can the idea, not yet expressed, which exists in the mind of the most foolish of men. "Not discoverable by reason;" does this mean that the divine reason did not discover the divine idea, or does it mean that human reason could not discover it? An idea in the mind of another being is not discoverable to man by reason, but by enunciation. The last expression is the most extraordinary; "as if immersed in sleep:" "an idea immersed in sleep!" An idea too in the divine mind immersed in sleep! What notion can be formed of this?

But it must be explained that this incoherence and absurdity is not the work of Menu, or of the author, whoever he was, of the treatise which goes by his name. It is a common plan in India, for a commentator who is explaining a book, to insert between the words of the text such expressions as to him appear necessary to render the sense of the author clear and distinct. This has been done by a commentator of the name of Culluca, in regard to the ordinances of Menu; and his gloss or commentary, interworded with the text, Sir William Jones has translated along with his author. As he has, very judiciously, however, printed the interwoven expressions of the commentator in italics, it is easy for the reader to separate them, and to behold the sense of the original unadulterated. According to this expedient, the words of Menu appear thus: "This existed only in darkness, imperceptible, undefinable, undiscoverable, undiscovered, as if it were wholly immersed in sleep." It seems remarkably the genius of the ancient Sanscrit writings to be elliptical, and the adjective pronouns especially are very frequently used without a substantive. "This," in the passage which we are now examining, is in that situation. The mind of the reader is left to supply the word which the sense of the context demands. This—every thing; this—whole; this—universe; such is the manner in which the mind easily here suggests the requisite idea; and when this is done, the incoherence and absurdity which the supplement of Culluca engendered, is entirely dispelled. The passage presents clearly and unambiguously, a description, a very vague and unmeaning description, it must be owned, of that chaos of which the Greeks and Romans drew so striking and awful a picture, and of which the belief appears to have been so widely and generally diffused. The notion which Culluca endeavoured to engraft, is remarkable. It is no other than the celebrated Platonic principle of the pre-existence of all things in the divine mind, which Culluca, it is evident, neither understood nor could apply, and with which he made such havoc on the genuine sense of his author. It is probable that he borrowed the idea from some foreign source, that it pleased him as preferable to the more rude conception of a chaos, and that he resolved, according to the invariable rule of the Brahmens, to give his own order the credit of it, by incorporating it with the doctrines of the sacred authors.

There is a remarkable coincidence, and there is a remarkable discrepancy, between this passage in the Institutes of Menu, and the following at the beginning of the book of Genesis: "In the beginning God created the heaven and the earth. And the earth was without form and void, and darkness was upon the face of the deep." The coincidence appears in the chaotic description here applied to the earth: the discrepancy consists in this, that the Jewish legislator informs us of the previous creation of the shapeless mass, the Hindu legislator describes it as antecedent to all creation.

This chaos, this universe, then, in its dark, imperceptible, undefinable state, existed, according to Menu, antecedent to creation. This too was the idea of the Greeks and Romans, who thence believed in the eternity of matter. It is doubtful, from the extreme vagueness of the Hindu language, whether they had carried their thoughts so far as to conceive the question respecting the origin of matter: but as its eternity is implied in several of their doctrines, so it appears to be recognised in some of their expressions. It appears, indeed, that they were unable to make any clear distinction between matter and spirit, but rather considered the latter to be some extraordinary refinement of the former. Thus even the Divine Being, though they called him soul and spirit, they certainly regarded as material. In the passage already quoted, it is said, "that he willed to produce various beings from *his own divine substance*." Now what can be meant by substance, if not material substance? Besides, from material substance alone can material beings be produced. But the first thing which we are told was produced from the divine substance, was water. It is worth remarking, at the same time, that in other places water appears to be spoken of as uncreated, and as the material out of which all other things were produced. A passage describing the creation, translated from the Yajur Veda by Mr. Colebrooke, commences thus: "Waters alone there were; this world originally was water. In it the lord of creation moved, having become air." [Asiat. Res. viii. 452.]—M.

If the incoherence and absurdity occasioned by the use of such an expression as existing in idea, is referable to the commentator, much of the previous criticism might have been spared, and the text of Menu acquitted, notwithstanding the charge with which it was first assailed, of being "nonsense." It is here admitted to be clear and unambiguous. But neither is the commentator open to cavil. The demerit of the confusion is Sir William Jones's. Not a syllable is said by Culluca about "idea," and the translator has misled the critic, both being influenced by European ideas, and unacquainted with the Hindu system. One of the philosophical schools, the Sankkya, which is chiefly followed by Menu, whose cosmogony, however, is by no means carefully described, maintains the eternity of matter or Prakriti. "This 'matter' existed, but without form, invisible, undefinable, inert, as if in sleep." There is nothing vague, ambiguous, or incoherent in this description. Culluca belongs to a different school, the Vedanta, that which maintains the unity of things; the identity of the elements of matter with its cause—and he explains the text agreeably to his doctrines. 'This' elementary matter existed, 'unseparated' from the divine cause. We may think what we please of the philosophy, but the notions are intelligibly expressed by both text and comment.—W.

NOTE B. p. 234.

Another and a very remarkable account of the creation of living creatures is found in the Vedas, and translated by Mr. Colebrooke. "This variety of forms was, before the production of body, soul, bearing a human shape. Next, looking round, that primeval Being saw nothing but himself; and he first said, *I am I.* Therefore his name was I: and thence even now, when called, a man first answers, *it is I*, and then declares any other name which appertains to him. —Since he, being anterior to all this which seeks supremacy, did consume by fire all sinful obstacles to his own supremacy, therefore does the man, who knows this truth, overcome him, who seeks to be before him. He felt dread; and, therefore, man fears, when alone. But he reflected, 'Since nothing exists besides myself, why should I fear?' Thus his terror departed from him; for what should he dread, since fear must be of another?—He felt not delight; and, therefore, man delights not when alone. He wished the existence of another; and instantly he became such as is man and woman in mutual embrace. He caused this his own self to fall in twain; and thus became a husband and a wife. Therefore was this body, so separated, as it were an imperfect moiety of himself: for so Yajnyawalcya has pronounced it. This blank, therefore, is completed by woman. He approached her; and thence were human beings produced.—She reflected, doubtingly; How can he, having produced me from himself, incestuously approach me? I will now assume a disguise. She became a cow; and the other became a bull and approached her; and the issue were kine. She was changed into a mare, and he into a stallion; one was turned into a female ass, and the other into a male one: thus did he again approach her, and the one-hoofed kind was the offspring. She became a female goat, and he a male one; she was a ewe, and he a ram: thus he approached her, and goats and sheep were the progeny. In this manner, did he create every existing pair whatsoever, even to the ants and minutest insect." See a curious discourse of Mr. Colebrooke on the Vedas, or Sacred Writings of the Hindus, Asiat. Research, viii. 440, 441.—M.

It is evident that from a very remote period different illustrative, rather than descriptive traditions of the origin and creation of the universe were current amongst the Hindus—even before the Vedas were compiled. Some of them, such as this cited from the Veda, were clearly allegorical—others were mystic, mythological and philosophical, and each should be considered by itself, for its character to be rightly understood. To attempt to force them into one system, is to place them in a condition to which they never pretended; and the confusion and contradiction that ensue is our work, not the error of the Hindus. —W.

NOTE C. p. 275.

DAILY CEREMONIES OF THE BRAHMENS.

As he rises from sleep, a Brahmen must rub his teeth with a proper withe, or a twig of the racemiferous fig-tree, repeating prayers. Should this sacred duty be omitted, so great a sin is incurred, that the benefit is lost of all religious rites performed by him. The next circumstance of importance is, the deposit of the withe after it has done its office. It must be carefully thrown away in a place free from impurities; that is, where none of those religious stains, which are so multiplied among the Hindus, and must infect so many places, have been imprinted. When the business of the teeth and of the twig is accomplished, ablution next engages the attention of the Brahmen. The duty of the bath, particularly in the months of Magha, Phalguna, and Cartica, is no less efficacious than a rigid penance for the expiation of sin. Standing in a river, or other water, the worshipper, sipping water, which is a requisite preliminary to all rites, and sprinkling it before him, recites inaudibly the gayatri, or holiest text of the Veda, with the names of the seven worlds. He next throws water eight times on his head, or towards the sky, and at last upon the ground, to destroy the demons who wage war with the gods, reciting prayers, of which the first may be received as a specimen: "O waters, since ye afford us delight, grant us present happiness, and the rapturous sight of the supreme God." When these ceremonies and prayers are performed, he plunges three times into the water, and each time repeats the expiatory text which recites the creation, and having then washed his mantle, the morning ablution is finished. If he is a householder, it is his duty to bathe again at noon; and if he belongs to an order of devotion, both at noon and in the evening, with ceremonies, differing somewhat in the words and forms, but the same in spirit and substance.[1]

An important part of the worship of the Brahmen then succeeds. Coming out of the water, and putting on his mantle, he sits down to worship the rising sun. This great duty is performed by first tying the lock of hair on the crown of his head, while he holds much cusa grass in his left hand, and three blades of it in his right, or wears a ring of it on the third finger of that hand, reciting at the same time the gayatri. He then sips water three times, repeats the mysterious names of the seven worlds, recites again the gayatri, rubs his hands as if washing them, touches with his wet hand his feet, head, breast, eyes, ears, nose and navel, and again three times sips water. If, however, he should sneeze, or spit, he must obey the text which says, "after sneezing, spitting, blowing his nose, sleeping, putting on apparel or dropping tears, a man should not immediately sip water, but first touch his right ear." The sipping, however, being at last performed, he passes his hand filled with water, briskly round his neck, while he prays: "May the waters preserve me!" He then shuts his eyes and meditates in silence. Till we got better information, very wonderful ideas were formed of the sublimity of the Brahmen's meditations. On this, one of the most sacred and solemn of all occasions, while he meditates in silence, with his eyes shut, and every mark of intense thought, we are informed, that he is only "figuring to himself, that Brahma, with five faces and a red complexion, resides in his navel; Vishnu with four arms and a black complexion, in his heart; and Siva, with five faces and a white complexion, in his forehead." Nor is this the whole of his meditation. He ponders next on the holiest of texts; and this sublime duty is performed in the following manner. Closing the left nostril with the two longest fingers of the right hand, he draws his breath through the right

[1] Colebrooke on the Religious Ceremonies of the Hindus. Asiat. Research. v. 345, 346.

nostril, and then closing it with his thumb, and suspending his breath, he repeats to himself the gayatri, the mysterious names of the worlds, and the sacred text of Brahme; after which, raising his fingers from the left nostril, he emits the breath which he had suppressed, and thus ends one part of his meditation. The same process is repeated three times, and the whole is then concluded. This meditation, says Yajnyawalcya, "implies, Om, (aum,) earth, sky, heaven, middle region, place of births, mansion of the blessed, abode of truth. We meditate on the adorable light of the resplendent generator which governs our intellects, which is water, lustre, savour, immortal faculty of thought, Brahme, earth, sky, and heaven."[1] He then stands on one foot, resting the other against his ancle or heel, and looking towards the east, while his hands are held open before him in a hollow form, and in that posture he recites prayers to the sun, of which the following is one of the most remarkable: "Thou art self-existent, thou art the most excellent ray; thou givest effulgence, grant it unto me." When all these ceremonies are performed, the oblation or offering is the next part of the service. It consists of tila, flowers, barley, water, and red sanders wood; it is put into a vessel of copper in the shape of a boat, and placed on the head of the votary, who presents it with fresh prayers and holy texts. In the last place comes the invocation of the gayatri. It is first addressed in these words: "Thou art light; thou art seed; thou art immortal life; thou art effulgent; beloved by the gods, defamed by none, thou art the holiest sacrifice." It is then recited measure by measure; next the first two measures are recited as one hemistich; and the third measure as the other; lastly, the three measures are repeated without interruption. It is addressed again in the following words: "Divine text, who dost grant our best wishes, whose name is trisyllable, whose import is the power of the Supreme Being; come, thou mother of the Vedas, who didst spring from Brahme, be constant here." It is then, along with the triliteral monosyllable, and the names of the three lower worlds, pronounced inaudibly a hundred, or a thousand times, or as often as practicable, while the repetitions are counted upon a rosary of wild grains, or of gems set in gold. Additional prayers are recited, and the morning worship of the sun is thus terminated.[2]

The religious duties which fill up the remaining portion of the day, are chiefly comprised in what are denominated the five sacraments. In a passage of the Institutes of Menu these are

[1] Colebrooke on the Religious Ceremonies of the Hindus. Asiatic Research. v. 348.

[2] Ibid. 347 to 358.

thus described: "Teaching and studying the scripture is the sacrament of the Veda; Offering cakes and water, the sacrament of the manes; An oblation to fire, the sacrament of the deities; Giving rice or other food to living creatures, the sacrament of spirits; Receiving guests with honour, the sacrament of men."[1] I shall endeavour, by a very short illustration, to convey an idea of each.

Preparatory to the study of the Veda must ablution be performed. Of this some ceremonies not yet described may be here introduced. "Let a Brahman at all times perform the ablution," says the law of Menu, "with the pure part of his hand, denominated from the Veda, or with the part sacred to the Lord of creatures, or with that dedicated to the gods; but never with the part named from the Pitris: The pure part under the root of the thumb is called Brahma; that at the root of the little finger, Caya; that at the tips of the fingers, Daiva; and the part between the thumb and index, Pitrya. Let him first sip water thrice; then twice wipe his mouth, and lastly touch with water the six hollow parts of his head, [or his eyes, ears, and nostrils,] his breast and his head. He who knows the law, and seeks purity, will ever perform the ablution with the pure part of his hand, and with water neither hot nor frothy, standing in a lonely place, and turning to the east or the north. A Brahmen is purified by water that reaches his bosom; a Cshatriya, by water descending to his throat; a Vaisya, by water barely taken into his mouth; a Sudra, by water touched with the extremity of his lips."[2] Having concluded this part of the ceremony, and walked in a circle beginning from the south, he proceeds to the pronunciation of the syllable Aum. "A Brahmen, beginning and ending a lecture on the Veda, must always pronounce to himself the syllable Aum; for unless the syllable Aum precedes, his learning will slip away from him; and unless it follow, nothing will be long retained. If he have sitten on culms of cusa grass, with their points toward the east, and be purified by rubbing that holy grass on both his hands, and be further prepared by three suppressions of breath, each equal in time to five short vowels, he may then fitly pronounce Aum. Brahma milked out, as it were, from the three vedas, the letter A, the letter U, and the letter M, which form by their coalition the triliteral monosyllable, together with three mysterious words, earth, sky, heaven."[3] Turning his face towards the east, with his right hand toward the south, and his left hand towards the north, he then sits down, having the cusa grass before him, holding two blades of it on the tips of his left fingers, and placing on them his right hand with the palm

[1] Institutes of Menu, ch. iii. 70.
[2] Ibid. ch. ii. 58 to 62.
[3] Ibid. ii. 74, 75, 76.

resting the sole of his right foot on his left ankle, sprinkles the grass with water, after which he places on it his Brahmen, made of cusa, saying to it, "Sit on this seat until thy fee be paid thee;" he then returns round the fire the same way by which he went, and sitting down again with his face towards the east, names the earth inaudibly. If no profane word should hitherto have been spoken, for which atonement is requisite, he must next spread leaves of cusa grass on three sides of the fire; he begins with the eastern side, and lays three rows of leaves in such a manner that the tip of the one shall cover the root of the other; after this be blesses the ten regions of space, and rising a little puts some wood on the fire with a ladle of clarified butter, while he meditates in silence on Brahma, the lord of creatures: next he takes up two leaves of the grass, and with another cutting off the length of a span, and saying, "Pure leaves be sacred to Vishnu," he throws them into a vessel of copper, or other metal; he then takes up other two leaves, and holding the tips of them between the thumb and ring-finger of his right hand, the roots between the thumb and ring-finger of his left, he takes up, having the one hand crossed over the other, clarified butter in the curvature of the leaves, and throws some of it three several times into the fire. He then sprinkles the leaves with water, and throws them away; next, having sprinkled the vessel containing the clarified butter, he puts it on the fire and takes it off again three several times, when, having recited the proper prayers with cusa grass in both his hands, the ceremony of hallowing the butter is finished. That of hallowing the wooden ladle is performed by describing three times with the tip of his fore-finger and thumb the figure 7 on the inside of it, and the figure 9 on the outside, by sprinkling water, having first dropped on one knee, from the palms of his hands, on the whole southern side of the fire, from west to east; on the western side from south to north; on the northern side, and then all around the fire, reciting prayers and sacred texts. Having next recited an expiatory prayer with cusa grass in both his hands, and having thrown the grass away, he has then finished the consecration of the sacrificial implements. It is only after all this is accomplished that he is prepared to begin the oblation to fire, of which the following is one of that variety of forms which it receives according to the rite intended to succeed. First, the priest burns silently a log of wood, smeared with clarified butter: next, he makes three oblations, by pouring each time a ladleful of clarified butter on the fire, and pronouncing severally the following prayers; "Earth! be this oblation efficacious."—"Sky! be this oblation efficacious."—"Heaven! be this oblation efficacious." On some occasions the oblation is made a fourth time, and he says, "Earth! Sky! Heaven! be this oblation efficacious." An offering of rice, milk, curds, and butter, is next performed, and the oblations accompanied with the names of the three worlds are repeated.[1] "In his domestic fire, for dressing the food of all the gods," says the law of Menu, "let a Brahmen make an oblation each day to these following divinities; first, to Agni, god of fire, and to the lunar god, severally; then, to both of them at once; next, to the assembled gods; and afterwards to Dhanwantari, god of medicine; to Cuhu, goddess of the day, when the new moon is discernible; to Anumati, goddess of the day after the opposition; to Prajapati, or the lord of creatures; to Dyava and Prithivi, goddesses of sky and earth; and lastly, to the fire of the good sacrifice. Having thus, with fixed attention, offered clarified butter in all quarters, proceeding from the east in a southern direction, to Indra, Yama, Varuna, and the god Soma, let him offer his gift to animated creatures."[2]

The fourth sacrament, or that of spirits, in the Institutes of Menu, is thus described: "Let him, saying, I salute the maruts or winds, throw dressed rice near the door: saying I salute the water gods, let him throw it in water; and let him throw it on his pestle and mortar, saying, I salute the gods of large trees. Let him do the like in the north-east, or near his pillow, to Sri, the goddess of abundance; in the south-west, or at the foot of his bed, to the propitious goddess Bhadracali: in the centre of his mansion, to Brahma, and his household god; to all the gods assembled, let him throw up his oblation in open air; by day, to the spirits who walk in light; and by night, to those who walk in darkness: in the building on his house-top, or behind his back, let him cast his oblation for the welfare of all creatures; and what remains let him give to the Pitris with his face towards the south."[3]

Of those diurnal sacraments, which constitute so great a part of the duty of the Hindus, receiving guests with honour, which is denominated the sacrament of men, is the fifth. This is commonly, by English writers, interpreted "hospitality." But we shall form a very erroneous notion of this sacramental service, if we confound it with the merely human and profane duty of receiving strangers beneficently from motives of humanity. This is a duty purely religious, confined to the twice-born and consecrated classes; and principally contrived for the benefit of the Brahmens; that for them, in all places, and on all occasions, every door may be open, and every table spread. "A Brahmen, coming as a guest, and not received with just honour, takes to

[1] Colebrooke on the Religious Ceremonies of the Hindus, Asiat. Res. vii 232 so 239.

[2] Institutes of Menu, ch. iii. 84 to 87. [3] Ibid. ch. iii. 88 to 91.

himself all the reward of the housekeeper's former virtue, even though he had been so temperate as to live on the gleanings of harvests, and so pious as to make oblations in five distinct fires."[1] A guest, in the Hindu sense, is not every man who may claim, or may stand in need of your hospitalities: A guest, according to the commentator, whom Mr. Colebrooke follows as his guide, is "a spiritual preceptor, a priest, an ascetick, a prince, a bridegroom, a friend."[2] "In the house of a Brahmen," says the law of Menu, "a military man is not denominated a guest; nor a man of the commercial or servile cast;"[3] so that a Brahmen, to whom are devoted the hospitalities of all the classes, is bound to return them to Brahmens alone. Among the religious ceremonies with which this sacrament is celebrated, a cow is tied on the northern side of the apartment, and a stool and other furniture placed for the guest, when the householder, rising up to bid him welcome, recites the prayer: "May she, who supplies oblations for religious worship, who constantly follows her calf, and who was the milch cow when Yama was the votary, abound with milk, and fulfil our wishes year after year." The guest then sits down on the stool or cushion prepared for him, reciting the text of the Yajurveda, which says: "I step on this for the sake of food or other benefits, on this variously splendid footstool." His host next presents to him a cushion made of twenty leaves of cusa grass, holding it up with both hands, and exclaiming, "The cushion! the cushion! the cushion!" which the guest accepts and places it on the ground under his feet, reciting prayers. This done, a vessel of water is presented to him, the host thrice exclaiming, "Water for ablutions!" Of this the guest declares his acceptance, and looking into the vessel cries, "Generous water! I view thee; return in the form of fertilizing rain from him from whom thou dost proceed." He then takes some of it in the palms of both hands joined together, and throws it on his left foot, saying, "I wash my left foot, and fix prosperity in this realm;" in the same manner on the right foot, with a similar declaration; and lastly, on both feet, saying, "I wash first one and then the other; and lastly both feet, that the realm may thrive, and intrepidity be gained." With similar formalities is next presented and received, an arghya; that is, a vessel shaped like a boat, or a conch, filled with water, rice, and durva grass; when the guest, pouring the water on his head, says, "Thou art the splendour of food; through thee may I become glorious." The host again presenting water, three times exclaims, "Take water to be sipped!" the guest, accepting it, says, "Thou art glorious, grant me glory!" These ceremonies being finished,

[1] Institutes of Menu. ch. iii. 100.
[2] Asiat. Res. vii. 289.
[3] Ibid. ch. iii. 110.

the host fills a vessel with honey, curds, and clarified butter, and, covering it with another vessel, presents it to his guest, exclaiming three times, "Take the Madhuparca!" He, receiving, places it on the ground, and looking into it, says, "Thou art glorious, may I become so:" he tastes it three times, saying, "Thou art the sustenance of the glorious; thou art the nourishment of the splendid; thou art the food of the fortunate; grant me prosperity;" and then silently eats until he be satisfied. When this is done he sips water: and touching his mouth and other parts of his body with his hand, he says, "May there be speech in my mouth; breath in my nostrils; sight in my eyeballs; hearing in my ears; strength in my arms; firmness in my thighs: may my limbs and members remain unhurt together with my soul." Presents are then presented to him, suitable to the rank of the parties: and a barber who attends for the purpose, now exclaims, "The cow, the cow." The guest then pronounces the following text: "Release the cow from the fetters of Varuna. May she subdue my foe. May she destroy the enemies both of my host and me. Dismiss the cow that she may eat grass and drink water." At this intercession she is released, and thus the guest addresses her: "I have earnestly entreated this prudent person, saying, Kill not the innocent, harmless cow, who is mother of Rudras, daughter of Vasus, sister of Adityas, and the source of ambrosia."[1] Such is the mode in which the ceremonial duty of entertaining guests is celebrated, and such is an idea of the ceremonies which are included in the five daily sacraments of the Hindus.

As the daily ceremonies, however, in their full detail, are sufficient to engross the whole time of the votary; for those on whom the functions of society devolve, some alleviation of the burden, or rather, in the Hindu notion, some restriction of the privilege, was necessarily devised; and while the sanctity of entire accomplishment is reserved for the holy men who maintain perpetual fires, those who are engaged in the affairs of life are obliged to content themselves with a rite, called Vaiswadeva, in which all the daily sacraments, excepting that of the Veda, are comprised. It consists of oblations to the manes, to the gods, and spirits, and of donations to guests, all out of the food prepared for the daily meal; and is thus performed. Sitting down in a place free from impurities, and setting a vessel containing fire on his right hand, the worshipper hallows the ground by throwing away a lighted piece of cusa grass, while he recites the appropriate text,[2] and then places his fire on the consecrated spot, repeating the prayer

1 Colebrooke on the Religious Ceremonies of the Hindus. Asiat. Res. vii. 288 to 293.

2 "I dismiss far away carnivorous fire," &c. quoted above, p. 355.

which is used, when the household and sacrificial fires are kindled by the attrition of wood.[1] He next lays cusa grass on the eastern side of the fire, with its tips pointed towards the north, exclaiming, "I praise divine fire, primevally consecrated, the efficient performer of a solemn ceremony, the chief agent of a sacrifice, the most liberal giver of gems."[2] He spreads it on the southern side, with its points towards the east, reciting the commencement of the Yajurveda. 1. "I gather thee for the sake of rain. 2. I pluck thee" (at this he is supposed to break off the branch of a tree) "for the sake of strength. 3. Ye are" (he touches calves with the branch he has pulled off) "like unto air. 4. May the liberal generator of worlds make you" (here he touches, or is supposed to touch, milch-cows with the same branch) "happily reach this most excellent sacrifice."[3] In like manner he lays grass on the two other sides of the fire, on the western side with the tips to the north, crying, "Fire! approach to taste my offering; thou who art praised for the gift of oblations; sit down on this grass, thou, who art the complete performer of the solemn sacrifice;"[4] and on the northern side with the tips pointed to the east, saying, "May divine waters be auspicious to us, &c."[5] When all these ceremonies are completed, he stirs the fire, and sprinkles water upon it, after which, having his hands smeared with clarified butter, he offers food three several times, repeating, "Earth! sky! heaven!" Five similar oblations are next performed: one to the regent of fire; one to the god of medicine; one to the assembled deities; one to the lord of created beings; and one to the creator of the universe. Six more oblations are then offered with six prayers, every oblation having its separate prayer. 1. "Fire! thou dost expiate a sin against the gods; may this oblation be efficacious. 2. Thou dost expiate a sin against man. 3. Thou dost expiate a sin against the manes. 4. Thou dost expiate a sin against my own soul. 5. Thou dost expiate repeated sins. 6. Thou dost expiate every sin I have committed, whether wilfully or unintentionally: may this oblation be efficacious." He next worships the fire, making an oblation with the following prayer: "Fire! seven are thy fuels; seven thy tongues; seven thy holy sages; seven thy beloved abodes; seven ways do seven sacrificers worship thee; thy sources are seven; be content with this clarified butter; may this oblation be efficacious." As the sacred lamp was lighted for the

[1] "Fire! this wood is thy origin, which is attainable in all seasons; whence' being produced, thou dost shine. Knowing this, seize on it, and afterwards augment our wealth,"

[2] This is the first verse of the Rig Veda, with which it is customary to begin the daily perusal of that Veda.

[3] A lecture of the Yajush is always begun with this text.

[4] The text with which a lecture of the Samaveda is begun,

[5] The prayer which precedes a lecture of the At'hervan.

repulsion of evil spirits, before the oblations to the gods and the manes were presented, it is now extinguished, while recitation is made of the following text: "In solemn acts of religion, whatever fails through the negligence of those who perform the ceremony, may be perfected solely through meditation on Vishnu." The oblations to spirits are next offered: the performer depositing portions of food in the several places prescribed for it, having previously swept each place with his hand and sprinkled it with water. Near the spot where the vessel of water stands, he makes three offerings, saying, "Salutation to rain! to water! to the earth!" He makes them at both doors of his house to Dhatri, and Vidhatri, or Brahma, the protector and creator. He presents them toward the eight points of the compass, adding salutation to them, and to the regents of them. To Brahm, to the sky, and to the sun, he makes oblations with salutation in the middle of the house. He then offers similar oblations to all the gods; to all beings; to twilight; and to the lord of all beings. After the sacrament of spirits thus performed, the worshipper, shifting the sacramental cord, and looking toward the south, drops upon one knee, and presents an oblation to the manes of ancestors, saying, "Salutation to progenitors: may this ancestral food be acceptable." Having performed a lustration, he should then present food to his guests. "When he has thus," says Mr. Colebrooke, "allotted out of the food prepared for his own repast, one portion to the gods, a second to progenitors, a third to all beings, and a fourth to his guests, he and his family may then, and not before, consume the remaining portion of the food.' This ceremony must be regularly performed in the forenoon, by those to whom the full celebration of the five sacraments is impracticable; and by some persons it is repeated again in the evening.[1]

After this tedious though greatly abridged account of the daily ceremonies of the Hindus, we come to those which are performed at certain great and chosen epochs. On these, however, I shall content myself with some very general notices.

The Brahmens wait not for the period of birth to commence the ceremonies which pertain to each individual. "With auspicious acts," says the holy text, "prescribed by the Veda, must ceremonies on conception, and so forth, be duly performed, which purify the bodies of the three classes in this life, and qualify them for the next." Oblations to fire are required during the mother's pregnancy, and holy rites are commanded on the birth of the child. "Before the section of the navel-string, a ceremony is ordained on the birth of a male child: he must be made, while

[1] Colebrooke on the Religious Ceremonies of the Hindus. Asiat. Res. vii. 271 to 275.

sacred texts are pronounced, to taste a little honey and clarified butter from a golden spoon."[1] The ceremony of giving a name is ordained to be performed on the tenth or twelfth day after the birth: "or on some fortunate day of the moon, at a lucky hour, and under the influence of a star with good qualities."[2] The ceremony of the tonsure, which is one of the distinguishing marks of the first three classes, is a rite of great solemnity, commanded to be performed in the first or third year after birth.[3] But of all the ritual ordinances of the Hindus, none are reckoned more essential or important than those relating to the investiture. "In the eighth year from the conception of a Brahmen," says the law of Menu, "in the eleventh from that of a Cshatriya, and in the twelfth from that of a Vaisya, let the father invest the child with the mark of his class: Should a Brahmen, or his father for him, be desirous of his advancement in sacred knowledge, a Cshatriya of extending his power, or a Vaisya of engaging in mercantile business, the investiture may be made in the fifth, sixth, or eighth years respectively. The ceremony of investiture, hallowed by the gayatri, must not be delayed, in the case of a priest, beyond the sixteenth year; nor in that of a soldier, beyond the twenty-second; nor in that of a merchant, beyond the twenty-fourth. After that all youths of these three classes, who have not been invested at the proper time, become vratyas or outcasts, degraded from the gayatri, and contemned by the virtuous. With such impure men let no Brahmen, even in distress for subsistence, ever form a connexion in law, either by the study of the Veda, or by affinity."[4] The investiture, or institution, is usually denominated the second birth; and it is from this ceremony that the three highest classes are denominated the twice-born.[5] It consists chiefly in bestowing upon the object of the rite, a mantle, a girdle, a sacrificial cord, and a staff, with numerous ceremonies, prayers, and holy texts. "Let students of the Veda," says the law of Menu,[6] "wear for their mantles, the hides of black antelopes, of common deer, or of goats, with lower vests of woven sana, of cshuma, and of wool, in the direct order of their classes. The girdle of a priest must be made of munja, in a triple cord, smooth, and soft; that of a warrior must be a bowstring of murva; that of a merchant, a triple thread of sana. The sacrificial thread of a Brahmen must be made of cotton, so as to be put on over his head in three strings; that of a Csha-

[1] Institutes of Menu, ch. ii. 26, 27, 29.
[2] Ibid. 30.
[3] Ibid. 35.
[4] Ibid. 36 to 40.
[5] "The first birth is from a natural mother; the second, from the ligation of the zone; the third, from the due performance of the sacrifice; such are the births of him who is usually called twice-born." Ibid. 169.
[6] Ibid. 41 to 48, and 64, 65, 68.

triya, of sana thread only; that of a Vaisya, of woollen thread.[1] A priest ought by law to carry a staff of Bilva or Palasa; a soldier, of Bata or C'hadira; a merchant, of Venu or Udumbara. The staff of a priest must be of such a length as to reach his hair; that of a soldier to reach his forehead; and that of a merchant to reach his nose. Let all the staves be straight, without fracture, of a handsome appearance, not likely to terrify men, with their bark perfect, unhurt by fire. His girdle, his leathern mantle, his staff, his sacrificial cord, and his ewer, he must throw into the water, when they are worn out or broken, and receive others hallowed by mystical texts. The ceremony of cesanta, or cutting off the hair, is ordained for a priest in the sixteenth year from conception; for a soldier, in the twenty-second; for a merchant, two years later. Such is the revealed law of institution for the twice-born, an institution in which their second birth clearly consists, and which causes their advancement in holiness."

The ceremonies of marriage, which next call for our attention, are extremely numerous. The bridegroom is first of all received by the father of the bride with all the ceremonies of hospitality which we have already described; and during this time the bride is bathed.[2] When these rules are finished, the hand of the bride is placed in that of the bridegroom, both having been previously rubbed with some auspicious drug, and a matron binds them with cusa grass amid the sound of cheerful music. The father of the bride then bidding the attendant priests begin their acclamations, pours water from a vessel containing tila and cusa grass, upon the hands of the united pair, and uttering the words, "God the existent," and pronouncing the names and designations of the bridegroom, the bride, and himself, says, "I give unto thee this damsel, adorned with jewels, and protected by the lord of creatures." The bridegroom replies, "Well be it." The bridegroom then having received from the father of the bride a piece of gold, and recited an appropriate text, the parties are affianced, and walk forth, while the bridegroom thus addresses the bride:

[1] The Persians also had a cincture which was given them as a grand religious emblem, about the period of manhood. See the Sadda in Hyde, p. 441.

[2] Three vessels of water are poured severally upon her head, and at each time one of the following prayers is in order pronounced: 1. "Love! I know thy name. Thou art called an intoxicating beverage. Bring the bridegroom happily. For thee was framed the inebriating draught! Fire! thy best origin is here. Through devotion wert thou created. May this oblation be efficacious."—2. "Damsel, I anoint this thy generative organ with honey, because it is the second mouth of the Creator: by that thou subduest all males, though unsubdued; by that thou art lively, and dost hold dominion. May this oblation be efficacious."—3. "May the primeval ruling sages, who framed the female organ, as a fire that consumeth flesh, and thereby framed a procreating juice, grant the prolific power that proceeds from the three-horned bull, and from the sun."

"May the regents of space, may air, the sun, and fire, dispel that anxiety which thou feelest in thy mind, and turn thy heart to me. Be gentle in thy aspect, and loyal to thy husband; be fortunate in cattle, amiable in thy mind, and beautiful in thy person: be mother of valiant sons; be fond of delights; be cheerful; and bring prosperity to our bipeds and quadrupeds."[1] A libation of water is afterwards made; and the father of the bride, having meditated the gayatri, ties a knot with the skirts of the mantles of the bridegroom and bride, saying, "Ye must be inseparably united in matters of duty, wealth, and love." The bridegroom next attires the bride, with a variety of ceremonies, of which the following are the most remarkable. Going to the principal apartment of the house, he prepares a sacrificial fire, and hallows the implements; when one friend of his bearing a jar of water, walks round the fire, and stops on the south side of it; and another, performing the same ceremony, places himself on the right of the first. The bridegroom then casts four double handfuls of rice, mixed with leaves of Sami, into a flat basket; and placing near it a stone and mullar, which with formality he had previously touched, he causes the bride to be clothed with a new waistcloth and scarf, while he himself recites a variety of prayers. This being done, the bride goes to the western side of the fire, and recites a prayer, while she steps on a mat made of virana grass, and covered with silk. She then sits down on the edge of the mat, and the bridegroom makes six oblations of clarified butter, reciting a prayer with each.[2] After this he names the three worlds separately and conjointly, presenting oblations; and makes four or five oblations to fire and to the moon. After these he rises up with the bride, and passing from her left to her right, makes her join her hands in a hollow form. The rice, which was previously put in the basket, being then taken up, and the stone which was laid near being placed before the bride, she treads on it with the point of her right foot, while the bridegroom recites this prayer: "Ascend this stone; be firm like this stone; distress my foe, and be not subservient to my enemies." He then pours on her hands a ladleful of clarified butter; another person gives her the rice; two ladlefuls of butter are poured over it; when she separates her hands, and lets fall the rice on

[1] The latter part of this address Mr. Colebrooke thinks proper to veil in a Latin dress, and certainly with good reason: for, if it be considered that this is a speech of a bridegroom to his virgin bride, while the marriage ceremony is yet in the act of performance, it is an instance of grossness to which there is probably no parallel: The speech is as follows. Illa redamans accipito fascinum meum, quod ego peramans intromittam in eam, multæ quâ illecebræ sistunt.

[2] Of these the first may be taken as a specimen: may fire come first among the gods; may it rescue her offspring from the fetters of death; may Varuna, king of waters, grant that this woman should never bemoan a calamity befallen her children.

the fire, while a holy text is recited. She treads again on the stone, again makes an oblation of rice, again a prayer is recited, again walking is performed round the fire, again four or five oblations are made with similar ceremonies and prayers, when the bridegroom pours two ladlefuls of butter on the edge of the basket, and then rice out of it into the fire, saying, "May this oblation to fire be efficacious." After the ceremony of ascending the stone and throwing the rice into the fire, the bride is conducted to the bridegroom, and by him directed to step successively into seven circles, while seven texts are repeated. This is the most emphatical part of the ritual; for no sooner is the seventh step of the bride performed, than the nuptial bond is complete and irrevocable. The bridegroom then in appropriate texts addresses the bride, and the spectators, dismissing them; after which his friend, who stood near the sacrificial fire, bearing a jar of water, advances to the spot where the seventh step was completed, and, while a prayer is recited, pours water on the head, first of the bridegroom and then of the bride. Upon this, the bridegroom, putting his left hand under the hands of his bride, which are joined in a hollow posture, takes her right hand in his, and recites six holy texts; after which he sits down with her near the fire, and makes oblations, while severally and conjointly he names the three worlds. On the evening of the same day, when the stars begin to appear, the bride sits down on a bull's hide of a red colour, placed with the neck towards the east, and the hair upwards; and the bridegroom, sitting down beside her, makes oblations, naming the three worlds as usual; then six other oblations, pouring each time the remainder of the clarified butter on her head, and reciting prayers.[1] After rising up, and contemplating the polar star as an emblem of stability, matrons pour upon them water mixed with leaves, which had been placed upon an altar prepared for that purpose, and the bridegroom again makes oblations with the names of the worlds. He then eats food, prepared without factitious salt, reciting prayers during the meal: and when he has finished, the remainder is given to the bride. During the three subsequent days, the married couple must remain in the house of the father of the bride, must abstain from factitious salt, must live chastely and austerely, sleeping on the ground. On the fourth day the bridegroom carries her to his house, reciting texts when he ascends the carriage, and when they come to cross-roads. Leading her into his own house he chants a hymn, when matrons hail, and seat her on a bull's hide

[1] As these prayers have something in them characteristic, they had better here be presented: 1. "I obviate by this full oblation all ill marks in the lines of thy hands, in thy eye-lashes, and in the spots of thy body. 2. I obviate by this full oblation all the ill marks in thy hair; and whatever is sinful in thy looking or in thy crying. 3. I obviate by this full oblation all that may be sin-

as before, and the bridegroom recites a prayer. They place next a young child in her lap, putting roots of lotus, or fruits, into his hand; when the bridegroom takes him up, and preparing a sacrificial fire with all the usual ceremonies, makes eight different oblations, with as many prayers. The bride then salutes her father-in-law, and the other relations of her husband. The bridegroom prepares another sacrificial fire, and sits down with the bride on his right hand: when with the usual preliminary and concluding oblations to the three worlds, he makes twenty oblations, with as many prayers, throwing the remainder of each portion of the consecrated butter into a jar of water, which is afterwards poured on the head of the bride.

If the ceremonies prescribed for marriage are thus multiplied, trivial, and tiresome, those allotted to funerals are in point of number still more exorbitant and oppressive. After a specimen, however, of the Hindu ceremonies, there is something exceedingly monotonous in the detail of the rest; and hardly anything is more ungrateful than to be obliged to go through them. The reader is, therefore, spared the task of stndying the funeral rites of the Hindus, of which, notwithstanding, he may form a sufficient conception, as, in point of character, they exactly resemble those which have already been described.[1]

Of the monthly ceremonies, one may suffice to afford an idea of the whole. "From month to month," says the law of Menu, "on the dark day of the moon, let a twice-born man, having finished the daily sacrament of the Pitris, and his fire being still blazing, perform the solemn sraddha."[2] Of the sraddhas, which are numerous but very similar, the following is exhibited as a specimen. The person who is to perform the ceremony having purified the place by smearing it with cow-dung, raises on it an altar of sand of certain dimensions and form, washes his hands and feet, sips water, and puts a ring of cusa grass on the ring-finger of each hand. He then sits down on a cushion of cusa grass, and lights a lamp, reciting a prayer. He next places the utensils and materials in order, sprinkles water on himself and all around, meditates on Vishnu, surnamed the Lotos-eyed, meditates the gayatri, and after some ceremonies proceeds to invite

---

ful in thy temper, in thy speaking, and in thy laughing. 4. I obviate by this full oblation all the ill marks in thy teeth, and in the dark intervals between them; in thy hands and in thy feet. 5. I obviate by this full oblation all the ill marks on thy thighs, on thy privy part, on thy haunches, and on the lineaments of thy figure. 6. Whatever natural or accidental evil marks were on all thy limbs, I have obviated all such marks by these full oblations of clarified butter. May this oblation be efficacious."

[1] See a very full delineation of these funeral rites in Mr. Colebrooke's Second Essay on the Religious Ceremonies of the Hindus, Asiat. Res. vii. 239 to 264.

[2] Institutes of Menu, ch. iii. 122.

and to welcome the assembled gods and the manes. Two little cushions, of three blades of cusa grass, he places on one side of the altar for the Viswadevas, and six in front of it for the Pitris, and strewing on them cusa grass, he asks, "Shall I invoke the assembled gods?" *Do so;* is the answer; upon which he exclaims, "Assembled gods! hear my invocation: come and sit down on this holy grass." After scattering barley and meditating a prayer to the gods, he invites the manes of ancestors with similar invocations; and welcomes the gods and manes wit oblations of water, &c. in vessels made of leaves. He puts cusa grass into the vessels, and sprinkles them with water, while he recites the prayer, beginning, "May divine waters be auspicious to us;" he next throws barley into the vessels intended for the gods, and tila into those intended for the manes, with a prayer appropriate to each. The vessels are then taken up in succession, a prayer being repeated for each; the cusa grass placed on the vessels is put into the hand of a Brahmen; that which was under them is held in the hand of the person by whom the sraddha is performed; and he pours through it, on the hand of the Brahmen, the water which the vessels contained, then piles up the empty vessels in three sets, and overturns them, saying, while he reverses the first, "Thou art a mansion for ancestors." Taking up food smeared with clarified butter, he next makes two oblations to fire, with two corresponding prayers. The residue of the oblation, the performer having consecrated it by prayers and other ceremonies, having sweetened it with honey and sugar, and having meditated the gayatri with the names of worlds, is distributed among the Brahmens; and when they have eaten till they have acknowledged that they are satisfied, he gives them water to rinse their mouths. He then offers the cakes, consisting of balls or lumps of food, mixed with clarified butter, observing the requisite ceremonies. In the next place, he makes six libations of water from the palms of his hands, with the salutation to the seasons; then places with due ceremonies and texts, a thread on each funeral cake, to serve as apparel for the manes. After this he takes up the middle cake and smells it, or his wife, if they are desirous of male offspring, eats it, while they recite a correspondent prayer. He takes up the rest of the cakes, and smelling them one after another, throws them into a vessel; which done, they are given to a mendicant priest, or a cow, or else cast into the water. He then dismisses the manes, reciting a holy text, and having walked round the spot, and recited a prayer, departs.[1] "Formal obsequies," says Mr. Colebrooke, "are performed no less than ninety-six times in every year."[2]

[1] Colebrooke on the Religious Ceremonies of the Hindus, Asiat. Res. vii. 264 to 270. [2] Ibid. 270.

NOTE D. By H. H. W.

Very grave faults disfigure the whole of this review of the manners and character of the people of India, and they not only render it valueless as authority, but expose it to the imputation of want of liberality and candour.

That the Hindu character is not without blemishes is undeniable, but it is not such a monstrous mass of vice as is here depictured; nor is it so utterly devoid of all redeeming virtues. If the picture were faithful, it would be impossible, as Colonel Vans Kennedy justly observes, for society to be held together. "Rend asunder the ties which unite husband and wife, parent and child, banish faith, honesty, and truth, and be the indulgence of every furious and malignant passion fostered and sanctioned by religion, and then by what bonds and what relations can society be maintained."—Trans. Literary Society of Bombay, ii. 124.

Mr. Mill's unjust representation of the Hindu character has arisen from his unfortunate choice of guides, and, in some respects, uncandid use of them. At the time at which Orme was in India, the opportunities of acquiring any knowledge of the Hindus were exceedingly defective, and his account of them is short and imperfect: it was also posthumous, and was possibly not intended by him for publication. Buchanan could not learn the language, and was prejudiced against the people because they did not understand him. Tennant is evidently a superficial, ignorant, and self-sufficient observer. Another of his authorities, Mr. Tytler, is of more weight, but he was a young and active magistrate of police, and his opinions were naturally biassed by his professional occupations. He had little leisure or opportunity to form a knowledge of the natives, except as they came before him in the course of criminal proceedings. Yet he bears testimony to the possession by the Hindus of virtues as well as vices, although hs is unfairly quoted only as a witness of the latter. "The natives," he says, "have in their character many faults and many excellencies: at present they have, at least, the following good qualities, patience, mildness, obedience, hospitality, sobriety, temperance."

In like manner the testimony of Dubois is cited whenever it is hostile to the Hindus; but it is not noticed, that as a set-off to meet that which he censures, the Abbé pronounces the highest possible panegyric upon them. "The Hindus," he remarks, "are not in want of improvement in the discharge of social duties amongst themselves. They understand this point as well as and *perhaps better than Europeans.*" To the Abbé, however, as well as to Ward, and other witnesses of the same class, there are obvious objections. As Missionaries, and therefore it is to be concluded, persons of much moral and religious sensitiveness, they see the errors and vices of a heathen people through a medium by which they are exaggerated beyond their natural dimensions, and assume an enormity which would not be assigned to the very same defects in Christians. All the evidence then upon which Mr. Mill solely and implicitly relies is good for little: it is either partially quoted, or it is influenced by false views, or it is palpably erroneous. It must be wholly set aside, and we must look to an estimate of the Hindu character from other sources. These are not deficient, and, as might be expected, they are utterly at variance with Mr. Mill's incompetent guides.

Men equally eminent in wisdom as in station, remarkable for the extent of their opportunities of observation, and the ability and diligence with which they used them, distinguished for possessing by their knowledge of the language and literature of the country, and by their habits of intimacy with the natives, the best, the only means of judging of the native character, and unequalled for the soundness of their judgment, and the comprehensiveness of their views—these men have left upon record opinions highly favourable to the character of the Hindus. To none of these has Mr. Mill made any allusion whatever, and as there is reason to think that some of them were accessible, having been published in 1813, and being for other purposes actually quoted by him, the omission reflects seriously upon either his industry or his candour. It is to be hoped that they escaped his research, and it is possible that the early pages of the history were written prior to the date of the parliamentary investigation, by which the opinions referred to were called forth. In the evidence given before parliament in 1813, many of the witnesses were interrogated respecting the Hindu character; the answers were very remarkable, both for the opinions which were uttered, and the persons by whom they were expressed. To a chapter like the present they furnish a wholesome correction, and they deserve to be perpetuated along with the history of British India. They were the following:—

Mr. Græme Mercer, who, during a period of twenty-five years, had filled important political stations in distant parts of India, thus pronounces the result of his experience. "It is difficult to form a general character of the natives of an empire which extends from near the equinoctial line to thirty-one degrees of north latitude: if called upon for a general characteristic of the natives of that empire, I would say, that they are mild in their dispositions, polished in their general manners; in their domestic relations kind and affectionate—submissive to authority, and peculiarly attached to their religious tenets, and to the observance of the rites and ceremonies prescribed by those tenets. In referring to any distinction in this general characteristic, I should say, that the inhabitants of the northern provinces of Hindustan, were of a more bold and decided character, and less submissive to authority than those of the southern provinces, but equally attached to the observance of their religious rites and ceremonies."

Captain Sydenham, who had also held high political appointments, thus answers the question of the committee, regarding the moral character of the Hindoos. "It is really very difficult to give the character of so large a portion of the human race, who, although they possess many qualities in common, are of course distinguished by strong shades of difference in different parts of India, arising from the climate under which they live; the government to which they are subject; the distinction of castes which prevails more in some parts of India than in others; their habits and occupations, and other circumstances, which in all countries produce a difference in the moral character of men——— To define the moral character of so extensive a nation within the compass of any answer which it is in my power to give to the committee, will be of course extremely difficult; but I think the general character of the Hindoo is submissive, docile, sober, inoffensive, as long as his religious prejudices and habits are not violated: capable of great attachment and loyalty, as long as they are well treated by their governors and masters; quick in apprehension, intelligent, active, generally honest, and performing the duties of charity, benevolence, and filial affeetion with as much sincerity and regularity as any nation with which I am acquainted."

Sir John Malcolm speaks in similar terms as the preceding, of a difficulty which never occurs to the calumniators of the people of India, that of giving a general character of the different races subject to the British government, who vary as much, if not more, than the nations of Europe do from each other. The people of Bengal he describes as weak in body and timid in mind, and those below Calcutta, to be in character and appearance among the lowest of our Hindu subjects, but "from the moment you enter the district of Bahar, the Hindoo inhabitants are a race of men, generally speaking, not more distinguished by their lofty stature and robust frame, than they are for some of the finest qaalities of the mind—they are brave, generous, humane, and their truth is as remarkable as their courage." At a subsequent examination he bears witness to the favourable character of the natives generally, for veracity, fidelity, and honour. "I have hardly ever known," he observes, "where a person did understand the language, or where a calm communication was made to a native of India, through a well-informed and trustworthy medium, that the result did not prove, that what had at first been stated as falsehood, had either proceeded from fear, or from misapprehension. I by no means wish to state, that our Indian subjects are more free from this vice than other nations that occupy a nearly equal condition in society, but I am positive that they are not more addicted to untruth. With respect to the honour of our native subjects, it is, as that feeling is understood in this country, chiefly cherished by the military tribes, among whom I have known innumerable instances of its being carried to a pitch that would be considered in England more fit for the page of a romance than a history: with regard to their fidelity, I think, as far as my knowledge extends, there is, generally speaking, no race of men more to be trusted——— I should state, that there are few large communities in the world, whose dispositions are better, or (speaking to the virtues described in the question) more praiseworthy: it may also be stated as a general proof of their possessing those qualities, the attachment which almost all European masters who reside in India feel for their native servants. This feeling amongst those who understand the language, and who are of good temper and character, is almost without an exception."

Sir Thomas Munro, when asked if he thought the civilization of the Hindoos would be promoted by the trade with England being thrown open, replied, "I do not exactly understand what is meant by the 'civilization' of the Hindus. In the higher branches of science, in the knowledge of the theory and practice of good government, and in an education, which by banishing prejudice—and superstition—opens the mind to receive instruction of every kind from every quarter, they are much inferior to Europeans. But if a good system of agriculture, unrivalled manufacturing skill, a capacity to produce whatever can contribute to either convenience or luxury, schools established in every village for teaching reading, writing, and arithmetic, the general practice of hospitality and charity amongst each other, and above all, a treatment of the female sex, full of confidence, respect, and delicacy, are among the signs which denote a civilized people—then the Hindoos are not inferior to the nations of Europe, and if civilization is to become an article of trade between the two countries, I am convinced that this country will gain by the import cargo."

A still more impressive reply was made by Warren Hastings. Being asked if he could give the committee any general description of the national character of the people of India, as contrasted with that of the English, he replied, "In answering to this question, it will not be easy to divest my mind of certain circumstances connected with it, which do not relevantly pertain to the question itself. Great pains have been taken to inculcate into the public mind, an opinion, that the native Indians are in a state of complete moral turpitude, and live in the constant and unrestrained commission of every vice and crime that can disgrace human nature. I affirm, by the oath that I have taken, that this description of them is untrue, and wholly unfounded. What I have to add must be taken as my belief, but a belief impressed by a longer and more intimate acquaintance with the people than has fallen to the lot of many of my countrymen. In speaking of the people, it is necessary to distinguish the Hindoos, who form the great portion of the people of India, from the Mohammedans, who are intermixed with them, but generally live in separate communities; the former are gentle, benevolent, more susceptible of gratitude for kindness shown them than prompted to vengeance for wrongs inflicted, and as exempt from the worst propensities of human passion as any people upon the face of the earth; they are faithful and affectionate in service, and submissive to legal authority; they are superstitious, it is true, but they do not think ill of us for not thinking as they do. Gross as the modes of their worship are, the precepts of their religion are wonderfully fitted to promote the best ends of society, its peace and good order; and even from their theology, arguments may be drawn to illustrate and support the most refined mysteries of our own." He then alludes to their unanimous and voluntary testimony in his own behalf when known to be the object of an iniquitous prosecution in England, and justly observes, "this effort of theirs affords as strong a proof as can be afforded or conceived, that they themselves possess in a very high degree the principles of gratitude, affection, honour, and justice." Minutes of Evidence before Committees of both Houses of Parliament, March and April, 1813.

To the high authorities here cited, no additional testimony can be required; but the opinions they have placed on record, have been since repeated by other witnesses, all of a very different stamp from the flippant travellers and prejudiced missionaries upon whom Mr. Mill depends, and who have contemplated Indian manners and the character of the people under very different aspects, and with very various qualifications. The opinions of Col. Vans Kennedy, a distinguished scholar in both Mohammedan and Hindu literature, and a man of extraordinary reading and research, have been already cited, as given in a paper in the Bombay Transactions, written for the express purpose of exposing Mr. Mill's mistakes. Of a no less active and cultivated mind was the lamented Bishop Heber, and he repeatedly bears favourable testimony to the manners and character of the people of India. "To say that the Hindoos or Mussulmans are deficient in any essential feature of a civilized people, is an assertion which I can scarcely suppose to be made by any who have lived with them; their manners are at least as pleasing and courteous as those in the corresponding stations of life among ourselves." Journal ii. 382. "I do not by any means assent to the pictures of depravity and general worthlessness which some have drawn of the Hindoos. They are decidedly by nature, a mild, pleasing, and intelligent race; sober, parsimonious; and where an object is held out to them, most industrious and persevering." Ibid. ii. 329. "Of the people, so far as their natural character is concerned, I have been led to form on the whole a very favourable opinion. They have unhappily, many of the vices, arising from slavery, from an unsettled state of society, and immoral and erroneous systems of religion. But they are men of high and gallant courage, courteous, intelligent, and most eager after knowledge and improvement; with a remarkable aptitude for the abstract sciences, geometry, astronomy, &c.; and for the imitative arts, painting and sculpture. They are sober, industrious, dutiful to their parents, and affectionate to their children; of tempers almost uniformly gentle and patient, and more easily affected by kindness and attention to their wants and feelings than almost any men I have met with." Ibid. ii. 369. And in his charge to his clergy at Calcutta in 1824, he observes, "I have found in India, a race of gentle and temperate habits, with a natural talent and acuteness beyond the ordinary level of mankind." A third witness is of a very different description from all who preceded him; a Hindu, one, the great object of whose life was to elevate the moral and intellectual character of his countrymen, and who was little inclined to veil or palliate their faults. Rammohum Roy's opinions on the moral condition of the people of India, are thus recorded in the first appendix to the Third Report of the House of Commons, 1831, p. 293, and they are well entitled to consideration for their modest, moderate, and candid spirit.

The question put to him was, "will you state your general views with respect to the moral condition of the people?"—to which he answered: "a great variety of opinions on this subject has been already afloat in Europe, for some centuries past, particularly in recent times; some favourable to the people of India, some against them. Those Europeans who, on their arrival in India, happened to meet with persons whose conduct afforded them satisfaction, felt prepossessed in favour of the whole native population; others again, who happened to meet with ill-treatment and misfortunes, occasioned by the misconduct or opposition, social or religious, of the persons with whom they chanced to have dealings or communication, represented the whole Indian race in a corresponding light; while some, even without being in the country at all, or seeing or conversing with any natives of India, have formed an opinion of them at second-hand, founded on theory and conjecture. There is, however, a fourth class of persons, few indeed in number, who, though they seem unprejudiced, yet have differed widely from each other in many of their inferences, from facts equally within the sphere of their observation; as generally happens with respect to matters not capable of rigid demonstration. I therefore feel great reluctance in offering an opinion on a subject on which I may unfortunately differ from a considerable number of those gentlemen: however, being called upon for an opinion, I feel bound to state my impression, although I may perhaps be mistaken.

"From a careful survey, and observation of the people and inhabitants, of various parts of the country, and in every condition in life, I am of opinion, that the peasants or villagers, who reside away from large towns, and head-stations, and courts of law, are as innocent, temperate, and moral in their conduct, as the people of any country whatsoever; and the further I proceed towards the north and west, the greater the honesty, and simplicity, and independence of character, I meet with. The virtue of this class, however, rests at present chiefly on their primitive simplicity, and a strong religious feeling which leads them to expect reward or punishment, for their good or bad conduct; not only in the next world, but like the ancient Jews—also in this. 2nd. The inhabitants of the cities, towns, or stations, who have much intercourse with persons employed about the courts of law, by Zemindars, &c., and with foreigners and others, in a different state of civilization, and generally imbibe from them their habits and opinions: hence, their religious opinions are shaken, without any other principles being implanted to supply their place; consequently a great proportion of these are far inferior in point of character to the former class, and are very often even made tools of, in the nefarious work of perjury and forgery. 3rd. A third class consists of persons who are in the employ of Zemindars, or dependent for subsistence on the courts of law, who much depend for their livelihood, upon their shrewdness; and who not having generally, sufficient means to enter into commerce or business, these are, for the most part, worse than the second class. But I have met, I must confess, a great number of the second class, engaged in a respectable line of trade, who were men of real merit, worth, and character. Even among the third class, I have known many who had every disposition to act uprightly, and some actually honest in their conduct; and if they saw, by experience, that their merits were appreciated, that they might hope to gain an independence by honest means; and that just and honourable conduct afforded the best prospect of their being ultimately rewarded, by situations of trust and respectability they would learn to feel a high regard for character and rectitude of conduct, and from cherishing such feelings, become more and more worthy of public confidence; while their example would powerfully operate on the second class before noticed, which is generally dependent on them, and under their influence."

If to the opinions thus cited I venture to add my own, it is not with the notion that any weight can or need be added to their incontestable preponderance over the authorities on which reliance has been exclusively placed in the text; but under the impression, that it may be expected of me to give the result of a long and intimate acquaintance with the natives of Bengal under circumstances of a peculiar nature. I lived, both from necessity and choice, very much amongst them, and had opportunities of becoming acquainted with them in a greater variety of situations, than those in which they usually come under the observation of Europeans. In the Calcutta mint, for instance, I was in daily personal communication with a numerous body of artificers, mechanics, and labourers, and always found amongst them cheerful and unwearied industry, good humoured compliance with the will of their superiors, and a readiness to make whatever exertions were demanded from them: there were among them no drunkenness, no disorderly conduct, no insubordination. It would not be true to say, that there was no dishonesty, but it was comparatively rare, invariably petty, and much less formidable, than, I believe, it is necessary to guard against in other mints in other countries. There was considerable skill and ready docility. So far from there being any servility, there was extreme frankness, and I should say, that where there is confidence without fear, frankness is one of the most universal features in the Indian character. Let the people feel sure of the temper and good-will of their superiors, and there is an end of reserve or timidity, without the slightest departure from respect. In these same workmen, and in all the natives employed in the mint, from the highest to the lowest, I invariably witnessed grateful attachment to those by whom they were treated with merited consideration.

The studies which engaged my leisure brought me into connexion with a very different class of natives, the men of learning, and in them I found the similar merits of industry, intelligence, cheerfulness, frankness, with others, peculiar to their avocation. A very common characteristic of these men, and of the Hindus especially, was a simplicity truly childish, and a total unacquaintance with the business and manners of life; where this feature was lost, it was chiefly by those who had been long familiar with Europeans. Amongst the Pundits, or the learned Hindus, there prevailed great ignorance and great dread of the European character. There is, indeed, very little intercourse between any class of Europeans and Hindu scholars, and it is not wonderful, therefore, that much mutual misapprehension should prevail.

Taking an active part in the education of the natives, both in their own and in English literature, I had many opportunities of witnessing the native character developing itself in boyhood and in youth, and the object was one of profound interest. There can be little doubt, that the native mind outstrips in early years the intellect of the Europeans, and generally speaking, boys are much more quick in apprehension, and earnest in application, than those of our own schools — they are also more amiable, more easily controlled, more readily encouraged, more anxious to deserve the approbation of their masters and examiners. The early age at which they are married and enter into active life, is unfavourable to the full improvement of their moral and intellectual faculties; but during the greater part of the period of tuition, there is a strikingly interesting manifestation of right feeling and of comprehensive intellect in native youth.

Occasions of public and private intercourse with another class of natives, men of property and respectability, were not unfrequent during a residence of twenty-four years in Calcutta, and they afforded me many opportunities of witnessing polished manners, clearness and comprehensiveness of understanding, liberality of feeling, and independence of principle, that would have stamped them gentlemen in any country in the world. With some of this class I formed friendships which I trust to enjoy through life.

Without pretending to deny, then, that there are many and grave defects in the native character, some inseparable from human nature, and others ascribable to physical constitution, to political position, and to an absurd and corrupt religion, my own experience satisfies me that it also presents many virtues, and that the natives of India are an estimable and amiable people, who deserve and will requite with attachment and improvement the kindness and justice, which they have a right to demand from the strangers who rule over them.

THE END.

WERTHEIMER AND CO., PRINTERS, CIRCUS PLACE, FINSBURY.

THE HISTORY OF

BRITISH INDIA.

BY JAMES MILL, ESQ.

FIFTH EDITION WITH NOTES AND CONTINUATION,

BY HORACE HAYMAN WILSON, M.A., F.R.S

MEMBER OF THE ROYAL ASIATIC SOCIETY, OF THE ASIATIC SOCIETIES OF PARIS, BOSTON AND CALCUTTA, AND OF THE ORIENTAL SOCIETY OF GERMANY; OF THE IMPERIAL INSTITUTE OF FRANCE, AND THE IMPERIAL ACADEMIES OF VIENNA AND ST. PETERSBURGH; OF THE ROYAL ACADEMIES OF BERLIN AND MUNICH, ETC., ETC.; AND BODEN PROFESSOR OF SANSCRIT IN THE UNIVERSITY OF OXFORD.

VOLUME II.

LONDON:

JAMES MADDEN, 8, LEADENHALL STREET;

PIPER, STEPHENSON AND SPENCE,

PATERNOSTER ROW.

M.DCCC.LVIII.

LONDON:

PRINTED BY WERTHEIMER AND CO.,
CIRCUS PLACE, FINSBURY CIRCUS.

CONTENTS.

BOOK II.—OF THE HINDUS.

(CONTINUED).

CHAPTER VIII.

CHAPTER IX.

CHAPTER X.

BOOK III.—THE MOHAMMEDANS.

CHAPTER I.

CHAPTER II.

CHAPTER III.

CHAPTER IV.

CHAPTER V.

HISTORY

OF

BRITISH INDIA.

BOOK II.—OF THE HINDUS.

CHAPTER VIII.

The Arts.

BOOK II.
CHAP. VIII.

WE come now to the arts, necessary or ornamental, known to the Hindus. As the pleasures, to which the arts are subservient, form one of the grounds of preference between the rude and civilised condition of man, the improvement of the arts may be taken as one of the surest indications of the progress of society.

Of the Hindus, it may, first of all, be observed, that they little courted the pleasures derived from the arts, whatever skill they had attained in them. The houses, even of the great, were mean, and almost destitute of furniture;[1] their food was simple and common; and their dress had no distinction (which concerns the present purpose) beyond certain degrees of fineness in the texture.

If we desire to ascertain the arts which man would first practise, in his progress upwards from the lowest barbarism, we must inquire what are the most urgent of his wants. Unless the spontaneous productions of the soil supplied him with food, the means of insnaring, or killing the animals fit for his use by clubs or stones, and afterwards by his bow

[1] "The buildings are all base, of mud, one story high, except in Surat, where there are some of stone. The Emperor's own houses are of stone, handsome and uniform. The great men build not, for want of inheritance; but, as far as I have yet seen, live in tents, or houses worse than our cottages." Sir T. Roe's Letter to the Archbishop of Canterbury. Churchill, i. 803.

BOOK II. CHAP. VIII.

and arrows, would first engage his attention. How to shelter himself from the inclemency of the weather would be his second consideration; and where cavities of the earth or hollow trees supplied not his wants, the rude construction of a hut would be one of his earliest operations. A covering for his person would probably be the next of the accommodations which his feelings prompt him to provide. At first he contents himself with the skin of an animal; but it is surprising at how early a period he becomes acquainted with the means of fabricating cloth.[1] Weaving, therefore, and architecture, are among the first of the complicated arts which are practised among barbarians; and experience proves that they may be carried, at a very early period of society, to a high state of perfection. It has been remarked, too, that one of the earliest propensities which springs up in the breast of a savage is a love of ornament, of glittering trinkets, of bits of shining metals, or coloured stones, with which to decorate his person. The art, accordingly, of fetching out the brilliancy of the precious stones and metals, and fashioning them into ornaments for the person; the art, in fine, of jewellery, appears at an early period in the progress of a rude people.

These three, architecture, weaving, and jewellery, are the only arts for which the Hindus have been celebrated; and even these, with the exception of weaving, remained in a low state of improvement.

In a few places in Hindustan are found the remains of ancient buildings, which have attracted the attention of Europeans; and have, where there existed a predisposition to wonder and admire, been regarded as proofs of a high civilization. "The entry," says Dr. Robertson, "to the Pagoda of Chillambrum, is by a stately gate under a pyramid 122 feet in height, built with large stones above forty feet long, and more than five feet square, and all covered with plates of copper, adorned with an immense variety of figures neatly executed. The whole structure extends 1332 feet in one direction, and 936 in another. Some of the ornamental

[1] It is curious to observe how Plato traces this progress. He is endeavouring to account for the origin of society. Ιθι δη (ην δ'εγω) τῳ λογῳ εξ αρχης ποιωμεν πελιν· ποιησει δ'αυτην, ὡς εοικεν, ἡ ἡμετερα χρεια. Πως δ'ου; Αλλα μεν πρωτη γε και μεγιστη των χρειων, ἡ της τροφης παρασκευη, δευτερα δη οικησεως, τριτη εσθητος και των τοιουτων. Εστι ταυτα' φερε δη (ην δ'εγω) πως ἡ πολις αρκεσει επι τοσαυτην παρασκευην; αλλοτι, γεωργος μεν, εἱς, ὁ δε οικοδομος· αλλος δε τις ὑφαντης. Plat. de Repub. lib. ii. p. 599.

parts are finished with an elegance entitled to the admiration of the most ingenious artists."[1] The only article of precise information which we obtain from this passage is the great size of the building. As for the vague terms of general eulogy bestowed upon the ornaments, they are almost entirely without significance—the loose and exaggerated expressions, at second-hand, of the surprise of the early travellers at meeting with an object, which they were not prepared to expect. Another structure still more remarkable than that of Chillambrum, the Pagoda of Seringham, situated in an island of the river Cavery, is thus described by Mr. Orme. "It is composed of seven square enclosures, one within the other, the walls of which are twenty-five feet high, and four thick. These enclosures are 350 feet distant from one another, and each has four large gates with a high tower; which are placed, one in the middle of each side of the enclosure, and opposite to the four cardinal points. The outward wall is near four miles in circumference, and its gateway to the south is ornamented with pillars, several of which are single stones thirty-three long, and nearly five in diameter; and those which form the roof are still larger; in the inmost enclosures are the chapels."[2] In this nothing is described as worthy of regard except the magnitude of the dimensions.

The cave of Elephanta, not far from Bombay, is another work which, from its magnitude, has given birth to the supposition of high civilisation among the Hindus. It is a cavity in the side of a mountain, about half-way between its base and summit, of the space of nearly 120 feet square. Pieces of the rock, as is usual in mining, have been left at certain distances supporting the superincumbent matter; and the sight of the whole upon the entrance, is grand and striking. It had been applied at an early period to religious purposes, when the pillars were probably fashioned into the sort of regular form they now present, and the figures, with which great part of the inside is covered, were sculptured on the stone.[3]

[1] Robertson's Histor. Disquis. concerning India, p. 225.

[2] Orme's Hist. of Milit. Transac. of Indostan, i. 178.

[3] The cave of Elephanta is not the only subterranean temple of the Hindus, exhibiting on a large scale the effects of human labour. In the isle of Salsette, in the same vicinity, is a pagoda of a similar kind, and but little inferior to it in any remarkable circumstance. The pagodas of Ellora, about eighteen miles from Aurungabad, are not of the size of those of Elephanta and Salsette, but

Antecedently to the dawn of taste, it is by magnitude alone that, in building, nations can exhibit magnificence, and it is almost uniformly in honour of the gods, that this species of grandeur is first attempted. Experience alone could have made us comprehend, at how low a stage in the progress of the arts, surprising structures can be erected. The Mexicans were even ignorant of iron. They were unacquainted with the use of scaffolds and cranes. They had no beasts of burden. They were without sledges and carts. They were under the necessity of breaking their

they surprise by their number, and by the idea of the labour which they cost. See a minute description of them by Anquetil Duperron, Zendavesta, Disc. Prélim. p. ccxxxiii. The seven pagodas, as they are called at Mavalipuram, near Sadras, on the Coromandel coast, is another work of the same description; and several others might be mentioned. Dr. Tennant, who has risen higher above travellers' prejudices in regard to the Hindus, than most of his countrymen, says, "Their caves in Elephanta and Salsette are standing monuments of the original gloomy state of their superstition, and the imperfection of their arts, particularly that of architecture." Indian Recreations, i. 6. The extraordinary cavern, the temple of Pusa, near Chas-chou-fou, in China, which was visited by Lord Macartney, and full of living priests, vies in wonderful circumstances with the cave of Elephanta. See Barrow's Life of Lord Macartney, Journal, ii. 374. "However these gigantic statues, and others of similar form, in the caves of Ellora and Salsette may astonish a common observer, the man of taste looks in vain for proportion of form, and expression of countenance." Forbes' Oriental Memoirs, i. 423. "I must not omit the striking resemblance between these excavations (Elephanta, &c.) and the sculptured grottoes in Egypt," &c. "I have often been struck with the idea that there may be some affinity between the *written mountains* in Arabia, and the excavated mountains in Hindustan." Ibid. i. 442, 449. It is difficult to say how much of the wonderful in these excavations may be the mere work of nature: "Left Sullo, and travelled through a country beautiful beyond imagination, with all possible diversities of rock; sometimes towering up like ruined castles, spires, pyramids, &c. We passed one place so like a ruined Gothic abbey, that we halted a little, before we could satisfy ourselves that the niches, windows, ruined staircase, &c. were all natural rock. A faithful description of this place would certainly be deemed a fiction." Mungo Park's last Mission to Africa, p. 75. "Between the city of Canton, and first pagoda, on the bank of the river, is a series," says Mr. Barrow, "of stone-quarries, which appear not to have been worked for many years. The regular and formal manner in which the stones have been cut away, exhibiting lengthened streets of houses with quadrangular chambers, in the sides of which are square holes at equal distances, as if intended for the reception of beams; the smoothness and perfect perpendicularity of the sides, and the number of detached pillars that are scattered over the plain, would justify a similar mistake to that of Mr. Addison's doctor of one of the German universities, whom he found at Château d'Un in France, carefully measuring the free-stone quarries at that place, which he conceived to be the venerable remains of vast palaces of great antiquity." Barrow's Travels in China, p. 599. The conclusions of many of our countrymen in Hindustan will bear comparison with that of the German doctor in France. It is not a bad idea of Forster, the German commentator upon the travels of P. Paolino, that the forming caverns into temples must naturally have been the practice when men as yet had their principal abodes in caverns. Voyage aux Indes Orien. par le P. Paolino, iii. 115. Volney says, "those labyrinths, temples, and pyramids, by their huge and heavy structure, attest much less the genius of a nation, opulent and friendly to the arts, than the servitude of a people, who were slaves to the caprice of their monarch." Travels in Egypt, &c. i. 282.

stones with flints, and polished them by rubbing one against another. Yet they accomplished works, which, in magnitude and symmetry, vie with any thing of which Hindustan has to boast. "The great temple," says Clavigero, "occupied the centre of the city. Within the enclosure of the wall, which encompassed it in a square form, the conqueror Cortez affirms that a town of 500 houses might have stood. The wall, built of stone and lime, was very thick, eight feet high, crowned with battlements in the form of niches, and ornamented with many stone figures in the shape of serpents. It had four gates to the four cardinal points. Over each of the four gates was an arsenal, filled with a vast quantity of offensive and defensive weapons, where the troops went, when it was necessary, to be supplied with arms. The space within the walls was curiously paved with such smooth and polished stones that the horses of the Spaniards could not move upon them withont slipping and tumbling down. In the middle was raised an immense solid building of greater length than breadth, covered with square equal pieces of pavement. The building consisted of five bodies, nearly equal in height, but different in length and breadth; the highest being narrowest. The first body, or basis of the building, was more than fifty perches long from east to west, and about forty-three in breadth from north to south. The second body was about a perch less in length and breadth than the first; and the rest in proportion. The stairs, which were upon the south side, were made of large well-formed stones, and consisted of 114 steps, each a foot high. Upon the fifth body (the top) was a plain, which we shall call the upper area, which was about forty-three perches long, and thirty-four broad, and was as well paved as the great area below. At the eastern extremity of this plain were raised two towers, to the height of fifty-six feet. These were properly the sanctuaries, where, upon an altar of stone, five feet high, were placed the tutelary idols."[1] The Tlascalans, as a rampart against the Mexican troops, erected a wall, "six miles in length, between two mountains; eight feet in height, besides the breast-work, and eighteen feet in thickness."[2]

Garcilasso de la Vega informs us that "the Incas, who

[1] Clavigero, Hist. of Mexico, book vi. sect. 10.
[2] Ibid. book vii. sect. 26.

BOOK II. CHAP. VIII.

were kings of Peru, erected many wonderful and stately edifices: their castles, temples, and royal palaces," says he, "their gardens, store-houses, and other fabrics, were buildings of great magnificence, as is apparent by the ruins of them. The work of greatest ostentation, and which evidences most the power and majesty of the Incas, was the fortress of Cozco, whose greatness is incredible to any who have not seen it, and such as have viewed it with great attention cannot but admire it, and believe that such a work was raised by enchantment, or the help of spirits, being that which surpasses the art and power of man. For the stones are so many and so great which are laid in the three first rounds, being rather rocks than stones, as passes all understanding, how, and in what manner, they were hewn from the quarry or brought from thence, for they had no instruments of iron or steel wherewith to cut or fashion them: nor less wonderful is it to think, how they could be carried to the building; for they had neither carts nor oxen to draw them with; and if they had, the weight was so vast as no cart could bear, or oxen draw; then to think that they drew them with great ropes, over hills and dales, and difficult ways, by the mere force of men's arms, is alike incredible; for many of them were brought ten, twelve, or fifteen leagues off. But to proceed further in our imagination of this matter, and consider how it was possible for the people to fit and join such vast machines of stones together, and cement them so close, that the point of a knife can scarce pass between them, is a thing above all admiration; and some of them are so artificially joined, that the crevices are scarce discernible between them. Then to consider that to square and fit these stones one to the other, they were to be raised and lifted up and removed often, until they were brought to their just size and proportion; but how this was done by men who had no use of the rule and the square, nor knew how to make cranes or pulleys, and cramps and other engines, to raise and lower them as they had occasion, is beyond imagination."[1]

[1] Royal Commentaries of Peru, by the Inca Garcilasso de la Vega, book vii. ch. xxviii. Acosta likewise says (see his Natural and Moral History of the Indies, book vi. ch. xiv), that of these stones he measured one, at Tiagunaco, which was thirty-eight feet long, eighteen broad, and six in thickness; and that the stones in that building were not so large as those in the fortress of Cuzco. He adds, " And that which is most strange, these stones, being not cut, nor squared to join, but contrariwise, very unequal one with another in form and greatness, yet did they join them together without cement, after an

Whatever allowance any preconceptions of the reader may lead him to make for exaggeration, which we may believe to be considerable, in the above descriptions, enough undoubtedly appears to prove, that no high attainments, in civilisation and the arts, are implied in the accomplishment of very arduous and surprising works in architecture; and it will be allowed that such comparisons between the attainments of different nations, are the only means of forming a precise judgment of the indications of civilisation which they present. The Gothic cathedrals reared in modern Europe, which remain among the most stupendous monuments of architecture in that quarter of the globe, were constructed, many of them, at least, at comparatively a very low stage of civilisation and science. To allude to Nineveh and Babylon, is to bring to the recollection of the historical reader, the celebrated works of architecture, in temples, walls, palaces, bridges, which distinguished those ancient cities. Yet it is demonstrated, that no high degree of improvement was attained by the people that erected them. The pyramids of Egypt, vast as their dimensions, and surprising their durability, afford intrinsic evidence of the rudeness of the period at which they were reared.[1] According to Strabo, the sepulchre of Belus, at Babylon, was a pyramid of one stadium in height. It appears to have been built of different bodies, or stages, one rising above another, exactly in the manner of the great temple at Mexico. A tower, says Herodotus, a stadium both in length and breadth, is reared at the base; and upon this is erected another tower, and

incredible manner." Acosta tells us, however (Ibid.), that they were entirely unacquainted with the construction of arches. Humboldt, who could have no national partialities on the subject, is almost as lofty in his praises of the remains of the ancient architecture of the Mexicans and Peruvians. "Au Mexique et au Pérou," says he, Tableaux de la Nature, i. 168, "on trouve partout dans les plaines élevées des montagnes, des traces d'une grande civilization. Nous avons vu, à une hauteur de seize à dix-huit cent toises, des ruines de palais et de bains." The ruins which he saw of a palace of immense size, are mentioned at p. 158.

[1] "Let us now speak," says the President Goguet, Origin of Laws, part iii. book ii. ch. i. "of the bridge of Babylon, which the ancients have placed in the number of the most marvellous works of the East. It was near 100 fathoms in length, and almost four in breadth, &c......... While we do justice to the skill of the Babylonians, in conducting these works, we cannot help remarking the bad taste, which, at all times, reigned in the works of the eastern nations. The bridge of Babylon furnishes a striking instance of it. This edifice was absolutely without grace, or any air of majesty......... Finally, this bridge was not arched." The first chiefs in Iceland built no inconsiderable houses. Ingulph's palace was 135 feet in length. Mallet. Introd. Hist. Denmark, vol. i. ch. xiii.

again another upon that, to the number of eight towers in all.[1]

Sonnerat informs us, "that the architecture of the Hindus is very rude; and their structures in honour of their deities are venerable only from their magnitude."[2] "Mail-cotay," says Dr. Buchanan, "is one of the most celebrated places of Hindu worship, both as having been honoured with the actual presence of an avatara, or incarnation of Vishnu, who founded one of the temples; and also as being one of the principal seats of the Sri Vaishnavam Brahmans, and having possessed very large revenues. The large temple is a square building of great dimensions, and entirely surrounded by a colonnade; but it is a mean piece of architecture, at least outwardly. The columns are very rude, and only about six feet high. Above the entablature, in place of a balustrade, is a clumsy mass of brick and plaster, much higher than the columns, and excavated with numerous niches, in which are huddled together many thousand images, composed of the same materials, and most rudely formed. The temple itself is alleged to be of wonderful antiquity, and to have been not only built by a god, but to be dedicated to Krishna, on the very spot where that avatara performed some of his great works."[3] Of the celebrated pagodas at Congeveram, the same author remarks, that "they are great stone buildings, very clumsily executed, both in their joinings and carvings, and totally devoid of elegance or grandeur, although they are wonderfully crowded with what are meant as ornaments."[4]

[1] Herodot. Clio. 181. Major Rennel, who was obliged to trust to Mr. Beloe's translation, was puzzled with the expression, "a tower of the solid depth and height of one stadium;" justly pronounces it incredible, and says, "Surely Herodotus wrote *breadth* and *length*, and not breadth and height," (Geog. of Herodot. pp. 359, 360), which is precisely the fact, the words of Herodotus being και το μηκος και το ευρος. The word στερεος, too, here translated *solid*, as if the tower was a mere mass of brick-work, without any internal vacuity, by no means implies a fact so very improbable. Στερεος means *strong*, *firmly built*, &c. This resemblance has been noticed by Humboldt (Essai Polit. sur la Nouv. Espagne,) p. 170, also that between the pyramids of Egypt, and the vast pyramids of which the remains are to be found in Mexico, p. 187. The palace of Montezuma bore a striking resemblance to that of the Emperor of China, p. 190.

[2] Voyage Sonnerat, liv. iii. ch. viii.

[3] Buchanan's Journey through Mysore, &c. ii. 70.

[4] Id. Ibid. i. 13. Sir James Mackintosh ingeniously remarks, that among the innumerable figures of men and monsters of all sorts exhibited at Ellora, you perceive about one in ten thousand that has some faint rudiments of grace, those lucky hits, the offspring of chance, rather than design, which afford copies to a rude people, and enable them to make gradual improvements.

Wonderful monuments of the architecture of rude nations are almost everywhere to be found. Mr. Bryant, speaking of the first rude inhabitants of Sicily, the *Cyclopes*, who were also called Lestrygons and Lamii, says, "They erected many temples, and likewise high towers upon the sea-coast; and founded many cities. The ruins of some of them are still extant; and have been taken notice of by Fazellus, who speaks of them as exhibiting a most magnificent appearance. They consist of stones which are of great size. Fazellus, speaking of the bay, near Segesta, and of an hill which overlooked the bay, mentions wonderful ruins upon its summit, and gives an ample description of their extent and appearance."[1] The old traveller, Knox, after describing the passion of the Ceylonese for constructing temples and monuments of enormous magnitude, in honour of their gods, drily adds, "As if they had been born solely to hew rocks and great stones, and lay them up in heaps;"[2] the unsophisticated decision of a sound understanding, on operations which the affectation of taste, and antiquarian credulity, have magnified into proofs of the highest civilisation.[3]

"Rude nations," (says Dr. Ferguson, Hist. of the Roman Republic, i. 18, ed. 8vo.) "sometimes execute works of great magnificence, for the purposes of superstition or war; but seldom works of mere convenience or cleanliness." Yet the common sewers of Rome, the most magnificent that ever were constructed, are assigned to the age of the elder Tarquin. Polybius tells us, that the city of Ecbatana, in Media, which contained one of the palaces of the Persian kings, far excelled all other cities in the world, πλουτῳ και τῃ της κατασκευης πολυτελειᾳ μεγα τι παρα τας αλλας δοκει διενηνοχεναι πολεις. With regard to the palace itself, he was afraid, he said, to describe its magnitude and magnificence, lest he should not be believed. It was seven stadia in circumference; and though all the wood employed in it was cedar or cypress, every part of it, pillars, cornices, beams, every thing was covered with plates of silver or gold, so that no where was a bit of wood visible; and it was roofed with silver tiles. Polyb. Hist. lib. x. 24.

[1] Bryant's Ancient Mythology, book v. p. 311. From p. 187 to 213, an ample and instructive collection will be found of instances to prove the passion of rude nations for erecting great buildings; and the degree of perfection in art which their works display. Priam's palace, according to Homer, was a magnificent building. That remarkable structure, the labyrinth of Crete, was produced at a very early age. Mr. Ward assures us, "that of the Hindu temples none appear to be distinguished for the elegance of their architecture: they are not the work of a people sunk in barbarism; neither will they bear any comparison with the temples of the Greeks and Romans." He adds, "We learn from the Ain Akburee, however, that the entire revenues of Orissa, for twelve years, were expended in erecting a temple to the sun." Introd. p. lx.

[2] Knox's Hist. of Ceylon, London, 1681.

[3] This laborious description of the architecture of the Hindus, affords some curious specimens of the inveteracy of the author's prejudices. In his zeal to undervalue the cavern-temples of the Hindus, he even insinuates that they are not artificial. "It is difficult to say, how much of the wonderful in these excavations, may be the work of nature." N. p. 4. And in the quarto edition, he seemed inclined, with Bryant, to think that it was not impossible that the

Of one very necessary and important part of architecture, the Hindus were entirely ignorant. They knew not the construction of arches, till they first learned it from their Moslem conquerors. In the description of the superb temple at Seringham, we have already seen[1] that no better expedient was known than great flat stones for the roof. "On the south branch of the river Cavery, at Seringapatam," says Dr. Buchanan, "a bridge has been erected, which serves also as an aqueduct, to convey from the upper part of the river a large canal of water into the town and island. The rudeness of this bridge will show the small progress that the arts have made in Mysore. Square pillars of granite are cut from the rock, of a sufficient height to rise above the water at the highest floods. These are placed upright in rows, as long as the intended width of the bridge, and distant about ten feet from each other. They are secured at the bottom by being let into the solid rock, and their tops being cut to a level, a long stone is laid upon each row. Above these longitudinal stones, others are placed contiguous to each other, and stretching from row to row, in the direction of the length of the bridge."[2] The celebrated bridge over the Euphrates, at Babylon, was constructed on similar princi-

pyramids had dropped from the clouds, or sprung out of the soil. "Mr. Bryant offers strong reasons to prove, that the pyramids in Egypt were, in a great measure, the work of nature, not of art." 4to. Ed. N. 335. It is quite as likely that the caves, as that the pyramids, were the work of nature—not of art, agreeably to Mr. Bryant's "strong reasons." Magnitude is not the only element of beauty in the cavern-temples. The columns are carved with great elegance and fitness of design, and many of the figures are graceful and expressive. No notice is taken of the numerous remains of temples, in various parts of India, in which extreme architectural beauty is to be found. And it may be doubted if those observers whom he has cited, have done justice to the edifices of which they speak so disparagingly. What is more to the purpose, however, is, that the Hindus did not "heap up stones" without a reason. They had reduced architecture to a science; and although they depart, in the variety, and sometimes grotesqueness of their details, from the stately simplicity of Grecian art, yet, their rules of proportion are very much the same. Ignorance of the arch, which is presently objected to them, is common to them and the Greeks. See Rám Ráz, on Hindu Architecture. Sykes on the Caves of Ellora. Trans. R. As. Soc. Grindlay's Architecture of Western India. Daniell's Engravings of the Caves of Ellora. J. Prinsep's Sketches of Benares, and a variety of pictorial works, which afford ocular demonstration, even to untravelled observers, of our author's injustice to Indian architecture.—W.

[1] See above, p. 3. "Their knowledge of mechanical powers," says Mr. Orme, is so very confined, that we are left to admire, without being able to account for, the manner in which they have erected their capital pagodas. It does not appear that they had ever made a bridge of arches over any of their rivers, before the Mahomedans came amongst them." History of Mil. Trans. of Indostan, i. 7.

[2] Buchanan's Journey through Mysore, &c. i. 61.

ples, and the president Goguet remarks "that the Babylonians were not the only people who were ignorant of the art of turning an arch. This secret," he adds, "as far as I can find, was unknown to all the people of remote antiquity."[1] Though the ancient inhabitants, however, of Persia, were ignorant of this useful and ingenious art, the modern Persians are admirably skilled in it; the roofs of the houses are almost all vaulted; and the builders are peculiarly dexterous in constructing them.[2]

Of the exquisite degree of perfection to which the Hindus have carried the productions of the loom, it would be idle to offer any description; as there are few objects with which the inhabitants of Europe are better acquainted. Whatever may have been the attainments, in this art, of other nations of antiquity, the Egyptians, for example, whose fine linen was so eminently prized, the manufacture of no modern nation can, in delicacy and fineness, vie with the textures of Hindustan. It is observed at the same time, by intelligent travellers, that this is the only art which the original inhabitants of that country have carried to any considerable degree of perfection.[3]

[1] Goguet, Origin of Laws, part iii. book ii. ch. i. He says, "it even appears to me demonstrated, that the Egyptians had not much more knowledge of architecture, of sculpture, and of the fine arts in general, than the Peruvians and the Mexicans. For example, neither the one nor the other knew the secret of building vaults. What remains of foundery or sculpture, is equally clumsy and incorrect. I think this observation absolutely essential." Origin of Laws, part iii. dissert. iii. Clavigero, however, asserts that the Mexicans did know the art of constructing arches and vaults, as appears, he says, from their baths, from the remains of the royal palaces of Tezcuco, and other buildings, and also from several paintings. Hist. Mex. book. vii. sect. 53.

[2] Chardin, Voy. en Perse, iii. 16. ed. 4to. Amsterd. 1785. "On est frappé [à Ispahan] de l'élégante architecture des ponts: l'Europe n'offre rien qui leur soit comparable pour la commodité des gens de pied, pour la facilité de leur passage, pour les faire jouir sans trouble, le jour, de la vue de la rivière et de ses environs, et, le soir, de la fraîcheur de l'air." Olivier, Voyage, &c. v. 180. "La sculpture est nulle en Perse......... Mais l'architecture, plus simple plus élégante, mieux ordonnée que chez les Turcs, est tout-à-fait adaptée au climat. Les plafonds et les dômes sont d'une recherche, d'un fini, d'un précieux, d'une richesse qui étonne ....Les Persans ont poussé fort loin l'art de faires les voûtes........Les toits de leurs maisons sont voûtés, leur planchers le sont aussi." Ibid. v. 298, 299. The skill in architecture of the Turks, a very rude people, is well known. "Perhaps I am in the wrong, but some Turkish mosques in Constantinople please me better than St. Sophia.—That of Validé Sultan is the largest of all, built entirely of marble; the most prodigious, and I think the most beautiful structure I ever saw. Between friends, St. Paul's Church would make a pitiful figure near it." Letters of Lady Mary Wortley Montague, Works, ii. 249, 250.

[3] "No art in Hindustan is carried to the same degree of perfection as in Europe, except some articles in which the cheapness of labour gives them an advantage, as in the case of the fine muslins at Dacca." Tennant's Indian Recreations, i. 104. The people are in a state of gross rudeness, Buchanan informs us, "in every part of Bengal, where arts have not been introduced by foreigners; the only one that has been carried to tolerable perfection is that of weaving." Journey through Mysore, &c. ii. 285.

To the skill of the Hindus, in this art, several causes contributed. It is one of the first to which the necessities of man conduct him:[1] it is one of those whichexperience proves to arrive early at high perfection; and it is an art to which the circumstances of the Hindu were in a singular manner adapted. His climate and soil conspired to furnish him with the most exquisite material for his art, the finest cotton which the earth produces. It is a sedentary occupation, and thus in harmony with his predominant inclination. It requires patience, of which he has an inexhaustible fund; it requires little bodily exertion, of which he is always exceedingly sparing; and the finer the production, the more slender the force which he is called upon to apply. But this is not all. The weak and delicate frame of the Hindu is accompanied with an acuteness of external sense, particularly of touch, which is altogether unrivalled, and the flexibility of his fingers is equally remarkable. The hand of the Hindu, therefore, constitutes an organ, adapted to the finer operations of the loom, in a degree which is almost, or altogether, peculiar to himself.[2]

Yet the Hindus possessed not this single art in so great a degree of perfection, compared with rude nations, as, even on that ground, to lay a foundation for very high pretensions. "In Mexico," says Clavigero, "manufacturers of various kinds of cloth were common everywhere; it was one of those arts which almost every person learned. Of cotton, they made large webs, and as delicate and fine as those of Holland, which were with much reason highly es-

[1] Mr. Park tells us that the arts of spinning, weaving, and dyeing cotton, are familiar to the Africans. Travels, p. 17.

[2] "A people," says Mr. Orme, "born under a sun too sultry to admit the exercises and fatigues necessary to form a robust nation, will naturally, from the weakness of their bodies (especially if they have few wants), endeavour to obtain their scanty livelihood by the easiest labours. It is from hence, perhaps, that the manufactures of cloth are so multiplied in Indostan. Spinning and weaving are the slightest tasks which a man can be set to, and the numbers that do nothing else in this country are exceeding." He adds: "The hand of an Indian cook-wench shall be more delicate than that of an European beauty; the skin and features of a porter shall be softer than those of a professed *petit-maître*. The women wind off the raw silk from the pod of the worm. A single pod of raw silk is divided into twenty different degrees of fineness; and so exquisite is the feeling of these women, that whilst the thread is running through their fingers so swiftly, that their eye can be of no assistance, they will break it off exactly as the assortments change, at once from the first to the twentieth, from the nineteenth to the second. The women likewise spin the thread designed for the cloths, and then deliver it up to the men, who have fingers to model it as exquisitely as these have prepared it." Orme, on the Gov. and People of Indostan, p. 409 to 413.

teemed in Europe. A few years after the conquest, a sacerdotal habit of the Mexicans was brought to Rome, which, as Boturini affirms, was uncommonly admired on account of its fineness. They wove these cloths with different figures and colours, representing different animals and flowers."[1] When the Goths first broke into the Roman empire, they possessed fringed carpets and linen garments of so fine a quality, as greatly surprised the Greeks and Romans, and have been thought worthy of minute description by Eunapius and Zosimus.[2] "Pliny, speaking of a carpet for covering such beds as the ancients made use of at table, says, that this piece of furniture, which was produced from the looms of Babylon, amounted to eighty-one thousand sestertia."[3] This proves the fineness to which that species of manufacture was then wrought, and the excellence which the Babylonians, who yet could not construct an

[1] Clavigero, Hist. of Mexico, book vii. sect. 57.

[2] See Gibbon (Hist. of the Decl. and Fall of the Rom. Emp. iv. 364), who says, "Yet it must be presumed, that they (the carpets and garments) were the manufactures of the provinces; which the barbarians had acquired as the spoils of war, or as the gifts or merchandise of peace." But had they been the manufactures of the provinces, the Romans must have known them familiarly for what they were; and could never have been so much surprised with their own manufactures, transferred by plunder, gift, or sale to the barbarians (of none of which operations, had they existed, could they have been altogether ignorant), as to make their historians think it necessary to place a minute description of them in their works.

[3] Goguet, Origin of Laws, part iii. book vi. ch. i. art. 2. That diligent and judicious writer says, "Of all the arts of which we have to speak in this second part, there are none which appear to have been more or better cultivated than those which concern clothing. We see taste and magnificence shine equally in the description Moses gives of the habits of the high priest and the veils of the tabernacle. The tissue of all these works was of linen, goat's hair, wool, and byssus. The richest colours, gold, embroidery, and precious stones, united to embellish it." Ibid. part ii. book ii. ch. ii. The following lofty description of the tissues of Babylon, by Dr. Gillies (see the description of Babylon, in his History of the World), is not surpassed by the most strained panegyrics upon the weaving of the Hindus. "During the latter part of Nebuchadnezzar's reign, and the twenty-six years that intervened between his death and the conquest of his capital by Cyrus, Babylon appears not only to have been the seat of an imperial court, and station for a vast garrison, but the staple of the greatest commerce that perhaps was ever carried on by one city. Its precious manufactures under its hereditary sacerdotal government remounted, as we have seen, to immemorial antiquity. The Babylonians continued thenceforward to be clothed with the produce of their own industry. Their bodies were covered with fine linen, descending to their feet; their mitres or turbans were also of linen, plaited with much art; they wore woollen tunics, above which a short white cloak repelled the rays of the sun. Their houses were solid, lofty, and separated, from a regard to health and safety, at due distances from each other: within them the floors glowed with double and triple carpets of the brightest colours; and the walls were adorned with those beautiful tissues called Sindones, whose fine yet firm texture was employed as the fittest clothing for eastern kings. The looms of Babylon, and of the neighbouring Borsippa, a town owing its prosperity to manufactures only, supplied to all countries round the finest veils or hangings, and every article of dress or furniture composed of cotton, of linen, or of wool."

arch, had attained in the art. The Asiatic nations seem to have excelled, from the earliest ages, in the manufactures of the loom. It is by Pliny recorded, as the opinion of his age and nation, that of the art of weaving cotton, Semiramis is to be revered as the inventress. The city Arachne, celebrated by the Greeks and Romans, as the place where weaving was first invented, and where it was carried to the highest perfection, is represented by Mr. Bryant as the same with Erech or Barsippa, and situated on the Euphrates, in the territory of Babylon.[1] One of the accomplishments of the goddess of wisdom herself (so early was the date), was her unrivalled excellence in the art of weaving; and Arachne, according to the poets, was a virgin, who, daring to vie with Minerva in her favourite art, was changed into a spider for her presumption.[2]

That ingenuity is in its infancy among the Hindus, is shown by the rudeness still observable in the instruments of this their favourite art. The Hindu loom, with all its appurtenances, is coarse and ill-fashioned, to a degree, hardly less surprising than the fineness of the commodity which it is the instrument of producing. It consists of little else than a few sticks or pieces of wood, nearly in the state in which nature produced them, connected together by the rudest contrivances. There is not so much as an expedient for rolling up the warp. It is stretched

[1] Bryant's Ancient Mythology, iii. 425. It was from this city the spider (Arachne), for its curions web, was said to have derived its name. The poet Nonnus thus celebrates its manufactures:

Και πορε ποικιλα πεπλα, τα περ' παρα Τιγριδος ὑδωρ
Νηματι λεπταλεῳ τεχνησατο Περσις Αραχνη.

Again:

Νηρευς μεν ταδε δωρα πολυτροπα· δωκε δε κουρῃ
Περσικος Ευφρητης πολυδαιδαλον εἱματ' Αραχνης.

Nonnus, lib. xviii. p. 326, Edit. 1569; et lib. xlii. p. 747. See the brilliant description which Chardin gives of the exquisite skill of the modern Persians in the art of weaving; of the extraordinary beauty and value of their gold velvets. They make not fine cottons, he says, only for this reason, that they can import them cheaper from India. Chardin, Voyages en Perse, iii. 119. Olivier says: "Ils excellent dans la fabrication des étoffes de soie pure, de soie et coton, de soie et or ou argent, de coton pur, de coton et laine. A Yesd, à Cachan, à Ispahan, on travaille, avec autant de goût que de propriété les brocards, les velours, les taffetas, les satins, et presque toutes les étoffes que nous connaissons." Olivier, Voyage, etc. v. 304, 305, 306.

[2] Ovid. We learn from Plato, that, when any fine production of the loom among the Greeks was represented as of the most exquisite fineness and beauty, it was compared to those of the Persians: την ζωνην του χιτονισκου ειναι με οἱαι αἱ Περσικαι των πολυτελων. Hippias Min. 255.

out at the full length of the web; which makes the house of the weaver insufficient to contain him. He is therefore obliged to work continually in the open air; and every return of inclement weather interrupts him.[1]

Among the arts of the Hindus, that of printing and dyeing their cloths has been celebrated; and the beauty and brilliancy, as well as durability, of the colours they produce, are worthy of particular praise. This has never been supposed to be one of the circumstances on which any certain inference with regard to civilization could be founded. It has been generally allowed that a great, if not the greatest part of the excellence which appears in the colours of the Hindu cloths, is owing to the superior quality of the colouring matters, with which their happy climate and soil supply them.[2] Add to this that dyeing is an early art. "It must have made," says Goguet, "a very rapid progress in the earliest times in some countries. Moses speaks of stuffs dyed sky-blue, purple, and double-scarlet; he also speaks of the skins of sheep dyed orange and violet."[3] The purple, so highly admired by the ancients, they represented as the invention of Hercules, thus tracing back its origin even to the fabulous times. In durability, it appears not that any thing could surpass the colours of the ancients. "We never," says Goguet, "find them complain that the colour of their stuffs was subject to alter or change. Plutarch tells us, in the life of Alexander, that the conqueror found, among the treasures of the kings of Persia, a prodigious quantity of purple stuffs, which, for one hundred and eighty years which they had been kept, preserved all their lustre, and all their primitive freshness. We find in Herodotus, that certain people, on the borders of the Caspian Sea, imprinted on

[1] Orme, on the Governments and people of Indostan, p. 409, etc. Tennant's Indian Recreations, p. 301. "The apparatus of the weaver is very simple; two rollers, placed in four pieces of wood, fixed in the earth; two sticks, which traverse the warp, and are supported at each of the extremities, one by two strings tied to the tree under which the loom is placed, and the other by two other strings tied to the workman's feet, which gives him a facility of removing the threads of the warp to throw the woof." Sonnerat, Voyag. liv. iii. ch. viii.

[2] "Perhaps their painted cloths are more indebted to the brilliancy of the colours, and the goodness of the water, than any skill of the artist, for that admiration with which they have been viewed." Tennant's Indian Recreations, i. 299. Chardin, who tells us how admirable the Persians are in the art of dyeing, adds, that their excellence in this respect, is principally owing to the exquisiteness of their colouring matters. Voyages en Perse, iii. 16.

[3] Goguet, Origin of Laws, part ii. book ii. ch. ii. art. 1.

BOOK II. CHAP. VIII.

their stuffs designs, either of animals or flowers, whose colour never changed, and lasted as long even as the wool of which their clothes were made."[1]

We shall next consider the progress of the Hindus in agriculture, which, though the most important of all the useful arts, is not the first invented, nor the first which arrives at perfection. It is allowed, on all hands, that the agriculture of Hindustan is rude; but the progress of agriculture depends so much upon the laws relating to landed property, that the state of this art may continue very low, in a country where other arts are carried to a high degree of perfection.

A Hindu field, in the highest state of cultivation, is described to be only so far changed by the plough, as to afford a scanty supply of mould for covering the seed; while the useless and hurtful vegetation is so far from being eradicated, that, where burning precedes not, which for a short time smoothes the surface, the grasses and shrubs, which have bid defiance to the plough, cover a large proportion of the surface.

Nothing can exceed the rudeness and inefficiency of the Hindu implements of agriculture. The plough consists of a few pieces of wood, put together with less adaptation

[1] Goguet, Origin of Laws, part ii. book ii. ch. ii. art. 1. "The linen manufactured by the Colchians was in high repute. Some of it was curiously painted with figures of animals and flowers, and afterwards dyed like the linen of the Indians. And Herodotus tells us, that the whole was so deeply tinctured, that no washing could efface the colours. They accordingly exported it to various marts, as it was everywhere greatly sought after." Bryant's Anc. Mythol. v. 109. Herodotus, however, represents the people of whom he speaks, as in a state of great barbarity: *μιξιν τε τουτων των ανθρωπων ειναι εμφανεα καταπερ τοισι προβατοισι.* Clio. cciii. The Chinese dye scarlet more exquisitely than any other nation. Lord Macartney says it arises "from their indefatigable care and pains in washing, purifying, and grinding their colouring matters." See Lord Macartney's Journal, Barrow's Life of Lord Macartney, ii. 516. The same expenditure of time and patience, commodities generally abounding in a rude state of society, are the true causes of both the fine dyeing and the fine weaving of the Hindus. Both Hindus and Chinese are indebted for all elegance of pattern to their European visitors.—" Pour ce qui est des arts méchaniques, celui où les Persans excellent le plus, et où ils nous surpassent peut-être, c'est la teinture. Ils donnent à leurs étoffes des couleurs plus vives, plus solides qu'on ne fait en Europe. Ils impriment celles de coton et celles de soie avec une netteté et une ténacité surprenantes, soit qu'ils emploient des couleurs, soit qu'ils procédent avec des feuilles d'or et d'argent." Olivier, Voyage, etc. v. 303. Mr. Park informs us, that the negroes of Africa have carried the art of dyeing to great perfection. Travels in Africa, p. 281: see also his last Mission, p. 10. The arts in which the Hindus have any pretensions to skill are the very arts in which so rude a people as the Turks most excel. "Presque tous les arts sont dans l'enfance, ou sont ignorés chez eux, si nous en exceptons la teinture, la fabrication de diverses étoffes, celle des lames de sabre et de couteau." Voyages dans l'Empire Ottoman, etc., par G. A. Olivier, i. 26.

to the end in view, than has been elsewhere found among some of the rudest nations. It has no contrivance for turning over the mould; and the share, having neither width nor depth, is incapable of stirring the soil. The operation of ploughing is described by the expressive term *scratching*.[1] Several ploughs follow one another, all to deepen the same furrow; a second ploughing of the same sort is performed across the first; and very often a third and a fourth, in different directions, before so much as an appearance of mould is obtained for the seed.[2]

The instrument employed as a harrow is described as literally a branch of a tree; in some places as a log of wood, performing the office partly of a roller, partly of a harrow; and in others as a thing resembling a ladder of eighteen feet in length, drawn by four bullocks, and guided by two men, who stand upon the instrument to increase its weight.[3] The hackery, which answers the purpose of cart or waggon, is a vehicle with two wheels, which are not three feet in diameter, and are not unfrequently solid pieces of wood, with only a hole in the middle for the axletree. The body of the machine is composed of two bamboos, meeting together at an angle between the necks of the two bullocks, by which the vehicle is drawn, and united by a few crossing bars of the same useful material. It is supported at the angle by a bar which passes over the necks of the two animals, and cruelly galls them. To lessen the friction between the wheel and axis, and save either his wretched cattle, or his own ears, the simple expedient of greasing his wheels, never suggested itself to the mind of a ryot of Hindustan.[4] Even this wretched vehicle can

1 What is meant by this? If it is intended, as may be supposed, to express the sense of the native term for ploughing, it is incorrect: and, as it appears to rest upon Mr. Tennant's authority, it is an additional proof of his ignorance. —W.

2 "You frequently see a field, after one ploughing, appear as green as before; only a few scratches are perceptible, here and there, more resembling the digging of a mole than the work of a plough." Tennant's Indian Recr. ii. 78.—M.

No allowance is made either here or in the text for the peculiarities of the soil or climate: the deep ploughing of England is not needed in a soil in which seeds take root upon the surface, and the reappearance of vegetation is scarcely to be prevented by any care; the assertion of the text, that repeated ploughings are necessary before an appearance of mould is obtained, seems to be a notion of his own, and shows strange unacquaintance with the peculiarities of the country, at least, of Bengal, where the whole soil is alluvial mould.—W.

3 Ibid. 124, 275.

4 Tennant's Ind. Recr. ii. 75. "You cannot, by any argument, prevail upon

BOOK II. CHAP. VIII.

seldom be employed for the purposes of husbandry, for almost total want of roads. It is in back loads that the carriage of almost all the commodities of the country is performed; and in many places the manure is conveyed to the fields in baskets on the backs of the women.[1]

Everything which savours of ingenuity, even the most natural results of common observation and good sense, are foreign to the agriculture of the Hindus. The advantages arising from the observation of the fittest season for sowing are almost entirely neglected. No attention was ever paid in Hindustan to the varieties of the grains; so as to select the best seed, or that fittest for particular situations. For restoring fruitfulness to a field that is exhausted, no other expedient is known, than suspending its cultivation; when the weeds, with which it is always plentifully stored, usurp undivided dominion. Any such refinement as a fallow, or a rotation of crops, is far beyond the reach of a Hindu. The most irrational practice that ever found existence in the agriculture of any nation, is general in India, that of sowing various species of seeds, mustard, flax, barley, wheat, millet, maize, and many others, which ripen at different intervals, all indiscriminately on the same spot. As soon as the earliest of the crops is mature, the reapers are sent into the field, who pick out the stalks of the plant which is ripe, and tread down the rest with their feet. This operation is repeated as each part of the product arrives at maturity, till the whole is separated from the ground.[2]

---

the listless owner to save his ears, his cattle, or his cart, by lubricating it with oil. Neither his industry, his invention, nor his purse, would admit of this, even though you could remove what is generally insurmountable—his veneration for ancient usage. If his forefathers drove a screeching hackery, posterity will not dare to violate the sanctity of custom by departing from their example. This is one instance of a thousand in which the inveterate prejudices of the Asiatics stand in the way of their improvement, and bid defiance equally to the exertions of the active, and the hopes of the benevolent." Ibid. 76. This characteristic mark of a rude people, a blind opposition to innovation, is displayed by persons among ourselves, as if it was the highest mark of wisdom and virtue.—The waggon wheels are one piece of solid timber, like a millstone. Tavernier, in Harris, i. 815.

[1] Into Oude are imported a variety of articles of commerce from the northern mountains, gold, copper, lead, musk, cow-tails, honey, pomegranate seeds, grapes, dried ginger, pepper, red-wood, tincar, civet, zedoary, wax, woollen cloths, wooden ware, and various species of hawks, amber, rock-salt, assafœtida, glass toys. What is carried back is earthenware. All this commerce is carried upon the backs of men, or horses and goats. Ayeen Akbery, ii. 33. Buchanan's Journey, i. 205, 434. Capt. Hardwicke, Asiat. Res. vi. 330.

[2] That there is much slovenliness in Indian agriculture, may be admitted;

Though, during the dry season, there is an almost total failure of vegetables for the support of cattle; of which every year many are lost by famine, and the remainder reduced to the most deplorable state of emaciation and weakness; none but the most imperfect means were ever imagined by the Hindu of saving part of the produce of the prolific season, to supply the wants of the barren one. Hay is a commodity which it would not always be convenient to make; but various kinds of pulse and millet might be produced at all seasons, and would afford the most important relief to the cattle when the pasture-grounds are bare. The horses themselves are often preserved alive by the grooms picking up the roots of grass with a knife from the ditches and tanks.[1]

---

but much that is here charged against it, is untrue. Hindu cultivators are by no means deficient in common observation and good sense, and are regulated in their proceedings by a knowledge of their soil and climate; in which the heavy implements and laborious culture of Europe, would be wholly out of place. To say that the Indian farmer is ignorant of the fittest season for sowing, is the contradiction of known facts; as nothing can be more regular than the periodical recurrence of the harvests. Nor is the Indian farmer unacquainted with the advantage of a rotation of crops; although, in general, the soil does not require it:—where, as in the case of sugar-cane, the produce exhausts the soil, we have Dr. Roxburgh's evidence, that the Indians "do not attempt to rear a second crop oftener than every third or fourth year; allowing the land either to rest, or employing it for the growth of such plants as are found to improve the soil; *of which the Indian farmer is a perfect judge.*" As. Annual Reg. 1802. Tracts, p. 8. Few persons had better opportunities of estimating the character of Indian agriculture than Sir Thomas Munro, and he calls it "a good system."—Evidence, 1813.—W.

[1] For this sketch of Hindu agriculture, the chief authorities are, a short treatise, entitled "Remarks on the Agriculture, &c. of Bengal;" Tennant's Indian Recreations, particularly the second volume; and Dr. Buchanan's Journey through Mysore, Canara, and Malabar. After describing the wretched state of agriculture in the neighbourhood of Seringapatam, Dr. Buchanan says; "I am afraid, however, that the reader, in perusing the foregoing accounts, will have formed an opinion of the native agriculture still more favourable than it deserves. I have been obliged to use the English words ploughings, weedings, and hoeings, to express operations somewhat similar, that are performed by the natives; and the frequent repetition of these, mentioned in the accounts taken from the cultivators, might induce the reader to imagine that the ground was well wrought, and kept remarkably clean. Quite the reverse, however, is the truth. Owing to the extreme imperfection of their implements, and want of strength in their cattle, a field, after six or eight ploughings, has numerous small bushes remaining as upright in it as before the labour, while the plough has not penetrated above three inches deep, and has turned over no part of the soil......... The plough has neither coulter nor mould-board, to divide and to turn over the soil; and the handle gives the ploughman very little power to command its direction. The other instruments are equally imperfect, and are more rudely formed than it was possible for my draughtsman to represent." Buchanan's Journey through Mysore, &c. i. 126. In another place he says, "In every field there is more grass than corn. Notwithstanding the many ploughings, the fields are full of grass roots." Ibid. p. 345. See also p. 15. Agriculture was almost universal among the American tribes. "Throughout all America, we scarcely meet with any nation of hunters, which does not practise some species of cultivation." Robertson's America, ii. 117. "The agriculture of the Peruvians was apparently superior to that of the Hindus." Ibid. iii. 341.

The only circumstance to captivate the fancy of those Europeans, who were on the look-out for subjects of praise, was the contrivance for irrigation. Reservoirs or excavations, known in India by the name of tanks, were so contrived as to collect a large body of water in the rainy season, whence it was drawn off in the season of drought for the refreshment of the fields. These tanks appear to have been at all times a principal concern of the government; and when it is considered that almost the whole revenue of the sovereign depended in each year upon the produce of the soil, and that the decay of the tanks ensured the decay of revenue, it is no wonder that of such care and wisdom as the government anywhere displayed, a large portion should appear to have been bestowed upon the tanks. In certain places much care and labour have been employed. But those authors were strangely mistaken who looked upon this as a proof of refined agriculture and great civilization. It is only in a small number of instances, where the whole power of an extensive government, and that almost always Mahomedan,[1] had been applied to the works of irrigation, that they are found on a considerable scale, or in any but the rudest state. In a country in which, without artificial watering, the crops would always be lost, the ingenuity of sinking a hole in the ground, to reserve a supply of water, need not be considered as great.[2]

[1] The most considerable works of this class, are in the South and West of India, where the Mohammedan rule was either not known at all, or not until a very recent date.—W.

[2] Frezier (see his Voyage to the South Sea, p. 213. London edition, 1718), says, "The ancient Indians were extraordinary industrious in conveying the water of the rivers to their dwellings: there are still to be seen in many places aqueducts of earth and of dry stones, carried on and turned off very ingeniously along the sides of hills, with an infinite number of windings, which shows that those people, as unpolished as they were, very well understood the art of levelling." There is something indicative of no little art in the floating gardens and fields which were on the lake of Mexico. (See the Description in Clavigero, Hist. Mex. book vii. sect. 27.) The cultivation of their fields, considering it was done by human, without the aid of animal labour, was remarkable, and their produce suprising. (Ibid. sect. 28.) The following passage from Garcilasso de la Vega deserves to be quoted as a monument of the labours of the Peruvians in agriculture· "They drained all wet moors and fens, for in that art they were excellent, as is apparent by their works which remain unto this day: and also they were very ingenious in making aqueducts for carrying water into dry and scorched lands." (He explains how careful they were to water both their corn-lands and pasture.).......... "After they had made a provision of water, the next thing was to dress, and cultivate, and clear their fields of bushes and trees; and, that they might with most advantage receive the water, they made them in a quadrangular form; those lands which were good on the side of hills, they levelled by certain alleys or walks which they

To separate the grain from the straw, the ancient method of treading with oxen has, in Hindustan, given way to no improvement; and, for the most part, the corn is still ground in handmills by the women.[1]

Of the arts which, at an early age of society acquire the greatest excellence, one, as we have already observed, is that of preparing brilliant trinkets for the ornament of the person. The Hindus cut the precious stones, polish them to a high degree of brilliancy, and set them neatly in gold and silver. It remains to be ascertained how much of civilization this faculty implies. So early as the time of Moses, the art of forming jewels had attained great perfection among the Jews. In the ephod of Aaron, and in the breast-plate of judgment, were precious stones set in gold, with the names of the twelve tribes engraved on them. The account of these jewels in the book of Exodus,

---

made. To make these alleys they raised three walls of friezed stone, one before, and one on each side, somewhat inclining inwards, so that they may more securely bear and keep up the weight of the earth, which is pressed and rammed down by them, until it be raised to the height of the wall. Then next to this walk they made another, something shorter and less, kept up in the same manner with its wall; until at length they came to take in the whole hill, levelling it by degrees in fashion of a ladder, one alley above the other. Where the ground was stony, they gathered up the stones, and covered the barren soil with fresh earth to make their levels, that so no part of the ground might be lost. The first quadrangles were the largest, and as spacious as the situation of the place could bear, some being of that length and breadth as were capable to receive a hundred, some two hundred, or three hundred bushels of seed. Those of the second row were made narrower and shorter. ...... In some part they brought the channels of water from fifteen or twenty leagues' distance, though it were only to improve a slip of a few acres of land, which was esteemed good corn-ground." Royal Commentaries of Peru, part i. book v. ch. i. The Mercurio Peruano describes extensive works for irrigation among the Peruvians, of which the vestiges are still to be seen. Mercur. Peruano, viii. 38. Acosta tells us, (Nat. and Mor. Hist. book iii. ch. xviii.) "The Indians do draw from these floods, that run from the mountains to the valleys and plains, many and great brooks to water their lands, which they usually do with such industry, as there are no better in Murcia, nor in Milan itself, the which is also the greatest and only wealth of the plains of Peru, and of many other parts of the Indies."

[1] Sonnerat, Voyag. liv. iii. ch. viii.; Tennant's Ind. Recr. i. 302. The country of the Seiks, a people confessedly barbarous, a well-informed author, Francklin, in his Memoirs of George Thomas, pp. 65, 66, informs us, is highly cultivated, and their arts and manufactures are on a level with those of any other part of India. "Les Tartares du Daghestan ont une coutume qu'ils observent soigneusement: sçavoir, que personne ne peut se marier chez eux, avant que d'avoir planté en un endroit marqué cent arbres fruitiers; ensorte qu'on trouve partout dans les montagnes du Daghestan de grandes forêts d'arbres fruitiers." (Hist. Généal. des Tartars, p. 313.) Zoroaster made the duties of agriculture part of his religion. "To sow grain with purity, is to fulfil the whole extent of the law of the Mazdeiesnans." (Anquetil, Zendav. ii. 610.) The Heruli and Lombards, in their native wilds, cultivated flax, "which supposes," says Gibbon, "property, agriculture, manufactures, and commerce." (Gibbon, vii. 276.)

BOOK II. CHAP. VIII.

suggests ideas of considerable magnificence.[1] Clavigero informs us, that the ancient Mexicans "set gems in gold and silver, and made most curious jewellery of great value. In short," says that author, "these sort of works were so admirably finished, that even the Spanish soldiers, all stung as they were with the same wretched thirst for gold, valued the workmanship above the materials."[2]

When Europeans have compared the extreme imperfection, the scantiness and rudeness of the tools by which the Hindu artist performs his task, with the neatness, and in some cases the celerity of the execution, they have frequently drawn an inference, the very reverse of that which the circumstances implied. This sort of faculty is no mark of high civilization. A dexterity in the use of its own imperfect tools is a common attribute of a rude society.

Acosta, speaking of some remarkable instances of this species of talent in the natives of Mexico and Peru, says,

[1] Exod. ch. xxviii. "I look upon engraving on fine stones," says Goguet, (Origin of Laws, part ii. book ii. ch. ii. art. 3.) "as the most remarkable evidence of the rapid progress of the arts in some countries. This work supposes a number of discoveries, much knowledge, and much experience." He adds, in a note, "It must be agreed, that the ancient Peruvians, whose monarchy had not subsisted above three hundred and fifty years, understood perfectly well the working of precious stones." (Hist. Gén. des Voyages, xiii. 578.)" Ibid.

[2] Clavigero, Hist. of Mexico, book vii. sect. 51. Even the most rude of the American tribes seem not to have been without some knowledge of the art of working the precious stones. M. de la Condamine, speaking of the green stones, found in some places bordering on the Amazons' River, in South America, says (Voyage dans l'Intérieur de l'Amérique Méridionale, p. 131), "La vérité est qu'elles ne diffèrent, ni en couleur, ni en dureté, du Jade Oriental; elles résistent à la lime, et on n'imagine pas par quel artifice les anciens Américains ont pu les tailler, et leur donner diverses figures d'animaux, sans fer ni acier."—In the same place, he mentions another phenomenon of the ancient Americans. "Ce sont," says he, "des Eméraudes, arrondies, polies, et percées de deux trous coniques, diamétralement opposés sur un axe commun, telles qu'on en trouve encore aujourd'hui au Pérou sur les bords de la Rivière de St. Jago dans la province d'Esmeraldas, à quarante lieues de Quito, avec divers autres monumens de l'industrie de ses anciens habitans." The Persians of the present day are eminent lapidaries. Chardin, Voy. en Perse, iii. 115.—Olivier says, "Ils taillent assez bien les pierres précieuses, et les montent avec assez de goût." Olivier, Voy. &c. v. 304, &c. "At this place I had an opportunity of seeing their mode of smelting gold. Isaaco had purchased some gold in coming through Konkodoo, and here he had it made into a large ring. The smith made a crucible of common red clay, and dried it in the sun. Into this he put the gold without flux or mixture whatever. He then put charcoal under it and over it; and, blowing the fire with the common bellows of the country, soon produced such a heat as to bring the gold into a state of fusion. He then made a small furrow in the ground, into which he poured the melted gold. When it was cold he took it up, and heating it again soon hammered it into a square bar. Then heating it again he twisted it by means of two pair of pincers into a sort of screw, and, lengthening out the ends, turned them up, so as to form a massy and precious ring." Mungo Park's Last Mission to Africa, p. 78.

"Hereby we may judge, if they have any understanding, or be brutish; for my part, I think they pass us in those things whereunto they apply themselves."[1] Mr. Forster himself, whose admiration was excited by the dexterity of the Hindus, affords an instance in the rude person of a Russian peasant, which might have suggested to him an appropriate conclusion. "At the distance," says he, "of a few miles from Choperskoy, the driver of the carriage alarmed me by a report of the hinder axle being shattered; an accident which gave me an opportunity of observing the dexterity of a Russian carpenter in the use of the axe. Without the help of any other tool, except a narrow chisel, to cut a space in the centre of it for receiving an iron bar which supports the axle, and to pierce holes for the linchpins, he reduced, in two hours, a piece of gross timber to the requisite form, and his charge was one shilling."[2]

But while dexterity in the use of imperfect tools is not a proof of civilisation: a great want of ingenuity and completeness in instruments and machinery is a strong indication of the reverse; nor would it be easy to point out any

[1] Acosta, Nat. and Mor. Hist. of the Indies, book vi. chap. viii.

[2] Forster's Travels, ii. 282.—Les habitans de Kamschatka, d'une stupidité sans égale à certains égards, sont à d'autres d'une industrie merveilleuse. S'agit-il de se faire des vêtemens? leur adresse en ce genre, dit leur Historien, surpasse celle des Européens. *Helvetius, de l'Homme*, i. 304.—"In general, the ingenuity of all their (*the Otaheitans'*) works, considering the tools they possess, is marvellous. Their cloth, clubs, fishing implements, canoes, houses, all display great skill; their mourning dresses, their war head-dress and breast-plates, show remarkable taste; their adjustment of the different parts, the exact symmetry, the nicety of the joining, are admirable: and it is astonishing how they can, with such ease and quickness, drill holes in a pearl-shell with a shark's tooth, and so fine as not to admit the point of a common pin." Missionary Voyage, p. 330. Observe the same remarkable coincidence in patience, rudeness of tools, and neatness of execution, in the following description by Robertson of the state of the arts in Mexico. "The functions of the mason, the weaver, the goldsmith, the painter, and of several other crafts, were carried on by different persons. Each was regularly instructed in his calling. To it alone his industry was confined; and, by assiduous application to one object, together with the persevering patience peculiar to Americans, their artisans attained to a degree of neatness and perfection in work, far beyond what could have been expected from the rude tools which they employed. Their various productions were brought into commerce; and, by the exchange of them in the stated markets held in the cities, not only were their mutual wants supplied, in such orderly intercourse as characterizes an improved state of society, but their industry was daily rendered persevering and inventive." Robertson's Hist. of America, iii. 286. Voltaire has a passage on this subject which shows philosophical discernment. "Il-y-a dans l'homme un instinct de méchanique que nous voyons produire tous les jours de très grands effets, dans des hommes fort grossiers. On voit des machines inventées par les habitans des montagnes du Tirol et des Vosges, qui étonnent les savans." Voltaire, Essai sur les Mœurs et l'Esprit des Nations, Introd. p. 32.

single circumstance which may be taken as a better index of the degree in which the benefits of civilisation are anywhere enjoyed, than the state of the tools and machinery of the artists. All European visitors have been vehemently struck with the rudeness of the tools and machinery used by the people of Hindustan.[1] Sonnerat, one of those travellers who have surveyed the state of the arts in that country with the greatest attention and the most enlightened eyes, informs us, that with his hands and two or three tools, the Hindu artisan has to perform that kind of task about which with us a hundred tools would be employed.[2] "When the rudeness of the tools," says Mr. Forster, "with the simplicity of the process, is examined, the degree of delicacy which the artisans have acquired in their several professions must challenge a high admiration."[3] Fryer, speaking of the mode in which coral is cut, says, "The tools of the workman were more to be wondered at than his art; his hands and feet being all the vice, and the other tools unshapen bits of iron."[4]

In the mode in which the Hindu artisans, of almost all descriptions, perform their work, is observed a circumstance, generally found among a rude people, and nowhere else. The carpenter, the blacksmith, the brazier, even the goldsmith and jeweller, not to speak of others, produce not their manufacture as in a refined state of the arts, in houses and workshops of their own, where the accommodations requisite for them can best be combined: they repair for each job, with their little budget of tools, to the house of the

[1] Crauford's Sketches, p. 328, 1st ed.

[2] Sonnerat, Voy. liv. iii. chap. viii. "The Indian carpenter knows no other tools than the plane, the chisel, the wimble, a hammer, and a kind of hatchet. The earth serves him for a bench, and his foot for a holdfast. He is a month in performing what our workmen will do in three days. Even after instruction he will not adopt our method of sawing. Placing his wood between two beams fixed in the ground, and sitting on a bench, a man employs three days, with one saw, to make a plank, which would cost our people an hour's work." Ibid. Among the Birmans the state of the more necessary and useful arts seems to be fully as much advanced as among the Hindus: in not a few cases more so. (See Mr. Symes' Embassy to Ava.) The waggons are more neat and commodious than the clumsy gauries or carts of India.

[3] Forster's Travels, i. 25. "Their artificers," says Stavorinus, "work with so little apparatus, and so few instruments, that an European would be astonished at their neatness and expedition." Stavorinus, Voy. p. 412. See, to the same purpose, Tennant, Indian Recreations, i. 301, 302, 303.

[4] Fryer's Travels, let. iii. chap. iii. They cut diamonds, he says, with a mill turned by men, the string reaching, in manner of our cutlers' wheels, to lesser that are in a flat press, where under steel wheels diamonds are fastened, and with its own bort are worn into what cut the artist pleases. Ibid.

man who employs them, and there perform the service for which they are called.[1]

With regard to the fine arts, a short sketch will suffice. Hardly by any panegyrist is it pretended that the sculpture, the painting, the music of the Hindus are in a state beyond that in which they appear in early stages of society. The merely mechanical part, that for which the principal requisites are time and patience, the natural produce of rude ages, when labour is of little value, is often executed with great neatness; and surprises by the idea of the difficulty overcome. In the province of genius and taste, nothing but indications of rudeness appear. The productions are not merely void of attraction: they are unnatural, offensive, and not unfrequently disgusting. "The Hindus of this day," says Mr. Forster, "have a slender knowledge of the rules of proportion, and none of perspective. They are just imitators, and correct workmen, but they possess merely the glimmerings of genius."[2] "The style and taste of the Indians," says Paolino, "are indeed extremely wretched; but they possess a wonderful aptitude for imitating the arts and inventions of the Europeans, as soon as the method has been pointed out to them."[3] Major Rennel himself informs us, that the imitative or fine arts were not carried to the height even of the Egyptians, much less of the Greeks and Romans, by the Hindus: that like the Chinese they made great progress in some of the useful arts, but scarcely any in those of taste.[4]

[1] The blacksmith goes from place to place carrying his tools with him. Beside his forge and his little furnace, a stone serves for an anvil, and his whole apparatus consists of a pair of pincers, a hammer, a mallet, and a file. They have not attained the art of polishing gold and silver, or of working gold in different colours. The goldsmith goes about with his tools, like the blacksmith. Sonnerat, Voy. liv. iii. chap. viii. The workmen in gold and silver are frequently only little boys, who sit every day in the bazaar or market waiting till they are called, when they go to your house, with their implements in a little basket, consisting of a very small anvil, a hammer, a pair of bellows, a few files, and a pair of pincers; a chafing-dish, or pan of embers, is then given to him with a model of what is to be made, and the material. He then sets about his work in the open air, and performs it with despatch and ingenuity. Other tradesmen go to your home in the same manner, the shoemaker and tailor. Stavorinus, Voy. p. 412. It is remarkable how exactly this description of the state of the arts among the Hindus tallies with that among the Persians; Chardin informs us that every where in Persia, the artisans of all descriptions go to work in the houses of those who employ them—that they perform their work with the poorest apparatus, and, comparing the tools with the work, to a surprising degree of perfection. Chardin, Voy. en Perse, iii. 98.

[2] Forster's Travels, i. 80.

[3] Bartolomeo's Travels, book i. chap vii.

[4] Rennel's Memoir, p. xxii.

BOOK II.
CHAP. VIII.

"In India," says Sonnerat, "as well as among all the people of the East, the arts have made little or no progress. All the statues we see in their temples are badly designed and worse executed."[1] We have the testimony of Mr. Hodges, which to this point at least is a high testimony, that the sculpture in the pagodas of Hindustan is all very rude.[2] In the description of a temple of Siva, at Hullybedu in Mysore, Dr. Buchanan says, "Its walls contain a very ample delineation of Hindu mythology; which, in the representation of human or animal forms, is as destitute of elegance as usual; but some of the foliages possess great neatness. It much exceeds any Hindu building that I have seen elsewhere."[3]

Whatever exaggeration we may suppose in the accounts which the historians of Mexico and Peru have given us of the works of sculpture in the new world, the description of them will not permit us to conclude that they were many degrees inferior to the productions of Hindustan. Clavigero says, "The Mexicans were more successful in sculpture than in painting. They learned to express in their statues all the attitudes and postures of which the human body is capable; they observed the proportions exactly; and could, when necessary, execute the most delicate and minute strokes with the chisel. The works which they executed by casting of metals were in still more esteem. The miracles they produced of this kind would not be credible, if, besides the testimony of those who saw them, curiosities in numbers, of this nature, had not been sent from Mexico to Europe."[4]

1 Sonnerat, Voy. liv. iii. ch. viii.—M. That this condemnation is too unqualified we have satisfactory testimony in some of the sculptures at Ellora, of which drawings are given by Captain Grindlay in the Trans. Royal Asiatic Society, vol. ii. 326.—W.

2 Hodges' Travels in India. Mr. Hodges says, "I am concerned I cannot pay so high a compliment to the art of sculpture among the Hindoos as is usually paid by many ingenious authors who write on the religion of Bramah. Considering these works, as I do, with the eyes of an artist, they are only to be paralleled with the rude essays of the ingenious Indians I have met with in Otaheite, and on other islands in the South Seas:" p. 26. He adds in the next page, that in point of carving, that is, the mere *mechanical* part, the ornaments in the Hindu temples are often beautiful. In another passage, too, p. 151, he speaks again of the same *mechanical* nicety, the peculiar sharpness of the cut in Hindu carvings. See, to the same purpose, Tennant's Indian Recr. i. 299.

3 Buchanan, Journey through Mysore, &c. iii. 391.

4 Clavigero, Hist. Mex. book vii. sect. 50. He adds, "The works of gold and silver sent in presents from the conqueror Cortez to Charles V. filled the goldsmiths of Europe with astonishment, who, as several authors of that period

The progress was similar, as we might presume, in the sister art of painting. The Hindus copy with great exactness, even from nature. By consequence, they draw portraits, both of individuals and of groups, with a minute likeness; but peculiarly devoid of grace and expression. Their inability to exhibit the simplest creations of the fancy, is strongly expressed by Dr. Tennant, who says, "The laborious exactness with which they imitate every feather of a bird, or the smallest fibre on the leaf of a plant, renders them valuable assistants in drawing specimens of natural history; but further than this, they cannot advance one step. If your bird is to be placed on a rock, or upon the branch of a tree, the draughtsman is at a stand; the object is not before him; and his imagination can supply nothing."[1] In one remarkable circumstance their painting resembles that of all other nations who have made but small progress in the arts. They are entirely without a knowledge of perspective, and by consequence, of all those finer and nobler parts of the art of painting, which have perspective for their requisite basis.[2]

---

attest, declared that they were altogether inimitable. The Mexican founders made, both of gold and silver, the most perfect images of natural bodies. They made a fish in this manner, which had its scales, alternately, the one of silver and the other of gold, a parrot with a moveable head, tongue, and wings, and an ape with a moveable head and feet, having a spindle in its hand in the attitude of spinning." Ibid. Garcilasso tells us, "that the Peruvians framed many figures of men and women, of birds of the air, and fishes of the sea; likewise of fierce animals, such as tigers, lions and bears, foxes, dogs, cats; in short, all creatures whatsoever known amongst them, they cast and moulded into true and natural figures of the same shape and form of those creatures which they represented. They counterfeited the plants and wall-flowers so well, that being on the walls they seemed to be natural; the creatures which were shaped on the walls, such as lizards, butterflies, snakes, and serpents, some crawling up and some down, were so artificially done, that they seemed natural, and wanted nothing but motion." Book vi. chap. i.)

1 Tennant's Ind. Rec. i. 299.

2 Dr. Tennant, at the place cited above, supports his own authority, by quoting the following passage of Sonnerat: "La peinture chez les Indiens est, et sera toujours, dans l'enfance; ils trouvent admirable un tableau chargé de rouge et de bleu, et dont les personnages sont vêtus d'or. Ils n'entendent point le clair-obscur, n'arrondissent jamais les objets, et ne savent pas les mettre en perspective; en un mot, leurs meilleures peintures ne sont que de mauvaises enluminures." (Voyages aux Indes, i. 99.) The Indian pictures, says Mandelsloe, are more remarkable for their diversity of colours, than any exactness of proportion. Harris's Collect. of Voy. i. How exactly does this correspond with the description which Chardin gives us of the state of the same art among the Persians! "En Perse les arts, tant libéraux que méchaniques, sont en général presque tous rudes et bruts, en comparaison de la perfection où l'Europe les a portés Ils entendent fort mal le dessin, ne sachant rien faire au naturel; et ils n'ont aucune connoissance de la perspective........ Pour ce que de la platte-peinture, il est vrai que les visages qu'ils représentent

BOOK II. CHAP. VIII.

It is anomalous and somewhat surprising that the music of the Hindus should be so devoid of all excellence. As music is, in its origin, the imitation of the tones of passion; and is most naturally employed for the expression of passion, in rude ages, when the power of expressing it by articulate language is the most imperfect; simple melodies, and these often highly expressive and affecting, are natural to uncultivated tribes. It was in the earliest stage of civilisation, that Orpheus is fabled to have possessed the power of working miracles by his lyre. Yet all Europeans, even those who are the most disposed to eulogise the attainments of the Hindus, unite in describing the music of that people as unpleasing, and void both of expression and art. Dr. Tennant, who founds his testimony both on his own, and other people's observation, says: "If we are to judge merely from the number of instruments, and the frequency with which they apply them, the Hindoos might be regarded as

---

sont assez ressemblans ; ils les tirent d'ordinaire de profil, parce que ce sont ceux qu'ils font le plus aisément ; ils les font aussi de trois quarts : mais pour les visages en plein ou de front, ils y réussissent fort mal, n'entendant pas à y donner les ombres. Ils ne sauroient former une attitude et une posture. .... Leur pinceau est fin et délicat, et leur peinture vive et éclatante. Il faut attribuer à l'air du pays la beauté des couleurs." Voy. en Perse, iii. 284. "La peinture est encore au berceau : les Persans n'ont fait aucun progrès dans cet art......... En général, leur manière de faire ressemble un peu à celle des Chinois : le dessin est très incorrect ; ils ne connaissent pas la perspective . ils ne savent pas employer les ombres....... Cependant on voit sortir de leurs mains des ouvrages assez jolis ; ils peignent assez bien les fleurs et les oiseaux de fantaisie ; ils réussissent dans les arabesques ; ils emploient très bien l'or ; ils font de très beaux vernis......... Les couleurs que les Persans emploient, et qu'ils font eux-mêmes, ont tout l'éclat, toute la solidité, qu'on peut désirer. Ce sont eux qui nous ont fait connaître l'outremer." (Olivier, Voyage, v. 301.) It is remarkable to find the state of the fine arts in China so exactly the same. "Quoique les Chinois ayent une passion extraordinaire pour tous les ouvrages de peinture, et que leurs temples en soient ornez, on ne peut rien voir néanmoins de plus borné, et de moins régulier. Ils ne sçavent point ménager les ombres d'un tableau, ni mêler ou adoucir les couleurs......... Ils ne sont pas plus heureux dans la sculpture, et ils n'y observent ni ordre, ni proportions. (Le Gentil. Voyage, ii. 111.) The painting of the Mexicans seems to have had the same perfections and imperfections with that of these eastern nations. The colours, Robertson (iii. 278) informs us, were remarkably bright, but laid on without any art, and without any regard to light and shade, or the rules of perspective. Clavigero, though the skill of the Mexicans in painting is not one of the points for which he most highly admires them, says, "We have seen, among the ancient paintings, many portraits of the kings of Mexico, in which, besides the singular beauty of the colours, the proportions were most accurately observed." (Hist. Mex. book vii. sect. 49.) "Les Mexicains," says Humboldt, "ont conservé un goût particulier pour la peinture et pour l'art de sculpter en pierre et en bois. On est étonné de voir ce qu'ils exécutent avec un mauvais couteau, et sur les bois les plus durs....... Ils montrent beaucoup d'aptitude pour l'exercice des arts d'imitation ; ils en déploient une plus grande encore pour les arts purement mécaniques. Cette aptitude deviendra un jour très précieuse, &c." Humboldt, Essai Politique sur le Royaume de la Nouvelle Espagne p. 9

considerable proficients in music; yet has the testimony of all strangers deemed it equally imperfect as the other arts.[1] Their warlike instruments are rude, noisy, and inartificial: and in temples, those employed for the purposes of religion are managed apparently on the same principle; for, in their idea, the most pleasant and harmonious is that which makes the loudest noise."[2] After a description of the extreme rudeness of the instruments of music of the people of Sumbhulpoor, Mr. Motte says, "the Rajah's band always put me in mind of a number of children coming from a country fair."[3]

[1] Europeans in general know nothing of Indian music. They hear only the accompaniments to public processions, in which noise is the chief object to be obtained, or the singing of Mohammedans, which is Persian, not Indian. That music was cultivated on scientific principles, is evident from the accounts given of it by Sir William Jones and Mr. Colebrooke, from which it appears that the Hindus had a knowledge of the gamut, of a mode of notation, of measurement of time, and of a division of the notes of a more minute description than has been found convenient in Europe. The practice of the art amongst them has declined, in consequence probably of its supersession by the Mohammedans, but occasionally Hindu performers are met with, whose instruments and execution might please more accomplished musicians than those whose opinions have been followed by the writer. See Willard, on the Music of Hindostan.—W.

[2] Indian Rec. i. 300.—Ces peuples n'ont aucune idée des accords. Leur chant commence par un bourdonnement sourd et fort bas, après lequel ils éclatent. Anquetil Duperron, Voyage aux Indes Orientales, Zendavesta, i. xxvi. Even Sonnerat himself informs us, that their music is bad, and their songs destitute of harmony. Voyages aux Indes, liv. iii. chap. viii.

[3] Motte's Journey to Orissa, (Asiat. An. Regist. i. Miscellaneous Tracts, p. 77.) "Their ideas of music, if we may judge from their practice, are barbarous." Orme's Hist. Milit. Trans. i. 3. The following passage from Garcilasso de la Vega is an important document in the history of music. It exhibits more nakedly the fact respecting its origin, than, perhaps, any other written monument; and it proves at the same time the power of expression which the art had attained. "In music," says he, "the Peruvians arrived to a certain harmony in which the Indians of Colla did more particularly excel, having been the inventors of a certain pipe made of canes glued together, every one of which having a different note of higher or lower, in the manner of organs, made a pleasing music by the dissonancy of sounds, the treble, tenor, and basse, exactly corresponding, and answering to each other; with these pipes they often played in concert...... They had also other pipes, which were flutes with four or five stops, like the pipes of shepherds; with these they played not in concert, but singly, and tuned them to sonnets, which they composed in metre, the subject of which was love, and the passions which arise from the favours or displeasures of a mistress........Every song was set to its proper tune; for two songs of different subjects could not correspond with the same air, by reason that the music which the gallant made on his flute was designed to express the satisfaction or discontent of his mind, which were not so intelligible, perhaps, by the words, as by the melancholy or cheerfulness of the tune which he played. A certain Spaniard, one night late, encountered an Indian woman in the streets of Cozco, and would have brought her back to his lodgings; but she cried out, 'For God's sake, sir, let me go, for that pipe which you hear in yonder tower calls me with great passion, and I cannot refuse the summons; for love constrains me to go, that I may be his wife, and he my husband.' The songs which they composed of their wars, and grand achievements, were never set to the airs of their flute, being too grave and serious to be intermixed with the pleasures and softness of love; for these

As the talent of the Hindus for accurate imitation, both in the manual and some of the refined arts, has excited much attention; and been sometimes regarded as no mean proof of ingenuity and mental culture, it is necessary to remark that there are few things by which the rude state of society is more uniformly characterised. It is in reality the natural precursor of the age of invention; and disappears, or at least ceases to make a conspicuous figure, when the nobler faculty of creation comes into play. Garcilasso de la Vega, who quotes Blas Valera in his support, tells us that the Peruvian Indians, "if they do but see a thing, will imitate it so exactly, without being taught, that they become better artists and mechanics than the Spaniards themselves."[1]

Sir William Jones, in pompous terms, remarks: "The Hindus are said to have boasted of three inventions, all of which indeed are admirable; the method of instructing by apologues; the decimal scale; and the game of chess, on which they have some curious treatises."[2] As the game of

---

were only sung at their principal festivals, when they commemorated their victories and triumphs." Royal Comment. book ii. ch. xiv. "The accounts of twenty-two centuries ago represent the Indians as a people who stood very high in point of civilization: but to judge from their ancient monuments, they had not carried the imitative arts to any thing like the degree of perfection attained by the Greeks and Romans; or even by the Egyptians. Both the Hindoos and the Chinese appear to have carried the arts just to the point requisite for useful purposes; but never to have approached the summit of perfection, as it respects taste or boldness of design." Rennel's Memoir, Introd. p. xxii. Our latest informants are the most intelligent. Mr. Ward (Introd. p. lxii.) assures us, "whatever may have been the case in other countries, idolatry in this has certainly not contributed to carry the arts of painting or sculpture to any perfection." The Abbé Dubois (p. 463) observes, "that the ornamental arts, such as painting, instrumental music, and the like, are extremely low in estimation. Hardly any but the low tribe of the Mushiers exercise the first of these; and music is nearly confined to the barbers and Pariahs: instrumental music wholly so. The small encouragement these two arts receive is, no doubt, owing to the little progress they have made. In painting, nothing can be seen but mere daubing, set off with bright colours and extravagant glare. And though all Hindus are great lovers of music, introducing it into all their civil and religious ceremonies, yet I can vouch that it is still in its infancy."

[1] Royal Comment. part ii. book ii. chap. xxx. Frezier (Voyage to the South Sea, p. 263) says of the same people, "They have a genius for arts, and are good at imitating what they see, but very poor at invention."

[2] See the Discourse, Asiatic Researches, i. 429. "Invented apologues!" as well might he tell us they invented language. And the "*decimal scale!*" as if they were the only nation that had ten fingers! or, as if most nations had not been led, by the simple and very natural process of counting by the fingers, to denominate and distinguish numbers by comparison with that sum! The Scandinavians, Mallet informs us, counted up the unities to twelve, and denominated higher numbers by comparison with twelve, which, he justly remarks, is preferable to ten, as being more divisible into fractions. Mallet, Introd. Hist. Denmark, vol. i. chap. xiii. The Swedes and Icelanders, as well as Scotch, retain a memorial of this in their great hundred. From

chess is a species of art, the account of it seems to belong to this place; and as it has been rated high among the proofs of the supposed civilisation of the Hindus, we must see what it really imports. Though there is no evidence that the Hindus invented the game, except their own pretensions,[1] which as evidence, are of very little value, it is by no means improbable. The invention of ingenious games is a feat most commonly displayed by nations in their rude condition. It is prior to the birth of industry that men have the strongest need for games, to relieve them from the pain of idleness: at that period they are most addicted to gaming; bestow upon it the greatest portion of time; and most intensely fix upon it all their faculties. It is, in fact, the natural occupation and resource of a rude mind, whenever destitute of the motives to industry. The valuable and intelligent historian of Chili observes of a tribe, but a few removes from the savage state, "If what the celebrated Leibnitz asserts is true, that men have never discovered greater talents than in the invention of the different kinds of games, the Araucanians may justly claim the merit of not being in this respect inferior to other nations. Their games are very numerous, and for the most part very ingenious; they are divided into the sedentary and gymnastic. It is a curious fact, and worthy of notice, that among the first is the game of chess, which they call *comican*, and which has been known to them from time immemorial. The game of *quechu*, which they esteem highly, has a great affinity to that of backgammon, but instead of dice, they make use of triangular pieces of bone marked with points, which they throw with a little hoop or circle, supported by two pegs."[2]

Mr. Park we learn that some of the negro tribes in Africa counted only five, the number of fingers on one of the hands, and then doubled; thus, instead of six, they said five and one; seven, five and two, &c. Park's Travels in Africa, p. 17.

[1] This is not true: we have not the evidence of their own pretensions. The evidence is that of Mohammedan writers: the king of India is said by Firdausi, in the Shah Nama, and the story is therefore of the tenth century at latest, to have sent a chess-board and a teacher to Naushirvan. Sir William Jones refers to Firdausi as his authority, and this reference might have shown by whom the story was told. Various Mohammedan writers are quoted by Hyde, in his Historia Shahiludii, who all concur in attributing the invention to the Indians.—W.

[2] Molina, Civil Hist. of Chili, book ii. chap. x. The Persians claim the invention of this game; and as their game is radically different from that of the Hindus, it is probable they are both inventions. See Chardin, Voy. en Perse,

BOOK II. CHAP. VIII.

Though the Hindus knew the art of making a species of rude glass, which was manufactured into trinkets and ornaments for the women, they had never possessed sufficient ingenuity to apply it to the many useful purposes to which it is so admirably adapted. In few climates is glass in windows more conducive to comfort than that of Hindustan, yet the Hindus had never learnt to afford this accommodation to themselves.[1] Of its adaptation to optical purposes they were so ignorant, that they were astonished and confounded at the effects of a common spy-glass. They are unable to construct furnaces sufficiently powerful to melt either European glass, or cast-iron.[2]

---

iii, 62. Gibbon, vii. 276, marks a fact in the narrative of Paul Diaconus, expressive of the manners of the Heruli: Dum ad tabulam luderet, while he played at draughts, says Gibbon; but he might as well have said chess; for the word as much expresses the one as the other: And we know that, among the Scandinavians, a game very closely resembling chess was known. The ancient chronicles of the Scandinavians frequently present us with young warriors endeavouring to acquire the good opinion of their mistresses by boasting of their accomplishments, such as *their skill at chess*, their dexterity in swimming and skating, their talents in poetry, and their knowing all the stars by their names. Mallet, Introd. Hist. Denmark, chap. xiii. Mr. Barrow informs us that the chess of the Chinese is totally different from that both of the Hindus and Persians. Travels in China, p. 158. It has been therefore probably, in each of those cases, a separate invention. The idea that chess was invented by the Hindus was, we believe, first started by Hyde (de Relig. Vet. Pers. ii. 1.), and thereafter it has been taken for granted. The curious reader may see an interesting description of a game at chess by four Brahmens, in Moor's Hist. of Capt. Little's Detachment, p. 139. That there are books in India containing the doctrine of chess proves nothing. There are books in Icelandic, on the art of poetry, but the Icelanders were not the inventors of poetry.

[1] The use of glass for windows, is a proof of civilization, that neither Greek nor Roman refinement presents.—W.

[2] "Buchanan's Journey through Mysore, &c." iii. 370. Dr. Tennant says, "Before the arrival of the Europeans, there was not a house in all India furnished with glass windows; even at present, when glass is so common here, I believe none of the natives have availed themselves of so obvious a remedy. Glass is considered by the Europeans as an indispensable requisite in the construction of every Bungalow at the upper stations: they have even introduced the use of it into the camp. Several officers carry, on their march, a frame of glass, which they fix in the windward door of their tents, during the hot winds, should the service call them into the field at that season." Indian Recreations, i. 325. See, too, Voyage aux Indes, par le P. Paolino, ii. 403, 404. The Jews first discovered the art of making glass. Tacit. Hist. lib. v. cap. vii.: Plin. lib. v. cap. xix.; also lib. xxxvi. cap. xxvi.; Strabo, lib. xvi; Josephus, Wars of the Jews, ii. 19, The Hindus seem to be considerably behind the perfection which the Japanese have attained in the useful arts. "As to all sorts of handicrafts," says Kæmpfer, "either curious or useful, they are so far from having occasion for masters, that they rather exceed all other nations in ingenuity and neatness of workmanship, particularly in brass, gold, silver, copper. What skill they have in working and tempering iron, is evident by the goodness and neatness of their arms. No nation in the East is so dexterous and ingenious, in making, carving, graving, gilding of servaas, which is a particular kind of a precious, blackish metal, made artificially of a mixture of copper with a little gold. They weave silken stuffs so fine, so neat and equal, that they are inimitable even to the Chinese." Kæmpfer, Hist. of Japan, Appendix, p. 62.—M.

In almost every manufacture, and certainly as a manufacturing people in general, the Hindus are inferior to the Chinese. Yet Sir William Jones says of that latter people, "Their mechanical arts have nothing in them characteristic of a particular family; nothing which any set of men, in a country so highly favoured by nature, might not have discovered and improved."[1] The partialities, which it was so much his nature to feel, prevented him from perceiving how much less entitled to any kind of admiration were the arts of another people, whom he had adopted it as a business to eulogise.

CHAPTER IX.

Literature.

As the knowledge of what conduces to the augmentation of human enjoyment and the diminution of human misery, is the foundation of all improvement in the condition of human life; and as literature, if not synonymous with that knowledge, is its best friend and its inseparable companion, the literature of any people is one of the sources from which the surest inferences may be drawn with respect to their civilisation.

The first literature is poetry. Poetry is the language of the passions, and men feel, before they speculate. The earliest poetry is the expression of the feelings, by which the minds of rude men are the most powerfully actuated. Before the invention of writing, men are directed also to the use of versification by the aid which it affords to the memory. As everything of which the recollection is valuable must be handed down by tradition, whatever tends to make the tradition accurate is of corresponding importance. No contrivance to this end is comparable to verse; which preserves the ideas by preserving the very words. In verse not only the few historical facts are preserved, to

---

"Casting iron" is not so simple a matter as our author seems to suppose. It is an art that has been practised in this manufacturing country, only within a very few years. The Hindus have the art of smelting iron, of welding it, and of making steel; and have had these arts from time immemorial. Ctesias notices the excellence of Indian steel.—W.

[1] Works of Sir W. Jones, Discourse on the Chinese.

BOOK II. CHAP. IX.

which the curiosity of a rude age attaches itself, but in verse are promulgated the maxims of religion, and the ordinances of law. Even after the noble art of writing is known, the habit of consigning to verse every idea, destined for permanency, continues, till certain new steps are effected in the intellectual career.[1]

At this first stage the literature of the Hindus has always remained. The habit of expressing everything in verse; a habit which urgent necessity imposes on a people unacquainted with the use of permanent signs,[2] and which the power of custom upholds, till after a certain progress in improvement, even among those to whom permanent signs are known; we trace among the Hindus to the present day. All their compositions, with wonderfully few exceptions, are in verse. For history they have only certain narrative poems, which depart from all resemblance to truth and nature; and have evidently no further connection with fact than the use of certain names and a few remote allusions. Their laws, like those of rude nations in general, are in verse. Their sacred books, and even their books of

[1] "It was long before mankind knew the art of writing; but they very early invented several methods to supply, in a good measure, that want. The method most commonly used was, to compose their histories in verse, and sing them. Legislators made use of this expedient to consign and hand down to posterity their regulations. The first laws of all nations were composed in verse, and sung. Apollo, according to a very ancient tradition, was one of the first legislators. The same tradition says, that he published his laws to the sound of his lyre, that is to say, that he had set them to music. We have certain proof that the first laws of Greece were a kind of songs. The laws of the ancient inhabitants of Spain were verses which they sung. Tuiston was regarded by the Germans as their first lawgiver. They said he put his laws into verses and songs. This ancient custom was long kept up by several nations." Goguet's Origin of Laws, i. 28. See the various authorities there quoted. The laws of the Druids were in verse. Henry. Hist. of Great Britain, i. 315.

[2] It is not clear what the writer means by "permanent signs." If he means the art of printing, the Hindus were, in that respect, situated similarly as the Greeks and Romans were; and they should have also retained the use of metre in their literature. If he means the art of writing, the Hindus have been in possession of that, as long as of a literature, for anything we know to the contrary—certainly long enough to have rendered the use of memorial stanzas as a substitute for writing, unnecessary and obsolete. A little consideration might have led the writer to suspect that his theory did not satisfactorily account for the singularity, for the practice has nothing in common with the carmina antiqua of the Germans. The principal reason for the continued use of metre, seems to be the greater facility of its composition. Sanscrit metre is unencumbered by rhyme—the prosody is infinitely varied—and the greater freedom of syntax, and the facility of forming compound terms, in which grammatical inflexions are merged, render it less laborious to construct metrical stanzas, than to attend to the niceties of a complex grammar, which are indispensable to the composition of intelligible prose. This seems to be the chief inducement to the continuation of the practice, and not the power of habit alone.—W.

science, are in verse; and what is more wonderful still, their very dictionaries.[1]

There is scarcely any point connected with the state of Hindu society, on which the spirit of exaggeration and enthusiasm has more signally displayed itself than the poetry of the Hindus. Among those whose disposition was more to admire than explore, scarcely any poetry has been regarded as presenting higher claims to admiration. Among the Hindus there are two great poems, the Ramayan, and the Mahabharat, which are long narratives, or rather miscellanies, in verse, and which their admirers have been puzzled whether to denominate histories, or epic poems. By the Hindus themselves, they are moreover regarded as books of religion; nay, further, as books of law; and in the Digest which the Brahmens, under the authority of the British government, have recently compiled, the text of these poems is inserted as text of the law, in the same manner as the text of any other legal authority and standard. They may even be regarded as books of philosophy; and accordingly the part of the Mahabharat, with the translation of which Mr. Wilkins has favoured us, he actually presents to his reader as one of the most instructive specimens of the philosophical speculations of the country.

It is incompatible with the present purpose to speak of these poems in more than general terms. They describe a series of actions in which a number of men and gods are jointly engaged. These fictions are not only more extravagant, and unnatural, less correspondent with the physical and moral laws of the universe, but are less ingenious, more monstrous, and have less of anything that can engage the affection, awaken sympathy, or excite admiration, reverence, or terror, than the poems of any other, even the rudest people with whom our knowledge of the globe

[1] "Le Dictionnaire Amarasinha est écrit en vers Sanscrit, comme tous les anciens livres, et n'est pas divisé par chapitres comme les nôtres, mais par classes de noms...... ainsi...... classe *Svarggavargga*, c'est à dire classe des noms qui apartiennent au ciel; *Manouchavargga*, de ceux qui apartiennent à l'homme," etc. Voyage aux Indes Orientales, par le P. Paolino, ii. 228. "Presque tous les livres Indiens sont écrits en vers. L'astronomie, la médecine, l'histoire, tout se chante." Ibid. p. 369. The same was the case with the ancient Germans: "Celebrant carminibus antiquis, quod unum apud illos memoriæ et annalium genus est, Tuistonem," etc. Tacit. de mor. Germ. cap. x.

BOOK II. CHAP. IX.

has yet brought us acquainted.[1] They are excessively prolix and insipid. They are often, through long passages, trifling and childish to a degree, which those acquainted with only European poetry, can hardly conceive. Of the style in which they are composed, it is far from too much to say, that all the vices which characterize the style of rude nations, and particularly those of Asia, they exhibit in perfection. Inflation: metaphors perpetual, and these the most violent and strained, often the most unnatural and ridiculous; obscurity; tautology; repetition; verbosity; confusion; incoherence; distinguish the Mahabharat and Ramayan.[2] That amid the numberless effu-

[1] Even Mr. Maurice, whose appetite for Hindu miracles is not easily overcome, could not digest the beauties of their historic muse. After an exhibition of some of these specimens in his history, he says, "I know not whether some of my readers may not be so insensible to the charms of the Indian historic muse as to rejoice that the Ramayan (only passages of it were then in an English dress) has not been translated; for certainly inflated accounts of the combats of giants, hurling rocks, and darting serpents at one another, and of monsters whose blood, spouting forth in torrents, is formed into considerable rivers, are not very consistent with the sober and dignified page of history." Maurice, Hist. of Hindustan, ii. 100. "To the above list of absurdities we may add monsters with ten heads and a hundred hands, which continue to fight after all their heads are cut off, and mow down whole battalions." Ibid. p. 248. "The minute accounts of incantations and combats of giants, that fill the Indian legends, however they may astonish the oriental literati, have no charm for the polished scholar of western climes, and are justly consigned to puerile reading." Ibid. p. 251. Yet Sir William Jones could say, "The first poet of the Hindus was the great Valmic; and his Ramayan is an epic poem on the story of Rama (or rather of the three Ramas), which, in unity of action, magnificence of imagery, and elegance of style, far surpasses the learned and elaborate work of Nonnus." See Asiat. Res. i. 258. We strongly suspect that Sir William Jones never read the poem; or more of it than scraps.

[2] At the time at which this was written, no other specimen of the Mahabharat had been translated, than the philosophical dialogue of the Geeta, and as there are certainly no such faults in that composition as those which Mr. Mill describes, he must have depended wholly upon his imagination for his knowledge of their existence in the rest of the poem. Some portions of the Ramayana had been rendered very uncouthly into English; but whatever may be the defects there so ruthlessly stripped of every redeeming grace, most certainly page after page will be searched in vain for "metaphors perpetual, and these the most violent, strained, unnatural, and ridiculous." It is clear, therefore, that Mr. Mill had not read even such portion of the Ramayana as was within his reach, but condemns both it and the Mahabharata upon the credit of some vague and superficial criticism, applicable not to Hindu, but to Mohammedan poetry; the characteristics of which are totally unlike. There is not so wide a contrast between Hindu and European poetry, as between Hindu and Persian. With respect to the particular poems under consideration, they are not to be judged of by a European standard, and that which to a person professing the Hindu religion, constitutes their greatest charm, is to us their main deformity; but, leaving the absurd inventions of mythology out of view, they both abound in poetical beauties of the first order, and particularly in delineations of picturesque manners and situations, and in the expression of natural and amiable feeling. On this subject we may take the opinion of a more competent judge of poetical merit than the historian. "Le Ramayana et le Mahabharata sont des monumens d'une antiquité vénérable; mais, abstraction faite de la valeur que cela leur donne, j'y trouve des choses

sions, which a wild imagination throws forth, in its loose and thoughtless career, there should now and then be something which approaches the confines of reason and taste, is so far from surprising, that it would be truly surprising if there were not. A happy description, or here and there the vivid conception of a striking circumstance, are not sufficient; the exact observation of nature, and the symmetry of a whole, are necessary, to designate the poetry of a cultivated people.

Of the poems in dialogue, or in the dramatic form, Sacontala has been selected as the most favourable specimen. The author, Calidas, though he left only two dramatic pieces, Sir William Jones denominates the Shakspeare of India, and tells us that he stands next in reputation to their great historic poets, Valmic and Vyasa.

Sacontala was the daughter of a pious king, named Causica, and of a goddess of the lower heaven; brought up by a devout hermit, as his daughter, in a consecrated grove. The sovereign of the district, on a hunting excursion, arrives, by accident in the forest. He observes Sacontala, and her two companions, the daughters of the hermit, in the grove, with watering pots in their hands, watering their plants. Instantly he is captivated. He enters into conversation with the damsels, and the heart of Sacontala is secretly inflamed. The king dismisses his attendants, and resolves to remain in the forest. In a little time the quality of the lover is ascertained, while the secret agitation in the bosom of Sacontala throws her into a languor which resembles disease. The king overhears a conversation between her and her companions, in which, being closely interrogated, she confesses her love. The king immediately discovers himself, and declares his passion. The two friends contrive to leave them together, and they consummate "that kind of marriage which two lovers contract from the desire of amorous embraces." So precipitate a conclusion, irreconcileable as it is with the notions of a refined people, is one of the numerous mar-

sublimes, d'autres pleines de charme et de grace, une fécondité inépuisable de l'imagination, l'attrait du merveilleux, de nobles caractères, des situations passionnées, et je ne sais quelle candeur sainte et ingénue, dans les mœurs qui y sont peints." Réflexions sur l'Etude des Langues Asiatiques, par A. W. de Schlegel.—W.

BOOK II. CHAP. IX.

riages legal among the Hindus. Presently, however, the king is summoned to his court. He promises to send for his wife in three days, and leaves a ring. In the meantime a Brahmen, of a proud and choleric temper, comes to the residence of the hermit, when his two daughters are at a little distance, and Sacontala has been overtaken with sleep. Finding no one to receive him with the expected honours, he utters an imprecation: "He on whom thou art meditating, on whom alone thy heart is now fixed, while thou neglectest a pure gem of devotion who demands hospitality, shall forget thee when thou seest him next, as a man restored to sobriety, forgets the words which he uttered in a state of intoxication." This malediction, which falls upon Sacontala, is overheard by her companions, and fills them with horror. They hasten to appease the angry Brahmen; who tells them his words cannot be recalled, but that the spell would be dissolved when the lord of Sacontala should look upon his ring. Her two friends agree to conceal the calamity from Sacontala, who now languishes at the neglect of her husband, and finds herself pregnant. The hermit Canwa, who at the time of the visit of the king was absent from home, returns, and is, by a voice from heaven, made acquainted with the events which have intervened. Encouraged by good omens, he soothes Sacontala, and resolves to send her to her lord. Her friends instruct her, should he not immediately recognise her, to show him the ring. Arrived at the palace, she is disowned by the king; thinks of the ring, but discovers it is lost. The king treats her, and the messengers who brought her, as impostors; and orders them into custody; but while they are conveying her away, a body of light, descending in a female shape, receives her into its bosom, and disappears; upon which the king regards the whole as a piece of sorcery, and dismisses it from his thoughts. After a time, however, the ring is found, and conveyed to the king; when his wife, and all the connected circumstances immediately rush upon his mind. He is then plunged into affliction; ignorant where Sacontala may be found. In this despondency, he is summoned by Indra, the god of the firmament, to aid him against a race of giants, whom Indra is unable to subdue. Having ascended to the celestial regions, and acquitted himself gloriously in the divine service, he is conveyed, in his descent to the earth, to the mountain Hemacuta, "where Casyapa, father of the immortals, and Aditi his consort, reside in blessed retirement." To this sacred spot had Sacontala, by her mother's influence, been conveyed; and there she had brought forth her son, a wonderful infant, whom its father found at play with a lion's whelp, and making the powerful animal feel the superiority of his strength. The king now recognises his wife and his son, of whom the most remarkable things are portended; and perfect happiness succeeds.

There is surely nothing in the invention of this story, which is above the powers of the imagination in an uncultivated age. With the scenery and the manners which the Hindu poet has perpetually present to his observation, and the mythology which perpetually reigns in his thoughts, the incidents, are among the most obvious, and the most easy to be imagined, which it was possible for him to choose. Two persons of celestial beauty and accomplishments meet together in a solitary place, and fall mutually in love: To the invention of this scene, but little ingenuity can be supposed to be requisite. To create an interest in this love, it was necessary it should be crossed. Surely no contrivance for such a purpose was ever less entitled to admiration than the curse of a Brahmen. A ring, with power to dissolve the charm, and that ring at the moment of necessity lost, are contrivances to bring about a great event, which not only display the rudeness of an ignorant age, but have been literally, or almost literally, repeated, innumerable times, in the fables of other uncultivated nations. To overcome the difficulties, which the interest of the plot rendered it necessary to raise, by carrying a man to heaven to conquer giants for a god, for whom the god was not a match, is an expedient which requires neither art nor invention; and which could never be endured, where judgment and taste have received any considerable cultivation.[1]

1 Much of what is intended for disparagement here is the highest commendation that criticism could have uttered. The incidents are natural and easy, and in accordance with national taste and belief. The hero and heroine are persons of the highest interest, not only for their rank, but their beauty and accomplishments. Yet, notwithstanding their exalted excellence, they are subjected to the usual fate of lovers. The course of true love runs not smooth,

BOOK II.
CHAP. IX.

The poem, indeed, has some beautiful passages. The courtship between Sacontala and Dushmantu is delicate and interesting; and the workings of the passion in two amiable minds are naturally and vividly portrayed. The friendship which exists between the three youthful maidens is tender and delightful; and the scene which takes place when Sacontala is about to leave the peaceful hermitage where she had happily spent her youth; her expressions of tenderness to her friends, her affectionate parting with the domestic animals she had tended, and even with the flowers and trees in which she had delighted, breathe more than pastoral sweetness. These, however, are precisely the ideas and affections, wherever the scene is a peaceful one, which may naturally arise in the simplest state of society; as the fables of the golden age, and of Arcadia, abundantly testify; and in whatever constitutes the beauty of these scenes, they are rivalled by the Song of Solomon, which is avowedly the production of a simple and unpolished age.[1] Beyond these few passages, there is nothing in Sacontala, which either accords with the understanding, or can gratify the fancy, of an instructed people.

Sir William Jones, who, on the subject of a supposed ancient state of high civilization, riches, and happiness among the Hindus, takes everything for granted, not only without proof, but in opposition to almost everything, saving the assumptions of the Brahmens, which could lead him to a different conclusion, says, "The dramatic species

---

and they are made unhappy by the most awful, in Hindu estimation, of all events, the imprecation of a Brahman. The interest is artfully kept up by a contrivance to which the only grave objection is, that it is not new, the consequence of its being popular; and a happy catastrophe is brought about by the most approved of all rules, the dignus vindice nodus. In all this there is great art, and the skill is evidenced by the success with which it has deceived the critic.—W.

[1] Of the Song of Solomon, Voltaire, notwithstanding all his prejudices against the Jews, confesses, "Après tout, ce cantique est un morceau précieux de l'antiquité. C'est le seul livre d'amour qui nous soit resté des Hébreux. Il y est souvent parlé de jouissance. C'est une églogue Juive. Le style est comme celui de tous les ouvrages d'éloquence des Hébreux, sans liaison, sans suite, plein de répétitions, confus, ridiculement métaphorique; mais il y a des endroits qui respirent la naiveté et l'amour." Voltaire, Diction. Philos., Mot *Solomon.* The criticisms would in most respects exactly suit Sacontala.—M.

Few, except the writer, would have had recourse to Voltaire, for a criticism on the Song of Solomon. Still fewer will find any resemblance between it and Sacontala.—W.

of entertainment must have been carried to great perfection, when Vicramaditya, who reigned in the first century before Christ, gave encouragement to poets, philologers, and mathematicians, at a time when the Britons were as unlettered and unpolished as the army of Hanumat."[1] Sir William forgets that, more than a century before Christ, the Britons had their Druids; between whom and the Brahmens,[2] in character, doctrines, and acquirements, a remarkable similarity has been traced.[3]

The mere existence, however, of dramatic entertainments has been held forth, in the case of the Hindus, as proof of a high state of civilization; and Sir William Jones, whose imagination on the accomplishments of the orientals delighted to gild, thinks the representation of Sacontala must have been something pre-eminently glorious; as the scenery must have been striking; and "as there is good reason," he says, "to believe, that the court of Avanti was equal in brilliancy, in the reign of Vicramaditya, to that of any monarch in any age or country."[4] To how great a degree this latter supposition is erroneous, we shall presently see. In the meantime, it is proper to remark, that nations may be acquainted with dramatic entertainments, who have made but little progress in knowledge and civilization. In extent of dominion, power, and everything on which the splendour of a court de-

[1] Preface to Sir William Jones's Translation of Sacontala.

[2] When the voluminous works of the Druids, or when any written specimens of them are produced, we shall be better able to compare their learning with that of the Brahmans. Even if the testimony of such superficial and credulous inquirers as the ancients undoubtedly were, be admitted, it will not be denied that Sir William Jones's parallel is allowable. The Britons were, if we may credit the same testimony, which vouches for "the learning" of the Druids, as unlettered and unpolished as the army of Hanumat: they certainly had no theatrical amusements.—W.

[3] The conformities in their religious system have already been remarked. All their doctrines, their narratives, and even the laws of which they were the promulgators, were delivered in verse. "They had made considerable progress," says Dr. Henry, "in several branches of learning. We shall be confirmed in this," he adds, "by observing the respectful terms in which the best Greek and Roman writers speak of their learning. Diogenes Laertius places them in the same rank, in point of learning and philosophy, with the Chaldeans of Assyria, the Magi of Persia, and the gymnosophists and Brachmans of India. Both Cæsar and Mela observe that they had formed very large systems of astronomy and natural philosophy; and that these systems, together with their observation on other parts of learning, were so voluminous, that their scholars spent no less than twenty years in making themselves master of them, and in getting by heart that infinite multitude of verses in which they were contained." Henry's Hist. of Great Britain. ii. 5, and i. 153.

[4] Preface to Sacontala.

pends, it will not, probably, be alleged, that any Hindu sovereign ever surpassed the present emperors of China. The Chinese, too, are excessively fond of dramatic performances; and they excel in poetry as well as the Hindus; yet our British ambassador, and his retinue, found their dramatic representations very rude and dull entertainments.[1]

As poetry is the first cultivated of all the branches of literature, there is at least one remarkable instance, that of Homer, to prove, that in a rude state of society it may acquire extraordinary perfection. At a point of civilization lower than that which we ascribe to the Hindus, poetry has been produced more excellent than theirs. From the effects produced by the poetic declamations of the Druids, it is certain that they must have possessed the faculty of working powerfully on the imaginations and sympathies of their audience. The Celtic poetry, ascribed to Ossian, and other bards, which, whatever age, more recent or more remote, controversy may assign for its date, is, beyond a doubt, the production of a people whose ideas were extremely scanty, and their manners rude, surpasses,

[1] "Wretched dramas," Lord Macartney calls them. Barrow's Life of Lord Macartney, ii. 286.

Garcilasso de la Vega, on the subject of the ancient Peruvians, says, "The Amautas, who were men of the best ingenuity among them, invented comedies and tragedies, which, in their solemn festivals they represented before their king and the lords of his court.—The plot or argument of their tragedies was to represent their military exploits, and the triumphs, victories, and heroic actions of their renowned men." Royal Commentaries of Peru, book ii. chap. xv.

"Dramatic as well as lyric poetry," says Clavigero, "was greatly in repute among the Mexicans." He then describes their theatres, and adds, "Boturini says, that the Mexican comedies were excellent." Clavigero, Hist. of Mexico, book vii. sect. 43. Carli (Lettres Américaines, i. 296) says, "Mais que direz vous si je vous assure que les Péruviens jouoient des comédies pendant ces fêtes, et qu'ils aimoient passionnément ce plaisir. Cela est cependant vrai. La comédie faisoit donc un des plaisirs du Péru; mais la tragédie étoit préférée à Tlascala, dont le peuple étoit républicain. Chez un peuple indépendant on se plait à produire les tyrans sur la scène pour en inspirer la haine à la génération actuelle, qui la transmet à la suivante........ Mais on a aussi remarqué ce goût du théâtre chez plusieurs peuples des îles du Sud." But an art which is known to the islanders of the South Sea, is not a proof of high civilization. The people in the Birman empire are fond of dramatic entertainments; but these entertainments among them are very rude. Dr. Buchanan, Asiatic Res. vi. 305.—M.

Of the Chinese drama, we are now qualified to judge, as well as of the Hindu, by translations; and the comparison is much in favour of the latter. The action of Chinese plays is unskilfully conducted, and they are wanting in the high poetic tone which distinguishes those of the Hindus; at the same time they are ingenious, often interesting, and represent manners and feelings with truth, and sometimes with force. They are the works of a civilized people. Of the Peruvian and Mexican theatre we may estimate the merits when specimens are produced.—W.

in every point of excellence, the sterile extravagance of the Hindus.[1] In so rude a state of society as that which existed in Denmark, Iceland, Sweden, at the time of our Anglo-Saxon monarchies, the number of poets, and the power of their compositions, were exceedingly great.[2]

Even in that figurative and inflated style, which has been supposed a mark of oriental composition, and is, in reality, a mark only of a low stage of society, uniformly discovered in the language of a rude people, the poetry of the northern bards exhibits a resemblance to that of the Hindus, the Persians, Arabians, and other eastern nations,[3] "The style of these ancient poems," says Mallet, "is very enigmatical and figurative, very remote from common lan-

1 The poems of Ossian are the impositions of a civilized age, founded upon a few ancient traditions; and their unnatural, and forced turgidity, their want of truth, as pictures of manners, their barrenness of incidents, and the absence of both simplicity and variety, render them unworthy to be named with the authentic, natural and rich, although, sometimes, extravagant inventions of the Hindus.—W.

2 "The poets of the north" (to use the words of Dr. Henry) "were particularly famous in this period, and greatly caressed by our Anglo-Saxon kings. 'It would be endless,' (says an excellent antiquary) 'to name all the poets of the north who flourished in the courts of the kings of England, or to relate the distinguished honours and magnificent presents that were heaped upon them.' The same writer hath preserved the names of no fewer than eight of those Danish, Norwegian, and Icelandic poets, who flourished in the Court of Canute the Great.—The poems of those ancient bards of the north, are said to have produced the most amazing effects on those who heard them, and to have roused or soothed the most impetuous passions of the human mind. Revenge, it is well known, rages with the greatest violence in the hearts of warlike, fierce barbarians, and is, of all their passions, the most furious and ungovernable: yet it is said to have been subdued by the enchanting power of poetry. Egil-Skallagrim, a famous poet of those times, had quarrelled with Eric Blodox, King of Norway; and in the course of the quarrel had killed the King's son and several of his friends; which raised the rage of Eric against him to the greatest height. Egil was taken prisoner, and sent to the King, who was then in Northumberland. No sooner was he brought into the presence of the enraged monarch, who had in his own mind doomed him to the most cruel tortures, than he began to sing a poem which he had composed in praise of his royal virtues, and conveyed his flattery in such sweet and soothing strains, that they procured him not only the forgiveness of all his crimes, but even the favour of his prince. The power of poetry is thus described in one of their most ancient odes: 'I know a song by which I soften and enchant the arms of my enemies, and render their weapons of none effect. I know a song which I need only to sing when men have loaded me with bonds; for the moment I sing it my chains fall in pieces, and I walk forth at liberty. I know a song useful to all mankind: for as soon as hatred inflames the sons of men, the moment I sing it, they are appeased. I know a song of such virtue, that were I caught in a storm, I can hush the winds, and render the air perfectly calm.'—Those ancient bards, who had acquired so great an ascendant over the minds of their ferocious countrymen, must certainly have been possessed of an uncommon portion of that poetic fire, which is the gift of nature, and cannot be acquired by art." —Henry's Hist. of Great Britain, book ii. chap. v.

3 This is repetition of an error already corrected. The poetry of England might be classed with those of Persia and Arabia, with equal propriety, as that of the Hindus.—W.

BOOK II. CHAP. IX.

guage; and for that reason, grand, but timid; sublime, but obscure. If everything should be expressed by imagery, figures, hyperboles, and allegories, the Scandinavians may rank in the highest class of poets."[1] For these peculiarities, too, this author philosophically accounts. "The soaring flights of fancy, may possibly more peculiarly belong to a rude and uncultivated, than to a civilized people. The great objects of nature strike more forcibly on their imaginations. Their passions are not impaired by the constraint of laws and education. The paucity of their ideas, and the barrenness of the language, oblige them to borrow from all nature, images in which to clothe their conceptions."[2] The poetry of the Persians resembles that of the Arabians; both resemble that of the Hindus; both have been celebrated in still higher strains, and are entitled to more of our admiration. The Persians have their

[1] Mallet, Introd. Hist. Denmark, i. 13. The following is a very soft but correct delineation of the rude features of Hindu poetry. "The poetical expression of the Hindus perhaps offends by too great loftiness and emphasis. One may understand their books and conversation in prose; but it is impossible to comprehend those in verse, until diligent study has rendered them familiar. Quaint phrases, perpetual allegories, the poetical terminations of the words, contracted expressions and the like, render the poetical style obscure and difficult to be understood, excepting to those who are inured to it. One of the principal defects of the Hindu poets is that their descriptions are commonly too long and minute. For example, if they are describing a beautiful woman, they are never contented with drawing her likeness with a single stroke.........Such a mode of expression would not be strong enough for the gross comprehension of a Hindu. The poet must particularize the beauty of her eyes, her forehead, her nose, her cheeks, and must expatiate on the colour of her skin, and the manner in which she adorns every part of her body. He will describe the turn and proportion of her arms, legs, thighs, shoulders, chest, and, in a word, of all parts, visible or invisible; with an accurate recital of the shape and form which best indicate their beauty and symmetry. He will never desist from his colouring till he has represented in detail every feature and part in the most laboured and tedious style, but at the same time with the closest resemblance. The epithets, in their poetical style, are frequent, and almost always figurative.—The brevity and conciseness of many modes of expression in the Hindu idioms does not hinder their style, upon the whole, from being extremely diffuse.—To give an exact idea of the different species of Hindu poesy would not be much relished by the greater number of readers, so different in their manner from ours. All their little pieces that I have seen are in general very flat." Description, &c. of the People of India, by the Abbé Dubois, p. 267.

[2] Mallet, ut supra. In the very subjects of their poems, as well as the style of them, the Scandinavian bards bore a great resemblance to the Hindu. Of the poetry of the Scalds, Mallet says (Ibid. ii. 183), "The same taste and mode of composition prevails every where: we have constantly allegories and combats; giants contending with the gods: Loke perpetually deceiving them; Thor interposing in their defence, &c." The Scandinavians had not only striking poems, but treatises on the art of poetry. Id. Introduction to the Edda, p. xix. Clavigero says of the Mexicans, "The language of their poetry was brilliant, pure, and agreeable, figurative, and embellished with frequent comparisons to the most pleasing objects in nature, such as flowers, trees rivers, &c." Hist. of Mex. book vii. sect. 42.

great historic poem, the *Shah Namu*, corresponding to the Mahabharat or Ramayan of the Hindus. It embraces a period of 3700 years, and consists of 60,000 rhymed couplets. On this poem, the most lofty epithets of praise have been bestowed; and a part of it, embracing a period of 300 years, Sir William Jones selects as itself a whole; a poem truly epic, of which the merit hardly yields to that of the Iliad itself.[1] We shall speak of it in the language of an oriental scholar, who has made the literature of Persia more peculiarly his study than Sir William Jones. The Shah Namu, says Mr. Scott Waring, "has probably been praised as much for its length, as its intrinsic merit. When we allow it is unequalled in the East, we must pause before we pronounce it to be equal, or to approach very nearly, to the divinest poem of the West. The stories in the Shah Namu," says he, "are intricate and perplexed, and as they have a relation to each other, they can only be understood by a knowledge of the whole. Episodes are interwoven in episodes; peace and war succeed each other; and centuries pass away without making any alteration in the conduct of the poem — the same prince continues to resist the Persian arms; the same hero leads them to glory—and the subterfuge of supposing two Afrasiabs or two Roostums, betrays, at least, the intricacy and confusion of the whole fable. The character of Nestor answered the most important ends, his eloquence and experience had a wonderful effect in soothing the contentions of a divided council; but the age of Zal or of Roostum answers no purpose, for they only share longevity in common with their fellow creatures." In many instances, he adds, "the poet is tedious and uninteresting. He is often too minute; and by making his description particular, makes it ridiculous. An example of this may be given in his description of Ukwan Deo; which, instead of expressing his immense size by some bold figure, gives us his exact measure: *He was one hundred yards high, and twenty broad*."[2] With respect to the style of this, as well as of

[1] The words of Sir William Jones are: "Nobilissimum interea, et longissimum (voluminis enim permagni, prope dimidiam partem constituit) est sine ulla dubitatione vere epicum, et profecto nullum est ab Europeis scriptum poema, quod ad Homeri dignitatem, et quasi cœlestem ardorem propius accedat." Works, ii. 502.

[2] Tour to Sheeraz, by Ed. Scott Waring, pp. 158, 159, 160, 198.

other Persian poets, the same author informs us, that "the style of the most admired Persian authors is verbose and turgid; the mind is filled with words and epithets, and you probably meet with several quibbles and monstrous images before you arrive at one fact."[1] And in another passage he says, "The Persian poets, in all their similes or comparisons, fall infinitely below mediocrity."[2]

As soon as reason begins to have considerable influence in the direction of human affairs, no use of letters is deemed more important than that of preserving an accurate record of those events and actions by which the interests of the nations have been promoted or impaired. But the human mind must have a certain degree of culture, before the value of such a memorial is perceived. The actions of his nation, or of his countrymen, which the rude and untutored barbarian is excited to remember, are those which he

[1] Tour to Sheeraz, by Ed. Scott Waring, p. 150. The author adds, "I shall give one instance, from an immense number, of the forced images of Persian historians; it would be disgusting to the reader to produce others:" —a style of which more than one instance would disgust, must be a bad style indeed. "Nous savons assez," says Voltaire, "que le bon goût n'a jamais été connu dans l'Orient.—Otez aux Arabes, aux Persans, aux Juifs, le soleil et la lune, les montagnes et les vallées, les dragons et les basiliscs, il ne leur reste presque plus de poésie." Voltaire, sur les Mœurs et l'Esprit des Nations, tom. i. ch. v.

[2] Ibid. p. 235. To the imagination of the eastern poets, and above all, of the Hindus, may be aptly applied, in many of its particulars, the description of the Demoness, Imagination, in the enchanted castle of Hermaphrodix:

> Sous les grands arcs — d'un immense portique,
> Amas confus de moderne et d'antique,
> Se promenoit un fantôme brillant,
> Au pied léger, à l'œil étincelant,
> Au geste vif, à la marche égarée,
> La tête haute, et de clinquans parée.
> On voit son corps toujours en action,
> Et son nom est l'*Imagination*.
> *Non cette belle et charmante déesse*
> *Qui présida dans Rome et dans la Grèce,*
> Aux beaux travaux de tant de grands auteurs,
> Qui repandit l'éclat de ses couleurs;
> *Mais celle-la qu'abjure le bon sens,*
> *Cette étourdie, effarée, insipide,*
> Que tant d'auteurs, approchent de si près.
> . . . .
> Près d'elle étoit le Galimatias,
> Monstre bavard caressé dans ses bras.
>
> La Pucelle d'Orléans, Chant 17me.

Gibbon well denominates the Koran, "an endless incoherent rhapsody of fable, and precept, and declamation, which seldom excites a sentiment or an idea, which sometimes crawls in the dust, and is sometimes lost in the clouds." Chap. l. p. 269. Yet it is a superior composition to any work among the Hindus.—M.

This is boldly said; especially as the means of comparison were wholly wanting. It would be as reasonable to compare the Koran with the Iliad, as with the Mahabharat; but a critic of the school of Voltaire is as little likely to exhibit diffidence of judgment, as purity of taste.—W.

wonders at and admires; and they are remembered solely for the pleasure of those emotions. Exaggeration, therefore, is more fitted to his desires than exactness; and poetry than history. Swelled by fiction, and set off with the embellishments of fancy, the scene lays hold of his imagination, and kindles his passions. All rude nations, even those to whom the use of letters has long been familiar, neglect history, and are gratified with the productions of the mythologists and poets.[1]

It is allowed on all hands that no historical composition existed in the literature of the Hindus; they had not reached that point of intellectual maturity, at which the value of a record of the past for the guidance of the future begins to be understood. "The Hindus," says that zealous and industrious Sanscrit scholar, Mr. Wilford, "have no ancient civil history." Remarking a coincidence in this characteristic circumstance between them and another ancient people, he adds, "Nor had the Egyptians any work purely historical."[2] Major Rennel says, that, founded on Hindu materials, there is no known history of Hindustan, nor any record of the historical events of that country prior to

[1] The mistake which runs through most of our author's generalisations, is here committed; that of drawing universal inferences from particular instances: because the Greeks early cultivated history, therefore all other people who have emerged from barbarism, cultivate history; the Hindus have neglected this branch of literature; therefore, they are still barbarians. But, as no one but the writer would so regard them, we must look to other causes to explain what may be admitted, with some reservation, to be true. It is not correct to say, that the Hindus never compiled history, particularly since the Mohammedan conquest. The literature of the south abounds with local histories by Hindu authors. Mr. Stirling found various chronicles in Orissa; and Col. Tod has met with equally abundant materials in Rajputana. The history of Cashmir has been brought down, by a succession of Hindu authors, from the remotest ages to the reign of Akbar; and an account of Acbar's reign is the work of a Hindu. See Mackenzie Collection. As. Res. vol. xv., and Tod's Rajasthan. It is, however, true, that the details of ancient times, though more authentic than they are presently represented to be, are few and imperfect; and there are various causes to account for this more satisfactorily than inapplicable generalities. The bias of the Hindu mind was from the first directed to matters of speculation; and it has never attached such value or interest to the concerns of ephemeral mortality, as to deem them worthy of record. The duty of preserving the memory of all such events, was transferred from the Brahman to an inferior order of men; the bard, the herald, the genealogist, whose compilations were never invested with any degree of importance; nor, in general, were they probably of much worth. India appears to have been, with perhaps some rare exceptions, parcelled out into a great number of petty states, whose transactions were of too insignificant a character, whose duration was too brief, whose influence upon the fortunes of the country was too confined, to have offered events that were deserving of commemoration. In later times, the Hindu has had still less inducement to cultivate history, as it would have been little else than a record of his own humiliation, a chronicle of centuries of subjection to foreign rule.—W.

[2] Wilford, on Egypt and the Nile, Asiat. Res. iii. 296.

BOOK II. CHAP. IX.

the Mohammedan conquests;[1] and since that period, it is not to Hindu, but Mohammedan pens that we are indebted for all our knowledge of the Mohammedan conquests, and of the events which preceded the passage to India by the Cape of Good Hope.[2] An inclination at first appeared among the warm admirers of Sanscrit to regard the poems Mahabharat and Ramayan, as a sort of historical records. A more intimate acquaintance with those grotesque productions has demonstrated the impossibility of reconciling them with the

[1] Rennel's Memoir, Introd. p. xl.

[2] "That no Hindu nation, but the Cashmirians, have left us regular histories," says Sir W. Jones, "in their ancient language, we must ever lament." Asiat. Res. iv. xvii. What he meant by excepting the Cashmirians, we know not. No history of them has ever been seen. "Although we have had recourse," says Dr. Tennant, "to the Sanscrit records at Benares for several years, no history of the country has been found, which is the composition of a native." Ind. Rec. i. 10. "Their poets," says Mr. W. Chambers, "seem to have been their only historians as well as divines; and whatever they relate is wrapped up in this burlesque garb, set off, by way of ornament, with circumstances highly incredible and absurd, and all this without any date, and in no order or method, than such as the poet's fancy suggested and found most convenient. Asiat. Res. i. 157. Such is the character of the Puranas, from which Mr. Wilford has exerted himself with such a waste of labour and credulity to extract some scattered fragments of history; or rather something, it is difficult to say what, on which some few historical inferences might be founded. "The department of ancient history in the East is so deformed by fable and anachronism, that it may be considered an absolute blank in Indian literature." Wilks's Mysore, Pref. p. xv. Mr. Dow's prejudices went far: "We must not," says he, (Preface to his Hist. of Hindostan) "with Ferishta, consider the Hindoos as destitute of genuine domestic annals, or that those voluminous records they possess are mere legends framed by the Bramins." Yet it has been found that all which Ferishta said was true, and all that Col. Dow believed was false.—"Seriously speaking, the turn and bent of the imagination of the people of India are such, that they can in no wise be excited but by what is monstrous. Ordinary occurrences make no impression upon them at all. Their attention cannot be gained without the introduction of giants and pygmies. The Brahmans, therefore, having studied this propensity, availed themselves of it to invent a religious worship, which they artfully interwove with their own private interests. This passion of the Hindus for the extraordinary and the wonderful, must have been remarked by every one who has ever so little studied their character. It continually leads to the observation I have so frequently repeated, that as often as it was necessary to move their gross imagination, some circumstance, altogether extravagant, but coloured with the hue of truth, was required to be added to the simplicity of narrative or fact. To give them any idea of the marvellous, something must be invented that will overturn, or at least alter the whole order of nature. The miracles of the Christian religion, however extraordinary they must appear to a common understanding, are by no means so to the Hindus. Upon them they have no effect. The exploits of Joshua and his army, and the prodigies they effected by the interposition of God, in the conquest of the land of Canaan, seem to them unworthy of notice, when compared with the achievements of their own Rama, and the miracles which attended his progress when he subjected Ceylon to his yoke. The mighty strength of Samson dwindles into nothing, when opposed to the overwhelming energy of Bali, of Ravana, and the giants. The resurrection of Lazarus itself is, in their eyes, an ordinary event, of which they see frequent examples, in the Vishnu ceremonies of the Pahvahdam.—I particularize these examples, because they have been actually opposed to me more than once by Brahmans, in my disputations with them on religion." Abbé Dubois, p. 421.

order of human affairs, and, as the only expedient to soften the deformities in which they abound, suggested a theory that they are allegorical.[1]

The ancient Persians, who used the Pehlavi language, appear in this respect to have resembled the Hindus. "I never," says Sir John Malcolm, "have been able to hear of the existence of any work in the ancient Pehlavi that could be deemed historical."[2]

The modern Persians, in this, as in many other respects, are found to have made some progress beyond the ancient Persians, and beyond the Hindus. The first step towards the attainment of perfect history is the production of prose compositions, expressly destined to exhibit a record of real transactions, but in which imagination prevails over exactness, and a series of transactions appears in which the lines of reality can but faintly be traced. With histories of this description the Persians abound; but "the Persians," says Mr. Scott Waring, "do not make a study of history; consequently their histories abound with idle tales, and extravagant fables."[3] Another celebrated Persian scholar says: "The Persians, like other people, have assumed the privilege of romancing on the early periods of society. The first dynasty is, in consequence, embarrassed by fabling. Their most ancient princes are chiefly celebrated for their victories over the demons or genii called dives; and some have reigns assigned to them of eight hundred or a thousand

[1] Such is the opinion of some of the best Sanscrit scholars; for example, of Mr. Wilkins. The same idea is encouraged by Sir William Jones, Asiat. Res. ii. 135. The good sense of Major Rennel rejected at an early period the notion of their historical truth. "The Mahabharat.......... supposed to contain a large portion of interesting historical matter: but if the father of Grecian poetry made so total a change in the story of Helen, in order to give a full scope to his imagination: what security have we that another poet may not mislead us in matters of fact." Memoir, p. xlii. A mind of greater compass and force has previously said, "It were absurd to quote the fable of the Iliad or the Odyssey, the legends of Hercules, Theseus, or Œdipus, as authorities in matter of fact relating to the history of mankind; but they may, with great justice, be cited to ascertain what were the conceptions and sentiments of the age in which they were composed, or to characterize the genius of that people, with whose imaginations they were blended, and by whom they were fondly rehearsed and admired." Ferguson, Essay on the Hist. of Civil Society, part ii. sect. 1.

[2] Hist. of Persia, i. 273. Yet the Jewish scriptures tell us, that the deeds of the kings of Persia were written in chronicles of that kingdom; and Ctesias, who was at the court of Artaxerxes Mnemon, says he had access to volumes contained in the royal archives. The Persians had no historians before the æra of Mohammed; Kinneir's Geog. Mem. of the Persian Empire, p. 49.—In Persia, there is now, as there has long been, a royal historiographer, whose business it is to record the glories of the reigning prince. Ibid.

[3] Tour to Sheeraz, p. 153.

BOOK II. CHAP. IX.

years."[1] On the comparison of the Grecian and native histories of Persia, he says, "There seems to be nearly as much resemblance between the annals of England and Japan, as between the European and Asiatic relations of the same empire." The names and numbers of the kings, as exhibited by the historians of the two countries, have no analogy. No mention in the Persian annals is made of the Great Cyrus, nor of any king of Persia, the events of whose reign can, by any construction, be tortured into a similitude with his. No trace is to be found of Crœsus, of Cambyses, or of his expedition against the Ethiopians; none of Smerdis Magus, or of Darius Hystaspes: "not a vestige of the famous battles of Marathon, Thermopylæ, Salamis, Platæa, or Mycale, nor of the mighty expedition of Xerxes."[2]

1 Richardson's Dissertations, p. 47.

2 Ibid. p. 47—60. He gives the following as the account, by the Persian historians, of the conquest of Alexander. Bahman, the King, had married his own daughter. When he died, leaving her pregnant, he appointed her his successor, if she had no son; and regent, if she had one. The lady wished to reign; and being delivered of a son, concealed his birth. He was exposed, but found, and brought up by a dyer. When grown to manhood he joined the Queen's army, which was marching against the Greeks, and performed prodigies of valour. The Queen sent for him; he was recognised, and the Queen resigned. He became King Darab. He marched against Philip of Macedon, and forced him to take refuge in a forest. Peace was granted, on Philip's giving his daughter to Darab, and paying annually a thousand eggs of gold. Philip's daughter ceased to please, and Darab sent her back after she was pregnant. The child she brought forth was the famous Alexander. The son of Darab, who succeeded him, proved so bad a king, that the nobles of Persia advised Alexander to assert his right to the throne. Alexander refused the annual tribute. Darab, the younger, marched against him, and was conquered. After the battle he was assassinated in his tent by his attendants. But Alexander protested his ignorance of the crime, and Darab named him his successor, requesting him to govern Persia by Persian nobles, which he did. Ibid. In another passage (Ibid. p. 326) he acknowledges that no account is found in the Persian historians of the expedition of Cyrus the younger. The story of Alexander, as told by Sir John Malcolm, in his late history of Persia, is similar, though not the same. Mr. Gibbon says well, "The art and genius of history has ever been unknown to the Asiatics.......... And perhaps the Arabs might not find in a single historian, so clear and comprehensive a narrative of their own exploits as will be deduced in the ensuing sheets." Gibbon. chap. li. Chardin, speaking of the ignorance of the Persians, in regard to geography and history, says, "On ne croiroit jamais que cette ignorance fut aussi outrée qu'elle l'est, et je ne l'aurois pu croire moi-même si je ne m'en étois convaincu par un long usage......... Pour ce qui est de l'histoire du pays, les livres qui en traitent ne sont clairs et sûrs, et ne se suivent, que depuis la naissance de la religion Mahométane: de manière qu'on ne se peut fier à rien de ce qui est rapporté de siècles précédents, surtout en matière de chronologie, où ces gens commettent les plus grossières erreurs, confondant les siècles, et mettant tout pêle-mêle sans se soucier du tems.—Toutes ces histoires, jusqu'au tems de Muhammed, sont des pièces où fabuleuses où romanesques, remplies de mille contes où il n'y a rien de vraisemblable." Voyage en Perse, iii. 256. And Gibbon says (Hist. of Decl. and Fall, ch. x. p. 442.), "So little has been preserved of Eastern history before Mahomet, that the modern Persians are totally ignorant of the victory of Sapor, an event so glorious to their nation."—"When the Romans had supplanted the Greeks, and extended their dominion over all Europe, they also engaged in endless wars with the Persian kings of the

On the geography and chronology, as parts of the literature of the Hindus, I shall express myself in the language of Mr. Wilford. "The Hindus," says that celebrated Hindu scholar, "have no regular work on the subject of geography, or none at least that ever came to my knowledge.[1] I was under a necessity of extracting my materials from their historical poems, or as they may be called more properly, their legendary tales." In another place, he says, "The Hindu systems of geography, chronology, and history, are all equally monstrous and absurd. The circumference of the earth is said to be 500,000,000 yojanas, or 2,456,000,000 British miles: the mountains are asserted to be 100 yojanas, or 491 British miles high. Hence the mountains to the south of Benares are said, in the Puranas, to have kept the holy city in total darkness, till Maha-deva, growing angry at their insolence, they humbled themselves to the ground, and their highest peak now is not more than 500 feet high. In Europe, similar notions once prevailed; for we are told that the Cimmerians were kept in continual darkness by the interposition of immensely high mountains. In the Calica Purana, it is said, that the mountains have sunk considerably, so that the highest is not above one yojana, or five miles high. When the Puranics speak of the kings of ancient times, they are equally extravagant. According to them, King Yudhishthir reigned 27,000 years; King Nanda is supposed to have possessed in his treasury above 1,584,000,000 pounds sterling in gold coin alone; the value of the silver and copper coin, and jewels, exceeded

---

Ashkanian and Sassanian dynasties, for these Asiatic provinces. The events of these early periods are not well described in our histories, as we have no authentic records prior to the time of Mohammed: But the Greeks, who have histories which extend back 2000 years, have minutely described all the circumstances of these wars." Travels of Mirza Abu Taleb Khan, translated by Charles Stewart, Esq., M.A.S., Professor of Oriental Languages, in the Hon. East India Company's College, Herts. iii. 23.

[1] Hindu literature is not devoid of sensible and correct geography, as far as India is concerned. The general geography of the Puranas, is mythology. But even they declare the topography of the country, mountains, and rivers, and cities, with perfect fidelity. Col. Wilford's later as well as his earlier notions, should have been cited. In the fourteenth volume of the Researches, is a paper on the ancient geography of India, from original sources, which had latterly come into his hands; and from which rational and accurate accounts of India were to be extracted. Col. Wilford announced his intention of making the originals over to the Asiatic Society of Bengal; but the intention was never fulfilled. The MSS. disappeared at his death, except a few loose leaves, from some of which I translated a description of the western districts of Bengal, containing much curious and authentic information. Oriental Quarterly Magazine. See also Vishnu Purána.—W.

BOOK II. CHAP. IX.

all calculation: and his army consisted of 100,000,000 men. These accounts, geographical, chronological, and historical, as absurd and inconsistent with reason, must be rejected. This monstrous system seems to derive its origin from the ancient period of 12,000 natural years, which was admitted by the Persians, the Etruscans, and, I believe, also, by the Celtic tribes; for we read of a learned nation in Spain, which boasted of having written histories of above six thousand years."[1]

It is an error to suppose, that for the origin of unprofitable speculations respecting the nature and properties of thought, great progress in civilisation is required. The fears and hopes, the conceptions and speculations, respecting the Divine Nature, and respecting a future state of existence, lead to inquiries concerning the invisible operations of the mind. If we consult but history, we shall be led to conclude that certain curious, and subtle, but idle questions, respecting the mental operations, are a mark, not of a cultivated, but a rude state of society.[2] It was during an age of darkness and barbarity, that metaphysical speculations engaged so passionately the minds of the European doctors; and called forth examples of the greatest acuteness and subtlety. It was prior to the dawn of true philosophy, that the sophists, whose doctrine was a collection of inge-

[1] See Wilford on Egypt and the Nile, Asiat. Res. iii. 295; and on the Chronology of the Hindus. Ibid. v. 241.

[2] Mr. Mill had no other key to the philosophy of the Hindus, than the imperfect views conveyed in a few verses of the laws of Manu. His opinion of its character and value, is necessarily erroneous. Of his criticism on the passages in the Code, it may be remarked, that besides being as usual uncandid, he makes no allowance for the difficulty of expressing terms, which in the original, have a determinate import, by others which have no precise and definite signification; and he forgets that in Manu, the ideas are enounced, not explained. The object of the writer not being to teach philosophy, but to detail the evolution of the mind, and the rest, in the order in which certain philosophical schools had arranged them. With regard to the writer's theory, that the cultivation of metaphysics is a proof rather of barbarism than of civilization, it may be asked if Locke, Descartes, Leibnitz, Kant, Schelling, were barbarians. That men when they begin to reason, should reason respecting their own being is natural; but time, and thought, and intellectual effort, are necessary before their reasonings can assume systematic and diversified classification. The metaphysical speculations of the Hindus are now more accurately known and estimated. "La philosophie Indienne est tellement vaste que tous les systèmes de philosophie s'y rencontrent, qu'elle forme tout un monde philosophique, et qu'on peut dire à la lettre que l'histoire de la philosophie de l'Inde est un abrégé de l'histoire entière de la Philosophie."—Cours de l'histoire de la Philosophie par M. V. Cousin. This opinion, it is important to observe, is founded not upon a few scattered and imperfect notions, but the elaborate dissertations of Mr. Colebrook. Trans. R. As. Society. Professor Cousin, was therefore acquainted with his subject.—W.

nious quibbles on abstract questions, enjoyed their celebrity in Greece. Pythagoras flourished at a very early age; and yet there is a high degree of subtle ingenuity in the doctrines he is said to have taught. Amid the rudeness of the Celtic inhabitants of Gaul and Britain, the Druids carried, we know not how far, the refinements of metaphysical speculation. Strabo, as quoted by Dr. Henry,[1] says, "The Druids add the study of moral philosophy to that of physiology.[2] Ammianus Marcellinus informs us, that the inhabitants of Gaul, having been by degrees a little polished, the study of some branches of useful learning was introduced among them by the bards, the Eubates, and the Druids. The Eubates made researches into the order of things, and endeavoured to lay open the most hidden secrets of nature. The Druids were men of a still more sublime and penetrating spirit, and acquired the highest renown by their speculations, which were at once subtle and lofty."[3] The progress which the Arabians made in a semblance of abstract science has been highly celebrated. The following observations, borrowed from one of the most intelligent of the Europeans by whom they have been studied, will enable us to appreciate their metaphysical science. Of the Arabians, he says, even at the brightest period of their history, the Europeans have been prone to form too favourable, indeed extravagant ideas.[4] Their best writers are the translators or copiers of the Greeks. The only study peculiar to them, a study which they continue to cultivate, is that of their own language. But by the study of language, among the Arabians, we must not understand that philosophical spirit of research, which in words investigates the history of ideas, in order to perfect the art by which they are communicated. The study is cultivated solely on account of its connexion with religion. As the word of God conveys the meaning of God, no conceivable nicety of investigation is ever too much to elicit that meaning in its divine purity. For this reason, it is of the highest moment to ascertain

[1] Hist. of Great Britain, ii. 4. [2] Strabo, lib. iv. p. 197.

[3] Ammian. Marcell. lib. xv. cap. ix.

[4] The high civilization, refined literature, beautiful language, profound philosophy, polished manners, and amiable morals of the Arabians, are celebrated in the highest strains, by M. de Boulainvilliers, Vie de Mahomet, p. 33; Ed. of Amsterdam, 1731. Pythagoras, after having studied the sciences of the Egyptians, travelled into Arabia to learn the philosophy of the Arabians. Porphyr. de Vit. Pythag.

BOOK II. CHAP. IX.

not only the exact signification of the words, but likewise the accents, inflections, signs, and pauses; in a word, all the most minute niceties of prosody and pronunciation; and it is impossible to conceive what a degree of complication they have invented and refined on this subject, without having heard their declamations in the mosques. The grammar alone takes several years to acquire. Next is taught the Nahu, which may be defined the science of terminations. These, which are foreign to the vulgar Arabic, are superadded to words, and vary according to the numbers, cases, genders and person. After this, the student, now walking among the learned, is introduced to the study of eloquence. For this, years are required; because the doctors, mysterious like the Brahmens, impart their treasures only by degrees. At length arrives the time for the study of the law and the Fikah; or science peculiarly so called, by which they mean theology. If it be considered that the object of these studies is always the Koran; that it is necessary to be acquainted with all its mystical and allegorical meanings, to read all its commentaries and paraphrases, of which there are 200 volumss on the first verse: and to dispute on thousands of ridiculous cases of conscience; it cannot but be allowed that one may pass one's whole life in learning much and knowing nothing.[1] It is vain, as the same author still further remarks, to tell us of colleges, places of education, and books. These words, in the regions of which we are treating, convey not the same ideas as with us.[2] The Turks, though signal, even among rude nations, for their ignorance, are not without speculations of a similar nature, which by superficial observers have been taken for philosophy. "Certain it is," says Sir James Porter, "that there are among the Turks many philosophical minds. They have the whole systems of the Aristotelian and Epicurean philosophy translated into their own language."[3]

[1] Volney's Travels in Egypt and Syria, ii. 434. "In two recent voyages into Egypt," says Gibbon, (Hist. of Dec. and Fall, &c. ix. 448.) "we are amused by Savary, and instructed by Volney. I wish the latter could travel over the globe." "The last and most judicious," he calls him, "of our Syrian travellers." Ibid. p. 224.

[2] Volney, ut Supra, p. 443.

[3] Observations on the Religion, Laws, Government, and Manners of the Turks, p. 39. Most, if not all, the Arabian versions of the Greek authors, were done by the Christian subjects of the caliphs. See Gibbon, ch. lii. The same is probably the origin of the Turkish versions. What use, if any, they make of them, does not appear. Mr. Scott Waring says, "The science of the

"The metaphysical questions," says Gibbon, "on the attributes of God, and the liberty of man, have been agitated in the schools of Mahomedans, as well as in those of the Christians."[1] And Mr. Elphinstone informs us, that if the rude Afghaun is ever stimulated to any degree of literary activity, it is when pursuing the subtleties of metaphysical speculation.[2]

These facts coincide with a curious law of human nature, which some eminent philosophers have already remarked. The highest abstractions are not the last result of mental culture, and intellectual strength; it is discovered, that some of our most general and comprehensive notions are formed at that very early period, when the mind, with little discriminating power, is apt to lump together things which have but few points of resemblance; and that we break down these genera into species more and more minute, in proportion as our knowledge becomes more extensive, more particular, and precise. The propensity to abstract speculations is then the natural result of the state of the human mind in a rude and ignorant age.[3]

Persians is, I believe, extremely confined. They have translations of Euclid, Ptolemy, the works of Plato, Aristotle, Pythagoras, and some other of the Grecian philosophers, which few of them read, and fewer understand." Tour to Sheeraz, p. 254.

[1] Hist. of Decline and Fall, &c. ch. i. Mr. Forster mentions a Mussulman fellow-traveller, a disputant, who, says he, "unhappily for himself, and his neighbours, had conned over some of those books of ingenious devices and quaint syllogisms, which are held in high note among the modern Mahometans, and have fixed among them a false distorted taste." Travels in India, p. 106.

[2] "There is generally a want of ardour in pursuit of knowledge among the Asiatics, which is partaken by the Afghauns; excepting, however, in the sciences of dialectics and metaphysics, in which they take much interest, and have made no contemptible progress." Elphinstone's Account of Caubul, p. 189.

[3] The clearest accounts I have seen of this important fact, which Mr. Dugald Stewart (Elements of the Philosophy of the Human Mind, ii. 231), appears not to have known that any body had noticed but M. Turgot, is in the following passage of Condillac. "Mais il faut observer, qu'une fois qu'un enfant commence à généraliser, il rend une idée aussi étendue qu'elle peut l'être, c'est-à-dire qu'il se hâte de donner le même nom à tous les objets qui se ressemblent grossièrement, et il les comprend tous dans une seule classe. Les ressemblances sont les premières choses qui le frappent, parce qu'il ne sait pas encore assez analyser pour distinguer les objets par les qualités qui leur sont propres. Il n'imaginera donc des classes moins générales, que lorsqu'il aura appris à observer par où les choses diffèrent. Le mot *homme*, par exemple, est d'abord pour lui une dénomination commune, sous laquelle il comprend indistinctement tous les hommes. Mais lorsque dans la suite il aura occasion de connoître les différentes conditions, il fera aussitôt les classes subordonnées et moins générales de militaires, de magistrats, de bourgeois, d'artisans, de laboureurs, &c.; tel est donc l'ordre de la génération des idées. On passe tout à coup de l'individu au genre, pour déscendre ensuite aux différentes

The Vedanti doctrine, which has caught the fancy of some of the admirers of Sanscrit, appears to be delivered *viva voce*, and solely in that mode.[1] As no passage implying it has been quoted from any Sanscrit work, it might, if it were any refinement, be suspected of being wholly modern. The following is the account of it by Sir William Jones. "The fundamental tenet of the Vedanti school consisted, not in denying the existence of matter, that is, of solidity, impenetrability, and extended figure (to deny which would be lunacy), but in correcting the popular notion of it, and in contending that it has no essence independent of mental perception, that existence and perceptibility are convertible terms, that external appearances and sensations are illusory, and would vanish into nothing, if the divine energy, which alone sustains them, were suspended but for a moment; an opinion which Epicharmus and Plato seem to have adopted, and which has been maintained in the present century with great elegance, but with little public applause; partly because it has been misunderstood, and partly because it has been misapplied by the false reasoning of some unpopular writers, who are said to have disbelieved in the moral attributes of God, whose omnipresence, wisdom, and goodness, are the basis of the Indian philosophy. I have not sufficient evidence on the subject to profess a belief in the doctrine of the Vedanta, which human reason alone could, perhaps, neither fully demonstrate, nor fully disprove; but it is manifest, that nothing can be further removed from impiety than a system wholly built on the purest devotion."[2]

"In some of these observations," Mr. Dugald Stewart very justly observes, "there is a good deal of indistinctness, and even of contradiction." He also remarks, that Sir William Jones totally misunderstands the doctrine of Berkeley and Hume.[3] We may suspect that he not less

espèces qu'on multiplie d'autant plus qu'on acquiert plus de discernement, c'est-à-dire, qu'on apprend mieux à faire l'analyse des choses." Cours d'Etude, i. 49, 50, Ed. à Parme, 1776. Vide note A. at the end of the volume.

[1] A strange assertion which Ward could have corrected, as he enumerates a long list of Vedanti writings, iv. 172.—W.

[2] Works of Sir Wm. Jones, i. 165. It may be remarked, that Sir William Jones, after all these praises, allows that the Vedanti doctrines are wild and erroneous. Asiat. Res. iv. 164, 165.

[3] Elements of the Philosophy of the Human Mind, vol. ii. note B.

widely mistakes the doctrine of the Brahmens, and fastens a theory of his own creation upon the vague and unmeaning jargon which they delivered to him. If in all minds the propensity be strong, and in weak minds irresistible, to *see* only through the medium of a theory; we need not wonder if theory manufactures the ideas of the other senses, of hearing, for example, after the same manner. "If the simplest narrative of the most illiterate observer involves more or less of hypothesis; and a village apothecary or a hackneyed nurse, is seldom able to describe the plainest case, without employing a phraseology of which every word is a theory,"[1] we may conclude with certainty that the same intrusion is very difficult to avoid, in making up our own conception of what we hear, and still more in clothing it with our own language. Of the ideas which we profess to report, and which we believe that we merely report, it often happens that many are our own ideas, and never entered the mind of the man to whom we ascribe them.

We have a more distinct account of the same doctrine from Sir James Macintosh, whose mind is more philosophical, and on oriental subjects less prepossessed and less credulous, than that of Sir William Jones. Presenting, in a letter to Mr. Dugald Stewart, an account of a conversation with a young Brahmen, "He told me," says he, "that besides the myriads of gods whom their creed admits, there was one whom they know by the name of Brim, or the great one, without form or limits, whom no created intellect could make any approach towards conceiving; that, in reality, there were no trees, no houses, no land, no sea, but all without was Maia, or allusion, the act of Brim; that whatever we saw or felt was only a dream; or, as he expressed it in his imperfect English, thinking in one's sleep; and that the re-union of the soul to Brim, from whom it originally sprung, was the awakening from the long sleep of finite existence."[2]

It will require few words, in application of the evidence adduced in the chapter on religion, to make it sufficiently appear, that this is a natural part of that language of

[1] The words in which this important observation is expressed, are borrowed from a happy application of it by Mr. Stewart, in the same volume, p. 443.
[2] The passage is transcribed by Mr. Stewart, in the note quoted above.

BOOK II. CHAP. IX.

adulation towards the deity, in which the Hindu theology mainly consists. One of the deities, who is chosen as the chief object of adoration, is first made to excel all the other deities; next to absorb all their powers; next to absorb even themselves; and lastly absorb all things.[1] The fancy of "Maia" is only a part of "the absorption of all things in God." There is nothing but God. All our supposed perception of things besides God is, therefore, only illusion; illusion created by God. Why, then, does God create such an illusion? This is a very necessary question. If it were put; and why it has not been put, we may a little admire; the Brahmens might very consistently reply, that as for a use, a design, a purpose, in the actions of their God, they never thought of ascribing to them any such quality. He pleases himself by his actions, and that is enough; no matter how fantastic the taste. It is with great pleasure I quote the following coincidence with my own opinion, expressed in a subsequent passage of the same letter. "I intend to investigate a little the history of these opinions; for I am not altogether without apprehension, that we may all the while be mistaking the hyperbolical effusions of mystical piety for the technical language of a philosophical system. Nothing is more usual, than for fervent devotion to dwell so long, and so warmly, on the meanness and worthlessness of created things, and on the all-sufficiency of the Supreme Being, that it slides insensibly from comparative to absolute language, and, in the eagerness of its zeal to magnify the Deity, seems to *annihilate* everything else. To distinguish between the very different import of the same words in the mouth of a mystic and sceptic, requires more philosophical discrimination than most of our Sanscrit investigators have hitherto shown."[2]

Sir James might have passed beyond a suspicion; if from nothing else, from the very words of the conversation he reports. Human life is there not *compared* to a sleep; it is literally affirmed to *be* a sleep; and men are not acting, or thinking, but only dreaming. Of what philosophical system does this form a part? We awake, only when we are re-united to the Divine Being; that is, when

[1] Vide supra, vol. i. p. 256.
[2] Stewart's Elem. ut supra.

we actually become a part of the Divine Being, not having a separate existence. Then, of course, we cease to dream; and then, it may be supposed, that Maia ceases. Then will there be anything to be known? anything real? Or is it the same thing, whether we are awake or asleep? But my reader might well complain I was only trifling with him, if I pursued this jargon any further. What grieves me is, that between the two passages which I have immediately quoted, Sir James (we must remember that it is in the negligence of private correspondence) has inserted the following words. "All this you have heard and read before as Hindu speculation. What struck me was, that speculations so refined and abstruse should, in a long course of ages, have fallen through so great a space as that which separates the genius of their original inventor from the mind of this weak and unlettered man. The names of these inventors have perished; but their ingenious and beautiful theories, blended with the most monstrous superstitions, have descended to men very little exalted above the most ignorant populace, and are adopted by them as a sort of articles of faith, without a suspicion of their philosophical origin, and without the possibility of comprehending any part of the premises from which they were deduced." Yet Sir James himself has described the origin from which they were deduced; namely, "the hyperbolical effusions of mystical piety;" and surely the Brahmens of the present day may understand these effusions as well as their still more ignorant predecessors.[1]

[1] Another circumstance is always to be remembered. If the Brahmens are once informed of the European doctrine, they will take abundant care to make their own conform to it. "With respect to the real tenets of the Hindus on subjects of theology, they are to be taken from their ancient books, rather than from the oral declarations of the most learned Brahmens of modern times, who have discovered that the opinions of Christians, concerning the nature of God, are far more rational than those currently entertained among them, and that the gross idolatry of the Hindus is contemned by the more intelligent natives of the western world. Bernier seems to have found occasion for the same remark in his time; for, after relating a conference between him and some learned pandits, in which the latter endeavoured to refine away the grossness of their image worship, 'Voilà (says he) sans ajouter ni diminuer, la solution qu'ils me donnèrent; mais, à vous dire le vrai, cela me sembloit un peu trôp bien concerté à la Chrétienne, aux prix de ce que j'en avois appris de plusieurs autres pandits.'" (Grant's Observations on the State of Society among the Asiatic Subjects of Great Britain, p. 73. Papers on India, ordered to be printed by the House of Commons, 15th June, 1813.) This supposed refinement, such as it is, Mr. Elphinstone found among the rude and uncivilized Afghauns. "Another sect in Caubul is that of the Soofees, who ought, perhaps, to be considered as a class of philosophers, rather than of religionists.

BOOK II. CHAP. IX.

With respect to morals or duty, it appears not that any theory has ever been constructed by the Hindus. In what regards the preceptive part, their ethics exactly resemble those of all other rude and uninstructed nations; an excellent precept, and a foolish or absurd one, are placed alternately, or mixed in nearly equal proportions, in all their books which treat upon the subject. For specimens of their ethical precepts, it is sufficient to refer to what we have already produced under the head of religion. If all the good precepts were selected from the rest, and exhibited pure by themselves, they would present a tolerably perfect code of the common duties of morality. As we have authors who have attached importance to this, without adverting to the fact that a soundness in detached maxims of morality is common to all men down to the lowest stage of society, it is necessary to give a specimen of the ethical rules of nations confessedly barbarous. We might, perhaps, be satisfied with a reference to the proverbs of Solomon, and other preceptive parts of the Jewish writings, which are not equalled by the corresponding parts of the books of the Hindus. We shall, however, produce another instance, which is less exposed to any objection. The Havamaal or sublime discourse of Odin, is a Scandinavian composition of great antiquity. It is a string of moral aphorisms, comprised in 120 stanzas; with which, as a

---

As far as I can understand their mysterious doctrine, their leading tenet seems to be, that the whole of the animated and inanimate creation is an illusion; and that nothing exists except the Supreme Being, which presents itself under an infinity of shapes to the soul of man, itself a portion of the Divine essence. The contemplation of this doctrine raises the Soofees to the utmost pitch of enthusiasm. They admire God in everything; and, by frequent meditation on his attributes, and by tracing him through all his forms, they imagine that they attain to an ineffable love for the Deity, and even to an entire union with his substance." (An Account of the Kingdom of Caubul, by the Hon. Mountstuart Elphinstone, p. 207.) See, for an account of a similar sect in Persia, Malcolm's Hist. of Persia, ii. 385.—How different is all this from the curious result of the refined and ingenious reasonings of Berkeley! And how shallow the heads that confound them!—M.

The whole of what is here said on the subject of the Vedanta doctrine, as founded on the brief notice of Sir Wm. Jones, and a private letter of Sir James Mackintosh, is necessarily imperfect and erroneous. The conclusion, too, is the reverse of what any one else would have drawn from the authorities cited, one of whom speaks of the Vedanta doctrine as built on the purest devotion; and the other calls the theory refined, abstruse, ingenious, and beautiful. As they are the sole authority for the premises, their conclusions are of equal weight. The Vedanta system has been since fully explained by Mr. Colebrooke, Dr. Taylor, Ram Mohun Roy, Sir Graves Haughton, Colonel Vans Kennedy. Trans. R. As. Society. Translation of the Prabodha Chandrodaya. Translations from the Vedas. Asiatic Journal, etc.—W.

whole, there is nothing in Hindu literature in any degree worthy to be compared. The following is a specimen:

"To the guest who enters your dwelling with frozen knees, give the warmth of your fire: he who hath travelled over the mountains hath need of food and well-dried garments:

"A man can carry with him no better provision for his journey than the strength of his understanding. In a foreign country this will be of more use to him than treasures; and will introduce him to the table of strangers:

"There is nothing more useless to the sons of the age than to drink too much ale; the more the drunkard swallows, the less is his wisdom, till he loses his reason. The bird of oblivion sings before those who inebriate themselves, and steals away their souls:

"I have never yet found a man so generous and munificent, as that to receive at his house was not to receive; nor any so liberal of his gifts as to reject a present when it was returned to him:

"They invite me up and down to feasts, if I have only need of a slight breakfast; my faithful friend is he who will give me one loaf when he has but two:

"Where is there to be found a virtuous man without some failing; or one so wicked as to have no good quality?"[1]

Among the parts of Hindu learning chosen by its admirers as the peculiar objects of their applause, are the niceties, the numerous and intricate subtleties, of the Hindu grammar. We are informed by an eminent Sanscrit scholar, that the grammatical precepts of one single treatise are no fewer than 3996. The reader will observe, that this number is composed of the digit 3 and its multiples, to which peculiar virtues are ascribed by the Hindus. It is not improbable that the rules may have been made to correspond with the number, rather than the number with the rules. Nevertheless, we learn from Mr. Colebrooke, that "those rules are framed with the utmost conciseness, the consequence of very ingenious methods." But it is added, that the studied brevity of the Paniniya Sutras renders them in the highest degree obscure; that even with the knowledge of the key to their interpretation, the student finds them ambiguous;

[1] See Mallet, Introd. Hist. Denmark, vol. ii. For additional illustrations we may refer to the maxims of Confucius and Zoroaster.

that the application of them, even when understood, discovers many seeming contradictions: and that, with every exertion of practised memory, the utmost difficulty is experienced in combining rules dispersed in apparent confusion through different portions of Paninis and lectures. The number of commentaries on the books of grammar is exceedingly great, and many of them very voluminous."[1]

As these endless conceits answer any purpose rather than that of rendering language a more commodious and accurate instrument of communication, they afford a remarkable specimen of the spirit of a rude and ignorant age: which is as much delighted with the juggleries of the mind, as it is with those of the body, and is distinguished by the absurdity of its passion for both.[2] It could not happen otherwise than that the Hindus should, beyond other nations, abound in those frivolous refinements which are suited to the taste of an uncivilised people. A whole race of men were set apart and exempted from the ordinary cares and labours of life, whom the pain of vacuity forced upon some application of mind, and who were under the necessity of maintaining their influence among the people, by the credit of superior learning, and if not by real knowledge, which is slowly and with much difficulty attained, by artful contrivances for deceiving the people with the semblance of it. This view of the situation of the Brahmens serves to explain many things which modify and colour Hindu society. In grammatical niceties, however, the Hindus but discover their usual resemblance to other nations in the infancy of knowledge and improvement. We have already seen that the Arabians on this subject carry their complex refinements to a height scarcely inferior to that of the Brahmens themselves.[3] Even the Turks, who are not in general a refining race, multiply conceits on this subject.[4] During the dark ages the fabrication of grammatical distinctions and subtleties furnished a favourite exercise to the European schoolmen.[5]

1 Colebrooke on the Sanscrit and Pracrit Languages, Asiat. Res. vol. vii.

2 Mr. Colebrooke still further remarks, that the Hindus delight in scholastic disputation; and that their controversial commentaries on grammar exhibit copious specimens of it.—Ibid.

3 Vide supra, p. 53—55.

4 Tout ce que le mauvais goût peut inventer pour fatiguer l'esprit, fait leur délices, et ravit leur admiration. Mémoires du Baron de Tott sur les Turcs et les Tartares, i. 8.

5 The following remarkable passage in the celebrated letter of our countryman, and (but for one exception) admirable countryman, Sir Thomas More, to

Not only the grammar; the language itself has been celebrated as the mark of a refined and elegant people. "It is more copious," we are told, "than the Latin. It has several words to express the same thing. The sun has more than thirty names, the moon more than twenty. A house has twenty; a stone, six or seven; a tree, ten; a leaf, five; an ape, ten; a crow, nine."[1]

That which is a defect and deformity in language is thus celebrated as a perfection.[2] The highest merit of language would consist in having one name for every thing which

---

Martin Dorpius, affords at once a proof of the fact, and a judgment on the practice: "At nunc absurda quædam portenta, ad certam bonarum artium nata perniciem, et luculenter ab antiquis distincta, commiscuerunt; et veterum purissimas traditiones suis adjectis sordibus infecerunt omnia. Nam in Grammatica (ut omittam Alexandrum, atque id genus alios; qui quamquam imperite, tamen grammaticam utcunque docuerunt) Albertus quidam, grammaticam se traditurum professus, logicam nobis quondam, aut metaphysicam, immo neutram, sed mera somnia, mera deliria grammaticæ loco substituit: et tamen hæ nugacissimæ nugæ in publicas academias non tantum receptæ sunt, sed etiam plerisque tam impense placuerunt, ut is propemodum solus aliquid in grammatica valere censeatur, quisquis fuerit Albertistæ nomen assequutus. Tantum auctoritatis habet, ad pervertenda bonorum quoque ingeniorum judicia, semel ab ineptis tradita, magistris, dein tempore corroborata persuasio. Quo fit ut minus mirer, ad eundem modum in dialecticæ locum nugas plus quam sophisticas irrepsisse quæ cultoribus suis argutiarum nomine tam vehementer, arrident." Caramuel says of the subtle doctor, Scotus, *Vix alibi subtilius scripsit quam cum de grammaticis modis significandi.* Mr. Horne Tooke, however, on this, remarks, that his *De modis significandi* should be entitled, An Exemplar of the subtle art of saving appearances, and of discoursing deeply and learnedly on a subject with which we are perfectly unacquainted. *Quid enim subtilius vel magis tenue quam quod nihil est?* (Diversions of Purley, Introd. p. 12.)

[1] Le Père Paolino (Bartolomeo) Voyage aux Indes, ii. 201.

[2] Mr. Gibbon quaintly says, "In Arabia as well as in Greece, the *perfection* of language outstripped the refinement of manners; and her speech could diversify the fourscore names of honey, the two hundred of a serpent, the five hundred of a lion, the thousand of a sword, at a time when this copious dictionary was intrusted to the memory of an illiterate people." Hist. of Decl. and Fall, etc. ix. 240. The German Professor Foster, who writes notes on the Voyage du Père Paolino, says not ineptly on the passage quoted in the text (Paolino, Voy. aux Indes, iii. 399), "Ce n'est pas de cette manière-là qu'on doit juger de la richesse d'une langue. On a coutume de dire que la langue Arabe est riche, parce qu'elle a je ne sais quel nombre de synonimes pour exprimer le mot *épée*. Un de ces synonimes, par exemple, signifie le meurtrier des hommes. Ce n'est là, dans la réalité, qu'une expression métaphorique et figurée, telle qu'on en peut former dans toutes les langues tant soit peu cultivées. On pouvait de même trouver plus de trente noms pour exprimer le soleil dans les poëtes Grecs; mais il n'est venu dans l'esprit de personne, de faire valoir cela pour prouver la richesse de la langue Grecque." Our own sagacious, and, in many respects, highly philosophical, Wilkins judges better when he names "*significancy, perspicuity, brevity,* and, consequently, *facility,*" among the perfections of a language; and says that the multitude of rules in the Latin "argues the imperfection of that language, that it should stand in need of such and so many rules as have no foundation in the philosophy of speech........If these rules be not *necessary* to language, and according to nature, but that words may signify sufficiently, and, in some respects, better without them, then there is greater judgment showed in laying them aside, or framing a language without them." Essay towards a Real Character,

BOOK II. CHAP. IX.

required a name, and no more than one.[1] Redundancy is a defect in language, not less than deficiency. Philosophy, and even common good sense, determine that every thing which can simplify language, without impairing it in point of precision and completeness, is a first-rate advantage. An ignorant and fantastical age deems it a glory to render it in the highest degree perplexing and difficult.

The other perfections which are ascribed to the Sanscrit, are its softness, or agreeableness in point of sound, and its adaptation to poetry. Of its completeness or precision, those who were the fullest of admiration for it, were too little acquainted with it to be able to venture an opinion. Yet completeness and precision would have been undeniable proofs of the mental perfection of the people by whom it was used; while a great multitude of useless words and grammatical rules were the very reverse. Nothing is more probable than that a language which has too many words of one description, has too few of another, and unites in equal degree the vices of superfluity and defect.[2] The adaptation of a language to poetry and the ear affords no evidence of civilisation. Languages, on which equal eulogies are bestowed to any which can be lavished on Sanscrit, are the languages confessedly of ignorant and uncivilised men. Nothing can surpass the admiration which is often expressed of the language of the modern Persians. Molina, the intelligent and philosophical historian of Chili, informs us, that of the language of the Chilians the grammar is as perfect as that of the Greek or Latin; that of no language does the formation and structure display greater ingenuity and feli-

---

etc. p. 448. Another writer, who speaks with as much boldness as he thinks with force on the subject of language, says, "Persons too dull or too idle to understand the subject, cannot, or will not, perceive how great an evil *many words* is; and boast of their *copiæ* verborum, as if a person diseased with gout or dropsy boasted of his great joints, or big belly." And again, "It cannot be too often repeated, that superfluous *variety* and *copia* are faults, not excellencies. Simplicity may be considered poverty by perverted understandings, but it is always of great utility; and to true judges it always possesses beauty and dignity." Philosophic Etymology, or Rational Grammar, by James Gilchrist, p. 110, 170. "If the Sanscrit is to be admired for its amplicated grammar, the Ethiopic should be admired for its 202 letters." Wilkins' Essay towards a Real Character, p. 14.

1 What would become of poetry, of eloquence, of literature, of intellect, if language was thus shorn of all that gives it beauty, variety, grace, and vigour? —W.

2 This is a gratuitous assumption in the case of the Sanscrit language. One of its merits is not here adverted to; its subservience to a sound theory of general philology and the affinities of languages.—W.

city.[1] The language of the Malays is described as remarkably sweet, and well adapted to poetry.[2] Clavigero knows not where to set a limit to his admiration of the Mexican tongue.[3] "Many extravagant things have been advanced concerning the great antiquity and superior excellency of the Anglo-Saxon language. According to some writers, it was the most ancient and most excellent in the world, spoken by the first parents of mankind in Paradise; and from it they pretend to derive the names, Adam, Eve, Cain, Abel, and all the antediluvian patriarchs."[4]

The same sacred volume which affords the most authentic materials for ascertaining the Hindu modes of accounting for the phenomena of mind, lends equal assistance in leading us to a knowledge of their modes of accounting for

[1] "Gi' indigeni Chilesi formano una sola nazione divisa in varie tribu, e tutti hanno la medesima fisionomia, e la medesima lingua chiamata da loro *Chiledugu*, che vuol dire lingua Chilese. Questa lingua è dolce, armoniosa, espressiva, regolare, e copiosissima di termini fatti ad enunciare non solo le cose fisiche generali, o particolari, ma anchè le cose morali, e astratte." Saggio Sulla Storia Naturale del Chili Del Signor Abate Giovanni Ignazio Molina, lib. iv. p. 334.

[2] Marsden's Hist. of Sumatra, p. 197, ed. 3rd.

[3] "It is so copious, polished, and expressive, that it has been esteemed by many superior to the Latin, and even to the Greek. It abounds," says he, "more than the Tuscan, in diminutives and augmentatives; and more than the English, or any other language we know, in verbal and abstract terms: for there is hardly a verb from which there are not many verbals formed, and scarcely a substantive or adjective from which there are not some abstracts formed. It is not less copious in verbs than in nouns; as from every single verb others are derived of different significations. *Chihua* "is to do;" *Chichihua*, "to do with diligence or often;" *Chihuilia*, "to do to another;" *Chihualtia*, "to cause to be done;" *Chihuatiuh*, "to go to do;" *Chihuaco*, "to come to do;" *Chiuhtiuh*, "to be doing," etc. Having mentioned the extraordinary variety with which the Mexicans express different degrees of respect, by adding adverbs and other particles to the names employed, Clavigero adds, "This variety, which gives so much civilization to the language, does not, however, make it difficult to be spoken, because it is subjected to rules which are fixed and easy; nor do we know any language that is more regular and methodical. The Mexicans, like the Greeks and other nations, have the advantage of making compounds of two, three, or four simple words; but they do it with more economy than the Greeks did; for the Greeks made use of the entire words in composition, whereas the Mexicans cut off syllables, or at least some letters from them. *Tlazotti* signifies *valued*, or *beloved; Mahuitzic, honoured* or *revered; Tespixqui, priest; Tatli, father*. To unite these five words in one, they take eight consonants and four vowels, and say, for instance, *Notlazomahuitzteopixcatatzin*, that is, *my very worthy father*, or *revered priest*, prefixing the *No*, which corresponds to the pronoun *my*, and adding *tzin*, which is a particle expressive of *reverence*. There are some compounds of so many terms as to have fifteen or sixteen syllables........In short, all those who have learned this language, and can judge of its copiousness, regularity, and beautiful modes of speech, are of opinion, that such a language cannot have been spoken by a barbarous people." Clavigero, Hist. of Mexico, book vii. sect. 41.

[4] Henry's Hist. of Great Britain, iv. 365.—"I know not a language spoken in Europe that hath words of more sweetness and greatness than theirs:" Penn's Letter on the American Indians, in Clarkson's Life of Penn, i. 385.

the phenomena of matter. "At the close of the night of Brahma, "intellect, called into action by his will to create worlds, performed again the work of creation; and thence first emerges the subtle ether, to which philosophers ascribe the quality of conveying sound." [1] Ignorant that air is the great agent in the conveyance of sound, the Hindus had recourse to a fiction; the imagination of a something, of whose existence they had no proof. Equally futile is their account of air. "From ether, effecting a transmutation in form, springs the pure and potent air, a vehicle of all scents; and air is held endued with the quality of touch."[2] The word touch is here ambiguous; it may mean either that air is tangible, or that it has the faculty, the sense of touch. The latter, I suspect, is the meaning of the original; for I can hardly credit that so great a master of language as Sir William Jones, would have explained a passage which only meant that air is tangible, by so exceptionable a term as that it is endued with the quality of touch. I can with less difficulty suppose, from other instances, that he endeavoured to cloak a most absurd idea under an equivocal translation.

With respect to light and heat, we are told in the immediately succeeding passage; "Then from air, operating a change, rises light or fire, making objects visible, spreading bright rays, and it is declared to have the quality of figure."[3] It sufficiently appears from these several passages, that the accounts with which they satisfy themselves, are merely such random guesses as would occur to the most vulgar and untutored minds. From intellect rose ether: from ether, air; from air, fire and light. It appears from this passage that they consider light and heat as absolutely the same: yet the moon afforded them an instance of light without heat; and they had instances innumerable of heat without the presence of light. What is the meaning, when it is declared that fire, alias light has the quality of figure, it is impossible to say. That fire, or, which is the same thing, light, is itself figured, is an affirmation wherein little meaning can be found. That fire, that is, light, is the *cause* of figure in all figured bodies, is an affirmation which, notwithstanding the absurdity, is in exact harmony with the

[1] Laws of Menu, ch. i. 75. [2] Ibid. 76. [3] Ibid. 77.

mode of guessing at the operations of nature, admired as philosophy among the Hindus.

The account of water and earth is a link of the same chain. "From light, a change being effected, comes water with the quality of taste; and from water is deposited earth with the quality of smell."[1] As from ether came air, so from air light, from light water, and from water earth. It is useless to ask what connexion appears between water and light, or earth and water. Connexion, reason, probability, had nothing to do with the case. A theory of successive production struck the fancy of the writer, and all inquiry was out of the question. Here occurs the same difficulty as in the case of air; air was endowed with the quality of touch; water and earth are said to have the qualities of smell and taste. In this we perceive a most fantastic conceit: To water is ascribed the quality of taste; to earth the quality of smell; to fire, the quality of *figure*, (I suspect it should be translated *sight*); to air, the quality of touch; and to ether, the quality (as Sir William Jones translates it) of conveying sound; I suspect it *should* be translated, the quality of hearing.[2]

We have thus seen the speculations respecting the origin and qualities of the principal parts of inanimate nature.

[1] Laws of Menu, ch. i. 78.

[2] It is not easy to apprehend the force of the technical terms of a system with which we are imperfectly acquainted, and it is still more impossible to express their purport in a foreign language in which no precise equivalents for the originals exist. We need not wonder, therefore, that the author sees nothing but absurdity in the imperfectly detailed evolution of the elements and their properties, although as far as relates to the connexion between the elements and their properties there is nothing irrational or absurd in the scheme. The Hindus early adopted the doctrine that there is no vacuum in nature, but observing that air was excluded under various circumstances from space, they devised, in order to account for the separation of particles, a subtle element or ether, by which all interstices, the most minute and inaccessible, were pervaded, a notion which modern philosophy intimates some tendency to adopt, as regards the planetary movements; and it was to this subtle element that they ascribed the property of conveying sound: in which they were so far right that in vacuo there can be no sound. Air, again, is said to be possessed of the faculty of touch, that is, it is the medium through which the contact of bodies is effected—ether keeps them apart—air impels them together. Fire, or rather light, has the property of figure. Mr. Colebrooke renders it of colour; in either case the theory is true, for neither colour nor form is discernible except through the medium of light. Water has the property of taste, an affirmation perfectly true, for nothing is sensible to the palate until it is dissolved by the natural fluids. The presence of odour as a property of earth, is less intelligible, but the notion was probably derived from observation of the fragrance of the vegetable world, which was assigned to the soil on which the flowers bloomed. That these views are open to philosophical objections is perfectly true, but they are not fantastic, not random guesses, they are founded on observation, and are not devoid of rationality.—W.

BOOK II. CHAP. IX

The same divine volume affords us a specimen of their ideas concerning the origin of at least one great department of animated nature. "From hot moisture are born biting gnats, lice, fleas, and common flies; these, and whatever is of the same class, are produced by heat."[1] If this be an idea natural enough to the mind of an uncultivated observer, it is at least not a peculiar proof of learning and civilisation.

Of the arbitrary style of deciding without inquiry, the natural and ordinary style of all rude minds, a curious specimen is afforded by the Hindu dogma, that vegetables, as well as animals, "have internal consciousness, and are sensible of pleasure and pain."[2]

Mr. Wilford, the industrious explorer of the literature of this ancient people, informs us: "The Hindus were superficial botanists, and gave the same appellation to plants of different classes."[3] To arrange or classify,[4] on this or any other subject, seems an attempt which has in all ages exceeded the mental culture of the Hindus.

Of all circumstances, however, connected with the state of Hindu society, nothing has called forth higher expressions of eulogy and admiration than the astronomy of the Brahmens. Mons. Bailly, the celebrated author of the History of Astronomy, may be regarded as beginning the concert of praises, upon this branch of the science of the Hindus. The grounds of his conclusions were certain astronomical tables; from which he inferred, not only advanced progress in the science, but a date so ancient as to be entirely inconsistent with the chronology of the Hebrew Scriptures. The man who invented a theory of an ancient and highly civilized people, now extinct, formerly existing in the wilds of Tartary, and who maintained it with uncommon zeal, and all the efforts of his ingenuity, is not to be trusted as a guide in the regions of conjecture. Another cause of great distrust attaches to Mons. Bailly. Voltaire, and other excellent writers in France, abhorring the evils which they saw attached to catholicism, laboured

[1] Laws of Menu, ch. i. 45. [2] Ibid. 49. See also Ibid. xi. 143 to 146.

[3] Wilford on Egypt and the Nile. Asiat. Res. iii. 310.

[4] The Hindus were certainly unacquainted with either the Linnæan or natural orders, but they were careful observers both of the external and internal properties of plants, and furnish copious lists of the vegetable world, with sensible notices of their uses, and names significant of their peculiarities.—W.

to subvert the authority of the books on which it was founded. Under this impulse, they embraced, with extreme credulity, and actual enthusiasm, the tales respecting the great antiquity of the Chinese and Hindus as disproving, entirely, the Mosaic accounts of the duration of the present race of men. When a case occurred, in which it appeared that this favourite conclusion could be established on the strength of astronomical observations and mathematical reasoning, the great object seemed to be accomplished. The argument was laboured with the utmost diligence by Mons. Bailly, was received with unbounded applause, and for a time regarded as a demonstration in form of the falsehood of Christianity.

The most eminent of all the mathematical converts, gained by Mons. Bailly, was Mr. Playfair, the professor of mathematics in the University of Edinburgh. A bias was probably created in his mind by the high reputation of Mons. Bailly for his attainments in that science in which Mr. Playfair himself was so great a master ; and any feeling of that nature could not fail to be greatly strengthened, by the loud applause, in which his countrymen, both those who were still in India, and those who had returned from it, at that time concurred, of the wonderful learning, wonderful civilization, and wonderful institutions of the Hindus ; applause which imposed implicit belief on minds such as that of his illustrious colleague, the author of the Historical Disquisition concerning the knowledge which the ancients had of India. In a paper published in the Transactions of the Royal Society of Edinburgh, Mr. Playfair stated, with skill and dexterity, the matter of evidence on which the proposition is founded;[1] and in an article lately published in the Edinburgh Review,[2] the arguments are controverted by which Mr. Bentley had endeavoured to overthrow his opinion; but a suspension of belief, till further information shall yield more satisfactory proof, is all that in this latter document is contended for.

Such a demand, however, is infinitely too much, and at variance with all the principles of reasoning. When an opinion is obviously contradicted by a grand train of cir-

[1] Transactions of the Royal Society of Edin. vol. ii.

[2] Of which he has over all Europe been recognised as the author; Vide infra, p. 105, note 1.

cumstances, and is not *entirely* supported by the special proof on which it pretends to rest, it is unproved; and whatever is unproved, and out of the known order of nature, is altogether unworthy of belief; deserves simple rejection.

Whoever, in the present improved state of our knowledge, shall take the trouble to contemplate the proof which we possess of the state of knowledge and civilization among the Hindus, can form no other conclusion, but that everything (unless astronomy be an exception) bears clear, concurring, and undeniable testimony to the ignorance of the Hindus, and the low state of civilization in which they remain. That such a people are masters of the science of astronomy to a degree which none but nations highly cultivated have elsewhere ever attained, is certainly not to be credited on any chain of proof that is not entire.[1]

Of the fitness of the proof to maintain any such conclusions as have been founded upon it, an idea may be formed from this; that Mr. Bentley, who had paid great attention to the books of Hindu astronomy, says they are all of modern date, and their pretensions to antiquity, founded only on forgery.[2] As his moderate knowledge of mathematics, however, and even the inelegancies of his style, have been sarcastically employed to throw discredit upon his conclusions, it is of importance to add that the two mathematicians whose reputation for profundity seems to exceed that of their contemporaries, Laplace, and an eminent ornament of our country, not only reject the inference of the great antiquity and perfection of the Hindu

[1] Mr. Playfair has himself given us a criterion for determining on his notions of the Hindu astronomy, which is perfectly sufficient. He says, in the conclusions of his discourse (Edin. Trans. ii. 192), " These conclusions are without doubt extraordinary; and have no other claim to our belief, except that their being false were much more wonderful than their being true." On this principle, the question is decided: for the wonder is little that they should be false, but mighty indeed were they true.

[2] Asiat. Res. vi. 577.—M. As presently mentioned, Mr. Bentley had but a moderate knowledge of mathematics. He had a still more moderate knowledge of Sanscrit, and was quite incapable of forming an opinion of the authenticity of Sanscrit writings, upon an accurate estimate of their contents. His notion that the astronomical works of the Hindus were all forgeries, was founded entirely upon prejudice, not upon inquiry. Having known him personally, the writer had various opportunities of appreciating his character, in this respect. Hindu forgery, was the engrossing idea of his mind, with which it was vain to argue, as it was the progeny of passion, not of reason.—W.

astronomy, but from the evidence offered, draw a conclusion directly the reverse; viz., that this science is in the very same state of infancy among the Hindus with all the other branches of knowledge. The Surya Sidhanta is the great repository of the astronomical knowledge of the Hindus. It is on the authority of our own countryman[1] I am enabled to declare, that this book is itself the most satisfactory of all proofs of the low state of the science among the Hindus, and the rudeness of the people from whom it proceeds; that its fantastic absurdity is truly Hindu; that all we can learn from it are a few facts, the result of observations which required no skill; that its vague allegories and fanciful reflections prove nothing, or everything; that a resolute admirer may build upon them all the astronomical science of modern times; but a man who should divest his mind of the recollection of European discoveries, and ask what a people unacquainted with the science could learn from the Surya Sidhanta, would find it next to nothing.[2]

1 No weight can be attached to an anonymous authority; what means has he had of forming an estimate of the Surya Siddhanta? The translation of a standard work on Hindu astronomy, is much wanted, to determine accurately the extent of their science. The conclusions founded on partial extracts from astronomical works, and dissertations, having certain circumscribed purposes, are necessarily imperfect, and are probably, in many respects, erroneous.—W.

2 Dr. Smith, with his usual sagacity, says, "There are various causes which render astronomy the very first of the sciences which is cultivated by a rude people: though from the distance of the objects, and the consequent mysteriousness of their nature and motions, this would seem not to be the case. Of all the phenomena of nature, the celestial appearances are, by their greatness and beauty, the most strikingly addressed to the curiosity of mankind. But it is not only their greatness and beauty by which they become the first objects of a speculative curiosity. The species of objects in the heavens are few in number; the sun, the moon, the planets, and the fixed stars. All the changes, too, which are ever observed in these bodies, evidently arise from some difference in the velocity and direction of their several motions. All this formed a very simple object of consideration. The objects, however, which the inferior parts of nature presented to view, the earth and the bodies which immediately surround it, though they were much more familiar to the mind, were more apt to embarrass and perplex it, by the variety of their species, and by the intricacy and seeming irregularity of the laws or orders of their succession. The variety of meteors in the air, of clouds, rainbows, thunder, lightning, winds, rain, hail, snow, is vast, and the order of their succession seems to be most irregular and inconstant. The species of fossils, minerals, plants, animals, which are found in the waters and near the surface of the earth, are still more intricately diversified; and if we regard the different manners of their production, their mutual influence in altering, destroying, supporting one another, the orders of their succession seem to admit of an almost infinite variety If the imagination, therefore, when it considered the appearances in the heavens, was often perplexed and driven out of its natural career, it would be much more exposed to the same embarrassment, when it directed its attention to the objects which the earth presented to it, and when it endeavoured to trace their progress and

BOOK II. CHAP. IX.

The Hindu astronomy is possessed of very considerable accuracy in regard to the mean motions. In other respects, it has no pretensions to correctness or refinement. Astronomy may acquire great accuracy in regard to the mean motions, without the help of any nice or delicate observations; and while the science can hardly be said to exist. If there is every reason to believe, and none whatsoever to disbelieve, that the mean motions of the Hindu astronomy have been gradually corrected in the same manner in which the calendars of ancient nations have been improved, the legitimate conclusion cannot be mistaken.

As far as a conclusion can be drawn respecting the state of astronomy among the Hindus, from the state of their instruments of observation (and an analogy might be expected between those closely connected circumstances,) the inference entirely corresponds with what the other circumstances in the condition of the Hindus have a tendency to establish. The observatory at Benares, the great seat of Hindu astronomy and learning was found to be rude in structure, and the instruments with which it was provided of the coarsest contrivance and construction.

Even Mr. Playfair himself observes that "regular observations began to be made in Chaldea with the era of Nabonassar; the earliest which have merited the attention of succeeding ages." The observation which he next presents is truly philosophical and important. "The curiosity of the Greeks," says he, "was, soon after, directed to the same object; and that ingenious people was the first that endeavoured to explain or connect, by theory, the various phenomena of the heavens."[1] This was an

---

successive revolutions." Essays by Dr. Adam Smith, p. 97, 98. Of the Persians, Mr. Scott Waring says, "Their perverse predilection for judicial astrology excites them to the study of astronomy, merely that they may foretell the conjunction of the planets; and when they are able to do this with any degree of accuracy, they are accounted men of considerable science. They have two descriptions of Ephemeris; the first containing the conjunction and opposition of the luminaries: and the second the eclipses, the longitude and latitude of the stars," &c. Tour to Sheeraz, p. 254. The pages of the historian being little adapted to mathematical and astronomical discussion, I have inserted, by way of Appendix, an examination of the arguments for the antiquity and excellence of the Hindu astronomy; with which the friendship of the great mathematician to whom I have alluded has enabled me to elucidate the subject. See Append. No. 1. at the end of the chapter.

[1] Playfair on the Astronomy of the Brahmens. Trans. Roy. Soc. Edin. ii. 135.

important step; all that preceded was mere observation and empiricism, not even the commencement of science.[1] He adds; "The astronomy of India gives no theory, nor even any description of the celestial phenomena, but satisfies itself with the calculation of certain changes in the heavens, particularly of the eclipses of the sun and moon, and with the rules and tables by which these calculations must be performed. The Brahmen, seating himself on the ground, and arranging his shells before him, repeats the enigmatical verses that are to guide his calculation, and from his little tablets and palm-leaves, takes out the numbers that are to be employed in it. He obtains his result with wonderful certainty and expedition; but having little knowledge of the principles on which his rules are founded, and no anxiety to be better informed, he is perfectly satisfied, if, as it usually happens, the commencement and duration of the eclipse answer, within a few minutes, to his prediction. Beyond this, his astronomical inquiries never extend; and his observations, when he makes any, go no further than to determine the meridian line, or the length of the day at the place where he observes."[2]

Scarcely can there be drawn a stronger picture than this of the rude and infant state of astronomy. The Brahmen, making his calculation by shells, is an exact resemblance of the rude American performing the same operation by knots on a string; and both of them exhibit a practice which then only prevails; either when the more ingenious and commodious method of ciphering, or accounting by written signs, is unknown; or when the human mind is too rude and too weak to break through the force of an inveterate custom.[3]

1 Dr. Smith says, "Nature, according to common observation, appears a chaos of jarring and discordant appearances, into which philosophy endeavours to introduce order by representing the invisible chains which bind together all these disjointed objects. It thus soothes the imagination, and renders the theatre of nature a more coherent, and therefore a more magnificent spectacle, than otherwise it would appear to be. Mankind in the first ages of society have little curiosity to find out those hidden chains of events which bind together the seemingly disjointed appearances of nature. A savage has no inclination to amuse himself with searching out what seems to serve no other purpose than to render the theatre of nature a more connected spectacle to his imagination." Essays, Hist. of Astron. pp. 20, 21, 23.

2 Playfair, on the Astron. of the Brahmens. Trans. R. S. E. ii. 138, 139.

3 Goguet, having mentioned the quipos of the Peruvians, says, "It is the same with the negroes on the coast of Juida. They know nothing of the art of writing, and yet they can calculate the largest sums with great facility, by

BOOK II. CHAP. IX.

But the rude state of the science of astronomy among the Brahmens of the present day, is supposed to have been preceded by a period in which it was cultivated to a high degree of perfection. It is vain to ask at what date this period had its existence; and where the signs of such ancient knowledge are to be found. To these questions, no answer can be returned. Sir William Jones himself admits, "it is improbable that the Indian astronomers, in very early times, had made more accurate observations than those of Alexandria, Bagdad, or Maraghah; and still more improbable that they should have relapsed without apparent cause into error."[1] Mr. Davis, one of the oriental inquirers to whom we are most indebted for our knowledge of Hindu astronomy, says, "I had been inclined to think with many others, that the Brahmens possess no more knowledge in astronomy, than they have derived from their ancestors in tables ready calculated to their hands, and that few traces of the principles of the science could be found among them; but, by consulting some Sanscrit books, I was induced to alter my opinion. I believe the Hindu science of astronomy will be found as well known now, as it ever was, among them."[2] In other words,

---

means of cords and knots, which have their own signification." Hist. Gén. de Voyage, iv. 283, 373, and 393. Origin of Laws, i. 224. We are informed by Herodotus, that the Egyptians, like the Brahmens, counted by shells; and, at one time at least the Greeks; but in an inverse order, the Greeks passing from left to right, the Egyptians from right to left. Herodot. lib. ii. cap. 36.

[1] Asiat. Res. ii. 115. The following is valuable from the pen of M. Delambre, "M. La Place, qui avoit quelque intérêt à soutenir la grande ancienneté de l'astronomie Indienne, et qui avoit d'abord parlé des mouvemens moyens et des époques des Hindous de la manière la plus avantageuse, a fini pourtant par croire et imprimer que leurs tables ne remontent pas au dela du 13me siècle. Mr. Playfair, en répondant à l'objection de M. de La Place, ne la détruit pas. Peu importe que Bailly ait affirmé plus ou moins directement et positivement la conjonction générale des planètes, qui a déterminé l'époque; ce qu'il fålloit éclaircir est un fait. Les tables indiquent-elles en effet cette conjonction, l'époque alors est fictive, et l'astronomie Indienne est beaucoup plus moderne. Les tables n'indiquent-elles pas cette conjonction, alors l'objection de M. La Place tombe d'elle-même. C'est ce que ne dit pas Mr. Playfair, et c'est ce que je n'ai pas le tems de vérifier. Mais quand même l'objection seroit sans force, il resteroit bien d'autres difficultés. Ce ne sont pas quelques rencontres heureuses parmi une foule de calculs erronés où incohérens, qui suffiroient pour prouver l'antiquité de l'Astronomie Indienne. La forme mystérieuse de leurs tables et de leurs méthodes suffiroit pour donner des soupçons sur leur véracité. C'est une question qui probablement ne sera jamais décidée, et qui ne pourroit l'être que par de nouvelles découvertes dans les écrits des Hindous." Letter from M. Delambe, dated Paris, July 21, 1814, published, Appendix, note D., of "Researches concerning the Laws, &c. of India, by Q. Craufurd, Esq."

[2] Asiat Res. ii. 226—228.

the ignorance of the present age is the same with the ignorance of all former ages."[1]

While we are thus unable, from all we have learned of the Hindu astronomy, to infer either its high antiquity, or great excellence, it is a matter of doubt whether even that portion of the science which they possess, they may not, to a certain degree, have derived from other nations more advanced in civilization than themselves.[2] The Hindu astronomy possesses certain features of singularity which tend to prove, and have, by various inquirers, been held sufficient to prove, its perfect originality. But it may very well be supposed, that in a science which so naturally fixes the attention of even a rude people, the Hindus themselves proceeded to a certain extent; and even if they did borrow the most valuable portion of all that they know, that it was constrained to harmonize with the methods they had already invented, and the discoveries they had previously made. The fact, moreover,

[1] Of that ignorance take the following specimens :—" The Bhagavat," (says Mr. Davis, Asiat. Res. iii. 225) " when treating of the system of the universe, places the moon above the sun, and the planets above the fixed stars."—" The prince of serpents continually sustains the weight of this earth." Sacontala, beginning of act v. " Some of them" [the Brahmens of the present day] " are capable," says Mr. Orme, Hist. of Indost. i. 3, " of calculating an eclipse, which seems to be the utmost stretch of their mathematical knowledge."

[2] As compared with the state of Astronomical science in modern times, Hindu Astronomy, of course, is far from excellence, as Schlegel remarks, " il n'est pas besoin de faire de gros livres pour le prouver ;" it is, perhaps, inferior to the Astronomy of the Greeks. but it exhibits many proofs of accurate observation and deduction, highly creditable to the science of Hindu Astronomers. The division of the ecliptic into lunar mansions, the solar zodiac, the mean motions of the planets, the precession of the equinoxes, the earth's self support in space, the diurnal revolution of the earth on its axis, the revolution of the moon on her axis, her distance from the earth, the dimension of the orbits of the planets, the calculation of eclipses, are parts of a system which could not have been found amongst an unenlightened people. That the antiquity of the Hindu Astronomy has been exaggerated is no doubt true, but there is no reason to conceive that it is not ancient. Even Bentley, himself, refers the contrivance of the lunar mansions to B. C. 1424, a period anterior to the earliest notices of Greek Astronomy, and implying a course of still earlier observation. The originality of Hindu Astronomy, if this era be granted, is at once established, but it is also proved by intrinsic evidence, as although there are some remarkable coincidences between the Hindu and other systems, their methods are their own. " If there be any resemblances," says Professor Wallace (Account of British India, Edinburgh,) they have arisen out of the nature of the science, or from what the Indians have borrowed from the Arabians, who were instructed by the Greeks, rather than from anything borrowed from the Indians by the Arabians or the Greeks." There is no occasion to suppose the Greeks were instructed by the Hindus, but the Arabians certainly were. Their own writers affirm that Indian Astronomers were greatly encouraged by the early khalifs, particularly Harun al Rashid and Al Mamun ; they were invited to Bagdad, and their works were translated into Arabic. The Hindus were, fully as much as the Greeks, the teachers of the Arabians. —W.

BOOK II. CHAP. IX.

is, that if the Hindu astronomy exhibits marks of distinction from other systems, it exhibits, on the supposition of its originality, still more surprising instances of agreement with other systems. "The days of the week" (I use the language of Mr. Playfair) "are dedicated by the Brahmens, as by us, to the seven planets, and, what is truly singular, they are arranged precisely in the same order. The ecliptic is divided, as with us, into twelve signs of thirty degrees each. This division is purely ideal, and is intended merely for the purpose of calculation. The names and emblems by which these signs are expressed, are nearly the same as with us; and as there is nothing in the nature of things to have determined this coincidence, it must, like the arrangement of the days of the week, be the result of some ancient and unknown communication."[1] From this striking circumstance, Montucla, the celebrated historian of mathematics, inferred, that the Hindu zodiac was borrowed from the Greeks; and from the vicinity of the Greek empire of Bactria, as well as from the communications which took place between the Hindus, the Persians, and Arabians, the facility with which the knowledge of the Grecian astronomy might pass into India is clear. Sir William Jones controverts the position that the Hindu ecliptic was borrowed from the Greeks; he contends that it was derived from the Chaldeans.[2] But this is the same in the end.[3]

[1] Playfair, on the Astronomy of the Brahmins. Trans. R. S. E. ii. 140, 141. See, to the same purpose, Colebrooke on the Indian and Arabian Divisions of the Zodiac, Asiat. Res. ix. 323, 376.

[2] Asiat. Res. ii. 289.

[3] The division of the zodiac among the Birmans as well as the Brahmens, resembles ours, the original Chaldean. "My friend Sangermano," (says Dr. Buchanan, Asiat. Res. vi. 204), "gave Captain Symes a silver basin, on which the twelve signs were embossed. He conceived, and I think justly, that this zodiac had been communicated to the Burmans from Chaldea by the intervention of the Brahmens. And I find, that in this conjecture he is supported by Sir W. Jones, (As. Res. ii. 306). Both, however, I am afraid, will excite the indignation of the Brahmens, who, as the learned judge in another place alleges, have always been too proud to borrow science from any nation ignorant of the Vedas. Of their being so proud as not to acknowledge their obligations, I make no doubt; but that they have borrowed from the Chaldeans, who were ignorant of the Vedas, Sir W. Jones himself has proved. Why, then, should he have opposed the sarcastic smiles of perplexed Pandits to the reasoning of M. Montucla (As. Res. ii. 303, 289), when that learned man alleged that the Brahmens have derived astronomical knowledge from the Greeks and Arabs. The expression of the Brahmens quoted by him as a proof, namely, 'that no base creature can be lower than a Yavan or Greek,' only exposes their miserable ignorance and disgusting illiberality."—On this pride, too great to learn (a sure sign of barbarity), it is also to be remarked, that a matrimonial connexion (among the Hindus the most sacred of all connexions) took place between Se-

At one time a disposition appeared to set the knowledge of the Hindus, in pure mathematics, very high. A very convenient, and even an ingenious mode of constructing the table of approximate signs, is in use among the Hindu astronomers. "But ignorant totally," says Professor Leslie, "of the principles of the operation, those

---

leucus and Sandrocottos. "On this difficulty," says Mr. Wilford, "I consulted the pundits of Benares, and they all gave me the same answer; namely, that in the time of Chandragupta, the Yavanas were much respected, and were even considered as a sort of Hindus." Asiat. Res. v. 286. What was to hinder the Brahmens from learning astronomy from the Greeks at that period? Mr. Wilford indeed says that a great intercourse formerly subsisted between the Hindus and the nations of the West. Ibid. iii. 297, 298. Sir William seems to have known but little of the intercourse which subsisted between the Hindus and the people of the West. Suetonius (in vit. Octav.) informs us, that the Indians sent ambassadors to Augustus. An embassy met him when in Syria, from king Porus, as he is called, with letters written in the Greek character, containing, as usual, a hyperbolical description of the grandeur of the monarch. Strabo, lib. xv. p. 663. A Brahmen was among those ambassadors, who followed Augustus to Athens, and there burned himself to death. Strabo, Ibid. and Dio Cass. lib. liii. p. 527. Another splendid embassy was sent from the same quarter to Constantine. Cedreni Annal. p. 242, Ed. Basil. 1566; Maurice, Hist. iii. 125. "I have long harboured a suspicion," says Gibbon, "that *all* the Scythian, and *some*, perhaps *much*, of the Indian science, was derived from the Greeks of Bactriana." Gibbon, vii. 294. A confirmation of this idea, by no means trifling, was found in China, by Lord Macartney and his suite, who discovered the mathematical instruments deposited in the cities of Pekin, and Nankeen, not constructed for the latitude of those places, but for the 37th parallel, the position of Balk or Bactria; Barrow's China, p. 289. The certainty of the fact of a Christian church being planted in India at a time not distant from that of the apostles, is a proof that the Hindus had the means of learning from the Greeks.—We learn the following very important fact from Dr. Buchanan: The greater part of Bengal manuscripts, owing to the badness of the paper, require to be copied at least once in ten years, as they will, in that climate, preserve no longer; and every copyist, it is to be suspected, adds to old books whatever discoveries he makes, relinquishing his immediate reputation for learning, in order to promote the grand and profitable employment of his sect, the delusion of the multitude. Asiat. Res. vi. 174, note. Anquetil Duperron, who had at an early period asserted the communication of Grecian science to the Hindus, (see Recherches Historiques et Philosophiques sur l'Inde) supported this conclusion at the end of his long life. "N'est il pas avoué," says he in his notes to the French translation of Paolino's Travels, iii. 442; "que, de tout tems, sans conquête, avec conquête, par terre comme par mer, l'Asie, l'Inde, et l'Europe, ont eu des relations plus ou moins actives; que les savans, les sages de ces contrées se sont visités, ont pu se faire part de leurs découvertes; et qu'il n'est pas hors de vraisemblance que quelques uns auront fait usage dans leurs livres, même sans en avertir, des nouvelles lumières qu'ils avaient reçues de l'étranger? De nos jours, le Rajah d'Amber, dans ses ouvrages astronomiques, parle des tables de la Hire. Le Rajah Djessingue, aura profité des leçons du P. Boudier, qu'il avait appelé auprès de lui. Si l'astronome Brahme, avec lequel M. le Gentil a travaillé à Pondicherri, écrit sur l'astronomie, sans abandonner le fond de ses principes, du systême Indien, il adoptera des pratiques qu'il aura remarquées dans son disciple, calculera, quoique Indou, à la Française, et donnera comme de lui, du pays des résultats réellement tirés de ses rapports avec l'astronomie Française. Nier ces probabilités, c'est ne pas connaitre les hommes."—"Il y a différentes époques dans les sciences Indiennes, dans la mythologie, les opinions religieuses de cette contrée. Les Indiens ont reçu ou emprunté diverses connaissances des Arabes, des Perses, en tel temps; des Grecs dans tel autre." Ibid. p. 451.

BOOK II. CHAP. IX.

humble calculators are content to follow blindly a slavish routine. The Brahmens must, therefore, have derived such information from people further advanced than themselves in science, and of a bolder and more inventive genius. Whatever may be the pretensions of that passive race, their knowledge of trigonometrical computation has no solid claim to any high antiquity. It was probably, before the revival of letters in Europe, carried to the East by the tide of victory. The natives of Hindustan might receive instruction from the Persian astronomers, who were themselves taught by the Greeks of Constantinople, and stimulated to those scientific pursuits by the skill and liberality of their Arabian conquerors."[1]

[1] Elements of Geometry, etc., by John Leslie, Professor of Moral Philosophy in the University of Edinburgh, note xxiv. All that can be said in favour of the mathematical science of the Hindus is very skilfully summed up in the following passage, by a mathematician of first-rate eminence, William Wallace, Esq., the Professor of Mathematics in the University of Edinburgh. "The researches of the learned have brought to light astronomical tables in India, which must have been constructed by the principles of geometry; but the period at which they have been formed has by no means been completely ascertained. Some are of opinion, that they have been framed from observations made at a very remote period, not less than 3,000 years before the Christian era; and if this opinion be well founded, the science of geometry must have been cultivated in India to a considerable extent, long before the period assigned to its origin in the West; so that many of the elementary propositions may have been brought from India to Greece. The Hindus have a treatise called the Surya Sidhanta, which professes to be a revelation from heaven, communicated to Meya, a man of great sanctity, about four millions of years ago; but setting aside this fabulous origin, it has been supposed to be of great antiquity, and to have been written at least two thousand years before the Christian era. Interwoven with many absurdities, this book contains a rational system of trigonometry, which differs entirely from that first known in Greece or Arabia. In fact, it is founded on a geometrical theorem, which was not known to the geometricians of Europe before the time of Vieta, about two hundred years ago. And it employs the sines of arcs, a thing unknown to the Greeks, who used the chords of the double arcs. The invention of sines has been attributed to the Arabs; but it is possible that they may have received this improvement in trigonometry, as well as the numeral characters, from India." Edinburgh Encyclopedia, Article Geometry, p. 191. The only fact here asserted, which bears upon the question of the civilization of the Hindus, is that of their using the sines of arcs instead of the chords of the double arcs. Suppose that they invented this method. It proves nothing beyond what all men believe, that the Hindus made a few of the first steps in civilization at an early period; and that they engaged in those abstract speculations, metaphysical and mathematical, to which a semi-barbarous people are strongly inclined. The Arabians were never more than semi-barbarous. The Greeks were no better, at the early age when they were acquainted with the elementary propositions of geometry. If the Greeks or Arabians invented, in the semi-barbarous state, the mode of computation by the chords, what was to hinder the Hindus from inventing, while semi-barbarous, the mode of computing by the sines of arcs? This is upon the supposition that the mode of computing by sines, and the elementary propositions on which it depends, really are original among the Hindus. But this seems not to rest upon very satisfactory proof, when it is barely inferred from the use of chords by the Greeks; and the *possibility* alone is asserted of the Arabians having derived the knowledge from the Hindus.—M.

The author has here shifted his ground; as his quotation from Professor

Arithmetic is a branch of mathematics; and among other inventions, of which the honour has been claimed for the Hindus, is that of numerical characters.[1] Whether the signs used by the Hindus are so peculiar as to render it probable that they invented them, or whether it is still more probable that they borrowed them, are questions which, for the purpose of ascertaining their progress in civilisation, are not worth resolving. "The invention of numerical characters," says Goguet, "must have been very ancient. For though flints, pebbles, and grains of corn &c., might be sufficient for making arithmetical calculations, they were by no means proper for preserving the result of them. It was, however, necessary on many occasions to preserve the result of arithmetical operations, and consequently it was necessary, very early, to invent signs for that purpose."[2] Under these motives, a people, who had communication with another people already acquainted with numerical signs, would borrow them: a people who had no such communication, would be under the necessity of inventing them. But alphabetical signs, far more difficult, were invented at a rude period of society; no certain proof of civilisation is therefore gained by the invention of arithmetical characters. The characters of which Europeans themselves make use, and which they have borrowed from the Arabians, are really hieroglyphics; and "from the monuments of the Mexicans," says Goguet, "which are still remaining, it appears that hieroglyphics were used by that people, both for letters and numerical characters."[3] That diligent and judicious inquirer says, in general, "The origin of ciphers or numerical characters was confounded with that of hieroglyphic writing. To this day, the Arabian

---

Wallace is hostile to the purport of his argument, and proves that the Hindus had an original method of computation, and one which anticipated modern discovery. The position that they must have been indebted to a people further advanced than themselves, as, for instance, the Greeks, is shown to be untenable. Obliged, however reluctantly, to admit that the Hindus may have invented this method, the author falls back upon the more general charge, and says, "it does not substantiate their civilization." The question at issue in this place is, not their civilization, but their proficiency in mathematics; and the instance given is favourable to the pretensions of the Hindus to very considerable progress effected by their own independent efforts.—W.

[1] Even Delambre, who disputes the originality of Hindu astronomy, concedes their claim to early progress in arithmetic, and the invention of numerical ciphers.—W.

[2] Origin of Laws, i. 221.

[3] Origin of Laws, i. 224.

BOOK II. CHAP. IX.

ciphers are real hieroglyphics, and do not represent words, but things. For which reason, though the nations who use them speak different languages, yet these characters excite the ideas of the same numbers in the minds of all.[1]

Algebraic signs, which were brought into Europe from Arabia, may, it is said, have originated in India. There is an assertion of the Arabian writers, that an Arabian mathematician in 959 travelled to India, in quest of information. He might, however, travel without finding. On this foundation, it is plain that no sound inference can be established. If, indeed, it were proved that the algebraic notation came from India, an invention which the Arabians could make, implies not much of civilisation wherever it was made. The shape, indeed, in which it was imported from Arabia, sets the question at rest. It cannot be described more clearly and shortly than in the words of Mr. Playfair. The characters, as imported from Arabia, "are mere abbreviations of words. Thus the first appearance of algebra is merely that of a system of short-hand writing, or an abbreviation of common language, applied to the solution of arithmetical problems. It was a contrivance merely to save trouble."[2]

The books of the Hindus abound with the praise of learning: and the love and admiration of learning is a mark of civilisation and refinement. By the panegyrics, however, in the books of the Hindus, the existence is proved of little to which admiration is due. On the pretensions of the Brahmens to learning, the title to which they reserved exclusively to themselves, a great part of their unbounded influence depended. It was their interest, therefore, to excite an admiration of it, that is, of themselves,

[1] Ibid. Mr. Gilchrist renders it highly probable, that not only the digits, but the letters of the alphabet, are hieroglyphics. Philosophic Etymology, p. 23.

[2] Second Dissertation, Supplement to the Encyclopædia Britannica, p. 12. It is a coincidence well worth remarking, that Diophantus, a Greek mathematician of Alexandria, about 150 years after Christ, employed a like expedient. "The questions he resolves," says Mr. Playfair, "are of considerable difficulty. The expression is that of common language abbreviated, and assisted by a few symbols." Ibid. p. 13. In a MS. of Diophantus, which Bombelli says he saw in the Vatican library, the Indian authors, he says, are often quoted. Nothing of this appears in the work of Diophantus, which was published about three years after the time when Bombelli wrote. Nor has any other work of Diophantus been produced. It is, besides, to be remembered, that the Greeks used the word *Indian* with great latitude. They applied it not merely to the people beyond the Indus: they applied it, also, to a people on the Euxine Sea; to a people in Ethiopia; in a general way, to all the people of the East. It is by no means clear that Diophantus would not apply it to the Arabians themselves. See Appendix, No. II., at the end of the chapter.

by every artifice. When we contemplate, however, the acquirements and performances on which the most lofty of these panegyrics were lavished, we can be at no loss for a judgment on their learning, or the motive from which the praises of it arose. To be able to read the Vedas was merit of the most exalted nature; to have actually read them, elevated the student to a rank almost superior to that of mortals. "A priest," says the sacred text of Menu, "who has gone through the whole Veda, is equal to a sovereign of the whole world.[1] What is valuable in learning could be

[1] Laws of Menu, ch. ix. 245. "Since the era of Halhed and Sir William Jones," says Mr. Scott Waring, "the existence of the precious manuscripts of Sanscrit learning has, like the chorus to a popular song, been echoed from author to author, who, though entirely ignorant of Sanscrit, have stamped with credibility a seemingly vague supposition; for what production have we yet seen to justify those extravagant praises?" Tour to Sheeraz, by Ed. Scott Waring, p. 5. Mr. Wilford, better acquainted with the Puranas than any other European, speaks of them with little respect. He talks "of the ignorant compilers of the Puranas, who have arranged this heterogeneous mass without method and still less judgment." As. Res. vi. 471. M. Bernier, than whom no European had better opportunities of observing the actual and present attainments of the Brahmens, who observed with a penetrating and judicious spirit, and wrote before the birth of theory on the subject, says, "Après le Purane quelques uns se jettent dans la philosophie où certainement ils réussissent bien peu;—je l'ai déjà dit, ils sont d'une humeur lente et paresseuse, et ne sont point animés dans l'espérance de parvenir à quelque chose par leur étude." Suite des Mémoires sur l'Empire du Grand Mogol, i. 184. "Leurs plus fameux Pendets," says he, "me semblent très ignorans." Ibid. p. 185. Mentioning their accounts of the world, he says, "Il y en a aussi qui veulent que la lumière et les ténèbres soient les premiers principes, et disent la-dessus mille choses à vue de pays sans ordre ni suite, et apportent de longues raisons *qui ne sentent nullement la philosophie*, mais souvent la façon ordinaire de parler du peuple." Ibid. p. 187. Though the Hindus abstain religiously from anatomy, they pretend to know most confidently anatomical facts. "Ils ne laissent pas d'assurer qu'il y a cinq mille veines dans l'homme, ni plus ni moins, comme s'ils les avoient bien contés." Ibid. p. 190. After a review of their whole knowledge, which would be reckoned no incorrect outline, by the best informed of the present day, he adds, "Toutes ces grandes impertinences que je viens de vous raconter m'ont souvent fait dire en moi-même que si ce sont là les fameuses sciences de ces anciens Bragmanes des Indes, il faut qu'il y ait eu bien du monde trompé dans les grandes idées qu'on en a conçues." Ibid. p. 193. "For some time a very unjust and unhappy impression appeared to have been made on the public mind, by the encomiums passed on the Hindoo writings. In the first place, they were thus elevated in their antiquity beyond the Christian Scriptures, the writings of Moses having been called the productions of yesterday, compared with those of the Brahmuns. The contents of these books, also, were treated with the greatest reverence; the primitive religion of the Hindoos, it was said, revealed the most sublime doctrines, and inculcated a pure morality. We were taught to make the greatest distinction between the ancient and modern religion of the Hindoos; for the apologists of Hindooism did not approve of its being judged of by present appearances. Some persons endeavoured to persuade us, that the Hindoos were not idolaters, because they maintained the unity of God; though they worshipped the work of their own hands as God, and though the number of their gods was 330,000,000. It is very probable, that the unity of God has been a sentiment amongst the philosophers of every age; and that they wished it to be understood, that they worshipped the One God, whether they bowed before the image of Moloch, Jupiter, or Kalee; yet mankind have generally concluded, that he who worships an image is an idolater; and I suppose they will continue to think so,

BOOK II. CHAP. IX.

little understood, where consequences of so much importance were attached to a feat of this description.

The Hindus have institutions of education; and the Brahmens teach the arts of reading and writing, by tracing the characters with a rod in the sand.[1] How extensively this elementary knowledge is diffused, we have received little or no information. This is a satisfactory proof of the want of intelligence and of interest with which our countrymen in India have looked upon the native population. The magistrates, however, who returned answers to the interrogatories of government in the year 1801, respecting the morals of the people, describe the state of education in general terms, as deplorable in the extreme. Mr. J. Stracey, magistrate of Momensing, says, "The lower sort are extremely ignorant." Mr. Paterson, magistrate of Dacca Jelalpore, recommends "a total change in the system of education amongst those who have any education at all:"

---

unless, in this age of reason, common sense should be turned out of doors.—Now, however, the world has had some opportunity of deciding upon the claims of the Hindoo writings, both as it respects their antiquity and the value of their contents. Mr. Colebrooke's Essay on the Védas, and his other important translations; the Bhuguvut Geeta, by Mr. Wilkins; the translation of the Ramayunu, several volumes of which have been printed; some valuable papers in the Asiatic Researches; with other translations by different Sungskritu scholars; have thrown a great body of light on this subject; and this light is daily increasing.—Many an object appears beautiful when seen at a distance, and through a mist; but when the fog has dispersed, and the person has approached it, he smiles at the deception. Such is the exact case with these books, and this system of idolatry. Because the public, for want of being more familiar with the subject, could not ascertain the point of time when the Hindoo Shastrus were written, they therefore at once believed the assertions of the Brahmuns and their friends, that their antiquity was unfathomable." Ward on the Hindoos, Introd. p. xcix. "There is scarcely anything in Hindooism, when truly known, in which a learned man can delight, or of which a benevolent man can approve; and I am fully persuaded, that there will soon be but one opinion on the subject, and that this opinion will be, that the Hindoo system is less ancient than the Egyptian, and that it is the most puerile, impure, and bloody, of any system of idolatry that was ever established on earth." Ibid. ciii.

[1] Anquetil Duperron, who lodged a night at the house of a schoolmaster at a Mahratta village, a little north of Poona, gives a ludicrous picture of the teaching scene. "Les écoliers, sur deux files, accroupis sur leur talons, traçoient avec le doigt les lettres, ou les mots, sur une planche noire couverte de sable blanc; d'autres répétoient les noms des lettres en forme de mots. Car les Indiens, au lieu de dire comme nous, a, b, c, prononcent ainsi—awam, banam, kanam. Le maître ne me parut occupé pendant une demi heure que la classe dura encore, qu'à frapper avec un long rotin le dos nud de ces pauvres enfans: en Asie c'est la partie qui paye; la passion malheureusement trop commune dans ces contrées, veille à la sureté de celle que nos maitres sacrifient à leur vengeance. J'aurois été bien aise de m'entretenir avec Monsieur le Pédagogue Marate, ou du moins d'avoir un alphabet de sa main; mais sa morgue ne lui permit pas de répondre à mes politesses." (Zendavesta, Disc. Prélim. p. ccxxx.)

adding that "the great mass of the lower ranks have literally none." The judges of the court of appeal and circuit of Moorshedabad say: "The moral character of a nation can be improved by education only. All instruction is unattainable to the labouring poor, whose own necessities require the assistance of their children as soon as their tender limbs are capable of the smallest labour. With the middle class of tradesmen, artificers, and shopkeepers, education ends at ten years of age, and never reaches further than reading, writing (a scarcely legible hand on the plantain leaf), and the simplest rules of arithmetic."[1] But if the Hindu institutions of education were of a much more perfect kind than they appear to have ever been, they would afford a very inadequate foundation for the inference of a high state of civilisation. The truth is, that institutions for education more elaborate than those of the Hindus, are found in the infancy of civilisation. Among the Turks and the Persians there are schools and colleges, rising one above another for the different stages of instruction."[2] And scarcely in any nation does the business of education appear to have been a higher concern of the government than among the Americans of Mexico and Peru.[3]

[1] Papers on India Affairs, No. iii. ordered to be printed by the House of Commons, 30th April, 1813.

[2] "There were in these times [the times of Aliverdi, nabob of Bengal] at Azimabad," says the author of the Seer Mutakhareen, "numbers of persons who loved sciences and learning, and employed themselves in teaching and in being taught; and I remember to have seen in that city and its environs alone, nine or ten professors of repute, and three or four hundred students and disciples; from whence may be conjectured the number of those that must have been in the great towns, and in the retired districts." SeertMutakhareen, i. 705, 4to. Calcutta, 1789. N.B. This with regard to the *Mussulmans* of Bengal. The translator says, in a note, "The reader must rate properly all these students, and all these expressions: their only object was the Coran and its commentaries; that is the Mahometan religion, and the Mahometan law." Ibid. A hint very different from those we are wont to receive from our guides in Hindu literature.—" In vain do some persons talk to us of colleges, of places of education, and books: these words in Turkey convey not the same ideas as with us." Volney's Travels in Syria and Egypt, ii. 443.—Chardin, who formed as high an opinion of the Persians as Sir William Jones of the Hindus, tells us (Voyage en Perse, iii. 130), "Le génie des Persans est porté aux sciences, plus qu'à toute autre profession; et l'on peut dire que les Persans y réussissent si bien que ce sont, après les Chrétiens Européens, les plus sçavans peuples du monde........ Ils envoyent les enfans aux collèges, et les élèvent aux lettres autant que leurs moyens le peuvent permettre." And at pages 137, 138, he adds that schools are distributed in great numbers in Persia, and colleges very numerous."

[3] "Inca Roca was reputed the first who established schools in Cozco, where the Amautas were the masters, and taught such sciences as were fit to improve the minds of Incas, who were princes, and of the chief nobility, not that they did instruct them by way of letters, for as yet they had not attained to that knowledge, but only in a practical manner, and by daily discourses: their

BOOK II. CHAP. IX.

As evidence of the fond credulity with which the state of society among the Hindus was for a time regarded, I ought to mention the statement of Sir W. Jones, who gravely, and with an air of belief, informs us, that he had heard of a philosopher "whose works were said to contain a system of the universe, founded on the principle of attraction and the central position of the sun."[1] This reminds the instructed reader of the disposition which has been manifested by some of the admirers of the Greek and Roman literature, and of these by one at least who had not a weak and credulous mind, to trace the discoveries of modern philosophy to the pages of the classics. Dr. Middleton, in his celebrated life of Cicero, says, that "several of the fundamental principles of the modern philosophy, which pass for the original dicoveries of these later times, are the revival rather of ancient notions, maintained by some of the first philosophers, of whom we have any notice in history; as the motion of the earth, the antipodes, a vacuum; and a universal gravitation or attractive quality of matter, which holds the world in its present form and order."[2] It is a well-known artifice of the Brahmens, with whose pretensions and interests it would be altogether inconsistent to allow there was any knowledge with which they were not

---

other lectures were of religion, and of those reasons and wisdom on which their laws were established, and of the number and true exposition of them; for by these means they attained to the art of government and military discipline; they distinguished the times and seasons of the year, and by reading in their knots they learned history and the actions of past ages; they improved themselves also in the elegance and ornament of speaking, and took rules and measures for the management of their domestic affairs. These Amautas, who were philosophers, and in high esteem amongst them, taught something also of poetry, music, philosophy, and astrology," &c. Garcilasso de la Vega, Royal Commentaries, book iv. ch. xix. This same Inca exhibited one stroke at least which will be reckoned high wisdom by some amongst us: "He enacted that the children of the common people should not be educated in the liberal arts and sciences, for that were to make them proud, conceited, and ungovernable, but that the nobility were those only to whom such literature did appertain, to render them more honourable, and capable of offices in the commonwealth." Ibid. "There is nothing," (says Acosta, book vi. ch. 27) "that gives me more cause to admire, nor that I find more worthy of commendation and memory, than the order and care the Mexicans had to nourish their youth." He tells us they had schools in their temples, and masters to instruct the young, "in all commendable exercises, to be of good behaviour," &c.

[1] Asiat. Res. i. 430, and iv. 169.

[2] Middleton's Life of Cicero, sect. 12. Considerable currency was obtained by a very learned work of a clergyman of the Church of England, Mr. Dutens, who undertook to prove that all the discoveries which the moderns have made in the arts and sciences, may be found distinctly broached in the writings of the ancients.

acquainted, or which was not contained in some of their books, to attach to the loose and unmeaning phraseology of some of their own writings, whatever ideas they find to be in esteem; or even to interpolate for that favourite purpose.[1] It was thus extremely natural that Sir William Jones, whose pundits had become acquainted with the ideas of European philosophers respecting the system of the universe, should hear from them that those ideas were

[1] Anquetil Duperron gives us a remarkable instance of the dispostion of the Brahmens to accommodate by falsification, even their sacred records, to the ideas of Europeans. " Si je n'avois pas sçu que le commencement de l'Amerkosh contenoit la description du lingam, peut-être m'eut il été impossible de découvrir que mes Brahmes, qui ne vouloient pas dévoiler le fond de leurs mystères, paraphrasoient et pallioient plutôt qu'ils ne traduisoient." Zendav. Disc. Prélim. i. ccclxix. Dr. Buchanan found the propensity general, to deceive him in their accounts both of their religion and history. See Journey through Mysore, &c. ii. 76, 79, 80. " The Brahmens," he says, " when asked for dates, or authority, say that they must consult their books, which may be readily done; but when I send my interpreter, who is also a Brahmen, to copy the date, they pretend that their books are lost." Ibid. i. 335. All information, he says, from the Brahmens, usually differs most essentially as derived from different individuals. Ibid. ii. 306. See an account of the imposition practised by his pundits upon Captain Wilford, by Lord Teignmouth, in the Introduction to his Life of Sir William Jones; also an account by Mr. Wilford himself, Essay on the Sacred Isles in the West, Asiat. Res. viii. 253.—In a letter to a friend, Sir. W. Jones said, " I can no longer bear to be at the mercy of our pundits, who deal out the Hindu law as they please, and make it at reasonable rates, when they cannot find it ready made." Life of Sir W. Jones, by Lord Teignmouth, 4to. Ed. p. 307.—Colonel Wilkes accuses the Hindu author of the Digest of Hindu Law, translated by Mr. Colebrooke, of substituting a false principle of law for a true one, out of " a courtesy and consideration, for opinions established by authority, *which is peculiar to the natives of India.*" Histor. Sketches, p. 116.—M.

These proofs " of a well-known artifice of the Brahmans," are for the most part proofs only of the ignorance or misconceptions of Europeans. Du Perron's instance is remarkable as an illustration of the former. There is no allusion to the " lingam," in a mythological sense, in the beginning of the Amerkosh, and the Brahmans must have been much amused and astonished at Du Perron's discovery; the word " linga " does occur, it is true, but only in its grammatical import of gender; the author intimating that his work (a lexicon) specifies the genders of the nouns which it contains. Buchanan insisted on the production of what rarely, if ever, exists in manuscripts—dates, and that they were not manufactured for him proves the integrity of his informers. Sir Wm. Jones's assertion is general, and purports no more than an undeniable truth, that it becomes those Europeans who administer Mohammedan and Hindu law, to know that law for themselves, and not be wholly dependent upon interpreters, who may have an interest in misleading them. Colonel Wilkes assumes, without any warrant, that Jagannatha was influenced by courtesy and consideration for established opinions, in pronouncing the earth to become the property of kings by conquest. It is much more probable that Jagannatha was quite honest, as he would attach great weight to the text on which he comments, however inconclusive it may appear to European critics, and whether well-founded or not, he expresses the general sentiment of his countrymen. The only one of these proofs then that will bear examination, is the case of Colonel Wilford, and he tempted imposition by his incaution and credulity. That instances of literary imposture occur in India, as elsewhere, is no doubt true, but they are not of a nature or extent to justify the unqualified attribution of dishonesty to all learned Brahmans whatever.—W.

BOOK II. CHAP. IX.

contained in their own books: The wonder was, that without any proof he should believe them.[1]

1 He might have got proofs, equal to those with which they presented him, of Plato's having been acquainted with the circulation of the blood; viz., because when speaking of that fluid he uses the word περιαγεσθαι which signifies to be carried round.—It is worthy of remark, that the philosopher, of whom Sir William heard, and whose works contained such important discoveries, was called Yavan Acharya, that is Gentile or Greek. By the argument of Sir William, we might believe that the Greeks anticipated Newton. When Copernicus, dissatisfied with the received account of the heavenly motions, addressed himself to discover a new arrangement, we are told that "he examined all the obscure traditions delivered down to us, concerning every other hypothesis which the ancients had invented. He found in Plutarch, that some old Pythagoreans had represented the earth as revolving in the centre of the universe, like a wheel round its own axis; and that others of the same sect had removed it from the centre, and represented it as revolving in the ecliptic, like a star round the central fire. By this central fire he supposed they meant the sun," &c. Dr. Ad. Smith, Essay on Hist. Astron. p. 51. We might prove that Parmenides had a just conception of the figure of the globe. Plato informs us that, according to that inquirer, Το όλον εστι

Παντοθεν ευκυκλου σφαιρας εναλιγκιον ογκῳ,
Μεσσοθεν ισοπελης παντη· του γαρ ουτε τι μειζον
Ουτε βεβαιοτερον πελει. Plat. Sophista, p. 171.

Herodotus mentions the opinion of a naturalist, even in his days, who supposed that the ocean flowed round the earth, (a bold step towards the conception of its right figure,) τον ωκεανον γην περι πασαν ρεειν, lib. ii. sect. 22. Dr. Vincent, giving an account of the knowledge possessed by the ancients of the globular form of the earth, and of the saying of Strabo, that nothing obstructed the passage from Spain to India by a westerly course, but the immensity of the Atlantic ocean, has the following note; "Aristotle seems the author of this supposition, as well as of most other things that are extraordinary in the knowledge of the ancients. See Bochart, Phaleg. 169. Συναπτειν τον περι τας Ἡρακλειους τηλας τοπον τῳ περι την Ινδικην. The parts about the pillars of Hercules join to those about India. This is a nearer approach still; but both suppositions arise from the contemplation of the earth as a sphere.—Aristotle has also preserved the opinion of the Pythagoreans, who made the sun the centre of our system, with the earth and the other planets revolving round it, which is the hypothesis adopted by Copernicus, and established by Newton. Strabo, likewise, who left the phenomena of the heavens, and the form of the earth, to the mathematicians, still thought the earth a sphere, and describes our system agreeably to the theory which was afterwards adopted by Ptolemy; but he adds the idea of gravitation in a most singular manner. Σφαιροειδης μεν ὁ Κοσμος και ὁ Ουρανος. Ἡ ΡΟΠΗ δ'επι το μεσον των βαρεων .... ὁ δ'ουρανος περιφερεται περι τε αυτην και περι τον αξονα, απ' ανατολης επι δυσιν. Lib. ii. 110. The earth and the heaven are both spherical; but the tendency is to the centre of gravity. The heaven is carried round itself, and round its axis from east to west. I barely suggest the extent of ancient knowledge on these questions; those who wish to gratify their curiosity may consult Stobæus, tom. ii. cap. 25, Ed. Heeren, Götting. 1792, 1794; and Diogenes Laertius in Anaximander, Pythagoras, and Zeno, lib. vii. sect. 155." Periplus of the Erythræan Sea, part ii. 517.—Sir William Jones tells us, in his Discourse on the Hindu zodiac, that the pundit Ramachandra had a correct notion of the figure of the earth.—So had the elder Hermes, of whom it was one of the established maxims, that the earth was oviform, and hence the oval form of many of the oldest temples of Egypt. The earth was called Brahma's egg. See Asiat. Res. i. 360. Or Ramachandra, like a common fortune-teller, might only repeat to Sir William what he had learned from Sir William.—Europeans will arrive in time to think justly respecting the Hindus: Thus speaks Dr. Buchanan; "No useful science have the Brahmens diffused among their followers; history they have abolished; morality they have depressed to the utmost; and the dignity and power of the altar they have erected on the ruins of the state, and the rights of the subject." Asiat. Res. vi. 166.

APPENDIX, No. I.

Remarks on the Arguments for the Antiquity of Hindu Astronomy.

THE knowledge of the Europeans concerning the astronomy of India is chiefly derived from different sets of astronomical tables brought to Europe at different times. All these tables are obviously connected with one another: for they are all adapted to one meridian; the mean motions are the same in them all; and their principal epochs are all deduced by calculation from one original epoch. The most ancient of the Indian epochs is fixed in the year 3102 before the Christian æra, at the commencement of the Cali-yug. On account of the mutual connexion which, it is allowed, subsists between the three remaining epochs, it is only necessary to discuss that one which seems to be the most important; it is comparatively of modern date, and goes back no further than to the year of Christ, 1491.

M. Bailly, in his Astronomie Indienne, has endeavoured to prove that the more ancient of the two epochs is fixed by actual observations; a proposition, which, if it were clearly made out, would confer the highest antiquity on the astronomy of India. In a paper in the Edinburgh Transactions, Mr. Playfair, who has adopted the opinion of M. Bailly, has given a clear and forcible summary of all the arguments that have been adduced in favour of the side he supports. M. Laplace, who is the only other author that has noticed the subject of the Indian astronomy since the publication of M. Bailly's work, does not accede to the opinion of his brother academician. In a very short passage in the "Système du Monde," Laplace states it as his own opinion, that the ancient epoch of the Brahmens was adopted with the view of making all the celestial motions begin at the same point of the zodiac: and he very briefly hints the reasons on which his opinion is founded. In drawing up the following remarks, the observations of Laplace have been kept in view.

1. If we set out from the epoch of 1491, and compute the places of the sun, moon, and the planets, for the ancient epoch in 3102 A.C., it is found that all the celestial bodies

BOOK II. CHAP. IX.

are then in mean conjunction with the sun in the origin of the moveable zodiac. Here then is an astronomical fact, which the Indian tables necessarily suppose to have taken place, and which, it must be allowed, appears to be very fit to bring the authenticity of the ancient epoch to the proof. For, although the tables of the modern astronomy, highly improved as they are, do not enable us to go back more than 2000 years with extreme accuracy, yet they are sufficiently exact to afford the means of judging whether the general conjunction, supposed in the Indian tables, was actually copied from the heavens or not. Now M. Bailly has computed the places of the planets at the time of the ancient epoch of the Indians, or for the commencement of the Cali-yug, from the tables of M. Lalande: and, although all the planets, except Venus, were then nearly in conjunction with the sun, yet they were by no means so near to one another as to render it probable that this epoch was fixed by observation. M. Bailly argues that the conjunction could not be determined by direct observation; because the planets are invisible when immersed in the sun's light: and he shows that fifteen days after the epoch all the planets, except Venus, were contained within seventeen degrees of the zodiac. But this is not satisfactory. Mr. Playfair admits that the Indian tables cannot be entirely vindicated in this respect. Laplace lays all the stress on this argument to which it seems fairly entitled.

The fiction of a general conjunction in the beginning of the moveable zodiac is the more remarkable, because it agrees precisely with the account which M. Bailly gives of the formation of the Indian astronomical systems.

The validity of the observations made by the critic in the Edinburgh Review, as far as they regard the accuracy of the mean motions, and other astronomical elements which do not depend on the epochs, cannot be disputed. There is but one way of determining the mean motions with accuracy: namely, by comparing together real observations of the places of the planets made at a sufficient interval of time. No fictitious, or assumed, epochs can be of the least use for this purpose. Indeed Mr. Bentley does not maintain that the Brahmens make any such use of their assumed epochs. The artificial systems of the Indian astronomy necessarily suppose the mean motions and other elements to be already determined and known. Mr. Bentley seems, in some measure, to have misconceived the nature of the arguments by which the Europeans endeavour to establish the antiquity of the Hindu astronomy. He seems to have imagined that nothing more was necessary for confuting all their reasoning on this subject, than to make them acquainted with the formation of the artificial systems of the Brahmens.

But considering Mr. Bentley as a person acquainted with the astronomy of the East, and as having access to the books in which it is contained, his testimony cannot but be allowed to be of great force in the present argument. He tells us that the Brahmens, when they would form an astronomical system, go back to a remote epoch, and assume as the basis of their system: that all the heavenly bodies are in a line of mean conjunction with the sun in the beginning of Aries: Now the Indian tables actually suppose such a conjunction at the commencement of the Cali-yug; and in this they are at variance with the most exact of the modern astronomical tables. Is it not then in the highest degree probable that the era of the Cali-yug is an assumed, or fictitious epoch in the astronomy of the Hindus?

If the ancient epoch, in 3102 A.C. be fictitious, the force of many of the arguments for the antiquity of the Indian astronomy will be greatly diminished. For that reasoning must needs be a good deal vague and unsatisfactory which rests entirely on the quantity of an astronomical element of an uncertain date, affected, as must be the case, by the errors of observation, of the limits of which we have no means of judging.

2. The equation of the sun's centre, according to the Indian tables, is $2° 10\frac{1}{2}'$; whereas the same quantity, according to modern observations, is only $1° 55\frac{1}{2}'$. It is one consequence of the mutual disturbances of the planets that the eccentricity of the solar orbit, on which the equation just mentioned depends, was greater in former ages than it is at the present time. From the quantity which the Hindus assign to this astronomical element, M. Bailly has drawn an argument in favour of the antiquity of the Indian tables, which, it must be confessed, is of great weight, when the difference of the Indian and European determinations is considered as arising from the gradual alteration of the pla-

BOOK II. CHAP. IX.

netary orbits. But Laplace has remarked that the equation which in the Hindu tables amount to 2° 10½′, is really composed of two parts; namely, the equation of the sun's centre, and the annual equation of the moon; both of which depend alike on the eccentricity of the sun's orbit, and complete their periods in the same interval of time. The Indians have naturally enough blended these two irregularities together; because, the great object of their astronomy being the calculation of eclipses, the relative places of the sun and moon are effected by the sum of both. The annual equation of the moon is nearly 11′: and, when added to the equation of the sun's centre, the amount (2° 6½′,) does not differ much from the quantity set down in the Indian tables. The force of M. Bailly's argument is therefore completely taken off.

But the remark of Laplace not only invalidates the argument for the antiquity, but it furnishes a powerful one on the opposite side. It is indeed in the situation of a perfidious ally, who not only deserts his friends, but marshals his whole force in the ranks of their opponents. The amount of the two irregularities which are blended together by the Indians is 2° 6½′ at the present time: but if we go back to the commencement of the Cali-yug, there must be added about 13½′, on account of the greater magnitude of the sun's eccentricity in that age above what it is in the present century; and thus we ought to have found 2° 20′, in place of 2° 10½′ in the Hindu tables, if their supposed antiquity be granted. It must be admitted that, in this instance at least, the Indian tables, when they are referred to the ancient epoch, are fairly at variance with the state of the heavens.

3. The quantities which the Indian tables assign to two other astronomical elements, viz. the mean motions of Jupiter and Saturn, have been found to agree almost exactly, not with what is observed at the present time, but with what the theory of gravity shows would have been observed at the beginning of the Cali-yug. This curious coincidence between the Hindu tables and the most abstruse theory of modern Europe, was discovered by Laplace after the publication of the Astronomie Indienne: and it was communicated to M. Bailly in a letter inserted in the Journal des Sçavans. The argument which this circumstance

furnishes in favour of the antiquity is not forgotten by Mr. Playfair; and it is also mentioned by the critic in the Edinburgh Review.

But the discovery of Laplace, although it cannot be disputed, is absolutely of no avail in establishing the antiquity of the Indian astronomy: for no inference can be drawn from it respecting the ancient epoch in 3102 A.C., which is not equally conclusive with regard to the modern epoch of 1491 of our era.

The theory of astronomy is indebted to Laplace for many interesting discoveries. Of these, two equations, affecting the mean motions of Jupiter and of Saturn, are not the least important. These irregularities are periodical, and they both complete their courses in 917¾ years: And while one of them augments the motion of one of the planets, the other diminishes the motion of the other planet. It is a consequence of this discovery of Laplace, that, after an interval of time equal to 917¾ years; or equal to twice, or thrice, or any exact number of times that period; the mean motions of Jupiter and Saturn will return, to be precisely of the same quantity that they were at the beginning of the interval of time. Now, if from the epoch 1491, we reckon back a number of years, equal to five times the period of Laplace, we shall arrive at the year 3095 A.C., which is so near the ancient epoch of the Indians, as to entitle us to infer, that an observer who lived in 1491, would agree in his determinations of the mean motions of Jupiter and Saturn, with an astronomer who had lived forty-six centuries before, at the beginning of the Cali-yug.

No reliance, then, can be placed on this argument, as a proof of the antiquity of the Hindu tables. On the contrary, if we admit, what it must be allowed is extremely probable, that the ancient epoch is a fictitious one, pointed out by superstition, or fixed upon for convenience in calculation, this argument will concur with the last in giving, to the astronomy of India, a modern date, rather than the high antiquity contended for.

4. M. Bailly has shown that the place of the aphelion of Jupiter's orbit, determined by the Indian tables for the beginning of the Cali-yug, agrees with the modern tables of Lalande, when corrected by the theoretical equations of La

Grange. The same thing is true of the quantity which the Hindus assign to the equation of Saturn's centre. It requires but little scepticism to raise up doubts of the validity of arguments founded on such coincidences. In the first place, we are ignorant of the limits of the errors that the Indian determinations may be susceptible of. In the second place, the dates of the observations on which the astronomical elements of the Indians depend, are unknown and merely conjectural: yet these are necessary data for calculating the corrections that must be applied to the modern tables, to fit them for representing the ancient state of the heavens. In the third place, the theoretical formulas themselves, by which the corrections are computed, cannot be supposed to enable us to go back with much accuracy to so remote an epoch as the Cali-yug; a circumstance which is not owing to any imperfection of the theory, but to the want of our knowing with precision the relative proportions of the masses of the planets that compose our system. When we reflect on these things, even the very exact coincidence of the Indian elements, with the calculated quantities (which is nearer than there is reasonable ground to expect) is apt to create a suspicion that the whole is owing to a happy combination of balancing errors.

But waiving these objections, fairness of reasoning requires that we should lay no more stress on such coincidences as those just mentioned, in favour of one side of the question, than we are willing to allow to discrepancies in similar circumstances, in support of the other side. M. Bailly allows that not any more of the elements of the planetary motions, contained in the Indian tables, agree so well with the determinations derived from the theory of gravity: and the quantities which are assigned to the equations of the centre, for Jupiter and Mars, are quite irreconcileable with the supposition of so remote an antiquity as the beginning of the Cali-yug. Such a contrariety of results justly invalidates the whole argument.

5. Another argument urged by the favourers of the antiquity of the Indian astronomy, is derived from the obliquity of the ecliptic, which the Indians state at 24°.

Both observation and theory concur in showing that the obliquity of the ecliptic has been diminishing slowly for many ages preceding the present. At the beginning of the

Cali-yug, this astronomical element, according to theory, was 23° 51′, which is still short of what the Indians make it. Twelve centuries before the Cali-yug, the actual obliquity of the ecliptic, as derived from theory, would coincide with the Indian quantity within 2′: and, by going back still further, the error may, no doubt, be entirely annihilated. Nothing, it must be confessed, can be more vague and unsatisfactory than this sort of reasoning.

Let us grant that the Hindus determined the obliquity of the ecliptic, 4,300 years before our era, which supposes that they made an error of 2′ only: How are we to account for the strange circumstance, that a quantity, which they were at one time able to determine with so much accuracy, should remain unaltered for a period of nearly 6,000 years; during which time the error of the first determination has accumulated to half a degree? Are we to suppose that, immediately after this imaginary epoch, the art of astronomical observation disappeared, and was entirely lost? This, we know, could not be the case, because many other astronomical elements necessarily suppose observations of a comparatively modern date: as, for instance, the equation of the sun's centre.

We shall account for the quantity which the Indians assign to the obliquity much more simply and naturally, if we trust to the authority of Mr. Bentley. According to him, the Hindu astronomers, (unless in cases where extraordinary accuracy is required) make it a rule, in observing, to take the nearest round numbers, rejecting fractional quantities: so that we have only to suppose that the observer who fixed the obliquity of the ecliptic at 24°, actually found it to be more than 23½°.

6. The length of the tropical year, as deduced from the Hindu tables, is $365^{d}\ 5^{h}\ 50'\ 35''$, which is 1′ 46″ longer than the determination of La Caille. This is certainly not a little accurate, and necessarily supposes some degree of antiquity, and the comparisons of observations made at a great interval of time. We shall be the better able to form a judgment of the length of time which such a degree of accuracy may require, if we consider the errors of some of our older tables, published before the art of making astronomical instruments was brought to its present perfect state. In the Alphonsine Tables, published about

BOOK II. CHAP. IX.

1252, the length of the tropical year, is —	365^d	5^h	49′	16″
Copernicus (about 1530) makes it . .	365	5	49	6
Kepler (about 1627)	365	5	48	57½

These quantities are determined by observations distant from one another about 1500 or 1600 years: and the differences between them and the year of La Caille, is about the fourth part of the error of the Indians.

If we suppose that the length of the year found in the Hindu tables was actually determined by observation at the beginning of the Cali-yug, the error, which has been stated at 1′ 46″, may be reduced to 1′ 5″. The reason of this is, that the year has been decreasing in duration, for all the intervening time, and the quantity, computed by theory, which must be added to the length of the year as observed in the present age, to have its length forty-nine centuries ago, is 40½″. Arguments of this kind carry but little force with them. For the time when the observations from which the length of the Indian year was deduced is totally unknown: and it seems highly probable, that the beginning of the Cali-yug is not an epoch settled by observation. Besides, the error of observation (which cannot be reduced under 1′ 5″) must be allowed to be, in this instance, nearly double of the correction applied: and there is nothing to prove that it may not amount to much more.

It is to be remarked that the Indian tables contain the sidereal motion of the sun, and not his motion in respect of the moveable equinox as our tables do. If we draw our comparison from the length of the sidereal, instead of the tropical year, the result will not be so favourable to the accuracy of the Hindu astronomy. The sidereal revolution of the sun, according to the Indians, is 365^d 6^h 12′ 30″; according to modern observation it is 365^d 6^h 9′ 11″; and the error is 3′ 19″, nearly double the former error. The difference of those errors arises from the quantity which they assign to the precession of the equinoxes, which is 54″ instead of 50½″.

7. Of all the arguments in support of the antiquity of the Hindu astronomy, the strongest and most direct is that which is derived from an ancient zodiac brought from India by M. le Gentil. This argument, therefore, deserves to be particularly considered.

It must be observed, that the force of an argument,

such as this, which turns on the magnitude of an astronomical quantity that accumulates slowly, and is perceptible only after a long lapse of time, will entirely depend on the authenticity of the observations, or facts, from which the argument is drawn, and on the precision and accuracy with which they are recorded. Anything uncertain, or arbitrary, or hypothetical, respecting these fundamental points, will greatly weaken the strength of the argument. We are told by Mr. Playfair, that the star Aldebaran has the longitude of 3° 20′ in the zodiac of M. le Gentil: and it is on the authenticity and precision of this fact, that the validity of his reasoning hinges. Now, if we turn to the passage of the Astronomie Indienne, which is cited by Mr. Playfair, it will appear that this position of Aldebaran is rather a conjecture, or hypothesis, of M. Bailly, than an authentic observation recorded with precision.

The Indian zodiac moves westward, at the same rate as the fixed stars, and it is divided into twenty-seven constellations, each of 13° 20′. The vernal equinox was 54° to the east of the beginning of the zodiac at the commencement of the Cali-yug; and it was therefore in the fifth constellation, being 40′ more advanced than the fourth. The Indians mark the fourth constellation, which they call Rohini, by five stars, of which the most easterly, or the most advanced in the zodiac, is the very brilliant star Aldebaran. These things being premised, M. Bailly thus proceeds: "Il est naturel que cette belle étoile ait marqué la fin ou le commencement d'une constellation. Je suppose qu'elle marque en effet la fin de Rohini, la quatrième des constellations Indiennes, et le commencement de la cinquième; il résulte de cette supposition que l'étoile Aldebaran étoit placée dans le zodiaque Indien à 1s 23° 20′ de l'origine du zodiaque." It appears, then, that the whole of the argument, which is stated so strongly by Mr. Playfair, and by the critic in the Edinburgh Review, rests on the conjecture of M. Bailly; that Aldebaran was exactly placed at the end of the fourth, and the beginning of the fifth constellation in the Indian zodiac. For this, no sort of proof is offered, except the conspicuousness of the star, which is certainly one of the most brilliant in the heavens. Are we to suppose, for the sake of this argu-

BOOK II. CHAP. IX.

ment, that the position of the Indian zodiac was entirely regulated by the star Aldebaran? For it must be admitted that when the beginning of one constellation is fixed, all the rest are thereby determined. Or, are we to suppose, what is still more improbable, that the beginning of the fifth constellation fell, by a lucky chance, exactly in the place of this conspicuous star?

But the Indians themselves afford us the means of correcting the supposition of M. Bailly. Mr. Bentley tells us that Brahma Gupta makes the longitude of the star, Spica Virginis, in the moveable zodiac of the Hindus, $6^s\ 3°$: According to De la Caille, the longitude of the same star in 1750, was

	6^s	20°	21′	18″
Of Aldebaran	2	6	17	47
Difference	4	14	3	31

which, substracted from $6^s\ 3°$, leaves $1^s\ 18°\ 56'\ 29''$ for the longitude of Aldebaran in the Indian zodiac, instead of $1^s\ 23°\ 20'$, which it is according to the hypothesis of M. Bailly. The error amounts to $4°\ 23'\ 31''$: a quantity which is nowise inconsistent with the configuration of the constellation Rohini, while it is sufficient to show that the Indians may have fixed the origin of their zodiac at the beginning of the Cali-yug, by calculating back from a modern epoch.

And indeed the Brahmens point out a modern epoch, a noted one in their astronomy, which is connected with the era of the Cali-yug by their precession, in the same manner that the modern epoch 1491, is connected with it by the mean motions. Mr. Bentley tells us that, according to Varaha, the year 3601 of the Cali-yug (A.D. 499) began precisely at the vernal equinox: which implies that the origin of the Indian zodiac did then coincide with the equinoxial point. Now if we deduct $1^s\ 24°$, the Indian precession for 3600 years, from 12^s, we shall have $10^s\ 6°$ for the origin of the zodiac, reckoned eastward from the vernal equinox, according to the practice of our astronomy: precisely as it comes out by the Indian tables.

The epoch, 3601 of the Cali-yug, is involved in all the Indian tables, insomuch that M. Bailly was led to discover it by calculation: and, in fact, there is no authority for fixing the origin of the Indian zodiac in $10^s\ 6°$ at the era of the Cali-yug, except by reckoning back from this epoch, according to the Hindu rule for the precession.

It appears, then, that the argument drawn from the zodiac of M. le Gentil, when closely considered, not only affords no evidence for the antiquity of the Indian astronomy, but rather favours the opinion that the beginning of the Cali-yug, is a fictitious epoch fixed by calculation. For it has been shown that the place of the origin of the Indian zodiac, at the era of the Cali-yug, is connected by the precession contained in the Hindu tables with the epoch 3601 of that age: and, indeed, all the epochs of the Brahmens, ancient as well as modern, are connected with the same fundamental epoch, in what regards the precession. The pretended position of the star Aldebaran is merely a conjecture of M. Bailly: and it is at variance with the place which Bramha Gupta, and other Indian astronomers, assign to the star "Spica Virginis."

8. In the preceding observations, all the arguments that have been adduced in favour of the antiquity of the Indian astronomy, as far as the question is purely astronomical, have been considered, excepting those drawn from the places of the sun and moon, at the beginning of the Cali-yug, (at midnight, between the 17th and 18th of February, of the year 3102 A.C.) With regard to the first of these, there is a difficulty which weighed so much with Mr. Playfair, as to induce him to set aside the argument entirely, and to lay no stress upon it. It is remarkable that the critic in the Edinburgh Review has brought forward this argument, without noticing the difficulty which, in Mr. Playfair's opinion, rendered it inconclusive. After all that has been urged to invalidate the opinion of M. Bailly, that the ancient epoch of the Indian tables was settled by observation, we shall be spared the task of examining the remaining argument drawn from the place of the moon: allowing to this argument all the force which the most sanguine supporters of the antiquity can demand, it can have but little weight in opposition to the many strong and concurring indications of a contrary nature.[1]

[1] Laplace has remarked, that the mean motions of the lunar orbit are quicker in the Indian tables than in those of Ptolemy: which indicates that

BOOK II. CHAP. IX.

9. If the author of the "Astronomie Indienne" has succeeded in establishing any of his positions, it is in proving that the astronomy of the Brahmens is original, or at least that it has not been borrowed from any of the astronomical systems that we are acquainted with. This was a preliminary point which his favourite system required him to examine: for if the astronomy of the Brahmens had turned out to have an obvious affinity to the astronomical systems of Arabia or Greece, it would have been in vain to bring proofs of its antiquity. But how does this prove the antiquity of the Indian astronomy? It only proves that the inhabitants of the eastern world, separated from the rest of mankind, have made the same progress to a certain extent, which, in the western world, has been carried to a far greater pitch of perfection.[1]

APPENDIX N°. II.

Colebrooke on Sanscrit Algebra.

SINCE the pages relating to the science of the Hindus were sent to the press, has appeared a work entitled, "Algebra, with Arithmetic and Mensuration, from the Sanscrit of Brahmegupta and Bhascara; translated by Henry Thomas Colebrooke, Esq." No person, who takes an interest in the history of the human mind, can fail to recognise that Mr. Colebrooke has added largely to the former obligations he had conferred upon us, not only by laying open to European readers the most approved production on Algebra, in the Sanscrit language, but by the research and ability with which, in a preliminary dissertation, he has brought together the materials for forming an opinion, both respecting the origin of that science among the Hindus, and their merit in the prosecution of it.

---

the former tables were constructed posterior to those of the Greek astronomer This argument is, at least, as strong as any of those by which the antiquity is supported.

[1] The question discussed in this Appendix is not the antiquity of Hindu astronomy, but the soundness of Bailly's views in assigning to it an improbable antiquity. This does not affect the probability of its being the oldest system of which we are able to judge from authentic materials furnished by itself. Even Bentley, as before noticed, places the invention of the lunar mansions 1426 B.C., implying, necessarily, previous observation of the heavens, and classification of the heavenly bodies.—W.

On mathematics I must speak superficially, because my knowledge does not permit me to speak profoundly. Enough, I think, however, appears on the face of this subject, to enable me to resolve the only question, in the solution of which I am interested.

Mr. Colebrooke thinks it possible, nay, probable, that the Hindus derived their first knowledge of algebra from the Greeks; that they were made acquainted with the writings of Diophantus, before they had, of their own accord, made any attempts in the science; and that it is in the accessions which Algebra received in their hands, that their title, if any, to our respect, must, in this particular, look for its foundation.[1] That the Hindus cultivated astronomy, and the branches of the art of calculation to astronomy, solely for the purposes of astrology, is not disputed by anybody, and least of all by Mr. Colebrooke. That candid and careful inquirer has brought to light a very important fact, that even on the subject of astrology, on which they might have been supposed original, the Hindus have been borrowers, and borrowers from the Greeks.[2] "Joining," he says, "this indication,

[1] "If it be insisted, that a hint or suggestion, the seed of their knowledge, may have reached the Hindu mathematicians immediately from the Greeks of Alexandria, or mediately through those of Bactria, it must at the same time be confessed, that a slender germ grew and fructified rapidly, and soon attained an approved state of maturity in Indian soil. More will not be here contended for: since it is not impossible, that the hint of the one analysis may have been actually received by the mathematicians of the other nation: nor *unlikely;* considering the arguments which may be brought for a probable communication on the subject of astrology." Dissertation, p. xxii. This is an important admission, which Mr. Colebrooke was too well informed to overlook, and too honest to conceal. His partialities, however, lead him to a very useless effort of extenuation. Why call the knowledge which the Hindus derived of the Diophantine methods a *hint?* What should confine it to a *hint?* Why make use of the word hint? when it is perfectly clear that if they had the means of receiving a hint, they had the means of receiving the whole. The communication was full and complete between the Hindus and the Greeks, both of Bactria and of Egypt; and the Hindus had the means of receiving from the Greeks all those parts of their knowledge, which the state of civilization among the Hindus enabled them to imbibe. Of the exaggerating language of Mr. Colebrooke, on the other side, about the growing and fructifying of the germ, and its attaining a state of approved maturity in Indian soil, we shall speak by-and-by.

[2] He had stated long ago, "That astronomy was originally cultivated among the Hindus solely for the purposes of astrology: That one branch, if not the whole of their astrological science, was borrowed from the Arabians: And that their astronomical knowledge must, by consequence, have been derived from the same quarter." Asiat. Res. ix. 376. And on the present occasion he says: "The position that astrology is partly of foreign growth in India; that is, that the Hindus have borrowed, and largely too, from the astrology of a more western region, is grounded, as the similar inference concerning a different branch of divination, on the resemblance of certain terms employed in both.

BOOK II. CHAP. IX.

to that of the division of the zodiac into twelve signs, represented by the same figures of animals, and named by words of the same import, with the zodiacal signs of the Greeks; and taking into consideration the analogy, though not identity, of the Ptolemaic system, and the Indian one of excentric deferents and epicycles, no doubt can be entertained that the Hindus received hints from the astronomical schools of the Greeks."[1]

To draw, then, from the tracts which Mr. Colebrooke has translated, an inference to any high state of civilization among the Hindus, the three following propositions must, first, be established;

1. That the Greeks did not teach to the Hindus as much of the science as the works in question contain.

2. That the works are sufficiently old to render it impossible that the knowledge could have been borrowed from any modern source.

3. That the accessions made to the knowledge derived from the Greeks are so difficult, as not to have been made except by a people in a high state of civilization.

If all these propositions are not fully and entirely made out; if any weakness appears in the evidence of any one of them, the inference falls to the ground. Upon inquiry, it seems to come out, that for not one of them is the evidence sufficient, or trustworthy.

1. That the Hindus received from the Greeks all that the latter knew, is admitted by Mr. Colebrooke. It is also admitted by Mr. Colebrooke, that "Diophantus was acquainted with the direct resolution of affected quadratic equations, and of intermediate problems of the first degree; that he displays infinite sagacity and ingenuity in particular solutions; and that a certain routine is discernible in them."[2] It is unfortunately from Diophantus

---

The mode of divination, called *Tájaca*, implies by its very name its Arabian origin: Astrological prediction, by configuration of planets, in like manner, indicates, even by its Indian name, a Grecian source. It is denominated *Hórá*, the second of three branches which compose a complete course of astronomy and astrology; and the word occurs in this sense in the writings of early Hindu astrologers...... The same term *hórá* occurs again in the writings of the Hindu astrologers, with an acceptation—that of hour—which more exactly conforms to the Grecian etymon. The resemblance of a single term would not suffice to ground an inference of common origin, since it might be purely accidental. But other words are also remarked in Hindu astrology," etc. Algebra, etc., from the Sanscrit, Dissert. Notes and Illust. p. lxxx.

[1] Algebra, etc., from the Sanscrit, Dissert. Notes and Illust. pp. x. and xvi.

[2] Ibid. pp. x. and xvi.

alone, that we derive any knowledge of the attainments of the Greeks in this branch of mathematics. It is no less unfortunate, that out of thirteen books which he wrote upon this subject, only six, or possibly seven, have been preserved. How does Mr. Colebrooke, know, that these other books of Diophantus did not ascend to more difficult points of the science?[1] He says, you have no right to infer that. True; but neither has he any right to infer the contrary. There is, however, another possibility, and a still more important one, which Mr. Colebrooke has altogether overlooked. Supposing that nothing more of Algebra was known to the Greeks, at the time of Diophantus, than is found in seven out of thirteen books of one author, which is a pretty handsome allowance; is it certain or is it probable, that when the Greeks had made so considerable a progress, they remained stationary? and, though the most ingenious and inventive people in the world, peculiarly at that time turned to mathematical and abstruse investigations, they made no addition through several generations, to what was taught them by Diophantus? This argument appears to be conclusive.

2. Mr. Colebrook has a very elaborate, complex, and in some parts obscure train of argument to prove the antiquity of certain points of algebraic knowledge among the Hindus. That it is not conclusive may be made to appear very certainly; it is only to be regretted that so many words are required.

The point is, to prove the antiquity of certain treatises which Mr. Colebrooke possesses; part under the name of Bhascara, one mathematician; part under that of Brahmegupta, another. He begins with Bhascara.

There are two treatises of astronomy, which bear the

[1] Dr. Hutton says, that Diophantus "knew the composition of the cube of a binomial...... In some parts of book vi. it appears that he was acquainted with the composition of the fourth power of the binomial root, as he sets down all the terms of it; and from his great skill in such matters, it seems probable that he was acquainted with the composition of other higher powers, and *with other parts of Algebra, besides what are here treated of*.... Upon the whole, this work is treated in a very able and masterly manner, manifesting the utmost address and knowledge in the solutions, and forcing a persuasion that the author was deeply skilled in the science of Algebra, to some of the most abstruse parts of which these questions or exercises relate. However, as he contrives his assumptions and notations, so as to reduce all his conditions to a simple equation, or at least a simple quadratic, it does not appear *what* his knowledge was, in the resolution of compound or affected quadratics." Mathematical Dictionary Art. Diophantus.

name of Bhascara, and which themselves affirm, that they were written at a particular time, corresponding to the middle of the twelfth century of the Christian era: Therefore the Treatise on Algebra, possessed by Mr. Colebrooke, was produced about the middle of the twelfth century. For this degree of antiquity, this is the whole of the evidence. Let us see what it is worth.

In the first place, the dates refer only to the astronomical treatises; not to the algebraic. The algebraic is indeed prefixed to the astronomic; but it is alleged by one of the commentators, and believed by Mr. Colebrooke, that it "may have been added subsequently." And then at what date subsequently, or by what hand, are questions to which we shall presently see that there is no answer.

In the next place, an important observation applies to the affirmations, with respect to their own age, found in the treatises on astronomy. From the known, the extravagant disposition of the Hindus to falsify with regard to dates, and make almost everything, with respect to their own transactions and attainments, more ancient than it is, such asseverations, found in books, or transcripts of books, are no proof of what is affirmed; and only deserve a moment's regard when fully corroborated by other circumstances. Not one circumstance is adduced to corroborate them by Mr. Colebrooke.

We come down, all at once, from the date of the work, to the date of the commentaries upon it. For none of them does Mr. Colebrooke claim a degree of antiquity beyond 200 or 300 years. Supposing this date to be correct, what reason has Mr. Colebrooke to infer that the work on which they comment, was, at the time of that commentary, 400 years? None, whatsoever. In nine instances out of ten, the commentator would be sure to speak of it as old, whether it was so or not. But further, what reason have we to believe that the date which he ascribes to these commentaries is the real one? Again the answer is, None; none that will bear examination. The date of the oldest is assumed upon the strength of an astronomical example, describing a particular state of the heavens: but this may be perfectly accidental; and, besides, the Hindus have the power of calculating backwards. Of the next two, the date is assumed upon the strength of their own assertion: this we have shown is of no value. Of the next two the date is assumed upon the assertion of other books. This, if possible, is of less value. There are three others to which no date is assigned: and there are two commentaries upon the astronomical treatises, the date of which, too, rests upon their own assertion.

Neither to the treatise, therefore, in the hands of Mr. Colebrooke, nor to the commentaries upon it, has anything appeared, in what we have yet mentioned, which enables us to assign, with any degree of certainty, any one date in preference to any other. We may, if we please, assume that all of them in a body are less than a century old.

Beside the Sanscrit commentaries, there is a Persian translation, of each of the two treatises of Bhascara. In general, what is testified by Persian, is far more trustworthy than what rests upon Sanscrit authority; because there was more publicity in the Persian writings; whereas the Sanscrit, being wholly secret, and confined to a small number of Brahmens, accustomed and prone to forgery, there is security for nothing which they had any interest, real or imaginary, to change. If there was any evidence, therefore, to fix the dates of the Persian translations, we could not reasonably dispute a degree of antiquity corresponding to them. I suspect that there is no evidence to fix the dates of these translations. Mr. Colebrooke says, the one was made by order of the emperor Acber, the other in the reign of Shah Jehan. But he subjoins no reason for this affirmation. The cause probably is, that he had none; and that he took the conjecture from some date written somewhere in the book, nobody knows at what time, nobody knows by whom.

Such is the whole of the evidence which is adduced by Mr. Colebrooke to prove the antiquity of Bhascara. "The age of his predecessors," he adds, "cannot be determined with equal precision:" that is to say, the evidence which can be adduced for the antiquity of the other treatise, that of Brahmegupta, is still less conclusive, and less satisfactory. As we have seen that the better evidence proves nothing, I shall spare the reader a criticism to show, what he will easily infer, that the worse evidence

BOOK II. CHAP. IX.

proves as little: evidence, which, as it is tedious and intricate, it would require a criticism of some length to unfold.

3. We come to the third of the propositions; that if the Hindus had discovered as much of algebra, as they know beyond what appears in the fragment of Diophantus, they must have been placed in a high state of civilization. That this proposition cannot be maintained, I expect to find universally acknowledged. I transcribe the passage from Mr. Colebrooke, in which he sums up the claims and pretensions of the Hindus. "They possessed well the arithmetic of surd roots; they were aware of the infinite quotient resulting from the division of finite quantity by cipher; they knew the general resolution of equations of the second degree, and had touched upon those of higher denomination, resolving them in the simplest cases, and in those in which the resolution happens to be practicable by the method which serves for quadratics; they had attained a *general solution* of indeterminate problems of the first degree; they had arrived at a method for deriving a multitude of solutions of answers to problems of the second degree from a single answer found tentatively."[1]

In all this it appears, that the only point in which there can be a pretence for their having gone beyond what we have in the fragment of Diophantus, is the *general* solution of indeterminate problems of the first degree. But, to quote Dr. Hutton once more, "Diophantus was the first writer on indeterminate problems. His book is wholly on this subject; whence it has happened that such kind of questions have been called by the name of Diophantine problems." Now, take the point at which the solution of indeterminate problems appears in the fragment of Diophantus, and the point at which it appears in the Sanscrit treatise, of whatever age, in the hands of Mr. Colebrooke; the interval between the two points is so very small, and the step is so easily made, that most assuredly far more difficult steps in the progress of mathematical science have been made in ages of which the civilization has been as low as that of the Hindus. Thales lived at a period when Greece was still uncultivated, and but just emerging from barbarism; yet he excelled the Egyptians in mathe-

[1] "Algebra;" &c. ut supra, Dissert. p. xiv.

matical knowledge, and astonished them by computing the height of the pyramids from the shadow. Pythagoras lived in the same age; and was a great inventor both in arithmetic and geometry. In astronomy, he made great discoveries, and maintained, we are told, the true system of the universe; that the sun is in the centre, and makes all the planets revolve about him. Regiomontanus was born in 1456, when the human mind was still, to a great degree, immersed in the darkness of the middle ages. Yet of him, Mr. Playfair says, "Trigonometry, which had never been known to the Greeks as a separate science, and which took that form in Arabia, advanced, in the hands of Regiomontanus, to a great degree of perfection; and approached very near to the condition which it has attained at the present day. He also introduced the use of decimal fractions into arithmetic, and thereby gave to that scale its full extent, and to numerical computation the utmost degree of simplicity and enlargement, which it seems capable of attaining."[1] Cardan was born in 1501, when assuredly much had not yet been gained of what deserves the name of civilization. "Before his time," says the same accomplished mathematician, "little advance had been made in the solution of any equations higher than the second degree. In 1545 was published the rule which still bears the name of Cardan; and which, at this day, marks a point in the progress of algebraic investigation, which all the efforts of succeeding analyists have hardly been able to go beyond."[2] Even Vieta, with all his discoveries, appeared at an early and ill-instructed age.

In looking at the pursuits of any nation, with a view to draw from them indications of the state of civilization, no mark is so important, as the nature of the *End* to which they are directed.

Exactly in proportion as *Utility* is the object of every pursuit, may we regard a nation as civilized. Exactly in proportion as its ingenuity is wasted on contemptible and mischievous objects, though it may be, in itself, an ingenuity of no ordinary kind, the nation may safely be denominated barbarous.

[1] Suppl. Encycl. Brit. Dissert. Second, p. 4.

[2] Ibid. p. 14.

BOOK II. CHAP. IX.

According to this rule, the astronomical and mathematical sciences afford conclusive evidence against the Hindus. They have been cultivated exclusively for the purposes of astrology; one of the most irrational of all imaginable pursuits; one of those which most infallibly denote a nation barbarous; and one of those which it is the most sure to renounce, in proportion as knowledge and civilization are attained.[1]

[1] The authority of Professor Wallace is recognised by Mr. Mill, and his conclusions from Mr. Colebrooke's publication are of a very different complexion from those of the text. The Surya Siddhanta, he states, contains a very rational system of trigonometry. In expressing the radius of a circle in parts of the circumference, the Hindus are quite singular. Ptolemy and the Greek mathematicians, in their division of the radius, preserved no reference to the circumference. The use of sines, as it was unknown to the Greeks, forms a difference between theirs and the Indian trigonometry. Their rule for the computation of the lines is a considerable refinement in science first practised by the mathematician Briggs. However ancient a book may be in which a system of trigonometry occurs, we may be assured it was not written in the infancy of the science. Geometry must have been known in India long before the writing of the Surya Siddhanta. The age of Brahmagupta is fixed with great probability to the sixth or beginning of the seventh century of our era, a period earlier than the first dawn of Arabian sciences. Aryabhatta appears to have written as far back as the fifth century, or earlier; he was therefore almost as old as the Greek algebraist Diophantus. The Lilavati treats of Arithmetic, and contains not only the common rules of that science, but the application of these to various questions on interest, barter, mixtures, combinations, permutations, sums of progression, indeterminate problems, and mensuration of surfaces and solids. The rules are found to be exact, and nearly as simple as in the present state of analytical investigation. The numerical results are readily deduced; and if they be compared with the earliest specimens of Greek calculation, the advantages of the decimal notation are placed in a striking light. In geometry, though inferior in excellence to the algebra, there is much deserving of attention. We have here the celebrated proposition that the square on the hypothenuse of a right-angled triangle is equal to the squares on the sides containing the right angle, and other propositions, which form part of the system of modern geometry. There is one proposition remarkable, namely, that which discovers the area of a triangle when its three sides are known. This does not seem to have been known to the ancient Greek geometers. In algebra the Hindus understood well the arithmetic of such roots, and the general resolution of equations of the second degree, which it is not clear that Diophantus knew—that they attained a general solution of indeterminate problems of the first degree—which it is certain Diophantus had not attained—and a method of deriving a multitude of answers to problems of the second degree when one solution was discovered by trial, which is as near an approach to a general solution as was made until the time of La Grange. Professor Wallace concludes by adopting the opinion of Playfair on this subject, "that before an author could think of embodying a treatise of algebra in the heart of a system of astronomy, and turning the researches of the one science to the purposes of the other, both must have been in such a state of advancement as the lapse of several ages and many repeated efforts of inventors were required to produce." This is unanswerable evidence in favour of the antiquity, originality, and advance of Hindu mathematical science, and is fatal to all Mr. Mill's references and conjectures. We have also historical evidence, that the Arabs derived their mathematical sciences in part from the Hindus; and we have every reason, from the differences of method, and in some instances superiority of progress, as well as from the absence of all evidence to the contrary, to conclude that the Hindus were as little indebted to the Greeks. A people who had pursued for ages researches of this nature, could not have been merely upon the threshold of civilization. The test of civilization proposed by Mr. Mill and the school to

CHAP. X.

General Reflections.

TO ascertain the true state of the Hindus in the scale of civilization, is not only an object of curiosity in the history of human nature; but to the people of Great Britain, charged as they are with the government of that great portion of the human species, it is an object of the highest practical importance.[1] No scheme of government can happily conduce to the ends of government, unless it is adapted to the state of the people for whose use it is intended. In those diversities in the state of civilization, which approach the extremes, this truth is universally acknowledged. Should anyone propose, for a band of roving Tartars, the regulations adapted to the happiness of a regular and polished society, he would meet with neglect or derision. The inconveniences are only more concealed, and more or less diminished, when the error relates to states of society which more nearly resemble one another. If the mistake in regard to Hindu society, committed by the British nation, and the British government, be very great; if they have conceived the Hindus to be a people of high civilization, while they have, in reality, made but a few of the earliest steps in the progress to civilization, it is impossible that in many of the measures pursued for the government of that people, the mark aimed at should not have been wrong.

The preceding induction of particulars, embracing the religion, the laws, the government, the manners, the arts,

---

which he belonged, "utility," will not be generally admitted in the restricted sense in which he employs the term; but even that is inapplicable, for in the estimation of those nations amongst whom astrology was credited, what could in their eyes be more useful, than rules of conduct derived from astrological calculation. It is not true, however, that the mathematical sciences of the Hindus were applied to astrology alone, as the greater number of the results which their arithmetic, algebra, and geometry, and even their astronomy afford, have no relation to that kind of knowledge, but are indispensable to the ordinary purposes of social life.—W.

[1] The measures of the British Government have very little concern with what the Hindus were in the days of Manu; what they are now is within their observation, and all that is required is to see them as they are without any bias from erroneous theories. Above all things, it is necessary for every purpose of wise and benevolent rule to see them with a bias rather in their favour than to their disadvantage. We shall not promote their advance in civilization by treating them as little better than barbarians.—W.

BOOK II. CHAP. X.

the sciences, and literature, of the Hindus, affords, it is presumed, the materials from which a correct judgment may, at last, be formed of their progress towards the high attainments of civilized life. That induction, and the comparisons to which it led, have occupied us long, but not longer, it is hoped, than the importance of the subject demanded, and the obstinacy of the mistakes which it was the object of it to remove.

The reports of a high state of civilization in the East, were common even among the civilized nations of ancient Europe. But the acquaintance of the Greeks and Romans with any of the nations of Asia, except the Persians alone, was so imperfect, and among the circumstances which they state so many are incredible and ridiculous, that in the information we receive from them on this subject, no confidence can be reposed.

Of the modern Europeans, the individuals who first obtained a tolorable acquaintance with any of the nations of the East, were the popish missionaries, chiefly the Jesuits, who selected China for the scene of their apostolical labours. Visiting a people who already composed a vast society, and exhibited many, though fallacious, marks of riches, while Europe, as yet, was everywhere poor; and feeling, as it was natural for them to feel, that the more they could excite among their countrymen an admiration of the people whom they described, the greater would be the portion of that flattering sentiment which would redound upon themselves, these missionaries were eager to conceive, and still more eager to propagate, the most hyperbolical ideas of the arts, the sciences, and institutions of the Chinese. As it is almost always more pleasing, and certainly far more easy, to believe, than to scrutinize; and as the human mind in Europe, at the time when these accounts were first presented, was much less powerful and penetrating, than it is at present, they were received with almost implicit credulity. The influence of this first impression lasted so long, that even to Voltaire, a keen-eyed and sceptical judge, the Chinese, of almost all nations, are the objects of the loudest and most unqualified praise.[1]

[1] "Any thing proposed to us which causes surprise and admiration, gives such a satisfaction to the mind, that it indulges itself in those agreeable emotions, and will never be persuaded that its pleasure is entirely without foundation." (Hume, Treatise of Human Nature, i. 53.)

The state of belief in Europe has, through the scrutiny of facts been of late approximating to sobriety on the attainments of the Chinese, and a short period longer will probably reduce it to the scale of reason and fact.[1]

It was under circumstances highly similar, that the earliest of the modern travellers drew up and presented their accounts of Hindustan. The empire of the Moguls was in its meridian splendour. It extended over the principal part of India; and the court, the army, and the establishments of Akber or Aurungzebe, exhibited that gorgeous exterior, that air of grandeur and power, which were well calculated to impose upon the imagination of an unphilosophical observer.[2]

It was unfortunate that a mind so pure, so warm in the pursuit of truth, and so devoted to oriental learning, as that of Sir William Jones, should have adopted the hypothesis of a high state of civilization in the principal countries of Asia. This he supported with all the advantages of an imposing manner, and a brilliant reputation; and gained for it so great a credit, that for a time it would have been very difficult to obtain a hearing against it.

Beside the illusions with which the fancy magnifies the importance of a favourite pursuit, Sir William was actuated by the virtuous design of exalting the Hindus in the eyes of their European masters; and thence ameliorating the temper of the government; while his mind had scope for error in the vague and indeterminate notions which it still retained of the signs of social improvement. The term civilization was by him, as by most men, attached to no

[1] To this good effect, if to no other, the embassy of Lord Macartney, and the writings to which it has given occasion, have largely contributed. See Barrow's two works, Travels in China, and Life of Lord Macartney; and, above all, that important document, a volume of the Laws of China, translated by Sir George Staunton. No one has more approximated to a correct judgment of the Chinese, than De Guignes. See Voyage.

[2] Many of the observations of Mr. Barrow upon the panegyrical accounts of the Chinese by the popish missionaries are very applicable to the flattering accounts which travellers have been so fond of giving us of the Hindus. "In the same breath that they extol the wonderful strength of filial piety, they speak of the common practice of exposing infants; the strict morality and ceremonious conduct of the people are followed by a list of the most gross debaucheries; the virtues and the philosophy of the learned are explained by their ignorance and their vices: if in one page they speak of the excessive fertility of the country, and the amazing extension of agriculture, in the next thousands are seen perishing with want; and whilst they extol with admiration the progress they have made in the arts and sciences, they plainly inform us that without the aid of foreigners they can neither cast a cannon nor calculate an eclipse." Barrow's Travels in China, p. 31.

BOOK II. CHAP. X.

fixed and definite assemblage of ideas. With the exception of some of the lowest states of society in which human beings have been found, it was applied to nations in all the stages of social advancement.[1]

It is not easy to describe the characteristics of the different stages of social progress. It is not from one feature, or from two, that a just conclusion can be drawn. In these it sometimes happens that nations resemble each other which are placed at stages considerably remote. It is from a joint view of all the great circumstances taken together, that their progress can be ascertained; and it is from an accurate comparison, grounded on these general views, that a scale of civilization can be formed, on which the relative positions of nations may be accurately marked.

Notwithstanding all that modern philosophy had performed for the elucidation of history, very little had been attempted in this great department, at the time when the notions of Sir William Jones were formed;[2] and so crude were his ideas on the subject, that the rhapsodies of Rousseau, on the virtue and happiness of the savage life, surpass not the panegyrics of Sir William on the wild, comfortless, predatory, and ferocious state of the wandering

[1] One of the chief circumstances from which Sir William Jones drew conclusions respecting the high civilization of the Hindus, was the supposition that they never went abroad, a supposition which is now well known to have been erroneous. See Asiat. Res. vi. 531, and i. 271.

[2] The writings of Mr. Miller, of Glasgow, of which but a small part was then published, and into which it is probable Sir William had never looked, contained the earliest elucidations of the subject. The suggestions offered in his successive productions, though highly important, were but detached considerations applied to particular facts, and not a comprehensive induction, leading to general conclusions. Unfortunately the subject, great as is its importance, has not been resumed. The writings of Mr. Miller remain almost the only source from which even the slightest information on the subject can be drawn. One of the ends which has at least been in view during the scrutiny conducted in these pages, has been to contribute something to the progress of so important an investigation. It is hoped that the materials which are here collected will be regarded as going far to elucidate the state of society in all the leading nations of Asia. Not only the Hindus, the Persians, the Arabians, the Turks, and Chinese of the present day, but the Hindus, Arabians, and Persians of ancient days, the Chaldeans, the Jews, and even the ancient Egyptians, may all be regarded as involved in the inquiry; and to these, with the sole exception of the wandering Tartars and the Hyperborean hordes, may be added the second-rate nations; the inhabitants of the eastern peninsula, and of the plains and mountains of Tibet. It is surprising, upon a close inspection, how extensively all these various nations, notwithstanding the dissimilarity in some of the more obvious appearances, resemble one another, in laws and institutions of government, in modes of thinking, in superstition and prejudices, in arts and literature, even in the external forms of manner and behaviour, and as well in ancient, as in modern times.

Arabs. "Except," says he, "when their tribes are engaged in war, they spend their days in watching their flocks and camels, or in repeating their native songs, which they pour out almost extempore, professing a contempt for the stately pillars and solemn buildings of the cities, compared with the natural charms of the country, and the coolness of their tents; thus they pass their lives in the highest pleasure, of which they have any conception, in the contemplation of the most delightful objects, and in the enjoyment of perpetual spring."[1] "If courtesy," he observes, "and urbanity, a love of poetry and eloquence, and the practice of exalted virtues, be a just measure of perfect society, we have certain proof that the people of Arabia, both on plains and in cities, in republican and monarchical states, were eminently civilized for many ages before their conquest of Persia."[2] We need not wonder if the man, who wrote and delivered this, found the Hindus arrived at the highest civilization. Yet the very same author, in the very same discourse, and speaking of the same people, declared, "I find no trace among them, till their emigration, of any philosophy but ethics;"[3] and even of this he says, "The distinguishing virtues which they boasted of inculcating, were a contempt of riches, and even of death; but in the age of the seven poets, their liberality had deviated into mad profusion, their courage into ferocity, and their patience into an obstinate spirit of encountering fruitless dangers."[4] He adds, "The only *arts* in which they pretended to excellence (I except horsemanship and military accomplishments) were poetry and rhetoric."[5] It can hardly be affirmed that these facts are less wonderful as regarding a people "eminently civilized;" a people exhibiting "a just measure of perfect society."[6]

1 Essay on the Poetry of Eastern Nations. Voltaire exclaimed, on reading Rousseau's panegyrics, "Jamais n'avais-je tant d'envie de marcher à quatre pattes."

2 Sir W. Jones, Asiat. Res. ii. 3. 3 Ibid. p. 9. 4 Ibid.

5 Sir W. Jones, Asiat. Res. ii. p. 14.—"On this occasion, as well as on many others, the sober historian is forcibly wakened from a pleasing vision; and is compelled, with some reluctance, to confess that the pastoral manners, which have been adorned with the fairest attributes of peace and innocence, are much better adapted to the fierce and cruel habits of a military life." Gibbon, Decline and Fall, ch. xxvi. p. 342.

6 In the same discourse Sir William further remarks: "That we have none of their compositions in prose before the Koran, may be ascribed, perhaps, to the little skill which they seem to have had in writing, to their predilection in favour of poetical measure, and the facility with which verses are committed

BOOK II. CHAP. X.

Among the causes which excited to the tone of eulogy adopted with regard to the Hindus, one undoubtedly was, the affectation of candour. Of rude and uncultivated nations, and also of rude and uncultivated individuals, it is a characteristic, to admire only the system of manners, of ideas, and of institutions to which they have been accus-

---

to memory; but all their stories prove that they were eloquent in a high degree, and possessed wonderful powers of speaking, without preparation, in flowing and forcible periods." Asiat. Res. ii. p. 14. "Who," says Dr. Ferguson, "would from mere conjecture suppose, that the naked savage would be a coxcomb and a gamester; that he would be proud and vain, without the distinctions of title and fortune; and that his principal care would be to adorn his person, and to find an amusement? Even if it could be supposed that he would thus share in our vices, and, in the midst of his forest, vie with the follies which are practised in the town; yet no one would be so bold as to affirm that he would likewise in any instance excel us in talents and virtue; that he would have a penetration, a force of imagination and elocution, an ardour of mind, an affection and courage, which the arts, the discipline, and the policy of few nations would be able to improve. Yet these particulars are a part in the description which is delivered by those who have had opportunities of seeing mankind in their rudest condition: and beyond the reach of such testimony, we can neither safely take, nor pretend to give information on the subject." Ferguson's Essay on the History of Civil Society, part ii. sect. 1.

The extreme inaccuracy and fluctuation of the ideas of European scholars, with respect to civilization, are curiously exemplified in their opinions of the Asiatic nations. Gibbon says, "The cavalry of Scythia was forced to yield to the admirable swiftness and spirit of the Arabian horses; their riders were skilled in the evolutions of irregular war; and the northern barbarians were astonished and dismayed by the inhuman ferocity of the barbarians of the south. A Gothic soldier was slain by the dagger of an Arab; and the hairy, naked savage, applying his lips to the wound, expressed a horrid delight, while he sucked the blood of his vanquished enemy." Gibbon, Hist. of the Decl. and Fall, etc , iv. 413. Of the various nations subject to the Persian sceptre, many of them still higher in civilization than the most civilized portion of the Arabians, the same author thus expresses himself: "It was here," says he, "in a place where the opposite banks cannot exceed 500 paces, that Xerxes imposed a stupendous bridge of boats, for the purpose of transporting into Europe 170 myriads of *barbarians.*" Ibid. iii. 9. Of the Syrians and Egyptians, who still more nearly than the Arabians resembled the Hindus, and were acquainted with more of the arts which attain their perfection in civilized life, he says, "The use of their ancient dialects, by secluding them from the commerce of mankind, checked the improvements of these *barbarians.*" Ibid. i. 62. (N.B. The same cause operated among the Hindus, and still more powerfully to the production of the same effects.) Mr. Halhed says, that the Jews, at the time of the Mosaic institutions, "were very little removed from a state of barbarism, gross in their conceptions, illiterate in their education, and uncultivated in their manners." Preface to Code of Gentoo Laws, p. xvii. And yet these institutions are not only superior to the institutions of the Hindus; they are in a high degree superior to the institutions of any other nation in Asia. But with the circumstances of Jewish society we become, through the medium of our religion, early and familiarly acquainted. No European is *early*, hardly any is ever *familiarly* acquainted with the other nations of Asia. No blind propensity, therefore, excites to admiration in the one case: several do so in the other. Among the authors who have followed Sir William Jones in his track of eulogy and admiration, it may be suspected, from the limited information of some, that they were unacquainted with the facts of uncivilized life, and wherever man exhibited the attributes of humanity believed he must there be civilized; ignorant of the intense exercise which is given to several of the human faculties even among savages, and of the strength which those faculties must hence acquire.

tomed, despising others. The most cultivated nations of Europe had but recently discovered the weakness of this propensity. Novelty rendered exemption from it a source of distinction. To prove his superiority to the prejudices of home, by admiring and applauding the manners and institutions of Asia, became, therefore, in the breast of the traveller, a motive of no inconsiderable power.[1]

The nations of Europe became acquainted nearly about the same period, with the people of America, and the people of Hindustan. Having contemplated in the one, a people without fixed habitations, without political institutions, and with hardly any other arts than those indispensably necessary for the preservation of existence, they hastily concluded, upon the sight of another people, inhabiting great cities, cultivating the soil, connected together by an artificial system of subordination, exhibiting monuments of great antiquity, cultivating a species of literature, exercising arts, and obeying a monarch whose sway was extensive, and his court magnificent, that they had suddenly past from the one extreme of civilization to the other. The Hindus were compared with the savages of America; the circumstances in which they differed from that barbarous people, were the circumstances in which they corresponded with the most cultivated nations; other circumstances were overlooked; and it seems to have been little suspected that conclusions too favourable could possibly be drawn.[2]

[1] None of them has confessed the existence of this motive with more frankness than Le Gentil, Voy. ii. 98. "Avant que j'eusse perdu mon clocher de vue, les François étoient mes héros........ Quant à moi je suis guéri de mes préjugés, et *je m'applaudis en secret de m'être détrompé.*" Col. Dow boasts of being actuated by the same sentiments and scruples not to call Goths, or worse than Goths, all those who are not so: "In love with our own times and country," says he, "we are apt to consider distant ages and nations as objects unworthy of the page of the historian........Some men of genius have entertained sentiments upon that subject too narrow and confined for the Goths of a much darker age. Had the translator of the following history thought so meanly of the affairs of the East," etc. Dow's Hindostan, Preface.

[2] The account which Robertson gives of the causes which led to exaggerated conceptions in the mind of the Spaniards, respecting the civilization of the Mexicans, applies in almost every particular to those of the English and French respecting the Hindus. "The Spaniards," says he, "when they first touched on the Mexican coast, were so much struck with the appearance of attainments in policy and in the arts of life, far superior to those of the rude tribes with which they were hitherto acquainted, that they fancied that they had at length discovered a civilized people in the New World. This comparison between the people of Mexico and their uncultivated neighbours, they appear to have kept constantly in view, and observing with admiration many things which marked the pre-eminence of the former, they employed, in de-

BOOK II. CHAP. X.

The progress of knowledge, and the force of observation, demonstrated the necessity of regarding the actual state of the Hindus as little removed from that of half-civilized nations. The saving hypothesis, however, was immediately adopted, that the situation in which the Hindus are now beheld is a state of degradation; that formerly they were in a state of high civilization; from which they had fallen through the miseries of foreign conquest and subjugation.

This was a theory invented to preserve as much as actual observation would allow to be preserved, of a pre-established and favourite creed. It was not an inference from what was already known. It was a gratuitous assumption. It preceded inquiry, and no inquiry was welcome, but that which yielded matter for its support.[1]

To this purpose were adapted the pretensions of the Brahmens, who spoke of an antecedent period, when the sovereigns of Hindustan were masters of great power and great magnificence. It was of importance to weigh these pretensions; because the rude writers of rude nations have almost always spoken of antecedent times as deserving all the praise with which their powers of rhetoric or song could exalt them. If the descriptions of antiquity presented by the Brahmens bore the consistent marks of truth and reality, a degree of intrinsic evidence would be attached to them. If these descriptions flew wide of all resemblance to human affairs, and were nothing but wild unnatural fictions, they would be so far from proving an antecedent state of knowledge and civilization, that they would prove the reverse. And, had the Hindus remained fixed from the earliest stages in the semibarbarous state, it is most certain that the Brahmens would

---

scribing their imperfect policy and infant arts, such terms as are applicable to the institutions of men far beyond them in improvement. Both these circumstances concur in detracting from the credit due to the descriptions of Mexican manners by the Spanish writers. By drawing a parallel between them and those of people so much less civilized, they raised their own ideas too high. By their mode of describing them, they conveyed ideas to others no less exalted above truth. Later writers have adopted the style of the original historians, and improved upon it." Hist. of America, iii. 320.

[1] "Le voyageur racontant ses aventures, cherche dans l'admiration de ceux qui l'écoutent, un dédommagement aux dangers qu'il a courus; il enfle la narration: Le sçavant, qui s'est donné beaucoup de peine pour apprendre des langues étrangères et lointaines, s'extasie sur la beauté des ouvrages qu'il est parvenu à entendre." Anquetil Duperron, Note, No. ii. Supplément aux Recherches, &c. sur l'Inde.

have given to us just such accounts of antiquity as those we have actually received at their hands.

As the Hindus have enlightened us by no record of antecedent events, and we thus have no immediate proof of their state of civilization, in the times that are past, the only sure ground of inference is the laws and institutions which they framed, the manners they adopted, and the arts and sciences to which they attended. If these great circumstances were at variance with the existing state of society, but adapted to one more advanced, the inference would certainly be a probable one, that to a period when society was in that improved condition, they really owed their birth. But in regard to the Hindus, their laws and institutions are adapted to the very state of society which those who visit them now behold. They are laws and institutions which, so far from importing any more perfect state of society, seem entirely inconsistent with it; such as could neither begin, nor exist, under any other than one of the rudest and weakest states of the human mind. As the manners, the arts and sciences of the ancient Hindus are entirely correspondent with the state of their laws and institutions, everything we *know* of the ancient state of Hindustan conspires to prove that it was rude.

It is another important fact, that, if the Hindus had ever been placed in this pretended state of civilization, we know of no such period of calamity, as was sufficient to reduce them to a state of ignorance and barbarity. The conquest of Hindustan, effected by the Mahomedan nations, was to no extraordinary degree sanguinary or destructive. It substituted sovereigns of one race to sovereigns of another, and mixed with the old inhabitants a small proportion of new; but it altered not the texture of society; it altered not the language of the country; the original inhabitants remained the occupants of the soil; they continued to be governed by their own laws and institutions; nay, the whole detail of administration, with the exception of the army, and a few of the more prominent situations, remained invariably in the hands of the native magistrates and officers.[1] The few occasions of the persecutions, to

[1] "The administration of justice has been almost universally, by the Mogul conquerors of Indostan, devolved upon the Mindus, the office of Duan being generally conferred upon one of that people. Orme on the Government and People of Indostan," p. 443. Although the Mogul Tartars under Tamerlane

which, under the reigns of one or two bigoted sovereigns, they were subjected on the score of religion, were too short and too partial to produce any considerable effects.[1]

When we look for the particulars of those pretended reigns of mighty kings, the universal lords of India, under whom science flourished, and civilization rose to the greatest height, we meet with nothing but fable, more wild, and inconsistent, and hyperbolical, than is any where else to be found. From this no rational conclusion can be drawn, except that it is the production of a rude and irrational age. Bharat or Bharata, is said to have been the first universal sovereign of India, which from him

---

and his successors have at last rendered themselves lords of almost the whole of it (India); yet the original inhabitants have lost very little of their original character by the establishment of these strangers amongst them." Orme, Hist. of Milit. Transact. in Indostan. i. 2.—M. Mr. Mill may be excused for making such a mistake as to assert that under the Mohammedan Government, the offices of "magistrates," were filled by Hindus; he follows the authority of Orme, but Orme, though an excellent guide in all that relates to the European transactions which he beheld, must have been exceedingly ignorant of the character, and apparently of the languages of the people. His remark that the administration of justice devolved upon the Hindus is most certainly erroneous, as no unbeliever could, consistently with the principles of the Mohammedan faith, have been intrusted with such duty, and the illustration he gives, that the office of Duan was generally conferred upon Hindus, is an amusing proof how little he understood what he was saying. The office of Duan or Dewan being entirely of a financial nature, and wholly unconnected with the administration of justice.—W.

[1] It seems to have been a rash and foolish assimilation of the conquest of Hindustan by the Moguls to the overwhelming of the Roman empire by the northern nations, that alone could have suggested so gratuitous a supposition as that of the degradation of the Hindus from an improved to a barbarous state of society by the calamities of conquest. The two cases are totally dissimilar. By the successive inundations of the barbarians, the ancient inhabitants of the Roman provinces were well-nigh swept from the face of the earth. Every where they were stript of the possession of the land, and commonly reduced to the state of bondsmen and slaves. The ancient institutions entirely gave way, and were replaced by a set of institutions altogether new. The language of the conquerors in most places entirely supplanted, in all it so much altered the language of the people subdued or exterminated, as to impose upon it a different structure. Another circumstance is never to be forgotten. To such a degree of barbarity were the inhabitants of the Roman provinces degraded, by the long-continued effects of a detestable government, that the invaders had really not so much to accomplish to reduce them to the same level with themselves. This was abundantly seen in the state of the Greeks of the eastern empire; who, upon their very first subjugation to the Turks, exhibited a condition not greatly different from that in which they grovel at the present day. The conquest to which, with greatest propriety, that of the Hindus by one tribe of Tartars might be compared would be the conquest of the Chinese by a similar tribe of Tartars. There is no reason to think that the one was a conquest of a more destructive nature than the other. If the Moguls did not adopt the religion and institutions of the Hindus, it was because the religion and institutions of the Hindus admitted of no participation, and because the Moguls had already embraced a more enlightened faith. See Francis's Minute, p. 30: also the treatise of Mr. Grant, on the Character of the Hindus, printed by order of the House of Commons in 1813.

derived its name; India being, in the language of the natives, Bharata Versh. In this, however, as usual, the Hindu accounts contradict themselves, since Bharat is represented as preceding Rama, the son of Cush, who, according to Sir William Jones, might have established the *first* regular government in India.[1] Judhishter is another of these universal sovereigns; but of him even the origin is allegorical; he is the son of Dherma, or the god of justice, and he reigned 27,000 years. The name, with which, chiefly, the idea of the universal sovereignship of India, and the glory of art and science, is combined, is that of Vicramaditya. Of him, let us hear what is represented; and then we shall be enabled to judge. "The two periods," says Captain Wilford, "of Vicramaditya and Salivahana are intimately connected; and the accounts we have of these two extraordinary personages are much confused, teeming with contradictions and absurdities to a surprising degree. In general the Hindus know but of one Vicramaditya; but the learned acknowledge four; and when, at my request, they produced written authorities, I was greatly surprised to find no less than eight or nine. Vicramaditya made a desperate *tapasya*, in order to obtain power and a long life from Calidevi, and as she seemingly continued deaf to his entreaties, he was going to cut off his own head, when she appeared, and granted him undisturbed sway over all the world for one thousand years, after which a divine child, born of a virgin, and the son of the great Tacshaca, carpenter or artist, would deprive him both of his kingdom and of his life. This would happen in the year of the Cali-yug, 3101, answering to the first of the Christian era. The history of these nine worthies, but more particularly when considered as a single individual, is a most crude and undigested mass of heterogeneous legends, taken from the apocryphal gospel of the infancy of Christ, the tales of the Rabbis and Talmudists concerning Solomon, with some particulars about Muhammed; and the whole is jumbled together with some of the principal features of the history of the Persian kings, of the Sassanian dynasty. Thus Vicrama is made contemporary with Solomon: and like him, he is said to have found the great *mantra*, spell or talisman; through

[1] Asiat. Res. i. 258.

BOOK II.
CHAP. X.

which he ruled over the elements, and spirits, of all denominations, who obeyed him like slaves. Like Solomon he had a most wonderful throne, supported and adorned with lions, who are endued with reason and speech. We read in the Vetala-pancha-vinsati,[1] that it was through the assistance of the great Vetala, or devil, that two Vicrama'-dityas obtained the empire of the world, a long life, with unlimited sway. They performed the puja in his honour, offered sacrifices, and in short dedicated or gave themselves up to him."[2] On this foundation of historical matter is built the magnificent fabric of a great and universal monarchy, the reign of the arts and sciences, all that embellishes human life, and augments the human powers. Such being the premises, and such the conclusion, are they not admirably adapted to one another? The legend speaks, and that loudly, and distinctly, what it is; the creation of a rude and uncultivated fancy, exerting itself to rouse the wonder of a rude and uncultivated age, by a recital of actions, powers, and events, swelled beyond the measure of human nature; profiting by all the hints which the legends or history of other nations supplied to furnish out its story, and by appropriating the wonderful deeds of all the world to gratify the barbarous vanity of the people to whom the story was addressed. If the historian gave to his hero a reign of a thousand years; it was quite in the same temper, and conducive to the same end, to give him the sovereignty of all India; and not only of all India, but, as we see was the fact, the sovereignty of the whole world. This is precisely the course which a wild and ignorant mind, regarding only the wonder which it has it in view to excite, naturally, in such cases, and almost universally, pursues. Such legends, if they existed in myriads, are no more a proof of a monarchy common to all India, which they do not assert, than of the universal monarchy of the whole world, or of the thousands or the myriads of years to one reign, which they expressly assert.[3]

[1] Here again the Historian is misled by his authority.—No Hindu ever proposed the twenty-five stories of a demon, as history; all the confusion, too, that arises out of multiplied Vikramadityas, is Wilford's work:—not that of the Hindu traditions, which are simple and consistent.—W.

[2] Essay on Vicramaditya and Salivahana, by Capt. Wilford, Asiat. Res. ix. 117 to 120.

[3] If we examine the chronological table of the Hindu kings, presented us by

The very lists which are found in the books of the Hindus, filled up with the names of successive monarchs, Mr. Wilford assures us, are the creation of the fancies of the writers, and are formed without any reference to facts. In enumerating the authorities from which he drew his materials, in the essay on Vicramaditya and Salivahana, he says, "The fourth list has been translated into all the dialects of India, and new-modelled at least twenty different ways, according to the whims and pre-conceived ideas of every individual who chose to meddle with it. It is, however, the basis and ground-work of modern history among the Hindus; as in the *Khalâset-ul-Tuwarikh* and the *Tudkerat-us-sulatin.* The latter treatise is a most perfect specimen of the manner of writing history in India; for, excepting the above list, almost everything else is the production of the fertile genius of the compiler. In all these lists the compilers and revisers seem to have had no other object in view, but to adjust a certain number of remarkable epochs. This being once effected, the intermediate spaces are filled up with names of kings not to be found any where else, and most probably fanciful. Otherwise they leave out the names of those kings of whom nothing is recorded, and attribute the years of their reign in some among them better known, and of greater fame. They often do not scruple to transpose some of those kings, and even whole dynasties; either in consequence of some pre-conceived opinion, or owing to their mistaking a famous king for another of the same name. It was not uncommon with ancient writers, to pass from a remote ancestor to a remote descendant; or from a remote predecessor to a remote successor, by leaving out the intermediate generations or successions, and sometimes ascri-

---

Sir William Jones, we shall find Vicramaditya placed at an era posterior to the Mussulman conquests.

	Years.
From Chandragupta to the end of the Maurya race (As. Res. ii. 139)....	137
From the beginning to the end of the Sunga (Ibid. p. 140)	112
From the ditto to ditto of the Canna (Ibid)........................	345
From ditto to ditto of Andra (ending with Chandrabija) (Ibid. p. 141) ..	456
From Chandrabija to Vicramaditya (Ibid. p. 142)	396
From Chandragupta to Vicramaditya................................	1446

Now Seleucus, who was contemporary with Chandragupta (Asiat. Res. iv. xxvi.), began to reign about 300 years before Christ. By this chronology, therefore, Vicramaditya began to reign about 1146 years after Christ.

bing the years of their reigns to a remote successor or predecessor. In this manner the lists of the ancient kings of Persia, both by oriental writers, and others in the west, have been compiled: and some instances of this nature might be produced from Scripture. I was acquainted lately, at Benares, with a chronicler of that sort; and in the several conversations I had with him, he candidly acknowledged that he filled up the intermediate spaces between the reigns of famous kings, with names at a venture; that he shortened or lengthened their reigns at pleasure; and that it was understood, that his predecessors had taken the same liberties. Through their emendations and corrections, you see plainly a total want of historical knowledge and criticism; and sometimes some disingenuousness is but too obvious. This is, however, the case with the sections on futurity in the Bhagavat, Vayu, Vishnu, and Brahmanda Puranas; which with the above lists constitute the whole stock of historical knowledge among the Hindus; and the whole might be comprised in a few quarto pages of print."[1]

Such is the mode, in which the authors of the Puranas supply themselves with a convenient quantity of *ordinary* kings: Mr. Wilford affords most satisfactory information with regard to the manner in which they further supply themselves with *extraordinary* ones. "The propensity," says he, "of the Hindus, to appropriate every thing to themselves, is well known. We have noticed before their claims to Bahram-Gûr and his descendants; and in the same manner they insist that Acbar was a Hindu in a former generation. The proximity of the time in which this famous emperor lived, has forced them, however, to account for this in the following manner:—There was a holy Brahmen, who wished very much to become emperor of India; and the only practicable way for him was to die first, and be born again. For this purpose he made a desperate *Tapasya*, wishing to remember then every thing he knew in his present generation. This could not be fully granted; but he was indulged with writing upon a brass plate a few things which he wished more particularly to remember; then he was directed to bury the plate, and

[1] Essay on Vicramaditya, and Salivahana, by Captain Wilford, Asiat. Res. ix. 132, 133.

promised that he would remember the place in the next generation. Mucunda, for such was his name, went to Allahabad, buried the plate, and then burned himself. Nine months after he was born in the character of Acbar, who, as soon as he ascended the throne, went to Allahabad, and easily found the spot where the brass plate was buried. Thus the Hindus claim Muhammed and Acbar as their own; exactly like the Persians of old, who insisted that Alexander was the son of one of their kings; so that after all they were forced to submit to their countrymen only."[1]

The account of the claim to Bahram-Gûr, mentioned in the beginning of the preceding passage, is extremely important on the present occasion; as it shows us that Vicramaditya, whom the legend makes sovereign of the world, and the believers in the great Hindu monarchy take for emperor of Hindustan, was in reality a King of Persia, borrowed by the Brahmens, from their propensity to appropriate every thing remarkable which they heard of in the world. "One of these Vicramas," says Mr. Wilford, speaking of the different persons in whom this Vicramaditya appears, "was really a Sassanian Prince: and the famous Shabour or Sapor, of that dynasty, who took the emperor Valens prisoner."[2] The story is as follows:—"In Gurjjara-mandalam are the Sabharamati and Mahi rivers; between them is a forest, in which resided Tamralipta-rishi, whose daughter married King Tamrasena. They had six male children and one daughter called Mandava-recha. The king had two young lads, called Devas'arma and Harisarma, whose duty chiefly was to wash, every day, the clothes of their master, in the waters of the nearest river. One day, as Devas'arma went, by himself, for that purpose, he heard a voice, saying, tell Tamrasena to give me his daughter; should he refuse me he will repent it. The lad on his return mentioned the whole to his master, who would not believe it, and the next day sent Harisarma to the river, who heard the same voice also, with the threats in case of a refusal. The King was astonished; and going himself heard the voice also

1 Essay on Vicramaditya, and Salivahana, by Capt. Wilford, Asiat. Res. ix. 158, 159.
2 Ibid. p. 149.

BOOK II. CHAP. X.

On his return he assembled his council; and after consulting together, it was agreed, that the king should go again, and ask him who he was. The supposed spirit being questioned, answered, I am a Gand'harva, or heavenly chorister; who, having incurred Indra's displeasure, was doomed to assume the shape of an ass. I was born in that shape, in the house of a cumbhacara, or potter, in your capital city; and I am daily roving about in quest of food. The king said that he was very willing to give him his daughter; but that he conceived that such an union was altogether impossible while he remained in that shape. The Gand'harva said, Trouble not yourself about that; comply with my request, and it shall be well with you. If, says the king, you are so powerful, turn the walls of my city, and those of the houses, into brass; and let it be done before sun-rise to-morrow. The Gand'harva agreed to it, and the whole was completed by the appointed time; and the king of course gave him his daughter. This Gand'harva's name was Jayanta, the son of Brahma. When cursed by Indra, he humbled himself; and Indra relenting, allowed him to resume his human shape in the night time, telling him that the curse should not be done away till somebody had burned his ass-like frame. The mother of the damsel spied them once in the night; and, to her great joy, found that the Gand'harva dallied with her daughter in a human shape. Rejoiced at this discovery, she looked for his ass-like form, and burned it. Early in the morning, the Gand'harva looked for this body of his, and found that it had been destroyed. He returned immediately to his wife, informing her of what had happened, and that his curse being at an end, he was obliged to return to heaven, and leave her. He informed her also that she was with child by him, and that the name of the child was to be Vicramaditya."[1] After the statement of some other particulars, Mr. Wilford says, "This is obviously the history of Yesdegird, son of Bahram-Gûr, or Bahram the ass, King of Persia: the grand features are the same, and the times coincide perfectly.[2] The amours

[1] Essay on Vicramaditya, and Salivahana, by Captain Wilford, Asiat. Res. ix. 147, 148,149.

[2] These are not the accounts of Vikramaditya, which the Hindus call upon us to believe. They are avowedly tales and fables having no connexion with a celebrated prince, except the employment of his name. There is no

of Bahram-Gûr, with an Indian princess, are famous all over Persia, as well as in India."[1] Such are the accounts of Vicramaditya, from which we are called upon for our belief of an universal monarchy, and a period of civilization and knowledge.[2]

---

reason whatever to confound him with Behram-Gûr. The story of the transformation of the Gand'harva is a mere popular tradition current in the west of India, the origin of which may be accounted for. The Puranas notice a dynasty of modern princes called Gardabhas, and the word happening to signify " an ass," has no doubt given rise to the tale of the transformation of the Gand'harba to that animal.—W.

[1] Essay on Vicramaditya, and Salivahana, by Captain Wilford, Asiat. Res. ix. p. 149.

[2] Mr. Wilford presents us also with the history which the Brahmens have manufactured for placing Mohamed among the great men of Hindustan. It is of much importance, to elucidate the accounts, which are given by the Hindus, not only of the actions, but of the very persons and existence of their pretended heroes. I should otherwise have been pleased to omit a story, tainted with that indelicacy which, even when they are inventing, and have the circumstances at their own selection, marks the writings of an uncultivated people. " The Hindus say, that the son of a certain King of India, being disgusted with the world, turned pilgrim, and went to Mocsheswarast'hana (or Mecca). In his way thither, and in Arabia, he stopped at the house of a Brahmen, who received him kindly, and ordered his daughter to wait on him as usual. Whilst asleep, the cloth with which his loins were covered was accidently defiled. When he awoke, he took it off, and concealed it in a corner of the house, in some hole, and out of the sight of the damsel, as he thought. Being from home, to perform his ablutions, in consequence of this nocturnal defilement, the damsel came at the usual hour; and her courses suddenly making their appearance, she was much distressed, and looking everywhere for some cloth, she spied the bundle—in short she conceived. He departed for Mecca: and some months after, the parents of the damsel and herself were thrown into the greatest confusion, as may be imagined. The holy man was considered as the author of their disgrace; though the damsel exculpated him: Yet she could not account for her present situation. She was like Hagar, turned out of the house into the wilderness with her son: where they were miraculously preserved, both being innocent. Some years after the holy man returned, unconscious of his having been the cause of so much uneasiness to the family of the hospitable Brahmen. After much abuse, the matter was explained; but the son of the damsel could not be admitted to share with his relatives, or even to remain in their communion. He was, however, honourably dismissed with his mother, after they had given him a suitable education, and rich presents; and they advised him to shift for himself, and to set up a new religion, as he could not be considered as a member of the old one, on account of his strange birth, or rather conception. When advanced in years, he wished to see his paternal relations and India; and to persuade them to conform to his new doctrine; but he died in his way thither, at Medina, near Candahar. This Medina is Ghazni, called emphatically the second Medina, from the great number of holy men entombed there: and it is obvious that the Hindus have confounded Muhammed with Sultan-Mahmood, whose sumptuous Mausoleum is close to that city. Thus we see, that the account they give of Muhammed is a mere rhapsody, retaining some of the principal features of the history of Ishmael, Hagar, Muhammed himself, and Sultan-Mahmood.—This *Samvat*, or era, of Maha'bhat (Muhammed), was early introduced into India, and the Hindus were obliged to use it, as they do now in all their civil transactions; and thus Muhammed became at least a Sambatica or Santica. According to the rules laid down by the learned in India, Muhammed is certainly a Saca and Saceswara, and is entitled to the epithet of Vicrama. He is a Saca, or mighty chief; and, like other Sacas, he killed his millions; he is Saceswara, or the ruler of a sacred period, still in use in India. For these reasons, the Pandits, who assisted Abul-Fazil, did

BOOK II. CHAP. X.

Our experience of human nature, and the phenomena which are exhibited under the manners, attainments, and institutions of the Hindus, are the only materials from which a rational inference can be drawn. It is by no means impossible for a people, who have passed but a small number of stages in the career of civilization, to be united extensively, under one government, and to remain steady for a great length of time in that situation. The empire of China is one conspicuous proof; the ancient kingdom of Persia, which for several ages stood exempt from revolution, is another. The Ottoman empire may be considered as a similar instance. And the Russians, a

---

not scruple to bestow the title of Vicramaditya upon him; and even to consider him as the real worthy of that name; and in order to make the era, or at least the time of Vicramaditya's appearance coincide with the era of Muhammed, they have most shamefully distorted the chronology of the appendix to the Agni-purana. Mr. Wilford, Asiat. Res. ix. 159, 160, 161. See a still more extraordinary attempt to foist the story of Jesus Christ, borrowed from the spurious gospels, into the Puranas; and to make Christ at one time Crishna, at another time Salivahana, at another time Buddhar. Essay on the Origin and Decline of Christianity in India, by Captain Wilford, Asiat. Res. x.

It would thus appear that Vicramaditya is a sort of an appellative, and is applied to any character, whether real or imaginary, whom it suited the Brahmens to erect into a hero; and whether it was originally the name of some Hindu prince who had greatly distinguished himself, or of pure iuvention, it is altogether useless to inquire. That this name has been attached to a particular era, in one of the numerous Hindu modes of dating, establishes nothing. What we do not know is—for what cause they adopted such an era: What we do know is—that they would very naturally apply to it the appellative Vicramaditya, whatever the cause. And no one can doubt the absurdity of supposing that the cause was a particular prince, contemporary at once with Solomon, with Jesus Christ, with Sapor, and with Mohammed.

What the Brahmens fable, about an universal monarchy, and the celestial glory of this or that pretended hero, can therefore be regarded as no evidence of the facts which they assert. The propensity of the Hindus to exaggeration is everywhere displayed. "The officers of government here," says Dr. Buchanan, "had the impudence to inform me, that according to Chica Deva Raya's valuation of the country which belonged to Nandi Raj, it contained 32,000 villages.. ....The account here given seems to be one of those gross exaggerations common in India, and is entirely contradicted by the accounts which I received from the revenue office at Seringapatam." Journey through Mysore, &c. ii. 97. In other places the native officers told him lies, contradicted by the very facts presented to their and his eyes, at the moment of delivering them. "Among the natives, however," he remarks, "similar departures from the truth are common." Ibid. p. 136, 137. Vicramaditya is indeed, expressly, at times asserted, not to have been King of all India, but only of a certain portion of it in the west. "The author of the Vicrama-Upac'hyana says, that he was a powerful prince, in the west of India, and possessed of the countries which we find, afterwards, constituting the patrimonial territories of the Balahara, which included Gurjjarasht'ra (or Gujjarat) with some adjacent districts." Essay on Vicramaditya, &c. by Captain Wilford, Asiat. Res. ix. 149.—M.

Where Wilford picked up all this nonsense cannot be ascertained; it was probably manufactured for him. No trace of it has been ever met with by any other Sanscrit scholar. I have elsewhere remarked that the appendix of the Agni Puránú has never yet made its appearance in any collection of Sanscrit manuscripts.—W.

barbarous people, have long formed a very extensive monarchy. It would, therefore, be far from evidence of any higher civilization, among the Hindus, than what they now manifest, had the existence of a great monarchy been proved.[1] Among uncivilized nations, however, it is most common to find a perpetual succession of revolutions, and communities in general small; though sometimes a prince or individual with uncommon talents arises; and, acquiring power, extends his authority over several of those communities; or even, as in the case of Charlemagne, over a great number; while, after his death the large empire which he had erected gradually dissolves, till the whole, or the greater part, is re-divided into small communities as before. Every thing which the Europeans have seen in Hindustan conspires to prove that such subdivision of communities, and occasional and temporary extensions of power in particular hands, have composed the history of that country. The Mahratta empire affords a striking example of those changes which seem natural to the circumstances in which the people are placed. Within the period of the modern intercourse of the Europeans with Hindustan, an aspiring individual was enabled to extend his authority partly by persuasion, partly by force, first over one district, and then over another, till at last he united under his command an extensive empire, composed chiefly of the separate and disjointed communities, who occupied the mountainous districts in the western and central parts of Hindustan.[2] Soon was this empire broken

[1] If the existence of a great monarchy be no proof of civilisation, the pains that are here taken to disprove its existence in India, have been somewhat superfluous; and, in any case, it is with the theories of European writers, not the assertion of the Hindus themselves, that the dispute is maintained. As to the question of civilisation, however, it in truth appears to be little influenced by extent of territory, and in some cases, as in ancient Greece, the division of the country amongst a number of petty principalities and communities, seems to have been favourable to social advancement.

The ancient state of India was, for the most part, no doubt, such as it has been known to be in later times: it was held by a number of independent princes, whose dominions varied in extent according to their personal character. At times, however, one more ambitious and able than the rest, does seem to have brought a very considerable portion of the country under 'one umbrella.' The edicts of Asoka are found engraven on the column of Delhi, the rocks of Orissa, and the mountains of Guzerat.—W.

[2] The word Hindustan is, in this work, generally used to signify, comprehensively, the land of the Hindus, from Cape Comorin to the farthest boundary of the country which they inhabited. It is necessary to mention, that in the oriental books, it has often a more limited signification, being appropriated to that part of the land of the Hindus which is north of the river Nerbudda.

BOOK II. CHAP. X.

into several different governments, the owners of which hardly acknowledged even a nominal homage to the throne of Sivajee; and had they been left to themselves, free from the irresistible operation of the British power, the empire of the Mahrattas, in all probability, would have been resolved ere this time, into its primitive elements. Even the empire of the Moguls itself, though erected on firmer foundations than it is reasonable to suppose that any Hindu monarchy ever enjoyed; though supported by a foreign force, and acted upon by peculiar motives for maintaining undivided power, had no sooner attained its greatest extension by the conquests of Aurungzebe, than it began immediately to fall to pieces; and a single century beheld it in fragments.

The monuments of the ancient state of Hindustan conspire in giving indication of a troubled scene. Every ancient writing, which bears any reference to the matter of history, the historical poems, the Puranas, hold up to view a state of society, the reverse of tranquil; perpetual broils, dethronements, injustice, wars, conquests, and bloodshed. Among the most important of all the documents of antiquity found in Hindustan, are the inscriptions, declaratory of grants of land, made by the ancient princes of the country. These princes are so far from appearing to have presided over a peaceful land, that they are all represented as victorious warriors; and as having been surrounded by enemies, over whom they have triumphed, and whom they have severely chastised.[1] Almost all the princes mentioned in these inscriptions, princes in all the parts of India, and not pretended to have been more than the sovereigns of some particular district, are described as the conquerors and sovereigns of the whole world.[2]

[1] See the inscription found at Monghir, and translated in the Asiat. Res. i. 123. That found at Buddal, Ibid. p. 130. That found at Tanna, Ibid. p. 357. Those from the Vindhya mountains, Ibid. ii. 168, 169. That on the staff of Feeroz Shah, Ibid. p. 382. That respecting a grant of land in the Carnatic, Ibid. iii. 40—47. That found in the district of Gorakhpur, Ibid. ix. 410. That found at Chitradurg, Ibid. p. 418, 419, 420. That found at Curugode, Ibid. p. 436, 437, 438. Those found at Nedigal and Goujda, Ibid. p. 447.

[2] See the inscriptions translated in the Asiat. Res. i. 360, 123, 125; iii. 48, 52; ix. 406, 418. The inscription, cut on a stone, upon the hill of Belligolo, in front of the great Jain image, bears a similar testimony. "In the year of the Saca, 1290 (A.D. 1367) . . . . be success and glory to the honourable monarch, the sovereign and destroyer of envious princes, lord of foreign kings, whose name is Buccaraya."—Asiat. Res. ix. 270.

Of the unsparing and destructive cruelty which accompanied the perpetual wars and conquests of the Hindus, among other proofs, the following may be considered as strong. In the inscription found at Tanna, part of the panegyric bestowed upon the donor Prince, is in these words: "Having raised up his slain foe on his sharp sword, he so afflicted the women in the hostile palaces, that their forelocks fell disordered, their garlands of bright flowers dropped from their necks on the vases of their breasts, and the black lustre of their eyes disappeared; a warrior, the plant of whose fame grows up over the temple of Brahma's egg (the universe) from the-repeated-watering-of-it-with-the-drops-that-fell-from-the-eyes-of-the-wives-of-his-slaughtered-foe."[1] It would be in the highest degree absurd to reject this, were it even a solitary instance, as evidence of a general fact; because the exterminating ferocity is described as matter of the highest praise; and panegyric, to be what it is, must be conformable to the ideas of the people to whom it is addressed.[2]

1 Asiat. Res. i. 360. It is a mere common place; and, after all, what does it mean? That the women of the prince, or the people of a subjugated country, will have cause to grieve for the loss of those killed in battle; a mere truism, denoting unsparing cruelty no more than the same event in all times and places. On the other hand, the Hindu 'laws' of war are very chivalrous and humane, and prohibit the slaying of the unarmed, of women, of the old, and of the conquered.—Manu, vii. Their practice has been found, in general, conformable to their laws; and for sanguinary cruelty, and the abuse of victory, Mohammedan, not Hindu princes, must be cited.—W.

2 The inscription on the Lat (staff) of Firoz Shah, celebrates the monarch, in whose honour it has been erected, "for having achieved conquest in the course of travelling to holy places—as resentful to haughty kings, and indulgent to those whose necks are humbled—making Ariaverta [the land of virtue or of respectable men] once more what its name signifies, by causing the barbarians to be exterminated.—Visala Deva, son of the fortunate Vella Deva, king of Sacambari, the situation of which the translator does not know, most eminent of the tribe which sprang from the arms of Brahma—boasts of having rendered tributary the region of the earth between Himavat (the Imaus of ancient geographers) and Vindhya (the range of hills which passes through the provinces of Bahar, Benares) and exhorts his descendants to subdue the remainder."—No proof, all this, of the peaceful state of Hindostan. The inscription continues—"May thy abode, O Vigraha, sovereign of the earth, be fixed, as in reason it ought, in the bosoms, akin to the mansions of dalliance, of the women with beautiful eye-brows, who were married to thy enemies."—The abuse of an enemy's wives is no great proof of a generous or civilized conqueror. The inscription then deifies this same Rajah. "Art thou not Vishnu himself? Art thou not he who slept in the arms of Lacshmi, whom thou didst seize from the ocean, having churned it?"—Are epithets of extravagant praise to the deity surprising, when they are thus heaped upon a mortal? (As. Res. ii. 382.) The account of the Sacas affords important proof of the glory that was attached by the Hindus to the shedding of blood. The Cali-yug is divided into six Sacas, so called from six glorious monarchs. Of these, three have made their appearance; three are yet to come. To become a Saca, each of these monarchs must have first killed 550,000,000 of a certain mighty tribe of heretics, called Sacas. The first of these blood-thirsty sovereigns was Judish-

BOOK II. CHAP. X.

The picture which Major Rennel, looking only to a limited period, drew of the state of Hindustan, may be taken, agreeably to every thing which we know of Hindustan, as the picture of it, to the remotest period of its history.[1] Rebellions, massacres, and barbarous conquests, make up the history of this fair country, (which to an ordinary observer seems destined to be the paradise of the world,)—the immediate effect of the mad ambition of conquering more than can be governed by one man."[2] "Revolutions," (says Sonnerat, directing his attention to the coast of Malabar, which had been little affected by foreign conquest) "have been more rapid in this than in any other part of the globe. A daring robber, possessed of policy and courage, in a short time gives laws to the whole coast, but in his turn becomes tributary to a bolder villain, who marching in the same path, subjects him to the lot he had inflicted on others."[3]

Notwithstanding, in other respects, the extreme scantiness and uncertainty of the materials for any inferences except the most general, in regard to the ancient state of Hindustan, there is a great body of evidence to prove the habitual division of the country into a number of moderate, and most frequently, petty sovereignties and states.[4] In the dramatic poem Sacontala, the daughter of the her-

ter, whose period was 3044 years; the second Vicramaditya, whose saca lasted only 135 years; the third, Salivahana, whose period is to last 18,000 years; the fourth Nandada, 10,000 years; the fifth Nargarjuna, 400,000 years; for the sixth, will re-appear the Antediluvian Bali, whose period will be 821 years, at which period a general renovation of the world will take place. Wilford, Asiat. Res. ix. 82.

1 Rennell, in speaking of India under the Mohammedans.

2 Rennell's Memoir, p. 1.

3 Sonnerat, Voy. liv. iii. ch. ii. Their very laws and religion encourage a spirit of restlessness, and warfare; "Fully performing all duties required by law, let a king seek to possess regions yet unpossessed." (Laws of Menu, ch. ix. 251.) This gives implicit encouragement to a spirit of conquest. The gloss of Culluca, the commentator, inserts the words *with justice*, a saving clause; but even then, the practical effect of the law is but too visible.

4 In the Bhagavat, (See Maurice, Hist. of Hindustan, ii. 395,) Creeshna says, he does not vaunt, "though he carried away Rokemenee from so numerous an assemblage of monarchs." When Creeshna fought with the seven bulls of Koosele, great numbers of rajahs and rajpoots were collected to see the conflict. Ib. p. 402. Bhoom Assoor had collected the daughters of 16,000 rajahs, Ib. p. 405. Rajah Doorjoodhen, sovereign of Hastanapoor, had a daughter who was courted by rajahs and rajpoots from every quarter, Ib. 413. Twenty thousand and eight hundred rajahs of eminence were held in confinement by Jarasaudha, and released upon his destruction by Creeshna and Rama, Ib. p. 433. When Creeshna carried away Rokemenee, Jarasanda said, "This is surely most astonishing, that, in the presence of so many crowned heads as are here assembled, this coward should make so bold an effort." Ib. p. 394.

mit asks the royal stranger, who had visited their consecrated grove; "What imperial family is embellished by our noble guest? What is his native country? Surely it must be afflicted by his absence from it?" The question undoubtedly implied that there were more royal families than one to which he might belong, and these at no remarkable distance, since the stranger was known to have come into the forest in the course of a hunting excursion. In the Hitopadesa, mention is made of a variety of princes. Thus in the compass of a few pages, we are told: "In the country of Calinga is a prince, named Rucmangada, who, advancing with preparations to subdue the adjacent regions, has fixed his station near the river Chandrabhaga."[1] Again, "In the country of Canyacubja is a prince named Virasena."[2] And further, "There is near the Bhagirathi, a city, named Pataliputra, in which lived a prince named Sudersana."[3] In the inscription, formerly quoted, found at Monghir, and bearing date 23 years B. C. there is sufficient proof of the division of Hindustan into numerous kingdoms. Gopal, the prince, or the father of the prince, by whom the grant is made, is panegyrized as the conqueror of many princes; and his son is, "He, who marching through many countries, making conquests, arrived with his elephants in the forests of the mountains Beendhyo, where seeing again their long-lost families, they mixed their mutual tears; and who going to subdue other princes, his young horses meeting their females at Kamboge, they mutually neighed for joy:—who conquered the earth from the source of the Ganges as far as the well-known bridge which was constructed by the enemy of Dosasyo, from the river of Luckeecool as far as the ocean of the habitation of Booroon."[4] If this prince overran the peninsula, and conquered a multitude of princes, the peninsula must have been possessed by a multitude of princes before. And we may form an idea of the exaggeration used in the account of his victories, when we are told that his father Gopal was king of the world, and possessed of two brides, the earth and her wealth.[5] The conquests by those princes, even when they took place,

[1] Hitopadesa, in Sir William Jones's Works, vi. 43.
[2] Ib. p. 44.
[3] Ibid. p. 51.
[4] Asiat. Res. i. 123.
[5] Ibid.

BOOK II. CHAP. X.

were but inroads, never to any considerable extent, effecting a durable possession. This prince himself, we are told, "when he had completed his conquests, released all the rebellious princes he had made captive; and each returning to his own country laden with presents, reflected upon this generous deed, and longed to see him again."[1] The laws frequently afford evidence to the same purpose. The penalty, so frequently imposed, of banishment from one kingdom to another, proves the vicinity of different kingdoms.[2] The following is another instance in point:—"If a lender of money says to a person, A debt due to me is outstanding in your hands, and that person denies the debt, if that time the bond is not in the lender's hands, but should be in some other kingdom, then until he brings the bond from such other kingdom, the suit shall not be determined."[3] In the code of Menu is a series of rules for behaviour to neighbouring princes; sufficiently proving, that Hindustan was in that state of subdivision which rendered these rules pertinent and useful.[4]

[1] Asiat. Res. 1. 123. The third stanza of this inscription, omitted by Mr. Wilkins, but translated by Sir W. Jones, affords additional proof that these conquests were but an irruption: "By whom, having conquered the earth as far as the ocean, it was left as being unprofitably seized." Ibid. p. 142. In the inscription on the pillar near Buddal, found by Mr. Wilkins, is described a race of princes, who originally, it is said, ruled over "but one quarter, and had no authority in other regions;" but one of the line, "being a virtuous prince, became supreme over every country without reserve, and the three worlds were held in subjection by his hereditary rank." The dominions of his son and successor extended from Reva Janak, to the father of Gowree, and to the two oceans, &c., and all this country, the prince Sree Devu Pal rendered tributary. Ibid. p. 134. Yet Sir W. Jones says, that this race of princes were all along only prime ministers to the House of Devu Pal: p. 142. Nothing can be more contradictory to the text; but it is necessary for Sir William's theory that the kings of Gaur, of whom Devupal was one, should be the lords paramount of India. Sir William, when he had a theory, seems to have had eyes to see nothing but what made in its favour. An additional proof of the small kingdoms of Hindustan is found in the inscription (As. Res. i. 133, stanza xiii.) "The king of Gowr" (Bengal) "for a long time enjoyed the country of the eradicated race of Ootkal" (Orixia,) "of the Hoons" (Huns,) "of humbled pride, of the kings of Draveer" (a country to the south of the Carnatic,) "and Goojar" (Goozerat,) "whose glory was reduced, and the universal sea-girt throne." Another grant of land (Ib. p. 357) affords evidence to the same purpose: a number of kings are actually named in the royal grant. As. Res. iii. 48.

[2] See Gentoo Code, passim.

[3] Halhed's Gentoo Code, ch. iii. sect. 6, p. 106, 107.

[4] Laws of Menu, ch. vii. p. 154, 155. Even Robertson, though a firm believer in the universal monarchy, is forced to allow that it had not yet existed in the time of Alexander. "In the age of Alexander, though there was not established in it any powerful empire, resembling that which in modern times stretched its dominion from the Indus almost to Cape Comorin, it was even then formed into monarchies of considerable extent." Robertson's Disq. concerning Ancient India, p. 21. But the times of Alexander, and times long antecedent, are the times fixed upon by the Brahmens, for this perpetually asserted, but never ascertained empire. To what modern

These articles, to which there is nothing whatsoever opposed, but the absurd fables of the Brahmens, constitute a degree of evidence to which we may with sufficient confidence attach our belief.[1]

We have already seen, in reviewing the Hindu form of government, that despotism, in one of its simplest and least artificial shapes, was established in Hindustan, and confirmed by laws of Divine authority. We have seen likewise, that by the division of the people into castes, and the prejudices which the detestable views of the Brahmens raised to separate them, a degrading and pernicious system of subordination was established among the Hindus, and that the vices of such a system were there carried to a more destructive height than among

---

times does Robertson allude? for he himself gives it as true information, that in the tenth century, there were four kingdoms in the north part alone of India. "The first was composed of the provinces situated on the Indus, and the rivers which fall into it; the capital of which was Moultan. The capital of the second kingdom was Canoge, which, from the ruins of it remaining, appears to have been a very large city. The third kingdom was Cachemire. Massoudi, as far as I know, is the first author who mentions this paradise of India, of which he gives but a short description. The fourth is the kingdom of Guzerate, which he represents as the greatest and most powerful; and he concurs with the two Arabian travellers, in giving the sovereign of it the appellation of Balhara." Ibid. Note xxxvii. p. 332.

[1] The inconsistencies of the believers in the great empire of Hindustan are miserable. Mr. Maurice tells us that Bali, "if that name imply not rather a dynasty of princes than an individual monarch," [a shrewd suspicion] "was the puissant sovereign of a mighty empire, extending over the vast continent of India; that under Rama, the next in succession, there is every appearance of its having remained unbroken; that Judishter is generally acknowledged to have been the sovereign of all India." Maurice, Hist. ii. 511. Yet both Mr. Maurice and Sir W. Jones believe Rama to be the Raamah of Scripture, the son of Cush, Genesis, ch. x. ver. 7, in whose days it was impossible that any considerable part of India could be peopled. See Sir W. Jones, Asiat. Res. ii. 401, and Mr. Maurice, Hist. iii. 104. Bali, the Baal, and Bel, of other eastern nations, who is also said to have been the first king of Assyria, was not a name of any particular person, but a title assumed by many, and those of different nations. It is in fact a title of the sun. (See Bryant's Myth.) Judishter, too, it is remarkable, was the contemporary of Rama, both being heroes in the war of the Mahabharat. For the performance of the Raisoo yug, it was not necessary, as they pretend, to conquer all princes, since at Judishter's yug, the father of Cansa, whom Creeshna, after the death of Cansa, seated on the throne of Mathura, was not conquered by Judishter. Nay, it is remarkable that this yug was celebrated while Judishter was yet a dependent upon Doorjoodhen, before the war of the Pandoos. Even after the war of the Mahabharat, when they assure us, for certain, that Judishter was king of all India, Ogur Sein, the grandfather of Creeshna, was reigning at Mathura; Creeshna and the Yadavas were all flourishing. See the Mahabharat, translated by Halhed; Maurice, History of India, ii. 463.—M. The Brahmans are here charged with "fables," which are almost wholly of European fabrication: although a prince may be sometimes termed in compliment a universal monarch, yet they almost always describe India as parcelled out amongst a number of independent rulers: the common division of India, according to Brahminical authorities, is into fifty-six principalities, but the Puránas and poems specify many more.—W.

BOOK II. CHAP. X.

any other people.[1] And we have seen that by a system of priestcraft, built upon the most enormous and tormenting superstition that ever harassed and degraded any portion of mankind, their minds were enchained more intolerably than their bodies; in short that, despotism and priestcraft taken together, the Hindus, in mind and body, were the most enslaved portion of the human race. Sir William Jones, in his preface to the translation of the Institutes of Menu, says, that this code exhibits "a system of despotism and priestcraft, both indeed limited by law, but artfully conspiring to give mutual support, though with mutual checks." The despotism and priestcraft of the system were, it seems, too glaring to be mistaken or denied; but, in order to palliate the deformity, Sir William is betrayed into nonsense. A despotism, he says, limited by law; as if a despotism limited by law were not a contradiction in terms; what is limited by law, so far as so limited, being not a despotism. A priestcraft, he also says, limited by law: A law of which the priests themselves were the sole makers, and the sole interpreters! A despotism, and a priestcraft, he says, with mutual checks. Yes, truly; it was the interest of the priestcraft to check the despotism, in all encroachments on the priestcraft; and it was the interest of the despotism to check the priestcraft, in all encroachments on the despotism. But who checked the despotism and the priestcraft in oppressing the people? Alas! no one. It was the interest of the despotism and the priestcraft to join together in upholding their common tyranny over the people; and it must be allowed that so commanding a motive had all the influence upon their conduct which it might be

[1] "In so far as the Hindu superstition tends to estrange mankind by creating artificial sources of mutual aversion and disgust; so far certainly does it counteract the real interests of society. Let it not be urged that the practical effects of the artificial separation of the Asiatics are not greatly felt in society; or that a Brahmin or Rajah will as readily supply the wants of the poorer classes as he would those of his own. The fact is otherwise; the Brahmin considers his order as in some measure a different race of beings; and imagines that the lower ranks are incapable of the same sensibility to suffering: he regards them as a race whose feelings are deadened by the meanness of their intellect, and therefore not entitled to the same share of compassion. That this is the idea of the princes and civil magistrates throughout India, their own conduct sufficiently evinces; hence the severity of their government, the rigour of their punishments, and their universal indifference to the comfort, and even the lives of their subjects." Tennant's Indian Recreations, i. 121.

expected to have.[1] Apply this remark of the splendid orientalist to the Turks ; *There* is a despotism and a priestcraft, limited, (if we may so abuse the term,) and still more strictly limited, by law ; for the Moslem laws are more precise and accurate than those of the Hindus: *There*, too, the despotism and priestcraft check one another: But has all this prevented the Turkish despotism and priestcraft from being the scourge of human nature ; the source of barbarity and desolation ?

That the Hindu despotism was not practically mild, we have a number of satisfactory proofs. We have seen the cruelty and ferocity of the penal laws ; itself a circumstace of the highest importance, "A thunderbolt," says the author of the Hitopadesa, "and the power of kings, are both dreadful ! But the former expendeth its fury at once, whilst the latter is constantly falling upon our heads."[2] Some of the observations are so comprehensive, and pointed, as to afford the strongest evidence. "In this world," says the same celebrated book, "which is subject to the power of one above, a man of good principles is hard to be found, in a country, for the most part, *governed by the use of the rod*."[3] "Princes in general, alas ! turn away their faces from a man endowed with good qualities."[4] "The conduct of princes, like a fine harlot, is of many colours. True and false ; harsh and gentle ; cruel and merciful ; niggardly and generous ; extravagant of expense, and solicitous of the influx of abundant wealth and treasure."[5] "An elephant killeth even by touching, a servant even by smelling, a king even by ruling."[6] All the gene-

[1] These notions of the condition of the people are all drawn from the history of Europe, and are in a great degree inapplicable to India. The people under their native princes know little of despotic government. They have determinate laws and fixed institutions, which no Raja can in any way modify or change, and which, therefore, set insuperable limits to arbitrary rule. With regard to the Brahmins, again, it must be always remembered that whatever influence they may have exercised, it has been entirely personal, proportionate to their individual reputation for sanctity and learning. They are no priesthood: they have never had, as a body, any common purpose, any organization, any head: and they can never, therefore, have prosecuted systematically, designs upon the liberties of the people. They are in fact the people ; not separated from them as monastic or clerical sections, but making up a very large proportion of the population, and giving the whole force of the consideration which their caste confers to the security of popular rights. A great mistake pervades all reasoning about the position of the Brahmins in Hindu society ; they are a tribe, a people, not an order or corporation.—W.

[2] Wilkins' Hitopadesa, p. 161.

[3] Ibid. p. 82.

[4] Ibid. p. 160.

[5] Ibid. p. 166.

[6] Ibid. p. 176. The following maxim, among many others in the book, is a proof of the idle and useless life of the Rajahs, who devolved all business

BOOK II. CHAP. X.

ral maxims of the Hindus import the extreme degradation of the great body of the people. "The assistance, O king, which is rendered to those of low degree, is like endeavouring to please bears. A low person should never be placed in the station of the great. One of low degree having obtained a worthy station, seeketh to destroy his master."[1] "The Hindus," says Dr. Buchanan, "in their state of independence, exacted deference from those under them, with a cruelty and arrogance rarely practised but among themselves. A Nair was expected instantly to cut down a Tiar or Mucua, who presumed to defile him by touching his person; and a similar fate awaited a slave, who did not turn out of the road as a Nair passed."[2] In Sacontala, Dushmanta is represented as a king who possessed every virtue, and made happiness flourish as in the golden age. Yet we have a specimen of the justice and legality which prevailed during this happy reign, in the passage relating to the innocent fisherman. He was found, by certain of the king's officers, offering to sale a ring with the king's name upon it. They instantly seize him, and drag him away to justice: all the while beating and bruising him; and loading him with opprobrious epithets. The victim of this brutal treatment offers only the most humble entreaties, making statement of the facts, and protestation of his innocence. Upon the sight of the ring, the king acknowledges that he is innocent; and orders him a sum of money, equal in value to the ring. Of this reward he is obliged to resign a half to the very men who had abused him, "to escape," it is said, "the effects of their displeasure."[3]

---

upon their ministers, and wallowed in sensuality and sloth. "The sovereign being a vessel for the distribution of happiness, and not for the execution of affairs, the minister, who shall bring ruin upon the business of the state is a criminal." (Ibid. p. 142.) The last article of the following character of a good minister is an abundant proof of the rapacious nature of the government; "A king should engage for his minister one who is a native of his own country; pure in all his ways, and cleanly in his dress; not one who is an outcast, addicted to idle pleasures, or too fond of women; but one of good repute, who is well versed in the rules of disputation, is of a firm mind, and expert in raising a revenue." Ibid. p. 179. See also the Inscription respecting a Royal Grant, Asiat. Res. iii. 48.

1 Wilkins' Hitopadesa, p. 242.

2 Buchanan's Journey through Mysore, &c. ii. 410.

3 Another remarkable circumstance. The fisherman informs the officers he gives them his present to purchase wine; on which they cry, "Oh! now thou art our beloved friend.—Good wine is the first object of our affection.—Let us go together to the vintner's." Sacontala, act v.

The laws for guarding the authority of the magistrate, exhibit a character of extreme severity, and indicate an habitual state of the most rigid domination. "If a man speaks reproachfully of any upright magistrate, the magistrate shall cut out his tongue; or, having confiscated all his effects, shall banish him the kingdom."[1] By this law, even the privilege of complaint was taken from the wretched Hindu. The victim of oppression was bound, under ferocious penalties, to suffer in silence.

The following is a law by which every act of despotism is legalized. "If a magistrate, for his own good, hath passed any resolutions, whoever refuses to submit to such resolutions, the magistrate shall cut out that person's tongue."[2] If every resolution which the magistrate chooses to pass for his own good, is by the very circumstance of his passing it, obligatory under violent penalties, the state of the government is not doubtful.

"If a man makes complaint before the magistrate against the magistrate's counsellor, without any real fault in him, or performs any business or service for the magistrate's accuser, the magistrate shall put him to death."[3] Under the operation of this law, the magistrate had little to fear from accusation. There could be no remedy for any grievance; because the existence of any grievance could hardly ever be told. If the magistrate was willing to hear of his own misconduct, or that of his servants, in that case he might hear of it; where he was unwilling, in that case it was death.[4]

Though all peaceable applications for the redress of grievances were thus precluded, any violence offered to the person of the magistrate was punished in a manner which none but the most savage people ever endured. "If a magistrate has committed a crime, and any person, upon discovery of that crime, should beat and ill-use the ma-

[1] Halhed's Gentoo Code, ch. xv. sect. 2. [2] Ibid.

[3] Halhed's Gentoo Code, ch. xxi. 10.

[4] The self-abasement of the Hindus, before their kings, is decisive proof of a merciless government. "The sovereign, although but a child, is not to be despised, but to be respected as a man; or as a mighty divinity who presideth in human form." Wilkins' Hitopadesa, p. 117. "They performed prostration to their princes, *falling down with eight members*, as they expressed their abject and grovelling mode of approach." Ibid, note 137. "Plus un gouvernement est despotique, plus les ames y sont avilies et dégradées; plus l'on s'y vante d'aimer son tyran. Les esclaves bénissent à Maroc leur sort et leur Prince, lorsqu'il daigne lui-même leur couper le cou." Helvetius de l'Homme, i. 318.

BOOK II. CHAP. X.

gistrate, in that case, whatever be the crime of murdering one hundred Brahmins, such crime shall be accounted to that person; and the magistrate shall thrust an iron spit through him, and roast him at the fire."[1]

The notices afforded us of particular sovereigns are exceedingly few. But, such as they are, most of them declare the misgovernment and cruelty of the individuals to whom they relate. "According to Plutarch, in his life of Alexander, Chandra-Gupta (I use the words of Mr. Wilford) had been at that prince's camp, and had been heard to say afterwards, that Alexander would have found no difficulty in the conquest of Prachi, or the country of the Prasians, had he attempted it, as the king was despised, and hated, too, on account of his cruelty."[2]

As the Hindu manners and character are invariable; according to their admirers, these admirers cannot consistently reject their present, as proof of their ancient, behaviour; and all men will allow that it affords strong ground of inference. "It is a remark," says one of the best-informed observers of Hindustan, "warranted by constant experience, that wherever the government is administered by Gentoos, the people are subject to more and severer oppressions than when ruled by the Moors. I have imputed this to intelligent Gentoos, who have confessed the justice of the accusation, and have not scrupled to give their opinions concerning it." The opinions of the Gentoos are as favourable to themselves as suiting the occasion, they could possibly make them. "A Gen-

[1] Halhed's Gentoo Code, ch. xvi. sect. 1.—M. These laws are all from Halhed's Code: their authority is questionable, and it may be doubted if in all respects the translation is accurate.—W.

[2] Wilford, on the Chronology of the Hindus, Asiat. Res. v. 284. There is a passage in Quintus Curtius which would lead us to conclude that India was not thickly inhabited in the times of Alexander. Speaking of Alexander's march into the interior of India, after the overthrow of Darius, he says: "Ad magnam deinde, *ut in ea regione*, urbem pervenit." (Curt. lib. ix. cap. i.) Not a syllable escapes from this author indicative of a populous country. He styles the inhabitants, "Barbari—operum militarium rudes." Ibid. cap. viii. The names of the separate nations which Alexander found in India are numerous.—M.

The inference deduced from an equivocal phrase of Curtius is contradicted by the positive testimony of the Greek writers. Megasthenes states that there are 120 nations in India; and Arrian, though he questions the accuracy of this enumeration, admits that the Indians are very numerous. On India, c. vii.: Strabo says, that Eukratides was master of 1000 cities between the Hydaspes and Hyphasis, xv. 3. To attach the general character of cruelty to Hindu princes because mention is made of one cruel sovereign, is a conclusion certainly not warranted by the premises.—W.

too," they say, "is not only born with a spirit of more subtle invention, but, by his temperance and education, becomes more capable of attention to affairs, than a Moor; who no sooner obtains power, than he is lost in voluptuousness; he becomes vain and lordly, and cannot dispense with satiating the impulse of his sensual appetites; whereas a Gentoo Prince retains, in his Durbar, the same spirit which would actuate him if keeping a shop." Mr. Orme adds, "Avarice is his predominant passion: and all the wiles, address, cunning, and perseverance, of which he is so exquisite a master, are exerted to the utmost in fulfilling the dictates of this vice; and his religion, instead of inspiring, frees him from the remorse of his crimes; for whilst he is harassing and plundering the people by the most cruel oppressions, he is making peace with the gods, by denying nothing to their priests." Mr. Orme exhibits an impressive example. "The present King of Travancore (an Hindu prince whose dominions had never been subject to a foreign government) has conquered, or carried war into all the countries that lay round his dominions, and lives in the continual exercise of his arms. To atone for the blood which he has spilt, the Brachmans persuaded him that it was necessary he should be born anew: this ceremony consisted in putting the prince into the body of a golden cow of immense value, where, after he had laid the time prescribed, he came out, regenerated and freed from all the crimes of his former life. The cow was afterwards cut up, and divided among the SEERS who had invented this extraordinary method for the remission of his sins."[1] No testimony can be stronger to the natural ten-

[1] Orme, on the Government and People of Hindustan, p. 434, 435, 436. "Quelques missionaires, tels que le P. de Magistris, le Danois F. Schwartz, le P. Jean de Brito, dans une relation manuscrite que j'ai entre les mains, accusent les rois payens d'exercer des oppressions intolérables envers leurs sujets. M. Anquetil du Perron tâche de justifier les souverains. * * * Je pourrais démontrer avec une historique évidence que M. Anquetil ne connait pas l'Inde. * * * Il est certain qu'il se commettait de grands abus dans l'exercice de l'autorité royale, et je pense que ce fut là la principale cause de la chûte des rois de Maduré, de Maiesour, de Tanjaur, et de Marava. Quoique ces rois fussent tous payens, de la première noblesse, et indigènes, sans cesse ils se faisaient la guerre réciproquement, et presque tous vexaient le peuple." Voyage aux Indes Orientales par le P. Paolin, de S. Bartelemy, i. 87. M. Anquetil Duperron, in a note, (Ibid. iii. 365,) falls into a curious coincidence with, and confirmation of, the above passage of Paolino, at the same time that he is controverting it:—"Le missionaire n'a pas lu l'histoire de l'Inde, n'est past même au fait de ce qui se passe tous les jours. Quoique le caractère propre de l'Indien soit la douceur, l'humanité, ou voit encore, dans cette contrée, comme ailleurs, des querelles entre les princes naturels Indiens, des querelles dans les

dency of the Hindu religion, and to the effects which their institutions are calculated to produce."[1]

---

familles; les chefs Marattes sont presque toujours devisés, et en guerres. Le Tanjaur, le Maduré, le Maissour, le Samorin, Narsingue, le Canara, offraient la même spectacle lorsque la puissance des Rajahs étoit dans sa vigueur; il en est de même de ceux de Bengale, du reste de l'Indoustan," Bernier, who had no theory on Indian affairs, but who displays more personal knowledge of the country than almost any other European, thus describes the Rajahs. "Ces sortes de rois barbares n'ont aucune véritable générosité, et ne sont guère retenus par la foi qu'ils ont promise, ne regardant qu'à leurs intérêts présents, sans songer même aux malheurs qui leur peuvent arriver de leur perfidie, et de leur brutalité." Révol. des Etats Mogol. p. 174. The ryots have every reason to dread the prevalence of the Mahratta power; of that power which yields them up to the tyranny and oppression of their chiefs; which affords no protection to its subjects; which is perpetually at war with its neighbours; and which has, in effect, laid waste the greatest part of Hindostan." Sir H. Strachey, Report as Judge of Circuit, Fifth Report of the Committee on Indian Affairs, 1810, p. 568, sect. 17. "La politique de leurs princes doit tenir de leur gouvernement.—D'une main on les voit signer un traité, et de l'autre ils jurent la perte de celui avec lequel ils font alliance." Anquetil Duperron, Zendavesta, cxxii. "The annals of Persia," says Mr. Scott Waring, "contain little more than a uniform tale of wretchedness and misery, of murder and treachery; and the mind, wearied and disgusted with this uniformity of vice, is hurried away to a contemplation of similar causes and events." Tour to Sheeraz, p. 267.

[1] There can be no rational doubt that what by European eyes has been seen to be the detail of government, in the hands of the Hindus, though under Mogul principals, was a fair picture of what had been the detail of government under Hindu principals; administration in the hands of Mogul magistrates being, according to all testimony, less oppressive than administration in the hands of Hindus. The same intelligent and unexceptionable witness, Mr. Orme, goes on to say: "Imitation has conveyed the unhappy system of oppression which prevails in the government of Indostan throughout all ranks of the people, from the highest even to the lowest subject of the empire. Every head of a village calls his habitation the Durbar, and plunders of their meal and roots the wretches of his precinct: from him the Zemindar extorts the small pittance of silver, which his penurious tyranny has scraped together; the Phousdar seizes upon the greatest share of the Zemindar's collections, and then secures the favour of his Nabob by voluntary contributions, which leave him not possessed of the half of his rapines and exactions: the Nabob fixes his rapacious eye on every portion of wealth which appears in his province, and never fails to carry off part of it: by large deductions from these acquisitions, he purchases security from his superiors, or maintains it against them at the expense of a war.—Subject to such oppressions, property in Indostan is seldom seen to descend to the third generation." Orme, on the Government and People of Indostan, p. 450, 451. The following is another stroke in the formation of the same picture. "The Havildar plunders the village, and is himself fleeced by the Zemindar; the Zemindar by the Phousdar; the Phousdar by the Nabob or his Duan. The Duan is the Nabob's head slave: and the Nabob compounds on the best terms he can make, with his Subah, or the throne.—Wherever this gradation is interrupted, bloodshed ensues." Ibid. p. 402. "In every city, and in every considerable town, is appointed a guard, directed by proper officers, whose duty it is to coerce and punish all such crimes and misdemeanours as affect the policy of that district, and are at the same time of too infamous or of too insignificant a nature to be admitted before the more solemn tribunal of the Durbar. These ministers of justice are called the Catwall; and a building bearing the same name is allotted for their constant resort. At this place are perpetually heard the clamours of the populace: some demanding redress for the injury of a blow or a bad name; others for a fraud in the commerce of farthings: one wants assistance to take, another has taken a thief; some offering themselves as bondsmen; others called upon for witnesses. The cries of wretches under the scourge, and the groans of expiring criminals, complete a scene of perfect misery and confusion. After

Among other expedients for saving the favourite system, it has been maintained that the petty states and princes in Hindustan were but subordinate parts of one great monarchy, whose sceptre they acknowledged, and whose mandates they obeyed. There is no definite limit to gratuitous suppositions.[1] If we are to be satisfied with opinions not only void of proof, but opposed by everything of the nature of proof, attainable upon the subject, we may conjure up one opinion after another; and nothing, except physical impossibility, or a defect of ingenuity, can set bounds to our affirmations. In the loose mode of thinking, or rather of talking without thinking, which has prevailed concerning Indian affairs, the existence of feudal institutions in modern Europe has constituted a sufficient basis for the belief of feudal institutions in India; though it would have been just as rational to conclude that, because the Saxon language forms the basis of most of the languages of Europe, therefore the Saxon language forms the basis of the language in India.

There are two modes in which the subordination of a number of petty princes, to a great one, may take place. The inferior states may exist merely as conquered, enslaved countries, paying tribute to a foreign government, obeying its mandates, and crouching under its lash. A second mode would be, where the inferior states were

---

these employments of the day, parties are sent from the Catwall to patrol and watch through the town by night. In such governments, where the superiors are lost to all sense of humanity, the most execrable of villanies are perpetrated by this institution, designed to prevent them. The Catwall enters into treaty with a band of robbers, who receive from hence the intelligence necessary to direct their exploits, and in return pay to it a stipulated portion of their acquisitions: besides the concessions necessary to secure impunity when detected, one part of the band is appointed to break into houses, another assaults the traveller upon the road, a third a merchant upon the rivers. I have seen these regulated villains commit murders in the face of day, with such desperate audacity as nothing but the confidence of protection could inspire." Ibid. p. 452, 453.—M. This picture is evidently exaggerated, and belief cannot be readily granted to Orme's assertion that he had been an eye-witness of "murders" perpetrated in the face of day by organised assassins.

[1] Yet something of the kind has been at various times the political state of India, a number of independent princes acknowledged the supremacy of one amongst them, to whom, on particular occasions, they offered a kind of feudal homage, by performing menial services to his person, and with whom they held consultations on points of common interest. The Rajasuya sacrifice was a case of the former, and repeated instances of the latter occur in the Mahabharata. In modern times it is not uncommon for one Hindu prince to receive from another the tíka, or mark on the forehead, which denotes sovereignty, and of which the grant is a proof of supremacy. See Annals of Mewar in Tod's Rajasthan, i. 211.—W.

connected together by confederacy, and acknowledged a common head for the sake of unity, but possessed the right of deliberating in common upon common concerns. It may, with confidence, be pronounced, that in neither mode is the supposed effect compatible with the state of civilization in Hindustan.

To retain any considerable number of countries in subjection, preserving their own government, and their own sovereigns, would be really arduous, even where the science of government were the best understood. To suppose it possible in a country where the science of government is in the state indicated by the laws and institutions of the Hindus, would be in the highest degree extravagant. Even the Romans themselves, with all the skill which they possessed, retained their provinces in subjection, only by sending thither their own governors and their own armies, and superseding entirely the ancient authorities of the country. The moderation of conquering, without seizing, is a phenomenon so rarely exemplified in the most civilized times, that to suppose it universal in India, is to make a supposition in contradiction to the known laws of human affairs, and even to particular experience. Wherever an Indian sovereign is able to take possession, he hastens to take it. Wherever he can make a plundering incursion, though unable to retain, he ravages and destroys. Now it sometimes happens, that a neighbouring prince, too weak to prevent or chastise these injuries, endeavours to purchase exemption from them by a composition. This, in the language of the Mahrattas, who, in modern times, have been almost the only people in India in a situation to exact it, is called *Chout*, of which the standard is a fourth part of the revenues of the district liable to be over-run. It has, in several instances, and these abundantly recent ones, been paid, for certain districts, by the British government itself, without the most distant idea of any lordship paramount in the Mahrattas. It is abundantly evident that this species of subordination, if subordination it can be called, never could have extended far; never could reach beyond the countries immediately contiguous to that from which the chance of mischief arose.

A confederation of princes, similar to that which was exemplified in Germany, and which no combination of circumstances has elsewhere produced, is a supposition, still more opposed to experience. Of all the results of civilization, that of forming a combination of different states, and directing their powers to one common object, seems to be one of the least consistent with the mental habits and attainments of the Hindus.[1] It is the want of this power of combination which has rendered India so easy a conquest to all invaders; and enables us to retain, so easily, that dominion over it which we have acquired. Where is there any vestige in India of that deliberative assembly of princes, which in Germany was known by the name of the Diet? Where is there any memorial of that curious constitution by which the union of the German princes was preserved; or of those elections by which they chose among themselves him who should be at their head? That nominal homage, which the Mahratta chiefs paid to the throne of Sivajee, was a temporary circumstance, entirely of a different nature. These chiefs were not subordinate princes, but revolted subjects, in a dismembered empire. There was among them no confederacy. When at war with Sindia, the British were at peace with the Peshwa and Holkar; when they were at war with Holkar, they were at peace with the rest. They acknowledged a subordination to the primary seat of government, only because their subjects had been accustomed to look to it; and because they were not yet secure of their obedience.[2]

They, who affirm the high state of civilization among

[1] They have always allowed themselves to be conquered in detail, just as the tribes of Gauls and Germans by the Romans. Gaul, however, cost Julius Cæsar himself five years to subdue; and it several times carried fire and sword to the gates of Rome. The Gauls must have known much more of the art of war than the Hindus. See the fine generalship of Vercingetorix, described by the conqueror himself, in the 7th book of his Commentaries; and analysed by Guischardt, Mémoires Militaires sur les Grecs et les Romains, ch. xvi.—"The most remarkable of these new states were the Polygars of Chittledroog, Raidroog, Harponelly, Tarrikera, with many others of inferior note, whose united efforts might have opposed a respectable barrier to Mohammedan encroachment, if united efforts could be expected from restless savages, perpetually occupied by intestine quarrels." (Wilks' Hist. Sketches, p. 63.) Wilks says (p. 23) that the Hindu character exhibits but few shades of distinction, wheresoever found. It follows, that nowhere is it far removed from the savage state.

[2] To some persons it may be of use to hear, that the sober good sense of Major Rennel makes him reject the theory of union. History gives us the most positive assurances, that India was divided into a number of kingdoms or states, from the time of Herodotus down to that of Acbar." (Rennel's Mem. Introd. p. xxxii.)

the Hindus previous to their subjugation to foreigners, proceed so directly in opposition to evidence, that wherever the Hindus have been always exempt from a dominion of foreigners, there they are uniformly found in a state of civilization inferior to those who have long been the subjects of a Mahomedan throne.[1]

It is in no quarter pretended, that the Hindu superstition was ever less gross than it now appears. It is remarkable, that in any quarter it should not be recollected, that superstition necessarily gives way as civilization advances. Powerful, at an early age, among the Greeks and Romans, it finally ceased to have almost any influence;[2] and Goguet had long ago declared, with philosophical truth, that "we wanted no evidence to prove the ignorance and rudeness of the Greeks in the heroic times; their credulity, and their respect for oracles, are proofs more than sufficient. This species of superstition has no force or dominion, but in proportion to the gross ignorance of the people: witness the savages, who do not undertake anything till they have previously consulted their divines and their oracles."[3]

So many regulations are found in the Hindu code of law respecting seasons of calamity; seasons when it is supposed that a great portion of the people are without the means of subsistence, that those dreadful visitations must

[1] Witness Nepaul, and the strong districts along the Malabar coast, where the reign of the Hindu princes had not been at all or very little disturbed. For an account of Nepaul, see the history of Col. Kirkpatrick's embassy; and of the Malabar coast, among other works, Voyage de P. Paolino; Sonnerat; and Anquetil Duperron; above all, the Journey of Dr. Buchanan through Mysore, Canara, and Malabar.—"Mr. Wilford states, in the ninth volume of the Asiatic Researches, that the kings of Behar or Magadha were for many ages the sovereigns or lords-paramount of India. If such was the case, their descendants must have degenerated exceedingly; for, at the period of the Mohammedan invasion, the Raja, instead of heading his army, in defence of his country and religion, shamefully absconded, leaving his capital, then a celebrated seat of Hindu learning (whence its name of Behar) so destitute, that it was taken by a detachment of 200 men, who put a number of the unopposing Brahmens to the sword, and plundered all the inhabitants." (Hist. of Bengal by Charles Stewart, Esq., p. 40.) Mr. Stewart speaks with judgment. Everything in the state of India, as it was originally found by the Mohammedans, bears testimony against the fiction of a great monarchy, great prosperity, and great civilization.—M. One great monarchy did not exist it is true: but there were many prosperous kingdoms. The Mohammedan conquest was not so simple a process as is here insinuated: it took them two centuries to get to Delhi.—W.

[2] "Quæ anus," says Cicero, "tam excors inveniri potest, quæ illa quæ quondam credebantur apud inferos portenta extimescat?" (De Nat. Deor. lib. ii. cap. 2.)

[3] Goguet, Origin of laws, part ii. book i. ch. iv. art. 8.

be very frequent. From which, soever, of these two great causes, famine, or the ravages of war, the frequency of those calamities arose, it equally bars the supposition of good government, and high civilization.[1]

If we apply the reflection, which has been much admired, that if a man were to travel over the whole world, he might take the state of the roads, that is, the means of internal communication in general, as a measure of the civilization; a very low estimate will be formed of the progress of the Hindus: "In India," says Rennel, "the roads are little better than paths, and the rivers without bridges."[2] "In Malabar," says Dr. Buchanan, speaking of the wretched state of the roads, "even cattle are little used for the transportation of goods, which are generally carried by porters."[3] The Emperor, Shah Jehan, constructed certain roads in Bengal, which were celebrated as prodigies; but the remains of them, Dr. Tennant remarks, sufficiently manifest that they can never have been good; and the admiration they excited proves nothing except the wretched condition of everything, under the name of road, which had been known in India before.[4] Another fact, of much importance, is, that a Mahomedan sovereign was the first who established Choultries; that is, Caravanseras, or houses of reception for travellers upon the road, of which, till that period, they had no experience. "This fact," says Mr. Forster, "also recorded in Dow's history, is well known amongst the natives."[5]

[1] In all parts of India, where things have not been altered by the influence of the Mohammedan government, the Hindus are found collected in villages, not in detached habitations; "a custom," says Millar, (English Gov. i. 70,) "introduced by necessity in times of extreme barbarity and disorder."—M. Famines still occasionally visit India: are they still ascribable to the same causes?—W.

[2] Rennel's Memoir, p. 6.

[3] Buchanan's Journey through Mysore, &c. ii. 434. "It is a fact, that there is not a road in the country made by Hindoos, except a few which lead to holy places." A View of the History, Literature, and Religion of the Hindus, &c. By the Rev. W. Ward, one of the Baptist Missionaries at Serampore, Introd. p. lviii.—M. The want of roads can scarcely be ascribed to the neglect of Hindu princes, seeing the greater part of the country had for so many centuries been under Mohammedan domination.—W.

[4] Tennant's Indian Recreations, ii. 13, 14, 323.—M. The road might have been a very good one when made by Shah Jehan. A very few years in India are sufficient to destroy any road that is not regularly kept in repair. Materials for "Roman roads" are deficient, and even they would not long resist the destructive effects of climate and vegetation.—W.

[5] Forster's Travels, i. 74.—Tennant's Indian Recreations, ii. 69.—M. The fact is more than doubtful. Had it been the case, they would have borne exclusively the Mohammedan appellation of Serai. Choultry and Dharamsálá are both Hindu names.—W.

Among the pretensions received without examination, that of enormous riches, found in India by the first Mahomedan conquerors, requires particular attention. If those accounts had not far exceeded all reasonable bounds, it would have been a matter of difficulty to prove the falsehood of them, except to those who were capable of estimating one circumstance, in any state of society, by its analogy with the rest. As the amount, however, stated by those authors, whose testimony has been adopted; by Ferishta, for example, followed by Dow; far exceeds the bounds, not of probability only, but of credibility; and affords decisive evidence of that Eastern exaggeration which, in matters of history, disdains to be guided by fact, the question is left free of any considerable difficulty.[1] These accounts refute themselves. We have, therefore, no testimony on the subject; for all that is presented to us in the shape of testimony, betrays itself to be merely fiction. We are left to our knowledge of circumstances, and to the inferences which they support. Now if the preceding induction, embracing the circumstances of Hindu society, is to be relied on, it will not be disputed, that a state of poverty and wretchedness, as far as the great body of the people are concerned, must have prevailed in India, not more in the times in which it has been witnessed by Europeans, than the times which preceded. A gilded throne, or the display of gold, silver, and precious stones, about the seat of a court, does not invalidate this inference. Only there, where gold and silver are scarce, can the profuse display of them about the monarch's person, either gratify the monarch's vanity, or dazzle, by its rarity, the eyes of the multitude. Perhaps there are few indications more decisive of a poor country, and a barbarous age, than the violent desire of exhibiting the precious metals and precious stones, as the characteristic marks and decorations of the chief magistrate.[2]

The science of political economy places this conclusion on the ground of demonstration. For the people to have

1 See some observations on Dow, by Mr. Edward Scott Waring, Tour to Sheeraz, p. 15.

2 Speaking of the Mohammedan governments in the Deccan, Colonel Wilks says: "These princes had arrived at that state of civilization in which gorgeous and awkward splendour covered the most gross political darkness.' (Historical Sketches, p. 65.)

been rich in gold and silver, these commodities must have circulated among them in the shape of money. But of gold and silver in the shape of money, no nation has more than what is in proportion to its exchangeable commodities. Now that ever the people of Hindustan were profusely supplied with commodities, everything in their manners, habits, government, and history, concur to disprove. There is, besides, a well-established fact, which ascertains the impossibility of their having abounded in gold and silver. Their commodities were not exchanged by the medium of the precious metals. The traffic of India, as in the rudest parts of the earth, was chiefly a traffic of barter;[1] and its taxes, as already seen, were paid in kind. It was not till the time of Akber that gold or silver was coined for circulation in the greatest part of India; antecedently to that period small pieces of copper were the only coin.[2] Up to the present hour, when the real signs of riches and civilisation are but just beginning to be understood, nothing has been more common with rash and superficial travellers, than to set down lofty accounts to the riches of almost every new country to which they repaired.[3]

[1] These assertions are all at variance with facts, but facts must give way to the "science of political economy." The trade of India with Rome and the Greek empire was maintained on their part, we know, from indisputable evidence, chiefly by the export of the precious metals. The passages of Tacitus and Pliny are well known, in which the prodigal exchange of silver for the spices and silks of India, is lamented as a national evil; and the author of the Periplus, and the laws of Justinian, both specify coin and bullion as articles of export to India. Nor is it more true that a gold and silver coinage was unknown till the time of Akbar. Great quantities of both, the date of which must commence long prior to the Mohammedan conquest, have been found in various parts of the country.—See Journal of the Asiatic Society of Bengal.—W.

[2] See the Analysis of Tooril Mull's System of Finance in British India Analyzed, i. 191. These copper pieces were called pulsiah or feloos, sixteen of which were reckoned equal to a Tunkah of base silver; a sort of coin, or rather medal, sometimes struck, at the pleasure of the king, not for use, but to make presents to foreign ambassadors, and others. "Trade must, therefore," says the author, "have been carried on chiefly by barter; the rents for the most part paid in kind."—In the Deccan, a gold and silver coin was known earlier; which the same author thinks must have been introduced by the intercourse of the Persians and Arabians, to whom the use of coin had been known nearly a thousand years before. (Ibid. p. 194.) See an instructive dissertation on this point in "Researches on India," by Q. Craufurd, Esq., i. 36—80. Yet this author, p. 80—84, is a firm believer in the great riches of India.

[3] Agatharchides gives the most magnificent description of the riches of the Sabæans. "Their expense of living, rivals the magnificence of princes. Their houses are decorated with pillars glistening with gold and silver. Their doors are crowned with vases, and beset with jewels; the interior of their houses corresponds with the beauty of their outward appearance, and all the riches of other countries are here exhibited in variety of profusion. (See the account extracted and translated, in Vincent's Periplus, part i. p. 33. See also Strabo,

BOOK II. CHAP. X.

As rude nations, still more than civilised, are incessantly harassed by the dangers, or following the gains of war, one of the first applications of knowledge is, to improve the military art. The Hindus have, at no period, been so far advanced in knowledge, as even to be aware of the advantage of discipline,[1] of those regular and simultaneous movements, upon which, in skilled warfare, almost everything depends. "In the Hindu armies," says Francklin, "no idea of discipline ever existed."[2] The rudeness of the military art in Indostan," says Mr. Orme, "can scarce be imagined but by those who have seen it. The infantry consists of a multitude of people assembled together without regard to rank and file."[3]

---

lib. xvi. p. 778.) In the barbarous state of the ancient Russian court at Moscow, there was the highest degree of magnificence and splendour. The Earl of Carlisle, giving an account of his embassy, says, that he could see nothing but gold and precious stones, in the robes of the Czar, and his courtiers.—The treasure of Sardanapalus, was a thousand myriads of talents of gold, at the lowest estimation, £44,174,999,760. (Herodot. lib. ii. cap. 150; Athenæi Deipnosop. lib. xii.; Gibbon sur la Monarchie des Medes, Miscel. Works, 8vo. Ed. iii. 68.)—"What is said to be given by David (1 Chron. xxii. 14, 15, 16, and xxix. 3, 4, 5,) and contributed by his princes, xxix. 6, 7, 8,) towards the building of the temple at Jerusalem, if valued by the Mosaic talents, exceeded the value of £800,000,000, of our money." (Prideaux, Connexion of the History of the Old and New Testament, i. 5. Edit. 5th.) The Arcadian who was sent ambassador to the court of the king of Persia, in the days of Agesilaus, saw through the glare of eastern magnificence. Ὁ δε Αντιοχος απηγγειλε προς τους μυριους, ὁτι βασιλευς αρτοκοπους, και οψοποιους, και οινοχοους, και θυρωρους παμπληθεις εχοι ανδρας δε, οἱ μαχοιντ' αν Ἑλλησι, πανυ ζητων ουκ αν εφη δυνασθαι ιδειν. προς δε τουτοις, και το των χρηματων πληθος αλαζονειαν οἱ γε δοκειν ειμαι εφη· επει και την ὑμνουμενην αν χρυσην πλατονον ουχ ἱκανην εφη ειναι τεττιγι σκιαν παρεχειν. Xenophontis Græcorum, &c. lib. vii. sect. 1, near the end.)

[1] Here again assertion and fact are at variance: whatever may have been the efficiency of the discipline in practice, there was no want of a theory of regular movements and arrangements for the march, array, encampment, and even the supply of troops. They are all repeatedly described in the Mahabhárata.—W.

[2] Francklin's Life of George Thomas, p. 103.

[3] Orme, on the Government and People of Indostan, p. 420. The exquisite ignorance and stupidity of the Mysoreans in the art of war, while yet a purely Hindu people, is strongly remarked by Orme. i. 207. In the following description appears the simplicity of the fortification of Hindu towns: "A place that hath eight cose in length and breadth, and on the skirts of which, on all the four sides. is a ditch, and above the ditch, on all the four sides, a wall or parapet, and on all the four sides of it are bamboos, and on the east or north side thereof, a hollow or covered way, such place is called Nigher, or a city; in the same manner, if it hath four cose in length and breadth, it is called Gherbut or a small city." Gentoo Code, ch. xiv. See also Motte's Journey to Orissa, As. An. Reg. i. 51, 67.—"The fortifications of places of the first order formerly consisted, and in many places still consist, in one or two thick walls, flanked with round or triangular towers. A wide and deep ditch is on the outside; but as the Hindus are unskilful in the construction of bridges, they always leave a causeway from the gate of the town over the ditch." The Abbé Dubois, p. 543. —See a curious testimony to the imperfection of the military art among the Mahrattas, (Broughton's Letters from a Mahratta Camp, p. 107, 108); and another still more remarkable, to the wretched pusillanimity of the Rajpoots,

Even medicine and surgery, to the cultivation of which so obvious and powerful an interest invites, had scarcely, beyond the degree of the most uncultivated tribes, attracted the rude understanding of the Hindus.[1] Though the leisure of the Brahmans has multiplied works on astrology, on the exploits of the gods, and other worthless subjects, to such a multitude "that human life," says Sir W. Jones, "would not be sufficient to make oneself acquainted with any considerable part of Hindu literature,"[2] he yet confesses, there is "no evidence that in any language of Asia, there exists one original treatise on medicine, considered as a science."[3] Surgery, says an author who believes in the high civilisation of the Hindus, is unknown among that people. In the case of gun-shot or sabre wounds, all they did was to wash the wound, and tie it up with fresh leaves; the patient, during the period of convalescence, eating nothing but the water-gruel of rice.[4]

---

those boasted descendants of the supposed magnanimous Cshatriyas, a pusillanimity, which, according to Mr. Broughton, forfeits their title even to pity, while "possessing so many advantages, they voluntarily bend their necks to one of the most galling yokes in the world." Ibid. p. 133.

[1] The expressions of Sir William Jones, to be properly understood, should have been quoted more in detail. He does not mean to say that the Hindus had not cultivated the practice of medicine; on the contrary, he says, "We have still access to a number of Sanscrit books on the old Indian practice of physic, from which, if the Hindus had a theoretical system, we might easily collect it." The value of a mere theoretical system of medicine is very small, and few medical men will condemn the Hindu works for containing only practical instruction. The real nature of the Hindu medical works is yet to be determined by translation. There is a very large body of medical literature in Sanscrit, and some of the principal works are named by Arabic writers, as having been known and translated at Bagdad, in the ninth century. These works comprise all the branches of medical science, surgery included; and, although mixed up with much that is irrational, contain numerous instances of accurate observation and judicious treatment. See *Calcutta Oriental Magazine*, 1823. Transactions, Medical and Physical Society of Calcutta, and Essay on the Antiquity of Hindoo Medicine, by Dr. Royle, London, 1837.—W.

[2] Asiat. Res. i. 354.

[3] Ibid. iv. 159.

[4] Craufurd's Sketches. Sir William Jones says, "We may readily believe those who assure us, that some tribes of wandering Tartars had real skill in applying herbs and minerals to the purpose of medicine;" the utmost pretended extent of the medical science of the Hindus. As. Res. ii. 40. See Tennant's Indian Recreations, for some important details, i. 357; Buchanan's Journey through Mysore, &c. i. 336.—"Medicine," says the last intelligent observer, "in this country has indeed fallen into the hands of charlatans equally impudent and ignorant." Ibid. "There are not indeed wanting several persons who prescribe in physic, play upon a variety of musical instruments, and are concerned in some actions and performances which seem at least to suppose some skill in nature or mathematics. Yet all this is learned merely by practice, long habit, and custom; assisted for the most part with great strength of memory, and quickness of invention." (Shaw's Travels, speaking of the people of Barbary, p. 263.) The good sense of Colonel Wilks has made that instructive

In comparing them with other people, it cannot, in a single word, be declared with which of the nations, more familiar to Europeans, the Hindus, in point of civilisation, may be regarded as on a level; because, in comparison with those whom they most nearly approach, while inferior to them in some, they are superior in other respects. Should we say that the civilisation of the people of Hindustan, and that of the people of Europe, during the feudal ages, are not far from equal, we shall find upon a close inspection, that the Europeans were superior,[1] in the first place, notwithstanding the vices of the papacy, in religion; and, notwithstanding the defects of the schoolmen, in philosophy. They were greatly superior, notwithstanding the defects in the feudal system, in the institutions of government and in laws. Even their poetry, if the observance of nature, if the power of moving the affections, or indeed ingenuity of invention, be regarded as the marks of excellence, is beyond all comparison preferable to the poetry of the Hindus.

---

writer use the followiug terms: " The golden age of India, like that of other regions, belongs exclusively to the poet. In the sober investigation of facts, this imaginary era recedes still further and further at every stage of the inquiry; and all that we find is still the empty praise of the ages which have passed.......... If the comparative happiness of mankind in different ages be measured by its only true and rational standard, namely, the degree of peace and security which they shall be found collectively and individually to possess, we shall certainly discover, in every successive step towards remote antiquity, a larger share of wretchedness to have been the portion of the human race...... The force of these observations, general in their nature, is perhaps more strongly marked in the history of India than of any other region of the earth. At periods long antecedent to the Mohammedan invasion, wars, revolutions, and conquests, seem to have followed each other, in a succession more strangely complex, rapid, and destructive, as the events more deeply recede into the gloom of antiquity. The rude valour, which had achieved a conquest, was seldom combined with the sagacity requisite for interior rule; and the fabric of the conquered state, shaken by the rupture of its ancients bonds, and the substitution of instruments, clumsy, unapt, and misapplied, either fell to sudden ruin, or gradually dissolved." Historical Sketches of the South of India, by Lieut.-Col. Mark Wilks, p. 1, 2.

[1] That Europeans in the feudal ages were superior in energy of character, may be admitted; but it may be doubted if they were equally advanced in civilization. They had, it is true, a better religion, but understood it little and practised it less. Education was less generally diffused; literature less honoured and less cultivated. They had no fixed standard of government, or written code of laws; their philosophy was less profound; their poetry more rude. In war, practically, they excelled the Hindus; they probably studied it less as a science. In manufactures, they were decidedly inferior, and so they were in agriculture and commerce. The manners of the higher ranks furnish abundant instances of profligacy, treachery, falsehood, and brutality; and those of the serf and bondsman, were not unlikely to afford examples of servility and deceit. Although, therefore, the state of civilization in Europe, in the feudal ages, contained in its restless activity the seeds of future improvement, yet there can be little doubt, that from the tenth to the twelfth century, the superiority of civilization was on the side of the Hindus.—W.

That, in war, the Hindus have always been greatly inferior to the warlike nations of Europe, during the middle ages, it seems hardly necessary to assert.[1] In some of the more delicate manufactures, however, particularly in spinning, weaving, and dyeing, the Hindus, as they rival all nations, so they no doubt surpass all that was attained by the rude Europeans. In the fabrication, too, of trinkets; in the art of polishing and setting the precious stones; it is possible, and even probable, that our impatient and rough ancestors did not attain the same nicety which is displayed by the patient Hindus. In the arts of painting and sculpture, we have no reason to think that the Europeans were excelled by the Hindus. In architecture, the people who raised the imposing structures which yet excite veneration in many of the ancient cathedrals, were not left behind by the builders of the Indian pagodas.[2] The agriculture of the Europeans, imperfect as it was, surpassed exceedingly that of the Hindus; for, with the climate and soil of most of the countries of Europe, agriculture, so imperfect as that of India, could not have maintained the population. In point of manners and character, the manliness and courage of our ancestors, compared with the slavish and dastardly spirit of the Hindus, place them in an elevated rank. But they

[1] The barbarians from Germany and Scythia quickly learned the discipline of the Roman armies, and turned their own arts against the legions. See Gibbon, vii. 377. The Hindus have never been able, without European officers, to avail themselves of European discipline.

[2] The monastery of Bangor, demolished by Adelfrid, the first king of Northumberland, was so extensive, that there was a mile's distance from one gate of it to another, and it contained two thousand one hundred monks, who are said to have been there maintained by their own labour. (Hume's England, i. 41.) "Les Etrusques, prédécesseurs des Romains, et les premiers peuples de l'Italie sur lesquels l'histoire jette quelque lueur.......... paroissent avoir devancé les Grecs dans la carrière des sciences et des arts, bien qu'ils n'aient pas pu, comme leurs successeurs, la parcourir toute entière. Les poètes ont placé au milieu d'eux l'age d'or sous le règne de Saturne, et leurs fictions n'ont voilé qu'à demi la vérité.—Comme nous ne savons pas même le nom des écrivains Etrusques ou Tyrrhéniens, et que ces peuples ne nous sont connus que par quelques fragmens d'historiens Grecs et Latins, ils resteront toujours enveloppés d'une grande obscurité. Cependant nous avons une indication de leur puissance, dans les murailles colossales de Volterra; de leur goût, dans les vases qui nous sont restés d'eux; de leur savoir, dans le culte de Jupiter Elicius, auquel ils attribuèrent l'art qu'ils connurent et que nous avons retrouvés, d'éviter et de diriger la foudre." Simonde de Sismondi, Hist. des Rép. Ital. Introd. p. iii. These Tuscans cannot have been advanced beyond the stage of semi-barbarism; and yet here are proofs of a progress in the arts, with which the Hindus have nothing to compare.—The Afghauns use a water-mill for grinding their corn. "It is also used in the north of India, under the Sireenugger hills; but, in general, no water-mills are known in India, where all grain is ground with the hand." Elphinstone's Caubul, p. 307.

BOOK II. CHAP. X.

were inferior to that effeminate people in gentleness, and the winning arts of address. Our ancestors, however, though rough, were sincere; but, under the glosing exterior of the Hindu, lies a general disposition to deceit and perfidy. In fine, it cannot be doubted that, upon the whole, the Gothic nations, as soon as they became a settled people, exhibit the marks of a superior character and civilisation to those of the Hindus.[1]

No one can take an accurate survey of the different nations of Asia, and of their different ages, without remarking the near approaches they make to the same stage of civilisation. This gives a peculiar interest and importance to the inquiry respecting the Hindus. There can be no doubt that they are in a state of civilization very nearly the same with that of the Chinese, the Persians, and the Arabians; who, together, compose the great branches of the Asiatic population; and of which the subordinate nations, the Japanese

[1] The Hindus are often found to be orderly and good servants at Calcutta, Madras, &c. This is but a fallacious proof of civilization. Hear Lord Macartney in his account of Russia. "All the inhabitants of Siberia, Casan, and the eastern provinces of Russia, to the sea of Kamschatka, who are not Christians, are confounded under the general name of Tartars. Many of these come to the capital in order to procure employment, either as workmen or domestics, and are exceedingly sober, acute, dexterous, and faithful." Barrow's Life of Lord Macartney, ii. 26. "Calmuck servants are greatly esteemed all over Russia, for their intelligence and fidelity." Mr. Heber's Journal, in Clarke's Travels in Russia, p. 241. "I recollect," adds Mr. Clarke, "seeing some of them in that capacity among English families in Petersburg. The most remarkable instance ever known of an expatriated Calmuck, was that of an artist employed by the Earl of Elgin, whom I saw (a second Anacharsis, from the plains of Scythia) executing most beautiful designs among the ruins of Athens. Some Russian family had previously sent him to finish his studies in Rome, where he acquired the highest perfection in design. He had the peculiar features, and many of the manners, of nomade Calmucks." Ibid. The negroes, when properly treated, make faithful, affectionate, and good servants.—But it is more than doubtful whether the Hindus do in reality make those good servants we have heard them called. Dr. Gilchrist says (Preface to his Hindostani Dictionary, printed at Calcutta, 1787, p. 27)—and Lord Teignmouth repeats, (Considerations, &c. on communicating to the Natives of India the Knowledge of Christianity, p. 82) "that he cannot hesitate about believing the fact—*that among a thousand servants of all descriptions whom he had intrusted and employed, he had the luck to meet with one only whom he knew to be upright in his conduct.*" By the author of that interesting little book, entitled Sketches in India, or Observations descriptive of the Scenery, &c. in Bengal, written in India in the years 1811, 1812, 1813, 1814, p. 13, we are told that when you are travelling in India, "An object of attention which must excite peculiar attention in every honourable mind, is the thefts and depredations which are apt to be committed at every bazaar or market, and indeed whenever opportunity offers, both by your own servants and the boatmen. Astonishing as this may seem, it is an undoubted fact that these people pillage every step they take; and, to escape the just indignation of the sufferers, shelter themselves under the name of their innocent masters, to whom these poor wretches are often afraid to refer."

Cochin-chinese, Siamese, Burmans, and even Malays and Tibetians are a number of corresponding and resembling offsets.

With regard to former ages, it is true, that the religion, and several circumstances in the outward forms of society, have been altered in Persia, since the days of Darius: but the arts, the sciences, the literature, the manners, the government, concur to prove, in a remarkable manner, the near approach of the two periods to the same points of civilisation. The ancient Persians, too, there is reason to believe, were placed in nearly the same state of society with the people whom they succeeded; the Chaldeans, Assyrians, and Babylonians. In contemplating, therefore, the state of Hindustan, curiosity is very extensively gratified. As the manners, institutions, and attainments of the Hindus have been stationary for many ages; in beholding the Hindus of the present day, we are beholding the Hindus of many ages past; and are carried back, as it were, into the deep recesses of antiquity. Of some of the oldest nations, about which our curiosity is most alive, and information the most defective, we acquire a practical, and what may be almost denominated a personal knowledge, by our acquaintance with a living people, who have continued on the same soil from the very times of those ancient nations, partake largely of the same manners, and are placed at nearly the same stage in the progress of society. By conversing with the Hindus of the present day, we, in some measure, converse with the Chaldeans and Babylonians of the time of Cyrus; with the Persians and Egyptians of the time of Alexander.

A judicious observer of Asiatic manners declares that "The leading customs of the various nations of Asia are similar, or but weakly diversified. When they sit, the legs are crossed or bent under them; they perform topical ablutions before and after meals, at which no knife or spoon is used, unless the diet be wholly liquid; they invariably adopt the like modes of performing natural evacuations."[1]

The account which Gibbon presents us, from Herodian and Ammianus Marcellinus, of the art of war among the Persians, in the time of the Roman emperors, is an exact description of the art, as practised by the Persians and

[1] Forster's Travels, ii. 135.

Hindus, and by most other nations of Asia, at the present day. "The science of war, that constituted the more rational force of Greece and Rome, as it now does of Europe, never made any considerable progress in the East. Those disciplined evolutions which harmonise and animate a confused multitude, were unknown to the Persians. They were equally unskilled in the arts of constructing, besieging, or defending regular fortifications. They trusted more to their numbers than to their courage: more to their courage than to their discipline. The infantry was a half-armed, spiritless crowd of peasants, levied in haste by the allurements of plunder, and as easily dispersed by a victory as by a defeat. The monarch and his nobles transported into the camp the pride and luxury of the seraglio. Their military operations were impeded by a useless train of women, eunuchs, horses, and camels; and in the midst of a successful campaign, the Persian host was often separated or destroyed by an unexpected famine."[1]

In the system of Zoroaster, and that of the Brahmens, we find the same lofty expressions concerning the invisible powers of nature; the same absurdity in the notions respecting the creation; the same infinite and absurd ritual; the same justness in many ideas respecting the common affairs of life and morality; the same gross misunderstanding in others; but a striking resemblance between the two systems, both in their absurdities and perfections. The same turn of imagination seems to have belonged to the authors of both; and the same aspect of nature to have continually presented itself; the deformities, however, of the Hindu system being always the greatest.

The Persians, in the time of Cambyses, had judges, select sages, who were appointed for life; and whose business it was, according to pre-established laws, to terminate all disputes, and punish crimes. This, like similar circumstances, in the state of the Hindus, presents part of the forms of a legal government.[2] These judges, however, when consulted by the king if he might perform an act, on which, for fear of popular odium, he hesitated to venture, gave a solemn opinion, *that for the king of the Persians it was law, to do*

[1] Gibbon, i. 342.

[2] The text shows clearly, that it is idle to compare the Hindus with the ancient Persians; the means of estimating the civilization of the latter are too defective.—W.

whatsoever he pleased.[1] "This *constitutional maxim*," says Gibbon archly, "was not neglected as a useless and barren theory."[2]

"Like Brimha, the Fo of the Chinese has various times become incarnate among men and beasts. Hence, he is represented in his temples as riding upon dragons, rhinoceroses, elephants, mules and asses: dogs, rats, cats, crocodiles, and other amiable creatures, whose figures he fancied and assumed. There are in some of these pagodas, a thousand of these monstrous statues, all most horribly ugly, and ill represented, and unlike anything in heaven or earth, or the waters under the earth."[3]

Under the reign of credulity, it is instructive to mark the inconsiderateness of a reflecting writer. After many praises of the Chinese husbandry, such as those which we have often heard of the agriculture of the Hindus, Lord Macartney adds, "The plough is the simplest in the world, has but one handle, is drawn by a single buffalo, and managed by a single person without any assistance."[4] And Mr. Barrow says, "Two-thirds of the small quantity of land under tillage is cultivated with the spade or the hoe, without the aid of draught cattle."[5]

Even of the principal route from Pekin to Canton, Lord Macartney remarks, "For horse and foot the road is excellent, but admits of no wheel-carriages."[6] Mr. Barrow more expli-

[1] Οι δε βασιληιοι δικασται κεκριμμενοι ανδρες γινονται Περσεων, ες ου αποθανωσι, η σφι παρευρεθη τι αδικον μεχρι τουτων· ουτοι δε τοισι δικας δικαζουσι και εξηγηται των πατριων θεσμων γινονται και παντα ες τουτους ανακειται· ειρομενου ὠν του Καμβυσεω ὑπεκρινοντο αυτω ουτοι .... τῳ βασιλευοντι Περσεων εξειναι ποιεειν τα αν βουληται. Herodot. Hist. lib. iii. cap. xxx. This, Sir William Jones would have said, is a despotism limited by law; and thus the government of the ancient Persians stood upon a foundation resembling that of the Hindus.

[2] Gibbon, Hist. Decl. and Fall, &c. vii. 304. Some ancient sculpture in the vicinity of Shahpoor in honour of Sapòr the First, "represents a king, seated in state, amid a group of figures standing before him, one of whom offers two heads to the monarch's notice. If we wanted other evidence, this alone would mark the state of civilization to which a nation had advanced, that could suffer its glory to be perpetuated by a representation of so barbarous a character." Sir John Malcolm, Hist. of Persia, i. 254. No historical writings in ancient Persia: none in Hindustan.

[3] Lord Macartney's Journal, Barrow's Life of Lord Macartney, ii. 279. In reading this passage, one seems to be reading an account of Hindu religion, temples, and sculpture.

[4] Lord Macartney's Journal, Barrow's Life of Lord Macartney, ii. 357.

[5] Barrow's China, p. 585. A large portion of the country, wet, swampy ground, the rich alluvium of rivers, which might be easily gained; if the Chinese had but the skill. Ibid. p. 70, 83, 208, 533.

[6] Barrow's Life of Lord Macartney, ii. 357.

BOOK II. CHAP. X.

citly declares, that except near the capital, and in some few places where the junction of the grand canal with navigable rivers is interrupted by mountainous ground, there is scarcely a road in the whole country that can be ranked beyond a foot-path.[1] Even the grand canal itself was opened by the Tartar conqueror Gingis Khan, in the thirteenth century; and that solely with a view to convey the taxes, paid in kind, from the southern part of the empire to the capital, a great part of them having been always lost by the unskilfulness of Chinese navigation, when conveyed by sea."[2]

Like the Hindus, before the improvements introduced among them by the Moguls, the Chinese have no coin, above a small one of copper; and the taxes of that immense empire are paid in kind.[3]

Lord Macartney remarks that the Chinese have no natural philosophy; no medical or chirurgical skill: that a fractured leg is usually attended by death.[4]

In the sciences and arts of the Hindus and Chinese there is manifested a near approximation to the same point of advancement. In respect to government and laws, the Chinese have to a considerable degree the advantage.[5] As they are a busy people, however; and have no idle class, whose influence depends upon the wonder they can excite by pretended learning, they have multiplied, far less than the Hindus, those false refinements, which a barbarous mind mistakes for science.[6] Both have made greater progress in

[1] Barrow's China, p. 513.

[2] Ibid. p. 43.

[3] Ibid. p. 561, 499.

[4] Barrow's Life of Lord Macartney, ii. 363.

[5] It would be difficult to prove where the advantage lies. Throughout this comparison, the analogies either do not exist at all, as in the case of the absence of a current coin, or they are too vague and universal to authorize a conclusion. There is one great advantage as a proof and means of civilization possessed by the Hindus, in the use of a perfect alphabet. The cumbrous contrivance of the Chinese symbols, must ever impede the advancement of knowledge amongst them. At the same time, the Chinese are in many respects a civilized people, with whom it is no discredit to the Hindus to be compared.—W.

[6] Lord Macartney remarks, that the Chinese had a very limited knowledge of mathematics and astronomy, "although from some of the printed accounts of China one might be led to imagine that they were well versed in them." "Their affectation of the science of astronomy or astrology (for they have but one word in their language to express both,) induced them at a very remote period to establish a mathematical college or tribunal, the duty of which is to furnish to the nation an annual calendar, somewhat like our ***Poor Robin's Almanack***, with lists of all the lucky and unlucky days of the year, predictions of the weather, directions for sowing and reaping, &c. This branch entirely belongs to the Chinese doctors, who are chosen for the purpose from among the most celebrated philomaths of the nation." Ibid. p. 481; See too Barrow's China, 284, 291, 292, 295, 323.

the refinement of useful arts, than in the advancement of science. But in these, too, the Chinese appear to have the superiority; for, though it may be doubted whether the Chinese manufacture of silk rivals in delicacy, the cotton manufacture of the Hindus, the latter people have nothing to set in competition with the porcelain of the Chinese; and in the common works in wood and iron, the Chinese are conspicuously preferable. In the contrivance and use of machinery both are eqnally simple and rude.[1]

In the state of the fine arts, there is a striking resemblance between the two nations. "The architecture of the Chinese," says Mr. Barrow, "is void of taste, grandeur, beauty, solidity, or convenience; their houses are merely tents, and there is nothing magnificent in the palace of the emperor."[2] Both nations were good at imitation.[3] Both were extremely defective in inventions. In painting and sculpture they were ignorant of perspective, of attitude, and proportion.

Even in manners, and in the leading parts of the moral character, the lines of resemblance are strong. Both nations are to nearly an equal degree tainted with the vices of insincerity; dissembling, treacherous, mendacious, to an excess which surpasses even the usual measure of uncultivated society. Both are disposed to excessive exaggeration with regard to everything relating to themselves. Both are cowardly and unfeeling. Both are in the highest degree conceited of themselves, and full of affected contempt for others. Both are, in the physical sense, disgustingly unclean in their persons and houses.[4]

1 Barrow's China, p. 311, 512.

2 Barrow's China, p. 101—330.

3 Ibid. p. 306, 323.

4 Similar traces are found in the following character of the Persians, drawn by a recent observer, Mr. Scott Waring, Tour to Sheeraz. "Mean and obsequious to their superiors and to their equals, if they have a prospect of advantage; but invariably arrogant and brutal in their behaviour towards their inferiors; always boasting of some action they never performed, and delighted with flattery, though they are aware of the imposition. I have repeatedly heard them compliment a person in his hearing, or in the presence of some one who would convey this adulation to his ears; and the instant that he has departed, their praises have turned into abuse." p. 101. "Not the least reliance is to be placed on their words or most solemn protestations." . . . . "They conceive it their duty to please; and to effect this, they forget all sentiments of honour and good faith." . . . . . "The Persians have but a faint notion of gratitude, for they cannot conceive that any one should be *guilty* of an act of generosity, without some sinister motive." p. 103. "Philosophers have held it for a maxim, that the most notorious liar utters a hundred truths for every falsehood. This is not the case in Persia; they are unacquainted with the *beauty of truth*, and only think of it when it is likely to advance their interests." . . . . "The generality of Persians are sunk in the lowest state of profligacy and infamy; and they seldom hesitate alluding to crimes

BOOK II. CHAP. X.

With respect to the inhabitants of another quarter of Asia, Turner, in his account of the embassy to Tibet, informs us, that the deportment of the Rajah of Bootan was exceedingly urbane, and his sentiments breathed that sort of humanity which seems to flow from the belief of the metempsychosis. "My food," said he, "consists of the simplest articles: grain, roots of the earth, and fruit. I never eat of anything which has had breath, for so I should be the indirect cause of putting an end to the existence of animal life, which, by our religion, is strictly forbidden.[1]

Though frequent ablutions are performed for religious purposes, the same author informs us that the people, in their persons, are extremely unclean.[2]

"Bootan presents to the view nothing but the most misshapen irregularities: mountains covered with eternal verdure, and rich with abundant forests of large and lofty trees. Almost every favourable aspect of them, coated with the smallest quantity of soil, is cleared and adapted to cultivation, by being shelved into horizontal beds; not a slope, or narrow slip of land between the ridges, lies unimproved. There is scarcely a mountain whose base is not washed by some rapid torrent, and many of the loftiest bear populous villages, amidst orchards, and other plantations on their summits, and on their sides. It combines, in its extent, the most extravagant tracts of rude nature and laborious art." [3]

Yet they have no discipline in their armies. In their

---

which are abhorred and detested in every civilized country in the universe.' The following is an important observation. (Voyage dans l'Empire Othomane l'Egypte, et la Perse, par G. A. Olivier, v. 120.) En Europe, il y a un espace immense entre les habitans des grandes villes et ceux des campagnes, entrs l'homme bien élevé et celui qui ne l'est pas. En Perse, nous n'avons pa- trouvé que cet espace fut bien grand: la classe pauvre des villes diffère très, peu, pour l'esprit, les connaissance et les mœurs, de l'habitant des campagnes et il n'y a pas non plus une grande difference, dans les villes, entre les riches et les pauvres. C'est presque partout la même conduite, la même allure, la même manière de s'exprimer; ce sont les mêmes idées, et j'oserais presque dire la même instruction. Ici l'habitant des campagnes, celui-là même qui se trouve toute l'année sous la tente, et qui conduit ses troupeaux d'un pâturage à un autre, nous a paru plus délié, plus rusé, plus poli, plus instruit, que le cultivateur Européen un peu éloigné des grandes villes."

[1] Turner's Embassy to Tibet, book i. ch. iv.

[2] Ibid.

[3] Turner's Embassy to Tibet, book ii. ch. ii. The agriculture is promoted by artificial irrigation, the water being conveyed to the fields through hollow cylinders, formed of the trunks of trees. Ibid. book i. ch. vi.

mode of warfare, stratagem is more practised than open assault.[1]

The appearance of the capital, Teshoo Loomboo, was in a high degree magnificent, and, together with the palace, afforded proofs of a progress in the arts which vied with that of Hindustan and China.[2]

The inhabitants of the great Peninsula, to the eastward of the Ganges, discover, as far as known, the uniform marks of a similar state of society and manners. The Cochin-Chinese, for example, who are merely a separate community of the Chinese race, appear by no means in civilization behind the Chinese and Hindus. A traveller from whom we have obtained a sensible, though short, account of some of the more striking phenomena of the country, both physical and moral, informs us, that it is "one of the most fruitful in the world. In many parts," he says, "the land produces three crops of grain in the year. All the fruits of India are found here in the greatest perfection, with many of those of China. No country in the East produces richer, or a greater variety of articles, proper for carrying on an advantageous commerce; cinnamon, pepper, cardamoms, silk, cotton, sugar, Aquila wood, Japan wood, ivory, &c."[3]

The following paragraph describes an important article of accommodation, to which no parallel can be found in all China and Hindustan. "In this valley we passed through three or four pretty villages pleasantly situated, in which, as well as on other parts of the road, were public houses, where tea, fruits, and other refreshments, are sold to travellers. At noon, we alighted at one of them, and partook of a dinner, which consisted of fowls, cut into small pieces, dressed up with a little greens and salt, some fish, &c."[4]

[1] Turner's Embassy to Tibet, book i. ch. vi.

[2] Ibid. book ii. ch. ii.

[3] Narrative of a Voyage to Cochin-China in 1778, by Mr. Chapman, in the Asiatic Annual Register for 1801, Miscellaneous Tracts, p. 85.

[4] Ibid. p. 72. Of China, Mr. Barrow says, "There are no inns in any part of this vast empire; or, to speak more correctly (for there are resting-places,) no inhabited and furnished houses where, in consideration of paying a sum of money, a traveller may purchase the refreshments of comfortable rest, and of allaying the calls of hunger. The state of society admits of no such accommodation. What they call inns are mean hovels, consisting of bare walls, where, perhaps, a traveller may procure his cup of tea for a piece of copper money, and permission to pass the night; but this is the extent of the comforts which such places hold." Barrow's China, p. 241. Such is the description of the Indian choultries; empty buildings into which the traveller may

BOOK II. CHAP. X.

The appearance of a king's court was not only splendid' but decorous: and even the little of the country which the travellers saw, discovered to them large cities, with streets laid out on a regular plan, paved with flat stones, and having well-built brick houses on each side.[1]

The people on the western side of that peninsula, whether known by the name of Birmans, Peguans, Assamese, or Siamese, partake strongly of the Hindu character, and exhibit only a variation of the religion, laws, institutions, and manners which prevail on the other side of the Ganges. The great difference consists in their having adopted the heresy, or retained the primitive faith of Buddha; and rejected the distinction of castes. But nothing appears among them which would lead to an inference of any inferiority in their progress towards the attainments of civilized life.

The Birmans, we are told by Symes, call their code generally Derma Sath, or Sastra; it is one among the many commentaries on Menu. "The Birman systêm of jurisprudence," he adds, "is replete with sound morality, and in my opinion, is distinguished above every other Hindoo commentary for perspicuity and good sense. It provides specifically for almost every species of crime that can be committed, and adds a copious chapter of precedents and decisions to guide the inexperienced in cases where there

---

retire, but into which he must carry with him every accommodation, of which he stands in need. "The Khans, or Caravanseras," says Volney, speaking of another Asiatic country, Syria, "afford only cells for the accommodation of travellers, with bare walls, dust, and sometimes scorpions. The keeper gives the lodger a key and a mat, and he must find everything else himself." Travels in Egypt, &c., ii. 420. "In the inland towns and villages of Barbary, there is, for the most part, a house set apart for the reception of strangers, with a proper officer (the Maharak, I think they call him) to attend it. Here persons are lodged and entertained, for one night, in the best manner the place will afford, at the expense of the community." Shaw's Travels, Pref. p. ii.

[1] Chapman's Voyage, ubi supra, p. 73, 76. Sir George Staunton says, Embassy of Lord Macartney, i. 389: "The Cochin-Chinese seemed sufficiently dexterous and attentive, though with scarcely any principles of science, to make, on any substances which promised to be of use or comfort to them in private life, such trials and experiments. as were likely to produce beneficial results. In the culture of their lands, and in the few manufactures exercised amongst them, they were not behind nations where the sciences flourish." "Though these people possessed not scientifically the art of reducing the metallic ore into the metal, they had attained the practice, for example, of making very good iron, as well as of manufacturing it afterwards into matchlocks, spears, and other weapons. Their earthenware was very neat. Their dexterity appeared in every operation they undertook," p. 387.

is doubt and difficulty. Trial by ordeal and imprecation, are the only absurd passages in the book." [1]

"There is no country of the East," says the same author, "in which the royal establishment is arranged with more minute attention than in the Birman Court; it is splendid without being wasteful, and numerous without confusion." [2]

Their literature appears to be as extensive and curious, as that of the Hindus.[3] They have numerous, and copious libraries: the books, says Colonel Symes, are "upon divers subjects; more on divinity, than on any other; but history, music, medicine, painting, and romance, had their separate treatises." [4]

Of the kingdom of Assam, we possess not many accounts; but what we have, yield evidence to the same effect. In the Alemgeernameh of Mohammed Cazim, is a description of Assam, which has been translated by Henry Vansittart, Esq., and presented to us in several publications. We are there told that the country, at least in many places, is "well inhabited, and in an excellent state of tillage; that it presents, on every side, charming prospects of ploughed fields, harvests, gardens, and groves." [5]

"As the country is overflowed in the rainy seasons, a high and broad causeway has been raised for the convenience of travellers from Salagereh to Ghergong, which is the only uncultivated ground to be seen: each side of this road is planted with shady bamboos, the tops of which meet and are entwined." [6] And this is more than seems to have been attained in Hindustan, before the improvements introduced by the Mohammedan conquerors.

"The silks are excellent, and resemble those of China.

[1] Symes' Embassy to Ava, ii. 326.—The following, too, are abundantly similar to corresponding features in the character of the Hindus. The Birmans, in some points of their disposition, display the ferocity of barbarians, and in others all the humanity and tenderness of polished life. They inflict the most savage vengeance on their enemies. As invaders, desolation marks their track: for they spare neither sex nor age. But at home they assume a different character. Ibid.

[2] Ibid.

[3] The civilization of the Burmese and the Tibetans, such as it is, is derived from India, along with the religion and literature of the Buddhists. Natural and political impediments have opposed their improvement to a much greater extent than similar obstacles in India.—W.

[4] Symes' Embassy to Ava, iii. 96.

[5] See description of the Kingdom of Assam, &c., Asiat. An. Register for 1800, Miscellaneous Tracts, p. 43.

[6] Ibid.

BOOK II.
CHAP. X.

They are successful in embroidering with flowers, and in weaving velvet, and tautband, which is a species of silk of which they make tents and kenauts."[1]

The bigoted and intolerant Mussulman, however, who finds no excellence where he finds not his faith; discovers no qualities but evil in the minds of the Assamese. "They do not adopt," he says, "any mode of worship practised either by heathens or Mahomedans: nor do they concur in any of the known sects, which prevail amongst mankind. They are a base and unprincipled nation, and have no fixed religion; they follow no rules but that of their own inclinations, and make the approbation of their own vicious minds the test of the propriety of their actions."[2] Such are the distorted views presented to an ignorant mind, through the medium of a dark and malignant religion, respecting a people cultivating the ground to great perfection, and forming a dense population. Among other particulars of the vileness which he beheld in them, is the following: "The base inhabitants, from a congenial impulse, are fond of seeing and keeping asses, and buy and sell them at a high price."[3] Yet he speaks in lofty terms of the royal magnificence of the court. "The Rajahs of this country have always raised the crest of pride and vain glory, and displayed an ostentatious appearance of grandeur, and a numerous train of attendants and servants." And he expresses himself with a mingled horror and admiration of the prowess and superiority of the Assamese in war. "They have not bowed the head of submission and obedience, nor have they paid tribute or submission to the most powerful monarch; but they have curbed the ambition, and checked the conquests of the most victorious princes of Hindustan." Several armies from Bengal, which had been sent to conquer them, having been cut off, of some of which scarce even tidings had ever been received, "the natives of Hindustan consider them wizards and magicians, and pronounce the name of that country in all their incantations and countercharms: they say that every person who sets his foot there, is

[1] See description of the Kingdom of Assam, &c., Asiat. An. Register for 1800., Miscellaneous Tracts, p. 43.

[2] See Description of the Kingdom of Assam, &c. p. 45.

[3] Ibid.

under the influence of witchcraft, and cannot find the road to return."[1]

The admiration which the Greeks, no very accurate observers of foreign manners, expressed of the Egyptians, and which other nations have so implicitly borrowed at their hands, not a little resembles the admiration among Europeans which has so long prevailed with regard to the Hindus. The penetrating force of modern intelligence has pierced the cloud: and while it has displayed to us the state of Egyptian civilization in its true colours, exhibits a people who, standing on a level with so many celebrated nations of antiquity, Assyrians, Babylonians, Persians, Arabians, correspond, in all the distinctive marks of a particular state of society, with the people of Hindustan. The evidence has been weighed by a cool and dispassionate judge, in the following manner: "I see nothing," says the President Goguet, "in the Egyptians that can serve to distinguish them in a manner very advantageous; I even think myself authorized to refuse them the greatest part of the eulogies that have been always so liberally bestowed upon them. The Egyptians did invent some arts and some sciences, but they never had the ingenuity to bring any of their discoveries to perfection. I have exposed their want of taste, and I venture to say, of talent, in architecture, in sculpture, and in painting. Their manner of practising physic was absurd and ridiculous. The knowledge they had of geometry and astronomy was but very imperfect. Their discoveries are far enough from entering into any comparison with those which the Greeks made afterwards in those two sciences. In fine, the Egyptians have had neither genius, ardour, nor talent, for commerce, or for the marine and military art.

"As to civil laws, and political constitutions, the Egyptians had indeed some very good ones; but otherwise there reigned in their government a multitude of abuses and essential defects, authorized by the laws and by their fundamental principles of government.

[1] See Description of the Kingdom of Assam, &c. Asiat, An. Register for 1800, Miscellaneous Tracts, p. 47, 48.—M. This picture of civilization in Assam, would much astonish the British officers, who are now charged with the management of the country: as it is given by Mohammed Kasim, however, it is confined to abundant population, extensive tillage, a causeway or bank, and the manufacture of a sort of silk, of which they make 'tents.' Assam silk, for such a purpose, must have been something like canvass.—W.

BOOK II. CHAP. X.

"As to the manners and customs of this people, we hve seen to what a height indecency and debauchery were carried in their religious feasts and public ceremonies. The public cult which a nation fixes to honour the Deity, bears the stamp of that nation's character. Neither was the morality of the Egyptians extremely pure; we may even affirm, that it offended against the first rules of rectitude and probity. We see that the Egyptians bore the highest blame of covetousness, of ill faith, of cunning, and of roguery.

"It appears to me to result from all these facts, thatthe Egyptians were a people industrious enough, but, as to the rest, without taste, without genius, without discernment; a people who had only ideas of grandeur ill understood; and whose progress in all the different parts of human knowledge never rose beyond a flat mediocrity,[1] knavish into the bargain, and crafty, soft, lazy, cowardly, and submissive; and who, having performed some exploits to boast of in distant times, were ever after subjected by whoever would undertake to subdue them; a people again vain and foolish enough to despise other nations without knowing them: superstitious to excess, singularly addicted to judicial astrology, extravagantly besotted with an absurd and monstrous theology. Does not this representation sufficiently authorise us to say that all that science, that wisdom, and that philosophy, so boasted of in the Egyptian priests, was but imposture and juggling, capable of imposing only on people so little enlightened, or so strongly prejudiced, as were anciently the Greeks in favour of the Egyptians?"[2]

[1] The monuments of the ancient Egyptians show them to have been well acquainted with the arts of civilized life, and to have carried them to a high degree of perfection. Of their literature, philosophy, and science, we know nothing but from imperfect report and conjecture; and we derive the pictures of their manners, chiefly from the Roman satirists. We are not qualified, therefore, to judge of their relation to the Hindus in these respects.—W.

[2] Goguet, Origin of Laws, part iii. book vi. ch. ii. He adds, "I should be greatly tempted to compare this nation with the Chinese. I think a good deal of resemblance and conformity is to be perceived between one people and the other." Ibid. Had the Hindus been then as fully described as they are now, he would have found a much more remarkable similarity between them and the Egyptians.—Exaggeration was long in quitting its hold of Egypt. At the time of the Arabian conquest, in the seventh century, "We may read," (says Gibbon, ix. 446) "in the gravest authors, that Egypt was crowded with 20,000 cities or villages: *that* exclusive of the Greeks and Arabs, the Copts alone were found on the assessment, six millions of tributary subjects, or twenty millions of either sex, and of every age: *that* three hundred millions

The sagacity of Adam Smith induced him, at an early period of his life, to deny the supposed proof of any high attainments among those ancient nations, and to declare, though with hesitancy, his inclination to the opposite opinion.

"It was in Greece, and in the Grecian colonies, that the first philosophers of whose doctrine we have any distinct account, appeared. Law and order seem indeed to have been established in the great monarchies of Asia and Egypt, long before they had any footing in Greece: yet after all that has been said concerning the learning of the Chaldeans and Egyptians, whether there ever was in those nations anything which deserved the name of science, or whether that despotism which is more destructive of leisure and security than anarchy itself, and which prevailed over all the East, prevented the growth of philosophy, is a question which, for want of monuments, cannot be determined with any degree of precision."[1] To leave the subject even in this state of doubt was but a compromise with popular opinion, and with his own imperfect views. The circumstances handed down to us, compared with the circumstances of other nations, afforded materials for a very satisfactory determination. The opinion by which he supports his disbelief of the ancient civilization of Asia is at once philanthropic and profound; that "despotism is more destructive of leisure

of gold or silver were annually paid to the treasury of the Caliph." He adds in a note, "And this gross lump is swallowed without scruple by d'Herbelot, Arbuthnot, and De Guignes. They might allege the not less extravagant liberality of Appian, in favour of the Ptolemies; an annual income of 185, or near 200, millions of pounds sterling; according as we reckon by the Egyptian or the Alexandrian talent." If this be wonderful, what is to be said of the lumps swallowed by the admirers of the Hindus? Voltaire remarks, "Que les Egyptiens tant vantés pour leurs lois, leurs connaissances, et leurs pyramides, n'avaient presque jamais été qu'un peuple esclave, superstitieux et ignorant, dont tout le mérite avait consisté à élever des rangs inutiles de pierres les unes sur les autres par l'ordre de leurs tyrans; qu'en bâtissant leurs palais superbes ils n'avaient jamais su seulement former une voûte; qu'ils ignoraient la coupe de pierres; que toute leur architecture consistait à poser de longues pierres plates sur des piliers sans proportion; que l'ancienne Egypte n'a jamais eu une statue tolérable que de la main des Grecs; que ni les Grecs ni les Romains n'ont jamais daigné traduire un seul livre des Egyptiens; que les élémens de géométrie composés dans Alexandrie le furent par un Grec, etc. etc....... on n'aperçoit dans les lois de l'Egypte que celles d'un peuple très borné." Voltaire, Supplément à l'Essai sur les Mœurs, &c. Remarque Premier.

[1] Essay on the History of Astronomy, p. 27.

and security, and more adverse to the progress of the human mind, than anarchy itself."[1]

[1] This question of the civilization of the Hindus, although discussed with disproportionate prolixity, irrelevancy of illustration, and tediousness of repetition, both in these concluding remarks, and in a variety of previous notes and observations, can scarcely be considered as satisfactorily determined. It may be admitted, that the Hindus were not a civilized people according to Mr. Mill's standard; but what that standard is, he has not fully defined. Civilization is used by him, however, as a relative term, and in this sense, we may readily grant that the Hindus never attained the advance made by modern Europe. It is not just to institute such a comparison; for, to say nothing of the advantages we possess in a pure system of religious belief, we cannot leave out of consideration the agency of time. The Hindus, by the character of their institutions, and by the depressing influence of foreign subjugation, are apparently what they were at least three centuries before the Christian æra. Two thousand years have done nothing for them, everything for us. We must, therefore, in fairness, compare them with their contemporaries, with the people of antiquity; and we shall then have reason to believe, that they occupied a very foremost station amongst the nations. They had a religion less disgraced by idolatrous worship, than most of those which prevailed in early times. They had a government, which, although despotic, was equally restricted by law, by institutions, and religion: they had a code of laws, in many respects wise and rational, and adapted to a great variety of relations, which could not have existed, except in an advanced condition of social organization. They had a copious and cultivated language, and an extensive and diversified literature; they had made great progress in the mathematical sciences; they speculated profoundly on the mysteries of man and nature, and they had acquired remarkable proficiency in many of the ornamental and useful arts of life. Whatever defects may be justly imputed to their religion, their government, their laws, their literature, their sciences, their arts, as contrasted with the same proofs of civilization in modern Europe, it will not be disputed by any impartial and candid critic, that as far as we have the means of instituting a comparison, the Hindus were in all these respects quite as civilized as the most civilized nation of the ancient world, and in as early times as any of which records or traditions remain.—W.

BOOK III.—THE MOHAMMEDANS.

CHAPTER I.

From the first Invasion of India by the Nations in the North, till the expulsion of the Ghaznevide dynasty.

AT the time when the nations of Europe opened their communication with India, by the Cape of Good Hope, the people whom we have now described had for a number of ages been subject to a race of foreigners. That subjection, though it had not greatly altered the texture of native society, had introduced new forms into some of the principal departments of state; had given the military command to foreigners; and had mixed with the population a proportion of a people differing from them considerably, in manners, character, and religion. The political state of India, at this time, consisted of a Mohammedan government, supported by a Mohammedan force, over a Hindu population.

It appears that the people of Hindustan have at all times been subject to incursions and conquest, by the nations contiguous to them on the north-west. The Scythians, that is, the rude nations on the east of Persia, conquered, we are told by Justin, a great part of Asia, and even penetrated as far as Egypt, about 1500 years before Ninus, the founder of the Assyrian monarchy. And we know that in the vast empire of Darius Hystaspes as much of India was included, as constituted one, and that the most valuable, of his twenty satrapies. The exact limits of the Indian satrapy are unknown; but from the account which Herodotus gives of its tribute, far exceeding that of any of the rest, the extent of it cannot have been small. Major Rennel supposes that it may have reached as far as Delhi,[1] and have included the whole of

[1] This is incorrectly quoted. Rennel's words are, "We may conclude, that Darius, in fact, possessed no more of India than what lay contiguous to the Indus and its branches;" 8vo. ed. i. 409. The amount of tribute, less than one million sterling, was not large absolutely; the only difficulty applies to its relative amount; it was nearly one-third of the whole revenue of the Persian empire; this is probably an exaggeration.—W.

BOOK III. CHAP. I.

the Punjab, or country watered by the five branches of the Indus, together with Cabul, Candahar, and the tract of country which lies along the Indus to the sea.[1]

The conquests of Alexander the Great, which succeeded to those of the Persian monarchs, seem not to have extended so far in India, as the previous possessions of Darius; since his career was stopped on the banks of the Hyphasis, or modern Beyah, the last of the five branches of the Indus; whence returning to the Hydaspes, he passed down the Indus to the sea. Seleucus, the successor of Alexander in Upper Asia, not only recovered, but endeavoured to augment, the acquisitions made by that conqueror in India. He gained victories over Sandracottos, the sovereign of a people living on the Ganges. But, as he was recalled to the defence of another part of his dominions against Antigonus, he made peace with the Indian: and the limits established between them are not ascertained.[2]

Among the kingdoms formed out of the vast empire of Alexander by the dissensions of his followers, was Bactria. This district was part of that great range of country, on the eastern side of Media and Persia, extending from the lake Aral to the mouths of the Indus, which the power of the Persian monarchs had added to their extensive dominions.[3] The people of this intermediate region seem to have possessed an intermediate stage of civilization between the Tartar or Scythian tribes which bordered with

[1] Rennel's Geography of Herodotus, p. 305. The Major, who is here puzzled with a mistranslation of 600 for 360, corrects the hyberbolical statement of the amount of the tribute, though he doubts not it was great. Herodot. lib. iii. cap. 94, 95. It is by no means impossible, or perhaps improbable, that Cyrus subdued part of India. Herodotus, who knew India, says that his general, Harpagus, subdued one part of Asia, and he another, παν εθνος καταστρεφομενος, και ουδεν παριεις ...... παντα τα της ηπειρου ὑποχειρια εποιησατο. Herod. lib. i. cap. 147. Justin says, that Cyrus having reduced Asia and *the East in general*, carried war into Scythia: lib. i. cap. 8. Xenophon says expressly, ηρξε δε και Βακτριων και Ινδων. Cyri institut. lib. i. cap. i. The Persian historians describe the Persians, in the early ages, as chiefly occupied by wars in Turan and India.

[2] The notices relating to the conquests of Alexander and his successors in India are collected in Robertson's Disquisition concerning Ancient India, and Gillies' History of the World. Strabo and Arrian are the authorities from whom almost everything we know of the transactions of the Greeks in India is borrowed.

[3] This is by no means an accurate statement. The political power of Bactria may, after its acquirement of independence, have extended over this space; but the Bactrian province of Persia lay entirely to the north of the Paropamisan mountains, and had Sogdiana and the Scythians between it and the Aral lake.—W.

them on the east, and the people of the Assyrian or Persian empire which was contiguous to them on the west. Among these people there is some reason for believing that the Bactrians were distinguished, and at an early period, by superior progress in the knowledge, and other acquirements of civilized men. Among the numerous Zoroasters, with whom Persian story abounds, one is said to have been king of Bactria, contemporary with Ninus; and to have invented magic; that is, to have been the object of admiration on account of his knowledge. Of the eastern nations added to the subjects of the Persian kings, the Bactrians were the nearest to India, and were only separated from it by that range of mountains, in which the Indus and the Oxus find their respective sources. Bactria as well as India were among the parts of the dominions of Alexander which fell to the share of Seleucus. In the reign, however, of his son or grandson, the governor of the Bactrian province threw off his dependence upon the Seleucidæ; and a separate Greek kingdom was erected in that country, about sixty-nine years after the death of Alexander. The Persian dominions in India seem to have fallen into the hands of the same usurper. The Greek sovereigns of Bactria became masters of an extensive empire, and assumed the proud title of *King of Kings;* the distinctive appellation of the Persian monarchs in the zenith of their power. They carried on various wars with India, and extended their conquests into the interior of the country.[1] The limits of their dominions in that direction we have no means of ascertaining. One of those great movements in central or eastern Tartary, which precipitates the eastern barbarians upon the countries of the west, brought an irresistible torrent of that people across the Jaxartes, about 126 years before the Christian era,

[1] Much additional light has been thrown upon the history of Bactria and the adjacent provinces of the Afghan country, by the recent discovery of large quantities of coins, bearing the effigies and names of Greek and Barbaric kings. They have been found in the tract between Balkh and the Panjab, and especially about Peshawar and Kabul, which were, no doubt, included in the dominions of the princes of Bactria, or of those principalities which were established in the direction of India by the Greeks. As most of these coins bear on one face an inscription which has been ascertained to be in a form of Prakrit, a derivative from Sanscrit; they prove that the Bactrians must have been an Indian people. See the descriptions and observations of Masson and Prinsep, J. As. Soc. of Bengal; of Jacquet, J. Asiatique, Raoul Rochette, J. des Savans; also Richter on the Topes (die Stupe) and Lassen, zur Geschichte der Griechischen und Indoskytischen Könige in Bactrien, Kabul und Indien.

BOOK III. CHAP. I

which, pouring itself out upon Bactria, overwhelmed the Grecian monarchy, after it had lasted nearly 130 years.[1]

About the same period that the successors of Alexander lost the kingdom of Bactria, the misconduct of a governor in the distant provinces bordering on the Caspian Sea, raised up a military chief who excited the rude and turbulent inhabitants to revolt, and laid the foundation of the Parthian kingdom; a power which soon possessed itself of Media, and finally stripped the descendants of Seleucus of almost all that they possessed from the Tigris eastwards. The rebellion of the Parthians is placed about the year 256 before Christ; and the kings of Syria maintained from that time a struggling and declining existence, till they finally yielded to the power of the Romans, and Syria was erected into a province sixty-four years before the commencement of the Christian era.[2]

The descendants of the Parthian rebel, known under the title of the Arsacides, held the sceptre of Persia till the year of Christ 226. The possession of empire produced among them, as it usually produces among the princes of the East, a neglect of the duties of government, and subjugation to ease and pleasure; when a popular enterprising subject, availing himself of the general dissatisfaction, turned the eyes of the nation upon himself,

[1] A curious history of the Greek kingdom of Bactria has been compiled by Bayer, entitled, Historia regni Græcorum Bactriani. In this, and in Strabo, lib. xi. Diod. lib. xv. and Justin, lib. xli. the only remaining memorials of this kingdom are to be found. The progress of the barbarians by whom it was destroyed has been traced by De Guignes, Mém. de Litérat. xxv. 17, and Hist. des Huns, *passim*. Herodotus says that those of the Indians, whose mode of life most resembled those of the Bactrians, were the most warlike of all the Indians (lib. iii. cap. 102), which would seem to indicate a nearer affinity between the Hindus, and their Bactrian neighbours, than is generally supposed. There is some confusion, however, in this part of Herodotus, nor is it easy to know whether he means the people called Indians on the Euxine Sea, or those beyond the Indus, when he says they were like the Bactrians. He distinguishes them from the Indians living *προς νοτου ανεμου*, by saying they were contiguous to the city Caspatyrus and the Pactyan territory, and lying *προς βορεου ανεμου* (lib. iii. cap. 102), but (cap. 93 of the same book) he says that the Pactyan territory is contiguous to Armenia, and the countries on the Euxine Sea. Yet in another place (lib. iv. cap. 44) he says that Scylax setting out from the city Caspatyrus, and the Pactyan territory, sailed down the Indus eastward to the sea. And Rennel places Caspatyrus and Pactya towards the sources of the Indus, about the regions of Cabul and Cashmere. Rennel's Mem. Introd. p. xxiii. Rennel's Herodot. sect. 12.—M.

Some illustrations of the position of these countries may be found in the As. Res. v. xv., Essay on Kashmir, and in Lassen's Pentapotamia.—W.

[2] What is known to us from the Greek and Roman authors, of the Parthian empire, is industriously collected in Gillies' History of the World; from the oriental writers by D'Herbelot, Biblioth. Orient. *ad verba* Arschak, Arminiah. See also Gibbon, i. 316.

and having dethroned his master, substituted the dynasty of the Sassanides to the house of Arsaces. As usual, the first princes of this line were active and valiant; and their empire extended from the Euphrates to the Jaxartes, and the mountainous ridge which divided the kingdom of Bactria from the Scythians of the East. To what extent their power was carried over the ancient soil of the Hindus, does not appear; but it is more than probable that the territory west of the Indus, from the time when it was first established into a Persian satrapy, in the reign of Darius, owned no more the caste who sprung from the arm of the Creator. Bactria was numbered as one among the four provinces of the great Chosroes, who reigned from the year 531 of the Christian era to the year 571, and was denominated King of Persia and of India. The grandson of Chosroes, who was deposed in 628, may be considered as closing the line of the Sassanides; for, after a few years of tumult and distraction, the irresistible arms of the successors of Mohammed were directed toward Persia, and quickly reduced it under the power of the Caliphs.[1]

In the year 632, Caled, the lieutenant of Abubeker, entered Persia. In a few years the standards of the Faithful were carried to the farthest limits of Bactria, and pushing once more the shepherds of the East beyond the Jaxartes, rendered the empire of the Caliphs in that direction conterminous with the Persian monarchy in its proudest days.[2]

The possession of empire required, as usual, but a few generations to relax the minds of the successors of Mohammed, and render them as unfit as their predecessors for any better use of power than the unrestrained indulgence of themselves in the pleasures which it commands.

The tribes of Tartar, or Scythian shepherds, from the centre of Asia, unsettled, fierce, and warlike, had from the

[1] In Gibbon, vols. vii. viii. ix. the reader will find a slight sketch, correctly but quaintly given, of this portion of the Persian history. Gibbon's first object unfortunately was to inspire admiration of the writer; to impart knowledge of his subject only the second. The results of the Persian records (if such they may be called) are carefully collected in D'Herbelot, Bibliothèque Orient., under the several titles.—M.

Further notices of the Arsacidan princes, have been subsequently published by Col. Vans Kennedy, Tr. Bombay, Lit. Soc. v. 3, and by M. St. Martin, in the J. Asiatique, and Mémoires de l'Académie.—W.

[2] Gibbon, ix. 364; D'Herbelot, Bibliothèque Orient. *ad verb.*

BOOK III. CHAP. I.

earliest ages proved dangerous and encroaching neighbours to the Eastern provinces of Persia. Pushed beyond the Jaxartes and Imaus by Cyrus and the more warlike of the successors of Cyrus, they were ever ready, as soon as the reign of a weak prince enfeebled the powers of government, to make formidable incursions, and generally held possession of the provinces which they over-ran, till a renewal of vigour in the government made them retire within their ancient limits. We are informed by Polybius that a tribe of *Nomades* or shepherds, whom he calls Aspasians, forced their way across the Oxus, and took possession of Hyrcania, even in the reign of Antiochus. We have already seen that a body of Tartars overwhelmed Bactria about 120 years before Christ. And about 100 years subsequent to the Christian era, a portion of the great nation of the Huns, who had been forced by a victorious tribe from their native seat behind the wall of China, penetrated into Sogdiana, the country between the Oxus and the Jaxartes, towards the shores of the Caspian Sea, and there established themselves under the titles of the Euthalites, Nephthalites, and White Huns. After these irruptions, the more vigorous of the princes of the Sassanian dynasty reduced Sogdiana, as well as Bactria, to occasional obedience; but without expelling the new inhabitants, and without acquiring any permanent dominion. In the cultivated provinces in which they settled, the savage Tartars acquired a degree of civilization; and when obliged to yield to the followers of Mohammed, felt so little attachment to their ancient religion, as immediately to recommend themselves to the favour, by adopting the faith of their conquerors.[1]

When the government of the Caliphs began to lose its vigour, a tribe of Tartars, originally situated in the Altai mountains, and known by the name of Turks, had acquired extraordinary power. They had, in a series of wars, subdued the neighbouring tribes, and extended their sway, that species of sway which it is competent to a pasturing people to exercise or to sustain, over a great portion of the Tartars of Asia.[2] When the military virtues of the Ara-

[1] Polyb. Hist. lib. x.; M. de Guignes, Hist. des Huns, tom. ii.; Gibbon's Roman Empire, iv. 367.

[2] The rise and progress of the power of the Turkish horde may be collected from Abulghazi, Hist. Genéalogique des Tartars; De Guignes, Hist. des Huns;

bians sunk beneath the pleasures which flow from the possession of power, the Caliphs sought to infuse vigour into their effeminate armies, by a mixture of fierce and hardy Turks. Adventurers of that nation were raised to the command of armies, and of provinces; and a guard of Turkish soldiers was appointed to surround the person of the monarch. When weakness was felt at the centre of the empire, the usurpation of independence by the governors of the distant provinces was a natural result. The first by whom this usurpation was attempted, was Taher, Governor of Khorasan, the province extending from the Caspian Sea to the Oxus. He and his posterity, under the title of Taherites, enjoyed sovereignty in that province from the year 813 to the year 872. The son of a brazier, called in Arabian, Soffar, who rose (a common occurrence in the East) through the different stages of military adventure, to be the head and captain of an army, supplanted the Taherites, and substituted his own family, called from their origin Soffarides, in the government of Khorasan and Transoxiana. The Soffarides were displaced by a similar adventurer, who established the house of the Samanides, after a period, according to the varying accounts, of either thirty-four or fifty-seven years, from the elevation of the Brazier. The Samanides are celebrated by the Persian historians for their love of justice and learning; they extended their sway over the eastern provinces of Persia, from the Jaxartes to the Indus, and reigned till after the year 1000 of the Christian era.[1]

The Taherites, the Soffarides, and Samanides usurped only the eastern provinces of the empire of the Caliphs, the provinces which, being the nearest to the turbulent and warlike tribes of shepherds, and most exposed to their incursions, were of the least importance to the sovereigns of Persia. Three adventurers, brothers, called, from the name of their father, the Bowides, rose to power in the provinces extending westward from Khorasan, along the shores of the Caspian Sea, about the year 315 of the Hegira, or 927 of Christ. This dynasty consisted of seven-

---

and D'Herbelot, Biblioth. Orient. Mr. Gibbon, vii. 284, throws a glance at the leading facts.

[1] See D'Herbelot, Biblioth. Orient. *ad verb. Thaher, Soffar,* et *Saman;* Gibbon, x. 80; De Guignes, Hist. des Huns, i. 404—406.

BOOK III. CHAP. I.

teen successive and powerful princes, who reigned till the year 1056. They conquered the provinces of Gilan, Mazenderon, Erak, Fars, Kerman, Khosistan, Ahvaz, Tabarestan, and Goorgian: and rendered themselves masters of the Caliphs, to whom they left only a shadow of authority.[1]

About the year of Christ 967, Subuctagi, a servant of the Samanides, was appointed governor of the Indian province of Candahar, or Ghazna, as it is called by the Persian writers; from the name of the capital Ghizni. Having raised himself from the condition of a Turkish slave to such a degree of power as made it dangerous to recall him from his government, he left it to his son Mahmood, who asserted his independence, and founded the dynasty of the Ghaznevides. Mahmood subverted the throne of the Samanides, reduced to a shadow the power of the Bowides, and reigned from the Tigris[2] to the Jaxartes. He also made extensive conquests towards the south; and, as he was the first who in that direction bore the crescent beyond the farthest limits of the Persian empire, and laid the foundation of the Mohammedan thrones in India, we are now arrived at the period when the Mohammedan History of India begins.[3]

The northern provinces of India, Cabul, Candahar, Multan, and the Punjab, appear, from the days of Darius Hystaspes, to have followed the destiny of Bactria, Khorasan, aud Transoxiana, the eastern appendages of Persia, and, excepting some short intervals, to have been always subject to a foreign yoke. Even the White Huns, who established themselves in Sogdiana, on the river Oxus, and in Bactria, about the end of the first century of the Christian era, advanced into India, and in the second century were masters as far as Larice or Guzerat.[4] Mahmood was already master of the dominions of the Samanides, and of all the eastern provinces that had occasionally owned allegiance to the Persian throne; when he first,

[1] D'Herbelot, Biblioth. Orient. *ad verb.* Buiah.

[2] This is not quite correct. Mahmood was content with the province of Khorasan in Persia.—W.

[3] D'Herbelot, Biblioth. Orient. *ad verb.* Sebecteghen, Mahmoud, Gaznaviah; Ferishta, by Dow, i. 41, 2d Ed. in 4to.

[4] The origin and progress of the Indo-Scythæ are traced in D'Anville sur l'Inde, pp. 18, 45, and 69, &c. His authorities are drawn from Dionys. Perieget. 1088, with the Commentary of Eustathius, and Cosmas, Topograph. Christ. lib. ix.

says the Persian historian, "turned his face to India." This expedition, of which the year 1000 of the Christian era is assigned as the date, seems to have been solely intended to confirm or restore the obedience of the governors who had submitted to his father, or been accustomed to obey the masters of Eastern Persia; and few of its particulars have been thought worthy of record. He renewed his invasion the succeeding year, and proceeded so far as to alarm a prince who reigned at Lahore, a city, on one of the most eastern branches of the Indus, which gave its name to a small kingdom. This prince, called by the Persian historians Jeipal, or Gepal, met him, with his whole army, and was defeated. It was, according to the same historians, a custom or law of the Hindus, that a prince, twice defeated by Mohammedan arms, was unworthy to reign; and as this misfortune had happened to Jeipal, who had formerly yielded to Subuctagi, he resigned the throne to his son Anundpaul, and burnt himself alive in solemn state.[1]

In the year 1004 Mahmood again marched into India to chastise, for defect of duty, a tributary prince on the Indus. His presence was still more urgently required the following year, when the king of Multan revolted, and was joined by Anundpaul. Mahmood was met by Anundpaul as he was descending through the pass in the intervening mountains. Anundpaul was conquered and obliged to fly into Cashmere: when the king of Multan endeavoured, by submission, to save what he could. As Mahmood had received intelligence that a body of Tartars had invaded his northern provinces, he was the more easily softened; and leaving Zab Sais,[2] a Hindu who had embraced the Mohammedan religion, his lieutenant, or governor in India, marched to repel the invaders.[3]

During this expedition against the Tartars, Zab Sais revolted; resumed the Brahmenical faith; and was on the point of being joined by a confederacy of Rajas, or Hindu sovereigns, when Mahmood hastened back to India, took

[1] Ferishta (*apud.* Dow, Hist. of Hindost. i. 40—42;) D'Herbelot, Bibl. Orient. *ad verb.* Mahmoud.

[2] This name is omitted in Col. Briggs's translation of Ferishta, and the MSS. give it variously, as Ab-sà or Ab-basa; the Hindu appellation is written Sewak-pal, or Sikh-pal.—W.

[3] Ferishta, ut supra, pp. 42—44; D'Herbelot, ut supra.

BOOK III. CHAP. I.

Zab Sais unprepared, and made him prisoner for life; after which, the season being far advanced, he returned to Ghizni. Early, however, in the following spring, some movements of Anundpaul recalled him to India, when the princes of Oogeen, Gualior, Callinger, Kanoge, Delhi Ajmere, the Guickwars, and others, joined their forces to oppose him. A general battle was fought, in which the Ghiznian monarch prevailed. He then reduced the fort of Nagracote or Nagarcote; and, having plundered the temple of its riches, very great, as we are told, returned to his capital. As the king of Multan still continued refractory, Mahmood returned to that province in the following year, and having taken the Raja prisoner, carried him to Ghizni, where he confined him for life.[1]

"In the year 402,[2] the passion of war," says the historian, "fermenting in the mind of Mahmood, he resolved upon the conquest of Tannasar or Tahnesir, a city about thirty coss north-west from Delhi; the seat of a considerable government; famous for its sanctity and subservience to the Brahmenical religion. Having taken Tannasar, and demolished the idols, he marched to Delhi, which he quickly reduced, and thence returned with vast riches."[3]

Two years afterwards, he drove from his dominions the king of Lahore, and overran Cashmere, compelling the inhabitants to acknowledge the prophet.[4]

In the beginning of the year 1018, the Sultan (Mahmood was the first on whom that title was bestowed) with a large army, raised chiefly among the tribes who possessed or bordered upon, the northern provinces of his empire, marched against Kanoge, the capital of a kingdom, situated on the Ganges, about 100 miles south-east from Delhi.[5] "From the time of Gustasp the father of Darab, to this period, this city (says the Persian historian) had not been visited by any foreign enemy; three months were necessary to complete the march between this kingdom and the

[1] Ferishta, ut supra, pp. 47—50; D'Herbelot, ut supra.

[2] Viz. of the Hegira; 1011, A.D.

[3] Ferishta, ut supra, pp. 51—58; D'Herbelot, ut supra.

[4] The chronicles of Kashmir take no notice of this event. Essay on the History of Kashmir, As. Res. vol. xv.—W.

[5] It may be necessary, once for all, to state, that in this sketch of Mohammedan history, the distances are given generally as in the native historians. Their very inaccuracies (where they do not mislead) are sources of information.

capital of Mahmood; and seven mighty streams rushed across the intervening space." The conqueror having with much difficulty forced a passage through the mountains by the way of Cashmere, arrived at Kanoge before the Raja was prepared for resistance. Placing his only hopes in submission, he threw himself upon the mercy of the invader. The magnitude and grandeur of the city is celebrated in poetic strains by the Persian historians. Mahmood, remaining but three days, proceeded against a neighbouring prince inhabiting a city called Merat; thence to another city on the Jumna, named Mavin, and next to Muttra, which is still a city of considerable extent, at a small distance from Agra. This last city was full of temples and idols, which Mahmood plundered and destroyed; and from which, according to the usual story, he obtained incredible treasure. Several other forts and Rajas being subdued, Mahmood returned from his eighth expedition into India, laden, we are told, with riches, and began to adorn and improve his capital. He built a mosque, so beautiful and magnificent, that it was called the *Celestial Bride*, and "struck every beholder with astonishment and pleasure. In the neighbourhood of this mosque he founded an university, which he furnished with a vast collection of curious books, in various languages: and with natural and artificial curiosities. He appropriated a sufficient fund for the maintenance of the students, and the learned men who were appointed to instruct the youth in the sciences."[1]

Mahmood's ninth expedition, in 1021, was for the purpose of protecting the Rajah of Kanoge, who now held the rank of one of his dependents. The Rajah of Callinger, a city in the province of Bundelcund, situated on one of the rivers which fall into the Jumna, was the most guilty of the assailants. As the Raja avoided Mahmood in the field, he plundered and laid waste the country, and, this done, returned to his capital.

Here he had not reposed many days, when he was in-

[1] D'Herbelot, ut supra; pp. 56—60. Ferishta says, that the taste of the sovereign for architecture being followed by his nobles, Ghizni soon became the *finest* city in the East. Ibid. p. 60. So that the grandeur, and riches, and beauty, he so lavishly ascribes to some of the Hindu cities, get an object of comparison, which enables us to reduce them to their true dimensions. The architecture of the Mohammedans was superior to that of the Hindus.

BOOK III. CHAP. I.

formed that two districts on the borders of Hindustan refused to acknowledge the true prophet, and continued the worship of lions.[1] The zeal of the religious sultan immediately took fire. Having speedily brought to reason the disrespectful provinces, he marched to Lahore, which he gave up to pillage. According to custom, it afforded enormous riches. Mohammedan governors were established in this and several other districts of Hindustan.

The twelfth expedition of the Ghiznian monarch was undertaken in the year 1024. He had heard not only of the great riches and supposed sanctity of the temple of Sumnaut, but of the presumption of its priests, who had boasted that other places had yielded to the power of Mahmood, by reason of their impiety; but if he dared to approach Sumnaut, he would assuredly meet the reward of his temerity. Mahmood, having arrived at Multan, gave orders to his army to provide themselves with water and other necessaries for crossing a desert of several days' march, which lay between this city and Ajmere. The Raja and people of Ajmere abandoned the place at his approach. They were invited to return, and experience the clemency of the victor; but not complying, beheld their country desolated with fire and sword. Arrived at Sumnaut, which was a strong castle, situated on the promontory of Guzerat, near the city of Diu,[2] washed on three sides by the sea, Mahmood met with a more serious resistance than any which he had yet encountered in Hindustan. Not only did the priests and guardians of the temple defend it with all the obstinacy of enthusiasm and despair, but a large army collected in the surrounding kingdoms was brought to its defence. Having triumphed over all resistance, the religious sultan entered the tem-

1 This incorrect expression, which refers to the fourth avatar, shows the carelessness and ignorance of Ferishta and the Persian historians, in regard to the Brahmanical faith.—M.

It is probably some blunder of the copyists, unless the mistake have originated in a misconception of the term " Sinh," in the name of Sakya Sinh, or Buddha, as its common import is "lion"; in that case, " Buddhists" may be intended. In some copies, the word is " But" an idol in general. The countries are called by Ferishta, Kuriat, and Nardein; names not verifiable, and probably inaccurate. They are said to lie amongst the mountains, on the borders of India, between it and Turkestan, and were possibly in the direction of the modern Kaferistan, or little Tibet.—W.

2 D'Herbelot, misled by some of the Persian historians, makes Sumnaut the same with the city of Visiapore in the Deccan. Biblioth. Orient. *ad verbum* Soumenat.

ple. Filled with indignation at sight of the gigantic idol, he aimed a blow at its head, with his iron mace. The nose was struck from its face. In vehement trepidation the Brahmens crowded around, and offered millions[1] to spare the god. The Omrahs dazzled with the ransom ventured to counsel acceptance. Mahmood, crying out that he valued the title of breaker, not seller of idols, gave orders to proceed with the work of destruction. At the next blow, the belly of the idol burst open: and forth issued a vast treasure of diamonds, rubies, and pearls; rewarding the holy perseverance of Mahmood, and explaining the devout liberality of the Brahmens.[2] After this Mahmood took vengeance on the rajas who had confederated to defend the temple, and reduced all Guzerat to his obedience. It is said that he was so captivated with the beauty of the country, the richness of the soil, and the salubrity of the climate, that he conceived the design of making it the place of his residence, and resigning Ghizni to one of his sons. Diverted from this design by the counsels of his friends, he placed a Hindu governor over the province, and after an absence of two years and six months, returned to Ghizni. A people whom the translator of Ferishta calls the Jits, afterwards better known under the name of Jaats, who inhabited part of the country bordering on the Indus, southward from Multan, either failed in respect or gave molestation, as he marched

[1] Ferishta says "some crores of gold. Dow says in a note, at the bottom of the page, "ten millions," which is the explanation of the word crore. Mr. Gibbon says, rashly and carelessly, that the sum offered by the Brahmens was *ten millions sterling*. Decl. and Fall. x. 337.

[2] The whole story of Mahmood's destruction of Somnath, is a curious specimen of the manner in which a story is embellished by repetition. According to earlier Mohammedan writers, the idol Somnath, was a straight solid block of stone, three cubits long; which, upon the temple being pillaged, was broken to pieces: they say nothing of the mutilation of its features, for, in fact, it had none: nothing of the treasures it contained; which, as it was solid, could not have been within it: nor do they speak of the sums offered for its ransom. Rozet-as Safa, Tabkat Akberi. Even Ferishta says nothing of any definite sum of money being offered for it. His words are, the Brahmans went to the attendants of Mahmood, and said, if the king will let the image alone, we will give as much gold, meaning, probably, an equal weight, to the public treasury. The crores and millions are due to Dow and Gibbon. Ferishta, however, invents the hidden treasure of rubies and pearls with quite as little warrant. Somnath was, in fact, a Linga, a Nath, or deity ascribed to Soma, the moon, as having been erected by him in honour of Sivà. It was one of the twelve principal types of that deity, which were celebrated in India at the time of the first Mohammedan invasion. Nandi Upapurana. See Calcutta Annual Register, 1821. Tracts, p. 34, and As. Res. vol. xvii., p. 194.

from Guzerat. Returning in the same year to chastise them, he defeated 4000 or 8000 (so wide are the accounts) of their boats, launched on the river to defend an island to which, as the place of greatest safety, they had conveyed the most valuable of their effects, and the most cherished of their people.[1] This was the last of the exploits of Mahmood in India, who died at Ghizni in the year 1028. Mahmood, the son of Subuctagi, the Turkish slave, is one of the most celebrated of eastern princes. He was supposed to possess in the highest perfection almost every royal virtue. He patronized learning, and encouraged the resort of learned men. Ferdosi, the author of the Shah Namah, the most celebrated poem of the East, was entertained at his court.

After a short contest between Mohammed and Musaood, the sons of Mahmood, Musaood mounted the throne of Ghizni, and the eyes of Mohammed were put out. Musaood entered India three times, during the nine years of his reign; and left the boundaries of the Ghaznevide dominions there in the situation nearly in which he received them. His first incursion was in the year 1032, when he penetrated by the way of Cashmere; and his only memorable exploit was the capture of the fort of Sursutti, which commanded the pass. In 1034, he sent an army which chastised a disobedient viceroy. And in 1035, he marched in person to reduce Sewalik, a kingdom or rajaship lying at the bottom of the mountains near the place where the Ganges descends upon the Indian plains. He assailed the capital, of great imputed strength; took it in six days; and found in it incredible riches. From this he proceeded against the fort of Sunput, a place about forty miles distant from Delhi on the road to Lahore, the governor of which abandoned it upon his approach, and fled into the woods. He proposed to march against another prince, called Ram; but Ram, understanding his intentions, endeavoured to divert the storm by gifts and compliments, and had the good fortune to succeed. Musaood was recalled from India to oppose an enemy, destined to render short the splendour of the house of Ghizni.

During several centuries, the movements westward of the

[1] Ferishta, *apud* Dow, Mahmood I.; D'Herbelot, Bibl. Orient. *ad verb.* Mahmoud.

hordes of Turkmans had been accumulating that people upon the barriers of the Persian empire. In the reign of Mahmood, three brothers, sons of Seljuk, solicited permission to pass the Oxus, with their flocks and herds, and to enjoy the unoccupied pastures of Khorasan. Mahmood, disregarding the advice of his best counsellors, granted their request. The example set, the number of Tartars in Transoxiana and Khorasan continually increased. During the vigilant and vigorous reign of Mahmood, the Turks behaved so much like peaceable subjects, that no complaint against them seems to have been raised. But in the days of his son and successor Musaood, the inhabitants of Khorasan and Transoxiana complained that they were oppressed by the strangers, and Musaood at last resolved to drive them back from his dominions, Togrul Beg, however, the son of Michael, the son of Seljuk. offered himself as a leader and a bond of union to the Turks; opposed Musaood; triumphed over him in the field; rendered himself master of the northern provinces of his empire, and established the dynasty of the Seljukides. Having baffled the power of the Sultan of Ghizni, Togrul found nothing remaining to oppose to him any serious resistance, from the Oxus to the Euphrates; he extinguished the remaining sparks of the power of the Bowides; and took the Caliph under his protection. Togrul was succeeded by his nephew Alp Arslan, and the latter by his son Malek Shah; both celebrated warriors, who pushed the limits of their empire beyond the Euphrates and the Jaxartes, and made deep inroads upon the Roman provinces and the Tartar plains. The provinces of Zabulistan or Candahar, of Segistan, or Seistan, and Cabul, with the provinces in India beyond the Hydaspes, were all that at last remained to the Ghaznevides.

Musaood, returning from the defeat which he, deserted by his troops, had sustained at the hand of the Turkmans, and hastening to India to recruit his forces, was deposed by a mutiny in the army, and his brother Mohammed, whose eyes he had put out, was placed upon the throne. Modood, the son of Musaood, who had been left by his father with an army at Balkh, marched against Mohammed, whom he dethroned. Modood made some efforts against the Seljukians, and for a time recovered Transoxiana. But the feebleness and distraction now apparent in the empire of the Ghaznevides encouraged the Raja of Delhi, in concert with some other rajas, to hazard an insurrection. They reduced Tannasar, Hansi the capital of Sewalik, and even the fort of Nagracote. The Rajas of the Punjab endeavoured to recover their independence; and the Mohammedan dominion was threatened with destruction.

In the year 1049 Modood died; and a rapid change of princes succeeded, violently raised to the throne, and violently thrown down from it. His son Musaood, a child of four years old, was set up by one general; and, after a nominal reign of six days, gave place to Ali, the brother of Modood, who was supported by another. Ali reigned about two years, when he was dethroned by Abdul Reshid, his uncle, son of the great Mahmood. Togrul, governor of Segistan, rebelled against Reshid, and slew him after reigning one year. Togrul himself was assassinated after he had enjoyed his usurpation but forty days. Furokhzad, a yet surviving son of Musaood, was then raised to the throne, who, dying after a peaceable reign of six years, was succeeded by his brother Ibrahim.

Ibrahim reigned a period of no less than forty-two years. After he had terminated his disputes with the dangerous Seljukians, by resigning to them all the provinces they had usurped of the Ghaznevide empire, he directed his ambition towards India. An army which he dispatched into that country is said to have reduced to his obedience many places which had not yet yielded to the Moslem arms. In the year 1080, he marched in person: and by the successful attack of several places of strength, added the territory they protected to his dominions.[1] Against the house of Seljuk, now reigning over Persia, Khorasan, and Bucharia, the latter comprehending the ancient provinces or kingdoms of Bactria, Sogdiana, and Transoxiana, he found protection chiefly by intermarriages and alliance.

Ibrahim was succeeded by his son Musaood, who enjoyed a peaceable reign of sixteen years. With the exception of one expedition, under one of his generals, who penetrated

[1] Ferishta mentions a city to which he came (the place not intelligibly marked,) the inhabitants of which came originally from Khorasan, having been banished thither with their families, for rebellion, by an ancient Persian king. See Ferishta, Dow, i. 117.

beyond the Ganges, India remained unmolested by his arms. But as the Indian provinces now formed the chief portion of his dominions, Lahore became the principal seat of his government.

"His son Shere," says the Persian historian, "placed his foot on the imperial throne; but within a year was assassinated by his brother Arsilla." Byram, one of the brothers of Arsilla, made his escape; and fled to the governor of Khorasan, who was brother to the king of Persia, and to his own, and Arsilla's mother. By the assistance of this prince, his uncle, who marched with an army to his support, he dethroned Arsilla, and assumed the reins of government, which had been held by the usurper for three years.

Byram, or Bahram, was twice called into India by the disobedience of the governor of Lahore, who aspired to independence. But he had no sooner settled this disturbance, than he was called to oppose the governor of another of his provinces, whose rebellion was attended with more fatal consequences. A range of mountainous country, known by the name of the mountains of Gaur, occupies the space between the province of Khorasan and Bactria on the west and north, and the provinces of Segistan, Candahar, and Cabul on the south. The mountaineers of this district, a wild and warlike race, had hardly ever paid more than a nominal obedience to the sovereigns of Persia. The district, however, had been included in the dominions of the Sultans of Ghizni; and had not yet been detached by the Seljukian encroachments. In the days of Byram, a descendant of the ancient princes of the country, Souri by name, was governor of the province. Finding himself possessed of power to aim at independence, he raised an army of Afghans, such is the name (famous in the history of India) by which the mountaineers of Gaur are distinguished, and chased Byram from his capital of Ghizni. Byram, however, having collected and recruited his army, marched against his enemy, and aided by his subjects of Ghizni, who deceived and betrayed their new master, gained a complete victory, and put the Gaurian to a cruel death. The power which he gained was but of short duration. Alla, the brother of Souri, who succeeded him in his usurped dominion, hastened to repair his loss. Byram was defeated in a decisive battle, and fled towards India; but sunk under his misfortunes,

BOOK III. CHAP. II.

and expired, after a languid, but gentle reign of thirty-five years.

He was succeeded by his son Khosroo, who withdrew to India, and made Lahore his capital. This prince cherished the hope of recovering the lost dominions of his house from the Gaurian usurper, by aid from his kinsman, the king of Persia: and collected an army for that purpose: but at this moment a fresh horde of Turkman Tartars rushed upon the Persian provinces, and inundated even Cabul and Candahar, from which the Gaurians were obliged to retire. The Turks, after two years' possession, were expelled by the Gaurians. The Gaurians were again defeated by the arms of Khosroo, and yielded up the temporary possession of Ghizni to its former masters. Khosroo continued to reside at Lahore, and having died after a reign of seven years, was succeeded by his son Khosroo the Second.

Mohammed, brother to the Gaurian usurper, pursued the same ambitious career. He soon rendered himself master of the kingdom of Ghizni or Candahar: and not satisfied with that success, penetrated even into India; overran Multan, with the provinces on both sides of the Indus; and advanced as far as Lahore. After an uninteresting struggle of a few years, Khosroo was subdued; and in the year 1184 the sceptre was transferred from the house of Ghizni to the house of Gaur. The same era which was marked by the fall of the Ghaznevides, was distinguished by the reduction of the house of Seljuk. The weakness and effeminacy which, after the vigour and ability of the founders of a new dynasty, uniformly take place among the princes their successors, having relaxed the springs of the Seljukian government, the subordinate governors threw off their dependence; and a small portion of the dominions of Malek now owned the authority of Togril his descendant.

CHAPTER II.

From the Commencement of the first Gaurian Dynasty to that of the second Gaurian or Afghan Dynasty.

MOHAMMED left the government of India after the defeat and death of Khosroo, in the hands of a viceroy and returned to Ghizni. After an absence of five years, he

1190.

marched towards Ajmere; and, having taken the city of Tiberhind, is said to have been on his way back, when he heard that the Rajas of Ajmere and Delhi, with others in confederacy, were advancing with a large army to relieve the city which he had just taken and left. He turned and met them a little beyond Tannasar. Having incautiously allowed his army to be surrounded by superior numbers, he was defeated, and, being severely wounded, escaped with great difficulty from the field of battle. He took such measures as the moment allowed, to secure his provinces and forts, and hastened to Gaur.

After little more than a year he was prepared to return to India with a formidable army of Turks, Persians, and Afghans. The combined Rajas had consumed their time in the siege of Tiberhind, which had resisted them for one year and one month. No fewer, it is said, than 150 kings, with their armies, amounting, by "the lowest and most moderate account, to 300,000 horse, 3000 elephants, and a great body of infantry," met him on the former field of battle. The Rajas sent him an insulting proposal that he might be permitted to march back unmolested, if he had the prudence to decline the combat. Mohammed had learned wisdom from experience. Sending an humble answer, that he was only the servant of his brother, bound to execute his commands, and praying for time, to learn the will of his master; he filled the Rajas, and their enormous camp with an ill-grounded and intemperate presumption. While they were spending the night in revelling and joy, Mohammed crossed the river with his army, and fell upon them before the alarm was spread. The extent of the camp was so great, that a part of the army had time to form itself, and advance to cover the flight. Mohammed immediately drew off his troops to meet them. Forming a strong reserve of his chosen horse, he ordered the rest of his army, drawn up in four lines, to receive the enemy calmly. The first line, having discharged its missile weapons, was made to withdraw to the rear; the next, coming in front, discharged in like manner its weapons, and in like manner gave place to another. By this stratagem were the enemy held in play, "till the sun was approaching the west," when Mohammed, placing himself at the head of his reserve, rushed upon the fatigued and now presumptuous multitude; who were im-

BOOK III. CHAP. II. mediately thrown into the greatest disorder, and "recoiled, like a troubled torrent, from the bloody plain."

1192. Shortly after this event, Mohammed returned to Ghizni, leaving the fruits of the victory to be gathered and secured by his favourite general, Koottub. The events of this man's life, though far from singular in the East, involved extraordinary changes of condition and fortune. In his childhood, he was brought from Turkestan to Nishapore, the capital of Khorasan, and there sold for a slave. It happened that the master by whom he was bought had the disposition to give him education, and that the quickness of his parts enabled him to profit by this advantage. The death of his patron, however, exposed him once more to the chance of the market; which fortunately assigned him to Mohammed the Gaurian. His intelligence and assiduity attracted in time the notice of the Prince. He advanced by gradual accessions of favour, till he rose to be Master of the Horse. Even misfortune, though he lost a detachment of men, and was taken prisoner by the enemy, did not lose him the kindness of Mohammed: or interrupt the career of his promotion.

Koottub improved, with diligence and ability, the advantages which his master had gained in India. He reduced the surrounding districts; took the fort of Merat; and invested Delhi. The garrison ventured to meet him in the field. He vanquished them; and, surmounting all opposition, obtained possession of the city.

Mohammed returned to India in 1193. Koottub was received with the highest marks of distinction; and being honoured with the command of the van of the army, he conquered the raja of Benares; where Mohammed destroyed innumerable idols, and obtained, of course, incalculable riches. The whole country submitted, to the confines of Bengal.

Upon the return of Mohammed to Ghizni, Koottub was declared his adopted son, and confirmed in the government of India. By various expeditions, he chastised repeatedly the refractory rajas of Ajmere and Guzerat; took the cities of Calinger and Kalpy, with their respective territories; and at last made himself master of the forts of Biana and Gualior.

In the year 1202, Mohammed was excited to try his for-

1202.

tune for a share in the dismemberment of the Seljukian empire. Among the provinces of which the governors had thrown off their dependence upon the Seljukian princes, that of Kharism, on the eastern side of the Caspian Sea, had risen to the rank of an independent kingdom. under a race of princes known by the name of the Kharismian dynasty. Against Takash, the reigning sovereign of this kingdom, Mohammed led an army. But Osman, a Tartar chief, who had assumed the rank of sovereign in another part of Transoxiana, and had Samarcand for his capital, marched to the assistance of Takash; Mohammed sustained a total defeat; and was fain, by a great ransom, to purchase return to his own country. Intelligence of his defeat was to his servants the signal for revolt. His slave Ildekuz, having assumed supremacy in his capital of Ghizni, refused him admittance. He continued his route to Multan, where another of his servants took arms against him. Being joined by many of his friends, he gave the traitor battle, and obtained the victory. He next collected such of his troops as were in the contiguous provinces of India, and marched back to Ghizni where the rebellious slave was delivered up by the inhabitants.

At the same time with the other rebellious attempts, to which his defeat by the Kharismians had given birth, a tribe of Indians, inhabiting the country about the sources of the Indus from the Nilab or western branch of that river upwards to the Sewalik mountains; called by the Persian historian, Gickers, and by him described as a people excessively rude and barbarous, putting their female children to death; attempted the recovery of their independence, and proceeded towards Lahore. Mohammed had no sooner recovered his capital than he marched against them; and Koottub at the same time advancing from Delhi, they were attacked on both sides, and speedily subdued. Mohammed was returning to Ghizni, when he was murdered in his tent by two Gickers, who penetrated thither in the night.

The death of Mohammed, who left no children, produced a contest for the succession, and a division of the empire. Mahmood, his nephew, retained Gaur, of which he was governor. Eldoze, another governor, took possession of Candahar and Cabul; and Koottub claimed the

BOOK III. CHAP. II. 1210.

sovereignty of India. Eldoze marched against him; but was met and conquered. Koottub, following up his victory, proceeded to Ghizni, where he was crowned. He now resigned himself to sloth and indulgence. Eldoze, who had retired to Kirman,[1] his former province, obtained intelligence of this degeneracy, and of the disgust to which it had given birth. He raised an army, and surprised Koottub, who withdrew to India, and made no effort for the recovery of Ghizni; but is celebrated for having governed his Indian dominions with great justice and moderation. During his administration, Bahar and Bengal were added to the Mohammedan dominions.[2] He died only four years after the death of Mohammed, in 1210. Takash, the Kharismian, who had extended his sway over almost the whole of Persia, shortly after marched against Eldoze, and added Ghizni, with all the possessions of the Gaurides, as far as the Indus, to his extensive empire.

Koottub was succeded by his son Aram; who proved unequal to the task of reigning. Multan and Sind were seized upon by one chief; Bengal by another; and in almost every province the standard of revolt was raised, or preparing to be raised; when the Omrahs of Delhi invited Altumsh, the son-in-law of Koottub, and governor of Budaoon, now the country of the Rohillas, to ascend the throne. The reign of Aram scarcely completed a year.

Altumsh, like Koottub, had been a slave from Tartary; but, being remarkable for the beauty of his person, was thought by his master worthy of a good education. He was sold to Koottub for a large sum, and appointed master of the chase. He rapidly made his way to great favour; was at last married to the daughter of his sovereign; and declared his adopted son.

Altumsh ascended not the throne in perfect tranquillity. Several of Koottub's generals aspired to improve their fortune by resistance; and Eldoze, being driven from Ghizni by the arms of the Kharismian monarch, made an effort to procure for himself a sceptre in India. But

[1] This is said by Ferishta, to be distinct from the province of Persia, so called, and to designate a town between Ghizni and India. Briggs, i. 152.—W.

[2] Hist. of Bengal, by Charles Stewart, Esq., sect. iii.

Altumsh prevailed over all his opponents; and reigned from the mouths of the Indus to those of the Ganges.

This prince died in 1235, and was succeeded by his son
Feroze; who appearing a weak and dissolute prince, sub- 1235.
servient to the cruel passions of his mother, was soon deposed; and Sultana Ruzia, the eldest daughter of Altumsh, was raised to the throne.

It is a rare combination of circumstances which, in the East, places sovereign power in the hands of a woman. Ruzia possessed manly talents and great virtues. The idea, however, of the weakness of her sex, encouraged the presumption of her deputies in the various provinces. She contended with success against more than one rebellious and usurping governor. But her difficulties continually increased; and at last a combination of the Omrahs set up her brother Byram, as a competitor for the throne. She was still able to meet the rebels with an army. But the Turkish or Tartarian mercenaries in her brother's pay were an overmatch for her Indian troops. She was conquered and put to death, after a reign of three years and six months.

Byram the Second, nursed in pleasure, and a stranger to control, was a weak, imprudent prince. The jealousies which he felt towards the great men in his court, he sought to relieve by assassination. His vizir, having escaped an intended blow, found means to regain his confidence: and being placed at the head of an army against the Moguls, he matured the dissatisfaction of the Omrahs, and, turning the army of Byram against himself, dethroned and killed him, about two years after he had ascended the throne.

It was during this reign that the Moguls, destined to erect in India the greatest empire it had ever seen, first penetrated into that country. Jangiz, the chief of a tribe of Tartars, distinguished by the name of Moguls, who roamed with their flocks and herds on the northern side of the wall of China, formed, by talents and good fortune, one of those combinations, among different tribes of Tartars, which more than once within the period of history had been witnessed before; and never without extensive revolutions and conquests. Partly by force, partly by intimidation, partly by hopes of sharing in the advantages

BOOK III. CHAP. II. 1210.

of conquest, Jangiz, about the year 1210, was acknowledged as Khan, by all the shepherd-hordes from the wall of China to the Volga. The presumption and pride of two such elevated neighbours as the emperor of China and the new sovereign of Tartary, could not fail to kindle the flames of war. Innumerable squadrons of Tartars surmounted the unavailing rampart which the Chinese had in former ages raised to exclude them. Pekin was taken; and the northern provinces of China were added to the empire of Jangiz.

About the same time a quarrel arose on the opposite side of his dominions. Mohammed was now king of Kharism, which from a revolted province had grown into the seat of a great empire, extending from the borders of Arabia to those of Turkestan. The monarch of so many provinces, which prided themselves in their riches and the acquirements of civilized life, made light, it seems, of the power of him who ruled over multitudes, indeed, but of men who had no riches except their cattle, and no cities except their camps. An injury done to some of the subjects of Jangiz, for which all reparation was haughtily refused, first drew upon western Asia the fury of his arms. Mohammed crossed the Jaxartes to meet his enemy in the plains of Turkestan, with no less, it is said, than four hundred thousand men. But these were encountered by seven hundred thousand Tartars, under Jangis and his sons, who in the first battle, which was suspended by the night, laid one hundred and sixty thousand Kharismians dead upon the field.

After this fatal blow, Mohammed expected to arrest the progress of the victor, by throwing his troops into the frontier towns. But the arms of Jangiz were irresistible: the places of greatest strength were obliged to surrender; and Kharism, Transoxiana, and Khorasan, soon acknowledged the sovereignty of the Mogul. He was withdrawn, by the wishes of his troops, from the further prosecution of his conquests in the West, and died in the year 1227; but left sons and grandsons to copy the deeds of their progenitor. In the year 1258, the conquest of Persia was consummated; and the last remains of the power of the Caliphs and Seljukians trampled in the dust.

It was but an incursion which, in the year 1242, the Moguls, during the reign of Byram II., made into India: they plundered the country as far as Lahore, and then retreated to Ghizni.

1242.

Upon the fall of Byram, the men in power thought proper to take from his prison Musaood, the son of Feroze, the late king, and set him upon the throne. In the second year of his reign, an army of Mogul Tartars made a descent into Bengal, by the way, says Ferishta, of Chitta and Tibet.[1] They met, we are told, with a total defeat. On the following year, however, another army of the same people crossed the Indus; but Musaood marching against them in force, they were pleased to retire. Musaood, however, in a reign of four years, had disgusted his nobles by his vices; and made them bold by his weakness. They combined to call Mahmood, his uncle, to the throne, and Musaood was thrown into prison for life.

Mahmood II., upon the death of his father Altumsh, had been consigned to a prison; but there exhibited some firmness of mind, by supporting himself with the fruits of his industry in copying books; while he often remarked that "he who could not work for his bread did not deserve it." He was released by his predecessor, Musaood, and received the government of a province; in which he acted with so much vigour and prudence, that the fame of his administration recommended him to the Omrahs, as the fittest person to cover, with his power and authority, their rebellious enterprise.

The infirm administration of the preceding princes had introduced much disorder into the kingdom. The tribes of Hindus, known by the name of Gickers, a more active and enterprising race than the general body of their countrymen, had been guilty of many acts of insubordination

[1] This fact; the passage of an army from Tartary, through Tibet, into Bengal (if real) is of no small importance. Ferishta gives us no further intelligence of the place; and it is in vain to inquire. Chitta may perhaps correspond with Kitta or Kitay, or Catay, which is one of the names of China, but is also applied by the Persian historians to many parts of Tartary; to the country, for example, of the Igoors: to the kingdom of Koten, south from Cashgar, &c. See D'Herbelot, Biblioth. Orient. articles *Igurs*, *Cara Calhai*, *Tarikh*, *Khatha*, *Khotan*.—Mr. Stewart, (See Hist. of Bengal, p. 62) says, that the invasion which is here spoken of by Ferishta, was an invasion of Orissians only, not of Moguls.—M.

No confusion is made by Ferishta. The events are clearly quite distinct. There is nothing very extraordinary in an incursion into India from Tibet, through Nepal. It is not long since Nepal was invaded by a Chinese army.—Kirkpatrick's Nepal.—W.

BOOK III. CHAP. II. 1257.

and violence towards the Mohammedan government and people, in the provinces near the Indus. One of the first enterprises of Mahmood, was to chastise this people; many thousands of whom he carried away into captivity. Of the Omrahs, who had received *Jagheers*, or estates in land, many declined or refused to furnish their quota of troops for the army; though it was for the maintenance of those troops, that the estates, says Ferishta, were bestowed. The chiefs who infringed this condition were carried prisoners to Delhi; and their sons, or other relations, gifted with the estates. Some places of strength, in the country lying between the Jumna and the Ganges, were taken. A governor of the Indus, who had rebelled was reduced to obedience, and received into favour. Shir, the king's nephew, viceroy of Lahore and Multan, expelled the Moguls from Ghizni, and once more annexed that kingdom to the Indian part of the Gaurian empire. Mahmood fell into the error of disgusting his Omrahs, by pampering a favourite; but recovered his authority, by sacrificing, with a good grace, the author of his danger. A fresh army of the Moguls crossed the Indus, in the year 1257; but retired upon the approach of Mahmood. In the following year, an ambassador from Hallaku, the grandson of Jangiz, who had just completed the conquest of Persia, arrived at Delhi. The grandest possible display of the power and wealth of the empire seems to have been studied upon this occasion. To meet the representative of the conqueror, before whom Asia trembled, the vizir went out at the head of 50,000 foreign horse, 200,000 infantry, 2000 elephants of war, and 3000 carriages of fireworks. With this magnificent escort, the ambassador was conducted to the royal presence: all the officers, dignitaries, and dependants of the empire, in gorgeous attire, surrounding the throne. This appears to have been a message of peace; since nothing of importance occurred till the death of Shah, which happened in the year 1265.

This prince carried to the throne that contempt of pleasure and show, and that simplicity of manners, which he had learned in his adversity. "Contrary," says Ferishta, "to the custom of princes, he kept no concubines. He had but one wife, whom he obliged to do every homely part of housewifery; and when she complained one day, that she had burned her fingers in baking his bread, desiring he would allow her a maid to assist her, he rejected her request, with saying — that he was only a trustee for the state, and that he was determined not to burden it with needless expenses. He therefore exhorted her to persevere in her duty with patience, and God would reward her in the end. As the emperor of India never eats in public, his table was rather that of a hermit, than suitable to a great king. He also continued the whimsical notion of living by his pen. One day, as an Omrah was inspecting a Koran, of the emperor's writing before him, he pointed out a word which he said was wrong. The king, looking at it, smiled, and drew a circle round it. But when the critic was gone, he began to erase the circle, and restore the word. This being observed by one of his old attendants, he begged to know his Majesty's reason for so doing; to which he replied, 'that he knew the word was originally right, but he thought it better to erase from a paper, than to touch the heart of a poor man, by bringing him to shame.'"

Mahmood died without leaving any sons; and his vizir, Balin, who even in his life-time engrossed the principal share of power, without opposition, mounted the throne. Balin was originally a Turk, of Chitta,[1] of the tribe of Alberi. He was taken, when very young, by the Moguls who overran his country, and sold to a slave-merchant, who carried him to Bagdad. The master into whose hands he fell, learning that he was a relation of Altmush, who then reigned at Delhi, proceeded with him to that city, and presented him to that monarch, who received him gladly, and liberally rewarded his conductor.

A brother of Balin had already made his way to the court of Delhi, and was considerably advanced in the road of favour and power. The young adventurer improved his advantages; and rapidly ascended the ladder of promotion. He took an active part in all the revolutions which placed so many successors on the throne. In the

[1] The names of persons and places are carelessly and inaccurately written in most of the MSS. of Ferishta, and Dow seems to have taken little or no trouble in collating copies, and determining the preferable reading. In this respect, the translation by Col. Briggs is much more exemplary. Accordingly, we find in this place, the name of the king, not Balin, but Bulbun; he was a Turk, and a native of Kara-Khutta, part of Chinese Tartary.—W.

BOOK III. CHAP. II. 1265-70.

reign of Musaood he was raised to the dignity of lord of requests; and in that of Mahmood obtained the vizirat.

The reign of Balin was severe; but vigilant, clear-sighted, and consistent. He punished disobedience with rapidity and cruelty; but he distinguished talents with care, and rewarded services with discernment and generosity. The fame of his government made his alliance be courted, even by the Mogul sovereigns who reigned over Tartary and Persia.

"He expelled," says Ferishta, "all flatterers, usurers, pimps, and players, from his court; and being one day told, that an Omrah, an old servant of the crown, who had acquired a vast fortune by usury and monopoly in the bazaar or market, would present him with some lacks of rupees, if he would honour him with one word from the throne; he rejected the proposal with great disdain. What, he said, must his subjects think of a king who should condescend to hold discourse with a wretch so infamous." As freedom of bargain respecting interest on loans is exceptionable, on principles of superstition alone, Balin was possibly mistaken in his instance, without being correct in his rule. The association of the king with persons infamous by their vices, sheds no moral depravity among the people, except in that proportion exactly in which it sheds contempt upon the throne.

The generosity of Balin made his court the resort and asylum of the various princes, whom the arms of Jangiz and his successors had rendered fugitives from their kingdoms. More than twenty of these unfortunate sovereigns, from Tartary, Transoxiana, Khorasan, Persia, Irak, Azarbijan, Persia proper, Roum, and Syria, among whom were two princes of the race of the Caliphs, had allowances assigned them from the revenues of Balin, with palaces, which took their names from their possessors, and admission, on all public occasions, to the presence and throne of their benefactor. The most learned men from all Asia, accompanying their respective princes, or seeking the same asylum, were assembled at Delhi. "And the court of India," says the historian, "was, in the days of Balin, reckoned the most polite and magnificent in the world. All the philosophers, poets, and divines, formed a society every night, at the house of the prince Shehid, the heir

1283.

apparent to the empire. Another society of musicians, dancers, mimics, players, buffoons, and story-tellers, was constantly convened at the house of the emperor's second son Kera, who was given to pleasure and levity. The Omrahs followed the example of their superiors, so that various societies and clubs were formed in every quarter of the city."

The hills to the south-east of Delhi were inhabited by Hindus,[1] who acted the part of banditti and plunderers; and advanced, in numbers resembling an army, sometimes to the very walls of the capital. Balin ordered operations against them; and they were massacred without mercy. The soldiers, who carried hatchets for the purpose, cut down, to the distance of one hundred miles, the woods to which the robbers retired. The cleared space proved excellent land, and was speedily peopled; the inhabitants being protected from the mountaineers by a line of forts erected at the bottom of the hills.

The Shah gave considerable employment to his army, in bridling the wild inhabitants of the mountains near the centre of his dominions; but he rejected the advice of his counsellors to regain the distant provinces of Malwa and Guzerat, which had asserted their independence from the time of Koottub;[2] wisely observing, that the cloud of Moguls, now gathered on his northern frontier, presented an object of more serious and anxious regard.

His accomplished and philosophical son, Mohammed Shehid, was appointed viceroy of the northern provinces, to hold in check those dangerous neighbours. And he assembled around him the men, most eminent for thought or action, whom the Asiatic world at that time contained.

Argun, the grandson of Hallaku who subdued Persia, and the fourth in descent from Jangiz, now filled the throne of Persia; and another descendant of that renowned conqueror, by name Timur, ruled over the eastern provinces, from Khorasan to the Indus. In revenge for some former check, as well as by desire for extension of

[1] They were not the people of the hills, but the inhabitants of the Do-ab, and either bank of the Ganges below it; as Bhojpoor and Benares; an active, vigorous, and courageous race of peasantry. Their numbers and boldness at this period show that the Mohammedan authority was far from established, even in the districts adjacent to the capital.—W.

[2] They had never been conquered, only invaded by the Mohammedans, and that with various success.—W.

BOOK III. CHAP. II. 1285.

empire, Timur invaded India with a large army, in 1283. They were met by the Indian prince, and battle was joined. Both leaders displayed the talents of great generals; but Mohammed at last prevailed, and the Moguls betook themselves to flight. Mohammed joined in the pursuit. He had just halted, in order to return; when he was surprised with only five hundred attendants, by a party of the enemy; and, being overpowered by superior numbers, was slain defending himself to the last. The army and the empire were filled with grief by his fall.

While the son was engaged in his arduous defence of the empire against the Moguls, the father was employed in subduing a dangerous rebellion in Bengal. Toghrul, governor of that rich and powerful province, had executed an expedition against the Raja of Jajnagur, a province bounded on the north by Bengal, and on the east by Orissa. Succeeding, and obtaining great treasure, he began to feel himself too great for a subject; delayed remitting the Emperor's share of the plunder; and, hearing that Balin was sick, and too ill to survive, raised the red umbrella, and assumed the title of king. Balin ordered the Governor of Oude to assume the office of Subahdar of Bengal, and, with an army which he committed to his command, to march against the rebel. The new Subahdar was defeated; and Balin was so enraged that he bit his own flesh, and commanded the general to be hanged at the gate of Oude. Another of his generals, whom he sent to wipe off the disgrace, had no better success; when Balin, deeply affected, resolved to take the field in person. Toghrul, hearing of his approach, thought proper to elude the storm, by retiring. He intended to remain in Jajnagur till the Shah retired; and then to resume the command of the province. With some difficulty Balin procured intelligence of his route. An exploring party, at last, discovered and surprised his camp. Toghrul fled and was killed, when Balin inflicted sanguinary punishment on his adherents.

But the death of his great and hopeful son was a blow to the heart of Balin, to which no success could yield a remedy. Oppressed at once with grief, with business, and with old age (he was now in his eightieth year,) he languished for a short time, and expired. He appointed

1285.

his grandson, by the deceased Mohammed, his successor. Kera[1], however, the second son of Balin, was governor of Bengal, the most affluent province of the empire ; and the Omrahs, respecting his present power, more than the will of their deceased master, raised his son Kei Kobad to the throne.

Kei Kobad was in his eighteenth year, handsome in his person, of an affable and mild disposition, and not slightly tinctured with literature. His mother was a beautiful princess, daughter of the emperor Altumsh. "He delighted," says his historian, "in love, and in the soft society of silver-bodied damsels with musky tresses." He adds : "When it was publicly known that the king was a man of pleasure, it became immediately fashionable at court ; and, in short, in a few days, luxury and vice so prevailed, that every shade was filled with ladies of pleasure, and every street rung with music and mirth. The king fitted up a palace at Kilogurry, upon the banks of the river Jumna, and retired thither to enjoy his pleasures undisturbed, admitting no company but singers, players, musicians, and buffoons."

The father of Kei Kobad remained contented with his government of Bengal. But Nizam-ud-din, who became the favourite minister of the young Shah, conceived hopes, from the negligence of his master, of paving for himself a way to the throne. He proceeded to remove the persons whose pretensions were likely to obstruct his career. The many acts of cruelty and perfidy, of which he was the cause, shed discredit upon the government. The father of Kei Kobad saw the danger, and forewarned his son ; but the prince could not attend to business, without sacrificing pleasure. He found it, therefore, more agreeable to repose upon the minister, and neglected the advice. Kera, alarmed for his own fate, as well as that of his son, thought it advisable to second his advice with his presence, and his presence with an army. This was construed an act of hostility ; and the Shah marched out from Delhi, at the head of an army, to oppose his father. The father, either conscious of his inferiority in point of strength, or unwilling to proceed to the last extremity, requested an inter-

[1] Ferishta. Mr. Stewart says, that in his MSS. the name is Bagora.—M. Briggs writes it Kurra.—W.

BOOK III. CHAP. II. 1289.

view. This was dreaded by the minister, who endeavoured to blow up the vanity and presumption of the young monarch to such a pitch, that he might hear of nothing but a battle. Kera was not easy to be repulsed, and renewed his application by a letter full of parental expostulation and tenderness. The heart of the young prince was corrupted, but not yet thoroughly depraved. He could not resist the letter of his father: and Nizam-ud-din, no longer able to defeat the interview by direct, endeavoured to elude it by artificial means. He prevailed upon the prince, as sovereign, to insist upon the first interview, in hopes that Kera would refuse. Kera was not a slave to points of ceremony, and readily consented to repair to the imperial camp, where the son was prepared to display his insolence at even his father's expense. The throne was set out with the greatest pomp and ceremony; and Kei Kobad ascending, commanded that his father should three times kiss the ground. At the first door, the aged prince was ordered to dismount; and, when he came in sight of the throne, to perform the abject obeisance of the East, the mace-bearer at the same time calling out, according to custom, "The noble Kera to the king of the world sends health!" The father, whose heart was full, was no longer able to restrain his tears. Upon sight of his father in tears, the young prince forgot his insolence, and rushing from the throne, threw himself upon his face at his father's feet, and implored his forgiveness.[1]

The presence and admonitions of Kera made an impression upon the mind of Kei Kobad, which it was too soft to retain. "When he arrived at Delhi," says Ferishta, "the advice of his father, for a few days, seemed to take root in his mind. But his reformation was not the interest of the minister." He accordingly plied him with pleasure in all the shapes in which it was known to have the greatest influence on the mind. The most beautiful and accomplished women whom it was possible to procure were made to present themselves to him at all the most accessible moments, and invention was exhausted to find an endless variety of modes to surprise and captivate the prince with new combinations of charms. The most ex-

[1] Mr. Stewart has greatly softened the account of the insolence of Kei Kobad.

quisite musicians, dancers, players, buffoons, were collected to fill up the intervals left vacant by love.

The hatred, however, which the success, the presumption, and insolence of the minister had engendered in his fellow-courtiers; or the suspicions and fears which, at last, though tardily, were excited in the breast of the sovereign, cut short the days and machinations of Nizam-ud-din. He was taken off by poison. The authority of the king did not long survive. His intemperance in the haram brought on a palsy; which disabled him in one side, and distorted his countenance. All attention was then absorbed by the scramble for power. Every Omrah of popularity set up his pretensions. The friends of the royal family brought out the son of Kei Kobad, a child of three years old, and set him on the throne. He was supported by the Tartars; a body of whom, as mercenaries, were generally kept by the Indian sovereigns, whom they became the common instruments of setting up and pulling down. On the present occasion, the Tartars had a formidable body of competitors. Of the Afghans, or mountaineers of Gaur and Ghirgistan, on the frontiers of Persia, a tribe named Chilligi[1] made war and depredation their business; and usually, in great numbers, served, as mercenaries, any power which chose to employ them. An adventurer of this tribe, of the name of Mallek, who subsisted by his sword, rose to distinction in the army of Balin: and left his talent and his fortune to his son Feroze, who at the time of the illness of Kei Kobad, was one of the chief Omrahs, and commanded a province. He was joined by the Chilligi mercenaries, who attacked, and cut to pieces, the Tartars. There was no longer any obstruction. Kei Kobad was killed upon his bed, after a reign of little more than three years. Such was the termination of the Gaurian, or rather of the first Gaurian dynasty; and such the commencement of the Afghan, or second Gaurian dynasty, in the year 1289. At the time of this revolution, Kubla, the grandson of Jangiz, sat on the throne of Tartary and China; another of his descendants on that of Persia; and a third possessed a kingdom in Transoxiana, and those provinces to the north-west of the Indus, which constituted the original dominions of the house of Ghizni.

[1] It is written Khuliji by Major Stewart. —M. Khilji, Briggs.—W.

CHAPTER III.

From the Commencement of the second Gaurian or Afghan Dynasty, to the Commencement of the Mogul Dynasty.

BOOK III. CHAP. III.

FEROZE was seventy years of age when he became the master of the kingdom. He was a man of intelligence; and though guilty of cruelty and injustice in acquiring or establishing his throne, he sought to distinguish himself by the justice, and also the popularity, of his administration. "For that purpose," says his historian, "he gave great encouragement to the learned of that age; who, in return, offered the incense of flattery at the altar of his fame."

Chidju,[1] however, a prince of the royal blood, nephew of the late Balin, and a nabob or governor of a province, obtained the alliance of several chiefs, and marched with an army towards Delhi. Feroze placed himself at the head of his army, and sent forward his son with the Chilligi cavalry. The prince encountered the enemy, and obtaining an advantage, took several Omrahs prisoners, whom he mounted upon camels with branches hung round their necks. When Feroze beheld them in this state of humiliation, he ordered them to be unbound, gave a change of raiment to each, and set an entertainment before them; repeating the verse, "That evil for evil it was easy to return; but he only was great who could return good for evil." In a few days Chidju was taken prisoner, and sent to the king; but instead of death, which he expected, received a pardon, and was sent to reside at Multan, on a handsome appointment for life. To the Omrahs of the Chilligi, displeased at so much lenity, Feroze replied, "My friends, I am now an old man, and I wish to go down to the grave without shedding blood."

The mind of this prince, however, did not, it seems, distinguish sufficiently between lenity and relaxation. The police of the empire was neglected; and robbery, murder, insurrection, ever ready to break loose in India, diffused insecurity over the nation. The Omrahs of the Chilligi "began," says Ferishta, "to lengthen the tongue

[1] Jujhoo is the reading of this name by Briggs.—W.

1291.

of reproach against their sovereign." The design was conceived of raising one of themselves to the throne; the project was even discussed at an entertainment, at which they were assembled; but one of the company privately withdrew and informed the emperor, who immediately ordered them to be arrested and brought before him. It occurred to one of them to represent the affair as a drunken frolic, and the words as the suggestion of intoxication. The prince was pleased to accept the apology; and dismissed them with a rebuke. He was not so lenient to a Dervish, or professor of piety, who by the appearance of great sanctity, and by the distribution of great liberalities to the poor, the source of which no one could discover, acquired immense popularity; and on this foundation aspired, or was accused of aspiring, to the throne. Though little or no evidence appeared against him, he was cruelly put to death.

With his expiring breath, the holy Dervish cursed Feroze and his posterity; nature was thrown into convulsions upon the death of the saint; and from that hour the fortunes of Feroze were observed to decline. His eldest son was afflicted with insanity, which no power of medicine could remove. Factions and rebellions disturbed his administration. In the year 1291, Hindustan was invaded by a prince of the house of Jangiz, at the head of 100,000 Moguls; and though Feroze engaged them, and obtained the advantage, he was glad to stipulate for the departure of the invaders, by consenting to let them retreat unmolested.

In this reign occurred an event of great importance in the history of Hindustan; the first invasion of the Deccan by Mohammedan arms. Deccan means the south; and is applied in a general manner to the kingdoms and districts included in the southern portion of India. It does not appear that the application of the name was ever precisely fixed. It has been commonly spoken of as indicating the country south of the Nerbudda river, which falls into the Gulf of Cambay, at Baroach; but as the Patan or Mogul sovereignties hardly extended beyond the rives Kistna, it is only the country between those two rivers which, in the language of India, commonly passes under the name of the Deccan.

1298. Alla, the nephew of Feroze, was Nabob, or Governor of Korah, one of the districts of the Doab, or country lying between the Ganges and the Jumna. Having distinguished himself in a warfare with some rajas who bordered on his province, he was gratified by the addition to his government of the province of Oude. His first success appears to have suggested further enterprise. He solicited and obtained the consent of Feroze to extend his empire over the Hindus. Having collected such an army as his resources allowed, he marched directly, by the shortest route, against Ramdeo, one of the rajas of the Deccan, whose capital was Deogur, now Dowlatabad.[1] Alla met with no inconsiderable resistance; but finally prevailed, and exacted heavy contributions (exaggerated by the pen of Oriental history into incredible sums), as the price of his return. He retreated many days through several hostile and populous kingdoms; the governments of which were too weak or too stupid to offer any obstruction to his march.

Feroze was not without uneasiness upon intelligence of the ambitious adventure of Alla; and of the great addition to his power which the vastness of his plunder implied. He rejected, however, the advice of his wisest counsellors, to take previous measures for the securing of his authority and power; and resolved to repose on the fidelity of his nephew. He was even so weak as to permit Alla, on feigned pretences, to entice him to Korah, where he was barbarously assassinated, having reigned only seven years and some months.

Alla made haste to get into his power the family of Feroze; of whom all who were the objects of any apprehension were unrelentingly murdered; and the rest confined. He had scarcely time, however, to settle the affairs of his government, when he learned that the Mogul sovereign of Transoxiana had invaded the Punjab with an army of 100,000 men. An army, commanded by his brother, was sent to expel them. A battle was fought in the neigh-

[1] Written Deogire, by Col. Wilks, and declared to be the Tagara of Ptolemy. The author of the Tibcat Nasiri says, that Alla left Korah on pretence of a hunting party, and passing through the territories of many petty rajas, too feeble to think of opposing him, he came upon Ramdeo by surprise. Ferishta. i. 231. The proofs of the division and subdivision of India into a great number of petty states meet us at every step in its authentic history.

1303.

bourhood of Lahore, in which the Indians were victorious, and the Moguls retreated. The successful general was sent into Guzerat, which he quickly reduced to the obedience of the Shah.

The Moguls returned the following year with much greater force; and marched even to the walls of Delhi, to which they laid siege. Alla at last collected his army, and gave them battle. Though his success was not decisive, the Moguls thought proper to retreat.

The king's arbitrary maxims of government, and the odious manner in which he arrived at the supreme command, engendered disaffection; and during the first years of his reign, he was harassed by perpetual insurrections and rebellions. He applied himself, however, with industry and intelligence, to the business of government; and though his administration was severe and oppressive, it was regular and vigorous, securing justice and protection to the body of the people. His education had been so neglected that he could neither read nor write; but feeling the disadvantages under which his ignorance laid him, he had firmness of mind to set about the work of his own instruction even upon the throne; acquired the inestimable faculties of reading and writing; made himself acquainted with the best authors in the Persian language; invited learned men to his court; and delighted in their conversation.

In 1303, he projected another expedition into the Deccan by the way of Bengal, but was recalled by a fresh invasion of the Moguls of Transoxiana; who advanced as far as Delhi, but retreated without sustaining a battle. After their departure, he resolved, by an augmentation of his army, to leave himself nothing to fear from that audacious enemy. But reflecting that his revenues were unequal to so great a burden, he resolved to reduce the soldiers' pay. Reflecting again, that this would be dangerous, while the price of articles continued the same, he ordered all prices to be reduced a half; by that means, says Ferishta, with an ignorance too often matched in more instructed countries, "just doubling his treasures and revenue." The Moguls were not discouraged by frequency of repulse. The armies of the king of Transox-

BOOK III. CHAP. III.

iana twice invaded Hindustan in 1305, and were twice defeated by Toghluk, the general of Alla.

1310. In the following year the design against the Deccan was renewed, and prosecuted with greater resources. Kafoor a slave and eunuch, his favorite, and, it was said, the instrument of his pleasures, was placed at the head of a grand army, and marched towards the south. He first "subdued the country of the Mahrattors,[1] which he divided among his Omrahs," and then proceeded to the siege of Deogur. Ramdeo endeavoured to make his peace by submission; and having agreed to pay a visit to the emperor at Delhi, and to hold his territories as a dependency, he was dismissed with magnificent presents, and his dominions were enlarged.

The division of the Deccan, known by the name of Telingana, is supposed to have extended, along the eastern coast, from the neighbourhood of Chicacole on the north, to that of Pulicat on the south; and to have been separated on the west from the country known by the name of Maharashtra, or by contraction Mahratta, by a line passing near Beder, and at some distance east of Dowlutabad, to the river Tapti.[2]

Alla was on his march against the Rajah of Warunkul, one of the princes in this district, in 1303, when he was recalled by another invasion of the Moguls. He made, indeed, a part of his army proceed in the expedition, for the purpose of reducing the fort of Warunkul, a place of great strength, and, by repute, of immense riches; but the project failed. In 1307, Kafoor was ordered to march into Telingana by the way of Deogur, and lay siege to Warunkul. Warunkul was taken by assault, after a siege of some months.[3] The Raja made his peace, by sacrificing largely to the avarice of his conquerors, and accepting the condition of a tribute.

The more Alla tasted of the plunder of the Deccan, the

[1] This is the first mention which we find of any of the tribes to whom the term Mahrattors or Mahratta, is applied, by the Moslem historians. From this statement we can only conjecture, that some district in the Deccan, inhabited by the description of Hindus to whom this name was applied, was overrun, and nominally parcelled out by Kafoor.

[2] Wilks, Hist. of Mysore, p. 6.

[3] The neighbouring Rajas, says Ferishta, hastened to the assistance of the Rajah of Warunkul; another proof of the division into petty sovereignties.

more he thirsted for additional draughts. In 1310, Kafoor was sent on a more distant expedition. He marched by Deogur; and penetrating as far as the Carnatic, took the Raja prisoner, and ravaged his kingdom. According to the historians, he returned with such wealth as no country ever yielded to a predatory invader.[1] Nor did he remain long at Delhi before he persuaded the Shah to send him once more into the Deccan, where he ravaged several countries, and sent the plunder to Alla. This prince had ruined his constitution by intemperance in the seraglio; and felt his health in rapid decline. He sent for Kafoor from the Deccan, and complained to him of the undutiful behaviour of his wife and his son. Kafoor, whose eyes had already turned themselves with longing to the throne, contemplated the displeasure of the emperor against his family as a means for realizing his most extravagant hopes. He prevailed upon Alla to throw his two eldest sons, and their mother, into prison, and to put to death several of the chiefs by whom his pretensions were most likely to be opposed. When things were in this train, Alla expired in the year 1316, in the twenty-first year of his reign.

The time was not yet come when Kafoor deemed it expedient to declare himself king. He produced a testament, genuine or spurious, of the late prince, in which he appointed Omar, his youngest son, then seven years of age, his successor, and Kafoor regent. The first act of Kafoor's administration was to put out the eyes of the two eldest of the sons of Alla: but there was a third, Mubarik, who escaped, till a conspiracy of the foot-guards put the regent to death, only thirty-five days after the decease of his master. The reins of government were immediately put into the hands of Mubarik; but he thought proper to act in the name of his young brother, already upon the throne, for the space of two months, till he had gained the Omrahs. He then claimed his birthright; deposed his brother; according to the Asiatic custom, put out his eyes, and sent him for life to the fort of Gualior.

Mubarik was a man of vicious inclinations, and mean

[1] Besides several *chests* of jewels, pearls, and other precious things, the gold alone amounted to about one hundred millions sterling. Col. Dow thinks this not at all incredible: Hist. of Hindost. i. 276: and Col. Wilks (Hist. of Mysore, p. 11) seems to have little objection.

BOOK III. CHAP. III. 1321.

understanding. He for a moment sought popularity, by remitting the more oppressive of the taxes, and relaxing the reins of government; but the last so injudiciously, that disorder and depredation overran the country.

The reduction of the revolted Guzerat was one of the first measures of Mubarik. The enterprise, being intrusted to an officer of abilities, was successfully performed.

The Rajas in the Deccan yielded a reluctant obedience; which, presuming on their distance, they imagined they might now, without much danger, suspend. Mubarik, in the second year of his reign, raised a great army, and marched to Deogur; where, not finding much resistance, he did little more than display his cruelty, in the punishment of those who, charged with enmity or disobedience, fell into his hands.

Among the favourites of Mubarik, was Hassan, formerly a slave, and according to Ferishta, the son of a seller of rags in Guzerat.[1] This man was an instrument of the pleasures of the Shah; and upon his accession to the throne, had been honoured with the title of Khosroo, and raised to the office of Vizir. Finding nothing more to perform in the region of Deogur, Mubarik placed Khosroo at the head of a part of the army, and sent him on an expedition against Malabar, while he himself returned with the remainder to Delhi.

The vices of Mubarik, and of his government, became daily more odious. He was the slave of every species of intemperance, and void of every humane or manly quality, which could procure the indulgence of mankind to his faults. Conspiracy succeeded conspiracy, and one insurrection another; till Khosroo, beholding the contempt in which his master was held, believed he might shed his blood with safety, and place himself upon his throne. The reputation and plunder derived from the success of his expedition to Malabar,[2] had added greatly to his power. He made use of his influence over the mind of the emperor, to fill, with his creatures, the chief places both in

[1] He was a converted Purwary or Hindoo outcast. Briggs's Ferishta, i. 387.—W.

[2] According to Wilks, what is here called Malabar was not the district which is now called by that name, but the hilly belt along the summit of the Ghauts, from Soonda to Coorg. Hist. of Mysore, p. 10.

1323.

the army and the state. In the year 1321, he conceived himself prepared for the blow; when in one night, Mubarik and his sons were destroyed.

On mounting the throne, Khosroo assumed the title of Nasir-ud-din, or defender of religion; a cause which has seldom been associated with that of government, except for the purpose of fraud; and Khosroo, it seems, was aware that, for his government, such a covering was required.

He put to death, without remorse, a great multitude of persons in the service of Mubarik; all those from whom he imagined that he had anything to fear, and distributed the offices of government among his creatures. "The army," says Ferishta, "loved nothing better than a revolution; for they had always, upon such an occasion, a donation of six months' pay immediately advanced from the treasury:" so exactly does military despotism resemble itself, on the banks of the Tiber, and those of the Ganges.

But though Khosroo met with no opposition in ascending the throne, he did not long enjoy his kingdom in peace.

Ghazi[1] was Governor of Lahore; and though, for the sake of securing him to his interest, Khosroo had bestowed high office and rank upon his son Jonah; Jonah made his escape from Delhi, and joined his father at Lahore.

Ghazi despatched circular letters to the Omrahs, exerted himself to raise forces, and was joined by several of the viceroys with their troops. Khosroo despatched an army to subdue the rebellion; but the soldiers of Ghazi were hardened by frequent wars with the Moguls; those of Khosroo, enervated by the debauchery of the city, were broken at the first onset; and the confederates marched with expedition to the capital. Khosroo was ready to receive them with another army. Though betrayed and deserted in the action by a part of his troops, he maintained the conflict till night; when he made a fruitless endeavour to fly with a few of his friends. Deserted by his attendants, and dragged from his lurking-place, he met the fate which he would have bestowed.

The Omrahs hastened to pay their respects to the victor;

[1] Ghazi Beg Toghluk is the appellation of this nobleman in Ferishta.—W

BOOK III. CHAP. III. 1323.

and the magistrates of Delhi presented to him the keys. Mounting his horse, he entered the city, and arriving at the gates of the palace, he addressed the people: "O ye subjects of this great empire! I am no more than one of you, who unsheathed my sword to deliver you from oppression, and rid the world of a monster. If, therefore, any of the royal line remains, let him be brought, that we, his servants, may prostrate ourselves before his throne. If not, let the most worthy of the illustrious order be elected among you, and I shall swear to abide by your choice." But the people cried out, with vehemence, that none of the royal family remained alive; and that he, who had protected the empire from the Moguls, and delivered it from the tyrant, was the most worthy to reign. He was then seized, and by a sort of violence, placed upon the throne; the people hailing him "King of the world."

Toghluk is the name by which the new emperor chose to be distinguished. It was the name of his father, who is understood to have been a slave in the service of Balin. His mother was of the tribe of the Jauts.

After appointing the instruments of his government, the first care of Toghluk was to secure his northern frontier against the formidable incursions of the Moguls; and so judiciously did he station his force, and erect his forts, that he was not once molested by those invaders during his reign.

This being accomplished, he sent his son Jonah into the Deccan to chastise the Raja of Warunkul, who, during the late disorders, "had withdrawn his neck from the yoke of obedience." Jonah, with the usual ease, hardly meeting with any resistance, overran the Hindu kingdoms: leaving everywhere behind him the cruel marks of imperial vengeance and avarice. After a few efforts in the field, the Raja of Warunkul shut himself up in his strong-hold, and was besieged. From the strength of the place, the siege was a work of time; during which, sickness, and along with sickness, desire to return, and from that desire, opposed disaffection, spread themselves in the Mohammedan army. Several of the Omrahs withdrew with their troops; when the Prince, no longer able to continue the siege, retreated first to Deogur, and thence to Delhi. The army was recruited with great expedition, and he marched again in a few months towards Warunkul, which soon yielded to his arms. Many thousands of the Hindus were put to the sword; and the Raja and his family were sent to Delhi. Appointing Omrahs to the government of Telingana, he marched against Cuttack, where he gained some advantages, and then returned by the way of Warunkul to Delhi.

Toghluk, receiving complaints of great oppression against his officers in Bengal, appointed Jonah governor of Delhi, and marched toward that province with an army. Nasir,[1] the grandson of the emperor Balin, had possessed the viceroyalty of Bengal, since the death of his father. He advanced to meet the Emperor with submission and presents; and was confirmed in his government. Jonah, with the nobles of Delhi, went out to meet his father with rejoicings upon his return. A wooden house was hastily erected to entertain him. When the entertainment was concluded, and the emperor was about to retire, the Omrahs hurrying out to be in readiness to attend him, the roof suddenly fell in, and crushed him, with several of his attendants; whether by the contrivance of Jonah, by the fault of the building, or a stroke of lightning, was variously conjectured and believed. He reigned but four years and some months, with the reputation of a wise and excellent prince.

Jonah mounted the throne by the title of Mohammed III.; and began his reign with acts of liberality and beneficence. He distributed profuse gifts, and made magnificent appointments. This prince was a compound of heterogeneous qualities. He was generous to profusion; a lover of literature, in which he had made considerable acquirements; he was not only temperate but austere in his manner of life, and an attentive performer of acts of religion; he had no regard, however, to justice, or to humanity; he was cruel and vindictive as a man; oppressive and tyrannical as a ruler. His plans proceeded on the supposition, that the happiness or misery of his subjects was a matter of indifference; and when their disaffection began to afford him uneasiness, their misery seemed to become an object of preference and a source of gratification. He displayed, however, no contemptible talents in supporting himself against the hatred and detestation of mankind.

[1] His name was Nasir-ud-din Kurra Khan, and he was the son of Bulbun, see p. 195.—W.

BOOK III. CHAP. III. 1324-51.

Immediately upon his accession he directed his attention to the further subjugation of the Deccan; but more, it would appear, with a view to plunder, than to permanent dominion. His generals appear to have overrun a large portion of its more accessible parts. He reduced the Carnatic; and in the hyperbolical language of Ferishta, spread his conquests to the extremity of the Deccan, and from sea to sea.

He adopted frantic schemes of ambition. He raised an army for the conquest of the kingdom of Transoxiana and Khorasan, and another for the subjugation of China. Previous to the grand expedition against China, 100,000 horse were sent to explore the route through the mountains, and to establish forts to the confines of China. The horse did, we are told, penetrate to the frontiers of China, but were met with an army which they durst not oppose; and the rains, covering with water the roads and the plains, obstructed their retreat. They perished through fatigue, famine, and disease; and scarcely a man survived to describe the disaster. The inaccurate and uninstructive genius of Oriental history gives us no information respecting the track which this ill-fated army pursued.

The expense of Mohammed's government led him to oppress his subjects by increase of taxes. To this great cause of misery and discontent, he added others by injudicious schemes of finance. "The King," says Ferishta, "unfortunately for his people, adopted his ideas upon currency, from a Chinese custom of using paper upon the emperor's credit, with the royal seal appended, for ready money. Mohammed, instead of paper, struck a copper coin, which, being issued at an imaginary value, he made current by a decree throughout Hindustan," This produced so much confusion and misery, and so completely obstructed the collection of the revenue, that Mohammed was obliged to recall his debased coin; and individuals acquired immense fortunes by the ruin of many thousands, the general misery of the people, and the impoverishment of the sovereign.

Being called into the Deccan, to suppress an insurrection raised by his nephew, whom he ordered to be flayed alive, and in that condition carried, a horrid spectacle, round the city; he took a fancy to the situation of Deogur, resolved to make it his capital, by the name of Dowlatabad, and to remove thither the inhabitants of Delhi. This caprice he carried into execution, unmoved by the calamities that were to fall upon the individuals, and unable to foresee the alienation in the minds of men to which the sight and the reports of so much unnecessary evil must of necessity expose him. "The emperor's orders," says the historian, "were strictly complied with, and the ancient capital was left desolate."

The provinces, one after another, began now to rebel. The Governor of Multan set the example. Scarcely was he subdued when Bengal broke into insurrection. This, too, the vigour of Mohammed quickly reduced. He was thence summoned by disturbances in Telingana, where he lost great part of his army by a plague, then raging at Warunkul. But what, to the mind of Mohammed, was of more importance than the lives of half the inhabitants of Hindustan, he himself was afflicted with the tooth-ache. He even lost a tooth. This he commanded to be buried with solemn pomp, and a magnificent tomb to be erected over it.

Calamity in every shape assailed the wretched subjects of Mohammed. Such was the excess of taxation, that in many parts, particularly in the fertile country between the Jumna and the Ganges, the cultivators fled from their fields and houses, and preferred a life of plunder and rapine in the woods. From this and from unfavourable seasons, famine raged about Delhi, and the neighbouring provinces; and multitudes of people perished from want. A chief of the Afghans came down from the mountains, and plundered the province of Multan. The fierce tribes of Hindus, called by Ferishta, Gickers, were combined by a leader, and ravaged the Punjab and Lahore.

Mohammed, struck at last with the calamities of his reign, had recourse to religion for a cure. He sent a splendid embassy to Mecca, that, his coronation being confirmed by the successor of the prophet, the blessing of Heaven might descend upon his throne.

The Rajas of Telingana and the Carnatic formed a confederacy; and within a few months expelled the Mohammedans from every place in the Deccan, except Dowlatabad.

Even the Viceroy of Oude rebelled. But the emperor, marching against him with expedition, brought him quickly

BOOK III. CHAP. III. 1324-51.

to his feet. Contrary to his usual practice, Mohammed pardoned the offender, and even restored him to his government; declaring, that he would not believe in his guilt, and ascribing his transgression to a temporary delusion, which the malice and falsehood of others had produced.

An effort was made to regain what had been lost in the Deccan, and governors and troops were despatched to the different districts: who in the way of plunder performed considerable feats. But in the mean time disturbances of a new description broke out in Guzerat. Of the mercenary troops, composed of Tartars, Afghans, and other hardy races from the North, in which consisted a great proportion of the armies of the Mohammedan emperors of Hindustan, a considerable number, during some ages, had been Moguls. Of these it would appear that a considerable body had been sent to keep in check the turbulent inhabitants of Guzerat. They began now to commit depredations, and to set the power of Mohammed at defiance. Mohammed resolved to punish and extirpate them. The presence of the emperor, and their fears, made them withdraw from Guzerat; but they retired into the Deccan, and took Dowlatabad by surprise. Mohammed allowed them little time to make an establishment. They ventured to meet him in battle, when they were partly slain and partly dispersed. Before, he could take the city, fresh disturbances arose in Guzerat. Leaving an Omrah to push the reduction of Dowlatabad, he hastened to the new insurgents. An army of no inconsiderable magnitude opposed him. He carried on his operations with vigour, and once more prevailed. But in the mean time the Moguls in the Deccan, gathering strength upon his departure, defeated his general, and pursued his troops towards Malwa. He resolved to march against them in person. But the settlement of Guzerat was an arduous and a tedious task. Before it was concluded, he fell sick, and died in the year 1351, after a reign of twenty-seven years.

His death was propitious to the Moguls in the Deccan; and afforded time for laying the foundation of a Mohamedan empire, which rose to considerable power, and preserved its existence for several centuries. Upon seizing Dowlatabad, the rebel chiefs agreed to elect a sovereign; when their choice fell upon Ismael, an Afghan, who had been commander of a thousand in the imperial army. Among the insurgents was a military adventurer of the name of Hussun. Wonderful things are recorded of his predestination to power; as usually happens in the case of those who, from a degraded station, rise to great command over the hopes and fears of mankind. He was an Afghan slave or dependent of a Brahmen, who professed astrology in Delhi. The Brahmen gave him a couple of oxen to cultivate a piece of waste ground near the city, as a means of livelihood, where his plough turned up a treasure. He informed the Brahmen; and the Brahmen, equally conscientious, or equally cautious, the emperor. The Emperor, struck with the honesty of Hussun, bestowed upon him the command of one hundred horse. The Brahmen told him, that he saw by the stars he was destined to greatness, and stipulated that, when king of the Deccan, he would make him his minister. Hussun offered his services to the first commander who was sent into the Deccan; joined the insurgents; and when Ismael was chosen king, he was decorated with the title of Zuffer Khan; and received a large jaghir for the maintenance of his troops.

After Mohammed was summoned from the Deccan, by the new disturbances in Guzerat, and after his general was obliged to raise the siege of Dowlatabad, Zuffer Khan marched with twenty thousand horse against Beder, a city on the Godavery, nearly a hundred miles north-west from Golconda, and about the same distance west from Warunkul. This had been the seat of a Hindu rajahship: it was at this time a station of one of the imperial generals. Zuffer Khan, obtaining the assistance of the Rajáh of Warunkul, who sent him fifteen thousand men; and being reinforced with five thousand horse, detached to his assistance by the new king of Dowlatabad, engaged and defeated the army of Mohammed. Returning with glory and plunder, he was met, before reaching the capital, by the king; who could not help observing, that more attention was paid to the general than to himself. Making a merit of what would soon be necessary: and taking the pretext of his great age, he proposed to retire from the cares of government, and recommend Zuffer Khan as successor. The proposition was applauded; and the slave or peasant Hussun, mounting the new throne by the style and title of Sultan Alla-ud-din, Hussun Kon-

BOOK III. CHAP. III. 1358-89.

goh Bhamenee, became the founder of the Bhamenee dynasty. Koolburga, or Culberga, which had been the place of his residence, he named Ahsunabad, and rendered it the capital of the Deccanee empire.

Sultan Alla was not unmindful of his ancient master; from whose name he added the term Kongoh,[1] and according to some authorities, that of Bahmenee, Brahmen being so pronounced, to his royal titles. He invited Kongoh from Delhi; made him lord of the treasury; and in his edicts associated the name of the Brahmen with his own. Hussun lived, after the acquisition of royalty, eleven years, two months, and seven days; having in that time reduced to his obedience all the regions in Deccan which had ever acknowledged the sway of the emperors of Delhi. He governed with wisdom and moderation, and died at Koolburga, in the year 1357, and the sixty-seventh year of his age.[2]

Upon the death of the Emperor Mohammed, his nephew Feroze, whom he recommended for his successor, was in the imperial camp, and without difficulty mounted the throne. The nerves of the state were relaxed by misgovernment: and it displayed but little vigour during the days of Feroze. The governor of Bengal aspired to independence: and the emperor, after several efforts, being unable to reduce him

[1] This word is more correctly, Gungoo.—W.

[2] A circumstantial history of the Bahmenee sovereigns was composed by Ferishta; and to Jonathan Scott we are indebted for an instructive translation of it. The above sketch of the origin of the Bahmenee dynasty is drawn partly from Ferishta's Deccan, translated by Scott; partly from his history of Delhi, translated by Dow. The facts are very shortly mentioned, or rather alluded to, by Lieut.-Col. Mark Wilks (Historical Sketches of the South of India, ch. i.); where the reader will also find all that research has been able to procure of Hindu materials, and all that sagacious conjecture has been able to build upon a few imperfect fragments of the history of the ancient Hindu governments in the south of India.—M.

It is not correet to say that Col. Wilks's work, however ably and industriously wrought out of imperfect materials, has exhausted those materials: his chief sources of information were the MS. collections of the late Col. Mackenzie, but a small part only of those MSS. were then accessible, nor was their extent or value understood. They are now in a much more serviceable condition, partly owing to the catalogue of the Mackenzie collection published by myself, and partly to a still more careful and competent examination of them by the Rev. Mr. Taylor, of Madras, now in progress. Besides these materials, valuable translations of inscriptions in the Deccan, and other documents relating to that part of India, have been published in the Journal of the Asiatic Society of Bengal, in the Madras Journal, and the Transactions of the Royal Asiatic Society; so that means exist of carrying on a more connected and comprehensive view of the political and religious history of the Peninsula, from an early date of the Christian era to modern times, than were those employed by Col. Wilks.—W.

to obedience, was forced to content himself with a nominal subjection.[1] Feroze, however, employed himself with laudable solicitude, in promoting agriculture, and the internal prosperity of his dominions. He lived till the age of ninety years; twenty-eight of which he spent upen the throne. He is celebrated in history for having constructed fifty great acqueducts or reservoirs of water; forty mosques; thirty schools; twenty caravanseras; an hundred palaces; five hospitals; one hundred tombs; ten baths; ten spires; one hundred and fifty wells; one hundred bridges; and pleasure-gardens without number.

Mohammed, a son of Feroze, had received the reins of government from his father, when the weight of them began to press heavily upon his aged hands. A conspiracy, however, of the Omrahs, had, after a time, obliged him to fly from the throne; and Feroze made Toghluk,[2] his grandson, successor. Toghluk was a friend to pleasure, and slenderly provided with talents. He made an effort to get into his power Mohammed his uncle, who had been chased from the throne; but Mohammed threw himself into the fort of Nagracote, which, for the present, it was deemed inexpedient to attack. The emperor, meanwhile, inspired so little respect, that Abu Beker, his cousin, in danger from his jealousy, found himself able to hurry him to his grave. By means of some Omrahs, he corrupted the imperial slaves; who assassinated their master, after he had reigned but five months.

Abu Beker was hardly more fortunate. Some of the Mogul mercenaries in the imperial service, conspired against him, and invited Mohammed from Nagracote, to place himself at their head. Mohammed succeeded; and Abu Beker resigned his life and his throne one year and six months after the death of Toghluk.

In the reign of Mohammed, the Mahrattors (Mahrattas) again appear in the field. They were soon brought to submission; and Narsing, their prince, waited upon the empe-

[1] Such is the account of Ferishta. Mr. Stewart (Hist. of Bengal, sect. iv.) follows other authorities, who represent Bengal as now erected into a Mohammedan kingdom, perfectly independent.—M.

Stewart's account is confirmed by coins struck by Sultan Sekander and his successors. J. Asiatique.—W.

[2] It should be Gheias-ud-din. Toghluk was the name of the family borne by all of the members.—W.

ror at Delhi. The six years of this emperor were chiefly employed in subduing or anticipating the insurrections of the principal Omrahs or governors, from whom he enjoyed scarce an interval of repose. His son Humayoon, who succeeded him, was seized with a fatal disorder, and survived his father not many days.

The Omrahs, after high dispute, at last raised Mahmood, an infant son of the late Mohammed, to the throne. The distractions in the empire increased.

Three of the most powerful Omrahs of the court, Mookurrib, Ekbal, and Sadut, fell into deadly feuds. The emperor, having left the capital, with the army commanded by Sadut, Mookurrib, fearing the resentment of Sadut, shut the gates of the city. The emperor was constrained to abandon Sadut, before he was allowed to re-enter his capital and palace. Joined by his sovereign, Mookurrib, the next day, marched out and gave battle to Sadut, but was worsted and forced back into the city. As the rains had commenced, Sadut was obliged to lead his army into quarters. He immediately sent for Noosrut, a prince of the blood, and set him up in opposition to Mahmood, by the name of Noosrut Shah. A conspiracy soon threw Sadut into the hands of Mokurrib, who put him to death. But a strong party adhered to Noosrut; and a most destructive contest ensued between the partisans of the rival kings. The balance continued nearly even for the space of three years, during which every species of calamity oppressed the wretched inhabitants. Some of the distant Subahdars looked on with satisfaction, contemplating their own elevation in the depression of the imperial power. But in the year 1396, Mohammed Jehangir, the grandson of Timur or Tamerlane, having constructed a bridge over the Indus, invaded Multan. The governor, who already regarded the province as his own, opposed him with no contemptible force; but was overcome, and resigned Multan to the conqueror. In the mean time the Omrah Ekbal obtained and betrayed the confidence of Noosrut, whom he obliged to fly to Paniput. He opened a deceitful negotiation with the Emperor. under cover of which he surprised and slew Mookurrib. All power now centred in Ekbal; and the emperor was converted into a cipher. In this situation were affairs at Delhi, when intelligence arrived that Timur himself had crossed the Indus.

1396.

The birth of Timur, or Tamerlane, was cast at one of those recurring periods, in the history of Asiatic sovereignties, when the enjoyment of power for several generations, having extinguished all manly virtues in the degenerate descendants of some active usurper, prepares the governors of the provinces for revolt, dissolves the power of the state, and opens the way for the elevation of some new and daring adventurer. At no preceding period, perhaps, had these causes enervated the powers of government over so great a part of Asia at once, as at the time of Tamerlane. The descendants of Jangiz had formed their immense conquests into three great kingdoms; of which Persia was one; the intermediate regions of Transoxiana, Khorasan, Bactria, and Zabulistan or Kandahar, and Kabul, lying between Tartary and Persia, were the second; and Tartary itself, or rather Tartary and China in conjunction, the third. The dynasties of the race of Jangiz, in all these several kingdoms, had been in possession of power so long, as now to display the effects which possession of power in Asia invariably produces. The reigning sovereigns had everywhere given themselves up to the vices which are the natural growth of the throne; the viceroys of the provinces despised their authority; and weakness and distraction pervaded the empire. About thirty years before the birth of Timur, the kingdom of Persia had undergone a species of dissolution; almost every province, under a rebel governor, had been erected into an independency, and the whole divided into a number of petty states. From nearly the same period, the kingdom of Zagatai, (this was the intermediate sovereignty, so called from that son of Jangiz whose inheritance it became,) had been contended for by a succession of usurpers. The Mogul throne of Tartary and China had been less violently agitated, but was greatly reduced in power. Into what confusion and weakness the Afghan empire of Delhi had fallen, we have seen in sufficient detail.

Timur was born forty miles to the south of Samarcand, in the village of Sebzar, where his fathers, enjoying the rank or command of a toman of horse, had possessed a local authority for some generations. Timur had, from a tender age, been involved in the warfare of a distracted period; and by his courage, activity, and address, had, at five-and-twenty fixed upon himself the hopes and esteem of a large

BOOK II. CHAP. III. 1396.

proportion of his countrymen. Amid the other calamities which had fallen upon the kingdom of Zagatai or Samarcand, upon the breaking up of the government of the descendants of Jangiz, the Tartars of Kashgar had been incited, by the apparent weakness of the state, to invade the country, where they now oppressed and massacred the wretched inhabitants. Timur stood forward as the deliverer of his country; but when the day for action arrived, the chiefs who had promised to support him betrayed their engagements, and he was constrained to fly to the desert with only sixty horsemen. Timur ran every sort of danger, and endured every sort of hardship for several months, during which he led the life of a fugitive or outlaw. By degrees, however, he collected a party of well-tried adherents. The soldiers of fortune, the most adventurous of the youth, gathered round him. He harassed the Tartars by daring, yet cautious onsets; whence he increased his reputation, and multiplied his followers. After a series of struggles, the invaders were finally driven from Transoxiana. But it was not till the age of thirty-four, and after a course of strenuous and fortunate activity, that he was raised by the general voice to the undivided sovereignty of his native country.

Placed on the throne of Samarcand, the eye of Timur perceived the situation of the neighbouring countries. The provinces or kingdoms which had become detached from the house of Zagatai; Kharism, and Khorasan, first tempted his restless ambition, and some years were spent in adding those important conquests to his dominion. The contiguous provinces of Persia; Mazenderan and Segistan, to which was added Zabulistan, the grand southern or Indian district of the kingdom of Zagatai, next employed his conquering arms. These enterprises successfully terminated, he passed into Fars, the Persia proper; into Persian Irak, and Azerbijian, the conquest of which he completed in two years. The princes or usurpers of the provinces, Shirvan and Gilan, sent to make their submissions, and to promise obedience. At Shiraz, in the year 1386, he received intelligence, that Toktamish Khan, a Tartar chief, whose authority waa acknowledged throughout the region known to the Persians under the title of Desht Kipchak, north of the Caspian, had made incursion into Transoxiana. He flew to

1397.

repel the invader: and the desire of chastising Toktamish was the primary cause of the conquests of Timur in Turkestan. He followed the enemy into regions, void of houses, where the men fled before him. When far driven to the north, they were at last constrained to fight; and the army of Timur, after severe suffering, repaid itself by a complete victory, which compelled Toktamish, with his remaining followers, to take shelter in the mountains on the western side of the Caspian Sea. From this enterprise, the victor returned to complete the conquest of Persia. He drove from the city of Bagdad, the last prince in Persia of the house of Jangiz; he conquered the whole of Mesopotamia; pushed his way into Tartary through Mount Caucasus, to chastise anew the insolence of Toktamish, who had passed Derbend and made an inroad in Shirvan; and, having settled these extensive acquisitions, was, in 1396, prepared to carry his army across the Indus.

Timur proceeded from Samarcand, by the city of Termed, and passing a little to the eastward of Balk, arrived at Anderob, a city on the borders of that stupendous ridge of mountains which separates Hindustan from the regions of the north. The difficulties of the passage were not easily surmounted; but everything yielded to the power and perseverance of Timur. He descended to the city of Cabul: whence he marched towards Attock, the celebrated passage of the Indus: and in the year 1397, commenced his operations against Mubarik, who governed the frontier provinces of the empire of Delhi. Mubarik betook himself to a place of strength, and resisted the detachment sent to subdue him: but, on the approach of the conqueror with his whole army, he fled, with his family and treasure. The attention of Timur was now called to the situation of his grandson, who had invaded Hindustan the preceding year. The solstitial rains had forced him to draw his army into Multan, after it had suffered much from the season: and no sooner was he enclosed within the city, than the people of the country invested it, preventing supplies. Mohammed was reduced to the greatest distress, when his grandfather detached a body of horse to support him, and soon after followed with his whole army. He ravaged Multan and Lahore, putting the inhabitants of such of the cities as presumed to offer any resistance indiscriminately to the sword. Without

BOOK III. CHAP. III. 1397.

further delay, he directed his march towards Delhi, and encamped before the citadel.

On the seventh day, though unlucky, Ekbal, and his ostensible sovereign marched out to engage him. But the enervated troops of Delhi scarcely bore to commence the action with the fierce soldiers of the north; and Timur pursued them with great slaughter to the walls of Delhi. Ekbal and Mahmood fled from the city in the night, the sovereign towards Guzerat, the minister towards Birren; upon which the magistrates and omrahs of the city tendered their submissions, and opened the gates. In levying the heavy contributions imposed upon the city, disputes arose between the Moguls of Timur and the inhabitants, when blood began to flow. One act of violence led to another, till the city was involved in one atrocious scene of sack and massacre, which Timur was either (authorities differ) careless to prevent, or pleased to behold.

Timur remained at Delhi fifteen days, and arrested the progress of conquest in Hindustan. Having received the submissions of several omrahs, the governors or subahdars of provinces, and confirmed them in their commands, he marched in a northern direction, overrunning the country on both sides of the Ganges, till he reached the celebrated spot where it issues from the mountains. He then advanced along the bottom of the hills to Kabul, and thence proceeded to Samarcand.

Delhi remained in a state of anarchy for two months after the departure of the Moguls. It was then entered by the pretended emperor Noosrut, with a small body of horse. Ekbal, however, by means of some Zemindars, was still able to dislodge him, and recovered the Doab, or country between the rivers, which, with a small district round the city, was all that now acknowledged the sovereign of Delhi. The governors or subahdars of the provinces all assumed independence, and adopted royal titles. Lahore, Dibalpore [Punjab,] and Multan, were seized by Khizer; Kanoj, Oude, Korah, and Jonpoor, by Khaja Jehan, then styled the king of the East; Guzerat, by Azim; Malwa, by Dilawur; and the other departments, by those who happened in each to have in their hands the reins of government. Ekbal made some efforts, but attended with little success, to extend his limits. He received Mahmood, who fled from the disre-

1413.

spectful treatment bestowed on him by the governor or king of Guzerat; but compelled him to live on a pension, without claiming any share in the government. At last he came to blows with Khizer, the powerful usurper of Multan and Lahore; when he was defeated, and lost his life in the action. Mahmood then recovered a small remainder of the power which once belonged to the Shahs of Delhi; but knew not how to employ it either for his own or the public advantage. Nothing but the struggles and contests which prevailed among the usurpers of the provinces prevented some one of them from seizing his throne, and extinguishing his impotent reign in his blood; when dying of a fever, in the year 1413, "the empire fell," says Ferishta, "from the race of the Turks [or Tartars] who were adopted slaves of the emperor Mohammed Gauri, the second of the race of the sovereigns of India, called the dynasty of Gaur."[1] An Omrah, who happened to be in command at Delhi, presumed to mount the vacant throne; but Khizer, with the troops and resources of Multan and Lahore, found little difficulty in throwing him down from his rash elevation.

Within a short period subsequent to the departure of Timur from Delhi, that conqueror had settled the affairs of Persia; reduced Syria, Egypt, and Asia Minor; defeated Bajazet the Turkish emperor on the plains of Galatia; and prepared a vast expedition against China, which he was conducting through the plains and across the mountains of Tartary, when he fell sick, and died, in the year 1405, leaving his vast empire to his son Sharokh.

Khizer, it seems, was of the race of the prophet. His father had been adopted as the son of a great Omrah, who was governor of Multan, in the reign of Feroze. Upon the death of this Omrah and his son, the father of Khizer succeeded as Subahdar of Multan, and from him the government descended to his son. At the time when Timur arrived in India, he was involved in difficulties, through the power of a neighbouring chief; and had the prudence, or good luck, to solicit the protection of the conqueror, who confirmed

[1] The two dynasties of Gaur are spoken of occasionally by the Oriental historians under the title of the Afghan and Patan government of India; Afghan and Patan, as also Abdaly, and several others, being names applied to the whole or a part of the people who inhabit the chain of mountains from Herat to the mouths of the Indus.

BOOK III. CHAP. III. 1420.

him in the government of Multan, and added to it several other important provinces.

Khizer affected to decline the title of sovereign; pretending that he held the government of India only as deputy of the house of Timur, in whose name he ordered the coin to be struck, and the instruments of government to be expedited. By this expedient, we are told, he obviated the jealousies and competition of the Omrahs, many of whom would have regarded their claim to the throne as preferable to his own. Khizer governed with considerable abilities; and the people again tasted the fruits of peace and protection under his reign. He made but little progress in re-annexing the revolted provinces to the empire of Delhi. He reigned, however, from the farthest branch of the Indus to the extremity of the Doab: and from the Kashmere and Himalaya mountains to the latitude of Gualior.

After a reign of seven years and some months, his death transferred the government to Mubarik his son. Mubarik was early involved in a contest with the Gickers, who, under a leader of the name of Jisserit, continued to molest the Punjab and Lahore during the whole of his reign. The Hindu tribes in the hill-country of Mewat, to the south of Delhi; those also in the hill-country to the north of Budaoon or Rohilcund, gave him at various periods no little disturbance. A war was at one time kindled between him and the governor who had usurped the provinces lying eastward from Delhi, and was then known by the title of the King of the East. Coming however to a drawn battle, the two sovereigns were contented ever after to leave each other in peace. A rebellious slave, in the northern provinces, drew him into a contest witb the Moguls of the empire of Samarcand; the rebel having invited the viceroy of Shahrokh, who resided at Kabul, to come to his assistance. The Moguls were defeated in battle and repelled. Mubarik, however, in consequence of a conspiracy, headed by the Vizir, was shortly after assassinated in the fourteenth year of a reign, during which he had displayed considerable talents for government, and more than usual attention to justice and humanity.

The Vizir placed Mohammed, a grandson of Mubarik upon the throne, expecting to govern the kingdom in his name, or in time to appropriate the shadow as well as the substance of command. But the Omrahs were disgusted with his

1446.

pretensions, and levied war; which enabled or compelled the king to rid himself by assassination of his domineering minister. The Omrahs returned to obedience; and the king, after making a parade of his power in a progress through several of the provinces, returned to Delhi, and resigned himself to pleasure. The temper of the times was not such as to permit a negligent hand to hold the reins of government with impunity. The Omrahs in the distant governments began immediately to prepare for independence. Beloli Lodi,[1] the governor of Sirhind, a town on the Sutlej, or eastern branch of the Indus, made himself master of Lahore, of the greater part of the Punjab, and the country eastwards as far as Paniput, within a few leagues of Delhi. Beloli retired before the imperial army, but preserved his own entire; and re-occupied the country as soon as the troops of Mohammed returned. Another Viceroy, who had become independent in Malwa, and assumed the title of its king, marched against the feeble sovereign of Delhi, who saw no hopes of safety, but in calling the rebel Beloli to his aid. An indecisive action was fought: and the monarchs of Delhi and Malwa, both suffering from their fears, made haste to quiet their minds by huddling up an adjustment; but Beloli attacked in its retreat the army of Malwa, which he plundered and deprived of its baggage. He was despatched by Mohammed against Jisserit, the Gicker chief, who still harassed the northern provinces. But Beloli made his own terms with the plunderer; and returned to besiege Delhi. It held out, however, so long, that for the present he abandoned the enterprise. Mohammed shortly after died, his power reduced to a shadow, after a reign of twelve years and some months.

In the same year, viz. 1446, died Shahrokh, son of Timur, and emperor of the Moguls. Upon his death, the vast empire of Timur, which had yet remained entire, underwent division. The eldest son of Shahrokh, the famous Ulug Beg, inherited the imperial titles, and the dominion of Western Tartary or Transoxiana. The eldest son of Basunker, another of the sons of Timur, possessed himself of Khorasan, Kandahar, and Kabul. The second son of Basunker held possession of the Western Persia. And Abul Kasem,

[1] The name is Bheilole in Briggs.—W.

BOOK III. CHAP. III. the third of Timur's sons, became sovereign of Georgia, and Mazenderan.

1446. Alla, the son of Mohammed, mounted the throne of Delhi, honoured now with the obedience of little more than a few of the contiguous districts.[1] Alla showed no talents for government; and after a few years, being attacked by Beloli, resigned to him the throne, upon condition of receiving the government of Budaoon, where he lived and died in peace.

Beloli was an Afghan, of the tribe of Lodi, which subsisted chiefly by carrying on the traffic between Hindustan and Persia. Ibrahim, the grandfather of Beloli, a wealthy trader, repaired to the court of Feroze at Delhi; and acquired sufficient influence to be intrusted with the government of Multan. When Khizer succeeded to the same command, he made the son of Ibrahim master of his Afghan troops; and afterwards bestowed upon him the government of Sirhind. Beloli was not the son of the governor of Sirhind, but of another of the sons of Ibrahim. Beloli, upon the death of his father, repaired to his uncle at Sirhind, and so effectually cultivated his favour, that he received the hand of his daughter in marriage, and his recommendation to succeed him in his government. But Ibrahim left a brother Feroze, and a son Koottub, who disputed the pretensions of the son-in-law of the governor of Sirhind. Beloli was the most powerful and adroit, and of course the successful competitor. The rest, however, excited against him the Emperor of Delhi. His country was attacked and overrun. But Beloli kept his army together, and speedily recovered his territory, and the imperial troops were withdrawn. By activity, valour, and skill, something was daily added to the power of Beloli: by indolence, effeminacy, and folly, something was daily detached from the power of the sovereign

[1] Ferishta's enumeration of the independent principalities now existing, shows accurately the limits to which the monarchy of Delhi was reduced. "The Deccan, Guzerat, Malwa, Jonpoor, and Bengal, had each its independent king. The Punjab, Depalpoor, and Sirhind, as far south as Paniput, formed the territory of Bheilole Khan Lody. Mehrowly and the country within seven cos (fourteen miles) of Delhi, was in the hands of Ahmud Khan Mewattí. Sumbhul, even to the suburbs of Delhi, was occupied by Durra Khan Lody. Kote-jalesur, in the south, by Eesa Khan. Joorb, and Rabery and its dependencies, by Kowuch Khan Afghan. Kampila and Pattialy, by Rajah Purtab Sinh, and Byana, by Dawood Khan Lody." Briggs' Translation, i. 541. We may be sure, that the Hindus, in all directions, took advantage of this dismemberment of the Patan sovereignty, to assert their own independence, and to augment the anarchy that must have prevailed.—W.

1480.

ef Delhi: till Beloli was able to measure strength with him on more than equal terms, and finally to seat himself on his throne.

The mother of Beloli was smothered, while pregnant, under the ruins of a falling house. Her husband, opening her body, saved the infant, afterwards emperor of Hindustan. It is related that when Beloli was yet a youth, in the service of his uncle, a famous Durvesh, whom he came to visit, suddenly cried out with enthusiasm, "Who will give two thousand rupees for the empire of Delhi?" Beloli had but one thousand six hundred rupees in the world. But he sent his servant immediately to bring them. The Durvesh, receiving the money, laid his hand upon the head of Beloli, and gave him salutation and blessing as the king of Delhi. Ridiculed by his companions as a dupe, Beloli replied, that if he obtained the crown it was cheaply purchased; if not, still the benediction of a holy man was not without its use.

Those Omrahs who regarded their own pretensions to the throne as not inferior to those of Beloli, were disaffected. A party of them joined Mahmood, who held the usurped sovereignty of Bahar, and the country towards Orissa,[1] and was called king of Jonpoor, the city, at which he resided, on the banks of the Goomty, about forty miles from Benares. The victory which Beloli gained over their united forces established him firmly on his throne.

Beloli made a progress through his unsettled provinces confirming or removing the several governors, as he supposed them affected to his interests. He was not long suffered to remain in peace. Between him and the rival sovereign of Jonpoor, or the East, an undecisive war was carried on during the whole of his reign. The advantage, partly through force and partly through treachery, was, upon the whole, on the side of Beloli, who at last drove the king of the East from Jonpoor, and severed from his dominions the district to which it belonged. In his declining years Beloli divided the provinces of his empire among his sons, relations, and favourites; and died at an advanced age, in the thirty-ninth year of his reign. He was a modest sovereign;

[1] Whence this is derived does not appear: it is not in Ferishta. The predecessor of Mahmood invaded Bengal, but it was only a predatory incursion. The kings of the East never had possession of any part of Orissa.—W.

and when reproved by his friends for showing so little of the prince, "It was enough for him," he replied, "that the world knew he was king, without his making a vain parade of royalty."

The partition which Beloli made of his dominions had no tendency to prevent those disputes about the succession which are so frequent in the east; but neither, perhaps, did it augment them. A strong party of the Omrahs declared for Sekunder, one of the younger sons of Beloli; and after some struggle of no great importance, he was seated firmly on the throne. The usual measures were pursued for placing the provinces in a state of obedience: and Sekunder was stimulated to endeavour the restoration of some of the districts which for several reigns had affected independence on the throne of Delhi. The tranquillity, however, of an empire, which had been so long distracted, was not so easily preserved; and Sekunder was perpetually recalled from the frontiers of his kingdom, to anticipate or to quell insurrections within. He waged, notwithstanding, a successful war with the king of the East, who had been driven from Jonpoor by the father, and was now driven from Bahar by the son. But he found himself unequal to a war for the recovery of Bengal, to the confines of which he had once more extended the empire of Delhi; and that important province still remained in the hands of the usurper. Sekunder reigned, with the reputation of abilities, and of no inconsiderable virtue, for twenty-eight years and five months, and was succeeded by his son Ibrahim.

Ibrahim had personal courage, and was not altogether destitute of talents; but he was a violent, capricious, unthinking prince; and quickly lost the affections and respect of his subjects. One of his maxims was, "that kings had no relations; for that all men equally were the slaves of the monarch." This, though perfectly constitutional doctrine in the East, was a language which had now become unusual to the proud Omrahs of the falling throne of Delhi. Ibrahim was involved in an uninterrupted struggle with rebellion, against which, however, he maintained himself, during a space of twenty years. His empire was then invaded by Baber, a descendant of the great Timur, who in 1525, deprived him at once of his throne and of his life.

CHAPTER IV.

From the Commencement to the Close of the Mogul Dynasty.

BOOK III. CHAP. IV. 1525.

UPON the death of Shahrokh, the son of Timur, and the division of the dominions of that conqueror among his descendants, quarrels and war ensued; the weakness and vice, which are the usual attendants upon long-inherited sovereignty, weakened the unsteady powers of Asiatic government; and in a few years the great empire of Timur was in a state of dissolution. The Turks, who had penetrated into western Asia, and who, under Bajazet, received a dreadful overthrow by the arms of Timur, no sooner felt the weakness of government in the hands of his successors, than they pressed upon the nearest provinces, and at an early period were masters of Mesopotamia. Ismael was a disgraced servant of Jacob Beg, the eighth in the Turkish dynasty of the white sheep. Pursuing the career of a military adventurer, he collected around him a number of those daring characters, so numerous in the turbulent and unsettled countries of the East, whose business it is to seek a livelihood by their sword; and after a period, spent in subordinate plunder, he conceived himself sufficiently strong to attack, in the year 1500, the governor or king (for he now affected independence) of the province of Shirvan. After the conquest of Shirvan, Ismael successively made himself master of Tauris, Media, Chaldea, Persia, and became the founder of the dynasty of the Sophis, who held the sceptre of Persia for a number of generations.

On the eastern side of the Caspian, Shaïbek Khan, a chief of the Usbeks, or Tartars of Desht Kipchak, entered Transoxiana, at the head of his horde, in the year 1494. In the course of four years, he rendered himself master of all Transoxiana and Khorasan; the last of which was, however, wrested from the Usbeks, by the arms of Ismael Sophi, in the year 1510.

Baber was the grandson of Abu Seid, the king of Zagatai; and Abu Seid was the son of Mohammed, the grandson of Timur, through Miran Shah. The dominions of Abu Seid were at his death divided among his sons. Ali

BOOK III. CHAP. IV.

1525.

became king of Kabul; Ahmed, king of Samarcand; Ahmer, king of Indijan and Fergana;[1] and Mahmood, king of Kunduz and Budukshan. Baber was the son of Ahmer, king of Indijan and Fergana; a district surrounded by mountains, lying between Samarcand and Kashgar. He succeeded his father, while yet very young, in the year 1493;[2] and was immediately involved in a war with his uncles, desirous to profit by his youth and inexperience. Baber maintained himself against them with varying fortune, sometimes reduced to the lowest ebb, at other times borne on a flowing tide; till the arrival of Shaïbek,[3] the Tartar. Shaïbek, after a struggle which was strenuously supported by Baber, swept the posterity of Timur from Transoxiana and Khorasan. Baber was compelled to retire towards Kabul; where the son of his uncle Ali had been dethroned by his Omrahs, and the greatest anarchy prevailed. The weak resistance opposed to Baber, in Kabul, he had means to overcome, and became master of that province in the year 1504. After spending some years in contending with the enemies who disputed with him the possession of Kabul, and resisted his efforts for obtaining Kandahar, he was fired with the hopes of recovering his paternal dominions, Ismael Sophi having defeated and slain his enemy, Shaïbek. In the year 1511, he marched towards Bokhara, of which, after some resistance, he made himself master. His next object was Samarcand, which surrendered upon his arrival. His ambition was to make this celebrated capital of the great founder of his house the place of his residence; and he appointed Nasir, his brother, governor of Kabul. But he had not enjoyed, above nine months, this coveted throne, when the Usbeks, under the successor of Shaïbek,[4] returned from the desert; and Baber, after an unavailing struggle, was forced back to Kabul.

Baber had not spent one year in re-establishing his au-

[1] A more accurate nomenclature, as well as a more precise account, is to be found in the introduction to the Memoirs of Baber, lvii. Ahmed was king of Samarkand; Mahmud, of Hisar, Kunduz and Badakhshan; Ulugh Beg, of Kabul and Ghizni; and Omar Sheikh Mirza, father of Baber, king of Ferghana.—W.

[2] It should be 1494. Mem. of Baber.—W.

[3] By Ferishta, as translated by Dow, he is called Shaibani, ii. 100.—M. And in Baber's Memoirs, Shaíbâk or Shaibani.—W.

[4] His son, Mohammed Taimur Sultan.—W.

1525.

thority, in Kabul,[1] when information received of the weakness at Delhi inspired him with the hopes of indemnifying himself in the south for the possessions which he had been constrained to relinquish in the north. In the year 1519 he took possession of all the countries on the further side of the Blue River, one of the branches of the Indus. He overran a part of the Punjab, levying contributions; and after chastising the Gickers, who had molested him in his progress, he returned to Kabul. Before the end of the same year, he renewed his march into Hindustan, and intended to reduce Lahore; but was interrupted, by news from the northern side of the mountains which separate Bokhara from Kabul, that a district there, of which he still retained possession, had been invaded by the Tartars of Kashgar. The following year, the conqueror was recalled, after he had made some progress in the invasion of Hindustan, by intelligence that Kabul itself was assailed by the people of Kandahar. Baber resolved to complete the conquest of this neighbouring country, before he again led out his armies to regions more remote. The vigour of the king of Kandahar, who held out for three years, procured, thus long, a respite to the kings and omrahs of Hindustan; or rather afforded three additional years[2] for the exercise of their mutual hostilities, and the oppression of the wretched inhabitants. But in the year 1523, Kandahar being at last reduced, Baber rendered himself master of Lahore and the Punjab. The next year, beginning to feel the seducements of luxury and ease, he contented himself with directing his troops in Hindustan to march against Delhi. But they were attacked and overthrown.[3]

1 An interval of three years elapsed, during which Baber was endeavouring to re-establish his authority in Kandahar. Mem. of Baber, 245.—W.

2 This is a mistake, the period being confounded with that previous to Baber's first invasion of India. It was in his third invasion, in 1520, that Shah Beg of Kandahar laid siege to Kabul, and Baber returned to its succour. During the following year, he completed his preparations for retaliation, and finally reduced Kandahar to his authority in 1522. Mem. of Baber, 286.—W.

3 This is not a correct representation of the events. Baber led his army into India in 1524, and was joined by several of the nobles of Delhi, with Alâ-ad-din, the brother of Ibrahim. Amongst others were Doulet Khan and his son, but they shortly deserted Baber, and raised an opposition in the Punjab, which rendered it advisable for him to fall back on Lahore, after having advanced to Sirhind. From Lahore he returned to Kabul, leaving Alâ-ad-din and several of his chiefs as his governors in the conquered provinces. They were almost immediately dislodged by Doulet Khan, and obliged to join Baber at Kabul. It was then that he sent a force into India, under the command of his officers and Alâ-ad-din, that the latter might be assisted

BOOK III. CHAP. IV. 1530.

In 1525 Baber resolved to repair this misfortune by his presence. Ibrahim marched out to defend his capital with an army as much inferior in bravery, as it was superior in numbers. It was speedily routed, Ibrahim was slain in battle, Baber entered Delhi, and mounting the throne of the Afghans, or Patans, began the Mogul dynasty in Hindustan.

Great efforts were still demanded for the reduction of the provinces, the Omrahs of which being Afghans, and expecting little favour under a Mogul monarch, held out and even formed themselves into an extensive and formidable confederacy, setting a son of the late Sekunder, as sovereign, at their head. Baber's principal officers, alarmed by the resistance which it seemed necessary to overcome, combined in offering him advice to return. The king, declaring that he would relinquish such a conquest only with his life, displayed so formidable a spirit of resolution and perseverance, that in a short time the confederacy began to dissolve. Many of the Omrahs, who were the weakest, or whose territories were the most exposed, came over to Baber, and entered into his service. At last a great battle was fought, which Baber with difficulty won, but which gave him so decided a superiority, that his enemies were no longer able to meet him in the field. Having reduced the provinces which latterly paid obedience to the throne of Delhi, he advanced against the Omrahs of the East, who for a length of time had affected independence. He had scarcely, however, conquered Bahar, when he fell sick and died, in the year 1530.

Humayoon succeeded to the throne of his father, but was not long suffered to enjoy it in peace. His brother Kamran, in the government of Kabul, formed a resolution of seizing upon the Punjab; and Humayoon was fain to confer upon him the government of all the country from the Indus to Persia, on condition of his holding it as a dependency. Mahmood, too, the son of the Emperor Sekunder, whom the confederated Omrahs had placed at their

---

to ascend the throne of Delhi; and his reason for not leading the army in person was, his being obliged to march to the relief of Balkh, which was besieged by the Uzbeks. Alâ-ad-din was defeated, and again took refuge, though rather reluctantly, with Baber, as he advanced on his fifth and final invasion of Hindustan, in the cold season of 1525. Mem. of Baber, 295.—W.

head, was again joined by some chiefs, and kindled the flames of war in the eastern provinces. A victory gained by the Emperor extinguished all immediate danger in that quarter. But Shir Khan, the regent of Bahar, refused to give up the fortress of Chunar. A conspiracy was formed in favour of Mohammed, a prince of the race of Timur; and Bahadur, king of Guzerat, was excited to hostilities by the protection Humayoon afforded to the Rana of Chitore. Bahadur was unequal to his enterprise; the war against him was pushed with activity and vigour, and he lost entirely the kingdom of Guzerat. Humayoon was now in favour with fortune; from Guzerat he marched to the eastern provinces, and reduced Chunar. Having gained the passes he then entered Bengal; the government of which had recently been usurped, and its sovereign expelled by the enterprising Shir. He took possession of Gour, then the capital of the province; and there resided for several months; but, his troops suffering from the humidity of the climate, and his two brothers now aspiring openly to his throne, he was compelled to proceed towards Agra, which he and his father had made the seat of government. In the meantime, Shir, though he had been defeated, was not subdued. He made himself master of the strong fortress of Rotas, after he had been obliged to retire from Gour; and he now threw himself in the way of Humayoon, whose presence was urgently required in another part of his empire. Humayoon, threatened with detention, if nothing worse, desired accommodation. After a negotiation, it was agreed that the government of Bahar and Bengal should be conferred upon Shir, on his paying a slight tribute in acknowledgment of dependence. The chance of finding the camp of the Emperor unguarded, under the negligence inspired by the prospect of peace, was one among the motives which led Shir to open the negociation. The perfidy succeeded; and Humayoon, having lost his army, was constrained to fly.

He repaired to Agra, and was joined by his brothers whose united strength was no more than sufficient to defend them against Shir the Afghan. But their conflicting interests and passions defeated every scheme of co-operation. The army with which Humayoon marched out to meet the assailant was overthrown; the capital no longer

BOOK III. CHAP. IV. 1536-54.

afforded him a place of refuge; he fled from one place to another, subject at times to the greatest hardships; and was at last obliged to quit the kingdom, and seek an asylum in Persia, where he was hospitably and honourably entertained.

The grandfather of Shir, the new sovereign of Hindustan, came from the district of Roh[1] in the mountains of Afghanistan, in quest of military employment, in the reign of Beloli, and entered into the service of an Omrah of the court. His son Hussun followed the Subahdar, who acquired the title of King of the East; and rose to considerable rank in his service. Ferid, the son of Hussun, received the name of Shir, which signifies lion, from killing with his own hand, in the presence of the King or Governor of Bahar, an enormous tiger which rushed from a thicket. When this monarch died, and his son, a minor, succeeded him, the government of Bahar rested chiefly in the hand of Shir; and a short time elapsed, when the young prince, having made his escape, left the name as well as the power of sovereign to the usurper. He had just accomplished the conquest of Bengal, when Humayoon, returning from Guzerat, invaded his dominions.[2]

Immediately after his victory, Shir assumed the imperial title of Shah, and exerted himself with great activity in reducing the provinces to his obedience. His mandates

[1] This district which gave its name to the Rohillas, a people considerable in the history of British India, is said by Major Stewart, on his Persian authorities, to have been the original seat of the Afghans, whose mountainous country (Roh signifies a mountainous country; and Rohillas, mountaineers or highlanders) extended, according to the same authorities, in length, from Sewad and Bijore to the town of Sui, in Bukharest, and in breadth, from Hussin to Rabul. Stewart's Bengal, p. 127.—M. There is some curious blundering, either by Stewart, or the authorities he has followed in these statements; and if the latter, it is extraordinary that he should have cited them without correction. What contiguity could Bukharest possibly have to any part of the Afghan country, and where are Hussin and Rabul? Ferishta furnishes a more accurate version. Roh extends in length, he says, from Swad and Bajour, to Sui, in the district of Bhukkur, and in breadth, from Husun Abdul to Kabul. According to him, Roh means mountain in the Afghan language, but no such term occurs in the list of Pushtu words collected by Mr. Elphinstone, nor in a Pushtu vocabulary, compiled by Mohabbet Khan, of which a MS. is in the library of the E. I. C.; Roh is there explained to be the name of an extensive country, intermediate between Iran and Turan; bounded on the north by Kashkar, on the south by Baluchistan, on the west by Herat, and Kashmir on the east; being, in fact, the country of the Afghans. It may be doubted if this description is very accurate. Roh seems to offer traces of the older appellation of a district of more limited extent, or Arachosia. A town called Roh-kaj is noticed by Ibn Hakil, not far from Ghizni.—W.

[2] What relates to Bengal, in these transactions, is extracted minutely by Mr. Stewart, (Hist. of Bengal, sect. 5.)

ran from the farthest branch of the Indus, to the Bay of Bengal; a more extensive dominion than for some ages had belonged to any sovereign of Hindustan. Besieging one of the strongly situated forts, which abound in India, he was killed by an accidental explosion of gunpowder, when he had reigned five years in Hindustan. What can be said of few sovereigns, even in still more enlightened ages, he left various monuments of public beneficence to prolong the memory, and the love, of his short administration. He built caravanseras at every stage, from the Nilab, or farthest branch of the Indus, to the shores of Bengal; he dug a well for the refreshment of the traveller at every two miles; he ordered that all travellers, without distinction of country or religion, should at every stage be entertained, according to their quality, at the public expense; he had trees planted along the roads to shelter the travellers against the violence of the sun; he established post-horses, the first in India, for the more rapid conveying of intelligence to government,[1] and for the accommodation of trade and correspondence; even the religious comfort of the traveller was not neglected; a number of magnificent mosques were erected along the road, and priests appointed for the performance of devotional services.

Shir left two sons, of whom the youngest, being with the army, was proclaimed king. A struggle, as usual, ensued, for the possession of the throne; a feigned accommodation was made up between the brothers; war again quickly broke out; the eldest lost a battle, from which he fled, and disappearing, was never heard of more. The youngest remained emperor, by the name of Selim. The Omrahs, however, or Subahdars of the provinces, who never neglected an opportunity that promised a chance of independence, rebelled in several quarters. In some instances they were not without difficulty subdued. After several years spent in reducing his dominions to order and obedience, Selim was roused from his dreams of future tranquillity, by intelligence that the exiled emperor Humayoon was on his way from Persia with an army for the

[1] This is a stage of civilisation to which the Hindus had not arrived.—M. It is one to which British India has not attained. There are obstacles to this arrangement which it is difficult to surmount.—W.

BOOK III. CHAP. IV. 1536-54.

recovery of Hindustan. Selim prepared for action with vigour. But Humayoon, instead of advancing, retired. Selim, shortly after, was seized with a violent distemper; and died suddenly, in the tenth year of his reign.

He left a son to succeed him, but only twelve years of age. There was a nephew to the late Emperor Shir, by name Mubarik, whose sister was mother of the young prince. Mubarik assassinated the boy in the arms of his mother, three days after he had been proclaimed as king.

Mohammed was the name which Mubarik thought proper to use upon the throne. Vice, profusion, and folly, the attributes of his character and administration, lost him speedily the respect of his people, and the obedience of his Omrahs. His brother Ibrahim raised an army, from which Mohammed fled to the eastern provinces, leaving Ibrahim to assume the style of royalty at Delhi. This was not all. Ahmed, another nephew of the Emperor Shir, laid claim to the sovereignty in the Punjab, assumed the name of Sekunder Shah, and marched towards Agra. Ibrahim met him, and was defeated. Ibrahim was attacked on the other side, by the vizir of Mohammed, and after several turns of fortune, fled to Orissa. Sekunder took possession of Agra and Delhi, while Mohammed was engaged in a war with the governor of Bengal; in which at first he was prosperous, but finally stript of his dominions and life.

In the meantime, Sekunder was summoned to oppose the exiled emperor Humayoon, who had now a second time returned for the recovery of his throne.

When Humayoon made his escape into Persia, Tamasp, the son of Ismael, second of the Sophis, ruled from beyond the Euphrates, to the farthest boundary of Transoxiana. The governor of the province, which first afforded shelter to Humayoon, received him with distinction; and he was conveyed, with the respect which seemed due to his rank and misfortunes, to the Presence at Ispahan. He was treated by Tamasp as a sovereign; and his misfortunes excited the compassion of a favourite sister of the king, and of several of his councillors. At their instigation an army of ten thousand horse was intrusted to Humayoon; with which he advanced towards

Kandahar, still governed, together with Kabul, by one of his rebellious brothers. After an obstinate resistance, the city of Kandahar fell into his hands, and the rest of the province submitted. Jealousy and dissatisfaction soon sprung up between him and the Persian commanders. But various Omrahs of the country now joined him with their troops; and, marching to Kabul, he was joined by the second of his rebellious brothers, and several other chiefs. Kabul was in no situation to resist; and his hostile brother fled to Bukker, a wild and desert province towards the mouth of the Indus, governed by a relation. When Kabul was subdued, Humayoon crossed the mountains to the north, for the purpose of reducing Budukshan, that district of the Mogul kingdom of Transoxiana which had remained united to the dominions of Baber. In the meantime his brother returned from Bukker, and in the absence of Humayoon and his army, obtained possession of Kabul. Humayoon hastened from Budukshan, gave battle to his brother's army, routed it, and laid siege to Kabul. His brother seeing no hopes of success, fled from the city by night, and made his way to Balkh, where he received assistance from the governor, marched against Humayoon's new conquest of Budukshan, and expelled his governor. Humayoon left him not to enjoy his acquisition in peace: he marched against him, and forcing him to submit, treated him with lenity and respect. Humayoon next involved himself in hostilities with the Usbeks of Balkh, over whom at first he gained advantages, but at last was routed, and obliged to retreat to Kabul. In this retreat he was deserted by his perfidious brother, whom he had recently spared. Some of the chiefs of his army wrote to that deserter, that if he could attack the army of Humayoon, they would betray him in the action. Humayoon was accordingly defeated; and obliged to fly towards Budukshan, leaving Kabul a third time to his foe. Being joined, however, by the second of his brothers, who now repaid, by great services, his former demerits; and by several other chiefs; he was speedily in a condition to march again to Kabul with a force which his brother was by no means able to withstand. After some resistance, the brother was obliged to fly; and though he continued

BOOK III. CHAP. IV.

for several years to raise disturbance, he was no longer able to endanger the sovereignty of Humayoon.

1555. That prince, though now in possession of part of his ancient dominions, though aware of the distraction which prevailed in the rest, and invited by the inhabitants of Agra and Delhi, paused at the thought of invading Hindustan. At first he was able to raise an army of only fifteen thousand horse. With that he began to advance towards the Indus, where he was joined by his veterans from Kandahar. The governors of the Punjab and Lahore fled before him; and those countries were regained without a contest. Sekunder detached an army, which advanced towards the Sutlej. But the general of the advanced division of the army of Humayoon surprised the camp of Sekunder in the night, and entirely dispersed the troops. This disaster made Sekunder hasten with his main army to meet the enemy; a great battle was fought under the walls of Sirhind, in which the young Akbar, son of Humayoon, showed remarkable spirit and resolution. Sekunder, being routed, fled to the mountains of Sewalik.

Humayoon re-entered Delhi in the year 1554; but was not destined to a long enjoyment of the power which he had regained. As he was supporting himself by his staff on the marble stairs of his palace, the staff slipped, and the emperor fell from the top to the bottom. He was taken up insensible, and expired in a few days, in the year 1555, the fifty-first of his age.

Tamasp still reigned in Persia. But the Usbeks had now possessed themselves of Bokhara, and of the greater part of Transoxiana.

Akbar, the son of Humayoon, though not quite fourteen years of age, was placed on his father's throne. He had been nursed in difficulty and misfortune, and, young as he was, those powerful teachers had done much in forming his mind.

When Humayoon, with the few friends who adhered to him first fled from India, they nearly perished in the sandy desert which lies between Ajmere and the Indus. With the utmost difficulty, and after the loss of many lives, they arrived at Amercot, the seat of a Hindu Raja, about two hundred miles from Tatta. It was here that

1557.

Akbar was born. Humayoon, proceeding to Kandahar, where he still hoped for support, was attacked by the governor of Kandahar, and obliged to fly, leaving his infant son and his mother behind him. Akbar was kept at Kandahar by the governor, till Humayoon was on his march from Persia, when he sent him to his uncle at Kabul. Humayoon, after Kabul was taken, again beheld his son and his wife, he took the child in his arms, then four years of age, and exclaimed; "Joseph, by his envious brethren, was cast into a well; but he was exalted by Providence to the summit of glory." Akbar once more fell into the hands of his uncle, when that rebellious prince regained possession of Kabul. When Humayoon returned to besiege him, Akbar was bound to a stake, and exposed upon the battlements. Humayoon made proclamation, that if injury happened to Akbar, every human being in Kabul should be put to the sword. The wretched uncle was deterred, or forcibly restrained, from exposing it to such a disaster.

Byram, the chief of the Omrahs in the service of Humayoon, a man of talents, but of a severe, or rather of a cruel disposition, was appointed regent during the minority; which, in so unsettled and turbulent an empire, was not likely to be attended with general submission and peace.

The first object of the new government was to exterminate the party of the late pretended emperor, Sekunder; and for this purpose an army, with the young sovereign at its head, marched towards the mountains. Sekunder fled; the Raja of Nagracote made his submission; and the rainy season coming on, the army retired into quarters.

In the meantime the governor, who had been left by Humayoon in the command of Budukshan, assumed independence; and presumed so far upon the weakness of the new government, as to march against Kabul. The city stood a siege of four months; but at last submitted, and acknowledged the authority of the invader.

This calamity arrived not alone. Himu, the vizir of Mohammed, the usurper, who retained a part of the eastern provinces, marched to the centre of the empire with a formidable army. He took Agra. He took Delhi. The young Shah still remained in his quarters. A council of

BOOK III. CHAP. IV. 1557-60.

war was held, in which Byram advised to march against the enemy. The principal part of the Omrahs, as the hostile army amounted to 100,000 horse, that of the king to scarcely 20,000, held it advisable to retreat. But the young Shah supported the opinion of Byram with so much ardour, that he kindled the enthusiasm of the Omrahs, who declared their resolution to devote their lives and fortunes to his service.

While the army was on its march, the governor of Delhi, he by whom the city had just been surrendered, joined the king. Waiting for a time when the presence of the prince offered no interruption, Byram called this governor into his tent, and beheaded him. It was to anticipate, he told the king, the clemency of the royal mind, that he had taken upon him, without consultation, to make this example; necessary to let the neglectful Omrahs know, that want of vigour was hardly less criminal than want of loyalty; and that, as meritorious services would be amply rewarded, so no failure in duty should pass with impunity. The prince, whatever were his thoughts, thanked the regent for the care he bestowed upon his person and government.

The brave Himu made the necessary dispositions for encountering the imperial army. The contending parties arrived in presence of one another in the neighbourhood of Paniput. The Moguls, who had been reinforced on the march, fought with great constancy, and the enemy were thrown into disorder. Himu advanced, conspicuous on a towering elephant, and endeavoured by his example to reanimate his troops. He was shot with an arrow through the eye; and his followers, believing him killed, endeavoured to save themselves by retreat. Himu drew the eye out of the socket with the arrow; and continued the fight wirh unabated constancy. But the driver of his elephant seeing a mortal blow aimed at himself, offered to direct the animal wherever he should be desired.[1] Upon this, Himu was surrounded and taken.

When the battle ended, he was brought into the pre-

[1] This is indistinct: Ferishta's account is, Shah Koolly Khan, (one of Akbar's officers,) levelled his lance at the driver, who, in order to save his own life, pointed to his master, and promised Shah Koolly Khan, to guide the elephant wherever he directed: he accordingly, it would seem, drove the animal amongst a body of Akbar's horse.—W.

1557-60.

sence of Akbar, almost expiring with his wounds. Byram, addressing the king, told him it would be a meritorious action to kill that dangerous infidel with his own hands. Akbar, in compliance with the advice of his minister, drew his sword, but only touching with it gently the head of his gallant captive, burst into tears. This movement of generous compassion was answered by the minister with a look of stern disapprobation ; and with one blow of his sabre he struck the head of the prisoner to the ground.

This important victory restored tranquillity to the principal part of Akbar's dominions. It is true, that in the same year the invasion of a Persian army, under the nephew of Tamasp, rendered that prince for a time master of Kandahar. And the late pretended emperor Sekunder advanced into the western provinces, and made the governor fly to Lahore. But the imperial standards were carried with expedition towards the Indus ; Sekunder was cooped up in a fort ; when, offering to surrender the place and all his pretensions, he was permitted to retire into Bengal, and Akbar returned to Lahore.

The overbearing pretensions of an imperious, though useful servant, and the spirit of a high-minded, though generous sovereign, could not long be reconciled. Mutual jealousies and discontents arose ; the minister used his power with cruelty to deliver himself from those who stood in his way ; he increased, by that means, the disgust of his master ; yet he contrived for a time to preserve himself in power, by occupying the mind of the king with military preparation and action. An expedition, which ended successfully, was planned against Gualior, at that time a place of the highest importance. In the same year, one of Akbar's generals subdued all the country about Jonpoor and Benares, hitherto retained by the Omrahs who had derived their power from the gift or the weakness of the late princes of the Afghan or Patan dynasty. Operations were commenced against Malwa, possessed by another of those Omrahs. But all this business and success served only to retard, not prevent, the fall of the minister. When the royal ear was found open to accusations against the harsh and domineering Byram, courtiers were not wanting to fill it. He was secretly

1560.

charged with designs hostile to the person and government of the Shah; and the mind of Akbar, though firm, was not unmoved by imputations against the man he disliked, however destitute of facts to support them. After some irresolution and apprehension, a proclamation was issued to announce that Akbar had taken upon himself the government; and that henceforth no mandates but his were to be obeyed. Byram, who had shown so much resolution when serving his master, was full of indecision when called upon to act for himself. The sovereign advised him to make a voyage to Mecca. At one time Byram proceeded to obey; at another time he resolved to render himself independent in some of the provinces which Akbar had not yet subdued; and at another time conceived the design of seizing and governing the Punjab itself. He attempted arms, but met with no support; and, driven to his last resource, implored the clemency of his master. Akbar hastened to assure him of forgiveness, and invited him to his presence. When the unfortunate Byram presented himself with all the marks of humiliation, and bursting into tears, threw himself on his face at the foot of the throne, Akbar lifted him up with his own hand, and setting him in his former place at the head of the Omrahs, "If the noble Byram," said he, "loves a military life, he shall obtain the government of a province in which his glory may appear; if he chooses rather to remain at court, the benefactor of our family shall be distinguished by our favours; but should devotion engage the soul of Byram to make a voyage to the holy city, he shall be provided and escorted in a manner suitable to his dignity." Byram, desiring leave to repair to Mecca, received a splendid retinue and allowance; but in his passage through Guzerat, an Afghan chief, whose father he had formerly slain in battle, pretending salutation, stabbed him with a dagger, and killed him on the spot.

In the year 1560, a son of the late Shah Mohammed, who had found means to raise 40,000 horse, advanced with a design to recover the province of Jonpoor. The generals of Akbar, who had the province in charge, vanquished him with the forces under their command. Presuming, however, on their services or strength, they delayed remitting the plunder. Akbar went towards them without a moment's delay; upon which they made haste to meet him with the spoils. He accepted their obedience; praised their valour; and bestowed on them magnificent gifts. This is a specimen of the behaviour of Akbar to his Omrahs. Their proneness to seize every opportunity of disobedience he restrained by prompt and vigorous interference; seldom punished their backwardness; but always bestowed on their services honour and renown.

Hussun, the governor of Ajmere, made some progress in subduing several forts in that hilly country, yet held by Hindu Rajas. The general, sent to reduce Malwa, had carried on the war in that province with so much success as to drive the pretended king out of his dominions. He fled, however, to the sovereigns of Kandesh and Berar; from whom he received such effectual support as to be able to defeat the army of the imperial general, which he pursued to the vicinity of Agra. Akbar gave commission to Abdallah, the Usbek, governor of Kalpy, a city and province on the Jumna, to prosecute the war; and by him was Malwa annexed to the Mogul dominions. About the same time the Gickers, those restless tribes of Hindus, who so often from their mountains disturbed the obedience of the upper provinces, were united under a warlike chief, and assumed the appearance of a formidable enemy. They were attacked with the usual vigour of Akbar's government; and compelled to receive, though of their own nation, a sovereign named for them by the Moguls.

Notwithstanding the virtues of Akbar's administration, the spirit of rebellion, inherent in the principles of Indian despotism, left him hardly a moment's tranquillity, during the whole course of a long and prosperous reign. Hussun revolted in Ajmere, and gained a victory over the imperial troops who were sent to oppose him. Hakim, brother of Akbar, a weak man, the governor of Kabul, began to act as an independent prince. A slave of his, approaching the king while marching with his troops, let fly an arrow which wounded him in the shoulder. Abdalla, the Usbek, master of Malwa, believed himself so strong, and the king, pressed by rebellion in various quarters, so weak, that he might erect a throne for himself. He contrived artfully to spread a rumour, that the Shah had contracted a general hatred of the Usbeks in his service, and meditated their destruction.

BOOK III. CHAP. IV. 1560-80.

This gained over Sekunder and Ibrahim, the governors of two of the eastern provinces. Asaph, who held the government of Korah, had obtained great wealth by subduing and plundering a rajaship or Hindu kingdom, between Berar and Bengal, which till this time had escaped the ravage of a Mohammedan conqueror.[1] Not wishing to part with any of this wealth and influence, he joined with the rebels, in hopes of being able to defy the imperial power. Even Zemaun, the captain-general of the empire, and his brother Bahadur, two chiefs of great power and renown, joined the enemies of Akbar, and hoped to raise themselves on the ruins of the king.

Akbar, whom neither exertion nor danger dismayed, opposed himself to his enemies with an activity, which often repaired the deficiencies of prudence. It would be tedious to follow minutely a series of expeditions, so much the same, to subdue one rebellious chieftain after another. Akbar had made considerable progress in reducing the eastern provinces to obedience, when he learned that Hakim, governor of Kabul,[2] in hopes of advantage from his absence, had advanced towards Lahore. The tranquillity of the northern provinces, whose inhabitants were hardy and warlike, was always regarded by Akbar as worthy of more watchful solicitude than that of the east, where the people were effeminate and more easily subdued. Leaving therefore the reduction of the Usbek rebels still incomplete, he hasted towards Lahore; and surprising his brother by the celerity of his appearance, he rendered opposition hopeless, and crushed the rebellion in its bud. In the mean time, the Usbeks increased their army, and extended their conquests. The expeditious movements of Akbar left them little time to enjoy their advantages.

[1] This is a very ungallant mode of passing over an instance of female heroism highly celebrated in the Hindu annals. The district in question was Gurra, or Gurrah Mundela, then under the regency of a queen-mother, Durgauti, or Durgavati. Upon the incursion of the Mohammedans, she led her forces in person against the invaders; a sanguinary conflict ensued, the event of which was long doubtful, until the queen, who was mounted on an elephant, was disabled by a wound from an arrow in her eye. Her troops then gave way, and fearing to fall into the hands of the victors, Durgavati snatched a dagger from the girdle of the elephant-driver, and stabbed herself. The story is told by Ferishta, and is confirmed by an inscription found at Gurra Mundala, and translated by Captain Fell. As. Res. xv. 427.—W.

[2] It was Akbar's brother Mohammed Hukeem Mirza, who had been driven out of Kabul by Soliman Mirza, and who endeavoured to obtain unauthorised possession of Lahore, as an equivalent.—W.

Having returned with a recruited army, he came to an action with the combined forces of the insurgents, and gained a great victory, which effectually quashed the rebellion in the east.

The unsettled state of the province of Malwa soon required the royal presence. Among other measures for the secure possession of that important district, he advanced to the attack of Chitore,[1] a fort of great natural strength, situated in a mountainous and difficult part of the province, inhabited by Hindus, who had been frequently subdued, by the more powerful of the Mohammedan princes, but had as often revolted when the reins of government were held by a feeble hand. After an obstinate resistance, Chitore was taken. Rantampore, in the Arrabarree hills, in the province of Ajmere, was also a hill-fort, of great strength, which had often been taken from the Hindus, and as often recovered. Having reduced Rantampore, as well as Callinger, another stronghold of similar description and importance, in the same range of mountains,[2] he directed his attention to Guzerat.

This was one of the provinces the governor of which, during the decline of the Patan or Afghan dynasty, had assumed independence; and it had been governed as a separate kingdom for a number of years. After a time it had fallen into the same confusion, which seems the common fate of Asiatic sovereignties whether great or small. The Omrahs became too powerful for the sovereign; the different districts or governments assumed independence; and the royal power was reduced to a shadow. In this situation the province offered but little resistance to Akbar; the different leaders, who felt their inferiority, courted favour by hastening submission. Hussun, in Ajmere, was able to take the field with an army; but as the king was now at leisure to push the war against him, he was driven from the province, and, with the remains of his army, fled to the Punjab. Attacked by a warlike tribe of the inhabitants, he was there taken prisoner, delivered up to the governor of Multan, and by him put to death. No sooner

[1] The particulars of this capture are narrated by Tod. Annals of Mewan, i. 325.—W.

[2] There is no range of mountains in this part of India. Calinjer, and some other elevations of a like character, are detached hills springing abruptly from a plain.—W.

BOOK III. CHAP. IV.

1580.

had the king turned his back on Guzerat, than some of the turbulent chiefs began to assemble armies, and prepare the means of resistance. The rainy season was now commenced, when the great army was unable to move ; but Akbar, selecting a small body of cavalry, pursued his way with the utmost expedition to Guzerat, surprised the rebels in the midst of their preparations ; offered them battle notwithstanding the inferiority of his force, and, contrary to all prudential calculation, gained a victory, which established his authority in Guzerat.

The province of Bengal paid a nominal submission to the throne of Delhi, but during several reigns had been virtually independent. After the other provinces of the empire were reduced to more substantial obedience, it was not likely that grounds of quarrel would long fail to be laid between Akbar and the King of Bengal. The governor or Subahdar of Oude being ordered, as contiguous, to begin operations against him, had gained some important advantages, and was besieging Patna, when he was joined by the Shah. The Bengal chief, seeing no chance of success, offered terms of accommodation. Akbar consented to engage for his life, but demanded that every thing else should be left to his clemency ; to spare, however, the blood of their subjects, he offered to decide their disputes by personal combat. In the following night the Bengal chief went secretly down the river in a boat, and his troops immediately evacuated the city. Akbar returned to Agra ; and the governor of Oude, to whose jurisdiction Patna was annexed, was ordered to complete the reduction of Bengal. The vanquished sovereign was allowed to retain Orissa. But, unfortunately for him, the Zemindars of Bengal still adhered to his interests, and speedily assembled a considerable army for his restoration. Having put himself at the head of this armament, he was taken prisoner, and, in the absence of Akbar, put to death in cold blood, upon the field.

For a short space, Akbar now enjoyed tranquillity and obedience throughout his extensive empire; and wisely made use of the interval to visit and inspect its several provinces. Soon was he recalled to his former troubles and exertions. The recently subdued Bengal furnished a variety of discontented spirits, who again appeared in

1593.

arms; and his brother, in Kabul, marched against Lahore. Akbar never allowed disobedience in the upper provinces to gain strength by duration. He hastened to Lahore, overcame his brother, followed him close to Kabul, and received a message from the vanquished prince, imploring forgiveness. Akbar, with his usual generosity, which was often inconsiderate, and cost him dear, replaced him in his government.

The peace of Bengal was in the mean time restored; but a formidable rebellion broke out in Guzerat, which the son of Byram, the late regent, was sent to subdue. He was opposed with great obstinacy; and some power. But being a man of talents, he restored the province in a little time to obedience, and was rewarded with its government.

The governor of Kabul, the king's brother, died. The state of the upper provinces seemed upon that occasion to require the presence of Akbar, and he marched towards the Punjab. Here he projected the conquest of Kashmere, and despatched an army for that purpose. The season being ill-chosen and provisions failing, that army found itself unequal to the enterprise. Akbar, however, was not willing to be foiled: he despatched a second army; and the conquest was made with little opposition. Soon after this, the Governor of Kandahar, a province which hitherto had paid but a nominal submission to the Mogul throne, unable to defend himself against his rebellious brothers, and the Usbeks, who had now rendered themselves masters of Transoxiana and Bactria, and were formidable neighbours to the northern provinces of Hindustan, offered to deliver up his government to Akbar; and received that of Multan in exchange.

Akbar, who now beheld himself master, from the mountains of Persia, and Tartary, to the confines of the Deccan, began to cast the eyes of ambition on that contiguous land. He gave directions to his governors, in the provinces nearest the Deccan, to prepare as numerous armies as possible; and to omit no opportunity of extending the empire. He despatched ambassadors to the kingdoms of the Deccan, more with a design to collect information, than to settle disputes. And at last a great army, under Mirza,[1] the son

[1] Mirza was his title; his name was Abdool Ruheem, but he was commonly called Mirza Khan: he was also entitled Khan-khanan.—W.

BOOK III. CHAP. IV. of Byram, who had reduced Guzerat, marched in execution of this project of unprovoked aggression, and unprincipled ambition.

1593. We have already observed the circumstances which attended the first establishment of a Mohammedan empire in the Deccan, and it will now be necessary to recount shortly the events which intervened from the death of Alla Bhamanee, in the year 1357, to the invasion of Akbar in 1593.[1] Alla was succeeded by his son Mohammed, who reigned seventeen years, and carried on successful wars against the Rajas of Telingana and Beejanuggur,[2] a city on the Tummedra or Toombuddra, the most southern branch of the Kistna or Krishna, and at that time the capital of a considerable kingdom.[3] He stript these sovereigns of part of their dominions, and rendered them tributary for the rest. A circumstance is recorded by the historian, which indicates but a thin population in that part of India. The number of lives which were destroyed by his wars was computed at near 500,000, among whom was the natural proportion of both sexes, and of all ages; for Indian wars spare neither sex nor age: And by this loss, the regions of the Carnatic, says the historian, were so laid waste, that they did not recover their natural population for several kerruns, or revolutions of ten years: yet they had never before been more than slightly overrun by a foreign invader; and the virtues or vices of Hindu policy were here to be traced in their natural effects.[4] Mujahid, the son of

[1] For the succeeding sketch of the history of the Mohammedan sovereignties in the Deccan, Ferishta's History of the Deccan, translated by Captain Jonathan Scott, and Wilks's Historical Sketches of the South of India, have been the principal guides.

[2] Called Bisnagar, in the common maps, and Vijeyanuggur by Col. Wilks. Bijanuggur was but a modern power, in the South of India, and had risen upon the ruins of the Rajaship of Warunkul. Historical Sketches, by Col. Wilks, ch. i.

[3] Col. Wilks thinks that the whole of the South of India, (i. e. India to the south of the Kistna,) had for a considerable space of time been comprised in the empire of Vijeyanuggur. Ibid. p. 20. After the ruin of the Rajaship of Warunkul, when was the time for such an aggrandisement?

[4] The premises are not of a character to warrant this conclusion. It is not true of 'Indian' wars, whether Mohammedan or Hindu, that they "spare neither age nor sex;" and, if the number be correctly stated, it consists for the most part of adult males, killed in battle, or in the sack of cities. It is not very likely, however, that the number is statistically precise, nor can the facts be admitted without further scrutiny; for, either the dates or names are irreconcileable with the authentic records of the Bijnagar kings as preserved in inscriptions. Cat. Mackenzie Collection, Introd. 139, and As. Res. vol. xx. p. 1. If at all correct, the injury to the country, however, and consequent depopulation, was not the result only of the numbers slain, but

Mohammed, was assassinated by his uncle after reigning three years. The murderer, Daood, placed himself on the throne, but lost his own life by assassination, after a month and five days. Of Alla, the first of the Bahmanee sovereigns, the youngest son was still alive, and had passed his life in confinement during the intermediate reigns. By the intrigues of the Haram, he was now acknowledged as King, and spent a mild and prudent reign of nineteen years, in almost uninterrupted tranquillity. His eldest son Gheause succeeded him; but, having affronted one of his Turkish Omrahs, who disguised his resentment the more effectually to secure his revenge, he lost his throne and his eyes, after a reign of little more than a month; and his brother Shums was made to possess it in his stead.

Shums was but fifteen years of age: and was a passive instrument in the hands of the Turk. Of Daood, however, the usurper, who had enjoyed royalty a month, several sons remained, who, under the odium attending the present state of the government, conceived hopes of profiting by the usurpation of their father. By an alternation of force and artifice, they secured the persons of the king and his minister, after a reign of only five months and seven days, and one of the brothers, by name Firoze, took possession of the throne. He reigned upwards of five and twenty years; and is the most celebrated of all the sovereigns of the Deccan. He was engaged in a variety of wars with the Hindu Rajas; but his acquisitions in point of territory were in-

---

of the ravages committed; the effects of which might possibly have been for some time visible; or, rather, similar effects might have been perpetuated by similar causes; as, up to the time the historian wrote, about 1596, the whole interval had been one of continual struggle with the Mohammedan kings. The desolate condition which Ferishta notices, may, however, have been the work of much more recent occurrences; Bijnagar had irrecoverably fallen about twenty years before, by the combined arms of the Mohammedans, and the capital had been destroyed and the country laid waste. The evidence of Ferishta applies to this season, if to any, and there is proof that it is not applicable to the whole intermediate time: we have evidence of the flourishing state of Bijnagar, ninety years before his time; so that the state must have recovered then from whatever blows it had previously sustained. It was well known to early European travellers, as the kingdom of Narsinha; several visited it in the beginning of the sixteenth century, Barbessa, for instance, in 1516, and he describes it as a city of considerable extent, and the seat of a still powerful, though declining monarchy. The king maintained 40,000 cavalry, and a very numerous body of foot. Ramusio, Collezione dei Viaggi, vol. i. As. Res. vol. xx. p. 3. There is no reason, therefore, to attach much weight to the vague assertions of the Mohammedan writer, and still less can the inference of scanty population, as the consequence of Hindu misrule, be derived from his statement.—W.

BOOK III. CHAP. IV. 1593.

considerable. His endeavours to secure the succession to his son, by the destruction of a brother of his own, whose power and talents excited his fears, involved the last months of his reign in trouble. But finding his efforts ineffectual he submitted to necessity, and appointing his brother successor, died in a few days.

The new sovereign, Ahmed, was a man of talents; governed with moderation and prudence; and enjoyed a prosperous reign of twelve years and two months. He overthrew the Raja of Warunkul, and added the city of Telingana to his dominions. The governors who, during the decline of the Afghan or Patan dynasty of Delhi, had assumed independence in the provinces of Malwa, Kandesh, and Guzerat, were now sovereigns, whose contiguity failed not to produce occasions of discord. At different times Ahmed was engaged in war with all those princes, but without any memorable result. He enlarged and beautified the city of Beder, which he called Ahmedabad, and removed to it the seat of government from Kalburga. Toward the conclusion of his reign he projected a partition of his kingdom among his sons. His acquisitions in Berar, with some contiguous districts, he assigned to Mahmood; he gave Telingana to Daood; and sent these princes to take possession of their shares. His two remaining sons Alla and Mohammed were destined to succeed him as colleagues on the throne of Koolburga.

They ascended the throne without opposition; but Mohammed, dissatisfied with the share of power which his brother allowed him, was soon excited to rebel. He was defeated, and treated with generosity by Alla. Their brother Daood having just died in Telingana, Mohammed was appointed governor of that kingdom, where he devoted himself to his pleasures, and lived in peace. Alla was at various times attacked, by the Raja of Beejanuggur in the south, and the kings of Guzerat, Kandesh, and Malwa, in the north; but defended himself with success. He sent an army to invade Malabar, which at first gained advantages, but being artfully drawn into a difficult recess of that mountainous and woody country, was almost totally destroyed. After a reign of nearly twenty-four years, he was succeeded by his son Humayoon, who meeting with opposition and rebellion, gave reins to the ferocity of a violent mind; but died, or was assassinated, it is uncertain which, after a reign of a little more than three years. His eldest son, Nizam, was only eight years of age at his accession; but the reins of government were directed by the queen-mother, a woman of talents, and though the surrounding sovereigns endeavoured to avail themselves of the weakness of a minority, and the king of Malwa penetrated to the very capital, he was repulsed, and the Bahmanee empire remained entire. Nizam died in little more than two years after his father, when the crown devolved upon his second brother Mohammed, who was then in his, ninth year. The abilities of the queen-mother, and of a faithful minister, conducted the state in safety through the difficulties and dangers of a second minority; and Mohammed, displaying, when he grew up, considerable talents for government, enjoyed prosperity for a number of years; took part of Orissa, and the island of Goa; and thus extended his dominion from sea to sea. At last, however, the jealous rivals of the minister forged an accusation, which they presented to the king at an artful moment, and surprised him into a sudden order for his destruction. Mohammed soon discovered, and soon repented, his fatal mistake. The ambitious Omrahs, whom the vigilance and talents of the minister had restrained began immediately to encroach on the royal authority. Mohammed died within a year of the execution of his minister, having languished both in mind and body, from the day of that unfortunate and criminal act.

His son Mahmood ascended the throne of the Deccan in the twelfth year of his age. The contentions of the Omrahs now filled the state with disorder. The sovereign himself displayed no talents for government, and was a slave to his indolence and pleasures. After plotting and struggling for several years, four of the great Omrahs declared themselves independent of their several governments; and a fifth, who remained at the court, reduced the power of the sovereign to a shadow, and ruled in his name. Mahmood's nominal sovereignty lasted for thirty-seven years; during which the Deccanee empire was divided into five several kingdoms; that of Beejapore or Visiapore, founded by Esuff Adil Khan; that of Ahmednugger, founded by Ahmed Nizam Beheree; that of Berar

BOOK III. CHAP. IV. 1593.

founded by Ummad al Mulk; that of Golconda, founded by Koottub al Mulk; their respective governors; and that of Ahmedabad Beder, founded by Ameer Bereed, who rendered himself master of the person and throne of his master, and retained the provinces which had not been grasped by the other usurpers. This revolution, after being several years in progress, was consummated about the year 1526. These sovereigns were engaged in almost perpetual wars with one another, with the Raja of Beejanuggur, and with the Sultan of Guzerat, who was so powerful as to hold in a species of subjection the Sultans of both Malwa and Kandesh. A temporary union of the Shahs of Beejapore, Golconda, and Ahmednuggur, in 1564, enabled them to subvert the empire of Beejanuggur, and reduce the power of its chief to that of a petty Raja. The kingdom of Beder, which had fallen to the share of Ameer Bereed, was conquered during the reign of his grandson; and its territories, which were not large, were divided among the other usurpers of the Bahmenee dominions. A similar fate awaited the portion of Ummad, which consisted of the southern part of Berar; it subsisted as a kingdom only four generations; and was annexed to his dominions by the King of Ahmednugger in the year 1574. The Deccan was, therefore, at the time when its invasion was projected by the Moguls, divided among the sovereigns of Beejapore, Ahmednuggur, and Golconda. At the time when the Bahmenee empire of the Deccan was first divided into separate kingdoms, the Portuguese began their conquests on the coast of Malabar, and took possession of the island of Goa.

In addition to the army which Akbar had despatched under Mirza Khan towards the Deccan, he sent orders to his son Morad, to whom he had committed the government of Guzerat, to join him with all his forces: Mirza had already been reinforced with the troops of Malwa, governed by another son of the Emperor, and by six thousand horse belonging to the king of Kandesh, who had endeavoured, by submission, to avert the ruin which resistance would ensure. The combined army marched upon Ahmednuggur, to which they laid siege. The place was defended with great bravery, till provisions began to fail in the Mogul army, when the generals opened a negotiation, and agreed, upon condition of receiving Berar, to raise the siege of Admednuggur, and evacuate the kingdom. The pain felt by the king at the loss of Berar soon prompted him to an effort for its recovery. His army fought a drawn battle with the Moguls. The resolution and ardour of Mirza led him to renew the engagement on the following day, when he defeated indeed the enemy, but was so weakened by his loss, as to be unable to pursue the fugitives, or to improve his victory, Mirza was soon after recalled. In his absence the Ahmednuggur arms gained some advantages; and the Mogul interests declined. But in 1598 Mirza was restored to the army in the Deccan, to which the Emperor proceeded in person. Ahmednuggur was again besieged; and at last compelled to open its gates. The territory of Ahmednuggur was formed into a province of the Mogul empire; and its government conferred upon Danial, one of the sons of Akbar. The Emperor did not long survive these new acquisitions. He returned to Agra, and died in the fifty-second year of his reign.

At the time of the death of this successful prince, his great empire was divided into fifteen vice-royalties, called Subahs; each governed immediately by its own viceroy called Subahdar. The names of the Subahs were Allahabad, Agra, Oude, Ajmere, Guzerat, Bahar, Bengal, Delhi, Kabul, Lahore, Multan, Malwa, Berar, Kandesh, and Ahmednugger.[1]

Shah Tamasp, the second in the line of the Sophis, held the sceptre of Persia till the twentieth year of the reign of Akbar; when there was a rapid succession of several princes, most of whom were cut off by violence. During these disorderly reigns, the Usbeks made dangerous inroads upon the eastern provinces of Persia, and even threatened the security of the northern provinces of India. At the time of the death of Akbar, Shah Abbas the Great was upon the throne, a prince who made both his neighbours and his subjects tremble at his name.

Selim was the only surviving son of Akbar; but even this fortunate circumstance did not save him from a rival. Selim's own son Khosroo was destined to supersede his father, by Azim Khan, whose daughter was the wife, and by Raja Man Sing, whose sister was the mother of Khos-

[1] Ayeen Akbery, ii. 2.

BOOK III. CHAP. IV. 1605.

roo. Azim Khan was vizir; Man Sing had a powerful government as an Omrah of the empire, and an army of twenty thousand Rajpoots, his countrymen, in his service. The schemes of these powerful chiefs were rendered abortive, by a decisive resolution of the commander of the city guards: who ordered the gates to be shut, and delivered the keys to Selim on his knees. Selim assumed the title of Mohammed Jehangir, or conqueror of the world, and dated his reign from October 21, 1605, being then in the thirty-seventh year of his age. Jehangir, for whom it would have been difficult, in the commencement of his reign, to contend with the power of Azim Khan, and Raja Man Sing, contented himself with sending them to their respective governments; the vizir to his Subah of Malwa; the Raja to that of Bengal; and Khosroo was received into favour. A short time elapsed, when Khosroo again rebelled, but, rejecting the advice of Azim Khan, and Raja Man Sing, to assassinate his father, he taught those artful chiefs to despair of his cause, and they abstained from lending him any open support. So many followers crowded to his standards, as enabled him to seize and ravage some extensive districts. Unable to contend with the army which pressed him, he retired towards the Indus, when his followers dispersed. His principal friends were punished with all the ferocity of Oriental despotism, and he himself was placed in confinement.

One of the circumstances which had the greatest influence on the events and character of the reign of Jehangir was his marriage with the wife of one of the Omrahs of his empire, whose assassination, like that of Uriah, cleared the way for the gratification of the monarch. The history of this female is dressed in romantic colours by the writers of the East. Khaja Aiass her father, was a Tartar, who left poverty and his native country, to seek the gifts of fortune in Hindustan. The inadequate provision he could make for so great a journey failed him before its conclusion. To add to his trials, his wife, advanced in pregnancy, was seized with the pains of labour in the desert, and delivered of a daughter. All hope of conducting the child alive to any place of relief forsook the exhausted parents; and they agreed to leave her. So long as the tree, at the foot of which the infant had been deposited, remained in view, the mother supported her resolution; but when the tree vanished from sight, she sunk upon the ground, and refused to proceed without her. The father returned; but what he beheld was a huge black snake, convolved about the body of his child, and extending his dreadful jaws to devour her. A shriek of anguish burst from the father's breast, and the snake, being alarmed, hastily unwound himself from the body of the infant, and glided away to his retreat. The miracle animated the parents to maintain the struggle; and before their strength entirely failed, they were joined by other travellers, who relieved their necessities.

Aiass, having arrived in Hindustan, was taken into the service of an Omrah of the court; attracted after a time the notice of Akbar himself; and by his abilities and prudence rose to be treasurer of the empire. The infant who had been so nearly lost in the desert was now grown a woman of exquisite beauty; and, by the attention of Aiass to her education, was accomplished beyond the measure of female attainments in the East. She was seen by Sultan Selim, and kindled in his bosom the fire of love. But she was betrothed to a Turkman Omrah; and Akbar forbad the contract to be infringed. When Selim mounted the throne, justice and shame were a slight protection to the man whose life was a bar to the enjoyments of the King. By some caprice, however, not unnatural to minds pampered, and trained up as his; he abstained from seeing her, for some years, after she was placed in his seraglio; and even refused an adequate appointment for her maintenance. She turned her faculties to account; employed herself in the exquisite works of the needle and painting, in which she excelled; had her productions disposed of in the shops and markets, and thence procured the means of adorning her apartments with all the elegancies which suited her condition and taste. The fame of her productions reached the ear, and excited the curiosity of the emperor. A visit was all that was wanting to rekindle the flame in his heart; and Noor Mahal (such was the name she assumed) exercised from that moment an unbounded sway over the Prince and his empire.

Through the influence of the favourite Sultana, the vizirat was bestowed upon her father; her two brothers

BOOK III. CHAP. IV. 1611.

were raised to the first rank of Omrahs, by the titles of Aetikâd Khan, and Asoph Jah; but their modesty and virtues reconciled all men to their sudden elevation; and though the emperor, naturally voluptuous, was now withdrawn from business by the charms of his wife, the affairs of the empire were conducted with vigilance, prudence, and success; and the administration of Khaja Aiass was long remembered in India, as a period of justice and prosperity.

The Afghans broke from their mountains into the province of Kabul, in the sixth year of the reign of Jehangir; but an army was collected with expedition, and drove them back to their fastnesses with great slaughter. About the same time, one insurrection was raised in the province of Bengal, and another in that of Bahar. But the springs of the government were strong; and both were speedily suppressed.

More serious hostility began in Odipore, a mountainous district lying between Ajmere and Malwa, the prince of which, though he had acknowledged subjection to the Mohammedans, yet, protected by his mountains, had never been actually subdued. Amar Singh, the present Rana or prince of Odipore, attacked and defeated the imperial troops in Kandesh. Purvez, the second son of the Emperor, at the head of 30,000 horse, was sent to take the command of all the troops on the borders of the Deccan, and to oppose him. But Amar Singh was no contemptible foe, possessing great authority among his countrymen, and the obedience of a great proportion of the people called Mahrattas, who inhabited the mountains on the south-west, adjoining those of Odipore. Dissensions prevailed among the Omrahs of the imperial army, which the youth and easy character of Purvez made him unable to repress. Encompassed with difficulties, and fain to retreat, he was pursued with loss to Ajmere. Purvez was recalled; a temporary general was sent to take charge of the army; the Emperor himself prepared to march to Ajmere, whence he despatched his third son Khurrum, to prosecute the war. Khurrum entered the mountains with a force which alarmed the Hindus, and induced the Rana after a few losses to offer terms of accommodation. It suited the views of Khurrum to show liberality on this occasion, and

1611-15.

to conclude the war with despatch. Peace was effected; and Sultan Khurrum returned to his father, with a vast increase of reputation and favour at the expense of Purvez, who was left, notwithstanding, governor of Kandesh, and lived in royal state at his capital Burrahanpore.[1]

It was at the time of which we are now speaking, that Sir Thomas Roe arrived at Surat, ambassador to the Great Mogul. In his way to the imperial presence, he repaired to Burrahanpore, to pay his respects to the Prince, and solicit permission for his countrymen to establish a factory in his province. Purvez, whose good-nature, affability, and taste, were better fitted for display, than his facility, indolence, and diffidence, for the duties of government, received the European messenger with magnificence and distinction. From Burrahanpore, Sir Thomas repaired to Ajmere, where the Emperor still remained. Jehangir was flattered by the compliments and solicitations of a distant monarch. But the rude court of India was not a place where the powers of an ambassador could be exerted with much effect.

In the year 1615, disturbances arose both in Guzerat and Kabul. In the most inaccessible parts of Guzerat lived a race of men, known by the name of Koolies, who exercised perpetual depredations and cruelties upon the inhabitants of the open and cultivated districts. The enormities of this people had lately risen to an extraordinary height, when Jehangir issued a sanguinary order for the utter extirpation of the race. Many were slaughtered; the rest hunted to their mountains and deserts. Kabul was again overrun by the Afghans, who issued from the mountains adjoining that province on the north. But the Subahdar, collecting an army, overcame them in battle, and drove them back to their own country.

The provinces of the south were still unquiet. Purvez was engaged in a war with the princes of the Deccan, which, from the dissensions and treachery of his Omrahs, was not successful, and encouraged the Rana of Odipore "to draw his neck from the yoke of obedience." The hopes of the Emperor were again cast upon his younger son; and though his counsellors set before him the danger of sending the younger to supersede the elder, he made light of

[1] Written also Brampore, and Boorhanpore.

BOOK III. CHAP. IV. 1615-28.

the menaced evil; bestowed upon Khurrum the title of Shah Jehan or King of the World, and vested him with the conduct of the war. The easy and unambitious Purvez contested not the royal appointment; fortune, rather than any merit of Shah Jehan, induced the opposing princes to offer terms of accommodation without trying the fortune of the sword: and the prudent desire of Shah Jehan to obtain the credit of terminating the war, without running any of its dangers, made him eagerly remove every obstacle to the conclusion of the peace. In the meantime the Emperor, accompanied by the English ambassador, departed from Ajmere to Mando, the capital of Malwa, where he presided at the settlement of the affairs of the south; and having spent at Mando seventeen months in business and pleasure, he conveyed the royal camp, which was a prodigious moving city, into the kingdom of Guzerat, and thence to Agra, where he arrived after an absence of little less than five years.

It was shortly after this arrival, that Khaja Aiass, the Vizir, now dear to the nation for the blessings conferred upon it, ended a life which had been chequered by so great a diversity of fortune. The sympathies of the Sultana with such a father appear to have been strong, in spite of that loss of heart which flows almost inevitably from the enjoyment of boundless power. She was inconsolable for his loss: and her inconsiderate mind and gaudy taste, made her conceive the design of raising a monument of silver to his memory, till reminded, by her architect, that one of less covetable materials stood a fairer chance for duration. Her brother Asaph Jah sustained the weight of administration, in the room of Khaja Aiass, and inherited the virtues and capacity of his father. But he dared not contend with the haughty and uncontrollable disposition of his sister. And from the death of her father, the caprices and passions of the Sultana exercised a calamitous influence over the fate of the empire.

As the other parts of his dominions were now at peace, Jehangir marched toward Sewalik, or that part of the mountains, separating Tartary from Hindustan, which lies near the spot where the Ganges descends upon the plain. In the recesses and valleys of these mountains, lived tribes of Hindus, which, protected by the strength of their country, had escaped subjection to a foreign yoke, and exercised the depredations, common to the mountaineers of Hindustan, upon the fertile provinces below. The Emperor wished to subdue them; his army penetrated into the mountains; and after enduring a variety of hardships, for nearly two years (so long the war continued), brought twenty-two petty princes to promise obedience and tribute, and to send hostages to Agra. During this expedition, the Emperor paid a visit to the delightful valley of Kashmir, where he spent several months. His partiality produced one good effect. A command was issued to improve the road, for the future visits of the Emperor; and this grand improvement, once begun, was extended to various parts of the empire.

In the meantime, the south engendered new disturbances, which led to important events. The princes of the Deccan withheld their tribute, and raised an army to make good their disobedience. Intelligence arrived that they had crossed the Nerbudda in great force, and were laying waste the adjacent provinces. A great army was placed under the command of Shah Jehan, with which he was despatched to repel and chastise the enemy. As the greatness of the force with which he advanced took from the confederates all hopes of successful resistance, they hastened to make their peace, paid arrears, and promised punctuality and obedience. The success and power of Shah Jehan encouraged him now to commence the execution of designs which had long existed in his mind. His eldest brother Khosroo, confined in a fortress at Malwa, from the time of his last rebellion, he prevailed on his father, before departing, to permit him to relieve from his confinement, and carry along with him. That prince was taken off by assassination; and all men ascribed the murder to Shah Jehan. The emperor loudly expressed his suspicions and resentment. Shah Jehan conceived the time for revolt to be now arrived; assumed the royal titles, and marched to attack his father. They came to action not far from Delhi, and the empire was staked on the turn of a die. After an obstinate struggle, the troops of the father prevailed; and the son, who in his rage and grief had with difficulty been restrained from laying hands on himself, fled in great consternation toward the moun-

BOOK III. CHAP. IV. 1615-28.

tains of Mewat. He was pursued to the Deccan; one province was wrested from him after another; and he lost a battle on the banks of the Nerbudda, which broke up his army, and obliged him to fly to Orissa. Here fortune seemed to dawn upon him anew. The governor of Orissa retired at his approach. He made himself master of Burdwan. He next entered Bengal, and defeated its Subahdar. He then marched to Bahar, which also yielded to his arms; and the impregnable fortress of Rotas, of which the governor came to deliver the keys into his hands, presented to him the inestimable advantage of a place of security for his family. In the meantime, the imperial army advanced. That of Shah Jehan was routed, in spite of all his exertions; and he again fled towards the Deccan. All men now deserted him. After some time spent in eluding his pursuers, his spirits sunk, and he wrote a contrite letter to his father. Pardon was obtained, but with an order to deliver up the forts which were held in his name, and to repair with his family to Agra. That part alone of the command which regarded his own person, he endeavoured to elude, alleging the shame he should feel to behold the face of an injured sovereign and father; and occupied himself under the guise of pleasure in travelling with a few attendants through different parts of the empire. During this rebellion, Abbas, the Persian Shah, attacked and conquered Kandahar. The Usbeks also penetrated to Ghizni, but were successfully resisted, and compelled to retreat.

The general, to whose valour and conduct, on the late extraordinary and critical occasions, the Emperor owed his success, was Mohâbet, from whom, also, on many former emergencies, he had reaped the most important services. The first movement in the breast of Jehangir was gratitude to his benefactor. But Mohâbet possessed a dangerous enemy in Noor Mahal. The slave, she said, who had power to keep the crown upon the head of the Emperor, had power to take it off. Fear is nearly allied to hatred in the breast of an emperor. The power of Mohâbet was curtailed; offensive mandates were addressed to him; a strong fort, which he held, was transferred to a creature of the Sultana. He was commanded to court. His friends represented the danger; but an angry and more peremptory order following his apology, Mohâbet resolved to obey. Five thousand Rajputs, who had served with him in the imperial army, offered themselves for his escort. When Mohâbet approached the imperial camp, he was ordered to stop, till he should account for the revenues of Bengal, and the plunder acquired in the recent battle. Mohâbet, deeply affected with this injurious treatment, sent his own son-in-law to the Emperor to represent his loyalty, and expose the injustice of his enemies. His son-in-law was seized in the royal square, stript of his clothes, bastinadoed, covered with rags, placed backwards on a horse of the most miserable description, and sent out of the camp amid the shouts and insults of the rabble. Mohâbet separated his retinue from the camp, and resolved to watch his opportunity. Next morning, the royal army began to cross the bridge which lay upon the river Jelum, or Behut, on the road between Lahore and Kabul. The greater part of the army had now passed, and the royal tents were yet unstruck; when Mohabet, with two thousand of his Rajputs, galloped to the bridge, and set it on fire. Hastening thence, with a few followers, to the royal quarters, he secured the person of the Emperor, and conveyed him without opposition to his camp. Noor Mahal, in the meantime, contrived to make her escape. Next day Asoph Jah, the vizir, made an obstinate attempt to ford the river and rescue the Emperor; but was repulsed with great slaughter. Unable after this to keep the army from dispersing, he fled to the castle of New Rotas on the Attock, where he was besieged and soon obliged to surrender at discretion, while his sister the Sultana fled to Lahore. The Emperor was treated by Mohâbet with profound respect, assured that no infringement of his authority was designed; that the necessity alone under which the enemies of Mohâbet had criminally placed him, was the lamented cause of the restraint which his imperial master endured. The generous Mohâbet, who really meant as he spoke, was well aware that for him there was no security under Jehangir, while influenced and directed by Noor Mahal. She was repairing to the Emperor upon his own request, when met by an escort of Mohâbet, who, under pretence of guarding, kept her a prisoner. He accused her immediately of treason and other high crimes; and the Emperor, on whose feeble

BOOK III. CHAP. IV 1615-28.

mind absence had already effaced in some degree the impression of her charms, signed without much reluctance the order for her execution. She only begged, that she might have leave, before her death, to kiss the hand of her lord. She was admitted, but in the presence of Mohâbet. She stood in silence. The Emperor burst into tears. "Will you not spare this woman, Mohâbet? See how she weeps." "It is not for the Emperor of the Moguls," cried Mohâbet, "to ask in vain." At a wave of his hand, the guards retired, and she was that instant restored to her former attendants. In a few months Mohâbet restored to the Emperor the full exercise of his authority, and, to show the sincerity of his obedience, dismissed the greater part of his attendants and guards. No sooner did the Sultana conceive him in her power, than she importuned the Emperor for his death. The Emperor had virtue to reject her proposal; but the consequence only was, that she resolved to employ assassination. Jehangir himself discovered to Mohâbet his danger, and he fled without attendants from the camp. The man who had saved the Emperor, and spared both his life and authority, when both were in his hands, was now the object of a command to all the governors of provinces to suffer him no where to lurk in existence; and a price was set on his head. Mohâbet seized a resolution which accorded with the boldness and generosity of his nature. In a mean habit, he secretly entered the camp of Asoph Jah when it was dark, and placed himself in the passage which led from the apartments of the vizir to the haram. He was questioned by the eunuch on guard, who recognised his voice, and carried to Asoph his request to see him on affairs of the utmost importance. Asoph was not ignorant of the baneful effects of his sister's passions, nor unmoved by the generosity with which Mohâhet had lately treated both her and himself. He took him in his arms, and conveyed him in silence to a secret apartment: Mohâbet opened his mind with freedom on the misconduct of the Sultana; the weakness of Jehangir; and the necessity of another sovereign to cure the evils of an afflicted state. "The elder of the princes," said he, "is a virtuous man, and my friend, but we must not exchange one feeble sovereign for another. I know the merit of Shah Jehan, for I have fought against him; and though his ambition knows no restraint either of nature or justice, his vigour will prevent intestine disorders, and give power to the laws." The views of Asoph, whose daughter was the favourite wife of Shah Jehan, corresponded, it seems, with those of Mohâbet: a plan of co-operation was concerted at that moment: and Mohâbet, with letters from the vizir, retired to the court of the Rana of Odipore, to wait for events.

The death of the prince Purvez, which happened soon after, of an apoplexy: and the death of Jehangir, which followed at a short interval, saved the conspirators from many difficulties, and probably crimes. It was found, when the will of the Emperor was opened, that he had named Shahriar, his youngest son, successor; at the instigation of the Sultana, whose daughter, by her first husband, that prince had espoused. As a temporary expedient, the vizir placed Dawur Buksh, the son of the late prince Khosroo, upon the throne; but at the same time despatched to Mohâbet the concerted signal for commencing operations in behalf of Shah Jehan. Asoph conquered the troops of Shahriar, and put out his eyes. Shah Jehan proceeded towards Agra; and every obstacle was removed by the death of Dawur Buksh. Shah Jehan was proclaimed Emperor of the Moguls in the beginning of the year 1628.

He began his reign by removing all danger of competition. The whole of the male posterity of the house of Timur, with the exception of himself and his sons, were despatched by the dagger or the bow-string. His sons were four in number; Dara surnamed Shêko, Shuja, Aurungzeb, and Morad; the eldest, at this time, thirteen; the youngest, four years of age. Even the daughters of Shah Jehan were important actors in the scenes of his eventful reign. They were three in number, women of talents and accomplishments, as well as beauty. The eldest, Jehânara, was her father's favourite, with a boundless influence over his mind; lively, generous, open; and attached to her brother Dara, whose disposition corresponded with her own. The second, Roshenrai Begum, was acute, artful, intriguing, and from conformity of character, favoured Aurungzeb. The gentleness of Suria Bânu,

BOOK III. CHAP. IV.

the youngest, kept her aloof from the turbulence of political intrigue and contention.

1632. The two chiefs, Asoph and Nohâbet, who had conducted Shah Jehan to the throne, and were the most able and popular men of the empire, were appointed, the first, vizir; the latter, commander-in-chief of the forces. Through the wide dominions of the Shah, Khan Jehan Lodi, who commanded the army in the Deccan, was the only disobedient chief. Even he submitted, as soon as an army approached.

The dissensions and weakness usually attending a change of sovereign in the disjointed governments of the East, persuaded the leader of the Usbeks, that conquests might be achieved in Hindustan. Though Abbas still reigned in Persia, and the Usbeks had lately shed their blood in torrents, in disputes about the succession to their throne, they still possessed the regions of the Oxus, of which Abbas had in vain attempted to deprive them. Ten thousand horse, with a train of artillery, penetrated through the mountains in Kabul. They first laid siege to the fortress of Zohâc; but, finding it strong and well defended, proceeded to Kabul. The city made a vigorous resistance, but was at last reduced to extremity. The defenders, resolving however upon one desperate struggle, sallied forth and repulsed the enemy, who evacuated the province, before Mohâbet, on his march from the Deccan, whither he had been sent for the subjugation of Lodi, could reach the scene of action.

The disobedience of the Raja of Bundelcund, who was so imprudent as to take offence at an increase of tribute, was chastised by an overwhelming force. But the heart of the generous Mohâbet was gained by the bravery of his enemy; and he obtained for him pardon and restoration.

All the merit of Mohâbet, and all his services, only inflamed the dark suspicions which usually haunt the mind of an Oriental despot. Shah Jehan regarded him with terror; and by such steps as it appeared safe to venture upon, proceeded to deprive him of his power.

The jealous and revengeful passions of the Emperor involved him in difficulties through another channel. When Lodi submitted upon terms, he was appointed to the go-

1632.

vernment of a province, but not forgiven. He was now ordered to court, and received with so much studied insult, that both his pride and his prudence taught him to look for safety in his independence alone. He escaped with much difficulty; was reduced to the deepest distress; but, having talents and perseverance, he baffled the imperial pursuers, and reached the Deccan. The resources which such a man as Lodi might find in the south made the Emperor tremble on his throne. He raised a large army; placed himself at its head; hastened to the scene of action; and engaged in those struggles for the subjugation of the Deccan, which formed so large a portion of the business of this, and of the following reign.

Since the fall of Ahmednuggur, at the close of the reign of Akbar, the following are the principal events which had taken place in the Deccan. The territories of the Nizam Shahee or Ahmednuggur sovereignty were divided between Mallek Umber, who possessed the country from the Telingana frontier to within eight miles of Ahmednuggur, and four of Dowlatabad; and Rajoo Minnaun,[1] who ruled from Dowlatabad northward to the borders of Guzerat, and southward to within twelve miles of Ahmednuggur, while Mortiza II. a prince of the royal house of Ahmednuggur, with the empty name of sovereign, was allowed to hold the fortress of Ouseh, with a few villages to yield him subsistence. Perpetual contests subsisted between the usurpers; and Umber succeeded at last in taking Rajoo prisoner, and seizing his dominions. Umber was now a sovereign of high rank among the princes of the Deccan, governed his dominions with wisdom, and, exacting something more than respect from the kings of Beejapore and Golconda, held in check the arms of Jehângir himself. He built the city of Gurkeh, now called Aurungabad, five coss from Dowlatabad, and died two years before the present expedition of Shah Jehan, at eighty years of age, leaving his dominions the best cultivated, and the happiest region in India. Futteh Khan, the son of Umber, succeeded him. Mortiza II., still alive, got him by treachery into his power; and recovered once more to the house of Nizam Beheree the remaining part of the Ahmednuggur territories. He did not retain them long; Futteh Khan regained his

[1] The name is Mian Rajoo with the epithet Dekhani.—W.

liberty and ascendancy; and, with the concurrence of Shah Jehan, whom he consulted, put Mortiza to death; and placed his son, only ten years of age, upon a nominal throne.[1]

The Beejapore and Golconda sovereignties remained nearly in the same situation in which they had been found and left by Akbar. Mohammed Adil Shah was now on the throne of the former; Abdoolla Koottub Shah, on that of the latter kingdcm.[2]

The Emperor arrived at Burrahanpore, the capital of Kandesh, and sent his mandates to the princes of the Deccan, to discard their forces, deliver up Lodi, and make their submissions in person, on pain of destruction. The celerity of the Emperor had allowed to Lodi too little time to make the preparations which resistance to so formidable an enemy required. But he had already engaged the three sovereigns of the Deccan in a confederacy for his support, and had influence to make them reject or evade the commands of the Emperor. He was intrusted with a body of troops, and, seizing the passes of the mountains, opposed the entrance of the Mogul army into Golconda. The Emperor, impatient of delay, removed his general, and commanded the vizir to take upon himself the charge of destroying Lodi, and chastising the insolence of the princes of the Deccan. The princes were already tired of the war, and alarmed by its dangers. The reputation and power of the vizir augmented their apprehensions. Lodi was deserted by all on the day of battle, except by a few chiefs, his friends, who adhered to him with their retinues. With these he posted himself on an advantageous ground, and long arrested victory against the whole might of the imperial arms. A neighbouring Raja, to gain the favour of the Emperor, set upon him unexpectedly, as he was pursuing his way to some place of safety, and he lost his brave son with the greater part of his followers. A party of those who were sent in all directions to scour the country at last came upon him in a place from which there was no retreat; and he fell defending himself to the last extremity. Shah Jehan

[1] Ferishta's History of the Deccan, by Scott, i. 400—403. Umber was one of the adventurers from Abyssinia, of whom so many sought, and obtained, their fortunes in the Deccan, during the existence of the Afghan dynasties.

[2] Ibid. p. 339, 340; and 409, 410.

exhibited the most indecent joy when assured of his destruction; the measure of his terrors, while this brave man was alive. After the conquest of Lodi, the war in the Deccan was little else than a series of ravages. The princes were able to make little resistance. A dreadful famine, from several years of excessive drought, which prevailed throughout India and a great part of Asia, added its horrid evils to the calamities which overwhelmed the inhabitants of the Deccan. The princes sued for peace, and the Emperor agreed to withdraw his army, which he now found it difficult to subsist, retaining, as a security for good behaviour, the forts which had fallen into his hands.

During the famine, religion had made the Hindus desert cultivation, and betake themselves to the supplications, penances, and ceremonies, pleasing to their gods. The calamities which sprung from this act of devotion raised the indignation of Shah Jehan. Though no fanatic in his own religion, he pronounced that "an army of divinities who, so far from benefiting their votaries, led them to inflict upon themselves worse evils than the wrath of an enemy, were unfit to be endured in his dominions." The Hindus, however, took arms in defence of their gods; and, after some unavailing and unhappy efforts, he desisted, declaring, "that a prince who wishes to have subjects must take them with all the trumpery and baubles of their religion."

The Portuguese, who had established themselves at Hoogley, in Bengal, and whose presumption rose with their success, gave displeasure to the Subahdar. He transmitted a complaint to the Emperor. "Expel those idolators from my dominions," was the laconic answer. The Portuguese defended themselves bravely. When compelled to lay down their arms, the principal evil which they were doomed to suffer, was to see their religious images broken and destroyed. To this affair succeeded a second revolt of the Raja of Bundelcund, who warded off the destruction now decreed for him with obstinate bravery for two years. The third son of the Emperor, Aurungzeb, with an experienced general for his guide, had the nominal command of the army, though only thirteen years of age; and showed that ardour in the work of destruction which distinguished his riper years.

BOOK III. CHAP. IV. 1640-55.

When the Emperor marched from the borders of the Deccan, he offered the government of Kandesh and of the frontier army, for which he saw that great talents were required, to the vizir, who, fearing the consequences of absence from the court, recommended successfully the virtues and capacity of Mohâbet. Adil Shah, the King of Beejapore, threatened to wrest Dowlatabad from the Futteh Khan, who governed in the name of the young Shah of Ahmednuggur. To prevent the annexation of this important fortress to the dominions of his rival, Futteh Khan offered it to Shah Jehan, and Mohâbet marched to receive possession. Futteh Khan repented of his offer; and Mohâbet laid siege to the fortress. Dowlatabad is a place of great natural strength, standing upon a detached and precipitous rock, and had been fortified with the highest efforts of Oriental skill; but famine at last made Futteh submit. The young prince, his master, was carried a prisoner to Gualior. Futteh Khan was allowed to retain his private property, and was destined to become one of the high Omrahs of the empire: but being seized with insanity, the consequence of a wound formerly received in his head, he was carried to Lahore, where he lived many years on a liberal pension. The fall of Dowlatabad put a period to the dynasty of Nizam Shah, which had swayed the sceptre of Ahmednugger for 150 years.[1] Mohâbet, resolving to pursue the reduction of the Deccan, marched towards Telingana, and laid siege to a fortress; but falling sick, and finding himself unable to superintend the operations of the army, he withdrew the troops to Burrahanpore, where he died at an advanced age.

The tranquillity of the empire permitted the ambition of Shah Jehan to attach itself to the subjugation of the Deccan. He began to march from Agra. That time might be afforded to the governors of the provinces for joining him with their troops, his progress was purposely slow. In rather less than a year he arrived at Dowlatabad with an accumulated army. This great host was divided into twelve bodies, and poured upon the kingdoms of Golconda and Beejapore, with orders not to spare the

[1] The fall of Dowlatabad is somewhat differently related by Dow in his history of Nizam Shah, p. 151. We have here followed the account of Ferishta. Scott's Deccan, i. 402.

severities of war : "because war (such was the reflection of Shah Jehan) was the scourge of humanity, and compassion served only to prolong its evils." One hundred and fifteen towns and fortresses were taken in the course of a year. The unfortunate sovereigns were overwhelmed with calamity, and solicited peace on any terms. It was granted ; but on condition that they should resign their dominions, and be contented to hold them as tributaries of the Mogul. The province of Kandesh, with the army in the Deccan, was left under the command of the son of the late Mohâbet, an accomplished chief. But he died in a little time, and Aurungzeb, the Emperor's aspiring son, was appointed to succeed him.

About this time, a refactory Raja, of Berar, drew upon himself the imperial arms. That large district of Hindustan was regularly subdued; and bestowed as a Subah upon the successful general. Another event yielded high satisfaction to the Emperor. The province of Kandahar, which had been wrested from the Moguls by the power of Abbas, Shah of Persia, was now recovered by the treachery of its governor, disgusted with the cruel and capricious sway of Sefi, the successor of Abbas on the Persian throne.

Of the operations next in order, it is to be lamented that our information is very imperfect. The province of Bengal, we are told, was invaded from the kingdom of Assam, the enemy descending the Brahmapootra in boats, till its junction with the Ganges below Dacca. The Subahdar of Bengal experienced little difficulty in repelling the invaders ; and, not contented with an easy triumph, pursued them into their own country, took possession of several forts, and reduced some provinces ; but he was obliged to return for want of subsistence, and suffered extremely in his retreat by the commencement of the rains and the badness of the roads. It is related also, that the kingdom of Tibet was reduced about this time by another of the generals of Shah Jehan, who was delighted to conquer in regions which the arms of his predecessor had never reached. But to these conquests no effects are ascribed; and of that which is said to have been accomplished in Tibet, we are told neither the place, nor the extent, nor the circumstances, neither the road by which the army was led to it, nor that by which it was conducted back.

BOOK III. CHAP. IV. 1640-55.

The numerous subjects of Shah Jehan now enjoyed a tranquillity and happiness, such as had seldom, if ever, been experienced in that portion of the globe. The governors and officers, in every part of his dominions, were strictly watched; aud not only their obedience to himself, but their duty to his subjects, was vigorously enforced. His reign is celebrated for the exact execution of the laws. And the collection of the revenue, which affects so deeply the condition of the people, and had, in the time of Akbar, been very much improved, was advanced to greater perfection under the diligent administration of Shah Jehan.[1]

This tranquillity was scarcely affected by an incursion of the Usbeks into Kabul, the governor of which not only repulsed them, but, following the invaders, he ravaged their country as far as Balkh, and returned with considerable booty. This success of the governor of Kabul encouraged him to make an incursion into the territory of the Usbeks the following year. But he was on the point of paying dear for his temerity, his communications being intercepted, and his retreat rendered, in the highest degree, dangerous and difficult. The Emperor himself was, at last, infected with the ambition of conquering the Usbeks. His youngest son, Morad, was sent with an army, and overran the country without much difficulty; but offended his father, by returning from his command, not only without, but contrary to, orders. The Usbek sovereign had fled into Persia, but one of his sons solicited and obtained the co-operation of the kindred tribes beyond the Oxus. Aurungzeb was sent to cope with the new adversary; and his talents, and persevering courage, were not more than necessary. In a desperate battle, victory hung suspended, and fortune was more than once on the point of declaring against the Moguls. After much difficulty and much loss, the country was indeed subdued; but its ancient sovereign, writing a most submissive letter

[1] We meet with boasts, in the Oriental historians, of kings, whose administration of justice was so perfect, that a purse of gold might be exposed on the highways, and no man would touch it. Never was justice better administered in India than under the reign of Shah Jehan; yet, knowing more of the circumstances of his reign, we know better what the general eulogies of the Oriental historians mean. Bernier, describing his situation at the time of his arrival at the court of Shah Jehan, speaks of "le peu d'argent qui me restoit de diverses rencontres de voleurs." Hist. des Estats du Grand Mogol, p. 5.

to the Emperor, was, on promise of a slight tribute, reinstated in his dominions.

It was mortifying to the Emperor, in so high a tide of his power, that Kandahar, regarded as the key of his dominions on the side of Persia, was wrested from his hands. Shah Abbas the Second had succeeded the wretched Sefi on the throne of Persia: and taking the advantage of the removal of the Mogul troops from the northern provinces, and of the subjugation of the Usbeks, which seemed to deliver those provinces from danger, he marched towards Kandahar with a great force, and obtained the city by capitulation, before the Mogul army was able to arrive. The strongest efforts were made for its recovery. Aurungzeb besieged it two several times; and Dara, the eldest son of the Emperor, once. It baffled the operations of both.

The most memorable transactions in the reign of Shah Jehan was the renewal of the war in the Deccan. The frontier provinces and the army appointed to hold in check the sovereigns of the south, had been intrusted to the command of Aurungzeb: but the suspicions and jealousy of his father and brothers had made them seek occasions to remove him, at one time to Guzerat, at another, in the war against the Usbeks; he had still, however, found means to regain that important government, and was at Dowlatabad when an occasion offered which a mind like his was not apt to despise. A chief, in the service of the king of Golgonda, who had carried the arms of that sovereign against the Rajas of the Carnatic, and added extensive districts to his dominions, fell at last, from apprehension of his power, under the hatred of his master; and perceived that his life was no longer safe. He transmitted private intelligence to Aurungzeb of his readiness to co-operate with him in surprising the city of Hyderabad, not far from Golconda, where the sovereign resided, and where his treasures were deposited. Aurungzeb, covering his designs under the pretence of an embassy, was admitted into the city; but the king discovered the treachery in sufficient time to make his escape to Golconda; and as Hyderabad was set on fire in the confusion of the attack, the greater part of the riches which had tempted Aurungzeb was consumed in the flames.

BOOK III. CHAP. IV. 1640-55.

Siege was laid to Golconda; but orders arrived from court, suggested by the jealousies which there prevailed, that the king of Golconda should be offered terms of peace. The troops were withdrawn, after the beautiful daughter of the king had been given in marriage to the eldest son of Aurungzeb.

The chief, at whose instigation Aurungzeb had undertaken the expedition, was the famous Emir Jumla, born in a village near Ispahan, in Persia, and of parents so extremely poor that they had scarcely the means of procuring him instruction to read. A diamond merchant, who travelled to Golconda, carried him to that city as a servant or clerk; at this place he left his master, and began to trade on his own account. With the first of his gains he purchased a place in the service of the king. His talents and address attracted favour; and he ascended by rapid gradations to the summit of command. During his public services he forgot not the arts of private acquisition; he had vessels trading to various places, and farmed under borrowed names the whole of the diamond mines. He greatly added to those riches by his successful wars in Carnatic; and was supposed to possess enormous treasures at the time when he connected himself with Aurungzeb. That prince immediately received him into his inmost friendship; and sought the benefit of his counsels and co-operation in his most important affairs. As it appeared that his talents might be employed advantageously for Aurungzeb at the court of his father, he was sent with such recommendations as helped him quickly to the highest rank. When the office of vizir became vacant, the remonstrances of Dara could not prevent the Emperor from bestowing it upon Jumla, in the sordid hope of receiving, upon his appointment, a magnificent present, suited to the riches he was supposed to possess.

Meanwhile, a new event demanded the presence of Emir Jumla in the Deccan. The king of Beejapore died: and his Omrahs, without consulting the Emperor, placed his son upon the throne. The Emperor, who now affected to reckon the sovereigns of the Deccan among his dependants, construed this neglect into a crime, which his new vizir was sent with an army to chastise. He joined Aurungzeb at Burrahanpore; and that ambitious, but artful prince, affected to act with profound submission under the orders of his father's vizir. These two leaders understood one another. The war was conducted with concert and ability. The city of Beder was taken. The Beejapore army was defeated in the field. Kalburga, the ancient capital of the Deccanee empire, submitted; and the king threw himself at the feet of the conqueror. After settling the terms of submission, which were severe, Aurungzeb returned to Burrahanpore, and the vizir was recalled to Agra.[1]

After these events, the health of the Emperor excited alarm;[2] when the flames, which had for some time been with difficulty compressed, broke out with irresistible fury. To every brother under an Oriental despotism the sons of the reigning monarch look as either a victim, or a butcher; and see but one choice between the Musnud and the grave. The usual policy of Oriental fear is to educate the royal youths to effeminacy and imbecility in the haram; but the sons of Shah Jehan had been led into action, and indulged with the possession of power. They were not all men of capacity; but they were all ardent, brave, and aspiring; and each thought himself worthy of empire. Dara, the eldest, gallant, open, sincere, but impetuous, thoughtless, and rash, was destined to the sovereignty by his father, and generally kept near himself; Shujah, the second, was now Subahdar of Bengal, with more prudence and discretion than his elder brother, but far inferior in those qualities to the deep and dissembling Aurungzeb, who had from an early age affected a character of piety, pretending to hate the business and vanities of the world, and to desire only a retreat where he might practise the austerities and devotions pleasing to God. Morâd, the youngest of the sons of Shah Jehan, was conspicuous chiefly for his courage; popular, from his affability and generosity; but credulous and weak. When his father's illness gave fire to the com-

[1] For these transactions of Aurungzeb and Emir Jumla, see Bernier, ut supra, p. 22—32, and the reign of Shah Jehan, chap. v. in Dow.

[2] Dow, who follows his Persian authority, says, the malady was paralysis and strangury, brought on by excesses in the harem; Bernier the physician speaks of it in the following terms; "Je ne parlerai, point ici de sa maladie, et je n'en rapporteray pas les particularitez. Je diray seulement qu'elle estoit peu convenable à un vieillard de soixante-dix ans et plus, qui devoit plûtôt songer à conserver ses forces qu'à les ruiner comme il fit." Ut supra, p. 33.

bustibles which filled the imperial house, this Prince was serving as Subahdar in Guzerat.

1655-58.

As the illness of the Emperor was from the first regarded as mortal, Dara took into his hands, without hesitation, the reins of government; and with his usual precipitation and violence began to show what he apprehended from his brothers, and what his brothers had to expect from him. All communication with them was interdicted on pain of death. Their agents, papers, and effects at the capital were seized. Jumla, and such of the other high officers of the state as were suspected of attachment to any of the younger princes, were removed from their situations. And orders were issued to place the imperial forces in a state of preparation for the field.

Shujah, who was nearest the scene of action, was the first to appear in hostile array. From the government of the richest province of the empire, which he had severely pillaged, he was master of a large treasure, the best sinew of war; and he had collected an army with a view to that very contest which was now impending. Solimân, the eldest son of Dara, was despatched without loss of time to oppose him; found means to cross the Ganges unexpectedly; surprised the camp of Shuja, and forced him to retreat precipitately to Mongeer; where he was immediately besieged.

In the mean time, Aurungzeb was employing the resources of his fertile mind for strengthening his hands, and making sure his blow. He persuaded Morâd, that with regard to himself his views were directed to heaven, not to a throne; but as his brothers Dara and Shujah, compared with Morâd, were unworthy to reign, he was desirous from friendship of aiding him with all his resources; after which the only boon he should crave would be to retire into obscurity, and devote his days and his nights to the service of his Maker.

Though Emir Jumla had been dismissed from the vizirat, he was sent, through some influence which Dara could not resist, to the command of an army in the Deccan, where it was the business of Aurungzeb to obtain the benefit of his talents and resources. But the family of Jumla, detained at Delhi, still retained that chieftain in bonds. The expedient which presented itself to the mind of Aurungzeb, fertile in contrivances, was, to seize the person of Emir Jumla. The appearance of constraint would deprive Dara of a pretext for taking revenge on his family. The sudden resentment of his army could be appeased by promises and bribes. The stratagem succeeded, and the talents and army of Jumla were both added to the resources of Aurungzeb.

Having concerted with his brother, from Guzerat, to join him at Oojein, he took the route from Burrahanpore, and arrived at the Nerbudda, where he learned that Jesswunt Sing, who had married the daughter of the Rana of Odipore, and through her succeeded to most of the dominions of her father, was in possession of the city of Oojein, and prepared to dispute the passage of the army. The Raja lost the favourable opportunity of attacking the troops of Aurungzeb, when, spent with heat and fatigue, they first arrived on the banks of the Nerbudda. The wily Mogul delayed some days, till joined by Morâd: when the brothers crossed the river, and, after a well-contested action, put the Raja to flight. Aurungzeb, who never trusted to force what he could effect by deceit, had previously debauched the Mohammedans in the army of the Raja, by disseminating among them the idea that help to the infidels was treason to the faithful.

In the mean time, the Emperor Shah Jehan had recovered from the violent effects of his disorder: and resumed the exercise of his authority. Dara, who during the royal illness had behaved with tenderness and fidelity truly filial, and delayed not a moment to restore the reins of government when his father was capable to receive them, was exalted to a still higher place in the affections of the Emperor; who despatched his commands to the Princes Aurungzeb and Morâd to return to their respective governments. Aurungzeb was little inclined to intermit the efforts he had so happily begun; but to make war upon his father, beloved both by the soldiers and people, was to ruin his cause, and make even his own army desert him. Under colour of refreshing his troops, he waited several days at Oojein; and the impetuosity of Dara, which the counsels of Shah Jehan were unable to restrain, speedily afforded him a pretext to cover his designs. The news of the passage of the Nerbudda, and of the defeat of the Raja, kindled Dara into a flame. He marched out of Agra at the head of the imperial forces; and enabled Aurungzeb to give out that he fought by necessity; against his brother merely, not his father; and in self-defence. Dara sent to his son Soliman, who was besieging Shujah in Mongeer, to make what terms he could with that Sultan, and march with all expedition to join him against Aurungzeb. Shujah was allowed to resume the government of Bengal: Soliman hastened toward the new scene of action; and, could the impatience of Dara have waited, till joined by his son, who was beloved by the soldiers, and at once prudent and brave, the career of Aurungzeb might perhaps have been closed. The emperor trembled at the prospect of a battle; he threatened to take the field in person, which would have been effectual; because no authority would have been obeyed in opposition to his. But the infatuated Dara found means to prevent the execution of this design; and marched to occupy the banks of the river Chumbul, and the passes of the mountains which extend from Guzerat to the Jumna. Aurungzeb found the passes so strongly guarded, and the enemy so advantageously posted, that he durst not attack them; and fearing the approach of Soliman, he was thrown into the greatest perplexity. In this situation he received, from a treacherous Omrah in the army of Dara, information of a by-road among the hills, which would conduct him to an unguarded part of the river. He left his camp standing to amuse the eyes of Dara; whose first intelligence was, that Aurungzeb was in his rear, and in full march towards the capital. By great exertion Dara threw himself before the enemy, and prepared for action. Dara appeared to most advantage in the field of battle. His bravery animated his troops. The impetuous gallantry of Morâd, and the cool and inventive intrepidity of Aurungzeb, were balanced by the spirit of the imperial army and its leader. The elephant of Dara was wounded; and in an evil hour he was persuaded to dismount. The troops, missing the imperial houda, suspected treachery, and the death of their general; and every man began to provide for himself. Aurungzeb found himself master of the field of battle, at the moment when he despaired of any longer being able to make his soldiers maintain the contest.

Dara fled to Agra, and, after a short interview with his

1658.

father, departed with his family and a few attendants to Delhi, where some imperial troops and treasures were placed at his disposal, and whence he proposed to effect a junction with Soliman. All the cunning and diligence of Aurungzeb were now exerted to the utmost, to improve his victory. He affected to treat Morâd as Emperor; and began to make preparations for himself, as intending immediately to set out on a religious pilgrimage to Mecca. In the mean time he wrote letters, and exhausted the arts of seduction, to detach the Omrahs from the cause of Dara. His principal solicitude was to debauch the army of Soliman; which he accomplished so effectually, that the unfortunate Prince found at last he could place no dependence on its obedience, and was not even safe in its power. He fled from his danger; and took shelter with the Raja of Serinagur, an unconquered kingdom of Hindus, among the northern mountains. The victorious army advanced towards Agra; but the Emperor ordered the gates of the citadel to be shut, and Aurungzeb was still afraid to offer violence to his father. He wrote a letter, replete with the strongest professions of loyalty, and of the most profound submission to his parent and sovereign. The Emperor, with the hope of drawing him into his power, affected to be satisfied, and invited him to his presence. Aurungzeb every day pretended that he was just about to comply; but every day found an excuse for delay. After a series of intrigues, he pretended that to set his mind at ease, in appearing under humiliation and abasement before his father, it was necessary that his son should previously be admitted into the citadel with a guard for his person. The Emperor, who was blinded by his desire to have Aurungzeb in his hands, assented to a condition which seemed indispensable. When he found himself a prisoner in the hands of his grandson, his rage and vexation exceeded bounds; and he offered to resign to him the crown, if he would set him at liberty, and join him in defeating the schemes of Aurungzeb. But the youth, though not averse to the prospect of reigning, and not much restrained by the sense of filial duty, refused to comply; and after some hesitation and delay, Shah Jehan sent the keys of the citadel to Aurungzeb. The hypocrisy of Aurungzeb was not yet renounced. By a letter, which was carefully made public,

BOOK III. CHAP. IV. 1658.

he declared; that with the utmost grief he had been reduced to these extremities; and that as soon as Dara, to whose crimes every evil was owing, should be disabled from future mischief, the happiest event of his life would be, to restore to his father the plenitude of his power.

To deliver himself from Morâd was the next study of Aurungzeb. The friends of that thoughtless prince had at last brought him to look with suspicion upon his brother's designs; and even to meditate an act which might deliver him finally from so dangerous a rival. The sagacity of Aurungzeb enabled him to discover the intended blow, which he contrived to elude at the very moment when it was aimed and ready to fall. In his turn he inveigled Morâd to an entertainment, and, having intoxicated him with wine, withdrew his arms while he slept; seized him without any commotion, and sent him a prisoner to the castle of Agra.[1]

It was now useless, if not hurtful to the cause of Aurungzeb, any longer to disavow his ultimate purpose. But he waited till he was importuned by his nobles; and then, on the second of August, 1658, in the garden of Azabad, near Delhi, pretending to be overcome by their entreaties, he submitted to receive the ensigns of royalty; and assumed the pompous title of Aulum-gir, or Conqueror of the World.

Aulum-gir allowed not what he had already achieved to slacken his efforts in finishing what remained to be done. Dara had taken the route towards Lahore; and had the resources of the northern provinces, Lahore, Multan, and Kabul, at his command: Soliman was ready to descend from the mountains with the assistance of the Raja of Serinagur, and with a body of adherents who still approached the size of an army: and Shujah was master of the rich province of Bengal. Aulum-gir saw, what every skilful leader has seen, that, in the coarse business of war, expedition is the grand instrument of success. He hastened toward the Sutlej, from the banks of which Dara retreated upon the news of his approach. Aurungzeb, pressing on, drove him first from the Beyah, then from

[1] Bernier had not heard of the attempt of Morad upon the life of Aurungzeb. It is here stated upon the Persian authorities of Dow, Bernier, ut supra, p. 109—114. Dow's Shah Jehan, ch. iii. Hist. of Hindustan, vol. iii.

Lahore, and next from Multan; the unfortunate prince BOOK III. who might have resisted with some chance of success, CHAP. IV. having lost his resolution together with his fortune. From Multan, he fled across the Indus to the mountains of 1658. Bicker, when Aurungzeb, declaring the war against him to be closed, left eight thousand horse to pursue him, and returned with haste to Agra.

He had no sooner arrived at Agra, than he learned, what he partly expected, that Shujah was already in force, and in full march toward the capital. He sent to his son Mohammed, whom he had left at Multan, to join him with all his forces; and in the mean time took the road to Bengal, but by slow marches, till Mohammed came up. Shujah intrenched himself near Allahabad; and waited for the arrival of his enemy. Though Shujah did not avail himself of all his advantages, he was able to join battle with a fair prospect of success. Nor was this all. In the very heat of the action, the Rajah, Jesswunt Sing, who had made his peace with Aurungzeb, and joined him with his forces, turned his arms against him, and fell upon the rear of his army. The dismay and desertion which every unexpected incident scatters through an Indian army began to appear. But the firmness of the usurper recovered the blow. His elephant, which was wounded, and began to be ungovernable, he ordered to be chained immoveable by the feet; the soldiers, still beholding the imperial castle opposed to the enemy, were rallied by the generals; Shujah committed the same fatal mistake which had ruined Dara; he descended from his elephant, and his army dispersed.

Emir Jumla, the ancient friend of Aurungzeb, who from his place of confinement, or pretended confinement in the Deccan, had joined him on the march, performed eminent service in this battle. It is even said, that Aurungzeb, when his elephant became ungovernable, had one foot out of the castle to alight, when Jumla, who was near him on horseback, cried out sternly, "You descend from the throne!" Aurungzeb smiled, had a moment for reflection, and replaced himself in the houda.

Shujah and his army fled during the night, while Aurungzeb was in no condition to pursue them. Jesswunt Sing and his Rajpoots, who had plundered the camp, had the

BOOK III. CHAP. IV. 1658.

audacity to wait the attack of Aurungzeb the following day; and were routed, but without being obliged to abandon their spoil. Leaving Mohammed with a force to pursue the vanquished Shujah, Aurungzeb hurried back to Agra.

The haste was not without a cause. Dara, after having arrived at Bicker, crossed the desert with his family, and arrived in Guzerat, where he gained the governor. Aurungzeb, aware how small a spark might kindle into a flame among the disaffected rajas of the mountains, and the distant viceroys and princes of the Deccan, was eager to allow the danger no time to augment. He courted Jesswunt Sing, who had so recently betrayed him, to prevent his co-operation with Dara: and marched with all expedition to Ajmere. Dara had already seized an important pass, and intrenched himself. Aurungzeb was not a little startled when he first beheld the advantages of the position and strength of his works. He set in motion his usual engines of treachery and deceit; and by their assistance gained a complete and final victory. Deserted by all, and robbed of his effects by a body of Mahrattas in his service, Dara fled towards the Indus with his family, who, nearly destitute of attendants, were on the point of perishing in the desert. After many sufferings, he was seized by a treacherous chief, who owed to him his life and fortune; and delivered into the hands of Aurungzeb. His murder was only a few days deferred; during which he was ignominiously exposed about the streets of Delhi.

While the emperor was engaged in opposing Dara, his son Mohammed, and Jumla the Vizir, prosecuted the war against Shujah. That prince had fled from the battle to Patna, from Patna to Mongeer, from Mongeer to Rajamahal, and from Rajamahal he was forced to retreat to Tanda. Shujah was still possessed of resources; his courage and resolution failed not; and an event occurred which promised a turn in the tide of his affairs. Mohammed had been formerly enamoured of the daughter of Shujah; and their union had been projected, before the distractions of the royal family had filled the empire with confusion and bloodshed. It is said that the princess wrote to Mohammed, reminding him of his former tenderness, and deprecating the ruin of her father. The impatient and

1658.

presumptuous Mohammed was little pleased with the treatment he sustained at the hands of Aurungzeb; his heart was touched with the tears of the princess; and he resolved to desert the cause of his own father, and join that of hers. He expected that the army, in which he was popular, would follow his example. But the authority and address of Jumla preserved order and allegiance. The news of his son's defection quickly reached Aulum-gir, who concluded for certain that he had carried the army along with him, and set out in the utmost expedition with a great force for Bengal. In the meantime Jumla attacked the army of Shujah, which he defeated; and the conquered princes retreated to Dacca. Aurungzeb, pursuing his usual policy, wrote a letter to Mohammed, which he took care that the agents of Shujah should intercept. It purported to be an answer to one received; offering to accept the returning duty of Mohammed, and to pardon his error, on the performance of a service which was nameless, but seemed to be understood. This letter smote the mind of Shujah with incurable disgust. After a time Mohammed was obliged to depart, and with a heavy heart to intrust himself to his unforgiving father. He was immediately immured in Gualior, where, after languishing for some years, he was intrusted with liberty, though not with power; but he died a short time after.[1] Shujah was speedily reduced to extremity in Dacca, and having no further means of resistance, fled from the province, and sought refuge in the kingdom of Arracan. But the wretched Raja, who at once coveted his wealth, and dreaded his pursuers, violated without scruple the laws of hospitality and mercy. Death, in some of the worst of its forms, soon overtook the family of Shujah.

During these transactions, rewards, which were too powerful for the virtue of a Hindu, had been offered to the Raja of Serinagur; and shortly after the ruin of Shujah, Solimân, the last object of the fears of Aulum-gîr, was delivered into his hands, and added to the number of the prisoners of Gualior.

[1] This account of the fate of Mohammed is given by Mr. Stewart, (Hist. Bengal, p. 276) on the authority of the Muasir Alumgiry, and varies from the account of Ferishta, who says he died in Gualior.—M.

Dow's supplement to Ferishta is here intended. Ferishta's history closes with the reign of Akbar, and there is reason to believe that he did not long survive A. D. 1611 - above 40 years before these events.—W.

BOOK III. CHAP. IV. 1661.

From the time when Aulum-gîr, having subdued all competition for the throne, found himself the undisputed lord of the Mogul empire, the vigilance and steadiness of his administration preserved so much tranquillity in the empire, and so much uniformity in its business, that the historians who describe only wars and revolutions, have found little to do. The most important series of transactions were those which occurred in the Deccan; which ceased not during the whole of this protracted reign; laid the foundation of some of the most remarkable of the subsequent events; and had a principal share in determining the form which the political condition of India thereafter assumed. That we may relate these transactions without interruption, we shall shortly premise such of the other transactions handed down to us (for we have no complete history of Aurungzeb) as fell near the beginning of his reign, and merit any regard.

When Aurungzeb marched from the Deccan to contend for the crown, he left Mohammed Mauzim, his second son, to command in his name. When established upon the throne, it was not altogether without apprehension that he contemplated so vast a power in hands which possibly might turn it against him. Mauzim, aware of the jealous disposition of his father, preserved the utmost humility of exterior; avoided all display, either of wealth or power; was vigilant in business; exact in obeying the commands of the Emperor, and in remitting the revenue and dues of his government. He was recalled, notwithstanding his prudence, and Shaista Khan made viceroy in the Deccan. At the same time, Aurungzeb, seeking security for the present, by directing hope to the future, declared Mohammed Mauzim heir to the throne, and changed his name to Shah Aulum, or King of the World.

The third year of his reign was visited with a great famine, a calamity which ravages India with more dreadful severity than almost any other part of the globe. It was occasioned by the recurrence of an extraordinary drought, which in India almost suspends vegetation, and, throughout the principal parts of the country, leaves both men and cattle destitute of food. The prudence of Aurungzeb, if his preceding actions will not permit us to call it his humanity, suggested to him the utmost activity of be-

1665.

neficence on this calamitous occasion. The rents of the husbandman, and other taxes, were remitted. The treasury of the Emperor was opened without limit. Corn was bought in the provinces where the produce was *least*, conveyed to those in which it was *most* defective; and distributed to the people at reduced prices. The great economy of Aurungzeb, who allowed no expense for the luxury and ostentation of a court, and who managed with skill and vigilance the disbursements of the state, afforded him a resource for the wants of his people.

It was before the commencement, perhaps, of this calamity, that the empire was agitated by the prospect of a fresh revolution from a dangerous sickness of the Emperor.[1] The court was full of intrigues; on one hand, for Mauzim, the declared successor; on the other, for Akbar, a young, and even infant son of Aurungzeb. Shah Jehan himself was still alive; and the people in general expected that he would resume the reins of government. But the nation was relieved from its terrors, and from the calamities which too certainly would have fallen upon it. The usurper recovered. But the efforts of Sultan Mauzim, to secure the succession, expressed to the suspicious mind of Aulum-gîr, more of the desire to obtain a throne than to preserve a father; and his purpose in regard to the succession, if his declaration in favour of Mauzim had ever been more than a pretence, was from this time understood to have suffered a radical change.

To forward his designs in favour of Akbar, he applied to Shah Jehan, to obtain for that prince, in marriage, the daughter of Dara, who remained in the seraglio of her grandfather. Shah Jehan, though strictly confined in the palace at Agra, had been treated with great respect; retaining his women and servants, and furnished with every amusement in which he was understood to delight. He had not, however, remitted his indignation against Aurungzeb, and now sent a haughty and insulting refusal. Aurungzeb had prudence not to force his inclination; and,

[1] Dow, (Hist. of Aurungzebe, chap. iv., places the Emperor's illness after the famine. But Bernier, who was on the spot, and mentions the arrival of ambassadors from the Khan of the Usbeks first among the events succeeding the termination of the civil war, says, that those ambassadors, who remained somewhat more than four months, had not departed from Delhi when the Emperor was taken ill. Bernier, Evénemens Particuliers des Etats du Mogul, p. 10.

BOOK III. CHAP. IV.

so far from showing any resentment, redoubled his efforts to soften his mind.

1665.

The services of Emir Jumla had been rewarded with the government of Bengal. But the mind of Aurungzeb, and indeed the experience of Oriental government told him, that he was never safe while there was a man alive who had power to hurt him. He wished to withdraw the Vizir from his government, but without a rupture, which might raise distrust in the breasts of all his Omrahs. To afford him occupation which would detain his mind from planning defection, he recommended to him a war against the king of Assam, who had broken into Bengal during the distractions of the empire, and still remained unchastised. Jumla, who promised himself both plunder and reputation from this expedition, and whose exploring eye beheld an illustrious path through the kingdom of Assam to the conquest of China, undertook the expedition with alacrity. He ascended the Brahmapootra in boats. The Assamese abandoned the country which lies on the side of the mountains facing Bengal; but the fortress of Azo was garrisoned, and stood an attack. After the reduction of Azo, Jumla crossed the mountains of Assam, vanquished the king, who took refuge in his capital, forced him to fly to the shelter of the mountains, and he became master of a great part of the kingdom. But the rains came on, which in that kingdom are peculiarly violent, and lay the greater part of the level country under water, Jumla found it impossible to subsist his army; and was under the necessity of returning to Bengal. Incredible were the difficulties with which he had to contend; necessaries were wanting, the roads covered with water, and the enemy everywhere harassing his retreat. The capacity of Jumla triumphed over all obstructions; he brought back the greater part of the army safe; and wrote to the Emperor that he would next year carry his arms to the heart of China. But the army, on its return, was afflicted with a dysentery, the effect of the hardships it had endured. The general escaped not; and, worn out as he was with years and fatigue, he fell a victim to the violence of the disease. "You," said the Emperor to the son of Jumla, whom he had recently made generalissimo of the horse, "have lost a father; and I

1665.

have lost the greatest and most dangerous of my friends."[1]

The next event is ludicrous, perhaps, in itself, but of high importance, as an instance of the power of superstition among the weak and credulous inhabitants of India. Of the professors of devotion and penance, going by the name of Fakîrs, one class is distinguished by wandering about the country in crowds, almost naked, pretending to live by mendicity, but stealing, plundering, and even committing murder, wherever prompted by the hope of advantage. In the territory of Marwar, or Jodpore, an old woman, possessed of considerable property, began to enlarge her liberalities towards the Fakîrs The sturdy beggars crowded around her, to the number of some thousands, and not satisfied with the wealth of their pious patroness, made spoil of the neighbouring country, and rioted in devotion and sensuality at her abode. The people, exasperated by these oppressions, rose repeatedly upon the saints ; but were defeated with great slaughter. The idea of enchantment was generated. The people regarded the old woman as a sorceress ; and believed that she compounded for her followers a horrid mess which rendered them proof against human weapons, and invincible. What they were not rendered by enchantments, they were rendered by the belief of them. The Fakîrs, finding themselves, under the auspices of an old woman, too formidable for resistance, assembled in great numbers, and spread their devastations to a wide extent. The Raja of Marwar attacked them, but was defeated. The collectors of the imperial revenue marched against thom with the troops under their command, but sustained a similar disaster. Becoming presumptuous from unexpected success, they

[1] Bernier, ut supra, p. 87.—M. A particular account of the invasion of Asam is given from the Hadiket-as-safâ in the Calcutta Quarterly Magazine, June 1825. The Mogul army suffered not only upon its retreat from disease, but from famine and sickness, during the rains whilst in the country. As an instance of their distress, it is stated that the battalion under Diler Khan was reduced from 1500 to 400 men. No such fort as Azo is mentioned ; the principal towns of Asam were Gergaon and Gohati, both which fell into the hands of the invaders, but were given up on their retreat, which was purchased by a present payment of money and elephants, and a promise, which no doubt was never fulfilled, of more. Mir Jumla was taken ill in Asam, and died at Khizerpore in Kooch Behar. According to the Asamese accounts of this occurrence, the Moguls were not only obliged to make a precipitate retreat, but were driven out of territories bordering on Asam, which had for some time been subject to the Emperor.—Account of Asam; Annals of Oriental Literature.—W.

BOOK III. CHAP. IV. 1665.

resolved on a march to the capital, to the number of twenty thousand plundering saints, with the sacred old woman at their head. About five days' journey from Agra, they were opposed by a body of imperial troops, under the collector of the district. Him they overcame; and now grasped in their imaginations the whole wealth and authority of the state. They set up their old woman as sovereign. Aurungzeb felt the danger to be serious; for the soldiers were infected with the superstition of the people; and it was hazardous to the last degree, from the terrors with which they might be disordered, to permit them to engage with the sainted banditti. What was first demanded, an antidote to the religious contagion, was invented by Aurungzeb. His own sanctity was as famous as that of the old woman; he pretended that by means of incantation, he had discovered a counter-enchantment; he wrote with his own hand, certain mysterious words upon slips of paper, one of which, carried upon the point of a spear before each of the squadrons, he declared would render impotent the spells of the enchantress. The Emperor was believed, and though the Fakîrs fought with great desperation, they were all cut to pieces, except a few whom the humanity of the general led him to spare. "I find," said Aurungzeb, "that too much religion among the vulgar, is as dangerous as too little in the monarch."[1]

[1] The whole of this story is a specimen of misrepresentation, for which, however, the author is no further censurable than in having too easily given credence to a tale which bears evident marks of inaccuracy and exaggeration. The best Mohammedan writers state the matter differently. They say nothing of the patronage by a rich old woman, of a set of sturdy beggars, of their riot and sensuality, or of their conflicts with the people, or of their setting up the old dame as sovereign. The story, as they tell it, wears every appearance of probability. The persons with whom the disturbance began were as unlike vagrant Fakirs as possible. They were a sect of quietists—Hindu quakers as they have been termed. Sádhs or Satnámis, who acknowledge one God only, offer worship to no idol or created thing; who enjoin truth as the first of virtues, who prescribe self-denial, temperance and continence, prohibit the use of all stimulating drugs and liquors, and forbid the assumption of the mendicant marks and raiment, and the acceptance of alms. Trans. R. As. Society, vol. i. 251; and As. Res. vol. xvi. 209. They of course follow a secular life; one of them was engaged in the cultivation of his land, when some dispute arose between him and the Peon or revenue watchman set to look after the government share of the crop; the dispute ended in an affray in which the Peon was worsted; he returned to the charge with some of his companions: the Satnámi was aided by his fellows, and the Revenue officers were put to the rout. This success inspirited the people of the country to make common cause with the Sadhs, and their strength became formidable; troops were sent against them, but they were defeated, and then a notion of their invincibility spread amongst the Mohammedans. It was they who reported that the insurgents were invulnerable, and amongst other stories asserted

BOOK III. CHAP. IV. 1665.

In the seventh year of the reign of Aurungzeb, his father died. The life of Shah Jehan had reached its natural period; but his death did not escape the suspicion of the *pousta*, that detestable invention of despotic fears.[1]

After the death of Jumla, the Raja of Arracan had invaded the contiguous quarter of Bengal, and possessed himself of Chittagong, and all the country along the coast of the Ganges. He availed himself of the Portuguese settlers, who were numerous at Chittagong, and of their ships, which abounded in the bay of Bengal, and it is said infested the coast and every branch of the Ganges as plunderers and pirates. These evils it consisted not with the vigilance of Aurungzeb to leave without a cure. A new deputy was appointed for Bengal; an army collected itself at Dacca; and descended the river. The enemy, though master of the forts and strong-holds of the country, without much resistance retired. The Portuguese were invited to betray them, and made no hesitation by their obedience to purchase for themselves privileges and settlements in Bengal.[2]

that they were led by a female upon a horse of wood, to which their magic had given animation. The Rajpoot Zemindars, near Delhi, joining the insurgents, Aurungzeb began to be alarmed, and sent a considerable force against them, directing the men to wear prayers and amulets upon their persons as counter-charms against the conjuration of the enemy. These were no mysterious slips written by his hand, but passages from the Koran, which the Mohammedans very commonly wear. There is very little authority for his supposed observation, and it is not likely that he would have spoken of the faith of infidels as "too much religion." The affair was clearly a sudden and aimless rising of the peasantry and landholders, originating in an insignificant quarrel, but expressing the prevailing feelings of the country, provoked by the exaction and tyranny of the imperial government. It owed neither its commencement nor its extent to "the power of superstition."—W.

[1] The Pousta is thus described by the physician, Bernier. Ce pousta n'est autre chose que du pavot écrasé qu'on laisse la nuit tremper dans de l'eau; c'est ce qu'on fait ordinairement boire à Goualeor, à ces princes auxquels on ne veut pas faire couper la teste; c'est la première chose qu'on leur porte le matin, et on ne leur donne point à manger qu ils n'en ayent bu une grande tasse, on les laisseroit plutôt mourir de faim; cela les fait devenir maigres et mourir insensiblement, perdant, peu à peu les forces et l'entendement, et devenus comme tout endormis et étourdis, et c'est par là qu'on dit qu'on s'est défait de Sepe-Chekouh, du petit fils de Morâd, et de Soliman même. Bernier, Hist. de la dernière Révolut. des Estats du Grand Mogul, p. 170. It is said, that when the gallant Soliman was, by the treachery of the Raja of Serinagur, delivered into the cruel hands of Aurungzeb, and introduced into his presence, when every one was struck with the noble appearance of the graceful and manly youth, he entreated that he might be immediately beheaded; and not reserved to the lingering destruction of the pousta; when the hypocritical Aurungzeb forbade him to fear, adding, that he was cautious, but not cruel. Bernier, Ibid, p. 168. Dow, Reign of Aurungzeb, ch. iv.

[2] Bernier, (Evénemens Particul. des Estats du Mogul, p. 88—101) speaks of these Portuguese as infamous buccaneers; and their own historian, Faria de Souza, countenances the assertion, which might have been founded upon the

BOOK III. CHAP. IV.

1668.

The mistake of a secretary was near involving the empire, not only in hostilities with the whole force of Persia, but in all the horrors of a civil war. Aurungzeb, who had been complimented upon ascending the throne by embassies from the Khan of the Usbeks, and from Abbas II. Shah of Persia, proposed, after settling the affairs of his government, to make the suitable return. The secretary who composed the letters, addressed to the respective sovereigns, inadvertently designated the Shah by no higher title than belonged to the Khan of the Usbeks. This was interpreted as a meditated insult; and resented by a declaration of hostilities. Aurungzeb wished to explain the mistake; but his ambassador was not admitted even to an audience. His own weapons were tried against him; and he added an illustrious instance to prove, that he who is practised in the arts of deception, is not always the hardest to deceive. Of the Mohammedan army and officers of the Mogul empire, as some were Moguls, some Afghans, some Turks, and some Usbeks, so a large proportion were Persians, among whom was the Vizir himself. The fidelity of this part of his subjects, Aurungzeb was by no means willing to try, in a war with their native country. A letter was intercepted from Abbas, addressed to the Vizir himself, importing that a conspiracy existed among the Persian nobles to seize the Emperor when he should take the field. Aurungzeb was transported with apprehension and rage. He issued a sudden order to the city guards to surround the houses of the Persian Omrahs, which they were forbidden to quit under pain of death. Aurungzeb found himself on the brink of a precipice. The Persian chiefs were numerous and powerful; a common danger united them; the descendants of the Afghan nobility, who formed a considerable proportion of the men in power, and hated the Moguls, by whom the Afghan dynasty had been driven from the throne, were very likely to make common cause with the Persians. Even if guilty, he beheld appalling danger in attempting to punish them; but he now reflected that he might have been deceived, and wished only for the means of a decent

reports of enemies. The Portuguese followed their merchandise as their chief occupation, but like the English and Dutch of the same period, had no objection to plunder, when it fell in their way.

1668.

retreat. He sent for some of the principal Omrahs; but they excused themselves from attendance. All had assembled their friends and dependents; fortified their houses, and waited the appeal to arms. After a suspense of two days, the princess Jehanara arrived. She had been sent for, express, upon the first alarm. The favourite daughter of Shah Jehan, by whom the Persians had always been distinguished and exalted, might render, by her mediation, the most important assistance. After a short conference with the Emperor, she presented herself in her chair at the door of the Vizir. This was an act of supreme confidence and honour. The door of the mansion flew open; the Vizir hastened to the hall of audience, and prostrated himself at the foot of the throne. Aurungzeb descended, and embraced him. Convinced that he had been deceived, he now sought only to obliterate all memory of the offence; and with some loss of reputation, and a remainder of disgust in the breasts of some of the Omrahs, he recovered himself from the dangerous position in which a moment of rashness had placed him. Shah Abbas, in the meantime, with a large army, was upon his march towards the confines of India; and Aurungzeb, who had sent forward his son Mauzim to harass the enemy, but not to fight, made rapid preparations to meet him in person. Shah Abbas, however, died in the camp, before he arrived at the scene of action. His successor wished to mount the throne, free from the embarrassment of an arduous war; and Aurungzeb was more intent upon gaining conquests in the Deccan, than in Persia. An accommodation, therefore, was easily made.[1]

These transactions were all contained within the first ten years of the reign of Arungzeb, during which several events had already occurred in the Deccan. A new enemy had arisen, whose transactions were not as yet alarming, but who had already paved the way to revolutions of the greatest importance. This was Sivajee, the founder of the Mahratta empire; a power which began when the empire of the Moguls was in its utmost strength; and rose to greatness upon its ruins. In the mountainous regions which extended from the borders of Guzerat to Canara, beyond the island of Goa, lived a race of Hindus,

[1] Dow, Reign of Aurungzeb, ch. vi.

who resembled the mountaineers in almost all the other parts of Hindustan, that is, were a people still more rude and uncivilised than the inhabitants of the plains, and at the same time far more hardy and warlike. They con-consisted of various tribes or communities, to some of which (it appears not to how many) the name of Mahratta, afterwards extended to them all, was applied.[1] Sivajee was the son of Shahjee, a Hindu in the service of Ibrahim Adil Shah, King of Beejapore, from whom he received a jaghir in the Carnatic, with a command of ten thousand horse.[2] Sivajee, when very young, was sent along with his mother to reside at Poonah, of which, as a zemindary, his father had obtained a grant, and of which he intrusted the management, together with the charge of his wife and son, to one of his officers, named Dadajee Punt. The mother of Sivajee was an object of aversion to her husband; and the son shared in the neglect which was the lot of his mother. He grew up under Dadajee to vigour. both of body and mind; and at seventeen years of age engaged a number of banditti, and ravaged the neighbouring districts. Dadajee, afraid of being made to answer for these enormities, and unable to restrain them, swallowed poison, and died; when Sivajee took possession of the Zemindary, increased the number of his troops,

[1] Mheerut, or Mharat, the name of a district, which under the Deccanee sovereigns was part of the province of Dowlatabad, may in former ages, says Mr. Jonathan Scott, have given name to a larger division of Dekkan and the original country of the Mahrattas. Scott's Deccan, Introd. p. x. Ibid. i. 32. The Mahratta language extends along the coast from the island of Bardez to the river Tapti. Orme, Histor. Frag. p. 57. It is said by Col. Wilks, (Hist. Sketches, p. 6) that "from Beder the Mahratta language is spread over the whole country to the northwestward of the Canara, and of a line which, passing considerably to the eastward of Dowlatabad, forms an irregular sweep until it touches the Tapti, and follows the course of that river to the western sea—but that in the geographical tables of the Hindus, the name of Maharashtra, and by contraction Mahratta desum (or country) seems to have been more particularly appropriated to the eastern portion of this great region, including Baglana, part of Berar and Kandeish; the western was known by its present name Concan."

[2] This is an error. Shahjee was never in the service oi Ibrahim Adil Shah: He was at first in the service of Nizam Shah of Ahmednagar, and held a principal command; he afterwards joined the Moguls, then transferred his assistance to Mohammed Adil Shah for a season, but returned to Ahmednagar, aspired to the regency, and set up a prince of the Nizam Shahi dynasty. In this character he was in alliance with the Sultan of Beejapore, and equally the object of the hostility of Shah Jehan. The power of the Emperor being more than he could oppose, he petitioned to be allowed to serve under the Mogul government, but he was told that he might take service with Beejapore. He accordingly passed the remainder of his life as a dependant upon the Beejapore prince, holding the districts of Poona and Sopa. Duff's History of the Mahrattas, vol. i. —W.

1668.

and raised contributions in all the neighbouring districts. Such was the commencement of the fortunes of Sivajee.[1]

Of his ancestry, the following is the account presented to us. His father was the son of Malojee; and Malojee was the son of Bauga Bonsla, a son of the Rana of Odipoor, by a woman of an inferior caste.[2] The degradation of Bauga Bonsla, from the impurity and baseness of his birth, drove him to seek, among strangers, that respect which he was denied at home. He served, during a part of his life, a Raja, possessing a Zemindaree in the province of Kandesh; and afterwards purchased for himself a Zemindaree in the neighbourhood of Poonah, where he resided till his death. His son Malojee entered the service of a Mahratta chief, in which he acquired so much distinction as to obtain the daughter of his master in marriage for his son. This son was Shahjee, and Sivajee was the fruit of the marriage. But Shahjee, having quarrelled with his father-in-law, repaired to the king of Bejapore, and received an establishment in the Carnatic. He here joined the Polygar of Mudkul in a war upon the Raja of Tanjore; and having defeated the Raja, the victors quarrelled about the division of the territory. Shahjee defeated the Polygar, took possession of both Mudkul and Tanjore; and having married another wife, by whom he had a son, named Ekojee, he left him and his posterity Rajas of Tanjore, till they sunk into dependants of the East India Company.[3]

[1] Aurungzebe's Operations in the Dekkan, translated by Scott, p. 6.

[2] Mallojee was the son of Bapjee, and married Deepa Bhye, the sister of Bunga or Bungo-Bhonslay. No person ever thought of making the latter the son of a Rana of Oudipore, although a legend is known intimating the descent of the Bhonslay family from the Raja of Mewar. Duff's Mahratta History, i. 89. See also Tod's Rajasthan, i. 235.—W.

[3] Aurungzebe's Operations in the Deccan, a translation from a Persian manuscript, by Jonathan Scott, p. 6;—Appendix A. to Lord Wellesley's Notes on the Mahratta war;—East India Papers, printed by the House of Commons, 1804, p. 255. Lord Wellesley seems to have followed Scott. Ekogee, as he is called by Mr. Orme and others, is written Angojee in Mr. Scott's translation, p. 32. The history and origin of the family is related with considerable variations, by Col. Wilks, on Mahratta authorities. (Hist. Sketches, chap. iii.) But if Hindu authority were better than Persian (and it is far inferior), the facts are not worth the trouble of a critical comparison. It is of some importance to state what is related (ibid.) by Wilks, that Shahjee went second in command in the army of the King of Beejapore which proceeded to the conquest of the Carnatic in 1638; that he was left provincial governor of all the Beejapore conquests in the Carnatic, when the general in chief returned to the capital: that his first residence was at Bangalore, but that he afterwards seems to have divided his time between Colar and Balapoor. Wilks infers by some grants of land by Shawjee, of which the writings still remain, that he affected independence of the declining govern-

BOOK III. CHAP. IV. 1668.

When Sivajee, upon the death of Dadajee, seized the Zemindaree of Poonah, his father was too much occupied in the East to be able to interfere. Aurungzeb was at the same moment hastening his preparations for the war with his brothers; and invited Sivajee to join his standards. The short-sighted Hindu insulted his messenger, and reproached Aurungzeb himself with his double treason against a king and a father. He improved the interval of distraction in the Mogul empire; took the strong fortress of Rayree, or Rajegur. which he fixed upon as the seat of his government; and added to it Porundeh, Jegneh, and several districts dependent on the king of Beejapore. The threats of that power, now little formidable, restrained not his career of plunder and usurpation. He put to death, by treachery, the Rajah of Jaowlee, and seized his territory and treasure; plundered the rich and manufacturing city of Kallean; took Madury, Purdhaungur, Rajapore, Sungarpore, and an island belonging to the Portuguese. At length, the Beejapore government sent an army, to suppress him. He deceived the general with professions of repentance and offers of submission; stabbed him to the heart at a conference; cut to pieces his army deprived of its leader; and rapidly took possession of the whole region of Kokun or Concan, the country lying between the Ghauts and the sea, from Goa to Daman.

When Aurungzeb, upon the defeat of his rivals, sent Shaista Khan, with the rank of Ameer al Omrah, or head of the Omrahs, to command in the Deccan, the Raja Jesswunt Sing, who had redeemed his treachery in the battle against Shujah, by his subsequent dereliction of the cause of Dara, was invested about the same time with the government of Guzerat. As soon as Aurungzeb had leisure to attend to the progress of Sivajee, the viceroy of Guzerat was commanded to co-operate with the viceroy of the Deccan, in reducing and chastising the Mahratta adventurer. Sivajee could not resist the torrent which

ment which he had served. The acquisition of Tanjore was made, as the Colonel thinks, not by Shawjee, but after his death by Ekojee his son; and his accomplice was not the Raja or Polygar of Mudkul, but the Naik of Madura, which however appears to have been called Mudkul by the Persian historians. Naik and Polygar were Hindu names of governors of districts, who, as often as they dared to assume independence, affected the title of Raja. Naik was a title of inferior dignity to Polygar.

1668.

now rolled against him. The strong fortress of Jegneh was taken. The Ameer al Omrah advanced to Poonah, where he took up his residence. Here a band of assassins made their way to his bed in the night. He himself was wounded in the hand, by which he warded off a blow from his head, and his son was slain. The assassins escaped, and Sivajee himself was understood to have been among them. Circumstances indicated treachery; and the suspicions of Shaista Khan fell upon Jesswunt Sing. These two generals were recalled; and after an interval of two years, during which the Prince Mohammed Mauzim, or Shah Aulum, held the government of the Deccan, two other generals, Jey Sing and Dilleer Khan, were sent to prosecute the war against the Mahratta chief. Jey Sing was the Raja of Abnir,[1] and Dilleer was a Patan Omrah, and both had obtained high rank as generals in the service of Shah Jehan; and being chosen for their merit as the fittest to guide and enlighten Soliman, when sent against Shujah, were the chiefs whom Aurungzeb had gained to betray their master, and debauch his army.

Before the arrival of these generals, Sivajee had, with great address, surprised and plundered Surat, a city of importance and renown; the chief port of the Mogul empire; and that from which the holy pilgrims commenced their voyage to the tomb of the prophet. The

[1] The mountainous districts, lying between the provinces of Agra and Guzerat, and forming part of the provinces of Malwa and Ajmere, were inhabited by a race of warlike Hindus, named Rajpoots, who, from pride of superior prowess, claimed to be of a higher caste than the mass of other Hindus. They had been divided into three principal Rajaships; that of Abnir or Ambeer, called afterwards Jeypore and Jyenagur, on the borders of Agra; that of Jodepore or Marwar, south-west from Abnir, approaching the centre of Ajmere: and lastly that of Chitore, called also Odeypore, from another city, lying further south. Of these Rajas the most powerful had been the Raja of Chitore, whose distinctive title was Rana. Jesswunt Sing, the Raja of Jodpore, having married the daughter of the last Rana, had merged those two kingdoms of Rajpoots into one. Mr. Orme seems not to have been aware of the marriage of Jesswunt Sing, and of its effects: as he mentions with some surprise, that the name of the Raja of Chitore nowhere appears in the history of the present transactions. Bernier, Revol. p. 52, 53; Dow, Reign of Shah Jehan, ch. v. p. 212; Scott, ut supra, p. 10; Memoirs of Eradut Khan, p. 18; Rennel's Memoir, Introd. p. cxxxii. To the above nations of Rajpoots should also be added those of Bondela, or Bundelcund, a district between the provinces of Agra and Malwa, extending from Jeypore, by Gualior and Callinger, as far as Benares. Memoirs of Eradut Khan, p. 17; Rennel, ut supra, p. cxxxii.—M.

For further and more accurate information regarding the states and tribes of Central and Western India, see Malcolm's Central India and Tod's Rajasthan. There is no such name as Abnir in Tod, and it is probably a misreading of Amber. The three principalities are more correctly termed Amber, Marwar and Mewar.—W.

BOOK III. CHAP. IV.

1668.

operations of the new commanders turned the tide in Mahratta affairs. The armies of Sivajee were driven from the field; his country was plundered; and Poorundeh, a strong fortress, in which he had placed his women and treasures, was besieged. It was reduced to the last extremity, when Sivajee, unarmed, presented himself at one of the outposts of the imperial camp, and demanded to be led to the general. Professing conviction of his folly, in attempting to contend with the Mogul power, he craved the pardon of his disobedience, and offered to the Emperor his services, along with twenty forts, which he would immediately resign. Jey Sing embraced the proposal; and Sivajee obeyed the imperial order, to wait upon the Emperor at Delhi. Sivajee had offered to conduct the war in Kandahar against the Persians. Had he been received with the honour to which he looked, he might have been gained to the Mogul service, and the empire of the Mahrattas would not have begun to exist, But Aurungzeb, who might easily have despatched, resolved to humble the adventurer. When presented in the hall of audience, he was placed among the inferior Omrahs; which affected him to such a degree, that he wept and fainted away. He now meditated, and with great address, contrived the means of escape. Leaving his son, a boy, with a Brahmen, whom he knew at Muttra, and who afterwards conducted him safe to his father, he travelled as a pilgrim to Juggernaut, and thence by the way of Hyderabad to his own country.[1]

The Prince Shah Aulum, and the Rajah Jeeswunt Sing, were sent to supersede the Raja Jey Sing, who was suspected of an understanding with Sivajee, and died on his way to the imperial presence.[2] The change was favourable to Sivajee; because Jesswunt Sing, who had but

[1] Scott, ut supra, p. 11—17. Mr. Orme, from scattered reports, has stated the circumstances differently. Historical Frag. p. 17, &c.

[2] Not without suspicion of poison. Mr. Scott's author, who probably wished to spare Aurungzeb, says, by his moonshee, or secretary (p. 17). Mr. Orme says, by order of Aurungzeb (p. 27). But the Raja was worn out with age and laborious services: and the only poison, perhaps, was the anguish of disgrace. He is praised by the Mohammedan historians as the most eminent, in personal qualities, of all the Hindus they had yet known; accomplished in Persian and Arabian learning. His successor, of whom more will be heard hereafter, was celebrated for his astronomical learning, and for the observatory which he erected at Jeypore. Memoirs of Eradut Khan, p. 18. Note (1) by Scott.

little affection to the imperial service, allowed the war to linger, and discontents and jealousies to breed in the army. Sivajee was not inactive. Immediately upon his arrival he took royal titles, and struck coins in his name. His troops, in consequence of his previous arrangements, had been well kept on foot during his absence; and he attacked immediately the Mogul territories and forts. Surat was again plundered; he recovered all the forts which he had resigned, and added some new districts to his former possessions.

The weakness of Beejapore made him look upon the territories of that declining state as his easiest prey. Neither upon that, however, nor any other enterprise, could he proceed with safety, till his forts were supplied with provisions; and provisions, while pressed by the Mogul arms, he found it difficult, if not impossible, to supply. He seems never to have distrusted his own address any more than his courage. By a letter to Jesswunt Sing, he averred, that only because his life was in danger had he fled from the imperial presence, where his faithful offers of services had been treated with scorn; that still he desired to return within the walks of obedience; and would place his son in the imperial service, if any command in the army, not dishonourable, was bestowed upon him. The stratagem succeeded to his wish; he obtained a truce, during which he supplied his forts; he dexterously withdrew his son from the Mogul army; with little resistance he took possession of several important districts belonging to Beejapore; compelled the king to pay him a contribution of three lacs of pagodas, and the King of Golconda to pay him another of four.[1]

The Emperor, displeased with Jesswunt Sing, as well on account of the ill success of the war, as the divisions and jealousies which reigned in the army, recalled him; and several generals were successively sent to conduct affairs under Aulum Shah. In the mean time, the Mahrattas plundered the adjoining countries, retreating with the spoil to their forts, in spite of all the efforts of the imperial commanders. At last, in 1671, the Prince him-

[1] Wilks, (p. 30) says nine, upon what authorities he, as usual, omits to state.

BOOK III. CHAP. IV.

1681.

self was recalled. An Omrah, titled Bahadur Khan,[1] succeeded him; and retained the government till the year 1676. During these years, the war produced no remarkable event, though it was prosecuted with considerable activity, and without intermission. The efforts of the Viceroy were divided and weakened by hostilities with Beejapore and Golconda; which, though they had contributed to the fall of those languishing states, had aided the rising power of Sivajee. In 1677, that chieftain affected to enter into an alliance with the King of Golconda against the King of Beejapore and the Moguls; and marched into the territory of Golconda at the head of an army of 40,000 horse. He proceeded to make conquests with great appearance of fidelity; but placed Mahratta governors in all the fortresses, and enriched himself by plunder. He obtained possession of the impregnable fortress of Gingee by treachery. He laid siege to Vellore, which defended itself during more than four months. An interview took place between Sivajee and Ekojee, the latter of whom, perceiving the insatiable appetite of his brother for power, trembled for his dominions. Before he had time, however, to conquer everything to the north of the Coleroon, he was recalled to his western dominions.[2] Dilleer Khan, who succeeded Bahadur, carried on the war in a similar manner, and was superseded by Bahadur, who received the command anew, in 1681. The most remarkable occurrence, during the administration of Dilleer, was the arrival in his camp of the son of Sivajee, who had incurred the displeasure of his father, and fled for protection to the Moguls. The event was regarded as fortunate, and a high rank was bestowed upon the young Mahratta; but Sivajee soon found means to regain his confidence, and he had the good fortune to make his escape a little time before his father terminated his indefatigable and extraordinary career.

During all the time of these great and multiplied transactions, a naval war, which we hear of for the first time

[1] His proper titles were Khan-jehan-Bahádar Kokaltash—though called by Scott, Bahadar Khan.—W.

[2] This expedition into the Carnatic is noticed by Scott, ut supra, p. 32; by Orme, Hist. Frag. p. 82—87. Col. Wilks, however, (ch. iii. ut supra) has given the most distinct account, and is here followed,

1682.

in the history of India, was carried on between Sivajee and his enemies. At the commencement of his exploits, a chief, distinguished by the name of Siddee Jore, had the government of the town of Dunda Rajapore, a seaport to the southward of Bombay, belonging to the King of Beejapore; and at the same time, the command of the fleet, which that sovereign had formed to protect his maritime dominions and their trade from the naval enemies which now infested the coasts of India. While Siddee Jore was endeavouring to signalize himself against Sivajee in another quarter, that ingenious adventurer arrived unexpectedly at Dunda Rajapore, and obtained possession of it by a stratagem. The loss of this important place so enraged the king against Sidde Jore that he procured his assassination. At the time of the capture of Dunda Rajapore, however, the heir of Siddee Jore was in the command of the fleet, which lay at the fortified island of Gingerah, before the town. When the outrage was committed upon his father by the King of Beejapore, he tendered his services to Aurungzeb, with the fort of Gingerah, and the whole of the Beejapore fleet. The offer, of course, was greedily accepted. Siddee, it appears, was a name, which was applied in common to those Abyssinian adventurers, who had passed over, in great numbers, from their own country into the service of the kings of the Deccan; and had there frequently engrossed a great proportion of the principal offices of state. Of this class of men was the admiral who had now enlisted himself in the Mogul service. He was joined by a great number of his family and countrymen. He himself was called *the* Siddee, by way of distinction; his principal officers had the term Siddee prefixed to their names; and his crews and followers were in general denominated the Siddees. They carried on an active warfare along the whole western coast of India, and were not only dangerous and troublesome enemies to Sivajee, but formidable even to the British and other European traders, who frequented the coast.[1]

Sivajee breathed his last in his fortress of Rayree, on the 5th of April, 1682, of an inflammation in his chest, at the early age of fifty-two; having displayed a fertility

[1] Orme's Hist. Frag. p. 2 to 11, 79 to 81.

BOOK III. CHAP. IV. 1682.

of invention, adapted to his ends; and a firmness of mind in the pursuit of them, which have seldom been equalled, probably never surpassed. With the exception of the few small districts possessed by the Europeans, his dominions, at the time of his death, comprehended, along the western coast of India, an extent of about 400 miles in length by 120 in breadth, and from the river Mirzeou in the south to Versal in the north. Of the detached forts, which at one time he had garrisoned in the Carnatic, only one or two appear to have at this time remained in his hands.[1]

During these transactions in the south, we are not informed of any other emergency which called the attention of Aurungzeb from the ordinary details of his administration, excepting a war with the Patans or Afghans, who infested the northern provinces, and another, which the Emperor himself provoked, with the Rajpoots of Ajmere and Malwa.

The Governor of Peshawur, to punish an incursion of the Patans, had, in 1673, pursued them to their mountains, where he allowed himself to be entangled in the defiles, and was cut off with his whole army. A Patan, who had served in the armies of Sultan Shujah, and bore a strong resemblance to his person, gave birth to a report, that the Sultan had made his escape from Arracan. The Patans proclaimed him King of India; and all the tribes of that people were summoned to join their forces to place him upon his throne. They were able, it is said, had they united, to bring into the field 150,000 men; and Aurungzeb was roused by the magnitude of the danger. He took the field in person, and crossed the Indus, about the close of the year 1674. The war lasted for about fifteen months, during which the Patans were driven from the more accessible country; and Aurungzeb was too cautious to penetrate among the mountains. A chain of forts was established to restrain them; and the governor, whom he left at Peshawur, having exerted himself to gain the confidence of the Patan chiefs, drew them to an entertainment at that place, and murdered them along with their attendants. Though Aurungzeb disowned the action, he obtained not the credit of being averse to it.[2]

[1] Ibid p. 133, 134. Wilks says he died in 1680, (ubi supra, p. 91.)
[2] Orme's Hist. Frag. p. 68—72.

1682.

It is probable that Aurungzeb, from political motives, projected the reduction of the Rajpoot states, viewing with jealousy the existence of so great an independent power (able, it is said, to bring 200,000 men into the field), in the heart of his dominions. He put on, however, the mask of religion, and began the execution of a project, or pretended project, for the forcible conversion of the Hindus to the religion of the faithful. Jesswunt Sing, the Maharaja, or Great Raja, as he was called,[1] having died, near Kabul, in 1681, his children, on their return to their native country, were ordered to be conducted to court, where he insisted on their being rendered Mohammedans. Their Rajpoot attendants contrived their escape, and fled with them to their own country. The Emperor revenged the disobedience by a war, which he conducted in person. His numerous forces drove the Rajpoots from the more accessible parts of their difficult country; but they held possession of their mountains and fastnesses; and the war degenerated into a tedious and ineffectual struggle. Aurungzeb sat down at Ajmere, where he superintended, at a less inconvenient distance, the operations in the Deccan, as well as the war with the Rajpoots.[2]

Samba, or Sambajee, the eldest son of Sivajee, succeeded to his throne, but not without a competitor, in a younger brother, whose adherents created him considerable danger, till the principal among them were all put to death. While the war was carried on between the Mahratta and the imperial generals in the Deccan, as it had been for several years, by sudden inroads on the one side, and pursuit on the other; but with few important advantages on either; Akbar, one of the younger sons of Aurungzeb, who was employed in the war against the Rajpoots, turned his standards against his father, being offered assistance by the enemy whom he was sent to subdue. One of Aurungzeb's tried artifices, that of raising jealousy between associates, enabled him to defeat the first attempt of Akbar, who fled from the country of the Rajpoots, and took refuge with Sambajee.

Both Sambajee and Aurungzeb knew the value of the

[1] The title was not peculiar to Jeswunt Sing. Every Hindu prince or Raja takes also the epithet of Mahá-raja.—W.

[2] Scott's Operations of Aurungzeb in the Deccan, p. 53. Orme, ut supra, p. 100—105, and 119—121.

BOOK III. CHAP. IV. 1687.

acquisition. The prince was received with extraordinary honours, by the Mahratta chief, who would not sit in his presence. And Aurungzeb, resolving to extinguish the enemy who had so long troubled his government in the south, arrived with a vast army at Aurungabad, in 1684. After the attack and defence of some forts, with no important result, the prince Shah Aulum was sent into the Concan, to reduce the Mahratta fortresses on the sea-coast. He found it impossible to procure provisions; the climate disagreed with the Mogul troops, and he was obliged to return with only a remnant of his army.[1]

In 1687, the Emperor resolved upon the final reduction of the Mohammedan kingdoms of the Deccan, Hyderabad or Golconda, and Beejapore, which displayed a greater residue of strength and resources, than their reduced condition had led him to expect, From Ahmednuggur, where the grand camp had already arrived, he moved as far as Sholapore, and sent one army towards Hyderabad, another towards Beejapore.

The general, who led the army of the King of Hyderabad, betrayed his trust, and passed over to the enemy, upon which the King abandoned the open country, and shut himself up in the fort of Golconda. Hyderabad was taken and plundered. That the Sultan Mauzim, however, who commanded, might not have the honour, which he was wise enough not to covet, of taking Golconda, Aurungzeb accepted the humble terms which were offered by the King, and reserved his destruction till another opportunity.

Beejapore made considerable resistance, which was aided by scarcity. After the city had been besieged for some time, the Emperor proceeded to the attack in person. Famine at last compelled the garrison to surrender; and the young King was delivered into the hands of Aurungzeb.[2]

He received, about the same time, intelligence of another agreeable event, the departure of Sultan Akbar, from the Mahratta country to Persia. As this lessened greatly, in the eyes of Aurungzeb, the importance of immediate operations against the Mahrattas, he turned from Beejapore

[1] Scott, ut supra, p. 54—64; Orme Hist. Frag. p. 134—162.
[2] Scott, ut supra, p. 65—73.

towards Golconda. Shah Aulum, with his sons, was seized and put in confinement, for remonstrating, it is said, against the treachery aimed at the unfortunate King of Golconda, who had submitted under pledge of honour to himself. Aurungzeb, in truth, was incurably jealous of his son, because heir to his throne, and was stimulated to ease his mind of a part of its load of terror and distrust. Golconda was invested, and, after a siege of seven months, fell by that treachery, the benefit of which Aurungzeb made it his constant endeavour to procure. He had now the two sovereigns of the Deccan in his hands, and the reduction of the outstanding forts wss all that remained to complete the extension of the Mogul dominion to the farthest limit of the Carnatic.[1]

This important success was immediately followed by an event which the Emperor regarded as peculiarly fortunate. His spies brought intelligence, that Sambajee, at one of his forts in the mountains not far distant, was spending his time in a round of his favourite pleasures, and very imperfectly on his guard. A body of troops was despatched to surprise him, and he was, in fact, taken prisoner. Sambajee was too formidable to be permitted to live; but the Emperor polluted his fortune by glutting his eyes with the butchery of his enemy, who relaxed not his haughtiness in the presence of death. The efficacy of Sambajee's talents, which were not inconsiderable, was obstructed by his immoderate passion for women, which his father predicted would lead him to his ruin.

The Emperor followed up his advantage with activity, and immediately sent an army into the Concan. Its operations were highly successful; and Rayree, which Sambajee and his father had made their capital, together with the wives and infant son of that chieftain, fell into the hands of the victor.[2]

Rama, however, the brother of Sambajee, escaped from the Concan, and, crossing by the way of Seringapatam to

[1] The greatest part of the Carnatic had belonged to the Rajas of Beejanugger, in the flourishing state of that empire. After the reduction of that state by the Mohammedan powers of the Deccan, it was divided between the states of Golconda and Beejapore. Aurungzebe's Operations in the Deccan, Scott, p. 73, 74, 75. Orme, p. 119—130.

[2] Scott, ut supra, p. 77—80; Orme, p. 230—234. Wilks (p. 215) says it was taken in 1698.

BOOK III. CHAP. IV. 1700-07.

the Carnatic, threw himself into the fort of Gingee, which was a place of great strength, and by the obstinacy of its resistance, or the interested delays of the imperial generals, retarded the settlement of the Deccan for several years. It gave occupation to a great part of the imperial army from the year 1692 to the year 1700; and during that period kept the reduction of the Carnatic incomplete.

The Emperor turned his whole attention to the final subjugation of the Mahrattas, and penetrated into the country with his principal army. But while he was employed in the reduction of forts, the Mahrattas, under various chiefs, issued from their mountains, and spreading over the newly-conquered countries of Beejapore and Golconda, and even the provinces of Berar, Kandesh, and Malwa, carried great plunder back with them, and left devastation behind. The imperial forces marched to oppose them in all directions, and easily conquered them in battle when they could bring them to an action. But the Mahrattas eluded rencounter, retired to their mountains when pursued, hung upon the rear of their enemy when obliged to return, and resumed their devastations whenever they found the country cleared of the troops which opposed them. The Emperor persevered with great obstinacy in besieging the forts in the accessible parts of the Mahratta country; the greater part of which fell into his hands. But during that time the Mahrattas so enriched themselves by plundering the imperial dominions, and so increased in multitude and power, being joined by vast numbers of the Zemindars in the countries which they repeatedly overran, that the advantages of the war were decidedly in their favour, and the administration of Aurungzeb betrayed the infirmities of age. The more powerful Omrahs, who maintained numerous troops, and were able to chastise invaders, his jealous policy made him afraid to trust with the command of provinces. He made choice of persons without reputation and power, who abandoning the defence of their provinces, to which they were unequal, were satisfied with enriching themselves by the plunder of the people. Under so defective a government, the Mahrattas found the whole country south from the Nerbudda open to their incursions. The Emperor persevered in his attempts to subdue them. In

1707.

that harassing and unavailing struggle were the years consumed which intervened till his death. This event took place in the camp at Ahmednuggur on the 21st of February, 1707, in the forty-eighth year of his reign, and ninety-fourth of his age.[1]

At the time when the last illness of Aurungzeb commenced, his eldest son Mohammed Mauzim, who at an early age had received the title of Shah Aulum, was at Kabul, of which, as a distant province where he would be least dangerous, he was made governor, upon his liberation from the confinement in which he had languished for several years. His two remaining sons, Azim Shah, who was subahdar of Guzerat, and his youngest son Kam Buksh, who had been recently appointed to the government of Beejapore, were both in the camp. Aurungzeb, who forgot not his caution to the last, hurried them away to their stations, either fearing lest under his weakness they should seize upon his person while yet alive, or lest they should fill the camp with bloodshed immediately upon his dissolution. Azim had not yet reached his province, when he received the news of the Emperor's decease. He hurried back to the camp, and, no competitor being present, received without difficulty the obedience of the army.

As it was not, however, expected that Shah Aulum would quietly resign his throne and his life, Azim began his march towards the northern provinces. On the news of the Emperor's illness, Shah Aulum had despatched his commands to his two sons, Moiz ad Din, the eldest, governor of Multan, and Azim oos Shaun, the second, governor of Bengal, to advance with their forces towards Agra. Azim oos Shaun had used so much diligence, that he was enabled to anticipate the arrival of Azim Shah, and got possession of Agra with its treasures. As the two armies were approaching one another in the neighbourhood of Agra, Shah Aulum addressed a letter to his bro-

[1] For the last seven years of the reign of Aurungzeb, the author of Aurungzeb's Operations in the Deccan, by Scott, (p. 73—123,) is our principal authority. The age of Aurungzeb is stated on the authority of Golam Hussein Khan (Seer Mutakhareen, i. 2). Mr. Scott's author mentions not the age. Both writers miscalculate the length of the reign (which began in August 1658, and ended in February 1707); the one calling it more than fifty, the other more than fifty-one years.

BOOK III. CHAP. IV. 1707.

ther, offering to divide the kingdom. The presumptuous prince rejected the proposal; and the armies came to action, when Azim Shah lost the battle, and he and his two eldest sons lost their lives. He had committed many important errors; among others offended the generalissimo, the famous Zulfikar Khan, the favourite general of Aurungzeb, and son of Assud Khan, his vizir. He rejected the advice of this commander at the commencement of the battle, and Zulfikar with his forces withdrew from the field.[1]

Shah Aulum, who now assumed the title of Bahadur Shah, was chiefly indebted to the prudence and wisdom of Monâim Khan, his minister of finance, for his victory and throne. He rewarded him with the office of vizir; but Assud Khan, the late vizir, and Zulfikar Khan, his son, were received with extraordinary favour, the former being created Vakeel Mutluk;[2] the latter Meer Bukshi;[3] and governor of all the Deccan, with the title of Ameer ul Omrah.

Another contest, however, still remained, The throne was promised to Kâm Buksh by his own vanity, and by his astrologers; and though his brother, even when near him with an irresistible army, invited him to enjoy in peace his kingdom of Beejapore, to which he offered to add that of Golconda, the infatuated prince was resolved upon his destruction. It had been the object of his father to render him, by his power in Beejapore, safe from the jealousy of any of his brothers who might ascend the imperial throne. For this purpose, he had placed in his service the Turanee Moguls, or that part of the army which consisted of the Mogul adventurers, newly arrived from Tartary, and distinguished from those who had been bred in Hindustan. The chief of these Moguls was Ghazee ad Din Khan, a man of great years and experience, who had acquired high reputation and influence in the Deccan during the wars of Aurungzeb. The light, inconsiderate, rash, and inconstant character of Kâm Buksh would have

[1] The reign of Shah Aulum is related by two Persian noblemen, both cotemparary with the events, Eradut Khan, (Mem. p. 11—64,) and Golâm Hussein Khan, Seer Mutakhareen, p. 1—23.

[2] This was the highest office in an Indian government, and seldom bestowed unless on some great emergency. Scott, Memoirs of Eradut Khan, p. 46.

[3] Chief paymaster; an office of great trust and dignity. Ibid.

1709.

discovered to a less discerning mind than that of Ghazee, the speedy ruin of that prince's hopes; he therefore listened to the friendly proposals of the Emperor, and was appointed Subahdar of Guzerat, while his son Cheen Koolich Khan, a man of great celebrity in the subsequent history of India, was favourably received at court. Kâm Buksh was gradually deserted by almost all his followers, but rushed desperately into battle near Hyderabad with not more than a few hundred attendants. He was taken prisoner, but not till he received a mortal wound, of which he died the same evening.

The Emperor seemed afraid of becoming, like his father, entangled in the labyrinth of Deccanee affairs; and leaving to his officers whatever remained for the settling of those newly-conquered regions, he began his march towards the capital, though in the middle of the rains. Zulfikar Khan, the subahdar of the Deccan, left Daood Khan Punnee, a native of the Deccan, his deputy; and followed his master, still further to push his ambitious designs.

The Emperor was not satisfied with the Rajpoot princes, whose disobedience had been provoked by the religious and mischievous war kindled against them at the end of the reign of Aurungzeb. Ajeet Sing, the successor of Jesswunt Sing, Raja of Odeypore; and Jey Sing, the successor of the Raja who had rendered himself famous in the wars of Aurungzeb, had formed an alliance, cemented by marriage; and without professing independence of the Mogul power, endeavoured to yield a very limited obedience. Some unavailing measures were taken to reduce them to more perfect subjection. But a new enemy, whose operations began to be serious, and even formidable, rendered it advisable to accept for the present the nominal obedience of the Rajpoots.

The Seiks, now ravaging the province of Lahore and the northern part of the province of Delhi, committing outrages on the persons of the Moslem, inflamed both the religious and political indignation of the Emperor and his Omrahs. This people, of whom the history is curious, were advancing rapidly to that importance, which renders them at present one of the principal powers in Hindustan. Their origin is to be traced back to the time of the Emperor Baber, when a celebrated Durvesh, being captivated

BOOK III. CHAP. IV. 1709.

with the beauty of the son of a grain-merchant of the Kshatriya caste, by name Nanuk, brought him to reside in his house, and instructed him in the sublime doctrines and duties of Islamism. Nanuk aspired beyond the merit of a learner. From theological writings which he perused, he selected, as he went on, such doctrines, expressions, sentiments, as captivated his fancy. At length his selections approached to the size of a book, and being written (it is said with elegance) in the Punjabee dialect, or language of the country, were read by various persons, and admired. The fame of Nanuk's book was diffused. He gave it a name, *Kirrunt*,[1] and, by degrees, the votaries of *Kirrunt* became a sect. They distinguished themselves by a peculiar garb and manners, which resembled those of the Moslem fakirs. They united so as to live by themselves apart from the other inhabitants; and formed villages or communities, called *Sangats*, in which some one, as head of the community, always presided over the rest. Nanuk was followed by nine successors in the office of chief, or patriarch of the whole sect; during whose time the Seiks led peaceable and inoffensive lives. Tej Bahadur, the tenth in order, was perpetually followed by a large multitude of the enthusiasts of the sect; and united himself with a Mussulman fakir who had a number of followers approaching that of his own. To subsist so numerous a body of idle religionists, the neighbouring districts were laid under contribution; and the saints having tasted the sweets of a life of plunder and idleness, pushed their depredations, and became the scourge of the provinces. Aurungzeb, who was then upon the throne, commanded the governor of Lahore to seize the two leaders of the banditti; to banish the Mussulman beyond the Indus; and to conduct the Hindu to the fort of Gualior; where he was put to death. The loss of their patriarch was far from sufficient to extinguish the religious flame of the Seiks. A son of Tej Bahadur, whose family name was Govind, was raised to the vacant supremacy, and was distinguished by the name of Gooroo Govind, Gooroo being the title bestowed by a Hindu on his religious instructor. The fate

[1] Sir John Malcolm writes it Grant'h. Sketch of the Sikhs, p. 25.—M. The word is Granth, or grunth, meaning in general a book, in this case, *the* book.—W.

1709.

of his father taught him audacity; he instructed his followers, hitherto unarmed, to provide themselves with weapons and horses; divided them into troops; placed them under the command of those of his friends in whose conduct and fidelity he confided; and plundered the country by force of arms. He was not, however, able to withstand the troops of the province, which were collected to oppose him; his two sons were taken prisoners, and he himself fled among the Afghans. After a time he came back, disguised as an Afghan devotee; but falling into mental derangement, was succeeded by Banda, one of his followers, who assumed the name of Gooroo Govind, and resolved to take vengeance on the Moslems for the slaughter of the father and sons of his predecessor. To the robbery and plunder which had become the business of the Seiks, he added cruelty and murder. The Moslem historians of these events are filled with horror as well as indignation at the cruelties which he exercised upon the faithful (to them alone, it seems, did they extend) and describe as one of the most sanguinary of monsters the man whose actions, had infidels been the sufferers, and a Mussulman the actor, they might not, perhaps, have thought unworthy of applause. It was this Banda whose enormities Shah Aulum hurried from the Deccan to interrupt and chastise. The rebels (so they were now denominated) deserted Sirhind upon the approach of the Emperor, and retired to Daber, a place of strength at the entrance of the mountains, and the principal residence of the Gooroo. When Daber was reduced to the last extremity, Banda, with his principal followers, retired to the mountains during the night. The presence of the Emperor suspended, but did not extinguish, the depredations of the Seiks.[1]

[1] Golâm Hussein, (Seer Mutakhareen, i. 87—93) who gives a pretty detailed account of the origin of the Seiks; and Scott (Hist. of Aurungzebe's Successors, p. 142). who gives an abridged one, agree pretty exactly in the facts. Eradut Khan (Mem. p. 61) describes the reduction of Daber. Some general remarkz are found in a paper of Mr. Wilkins, in the first vol. of the Asiatic Researches. The more detailed account of Sir John Malcolm, (Sketch of the Sikhs, p. 1—85,) taken from Seik authorities, differs widely in the history of Nanuk; but though the inaccurate Persians are not much to be trusted, the fabling Seiks, making everything miraculous in the origin of their sect, are still less.—M.

Without attaching more credit to the Sikh accounts than they deserve, their authority is preferable to those of the Mohammedan writers, whose defect is not inaccuracy only, but religious bigotry also; the Sketch of the Sikhs, by Sir J. Malcolm, first published in the As. Researches, vol. xi. is a much safer guide than even the Seir Mutakhareen.—W.

1712.

Shah Aulum had reigned five years, counting from the death of Aurungzeb, with the praise of great humanity, having spilt the blood of no rival but in the field, and treating the sons of his rebel brothers like his own; when he was seized with a violent illness, and expired suddenly in his camp, near Lahore, in the year 1712.

The four sons of Shah Aulum, each with his army and retainers, were in the camp; Moiz ad Dien Khan, the eldest; Azim oos Shaun, the second, the favourite of his father; Ruffeh oos Shaun, the third; and Kojesteh Akter, the youngest. Of all the Omrahs, the vizir Monaim Khan being dead, Zulfikar Khan was by far the most powerful; and doubted not to place on the musnud any of the princes whose cause he should espouse. Azim oos Shaun, who had in the camp a large treasure of his own, and from his situation near his father was enabled to possess himself of all the imperial treasure and effects, assumed the sceptre without hesitation. Zulfikar Khan sent to him a confidential messenger, to ask if, in that emergency, he could render him any service; and receiving a careless and disdainful answer, took his resolution. He passed to the camp of Moiz ad Dien, and formed or confirmed a union of the three brothers, who agreed to oppose Azim oos Shaun, and afterward to divide the empire. Azim oos Shaun lost the favourable opportunity of attacking his brothers. He allowed the time to pass, till they made their preparations; and till his own army, becoming uneasy and dispirited, began to disperse. When the inevitable hour arrived, he was conquered without much difficulty, and disappeared in the battle; his wounded elephant, it is supposed, rushed with him down the precipice into the river, where both sunk to appear no more.

To the surviving princes it remained to settle the partition on which they had agreed; but Zulfikar Khan had other designs. Whether from selfish motives, or a patriotic dread of the consequences of division; whether because that prince was the weakest, and might be governed, or the oldest, and had the better title, the Ameer ul Omrah resolved to make Moiz ad Dien sole Emperor, and to defeat the expectations of the other two. By various artifices, creating difficulties and delay, he contrived to secure the greater part of the treasure to Moiz

1712.

ad Dien. This roused the jealousy of Kojesteh Akter, and he prepared for action; but the night before the projected battle a fire broke out in his camp, and he lost the greater part of his ammunition. He and his son fought with gallantry, but his soldiers deserted him during the engagement, and gave an easy victory to his more fortunate brother. Ruffeh oos Shaun stood aloof during this action; still confiding in the friendship of Zulfikar Khan, and reserving himself to fall upon the victor. While he waited with impatience for the morning, having been dissuaded from attacking the successful army the same night, intelligence of his design was carried to the Ameer ul Omrah, who made preparations to receive him. The victory was not a moment doubtful; for the army of the prince almost immediately dispersed, and he was slain, fighting bravely amid a few attendants.[1]

Moiz ad Dien was proclaimed Emperor, with the title of Jehandar Shah. He possessed not abilities to redeem the weaknesses by which he exposed himself to the disapprobation of his people; and his government and person fell into contempt. He was governed by a concubine, who had belonged to the degraded and impure profession of public dancers, and shed infamy upon the man with whom she was joined. The favours of the crown were showered upon the mean relations, and ancient companions of Lall Koor (such was the name of the mistress), who did not always enjoy them with moderation. The Emperor, who loved the jollity of debauch, exposed himself about the city in company with Lall Koor and her favourites, in situations where dignity was apt to be lost. The nobles were offended, because a new set of favourites intercepted the rays of imperial favour; and the people were disgusted at the sight of vices in their sovereign, which shed degradation on the meanest of themselves.

Jehandar Shah was, from these causes, ill prepared to meet the storm which shortly after he was summoned to face. When Azim oos Shaun marched from Bengal to assist his father in the struggle for the crown, he left behind him his son Ferokhser. Upon the defeat of Azim

[1] Eradut Khan, (Memoirs, p. 65—67,) and GolamHussein Khan, (Seer Mutakhareen, i. 23—36,) agree in the general points of this struggle for the crown; the former describing it like an eye-witness, but not a very curious one; the other from report merely, but not without diligence and criticism.

BOOK III. CHAP. IV. 1712.

oos Shaun, and the elevation of Jehandar Shah, it became necessary for Ferokhser to think either of flight or of resistance. There were two brothers, Abdoolla Khan, and Hussun Khan, of the high birth of Syeds, or descendants of the prophet, who had distinguished themselves in the service of Azim Shah, and having afterwards attached themselves to Azim oos Shaun, were by him appointed, the one to the government of Allahabad; the other, to that of Bahar. Ferokhser succeeded in gaining the support of these brothers, whose talents were powerful, and their reputation high. The counsels of Jehandar were divided. The powers and services of Zulfikar Khan were eclipsed by the favour of Kokultash Khan, the foster-brother of the Emperor. The talents of Kokultash were unequal to the conduct of any important affair. The abilities of Zulfikar were restrained, and his ardour cooled, by the success with which Kokultash thwarted his designs. Neither wished to take the command of the army, which, compelling him to quit the Emperor, left the imperial power in the hands of his rival. Time was consumed during these intrigues. In the end, Aiz ad Din, the eldest son of the Emperor, and with him, for his guide, a relation of the foster-brother, a man without talents or experience, proceeded to the reduction of Ferokhser. The two armies met at Kudjwa, a town in the district of Korah, where Aurungzeb and Shujah had formerly engaged. But the conductor of Aiz ad Din fled with him during the night which was expected to precede the battle; upon which the army either dispersed or joined Ferokhser. By an advice of Syed Abdoolla, for which it is difficult to account, Ferokhser halted for several days, instead of rapidly improving his advantage. Jehandar Shah had now to put life and empire upon the fate of a battle. All that could be assembled of the imperial forces marched towards Agra, with the Emperor himself at their head. Ferokhser also arrived on the opposite side of the river, and the two armies faced one another for several days. At last Ferokhser unexpectedly crossed the river in the night; and battle was joined the following day. The line of the imperial army was soon broken, and confusion ensued. Zulfikar Khan, indeed, fought with a gallantry not unworthy of his former renown, and kept the field when he and his

1713.

followers remained alone. Not despairing to rally the army, and renew the action on the following day, he despatched messengers in all directions, but in vain, to search for the Emperor during the night. That unhappy prince had taken the road in disguise toward Delhi, of which Assud Khan, the father of Zulfikar, was governor. After intelligence of his arrival, the friends of the late Azim oos Shaun surrounded his palace. and demanded the custody of his person. To quiet their clamours, or to lay a foundation of merit with the future sovereign, Assud Khan placed him in confinement; and wrote to Ferokhser that he waited for his commands to dispose of the prisoner. So gracious an answer was received, as dissipated the fears of Assud Khan, and enabled him to prevail upon his son, who had arrived at Delhi, to trust himself in the hands of Ferokhser. The credulity of Zulfikar deceived him; for he might have escaped to his government of the Deccan, where his talents would have enabled him to set the imperial power at defiance. He was strangled by order of Ferokhser, and his dead body was exposed about the streets of Delhi, at the same time with that of his master, Jehandar Shah.[1]

Ferokhser began his reign in the year 1713, with the usual performances of an Oriental despot; that is, the murder of all who were the objects of his apprehension. After this the two Syeds, to whom he owed both his life and his throne, were elevated; Hussun to the post of Bukshi, or paymaster of the forces, with the title of Ameer ul Omrah; and Abdoolla to that of Vizir, with the title of Koottub al Mulk, or axis of the state. Cheen Kulich Khan, the son of Ghazee ad Din Khan, who was chief of the Tooranee Moguls in the Deccan at the end of the reign of Aurungzeb, was known to have lived on adverse terms with Zulfikar Khan; and by this circumstance, as well as by the weight which was attached to his reputation for talents, and his connexion with the Tooranee lords, was recommended to the attention of the new government. He was appointed to the regency or subahdarry of the

[1] The Memoirs of Eradut Khan finish with the reign of Jehandar Shah. He describes the scenes with the knowledge of an eye-witness, but with little favour to Jehandar Shah or Zulfikar, the victims of the severity or cruelty of the prince under whom he wrote, and whom it was advisable not to offend. Gholam Houssein is more candid and more discerning. Seer Mutakhareen, i. 42—63.

BOOK III. CHAP. IV. 1713.

Deccan, and decorated with the title of Nizam al Mulk, or composer of the state ;[1] a common title, which he rendered remarkable, in the modern history of India, by transmitting it to his posterity, and along with it a kingdom, in that very region which he was now sent, and but for a little time, to superintend.

Ferokhser was a weak prince, governed by favourites. The two Syeds had laid such obligations upon their sovereign, and possessed such power, chiefly from the inconsiderate cruelty of Ferokhser, who had killed Zulfikar and others by whom they might have been restrained, that they could brook neither rival nor partner in disposing of the state. Their chains soon became heavy on Ferokhser. Aware of his impatience, they made such efforts to render themselves secure against the effects of his malice, as embroiled the state from the very commencement of his reign.

The first of the contrivances of Emir Jumla (this was the name of the favourite, a man who had formerly been Kauzy at Dacca), was to separate the brothers. under the pretence of honourable employment. The Raja Ajeet Sing, whom we have already mentioned as the successor of Jesswunt Sing, in that district or division of Rajpootana which was known by the name of Marwar ar Rhatore,[2] and of which Chitore and Odeypore had been successively the capitals, had stood out against the operations of Aurungzeb, and remained in a state little short of independence, during the reigns of Shah Aulum and Jehandar Shah. Hussun, the Ameer al Omrah, was required to undertake the reduction of the rebellious Hindu. He marched with so great a force that the Raja deemed it better to yield than contend ; and though he received private encouragements from the court, where he was assured that opposition would be gratefully considered, he concluded an agreement with Hussun, impatient to return to the capital, where his brother's letters assured him, that designs were ripening for their common destruction.

Though Abdoola, the Vizir, had talents and other eminent qualities ; he was so addicted to women and other

[1] Rather, regulator or governor of the state.—W.

[2] Rhatore is the name, not of the country, but of the Rajput tribe to which the Rajas of Màrwar belong.—W.

1713.

pleasures, that he neglected business; and let the affairs of his high office devolve into subordinate hands, whose mismanagement shed discredit and unpopularity on himself. His enemies, therefore, enjoyed advantages, which in the absence of his brother they were eager to improve. Upon the return of Hussum from Marwar, he demanded the regency of the Deccan, with a view to govern it by deputy, and remain at court; and he received the appointment, in expectation of his being called to that distant province by the duties of his trust. When it was found, at last, that he had no intention to depart for the Deccan, the misunderstanding between the court and the brothers became public and undisguised. They forbore attendance upon the Emperor; assembled their followers, and fortified themselves in their palaces; while the weak and timid Ferokhser, who desired, without daring to attempt, their destruction, formed and abandoned twenty resolutions in a day. After a period of anxiety and alarm, a reconciliation was effected by mediation of the Empress-mother, who was favourable to the Syeds, and by whom, it is said, that intelligence was sometimes conveyed to them of the plots by which their lives were essayed. The argument was, that Meer Jumla, being appointed to the government of Bahar, should depart for that province, at the same time that the Ameer al Omrah should proceed to the Deccan.[1]

Hussun told the Emperor, that if mischief were aimed at his brother, he would in twenty days be in the capital from the Deccan. The first danger, however, regarded himself. Daood Khan Punnee, the Afghan, who had been left deputy by Zulfikar, and obtained the province of Guzerat, upon the appointment of Nizam al Mulk to the regency of the Deccan, was ordered to Boorahanpore, ostensibly to wait upon the Subahdar of the Deccan, and receive his commands; but with secret instructions to

[1] Before the departure of Hussun, the marriage of the Emperor was celebrated with the daughter of Maharaja Ajeet Sing, stipulated for, in the conditions lately imposed by Hussun upon the Raja. She had been conveyed from her father's palace to that of Hussun, as her adopted father, who graced her nuptials with a magnificence which surpassed all that hitherto had been seen in Hindustan.

An indisposition of the Emperor, rather inconvenient at the time of a marriage, cured by a medical gentleman of the name of Hamilton, is said to have been the cause of obtaining the first firmaun of free trade for the East India Company. Scott's Successors of Aurungzebe, p. 139.

BOOK III. CHAP. IV. 1719.

assail the Syed and cut him off. Great expectations were entertained of the Afghan, who, being a man of prodigious bodily strength, great courage, and not devoid of conduct, had risen to the highest repute as a warrior. It is not unworthy of remark, that he had associated with himself a Mahratta chief, named Neemajee Sindia, who had been taken into the imperial service by Shah Aulum, honoured with a high rank, and gifted with several jagheers in the vicinity of Aurungabad. Hussun had a severe conflict to sustain; and had not a matchlock ball struck Daood, at the moment when the advantage seemed hastening to his side, the day might have been fatal to the fortune of the brothers. When the Emperor heard of the failure of his project, he could not, even in the presence of Abdoolla, suppress his chagrin; and observed that Daood was a brave man unworthily used. Abdoolla replied, that if his brother had fallen the victim of perfidy, the imperial mind would have experienced more agreeable sensations.

About this time, Banda, the patriarch and captain of the Seiks, fell into the hands of his enemies. He had soon collected his followers, after they were dispersed by Shah Aulum, and spread more widely his depredations and authority in the contiguous provinces. The Subahdar of Lahore had been sent against him, shortly after the accession of Ferokhser; but was defeated with great slaughter. The Faujdar, or military and judicial chief of Sirhind, was next commanded to take the field; but was assassinated in his tent by a Seik, especially commissioned for that purpose. The governor of Kashmere was then removed to the government of Lahore, and appointed to act against the heretics or infidels, with a great army. After many severe engagements, Banda was driven to seek refuge in a fort; where famine at last compelled him to surrender. Great cruelty was exercised upon his followers; and he himself was carried to the capital, where he was ignominiously exposed, and afterwards put to death by torture.

It would be useless and disgusting to describe the scenes to which the hatred of the Emperor, and the jealousy of the Vizir, gave birth in the capital. When the Ameer al Omrah arrived in the Deccan, he found the power of the Mahrattas arrived at a height which was not only oppressive to the provinces, but formidable to the imperial

1719.

throne. Sahoo Raja, or Sahojee, the son of Sambajee, had succeeded to the authority of his father and grandfather, as the head of the Mahrattas, and had, during the distractions in the Mogul empire, experienced little resistance in extending the sphere of his domination and exactions. Towards the close of the reign of Aurungzeb, the widow of Rama, the brother of Sambajee, who during the minority of Sahogee, enjoyed a temporary authority, had offered to put a stop to all the predatory incursions of the Mahrattas, under which the imperial provinces in the Deccan so cruelly suffered, on condition of receiving a tenth part, which they call Desmukhee, of the revenues of the six provinces which composed the viceroyalty of the Deccan. The pride of Aurungzeb revolted at the humiliating condition; and the offer was rejected with scorn.[1] Daood Khan Punnee, however, who governed the country, as deputy to Zulfikar, during the reigns of Shah Aulum and Jehandar, and who cultivated the friendship, rather than the enmity, of the Mahrattas, agreed to purchase deliverance from their incursions by the payment of even the chout, or fourth part of the revenues of the Deccanee provinces, reserving only such districts as were held in jagheer by any princes of the blood royal, and excluding the Mahrattas from the collection, which was to be performed by his own officers alone. Upon the arrival of Nizam al Mulk as Viceroy of the Deccan, the chout gave rise to dispute and hostilities; in which the Viceroy gained a battle, and might have further checked the pretensions of the freebooters, had he not been recalled, after enjoying the government one year and some months. The Ameer al Omrah sent a force to dislodge a Mahratta chief who had established a chain of mud forts along the road from Surat to Boorahanpore; and by means of them plundered or levied a tax upon the merchants who trafficked between the two cities. The commander allowed himself to be drawn by the wily Mahratta into a place of difficulty; where he and the greater part of his soldiers lost their lives. A still stronger force

[1] In the first instance these claims had been made by Sivaji, and were confined to the district dependant on Bijapur. Aurungzeb tacitly recognised them on the occasion of the treaty into which he entered with Sivaji, and although that treaty was not long unviolated, the recognition formed the basis of the similar claims subsequently extended to other provinces.—Duff, Mahrattas, 210.—W.

BOOK III. CHAP. IV. 1719.

was sent to dislodge the plunderer, who declined an action, and was followed by the imperial general as far as Sattara, the residence of Sahojee. But before Sattara was besieged, the Ameer al Omrah, understanding that danger was increasing at Delhi, and that even Sahojee had received encouragement from the Emperor to effect his destruction, resolved, on any terms, to free himself from the difficulties and embarrassment of a Mahratta war. He not only granted the chout, but he added to it the desmukhee; nay, admitted the Mahratta agents, with a respectable force at Aurungabad, to perform the collection of their own portion of the taxes. The provinces were thus freed from the ravages of military incursion; but the people were oppressed by three sets of exactors, one for the imperial revenue, one for the chout, another for the desmukhee.[1]

Meanwhile a new favourite had risen at court, recommended to the Emperor by a double tie, a fellowship in disreputable pleasures, and promises to cut off the Syeds without the danger of a contest. By his advice, the most powerful chiefs in the empire were invited to court; Nizam al Mulk, from his government of Morâdabad; Sirbullund Khan, from that of Patna; and the Rajpoot princes, Jey Sing of Ambere or Jagenagur; and the father-in-law of the Emperor, Ajeet Sing of Rhatore. Had these chiefs perceived a prospect of sharing among themselves the grand posts of the empire, they would have undertaken the destruction of the Syeds; but they found the despicable Ferokhser so infatuated with his unworthy favourite, that he alone was destined to be the organ of power. Ajeet Sing, perceiving the miserable state of the imperial councils, lost no time in uniting himself with the Vizir.

The increasing violence of the councils pursued for the destruction of the Syeds, and the union, which the removal of the favourite would suffice to form against them, of so many powerful chiefs, induced Abdoolla to summon his brother from the Deccan, and to meditate a decisive step. No sooner did the Emperor hear that Hussun was

[1] The circumstances leading to this arrangement, as well as the particulars, are somewhat differently related by Duff. Hist. of the Mahrattas, i. 444.—W.

1720.

in motion, than, struck with apprehension, he solicited reconciliation with the Vizir. They exchanged turbans, and vows of fidelity, which were equally sincere on both sides. A messenger of rank was despatched towards Hussun, to declare the reinstatement of his family in the plenitude of imperial favour; while Hussun, giving up to the Mahrattas such forts as he could not garrison, proceeded to the capital with an army, of which ten thousand were Mahrattas; attended by a youth, whom he received from Sahojee as a son of Sultan Akbar, and treated with all the respect due to a grandson of Aulumgir, and a competitor for the imperial throne. In the meantime the Vizir had found little difficulty in detaching from the hopeless cause of the Emperor, Nizam al Mulk, and the other chiefs of the intended conspiracy. Jey Sing alone adhered to Ferokhser, advising him to take the field in person, and, by the weight of the imperial name, bear down the cause of rebels and traitors. The pride and the resentments of Ferokhser made him incline to violent measures during one moment; his fears and pusillanimity made him incline to submissive measures the next. After an interval, during which these passions violently alternated in his breast, he threw himself upon the mercy of the Syeds, and submitted to all their demands. It is not certain that they meant to depose him; but during these violent proceedings, tumults arose in the city; Ferokhser shut himself up in the women's apartments, and refused to come out; his friends and servants took arms; the commotions became alarming, and a moment might be productive of fatal events. After repeated entreaties, the Vizir was at last compelled to violate the sanctity of the secret apartments; Ferokhser was dragged forth, and put in confinement; Ruffeh al Dirjaut, son of Ruffeh al Kudder, a grandson of Aurungzeb by a daughter of Akbar, was taken from among the confined princes, and seated on the throne; his accession was announced by the sound of the nobut, and firing of cannon; and, in a few hours, the commotions, which seemed ready to overwhelm the city, gave place to tranquillity and order.

Ferokhser was rather more than six years on the throne. His successor was labouring under a consumption, and died in five months after his exaltation. During this in-

BOOK III. CHAP. IV. 1720.

terval, Ferokhser suffered a violent death, but whether at his own hand, or that of the brothers, is variously affirmed. Except in the palace, the offices of which were filled entirely with the creatures of the Syeds, the different functionaries of the state were confirmed in their situations. Nizam al Mulk, who liked not the complexion of the times, desired leave to retire; but he was prevailed upon to accept the government of Malwa.

Ruffeh al Dowlah, the younger brother of Ruffeh al Dirjaut, was chosen to supply the vacancy of the throne. But the governor of the citadel of Agra had under his charge a son of Akbar, the youngest son of Aulumgîr; and, in hopes of being joined by other lords, inimical to the Syeds, as well as by Jey Sing, who, through influence of the brothers, had been dismissed to his own country before the dethronement of Ferokhser, proclaimed the son of Akbar king. The Syeds left no time for the disaffected to combine; and the governor, finding his undertaking desperate, put an end to his life. The sickly youth, who this time also was placed upon the throne, followed his predecessor in three months. Roshun Akter, a son of Kojesteh Akter, the youngest son of Shah Aulum, was the prince who now was taken to fill the dangerous throne.

Mohammed Shah (that was the name which the new sovereign adopted) began his reign in the year 1720. He was in his seventeenth year; had been confined along with his mother, a woman of judgment and prudence, from the beginning of the reign of Jehandar Shah, and reared by her in great silence and obscurity.

The Syeds were now deprived of all grounds of jealousy and resentment towards the throne; for the Empress-mother advised, and the Emperor practised the most perfect submission to their will. But among the great lords of the empire were some, who beheld not their triumphs and power, without envy and hatred. The governor of Allahabad had been guilty of some marks of disrespect. Shortly after the accession of Mohammed, Hussun marched to chastise him. The Governor died while Hussun was yet upon the march; and his nephew, though he stood upon the defensive, offered to lay down his arms, provided Rajah Ruttun Chund, the famous Dewan of the Vizir, were sent

1720.

to negotiate the terms of his submission.[1] The difficulty of besieging Allahabad, strongly defended by the Jumna and the Ganges, which meet under its walls, allayed in the bosom of Hussun the thirst of revenge. He listened to the proposition of the nephew, and gave him the government of Oude, in exchange for that which his uncle had enjoyed.

Mohammed Ameen Khan, one of the Toranee Omrahs, remaining at court, began to excite the suspicions of the Syeds; but Nizam al Mulk soon became the principal object of their attention and fears. Upon taking possession of his government of Malwa, he found the province, owing to the late distraction of the empire, overrun with disorder; the Zemindars aiming at independence, and the people either become robbers themselves, or suffering from bands of robbers, who plundered the country with impunity. The vigorous operations demanded for the suppression of these enormities, justified the Nizam in raising and maintaining troops; in providing his garrisons; in adopting all the measures, in short, which were best calculated to strengthen his position. The Syeds were not slow in discerning that these preparations looked beyond the defence of a province. Policy required the removal of the Nizam. The most respectful intimations were conveyed to him, that, as Malwa lay half way between the Deccan and the capital, it was pointed out as peculiarly convenient to form the place of residence for the Ameer al Omrah, who, from that station, could both superintend his viceroyalty in the Deccan, and watch the operations of the court; and four Subahs were pointed out to Nizam al Mulk; Multan, Kandesh, Agra, and Allahabad, of which he was invited to make his election in exchange. Policy might counsel the non-compliance of the Nizam; but pride and vanity counselled an insolent reply, which precipitated hostilities on both sides. The brothers sent an army against Malwa. The Nizam resolved to take possession of the Deccan. He crossed the Nerbudda; got, through bribery, possession of the strong fortress of Asere, and the city of Boorahanpore; was joined by Eiwuz Khan,

[1] The governor of Allahabad, Girdhar Bahadar, was a Hindu, which explains his object in requiring Katan Chund, also a Hindu, and in whom therefore he had confidence, to negotiate for his surrender.—W.

BOOK III. CHAP. IV. 1720.

Subahdar of Berar, his relation; by a Mahratta chief, who had quarrelled with Sahojee; and by a variety of Zemindars. He encountered and defeated the army which the the brothers had sent to oppose him; conquered, and slew in battle the governor of Aurungabad, who marched out to meet him: and remained without a rival in the Deccan. The Governor of Dowlatabad held out; but the Governor of Hyderabad joined him with 7,000 horse. In addition to all these fortunate events, he was encouraged by messages from the court, from Mohammed Ameen Khan, and from the Emperor himself, that his opposition to the Syeds should meet with their support.

The brothers wavered, and permitted time to be lost. Ruttun Chund recommended, what was probably wise, to gain Nizam al Mulk by resigning to him the Deccan; and, with vigilance, to guard the rest of the empire. Pride rejected this proposal. It was at last determined that Hussun, accompanied by the Emperor, should proceed with a great army to the Deccan, while Abdoolla should remain to guard the capital. The troops were assembled; the march began, and had continued during four or five days, when Mohammed Ameen Khan conceived his plan to be ripe for execution. He had associated with himself Sadut Khan, afterwards Nabob of Oude, progenitor of the now reigning family; and another desperado, named Hyder Khan, in a conspiracy, with the privity of the Emperor, to assassinate the Ameer al Omrah. The lot fell upon Hyder to strike the blow. Hussun, who received a mortal stab, had strength to cry, "Kill the Emperor!" but the conspirators had taken measures for his protection; and, though the nephew of the deceased armed his followers, and endeavoured to penetrate to the Emperor, he was overpowered and slain, while his tents were plundered by the followers of the camp.

The dismal news was speedily conveyed to Abdoolla, who was on his march to Delhi. He advanced to that city; took one of the remaining princes, and proclaimed him Emperor; found still the means to assemble a large army, and marched out to oppose Mohammed. A great battle was fought at Shahpore; but the Vizir was vanquished and taken prisoner. The Emperor, after a little more than a year of tutelage, entered his capital in great pomp and ceremony, and was hailed as if it had been his accession to the throne.

The weakness of Mohammed Shah's administration, whose time was devoted to pleasure, and his mind without discernment and force, was soon felt in the provinces. The Raja, Ajeet Sing, with a view to bind him to the cause of Mohammed, had, through the hands of the Empress-mother, at the time of the accession, received a firman appointing him Governor of Guzerat and Ajmere during life. The grant was now revoked, and Ajeet Sing rebelled. After some vain demonstrations of resentment, the Emperor was obliged to submit to concessions and indulgence.

The Afghans about Peshawur rose in arms; and, after an obstinate engagement, defeated and took prisoner the son of the Governor of the province.

These, and other disorders, were expected to be redressed upon the arrival of Nizam al Mulk, who was invited from the Deccan to receive the office of Vizir. He earnestly exhorted the Emperor to apply his own mind to affairs, and to infuse vigour into government, now relaxed and dissolving, through negligence and corruption. But the pleasantries of his gay companions, who turned the person and the counsels of the old and rigid Vizir into ridicule, were more agreeable to the enervated mind of Mohammed; and the Nizam, in disgust, under pretence of coercing a refractory Governor in Guzerat, withdrew from the capital. Sadut Khan was about the same time appointed Subahdar of Oude.

The Nizam, having reduced to his obedience the province of Guzerat, and taken possession of Malwa, which was also added to his extensive government, paid another visit to the capital, where he found the temper of administration as negligent and dissolute as before. Despairing, or careless of a remedy, and boding nothing but evil, he only thought of securing himself in his extensive dominions; and, under pretence of a hunting excursion, left the capital without leave, and pursued his march to the Deccan. The Emperor, who now both hated and feared him, despatched a private message to the Governor of Hyderabad to oppose and cut him off, with a promise of all his government of the Deccan, as the reward of so meritorious a service. The bribe was too great to be resisted; but the undertaker paid the forfeit of his temerity with his life. The Nizam, however, was deprived of his Vizirat, and of his new governments of Malwa and Guzerat. To be revenged, he encouraged his deputy in Guzerat to resist the imperial commands; and the Mahratta chiefs Pilajee and Kantogee to invade the provinces. Some inadequate and unavailing efforts were made to oppose the progress of these Mahratta chiefs; who were afterwards joined, still at the instigation, it is said, of the old Nizam, by Baji Rao, the general of Sahojee. The struggle was upheld with more or less of vigour, by the imperial deputies, till about the year 1732, when the provinces of Guzerat and Malwa might be regarded as completely reduced under Mahratta dominion. Never contented with present acquisitions, the Mahrattas made endless encroachments; and, by degrees, seized upon several districts in the Subahs of Agra and Allahabad, plundering even to the vicinity of Agra. When opposed by an army, they retreated, scoured the country, cut off supplies, and made flying attacks. When the opposing army was obliged to retrace its steps, they immediately re-seized the country, and still more extensively diffused their depredations.

During the calamities of the empire, Sadut Khan alone, among the different Omrahs and Governors, exhibited any public spirit, or any manliness and vigour. Though his province, placed beyond the Ganges, was little exposed to the devastations of the destructive Mahrattas, he marched out, in 1735, to chastise a body of them, who were plundering to the very walls of Agra; overtook them by forced marches, brought on a battle, and gave them a signal overthrow.[1] The wreck of the army joined Baji Rao, in the neighbourhood of Gualior. Sadut Khan intended to follow up his blow, to pursue the marauders to their own country, and redeem the lost honour of the imperial arms. But the Ameer al Omrah, jealous of the glory, sent him orders to halt, till he should join him with the troops of the capital. Baji Rao, having time to restore animation to the Mahrattas, and learning the removal of the troops

[1] This is a greatly exaggerated account of the transaction furnished by Mohammedan writers. Sadut Khan, merely repelled a detachment of Mahrattas, under Holkar and other leaders, who were committing ravages, not only near Agra, but in the Doab. Baji Rao, with the main army, proceeded to Delhi. Hist. of the Mahrattas, i. 531.—W.

1736.

from Delhi, marched with Mahratta speed towards that capital, and communicated the first intelligence of his stratagem by the fires which he lighted up in the suburbs. He was in possession of the outskirts of the city for three days before the approach of the imperial army made it necessary for him to decamp. He took the road to Malwa; and the pusillanimous monarch was advised by his dissolute courtiers to purchase the promise of peace by paying the chout, or fourth, of his revenues to the Mahrattas.

A more dreadful enemy was now about to fall upon the misgoverned empire. The Sophis, whom in the reign of Shah Jehan we left sitting upon the throne of Persia, had sunk into that voluptuousness and neglect of the business of government, which so uniformly accompany the continued possession of power, relax the springs of the existing government, and prepare the way for an usurper. In this state of the country, the range of mountains placed near the confines of Persia and India, which had already given a race of sovereigns to Hindustan, produced a chief who with his rude and hardy countrymen, the mountaineers of Afghanistan, invaded Persia, and pushed his conquests against the feeble Hussun Shah, whose government was, moreover, distracted, by the wretched factions of the black eunuchs, and the white. Though the Afghan was assassinated, he was succeeded by a nephew, an enterprising youth of eighteen years of age. The provinces near the Caucasus and the Caspian, as well as those near the Indus, revolted. The Afghan in 1722 laid siege to Ispahan itself, and the wretched Hussun laid his crown at his feet. In the meantime a son of Hussun, whose name was Thamas,[1] escaped from massacre, and was joined by as many people as still adhered to his family or person, in the neighbourhood of Tauris; among others by Nadir, the son of a shepherd of Khorasan, who, by the sale of part of his father's flocks, had hired a banditti, with whom he scoured and plundered the country. By his daring courage and indefatigable activity, he soon distinguished himself among the followers of the fugitive prince. He took the name of Thamas Koolee Khan, or Khan the slave of Thamas. Such a man found it easy in Persia to increase the number of his followers, whom he subsisted and rewarded

[1] Tamasp is the more correct form of this name.—W.

BOOK III. CHAP. IV. 1739.

by the plunder of the country. In a short time he was daring enough to measure swords with the Afghan himself, and prevailed. In 1729, he re-took Ispahan, pursued the usurper to Afghanistan itself, vanquished and took him prisoner. Thamas, whom he acknowledged as king of Persia, he retained in confinement, and, governing in his name, turned his arms against the Turks, who had made encroachments on the eastern provinces of Persia during the declining vigour of the Sophis. Having conducted this war with success, he felt his power sufficient to pull off the mask. He proclaimed himself King, by the title of Nadir Shah, in the year 1736, and put out the eyes of the unfortunate Thamas.

The restless and enterprising Afghans, who regretted the loss of Persia, still kept up disturbance on its eastern frontier; and they provoked the proud and furious Nadir to undertake a war of little less than extermination. Not satisfied with driving them from all the accessible parts of their own country, he made his way into Kandahar, which had for some generations been detached from the Mogul empire, and annexed to that of Persia. Kabul, which already contained a great mixture of Afghans, was now crowded with that people, flying from the cruelties of the foe. Nadir was not soon tired in the pursuit of his prey. He had reason to be dissatisfied with the government of Hindustan, to which he had sent repeated embassies, received with something more than neglect. In the general negligence and corruption which pervaded the whole business of government, the passes from Persia into Kabul were left unguarded. The Persian protested that he meant neither hostility nor disrespect to his brother of Hindustan; and that, if not molested, he would chastise the accursed Afghans, and retire. The opposition he experienced was, indeed, so feeble, as hardly to excite the resentment of Nadir; and, after slaughtering the Afghans in Kabul, he was ready to withdraw; when a circumstance occurred which kindled his rage. A messenger and his escort, whom he had dispatched from Kabul to the Emperor of Delhi, were murdered at Jellalabad by the inhabitants; and, instead of yielding satisfaction for the injury, the silken courtiers of Mohammed counselled approbation; and ridiculed supposition of danger from the shepherd and freebooter of Khorasan.

That furious warrior hastened to the offending city, and slaughtered the inhabitants without mercy. From this he pursued his route to Peshawur, and thence to Lahore; at both of which places he experienced but little opposition. He then turned his face directly to the capital, where Mohammed and his counsellors, wrapped in a fatal security, were not prepared to believe that the Persian usurper would dare to march against the Majesty of Hindustan. The Hindustanee army, which had been two months in the field, had only advanced to Karnal, four days' march from Delhi, where it was surprised by the appearance of the enemy, while Mohammed and his friends were yet ignorant of his approach. The hardy and experienced valour of Nadir's bands quickly spread confusion among the ill-conducted crowds of Mohammed. The Ameer al Omrah was mortally wounded, and died after leaving the field of battle. Sadut Khan fought till he was deserted by his followers, and taken prisoner. Nadir, who had no project upon Hindustan, left the disordered camp the next day without an attack; and readily listened to the peaceful counsels of his prisoner, Sadut Khan, who hoped, if now set free, to obtain the vacant office of Ameer al Omrah. Mohammed honoured the Shah with a visit in his camp, and the Shah consented to evacuate Hindustan, upon receipt of two crores of rupees. The insatiable avidity, however, of Nizam al Mulk fatally defeated this happy agreement. He demanded, and was too powerful to be refused, the office of Ameer al Omrah. The disappointed and unprincipled Sadut hastened to inform Nadir, that two crores of rupees were no adequate ransom for the empire of Hindustan; that he himself, who was but an individual, would yield as great a sum; that Nizam al Mulk, who alone had power to offer any formidable resistance, ought to be secured; and that Nadir might then make the wealth of the capital and empire his own. A new and dazzling prospect was spread before the eyes of the ravager. Mohammed Shah, and Nizam al Mulk, were recalled to the Persian camp; when Nadir marched to Delhi, the gates of which were opened to receive him.[1]

[1] This is the story told by the writers of Hindustan; and no doubt, various intrigues were at work to influence the decision of Nadir Shah, but it is little likely that he would have withdrawn, without laying Delhi under contribution.

BOOK III. CHAP. IV. 1739.

For two days had the Persians been in Delhi, and as yet observed the strictest discipline and order. But on the night of the second, an unfortunate rumour was spread that Nadir Shah was killed; upon which the wretched inhabitants rose in tumult; ran to massacre the Persians; and filled the city throughout the night with confusion and bloodshed. With the first light of the morning, Nadir issued forth; and dispersing bands of soldiers in every direction, ordered them to slaughter the inhabitants without regard to age or sex in every street or avenue where the body of a murdered Persian should be found.[1] From sun-rise to mid-day the sabre raged; and by that time not less than 8000 Hindus, Moguls, or Afghans, were numbered with the dead. During the massacre and pillage, the city was set on fire in several places. The destroyer at last allowed himself to be persuaded to stay the ruin; the signal was given, and in an instant, such was the authority of Nadir, every sword was sheathed. A few days after the massacre, a nobleman was despatched by Nadir, to bring from Oude the two crores of rupees, promised by its governor, Sadut Khan; who, in the short interval, had died of a cancer in his back. On the same day he commenced his seizure of the imperial treasure and effects; three crores and fifty lacks in specie;[2] a crore and fifty lacks in plate;[3] fifteen crores in jewels;[4] the celebrated peacock throne, valued at a crore;[5] other valuables to the amount of eleven crores;[6] besides elephants, horses, and the camp-equipage of the Emperor. The bankers and rich individuals were ordered to give up their wealth, and tortured to make discovery of what they were

Sir J. Malcolm observes, "our knowledge of the character of Nadir Shah, forbids our granting any belief to a tale, which would make it appear, that the ultimate advantages to be obtained from this great enterprise, and the unparalleled success with which it had been attended, depended less upon his genius than upon the petty jealousies and intrigues of the captive ministers of the vanquished Mohammed Shah." History of Persia, ii. 78.—W.

[1] Nadir at first, it is said, endeavoured to allay the tumult, both by messengers sent to pacify the people, and by his personal interference; and it was not till his agents were slain, and he himself endangered, that he gave orders for a general massacre. History of Persia, ii. 83.—W.

[2] £ 3,500,000.
[3] £ 1,500,000.
[4] £15,000,000.
[5] £ 1,000,000.
[6] £11,000,000.

I all, if we believe our authorities, £32,000,000.

1396.

suspected to have concealed. A heavy contribution was demanded of the city, and exacted with cruel severity; many laid violent hands upon themselves to escape the horrid treatment to which they beheld others exposed. Famine pervaded the city; and pestilential diseases ensued. Seldom has a more dreadful calamity fallen upon any portion of the human race, than that in which the visit of Nadir Shah involved the capital of Hindustan. Yet a native and contemporary historian informs us, such is the facility with which men accommodate themselves to their lot, "that the inhabitants of Delhi, at least the debauched, who were by far the most numerous part, regretted the departure of the Persians; and to this day, (*says he*), the excesses of their soldiery are topics of humour in the looser conversation of all ranks, and form the comic parts of the drolls or players. The people of Hindustan at this time regarded only personal safety and personal gratification. Misery was disregarded by those who escaped it; and man, centered wholly in himself, felt not for his kind. This selfishness, destructive of public and private virtue, was universal in Hindustan at the invasion of Nadir Shah; nor have the people become more virtuous since, consequently not more happy, nor more independant."[1]

Nadir having ordered, as the terms of peace, that all the provinces on the west side of the Indus, Kabul, Tatta, and part of Multan, should be detached from the dominions of the Mogul, and added to his own, restored Mohammed to the exercise of his degraded sovereignty; and, bestowing upon him and his courtiers some good advice, began, on the 14th of April, 1739, his march from Delhi, of which he had been in possession for thirty-seven days.[2]

[1] Aurungzeb's Successors, by Scott, p. 214.

[2] The most valuable of the details respecting the invasion of Nadir are furnished us by Golam Hussein, (Seer Mutakhareen, i. 325—344.) Scott as usual, gives chiefly an abridgement of the Seer Mutakhareen, but here, enriched with some particulars from the known historians of Nadir. An interesting account of the march of the Persian army back, and its operations in Bucharia, and Kharism, to which Nadir immediately proceeded, is given us by an eye-witness, Khojeh Abdulkurreem, a Kashmerian of distinction, who accompanied him from Hindustan, and whose narrative has been translated for us by Mr. Gladwin. Khojeh Abdulkurreem differs from Scott, in the day of the conqueror's departure from Delhi, which he makes the 4th of May. Memoirs of Khojeh Abdulkurreem, p. 1. A curious letter of Nadir Shah himself, giving an account to his son of his march towards Delhi, of the battle, and of his in-

BOOK III. CHAP. IV. 1739.

In regulating the offices of state, Mohammed was obliged to confirm the vizirat, which he intended for other hands, to Kummur ad Din Khan, the relation and partisan of Nizam al Mulk. At the request of that domineering chief, the office of Ameer al Omrah was transferred to Ghazee ad Din Khan, his eldest son, while he himself was in haste to depart for the Deccan, where Nazir Jung, his second son, whom he had left his deputy, was already aspiring at independence. After several months spent without avail in messages and negotiations, the father was obliged to draw his sword against the son. A victory, gained in the neighbourhood of Ahmednuggur, restored his government to the Nizam, and made Nazir Jung his prisoner. To compose the provinces subject to his command, which had been governed so irregularly and feebly for many years, and were overrun by innumerable disorders, required both vigour and time. The war which he carried on in the Carnatic was the most remarkable of his subsequent transactions. Its result is the only circumstance material to us. Nearly the whole of that great province was reduced to his obedience.[1]

Sadut Khan Boorahan al Mulk, the deceased governor of Oude, was succeeded by his son-in-law, Abul Mansoor Khan Suffder Jung; who subsequently received the dignity of grand master of the household. A new governor was appointed for Guzerat, and an effort was made, without success, to ravage that important province from the Mahrattas.

A refractory chief called the Emperor into the field, in the year 1745. This was Ali Mohammed Khan, the founder of the power of the Rohillas, a name of some celebrity in the modern history of Hindustan. The Afghans, inhabiting the district of Roh, bordering on Cabul, were known by the name of Rohillas.[2] Ali Mohammed himself is said to have been of Hindu extraction; the son of a man of the caste of cow-keepers. He was

tention not to seize the crown of Mohammed, has been translated by Sir John Malcolm. (Asiat. Res. x. 539.)—M. Other authorities might have been cited, particularly Fraser's Life of Nadir Shah, and Hanway's Travels. Malcolm's History of Persia was perhaps not available when these pages were written, though the work was published before the History of India.—W.

[1] For the circumstances of Nizam ul Mulk's resumption of his government in the Deccan, see Seer Mutakhareen, iii. 3, 8.

[2] Memoirs of Khojeh Abdulkurreem, p. 183.

adopted, however, and reared by an Afghan of the Rohilla clan; a man of a rank no higher than his own. He entered into the army as a common soldier; and after a time acquired the command of a small body of Afghan cavalry, with which he served in the army of the Vizir, governor of Moradabad. His conduct gained him distinction; he was recommended to promotion by the Vizir; received some lands in grant from the Emperor; and was appointed to manage certain districts in Moradabad by the Vizir. Under the negligent government of Mohammed, and the disorders which ensued upon the invasion of Nadir Shah, scope was afforded to the ambition of such a man as Ali Mohammed, the Rohilla. He acquired possession of the lands of some neighbouring jagheer holders, under pretence of taking them in lease: he increased the number of Afghans in his pay; many of whom the severities of Nadir Shah had driven to look for a home beyond the reach of his destructive sword, and to seek employment and protection under Ali Mohammed their countryman. The supposition of power produced its usual consequence. The remittances from his government were delayed and evaded. The Vizir sent a new governor with an army to enforce obedience. Him the Rohilla conquered and slew; and the Vizir, who hated everything which disturbed his pleasures and ease, thought it better to make an accommodation with Ali than contend with him. He was confirmed in the government of certain districts; and by one acquisition after another, extended the limits of his authority, till they comprehended Moradabad, Bareilly, Aunlah, Sambal, Bangur, Budaoon, and Amroah, districts of Kutter, a province henceforward known by the name of Rohilcund, from the Afghan clan, to whom more particularly, Ali and his followers were regarded as belonging. The progress of this adventurer alarmed at last the Viceroy of Oude; whose representations of danger prevailed upon the Emperor to take the field in person. The Rohilla was unable to resist the imperial army, but was underhand supported by the Vizir, in opposition to the Viceroy of Oude. He was besieged in one of his fortresses; but receiving the promise of the Vizir to make his peace with the Emperor, he sent away his treasures to a place of safety, and surrendered. As a

BOOK III. CHAP. IV. 1747.

compensation for the territory which he had governed, he received the foujdary, or military and judicial authority of Sirhind, a district in the upper part of the province of Delhi.[1]

In the second year after this imperial expedition, happened the invasion of Ahmed Abdallee, a man destined to be the founder of a formidable empire in the contiguous provinces of Persia and Hindustan. He was an Afghan chief of the tribe of Abdal, inhabiting a district of the mountains of Gaur, near the city of Herat. When yet very young he was taken prisoner by Nadir Shah, and was for some time one of the slaves of the presence; till, attracting the attention of his master, he was raised to the office of Yessawal, or mace-bearer. He was by degrees promoted to a considerable rank in the army, and accompanied Nadir in his invasion of India. Nadir Shah was massacred in his tent, not far from Meshed, on the 8th of June, 1747. Ahmed Abdallee had acquired so great an ascendancy among the troops, that upon this event several commanders and their followers joined his standard; and he drew off towards his own country. He fell in with and seized a convoy of treasure, which was proceeding to the camp. This enabled him to engage in his pay a still larger body of his countrymen. He proclaimed himself king of the Afghans: and took the title of Doordowran, or pearl of the age, which being corrupted into Dooranee, gave one of their names to himself and his Abdallees.[2] He marched towards Kandahar, which submitted to his arms; and next proceeded to Kabul. The inhabitants had resisted the proposal of the governor to purchase tranquillity by the payment of a contribution, but they deserted him on the approach of danger; and this province also fell into the hands of the Afghan. The governor of Lahore sent him a proposal, offering to betray his trust, and become the servant of Ahmed, on condition of being appointed his Vizir; and though he repented of his engagement and came to blows, his troops made a feeble

[1] Seer Mutakhareen (iii. 20—26); Memoirs of Khojeh Abdulkurreem, (p. 183—185). Scott gives a very short and unsatisfactory abridgement of the passage in the Seer Mutakhareen; Aurungzeb's Successors, p. 218.—M.

A more detailed account is given in Hamilton's History of the Rohilla Afghans.—W.

[2] Memoirs of Khojeh Abdulkurreem, p. 204.

1747.

resistance; and Lahore was added to the dominions of the conqueror. He now directed his ambitious thoughts to the capital of Hindustan, with the feeble government of which he was not unacquainted. A large army, under the Emperor's eldest son, the Vizir, and other distinguished chiefs, advanced as far as the Sutlej to repel him; but he passed them artfully, and plundered the rich city of Sirhind, where the heavy baggage of the prince was deposited. The imperialists made haste to overtake him; and after several days of skirmishing, the Vizir was killed by a cannon ball in his tent. The brittle materials of an Indian army were nearly broken asunder by this event; the Rajpoots, under their princes, "stretched," says the historian, "the feet of trepidation on the boundless plain of despondency, and marched back to their homes." However, the remaining chiefs, and among the rest the sons of the late Vizir, exerted themselves with constancy and judgment; and on the following day a still more disastrous accident took place in the camp of the Abdallees. A magazine of rockets and ammunition which had been taken at Sirhind accidentally exploded, and killing a great number of people, shed through the army confusion and dismay. Ahmed, no longer willing to risk an engagement, drew off his troops, and marched unmolested to Kabul.[1]

The Emperor, who only survived a sufficient time to receive intelligence of this joyful event, expired in the thirtieth year of his reign, and forty-ninth of his age; his constitution exhausted by the use of opium.[2]

Ahmed Shah, his eldest son, succeeded him without opposition. The great character and power of Nizam al Mulk removed all competition for the vizirat, but he excused himself on account of this years, and actually died, about a month afterwards, in the hundred and fourth year

[1] Seer Mutakhareen (iii. 38—52); Memoirs of Khojeh Abdulkurreem, p. 186, 203—207. Life of Ahmed Shah, king of the Abdallees, who are also called Duranees, from the custom of wearing a pearl in one of their ears, translated from the Persian by Henry Vansittart, published in Gladwin's Asiatic Miscellany.

[2] The Seer Mutakhareen is the great authority for this reign; Mr. Scott giving little more than an abridgement of the narrative in that work. Some curious facts are contained in the memoirs of Khojeh Abdulkurreem. Frazer's Nadir Shah; and the history of that ferocious conqueror, translated into French by Sir William Jones, are to be consulted for the details on the Persian side. In Frazer, there is an abridgement of the Mogul history, from Aurungzeb to Mohammed Shah, which is given in a still more abridged form by Holwell in his "Interesting Historical Events." Frazer's materials were mperfect.

BOOK III. CHAP. IV. 1749-50.

of his age, leaving his government of the Deccan to be seized by his second son Nazir Jung, whose good fortune it was to be present on the spot. After the refusal of the Nizam, the vizirat was bestowed upon Suffder Jung, the Viceroy of Oude, for whom it was originally intended.

The Rohillas and Abdallee Afghans gave occasion to the most remarkable transactions of the reign of Ahmed Shah. Ali Mohammed, though removed from Rohilcund to Sirhind, found means to return upon the invasion of the Abdallees, and being joined by the Afghans, great numbers of whom had still remained in the country, he regained possession, and expelled the imperial governor, much about the time of the death of Mohammed Shah. He enjoyed not his prosperity long; but, dying of a cancer in his back, left discord and contention in his family. This circumstance encouraged the governor of Oude, who was now Vizir, and commanded the remaining resources of the state, to form the design of relieving himself from the dread of an aspiring neighbour, and of increasing his power and dominion by the country which that neighbour possessed. The district of Furruckabad was governed by an Afghan of the Bungush tribe. This man the Vizir endeavoured to made his instrument in the destruction of the Rohillas. But the Bungush chieftain lost his life in the contest. The Vizir was not less greedy of the country of his Bungush friend, than he was of that of his Rohilla antagonist. The family of the Bungush chieftain, perceiving the designs of the Vizir, formed a confederacy with the neighbouring Afghans. The Vizir was defeated in a great battle; after which the Afghans proceeded in two bodies, one to Allahabad, where they plundered the city and besieged the citadel; the other to Lucknow, which they expected to surprise. The Vizir, now trembling for his own possessions, could think of nothing better than the wretched resource of calling in the Mahrattas to his aid. They fell upon the country with their usual rapidity; took the Afghans in a great measure by surprise; and compelled them, after much slaughter, to take shelter in the neighbouring hills. This done, the Mahrattas had no inclination to depart. They took up their quarters during the rainy season in the country which they had cleared; and the Vizir was fain to assign them a large portion of it in the name of a reward for their service. The Afghans, as a welcome counterpoise, were allowed to re-occupy the remainder. These events occurred before the end of the year 1750.

In 1749, Ahmed Abdallee marched from Kabul, and advanced as far as Lahore. Meer Munnoo, the eldest son of the late Vizir, had been appointed Governor of Multan, and of as much of the other provinces of Upper India, as could be recovered from the Persians or Afghans. Being unprepared for adequate resistance, he offered to purchase the retreat of the Dooranee by assigning to him the revenues of four districts; with which Ahmed, for the present, thought proper to content himself.[1] In two years he repeated his visit; when Meer Munnoo, after some months of vigorous resistance, was betrayed by one of his generals, and defeated. The Dooranee Shah was not incapable of generosity; he soothed the vanquished leader by obliging expressions, and appointed him his deputy in the two provinces of Multan and Lahore, which were now finally severed from the dominion of the Moguls. A messenger was sent to Delhi to demand even a formal cession of the conquered territory; and, though Suffder Jung was summoned from his government, with a view to resist the Afghans, the favourite eunuch, jealous of the honour which he might acquire by recovering those important provinces, persuaded the emperor to ratify the cession before he arrived. About the same time an expedition was undertaken against one of the nations of Rajpoots, who had seized, with a disputable title, upon certain districts in Ajmere. The war was ill conducted, and ended in disgrace.

A youth now appeared on the stage, who was destined to play a conspicuous part in the closing scenes of the Mogul sovereignty. This was the only son of Ghazee ad Din Khan, the eldest son of Nizam al Mulk. Upon the death of Nazir Jung in the Deccan, Ghazee ad Din, his elder brother, solicited the Viceroyalty of that important country for himself; and taking with him the Mahratta army, which had been in the pay of the Vizir, marched unmolested to Aurungabad. At this place he died only a few days after

[1] Seer Mutakhareen (iii. 79). Mr. Scott speaks of a vigorous resistance on the part of the Governor (p. 225); but Golâm Hussein says, there was no fighting; and so doés Kojeh Abdulkurreem (p. 236).

BOOK III. CHAP. IV. 1752.

his arrival. His army immediately dispersed; and the Mahratta general took possession of Kandesh, the government of which the deceased Viceroy had been obliged to assign him in security for the pay of his troops. His son Shuhab ad Din, whom he had left in the capital, made so good a use of his interest, chiefly with the Vizir Suffder Jung, that he received his father's titles of Ghazee ad Din Khan Bahadur, and was raised to his office of Ameer al Omrah. This did not prevent him from joining immediately the party of the Emperor, and from seconding, with all his power, the machinations intended for the destruction of the Vizir. The military command of the palace was artfully taken out of the hands of that officer; and he and his dependants were refused admittance. The Vizir was alarmed at the prospect of a war with his master. He therefore solicited permission to retire to his government beyond the Jumna. This was refused. He marched out of the city, and encamped at a few miles' distance, with an intention of proceeding to his government without leave, but without drawing the sword, unless in self-defence. Learning that an attack was certainly intended, he invited to his assistance the Jaat Raja Soorâje Mul. This chief had already fought in his service, and readily joined his old friend and commander.[1] The Vizir set up a new Emperor, a youth whom he represented as one of the royal princes; and laid siege to the castle. It was vigorously defended by the spirit and bravery of the young Ameer al Omrah; and, after a fruitless contest of six

[1] The Jaats or Jauts, inhabiting the mountainous region, from the Chumbul and Jumna eastward, to the Jeypoor Rajaship on the west; and from twenty coss to the southward of Agra, to the province of Delhi on the north, were known as a formidable predatory tribe from the earliest period of the Mohammedan history. The original seat of the Jaats appears to have been near the Indus, in the lower part of Multan. Their chief, or one of their chiefs, was received into the service of Jehandar Shah, and behaved with gallantry in the war between that Prince and Ferokshere. Upon the ascendancy gained by the latter Prince, the Jaat retired with his plunder to his fortress of Bhurtpore. This chief was succeeded by his son, who was obliged to become tributary to the Raja of Jeypoor. To him succeeded his brother, who contrived to throw off his dependence upon the Rajpoot; and, first of his race, assumed the title of Raja. During the weakness of Mohammed Shah's administration, he spread his incursions to the very walls of Agra, and left to his son and successor, Sooraje Mull, a considerable kingdom. His power, and vicinity to the capital, rendered him an object of consequence; and the Vizir had attached him to his interests by placing him among the Omrahs of the empire, and other favours. See an account of the Jaats, Asiat. An. Reg. 1802; Characters, p. 12. Also "A Sketch of Rajahpootaneh," translated from the Persian, in "Tracts, &c." by William Francklin, a small volume, published in 1811.

1753.

months, both parties were glad to negotiate. Suffder Jung gave up his pretended Prince, and was allowed to retire to his government, but was deprived of the Vizirat, which was bestowed upon Intizam ad Dowlah, son of the late Vizir Kummur ad Din Khan.

The Jaat Raja, Sooraje Mul, had given sufficient umbrage by his support of the rebellious Vizir; but, during the weakness of the Mogul government, the Jaats had also extended their encroachments over a great part of the province of Agra. The youthful ardour of Ghazee ad Din suggested to him an expedition for the entire reduction of the Jaat country. He called to his assistance a Mahratta general, Holkar Mulhar Rao; and the Jaats, unable to keep the field, retired to their strong-holds. To reduce them speedily, heavy cannon was required. For this Ghazee ad Din applied to the Emperor. But the aspiring temper of the Ameer al Omrah was already formidable to both the Emperor and Intizam ad Dowlah. Sooraje Mul, aware of their sentiments, conveyed intimation to the Emperor, that if he would meet him at Secundra, he would join him with all his forces, and deliver him at once from the dangers which, from the ambition of his Ameer al Omrah, impended over his person and throne. The scheme was relished; and the Emperor, under pretence of a hunting-party, set forward with as great a force as possible on the road to Secundra. He had advanced as far as that city, when Holkar Mulhar Rao surprised his camp in the night. The Emperor, the Vizir, and other leading officers, fled, disguised as women; leaving even their wives and daughters behind them. Upon this, the army disbanded, and Ghazee ad Din marched to the capital, where nothing remained to oppose him. He invested himself with the office of Vizir; seized the Emperor and his mother; blinded them both; and bringing forth Yezziz ad Din, son of the late Jehandar Shah, proclaimed him Emperor, by the title of Aulumgeer the Second. This revolution occurred in the year 1753.[1]

During the same year died Suffder Jung, Subahdar of Oude; and was succeeded by Sujah ad Dowlah, his son. About the same time died also Meer Munnoo, Viceroy

[1] The Seer Mutakhareen is followed in the text. Francklin (Hist. of Shah Aulum, p. 4) says, 1755.

BOOK III. CHAP. VI. 1754.

under the Abdallee King, of the provinces of Multan and Lahore. By the severe exactions of the government, and the interruptions of agriculture through the ravages and terror of war, these provinces had for some time been severely afflicted with scarcity. Of this, one important consequence was, an accession to the numbers and power of the Seiks; for that people making it a rule to provide maintenance and occupation for one another, great numbers of persons in distress were tempted to join them; and all were readily received, upon adopting the garb and principles of the sect.[1] The Abdallee Shah withdrew not the government of Multan and Lahore from the family of Meer Munnoo. His son was a minor; but, in quality of guardian of the minor, his mother was allowed to act in his stead. Under this arrangement, the disorder of the provinces increased. The weakness of the administration suggested to the Vizir, who now had changed his title from that of Ghazee ad Din Khan to that of Umad al Mulk, the project of wresting the provinces at once from the hands of this female superintendent, and from the dominion of the Afghans. During the life of Meer Munnoo, the daughter of the Governess had been promised in marriage to Ghazee ad Din Khan, who now claimed fulfilment of the contract. The mother, to whom few events could yield greater pleasure, conveyed to him his bride, with all the magnificence which the importance of the nuptials appeared to require. Under the confidence and security which this alliance inspired, the Vizir detached a body of troops to Lahore, who seized, and conveyed to his camp, the deluded Governess, inveighing against his perfidy, and denouncing the vengeance which Ahmed Shah, her sovereign, would speedily exact.

The fulfilment of her angry predictions was not long deferred. The exasperated Afghan hastened from Kandahar to Lahore, which was evacuated on his approach; and thence directed his march to Delhi. The Vizir, sensible of his inability to contend with the storm, eagerly solicited reconciliation with his mother-in-law, and employed her as a mediator with the Shah. The invader rejected not the prayer, but demanded a large contribution as the price of his clemency; and in the mean time continued his march

[1] Seer Mutakhareen, iii. 137.

1756.

to Delhi. The wretched Aulumgeer, having no means of resistance, opened to him the gates of the capital; and affected to receive him as a royal guest. For some weeks, Delhi was subject to all the enormities which are practised by a barbarian soldiery on a prostrate foe. To gratify more fully the rapacity of the invader, Umad al Mulk offered to go in person to raise contributions in the Dooab, or country between the Jumna and Ganges; while the Dooranee Shah was to march against the country of the Jaat Raja Sooraje Mul. He had reduced some fortresses, and was employed in besieging the citadel of Agra, when a plague broke out in his camp. Upon this he formed the resolution of returning immediately to his own country, without even waiting for the return of the Vizir. An interview, as he passed Delhi, again took place between him and Aulumgeer. The fallen Mogul entreated the invader of his country, not to leave him in the hands of his overbearing Vizir. Nujeeb ad Dowlah, a chief of Rohillas, who had lately acted a conspicuous part in the imperial service, was, at the request of the Emperor, appointed Ameer al Omrah; and to him the Dooranee recommended the protection of his master.

The Vizir, upon the retreat of the Abdallees engaged in his party Ahmed Khan, the Bungush chief of Furrukhabad, whose father had lost his life in the contest with the Rohillas. To him and his Afghans he joined an army of Mahrattas, under Ragonaut Rao and Holkar. With this force he marched to Delhi. The Emperor and Nujeeb ad Dowlah shut the gates of the city; but after a siege of forty-five days, the Emperor was obliged to submit; while Nujeeb ad Dowlah, by bribing the Mahrattas, obtained the means of escaping to his own district in Rohilcund; and his office of Ameer al Omrah was bestowed upon Ahmed Khan. Alee Gohur, the eldest son of Aulumgeer, was in the vicinity of Delhi, supporting himself with a small body of cavalry in some districts which he had in Jaghire. The Vizir made his father recall him; and the Prince repaired to Delhi, but refused to enter the citadel, where he might easily be confined. He was, accordingly, besieged in his palace; but a few of his followers cut a passage for him through the troops of the Vizir, and he made his escape to Nujeeb ad Dowlah, with whom, and

BOOK III. CHAP. IV. 1756.

with the Subahdar of Oude, he remained for some months; and then betook himself for an asylum to the English in Bengal.

The settlement which, with short-sighted policy, the viceroy of Oude had given to a body of Mahrattas in part of Rohilcund, had fired other Mahrattas with a passion for the fertile country beyond the Ganges. Of this passion, in labouring the ruin of Nujeeb ad Dowlah, and of the Nabob of Oude,[1] whose power he dreaded and whose government he desired, Umad al Mulk resolved to make his account. At his instigation, two chiefs, Junkojee and Duttah Sindia, set out from the Deccan, meditating no less than the entire subjugation of Hindustan. They crossed the Jumna; and, driving Nujeeb ad Dowlah from the open country, besieged him in one of his forts, where he defended himself with obstinate bravery. Sujah ad Dowlah saw that the danger was common; and, collecting an army, marched to support him. He encountered the Mahratta army; gained the advantage, and forced it to cross the Jumna, where a considerable portion of it perished in the waters. Hearing, at the same time, of the march of the Abdallee Shah, its leaders were sufficiently disposed to accommodation.

As soon as Umad al Mulk, the Vizir, was made acquainted with the alliance of Sujah ad Dowlah and the Rohillas, it was his desire, as his interest, to march to the assistance of his Mahratta allies. But he was now beset with a number of difficulties. The Abdallee Shah, whom he had twice offended, was in motion: The Rohillas, with the Nabob of Oude, were opposing the Mahrattas; and Aulumgeer was in correspondence with all his enemies. He resolved, without scruple, to deliver himself from the last of these difficulties. A trusty Cashmerian having received his commission, the Emperor was stabbed with poignards, and his body thrown out upon the strand of the Jumna, where it was stripped by the people, and

[1] The term Nabob, as equivalent to Subahdar, is very modern in Hindustan; and is said to have begun with Sujahad Dowlah. Formerly it was not applied to the Subahdar or governor of the Subah, but to the Subahdar's deputy, or *locum tenens;* the literal meaning of the word being *deputy.* The new use of the term is thus accounted for in the Seer Mutakhareen (iii. 167): When the Prince Alee Gohur was on the visit just mentioned, to Sujah ad Dowlah, and received the compliments of that Governor, he addressed him by the title of *brother Nabob,* which being reckoned an elegant compliment, passed into conversation, when the name was afterwards currently applied to him, and also to other governors.

1759.

remained exposed for eighteen hours. Mohee al Sunnut, a son or grandson of Kaum Buksh, the youngest son of Aurungzeb, was taken from confinement, and set up as the pageant of royalty; after which the Vizir hastened to join the conflict against Nujeeb ad Dowlah and the Nabob of Oude. He was on his march when he heard that peace was concluded, and that the Mahrattas were gone to oppose themselves to the approach of the Abdallee King. The means of personal safety now engrossed the mind of Umad al Mulk. He retired to the country of Suraje Mul, and shut himself up in one of the strongest of his forts.

Upon the last retreat of Ahmed Dooranee Shah from Hindustan, he had left his son Governor of Lahore and Multan; disordered by revolutions, wasted and turbulent. A chief who had served with distinction under the late Meer Munnoo incited the Seiks to join him in molesting the Dooranees; and they gained several important advantages over their principal commanders. They invited the Mahratta generals, Ragonaut Rao, Shumsheer Bahadur, and Holkar, who had advanced into the neighbourhood of Delhi, to join them in driving the Abdallees from Lahore.[1] No occupation could be more agreeable to the Mahrattas. After taking Sirhind, they advanced to Lahore, where the Abdallee prince made but a feeble resistance, and fled. This event put them in possession of both Multan and Lahore. Placing the country under a temporary government, they marched homeward at the approach of the rains; but left a Mahratta Subahdar, who next season extended his acquisitions as far as the river Attok. It was at this very time that the army, of which we have already spoken, marched to take possession of Rohilcund and Oude; and the whole Indian continent appeared now about to be swallowed up by the Mahrattas. Had not Ahmed Shah, the Abdallee, whose empire was in its youth and vigour, been upon the stage: had not the Mahrattas at that time been possessed of extraordinary power, the Mahrattas in the one case, the Abdallees in the other, might have extended their dominion from Thibet and Persia to Cape Comorin. The opposition which they made to one another opened a way for a maritime nation to in-

[1] The Mahratta General was Ragunath Rao, Holkar was serving under him. Duff's Mahrattas, ii. 132.—W.

BOOK III. CHAP. IV. 1760.

troduce itself from the other side of the globe, and to acquire by rapid strides a more complete ascendant over that extensive region than any single government had ever attained.

Ahmed Shah was not only roused by the loss of his two provinces, and the disgrace imprinted on his arms, but he was invited by the chiefs and people of Hindustan, groaning under the depredations of the Mahrattas, to march to their succour, and become their king. The Mahrattas, flying before him, evacuated the two provinces at his approach; and assembled together from all quarters in the neighbourhood of Delhi. The Dooranee army was joined by the chiefs of Rohilcund, Nujeeb al Dowlah, Saadoollah Khan, Hafiz Rahmut, and Loondee Khan. For some days the Dooranees hovered round the Mahratta camp; when the Mahrattas, who were distressed for provisions, came out and offered battle. The army, consisting of 80,000 veteran cavalry,[1] was almost wholly destroyed; and Duttahjee Sindia, their general, was among the slain. A detachment of horse sent against another body of Mahrattas, who were marauding under Holkar in the neighbourhood of Secundra, surprised them so completely that Holkar fled naked, with a handful of followers; and the rest, with the exception of a few prisoners and fugitives, were all put to the sword.

During the rainy season, while the Dooranee Shah was quartered at Secundra, the news of this disaster and disgrace excited the Mahrattas to the greatest exertions. A vast army collected; and Suddasheo Rao, commonly called Bhao,[2] the nephew of Ballejee, the Peshwa, and other chiefs of the greatest note, assuming the command, the Mahrattas marched to gratify the resentments, and fulfil the unbounded hopes of the nation. Having been joined by Sooraje Mul, the Jaat, and Umad al Mulk, the Vizir, they arrived at the Jumna before it was sufficiently fallen to permit either the Mahrattas on the other side, or the Dooranees, to cross. In the meantime they marched to Delhi, of which, after some resistance, they took possession; plundered it with their usual rapacity, tearing away even

[1] Holkar and Sindhia, had not 30,000 men in the whole, and these were acting in separate divisions. Hist. of the Mahrattas, ii. 136.—W.

[2] The term means "brother," but is applied to a cousin, and Sadasheo was so termed, because he was the cousin of the Peshwa.—W.

the gold and silver ornaments of the palace; proclaimed Sultan Jewan Bukht, the son of Alee Gohur, Emperor; and named Sujah ad Dowlah, Nabob of Oude, his Vizir. Impatient at intelligence of these and some other transactions, Ahmed Shah swam the Jumna, still deemed impassable, with his whole army. This daring adventure, and the remembrance of the late disaster, shook the courage of the Mahrattas; and they intrenched their camp on a plain near Paniput. The Dooranee, having surrounded their position with parties of troops, to prevent the passage of supplies, contented himself for some days with skirmishing. At last he tried an assault; when the Rohilla infantry of Nujeeb ad Dowlah forced their way into the Mahratta works, and Bulwant Rao with other chiefs was killed; but night put an end to the conflict. Meanwhile scarcity prevailed, and filth accumulated, in the Mahratta camp. The vigilance of Ahmed intercepted their convoys. In a little time famine and pestilence raged. A battle became the only resource. The Abdallee restrained his troops till the Mahrattas had advanced a considerable way from their works; when he rushed upon them with so much rapidity, as left them hardly any time for using their cannon. The Bhao was killed early in the action; confusion soon pervaded the army; and a dreadful carnage ensued. The field was floated with blood. Twenty-two thousand men and women were taken prisoners. Of those who escaped from the field of battle, the greater part were butchered by the people of the country, who had suffered from their depredations. Of an army of 140,000 horse, commanded by the most celebrated generals of the nation, only three chiefs of any rank, and a mere residue of the troops, found their way to the Deccan.[1] The Dooranee Shah made but little use of this mighty victory. After remaining a few months at Delhi, he recognised Alee Gohur, as Emperor, by the title of Shah Aulum the Second: and intrusting Nujeeb ad Dowlah with the superintendence of affairs, till his master should return from Bengal, he marched back to his capital of Kabul in the

[1] This account of the famous battle of Panipût; the consequences of which were so momentous to the future fortunes of India, is not altogether correct: one great cause of the defeat of the Mahrattas, was, the defection of Suraj Mull and the Jaats. See account of the battle by an eye-witness. As. Researches vol. iii. p. 91, and Duff's Mahratta History, ii. 144.—W.

BOOK III. CHAP. V.

end of the year 1760. With Aulumgeer the Second, the empire of the Moguls may be justly considered as having arrived at its close. The unhappy prince who now received the name of Emperor, and who, after a life of misery and disaster, ended his days a pensioner of English merchants, never possessed a sufficient degree of power to consider himself for one moment as master of the throne.[1]

CHAPTER V.

A Comparison of the State of Civilization among the Mohammedan Conquerors of India with the State of Civilization among the Hindus.

AFTER this display of the transactions to which the Mohammedan nations have given birth in Hindustan, it is necessary to ascertain, as exactly as possible, the particular stage of civilization at which these nations had arrived. Beside the importance of this inquiry, as a portion of the history of the human mind, and a leading fact in the history of India; it is requisite for the purpose of ascertaining whether the civilization of the Hindus received advancement or depression from the ascendancy over them which the Mohammedans acquired.

We have seen, in the comparisons adduced to illustrate the civilization among the Hindus, that the nations, in the western parts of Asia; the Persians, the Arabians, and even the Turks; possessed a degree of intellectual faculties rather higher than the nations situated beyond them toward the East; were rather less deeply involved in the absurdities and weaknesses of a rude state of society; had

[1] The events of Aulumgeer's and the preceding reign are found in considerable detail in the Seer Mutakhareen (iii. 62—193), which is abridged by Scott, Hist. of Aurungzeb's Successors, p. 224—246. The principal facts are noticed, but in certain respects somewhat differently, by Francklin, Life of Shah Aulum, p. 7—27.—M.

This summary of Mohammedan History, though too concise to be of all the interest of which it is capable, is, in most instances, as correct as the imperfect materials at the author's command permitted. Some valuable additions to the authorities on this subject have been made since it was written; but a more extensive reference to native histories, many of which, of great merit, exist, is still indispensable to a faithful and interesting view of the History of Mohammedan India.—W.

in fact attained a stage of civilization, in some little degree, higher than the other inhabitants of that quarter of the globe.

This is a statistical fact, to which it is not probable that much contradiction will hereafter be applied. The point of chief importance, for the present inquiry, is, to shew, that the people who actually invaded Hindustan, and assumed the government over so large a portion of its inhabitants, were perfectly on a level with the Arabians and Persians, in the highest state of their civilization.

The Mohammedans, who established their dominion in Hindustan, were principally derived from the eastern portions of that great country which was contained within the limits of the Persian empire in its greatest extent.

These eastern provinces of the great Persian empire, Bactria and Transoxiana, with the contiguous regions, at the time when those men were formed who established the Mohammedan dominion in Hindustan, were remarkable rather for exceeding than falling short of the other parts of that empire, in the attainments of civilized life. The language of Balkh was reckoned the most elegant dialect of the Persian tongue; and when God speaks mildly and gently to the cherubim surrounding his throne, this, according to the Mohammedans, is the language he employs. A large proportion of the men who have been most distinguished in all the different walks of Persian literature, have been natives of Balkh; of whom it may suffice to mention Mohammed Ebn Emir Khowând Shah, better known to Europeans under the name of Mirkhond, the author of a great historical work, to which Europeans have been indebted for much of their knowledge of Persian history; Rashîd, a celebrated poet; and Anwari, famous both as a poet and astronomer. So greatly was Balkh distinguished during the reigns of the immediate successors of Jangiz Khan, that it was denominated Kobbat al Islâm, the Metropolis of Islamism. Bokhara was one of the greatest seats of learning in the East. Students flocked from all parts to the celebrated university of Bokhara. In the Mogul language, Bokhâr, we are told, is a common appellation for a learned man. Among the celebrated men who have made illustrious the studies of Bokhara, is found a name, ranked high among his contemporaries in all the quarters of the globe, Ebn Sîna, or Avicenna, who wrote above one hundred volumes, and died 1036, at the early age of fifty-eight.

The Moguls were not perfectly barbarous when they advanced upon the countries of the West. It is sufficiently proved that they had the use of letters; they had an alphabet of their own, in no degree corresponding with the troublesome characters of the Chinese, but as ingenious and simple as that of the Romans.[1] The degree in which they approximated to the mental capacity of the most enlightened nations of Asia, is abundantly proved, not only by that power of combined action which enabled them to effect their conquests, but by the skill with which they regulated the government of China, as well as that of Persia and Transoxiana, to which they subsequently advanced. It appears not that the government in those several countries was more skilfully conducted in any hands, than in those of the immediate successors of Jangiz. The Moguls, at the time of their conquests, were so fully prepared for a new step in civilization, that they assimilated themselves with wonderful rapidity, both in China and Persia, to the more cultivated people among whom they had arrived; and, in a short time, were to be distinguished from them rather by slight shades of character and manners, than any difference in point of civilization.[2] In their new acquisitions in Persia and Transoxiana, they were celebrated for prosecuting the sciences with great ardour; and, in particular, for having laid astronomy, geography, and the mathematical sciences, under great obligations. In the city of Samarcand, the seat of government of one of

[1] It was not their own, but the Syriac, introduced by Nestorian missionaries Remusat Langues, Tartares, p. 29.—W.

[2] This is by no means satisfactorily proved, and at any rate the people were in a state as remote from that of civilization as can be well imagined, unless by that term be understood the condition of nomadic races. The Mongols of Jangiz Khan were shepherds and robbers, whose migratory life and predatory habits rendered it easy to collect them into large moving masses, and to precipitate them upon other countries in quest of plunder. That they readily adopted the arts and civilization of those they subdued, is a proof of their capacity for civilization, not of their being civilized. It is true, however, only of their princes, upon their adoption of the Mohammedan faith; the people remain to the present day what they always were—shepherds and freebooters. The Turkman representative of the original Turk, and the Uzbek representative of the early Mongol, offer in the pages of Conolly, Burnes, and Moorcroft, no such examples of civilization as are imagined in the text.—W.

the sons of Jaugiz and his successors, "the academy of sciences," to use the words of the writer in the Universal History, "was one of the most eminent to be found among the Mohammedans, who resorted thither to study from all the neighbouring countries." Abulfeda mentions two decisive marks of a considerable degree of civilization. In his time the streets were paved, and water was conveyed into the city by leaden pipes. The silk-paper made here was the most beautiful in Asia; and in great request over all the East.[1]

Mohammed, of Ghizni, the founder of the first Mohammedan dynasty in Hindustan was the most accomplished Prince in Asia. His court contained an assemblage of learned men. The greatest poet of Asia wrote in his capital, and was fostered by his bounty. He and his nobles adorned Ghizni with an architecture which rendered it the finest city in the East. He there erected a university, which he richly endowed, and made it one of the principal seats of learning in that quarter of the globe.[2]

Under Mohammed of Ghizni, the great sovereign of Persia,[3] who combined in his service all the finest spirits that Persian civilization could produce, the Hindus could not be said to be overrun, or held in subjection by a people less civilized than themselves. As little could this be said under the descendants of Mohammed, who, though inferior to him in personal qualities, were themselves formed, and served by men who were formed, under the full influence of Persian arts and knowledge. The same was undoubtedly the case with the princes of the Gaurian dynasty. They, and the leaders by whom they were principally served, were, in respect of training and knowledge, in reality Persians. It will not be denied, that the Moguls, the last of the Mohammedan dynasties of Hindustan, had remained a sufficient time in Transoxiana and Persia, to have acquired all the civilization of these two countries, long

1 For these facts, the reader will find the original authors faithfully quoted and extracted, in the Universal History, ii. 352, 354; iv. 309, 393; v. 123. Modern Part, 8vo. Ed. In exploring the Persian and Arabian Authorities, the authors of the Universal History are not the worst of our guides.

2 Vide supra, p. 178.

3 Mahmud never was sovereign of Persia. That country was divided among the houses of Saman and Dilem, from the former of whom Mahmud obtained some advantages, but not such as to justify the designation here assigned to him.—W.

BOOK III. CHAP. V.

before they attempted to perform conquests in India. The Persian language was the language they used; the Persian laws, and the Persian religion, were the laws and religion they had espoused; it was the Persian literature to which they were devoted; and they carried along with them the full benefit of the Persian arts and knowledge, when they established themselves in Hindustan.

The question, therefore, is, Whether by a government, moulded and conducted agreeably to the properties of Persian civilization, instead of a government moulded and conducted agreeably to the properties of Hindu civilization, the Hindu population of India lost or gained. For the aversion to a government, because in the hands of foreigners; that is, men who are called by one rather than some other name, without regard to the qualities of the government, whether better or worse, is a prejudice which reason disclaims.[1] As India was not governed by the Moguls, in the character of a detached province, valued only as it could be rendered useful to another state, which is the proper idea of foreign conquest, but because the sole residence and sole dominion of the Mogul government, which thereby found its interest as closely united to that of India, as it is possible for the interest of a despotical government to be united with that of its people, the Mogul government was, to all the effects of interest, and thence of behaviour, not a foreign, but a native government.[2] With these considerations before the inquirer, it will not admit of any long dispute, that human nature in India gained, and gained very considerably, by passing from a Hindu to a Mohammedan government. Of this, without

[1] It is something more than a prejudice; a government of foreigners excluding natives in their own country from power, can never be reconciled to their feelings or opinions by abstract considerations of its goodness. The difference implied by the term *foreigners* is also something more than one of name alone; it is a difference of sympathies and of interests which cannot be concealed by the most conscientious and philosophical perfection in the discharge of its public obligations.—W.

[2] Then of course all objection to it as a government of foreigners ceased, but even to the last there were vestiges of its foreign origin at the court of Delhi. As regards the Hindus, there was the essential difference of law and religion, but even the Indian Mohammedans had reason to complain of the partial encouragement given to adventurers from Persia and Turkestan, many of whom rose to great wealth and power, and they suffered a more permanent and extensive injury in the patronage bestowed upon the languages and literature of Arabia and Persia, to the neglect and corruption of their own forms of speech, and the consequent depression of the intellectual state of the people.—W.

descending to particulars, the situation of human nature, under the Hindu governments which we have seen; that of the Mahrattas, for example; that of Nepaul; that of Mysore, before the time of Hyder Ali; or that of Travancore; affords a very satisfactory proof. The defects of Mohammedan rule, enormous as they justly deserve to be held, can by no means be regarded as equal to those which universally distinguish the government of Hindus.

The same minute analysis might here be instituted of the grand circumstances which constitute the marks of civilization among the Mohammedans of India, as has been already executed in regard to the Hindus. But it is by no means necessary. The state of civilization among the Hindus has been mysterious, and little known. With the state of civilisation in Persia, the instructed part of European readers are pretty familiar. Besides, in analyzing the circumstances which constitute the marks of civilization among the Hindus, such comparisons, for the sake of illustration, were made with the corresponding circumstances among the Persians, as served to throw some light upon the state of civilization among the latter people, and to show in what position they stood as compared with the Hindus. A few short reflections under each of the heads will therefore suffice.

I. CLASSIFICATION AND DISTRIBUTION OF THE PEOPLE.—In this grand particular, the superiority of the order of things among the Mohammedans, over that among the Hindus, was inexpressibly great. The Mohammedans were exempt from the institution of caste; that institution which stands a more effectual barrier against the welfare of human nature than any other institution which the workings of caprice and of selfishness have ever produced.[1]

[1] The effects of caste, as a barrier to the happiness or advancement of society have been shown to be exceedingly exaggerated; and it may be safely asserted, that it is much more propitious to social advancement, than the rapid vicissitudes of Mohammedan society, in which there is no security for the permanent possession of either station or property. That condition of equality which Mr. Mill admires is a condition of equal abjectness, men may rise daily from the lowest ranks to the highest command, but how are they raised? by the will of one individual; in all probability they are wholly unfit for their elevation, and it is certain that they are liable every day to be pushed down again to their original insignificance, happy if they escape with life. There was much more real equality under the Hindu system in which each man knew and could maintain his position, and could rely upon the laws and their hereditary expounders, for protection against despotic caprice and cruelty.—W.

Under the Mohammedan despotisms of the East, nearly as much as in republics themselves, all men are treated as equal. There is no noble, no privileged class. Legally, there is no hereditary property, as the king is the heir of all his subjects. The only thing which creates distinction is office, or the exercise of some portion of the powers of government. For office, there is no monopolizing class. Men from the very lowest ranks in life are daily rising to the highest commands, where each of them is honoured in proportion, not to the opulence of his father, but the qualities which he himself displays. Though here there is wanting that barrier to the unlimited progress of the power of the king which was found in the hereditary nobility of Europe, yet the situation of Spain, of Poland, and, in a greater or less degree, of every country in Europe, shows that the body of the people is not much benefited when the unlimited power of oppressing them, instead of being confined to the hands of the king and his servants, is shared between him and a body of nobles.

II. The Form of Government.—In the simplicity of Oriental despotism there is not much room for diversity of form. Yet there are circumstances which distinguish to a considerable extent the state of government among the Mohammedans from that among the Hindus, and all of them to the advantage of the former.

Under the Mohammedan sovereigns there was a regular distribution of the functions of government to certain fixed and regular officers; that of the Vizir, that of the Bukshee, Ameer al Omrah, and so on. Under the Hindu sovereigns, there appears to have been a confusion of all things together in one heterogeneous mass.[1] The sovereign governed by a sort of council, composed of Brahmens, who exercised the powers of government according to no pre-established plan, but according as each, by intrigue or by reputation, could obtain an ascendancy among the rest.[2]

[1] This has been shown to be a mistake; the functions of the several officers under the Hindu form of government were in fact more accurately and carefully appropriated, than under the Mohammedan, and the instrumentality of a cabinet council, was no disadvantage, it may be apprehended, to the Hindu prince or his people.—W.

[2] Mr. Grant remarks that Kirkpatrick's account of Nepaul exhibits a form of government, state officers, civil, and military, nearly the same as were established in Hindustan, under the rule of the Moguls. Grant's Observations on the Hindus, p.41.—M. But Kirkpatrick's account is very imperfect, and he appears to have

The natural and common order of things, in this situation, was, that some one individual acquired a predominant influence, and employed the rest as merely his instruments. This man became, by way of distinction, *the* minister—Peshwa, as he is called by the Mahrattas. Where the council of Brahmens is not a regular establishment, the sovereign chooses a minister, that is, a depositary of all his power, who disposes of it in portions regulated by no rule, and by not much of established custom and habit.

To the abuse of the power which is placed in the hand of absolute sovereigns there is no limit, except from three circumstances: 1. Religion; 2. Insurrection; 3. Manners.

1. When it is said that *Religion* opposes the will of the sovereign, it is meant that the ministers of religion oppose it—the priests; for, as a political engine, religion, without somebody to stand up for it, is a dead letter. Now the priests can only oppose the will of the sovereign when, by their influence over the minds of men, they have acquired a great portion of power, a power which the king is afraid to provoke. Again, this power of the priests will, or will not, be applied in a way to protect the people from the abuse of the sovereign power, according as the sovereign allies himself with it, or does not ally himself with it. If he allies himself with it, that is to say, if he associates the power of the priests with his own, and admits them to a due share of the benefits which he pursues, the power of the priests is employed, not in checking, but in supporting him in the abuse of his power. Now, so completely was the power of the priests associated with that of the sovereign under the Hindu system of government, that the power of the sovereign was almost wholly transferred into the hands of the priests. As the benefit of abusing the sovereign power was shared so largely with themselves, they had no motive to check, but every motive to support.[1] To misgovernment, accordingly, under Hindu

supplied his want of information, by ideas borrowed from what he knew in other parts of India. Besides, the Nepaulians, as well as the Mahrattas, were in a situation to borrow from the Mohammedans.—W.

[1] The mistake is here repeated of confounding Brahmans with priests. The alliance of church and state is much more intimate with the Mohammedans where the sovereign should properly even perform the office of public preacher in the temples; he has also the whole patronage of the Moollas in his hands. With the Hindus the Raja can perform no sacred offices, nor can he exercise any control over the Brahmanical caste.—W.

sovereigns, we find nowhere any symptoms of opposition from religion.

Under Mohammedan sovereigns the alliance between the Church and the State is much less complete. The Caliphs, it is true, were at once head magistrates and head priests: in other situations, under Mohammedan sovereigns, the priests have had little political power. Except in some matters of established custom, which by themselves are little capable of mending the condition of the people upon the whole, they have never had sufficient influence, nor apparently any inclination, to protect the people from the abuses of sovereign power. Herein they differ from the Hindu system of priesthood, and the difference is an important one, that they are not allied with those who abuse the sovereign power, and yield them no protection.

2. *Insurrection* is a principle of salutary operation under the governments of the East. To that is owing almost everything which the people are anywhere left to enjoy. I have already had some opportunities, and as I proceed shall have more, to point out remarkable instances of its practical effects. In a situation where there is no regular institution to limit the power of gratifying the will, the caprices, and the desires of the sovereign and his instruments, at the expense of the people, there is nothing which hinders the people from being made as completely wretched as the unbounded gratification, at their expense, of the will, caprices, and desires of those who have sovereign power over them can render human beings, except *the dread of insurrection.* But, in a situation where the mass of the people have nothing to lose, it is seldom difficult to excite them to insurrection. The sovereigns of the East find, by experience, that the people, if oppressed beyond a certain limit, are apt to rebel, never want leaders of capacity in such a case to conduct them, and are very apt to tread their present race of oppressors under their feet. This prospect lays these rulers under a certain degree of restraint, and is the main-spring of that portion of goodness which anywhere appears in the practical state of the despotisms of the East. But the dread of insurrection was reduced to its lowest terms, among a people whose apathy and patience under suffering exceeded those of any other

specimen of the human race. The spirit, and excitability, and courage of the Mohammedan portion of the Indian population, undoubtedly furnished, as far as it went, an additional motive to good government on the part of the sovereigns of Hindustan.[1]

3. It is in a higher state of civilization than that exemplified, either among the Mohammedans or among the Hindus, that *Manners* have great influence in limiting the abuses of sovereign power. It is only in proportion as the mind of man is susceptible of pleasure from the approbation, pain from the disapprobation, of his fellow-creatures, that he is capable of restraint from the operation of manners; unless in so far as they increase or diminish the chance of insurrection. Though no great amount of salutary effects is, therefore, to be ascribed to the operation of manners, under the sovereigns, either of Hindu or Mohammedan breed, the benefit, so far as it went, was all on the side of the Mohammedans.[2] There was, in the manners of the Mohammedan conquerors of India, an activity, a manliness, an independence, which rendered it less easy for despotism to sink, among them, to that disgusting state of weak and profligate barbarism, which is the natural condition of government among such a passive people as the Hindus.

Further, along with those remains of barbarism which in considerable amount adheres to the best of the Mohammedan nations, as well as to all the other inhabitants of Asia, a considerable portion of plain good sense marked the character of the conquerors of India; while the natives of that country are distinguished by a greater deficiency in the important article of practical good sense,

[1] We may grant the greater aptitude of the Mohammedans to rebellion; but instances are not wanting to show that the Hindus can resent violence offered to their religion, if not to themselves: the history of the Sikhs is a continual series of Hindu insurrections against the Mogul government, terminating in national independence.—W.

[2] The contrary was the case: the Mohammedan princes were, with a few honourable exceptions, remarkable for profligacy and contempt of opinion; in scarcely any instances, indeed, did they attach any importance to the opinions of their Hindu subjects. The natural mildness of the Hindu prince, and the restriction of caste, tended to preserve him from indecorous excess. If it was true that profligate barbarism was the natural condition of the government among such a passive people as the Hindus, we cannot expect that our own government of them should be free from the imputation. It scarcely follows, as a matter of course, that because the people are submissive their rulers must naturally be barbarous or profligate.—W.

than any people, above the rank of savages, of whom we have any record. The practical good sense of any people is not without its influence upon the mode of employing the powers of government, and upon the minds of some at least of the princes that wield them. Before the Moguls proceeded to Hindustan, we have a proof, in the Institutes of the conqueror Timur,[1] of the degree of beneficent contrivance, with which he laid down the plan of his administration.

"I appointed a Suddur, a man of holiness, and of illustrious dignity, to watch over the conduct of the faithful; that he might regulate the manners of the times, and appoint superiors in holy offices; and establish in every city, and in every town, a judge of penetration, and a doctor learned in the law, and a supervisor of the markets, of the weights, and the measures.

"And I established a judge for the army, and a judge for the subjects: and I sent into every province and kingdom, an instructor in the law, to deter the faithful from those things which are forbidden, and to lead them in the truth.

"And I ordained that in every town, and in every city, a mosque, and a school, and a monastery, and an almshouse for the poor and the indigent, and an hospital for the sick and infirm, should be founded, and that a physician should be appointed to attend the hospital; and that in every city a government-house, and a court for the administration of justice should be built; and that superintendents should be appointed to watch over the cultivated lands, and over the husbandmen.

"And I commanded that they should build places of worship, and monasteries in every city; and that they should erect structures for the reception of travellers on the high roads, and that they should make bridges across the rivers.

"And I commanded that the ruined bridges should be repaired; and that bridges should be constructed over the rivulets, and over the rivers; and that on the roads, at the distance of one stage from each other, Kauruwansarai

[1] The Persian version was translated by Major Davy; and edited, with a preface and other additions, by Mr. White, the Arabic Professor at Oxford, in 1783.

should be erected; and that guards and watchmen should be stationed on the road, and that in every Kauruwan-sarai people should be appointed to reside; and that the watching and guarding of the roads should appertain unto them; and that those guards should be answerable for whatever should be stolen on the roads from the unwary traveller.

"And I ordered that the Suddur and the Judge should, from time to time, lay before me all the ecclesiastical affairs of my empire; and I appointed a Judge in equity, that he might transmit unto me all civil matters of litigation, that came to pass amongst my troops and my subjects."

Here is a selection of four of the most important objects of government, in making a provision for which, the first care and attention of the Mogul sovereign are employed: the administration of justice, the instruction of the people, the facilitation of intercourse, and his own knowledge of all that is transacted in his name. That the provision for these objects was very incomplete, we have sufficient assurance; but some progress was made in the art and science of government, when they were pointed out as primary objects of regard; still more, when something considerable was really done for their attainment.

Of the twelve maxims of his government, the following is a selection:

"Persons of wisdom, and deliberation, and vigilance, and circumspection, and aged men endowed with knowledge and foresight, I admitted to my private counsels; and I associated with them, and I reaped benefit, and acquired experience from their conversation.

"The soldier and the subject I regarded with the same eye. And such was the discipline which I established amongst my troops and my subjects, that the one was never injured or oppressed by the other.

"From amongst the wise and the prudent, who merited trust and confidence, who were worthy of being consulted on the affairs of government, and to whose care I might submit the secret concerns of my empire, I selected a certain number, whom I constituted the repositories of my secrets: and my weighty and hidden transactions, and my secret thoughts and intentions, I delivered over to them.

"By the vizzeers, and the secretaries, and the scribes, I gave order and regularity to my public councils: I made them the keepers of the mirror of my government, in which they showed unto me the affairs of my empire, and the concerns of my armies and my people: and they kept rich my treasury; and they secured plenty and prosperity to my soldiers and to my subjects; and by proper and skilful measures they repaired the disorders incident to the empire; and they kept in order the revenues and the expenses of government; and they exerted themselves in promoting plenty and population throughout my dominions.

"Men learned in medicine, and skilled in the art of healing, and astrologers, and geometricians, who are essential to the dignity of empire, I drew around me: and by the aid of physicians and chirurgeons I gave health to the sick: and with the assistance of astrologers I ascertained the benign or malignant aspect of the stars, their motions, and the revolutions of the heavens; and with the aid of geometricians and architects, I laid out gardens, and planned and constructed magnificent buildings.

"Historians, and such as were possessed of information and intelligence, I admitted to my presence: and from these men I heard the lives of the prophets and the patriarchs, and the histories of the ancient princes, and the events by which they arrived at the dignity of empire, and the causes of the declension of their fortunes: and from the narratives and the histories of those princes, and from the manners and conduct of each of them, I acquired experience and knowledge: and from those men I heard the descriptions and the traditions of the various regions of the globe, and acquired knowledge of the situations of the kingdoms of the earth.

"To travellers, and to voyagers of every country, I gave encouragement, that they might communicate unto me the intelligence and transactions of the surrounding nations: and I appointed merchants and chiefs of Kauruwauns to travel to every kingdom and to every country, that they might bring unto me all sorts of valuable merchandise and rare curiosities, from Khuttau, and from Khutton, and from Cheen, and from Maucheen, and from Hindustaun, and from the cities of Arabia, and from Missur, and from Shaum, and from Room, and from the islands of the Christians, that they might give me information of the situation, and of the manners, and of the customs of the natives and inhabitants of those regions, and that they might observe and communicate unto me the conduct of the princes of every kingdom and of every country towards their subjects."

All these different points laid down, in writing, as main objects of attention in the conduct of government, undoubtedly indicate a state of the human mind very considerably removed from the lowest barbarism.

The following regulations respecting the collection of the revenues; of all the parts of an imperfect government that which most deeply affects the happiness of the people; indicate no common share of excellence in the spirit of administration.

"And I commanded that the Ameers, and the Mingbaushees, in collecting the revenues from the subjects, should not, on any account, demand more than the taxes and duties established.

"And to every province on which a royal assignment was granted, I ordained that two supervisors, should be appointed; that one of them should inspect the collections, and watch over the concerns of the inhabitants, that they might not be impoverished, and that the Jaugheerdaur might not ill-use or oppress them, and that he should take an account of all the sums which were collected in the province; and that the other supervisor should keep a register of the public expenses, and distribute the revenues among the soldiers.

"And every Ameer who was appointed to a jaugheer, I ordained that for the space of three years it should remain unto him, and that, after three years, the state of the province should be inspected. If the inhabitants were satisfied, and if the country was flourishing and populous, that he should be continued therein; but, if the contrary should appear, that the jaugheer should return unto the crown, and, that for the three following years, subsistence should not be granted to the holder thereof.

"And I ordained that the collection of the taxes from the subject might, when necessary, be enforced by menaces and by threats, but never by whips and by scourges. The governor, whose authority is inferior to the power of the scourge, is unworthy to govern.

"I ordained that the revenues and the taxes should be collected in such a manner as might not be productive of ruin to the subject, or of depopulation to the country."

Of the produce of the fertile and cultivated lands, one third was taken for the government; and this was the principal, and almost the only source of the revenue.

"And I ordained, whoever undertook the cultivation of waste lands, or built an aqueduct, or made a canal, or planted a grove, or restored to culture a deserted district, that in the first year nothing should be taken from him; and that in the second year, whatever the subject voluntarily offered should be received; and that in the third year the duties should be collected according to the regulation.

"And I ordained, that if the rich and the powerful should oppress the poorer subject, and injure or destroy his property, an equivalent for damage sustained should be levied on the rich oppressor, and be delivered to the injured person, that he might be restored to his former estate.

"And I ordained, that in every country three Vizzeers should be stationed. The *first*, for the subject—to keep a regular account of the taxes and the duties received, and what sums, and to what amount, were paid in by the subject, and under what denomination, and on what account, and to preserve an exact statement of the whole. The *second*, for the soldier—to take account of the sums paid to the troops, and of the sums remaining due unto them." The *third*—was for certain miscellaneous services, too tedious to be specified.

These details are sufficient to show, that among the Moguls, even at their first irruption into Hindustan, the arts of government were considerably advanced; and that the Hindus had much to gain by a change of masters. In the hands of some of the most eminent of the Mogul princes, the Emperor Akbar, for instance, the powers of government were distributed, and employed with a skill which would not disgrace a period of considerable knowledge and refinement.

Though in a pure despotism much depended on the qualities of the sovereign, yet when a good plan of administration was once fully introduced, a portion of its excellence always remained, for a time ; and had a strong tendency to become perpetual.

III. THE LAWS. — The laws of the Hindus, we have already seen, are such as could not originate in any other than one of the weakest conditions of the human intellect; and, of all the forms of law known to the human species, they exhibit one the least capable of producing the benefits which it is the end and the only good consequence of law, to ensure.[1]

The Mohammedan law, as introduced into India by its Mogul conquerors, is defective indeed, as compared with any very high standard of excellence; but compare it with the standard of any existing system, with the Roman law for instance, or the law of England, and you will find its inferiority not so remarkable, as those who are familiar with these systems, and led by the sound of vulgar applause, are in the habit of believing. In the following view of the most remarkable particulars in the state of Mohammedan law, a reference to the system of English law is peculiarly instructive, and even necessary ; as it is by the English system that the Mohammedan has been superseded.

1. The civil, or non-penal branch of law, lays down the rights which, for the good of the species, should be constituted in behalf of the individual ; in other words, prescribes the power which the individual, for the good of the species, ought exclusively to possess, over persons, and over things.

The particular powers or privileges which it is expedient to constitute rights, are, in the great points, so distinctly

[1] It has been shown that the view taken of the laws of the Hindus is exceedingly imperfect: and that which follows of Mohammedan law resting upon the Hedaya alone is not much more comprehensive, but being influenced by a different feeling it is more candid. During the flourishing periods of Mohammedan rule in Asia, the law was very diligently cultivated by a number of ingenious writers, some of whom were not improbably acquainted with the compilations of Justinian, which will account for its analogy in classification to Roman law. In this respect, it may be allowed to have an advantage over Hindu law, but in the civil branch, in the laws of contracts and inheritance, it is not so exact or complete as the latter. The penal law has the advantage also of being framed without regard to persons, but its spirit of barbarous retaliation is unknown to the Hindu code.—W.

and strongly indicated by common experience, that there is a very general agreement about them among nations in all the stages of civilization. Nations differ chiefly in the mode of securing those rights.

One instrument, without which they cannot be secured, is strict and accurate definition. In affording strict and accurate definitions of the rights of the individual, the three systems of law, Roman, English, and Mohammedan, are not very far from being on a level. Completeness, in point of definition, it seems, is a perfection in the state of law, which it requires a very advanced state of civilisation to bestow. At first, experience has provided no record of all the variety of material cases for which a provision is necessary. Afterwards, the human mind is not sufficiently clear and skilful to classify accurately a multitude of particulars; and without accurate classification, useful definitions and rules can never be framed. Lastly (and that is the state in which the more civilized nations of Europe have long been placed) custom and habit acquire a dominion which it is not easy to break; and the professors of law possess an interest in its imperfections, which prompts them to make exertions, and a power, which enables them for a long time to make successful exertions, to defeat all endeavours for its improvement.

Until very late, there was no civil code, that is to say, there was no description, good or bad, in a permanent set of words, of almost any of the rights belonging to individuals, in any country in Europe. The whole was traditionary, the whole was oral; there was hardly any legislative writing. Of course, in the greater number of cases, nobody knew exactly what was right. The judge, having no fixed definition for his guidance, made for himself, on each particular occasion, a definition to suit that particular occasion. But these numerous definitions, made by numerous judges on numerous occasions, were more or less different one from another. All the approximation to accuracy that was attained, or that was attainable, consisted in this, that the routine of decision fixed a certain sphere, within which the variation of the arbitrary definitions which the judges on each occasion made for themselves was, with a certain force, confined; as he, by whom a wider range was taken for injustice than what was usually taken, would expose himself to the consequences of blame. Within a few years some attempts have been made, in some of the German states, to supply a code; that is, to give fixed and determinate words to the laws, by the only instrument of permanency and certainty in language, writing. These attempts have been partial, and exceedingly imperfect, even as far as they went. The Emperor Napoleon was the first sovereign in modern Europe, who bestowed upon his subjects the inestimable benefit of laws, in written, fixed, and determinate words. Many are the faults which might be discovered in this code, were this the place to criticize the execution; but with all its imperfections, it placed the French people, with respect to law, in a situation far more favourable than that of any other people upon the globe. In England, the whole portion of the field, occupied by what is denominated the common law; that is, almost all the civil, and a great proportion of the penal branch, is in the unwritten, that is, the oral, and traditionary, or barbarous state. Lastly, that portion, which bears the character of written, or statute law, is so overloaded with useless words; so devoid of classification; and the expression is so ambiguous and obscure, that the lawyers declare it as far more polluted with the vice of uncertainty, than that which is in a state of necessary and perpetual fluctuation, the common law itself.

The form of the Mohammedan law, as exhibited to us in some of the best of its digests, as the Hedaya, for instance, is not much more rude and barbarous than this. To give any intelligible account of the powers which law converts into rights, it is necessary to make a distribution of the existences which are the subject of those rights, or over which the powers, converted into rights, are granted. This distribution is the same, in the Mohammedan, as in the European systems. The subjects of those rights, or the existences over which the powers are granted, are either, first, Persons; or, secondly, Things. In the case in which *Persons* are considered as the subject of rights; 1. Individuals, as individuals, are allotted rights, or exclusive powers, with respect to their own persons; 2. As husbands, fathers, sons, masters, servants, judges, suitors, kings, or subjects, &c., they are allotted rights or exclusive powers, with respect to the persons (including the services) of others. In the case in which *Things* are considered as the subject of right, two circumstances principally require to be ascertained; first, the powers which are included in each right; secondly, the events which cause, or give origin to the existence of a right. These points are determined upon the same principles, and nearly in the same way, by the Mohammedan, as by European legislation. Every where law has been formed, not by a previous survey and arrangement of the matters which it belongs to a system of law to include; but by the continual aggregation of one individual case to another, as they occurred for decision. The only classifications, therefore, which have ever been attempted, are those of the cases which occur for decision; the states of circumstancss which most frequently give occasion to disputes about rights. Now, these states of circumstances are the more common of the events which constitute change of ownership, or affect the transfer of property: of these events, one set, which obviously enough fall into a class, are those of bargain and sale, or the exchange of one article of value for another; this constitutes a large chapter in the Mohammedan code. Another important class of such events are those which relate to inheritance: a third class are those which relate to wills; a fourth, those which relate to engagements either to pay a sum of money, or to perform a service. There are other inferior titles, of which those relating to deposits and to bail are the most considerable: and under these heads is the matter of civil law distributed in the Mohammedan code.

It will not be denied that this distribution very closely resembles that which is made of the same subject in the legal systems of Europe. It will hardly be denied that this combination of heads as completely includes the subject, or all the cases of dispute respecting ownership or right, as that combination of heads which we find in the codes of the West. To show the exact degree in which the Mohammedan system falls short of the Christian system, but exceeds the Hindu, in making clear and certain the rights which it means to create and uphold, would require a development far too long and intricate for the present occasion. From the delineation of the great lines to which the present aim has been confined, it will appear, that a much higher strain of intelligence runs through the whole, than is to be found in the puerilities, and the worse than puerilities, of the Hindus.

2. So much for the comparison of Mohammedan law with that of Hindus and Europeans, in regard to the civil branch, or the constitution of rights. In the penal branch, besides a selection of the acts which shall be accounted offences, in which selection there is great uniformity all over the globe, two things are necessary, an exact definition of the act which the law constitutes an offence, and an exact specification of the punishment which it adopts as the means of preventing that offence.

On the penal branch of law, the Mohammedan, like the Roman system, is exceedingly scanty. In the Institutes of Justinian, for example, three short titles or chapters, out of eighteen, in the last and shortest of four books, is all that falls to the share of this half of the field of law; and the whole is brought in under the subordinate title of "Obligations arising from delinquency." The arbitrary will of the judge (a wretched substitute) was left to supply the place of law. The same disproportion, (and it is one of the most remarkable points of inferiority in the ancient Roman as compared with the modern systems of jurisprudence,) is observable in the Mohammedan books of law: the portion which relates to the penal is very small, in comparison with that which relates to the non-penal branch of the subject.

The Mohammedan system contained, indeed, one law comprehensive enough to supersede a number; viz., that, in all cases of injury to the person, retaliation should be the rule; an eye for an eye, and a tooth for a tooth. This recommends itself to a rude age by the appearance of proportion. But it recommends itself to no other but a rude age, because it possesses nothing but the appearance of proportion, and grossly violates the reality. In this the Mohammedan more nearly approached the Hindu, than the European systems of penal law. By this, however, it avoided the atrocity of some modern systems, particularly the English, inasmuch as it limited capital punishment, never allowed for offences against property, to the single case of murder. In practice, too, "the Mussulman courts," says the translator of the Hedaya, "in all cases short of life, understand the words of the Koran, not as awarding an actual retaliation according to the strict literal meaning, but an atonement in exact proportion to the injury."[1] This indicates a considerable refinement of thought on the subject of penal law: far removed from the brutality which stains the code of the Hindus.

The most atrocious part of the Mohammedan system of punishment is that which regards theft and robbery. Mutilation, by cutting off the hand, or the foot, is the prescribed remedy for all higher degrees of the offençe. This savours strongly of a barbarous state of society: and in this the Mohammedan and Hindu systems resemble one another. The translator of the Hedaya, though he laments the *inhumanity*, *inconvenience*, and *inefficiency*, of this mode of punishment, yet tells his British countrymen, "They have nothing better to offer by way of substitute; for surely their penal laws are still more sanguinary." This is a heavy imputation on the legislature of his country; but surely no good reason hinders a better system of penal remedies, than that of either English or Mohammedan law, from being introduced into India, by an enlightened legislature, if such a thing were to be found.

One peculiarity, indicating the work of an immature state of the human mind, strongly distinguishes the Mohammedan system; while it distinguishes the English, in a degree scarcely, if at all, inferior. In framing the several rules or ordinances; which, of course are intended each to include not a mere individual case (for then to be complete they must be innumerable,) but sets or classes of cases; it is not the specific, or the generic differences, but the individual differences, upon which a great proportion of the rules are founded. Their mode of proceeding is the same as if (taking a familiar case for the sake of illustration) they were to make one law to prohibit the stealing of a sheep; another to prohibit the stealing of a cow: a third, the stealing of a horse; though all the cases should be treated as equally criminal, and all subjected to the same penalty. Not merely a good logic, but a good talent for expediting business, would teach that all such cases as could be comprehended under one description, and were to be dealt with in one way, should

[1] The Hedaya, or Guide: a Commentary on the Mussulman Laws: Translated by order of the Governor-General and Council of Bengal, by Charles Hamilton, in 4 vols. 4to. Preliminary Discourse, by the translator, p. lxxxiii.

be included in one comprehensive law. This would have two admirable effects. The laws would be less voluminous; hence less obscure, and difficult to administer. In the second place, being founded upon the generic and specific differences, they would include all individual cases without exception; whereas in so far as they are founded upon individual distinctions, they may rise to the number of millions, and leave as many cases (no individual case resembling another) without an appropriate provision.

3. Besides the laws which mark out rights and punishments, are a set of laws on which the execution of the former branches altogether depends. These are the laws which constitute the system of procedure, or the round of operations through which the judicial services — inquiry, sentence, and enforcement — are rendered.

In this part of the field of legislation there is a most remarkable difference between the Indian and European systems. In the European system, the steps of procedure are multiplied to a great number, and regulated by a correspondent multiplicity of rules. In the Mohammedan (and in this the Mohammedan and the Hindu systems concur) the mode of procedure is simple, and not much regulated by any positive rules; the Judge being left to conduct the judicial inquiry in the mode which appears to him most conducive to its end, and falling, of course, into the natural and obvious train of operations, recommended to every individual by ordinary good sense, when he has any private inquiry, analogous to the judicial, to perform. The parties are summoned to appear before him: they state, in their order, the circumstances of the case, subject to examination of all sorts, for the elucidation of the facts: the evidence which they have to adduce, whether of testimony or of things, is received: when all the evidence is before the Judge, he balances the weight of that which affirms with the weight of that which denies the point in dispute; and according as either preponderates, decision is pronounced.

In this department, the advantage is all on the side of the Indian systems. The inconvenience to which the Indian mode of procedure is liable, consists in the arbitrary power intrusted to the Judge, which he may employ either negligently, or partially and corruptly. Two things may here be observed: first, that this inconvenience is not removed from the system characterized by the great number of steps and rules, which may be called the technical system; secondly, that it may, to a great degree, be easily removed from the system which is characterized by the small number of steps and rules, which may be called the natural system.

It is not removed from the technical system, for that binds the Judge to nothing but an observance of the technical rules: now *they* may all be observed in the most punctilious manner, while the real merits of the case may have been most imperfectly brought to light through negligence, or purposely disguised through corruption. The observance of the technical rules by no means forces the inquiry upon the merits of the case, and affords no security whatsoever that, in regard to *them*, the inquiry shall be complete.

In the next place, the power of the Judge may be restrained from abuse, in the natural mode of procedure, by very easy expedients. As the steps are simple, they can be clearly described, and a standard of perfection may be rendered perfectly familiar to the minds of the people: with this standard in their minds, the conduct of the Judge may be subjected to perfect publicity, and held open to the full view and unrestrained criticisms of the people; as no misconduct would thus escape detection, an efficient method might be easily provided to render it very difficult, or impossible, that it should escape the due measure of punishment. This is the mode of obtaining good conduct from the Judge, as from every other servant of the public; not the prescription of numerous ceremonial observances, few of them having any connexion with the merits of the case; many of them obstructing, rather than aiding, the efficient operations of a rational inquiry; and all, taken together, far better calculated for screening the Judge in a course of misconduct, than for imposing upon him any necessity of good and faithful service.

If the technical affords no security for good conduct in the Judge above the natural system, it possesses other qualities which render it infinitely hurtful to the interests of justice. By multiplying the operations of judicature, it renders the course long, intricate, obscure, and treacherous.

It creates delay, which is always a partial, often a complete denial of justice. It creates unnecessary expense, which is always positive robbery; and, as often as it is above the means of the suitor, is complete and absolute denial of justice; expense, which is almost always above the means of the indigent, that is, the most numerous class; which possesses, therefore, this peculiar property, that it *outlaws* the great body of the people; making law an instrument which any one may employ for the oppression of the most numerous portion of the species, an instrument which they can scarcely at all employ for their protection.

It is instructive, and not difficult, to trace the causes which gave birth to such different modes of judicial procedure in the two countries. The difference arose from the different situations of the judges. It rose from the different means presented to the judges of drawing a profit out of the business which they had to perform. In India as the state of manners and opinions permitted them to receive bribes, they had no occasion to look out for any other means of drawing as much money as possible from the suitors; and, therefore, they allowed the course of inquiry to fall into the straight, the shortest, and easiest channel. In England, the state of manners and opinions rendered it very inconvenient, and in some measure dangerous, to receive bribes. The judges were, therefore, induced to look out for other means of rendering their business profitable to themselves. The state of manners and opinions allowed them to take fees upon each of the different judicial operations. It was, therefore, an obvious expedient, to multiply these operations to excess; to render them as numerous, and not only as numerous, but as *insnaring* as possible. For, with a view to fees, it was of prodigious importance, after the operations had been rendered as numerous as possible, to create pretexts for performing them twice over. This was easily done, by rendering the operations, imposed upon the suitors, so nice, and intricate, and equivocal, that it was hardly possible to observe them in such a manner as to preclude exception; and, by making it a rule, that as soon as any misobservance was laid hold of by the judge, the whole of the preceding operations, how exactly soever performed

BOOK III. CHAP. V.

should be set aside, and the suit ordained to commence anew. This recommencement, accordingly, this double performance of the ceremonies, double payment of the fees, is one of the most remarkable features in the English system of procedure.[1]

Two persons in the Mohammedan courts, the Cauzee and Mooftee, share between them, on each occasion, the functions of the judge. The Mooftee attends in order to expound the sacred text; the Cauzee is the person who investigates the question of fact, and carries into execution what he receives as the meaning of the law.[2]

The following passage discovers a correct mode of thinking, whatever disconformity may have been found between the rule and the practice. "It is incumbent on the Sultan to select for the office of Cauzee, a person who is capable of discharging the duties of it, and passing decrees; and who is also in a superlative degree just and virtuous; for the prophet has said: *Whoever appoints a person to the discharge of any office, whilst there is another among his subjects more qualified for the same than the person so appointed, does surely commit an injury with respect to the rights of God, the prophet, and the Mussulmans.*"[3]

Publicity was an important principle in the Mohammedan jurisprudence. For the hall of justice, "the principal mosque," says the law, "is the most eligible place, if it be situated within the city; because it is the most notorious."[4]

There is no part of the rules of procedure which more strongly indicates the maturity or immaturity of the human mind, than the rules of evidence. There is scarcely any part of the Mohammedan system, where it shows to greater advantage. On many points, its rules of evidence are not inferior; in some, they are preferable to those of the European systems. Its exclusion of evidence, for example, is not so extensive, and, in the same proportion, not so mischievous as the English. There are other cases, however, in which inferiority appears. Reckoning women's

[1] This explanation of the causes of complex procedure in the English courts of law is an amusing exemplification of one of our author's peculiarities; his horror of English is even more strong than of Hindu law. According to his theory, the corruption of the judge is the best security for justice. It would be dangerous to reduce this to practice.—W.

[2] Hedaya, ii. 614.

[3] Hedaya, ii. 615.

[4] Hedaya, ii. 620.

testimony inferior to that of men (they have less correctness, says the law, both in observation and memory—which, so long as their education is inferior, will no doubt be the case), the Mohammedan law makes some very absurd rules. In all criminal cases, the testimony of the woman is excluded; and in questions of property, the evidence of two women is held only equal to that of one man; as if one class of women may not be better educated than another class of men, and their testimony, therefore, more to be depended upon. Under Mohammedan customs, indeed, which exclude the women from the acquisition of knowledge and experience, the regulation had less of impropriety than it would have in a state of things more favourable to the mental powers of the sex. There is nothing, however, in the Mohammedan laws of evidence, to compare with many absurdities of the Hindu system, which makes perjury, in certain cases, a virtue.[1]

IV. The Taxes.—To a great extent the Mohammedans followed the plan of taxation which was established under the native government of the Hindus. The great source of the revenue was the proportion, exacted by the sovereign, of the gross produce of the land. The Emperor Akbar was celebrated as having placed the details of collection in a better state, than that important business had ever been seen in before. From what has been observed of the practice of existing Hindu governments; and, from the superior share of intelligence which the Mohammedans brought to the business of state, we may infer, with sufficient assurance, that the improvement introduced by that people was not inconsiderable. That the Mohammedan princes generally made use of Hindus in affairs of revenue; and even employed them as their instruments, in the reforms to which they were led, is not inconsistent with the supposition, that the business was better managed under the Mohammedans than under the Hindus.[2] For the details

[1] This, as we have seen, is a mistake; truth in evidence is as strenuously enjoined in Hindu as in Mohammedan law, and the disregard of it is as common among the unprincipled of one as of the other faith.—W.

[2] The Mohammedans have always been in India, and are, to the present day, notorious for incapacity as officers of account. Under the English as under their own administrations, all the chief appointments in the revenue department are filled by Hindus. Both as instruments and as principals, whatever merit there may have been in the financial arrangements of Akbar it belonged to the Hindus. See Ayeen Akbery.—W.

of collection; which a revenue chiefly derived from a proportion of the gross produce of the land rendered excessively operose and complex; an intimate acquaintance with the language and manners of the people was indispensably required; and that acquaintance Hindus alone possessed. There is nothing to hinder the Hindus, as any other people, from being well qualified to be used as instruments in a business, in which they might have been utterly incapable of being the principals. The methods devised, with considerable skill, under the Emperor Akbar, for preventing the two great abuses incident to the machinery of collection; the oppression of the people; and embezzlement of the king's revenue; appear to have preserved their virtue, not much impaired, during the time when any vigour remained in the Mogul government; and to have become altogether neglected, only when each province, as the empire fell to pieces, became an independent petty state; and when the feeble and necessitous sovereign of each petty state was unable to contend either with his own vices, or those of his agents.[1]

V. Religion.—Under this head very few words are required; because the superiority of the Mohammedans, in respect of religion, is beyond all dispute. To the composition of the Koran was brought an acquaintance with the Jewish and Christian scriptures; by which the writer, notwithstanding his mental rudeness, appears to have greatly profited; and assigning, as we are disposed to assign, very little value to the lofty expressions regarding the Divine perfections, in the Koran, as well as to those in the Vedas, we find the absurdities in the Koran, by which those lofty ideas are contradicted, inconsiderable both in number and

[1] "The moderation of the tribute imposed by all Mohammedan conquerors, and the simplicity of their method of collecting it, accounts for the surprising facility with which they retained possession of their conquests. The form of their government was despotic; but in fact it was not oppressive to the mass of the conquered people. In general they introduced no change, but in the army, and in the name of the sovereign." Francis, Plan for a Settlement of the Revenues of Bengal, par. 9. "The gentiles (Hindus) are better contented to live under the Mogul's laws than under Pagan princes, for the Mogul taxes them gently, and every one knows what he must pay; but the Pagan kings or princes tax at discretion, making their own avarice the standard of equity: besides, there were formerly many small Rajas, that used upon frivolous occasions to pick quarrels with one another, and before they could be made friends again, their subjects were forced to open both their veins and purses to gratify ambition or folly." Hamilton's New Account of the East Indies, ii. 26.

degree, compared with those which abound in the religious system of the Hindus.[1]

VI. Manners. In this respect the superiority of the Mohammedans was most remarkable. The principal portion of the manners of the Hindus was founded upon the cruel and pernicious distinction of castes. A system of manners proceeding, like that of the Mohammedans, upon the supposition of the natural equality of mankind, constituted such a difference in behalf of all that is good for human nature, as it is hardly possible to value too high. Another great portion of the manners of the Hindus consisted in the performance of religious ceremonies: in ceremonies to the last degree contemptible and absurd, very often tormenting and detestable, a great proportion of the life of every Hindu is, or ought to be, consumed. The religion of the Moslem is stript of ceremonies to a degree nowhere else exemplified among nations in the lower stages of civilization.

As so great a portion of human life is devoted to the preparation and enjoyment of food, the great diversity between a diet wholly vegetable, and one which may in any degree consist of animal food, implies a considerable diversity in one grand portion of the details of ordinary life. Abstinence from intoxicating liquors, is a feature almost equally strong in the manners of both Mohammedans and Hindus.

In point of address and temper, the Mohammedan is less soft, less smooth and winning than the Hindu. Of course he is not so well liked by his lord and master, the Englishman: who desires to have nothing more to do with him than to receive his obedience. In truth, the Hindu, like the Eunuch, excels in the qualities of a slave. The indolence, the security, the pride of the despot, political or domestic, find less to hurt them in the obedience of the Hindu than in that of almost any other portion of the species. But if less soft, the Mohammedan is more manly, more vigorous. He more nearly resembles our own half-

[1] In some respects, the superiority may be granted to the Mohammedan religion, but there are two important principles by which its advantages are more than counterbalanced, its promise of sensual delights as the reward of virtue, and its bigoted Intolerance. The Hindu sees truth in every form of religious worship, and holds the pleasures of Paradise unworthy of a wise or pious hope.—W,

civilized ancestors; who, though more rough, were not more gross; though less supple in behaviour, were still more susceptible of increased civilisation, than a people in the state of the Hindus.

In the still more important qualities, which constitute what we call the moral character, the Hindu, as we have already seen, ranks very low; and the Mohammedan is little, if at all, above him. The same insincerity, mendacity, and perfidy; the same indifference to the feelings of others; the same prostitution and venality,[1] are conspicuous in both. The Mohammedans are profuse, when possessed of wealth, and devoted to pleasure; the Hindus are almost always penurious and ascetic.[2]

VII. THE ARTS. The comparison has been so fully exhibited between the Persians and Hindus, in respect to progress, in the arts, in that chapter of the preceding book, in which the arts of the Hindus have been described; and it is so well known, that the Mohammedan conquerors

[1] Sir Thomas Roe, speaking of even the Mogul Emperor and his court, says, "Experience had taught me that there was no faith among these barbarians." Journal in Churchill's Voyages, i. 799. Contrasting the opposition he met with, when he had not, and the obsequiousness when he had something to give, he says, "This made me sensible of the poor spirits of those people. Asaph Khan [the minister] was become so much our friend, in hopes to buy some trifles, that he would have betrayed his own son to serve us, and was my humble servant." Ibid. Sir Thomas Roe said it was better not to send ambassadors to the Mogul's court, but to employ the money in bribing. "Half my charge," said he, "shall corrupt all this court to be your slaves." Letter to the E. I. Company, Ibid. p. 809.

[2] In this comparison of manners, a variety of assertions is made, wholly unfounded. The distinction between the Moslem and the unbeliever, has everywhere rendered the former inclined to be brutal in his treatment of the latter, to an extent much beyond the ordinary effect of the distinction of caste. This was a matter of importance in India, where nine-tenths of the people were unbelievers, and were constant food for the insolence and cruelty of the faithful. The Mohammedan doctrine of equality was not incompatible with slavery to a very great extent, with all its debasing effects upon the manners of the slave-owner. Although not unknown to the Hindu system, it is in so modified a form, and is so little in harmony with Hindu manners, that it scarcely exists in most parts of India. The Hindus are not restricted to a vegetable diet any more than the Mohammedans, whilst it is not true that the Mohammedans abstain from spirituous liquors as rigidly as the Hindus. There are no such confessions in Hindu writings as in Baber's honest accounts of his drinking bouts, no such panegyrics upon wine, as in the poetry of Hafiz. With regard to deportment, there is not much difference between a well-bred Mohammedan and Hindu; but, generally speaking, there is more sincerity in the latter. The morals of the Mohammedans are much lower than those of the Hindus, from their stronger propensity to personal gratification ascribable partly to the spirit of their religion, and partly to greater physical vigour. The only superiority possessed by the Mohammedan over the Hindu is energy; they are, in general, a more resolute and enterprising race, retaining some of the physical qualities of their Turkish or Persian origin. This applies only to the better classes of them. The lower orders of Indian Mohammedans, are in general inferior to the lower orders of the Hindus.—W.

of India carried with them in perfection the arts of the Persians, that under this head scarcely anything remains to be adduced.

Of the mechanical arts, those of architecture, jewellery, and the fabrication of cloth, appeared to be the only arts for which admiration has been bestowed upon the Hindus. In the first two, the Hindus were found decidedly inferior to the Mohammedans.[1] Of the Mohammedan structures, some are hardly exceeded by the finest monuments of architecture in Europe. The characteristic circumstance of building an arch, the Hindus were totally ignorant of; the Mohammedans excelled in it.[2] If in anything the Mohammedans were inferior to the Hindus, it was in the productions of the loom; though it is doubtful whether, as high specimens of art, the silks and velvets of the Persians are not as wonderful as the fine muslins of the Hindus.

In making roads and bridges, one of the most important of all the applications of human labour and skill, the Hindus, before the invasion of the Mohammedans, appear to have gone very little beyond the state of the most barbarous nations. We have seen in the extract lately produced from the Institutes of Timur, that this was a primary care of government among the Moguls, before they became the conquerors of Hindustan.

In the fine arts, as they are usually called, or those of music, painting, and sculpture, the reader has already traced, with me, a remarkable coincidence in the progress of the Mohammedans, the Chinese, and the Hindus. In painting, the taste, as well as the mechanical faculty of all these nations, exhibit a resemblance which is singular and surprising. In music, the Hindus appear to be inferior; as, in sculpture, the Persians superior to the other two.

Whether war is to be ranked among the fine or the coarse arts; and whatever the relative portion of the powers of the mind which it requires; the art may be

[1] This is quite gratuitous; what do we know of the works of Hindu princes in those respects? In a country like India, edifices of the most stately character soon fall into decay, if left to such neglect as could not fail to be the fate of Hindu monuments under the scourge of foreign aggression. There are, however, remains of magnificent causeways in Behar, the Dekhin, and Guzerat, which must have been the work of Hindu princes, and sufficiently prove that they were not unmindful of the construction of roads and bridges.—W.

[2] Vide supra, p, 13, 14.

expected to exist in a state of high perfection among a people who are more, than a people who are less advanced in the scale of intelligence. When a number of people, comparatively few, overcome and hold in subjection a number of people, comparatively large, the inference is a legitimate one (unless something appear which gives the small number some wonderful advantage), that the art of war is in a state of higher perfection among the conquering, than the conquered. This inference, in the case of the Mohammedans aud Hindus, is confirmed by everything which we know with respect to both those people.

VIII. Literature.—In this important article, it will be impossible to show that the Hindus had the superiority in one singular particular. It will not be disputed, it is probable, that in almost every respect a decided superiority was on the side of their invaders. The only branches of Hindu literature of which the admirers of Hindu civilization have called for any admiration, are the mathematics and the poetry.

With regard to the mathematics, it is rather the supposed antiquity than the high progress of the science among the Hindus at which any wonder has been expressed. Whatever the case in regard to antiquity, it is abundantly certain that the science existed among the Mohammedans, acquainted to a considerable degree with the mathematics of Europe, in a state not less high than it was found among the Hindus, and that point is all which is material to the present purpose.

Of the poetry of the Hindus I have already endeavoured to convey a precise idea. On the present occasion it appears sufficient to say, that even those who make the highest demand upon us for admiration of the poetry of the Hindus, allow, as Sir William Jones, for example, that the poetry of the Persians is superior.[1] Compare the Mahabharat, the great narrative poem of the Hindus, with the Shah Namah, the great narrative poem of the Persians; the departure from nature and probability is less wild and

[1] Who makes any such admission? A more specific reference to the opinion of Sir William Jones is necessary, as it may be doubted if it is accurately quoted. The Shah Namah has some interesting narrative, but little that can be called poetry. The Mahabharat is no doubt inartificial, and often tiresome, but it abounds with poetical beauties.—W.

extravagant, the incidents are less foolish, the fictions are more ingenious, all to a great degree, in the work of the Mohammedan author than in that of the Hindu.

But the grand article in which the superiority of the Mohammedans appears is history. As all our knowledge is built upon experience, the recordation of the past for the guidance of the future is one of the effects in which the utility of the art of writing principally consists. Of this most important branch of literature, the Hindus were totally destitute. Among the Mohammedans of India, the the art of composing history has been carried to greater perfection than in any other part of Asia. In point of simplicity and good sense, there is no specimen, even of Persian history, known to the European scholar, which can vie with the works of Ferishta, or the interesting Memoirs of Gholam Hussein, the Seer Mutakhareen.[1] Beside the best specimens of Persian history, it is worthy of remark, that the best specimen of Persian poetry, the celebrated Shah Namah, was produced among the Mohammedan conquerors of Hindustan.[2]

[1] It may be shrewdly suspected, that our author would not have spoken so highly of Ferishta, or even of that much more intelligent chronicler Gholam Hosein, had not his purpose been to disparage the Hindus by exalting the Mohammedans.—W.

[2] The answer to this, in all, except in history, is, that the superiority is with the Hindus.—W.

NOTES.

NOTE A.

The most authentic source of information, yet open to the research of the European scholar, on the metaphysical, as on other ideas of the learned Hindus, is the volume of the Institutions of Menu. This celebrated, authoritative, and divine work, contains, as is usual with the sacred books of the Hindus, a specimen of all their knowledge; cosmogony, theology, physics, metaphysics, government, jurisprudence, and economics. From the account which in this work is rendered of the origin of the mind and its faculties, very sure conclusions may be drawn respecting the extent and accuracy of the psychological knowledge of the people by whom that account is delivered and believed.

The inspired author of this divine work informs the believing Hindu that, "From the supreme soul, Brahma, the Creator, drew forth mind, existing substantially, though unperceived by sense, immaterial."[1] The principal words here employed are vague and obscure, and no distinct meaning can be assigned to them. What is meant by "existing substantially?" What is meant by "immaterial?" "To exist substantially," if it have any meaning, is to be a substance. But this is inconsistent with the idea which we ascribe to the word immaterial; and there is in many other passages, abundant reason to conclude that the word, with its usual leanings, here translated, "immaterial," by Sir William Jones, meant nothing, in the conception of a Hindu, but a certain air, or ether, too fine to be perceived by the organs of sense.

Immediately after the words we have just quoted, it is added; "And before mind, or the reasoning power, he produced consciousness, the internal monitor, the ruler."[2] Consciousness, a faculty of the mind, is here represented as created before the mind, the quality before the substratum. It is subjoined in the

[1] Laws of Menu, ch. i. 14. See the passage quoted at length, supra, vol. i. ch. vi.

[2] Laws of Menu, ch. i. 14.

next words; "And before them both" (that is, before the mind and consciousness) "he produced the great principle of the soul, or first expansion of the divine idea."[1] Here is a third production, which is neither the mind, nor consciousness. What is it? To this we have no answer. As to the term "first expansion of the divine idea," which may be suspected to be a gloss rather than a translation, it is mere jargon, with no more meaning than the cawing of rooks. "In the same manner"—(that is, according to the construction of the sentence, before mind and consciousness—) "he created the five perceptions of sense, and the five organs of perception."[2] Another faculty of the mind, perception, is thus a creation antecedent to mind. The organs of perception, too, or bodily part, are a separate creation; perceiving organs which belong to no perceiving being.

The following text, which are the words next in order, exhibits a curious sample of metaphysical ideas. "Having at once pervaded, with emanations from the supreme spirit, the minutest portions of six principles immensely operative, consciousness, and the five perceptions, the Creator framed all creatures."[3] Consciousness, and the five perceptions, existed antecedently to all creatures; consciousness and perception, without conscious and perceiving beings. What is meant by the minute portions of consciousness? How can consciousness be supposed divided into portions either minute or large; especially when we are told that the mind is immaterial? What, too, are we to understand by the minute portions of a perception? As to the mere jargon, such as "pervading consciousness, and the five perceptions with emanations from the supreme spirit," it is unnecessary to offer on it any remarks.

We are next informed, "that the minutest particles of visible nature have a dependence on those six emanations from God."[4] What is meant by these six emanations is not very definitely expressed. The six things that are spoken of are consciousness and the five perceptions; and it is probable that they are meant. But how visible nature should depend upon consciousness and the five perceptions, does not appear. Certain other emanations from God, however, are spoken of, with which consciousness and the five perceptions were pervaded: and perhaps it was meant that the minutest particles of matter depend on them. But this is only barbarous jargon.

In the following verse, it is said, that "from these six emanations proceed the great elements, endued with peculiar powers, and mind with operations infinitely subtle, the unperishable cause

[1] Laws of Menu, ch. i. 15. [3] Ibid. [3] Ibid. 16.
[4] Ibid. 19.

of all apparent form."[1] It is still a difficulty, what is meant by the six emanations. If those are meant with which consciousness and the five perceptions are pervaded, no ideas whatever can be annexed to the words; they are totally without a meaning ; and that is all. If consciousness and the five perceptions be, as seems probable, the emanations in question; in what manner do the great elements and mind proceed from consciousness and the five perceptions? Mind would thus proceed from certain of its own operations.

It is added, in the succeeding sentence, " This universe, therefore, is compacted from the minute portions of those seven divine and active principles, the great soul, or first emanation, consciousness, and five perceptions; a mutable universe from immutable ideas."[2] Here it appears that the great soul, as well as consciousness and the perceptions, can be divided into portions. The great soul is not therefore immaterial, according to our sense of the word: and still less can either that, or the perceptions and consciousness be immaterial, if the universe, a great part of which is surely material, can be compacted from portions of them. " A mutable universe," it is said, " from immutable ideas;" therefore, the great soul, consciousness, and the five perceptions, are not realities, though divisible into portions; they are only ideas! What conclusions are we entitled to form respecting the intellectual state of a people who can be charmed with doctrine like this?[3]

In the following passage, and there are others of a similar import, we find a specimen of those beginnings which are made at an early stage of society, to refine in the modes of conceiving the mental operation. " Self-love," it is said, " is no laudable motive; yet an exemption from self-love is not to be found in this world: on self-love is grounded the study of scripture, and the practice of actions recommended in it."[4] The absurdity lies, in not perceiving, that if no action proceeding from self-love is virtuous; and if there is no action which does not proceed from self-love; then there is no virtue in the world, which is far from being the subject of Hindu belief.—M.

[1] Laws of Menu, ch. i. 17. [2] Ibid. 18.

[3] Not only are consciousness and the five perceptions regarded as separate existences, and separate products of creative power, but various other operations of the mind, and even states of the affections. Thus, among the other creations, it is said, that the Creator " gave being to devotion, speech, complacency, desire, and wrath." (Laws of Menu, ch. i. 25.)

[4] Ibid. ch. ii. 2.

NOTE B. p. 351.

This superior intellectual advancement of the Mohammedan nations, so confidently asserted, as a fact, is no fact at all, nor has any proof of it been adduced. The analogies upon which it is based, have been shown to be inaccurate, and the comparison involves a total disregard of time and circumstance. The question formerly discussed, was not what the Arabs, Persians, Turks, and Hindus now are, but what they were. Admitting that the three former have attained since the eighth century a level with the Hindus, it may most confidently be denied that the Arabs before the time of the Khalifat, or the Turks before that of Jangiz, were on a par with Hindu civilization. It would be equally consistent to assert, that because the progress made by the inhabitants of Great Britain, has left the Hindus behind; therefore the Britons in the days of Cæsar were more civilized than the people of India. Whatever, therefore, may have been the case in modern times, the nations of Western Asia had not at an earlier period a stage of civilization higher than the other inhabitants of the East. In truth the fact is disputable, even in all times. Mohammedan civilization is one, whatever be the nation, the same literature and science are cultivated from the Hellespont to the Oxus, the same laws and the same religion prevail. The literature is in some degree original, but with the exception of the historical portion, is much less agreeable to European taste than that of the Hindus: the science is borrowed, not only from the Greeks, but from the Hindus, and it is not true that the disciple has surpassed his masters. The magnificence of the Khaliphs rose suddenly and soon disappeared; their bounty created, and their example continued, a race of men of letters, who justly reflect great celebrity and credit upon the Mohammedan name; but literature was always confined to the court and the camp, it never enlightened the people. Nor were they brought within reach of civilization by the nature of their governments, the prevailing form of which has always been a military despotism, depending for its administration wholly on the character of the reigning prince. Neither now nor before the birth of Mohammed, were Arabs, Turks, or Persians, elevated above the Hindus by their political condition. They have had an advantage subsequently in their religion, the principles of which approached nearer to truth than Hindu idolatry. In practice, however, it is quite as full of unmeaning and trifling observances, and in its ferocious intolerance contributes less to humanize its professors, than the universal toleration of Hindu polytheism.—W.